MW01026242

IAMS OF AMERICA:

LANDED GENTRY OF MARYLAND:

PATRIOTS, PIONEERS, AND SUCCESSFUL AMERICANS

Includes Iiams, Ijams, Iames, Eyoms, Jiames,
Ijames, Ijems, Jiams, Jiemes, Iiames, Imes, Hioms,
Eyeams, Ijemes, Yams, Iimes, Ims, Emson,
Ems, Eyoms, Eyans, Jams, Iioms, etc.

Edited by
Ralph D. Reynolds, M.D.
319 Paoli Pointe Drive
Paoli, PA 19301

1998

IAMS OF AMERICA

Copyright © 1998 by
Ralph D. Reynolds, M.D.
516 North Baltimore Street, Suite A305
Kirksville, MO 63501

Printed in the United States of America.

Library of Congress Number: 97-76171

International Standard Book Number: 1-883294-63-0

First Edition

Printed by
Masthof Press
R.R. 1, Box 20, Mill Road
Morgantown, PA 19543-9701

TABLE OF CONTENTS

Chapter 1: William Ijams (d. 1703, Maryland), Progenitor in America. He first appears as a landed gentry in Anne Arundel County, Maryland. Includes early history, family of William Iams (b. 1670), Charity Iams (b. 1698), and Thomas Iams.   **Page 1**

Chapter 2: Richard Iiams (b. 1673, Maryland), son of William (d. 1703). He lived in Maryland and had twelve children. Chapter includes slave Jack Imes, Williams Iams (b. 1800) family, Francis Marion Iams (b. 1830, Ohio), William Iams (b. 1750), John Iiams (b. 1712), Thomas Iiams (b. 1745), Dennis Iams (b. 1808, Pennsylvania), Benjamin Iams (b. 1839, Pennsylvania), and Charles Iams (b. 1873, Pennsylvania). **Page 55**

Chapter 3: George Iiams (b. 1676, Maryland), son of William (d. 1703). Began the Ijams migration to North Carolina. Chapter includes John Iames (b. 1725, Maryland), Brice W. Ijams, Beale Ijams (b. 1767, Maryland), Joseph Marion Ijames (b. 1855, North Carolina), Jerry Lucio Ijams (b. 1884, North Carolina), Denton Ijams (b. 1811, North Carolina), Basil Gaither Ijams (b. 1845, North Carolina), William Iiams (b. 1722, Maryland), Vachel Ijams (b. 1759, Maryland), and Burgess Ijams (b. 1801, North Carolina). **Page 93**

Chapter 4: John Ijams (b. 1712, Maryland), son of William (d. 1703). Includes their eight children, William Ijams (b. 1760, Maryland), Richard Daniel Ijams (b. 1811, Fairfield County, Ohio), William Howard Ijams (b. 1780, Maryland), John Howard Ijams (b. 1783, Maryland), Sarah Howard Ijams (b. 1798, Maryland), Isaac Beall Ijams (b. 1849, Ohio), Isaac Plummer Ijams (b. 1765, Maryland), John Wesley Iiams (b. 1805, Fairfield County, Ohio), Edwin Clayton Ijams (b. 1886, Kansas), Sheldon L. Ijams (b. 1884, Arizona), Edward T. Ijams (b. 1846, Ohio), Thomas Plummer Ijams (b. 1773, Maryland), Lewis Ijams (b. 1798, Maryland), James Wallace Shaw (b. 1898), William Fletcher Ijams (b. 1816, Ohio), William Henry Harrison Ijams (b. 1840, Illinois), Thomas LeRoy Ijams (b. 1842, Ohio), John Ijams (b. 1755, Maryland), John Waters Ijams (b. 1807, Maryland), Plummer Iiams (b. 1716, Maryland), Plummer Ijams (b. 1781, Maryland), John Ijams (b. 1789, Maryland), Richard Ijams (b. 1800, Maryland), Thomas Musgrove Ijams (b. 1812, North Carolina), Richard Iams (b. 1786), Thomas Iams (b. 1780, Pennsylvania), William Iiams (b. 1825, Pennsylvania), Ross Lindsey Iams (b. 1879, Pennsylvania), Richard Iams (b. 1817, Pennsylvania), Rezin Iams (b. 1850, Pennsylvania), Richard Iams (b. 1811, Ohio), Eli Iiams (b. 1790, Maryland), and Rufus Putnam Ijams (b. 1818, Ohio).   **Page 105**

Chapter 5: William Iams (b. 1745, Maryland), son of Thomas (b. 1708). The family migrated to Western Pennsylvania. Includes Isaac Iams (b. 1795, Pennsylvania), John Iams (b. 1792, Pennsylvania), Samuel Iams (b. 1817, Pennsylvania), Graham Peter Iams (b. 1852, Pennsylvania), John T. Iams (b. 1846, Pennsylvania), John Iiams (b. 1825, Pennsylvania), Thomas Iams (b. 1858, Pennsylvania), Thomas Iiams (b. 1784, Pennsylvania), John Iiams (b. 1816, Pennsylvania), George L. Iiams (b. 1846, Auglaize County, Ohio), Birt Elmer Iiams (b. 1875, Ohio), William E. Morson Iiams (b. 1837, Shelby County, Ohio), Samuel Iiams (b. 1843, Ohio), and Guy Ralston Iiames (b. 1897, Lima, Ohio).   **Page 165**

Chapter 6: Richard Iiams (b. ca1745, Maryland), son of John (b. 1720). The family moved to Western Pennsylvania, and then to all corners of the country. Chapter includes John Iiams (b. 1780, Maryland), William Iiams (b. 1786, Maryland), John Iams (b. 1814, Pennsylvania), Jeremiah H. Iams (b. 1832, Columbiana County, Ohio), Richard Iams (b. 1817, Pennsylvania), Isaac Iams (b. 1809, Pennsylvania), John Iams (b.1819, Pennsylvania), Dennis Iams (b. 1808, Pennsylvania), Charles Robert Iams (b.1931, Pennsylvania), George W. Iams (b. 1860, Pennsylvania), Richard Iams (b. 1787), Rufus Putnam Iams (b. 1818, Ohio), Richard Iams (b. 1822, Pennsylvania), John Iams (b. 1809, Pennsylvania), George Iams (b. 1871, Iowa), Richard Iams (b. 1831, Licking County, Ohio), Charles Iams (b. 1859, Iowa), Otho Iams (b. 1791, Maryland), William Iams (b. 1755, Maryland), and Franklin Pierce Iams (b. 1852, Pennsylvania). Ervin F. Bickley, Jr. includes Eli Iams (b. 1796, Pennsylvania).   **Page 203**

Chapter 7: John Iams (b. 1750, Maryland) son of Thomas (b. 1708). Chapter shows the family migration to Western Pennsylvania, and includes William Iams (b. 1792), Isaac Iams (b. 1828), Robert Imes (b. 1822), Samuel Enock Imes (b. 1871, Preble County, Ohio), Zebulon Ferrell Iams (b. 1856, Pennsylvania), Isaac Weller Iams (b. 1874, Pennsylvania), Evelyn Morrison Iams (b. 1903, Pennsylvania), James Dorsey Iams (b. 1860, Pennsylvania), Charles Shirk Iams (b. 1891, Pennsylvania), William Iams (b. 1830, Pennsylvania), Miller Iams (b. 1811, Pennsylvania), Elisha Iams (b. 1822, Pennsylvania), William Owen Iams (b. 1855, Pennsylvania), and Elisha Bernard Iams (b. 1892, Pennsylvania).   **Page 241**

iv

v

EDITOR

Ralph D. Reynolds, M.D., and Norita Rose Sholly (1995)

Ralph D. Reynolds, M.D., FACP, was born along the Ohio River in the coal mining town of Powhatan Point in Southeastern Ohio on February 22, 1934. He graduated from Hubbard High School, near Youngstown, where he played in football, basketball, baseball, and track. He graduated with a mathematics major from Muskingum College where he was named to the men's honorary society, *Who's Who in America*, and played football, basketball, and track. He graduated from The Ohio State University School of Medicine in 1960 and served his internship at Madigan General Hospital in Tacoma, Washington. He finished his internal medicine residency and fellowship in hematology and oncology at Wilford Hall USAF Medical Center in San Antonio, Texas. In 1968-1969, he served as Chairman, Department of Medicine and Senior Consultant to Surgeon General at Cam Ranh Bay, South Vietnam. He returned to David Grant USAF Medical Center at Travis AFB, California, where he developed an NCI-sponsored cancer program, a residency and fellowship program in internal medicine and the various subspecialties, and assisted in the development of University of California Davis School of Medicine. Ralph remained there until 1982, when he retired from the Air Force at the rank of Colonel and as Clinical Professor of Medicine at University of California. He served as Chairman of the New Agents Committee and Board of Directors of WCSG and as Chairman of the Lung Committee, Acting Chairman of the Institutional Review Board and member of the Board of Directors of NCOG. He was awarded the Surgeon General's Award for Clinical Research, the "W" Suffix (Professor) rating and the Physician of the Year Award while in the Air Force. In 1982, he became Medical Director of Ellis Fischel Cancer Center, Professor of Medicine, Director of the Missouri Women's Cancer Control Program and Medical Director of the Cancer Research Center at University of Missouri and State Cancer Center in Columbia, Missouri. In 1987, Ralph moved to Columbus, Ohio, as Associate Director for Oncology Research for Adria Laboratories as well as a member of the staff at the Ohio State University where he managed the oncology program for the state correctional system. In 1993, he was recruited as Vice President for Research and Development at U.S. Bioscience. Most of Ralph's professional career has been involved in cancer research, conducting clinical studies, and writing scientific articles. Most recent oncology clinical trials have been directed toward the development of chemotherapy agents and agents which modify the toxicities of therapy. He is board certified in both internal medicine and medical oncology, and is board eligible in nuclear medicine, hematology, preventive medicine, aerospace medicine, and geriatrics. He is married to the former Norita Rose Sholly, and they have five mature professional children. Ralph and Norita now live in Kirksville, Missouri. He authored the book, *John Hobbs: 1600-1732* in 1994. He is currently Director of Oncology, Kirksville Osteopathic Medical Center, the founding osteopathic institution.

ASSOCIATE EDITORS

Lois Ijams Hartman, born in Kansas, the daughter of Edwin C. Ijams, lives in Pasadena, California.

Lois Ijams Hartman, of Pasadena, California, is well known for her genealogy of the Ijams/Iiams/Iams family and for such published works *as Remembered in This Land* and *Footprints Beside Him*. In spite of her many wonderful contributions and her lasting scholarly works on the family tree, she readily admits to some of the recognized frustrations encountered in establishing the family lines. For example, she described her experiences working on the Iams families of Western Pennsylvania, an effort that was "stopped because there were so many John and Thomas Iiams that it was difficult to try to pin-point them to the right family. . . . Newman's 1970 and Howard Leckey accounts vary in dates of birth." She and Roberta Wright Iiames have expressed such ideas as "I go through the (census) pages line by line... since the Iiams name is many times written incorrectly, the

Lois Ijams Hartman 1977 standing in the front doorway of the oldest home in North Cornwall, England. This was the summer home of I'Ans, and was later the home for the last four spinster sisters.

Lois Ijams Hartman in the churchyard at Moroentow Parish, North Cornwall, where Charlotte I'Ans Hawher was the vicar's wife for many years and which served as the setting for the book Footprints *by Lois Ijams Hartman.*

person making up the index doesn't always write down the name the way it should be. (This is) time consuming but I have found an awful lot of data in this manner." "Genealogy is not an exact science and there are probably some errors in compiling this data; however, we have tried to correct any such errors and will continue to do so." (Roberta Wright Iiames and Guy Ross Iiames). Lois Ijams Hartman has had some disagreements with James B. Meighen and states that "we have some different understanding of the Scottish line. I did a lot of research on that and gave it up as an error in plotting. I believe there were too many years between Sir Robert Innes (I'Ans) and the Cornish I'Ans and that they were not the same man. Others differ, and it is all so easy to misinterpret."

Early History of Iams Family

Lois Ijams Hartman has spent considerable time and made many trips to England and Europe in an attempt to define the branches of the tree that led members of the family to settle in Maryland during the seventeenth century. While her work has been the best effort made to date, there still remain several questions that should be resolved before the final "die is cast" with regard to the trans-Atlantic bonds of kinship within the Iams family tree.

At the West Counties Library in Exeter, she found what she deemed to be a fragmented pedigree of the family whose name was spelled I'Ans. The earliest record of the family name may be that of David Ion from 1370 or perhaps to Abraham Johns of that same era. Other early spellings include Ijams and Iianes. Lois Ijams Hartman found most references to the I'Ans name to be centered around Cornwall and North Devon and especially near the western seacoast areas of Ilfracombe, Bideford, Bude, and Barnstaple (formerly called Barum). Walter I'ans married Amy Redford, according to the records of Bideford. A Walter I'ans, Gentleman, was buried in 1749 at Ilfracombe. The children may have included Thomas (b. October 20, 1720), Elizabeth (b. November 24, 1719), and Amy (b. 1724; d. 1725). A Joseph I'Ans marker reads July 29, 1765. An Edward I'Ans of Bennetts, Whitstone, was buried 1745, and an Edward I'Ans of Whitstone House was buried 1772. A Mr. William Carder and Mrs. Elizabeth I'Ans buried a Joseph I'Ans April 16, 1732. A review of the listing of the graduates of Oxford University shows the presence of at least two I'Ans: George at Edin Hall March 1694 with M.A. on June 11, 1695; and Francis, later the Rector of Cruys Morchard, Devon, who graduated May 30, 1782.

Lois Ijams Hartman also explains how the name has changed since the first arrival of family members in Maryland. The use of the spelling of I'Ans, and the use of the letter "n" was believed to be favored by those with close ties to England, while early life in America resulted in the spelling of the name as "Eyoms." She further subscribes to the beliefs expressed by Newman that the spelling "I'ams" and "Ijams" are versions that originated within Maryland, and that there is some belief that the name may have been derived from "James," "Ian" (Scottish version), or "Ion" (Welsh). The connection to the "James" version of the name is based on the former interchangeable use of the letters "I" and "J." The name is believed to have been converted from the Maryland version to the southwestern Pennsylvania version of "Iams," or the western version of "Ijams," or the North Carolina version of "Ijames." Newman used Lois Ijams Hartman as a reference in his writing.

Newman describes I'Ans during the time of Henry VIII (1491-1547) in Stratton, Cornwall. Arms were presented to "Robert I'Ans of Whitstone by Elizabeth, her Master of Ordance and Her Majesty's Privy Council in Ireland," with the family pedigree dating to February 1640. Colonel Wrey I'Ans of Whitstone House, Cornwall, died 1816; and had been Justice of the Peace for Cornwall and Devon.

In March 1934, E. Jay Iiams of Donora, Pennsylvania, wrote that the name was believed to have been derived from the expression "Emma's son," and was subsequently contracted to such variations as Emson, Ems, and Ims. He felt that the family was of Welsh origin, with probably earlier migration from Germany to Wales. He agrees that the Iiams were among the earliest settlers of the state of Maryland, though the exact date and location of their settlement is not known. He acknowledges that a William Yams was a "resident of Anne Arundel County as early as October 2, 1696." William Eyams/Iiams, the pioneer, died in 1703. He had "married Elizabeth Cheyney, daughter of Richard Cheyney, about 1669, in Anne Arundel County, Maryland. He was a member of the Established Church in All Hallows Parish and buried from the church, July 29, 1703. His will was probated in Anne Arundel County, Maryland, November 10, 1703, and shows that he was a land owner."

Listed herein, as separate entities, are items of potential useful information that have been compiled by Lois Ijams Hartman during her international travels and her intensive searches through various archives in America.

From Enstone, Oxfordshire, England:

1. Elizabeth Eyans, b. December 3, 1660, to Richard and Margaret Eyans.
2. Eleanor Eyans, b. April 17, 1664, to Richard and Margaret Eyans.
3. Margaret Eyans, b. December 20, 1666, to Richard and Margaret Eyans.
4. Asgyle Eyans, a son, b. January 3, 1667, to Richard, gent. and Margaret.
5. Dorothea Eyans, b. October 25, 1672; d. December 16, 1672, of Richard and Margaret.
6. Elizabeth Eyans, b. December 9, 1680, to Richard and Elizabeth Eyans.
7. Richard Eyans, b. January 5, 1681, to Richard and Elizabeth Eyans.
8. Hester Eyans, b. September 7, 1686, to Richard and Elizabeth Eyans.
9. Joseph Eyans, b. March 24, 1687, to Richard and Elizabeth Eyans.

10. Anty Eyans, baptized July 31, 1690, son of Richard and Elizabeth Eyans.
11. Elizabeth Hyans, b. March 16, 1724, to William and Elizabeth Hyans.
12. My Hyans, daughter, b. April 6, 1726, to William and Elizabeth Hyans.
13. William Hyans, b. April 1728, to William and Elizabeth Eirrons.
14. My Hyans m. November 8, 1724, Enstone, to Richard Ryman.
15. Dorothea Eyans, d. December 16, 1672, Enstone.
16. Richard Eyans, Gentleman, d. October 5, 1677, Enstone.
17. Elizabeth Eyans, wife of Richard, Esq., d. September 24, 1707.
18. Richard Eyans, Esq., d. August 1, 1709.

In separate works, Lois Ijams Hartman has reviewed accounts of the King George's War (1742) and Proceedings of the Council of Maryland in the Maryland Archives. In March 1742/3, a Captain Richard I'on commanded the privateer *Eagle* out of the port at Charleston which captured a 200-ton French ship bound from Spain to Havana and which contained 25,000 pieces-of-eight concealed in bags of snuff. Captain I'on later commanded the privateer *Assistance*, with fourteen guns and one hundred men, that was built in Charleston and which patrolled the East Coast with the Philadelphia privateer *Cruizer*. By May 14, 1745, Captain I'on and Captain Lampiere had captured the *Isabella* or *St. Isabel*, valued at more than 331 pounds.

From the Proceedings of the Council of Maryland, a 1752 Anne Arundel County account of court examinations of Stockett Williams and John Ijams is reviewed. A deposition talked him out of free cloth and thread from the family store on repeated occasions; then, presumably under the influence of proffered rum, Jeremiah Williams and an accomplice, John Jones, led this Stockett Williams to attempt robbery of a warehouse, to steal and slaughter some sheep, to steal some 300 pounds of tobacco, to steal clothing from a dry goods store by breaking and entering, to steal cherry rum and a dozen large felt hats from another store by digging a tunnel-type entrance and then burying the rum in order to hide it, to steal half a firkin (sic) of hogs, lard, and some bacon from a locked milk house, to steal two or three pieces-of-eight from another store, and to plan a robbery of the store and cash reserves of one John Ijams, Jr. John Ijams, Jr. gave his testimony on July 22, 1752, before the judge, John Brice.

This John Ijams, Jr. described an episode where a Jerome Williams had approached him (Ijams) to inquire when he (Ijams) would be leaving a neighbor's home and going to his (Ijams) own home. John Ijams later took his horse and headed toward home, but before he came to the William Ijams home (Anne Arundel County), he was overtaken by this Jerome Williams. This Jerome Williams diverted John Ijams, Jr. under the pretense of wanting to complete a trade. John Ijams, Jr., went along with him and became more and more involved with things related to the activity of the thieves: observing the stolen goods, unknowingly partaking of the stolen cherry rum, etc. John Ijams, Jr. was eventually convinced by the thieves that since he was already an accomplice, that he may as well join with them in their illegal activities. John Ijams, Jr. described that he was under a threat of death if he did not comply, so he put on the old red jacket supplied to him and helped rob a home of shoes, dry goods, some equipment, two large copper kettles, a large skillet, a spice pestle and mortar, and six candlesticks. After hearing the testimony, the judge gave pardons to both John Ijams, Jr. and to William Stockett so that their confessions could be used to convict the ringleader and influential Jerome Williams.

In another matter brought before the court on May 13, 1777, by a letter from Christian Loundes, Esquire, a Sergeant Ijams was described as having been accused of some disorderly conduct that had not yet been fully investigated. Then, in the

Calendar of Maryland State Papers—Executive Miscellanea (p. 92), on May 14, 1777, Thomas Ijams was identified as "the officer of the recruiting party mentioned in Christopher Loundes' letter of May 12, appeared before the Council; he confessed he had ordered his men to fire and afterwards to fix their bayonets as described in the letter; he was ordered to give bond for his appearance before the Prince George's County Court to answer for his conduct towards Loundes." Also, on May 14, 1777, "Bond of Thomas Ijams (Jiams), Anne Arundel County, State of Maryland. The condition is that Ijams made his personal appearance before the Prince George's County Court on the third Tuesday in May."

In records of the 1777 Council of Maryland (pp. 371, 372), a letter of September 9, 1777, from George Washington at Wilmington, described plans to attempt to capture Philadelphia but asked for more troops. Council of Maryland records of September 12, 1777, show a quick response to General George Washington's request, by describing rations being allocated and men, including Ensign John Iiams having been conscripted. Records of the same day also describe "That the Commissary of Stores deliver to Thomas Ijams stript linnen for two p' trousers and two jackets, white linnen for two shirts, brown linnen for a coatee and trimmings suitable."

In another area, Lois Ijams Hartman described how the Tennessee School for the Deaf was refurbished after the Civil War, and had elected J. H. Ijams, a teacher from Iowa, as principal of the school in 1866, at a salary of $1200 per year. Mr. Ijams remained at the school until 1882.

Lois Iams Blake was born in the evening of a Saturday, on August 13, 1910, after her mother had canned peaches all day long. At the age of four, she contracted polio, leaving a slight right-sided weakness. She attended a one-room public school for the first eight grades, and then graduated as Salutatorian of her high school class before graduating in 1930 from Marietta Commercial College in nearby Marietta, Ohio, after taking the complete business course. She worked from 1933 to 1936, with the Home Owner Loan Corporation, a federal organization designed to aid families in retaining their homes after the depression. On February 25, 1937, she was married in Washington, D.C., where her husband worked in the House of Representatives. She and her husband returned to Ohio, where he managed a retail auto parts store before dying in June 1964. Her daughter married and her son went off to college, so she then began her full-time pursuit of genealogy. She initially began working on her own Blake and Iams families, but as she gained expertise and learned of the needs of others, her avocation soon became a blossoming profession. For a change of pace from her hectic genealogy routine, she pursued hobbies of knitting, crocheting, sewing, and reading. She has been a member of Olive Green Christian Church, has pursued all seven Degrees of the Patrons of Husbandry (including Subordinate, Pomona, State, and National), member Noble County Chapter Ohio Genealogical Society, member Noble County Historical Society, Honorary Member of the Women's Literacy Society, member Marietta Chapter of Daughters of American Revolution, member of Caldwell Merrimaker's Group, member of First Families of Guernsey County, and member of First Families of Noble County. Locally, she is known as "Mrs. Genealogy."

Lois Iams Blake of Caldwell, Ohio, began her genealogy search of the Iams family tree approximately sixty years ago, as a teenager. A native of Southeastern Ohio, she is generally recognized as the leading genealogist of that area. She has spent her entire life in and around the village of Caldwell in Noble County, Ohio.

Lois has written that "the name Innes originated by the village of Innes in Morayshire, and the name means 'green.' ...The father of Robert Bruce, first Scottish

Lois Iams Blake,
Caldwell, Ohio,
May 1995.

Lois Iams Blake, Caldwell, Ohio,
1980, at home with filing cabinet
and book shelves in background.

Lois Iams Blake, guest speaker at Betsy Mills
DAR, November 2, 1985, Marietta, Ohio.

Lois Iams Blake, holding crewel embroidery
on linen cloth, flax grown, made into thread
and woven by Mary Myers Iams (1808-1904),
wife of Rezin Iams (1807-1873), who mi-
grated to Morgan County, Ohio, in 1830s.

xii

Joy Imes Hannon and Jack Hannon (1994).

King of Scotland, was Adam deBrus, from the French town of Brix, (and) who came to England with William the Conquerer."

In 1619, there is an entry into the record of the Virginia Company records (Volume 3) that states a transaction of 37.10 paid by Edward Iams/James, to Sir Thomas Smith, tale Treasurer; and on June 22, 1620, both Edward Iames and William Ianson, are mentioned as names "said to" Sir Thomas Smith, Knight, Treasurer of Virginia Company.

Joy Imes Hannon has written:

"Legend has it that "the 'A' was dropped from our name, because of the confusion with the James family." EFB recorded that John Iiams (Jefferson County, Ohio, ca1747-1816) had a son Richard (Perry) Iiams (ca1786-1848); but with the

The Isaac and Ruth Iams Family: Rear (left to right) James, Bill, David, and Richard Iams; front (left to right) Judy, Isaac, Ruth Clinton, and Kim Iams. (1981)

next generation to Richard Perry Iams (1814-ca1879), the name changed to Iams and/or Imes, with Imes being passed down to subsequent generations."

Joy Imes Hannon is a native of Zanesville, Ohio, where she now lives. She has spent about thirty years collecting information on her family, and on other Ohio Imes/Iams family members. At one time she had identified each Imes/Iiams/Iams family that was located in Ohio, and had constructed an Ohio county map with a listing of each representative family. She also pursued a branch of her family that played a significant part in the early "Cowboy and Indian" activities during the settlement of the upper midwestern part of the United States. Marjorie Dixon has recently assumed her duties.

Ervin F. Bickley, Jr. has devoted much of a complete lifetime in the pursuit of the Iams/Ijams/Iiams family. His work has been exacting, complete, and extremely well documented, in keeping with his training as an astute businessman. In some ways, he found the work frustrating. He, like Lois Ijams Hartman and James B. Meighen, had several disagreements with Harry Wright Newman. While they were to win some of the arguments with Mr. Newman, there were many issues which remained unsettled, and several questions which remained as they were. Mr. Bickley, perhaps more than the others, engaged numerous persons throughout the country to participate in the search to complete the Iams picture puzzle. While the cost of the efforts of Mr. Bickley ran into the thousands of dollars, no exact accounting of this effort was ever made. The names of many of his collaborators, however, do remain: Charlotte Calhoun (Oregon), Reverend Ralph B. Imes (Eldora, Iowa), Joy Imes Hannon (Ohio), Jennie Kay (Indiana), E. E. Arnold (Medicine Hat, Alberta), E. F. Trojan (Clarkson, Nebraska), Mildred Wood (Kokomo, Indiana), John E. Evans (Walton, Indiana), Mary D. Kemp (Wichita, Kansas), Elizabeth Landers (Bakersfield, California), Alice Williams (Tulsa, Oklahoma), Frances Iams (Upper Sandusky, Ohio), Harley Iams (McConnellsville, Ohio), Harley G. Roby (Marion, Ohio), John V. Iams (West Virginia), Janice Sharp (Defiance, Ohio), Ruth M. Watts (Odenten, Maryland), Marjorie S. Dickson (Oregon, Illinois), Robert Elton Iams (Seattle, Washington), Elisha B. Iams (Washington, Pennsylvania), Lois Iams Blake (Caldwell, Ohio), M. K. Ijams (Terre Haute, Indiana), Gilbert Imes (Ohio), Edith Rector (Marietta, Ohio), Jean Van Fossen (Stark County, Ohio), Chester R. Imes (New Boston, Ohio), William A. Ijams (Corinth, Michigan), Lillian T. Taylor (Columbus, Ohio), Nettie Leitch Majors (Washington), Kathryn Shipley (Wheeling, West Virginia), Reverend Fred Cochran (Waynesburg, Pennsylvania), Winifred Van Seters (Salt Lake City, wrote "lots of effort, lots of money, many letters, little value"), Clifford H. Iams (Washington, Pennsylvania), Omer Ingersol Imes (Waverly, Indiana), Dolores N. Larson (Woolstock, Iowa, correspondent with greatest sense of humor), Mildred H. Russell (Waynesburg, Pennsylvania), Grace M. Hirschauer (Batavia, Ohio), Grace Ochsenbein (Bridgeport, Ohio, a noted Eastern Ohio genealogist and historian), Eliza E. Imes (Sidney, Montana), and Phillinda K. Naegle (Phoenix, Arizona), among others, most of whom were involved in correspondence with Mr. Bickley between 1951 and 1997.

After reviewing this manuscript, Mr. Bickley pointed out that there were many areas in the lineage that must be considered to be tentative, since absolute proof may be lacking. With his assistance, it is hoped that many of these have been omitted from the final text. Where publications are cited, the information is listed as being from a given source. In spite of this, a "very large number of inconsistencies and inaccuracies" have become part of the published material.

Mr. Bickley states that "any further mention of Eli Iams, born in Maryland in 1790, as having any direct relationship to Richard of Greene County, Pennsylvania, should be stopped. Richard's son, Eli, was born in Pennsylvania on March 4, 1799. His tombstone and death certificate, and the 1850 census, give his birth at about that time. Eli of Washington County, Ohio, born 1790, presumably in Frederick County, Maryland, remains a mystery as far as names of his parents are concerned, after decades of search by many interested searchers. Any further showing of this Eli (m. Catherine Crawford) or any of his children, such as Rufus Putnam Iams, in connection with Greene or Washington Counties, Pennsylvania, is only perpetuating a mistake and confusion.

"The *Anne Arundel Gentry* and others have thoroughly confused and intermixed the various Williams who had connection with either Washington County, Maryland; Allegany County, Maryland; and Bedford County, Pennsylvania; and perhaps others. On page 326 of *Anne Arundel Gentry*, the William mentioned as from Allegany County, Maryland, is separate from the William who married Elizabeth Howard and settled in Washington County, Maryland. Practically all the entries of real estate transactions on page 326 actually related to the William who married Elizabeth Howard and to properly be included in his notes on page 307.

"Some confusion still seems to exist about the parents of Richard Daniel Iams and William Howard Iams. These two are definitely the sons of William Iams, Jr. (m. Catherine Ruffner), who died in Ohio about 1817. Guardians were appointed for the children of William Iams, Jr. on September 30, 1817, so obviously he had died by that time." Also, "it is long past the time when any connection should be made between Thomas Iams (b. 1708) and the Richard, Thomas, William, and John who went to Greene or Washington Counties, Pennsylvania. The Bible record shown by Newman for Thomas (b. 1708) must be given credence. The birth dates in that record do not match for any of the aforementioned who were in Pennsylvania by 1795 or earlier.

"Another William (m. Charity Ryan) went to Greene County, Pennsylvania, some years later and died there about 1809. This William was very probably the son of Thomas (b. 1708), and William was born in 1755, according to the Bible record.

"Richard (b. ca1745) and Thomas (b. 1754) were either brothers or first cousins, given the highly probable best interpretation of the court record referred to on page 327 of *Anne Arundel Gentry*. Incidentally, this court record confirms that the wife of Richard (b. ca1745) was named Eleanor. Various names, such as Elizabeth Hill and others have been mentioned for the wife of Richard (b. ca1745). To this date, I have never seen a single item of proof for these statements and I think it is time that they were removed."

The revision of the family of William Ijams (17__-1816) and Elizabeth (Howard) Ijams (pages 306 and 307, *Anne Arundel Gentry*) give the children as: Richard D. Ijams (m. J. E. Alford, Fairfield County, Ohio) and William Howard Ijams. The remaining listed children are believed to be children of William, Jr. The remainder of the text about this family should read:

"William Ijams, son of John and Rebecca (Jones) Ijams, was born in All Hallow's Parish. By the will of his father, he received several Negro slaves, and resided in his native parish, but later settled in Frederick County. He married Elizabeth, daughter of Joseph and Rachel (Ridgely) Howard of Anne Arundel County. On March 12, 1785, Rachel Howard devised her daughter, Elizabeth Ijams, several slaves, stating in the deed that they were from the estate of her deceased husband, Joseph Howard. From his deceased cousin, William Ijams, he inherited 400 acres of Cheyney's Resolution, which he mortgaged to Nicholas Maccubbin, Gent. On June 3, 1778, Nicholas Maccubbin released him from the lien, stating in the indenture that William Ijams had inherited the plantation as the residuary heir of his cousin,

"On July 15, 1789, of Anne Arundel, declaring himself as the son of John and Rebecca Ijams, he sold his portion of Cheyney's Resolution to Edward Hall, son of Henry, Gent., for £1,987/10/-. The conveyance contained 400 acres of the plantation near the head of South River except 150 acres then in the possession of Gassaway Rawlings and the heirs of Isiah Cheney. He signed the deed of conveyance, while his wife, Elizabeth, waived all rights of dower. In March 1778, he manifested his loyalty to the Colonies by taking the Oath of Allegiance to the State of Maryland before Judge Richard Harwood, Jr., signing his name as 'William Ijams of John.' In 1806, he was a tithable in Richland Township, Fairfield County, Ohio, where he and his two brothers settled a couple of years previously. He died intestate in Fairfield County in 1816. His last will and testament mentioned sons John, Isaac, Joseph, Frederick, a widow, and unnamed daughters.

"Before March 5, 1787 (from page 325), he settled in Washington County, when he purchased personalty from John Donnachy. Undoubtedly he was the William James who was domiciled in Washington County at the first Federal Census, with himself over 16 years, 4 males under 16 years and 4 females, and 7 negroes. On March 30, 1793, he purchased of Thomas Worley, of Washington County, Maryland, for £800 a tract of land whereon the said William Iiams was then residing in Washington County, known as Chance, of 58 acres, which had originally been rented to John Bowling on August 11, 1753. Susannah Worley, wife, waived all dower rights.

"On September 10, 1803, styled William Iiams of Washington County, Maryland, he deeded to Abraham Ditto, of the same county, for £1,882/10/- The Chance of 110 acres, and also Hole in the Hole, containing 58 acres which had been granted to the said William Iiams by patent of March 13, 1793; also land conveyed by Richard Barnes on April 11, 1793; and also Addition to Chance, of 9 acres, granted to him, with all five tracts of 251 acres with houses and other improvements. Elizabeth Iiams, wife of William, waived her dower interest.

"The fact that he disposed of his realty in Washington County by 1803 is indicative of his preparing to settle elsewhere. At the 1830 census of Fairfield County, his sons, Joseph Howard Ijams and William Howard Ijams, were heads of families (from page 307). His son John Howard Ijams held a commission during the War of 1812. The latter's son-in-law, William J. Hester, of Sarahsville, Noble County, Ohio, addressed a letter to the Commissioner of Pensions, dated January 25, 1884, stating that the widow of John Howard Ijams was still alive." (EFB)

Roberta Wright Iiames and **Guy R. Iiames** of Springboro, Ohio, have been extremely active in their pursuit of the Iiames/Iams/Iiams family tree. They have specialized in the pursuit of the Ohio families, and especially in the families of Western and Southwestern Ohio. Their contribution to this work has been invaluable and their efforts have been both thorough and exhaustive. In Allen County, Ohio, they pursued sources in the Allen County Public Library, Allen County Historical Museum, Allen County Probate Court Records, Allen County Death Records, Allen County Public Health Records, and Allen County Birth and Marriage Records. In Auglaize County, Ohio, they pursued Probate Court Records, Birth Records, and Death Records. In Clinton County, Ohio, they searched Probate Court Records, Birth Records, Death Records, Marriage Records, and sources in the Clinton County Public Library. In Greene County, Ohio, they searched the Greene County Public Library and the Friends of the Greene Room. In Hardin County, Ohio, they reviewed the Probate Court Records, Birth Records, Death Records, and Marriage Records. In Selby County, Ohio, they reviewed Probate Court Records, Birth Records, Death Records, records of the County Public Library. In Preble County, Ohio, they searched the Probate Court Records, Birth Records, Death Records, and Marriage Records. They, too, found materials in the Ohio State Library (Columbus) and the Ohio State Historical Society (Columbus) to be helpful. In Montgomery County, Ohio, they reviewed Birth Records, Marriage Records, Probate Court Records, and materials in the Montgomery County Public Library. In Mercer County, Ohio, they reviewed material in the Mercer Public Library, and in the Warren County, Ohio, Historical Society, they reviewed stored material at that facility. They also received vauable information from the following family members: Descendants of James Arthur Iiams, Harvey Enos Iiames, Guy Ralston Iiames, Sr., Helen Irene Iiames Custer, William E. Iiams, and Barbara Locker.

In April 1994, **James B. Meighen** (808 Sampson Street, Monongahela, Pennsylvania, 15063), formerly of Waynesburg, Pennsylvania, with a life-long obsession in tracing the Iams and other Western Pennsylvania families, related how he became interested in genealogy and how it led to tracing family roots of a Frances White (b. ca1625 in County Essex in England, married a surgeon, Captain Richard Wells, and lived in Upper Norfolk County, Virginia) to King Edward III (Charles Martell) and to 80 B.C. Egypt (Mark Anthony). As a young man, James B. Meighen was interested in athletics but, because of severe, chronic osteomyelitis of the right femur in the 1930's, was forced to seek more sedentary activities. His father did abstract work for Consolidated Natural Gas, so often went to the Greene County Courthouse in Waynesburg. James often accompanied his father on this work, and soon became aware of the various records stored in the archives of the courthouse. Also, because of his chronic illness, he also became acquainted with Howard Leckey, a Waynesburg pharmacist and well-known local genealogist whose work is also referenced in this text. This association soon had James Meighen hooked, and he has spent most of his non-working hours on genealogical projects. His work has become widely accepted as being among the most carefully prepared and with only the most accurately described names, dates, places, and events. James B. Meighen is a graduate of Waynesburg College who spent a career working for Peoples Gas Company. After retirement, he worked as a geological consultant for an oil company. Among his other works is a published pamphlet which studies the energy patterns of tree movements that became a project of interest to Major General USAF MC Walter Tkasch, personal physician to President Richard M. Nixon, who is reported to have said, "Jim, I know you know what you are doing." Mr. Meighen has also studied effects of the various energies, including atomic energy plant locale, on surrounding plant and animal life. He has perfected a rod which has been used for at least three years to detect changes in energy pressure areas. Ahead of his time, and as described by Doctor Tkasch, it would be pointless to debate these issues in the current scientific world because if they did "call in the experts, all they would do would be to defend their own theses." Mr. James B. Meighen has graciously consented to provide much of his personal files on the Iams family for inclusion in this publication:

Frances White (b. ca1625, County Essex, England) married Captain Richard Wells (a surgeon, born in England in 1609) and they lived in Upper Norfolk County, Virginia. The daughter of Richard Wells (b. 1609) and Frances White (b. ca1625) was Mary Wells (b. 1642, Upper Norfolk County, Virginia) who married Captain Thomas Stockett. The daughter of Captain Thomas Stockett and Mary Wells (b. ca1642) was Elizabeth Stockett (b. ca1662, Anne Arundel County, Maryland). Elizabeth Stockett (b. ca1662) married Thomas Plummer (b. before 1630, England). Children of Thomas Plummer (b. before 1630) and Elizabeth Stockett were: Thomas Plummer, Margaret Plummer, Mary Plummer, Susanna Plummer, and Elizabeth

Plummer (b. ca1679, Anne Arundel County, Maryland). Elizabeth Plummer (b. ca1679) married William Ijams, a farmer (b. 1670, Anne Arundel County, Maryland). William Ijams (b. 1670) and Elizabeth Plummer (b. ca1679) had children, including 1) William Ijams (b. December 22, 1699, Anne Arundel County, Maryland, who married Elizabeth Jones (b. ca1679, Anne Arundel County, Maryland); 2) Elizabeth Ijams; 3) Richard Ijams; 4) Mary Ijams; 5) Thomas Ijams; 6) Captain John Ijams (b. 1712, Anne Arundel County, Maryland, who m. Rebecca Jones); 7) Plummer Ijams; 8) Annie Ijams; and 9) Charity Ijams.

This William Ijams (child number 1, b. December 22, 1699, Anne Arundel County, Maryland, who m. Elizabeth Jones who was b. 1704 in Harford County, Maryland) and Elizabeth Jones had the following children: 1) William Ijams; 2) Margaret Ijams; 3) Cassandra Ijams; 4) Thomas Plummer Iiams (b. ca1726); and 5) Sarah Ijams. The fourth child, Thomas Plummer Iiams (b. ca1726, Anne Arundel County, Maryland) married Mary Ijams (b. ca1735, daughter of Captain John Iiams, b. 1712, and Rebecca Jones). Children of Thomas Plummer Iiams (b. ca1726) and Mary Ijams (b. ca1735) included: 1) John Ijams (moved to Ohio); 2) Rebecca Ijams; and 3) Mary Plummer Ijams.

Mary Plummer Ijams (b. 1768, Anne Arundel County, Maryland) married William Penn (b. 1762, Baltimore County, Maryland, Revolutionary War) and died 1848 in Morris Township, Greene County, Pennsylvania. Children of William Penn (b. 1762) and Mary Plummer Ijams (b. 1768) included: 1) Richard Penn; 2) Mary Penn; 3) Nancy Penn; 4) Susannah Penn; 5) William Penn; 6) Nathan Penn; 7) Thomas Penn; 8) Matilda Penn; 9) John Penn; 10) Margaret Penn; 11) Sarah Penn; and 12) Ruth Penn.

John Iiams (b. 1712, Bridge Hill, Anne Arundel County, Maryland, Captain Revolutionary War effort, brother of William, b. December 22, 1699) married Rebecca Jones (daughter of Isaac Jones). John Iiams (b. 1712) was a prosperous merchant along South River, member of the South River Club, Warden in All Hallows Parish, a loyal patriot who took Oath of Fidelity in 1778, a Captain in the Colonial Militia who recruited soldiers for the Revolution and whose estate papers refer to him as Captain John Iiams. A daughter of Captain Thomas Iiams and Rebecca Jones was Mary Ijams (b. ca1735) who married her first cousin Thomas Plummer Ijams (b. ca1726), the son of William Ijams (b. 1699). William Ijams (b. 1699) and John Iiams (b. 1712) were brothers and sons of William Ijams (b. 1670), listed above.

James B. Meighen has written:
"Many years ago, Harry Wright Newman overwhelmed me with a very strong letter, stating that the genealogist Elisha Iams was incorrect in stating that William Iiams was the son of Robert Innes, (and that) this letter was so strong that I (even) withdrew my 3rd great-grandmother from the family of Thomas Iiams, and placed her as the daughter of (another) Thomas Iiams (b. 1708). After reviewing my notes, I am now convinced (that Harry Wright Newman was incorrect and) Elisha Iams was -correct." Mr. Meighen felt that the Cromwell Revolution resulted in several Catholic Scots, including the brother James of Progenitor William Iiams (d. 1703) in Innes, and that many of the followers of King Charles 1st, fled to Europe and on to Maryland between 1645 and 1660, thus illustrating the power of the "wrath of the Presbyterian Ministers and Cromwell." Additionally, Mr. Meighen pointed out some potential conflicts within the Newman outline of the Iams lineage, and also pointed out that Mr. "Newman (had) said Howard Leckey was incorrect in his book *The Ten Mile Country* when he placed Richard as the son of Richard (p. 482). Howard Leckey was described by James B. Meighen as being a "very thorough man and excellent researcher." Mr. Meighen further pointed out that Howard Leckey and Elisha Iams never got to compare notes, even though they both lived in Western Pennsylvania during the same era.

James B. Meighen, a life-long researcher of the Iams family tree has traced the family line to Edward III, King of England (b. 1312). Children of King Edward III included:

1. The Black Prince (b. 1330) who m. Joan Maid of Kent (b. 1328)
2. William (b. 1330), died in infancy
3. Prince Lionel (b. 1338) m. Lady de Burgh (b. 1332)
4. Sir Edmund Plantagenet m. Isabel Princess
5. Prince E. John of Gaunt (b. 1340) m. Lady Scoynford (b. 1350)
  1. John Beaufort (b. 1372) m. Margaret de Holand
    1. Joan Beaufort m. Sir Ralph de Neville m. Elizabeth de Beauchamp (b. 1415)
      1. Sir George de Neville (b. 1440) m. Lady Margaret Fenn
        1. Sir George de Neville m. Lady Mary Stafford
          1. Lady Ursula de Neville
        2. Sir Edward Neville m. Eleanor Windsor
          1. Frances Neville (b. 1519) m. Sir Edward Waldegrave (b. 1517)
            1. Nicholas Waldegrave m. Catherine Browne
              1. Frances Waldegrave m. Sir Richard Weston
                1. Lady Catherine Weston (b. 1607) m. Richard White
                  1. Frances White (baptized 1625) m. Richard Wells
                    1. Richard Wells (baptized 1641)
                    2. Anne Wells (baptized 1641)
                    3. Benjamin Wells (baptized 1641)
                    4. Elizabeth Wells (baptized 1641)
                    5. Frances Wells (baptized 1641)
                    6. George Wells (baptized 1641) - line of Helen Murdock
                    7. John Wells (baptized 1641)
                    8. Mary Wells (baptized 1642) m. Capt. Thomas Stockett
                      1. Thomas Stockett (baptized 1671)
                      2. Frances Stockett (b. 1671)
                      3. Elizabeth Stockett (b. 1662) m. Thomas Plummer
                        1. Thomas Plummer
                        2. Margaret Plummer
                        3. Mary Plummer
                        4. Susanna Plummer
                        5. Elizabeth Plummer (b. 1679) m. William Ijams (b. 1670)
                          1. Elizabeth Ijams (b. 1697)
                          2. William Ijams (b. 1721) m. Elizabeth Jones (b. 1764)
                            1. William Ijams (b. 1721)
                            2. Margaret Ijams (b. 1724)
                            3. Cassandra Ijams (b. 1722) m. Henry Leeke
                            4. Thomas Plummer Iiams (b. 1726)
      2. Edward Neville (b. 1516) m. Catherine Broune
      3. Lady de Neville (b. 1415) m. Richard Plantagenet (b. 1411)
      4. Richard E. de Neville
      5. Alice de Neville
    2. John Beaufort
  2. King Henry IV (b. 1367)
    1. King Henry V (b. 1387) m. Lady Catherine
      1. King Henry VI (b. 1421)
    2. Thomas D. Beaufort
    3. John Duke of Bedford

3. Philippa
4. Elizabeth Plantagenet
6. Thomas Plantagenet (b. 1355)

James B. Meighen has also written (1994) a proposed earlier extension to the accepted lineage of the American Progenitor William Eyams/Iiams (d. 1703) who m. Elizabeth Cheyney (b. 1652).

The parents of William Eyams/Iiams (d. 1703) were Robert Innes (b. 1621 in Scotland, House of Gordon) and Lady Grezil Stewart, daughter of the Earl of Murray.

The parents of Robert Innes (b. 1621) were Alexander Innes and Marjorie Gordon, who m. before 1587, and who had six children.

The parents of Marjorie Gordon were William Gordon and Isabel Ochterlony, the daughter of W. of Kelly.

The parents of William Gordon were John Gordon Laird of Gight and Marjory Gordon, daughter of First Laird of Lesmoir.

The parents of John Gordon Laird of Gight were William Gordon and Janet Ogilvie, the daughter of the Laird of Boyne.The parents of William Gordon were George Gordon, Second Earl of House of Stuart and Princess Annabella Stuart. The parents of Princess Annabella Stuart were James I, King of Scotland (b. 1394) and Joan Beaufort, the second wife of Ralph de Neville.

Additional children of Alexander Innes and Marjorie Gordon were: John Innes, Alexander Innes, James Innes, Patrick Innes, and George Innes.

On June 17, 1994, the editor received the following note, with the accompanying table, from noted Iams biographer and historian James B. Meighen. It is being included for future reference:

"Dear Dr. Reynolds:
Our visit as of the 15th was the most enjoyable experience for Helen and I.The chart shows the beginning of matter, when God concentrates and builds up to material and keeps building until the incoming force can no longer support the outgoing. As you can see, the world has not recognized the incoming current to matter.
Most sincerely yours, James B. Meighen"

Atomic Number	Sex	Valence	CPS Incoming Speed	Pressures motion	CPS Outgoing Speed	Color	Potential Voltage	Atomic Name	Vibrates to Note
1	F	-1	15483	2 length	.493	Blue		Unknown	G
2	F	-2	15957	3 breadth	.967	Blue		Unknown	A
3	F	-3	16541	4 thick	.45	Blue		Unknown	B
4	N		1451	4	16541			Inert Gas	
5	M	+1	1935	5 chakra	16935	Red		Survival	C
6	M	+2	2419	6 chakra	17419	Red		Creative	D
7	M	+3	2903	7 chakra	17903	Red		Emotional	E
8	M/F	+4 or -4	17903	8 chakra	2903				F
9	F	-1	18387	16 chakra	3387	Blue	.0000002	Throat	G
10	F	-2	18870	24 chakra	3870	Blue	.0000004	3rd., Eye	A
11	F	-3	19354	32 chakra	4354	Blue	.0000005	Crown	B
12	N		4354	32	19354		.0000005	Inert Gas	
13	M	+1	4839	40	19838	Red	.0000007	Radio	C
14	M	+2	5322	48	20322	Red	.0000009	Emotional	D
15	M	+3	5806	56	20806	Red	.0000010	Infrared	E
16	M/F	+4 or -4	20806	64	5806		.0000011	Ultraviolet	F
17	F	-1	21290	128	6290	Blue	.0000022	X-Ray	G
18	F	-2	21744	192	6774	Blue	.0000034	Gamma	A
19	F	-3	22528	256	7258	Blue	.0000045	Cosmic	B
20	N		7256	256	22528		.0000045	Inert Gas	
21	M	+1	7741	320	22741	Red	.0000057	Hydrogen Gas	C

22	M	+2	8225	384	23225	Red	.0000068	Unknown	D
23	M	+3	8709	448	23709	Red	.0000080	Unknown	E
24	M/F	+4/-4	23709	512	8709		.0000091	Unknown	F
25	F	+-1	24193	1024	9193	Blue	.0000183	Unknown	G
26	F	-2	24679	1536	9677	Blue	.0002749	Ozone	A
27	F	-3	25161	2048	10161	Blue	.000366	Unknown	B
28			10161	2048	25161		.000366	Inert Gas	
29	M	+1	10625	2560	25645	Red	.000458	Lithium Gas	C
30	M	+2	11129	3072	26129	Red	.005496	Berylium Gas	D

The Speeds are expressed in millions of centimeters per second

31	M	+3	11612	3584	26512	Red	.006412	Boron Gas	E
32	M	+4/-4	26612	4096	11612		.007324	Carbon Gas	F
33	F	-1	27076	8192	12096	Blue	.01464-V	Nitrogen Gas	G
34		-2	27580	12228	12580	Blue	.02197-V	Oxygen Gas	A
35		-3	28064	16384	13064	Blue	.02929-V	Flourine Gas	B
36	N		13064	16384	28064		.02929 V	Helium Inert	
37	/ M	+1	13549	20480	28549	Red	.03662	Lithium	C
38	M	+2	14032	24576	29032	Red	.04394	Berylium	D
39	M	+3	14516	28672	29516	Red	.05126	Boron	E
40	M	+4/-4	30000	32768	15000		.05859-V	Carbon Diamond	F
41	F	-1	29516	65536	15484	Blue	.001162	Nitrogen	G
42	F	-2	29032	98304	15968	Blue	.001752	Oxygen	A
43	F	-3	28548	131072	16451	Blue	.002342	Flourine	B
44	N		16451	131072	16451	Neither	.002342	Neon	
45	M	+1	16935	163804	28064	Red	.002914	Sodium	C
46	M	+2	17419	196608	27580	Red	.003504	Magnesium	D
47	M	+3	17902	229376	27096	Red	.004094	Aluminum	E
48		+4 or -4	27096	262144	17902	Either	.004684	Silicon	F
49	F	-1	26612	524288	18387	Blue	.009369	Phosporus	G
50	F	-2	26129	736432	18870	Blue	.014054	Sulfur	A
51	F	-3	25645	1048576	19354	Blue	.018739	Chlorine	B
52			19354	1048576	19354	Neither	.019739	Argone	
53	M	+1	19838	1572864	25161	Red	.023424	Potassium	C
54	M	+2	20322	1835008	24677	Red	.028109	Calcium	D
55	M	+3	20806	1867776	24193	Red	.032812	Scandium	E
56			21338	1900544	24161		.033384	Titanium	
57			21870	1900544	24129		.033974	Vanadium	
58			22403	1933312	24096		.034564	Chromium	
59			22935	1966080	24064		.035154	Manganese	
60			23467	1998848	24032		.035548	Iron	
61		+4 or -4	24193	2097152	23467	Either	.037497	Cobalt	F
62			23951	2883584	23548		.051552	Nickle	
63			23903	3145728	23095		.056237	Copper	
64			23954	3407872	22645		.060921	Zinc	
65			23806	3670016	22193		.065624	Gallium	
66			23758	3932160	21741		.070309	Germanium	
67	F	-1	23709	4194304	21290	Blue	.074994	Arsenic	G
68	F	-2	23225	6291456	21774	Blue	.112491	Selenium	A
69	F	-3	22741	8388606	22258	Blue	.149989	Bromine	B
70			22258	9388606	22258	Neither	.149989	Krypton	
71	M	+1	22528	10485760	22741	Red	.187485	Rubidium	C
72	M	+2	21744	12582912	23225	Red	.224993	Strontium	D
73	M	+3	21290	14680064	23709	Red	.262499	Yttrium	E
74			21241	14942208	23258		.267184	Zirconium	
75			21193	15204352	22806		.271868	Niobium	
76			21145	15466496	22354		.273524	Molybdenum	
77			21095	15728640	21902		.281238	Technetium	
78			21048	15990794	21451		.286057	Ruthenium	
79		+4 or -4	23709	16777216	21048	Either	.299995	Rhodium	F
80			21532	23068672	20967		.412468	Palladium	
81			22064	25165824	20935		.449996	Silver	
82			22596	27262976	20903		.487483	Cadmium	
83			23129	29360128	20370		.524998	Indium	
84			23661	31457280	20838		.562495	Tin	
85	F	-1	24193	33554432	20806	Blue	.599990	Antimony	G
86	F	-2	24667	50331648	20322	Blue	.899998	Tellurium	A
87	F	-3	25161	67108864	19838	Blue	1.999855	Iodine	B
88									
89	M	+1	19354	83886080	25645	Red	1.500000	Cesium	C
90	M	+2	18870	100663296	26129	Red	1.722977	Barium	D
91	M	+3	18387	117440512	26612	Red	2.099992	Lanthanum	E

92			18359	118638384	25997		2.121414	Cerium
93			18331	119937256	25382		2.142854	Praseodymum
94			18304	121035628	24767		2.164276	Neodymium
95			18276	122234000	24125		2.185716	Promethium
96			18248	123432372	23536		2.207138	Samarium
97			18221	124630744	22921		2.228560	Europium
98			18193	125829116	22306		2.25	Gadolinium
99			18165	127027489	21691		2.271421	Terbium
100			18138	128225860	21076		2.292843	Dysprosium
101			18110	129424232	20460		2.314283	Holmium
102			18082	130622604	19845		2.336420	Erbium
103			18055	131820976	19230		2.357127	Thulium
104			18027	133019348	18615		2.378567	Yttrium
105		+4 or -4	26612	134217728	18027	Either	2.399989	Lutecium F
106			18758	145402538	17991		2.599992	Hafnuim
107			19516	156587348	17698		2.799996	Tantalum
108			20274	167772158	17975		3.000000	Tungsten
109			21032	178956968	17967		3.199982	Ytterbium
110			21790	190141778	17959		3.399989	Osmium
111			22548	201326588	17951		3.599992	Iridium
112			23306	212511398	17943		3.799996	Platinum
113			24064	223696208	17935		4.000000	Gold
114			24822	234881108	17927		4.200003	Mercury
115			25580	246065828	17919		4.399989	Thallium
116			26338	257250638	17911		4.599992	Lead
118	F	-2	27580	402653184	17419	Blue	7.2000	Polonium A
119	F	-3	28064	536870912	16935	Blue	9.4211	Astatine B
120			16935	536870912	16935	Neither	9.4211	Radon
121	M	+1	16451	671088640	28548	Red	12.0000	Francium C
122	M	+2	15967	805306368	29032	Red	14.4000	Radium D
123	M	+3	15483	939524096	29516	Red	16.8000	Astatine E
124			15446	949848536	29553		16.9667	Thorium
125			15409	960172976	29590		17.1692	Protactium
126			15372	970497416	29627		17.3538	Uranium
127			15334	980821856	29665		17.538	Neptuniumnum
128			15297	991146296	29702		17.7271	Plutonium
129			15260	1001470736	29739		17.9076	Americanium
130			15223	1011795176	29776		18.0923	Cerium
131			15186	1022119616	29813		18.2769	Berkelium
132			15148	1032444056	29851		18.4615	Carifornum

Carmen Harleston has written:

Ijames came form Wales to London. He had two sons. Either those two boys or their two sons came to the United States around the year 1790. One son bought 400 acres of land west of Philadelphia, about 30 miles west of Jamesville.

The second son was married and had four sons. They came west and: 1) one son moved to Washington County; 2) one went to Greene County; 3) one moved to Monroe County, Ohio; 4) and one moved to Indiana. One of the original two married at age 35, but prior to his getting married, he fathered three children with a high yellow slave. The female and the children moved to Baltimore.

One of their descendants is Doctor Lake Iams, who was working at Johns Hopkins Hospital when he gave this story to John Iams of New Martinsville, West Virginia.

CONTRIBUTING EDITORS

Paul Iams, Sun City, Arizona
Margaret Iams, San Diego, California
James Iams Cerney, M.D., Zanesville, Ohio
Dorothy Iams, North Canton, Ohio
Jean Griffen, Canton, Ohio
Ken (Eileen) Bame, Findlay, Ohio
Sue Rulfs, Ann Arbor, Michigan
Donald Iams, Washington, Pennsylvania
Sherwin W. Iams, Waynesburg, Pennsylvania
Ohlin R. Iiams, Hemet, California
Evelyn Magnuson, Albert Lea, New York
Mary Iams Grimes, Waynesburg, Pennsylvania
Thomas Imes, Kendallsville, Indiana
Harriet Imes Haase, Winthrop, Washington
Jeffrey Lynn Imes, Rolla, Missouri
Nellie Mae Imes, Columbus, Ohio
James Iams, Troy, Ohio
Russell F. Iiams, Los Alamitos, California
Wilda L. Iams, Marietta, Ohio
Edward Iames, Cape May, New Jersey
Duane Iams, Plum, Pennsylvania
Jan Sharp, Defiance, Ohio
Conchetta Geis, Red Key, Indiana
Charlotte Corbett, Bellaire, Ohio
Meek Corbett, Key, Ohio
George E. Iams, Mishawaka, Indiana
Robert Elton Iams, Seattle, Washington
David Aveling Iams, Philadelphia, Pennsylvania
Lois M. Neely, Conover, South Carolina
Mildred C. McKelvey, Lebanon, Ohio
Edna Corbett Reynolds, Columbus, Ohio
Bill Iams, M.D., Cumberland, Maryland
William B. Iams, M.D., Camp Hill, Pennsylvania
Jay D. Iams, M.D., Columbus, Ohio
Jennifer Iams, Hillsboro, Ohio
Ray E. Iams, Ada, Ohio
Earl Iams, Mount Blanchard, Ohio
Zail E. Spear, Caldwell, Ohio
Wendell Iams, Geneses, Illinois
Rodger A. Hagmaier, Hudson, Ohio
Wilma Bircher, Harrisville, West Virginia
Betty Iams Kromi, Canton, Ohio
Mildred P. Beck, Columbus, Ohio
Jeanne K. Starkey, Marietta, Ohio
Rev. Harold N. Imes, Mifflintown, Pennsylvania
Mary Iams Dobich, Bridgeport, New Jersey
Pauline Z. Imes, New Athens, Illinois
Betty C. Iams, Washington, Pennsylvania
Jack S. Iams, Silver Spring, Maryland

Paul C. Iams, Pittsburgh, Pennsylvania
Betty Iams, San Diego, California
Joan M. Iams, Canton, Ohio
William A. Iams, Washington, Pennsylvania
Mary S. Iams, Indianapolis, Indiana
John W. Iams, South Bend, Indiana
Robert T. Forest, Sparks, Nevada
Ruth Scott McCord, Washington, Pennsylvania
Donald D. Imes, Roaring Springs, Pennsylvania
Carol C. Paprocki, Columbus, Ohio
William (Ruby) Iams, St. Matthews, South Carolina
Chris Iams, Berkeley, California
Mary C. Iams, McMinnville, Tennessee
Elmer Iams, Flagstaff, Arizona
W. Roger Iams, Hamilton, Ohio
Sandra J. Wright, Mt. Carmel, Illinois
Sally Iams Ross, Long Beach, California
Ivan E. Imes, Baton Rouge, Louisiana
Sandra M. Iams, Indianapolis, Indiana
Jim Ijams, Tucson, Arizona
Wilda L. Iams, Marietta, Ohio
Bill Iams, Bedford, Ohio
Sarah Iams Cain, Crucible, Pennsylvania
Norita S. Reynolds, Kirksville, Missouri
Isabel B. Iams Griffith, Helena, Montana
Dr. Howard (Ella) Iams, Bethesda, Maryland
Allen Bare, Macon, Georgia
John Frederick Iams, Poway, California
John W. Iams, South Bend, Indiana
Stanley (Virginia) Braxton, Wynnewood, Pennsylvania
Kathryn Shipley, Wheeling, West Virginia
G. David (Mrs.) Koch, Terre Haute, Indiana
Ann A. Heckathorne, Carlsville, Illinois
Rev. Carl P. Ijams, Tucson, Arizona
James Oscar Ijams, Lennox, California
Mary Lou Iams
Martha K. Anspaugh
Dorothy L. Iams
Stanley Iams
William "Bob" Iams
Sarah Iams Hoagland
John E. Iams
Charles E. Buckingham
Geraldine E. I. Cheslick
Tim Duke
Robert F. Iams
Suzanne G. Long
James Frank Iams
Eleanor Jones
Elsie W. Ijams
Linda Amey

Barbara Locker
Jack L. Iams
Jeanne Iams Kilmer

LEGEND

b. "born on date," or earliest date known
d. date of death
m. date of marriage, or date of license

Every effort has been made to minimize abbreviations, except for those listed above. Some slip-ups will be noted, just as errors and disagreements will be found. Apologies are offered for omissions that are found. A friendly note of additions and corrections will be appreciated. While there is no perfect style in presenting vital data, it is hoped that the reader will enjoy the narrative style used in this book. There turned out to be more Iams, etc., than was anticipated. Hopefully, the Index will help you become oriented with regard to your personal Iams family connection. Corrections for early calendar dates will be necessary for the purists. Literally hundreds of persons have contributed to this works. Hopefully, most have been listed.

BACKGROUND INFORMATION

Harley Iams
Harley Iams, an inventor of television, primarily quoting the work of Newman, felt that the Iams were originally from Scotland or Wales and that the English spelling had been Ian, the Scot equivalent of John, or Ion, the Welsh variant. The most common early American version used the Iiams version of the spelling. The branch of the family that settled in Davidson, Davies Counties, in North Carolina are said to have come under the teachings of Marshall Ney, who convinced them both that they were originally French and that the spelling should be Ijams. This spelling also became more common in the West. The family branch migrating from Maryland to Western Pennsylvania, Ohio, West Virginia, and points West kept the Iiams spelling for a time, but most changed to Iams by the time they had reached Western Pennsylvania.

In a letter from Governor Ogle, South Carolina, to Charles, Lord Baltimore, in 1731, describes a "Mr. Eyoms, who was recommended...is exacting, such a one as your Lordship guessed him to be. He talks a great deal of husbandry and improving land, and at the same time is perfectly indolent and incapable of serving either himself or family...." Also, a will of a Richard Eyams, "late of Enstone in Oxford and now of city of Annapolis," was proved in Annapolis, February 18, 1734, and he named wife Jane and children Richard and Jane.

Harley Iams also pointed out that there is a town in Denmark by the name of "Ans," and pointed out that the initial "I" was sometimes used to mean "mountain" or "mount," hence the name "I'ans," as can be found in the British Isles.

Harley Iams and wife Margaret, San Diego, California, wrote in 1971, based on E. B. Iams correspondence with Harley Iams and sister Gertrude Iams Bennett:

William Iiams of Wales m. Miss Jones and they moved to Maryland 1660 and the family lived in Anne Arundel County. From this settlement, five brothers moved to Washington County, Pennsylvania, area (then called Manongahela County, Virginia) after the Revolutionary War. Richard Iiams settled at Niniveh (now Greene

County, Pennsylvania); Jeff Iiams, a bachelor, lived with Richard; John Iiams lived on Ten Mill and built the first mill west of the Monongahela River and Allegheny Mountains (later called Martin's Mill); William Iiams and John Iiams who both settled along the Kentucky Trail in West Bethlehem Township, Washington County, Pennsylvania, where they operated a linseed oil mill. John Iiams married Elizabeth Hampton; William Iiams married Mary Hampton; and Thomas Iiams married Catherine Hampton. E. B. Iiams descended from John Iiams, and Wesley Iiams descended from Thomas Iiams (a Sgt., Revolutionary War). A son of Thomas and Catherine Hampton Iiams was William Iiams who married Susannah Sharp who lived at Amity, Amwell Township, Washington County, Pennsylvania. Children of William and Susannah Sharp Iiams were: Salam, Jehu, Franklin, Wesley, Elizabeth, Jane, Elenor, and Delilah. This Wesley was the father of John Iiams, father of Harley Iiams; and of Iola Ellen Iams, mother of Edna Louise Corbett Reynolds.

William Eyams belonged to All Hallow's Parish where the marriage and baptisms of descendants were held. William Eyams "was buried from the parish church on July 29, 1703." His will was dated February 16, 1698 and was probated in Anne Arundel County, Maryland, on November 10, 1703, with Richard Cheyney and Robert Davis as witnesses. He left 100 acres of land near the Patuxent River in Prince Georges County to son Richard certified they were brothers, aged 59 and 56, respectively. In 1726, widow Elizabeth vowed to being aged 74, remembered her father saying that the land should go to her brothers Thomas and Charles.

William Iiams (b. 1670), the son of Pioneer William Eyams, was born in the South River Hundred in Anne Arundel County, and married Elizabeth Plummer, or Ploummer, a Quaker, on August 27, 1696. This William Iiams (b. 1670) lived at Bridge Hill, originally surveyed in 1669 for Henry Stockett, and also owned 64 acres of Dodon, the land of Burgess Choice and of Cheyney's Resolution. The will of this William Iiams (b. 1670), in 1738, left the land first to his wife Elizabeth Plummer Iiams, and secondly to children John, Plummer, and Anne (Iiams) Williams.

Thomas (b. 1708), the son of William (b. 1670) and Elizabeth Plummer Iiams, was born at Bridge Hill, All Hallow's Parish, Anne Arundel County, Maryland, and with his brother Captain John Iiams (b. 1712) was the executor of the estate of their father. On April 17, 1730, Thomas (b. 1708) purchased a portion of Duval's Delight from Charles Carrol of Annapolis, Maryland, and ten years later purchased a second part of that same property, from Charles and Mary Hogan. In his will of 1768, Thomas (b. 1708) left his estate to his four sons and one daughter: John (b. 1750), Thomas, Richard, William (b. 1750) and Susannah Iiams Pumphrey. Not named were three other children. Son Thomas was the executor of the will, with the estate inventory entered into the Annapolis court record July 14, 1769. Elizabeth and John signed as kinsmen. At the 1770 settlement, the estate was divided among seven unnamed representatives. Son Thomas (b. 1754) had been born in All Hallow's Parish, Anne Arundel County, Maryland (Newman, 1933), and was in attendance at the 1770 court settlement of the estate of his father when 97 pounds each was distributed to the seven representatives. On January 10, 1777, Thomas (b. 1754) enlisted in the Maryland Line with the company commanded by Captain Richard Stringer, and by March 20, 1777, had been promoted to Sergeant and was in charge of a recruiting party. In May 1977, Thomas (b. 1754) created something of a stir when he ordered his men to "fire and fix their bayonets," but the details are unknown. This episode resulted in posting a bond of 100 pounds and an appearance at the Prince George's Court House before Judge Christopher E. B. Loundes. The outcome of this trial is not known, but he remained a Sergeant, and on July 17, 1778, he received "linen for two pairs of trousers, two jackets, two shirts and for one coatee and trimmings suitable," making it appear that his order to "fire and fix bayonets" was justified. Thomas (b. 1754) was discharged January 1, 1780, and was granted a pension. Thomas (b. 1754) also played a big part in the organization of the Methodist Church in Anne Arundel County, Maryland. On April 5, 1783, Thomas (b. 1754) and others of Anne Arundel County and Prince George's County purchased one acre of land owned by Richard Jones for the building of a house "for the use of Methodist Preachers." Other collaborators included Nicholas Ridgely, Greenbury Ridgely, Seth Hyatt, Shadrick Turner, Benjamin Waters, and Thomas Duval. A Baltimore County, Maryland, marriage license lists the marriage of Thomas Iiams and Catherine Gill Hampton, daughter of Thomas Gill Hampton of Anne Arundel County, Maryland, on November 29, 1785. The Hamptons later moved to Washington County, Pennsylvania, as did many of the Iiams family, including Thomas (b. 1754) and his wife Catherine Gill Hampton Iiams. Thomas (b. 1754) moved to Bethlehem Township, Washington County, Pennsylvania, in 1793. This Thomas (b. 1754) apparently sold the land called Duval's Delight, in Anne Arundel County, Maryland, to his sister and son-in-law Mary Iams Penn and Joseph Penn for 200 pounds, in 1786; and in 1792 he had been named as one of the sureties for the estate of Joseph Penn of Anne Arundel County. This estate was not settled until May 29, 1792, the year before the westward migration of Thomas (b. 1754). In 1833, Thomas (b. 1754) moved to Richland Township, near Glencoe, Belmont County, Ohio, where he died on June 24, 1834. He is buried at the now-abandoned Old Dutch (or Ault Cemetery) in Richland Township, Belmont County, Ohio, with his wife and son Samuel (b. 1795). The Revolutionary Pension Act was passed in 1832 and although he applied for and was granted a pension, he never lived long enough to receive any of the money. He had promised his first pension to his youngest grandson, Thomas Ault, the son of his daughter Catherine Iiams Ault and Michael Ault of Belmont County, Ohio. Thomas (b. 1754) is often referred to in the family discussion as "The Revolutionary War" soldier and serves as a pivotal reference for the various branches of the Iiams family to determine their inter-relationships. Sons of Thomas (b. 1754) included John, Samuel, Thomas, Richard, William and Rezin. Daughters included Elizabeth, Charity, Polly, Rebecca, and Catherine.

PATRIOTS OF THE AMERICAN REVOLUTION

Several members of the Iams/Ijams/Iiams family served their country during the American Revolution. Each of these patriots can trace their origin to the state of Maryland, and nearly all were from Anne Arundel County, Maryland. The following listing was taken from three sources: 1) Henry C. Peden, Jr., *Revolutionary Patriots of Anne Arundel County, Maryland*, Family Line Publishers, Westminster, Maryland, 1992; 2) J. D. Warfield, *The Founders of Anne Arundel and Howard Counties, Maryland*, Kohn and Pollock Publishers, Baltimore, 1905; and 3) F. B. Heitman, *Historical Register of Officers of the Continental Army During the War of the Revolution, April 1775 to December 1783*, Washington, 1893.

1. Ijams, John, Jr. From Maryland, 3rd Lieutenant of Watkins Independent Maryland Company of Cannoneers, January 1776.

2. Ijams, John, I. Recommended for rank of ensign, Anne Arundel County, Maryland, 1776.

3. Ijams, Jacob. Son of George and Elizabeth Ijams and father of William Ijams. Took Oath of Allegiance before Honorable Richard Harwood, Jr., March 1, 1778, in Anne Arundel County, Maryland.

4. Ijams/Iiams, John. Born 1712 and died 1783. Son of William Ijams and Elizabeth Plummer. Married Rebecca Jones. Father of Elizabeth Ijams Fenley, Anne Ijams Stockett, Mary Ijams Ijams, William Ijams, Isaac Ijams, Thomas Plummer Ijams, John Ijams, and Rebecca Ijams Sunderland. A wealthy merchant who was elected to the prestigious South River Club in Anne Arundel County in 1744. Called Captain because of his service in the colonial militia. Took Oath of Allegiance before Honorable Richard Harwood, Jr., March 1, 1778.

5. Ijams, John, Jr. Born about 1755 and died 1823. Son of John Ijams and Rebecca Jones. Married in 1782, Frederick County, Maryland, to Mary Waters. Father of Jacob Ijams, John Waters Ijams, Plummer Ijams, Anne Ijams McLaughlin, Jane Ijams Burgee, Elizabeth Ijams Duvall, and Mary Ijams Montgomery. Recommended for Ensign, September 16, 1776, in Anne Arundel County. Served as 2nd Lieutenant in Thomas Watkins' Company in West River Battalion in 1778; was Captain 1780-1781, involved in recruiting. Took Oath of Allegiance before Honorable Richard Harwood, Jr., March 1, 1778.

6. Ijams, John. Born November 18, 1725, and died 1789. Son of George and Elizabeth Ijams. Married the widow of Nicholas Watkins, Ariana Worthington, in 1758. Father of Vachel Ijams, Brice Ijams, Ariana Ijams Hendren, Beale Ijams, Denton Ijams, and Nicholas W. Ijams. Took Oath of Allegiance in 1778 in Anne Arundel County, but later moved to Prince George's County.

7. Ijams, John. Born October 20, 1747, and died June 2, 1785. Son of Thomas and Artridge Ijams. Married Susanna Taylor (Watkins) in 1778. Took Oath of Allegiance before Honorable Richard Harwood, Jr., March 1, 1778, Anne Arundel County.

8. Ijams, John. Born June 5, 1756, and died 1791. Son of Plummer Ijams and Ruth Childs. Never married. Took Oath of Allegiance before Honorable Richard Harwood, Jr., March 1, 1778, in Anne Arundel County.

9. Ijams, John. Resigned 3rd Lieutenant Commission of an Artillery Company, May 31, 1777, Anne Arundel County.

10. Ijams, John Frederick. Born in Maryland 1765 and died in Tennessee on January 24, 1839. Lived in Prince George's County, Maryland, when he enlisted in 1780 at Annapolis. He served at Yorktown in 1781, under Colonel Peter Adams' First Maryland Regiment and was discharged in 1783. Moved to Virginia, then married Mary Johnson about 1789 in Wilkes County, Georgia. Applied for a pension from Grainger County, Tennessee, in 1833.

11. Ijams/Iiams, Plummer. Born 1716 and died November 26, 1792. Son of William Ijams and Elizabeth Plummer. Married Ruth Childs about 1747. Father of Plummer Ijams, Elizabeth Ijams Drury, Margaret Ijams Selby, John Ijams, and Ann Ijams Drury. Took Oath of Allegiance on March 1, 1778, in Anne Arundel County, before Honorable Richard Harwood, Jr.

12. Ijams, Plummer, Jr. Born October 29, 1748, and died in February 1795. Son of Plummer Ijams and Ruth Childs. Married in 1760 to Jemima Welsh. Father of Anne Ijams Sacks, Plummer Ijams, Ruth Ijams Mussetter, Rebecca Ijams Duvall, and John Ijams. Took Oath of Allegiance in Maryland, in March 1778, before Honorable Nicholas Worthington.

13. Ijams, Thomas. Born in Maryland December 26, 1754, and died in Belmont County June 24, 1834. Son of John Ijams and grandson of Richard Ijams. Served three months under Colonel Thomas Dorsey as a private in the state militia. Married Catherine G. Hampton in 1785 in Baltimore County, Maryland. Had moved to Washington County, Pennsylvania, by 1793. Applied for pension in 1834 from Belmont County, Ohio. He and his wife are buried in Old Dutch Cemetery, South of Saint Clairsville, near Glencoe, Ohio.

14. Ijams/Iiams, Thomas. Two men of this name took Oath of Allegiance in March 1778. One was born in 1745, died in 1806, and had married Mary Ijams.

15. Ijams, Vachel. Born in Maryland in January 1759 and died in Alabama on January 20, 1833. Son of John Ijams and Ariana Worthington. Enlisted in Captain Watkins Company in September 1776 and discharged December 18, 1776. His second enlistment was in August 1777, and served at Battle of Germantown in Captain Brogdeu's Company, being discharged in October 1777. His third enlistment was in the militia in Prince George's County, Maryland, in 1781, receiving his discharge December 11, 1781. His fourth enlistment, from Rowan County, North Carolina, was as a Sergeant in Captain Sharpe's Company in 1782 and 1783, married in 1789 to Lilah Gaither, who died shortly after their marriage; and in 1791 he married Martha Cunningham. Father of Joseph Ijams, Basil Gaither Ijams, Burgess Ijams, Wilson Ijams, Pearson Ijams, Nancy Ijams Bollen McDamrock, Elizabeth Ijams Hernden and Margaret Ijams Edwards. Died in Lauderdale County, and buried in private cemetery near Florence, Alabama.

16. Ijams/Iiams, William. Took Oath of Allegiance, Anne Arundel County, Maryland, March 2, 1778, before Honorable Thomas Dorsey.

17. Ijams, William. Born November 26, 1755. Son of Thomas and Artridge Ijams. Married in 1782 to Charity Ryan. Took the Oath of Allegiance February 28, 1778, before Honorable Thomas Worthington.

18. Ijams, William. Born December 22, 1723, and died in November 1780, son of George Ijams and Elizabeth Basford. Married to Elizabeth in 1764, and to widow Anne Ijams Williams in 1770. No known children. Took Oath of Allegiance in Anne Arundel County on March 1, 1778, before Honorable Richard Harwood, Jr.

19. Ijams, William. Son of John Ijams and Rebecca Jones. Married to Elizabeth Howard. Father of Richard D. Ijams, William Howard Ijams, Rebecca Ijams, Rachel Ijams, Mary Ijams, Comfort Ijams, Sarah Ijams, John Ijams, Joseph Howard Ijams, Frederick Ijams, and Isaac Ijams. Took Oath of Allegiance in Anne Arundel County, Maryland, before Honorable Richard Harwood, Jr. on March 1, 1778. Died in Faufield County, Ohio, in 1816.

THE NATIONAL IAMS ASSOCIATION

Elisha B. Iams, J. Howard Iams, E. Jay Iams, and other members of the Iams clan of Western Pennsylvania organized the National Iams Association in the early 1930's, but the organization became inactive after the outbreak of the second World War and the subsequent death of Elisha B. Iams in 1944. At one time, the organization was reported to be ten thousand members strong. At the second annual reunion held in Washington, Pennsylvania, August 27, 1932, five hundred people attended

A deteriorated newspaper account of the event was published in the Washington, Pennsylvania, newspaper, and described the events held under the direction of James S. Iams and Mr. J. L. Hook of Waynesburg, Pennsylvania. Entertainment included an orchestra of students of the Washington Seminary, under the direction of Miss Marjorie Patterson. The invocation was given by Reverend John Myers of Toledo, Ohio. Mrs. Gladys Blackburn, a graduate of King's School of Oratory gave several humorous readings; as did Mrs. Mary Miller Smith, a former school teacher. Miss Hilda Conner, a graduate of Waynesburg Conservatory of Music, provided a piano solo. The keynote speaker was Harry Wright Newman, noted author and researcher of the Iams family background. Mr. Newman, of the United States Department of Commerce in Washington, D.C. gave a scholarly description of the early colonial history of William Iams, the pioneer. William Iams was a vestryman in the South River district of Maryland, and that church remains standing today. Mr. Newman commended the efforts of the Western Pennsylvania group in organizing the reunion, and agreed to serve as President of the Maryland branch of the Iams clan. Other speakers included Mrs. Browning and Reverend John Iams Myers of the Ohio clan; Roy Lee Iams of the Topeka, Kansas, clan; Doctor John Robb of Pittsburgh; and John Howdenshield.

James Monroe Ijames of Kansas was elected unanimously as the honorary president of the Association, the organization's highest honor. Mr. James Monroe Ijames was born in North Carolina on May 4, 1843, and served in the Civil War in the Fifth Carolina Infantry. He reportedly saw action for the Confederacy from Antietam to Petersburg. He was a member of Pickett's charge at Gettysburg in July 1863. He was 89 years old at the time of his election in 1932. He was one of 43 survivors of his regiment, and had been taken prisoner. Two of his brothers were killed at the battle of Seven Pines. After his return to his home, he found his parents were being cared for by a Union/Yank soldier who had escaped a Southern prison camp. Gifts to the Association were also made by W. C. Iams of Missouri, Cass M. Iams of South Carolina (a case of plug tobacco from his plantation), and by Earl R. Buys, representing the Goodyear Rubber Company of Akron.

The **Elsie Iams Narrative** (pp. 29-31) (from *The Tower, North Ten Mile Baptist Church*, March 1972):

Elsie White Iams and her sister Hazel White McCullough, daughters of Omer D. White, remember making trips to the Martin Mill with loads of wheat in their heavy road wagon pulled by a team of Percheron horses. "Sitting on the high seat with legs dangling in mid air would not be considered the best ride in the world today, but it was exciting. Mr. Martin was always very helpful and kind in helping us off and on the big high seat. In the meantime, the flour dust, the noise, and the movement of the machinery were a never-ending fascination to two country lassies."

The original mill is believed to have been built by a Mr. Keys in the 1780's, and he sold the land to John Iams (b. 1750) who built a new, more substantial mill by 1840. The land, called "Industry," had been patented by John Keys on May 15, 1790, with survey made February 12, 1788, and contained 400 acres, probably including a November 17, 1787, claim by a John Chamberlain. John Iams bought the land on June 3, 1816, and on May 17, 1839, the heirs of John Iiams sold the land to John Iiams, Jr. John Iiams, Sr. was a well-known miller and millright. Included in the deed, as heirs of John Iiams, Sr. were: William Iams and wife Delilah, Joseph Martin and wife Nancy Iams, John D. Smith and wife Mary Iams, and John Iams, Jr.

Each of the five shares were believed to consist of 74 acres and 73 perches, and all conveyed their shares to John Iams, Jr. who operated the mill until May 31, 1844, when he conveyed the land to Joseph Martin and his wife Nancy Iams Martin, the latter being the sister of John Iams Jr. The deed of this transaction described the property as being "a log house 30 ft. by 20 ft., one and a half stories high, with a cellar under the whole house; a frame barn 36 ft. by 22 ft., and a grist mill 4-1/2 stories high with four run of stone, two pairs of which are French Buhrs and two pairs of Laurel Hill Buhrs (sandstone), five bolting clocks, three of which are merchant and two common, a ___ machine, a double rolling screen and a sawmill." The transaction brought $3,250. Joseph Martin ___ passed the mill on to William R. Martin and Morgan Martin, with William R. Martin operating the mill for 60 years, before dying and being buried in Franklin Cemetery. The mill has recently been known as the Martin Mill, and was earlier called the Iiams Mill. The earliest name was undoubtedly the Keys Mill. The mill was originally water powered, and some evidence of the old mill race may still be found along Ten Mile Creek.

Joseph Martin was b. March 15, 1790, d. December 25, 1850, m. December 27, 1821 to Nancy Iams (d. January 21, 1871, age 84 years and 11 days), daughter of John Iams (b. 1750) and Elizabeth Hampton. Children of Joseph Martin and Nancy Iams included: Morgan Martin (b. October 19, 1823, m. Anna Rees), Elizabeth Martin, John Martin, Joseph Martin, Jr., Anna Martin, and Jacob Martin.

EARLY NEWSPAPER ACCOUNTS

1670 Iiams Reunion 1931
North Ten Mile Baptist Church
Saturday, August 29, 1931

Morning Observer, Washington, Pennsylvania, August 31, 1931

The first national reunion of the Ijams clan descendants of William Ijams, who came to the United States from Wales, was held at North Ten Mile Baptist Church Saturday. About 500 persons representing Iamses from various sections of the United States attended. The forenoon was spent in exchanging greeting and visiting places of interest to the clan assembled. Dinner was served at 2:00, and were entertained by the Garrett Orchestra, who are members of the clan, and a local quartet, and speakers from Kansas, North Carolina, Tennessee, Florida, West Virginia, Ohio, and Pennsylvania. Many have won distinction in their professions. Members have participated in every war of this country.

William Iiams, a descendant of the Royal family of England, settled in Maryland in 1670, had three sons from whom there are thousands of descendants. These sons migrated to North Carolina, Pennsylvania, and the middle west, and from there to all parts of the union. A member from each branch was present. In the Civil War, those of the North fought for the Union and those in the South for the Confederacy. On each side, some were killed in action, others wounded, and numerous died in prison. A representative from the South told of an interesting experience that his father had with his slaves. When he dismissed them and told them that they were to care for themselves and look after their own business, they refused to leave. Homes were erected for them on the plantation where they lived the rest of their lives. They were buried at their master's feet, which was the custom of the South.

At the business meeting, a national organization known as the Iams Association was affected. A Board of Directors representing each of the three branches of the clan met and elected the following officers: President E. H. Ijams; Secretary Mrs. G. A. Barnes; Treasurer Doctor ___ Iams. Each local association is to elect its own officers.

1933 Iams Reunion/*Morning Observer*

The third annual national reunion of the Iams clan was held in Washington Park, Pennsylvania, Saturday, August 26, 1933. Over 350 representatives from 36 cities attended and enjoyed the abundant picnic dinner and program. It was a perfect day for a reunion. The youngest ones played musk ball, pitched horseshoes, and swam. Many who attended last year sent telegrams and good wishes.

A rare treat was afforded those present in the afternoon by instrumental music by the Garrett Orchestra of Salesbury, directed and assembled by three Garrett sisters of Uniontown, radio artists from Wheeling and Pittsburgh stations.

The program was in charge of E. J. Iams of Donora, who gave a hearty welcome followed by an address by his grandson Elmer Iams. Mrs. Isabel McPherson of Sonora read; Miss Gladys Miller of Evans City rendered several intricate piano solos. Addresses were given by John Robb, The Rev. C. M. Iams of Pittsburgh, the Rev. J. E. Iams of Harrisonville, and Victor Iams, prominent attorney of New Martinsville. Mrs. G. E. Iams and her niece Miss Ella of Baltimore gave talks. Mrs. G. E. Iams has spent much time in research and has founded the Division of D.A.R. known as C & R as a memorial to her famous husband. She spoke at length urging parents to see that their children join. At age 21 they can be transferred to D.A.R. and S.A.R. It was suggested by many that the order of program be changed for next year, and that the entertainment consist of music and social time. A vote of thanks was extended. It was decided to hold the reunion next August.

An article, September 25, 1932, in *Topeka* (Kansas) *Daily Capital*, was headed "Good Speller Needed when Imes Clan Meets: Name May Be Spelled Six Different Ways, All Correct: James Monroe Ijames, Concordia, Elected Head of Iams Clan of Which Harry Imes Is Member." The article outlined how the name is spelled in various ways. Harry Imes of Topeka had an Uncle James Ijames, and accepted spellings at the 1932 Reunion included "Iams, Ijams, Ijames, Iiams, Hioms, Imes, and Eyoms" among others. "The variation in spelling has kept genealogists busy for years trying to trace down the various branches of the Iiams clan." Examples of local Kansas families included: W. H. Imes of the Imes Motor Co. and C. C. Ijames also of Topeka, of the Vachel Iams branch; members of the Thomas Iiams branch of Pennsylvania (Mrs. W. H. Rutter and Mrs. George Hoyes); and John Ijams (Capt. Rev. War) descendants: Edwin Ijams of Oskaloosa, John Ijams of Grantville, Mrs. Charles Gramse of Perry, Shelby Ijams of Topeka, Roy Ijams of Topeka, John Hogue of Topeka, Mrs. Fred Bigham of Topeka; Earl Manning of Capper Publications; and Mrs. Mabel Stark, wife of S. H. Stark, Principal of Curtis School. James Monroe Ijames was a Confederate soldier during the Civil War and was captured by the Union Army, but later escaping with 43 other prisoners, and later settled in Concordia, Kansas, and voted Republican. Judge Isaac Ijams, age 92 and living in North Hollywood, California, in 1932, descendant of Captain John Ijams, went west after the Civil War, was Captain of many Emigrant Trains over the Oregon and California trails, before settling on the Pacific Coast.

July 20, 1932, *The Leader* (a Noble County, Ohio, weekly):
Iiams Reunion

The second annual reunion of the Iiams Clans in America was planned at a meeting of the Directors of the National Association of Iiams Clans, which was held in Washington, Pa., June 16. The reunion will be held August 27, 1932, in the City Park at Washington, Pa., and all descendants of William Iiams, who settled in Maryland about 1664, will be expected to attend. However, the name has been changed to various spellings—Imes - Iams - Ijams - Ijames and Hyams.

Provision has been made for speeches, sports, and musical entertainment. A full day basket picnic is arranged for and a pleasant gathering is looked forward to.

The Iiams clan is one of the oldest American families and is ranked as one of the Empire builders. Their charts show many who were in the Indian Wars, Revolutionary War, and the Civil War, both with the south and the north.

For the convenience for those from a distance who wish to attend, it is suggested they notify the National Secretary Mrs. George Bovier, 700 Deacon Avenue, Washington, Pa., at an early date, so that housing arrangements may be made.

- - - - - - - - - - - -

Note: Those who attended the reunion in 1933 from Noble County:

Thomas Bliss Iams, wife, Ethel, daughter, Wava, age 3 mo.

Mr. and Mrs. Rezin E. Iams

Miss Lois Iams and fiance, Robert Blake

Mr. and Mrs. Madison Iams

Mr. John M. Iams

Mrs. Lydia (Iams) Combs

Rudy Combs (son)

Frank and Grace Combs Radcliff

Rezin, Madison, John M. and Lydia (ch. of Thomas Iams and Nancy Jane Parks)

Bellaire, Ohio
Give Interesting Story of Ancestor of 5 D.A.R. Members
A charter member of N.S.D.A.R. presents an interesting story of the revolutionary ancestor of five members of the chapter, namely: Edna Myers Browning, Elizabeth Haines Albright, Iva Myers, Blanche Thomas, and Roberta Hagmaier.
THOMAS IAMS
Thomas Iams was born in All Hallow's Parish, Anne Arundel County, Maryland, in the year 1754. He was the son of William Iams who married Elizabeth Plummer in 1696. This William was the son of another William Iams who died July 29, 1703, and he was married to Elizabeth Cheney in 1669.

Iiams, Iimes, Ims, Yams, Iams are some of the many ways of spelling this name. It is supposed to mean Emma's son, Emmason, Emson, Ems, Ims. The family is of Welsh origin and the first of the line in America came from the earliest settlers of the state of Maryland. The exact date and place of settlement of the immigrant is unknown but the records of Anne Arundel County abound with references to the family from the year 1696.

On January 10, 1777, Thomas Iiams enlisted as a private in the Revolutionary Army. He must soon have become a sergeant for the records show on March 20, 1777, he was in charge of a recruiting party and while in charge of this party in May 1777, he ordered his men "Fire and fix bayonets," but at whom or for what reason the records do not state.

In the archives of *Maryland Journal and Correspondence of the Maryland Council of Safety 1777-1778* this notation is found. "Council of Safety in Council at Annapolis to C. Lowndes, May 13, 1777: We are obliged to you for the trouble you took in stating the officers. We understand Sergeant Iiams conduct in so full and circumstantial a manner, he is not yet come to town, we expect him and shall make proper inquiry and act accordingly. We are sorry that there should happen ground for complaint, but shall surely duly attend to any that is well founded."

And again from the same *Journal*, "Thomas Iiames, the person mentioned in the letter of Mr. Christopher Lowndes dated the 12th inst. as the officer of the recruiting party therein mentioned appeared before the council according to order, and confessed that he ordered the men of his party to fire and afterwards to fix bayonets nearly in the manner and on the occasion mentioned in the said letter. It is therefore ordered that the said Thomas Iimes enter into bond with sufficient security in the sum of 100 pounds currency for his appearance at Prince George's county court to be held in upper Marlbora the 3rd Tuesday Inst to answer for his conduct toward and in the presence of the said Christopher E. B. Lowndes Magistrate in the execution of his office."

Just what was the outcome of this trial is not told but one may conclude that the court found his orders justifiable, since the records also state that on July 11, 1778, "That the commissary of stores deliver to Thomas Iiams—stript linen for two pr. trousers and two jackets, white linen for two shirts, brown linen for coatee and trimmings suitable."

He was discharged from the army January 1, 1780, having served three years in the war that brought independence to our country.

Thomas Iams was married to Catharine Hampton, daughter of Thomas Gill Hampton, in Maryland, November 29, 1785.

It is known that Thomas and Catharine lived for a time in Frederick County, Maryland, for it is recorded that on the 19th day of November 1796, he voted for George Murdock at the courthouse at Frederick Town, Murdock, was a candidate for presidential elector on the Republican (now Democratic) ticket. Therefore, it was later than the year 1796 that he moved to Washington County, Pennsylvania.

Twelve children, six boys and six girls, were born to them and the records show that at least three were born before they left Maryland. It has not been determined when he came to Pennsylvania nor when or why he came on to Ohio. It seems that all his children came to Ohio except William who remained at Amity, Washington County, Pennsylvania.

The Thomas Iams homestead in Ohio was located on a road that leads off from Route 147 between Jacobsburg and Key in Belmont County and follows into Glencoe. At present the road is little used. It is said that at one time a flour mill was located near Glencoe, owned and operated by the Iamses. There are a number of other branches of the Iams family.

Thomas and Catharine must have lived in this home until their death and likewise their son, Samuel, and his wife, Elizabeth. There was, also, another Elizabeth, daughter of Thomas and Catharine who never married and she lived to the age of eighty years. She, too, probably spent her life in this homestead. All are buried in "Old Dutch Cemetery." Since Samuel and his wife, Elizabeth, had no children, there are no descendants of that name left in the neighborhood of the original home.

Several weeks before his death on May 12, 1838, Thomas Iams received word that a pension had been voted him for his service in the Revolutionary Army. The first installment of his pension he promised to his youngest grandson and namesake Thomas Ault (Bellaire, Ohio) but he died before any payment was received.

Old Dutch Cemetery where Thomas and Catharine are buried is not far from Glencoe and a few miles south of St. Clairsville, near a road which leads off from Route 35 toward Glencoe. There is erected to their memory a monument which is about nine feet in height with a two-foot-square base. The stone bears rather unique carving. On the south side is an opened ear of corn, on the north side fruit—peaches, pears, plums, on the west side is a branch with grapes, and on the east side blossoms of flowers. Whether this carving is merely decorative or whether it is meant to represent the occupation of Thomas Iams while living or the different stages of development of the many years of his life, is not known.

Until a year or two ago, no marker showing his army service had been placed on his grave. This has now been done by his descendents from the Little Washington, Pennsylvania, D.A.R.

REFLECTIONS OF THE EDITOR

The compilation and sorting out of the various members in the Iams ancestral tree has been difficult, though many have devoted many years and committed an enormous amount of dollars to the challenge. There are undoubtedly several reasons why this process has been such a difficult task, and the reasons probably combine to create the fact that publications on the subject have been lacking.

The focus of attention on the Iams family tree probably occured at about 1930. At that time, the Iams Family Association was being formally organized, and there were three sources of Iams information that had been compiled. At the time of the first Iams Reunion at North Ten Mile Baptist Church, Amwell Township, Washington County, Pennsylvania, both Elisha B. Iams, the founder of the Iams Family Association, and Harry Wright Newman, author of *Anne Arundel Gentry* (1930), had been proven to be valuable sources of publications of the Iams family tree. Both E. B. Iams and H. W. Newman attended the Iams Reunion in Washington County, Pennsylvania. Mr. Newman was the keynote speaker for the occasion, but the recorded references of his discussion centered as much on other Anne Arundel County members such as the Waters family, as it did about the Iams family. Although there are no recorded comments about Mr. Newman by Elisha B. Iams, the reverse was not true. Mr. Elisha B. Iams, a worthy researcher and local historian responsible for a significant portion of the extant information compiled during the time of his active period, never published additional information. He did, however, compile an enormous amount of material about the local area as well as the Iams family, and this was subsequently given to the local historical societies. Mr. H. W. Newman is known to have had some disagreements with the recorded work of Elisha B. Iams, and those differences of opinion and conclusions have been addressed at key points throughout this book. In most instances, the problems cannot be resolved, primarily because records have been burned or otherwise lost over the years.

The third source of information that had been developed during the early period of the 1930's and 1940's was that of James B. Meighen. As a young lad, Jimmy Meighen used to accompany his father on frequent visits to the Greene County Court House in Waynesburg, Pennsylvania, to assist in the retrieval of records that were required in his father's business. At about this same time, Jimmy Meighen had the good fortune to become acquainted with the local pharmacist, Howard Leckey. The relationship most likely developed as a result of the many drugstore visits that were required as Jimmy Meighen and his family attempted to control a serious, chronic problem of osteomyelitis of one of Jimmy Meighen's legs. Doctor Howard Leckey encouraged young Jimmy Meighen, a teenager, to pursue the genealogy of the Iiams family, and a result of this work was subsequently published in Howard Leckey's important book on the popular area of "Ten Mile" and Amity. While James B. Meighen and Mr. H. W. Newman corresponded a few times, the differences that they had uncovered with each other's work could never be resolved. Those issues are also addressed in this book.

The works of Misters Newman, E. B. Iiams, and J. B. Meighen were subsequently criticized during the period 1952-1975 by Ervin F. Bickley, Jr., a bright young businessman from the Main Line and Drexel University, in Philadelphia. Mr. Bickley became an ardent researcher in pursuit of the Iams family line, and has undoubtedly spent more time and money attempting to complete this project to everyone's satisfaction, than anyone else. In addition, Mr. Bickley personally contacted all family members that became known to him, and actually hired many of the family to perform various research tasks. In addition, Mr. Bickley hired numerous local professional genealogists to pursue his goals of excellence in the compilation of the Iams family tree. As part of this exhaustive search, he collected certified copies of numerous original documents such as wills, deeds, rent rolls, and court records. In spite of this effort, he never published his work. Fortunately, he has made this vast collection (6,000 sheets) available for review, and copies were made for inclusion into this publication. The transcriptions and conclusions of Mr. Bickley and his staff have been recorded in the book. While this may be interpreted as demonstrating some discrepancies since the conclusions changed as the years progressed, they more accurately display the thinking created by the proliferation of information that has been gathered as a result of diligent research from numerous sources; each attempting to seek the truth with regard to the description of the Iams family tree.

Although living in the Philadelphia and Connecticut areas, Mr. Bickley made numerous trips, especially to the Western Pennsylvania and Maryland areas, to review original documents and to record cemetery information. As he subsequently began to compare his work with the work of others, various discrepancies emerged. Mr. Bickley attempted to confront each of the previously mentioned authors, as these differences were uncovered. Many of the discrepancies between Mr. Bickley and Mr. Newman never were resolved, even when Mr. Newman published the second version of the Anne Arundel Gentry in 1970. Much of this correspondence has been reviewed, and it is the editor's (RDR) opinion that most of these issues can never be resolved. The various conflicts remain to this day and are probably the reason why none of these authors have published any major work on the Iams family in almost 30 years. The published works of Harry Wright Newman remain as the only extensive published work of the Iams family, except for the personalized family history, and family mythology published by the brilliant Lois Ijams Hartman of Pasadena, California. While Mrs. Hartman and Mr. Bickley have corresponded, there are some conflicts that exist when their works are compared.

Lois Iams Blake of Caldwell, Ohio, and Joy Iiams Hannon of Zanesville, Ohio, have also made the pursuit of the Iiams family a life-long avocation and have made enormous contributions, both to this book, and as researchers earlier directed and financed by Mr. Bickley. Numerous other researchers have also made major contributions to this work. It is my intention to acknowledge each of these persons either in the reference listing or in the text of the material being presented. Probably none has contributed more about the local history than have Isaac and Ruth Iams who continue to live and promote the Ten Mile of Amwell Township, Washington County, in Western Pennsylvania. As Trustees of the Township, and leaders in the North Ten Mile Church community, they have authored numerous publications and held several celebrations that promote the beautiful area that has been the home of many of the Iams families since late in the eighteenth century. The work of the youthful, brilliant Michael Iams of Phoenix has been an encouraging example of the interest of the next generation in preserving the Iams legacies. The legacy of the black slaves that descended from the legendary Jack Imes (b. 1777) has been the dedicated work of Carmen Henrietta Cecile White Wright Harleston.

Returning to the work of Ervin F. Bickley, Jr., it seems worth recording some of the thoughts and conclusions, some of which must be considered tentative, that have been proposed during the 40-year process of compiling information on the Iams family by Mr. Bickley and his numerous friends, family members and professional researchers who assisted him. Certain insights are provided by these recordings:

Recorded December 18, 1962, "One of these fine days I am going to unravel the puzzle or probably work myself into a state of complete frustration while trying." Also in 1962, Richard (Greene County, Pennsylvania) was declared to be the father of Thomas, Richard, Jr., Otho, Reason, Eli, Basel, William, and probably of John; with the death records of Richard, Jr., Otho, and Reason in the possession of Mr. Bickley. He also declared that the Washington County, Pennsylvania, tax lists listed men's names after they had attained the age of 21, and that their names remained on the tax lists for about two years after their death. As early as August 5, 1953, Mr. Bickley had declared that the Washington and Greene County, Pennsylvania, accounts of the Iams families by H. W. Newman were somewhat incorrect, and that some locally published newspaper accounts were actually taken almost verbatim from the work of Mr. Newman. Mr. Bickley, Mrs. McIlvane and Mrs. Mildred Russell apparently agreed that Mr. Leckey erroneously listed the son of Thomas and Mary Iiams as marrying Priscilla Hopkins, rather than the preferred listing of the marriage to Matilda Huffman. Additionally, Thomas (d. 1862), the son of Thomas (b. 1754), married June 6, 1823, to Mary Hardesty, said to have been born near St. Clairsville December 27, 1805, and died south of Galion, Ohio, August 11, 1903. In a 1957 letter to Rev. Fred Cochran of Western Pennsylvania, Mr. Bickley compares his work with the work of Meighen, Leckey and Newman, and 1) agrees that the four brothers (John, Thomas, Richard, and William) went to Washington and Greene Counties by 1794; 2) that Thomas (b. 1708; d. 1768) was not their father, but was instead the father of Richard Iams (d. 1800, m. Eleanor); and 3) felt that Richard (m. 1737 to Mary Nichols in Maryland) was the father of the four brothers.

Mr. Bickley had several questions that were posed to H. W. Newman. Among those were: 1) Richard (HWN, 1970, p. 323) (baptized 1712) didn't marry Mary Nichols; Richard's 1747 will did not mention a son Richard; and Richard listed John as the eldest son in a deed where Richard of Pennsylvania transferred land to Thomas of Pennsylvania; 2) the John that approved the estate (p. 325) was Captain John and not a son named John; that John did not have a son named Richard; and that the will of William of Washington County, Pennsylvania, had sons named Thomas and William; 3) questioned the report (p. 328) that Richard, Sr. had a son William that lived in Allegany County, Maryland, and signed a 1792 document, since this William would also be the father of William, Jr.; but that this William, Sr. was known to have married Elizabeth Howard, settled in Washington County, Maryland, purchased land from John Donnacky, was listed in the 1790 Federal Census of Washington County, Maryland; purchased land from Thomas Worty in Washington County, Maryland, and sold the land in 1803 to Abraham Ditto; and who settled in Fairfield County, Ohio in 1808; 4) doubts that 1745 was the birth year of Richard, son of John (p. 326); 5) while there were two Eli Iams, the listing that Eli married Catharine Crawford (p. 327) rather than Phoebe Heckathorne is in error, since the Eli was the son of Richard and Eleanor Pottenger; and pointed out that both Richard, Sr. and Richard, Jr. took the Oath of Allegiance in Washington County, Maryland March 1778; 6) it was Samuel who wrote a letter to William, rather than vice versa (p. 328); 7) that DAR-28919 claim of Henrietta Adamson Conover that Thomas (b. 1781-90) was the son of Thomas, rather than the son of Richard (pp. 402-3, 410, and E. B. Iams); 8) that Catherine, widow of Sgt. Thomas (p. 329), died in Belmont County, Ohio, in 1838; that Richard and Eleanor Pottenger Iams had a son Richard, Jr. that married Mary Shidler (died Monticello, Indiana, February 15, 1868) and had 10 children: John, Reason, Peter, Nancy, Sally, George, Richard, Susannah, William, and Mary. In 1970 and again in 1973, Mr. Bickley cites correspondence with Mr. Newman of "several years ago," "to make available the information I have collected over several years" to clarify some of the lines in the 1933 edition, and cites work done on behalf of Mr. Newman. Mr. Bickley proposed to "sit down together and compare notes as that is probably the only way to reach a common conclusion on such a complicated family line." Mr. Newman's known reply included references to "negotions" and asked for proof of questions that had been raised.

In 1934, Elisha B. Iams claimed Richard to be a son of Thomas and a grandson of William and Elizabeth Plummer Iams, and that Thomas (1708-1768) who m. Artridge had four sons: Richard, Thomas, John, and William. In 1966, Clifford H. Iams, brother of Elisha B. Iams and the noted painter Howard Iams, in his own right a talented woodcrafter, wrote to Mr. Bickley stating that he (Clifford) had the records of Elisha B. Iams, but their whereabouts since then are not fully known. Mr. Bickley stated that Richard m. Elizabeth Pottenger and lived in Greene County, Pennsylvania. Richard, Sr. was listed on the Greene County Tax Records of 1830, and the Tax Records suggest that he died in 1833; and that Eli, the son of Richard, Sr. of Greene County, Pennsylvania, moved to Montgomery County, Ohio, while another Eli (b. 1790, Maryland) married Catherine Crawford and lived in Washington County, Ohio, in 1813. A Chancery Court Record of Annapolis, Anne Arundel County, Maryland (pp. 51-54, 1797) recorded that Richard Iiams had moved from Maryland and was now living at Redstone in Western Pennsylvania as of June 25, 1796, and this statement was part of a court proceeding to correct an error of Thomas Iiams, who misplaced the deed to the property by placing it in his billfold and then losing the billfold/pocket book, for the land formerly known as "Richard Iiams Dwelling Plantation" or "New Birmingham" with the correction being made February 17, 1797.

In an October 8, 1931 letter to Miss E. K. Evans, Terre Haute, Indiana, Mr. E. B. Iams stated 1) that there were now 20 Iams Clans within the Iams Family Association and that the first National Family Reunion had been held in Washington County, Pennsylvania, in August 1931; and 2) that, with regard to the origin of the family name, that Ievans was an old Welsh or Saxon King in 1040 AD, and that various name spellings since that time have included I'ans (Welsh); Eyoms, Eyams, and Iiams in Maryland; and subsequently Ijams, Iams, Imes, and Ijames. On August 3, 1932, Mr. Elisha B. Iams wrote to Mr. L. C. Jordan of South Olive, Ohio, stating that "Thomas, John and William married these sisters Catherine, Elizabeth, and Mary Hampton, and settled in Washington County, Pennsylvania, with another brother Richard and a sister Susannah, who married William Penn. William Penn was related to the Quaker William Penn, and the Hamptons were related to General Hampton of the Confederate Army." A deed (1-3, p. 153, January 16, 1791, Washington County, Pennsylvania) lists William Iiams as having sold 153 acres to Thomas Gill Hampton, father of the three Hampton girls, of Anne Arundel County, Maryland, for the sum of 94 pounds, with the land originally patented by John Grant on November 17, 1784, and subsequently (June 4, 1788) sold to William Iiams, with the land known as "Brusky Ridge" on Ten Mile Creek; recorded February 15, 1791, with Thomas Iiams and William Mutlicte as witnesses. Records of the Pennsylvania Land Office, from the Historical Collection of Land Warrants 1784-1797 at Washington and Jefferson College of Washington, Pennsylvania, lists Richard Imes, Jr. as having been granted 150 acres in 1785, with the land within the area south of the Ohio River and west of the Monongahela River (Washington County). The Tax Lists of Washington County, Pennsylvania, list John Iiames (Amwell Township.) from 1791-1798 (100 acres, grist mill, 300 acres, miller, also spelled Iams) and John Iams, Jr. (Amwell Township) in 1815; Thomas Iams (West Bethlehem Township) from 1800-1810 (240 acres); Mary Iams (West Bethlehem Township), 1800-1806 at which time she was "removed" and transferred the land to Thomas Iams, Jr.; Thomas Iams, Jr. (West Bethlehem Township) 1805-1810, listed as tenant in 1806, and with 150 acres in 1807; Richard Iams (West Bethlehem Township) 1807-1811, listed as single, son of Sgt. Thomas in 1807, as having one horse in 1810, and as being single, having 200 acres and a distillery in

1810; and William Iams (West Bethlehem Township) 1817-1818. The 1800 Western Pennsylvania Census listed the following Iiams as heads of household: Mary (age 16-26), Thomas (over age 45), Isaac, John, Robert, Thomas, Thomas, William, and William Iames.

Elisha B. Iams reviewed the tombstones of those family members buried at the cemetery at Amity, Washington County, Pennsylvania, with the following comments: William Iams (September 18, 1793-April 30, 1859) and wife Susannah Iams (April 27, 1795-February 6, 1883); Brothers William H. Iams (February 10, 1866-February 2, 1877), and George L. Iams (February 28, 1868-February 17, 1913); father Franklin F. Iams (July 11, 1836-May 3, 1906) and his wife Mary Iams (February 11, 1889-July 26, 1913); sister of Franklin Iams was Charity J. (Iams) Eliot (November 23, 1830-December 13, 1931) and children Bastian Eliot (May 28, 1885-1909), John Alonzo Eliot (1869-1917) and Saddie Eliot (1861-1865).

Correspondence in 1969 and 1970 between Alice Williams, descendant of Eli Iams of Marietta, Ohio, and Mr. Bickley sheds some light surrounding the work of Mr. Newman. Mr. Bickley stated that he considered the William of Shelby County, Ohio, as having migrated from Washington County, Pennsylvania; while Mr. Newman has "continued to show Alice Williams' Eli as a son of Richard of Greene County, Pennsylvania" even though this "can't be," that William and Elizabeth continue to be shown erroneously as being in Allegany County, Maryland, in 1792; that Mr. Newman "has perpetuated a second time many errors in the various Iiames family lines," even though he "asked if I could substantiate the questions and statements I (Mr. Bickley) made," and wondered if Alice Williams was "as unhappy with Newman as I am;" to which Mr. Williams of Tulsa, Oklahoma, replied that "he (Mr. Newman) continues to make mistakes and I don't think the new book should be published." She further commented that "I (Mrs. Williams) am absolutely amazed that Mr. Newman still places my Eli as the son of Richard of Greene County," even though "I sent them to Mr. Newman and told him that this proved that they were two different Elis," and that "He must be a stubborn person," closing with "Really, this upsets me no end." Mrs. Williams further cites the will of Lucy Putnam (1813, Marietta, Ohio) that mentions Katherine Crawford (alias Imes); and the will of Catherine Crawford, wife of George Crawford (Marietta, 1862) listing John L. Crawford (a son, b. 1810 in Pennsylvania, according to 1850 Census of Marietta, Washington County, Ohio) as executor and R. P. Iams as witness.

While it is expected that all work of this type will generate lively discussion, and much will be found to be duplicative, redundant, imprecise, and erroneous, the conflicts over the Iams family lines were often deep seated, and may indeed be associated with some degree of stubbornness. Some have felt that the motivations may need to be evaluated in such situations, with the thought that those pursuing goals for money may inadvertently make genetic connections to satisfy needs of a client that may not be acceptable to others. Mr. Bickley acknowledged that Mr. Newman had agreed that the Newman line of Iams in both Washington and Greene Counties in Pennsylvania were incorrect, as far back as August 5, 1953; and that in spite of continuing negotiations through the time of the 1970 publication by Mr. Newman, many of the corrections were never made. The current work has asked for and has received all information that all serious Iams researchers, living or dead, were willing to contribute for this purpose. For the most part, the work of each researcher, including Mr. Newman, has been received by the editorial panel. The critique of each of the panel members has also been made part of this book. These differences represent reasons why a previous account has not been published.

Harry Shipp Truman (b. May 8, 1884, Lamar, Missouri; d. December 26, 1972) married in 1934 to Bess Wallace (b. February 13, 1885, Independence, Missouri). They had a daughter, Mary Margaret Truman (p. 7).

Harry S. Truman was the son of John Anderson Truman (b. 1851; d. 1915) and Martha Ellen Young (b. 1853; d. 1947). John Anderson Truman was the son of Anderson Shipp Truman (b. 1816; d. 1887) and Mary Jane Holmes (b. 1821; d. 1879). Mary Jane Holmes was the daughter of Captain Jesse Holmes (b. 1775; d. 1840) and Ann Drusilla Tyler (b. 1780; d. 1875). Ann Drusilla Tyler was the daughter of Captain Robert Tyler (b. 1751 in Maryland; d. 1815) and Margaret Tyler (b. 1755; d. 1840). Captain Robert Tyler was the son of Edward Tyler (b. 1719, Maryland; d. 1802) and Ann Langley (b. 1732, Maryland; d. 1800). Edward Tyler was the son of William Tyler (b. 1696, Maryland) and Elizabeth Duvall (b. 1697). Elizabeth Duvall was the daughter of Samuel Duvall (b. 1665) and Elizabeth Ijams (b. 1670, Anne Arundel County, Maryland); she married 2) June 18, 1697. Elizabeth Ijams was the daughter of the first known Iiams in Maryland, William Eyams and Elizabeth Cheyney (b. 1652). Thus, as James B. Meighen has said, "Give 'em Hell Harry was part Iams!" (SR).

Pinkethman reports that Captain Robert Tyler (b. 1751; d. 1815), the son of Edward Tyler (b. 1719; d. 1802) and Ann Langley (b. 1732; d. 1820), married his first cousin, Margaret Tyler (b. 1755; d. 1840), the daughter of Robert Tyler (the brother of Edward Tyler, b. 1719) and Eleanor Bradley. The parents of Edward Tyler and Robert Tyler were Edward Tyler (b. 1696; d. 1735) and Elizabeth Duvall (b. 1697) were also first cousins. The parents of this Edward Tyler was Robert Tyler (b. 1671; d. 1738) and Susanna Duvall (b. 1678; d. ca1717); while the parents of this Elizabeth Duvall (b. 1697) were Samuel Duvall (b. 1667; d. 1741) and Elizabeth.

FAMILY CIRCLE

Iams, Ijams, Iiams, Imes, Ijames, etc., family circle. An example of the relationship of the early family members in America. While there are areas of contention, it appears clear that all early families are related, regardless of the individual choices of the surname spelling. The exact date and place of birth of William, the progenitor, remains unknown. His earliest known whereabouts is in Anne Arundel County, Maryland, during the late 1600s. The period from 1800 to 1850 remains as the most controversial and may never be resolved.

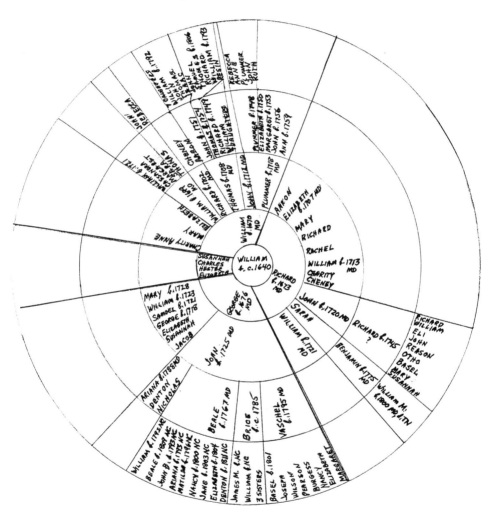

CHAPTER 1

WILLIAM IJAMS (D. 1703, MARYLAND),

PROGENITOR IN AMERICA

William Iiams/Ijams/Eyams of Maryland married Elizabeth Cheyney. Early family history and family lines of their children Elizabeth and William, including several controversial areas.

Contains lines of President Harry S. Truman, Senator/Astronaut John Glenn, Joy Imes Hannon, James B. Meighan, Roberta Wright Iiames and Guy Iiames, and Paul Iams (Iams Pet Food).

Harry Wright Newman is generally considered to be the gold standard by which all writings about early Maryland settlers are compared. A noted researcher, he devoted his life to the definition of the various family lines that began in seventeenth-century Maryland. His delineation of the Iams/Ijams family lines are among his greatest works. In many instances, records are no longer available for comparisons or rebuttals of the inheritance lines as he saw them. Nevertheless, members of this editorial staff have had honest disagreements with the work of Mr. Newman, and these views have been expressed elsewhere in this book.

Mr. Newman has identified William Iiams as the earliest American progenitor. This William Iiams lived in the South River Hundred neighborhood, Anne Arundel County, Maryland, by 1665, where he farmed. Records of his transportation or arrival in Maryland have been conspicuously absent. While he owned land, there is no record of how he acquired this land, or how he had acquired the wealth necessary to purchase his multiple plantations. It is known that he married well and that his land acquisitions were enhanced as a result of his marriage. His wife, Elizabeth Cheyney, was the daughter of Richard and Charity Cheyney, and they had at least six children:

1. William Iiams, b. 1670; m. Elizabeth Plummer
2. Elizabeth Iiams, m. 1st, Daniel Clark; m. 2nd, in 1697, Samuel Duvall
3. Richard Iiams, m. 1st, Anne Cheyney; m. 2nd, Elizabeth Gaither
4. George Iiams, m. Elizabeth Basford
5. Hester Iiams, m. 1708, John Nicholson
6. Susannah Iiams, m. 1st, 1696, Thomas Fowler; m. 2nd, 1716, Mark Brown

In his February 16, 1698/9 will, William Iiams named sons William Iiams, Richard Iiams, and George Iiams; and daughters Elizabeth, Hester, and Susannah, in addition to his wife, Elizabeth. The will was probated November 10, 1703, and he was buried July 29, 1703.

R.W.I. and B.L. have suggested that William Iiams/Ijams/Eyams was born in 1652 in Stratton, Cornwall, England. Newman has pointed out that the name Iiams is more Flemish/Dutch in origin than Great Britain/England. All Hallow's Parish records are clear about his burial and indicate that he was buried in the cemetery of that parish, in which he was a member. His will is filed in the Anne Arundel County Wills, Liber 3, Folio 122. His wife, Elizabeth Cheyney Iiams, had inherited 400

1

acres on the south side of South River from her father on May 29, 1663. This land went by the title Cheyney's Resolution and was part of a larger plot of 4,300 acres. This land was given for "the consideration of natural love and affection" to William Iams and wife Elizabeth, surveyed again on March 1, 1674.

Evelyn Bott (1950) considered 1650 to have been the year that Richard Cheyney had been settled on Cheyney's Hill in Anne Arundel County, Maryland, on a tract of land of 1,100 acres along South River. Guy R. Iiames has placed the birth of William Iams as 1652 in Stratton, Cornwall, England. Elizabeth Cheyney Iiams, wife of William Iiams, was the daughter of Richard and Charity Cheyney. After Charity Cheyney died, Richard Cheyney married Eleanor and had additional children.

The will of William Iiams/Eyams, written in 1689 and probated in 1703, identified daughter Elizabeth Iiams Duvall, to whom he left five shillings; son George Iiams, to whom he left 100 acres on the south side of Western Run; son Richard Iiams, to whom he left 100 acres near the Patuxent River in Prince George's County; widow Elizabeth Iiams, to whom he left dower rights; with the residual of the estate to be divided among children Richard Iiams, George Iiams, Hester Iiams, and Susannah Iiams.

Widow Elizabeth Cheyney Eyams filed an estate account on February 7, 1706, showing a balance of 37 pounds, 8 shillings, and 4 pence. James Frank Iiams (b. 1928) has written that William Iiams/I'Ans/Eyoms/Hyime/Jams/Ijams was born in Wales in 1640; married 1669 in Wales to Elizabeth Cheney; died in Anne Arundel County, Maryland, on July 29, 1703. Elizabeth Cheney was said to have been born in 1652 and died in 1726.

Elisha B. Iams, one of the founders of the National Iams Family Association in 1930, wrote that William Iiams/Eyams, Sr., born in Wales, was a colonial agent for Lord Baltimore, a vestryman at All Hallow's Parish in 1668; the son of Sir Robert Iiam, Chief Ordnance for the Queen as Quartermanster General. Sir Robert Iiams was also listed as I'ams, I'ans, and Innes, and married Lady Grizil Stewart, daughter of Earl of Murray. Robert Innes, Quartermaster General, was the son of Alexander Innes (d. 1634), who married a cousin, Marjory Gordon, oldest daughter of William Gordon, Baron of Gight; and great-great-grandson of George, the second Earl of Huntley, and his countess, Princess Annabella Stewart, the youngest daughter of King James I of Scotland.

Alexander Innes (d. 1634) was the son of Robert Innes of Crony and Path Makenzie, who married the daughter of William Molerum, Baron of Fyvie. Robert Innes was the son of James Innes, Laird of Innes, who entertained King James IV in 1490. James Innes married Janet Gordon, daughter of Alexander Gordon, first Earl of Huntley. James Innes was also the sixteenth Feudal Baron of Innes and held the appointment of Esquire to King James III. Burke's English Gentry relates that the First Feudal Baron, Lord Innes, by a Crown Charter of King Malcolm IV Borewald, in 1160, was "styled Flanders."

After a fire in the Anne Arundel County, Maryland, Courthouse between 1703 and 1726, many of the local land records were destroyed. As a result, owners were invited to bring in copies of their deeds to be re-recorded. Widow Elizabeth Cheyney Iiams was one such land owner who had her land records copied.

Richard Cheyney, Sr. (I), father of Elizabeth Cheyney Iiams, is believed to have had two wives (EFB). The Cheyney family is mentioned in the Maryland Archives (Vol. 51, page 264) several times. On April 20, 1679, for example, Richard Cheyney, Sr., Richard Cheyney, Jr., and John Jacobs served as jurors in Anne Arundel County, Maryland. On March 6, 1685/1686, Richard Cheyney, Sr., wrote his will, but it was not probated until May 14, 1724.

In his will, Richard Cheyney, Sr. (I) named eleven children. By his first marriage were:

1. Elizabeth Cheyney
2. Richard Cheyney, Jr.
3. Mary Cheyney
4. Anne Cheyney

By his second marriage were:

5. Thomas Cheyney
6. Charles Cheyney
7. Sarah Cheyney
8. Katherine Cheyney
9. Charity Cheyney
10. John Cheyney
11. Richard Cheyney, the younger

Daughter **Elizabeth Cheyney**, born ca1651, Maryland; living on January 26, 1725/6; was married by March 1, 1674/5, to William Iiams, who died after 1698, when his will was written. The will was probated November 10, 1703, Anne Arundel County, Maryland. On January 26, 1725/1726, Widow Elizabeth Cheyney Iiams, age about seventy-four, testified that her father had left the family plantation and land to her brothers, Thomas Cheyney and Charles Cheyney (Maryland Proceedings, Vol. 27, pp. 290-291).

Richard Cheyney, Jr., born 1658; died December 6, 1704; and wife Mary, had ten children:

1. Mary Cheyney, b. August 3, 1688(?); m. December 1, 1702, to Walter Phelps, Jr.; d. before January 2, 1717
2. Richard Cheyney III, b. March 8, 1682/1683; m. December 11, 1707, to Rachel Nicholson; buried March 1716
3. John Cheyney, b. March 8, 1682/3; m. 1st, Elizabeth Tylley, September 22, 1709; m. 2nd, Ann ___
4. Joseph Cheyney, b. May 25, 1686
5. Benjamin Cheyney, b. October 10, 1687; m. June 23, 1719, to Ruth Cheyney, daughter of Thomas and Sarah Westhall Cheyney
6. Elizabeth Cheyney, b. March 25, 1688(?); m. August 8, 1706, to William Phelps
7. Ann Cheyney, b. May 18, 1691; m. January 16, 1706/7, to Richard Eyoms, son of William and Elizabeth Cheyney Iiams, Sr.
8. Samuel Cheyney, b. September 25, 1694
9. Hannah Cheyney, b. May 8, 1697
10. Susannah Cheyney, b. August 22, 1700; m. January 11, 1727, to Thomas Mackelfish

Anne Cheyney, born 1660; died April 28, 1730; daughter of Richard Cheyney I; married by March 1, 1674, to John Jacob, born 1631; died October 1726, Anne Arundel County, Maryland.

Thomas Cheyney, born March 1, 1669/70; died 1738, son of Richard Cheyney I, married 1st, August 19, 1697, to Sarah Westall, born August 31, 1680; buried September 14, 1713), daughter of George and Sarah Westall. He married 2nd, June 7, 1716, to Susannah Hoffer. Thomas Cheyney had seven children by his first marriage and five children by his second marriage.

First marriage:

1. Sarah Cheyney, b. October 4, 1698
2. Elizabeth Cheyney, baptized October 19, 1700; m. April 22, 1716, to Thomas Joyce

3. Thomas Cheyney, baptized October 19, 1700
4. Ruth Cheyney, b. March 16, 1702; m. June 23, 1719, Benjamin Cheyney, son of Richard Cheyney, Jr.
5. Moses Cheyney, b. March 20, 1705
6. Elinor Cheyney, baptized October 18, 1711
7. Sarah Cheyney, 2nd, baptized October 18, 1711; d. before November 1765; m. May 17, 1733, to John Hatton

Second marriage:
8. Richard Cheney
9. Lewis Cheney, baptized April 6, 1724; m. February 16, 1743, to Mary Donaldson
10. Susannah Cheyney, baptized March 5, 1718
11. Rachel Cheyney
12. Rebecca Cheyney, baptized August 13, 1727; m. August 19, 1742, to Richard Ricketts

Charles Cheyney was born June 6, 1673, and died 1744/5. He m. 1st, July 15, 1701, to Anne Jones Pattison, widow of Gilbert Pattison, and daughter of William and Elizabeth Jones, Sr. He m. 2nd, before 7, 1718, to Elizabeth ___; and 3rd, Agnes ___. Charles, son of Richard Cheyney I had eleven children:

1. Charles Cheyney, Jr., b. September. 20, 1703; d. March 7, 1781
2. Ann Cheyney, d. young
3. Dinah Cheyney, baptized September 27, 1710; d. young
4. Greenbury Cheyney, baptized September 14, 1713; m. November 16, 1725, to Elizabeth Cheyney, daughter of Richard and Rachel Nicholson Cheyney
5. Jacob Cheyney
6. Mordecai Cheyney
7. Isiah Cheyney, m. 1st, Sarah ___; m. 2nd, Rachel ___
8. Shadrack Cheyney
9. Mary Cheyney, m. February 3, 1729, to Edward Ricketts
10. Rachel Cheyney
11. Elizabeth Cheyney

John Cheyney, born May 1, 1684, m. January 3, 1705, to Mary Williams Beadle, widow of William Beadle and daughter of Benjamin Williams. John, son of Richard Cheyney I, had at least three children.

1. Ann Cheyney, b. October 6, 1706
2. Mary Cheyney, b. July 28, 1708
3. Rachel Cheyney, b. December 1, 1709; m. January 26, 1726/7 to James Bryan

Richard Cheyney, the Younger, son of Richard Cheyney I, was a twin who was born May 1, 1684, and died 1759. He married September 11, 1722, to Mary Penn, and had eleven children:

1. Richard Cheyney, Jr., baptized October 28, 1724
2. Edward Cheyney
3. John Cheyney
4. Joseph Cheyney
5. James Cheyney
6. Sarah Cheyney
7. Mary Cheyney
8. Rachel Cheyney
9. Jemima Cheyney
10. Jane Cheyney
11. Catherine Cheyney

Other children of Richard Cheyney I:
1. Mary Cheyney
2. Sarah Cheyney, b. October 15, 1677; m. 1) James Chickly
3. Katherine Cheyney, b. March 12, 1679; m. 1st, September 1, 1701, to Widower James Parnell; m. 2nd, June 18, 1702, Robert Broune, son of Anne Arundel County Sheriff, Abel Broune
4. Charity Cheyney, b. March 16, 1681; m. November 7, 1706, to John Patten

The children of William Iams, Sr. (d. 1703) and Elizabeth Cheyney, daughter of Richard Cheyney I, were (RWI, BF, R1, LIH, EFB, CR1, HWN, LDS):
1. Richard Iiams, b. South River, Anne Arundel County, Maryland; d. 1761, age 85. He m. 1st, January 16, 1706, at South River, to Anne Cheyney, daughter of Richard (b. 1691; d. 1713) and Mary Cheyney; m. 2nd, Elizabeth Gaither (FEW). Richard inherited land in Prince Georges County, Maryland, from his father. Children:
   1. Elizabeth Iiams
   2. Mary Iiams
   3. Richard Iiams
   4. Rachel Iiams
   5. William Iiams
   6. Cheney Iiams

The genealogy of this Richard Iiams family may be found later in the book.
2. Elizabeth Iiams, b. South River, Anne Arundel County, Maryland, in 1670 or 1675 (LDS, BL); m. 1) Captain Daniel Clare, b. 1675; d. 1696; m. 2) July 16, 1697, to Samuel Duvall. This forms the family line association that includes Harry S. Truman, 32nd President of the United States (p. xxxix). The genealogy of the family of this Elizabeth Iiams may be found later in this chapter.
3. George Iiams, b. 1676/7, South River, Anne Arundel County; m. Elizabeth Basford, b. 1676. The description of the family of George Iiams is described on later pages.
4. William Iiams II, b. 1670, South River, Anne Arundel County, Maryland; d. 1738; m. August 27, 1693, at All Hallows Parish, Anne Arundel County, Maryland, to Elizabeth Plummer, b. 1670; baptized June 19, 1698; d. 1762. Elizabeth is the daughter of Thomas Plummer and Elizabeth Yates (LDS, EFB, LIH, CR1). In 1726, William Iiams (age 59), brother Richard Iiams (age 50), and their mother Elizabeth Cheyney Iiams, testified that the brothers were sons of William Iiams, Sr., in a lawsuit over land known as Iiams Choice in Anne Arundel County. The will of William Iiams, Jr., was probated in Anne Arundel County in 1738. The line of this William Iiams (b. 1670) includes the noted genealogist and author Lois Ijams Hartman, and of Marine Colonel, Astronaut, US Senator, and fraternity brother of the editor, John H. Glenn, Jr.

The family genealogy of William Iiams II (b. 1670) is expanded later in the book.
5. Hester Iiams, also called Esther Iiames, b. 1679, South River, Anne Arundel County, Maryland; m. December 23, 1708, to John Nicholson at South River. Hester, described as the romantic one, is believed to have received monetary support for her early children from Captain John Duvall, husband of Elizabeth Jones, until Hester married John Nicholson in 1708. Newman described Hester as having "a romantic nature" and as having an affair with Captain John Duvall, a leading military officer of the Province, and son of the famous Mareen Duvall, the Huguenot.

5

John Duvall deeded a portion of the plantation Burgess Choice to Hester Iiams, spinster, April 16, 1705. Early children of Hester Iiams included:

1. Anne Iiams, baptized March 25, 1706, All Hallows Parish
2. Elizabeth Iiams, "daughter of Ester," b. August 15, 1703; baptized January 3, 1705, All Hallows Parish
3. John Iiams, "son of Ester," baptized September 19, 1702, at All Hallows Parish, Anne Arundel County, Maryland

Children of Hester Iiams and John Nicholson may have included:

1. Rachel Nicholson, b. April 28, 1709
2. John Nicholson, Jr., b. July 11, 1710; baptized July 14, 1711
3. Richard Nicholson, b. November 11, 1712
4. Rebecca Nicholson, b. January 16, 1713
5. Joseph Nicholson, b. September 7, 1715; baptized July 28, 1717
6. Nicholas Nicholson, b. March 11, 1717
7. Sarah Nicholson, b. September 7, 1720; baptized April 3, 1724

and, perhaps,

8. Benjamin Nicholson, b. June 4, 1723 (RWI)

6. Susannah/Susan Iiams, b. 1677 (1681, LDS), South River, Anne Arundel County, Maryland; m. 1677 (BF) or October 15, 1696, to Thomas Fowler; or October 15, 1697, to Thomas Pfloueller (FEW), and had at least two children:

1. Elizabeth Fowler, b. June 13, 1697; baptized June 19, 1698
2. William Fowler, b. February 16, 1698/9; baptized July 26, 1700

Susannah m. 2) November 8, 1716, to Mark Broun. Susannah Iiams Fowler Broun (BF, LIH) is also reported to have had thirteen children:

1. William Fowler, b. Prince Georges County, Maryland, on either June 14, 1697, or February 16, 1699; m. Susannah Duvall, b. September 12, 1704, Anne Arundel County, Maryland
2. Elizabeth Fowler, b. June 14, 1697, Prince Georges County, Maryland
3. William Fowler, b. February 16, 1699, or June 14, 1697 (LDS), Prince Georges County, Maryland; m. Susanna Duvall
4. Thomas Fowler, b. September 11, 1700, Prince Georges County, Maryland
5. Susannah Fowler, b. March 22, 1702, Queen Anne Parish, Prince Georges County, Maryland
6. John Fowler, b. September 12, 1703, Prince Georges County, Maryland
7. Benjamin Fowler, b. May 30, 1705, Prince Georges County, Maryland
8. Samuel Fowler, b. October 13 or 19 (LDS), 1706, Prince Georges County, Maryland
9. Mary Fowler, b. April 3, 1708, Prince Georges County, Maryland
10. Richard Fowler, b. May 12, 1711, or October 6, 1709 (LDS), Prince Georges County, Maryland
11. Jeremiah Fowler, b. May 12, 1711, Prince Georges County, Maryland
12. Ann Fowler, b. June 14, 1713, Prince Georges County, Maryland; m. John Duvall, b. February 20, 1712
13. Benoni Fowler, b. November 15, 1715, Prince Georges County, Maryland, m. Mark Broun, and they had four children:

6

1. Mark Broun
2. Alice Broun, m. 1st, Frances Hardesty; m. 2nd, Lewis Duvall; 5 children:
    1. Frances Hardesty, Jr.
    2. Elizabeth Hardesty
    3. Alice Hardesty
    4. Henry Hardesty
    5. Thomas Hardesty, m. Elizabeth Knapp
3. Mark Broun, m. Elizabeth Gaither
4. Frances Broun, m. ___ Sappington

Mareen Duvall was a much talked about Frenchman who left Nantes around 1650 and was one of 150 members of the Colonel William Burgess ship that settled in Anne Arundel County along the South River. During the 1689 Revolution, Mareen Duvall was among the leaders who "sustained the Lord Proprietary." This Huguenot planter and merchant held vast land tracts in Anne Arundel and Prince Georges Counties. A daughter, Susanna Duvall, married Robert Tyler about 1695; and a son, Samuel Duvall, born ca1667, Anne Arundel County, married Elizabeth Iiams Clarke, widow of Captain Daniel Clark, on June 12, 1696, in All Hallows Parish, Anne Arundel County, daughter of William and Elizabeth Cheyney Eyams/Iiams.

Ann Ijams Callahan of Baltimore, Maryland, has determined that Richard Wells, born in England, died in Maryland, 1667, moved to Virginia in 1635, and with his wife Frances and eleven children to Anne Arundel County, Maryland, in 1652. Richard Wells was a member of Maryland General Assembly, 1654; a governing commissioner from July 22 1654 to 1655; a justice, including Presiding Justice of Anne Arundel County, Maryland, July 12, 1658 to 1661; who had a daughter, Mary Wells.

This Mary Wells married 1st, a seafaring Captain, John Stockett, and after his death married 2nd, Joseph Yates. Joseph and Mary Wells Stockett Yates had four children before his death in 1691. A daughter, Elizabeth Yates, married Thomas Plummer who had moved from Boston to Prince Georges County, Maryland, in 1667. Elizabeth Plummer, the daughter of Elizabeth Yates and Thomas Plummer, married William Ijams and they had nine children.

Ann Ijams Callahan is a proponent of the theory that the first William Ijams was a native of Whitestone, England, and that he journeyed first to Boston before settling in Anne Arundel County, Maryland. Further, Ann felt that their William Ijams may have been a grandson of Robert Ijams, Esquire, Master of Ordnance to Queen Elizabeth; member of Privy council of Ireland; and formerly in charge of a combined military and civil board that managed all matters concerning artillery, engineers, and material of the army.

Elizabeth Iiams, listed as the second child of William Iams, Sr., and Elizabeth Cheyney, above, b. 1670 or 1675, m. 1st, Captain Daniel Clark (b. 1675; d. 1696) and m. 2nd, July 16, 1697, Samuel Duvall. This includes the family line of U.S. President Harry S. Truman. The eight children of Elizabeth Iams were:
1. Thomas Clarke, b. September 28, 1688, Anne Arundel County, Maryland
2. William Clarke, b. September 11, 1691
3. Richard Clarke, b. July 30, 1694
4. Elizabeth Duvall, m. Edward Tyler; had two sons: Samuel Tyler and Edward Tyler, Jr.
5. Susannah Duvall, m. Alexander Falconer
6. Esther Duvall, m. William West
7. Sarah Duvall, m. James Beck; one son, Samuel Duvall Beck
8. Lucy Duvall, m. William Forest; one daughter, Elizabeth Forest

7

Elizabeth Duvall (b. October 6, 1697, Anne Arundel County, Maryland; d. after 1770); m. 1713, Edward Tyler, Sr. (b. October 2, 1696, Prince George's County, Maryland; d. by 1726). Edward Tyler, Sr. (b. 1696) was the son of Robert Tyler, Jr. (b. January 6, 1671, Calvert County, Maryland; d. by 1738) and Susannah Duvall (b. ca1676, Anne Arundel County, Maryland; d. 1716, Prince Georges County, Maryland). Robert Tyler, Jr. (b. 1671) was the son of Robert Tyler, Sr. (b. 1637, England; m. 1668, d. 1674, Calvert County, Maryland) and Jean Reade (her second marriage). Susannah Duvall (b. 1676) was the daughter of Mareen Duvall (b. ca1630) and Susannah Brasseur (her second marriage), daughter of Benjamin and Marie Braseur of France.

Elizabeth Duvall (b. 1697) was the daughter of Samuel Duvall (b. ca1667, Anne Arundel County, Maryland; m. June 18, 1697; d. 1742, Prince George's County, Maryland) and Elizabeth Ijams Clark (her 2nd marriage, with first m. to Daniel Clark). Elizabeth Ijams (b. ca1671, Anne Arundel County, Maryland) was the daughter of William Ijams (d. 1703, Anne Arundel County, Maryland) and Elizabeth Cheyney (b. 1652; d. ca1726, daughter of Richard and Charity Cheyney).

Samuel Duvall (b. 1667) was the son of Mareen Duvall (b. ca1630), and the brother of Susannah Duvall (b. ca1676), wife of Robert Tyler, Jr. (b. 1671). The child of Elizabeth Duvall (b. 1697) and Edward Tyler, Sr. was Elizabeth Tyler (b. 1721; d. Berkeley County, Virginia, 1795); who m. 1740, in Prince Georges County, Maryland, to Stephen Rawlings (b. 1713, Anne Arundel County, Maryland). Stephen Rawlings (b. 1713) was the son of Aaron Rawlings (b. 1667; d. 1741) and Susannah Jones (daughter of Dr. William Jones of Anne Arundel County, Maryland); and the brother of William Rawlings, Jonathan Rawlings, Aaron Rawlings, and Ann Rawlings. The child of Stephen Rawlings (b. 1713) and Elizabeth Tyler (b. 1720) was Edward Rawlings (b. 1745, Berkeley County, Virginia; m. 1765, Berkeley County, Virginia, to Rebecca Van Meter, daughter of Jacob Van Meter and Letitia Strode. The families had moved to Redstone (Brownsville) in western Pennsylvania by 1779, and then to Louisville, Kentucky, shortly thereafter.

The will of Edward Rawlings (b. 1765) was written in July 1792 and proven on July 26, 1796, in Hardin County, Kentucky, and named wife Rebeckah, daughter Elizabeth Hart, daughter Ann Hart, daughter Letitia Fairleigh, and daughter Rebeckah Rawlings. Letitia Rawlings (b. 1769; d. 1794, Hardin County, Kentucky), m. 1st on September 3, 1787, Nelson County, Kentucky, to Silas Hart (killed by Indians), and m. 2nd, on August 2, 1791, in Nelson County, Kentucky, to Andrew Farleigh, Sr. (b. 1761; d. 1823).

Elizabeth Rawlings (b. 1766, Berkeley County, Virginia; d. 1844, Hardin County, Kentucky), m. 1st, to Miles Hart, in 1780, and m. 2nd, March 7, 1797, in Nelson County, Kentucky, to Peter Gunterman (b. 1760; d. 1817, son of Henry Gunterman and Elizabeth Cass). The will of Miles Hart was written September 6, 1786; proved June 8, 1790. Elizabeth Rawlings and Miles Hart, and the children of Elizabeth Rawlings and Miles Hart were captured by the Indians. A son, Joseph Hart, was rescued by Josiah Hart, an uncle, but Elizabeth Rawlings Hart was taken to Detroit. En route to Detroit, she delivered a baby which died a few months later in Detroit. She later convinced a French fur trader to purchase her from the Indians and return her to Kentucky. The estate of Miles Hart (September 6, 1786) included payment for expenses to Josiah Hart for his part in the rescue process (SR). Known children of Elizabeth Rawlings Hart and Miles Hart were Joseph Hart and Edward Hart, plus those killed at the time of the capture. Children of Elizabeth Rawlings Hart and her second husband, Peter Gunterman, were:

1) Nancy Gunterman (b. November 24, 1797, Kentucky; d. August 22, 1842; m. August 23, 1816, in Bullitt, Kentucky, to Samuel Price (b. 1795; d. 1868, Lincoln

County, Missouri); 2) Sarah Gunterman (b. January 2, 1802, Kentucky; d. March 11, 1839, Hardin County, Kentucky; m. August 2, 1819, to Reverend Bailey Seaton Tabb (b. 1799; d. 1876, Cass County, Missouri); and 3) Katherine Gunterman (b. 1807, Kentucky; d. 1853, Spencer County, Indiana; m. 1827 to John Kellams who was b. 1806; d. 1886, in Orange County, Indiana).

The child of Katherine Gunterman and John Kellams was Gideon Riley Kellams who was a colonel in the 42nd Indiana Volunteers in the Civil War, who served from Chickamauga to Atlanta, and who was buried in Spencer County, Indiana. Gordon Riley Kellams had a son, Wesley W. Kellams, who owned and edited the *Rockport Democrat* newspaper in Rockport, Indiana, and who was buried in Spencer County, Indiana (SR). The son of Wesley W. Kellams was W. Wayne Kellams, a graduate in Electrical Engineering from Purdue in 1911, who lived in St. Louis, Missouri; and who worked for Union Electric of Missouri. The daughter of W. Wayne Kellams was Sue Kellams Rulfs, who lived in Ann Arbor, Michigan, and who contributed to this family history. Sue Kellams Rulfs had five children (four daughters and one son) and ten grandchildren (nine boys and one girl).

William Iiams, number four above, the oldest son of William Iiams and Elizabeth Cheyney, was born in Anne Arundel County, Maryland, in 1670, and died in Anne Arundel County, Maryland, in 1738 (LIH, RNI, CWH). William Iiams (b. 1670) m. August 27, 1696, to Elizabeth Plummer, the only daughter of Thomas Plummer and second wife, Elizabeth Yates Stockett, a Quaker of West River, Maryland. Elizabeth Plummer was baptized at All Hallows Parish, Anne Arundel County, Maryland, July 19, 1698, after their marriage, and she died in 1762. Elizabeth Yates was the granddaughter of George Yates and Mary Wells (b. 1652). George Yates was the founder of Annapolis, Anne Arundel County, Maryland. Elizabeth Yates was the daughter of Joseph Yates.

William Iiams (b. 1670) was a vestryman at All Hallows Parish. William Iiams lived on the homestead on a portion called Bridge Hill, surveyed in 1669 for Henry Stockett. He also managed a tract of 64 acres called Dodon, which was purchased from Henry and wife Katherine Stockett on May 20, 1696, for three thousand "pounds" of tobacco. The will of William Iiams (b. 1670) was written June 28, 1734, and proved May 17, 1738, in Anne Arundel County, Maryland, was witnessed by Richard Williams, Richard Welch, John Nicholson, Jr. and Richard Williams, Jr. The will named sons John Iiams, Plummer Iiams, Richard Iiams, William Iiams, and Thomas Iiams; and daughters Ann Iiams, Elizabeth Iiams, Mary Iiams, and Charity Iiams; with Thomas Iiams and John Iiams named executors. In the will, the name of the wife is spelled Elizabeth Jiams, and she was left the estate, except as specifically named. Son William Jiams was willed the 100-acre plantation called Cheyney's Resolution, plus five shillings. Son John Jiams was given a 100-acre parcel called Bridge Hill, with the land to go to son Plummer Jiams should John Jiams have no heirs, and likewise, John was to inherit Plummer's land should Plummer have no heirs. Plummer Jiams was willed the homestead of 64 acres, adjacent to Bridge Hill, after the death of widow Elizabeth Cheyney Jiams. Sons Richard Jiams, Thomas Jiams and William Jiams; and daughters Mary Jiams as well as Charity Jiams were all willed five shillings. Sons Thomas Jiams and John Jiams were named as executors.

The will of the mother, Elizabeth Plummer Iiams (Folio 31, Maryland Archives), was written May 5, 1762, and probated in Anne Arundel County, Maryland, September 22, 1762. That will declared that sons John Iiams and Plummer Iiams, as well as daughter Ann Williams were to divide the negroes and the plantation originally designated to son John Ijams. Daughter Ann Ijams was to receive the wearing apparel, and daughter-in-law Ruth Ijams was to receive the earthenware and the side saddle. Son John Ijams was also to receive the furniture and the "great looking glass." Son Thomas Ijams was to be given 10 pounds of money from the other three children. The small looking glass was for son Plummer Ijams. John Ijams was executor; and witnesses were Ariana Ijams, Mary Tull, John Phelps and Richard Harwood, Jr. Elizabeth Plummer Ijams was the daughter of Thomas Plummer and Elizabeth Yates. Elizabeth Yates was the daughter of George Yates (d. 1691) and Mary Wells (she m. 1st, Thomas Stockett). Mary Wells was the daughter of Richard Wells (d. 1667) and Frances of Herring Bay Hundred, Virginia. Richard and Frances White Wells had eleven children:

    1) Richard Wells (m. Sophia Erven)
    2) Anne Wells (m. Dr. John Stansby)
    3) Benjamin Wells (m. Frances Hanslap)
    4) Elizabeth Wells (d. young)
    5) Frances Wells (d. young)
    6) George Wells (m. Blanche Goldsmith)
    7) John Wells
    8) Mary Wells (see above)
    9) Martha Wells (m. Anthony Salloway)
    10) Robert Wells
    11) William Wells.

Elizabeth Plummer (m. William Iiams) was the daughter of Thomas Plummer (b. before 1630, England). The will of Thomas Plummer was written July 12, 1694, Anne Arundel County, Maryland, and left son Thomas Plummer, Jr. 100 acres, Domon's Delight, in Calvert County, Maryland, and 300 acres. Scott's Lot was willed to daughters Mary Plummer (m. William Jackson) and Margaret Plummer (m. Hugh Reilly). Daughter Susanna Plummer (m. Francis Swansen) was willed personal items. Widow Elizabeth Plummer, executor, was willed the 164-acre plantation, Bridge Hill. Daughter Elizabeth Plummer (m. William Iiams) was left the remainder of the estate. Children of Thomas Plummer (b. before 1630) and Elizabeth Stockett (JBM) were: 1) Thomas Plummer; 2) Margaret Plummer; 3) Mary Plummer; 4) Susanna Plummer; and 5) Elizabeth Plummer.

Children of Thomas Stockett and Mary Wells were: 1) Thomas Stockett; 2) Frances Stockett; 3) Elizabeth Stockett (see above); and 4) Mary Stockett. The family of Frances White (m. Captain Richard Wells, surgeon, father of Mary Wells) has been traced to King Edward III of England (alias Charles Martill) and on back to 80 B.C. Egypt of Mark Anthony (JBM).

The children of William Iiams (b. 1670) and Elizabeth Plummer:

    1. Elizabeth Iiams (b. June 15, 1697; christened June 19, 1698); m. Gassaway Watkins (b. 1697) (FEW, JFI).
    2. William Iiams (b. December 22, 1699; baptized July 26, 1700; lived on Cheyney's Resolve, South River, Anne Arundel County, Maryland); m. October 9, 1720, at South River, to Elizabeth "Liza" Jones (b. 1699), daughter of William Jones. They had five children. On April 20, 1751, William Iiams purchased part of Cheney's Resolution from John and Samuel Jacob. This line is continued later in this chapter (FEW, LDS).
    3. Richard Iiams (b. 1701, christened March 4, 1702, South River, Anne Arundel County, Maryland), m. January 19, 1737, to Mary Nichols (FEW) or Eleanor Pottenger (b. 1702) (LDS). This line is also continued later in this chapter.
    4. Mary Iiams (b. May 6, 1705; baptized August 26, 1705, or October 13, 1705) (IGI); m. 1st, to John Waters, a Quaker and son of John Waters and

Elizabeth Gates, or to Richard Wright (RWI), with daughter Margaret Wright, born Septembert 18, 1729. This line is continued later in the chapter.

5. Thomas Iiams [b. August 7, 1708 (RWI, HWN) or 1710 (LIH), at Bridge Hill plantation, Anne Arundel County, Maryland; d. 1768, Washington County, Pennsylvania (RWI)]; m. Artridge Waters (LDS, RWI) who was born 1708; or m. Elizabeth Hill (b. 1730), daughter of John Hill of Prince Georges County, Maryland (JBM). This line, with modifications, is expanded elsewhere in the book.

6. John Iiams (b. 1712, South River, Anne Arundel County, Maryland; baptized at All Hallows Parish, 1718; d. 1783 in Anne Arundel County, Maryland), m. Rebecca Jones (b. 1712; d. 1783), daughter of Isaac Jones (one of eight children). John Iiams was a Captain in the Revolutionary War militia, a member of the prestigious South River Club (organized 1740) by 1742, and father of John (Jack) Imes, famous progenitor of the Imes family featured later in the chapter and son of a slave woman owned by an Anne Arundel County neighbor and plantation owner, Joseph Howard. This remarkable lineage has been chronicled by Carmen W. Harleston and is presented later in this book. Captain John Iiams (b. 1712) and wife Rebecca Jones had eight children.

7. Plummer Iiams (b. 1716, South River, Anne Arundel County, Maryland; or August 6, 1718 (LDS); baptized at All Hallows Parish, Anne Arundel County, Maryland, August 6, 1718; lived at Dodon (JIH, FEW); d. November 26, 1792 (or 1772) in Anne Arundel County Maryland); m. South River, Anne Arundel County, Maryland, in 1747 (HCP), to Ruth Childs [d. November 26, 1792 (SH), or December 24, 1794 (LIH)], and they had five children. Brothers Plummer Iiams and William Iiams were vestryman at All Hallows Parish in 1768, when John Galloway deeded the parish land to Reverend David Lent. Plummer Iiams' family settled the area of Maryland, near Frederick, now known as Ijamsville (JH, HWN, HCP, LIH, FEW, LDS). This line is continued in later pages.

8. Charity (or Rebecca) Iiams [b. 1698 (LDS) or 1707, South River, Anne Arundel County, Maryland; m. January 28, 1724, Prince Georges County, Maryland, to John Waters (b. 1698 (LDS)), son of Samuel Waters and Sarah Arnold, and lived in Prince Georges County, Maryland]. The line is continued in later pages.

9. Anne B. (or M., per JFI) Iiams (b. 1709, South River, Anne Arundel County, Maryland, or 1700 per LDS); m. 1st, to Richard Williams (or Willis); and m. 2nd, to William Iiams (d. 1780), son of George B. Iiams (d. 1732). Geroge B. Iiams and her father William Iiams (b. 1670) were brothers.

Children of Second Child of William Iiams (b. 1670) and Elizabeth Plummer, William B. Iiams (b. 1699) and his Wife Elizabeth Jones

1. William Ijams III (b. November 22, 1721, South River, Anne Arundel County, Maryland; d. 1774), single, a carpenter; heir of the Cheyney's Resolution plantation, but a 1750 legal battle cost him the property. On November 27, 1750, he purchased 100 acres from John Jacob for the sum of 80 pounds. He executed his will on January 25, 1774, and it was probated in Anne Arundel County, Maryland, on August 26, 1774. William Ijams was executor; John Ijams and Thomas Ijams were sureties; and he left bequests to his mother Elizabeth Jones Ijams, his single

sister Sarah Iiams, and the residual of his estate to his cousin William Iiams, son of John Iiams and Rebecca Jones. The estate was appraised by Thomas Iiams and John Ijams, Jr., kinsmen, at 245 pounds, 7 shillings.

2. Cassandra Ijams (b. September 20, 1722, South River, Anne Arundel County, Maryland); m. December 13, 1735 (FEW) or December 16, 1736 (IGI), South River, Maryland, to Henry Leeke. This line has been compiled in detail by James B. Meighen, and will be described below.

3. Margaret Ijams (b. August 13, 1724, South River, Anne Arundel County).

4. Sarah Ijams, named as being single in 1714 will of her brother.

5. Thomas Plummer Ijams [b. 1726 (or 1728, EFB), Anne Arundel County, Maryland], m. Mary Ijams (b. 1735), daughter of John Iiams (b. 1712) and Rebecca Jones (AIC), and thus, a first cousin. James B. Meighen acknowledges that while this may be true, the family never acknowledges this fact. They are believed to have had three children: 1) John Iiams (b. 1775, Maryland), m. 1794, to Rachel Marriott. John Iiams (b. 1775) was a captain during the seige of Fort McHenry, Maryland, during the War of 1812; was known by the title, "The Old Defender;" later moved to Ohio; had 7 children, including: Franklin (or Fayette) Ijams, who m. Harriet Brown and they had a child, Charles Plummer Ijams who m. Rebecca Clay; and they had three children: Margaret Ijams (m. William Tucker), Maud Ijams (m. Judson Hunt), and Franklin Ijams [m. Olivia Nuez, and they had four children: Anna Ijams Sutton (d. 1917), Emma Ijams, Margaret Ijams (m. Walter Oggessen), and John Plummer Ijams (m. Helen Bernheimer, and their child was Ann Alicia Ijams), per AIC, EIL, JO1, JBM]; 2) Rebecca Ijams; and 3) Mary Plummer Ijams (b. 1768, Anne Arundel County, Maryland; d. 1848, Morris Township, Greene County, Pennsylvania), m. William Penn (b. 1762, Baltimore County, Maryland). This Mary Plummer Ijams has been the subject of heated debates, but is placed here as a result of the research of James B. Meighen, who feels that she was not the daughter of Thomas Iiams (b. 1798; d. 1868) as listed by Harry Wright Newman, and others; or daughter of John Iiams (b. 1712). Children of Mary Ijams and William Penn, included: Richard Penn, Mary Penn, Nancy Penn, Susannah Penn, William Penn, Nathan Penn, Thomas Penn, Matilda Penn, John Penn, Margaret Penn, Sarah Penn, and Ruth Penn.

Cassandra Ijams (b. 1722), second child of William Iiams (b. 1699) and Elizabeth Jones (see above); and her husband Henry Leeke (b. 1711), son of Henry Leeke, Sr. (JBM) had six children: 1) Joseph Leeke (d. 1805); 2) Mary Leeke [b. February 10, 1747, m. Capel Holland (b. August 8, 1723; d. 1823), and this line is continued below]: 3) Henry Leeke III (b. 1749, served in Revolutionary War); 4) Obed Leeke (son of second wife); 5) Lucy Leeke Moore; and 6) Ann Leeke (m. James Brown).

Mary Leeke, second child above (b. 1747), m. Capel Holland (b. 1733), and they had seven children: 1) Jacob Holland [(b. 1764, m. Mary Gordon of Fayette County, Pennsylvania, and they moved to Indiana. Their daughter was Cassandra Holland Powers]; 2) Mercy or Messey Holland (b. 1764, m. Solomon Pelly or Brown, and lived in Harrison County, West Virginia); 3) Elizabeth Holland [(m. April 29, 1804, to Reverend John Nowell or Howell (b. 1785), and children were Capel Howell and Sarah Howell); 4) Cassandra Holland [(b. May 4, 1771; d. December 2, 1805) m. 1789 to John Adam Gordon (b. November 3, 1762; d. January 22, 1816); this line is continued below]; 5) Reezin Holland [b. February 23, 1776; d. September 9, 1851, in Monongalia County, West Virginia); m. January 11, 1807, to Joann Hanna Wilson (b. 1786), and they had 13 children: Capel Holland (b. 1808), Mary Holland (b. 1809), William Holland, (b. 1811), Sarah Ann Holland, Anna Holland (b. 1813), Eli Holland (b. 1815), Sarah Holland (b. 1818), Reezin Holland, Jr. (b. 1822, m. Leah Way, also b. 1822), John Holland (b. 1822), Joann Holland (b. 1824), Amelia Holland (b. 1828), Solomon Holland (b. 1831), and Elizabeth Holland (b. 1826) who m. H. G. West (b. 1825) and they had nine children: William Holland West (his children were Elizabeth West and John West), Lancelot John West, Joannah H. West, Sallie J. West, Hamilton G. West, James H. West, Sarah West, Jane West and Esther West (b. 1861)]; 6) Brice Holland; and 7) Eli Holland (d. Greene County, Pennsylvania, in 1816; single).

Cassandra Holland (b. 1771), who m. John Adam Gordon (b. 1762), had seven children:

1) Delilah Gordon [(b. June 20, 1790), m. Adam Shriver (b. June 29, 1788), lived in Ohio, a line of Air Force Colonel, Astronaut and United States Senator from New Concord, Muskingum County, Ohio, John Glenn, Jr., a line which continues below];
2) Lucy Gordon (b. February 9, 1792; m. Isaac Shriver);
3) Ara Gordon [(b. July 1, 1796; m. 1st, Solomon Cain, m. 2nd, Squire Clark, m. 3rd, Reverend Barnet Whitlatch), whose four children were: a) Sarah Ann Cain, who m. Joe Guinn, and had five children: Haddie Guinn (m. William Hall and had five children: Guinn Hall, Duite Hall, Raymond Hall, Mary Hall, and Lylian Hall), Leasure Guinn, Ella Guinn, Eva Guinn and Linnie Guinn; b) Kathryn Cain Filbey (whose four children were: Albert Filbey, Rebecca Filbey, Nora Filbey and Hadie Filbey); c) Maria Cain (m. Owen Pitcock and had six children: William Pitcock, Brice Pitcock, Alberta Pitcock, Plezzy Pitcock, Ray Pitcock and Bertha Pitcock); d) Caroline Cain, m. Thomas J. Morris, and had eight children: Emma Morris Glennen (had two children: Helen Glennen Jacobs, whose children were Charles Walter Jacobs and John W. Jacobs; and Walter Glennen); George Morris (m. Lizzie Kennedy and had seven children: Alice Morris, Lawrence Morris, Helen Morris, George Morris, Winifred Morris, Elizabeth Morris and Edward Morris); Florence Morris Lippencott (b. 1893; had three children: Herbert Lippencott, Ruth Lippencott Schuck and Robert Lippencott); Frank Morris (b. 1877; m. Bell Kennedy and had three children: Paul Morris, Russell Morris and John K. Morris); Mark Morris (b. 1880; m. Nettie Rinehart who was b. 1882, and had two children: Nell Morris, who m. Glenn Canen; and Elizabeth Morris); Lula Morris (m. William Baynham, and their daughter was Ruth Baynham); Thomas J. Morris (had three children: Dorothy Lee Morris, Jack Morris and Burdette Morris); and Edith Morris];
4) John Brice Gordon [(b. December 4, 1798; d. 1876), m. Delilah Inghram (b. 1821; d. 1898), and had five children: a) Carrie Lee Gordon (b. 1848); b) George W. Gordon (b. 1853), m. Helen M. Scott (b. 1855), and they had two children: Lucy Delilah Gordon (b. 1880) and Carrie Lee Gordon; c) Elizabeth Gordon (b. 1850); d) Lucy Emma Gordon Brock (b. 1855, m. a physician), whose daughter, Delilah Brock Shannon had a son Herbert Shannon; e) John Brice Gordon (b. 1864), m. Amanda Cowell (b. 1879), lived in Greene County, Pennsylvania, and had three children: George W. Gordon (b. 1899, m. Lula Shannon Everly);

13

Elizabeth Gordon, and Ethel Gordon (m. Carl Spragg), whose daughter Joann Spragg m. David Wermlinger, and had five children: Rebecca Jane Wermlinger (b. 1949), Betsy Carol Wermlinger (b. 1951), Brenda T. Wermlinger (b. 1953), Bruce Wermlinger (b. 1955), and Barbara Ann Wermlinger (b. 1959);

5) Solomon Gordon [(b. April 2, 1801), m. Sarah Inghram (b. 1805), had seven children: a) John Brice Gordon (b. 1830); b) James M. Gordon [(b. 1839), m. Delilah Adamson and had ten children: Lettie Gordon, Clarence Gordon, Ella Gordon, William Gordon (b. 1825), George Gordon, John Brice Gordon (m. William Knox), Mettie Gordon, and Joseph Solomon Gordon (m. Matilda Ammons), had three children: Martha Marie Gordon (b. 1908, m. Frank Davis), Joseph Ammons Gordon (b. 1914, m. Marie Dee Baker, and whose son was Brian Lee Gordon), and Delilah Gordon, b. 1911, m. John Summersgill, and had three children: Martha E. Summersgill, b. 1932, m. Albert Lackney and had two children: Linda Lou Lackney, b. 1952, and Lela Michelle Lackney, b. 1956; John Gordon Summersgill, b. 1934, m. Sally Hay, and had four children: John J. Summersgill, b. 1955, Stacy Sue Summersgill, b. 1958, Stuart G. Summersgill, b. 1959, and Patrick C. Summersgill, b. 1961; and Charles W. Summersgill, b. 1942, m. Carol Sue Sato and had two children: Shelly Sue Summersgill, b. 1964, and William S. Summersgill, b. 1970]; c) William Gordon (b. 1828); d) Adam S. Gordon [(b. 1829, m. 1st, L. Ann Rhodes, and had three children; then m. 2nd, Nancy Hannah Rinehart, b. 1831, and had three additional children), who had six children: Emma L. Gordon; Ankrom Gordon (m. Dasie Harrington, and had two children: Kenneth H. Gordon, who m. Mary Sutton; and Helen Margaret Gordon, who m. Carl Hoffman, and had three children: Eleanor Lee Hoffman, John Lynn Hoffman and Allan Hoffman); James W. Gordon (m. Cora Vanetta, and had six children: Lydia Gordon, who m. Charles Stansell; Hazel Gordon; James Clark Gordon; Gail Gordon, Vanetta Gordon, and Wilson Gordon); Thomas Franklin R. Gordon (b. 1869, m. Josephine Adamson, and had two children: Erving Gordon, who m. Margaret Scott, and had two children: Virginia Gordon, who m. Paul Inghram; and Harold Gordon; and Adam Byron Gordon, b. 1905, m. Helen Dodd Morris, and whose daughter, Carolyn Jean Gordon, m. Clyde Barger, and had two children: Debra Lynn Barger, who m. David Anthony Young, and Sandra Barger); Solomon Gordon (b. 1870, m. Charlotte Sproat, and had two children: Margaret Sproat Gordon, and Adam Randolph Gordon, who m. Lillian Phillips); and Lafayette Gordon]; e) Elizabeth Gordon (b. 1826); f) Margaret Gordon (b. 1834); and g) Cassandra Gordon [(b. 1833), who m. J. R. Tygart, and their daughter Sadie Tygart (m. Andrew J. Waychoff) had eight children: Rose Waychoff (m. John Shriver, and had six children: Cassie Sarah Shriver, Cecil Donley Shriver, Charles Ray Shriver, Russell James Shriver, Edward Paul Shriver, and Allen William Shriver), Nancy Waychoff (m. Nort Reese and had three children: Elizabeth Reese, Doris Jean Reese and Mary Jane Reese), Margaret Waychoff (m. Perry Thompson and had three children: Lucy Thompson, Earnest Thompson and Floyd Thompson), Emma Waychoff (m. William Clayton and had two children: Dorothy Clayton and Aldine Clayton), Albert Waychoff (two children: Edith Waychoff and Opal Waychoff), William Waychoff (five children:

Marie Waychoff, Sarah Waychoff, Martha Joan Waychoff, Charles Waychoff and Ralph Waychoff), Lucy Waychoff, and James Waychoff];
6) Elizabeth Gordon Shriver (b. December 10, 1803); and
7) Judge Marquis "Mark" Lafayette Gordon (b. January 22, 1794; d. 1886), m. 1st to Susannah Shriver (b. December 28, 1796; d. 1837), and m. 2nd to Eliza Shultz. This line is continued following the paragraph that follows the Delilah Gordon (b. 1790) line through the line to John H. Glenn, Jr.

Delilah Gordon (b. 1790), the daughter of Cassandra Holland (b. 1771) and John Adam Gordon (b. 1762, see above), m. Adam Shriver (b. 1788) and they had nine children: 1) Eliza Shriver, 2) Elijah Shriver, 3) Michael Shriver (m. Martha Woodrow), 4) Cassandra Shriver, 5) Margaret Shriver (m. John Deets), 6) Mary Shriver (m. Henry Pipes), 7) Mark Gordon Shriver (m. Rachel Kirkpatrick), 8) Solomon Shriver, and 9) Jane Shriver (m. Thomas White) whose daughter Mary White m. John C. Glenn. This John C. Glenn and Mary White had a son, John H. Glenn, Sr., who m. Clara Sproat, and who lived in New Concord, Muskingum County, Ohio, where he owned and operated the Glenn Plumbing Company. A son of John H. Glenn, Sr. and Clara Sproat was John H. Glenn, Jr., who m. Anna Castor, and her father was a pharmacist and owner of Castor Drugs of New Concord, Ohio. John H. Glenn, Jr., Marine Colonel, astronaut, and United States Senator, and his wife Anna "Annie" Castor, both attended Muskingum College, and had two children.

Judge Marquis "Mark" Lafayette Gordon, from above (b. January 22, 1794; d. 1886) m. 1st to Susannah Shriver (b. December 28, 1796; d. 1837), and had ten children:
1) John Adam Gordon [(b. 1816, Greene County, Pennsylvania), m. 1st, Rebecca Crawford; m. 2nd, Margaret Crawford, or Susannah Shriver; was a merchant in Greene County, Pennsylvania, and had ten children: Marquis L. Gordon (b. 1843, m. Agnes H. Donald, and had four children: Fannie Gordon, Donald Gordon, Mary Gordon and Crawford Gordon); John Crawford Gordon (b. 1846, m. Margaret Harper); Basil Jennings Gordon (b. 1848); William Lynn Gordon (b. 1850, m. Belle Hunt and had two children: Frances Gordon and Alice Gordon); Rebecca Alice Gordon (b. 1853); Solomon Gordon (m. Catherine Carson); Stephen D. Gordon; Robert H. Gordon; Edgar C. Gordon; and James R. Gordon];
2) Godfrey Gordon [(b. 1821, Greene County, Pennsylvania, a stockman), m. Elizabeth Crayne (b. 1820), and had seven children: Jerome Gordon (b. 1844, m. Julia Cosgray), Josephine Gordon (b. 1879, m. C. Bower, had two children: Ollie Bower and Jerome Bower), Robert Gordon (b. 1850, m. Jennie Allen, and their child was Allen Gordon), Emma Gordon (m. David Lemley), Lucy Crayne Gordon (m. John Eby, M.D. and their child was Mary Eby), and two Gordon children died as infants;
3) Basil Gordon [(b. 1822, Greene County, Pennsylvania), m. Mariah Inghram (b. 1828), and they had seven children: John Adam Gordon (b. 1848) who m. Mariah Bell and their two children were Jessie Gordon (m. Wesley Smith, and their daughter Dorothy Smith m. John Davis, and had three children: Joretta Davis, Dianne Davis and Coleen Davis), and Frederick Gordon; Virginia Gordon (second child of Basil Gordon), who m. Thomas Montgomery, and they had six children: 1) Walter Montgomery (b. 1879), who m. Grace Sayers (b. 1880) and they had four children: Virginia Montgomery (m. William C. McDermott and their child, b. 1944, was Grace M. McDermott), Thomas F. Montgomery (b. 1911), m. Nancy Slaugherhaupt, and their child, b. 1942, was Thomas Ford Montgomery II, Hugh Montgomery (b. 1920, m. Margaret

15

Dinsmore, and their two children were Michael G. Montgomery and Susan W. Montgomery), and Walter C. Montgomery (b. 1918, m. Mavis Terry, and their child was Terry Montgomery); b) Bernice Montgomery (m. Earl Moredock); c) Florence Montgomery (m. Forrest Moredock); d) Bazil Montgomery; e) Pauline Montgomery; and f) Erving Montgomery; Sadie E. Gordon (third child of Basil Gordon) m. James Hatfield; Joseph A. L. Gordon (fourth child of Basil Gordon, b. 1856, m. Emma Cox, and their child was John Brice Gordon; Alice D. Gordon (fifth child of Basil Gordon) m. William Wood, and their child Gordon B. Wood m. Sadie Ocie Shultz, who was born 1889, and they had three children: Carlos G. Wood, Donald G. Wood (m. Emma Grimes), and William R. Wood (m. Margaret Kilcoyne, and their four children were: Isaac Wood, Nancy Wood, Rita Mae Wood and Linda Wood); Mack Gordon (sixth child of Basil Gordon); and an infant son of Basil Gordon who died early];

4) Alice Ellen Gordon [(b. 1828, m. Uriah Inghram (b. 1818), and they had nine children: a) Susan Inghram (m. Thomas Hook; children: Helena Hook and Jane Hook); b) Josiah A. Inghram (b. 1859, m. Laura M. Everly, and their child Mary Duke Inghram was born 1894); c) Delilah Inghram (m. Abner Hoge, and their child was Furman Hoge); d) Rebecca Inghram (m. Frank Inghram, and their children: Mark Inghram and Alice Inghram); e) Emma Inghram; f) Catherine Inghram; g) Thomas Inghram; h) Frances Inghram (m. Dr. Spragg, and their daughter was Kathryn Spragg); and i) William Inghram (m. Haddie Bell, and their three children were: Crawford Inghram, James Inghram and Frances Inghram)];

5) Delilah Gordon (m. 1st, Harvey Higgens; and m. 2nd, John I. Worley, but had no children);

6) Elizabeth Gordon (single);

7) Katherine Gordon [m. Thomas Porter, and they had two children: William A. Porter (m. Jennie Strosnider, and they had three children: Thomas Porter, Charles Porter and Helen Porter Hiller), and Emma Inghram Porter (m. Frank Lapping, and their son was John Lapping)];

8) John Brice Gordon [(b. 1817), m. Hannah Shultz (b. 1821), and they had six children: Mack Gordon (b. 1839), Susan E. Gordon (b. 1841), Delilah Gordon (b. 1844), Sarah J. Gordon (b. 1846), Margaret Gordon (b. 1846), and Frances E. Gordon (b. 1850)]];

9) Cassandra Gordon [(b. 1825) m. Hamilton Maple (b. 1821), and they lived in Greene County, Pennsylvania, where they had nine children: a) Mark Maple, b) Adam Maple (m. Sadie Day, and had two children: Raymond Maple and Harvey Maple), c) Basil Maple, d) Sidney Maple, e) Lafayette Maple, f) Sarah Maple, g) Elijah Maple (m 1st, Lyde Clark, and m. 2nd, Mary Orndorff), b) Ida Maple (m. Melvin Nichols), and i) Susan Maple, who was b. 1848, m. Eli Newton Duvall, who was b. 1854, who lived in Greene County, Pennsylvania, and who had four children: Alice Cassandra Duvall (b. 1875), Charles Leonard Duvall (b. 1877, m. Ida Ora Clark, and had five children: Charles Duvall, Orville Russell Duvall, Samuel John Duvall, Harry Pershing Duvall, and Melvin Richard Duvall), Mark B. Duvall, and Fanny O. Duvall (b. 1887). Samuel John Duvall (b. 1917) m. Rita Boyle, had four children: John Samuel Duvall, Karen Ruth Duvall, Mary Rita Duvall and David Mark Duvall. Harry Pershing Duvall (b. 1919) m. Emma Stephans, and had three

children: Sammye Duvall (b. 1943, m. Eleanor Vivian Dzurian), Charles John Duvall (b. 1944), and Tanya Jeannette Duvall (b. 1948). Melvin Richard Duvall (b. 1921) m. Elizabeth Jane Durbin (b. 1932) and their three children were: Joseph Richard Duvall (b. 1952), Lawrence Edward Duvall (b. 1956), and Charlene Sue Duvall (b. 1958)];

10) William Holland Gordon [(b. March 10, 1833; d. June 12, 1901, lived in Greene County, Pennsylvania), m. December 24, 1856, to Margaret Maria Whitlatch (b. April 3, 1834; d. May 23, 1910), and they had seven or eight children, including: a) Lucinda Gordon (b. April 14, 1858; d. December 26, 1943, a schoolteacher), m. January 22, 1881, to John Meighen (b. July 19, 1843; d. 1933), whose family line is continued in the following paragraph; b) Katherine Gordon (b. April 14, 1858), m. James Jones Sammons (b. 1855; d. 1936, lived in Moundsville, West Virginia, who had three children: Gordon Sammons (b. 1896), Margaret Sammons (m. Walter Hartman and had three children: Elizabeth Hartman, Catherine Hartman, and Johanna Hartman) and Elizabeth Sammons); Harriet Gordon (b. 1867; d. 1925) m. George B. Orndorff (b. 1863), lived in Greene County, Pennsylvania, and they had five children: Elizabeth Orndorff (m. Floyd Miller, newspaper editor, and their four children were: Virginia Miller, Richard Miller, Harriet Miller, and Mary Miller), Ruth Orndorff (m. James Taylor, and their three children were: Marie Taylor, James Taylor, and Charles Taylor), Florence Orndorff (b. 1899, m. Harvey Higgins, and their four children were: William Gordon Higgins, Ruth Ann Higgins, who m. Charles B. Blair, Betty Joe Higgins who m. Dwight Blair, and John Higgins), Ralph Orndorff (b. 1895), and Edith M. Orndorff (b. 1897); d) Elizabeth Gordon (b. October 5, 1871; d. May 9, 1925), m. William A. Elms (b. October 15, 1869; d. October 7, 1959), lived in Greene County, Pennsylvania, where they had four children: Laura Elms (m. Thomas H. Morris, b. 1915, and they had two children: Andrew Jackson Morris and Ruth Lynette Morris), George Gordon Elms (b. 1897, m. Bessie Lewis, and their daughter Elizabeth Jane Elms was born 1925), Anna Elms, Alice Elms, and Helen Elms (b. 1896); e) Mary Gordon (b. July 11, 1865) m. Newton Brown (b. November 13, 1860), a farmer, lived in Greene County, Pennsylvania, and had nine children, including: George Brown (an engineer, whose children were Granley Brown, Violet Brown, Walter Brown, and Mary Brown), Barnet W. Brown (an engineer, b. 1888, son Allen Brown), Margaret Brown (b. 1890), Mark Gordon Brown (m. Jessie G. Thomas, children: Margaret Brown and James Davis, a tailor), Ambrose Brown (m. Evelyn Davis, and their children were Evelyn Brown, Wilma Brown, Kenneth Brown and Martha Brown), Benjamin Brown (died in infancy), Anna Brown (m. Raymond Mason, lived in Greene County, had four children: Everett Mason, John Ray Mason, George Mason and Ruth Anna Mason), Dorothy Brown (m. William Phillip, and their three children were: William Phillip, Elizabeth Phillip and Robert Phillip), Harriet Brown (b. 1897, m. Sherman Roberts, and their five children were Phyllis Roberts, Delilah Roberts, Wilma Roberts, James Roberts, and Sherman Roberts), and Edgar Brown (b. 1903); Sherman Roberts (b. 1922, m. Mary Emma Morris and their two children were: Robin B. Roberts and Rick B. Roberts; John Ray Mason (m. Helen Headley, and their daughter was Sheila Kay Mason, b. 1943); f) Sadie Gordon (d. age 16); and g) Margaret Gordon (m. Quincy Arthur Jones, but they had no children).

17

Lucinda Gordon (b. April 14, 1858; d. December 26, 1943), daughter of William Holland Gordon (b. 1833), m. January 22, 1881, to John Meighen (b. July 19, 1843; d. 1933), a Union soldier in the Civil War. Lucinda Gordon (b. 1858) and John Meighen (b. 1843) had twelve children:

1) William Gordon, or Holland, Meighen [b. October 22, 1881, Greene County, Pennsylvania; a schoolteacher, killed in France during World War I), m. Laura Armstrong (b. 1885)];

2) Lucy Holland Meighen [(b. April 11, 1883), a schoolteacher, m. David Edward Porter (b. 1884), and their child Glenn Edward Porter (b. 1911) m. Annette Mae Burry (b. 1910) and had thirteen children including Eleanor Kay Porter (b. 1942), Carol Jean Porter (b. 1944) and Glenn Edward Porter (b. 1946)];

3) Mark Meighen [(b. January 13 1885), a farmer, m. Olive Hughes (b. 1892), and they had six children: a) John Hughes Meighen (b. 1910, m. Mary Catherine, their three children: John Martin Meighen, Michael Meighen and Sandra Meighen), b) Frank Meighen (b. 1912, wife Catherine, had two children: Patricia Meighen and Robert Frank Meighen), c) Harold Meighen (b. 1914), d) Bernice Meighen (b. 1915, m. Dale Stollar, and their three children were: Wayne Stollar, William Stollar and Ronald Stollar), e) Jane Meighen (b. 1917, m. Harry Flynn, child: Terri Flynn), and f) Margaret E. Meighen (b. 1920)];

4) Frank Whitlatch Meighen [(b. March 30, 1886; d. November 1, 1960), a schoolteacher and banker, m. March 11, 1912, to Mary Luvina Huffman (b. February 17, 1888; d. July 14, 1971, a schoolteacher, and they had two children: a) Anne Gordon Meighen (b. February 25, 1913, school-teacher, graduate of Waynesburg College), and b) James Brice Meighen (b. April 21, 1915, Waynesburg, Pennsylvania, noted genealogist and scientist, who had prepared the Iams genealogy as a teenager, with works published by his mentor and pharmacist, Howard Lecke; an engineer who worked out concepts in theoretical physics, graduate of Waynesburg College in 1938), m. June 23, 1944, to Helen Elizabeth Murdock (b. March 15, 1917; graduate of Carnegie Tech, 1938), and who had four children: Nancy Ann Meighen (b. 1946, m. Jack Harold Biel, and had three children: Dana Leigh Biel in 1970, Tracy Elizabeth Biel in 1973, and James Gordon Biel in 1979), Mary Elizabeth Meighen (b. 1950, m. Ross Howard Carnes, and their three children were: Heather Elizabeth Carnes in 1976, Ross Christopher Carnes in 1978, and Jennifer Lynn Carnes in 1986), John Murdock Meighen (b. 1952), and Helen Marie Meighen (b. 1957, m. Steven Ray Ultested, and their two children were: Matthew Donald Ultested in 1985 and Jesica Marie Ultested in 1987)];

5) John Lynn Meighen [(b. May 15, 1888, a banker in Pittsburgh, Pennsylvania; m. Lucy Elizabeth Ely (b. 1891) and they had three children: a) Ida Martha Meighen (b. 1920), m. Robert Lester Jamison, lived in Oklahoma, had two children: Robert Lee Jamison in 1941, and John Paul Jamison in 1944, the latter married Bertha Eleanor Penske), b) George Allen Meighen (b. 1929, m. Barbara Annella Hiott, and they had two children: Ann Garrison Meighen in 1957, and George Allen Meighen in 1959), c) John Lynn Meighen, Jr. (b. 1933, m. Mary Rose Dodson, and they had two children: Lyn Ann Meighen in 1963, and Betty Jean Meighen in 1965)];

6) Alice Margaret Meighen [(b. August 4, 1889), m. Elzie Lee McGlumphy (b. 1888), lived in Washington, Washington County, Pennsylvania, and

had seven children: a) Earl Gordon McGlumphy (b. 1910, m. Kathleen Coggins, and their son Earl Gordon McGlumphy II was b. 1942, m. 1st to Delores Jean Jedlowski, and m. 2nd, Faynella R. Zetoo; with two children by first marriage: Kelly Jean McGlumphy in 1977 and Debra Ann McGlumphy in 1980; and one child by second marriage: Earl Gordon McGlumphy III); b) Helen Mae McGlumphy (b. 1913, m. John Harry Frazier and had one child: Robert Lee Frazier, in 1936, who m. Barbara Comfort, and they had two children: John Douglas Frazier and unknown); c) William Lee McGlumphy (b. 1915); d) Naomi Ruth McGlumphy (b. 1916, m. Arthur Beden Morris; their child: Richard Lynn Morris in 1952); e) Mary Alice McGlumphy (b. 1918, m. William Quay Johnston and their son was John William Johnston); f) Vera Lucinda McGlumphy (b. 1926, m. William J. Brown, and their two children were: Timothy Mack Brown in 1949, and Alice Arletta Brown in 1952); and g) John Ralph McGlumphy (m. Patricia Ann McNabb, and their son Brian Edward McGlumphy was b. 1967)];

7) Catherine Jane Meighen [(b. July 4, 1891), m. William H. Minton, lived in Greene County, Pennsylvania; they had seven children: a) Dorothy Minton (b. 1912, m. John Wilbur Thompson, their daughter Nancy Thompson m. Robert D. Worstell and had child Karen Lynn Worstell); b) a daughter, b. 1914, m. Harvey Ferrell, amd they had two daughters; Mary Ferrell (a twin, m. Richard Bayard, and their daughter was Rita Bayard), and Martha Ferrell (a twin, m. William Urban, and their two sons were William Urban and Gary Urban); c) James W. Minton (b. 1916, m. Mildred Murray, and their three children were: William Minton, Linda Minton and Lisa Minton); d) John Gordon Minton (b. 1919, m. Inez Clutter, their two children: Susan Arlene Minton and Jerry L. Minton); e) Robert Lynn Minton (m. Wahnetta Clark and their two children were: Robert Lynn Minton Jr. and Bonnie Jean Minton); f) Edward M. Minton (m. Patricia Rutan, and their two children were: Jody Minton and Edward Douglas Minton); and g) R. Frank Minton (m. Evelyn Whipkey, and their three children were: Christine Minton, Carol Minton and Sharon Kay Minton)];

8) Robert Pattison Meighen [(b. August 12, 1892), m. Cora Lapping, lived in Greene County, Pennsylvania; they had two children: a) Harvey David Meighen (b. 1917, m. Helen Brook, and their twins were: Donald David Meighen and Donna Kay Meighen), and b) Anna Helen Meighen (m. Lee W. Wise, and their daughter Sara Leanne Wise m. Edward T. Warren, Jr., and they had two sons: Frederick Warren and Albert Warren)];

9) James Lewis Meighen [(b. July 26, 1894), a schoolteacher, m. Olive P. Murphy (b. 1901), lived in Greene County, Pennsylvania; their two children were: a) William Edward Meighen (b. 1921, m. Jesse L. Reed), and they had two children: James William Meighen (b. 1944, m. Sharon Ann Inghram, and they had two children: Jamie Lynn Meighen in 1968; and Patrick James Meighen), and Leslie Ann Meighen (m. Richard Ross, and their four children were: Kimberly Jane Ross in 1964, Deborah Suzanne Ross in 1968, John Ross and Rebecca Ross); and b) Margaret Jean Meighen (b. 1925; m. 1st to Raymond Carl Gray, and their daughter Beverly Ann Gray, b. 1947, m. Ray Douglas White; and m. 2nd to William Harry Barnhart, and their son William D. Barnhart was b. 1965)];

10) Adalyn Elizabeth Meighen [(b. October 14, 1895, m. 1st, John Hughes (b. 1885), lived in Washington, Pennsylvania, and they had one daughter

Carolyn Hughes (Jones) in 1915, who m. Herbert R. Staggers, and they had seven children: 1) Carolyn Rae Staggers (b. 1939, m. Robert Thomas Andersen, and they had two children: Susan Lynn Andersen and Scott Robert Andersen); b) Peggy Ann Staggers (b. 1941); c) Richard H. Staggers (b. 1946); d) Sarah Sue Staggers (b. 1945); e) David Lee Staggers (b. 1946); f) Donna Joe Staggers (b. 1948); and g) Ralph Lynn Staggers (b. 1950, m. Janice Phillips, and their daughter was Melissa Lynn Staggers); m. 2nd, to Walter McCarrihan, and their son was Donald W. McCarrihan (b. 1917, m. Josephine McClay, and their two children were Donald McClay Meighen and John Price Meighen, b. 1949); and m. 3rd to Lawrence Thomas (and their daughter, Lois Thomas, m. Edward Devlin, and they had three children: Patrick Michael Devlin, Sharon Kelly Devlin, and Lucinda Lynn Devlin)];
11) Mary Frances Meighen (b. October 21, 1896); and
12) Glenn Edward Meighen (b. August 18, 1904, a schoolteacher).

Charity (or Rebecca) Iiams (b. 1698, South River, Anne Arundel County, Maryland), m. January 28, 1724, in Prince Georges County, Maryland, to John Waters (b. 1698). Charity Iiams (b. 1698) is listed above as the eighth child of William Iiams (b. 1670) and Elizabeth Plummer.

Charity Iiams, daughter of William Iiams (b. 1670) and Elizabeth Plummer, was born December 10, 1698 (LDS) or after 1718 (HWN, RWI), and m. John Waters (b. October 10, 1698, Anne Arundel County, Maryland), son of Samuel Waters and Sarah Arnold. They lived in Queen Anne's Parish of Prince Georges County, Maryland. The will of John Waters was dated March 17, 1768, and probated October 27, 1776, in Prince Georges County, and named a son, Samuel Waters, of Anne Arundel County, Maryland, Sarah Arnold was the daughter of Richard Arnold, planter, and Martha Thomas. Charity Iiams and John Waters had eleven children:
1) Samuel Waters [(b. January 28, 1726, Prince Georges County, Maryland), m. Sarah Arnold or Elizabeth Burton (b. 1726). The will of Samuel Waters (dated November 27, 1703: probated in Anne Arundel County, June 13, 1700) (sic), named sons Samuel Waters, John Waters, William Waters, an unborn child; daughers Mary Waters; and Elizabeth, wife of John Giles]:
2) Elizabeth Waters (b. January 27, 1729, Prince Georges County, Maryland; or February 12, 1729), single (LDS, RWI);
3) John Waters II (b. December 11, 1735, Prince Georges County, Maryland);
4) Thomas Waters;
5) Arnold Waters (b. 1737, Prince Georges County; m. Rachel Franklin);
6) Mary Waters (m. 1773 to Stockett Williams);
7) Sarah Waters Norris (b. 1749, Prince Georges County, Maryland);
8) Ann Waters (b. 1751, Prince Georges County, Maryland; m. Nathaniel __man);
9) Susannah Waters (b. 1753; m. George Roberts);
10) Charity Waters [b. 1755, Anne Arundel County (BL), m. Edward Collinson (b. 1745, Anne Arundel County), and they had seven children: a) Alice Collinson (b. December 22, 1772, Anne Arundel County; m. Samuel Harper, b. 1772); b) William Collinson (b. April 29, 1781, Anne Arundel County; m. Elizabeth Whittington, b. 1781); c) Sarah Collison (b. March 20, 1784, Anne Arundel County; m. Richard Gott, b. March 25, 1776, Anne Arundel County); d) Edward Collinson (b. 1786);

e) John Collinson (b. 1788); f) Mary Collinson (b. 1790); and g) Benjamin Collinson (b. 1792)]; and
11) William Waters.

Thomas Iiams (b. August 7, 1708, Anne Arundel County, Maryland), listed as fifth child of William Iiams (b. 1670) and Elizabeth Plummer; m. a woman whose first name was Artridge, and was introduced above (HWN).

Thomas Iiams (b. August 7, 1708, Anne Arundel County, Maryland) purchased a part of Duvall's Delight, Anne Arundel County, in 1730, from Charles Carrol; and an additional 100 acres of Duvall's Delight, in 1741, from Charles and Mary Hogan. In his will of October 27, 1766, the witnesses were John Iiams and Mary Iiams; with John Iiams and Plummer Iiams witnesses to a codicil. The will, probated November 28, 1768, listed son Thomas Iiams, executor; sons John Iiams, Thomas Iiams, Richard Iiams and William Iiams, and daughter Susanna Pumphries, all to share in the estate. As the estate was being settled, Elizabeth Ijams and John Ijams were named as next of kin. Newman lists ten children of Thomas Iiams (b. 1708):
1) Elizabeth Iiams (b. August 19, 1732); 2) Sarah Iiams (b. December 8, 1734); 3) Artridge Iiams (b. February 6, 1736); 4) Charity Iiams (b. January 15, 1739); 5) Susanna Iiams (b. December 15, 1742; m. Mr. Humphreys); 6) Thomas Iiams (b. April 20, 1745; m. Mary Iiams and Sarah Marriott); 7) John Iiams (b. October 20, 1747; m. Susannah Watkins); 8) Richard Iiams (b. February 15, 1749; m. Eleanor Musgrove); 9) Mary Iiams (b. June 10, 1752; m. Thomas Ijams or Joseph Penn); and 10) William Iiams (b. November 26, 1755; m. January 5, 1782, to Charity Ryan).
This family line has been the subject of considerable controversy, and all proposals should be considered as tentative. The birth date of Thomas Iiams has also been set at 1710 (LIH), his wife as Artridge Waters (MI), or Elizabeth Hill, daughter of John Hill of Prince Georges County, Maryland (JBM). On May 7, 1795, Benjamin Penn and wife Rebecca, of Hopewell, Bedford County, Pennsylvania, sold Duvall's Delight to William Iiams, a blacksmith, for 100 pounds, with the plantation being occupied by Vachel Warfield. Children of Richard Iiams and Eleanor Musgrove (EFB) include: 1) Thomas Musgrove Ijams (b. 1774; d. 1848, in North Carolina; m. Nancy Carvel); 2) Nancy Ijams (b. March 10, 1792, Frederick County, Maryland; d. February 11, 1858, in Cornelice, Missouri; m. December 18, 1812, to John B. Cecil); and 3) Amelia Fisher Ijams (inherited one-third of the family estate, Frederick County, Maryland, in 1800).
Roberta Wright and Guy R. Ijames have listed son John (b. 1751; d. 1873) as the spouse of Elizabeth Hampton, who was buried at Franklin Cemetery in Washington County, Pennsylvania; son Thomas (b. 1754 in Maryland; d. 1836, in Belmont County, Ohio) as spouse of Catherine Hampton; son Richard (d. 1800), as spouse of Eleanor Jones, and with his will probated November 7, 1800, in Frederick County, Maryland; son William as spouse of Mary Hampton; and daughter Mary as spouse of William Penn, of Baltimore, Maryland, who moved to Washington County, Pennsylvania.
This son Richard (d. 1800, in Frederick County, Maryland), had at least three children, including a Richard Iiams (m. Eleanor Pottenger and moved from Frederick County, Maryland, to Bates Fork, Greene County, Pennsylvania, in 1790, where they raised their seven children: 1) Thomas Iiams (m. Mary Smith); 2) Richard Iiams (m. Mary Shidler); 3) Otha Iiams (m. Nancy Cole); 4) Resin Iiams (m. Phoebe Clark); 5) John Iiams (m. Ruth Bacher) who lived in Athens County, Ohio; 6) Bazil Iiams, who was single; and Eli Iiams (m. Phoebe Heckathorn). William Iiams (m. Mary Hampton) had four children: 1) Elizabeth Iiams (m. Daniel Smith), 2) Mary Iiams; 3) Thomas Iiams (b. 1784 in Washington County, Pennsyl-

21

vania; m. Mercia Walton); and 4) John Iiams (b. 1792; m. Ann Coulson). Thomas Iiams (b. 1784) may have m. Mercia Bonnell (RWI).

Harry Wright Newman described the lines of three of the sons of Thomas Iiams (b. 1708): Thomas Iiams (b. 1745), John Iiams (b. 1747) and Richard Iiams (b. 1749). **Thomas Iiams** (b. 1745), inherited part of the estate Duvall's Delight in 1766; married first to his first cousin Mary Iiams (daughter of John and Rebecca Iiams), and had at least two children (John Iiams, b. 1775, m. Rachel Marriott; and Rebecca Iiams, b. 1777, m. Joseph Marriott); and m. 2nd to Sarah Marriott, daughter of Joseph Marriott (b. 1774). The son John Iiams (b. 1775, m. Rachel Mariott, daughter of Joshua Marriott and Anne Homewood), remained in Anne Arundel County, Maryland; had seven children: 1) Franklin Lafayette Ijams (m. 1824 to Harriet Brown); 2) Rebecca Marriott Ijams (m. John Ijams); 3) Richard William Ijams (m. Rebecca H. Marriott, in 1832); 4) Isaac Plummer Ijams (m. Cecelia Smith Moxley); 5) Joshua Barney Ijams; 6) Rachel Maria Ijams (m. Voltaire Willett, in 1836); and 7) Anne Homewood Ijams (m. 1824, to Benjamin Brown), but these lines are not followed further (HWN).

John Iiams (b. 1747) is believed to have married Susannah Watkins Taylor, widow of Joseph Taylor, but the line is not followed beyond that marriage (HWN). **Richard Iiams** (b. 1749) m. Eleanor Musgrove, settled in Frederick County, Maryland, where he was a millwright, owned a portion of Duvall's Delight in 1777, is inconsistently portrayed (HWN) as having died in 1800, and having been married twice, with one child by each marriage: Thomas Musgrove Ijams (m. Nancy Carvel), and Nancy Ijams (b. March 10, 1792; m. December 18, 1812, in Rowan County, North Carolina, to John B. Cecil, and she died February 2, 1858, in Johnson County, Missouri, where he also died January 21, 1861). HWN also lists a William Iiams as a fourth brother of Thomas, John, and Richard Iiams), but this merely emphasizes the inconsistencies of the lineages described for Thomas Iiams (b. 1708).

James B. Meighen and Howard Leckey have described Thomas Iames (b. 1708) to m. Elizabeth Hill. While most researchers agree that there were four brothers who migrated to southwestern Pennsylvania (Richard, Thomas, William and John Iiams) just prior to 1800, the problems remain to specifically identify the earlier lineages of these brothers and to separate them from the many relatives with the same given names. The names of these brothers appear on early tax records of Greene and Washington Counties of western Pennsylvania. The Reverend Fred Cochran, Howard Leckey, James B. Meighen and Ervin F. Bickley, Jr. have accepted the times for this migration: William Iiams (1791), John Iiams (1791), Richard Iiams (1794), and Thomas Iiams at about the same time.

While modern day Iiams (Iams, Ijams, Imes, etc.) continue to define the spelling of their name with variable difficulties, Jay D. Iams, M.D., well-known physician and medical researcher at the Ohio State University School of Medicine, has expressed his appreciation for the emergence of the Iams Pet Food Company as a means of ready reference for his patients to know how he spells his name. This prosperous Ohio pet food company was founded by Paul Iams, now living near Phoenix, Arizona. It is now a probability that the exact lineage in the pre-1850 era will never be resolved to the satisfaction of all researchers, in spite of the outstanding contributions of careful, diligent, and thorough workers, including Newman, Bickley, Hartman, Meighen, Lecley, Cochran, and others; as pointed out by Mrs. Allen Iams of southwestern Pennsylvania.

Oral history often plays an important part of the eventual recording of the various family lines. As a case in point, Paul Iams, founder of the Iams Pet Food Company, wrote in 1994 that his family line was believed to be traced to the Revolutionary

War days in Maryland, when two brothers (James Iams and Thomas Iams) wished to cross a river, but found two Hessian soldiers guarding that crossing. During the ensuing argument, the two soldiers were killed. Rather than return, the two Iams brothers continued west to Erie, Pennsylvania, and then to Trotwood area in Ohio (near Dayton, Ohio). This Thomas Iams had a son, Eli Iams, who purchased "160 acres of good land for a song," and had twelve children, including nine sons: Martin Iams, Richard Iams, George Iams, Alfred Iams, Jacob Iams, David Iams, Harvey Iams, Howard Iams, and Loren Iams.

Loren Iams, at a height of 73 inches, was the "smallest of the bunch" of "big powerful men," described by Paul Iams as "I guess they raised a lot of hell according to some people I talked to." This Loren Iams was the grandfather of the pet food founder who recognizes that "I have given the name some publicity since I started the Iams Pet Food Company who have advertised the name pretty extensively. "Because of the wide variations in individual researcher results, this author has taken an editorial approach so that the recognized works on the family lines will not be discredited; but instead, to present the various lines as alternative lines of relationships between family members, and to acknowledge this work through references, as reported by the authors.

Leckey, Meighen and Cochran have expressed the belief that the Richard Iiams who married Eleanor Pottenger was not one of the four brothers that migrated to Greene and Washington Counties, Pennsylvania, and that this Richard Iiams married Eleanor Jones. Leckey describes the migrating Richard Iams as a Revolutionary War soldier; Thomas Iams as being buried in Greene County, Pennsylvania, in 1843; and Richard Iams as having died in 1825 and buried in Bates Fork Cemetery, Greene County, where the grave is marked by "rude sandstones" marked with the initials "RI" and "EI" (for his wife).

Leckey gives the offspring of Richard Iams and Eleanor Pottenger as: Thomas Iams (m. Mary Smith), Richard Iams, Otho Iams (the Allen Iams family line), Rezin Iams, John Iams, William Iams, Boyd Iams, and Eli Iams. Bickley had corresponded with H.W. Newman and was apparently able to convince Newman that there were errors in the reporting of the Iams family lines in his published texts. Bickley had proposed (later disproved) that a Richard Iams (m. Mary Nichols in 1737 in Maryland) was the father of the four migrating brothers. In another version, the seven children of Thomas Iams (b. 1708) were listed (EFB) as follows:

1) John Iams (b. July 2, 1751 or 1750; d. September 12, 1823), m. Elizabeth Hampton (EFB, LIH) and one of their children, William Iiams (b. 1790) m. June 6, 1816, to Delilah Meeks (b. June 6, 1793; d. September 6, 1876);

2) Thomas Iiams (b. 1754 or December 26, 1754; d. June 28, 1834, or 1836) m. November 29, 1785, in Baltimore, to Catherine Hampton (EFB, JIH), b. 1765, d. May 12, 1834, and among their children were: John Iiams, Samuel Iiams (b. 1795, d. August 21, 1860, m. Elizabeth Meek), Thomas Iiams (m. Mary Hardesty), William Iiams (m. Susanna Sharp) and Rezin Iiams (b. December 13, 1807; m. Mary Iams);

3) Richard Iiams (d. 1800, Maryland), m. ___ ___, to (EFB) Elinor Jones, Elinor Musgrave (JIH), or Elizabeth Pottinger (EBI) of Hagerstown, Maryland;

4) William Iiams (b. 1751; d. February 23, 1795, in Washington County, Pennsylvania), m. February 21, 1795(?) (EFB) to Mary Hampton (EBI), and their children included Thomas Iiams (b. 1790), John Iiams (b. January 25, 1792; d. December 12, 1866), who m. Anne Coulson (EFB);

5) Susannah Iiams (m. Mr. Pumphreys);

6) Mary Iiams (b. 1769), m. April 8, 1788, to William Penn, son of John Penn, of Baltimore, Maryland; and who had six children (one of their grandchildren m. Thomas Iams in 1850) (LIH, EBI); and

7) Prudence Iiams (EBI, JCW), m. John Sargent (b. 1756; d. 1852, at age 95, Guernsey County, Ohio) who moved to a farm about ten miles east of Cambridge, Ohio, about 1835; and their children included Jeremiah Sargent (b. December 31, 1797; m. Mary Smith, daughter of Thomas Smith and Mary Rupp of Washington County, Pennsylvania, and whose daughter Ellen Sargent m. George Emerson; Mary Rupp, being the daughter of John Rupp and Ann Ro__ of West Alexandria, Washington County, Pennsylvania; and John Rupp, being famous for having been shot by Indians in 1782, Washington County, Pennsylvania); and second child, daughter, Margaret Sargent (m. Mr. Potts and lived in Guernsey County, Ohio).

Other researchers (JM, GRI, HL, REI) have accepted these seven children of Thomas Iams (b. 1708) with some reservations. John Iiams could have been born 1750, 1751, 1752, or 1756; and could have died 1822, and buried in Franklin Cemetery, Ten Mile, Washington County/Greene County, Pennsylvania.

Richard Iiams could have been born in 1745. William Iiams could have been born 1745. The tombstone of Thomas Iiams in Richland Township, Belmont County, Ohio, appears to give his death as June 24, 1834, and his wife Catherine Gill Hampton was the sister of both Elizabeth Hampton and Mary Hampton, each of whom married one of these Iiams brothers. Mary Iiams was probably called "Elizabeth" and may have had the middle name "Plummer" (JBM), with birth dates of 1758, or June 10, 1752 (REI), and m. Captain William Penn in Saint Paul's Church, Baltimore County, Maryland (license April 8, 1788); though some have doubted that she was the daughter of Thomas Iiams (b. 1708), electing instead for placing her as the daughter of Richard Iiams (b. 1745). Patience Iiams (m. John Sargeant) could have been the given name for Prudence Iiams. Captain William Penn (m. Mary Iiams) was a member of Captain Ezekial Rose's Company of 5th Battalion in the Washington County, Pennsylvania Militia, and was a member of the Sandusky (Ohio) Expedition (*Pennsylvania Archives, Series VI*, Volume 2, pp. 203 and 399). This Mary Iiams is permitted by James B. Meighen to be listed here, but he prefers considering her as the daughter of Thomas Plummer Ijams (b. 1726), and has repeatedly found himself frustrated over the years by what he considers to be lack of consistency in the decision-making process by the various researchers of the Iams family lines.

Of the four brothers that settled in southwestern Pennsylvania, Richard Iams is believed to have been the earliest, settling at Bates Fork in Greene County in 1775, followed by John Iams, William Iams and Thomas Iams, each of whom settled in Washington County, Pennsylvania. (JBM)

One of the four brothers, Thomas Iiams (b. December 26, 1754, in Maryland; d. June 24, 1834, Belmont County, Ohio), m. Catherine Hampton, and one of their sons was William Iiams (b. September 8, 1793; d. April 20, 1859, in Washington County, Pennsylvania) who m. Susannah Sharp (b. 1795). One of the sons of this William Iiams (b. 1793) was John "Wesley" Iams (b. 1828, Washington County, Pennsylvania) who lived in eastern Ohio before settling in Ritchie County, West Virginia, where one of his daughters was Iola Ellen Iams (b. March 9, 1879, Ritchie County, West Virginia; d. April 15, 1959, in Ohio) who married William "Milton" Corbett. A daughter of Iola Ellen Iams (b. 1879) and Milton Corbett was Edna Louise Corbett (b. June 29, 1906, Noble County, Ohio) who m. Ray Campbell

Reynolds. Their son was Ralph D. Reynolds (b. February 22, 1934, Powhatan Point, Belmont County, Ohio) and his three sons were: Daniel Ralph Reynolds (b. October 21, 1960, Tacoma, Washington), Barry Duane Reynolds (b. March 31, 1962, San Antonio, Texas), and Ronald Arthur Reynolds (b. March 20, 1966, Fairfield, Solano County, California).

William (b. 1755) and Charity Ryan Ijams were said to have had:

1. William Ijams, Jr. (b. ca1783, Anne Arundel County) had five children: a son George (b. ca1803) plus three other sons and a daughter (b. 1805 to 1815).
2. John Ijams (b. ca1785, Anne Arundel County) who m. ca1808, Mary ___ (b. 1784-94; d. ca1830) who had 6 children between 1813 and 1833, including John J., Anne, Mary, ?Henry and ?Andrew; and ___.
3. Isaac Ijams (b. ca1798) who m. Margaret ___.

REI has recorded the children of Mary Iiams (b. 1752) and William Penn to include John Penn (b. 1808; d. September 5, 1872), m. 1832 to Deborah Iams (b. September 27, 1812; d. February 20, 1856), daughter of Reason Iiams (b. 1789; d. February 19, 1888), whose first wife was Phoebe Clark (b. June 30, 1789; d. November 2, 1845), and second wife was Nancy McClung (b. March 24, 1804; d. January 9, 1876).

The daughter of John Penn (b. 1808) and Deborah Iams (b. 1812) included Phoebe Penn (b. 1833; d. 1890) who m. Thomas Iams, Jr. (b. 1821; d. 1906), the son of Thomas Iams, Sr. (b. 1783) and Mary Smith. The son of Thomas Iams, Jr. (b. 1821) was George Iams (b. June 7, 1860; d. March 11, 1935), who m. Nancy Longdon (b. March 14, 1862; d. November 29, 1941). The son of George Iams (b. 1860) was Bryan Iams (b. 1895; d. 1956) who m. Hilda Wiese (b. 1896; d. 1974). The son of Bryan Iams (b. 1895) was Robert Elton Iams (b. 1925) who m. Shirley Branton (b. 1927).

Thomas Ijams (b. April 20, 1745, Anne Arundel County, Maryland; d. December 1806, Anne Arundel County, Maryland), son of Thomas (b. 1708) and Artridge Ijams; m. 1st, Mary Iiams (b. 1755), daughter of Captain John Ijam (b. 1712) and Rebecca Jones; and m. 2nd, Sarah Marriott. RWI has listed Thomas Ijams (b. 1745) as the son of William B. Iiams III (b. 1699). Children of Thomas Ijams (b. 1745) and Mary Iiams (EFB) include: John Ijams (b. June 1775, Anne Arundel County, Maryland; d. 1831, Anne Arundel County, who m. February 5, 1794, to Rachel Marriott, daughter of Joshua Marriott and Ann Homewood; and Rebecca Ijams (b. September 5, 1774, Anne Arundel County, Maryland), m. March 25, 1796, to Joseph Marriott.

The seven children (RWI) of John Ijams (b. 1775) and Rachel Marriott were: Franklin Lafayette Ijams (m. Harriett Brown); Rebecca Marriott Ijams (b. February 4, 1806; d. October 25, 1885; m. May 29, 1827, to John Waters who was b. November 21, 1807, in Fairfield County, Ohio; d. February 16, 1875); Richard William Ijams (m. Rebecca H. Marriott); Isaac Plummer Ijams (b. 1812; d. 1877; m. 1834 to Cecelia Smith Moxley or Moyley); Joshua Barney Ijams; Rachel Marie Ijams (m. January 7, 1835, to Voltaire Willett); and Ann Homewood Ijams (m. Benjamin Brown).

RWI and GRI have outlined extensive lineage for the family line of Thomas (b. 1708) and Artridge Waters Ijams and their six children: John Iiams (b. 1751, m. 1st, Susannah Watkins, and m. 2nd, Elizabeth Hampton); Richard Iiams (b. 1755; m. Eleanor Jones); William Iiams (b. 1756; m. Mary Hampton); Mary Iiams (b. 1762; m. William Penn); Susannah Iiams (m. Mr. Pumphreys); and Thomas Iiams, Jr. (b. 1754; m. Catherine Hampton).

In this line (RWI, EBI, GRI), John Iiams (b. 1751) had nine children:

1) William Iiams [(b. 1792; d. April 1869, Ten Mile, Washington County, Pennsylvania); m. Delilah Meeks (b. 1783; d. September 6, 1876), and they had ten children:

25

a) Miller James Iiams (b. July 4, 1819) who m. Sarah Eggy, and their six children were: William Lyman Iiams (m. Hannah M. Harkinson), Joseph Martin Iiams (m. Sarah Piatt), Thomas Morgan Iiams (m. Nancy Adamson), Alonzo Iiams, Frank Iiams, and Mary Iiams (m. Romeo Frier of Harrisonville, West Virginia);

b) John Hill Iiams (b. June 2, 1821; d. February 26, 1890; m. Rebecca McKenna);

c) Elisha Iiams (b. December 16, 1822; d. 1895; m. Cynthia Garber who was b. May 6, 1828; d. October 11, 1877), who had ten children: 1) Demas Garber Iams (m. Anne Dunn) who had three children: Winfield Scott Iams (b. September 18, 1882; m. Mable Phillips), William Wylie Iams (m. Laura Steele), Sarah Margaret Iams (m. M. P. Rush), Elisha B. Iams (m. Rowena Denman), John Howard Iams (b. 1879), and Clifford Haldon Iams (m. Bertha Waugaman); 2) William Owen Iiams (b. October 19, 1855; m. Katherine Shidler); 3) Delilah Iiams (m. Peter Voorhees); 4) Emma Iiams (m. William Hufford); 5) Lucy Idama Iiams (died young); 6) Reuben Iiams (died young); 7) Clara Iiams (b. 1868); 8) Cynthia Annabel Iiams (m. Norton Reese); 9) Margaret Pleasane Iiams (m. Lebius G. Garrett); 10) Elizabeth Iiams (m. J. M. Cowan);

d) Thomas P. Iiams, fourth child of William Iiams (b. September 24, 1824; d. June 2, 1902; m. Sarah Johnson (b. June 28, 1831; d. April 30, 1907);

e) Isaac Iiams (b. July 28, 1828; d. July 24, 1907), m. Anne Ferrell (b. 1832; d. March 20, 1905);

f) William P. Iiams (b. March 2, 1830; d. May 14, 1899), m. Elizabeth Farrell (d. July 8, 1863) and their three children were: Sarah F. Iams (b. 1854), John H. Iams (b. 1856), and Laura A. Iams (b. 1862);

g) Delilah Iiams (b. September 24, 1832; m. James Loudon-Johnson);

h) Mary Iiams (b. April 24, 1834; m. Jacob Bigler);

i) Abraham Iiams (b. September 24, 1836; d. Civil War); and

j) Rachel J. Iiams (b. April 11, 1839; m. Daniel Smith)].

2) Elizabeth Iams (b. 1792; d. age 21);

3) Anna Iams (b. 1793; d. age 6);

4) Sabina Iams (b. 1794; d. age 4);

5) Nancy Iams [(b. 1787; d. 1871), m. Joseph Martin (b. March 15, 1790; d. December 25, 1850, Washington County, Pennsylvania) who had four children: Anne Martin (m. Andrew Van Dyke), Sarah Martin (m. Neal Zollars), John Iiams Martin (m. Elizabeth Bane), and Morgan Martin];

6) John Iiams, Jr. [(b. August 1797; d. April 30, 1846];

7) Charity Iams [(b. 1799; d. January 19, 1876); m. John Smith (d. March 12, 1876, Washington County, Pennsylvania)];

8) Sarah Iiams [(b. 1804; d. April 15, 1838, Washington County, Pennsylvania)];

9) Mary Iams [(b. April 20, 1810); m. Moses Smith (b. 1806, Washington County, Pennsylvania; d. September 14, 1848)].

In the same line (RWI, GRI), Richard Iiams (b. 1755) had three children:

1) Richard Iams [(b. 1825, m. Elizabeth Pottenger) who had eight children:

a) Thomas Iams (b. 1843, Pennsylvania; m. Mary Smith); b) Richard Iams (b. 1829, Greene County, Pennsylvania; m. Mary Shidler, who d. 1868, Indiana); c) Otho Iams (m. Nancy Cole); d) Resin Iams (b. 1791; m. Phoebe Clark), and they had six children: Reason Iiams (b. 1821; m. Nancy Iiams), Richard Iiams (m. Lucinda Forner); Isaac Iiams (m. Elizabeth Williams); Ellen Iiams (m. Ephraim Conger); John Iiams (m. ___ Miller); and Deborah Iiams (m. John Penn; b. June 9, 1808); e) John Iiams (b. Athens County, Ohio; m. Ruth Barker); f) William Iiams (m. Charity ___); g) Bazil Iiams: h) Eli Iiams (m. Phoebe Heckathorn); and they had a son Richard Iiams (b. 1823 in Pennsylvania, who m. Phebe Jane Thompson, b. Montgomery County, Ohio; and they had five children: Alfred Iams, Richard Iams, Charles Iams, Alva Iams, and Howard Iams)].

2) Thomas M. Iams [(b. 1774; d. 1848; m. Nancy Carval) who had twelve children:

a) Ellen Ijams; b) John Ijams; c) Rachel Ijams; d) Henrietta Ijams (b. 1796, North Carolina; m. Samuel Cecil); e) Sarah Ijams (d. Johnson City, Missouri; m. Daniel Livingood); f) Richard Iiams (m. Ellen Collett; d. Davidson County, Missouri); g) Thomas Ijams (b. 1812; d. 1874, Johnson County, Missouri); h) Nancy Ijams (b. 1815; d. 1901, in Missouri; m. Salathial Stone); i) George Washington Ijams (b. 1817; d. Johnson County, Missouri; m. Elizabeth Cecil); j) Richard Iiams (b. 1831, North Carolina; d. 1906, Missouri; m. Charity Roberts); k) Mary Ijams (m. Philip Clinard); and l) William Ijams (m. Mary Leonard)].

3) Nancy Iams [(b. March 10, 1792, Frederick County, Maryland; d. February 11, 1858, Johnson County, Missouri); m. John Cecil (b. October 29, 1785, Frederick County, Virginia; d. January 21, 1801, Johnson County, Missouri)].

Also, in the same line (RWI, JBM, GRI), William Iiams (b. 1756, Maryland) had four children:

1) John Iiams [(b. January 25, 1792; d. December 12, 1866, Washington County, Pennsylvania); m. Anne Coulson; had son Samuel Iiams (b. April 8, 1817, Washington County, Pennsylvania; m. Nancy Grimes)];

2) Elizabeth Iams [(b. 1780), m. Daniel Smith];

3) Mary Iams; and

4) Thomas Iams [(b. 1785, Washington County, Pennsylvania; d. April 4, 1855, Shelby County, Ohio), m. 1st, Mercia Walton; m. 2nd, Mercy "Mercy" Bonnell (b. February 25, 1784, New Jersey; d. May 21, 1867, Shelby County, Ohio). Thomas Iams (b. 1785) had several children: 1) William R. Iiams [(b. February 13, 1807, Washington County, Pennsylvania; d. October 18, 1844, Shelby County, Ohio), m. Martha McClure, and they had seven children:

a) Thomas A. Iams (b. October 10, 1832, Shelby County, Ohio; d. March 16, 1868, Shelby County, Ohio), m. Mary F. Ellis, and they had three children: Frances J. Iiams (b. 1855, Shelby County, Ohio; d. 1925), m. Benjamin F. Parks (b. 1848); Martha C. Iams (b. July 6, 1858, Shelby County, Ohio; d. 1880), m. Hiram Howard Varner (b. 1843); and William W. Iiams (b. July 19, 1860, Shelby County, Ohio; d. October 14, 1927, Montgomery County,

27

Ohio), m. 1st, Freda Jaeger, and m. 2nd, Angela Catherine Hilbrant (b. 1861, Shelby County, Ohio; d. 1930, Montgomery County, Ohio) and their two children were: Guy Harrison Iiams (b. 1888, Ohio; m. Clara Bentrop) and Clyde Vernon Iiams (b. 1892);

b) T. John Iiams (b. 1834 or 1835, Shelby County, Ohio; d. March 13, 1907, Landes, Crawford County, Illinois), m. 1st, Mary R. Kraft (b. 1838, Shelby County, Ohio; daughter of John Jacob Kraft and Catharine Frank); m. 2nd, Mary A. Donaldson (b. June 2, 1846, Bicknell, Knox County, Indiana; d. August 12, 1885, Crawford County, Illinois. Sold land to brother Thomas in 1858 and donated land for Watts Cemetery. Three children by first marriage:

  1) Laura A. Iiams (b. 1859, Shelby County, Ohio; m. March 15, 1885, in Knox County, Indiana, to C. G. Davis;

  2) Ira Russell [(b. December 15, 1861, Champaign County, Illinois; d. March 6, 1949, Oblong, Crawford County, Illinois), m. September 13, 1883, Oblong, Illinois, to Huldah Jane Kieffer (b. September 24, 1864, Wapakoneta, Auglaize County, Ohio; d. March 5, 1922), daughter of Thomas D. Kieffer and Mary Catherine Orr; and had three children: S. Emma Iiams (m. 1st to Oren S. Strain, and had son John E. Strain; m. 2nd to Frank Fowler), Edith Effie Iiams (b. August 28, 1884, Oblong, Illinois; d. September 17, 1885, Oblong, Illinois; buried Watts Cemetery), and Mary Marguerite Iiams (b. August 7, 1907; d. Kansas; m. 1st to Roy Smith; m. 2nd June 12, 1940, to Lester Kintner)];

  3) Hettie Rose Iiams [(b. August 27, 1864, Champaign County, Illinois; lived in Marion, Indiana), m. December 24, 1884, Knox County, Indiana, to John Woodward Jackson (b. ca1855, Owensburg, Greene County, Indiana); and they had nine children: Omar Earl Jackson, Quince Dolphus Jackson, Myrtle Jackson, William V. Jackson, Sattie Velma Jackson, Opal F. Jackson, Joy Wilma Jackson, and twins Bonner Jackson and Bonnie Jackson].

There were five children of the second marriage of T. John Iiams (b. 1834 or 1835):

  1) Albert Iiams (b. November 1, 1867; d. December 22, 1878, Crawford County, Illinois; buried Watts Cemetery);

  2) Cora Ellen Iiams [(b. March 23, 1870, Bicknell, Knox County, Indiana; d. December 21, 1930, Oblong, Illinois), m. December 23, 1889, Oblong, Crawford County, Illinois, to William Henry Forcum (b. July 16, 1859, Oblong, Illinois); and their four children were: Martha Cleo Forcum (b. October 4, 1890, Oblong, Illinois; d. July 4, 1978; had son: Wilbur Malcolm Forcum, b. July 26, 1910, in Oblong, Illinois); Edith May Forcum (b. March 12, 1893, Oblong, Illinois; m.

P. V. Morris); Cecil Loy Forcum (b. July 5, 1895, Oblong, Illinois; d. November 27, 1982, Waco, McLennan County, Texas, m. February 12, 1923, Tulsa County, Oklahoma, to Margaret Eliza Taylor, b. March 6, 1898, Lucas County, Ohio; d. April 18, 1988, Waco, Texas; and their two children were: Phyllis Ann Forcum, b. November 20, 1926, and William Richard Forcum, b. August 25, 1927, Blackwell, Oklahoma); and Eva Leona Forcum (b. October 28, 1897, Oblong, Illinois; d. February 19, 1974, Monterey, California; m. Homer Glen Henderson; had seven children)];

3) Sarah Jane Iiams [(b. February 19, 1873, Bicknell, Crawford County, Illinois; d. June 25, 1956, Robinson, Illinois), m. B. W. Griffey (b. June 17, 1903); had two children: B. W. Griffey (b. 1903, a dentist in Robinson, Illinois, and Valeria Eileen Griffey (b. 1907, Illinois; m. October 31, 1926, Oblong, Illinois, to Rhoney Ray Saulsberry)];

4) Otis Hayden Iiams [(b. January 7, 1881, Illinois; d. May 12, 1959, Robinson, Illinois), m. 1st February 14, 1904, to Julia Myrtle Shipman (b. December 20, 1885, Crawford County, Illinois, daughter of Jesse Shipman and Sarah Littlejohn); and their four children were: Clara Iiams (m. Mr. Davis); Floyd Iiams, Harold Iiams, and Mildred Iiams (m. 1st Mr. Tatum; m. 2nd Frank Burchett); Otis H. Iiams m. 2nd to Ethel Clesta Williams (b. 1894, Iowa); and their two children were: Arthur Raymond Iiams (b. July 15, 1916; d. January 19, 1981), and John Murray Iiams (b. May 29, 1918; d. December 1977, in Missouri)];

5) Ida Leila Iiams [(b. October 3, 1883, Oblong, Illinois; d. October 2, 1973, Crawford County, Illinois), m. Harry O. Fowler (b. May 5, 1879, Crawford County, Illinois, son of James Fowler and Susan McCrillis); and their son was Howard M. Fowler (b. October 16, 1911; d. August 5, 1921, Crawford County, Illinois)].

c) William E. Iiams [(b. September 24, 1837, Shelby County, Ohio; d. 1913, Allen County, Ohio), m. July 22, 1858, Shelby County, Ohio, to Martha Anna Moyer (b. December 24, 1841, Port Jefferson, Ohio; d. March 24, 1905, Lima, Allen County, Ohio), daughter of George Moyer and Ann Consolver; and had twelve children: Alonzo Phillip Iiams (b. September 15, 1859, Shelby County, Ohio; d. December 13, 1952, Shelby County, Ohio; m. November 4, 1880, Shelby County, Ohio, to Ruth Ella Taylor; nine children, listed below); Emma Jane Iiams (b. September 22, 1861, Shelby County, Ohio; d. April 11, 1939, Lima, Ohio; m. July 27, 1880, Shelby County, Ohio, to Frank Marion Taylor; had five children); Elmer Rodifus Iiams (b. November 1863, Shelby County, Ohio); Charles Riley Iiams (b. April 12, 1866, Shelby County, Ohio; d. July 10, 1951, Lima, Ohio; m. March 15, 1895, Lima, Ohio, to Mary Elizabeth Watkins; four children, listed below); George Milton Iiams (b. September 17, 1867, Shelby County, Ohio; d. January 25, 1934, Allen County, Ohio; m. Minnie Decker; one daughter, Luella Iiams); William Edward Iiams (b. July 24, 1869, Shelby County, Ohio; d. June 5, 1954); Nora Della Iiams (b. and d. December 5, 1871, Shelby County, Ohio); Joseph N. Iiams (b. July 17, 1873, Shelby County, Ohio; d. July 9, 1953, Tiffin, Ohio; m. Alice Mary Hayes); Ida May Iiams (b. July 1876, Shelby County, Ohio; d. July 1941 in California); Cordelia Mattie Iiams (b. February 25, 1877, Shelby County, Ohio; d. July 24, 1879, Shelby County, Ohio); d. January 1, 1949, Compton, California; m. James Parsons; two daughters: Ruth Parsons, b. March 1898; and Ethel Parsons, b. August 1899); and Harry Early Iiams (b. April 11, 1882, Shelby County, Ohio; d. November 16, 1918, Lima, Ohio; m. Evangeline "Eva" Susanna Peterson; six children listed below)].

Alonzo Phillip Iiams [(b. September 15, 1859, Shelby County, Ohio), m. Ruth Ella Taylor; and their nine children were:

1) Ollie C. Iiams (b. February 20, 1882, Botkins, Ohio; m. October 1, 1903, Botkins, Ohio, to Lowell E. Blakely, b. March 10, 1882, Botkins, Ohio; son of Adam Blakely and Emma Cocklin);

2) Ertie Leona Iiams (b. September 24, 1884; m. Harvey B. Parke; and their four children were: a) Harold Ralph Parke, b. 1970; m. Elsie L. Heiland; b) Gerald Paul Parke, b. 1913; m. Ruth Lenox; c) Erma Eileen Parke, m. Gordon Eldon Baxter; and d) Donald Emerson Parke, m. Marian Busse);

3) Urril Vincent Iiams (b. May 12, 1886; d. December 8, 1965, Shelby County, Ohio; m. Pearl E. Griffis, and each of their two children had three additional children: Doyle Keith Iiams, b. November 20, 1928; m. Margaret Frances Toller; and their three children were: Kurt Allen Iiams, b. April 7, 1954; Pamela Lynn Iiams, b. June 21, 1956; and Elaine Susan Iiams, b. August 1, 1959, Shelby County, Ohio; and second child Myron Gale Iiams, b. February 24, 1921; m. Janice Elizabeth Roth; and their three children were: Gregory Keith Iiams, b. March 24, 1947; James Stephen Iiams, b. December 17, 1954; and Thomas Wayne Iiams, b. April 7, 1948, Shelby County, Ohio);

4) Winfred Ramond Iiams (b. August 31, 1890; d. February 21, 1967, Anna, Shelby County, Ohio; m. Edna Catharine Arnold; four children: a) Gerald Ralph Iiams, b. January 17, 1920; m. Thelma Pauline Everett; son was Richard Lee Iiams, b. July 24, 1951; b) male infant Iiams, b. September 11, 1921, Shelby County, Ohio; d. September 12, 1921; c)

Lester Charles Iiams, b. September 30, 1922; d. February 22, 1949, Shelby County, Ohio; and d) Marion "Pete" Iiams, b. October 29, 1925, Botkins, Ohio; d. October 1977, Ohio; m. Carmen Yount; child was: Charles Iiams);

5) Mandy Iiams (b. June 17, 1891; d. November 8, 1892, Shelby County, Ohio);

6) Florence L. Iiams (b. ca1893, Shelby County, Ohio);

7) Martha J. Iiams (b. October 31, 1894, Botkins, Ohio; m. October 31, 1916, to Harold N. Daugherty);

8) Alma G. Iiams (b. May 9, 1898, Botkins, Shelby County, Ohio; m. December 7, 1917, to Edward A. Sollman); and

9) Grace Iiams (b. October 23, 1901, Botkins, Ohio; m. September 24, 1921, to Edwin Nevin, b. December 4, 1899, New York City)].

Emma Jane Iiams [(b. September 22, 1861, Shelby County, Ohio), m. Frank Marion Taylor; had five children;

1) Walter Wilber Taylor (b. June 29, 1881; m. December 12, 1906, Lima, Ohio, to Iva Gertrude Leffler);

2) Bertha M. Taylor (b. November 7, 1883);

3) Charles B. Taylor (b. December 6, 1886);

4) Clevely O. "Pete" Taylor (b. September 10, 1888); and

5) Evy Taylor (b. December 21, 1894, Lima, Allen County, Ohio)].

Charles Riley Iiams [(b. April 12, 1866, Shelby County, Ohio), m. March 15, 1895, Lima, Ohio, to Mary Elizabeth Watkins, and they had four children:

1) Frank M. Iiams (b. August 1893);

2) Cordelia Bernice Iiams (b. August 7, 1901, Lima, Ohio; m. February 17, 1917, to John Charles Schwartz, b. February 11, 1900, Lima, Ohio);

3) Alice Irene Iiams (b. September 6, 1904; d. November 9, 1994, Toledo, Lucas County, Ohio; m. February 8, 1922, Lima, Ohio, to Charles Clyde Hanthorn, and their seven children were: Dorothy Hanthorn, Mary Hanthorn, Delores Hanthorn, Bertha Hanthorn, Harold E. Hanthorn, Charles C. Hanthorn, and Harry William Hanthorn);

4) Charles Ralph Iiams (b. December 28, 1907; d. May 1969; m. Bonnie L. Buck; their son was: Charles W. Iiams)].

Harry Early Iiams [(b. April 11, 1882, Shelby County, Ohio), m. Evangaline "Eva" Susanne Peterson, b. July 27, 1881, Mercer County, Ohio; and they had six children;

1) Martha Ida Iiams (b. ca1908, Lima, Ohio; m.

31

Robert Krause; two children: Robert Krause, Jr., and Dorothy Krause);

2) James Earl Iiams (b. September 10, 1907, Lima, Ohio; d. January 23, 1970, Toledo, Ohio; m. 1st, Rosella Mae Stevens; d. 1965; m. 2nd, 1929, Margaret Krause, no issue; m. 3rd, 1931, Leah Hopkins, no issue; two children: a) James Earl Iiams (b. August 16, 1926, Toledo, Ohio; d. November 6, 1926, Toledo, Ohio); and b) Donald Edward Iiams (b. April 5, 1928, Dayton, Montgomery County, Ohio; m. 1st, January 10, 1948, Toledo, Ohio, to Elaine Marie Van Tassel; two children; m. 2nd, 1958 to Mary Catherine Cramer; m. 3rd, 1968, to Constance Bondy; no issue; m. 4th, 1973, to Shirley Weller; no issue; m. 5th, 1981, to Linda Iiams, no issue; and the five children of Donald Edward Iiams, b. 1928, were: Barbara Ann Iiams, Donald Edward Iiams, Jr., Patrick Michael (Frayer) Iiams, Candace Susan Iiams, and Bruce William Iiams); Barbara Ann Iiams (b. January 10, 1848, Toledo, Ohio; m. March 15, 1968, to James K. Kent Eichner; and their five children were: Amy Lee Eichner, Holly Ann Eichner, John Daniel Eichner, Ashley Noel Eichner, and Whitney Rae Eichner); Donald Edward Iiams, Jr. (b. August 16, 1949, Toledo, Ohio; m. 1st, Jill Klulter; m. 2nd, 1987, to Tammy Hill; four children: a) Kelly Anne-Marie Iiams, b. April 15, 1973, Toledo, Ohio; m. 1994, to Justin Canfield, and their child was: Haley Kay Canfield, b. June 17, 1991, Toledo, Ohio; b) Andrew Edward Iiams, b. July 4, 1974; c) Jessica Lynn Iiams, b. January 22, 1975, Toledo, Ohio; and d) Loren Ashley Iiams, b. November 16, 1990; Patrick Michael (Frayer) Iiams (b. November 18, 1951, Toledo; m. January 27, 1979, Monroe County, Michigan, to Lisa Carol Della Contrada, and their three children were: Nicholas James (Frayer) Iiams, Laura Avery (Frayer) Iiams, and Patrick Joseph (Frayer) Iiams); Candace Susan Iiams (b. September 26, 1953, Toledo; m. April 24, 1970, Monroe County, Michigan, to Ronald Baron, and their two children were: Tracy Marie Baron and Richard Ronald Baron); Bruce William Iiams (b. May 15, 1958, Toledo, Ohio; m. Maria O'Brian; their two children were: Maura Iiams, b. October 14, 1987, Toledo, Ohio; and Eren Iiams, b. October 5, 1989, Toledo, Ohio);

3) Vista Florine "Flora" Iiams (b. ca1907, Lima, Ohio; d. ca1947, Toledo, Ohio; m. Mr. Hitz; son: Richard Inman Hitz);

4) Everett Milton Iiams (b. March 21, 1912, Lima, Ohio; d. February 6, 1977, Las Vegas, Nevada);

5) Evaline Alice Iiams (b. August 6, 1915, Allen County, Ohio; m. Harry Cressman Gregg; and their two sons were: Harry Cressman Gregg, b. January 17, 1945; and Allen Albert Gregg, b. January 5, 1949; m. Bonnie Lou Leonard); and

6) Flossie Ruth "Rosemary" Iiams (b. ca1917; m. Raymond Hess; and their three children were: Robert Collins Hess, Roberta Hess, and Timothy Hess).

d) Richard Iiams (b. August 23, 1839, Shelby County, Ohio; d. May 2, 1923, Corvallis, Oregon), m. June 16, 1863, Anna, Ohio, to Martha Ann Hardnock (b. February 5, 1843, Hagerstown, Maryland; d. April 14, 1920, Custer County, Nebraska; ten children:

1) Alice Iiams [(b. March 7, 1864, Sterling, Illinois; d. July 26, 1916, Lincoln, Nebraska), m. 1st, March 18, 1887, Lincoln, Nebraska, to Jefferson Harper Foxworthy; m. 2nd, August 15, 1899, Lincoln, Nebraska, to Ferdinand A. Truell)];

2) Samuel B. Iiams [(b. October 12, 1865, Anna, Ohio; d. September 12, 1921, Lincoln, Nebraska)];

3) Eliza Iiams [(b. August 24, 1867, Cass County, Nebraska; d. May 12, 1941, Salem, Oregon), m. March 11, 1889, Lincoln, Nebraska, to William J. Albright; son: Weldon Iiams];

4) William Marshall Iiams (b. December 21, 1869, Cass County, Nebraska; d. June 1930, Salem, Oregon), m. 1st, December 13, 1889, Kearney, Nebraska, to Lucy Ward (son Thomas J. Iiams, b. October 2, 1890; m. Alta Leda Graves); m. 2nd, March 3, 1898, Lincoln, Nebraska, to Harriet E. Ford; m. 3rd, March 9, 1874, Union County, Iowa, to Josefina Andreasdotter Burdette; children: A) Lois Rosalind Iiams (b. December 21, 1902, Adair County, Iowa; d. March 28, 1951, Salem, Oregon; m. Wallace Lawson); B) Mildred Burdette Iiams (m. April 25, 1909; m. Stanley Roscoe Busch; four children: James A. Busch, Karen M. Busch, Sandra S. Busch, and Linda Lou Busch; C) Manly William Iiams (b. October 30, 1910, Genoa, Nebraska; d. September 21, 1980, Adams County, Iowa), m. May 26, 1934, Clarke County, Iowa, to Jessie Nevada Johnson; six children: 1^1) Carole Ann Iiams [(b. April 4, 1936), m. Larry McLaughlin; three children: Kelly Kane McLaughlin, Lori Lei McLaughlin, and Ricky Ray McLaughlin]; 2^1) Donald Lawrence Iiams [(b.

33

November 18, 1937), m. 1st, Carol Sue Allen; m. 2nd, 1968, Frances Jean Rowley; five children: Barbara Sue Iiams (b. 1956); John David Iiams (b. 1957; d. 1984); m. Ellie Rodriguez; daughter Jennifer Iiams, b. 1975); Billy Gene Iiams (m. Michell Francis; child: Nicholas Allen Iiams, b. 1978); James Donald Iiams (m. Ginger Lee Headrick); and Joseph Daniel Iiams (b. 1973; m. Tricia ____; child: Stephanie Iiams)]; 3[1]) Dennis William Iiams [(b. July 6, 1941), m. Patricia Elaine Shawler; three children: Crystal Rae Iiams (b. November 16, 1962; m. Chris Harwood Johnson); Brian William Iiams (b. January 18, 1965; m. Jacqueline Frey); and Randall Wayne Iiams (b. October 29, 1972; m. Melanie Swigart; two children: Alison Dawn Iiams and Patrick Riley Iiams)]; 4[1]) Donald Eugene Iiams [(b. September 5, 1943), m. 1st, Miriam Delores Buckroyd Cowman (child: Michael Gregory Cowman Iiams); m. 2nd, Linda Marie Hitchcock; two children: John Christian Iiams (b. ca1968) and Curtis Eugene Iiams)]; 5[1]) Janet Kay Iiams [(b. April 6, 1947), m. Steven Ouada; four children: Gregory Thomas Ouada, Susan Elaine Ouada, Julie Ann Ouada, and Deborah Lea Ouada)]; 6[1]) [Sharon Elaine Iiams];

5) Elizabeth Martha Iiams [(b. August 24, 1873, Cass County, Nebraska; d. California), m. September 24, 1897, Lincoln, Nebraska, to Clarence Coombs Drummond (b. February 15, 1867, Mount Pleasant, Henry County, Iowa; medical missionary to India); four children: Donald L. Drummond (b. September 30, 1898, Landour, India; m. Dorothy Canan); Lois Maude Drummond (b. July 29, 1900, Conoor, India; m. Hugh W. Milner); Clarence Iiams Drummond (b. December 5, 1903, Mahoba, India; m. 1926, Nebraska, to Helen Elta Oberlies; and Helen Elizabeth Drummond (b. March 20, 1911, Haroa, India; m. 1937, Nebraska, to Linus Southwick II)];

6) Luther Richard Iiams [(b. August 30, 1876, Cass County, Nebraska; d. July 28, 1945, Salem, Oregon), m. December 25, 1900, Gothensburg, Nebraska, to Della Blanche Thompson (b. September 15, 1873, Russel, Iowa; five children: a) Gladise Iiams (b. ca1901; m. Anton Hibson; two children: Wallace Anton Hibson and Marilyn Hibson); b) infant boy Iiams (b. and d. August 16, 1902, Custer County, Nebraska); c) Virgil Truell Iiams (b. May 7, 1904, Custer County, Nebraska; d. September 27, 1916, Custer County, Nebraska); d) Jessie Pearl Iiams (b. January 1, 1907, Custer County, Nebraska; d. February 23, 1983, Salem, Oregon; m. 1st, October 14, 1929, to Lorents E. Hill; m. 2nd, December 17, 1942, Salem, Oregon; three children: Vern E. Hill, Charles Stanley Gadack, and

34

Mike James Gadack); e) Helen Blanche Iiams (b. ca1909, Nebraska; m. 1st, Floyd McCurdy; four children; m. 2nd, to Ivan Murphy; one child; the five children were: Floyd Lonnell McCurdy, Marquita Colleen McCurdy, Rita Colleen McCurdy, and Tynne Ivana "Lennie" Murphy)];

7) Arthur Conrad Iiams [(b. August 16, 1878, Cass County, Nebraska; d. February 21, 1951, Custer County, Nebraska), m. 1st, June 20, 1906, Nebraska, to Myrtle June Cowers; three children; m. 2nd, November 17, 1931, Nebraska, to Lucille Richie (no issue); the children of first marriage: Stanley Bernard Iiams, Lethia Rose Iiams, and Glenn Richard Iiams];

8) Edgar E. Iiams [(b. April 17, 1880, Cass County, Nebraska; d. February 26, 1883, Cass County, Nebraska)];

9) Austin Henry Iiams [(b. October 10, 1882, Cass County, Nebraska; d. August 26, 1953, Corvallis, Oregon), m. February 19, 1908, Turner, Oregon, to Elizabeth Katherine Hohl; two children: a) Edna Iiams (b. February 12, 1918, Benton County, Oregon; d. California), m. James Skrable; child: Mary Lou Skrable, b. ca1946); b) Meryl Austin Iiams (b. January 1, 1922, Corvallis, Oregon; career U. S. Navy pilot); m. December 24, 1949, Rhode Island, to Vera Garlow; three children: 1¹) Jeffrey Allan Iiams (b. April 1951, Monterey, California; d. 1978, Japan, U. S. Naval Academy graduate; pilot); 2¹) Gordon John Iiams (b. February 27, 1953, Alameda County, California; orthopedic hand surgeon, career U. S. Navy; m. May 26, 1988, Norfolk, Virginia, to Barbara Lee; three children: Jeffrey Allan Iiams, Joshua Austin Iiams, and Jaime Lynn Iiams); and 3¹) Vera Elizabeth Iiams (b. March 4, 1955, Honolulu, Hawaii; m. Santa Fe, New Mexico, to Terrence John Dooling; one child: Emily Michell Dooling, b. June 11, 1990, Santa Fe, New Mexico); and

10) Oscar Harry Iiams [(b. October 10, 1882, Cass County, Nebraska; d. September 20, 1971, Salem, Oregon), m. June 2, 1909, Benton County, Oregon, to Effie Mabel Sheldon (b. November 10, 1890); three children: a) Irum Turner Iiams (b. March 31, 1912, Oregon; m. 1st, May 17, 1934, Astoria, Oregon, to Stella Mason; one child: Edgar Iiams: m. 2nd, March 29, 1944, Vancouver, Washington, to Lela E. Hurst; two children: Carol Ann Iiams and Darrell Lee Iiams, b. ca1948, Oregon); b) George Richard Iiams, Sr. (b. April 1, 1916; d. May 1971, Oregon; m. Geraldine Iola Peterson; child: George Richard Iiams, Jr.); and c) Howard Leslie Iiams (b. August 11, 1917, Salem, Oregon; d. May 19, 1996, Eugene, Oregon; m. 1st, 1938, Lueata Eulalie White; three children: Howard Leslie Iiams, Gregory Lance Iiams, and Bryon Linn Iiams; m. 2nd, Shirley Henry;

no issue)];

e) Martha J. Iiams (b. July 8, 1841, Shelby County, Ohio; d. December 8, 1858, Ohio);

f) Samuel Iiams [(b. April 20, 1843, Shelby County, Ohio; d. January 30, 1919, Lima, Ohio), m. Mary Ann Abbott (b. 1847, Pennsylvania) and they had eight children: 1[11]) Martha J. Iiames (b. July 11, 1867, Shelby County, Ohio; d. November 13, 1889, Shelby County, Ohio); 2[11]) Harvey Enis Iiams (b. July 5, 1871, Auglaize County, Ohio; d. July 9, 1947, Allen County, Ohio; m. Martha Myrtle Drew, and they had five children: a[1]) Lila Vesta Iiames (b. April 19, 1893, Allen County, Ohio; m. Harry Lovell, b. January 22, 1890, Allen County, Ohio); b[1]) Guy Ralston Iiames (b. February 23, 1897, Allen County, Ohio; d. August 12, 1984, Montgomery County, Ohio; m. Vida Iantha, and they had sixteen children: 1[1]) Juanita Vida Iiames, b. April 6, 1921, Allen County, Ohio; m. Robert Graham True, b. 1922, Ohio; 2[1]) Helen Irene Iiames, b. April 7, 1922, Allen County, Indiana; m. Roy Hollon; 3[1]) Betty Ruth Iiames, b. January 11, 1923, Allen County, Ohio; 4[1]) Guy "Chick" Ross Iiames, b. June 28, 1924, Allen County, Ohio; m. Roberta "Bert" Wright, b. November 7, 1928, Ohio; three children: William Lee Iiames, b. June 23, 1950, Montgomery County, Ohio, m. Carol Ann Frost; Patricia "Tish" Iiames, b. November 27, 1953, Montgomery County, Ohio, m. Timothy Alan Crouch; and George Marcus Edward Trapp, b. November 14, 1968, Montgomery County, Ohio, m. Barbara A. Long; 5[1]) James Edward Iames, b. November 27, 1926, Allen County, Indiana; d. 1996; m. Betty Eileen Rist, and they had two children: David Leslie Iiames, b. February 7, 1947, Lawrence County, Ohio, m. Mary Struck; and Debra Leone Iiames, b. December 6, 1953, Lawrence County, Ohio; 6[1]) Ray Leo Iames, b. October 26, 1927, Allen County, Indiana, m. Laura Nell McMullen, b. 1931; 7[1]) Joan Iiames, b. January 30, 1929, Allen County, Indiana, m. 1st, Ray Bailey; 8[1]) Bonnie Jean Iiames, b. December 22, 1931, Indiana, m. Lee Wayne Farley; 9[1]) Lois Ann Iiames, b. November 10, 1933, Montgomery County, Ohio, m. Bernard Lloyd Bise; 10[1]) Robert Wayne Iames, b. November 29, 1936, Indiana, m. Pauline Marie Bauer, b. 1937, Ohio; 11[1]) Judith Beth Iiames, b. April 5, 1937, Montgomery County, Ohio; d. 1945, Ohio; five children; 12[1]) William Lee Iiames, b. March 4, 1940, Montgomery County, Ohio, m. Peggy K. Lucus; 13[1]) Linda Lou Iiames, b. April 30, 1941, Montgomery County, Ohio, m. Benjamin F. Clark, b. 1937; 14[1]) Samuel Edward Iiames, b. September 4, 1942, Montgomery County, Ohio, m. Nancy Rose Moore; 15[1]) Barbara Jean Iiames, b. March 14, 1944, Montgomery County, Ohio; 16[1]) Michael Allen Iiames (b. March 19, 1949, Montgomery County, Ohio, m. Sandra Elaine Glass, b. 1947); c[1]) Irene Adele Iiames (b. August 31, 1899, Allen County, Ohio; d. September 7, 1971, Allen County, Ohio), m. Clyde R. Cluster; d[1]) Olive Ruth Iiames (b. March 25, 1904, Allen County, Ohio), m. Clarence E. Dohme (b. 1900); and e[1]) Esther Blanche

Iiames (b. June 17, 1906, Allen County, Ohio), m. Paul Myron Kelly; 3[11]) Minnie E. Iiams (b. August 15, 1874, Shelby County, Ohio; d. July 27, 1959, Allen County, Indiana), m. George Anspach; 4[11]) James Arthur Iiames (b. February 9, 1877, Shelby County, Ohio; d. April 14, 1967, Allen County, Ohio), m. Myrtle Mae Wood; and they had three children: a[1]) Howard Theodore Iiames (b. October 11, 1907, Allen County, Ohio); m. Edith Dempster (b. June 21, 1909, Allen County, Ohio) and they had a daughter: Norma Jean Iiames (b. June 23, 1931), who m. Albert James Kihm (b. 1931, Lorain, Ohio); and b[1]) Raymond Merle Iiames (b. February 1, 1911, Allen County, Ohio; d. January 3, 1981, Allen County, Ohio), m. Emerald G. Critchfield, and they had three children: 1[1]) Sharon Rae Iiames (b. July 18, 1938, Allen County, Ohio; m. Emil Ralph White, b. 1937, Ohio), 2[1]) Linda Sue Iiames (b. July 6, 1940, Allen County, Ohio; m. 1st, David Lester Becker, and m. 2nd, Donald G. Staley); 3[1]) James William Iiames (b. March 22, 1942, Allen County, Ohio); m. Iva Joyce Plaugher, b. 1943, Allen County, Ohio, and they had two children: Jeffrey Alan Iiames (b. January 30, 1969, Allen County, Ohio; m. Mary C. Steiner), and John William Iiames (b. October 8, 1971, Allen County, Ohio); and c[1]) Ruth May Iiames (b. April 12, 1916, Allen County, Ohio), m. Donald E. Brown (b. May 18, 1918, Allen County, Ohio); 5[11]) Thomas E. Iiames (b. December 16, 1878, Shelby County, Ohio; d. August 22, 1933, Lucas County, Ohio), m. Wilma A. Wright (b. 1882, Indiana); 6[11]) Berthey P. Iiames (b. April 1, 1882, Shelby County, Ohio; d. May 2, 1890, Shelby County, Ohio); 7[11]) Frank Merle "Tinker" Iames (b. January 12, 1885, Auglaize County, Ohio), m. Minnie D. Betz (b. 1889, Ohio), and they had two children: a[1]) Arthur Ray Iiams (b. January 3, 1905, Allen County, Ohio; d. 1905, Allen County, Ohio); b[1]) Kenneth Milton Iiams (b. July 7, 1907, Allen County, Ohio; d. October 2, 1944, while flying over China), m. Edna R. Frock, and they had four children: 1[1]) Jackie Lamar Iiams (b. August 2, 1927, Allen County, Ohio; 2[1]) Franklin Robert Iiams (b. March 31, 1935, Allen County, Ohio); 3[1]) Terry Joseph Iiams (b. June 4, 1944, Lima, Allen County, Ohio); and 4[1]) Don Iiams; and 8[11]) William R. Iiams (b. January 27, 1887, Kenton, Ohio; d. March 20, 1958, Allen County, Ohio), m. Hazel L. Upperman, and they had three children: a[1]) William Harold Iiams (b. January 21, 1911, Van Wert County, Ohio; d. January 26, 1911, Van Wert County, Ohio); b[1]) Robert E. Iiams (b. May 28, 1912, Ohio) m. 1st, Romain Heite (b. August 20, 1914, Indiana, m. 2nd, D. Henderson; and c[1]) Valerie Iiams; and

g) James E. Iiams (b. May 30, 1844, Shelby County, Ohio; d. February 28, 1911, Shelby County, Ohio).

2) Rebecca Iiams (b. 1808) m. Howard Hartford. Sarah Iiams (b. May 6, 1810, Pennsylvania; d. September 23, 1875, Jay County, Indiana), m. George Washington Harford.

3) Mary Iiams (b. December 11, 1811, Washington County, Pennsylvania), m. Erasmus B. Toland (b. 1808, Virginia).

4) John Iiams (b. November 21, 1816, Washington County, Pennsylvania; d. June 30, 1878, Shelby County, Ohio), m. Deborah A. Scott (b. 1818, New Jersey), and they had twelve children:
- a) Mary E. Iiams (b. 1842, m. Henry Beckdolt);
- b) William Iiams (b. 1844);
- c) George L. Iiams (b. September 16, 1846, Auglaize County, Ohio; d. February 20, 1908, Auglaize County, Ohio), m. Mary Jane Snyder, and they had five children: a^1) Lola Emma Viola Iiams (b. October 24, 1872; d. January 7, 1949), m. Charles F. Morris; b^1) Bert Elmer Iiams (b. March 13, 1875, Auglaize County, Ohio; d. July 24, 1939, Ohio), m. Sarah A. Ingmire, and they had eight children: 1^1) Elmer William Iiams (b. December 23, 1914; Auglaize County, Ohio; d. 1994, Ohio), m. Marjorie Frysinger, and their child was Warren William Iiams (b. December 13, 1942); 2^1) Helen Olive Iiams (b. January 19, 1917, Freeport, Michigan), m. Donald L. Shrider; 3^1) Martin Lewis Iiams (b. September 9, 1919, Allen County, Ohio; d. September 19, 1920, Allen County, Ohio); 4^1) Franklin Carl Iiams (b. October 9, 1920, Allen County, Ohio; d. October 31, 1987, Putnam County, Ohio), m. LaDonna Carrino, and they had four children: Helen Marie Iiams (b. January 11, 1942, Allen County, Ohio), Franklin Paul Iiams (b. December 17, 1942); Female Iiams (b. March 27, 1949, Allen County, Ohio), and Philip William Iiams (b. March 28, 1954, Auglaize County, Ohio); 5^1) Alice Luella Iiams (b. April 7, 1923, Allen County, Ohio; d. February 26, 1994, Indiana), m. Calvin C. Moore; 6^1) Edna Phyllis Iiams (b. May 1, 1925, Allen County, Ohio), m. Gerald E. White (b. 1922, Allen County, Ohio); 7^1) Louise Catherine Iiams (b. October 12, 1932; Allen County, Ohio), m. Ben D. King; 8^1) Thomas Levi Iiams (b. November 28, 1932; d. May 20, 1976), m. Joyce Webb; c^1) Joseph William Iiams (b. March 20, 1877; d. 1942, Auglaize County, Ohio), m. Flossie Fern McClory (b. 1888, Ohio); d^1) Eva Mae Iiams (b. September 8, 1879; d. 1952, Ohio), m. George Kaeck; e^1) Ella Sarah Iiams (b. 1882), m. Homer Smith;
- d) Sarah Jane Iiams (b. 1850; d. December 6, 1895, Shelby County, Ohio);
- e) July Iiams (b. March 1850);
- f) Margaret Iiams (b. 1855), child of John Iiams (b. 1816) and second wife Margaret Ann Bitner (b. December 12, 1827, Virginia);
- g) Deborah Iiams (b. 1857), m. Oscar Sands;
- h) John Henry Iiams (b. September 24, 1858, Ohio; d. November 30, 1899, Ohio), m. Della E. Carter (b. 1866, Ohio; d. 1902, Ohio);
- i) Naoma Iiams (b. July 23, 1861, Auglaize County, Ohio; d. August 18, 1882, Auglaize County, Ohio);
- j) Rebecca Iiams (b. 1863, Auglaize County, Ohio), m. James Tippie;
- k) Minerva Iiams (b. April 24, 1866, Auglaize County, Ohio; d. October 6, 1872, Auglaize County, Ohio; and
- l) Louisa E. Iiams (b. 1869); m. February 21, 1886, to William Henry Carter;
5) Elizabeth Iiams (b. April 18, 1820, Warren County, Ohio) m. William

Frushour; Thomas Iiams (b. June 22, 1822, Morrow County, Ohio; d. March 5, 1888, Jay County, Indiana), m. 1st, Elizabeth Jane Scott, and m. 2nd, Amanda Wolary, and had eight children:

    a) Absalom "Abner" H. Iiams (b. October 31, 1847, Shelby County, Ohio; d. June 2, 1928, Van Wert County, Ohio), m. Sarah E. Crawford, and they had four children: a[1]) Percella Iiams (b. 1868); b[1]) Mary R. Iiams (b. 1868); c[1]) Emma V. Iiams (b. February 11, 1872, Ohio; m. James S. Snodgrass); d[1]) Clara Estella Iiams (b. January 1882, Indiana; m. C. E. Morris, b. October 29, 1869, Ohio);

    b) Mary Jane Iiams (b. March 29, 1852; m. Francis J. Edgerly);

    c) Ivan Roger Iiams (b. November 24, 1853; d. young);

    d) Elizabeth Georgia Iiams (b. September 22, 1856; m. 1st, Mr. Mock; m. 2nd, Mr. Cushing);

    e) Sarah Rebecca Iiams (b. 1860);

    f) William Henry Iiams (b. September 30, 1863, Auglaize County, Ohio; d. May 1936, Kalamazoo, Michigan), m. Effie J. Lanning, and their child Samuel Francis Iiams (b. March 12, 1891, Indiana; d. December 5, 1966, Michigan; m. 1st, Mina Brown, and m. 2nd, Ada Alice Jones); had seven children: 1[1]) Iris Rebecca Iiams (b. August 31, 1913; d. April 1964, Michigan; m. Willis Allen Parker); 2[1]) Francis Basil Iiams (b. July 30, 1918); 3[1]) Elon Alton Iiams (b. January 15, 1921); 4[1]) Henry Iiams; 5[1]) Female Iiams (b. January 1922; d. 1922, age 2 weeks); 6[1]) Dorothea Jean Iiams (b. January 11, 1924); and 7[1]) Donald Eugene Iiams (b. August 12, 1927);

    g) Nancy Rachel Iiams (b. 1868, Jay County, Indiana; m. James H. Phillips);

    h) Georgia Anne Iiams (b. May 1870).

6) Eleanor Iiams (b. September 11, 1824, Ohio; d. December 30, 1908, Auglaize County, Ohio; m. Absalom Scott, b. 1820, Ohio); and Charity Iiams (b. July 7, 1832, Ohio; d. July 15, 1910, Shelby County, Ohio; m. Aaron Lambert).

The *International Genealogical Index* (IGI) lists, as a son of Thomas (b. 1708) and Artridge Ijams of South River, Anne Arundel County, Maryland, as being John Iiams. John Iiams (b. October 20, 1747; d. May 23, 1817, Jefferson County, Ohio, or August 5, 1816) (HWN, EFB) lived in Bedford County, Pennsylvania, until September 5, 1797, when he purchased land in Brooke County, Virginia (now West Virginia) (KIC, JH). Richard Iiams of Bedford County, Pennsylvania, has also been proposed as the father of John Iiams (b. 1747). This Richard Iams, proposed father of John Iiams (b. 1747), purchased land in Brooke County, Virginia, on September 5, 1799, while John Iiams purchased land in Brooke County, Virginia, on September 5, 1797; April 7, 1798; June 8, 1802 and June 26, 1815; as well as in Bedford County, Pennsylvania, on April 2, 1800; and in Jefferson County, Ohio December 24, 1802; May 23, 1807; September 2, 1807 and June 12, 1809).

Jefferson County, Ohio, records, March 29, 1821, list widow Ann James as wife of the late John James, formerly of Brooke County, Virginia, deeded land to Richard James of Jefferson County, Ohio, and declares that this Ann James is the attorney for Plummer James of Clermont County, Ohio, one of the heirs of deceased John James. This legal action was taken on behalf of Lot 17 in Steubenville which was Plummer James' share of the inherited estate.

John Iiams (b. 1747) is believed to have had a wife named Ann (d. 1821, Brooke County, Virginia), and their children have been described (EFB, KIC, JH) as including:

1) Plummer Iiams (b. 1780, Frederick County, Maryland; d. ca1850, Clermont County, Ohio), and this line is continued below;

2) John Iiams II (b. Frederick County, Maryland; m. Mary ___);

3) Mary Iiams (b. Frederick County, Maryland; m. John J. Stoudtstout);

4) Richard Perry Iiams, Sr. (b. 1786, Frederick County, Maryland; d. 1848, Jefferson County, Ohio; File 1293, Jefferson County, Ohio, states that widow Mary Ann Iiams declined to be the administrator of the estate of Richard Perry Iiams, so a Robert Sherrard was appointed; and also mentioned was a son, Amos Iiams, a daughter called Mary Ann Iiams, Jr., and a daughter, Ella Iiams, all of Cross Creek Township, Jefferson County, Ohio; with Ella Iiams, m. Lewis Anderson February 1846; Plummer J. Iiams was mentioned in the Jefferson County Common Pleas Court Record of 1839; 1830 Census of Jefferson County lists Richard Iiams as head of household that included one male 40-50, one female 40-50, two males and one female age 15-20, one male 10-15, one male and one female 5-10 years; and the 1850 census of Jefferson County, Ohio, lists Mary Ann Imes, age 61, b. Ohio, living with Anderson (age 35) and Ellen (age 35) Lewis; and the 1850 Ohio Mortality Schedule lists Mary Ann Ijams of Jefferson County as having died at Steubenville.

A Gassaway Iiams (b. 1780; d. 1845, m. 1804, Ann Pearce) has been proposed (EFB, MI) as a son of John Iiams (b. 1747), and also proposed (MI) as children of John Iiams (b. 1747) are: Nancy Iiams (b. 1787), William Iiams (b. 1792, see below), Elizabeth Iiams, Anna Iiams, Sabina Iiams, John Iiams (b. 1789), Charity Iiams (b. 1789), Mary Iiams (b. 1800), and Sarah Iiams (b. 1801). This William Iiams (b.1792) is reported (MI) to have had the following children: Betsy Iiams, Miller Iiams (b. 1819, lived in West Virginia, m. ___ Eggy and had two sons: Thomas Iiams, b. 1851, and James H. Iiams, b. 1874, who had two children: Hillis D. Iiams, b. 1904, and lived in Western Pennsylvania where he had a son Jack L. Iiams, b. 1924; and Ilda I. Iiams, b. 1906), James Iiams, John H. Iiams (b. 1821), Elisha Iiams [b. 1822, lived in Western Pennsylvania, and had five children: Elizabeth Iiams, Delilah Iiams, Demas G. Iiams, b. 1851 (and had children Winfield S. Iiams, b. 1882; William W. Iiams, b. 1883; Sarah Iiams, Elisha B. Iiams, b. 1892; John H. Iiams, b. 1897; and Clifford H. Iiams, b. 1903), Thomas Iiams (b. 1824, lived in Greene County, Pennsylvania), Isaac Iiams (b. 1828, lived in Washington County, Pennsylvania), and William Iiams (b. 1830, and had children: Sadie F. Iiams, John H. Iiams, Laura A. Iiams, infant Iiams, Ella R. Iiams, Lizzie B. Iiams, William J. Iiams, Mary E. Iiams, Miller A. Iiams, Clark J. Iiams, Isaac W. Iiams, Charlie P. Iiams, and Iris M. Iiams), Delilah Iiams (b. 1831), Mary Iiams (b. 1834), Abraham Iiams (b. 1846; d. Civil War), and Rachel Iiams (b. 1839)].

Work in West Virginia (Ohio County) and Eastern Ohio (IMO) has added additional information, most of which is probably related to the offspring of this elusive Thomas Iiams (b. 1708). John and wife Ann Iiams had a son John Iiams, whose wife was Mary. Brooke County, West Virginia, deeds show that: John Ims of Bedford County, Pennsylvania, purchased land on Buffalo Creek from Walter Cain, September 5, 1797; John Ijams of Bedford County, Pennsylvania, purchased land on Buffalo Creek from Arthur Griffith on April 17, 1798; John and Ann Iiams of Brook County, Virginia (now West Virginia) sold land (21 acres) on Buffalo Creek to Walter Cain, June 8, 1802; John and Ann Iams of Brooke County, Virginia, sold 100 + 28 acres to Joseph Henning, June 26, 1815; Plummer Iams of Clermont County, Ohio, gave Ann Iams of Jefferson County, Ohio, power of attorney with regard to the estate inventory of John Iiams of Jefferson County, Ohio (across the Ohio River from Brooke County, Virginia), with settlement date of May 1, 1817, and entry date of July 9, 1819; original land patent from Thomas Jefferson, President of the United States, dated December 24, 1802, to John Ieams, Sr. of Brooke County, Virginia, for 640 acres in Section 3, Township 6, Range 2, of the "Seven Ranges" located in Jefferson County, Ohio, and not entered into the Jefferson County, Ohio, records until June 19, 1917; land deeded to John Iiams, Jefferson County, Ohio, from Robert Carrell July 20, 1815, and from Bernard Lucas on August 5, 1816, suggesting that John Iiams moved form Brooke County, Virginia, to Jefferson County, Ohio, in 1815.

John and Ann Ijams (IMO) were probably parents of four children: John Ijams, Jr., Richard Ijams, Plummer Ijams, and Mary Ijams Stoudt. (Plummer Ijams moved to Clermont County, Ohio, and had one child, a daughter.) The children of Richard and Mary Ann Ijams (IM)) were: Mary Ann Ijams, Eleanor Ijams, Amos Ijams, Andrew Ijams, and Richard P. Ijams. A Joseph Iiams of Bedford County, Pennsylvania, married a Sarah Moore in Jefferson County, Ohio, on December 25, 1827 (IMO); a William Iiams was present in Jefferson County, Ohio, in 1830 (EFB); Richard Iiams of Belmont County, Ohio, deeded two acres in Section 36, Township 5, Range 3, of the "Ohio Seven Ranges," November 29, 1837.

Belmont County, Ohio, early marriage licensed include Catherine Ijams to Michael Ault, March 10, 1831; Reason Imes to Mary Myres, October 12, 1831; and Charity Imes to Jacob Myres. The 1850 Federal Census of Ohio County, Virginia, lists Isaac Imes (age 27, born Pennsylvania), as head of household, with Elizabeth Imes (age 24, Pennsylvania), Thomas Imes (4, Virginia) and Sarah Imes (2, Virginia). In Stock Township, Monroe County, Ohio, the 1850 Census lists Isaac Iams (41, Pennsylvania) with Elizabeth Iams (38, Pennsylvania), Eleanor Iams (14, Ohio), George Iams (12, Ohio), Rebecca (10, Ohio), Isaac Iams (8, Ohio), Sarah Iams (7, Ohio), and Demas Iams (25, Pennsylvania). Also, in Stock Township at this same time were Martha Iams (4, Pennsylvania) and Rezin Iams (5 months, Pennsylvania) listed with Joseph and Sally Wilson.

Jefferson County, Ohio, deeds include: 196 1/2 acres to John Iiams, Sr., Section 3, Township 6, Range 2 in 1802; 65 acres to John Iiams, Sr., Section 3, Township 6, Range 2, on December 4, 1802; sold by John and Ann Iiams of Brooke County, Virginia, to John Riddle, part of Section 3, Township 6, Range 2; from John Iiams, Sr. to John Iiams, Jr. for land patented to John Iiams, Sr. on September 10, 1817, for land in Section 19, Township 6, Range 2; Power of Attorney of John Iiams of Gallatin County, Kentucky, to John Stoudt of Beaver County, Pennsylvania, on October 11, 1817, to dispose of 270 acres claimed by John Iiams on May 12, 1809, as part of Section 19, Township 6, Range 2; from John and Mary Iiams of Jefferson County, Ohio, to Thomas Mansfield, for part of Section 19, Township 6, Range 2, on June 9, 1809; from John and Mary Iiams Stoudt of Jefferson County, Ohio, to brother Richard Iiams in about 1820.

Richard and wife Mary Ann Iiams sold lot 17, Steubenville, Jefferson County, Ohio, to Thomas Blackburn on July 7, 1834; Richard and wife Mary Ann Iiams of Jefferson County, Ohio, sold 52 acres in Section 3, Township 6, Range 2, of "Seven Ranges" to Plummer J. Iiams and Richard P. Iiams, Jr. of Jefferson County, Ohio, June 11, 1839; Richard P. Iiams and wife Elizabeth Iiams, and Susannah L. Iiams of Jefferson County, Ohio, sold land to William Ekey, May 28, 1840; Richard and wife Mary Ann Iiams of Jefferson County, Ohio, sold Lot 5 of Bernard Lucas Addition, Steubenville, Jefferson County, Ohio, to Mary Ann Iiams of Jefferson County, Ohio,

April 18, 1842; and Richard and Mary Ann Iiams sold 84 acres of Section 3, Township 6, Range 2, to Amos W. Iiams and Andrew Iiams, April 18, 1844, among other later Jefferson County, Ohio, land transactions involving the Iiams family.

Noted Eastern Ohio genealogist and professional researcher, Irene M. Ochsenbein, in 1967, declared that while working on the Iams family for Ervin F. Bickley, Jr. for the rate of one dollar an hour, "I nearly wore my eyes out...," and that, "This is surely a mixed-up family, (but) not half as mixed up as this researcher though!!!"

Tax records of Brooke County, Virginia (now West Virginia) show (EFB) that John Iimes paid taxes on 150 acres of land in 1798, 128 acres in 1803, and 119 acres from 1804 to 1814. The 1810 Federal Census of that area show John Aaims as head of household and age over 45 years with one female of the same age, two slaves, one loom, and 40 yards of cloth. In 1820, there are two families: Isaac Iames at age over 45 years, a female over 45 years, one female between the age of 26 and 45 years, four males and three females between the age of 16 and 24, two males between ages of 10 and 16 years, one male and one female under 10 years; and Daniel Iames at age 26 to 45 years, one female age 26 to 45 years, one male and one female between ages 16 and 26 and two females under age 10 years, and with two household members listed as being in manufacturing. Also, in 1820 Brooke County, Virginia, was Samuel Iams, age 26-44, with a female of the same age group, one male and three females of the under ten-year-old age group.

Other work by EFB, regarding a Richard Ijams of Frederick County, Maryland, shows that at age 40, and then listed as being a resident of Ohio, married Elizabeth Miller, age 39, in Berkely County, Virginia (now West Virginia). On April 15, 1848, Richard Ijams of Frederick County, Maryland, received 325 acres in Berkely County, Virginia, and on December 31, 1847, had purchased a house and lot in Hedgesville, Virginia, from Conrad M. Hedges. The estate settlement of Richard Ijams, June 24, 1856, by executrix Elizabeth A. Ijams, included deeding a house and lot in Hedgesville to Conrad Robbins and Henry J. Siebert. Also in Berkely County, Virginia, 1) a James Ijams purchased a lot in Gerardstown from John W. Stewart on March 10, 1852; 2) James and Dorcas S. M. Ijams granted 151 acres of land that had been given by her father John Tabb on February 11, 1853; 3) James and Dorcas Ijams conveyed a lot in Gerardstown to James Parks on March 22, 1856; 4) James Ijams paid several debts on June 7, 1856, and these included $200 to Margaret Kreglow, $200 to David Conrad, $140 to James Wilson, $500 to Israel Robinson; and to pay debts, he agreed to sell a) Negro man Lewis, 45, slave for life; b) Negro named Harriet, age 24, to serve to age 35; c) Negro William, age 8, to serve to age 35; d) 22 bedsteads and bedding; e) 6 stones; f) 20 washstands; g) a stock of liquor; h) all the ice in the icehouse; i) crop of oats now growing; and j) other household furniture.

In Clermont County, Ohio, Plummer Ijams bought land in New Richmond from Jacob Light, also of Clermont County, in 1815; and Plummer Imes was listed in the 1820 and 1830 Census of Ohio Township of Clermont County. On April 18, 1820, William H. Iams, Clermont County, heir of Joseph Iams, filed a petition for 500 acres of the land of the deceased Joseph Iams, with the land being located on the East Fork of the Little Miami River, and the widow of Joseph Iams was listed as being Catherine Iams. On April 28, 1820, William H. Iamas, formerly of Warren County, Ohio, sold land in Jackson Township for $283 to Elijah Hankins and Obadiah Williams. On October 21, 1824, John and wife Anne Iams of Washington County, Pennsylvania, sold land on Ullery's Run to William Ross; in 1827, this John Ijams bought land from William Coulson of Warren County, Ohio, for $158; in April 1827, John Ijams and others recovered damages from William Ross at a sheriff's sale in the amount of $559.13, resulting from a "bad deed;" and John Iams is listed on the 1826 tax list of Monroe Township.

A Ralph Iams reported in 1965, that he was the son of Thomas Iams and the sister of Mrs. James Gundstaff of Knoxville, Tennessee; and that he (Ralph) had lived in Williamsburg, Clermont County, Ohio, for 64 years, believing that his family had moved there from Knoxville, Tennessee.

Roberta Wright Iiames has listed twelve children of Rebecca Marriot Ijams (b. February 4, 1806, daughter of John Iiams, b. ca1775, and Rachel Marriott) and John Waters Ijams (b. November 21, 1807, Fairfield County, Ohio; d. February 16, 1875): 1) John Richard Ijams (b. March 13, 1828; d. November 29, 1831); 2) Van Buren Ijams (b. June 28, 1829; d. February 10, 1892, m. Florilla Spears); 3) Rachel Ann Ijams (b. January 20, 1831; d. November 10, 1831); 4) Maria Antionette Ijams (b. September 11, 1832; d. April 15, 1904); 5) Richard William Ijams (b. August 20, 1834; d. June 10, 1889); 6) Sprigg Homewood Ijams (b. August 19, 1836; d. January 4, 1918; m. Ann Rebecca Brown); 7) Jacob Waters Ijams (b. July 26, 1838); 8) Josephine Ijams (b. October 12, 1840; d. November 1925); 9) Dewitt Clinton Ijams (b. April 13, 1842, Anne Arundel County, Maryland; d. October 24, 1862); 10) John Barney Ijams (b. September 10, 1844; d. May 27, 1849); 11) Victoria Ijams (b. March 15, 1847; d. June 8, 1849); and Jane Rebecca Ijams (b. March 3, 1849; d. April 21, 1858).

Another child of John Iiams (b. ca1775) and Rachel Marriott was Isaac Plummer Ijams (b. 1812; d. 1877, Maryland) who m. 1834 to Cecelia Smith Moxley, and they had ten children: 1) Frances E. Ijams (b. ca1836); 2) Mary V. Ijams (b. ca1837); 3) John T. Ijams (b. ca1838); 4) Joseph A. Ijams (b. ca1840; m. Violette Waters); 5) William H. Ijams (b. ca1841; d. December 23, 1932, Baltimore County, Maryland); 6) Jerusha H. B. Ijams (b. ca1844); 7) Cecelia R. Ijams (b. ca1846); 8) Ann H. Ijams (b. ca1849); 9) George Walter Ijams; and 10) James Ijams (b. ca1851). Harry Wright Newman lists John Iiams (b. June 1775; m. Rachel Marriott) and Rebecca Iiams (b. September 5, 1777; m. Joseph Marriott) as children of Thomas Iiams (b. 1745; son of Thomas and Artridge Iiams).

John Iiams (b. 1747), also a son of Thomas and Artridge Iiams (EFB), had a son Plummer Iiams (b. 1780, Frederick County, Maryland; d. ca1850, Clermont County, Ohio). The wife of Plummer Iiams (b. 1780) had died before the listing of the 1820 Federal Census of Clermont County, Ohio, listed Plummer Imes as being age 26-45, as head of household which also contained one female age under ten and one female age 16 to 26 (EFB). Plummer Iams was mayor of New Richmond, and was one of the first to serve as Justice of Peace in New Richmond, Clermont County, Ohio (1814). Both Plummer Iams and John Iams are listed on the 1826 Clermont County, Ohio, tax lists. Plummer Iams had a daughter Ann Iams (b. November 11, 1816, Clermont County, Ohio; d. May 23, 1851, and buried in Green Mount Cemetery near Richmond, Clermont County, Ohio), who m. October 11, 1836, to William Ross, Jr. (b. April 10, 1811, Brownsville, Pennsylvania; d. Jacksonville, Florida), the son of William Ross, Sr. and Margaret Milligan of Pennsylvania. The 1850 Federal Census of Ohio Township, Clermont County, Ohio, lists William Ross (age 39, b. Pennsylvania), Ann Ross (age 33, b. Ohio), Albert Ross (age 12, b. Ohio), Margaret Ross (age 10, b. Ohio), Harriet B. Ross (age 7, b. Ohio), Martha Ross (age 4, b. Ohio), Charles Ross (age 1, b. Ohio), and Plummer Iams (age 70, b. Pennsylvania).

After the death of his first wife Ann, William Ross, Jr. m. 2nd, on October 11, 1836, at New Richmond, Clermont County, Ohio, to Mrs. Mary A. (Emmerson) Collard. The parents of William Ross, Sr. were Alexander and Nancy Ann Ross, and they had moved from eastern Pennsylvania to the Washington County, Pennsylvania, area after the birth of William Ross, Sr. (b. September 22, 1772). William Ross, Sr. moved to Clermont County, Ohio, in 1818, where he was a gunsmith. William Ross, Sr. had ten children:

1) Andrew Ross (b. April 16, 1797, Pennsylvania, single); 2) Eli Ross (b. April 29, 1799, Pennsylvania, single); 3) James Ross (b. February 12, 1801, Pennsylvania, m. Ann Simpson); 4) Harriet Ross (b. February 3, 1803, m. 1st, Elijah Rossberry, and m. 2nd, Robert Davis); 5) Alexander Ross (b. January 20, 1805; m. Evaline Fowler and moved to Iowa); 6) Ann Ross (b. December 14, 1807; m. William B. Pease); 7) Samuel Ross (b. May 16, 1809, single); 8) William Ross, Jr. (b. April 10, 1811; m. Ann Imes, and they had seven children); 9) Margaret Ross (b. July 5, 1814; d. Batavia, Ohio; m. Reader W. Clarke and had daughter Missouri Reader); and 10) Ruth Ross (b. August 11, 1816; d. July 18, 1912, at age 96) who m. George W. Salt of Bethel, Ohio (d. March 20, 1874, age 61).

William Ross, Jr. and Ann Imes had seven children: 1) Albert G. Ross (b. 1838, Clermont County, Ohio); 2) Margaret M. Ross (b. 1840, Clermont County, Ohio, m. ___ Harris); 3) Virginia Ross; 4) Harriett B. Ross (b. 1843, Clermont County, Ohio); 5) Eli Ross (b. 1845, d. 1845); d. Martha Ross (b. 1846); and 7) Charles Ross (b. 1848, Clermont County, Ohio).

John Iiams (b. 1747) also had a son, Richard Perry Iiams, Sr. (b. ca1786; d. ca1848, Jefferson County, Ohio; m. ca1809, to Mary Ann Wayman). Jefferson County, Ohio, probate records are known to exist (EFB) for Plummer J. Iams (1839), Richard Iams (1852) and Mary Ann Iams (1860). The 1830 Federal Census of Jefferson County, Ohio, lists Richard Iams as head of a household; and the 1850 Census of Jefferson County, Ohio, lists Mary Ann Ijams/Jiams/Iiams of the city of Steubenville, Jefferson County, Ohio; and also of Cross Creek Township, Jefferson County, Ohio. Richard Perry Iiams, Sr. (b. ca1786) and Mary Ann Wayman (b. 1788) had six children: 1) Plummer John Iiams (b. ca1812, Jefferson County, Ohio; d. 1839, Jefferson County, Ohio; m. Susannah L.); 2) Richard Perry Iiams, Jr. (b. Jefferson County, Ohio, ca1817; d. October 1879, age 62, in Labette County, Kansas; after living in Henry County, Iowa; m. ca1835, to Elizabeth ___); 3) Mary Ann Iiams (b. ca1819; d. 1885); 4) Eleanor Iiams (b. ca1823, Cross Creek Township, Jefferson County, Ohio; m. February 1846, to Lewis Anderson); 5) Andrew Iiams (b. ca1825, Jefferson County, Ohio); and 6) Amos W. Iiams (b. ca1815, Jefferson County, Ohio).

Richard Perry Iiams, Jr. (b. ca1817, Jefferson County, Ohio) and his wife Elizabeth had eleven children. They were among the first of the Iiams family to move to Iowa, and in 1854, was registered in the census of Trenton Township, Henry County, Iowa. In the 1860 census of the same township, he is listed as R. P. (age 45, b. Ohio), with wife Elizabeth (age 42, b. Pennsylvania), Plummer Iiams (23, b. Ohio), Eli Iiams (age 21, b. Ohio), Rebecca Iiams (age 19, b. Ohio), Richard Iiams (age 17, b. Ohio), Mary Iiams (age 15, b. Ohio), Maria Iams (age 12, b. Ohio), Louise Iiams (age 9, b. Ohio), Lucretia Iiams (age 8, b. Ohio), Matilda Iiams (age 6, b. Iowa), and George Iiams (age 4, b. Iowa). Son Richard Perry Iiams III (b. Jefferson County, Ohio, March 13, 1841 or 1843; d. August 11, 1905, at Idaho Soldiers Home in Boise), m. September 15, 1872, to Elizabeth "Liz" Esther Reynolds (b. October 26, 1853; d. February 9, 1939, at Hot Springs, South Dakota; the daughter of George Reynolds (b. 1812; d. December 6, 1876) and Emily Roderick (b. 1823, St. Louis, Missouri; d. December 4, 1862), and the sister of Thomas Reynolds (b. March 29, 1843), Jane Reynolds (b. December 2, 1845; m. Phillip Sappington), Mary Reynolds (b. May 7, 1848; m. William Trout); Emily Reynolds (b. December 3, 1850; m. Henry Scott); Margaret Reynolds (d. age 2, 1844); George Reynolds, Jr. (b. March 8, 1855), Louis Reynolds (b. December 4, 1857); and Susan Eva Reynolds (b. 1859).

The Reynolds family lived in Rock Spring, Missouri. Richard Perry Iiams III (b. 1841) was a private, Company B, 25th Iowa Infantry in the Civil War, and had pension inventory numbers of 655416, 498017, XC2678311, wid 835749 and 647558.

The initial pension application was made on May 1, 1888, from Custer County, South Dakota, as a resident of Hermosa, South Dakota. He enlisted August 13, 1862, at Mount Pleasant, Iowa, under Captain J. B. Smith, and was discharged at Davenport, Iowa, June 22, 1865; and his age was given as 46 in the 1888 application. He declared that he had lived in the states of Missouri, Kansas, and South Dakota since his discharge. The widow, age 52, applied as a resident of Rockford, Pennington County, South Dakota, stating that the soldier had left a wife and children in Pennington County in 1892.

A Thomas Reynolds living in Potosi, Missouri, in 1906 was listed as an uncle. When admitted to the Boise, Idaho, Soldiers Home, Richard Perry Iiams III (b. 1841) listed a wife in Oneida County, Idaho, and a son Carl Imes of American Falls, Idaho. He also stated that he had lived as a volunteer inmate at Western Branch of National Military Home in Leavenworth, Kansas, from February 23, 1892 and October 6, 1893. The military records show that he lived alone in Aldrick, Polk County, Missouri, from October 1893 to October 1898, while the family lived in the Black Hills of South Dakota. On June 2, 1865, the records show that he was age 21, height 5' 10 1/2", dark complexion, with grey eyes and dark hair. After his marriage in 1872, he lived three years in Parsons, Kansas; then six years near Avon, Missouri; then 3 years at Tarkio, Missouri; then at Herman, South Dakota, from 1885 to 1889; then at Hill City, South Dakota, until 1891; and then left the family behind.

The four children of Richard Perry Iiams III (b. 1841) and Elizabeth Esther Reynolds (b. 1853) were: 1) Carroll "Carl" B. Imes (b. April 10, 1874; worked for U.S. Forestry Service in Boise, Idaho); 2) Jennie Mae Imes (b. November 7, 1875; d. April 3, 1907, had congenital blindness); 3) Richard Perry Iiams IV [(b. November 4, 1878, St. Louis, Missouri; d. September 19, 1931, Billings, Montana), m. December 31, 1903, at Lincoln, Nebraska, to Hannah Charlotte Christianson (d. September 16, 1973, at Billings, Montana, where she had moved in 1955); with an affidavit issued by his father on June 4, 1907, declaring him to be age 28, and a resident of Spearfish, Montana]; and 4) Charlotte K. Imes (m. Carl Calhoun and lived in Sidney, Montana, in 1954, and who wrote a 1954 letter to Reverend Ralph B. Imes, First Congregational Church, Eldora, Iowa, giving some of the above information).

Another son of Richard Perry Iiams, Jr. (b. ca1817) was Plummer J. Imes (b. August 6, 1836, Jefferson County, Ohio; d. December 15, 1875, in Indiana, after living in places such as Iowa and the west), who m. December 21, 1861, to Sarah Ann McDaniel (b. March 21, 1844; and later disappeared). Sarah Ann McDaniel (b. 1844) has been said to have been from Princeton/Rushville, Indiana, and from Fultonham, Muskingum County, Ohio; and after the death of Plummer J. Imes, was reported to have returned to Fultonham with her six children. The children were placed in foster homes. One son, James (b. 1868), was taken out west, and later returned to Ohio to write his account of his adventures and hardships. Sarah Ann Imes (b. 1844) became depressed over the situation and disappeared, being quoted as saying, "I can't stand this.... I'm going away." In the 1860 Federal Census of Trenton Township, Henry County, Iowa, Plummer Imes (age 23, b. Ohio) was listed with his father, Richard Perry Imes (b. 1817) as head of household. Many of the family moved to Kansas, but Plummer J. Imes (b. 1836) returned to Ohio where he married Sarrah Ann McDaniel, and they then moved to Indiana where he died (Family line of Joy Iiams Hannon). The June 11, 1860, Federal Census of Fultonham, Newton Township, Muskingum County, Ohio, lists Plummer Imes (age 24, b. Ohio); and the July 6, 1860, Federal Census of Trenton Township, Fulton County, Iowa, lists Plummer Imes (age 23, b. Ohio) with R. F. Imes family. EFB and others have decided that the same Plummer Imes was counted twice (JIH).

Plummer J. Imes (b. 1836) and Sarah Ann McDaniel (b. 1844) had seven children:

1) Ella or Etta Imes (b. December 21, 1862, Muskingum County, Ohio; lived in Indiana; d. February 23, 1950; m. William Hummell);

2) Ulysses S. Grant Imes [(b. December 26, 1864, Princeton, Indiana; d. September 10, 1922, Somerset, Perry County, Ohio); m. Mary Hester "Hattie" Rose (b. December 21, 1864, Zanesville, Muskingum County, Ohio; d. December 12, 1932, Zanesville, Ohio, and buried in Somerset), daughter of George Washington Rose and Caroline Black of Zanesville, Ohio];

3) William T. "Will" Imes (b. December 7, 1866, or July 12, 1866; d. August 7, 1892, Ohio, single; lived with sister Eliza);

4) James Imes [(b. August 3, 1868, Rushville, Rushville County, Indiana; d. September 18, 1933, Columbus, Ohio; single); wrote autobiography of questionable accuracy that described being taken to Iowa at age 10 by J. W. Plummer, a Methodist minister from Council Bluffs, Iowa, who moved to Rock Rapids, Little Rock County, Iowa, in 1878, to Esterville, Emmet County, Iowa, before 1880 (described meteorite there in 1879), to Dakota Territory with Lewis Wells at age 12, because he had been mistreated by the minister; with Dakota travels to Central City in Black Hills; then to a claim by "Old Pete" on the Belle Fourche River; then returned to Central City to stay with schoolteacher Wyamond Richard, picking up nicknames used by local writers, including "Spearfish Jim" and "The Deadwood Kid;" becoming acquainted with such Wild West characters as "Deadwood Dick," "Coyote Bill," "Texas Jack Cheyenne," "John Cole," "Calamity Jane," and "Wild Bill Hickock," claiming to have seen "Wild Bill" killed, or at least shot, in a saloon where he had been gambling before being buried in"Deadwood Cemetery," and claimed that "Calamity Jane" was General Cook's scout, and was some-what of a personal friend who bought James' (b. 1868) clothes, who dressed in men's clothes, who "was a good shot" as legends have stated, and that she went by the name "Cattle Kate," and with James Iiams (b. 1868) returning to Ohio in hopes of reuniting the children, only to find that two had died of tuberculosis at young ages; and he himself died in Columbus, Ohio, where he had worked as a janitor, after finally seeing his living brothers and sisters];

5) Elizabeth Imes (b. October 13, 1870; known as "Eliza;" d. November 30, 1894, Perry County, Ohio; single);

6) Richard Iiams or Imes (b. January 11, 1872; d. July 24, 1874, died young); and

7) Rose or Rosa Iiams or Imes [(b. April 17, 1876, Fultonham, Ohio; d. December 17, 1958); m. Ezra Leckrone/Lecrone or/Lecroke (b. November 29, 1878; d. May 1952), son of Jacob Leckrone and C. Shrider; with Rose Imes and Ezra Leckrone having eight children: a) Carnet Paul Leckrone (b. September 1, 1896, Perry County, Ohio; m. Cleno Lover); b) Vera Marie Leckrone (b. January 6, 1899, Perry County, Ohio; m. Lester Cotterman); c) Ralph Leckrone (b. July 18, 1901, Perry County, Ohio; d. February 7, 1976; m. Gladys Westal); d) Merle Leckrone (b. May 6, 1903, Perry County, Ohio; d. May 1960; m. Kathleen ___); e) Edgar Leckrone (b. October 19, 1905, Perry County, Ohio; m. Faye Clark; f) Willard Leckrone (b. August 30, 1907, Perry County, Ohio; m. Margurite Lowrie); g) Carl Leckrone (b. April 4, 1911, Perry County,

Ohio; m. Bonnie Sthrol); and h) Eloise Leckrone (b. May 5, 1917, Perry County, Ohio; m. Fred Beem)].

From above, Ulysses S. Grant Iiams or Imes (b. 1864) and Mary Hester "Hattie" Rose (b. 1864) is reported to have been a farmer, and he was given an expensive violin by his father, Plummer Imes (b. 1836); but who lived with another farmer as a child, and that farmer heavily favored his own two sons, so that his schooling was minimal. He often went without socks or other clothing items; but who fondly remembers the kindness of the wife of the farmer, who saved up some "butter money" to buy Grant an orange—which he admired by smelling it for several days before eating it. Grant Imes was a farmer, a butcher, and a cemetery caretaker. Ulysses S. "Grant" Imes and Mary Hester "Hattie" Rose had eight children:

1) Mary Grace Imes [(b. March 23, 1888, Ohio; d. April 1, 1967); m. Walter Sutton (b. February 23, 1891, Ohio; d. February 13, 1961, buried Somerset, Perry County, Ohio), and they had three children: a) Donald Eugene Sutton (b. March 22, 1914, Ohio; d. September 10, 1933); b) Kenneth Sutton (b. November 1, 1915, Ohio; d. July 25, 1933), and c) Robert Walter Sutton, Sr. (b. April 26, 1919, Ohio; d. March 7, 1990, Zanesville, Muskingum County, Ohio; m. Virginia M. Krause, and they had three children: 1^1) James Imes Sutton, b. August 4, 1941; m. Carolyn Flora Epply, b. April 22, 1944, daughter of Wilber Eppley and Elsie Friesinger; and they had Shawn Ryan Sutton, b. February 21, 1973; 2^1) Robert Walter Sutton, b. August 22, 1943; m. Janet Marie Crum; and they had two children: Lisa Suzette Sutton, b. September 13, 1967; and Robert Aaron Sutton, b. February 19, 1973; and 3^1) Kenneth Kevin Sutton, b. December 17, 1954);

2) James William Imes [(b. June 11, 1890, Ohio; d. January 15, 1966), m. Bertha M. Buchanan (b. October 11, 1892; d. July 15, 1980, Zanesville, Muskingum County, Ohio), and they had two children: a) Janet Evelyn Imes (b. May 15, 1918); m. Clifford Franklin Davis (b. February 8, 1911; d. November 14, 1990, Zanesville, Ohio), and they had two children: Stephen Lynn Davis, b. July 6, 1943; m. Martha Handy, b. February 9, 1947 (and their three children were: Amy Elizabeth Davis, b. February 2, 1971; Barry Allen Davis, b. October 8, 1976; and Adam Andrew Davis, b. December 31, 1978); and Philip Alan Davis, b. March 5, 1947; m. 1st, Phyllis Ann Moran, and m. 2nd, Konnie Campbell; (and Phyllis had two children: Mark Alan Davis, b. January 20, 1967; and Michael Brent Davis, b. September 18, 1970; d. February 19, 1987, of leukemia); and b) Loren Grant Imes (b. September 11, 1923), m. Jeanne Harris (b. May 21, 1927), and they had three children: Cynthia Lynne Imes (b. October 7, 1953; m. 1st, Barry ___; and m. 2nd, Richard Anderson, and had one son, Andrew Michael Anderson, b. April 23, 1989); Grant Harris Imes (b. February 15, 1960, single); and David Ross Imes (b. April 29, 1963; m. Vickie Helms, b. July 8, 1958; and they had a son, Aaron Imes, b. April 1, 1990);

3) Bertha "Inez" Imes [(b. February 22, 1893, Perry County, Ohio; d. November 1, 1969), m. June 1, 1916, to Carl Henry Mautz (b. September 3, 1892, Zanesville, Ohio; d. January 6, 1984, Zanesville, Ohio), son of Carl Christian Godfrey Mautz and Anna Eisen; and they had six children:

a) Carl Myron Mautz (b. March 24, 1918, Zanesville, Ohio; d. January 4, 1985, Zanesville, Ohio; buried Memorial Park in Zanesville; m. 1st, Marjorie Fisher, b. December 31, 1922, daughter of Mike and Myrtle Fisher; and m. 2nd, Alma Forker Kirk; and had two children: Kenneth Myron Mautz, who had: 1¹) Philip Myron Mautz, b. March 29, 1963; m. October 26, 1991, to Carin Schultz, b. September 19, 1969; and they had a son Aaron Myron Mautz, b. April 28, 1994, in Michigan; 2¹) Paul Michael Mautz, b. March 5, 1965, Michigan; m. 1st, Gwen Murray, and m. 2nd, to Jill Woodman, b. July 3, 1957; and they had a daughter, Courtney Rochelle Mautz, b. June 7, 1992, Michigan; and 3¹) Timothy Wayne Mautz, b. May 21, 1969, Michigan; m. May 25, 1991, to Nancy Ann Deason, b. April 13, 1968; and their son was Scott Christopher Mautz, b. January 14, 1993; and daughter Stephanie Ann Mautz (b. February 19, 1996, Michigan); and Gerald Eugene Mautz (b. July 28, 1942, Zanesville, Ohio; d. January 16, 1990), m. 1st, to Judy Opperlander, and m. 2nd, to Marti Hedges);

b) William Eugene Mautz (b. April 6, 1922, Zanesville, Ohio; m. January 28, 1946, Zanesville, to Jessie Irene West, b. July 29, 1921); and they had four children: 1¹) Judith Ann Mautz (b. November 9, 1946, Zanesville, Ohio; m. 1st, Bruce Phipps, and m. 2nd on December 12, 1976, to Michael Anthony Conner, his second, b. April 13, 1942; and Judith had one son: Christopher Duane Phipps, b. October 2, 1971, Zanesville, and m. August 18, 1992, to Tracy Maureen Potts, b. September 8, 1973; and they had two children: Adam Duane Phipps, b. September 10, 1993; and Megan Denise Phipps, b. August 24, 1994); 2¹) Ronald Eugene Mautz (b. June 24, 1949, Zanesville, Ohio; m. 1st m.Anna Louise Hutcheson, and m. 2nd, December 12, 1984, to Billie Kay Hawkins Penny, b. June 25, 1953); 3¹) Janice Irene Mautz (b. December 7, 1951, Zanesville, Ohio; m. 1st to Arthur Francis Mercer, and m. 2nd to Stefen Rhys Chapman; and her son was Jesse Aaron Mercer, b. February 22, 1977; and 4¹) Richard Alan Mautz (b. April 17, 1953, Zanesville, Ohio; m. 1st to Ginger Jean Boggs, and m. 2nd, February 19, 1994, to Jane Elizabeth Knieriemen, b. October 22, 1948);

c) Dale Henry Mautz (b. September 26, 1924, Zanesville, Ohio; m. September 8, 1946, in Zanesville, to Juanita Marie Bailey, b. January 28, 1927, daughter of Edward and MargaretBailey), and they had four children: 1¹) Anita Louise Mautz, b. February 23, 1948, Zanesville, Ohio; m. September 1969 to Kenneth Francis Friel, and they had two children (Kimberly Lynn Friel, b. September 14, 1969, Zanesville, Ohio; d. cystic fibrosis, May 20, 1970; and Brian Matthew Friel, b. December 10, 1974, Zanesville, Ohio); 2¹) Loren Edward Mautz, b. March 9, 1951, in Zanesville, Ohio; m. July 8, 1972, at St. Nicholas Church, Zanesville, to Kathleen Marie Greulich, b. July 1, 1951, daughter of Edward and Barbara Greulich, and they had two children (Dale Edward Mautz, b. January 3, 1975, Zanesville, Ohio; m. Kim Morgan; and Kathryn Ann "Kay" Mautz, b. August 12, 1976, Zanesville, Ohio); 3¹) Shirley Ann Mautz, b. October 25, 1954, Zanesville, Ohio; m. 1st, March 17, 1974, Kevin Lee Peters, b. May 30, 1952, son of Tom and Norma Peters, and they had three children: (Beth Ann Peters, b. July 19, 1974, m. August 13, 1994, to John Douglas Stiefel; Amy Katherine Peters, b. June 11, 1976; and Jason Lee Peters, b. February 11, 1978), m. 2nd, Glen Parker; and 4[1]) Donna Jean Mautz, b. February 3, 1957, Zanesville, Ohio; (m. 1st to James Alan Young, and m. 2nd, June 26, 1986, to James Taylor Davis, b. January 19, 1960);

d) Roger Paul Mautz (b. November 21, 1927, Zanesville, Ohio), m. 1st, December 26, 1946, to Alice Arlene Hanks (d. May 16, 1982); m. 2nd, August 24, 1984, to Roma Jean Hazlett Swinehart, b. July 1, 1928 (she m. 1st to Dwight Swinehart), and he had three children: 1[1]) Thomas Roger Mautz, b. July 2, 1952, in Zanesville, Ohio; m. August 26, 1972, to Ellen Lynn Swinehart, b. June 6, 1953, daughter of Dwight Swinehart and Roma Jean Hazlett, and they had three children: (Cheryl Lynn Mautz, b. May 20, 1973, Zanesville, d. October 16, 1979, of cystic fibrosis; Robert Thomas Mautz, b. July 24, 1978, Zanesville; and Elizabeth "Beth" Yvonne Mautz, b. January 30, 1982, Zanesville); 2[1]) Linda Diane Mautz, b. September 29, 1954, Zanesville, Ohio; m. September 21, 1974, to Dennis Lee Carter, b. July 14, 1953, son of Robert and Ruby Carter; and they had two children: (Bruce Edward Carter, b. August 2, 1977; and Teri Kathleen Carter, b. September 23, 1980); and 3[1]) Pamela Arlene Mautz, b. February 12, 1957, Zanesville, Ohio; m. November 19, 1977, to Johnny Lee Dooley, b. February 2, 1952; and they had two children: Heather Janelle Dooley, b. June 21, 1978; and Rachel Caryn Dooley, b. June 25, 1981);

e) Glen Eldon Mautz, b. January 8, 1933, Zanesville, Ohio; m. 1st, Jo-Ann Carter; and m. 2nd, December 30, 1979, to Gloria Susan Robinson Gordon; and he had three children: 1[1]) Carl Eugene Mautz, b. November 25, 1954, Texas; m. 1st, Virginia Condon; m. 2nd, Denise Autry; and m. 3rd, Debbie Ann Ham Workman; 2[1]) Randall Alan Mautz, b. April 17, 1958, in Texas; m. May 3, 1980, in Texas to Sharon Kay Polk, b. June 19, 1958, and their son was Stephen Glen Mautz, b. January 5, 1988; and 3[1]) Jason Michael Mautz, b. May 21, 1981, in Texas; and

f) Marjorie Inez Mautz, b. June 30, 1937, Zanesville, Ohio; m. December 31, 1955, in Zanesville, to Raymond Earl Dixon, b. January 11, 1935, son of Roy Albert Dixon and Christena Mae Wilson of Zanesville; and they had two children: 1[1]) Raymond Michael "Mike" Dixon, b. December 14, 1956, in Zanesville; m. September 17, 1977, First Baptist Church in Zanesville, to Bonnie Lou Rogers, b. January 3, 1958, daughter of Edward Rogers and Ruth Ann Barker, and they had two children: Jennifer Marie Dixon, b. March 11, 1980, Zanesville; and Stephanie Ann Dixon, b. January 10, 1984, Zanesville); and 2[1]) Jeffrey Alan Dixon, b. September 9, 1958, Zanesville; m. June 20, 1981, to Cynthia Jane Bell, b. July 7, 1959, daughter of Rhudy and Janet Bell, and they had two children: (Susan Ruth Dixon, b. May 3, 1984, in Zanesville, Ohio; and Erin Rachel Dixon, b. May 23, 1986, in Zanesville, Ohio). Family of Bertha Inez Imes (b. 1843) and Carl Henry Mautz prepared by Marjorie Inez Mautz Dixon (b. 1937);

4) Carrie May Imes (b. May 14, 1896, Zanesville, Muskingum County, Ohio; d. September 9, 1898 or 1899, of typhoid fever);
5) LaVerna Imes (b. May 4, 1898, Zanesville, Ohio; d. July 28, 1976, in New Hampshire and buried in Memorial Park, Zanesville); m. to Karl Yost (b. April 12, 1899; d. February 6, 1986, in Zanesville, Ohio), had three children:
    a) Rita Gail Yost (b. May 23, 1924), m. Jack Anthony Martin, and they had five children: 1^1) Rachel Ann Martin, b. November 21, 1950, Ohio; m. Kenneth Barnes, and their child was Patrick Anthony Barnes, b. February 11, 1972; 2^1) Karl Whitmer Martin (b. July 28, 1952, Ohio), m. Toni Spangler and they had two children: Benjamin Whitmer Martin, b. April 5, 1973; and Yvonne Marie Martin, b. November 2, 1974; 3^1) Rebecca Gail Martin (b. March 3, 1954, Ohio), m. December 31, 1976, to Floyd Thomas, Jr., and they had one son and one daughter; 4^1) Deborah Sue Martin (b. August 16, 1956, Ohio); m. 1st to John Scott Boughner, and m. 2nd to Peter MacGregor; son: Ryan MacGregor, b. October 11, 1995; and 5^1) Sarah Jane Martin (b. November 14, 1957, Ohio), m. Dale Randy Mayle, and they had two children: Tory Justin Mayle, b. July 19, 1980; and Eden Nicole Martin-Mayle, b. June 14, 1988;
    b) Theda Maryanna Yost, b. September 12, 1928; m. September 4, 1953, to Phillip Pierce Clemans, b. March 18, 1928; and they had three children: 1^1) Phillip Michael Clemans, b. July 28, 1954; and they had two children: (Jennifer Jo Clemans, b. May 19, 1972; and Cassandra Rose Clemans, b. July 23, 1982); 2^1) Kristie Suzanne Clemans, b. April 27, 1957, Ohio; m. Mark Richard Rausch, b. March 30, 1956, and they had three children: (Nicholas Mark Rausch, b. May 6, 1979; Stacy Elizabeth Rausch, b. May 26, 1982; and Nathan Phillip Rausch, b. March 10, 1984); and 3^1) Matthew Vernon Clemans, b. February 6, 1959, Ohio; m. Sharon Burns, b. July 20, 1959, and they had three children: (Tyler Matthew Clemans, b. October 12, 1987; Andrew William Clemans, b. March 3, 1993; and Aaron Michael Clemans, b. March 3, 1993, twin); and
    c) Karl Zane Yost, b. May 3, 1930; m. Megan Owen, and they had four children: 1^1) Owen Yost, b. July 30, 1959; m. Dawn ___, June 10, 1994; 2^1) Dierdre Yost, b. March 14, 1961; m. and two children; 3^1) Jason Yost, b. August 25, 1962; and 4^1) Molly Yost, b. May 2, 1965;
6) Clarence Aaron Imes (b. July 26, 1902, Somerset, Perry County, Ohio; d. April 9, 1969, Zanesville, Muskingum County, Ohio); m. Ada Lillian Luman, and they had one daughter, Roberta LaJoy Imes (b. January 30, 1928, in Zanesville, Ohio) who m. 1st, Dallas Cale, and m. 2nd, December 8, 1979, to Jack Hannon after death of Dallas Cale, by whom she had two children: Mark Aaron Cale (b. January 8, 1956, Zanesville, Ohio; m. Roseanna X. Curl, b. April 15, 1956; and they had a daughter, Megan Elizabeth Cale, b. July 14, 1991); and Melissa Lynn Cale (b. June 7, 1958, Zanesville, Ohio; m. 1st, Mark Sells; and m. 2nd, Keith Kent; and she had a son Aaron Andrew Kent, b. April 22, 1986); m. 3rd, August 16, 1997, to Bob Paap. Roberta LaJoy Imes Cale Hannon

contributed major portions of the text, and is known as Joy Imes Hannon (JIH);

7) Jesse Orren Imes (b. May 4 or 31, 1905 or 1907, Ohio), m. Edith Caroline Voght, b. April 20, 1905, and they had two children: a) Jerry Orren Imes, b. June 13, 1937, Zanesville, Ohio; m. 1st, Helen Moses, and m. 2nd, Kathryn Bauer Clayton; and b) Carolyn Sue Imes, b. August 28, 1939, Zanesville, single; and

8) Charles Clinton Imes (b. August 24, 1900, Ohio; d. January 19, 1901, of pneumonia).

REFERENCES

- Harry Wright Newman: *Anne Arundel Gentry*, Volume 1, published by Author, 1970.

- James Frank Iams: Personal communication, 1993.

- Elisha B. Iams: Lifelong personal files, Washington County Historical Society, Washington, Pennsylvania.

- Ervin F. Bickley, Jr.: Personal notes 1935-1995, New Canaan, Connecticut.

- F. D. Wright: *Anne Arundel Church Records of the Seventeenth and Eighteenth Centuries, Annapolis, Maryland*, Family Line Publishers, Westminster, Maryland, 1993.

- Latter Day Saints Files, Salt Lake City, Utah, microfilms.

- Barbara Locker: Personal files.

- Ruth Iams: Personal files, Ten Mile, Pennsylvania, 1994.

- Lois Ijams Hartman: *In His Steps and Remembered in this Land*, Hillcrest Books, Pasadena, California, 1978; and personal files, 1994.

- Roberta Wright Iiames and Guy R. Iiames, Jr.: *The Iiames Family Genealogy*, Springboro, Ohio, 1994.

- Barbara Fowler: Personal files, Toledo, Ohio, compiled by Roberta E. Wright Iiames, Springboro, Ohio, 1994.

- Sueki Rulfs: Personal files, Ann Arbor, Michigan, 1995.

- Carmen W. Harleston: *A Brief History of the Imes Family, 1660-1916*, Gaithersburg, Maryland, 1982; U. S. Archives.

- Maryland Archives, Volume 17, p. 246; Folio 21, pp. 828-829, 1734; Folio 31, pp. 741-742;

- James B. Meighen: Personal files of Iams family, Western Pennsylvania, 1994.

- John C. Weaver: Personal correspondence to George D. Iams of Washington, Pennsylvania, from Shaker Heights, Ohio, 1939.

- Howard Leckey: *Ten Mile Country, Washington and Greene Counties, Pennsylvania*.

- E. Jay Iiams: Personal files of Iams family, Washington County, Pennsylvania, 1934.

- Michael Iams: Personal files of Iams family line, Philadelphia Imes Reunion, Philadelphia, 1994.

- Robert Elton Iams: Personal records of Iams family line of Phoebe Penn and Thomas Iams, Jr.

- Property Records of Brooke County, West Virginia (formerly Virginia): Volume 1, p. 135; Volume 3, p. 9; Volume 5, p. 405.

- Property Records of Bedford County, Pennsylvania, and Allegany County, Maryland; County Court House.

- Property Records of Jefferson County, Ohio; Court House, Steubenville, Ohio.

- Irene M. (Mrs. M. T.) Ochsenbein: Personal paid genealogical search on behalf of requests by Ervin F. Bickley, Jr., Eastern Ohio, West Virginia, 1967.

- Deeds, Brooke County, West Virginia (Virginia), Book 1, pp. 135, 225, 1797; Book 3, p. 9, 1802; Book 5, p. 405, 1815; Book 6, p. 404, 1819; Book E, p. 333, 1917; Book E, p. 696, 1816.

- Deeds, Belmont County, Ohio, Book Y, p. 166, 1837.

- Marriage Licenses of Belmont County, Ohio, Book 3, p. 41, 1831; Book 3, p. 87, 1831; Book 3, p. 168, 1831.

- Deeds of Jefferson County, Ohio: Book B, pp. 91, 284, 612, 644; Book C, pp. 13, 79; Book F, p. 311; Book H, pp. 92, 161; Book P, p. 388; Book U, p. 185; Book V, pp. 159, 160; Book W, pp. 315-317; Book A-2, pp. 218, 388; Book B-2, p. 82; Book C-2, p. 536; Book D-2, p. 629; Book E-2, pp. 275, 343.

- Land, tax, and marriage records of Berkeley County, West Virginia, as searched by Ervin F. Bickley, New Canaan, Connecticut.

- Tax Census Records, Brooke County, West Virginia.

- Joy Imes Hannon: Personal files of Iiams family, Zanesville, Ohio, 1994, by Roberta LaJoy Imes Cale Hannon.

- Marjorie Inez Mautz Dixon: Personal contributions on family of Bertha Inez Imes (b. 1893), and Ulysses Grant Imes; Zanesville, Ohio, 1997.

CHAPTER 2

RICHARD IIAMS

(B. 1673, MARYLAND; D. MARYLAND)

Richard Iiams, born 1673, son of William Iiams (d. 1703) and Elizabeth Cheyney, had twelve children: 1. Elizabeth Iiams, 2. Richard Iiams, 3. Rachel Iiams, 4. Mary Iiams, 5. William Iiams, 6. Cheyney Iiams, 7. John Iiams, 8. John (the Second) Iiams, 9. Charity Iiams, 10. Sarah Iiams, 11. Aaron Iiams, and 12. William (the Lesser) Iiams.

The family lived in Maryland, while offspring including the family of slave Jack Imes, born 1775, lived in Pennsylvania. Later offspring moved to Tennessee, Ohio, West Virginia, Illinois, and Wisconsin.

Richard Iiams, born August 1673, Anne Arundel County, Maryland; died 1761, South River Hundred, Anne Arundel County, Maryland; son of William Iiams (b.1640) and Elizabeth Cheney. He married first, January 16, 1706, Anne Arundel County, Maryland, to Anne Cheyney, born March 18, 1691, Anne Arundel County Maryland; buried October 16, 1713, Anne Arundel County, Maryland. They had seven children. Richard Iiams married second Elizabeth Gaither, born 1698, Anne Arundel County, Maryland; died after 1761; daughter of John Gaither and Elizabeth Duvall. Richard Iiams and Anne Cheney had five children.

First marriage:
1. Elizabeth Iiams, b. August 12, 1707, Anne Arundel County, Maryland; christened January 29, 1708; d. after 1747
2. Richard Iiams, baptized September 1712, South River, Anne Arundel County, Maryland; m. January 19, 1737, to Mary Nichols
3. Rachel Iiams, baptized September 1712, South River, Anne Arundel County, Maryland; probably d. young
4. Mary Iiams, baptized September 1712, Anne Arundel County, Maryland; m. December 22, 1726, South River, Anne Arundel County, Maryland, to Richard Wright
5. William Iiams, baptized July 22, 1713, South River, Anne Arundel County, Maryland; d. young
6. Cheyney Iiams, baptized November 14, 1718, South River, Anne Arundel County, Maryland; d. young
7. John Iiams the First, b. 1708, Anne Arundel County, Maryland; d. 1747, per EFB

Second marriage:
8. John Iiams, b. 1716/20, All Hallow's Parish, Anne Arundel County, Maryland; d. May 17, 1778
9. Charity Iiams, baptized November 14, 1718, Anne Arundel County, Maryland; d. 1747
10. Sarah Iiams, d. after 1747
11. Aaron Iiams, baptized June 24, 1721, South River Hundred, All Hallows Parish, Anne Arundel County, Maryland; d. after 1803

12. William Iiams, baptized July 22, 1713; d. 1778/82; m. Elizabeth Howard. He shared 100-acre plantation of New Birmingham in Upper Patuxent River area with his brother John Iams according to the 1747 will of his father, Richard Iiams (b. 1673). (HWN added this to his 1970 edition.) He is believed to have lived in Washington County, Maryland, by 1787 and sold land there as late as 1803, though LIH has William Iiams settled in Washington County, Pennsylvania, by 1787 and "styled himself in 1792 as of Allegany County, Maryland. Purchased Chance. In 1803 William of Washington County sold property and prepared to move elsewhere." (LIH, HWN, EFB, REI, FEW, RI)

Anne Cheyney (b. 1691; d. 1717) was a cousin of Richard Iiams (b. 1673). Richard Iiams (b. 1673) purchased the plantation Iiams Purchase from Benjamin Burgess, South River, on October 1, 1700. He purchased Iiams Last Purchase, formerly known as Burgess Choice at about that same time. Richard Iiams sold a portion of Iams Choice on June 7, 1710, to Henry Fitch; sold both Iiams Purchase and Iiams Last Purchase on June 8, 1727, to Richard Snowden; purchased the 100-acre plantation Birmingham in 1742 from Richard Snowden.

Richard Iiams wrote his will March 30, 1747 (Folio 31, pp. 463-465, Ann Arundel County), fourteen years before his death, leaving his personal estate to his wife Elizabeth Gaither Iiams, and mentions his children: John Iiams, William Iiams, Jr., Mary Iiams, Charity Iiams, Sarah Iiams, and Elizabeth Iiams. The plantation was divided equally between John Iiams and William Iiams, Jr. The will was probated August 1761 in Anne Arundel County and witnessed by Thomas Iiams, John Iiams, Rebecca Iiams, Plummer Iiams, and Thomas Donaldson. After initial refusals, Elizabeth Gaither Iiams accepted administrative bond on December 14, 1763, with John Iiams and Thomas Elliott as sureties. The estate "passed at court" March 14, 1764, with Thomas Iiams and John Iiams as kinsmen.

A William Iiams purchased land in Washington County, Maryland, March 5, 1787, from John Donnachy, and the 1790 census of Washington County, Maryland, lists William Iiams with four males under age sixteen, 4 females, and seven negroes.

As a resident of Allegany County, Maryland, on October 1, 1792, William Iiams deeded his portion of the family plantation New Birmingham to John Snowden of Anne Arundel County, Maryland. On March 30, 1793, he purchased fifty-eight acres called Chance from Thomas and Susannah Worley in Washington County, Maryland. On September 10, 1803, he deeded several tracts of land in Washington County, Maryland, including 110 acres for £1,882 (Chance); fifty-eight acres (Hole in the Hole); nine acres (Addition to Chance), and a "total of 251 acres with houses and other improvements." Mr. Newman (HWN) has taken these transactions to represent evidence of the preparation to move to Washington County, Pennsylvania.

A slave, John "Jack" Howard Imes, born January 1, 1775, Anne Arundel County, Maryland; died July 2, 1871, Spruce Hill, Juniata County, Pennsylvania, is believed to be the son of John Iiams (b. 1720), brother of William Iiams (b. 1713), and a mulatto slave woman at the Howard Plantation, became fabled as the propositus of the highly successful, respected, and endeared Jack Imes branch of the family tree.

Jack Imes was buried in the Ebenezer Church Cemetery near Port Royal, Juniata County, Pennsylvania. Although given his freedom by legal decree, Jack Imes (b. 1775) elected to remain with the family of William Iiams and Elizabeth Howard until about 1824 when he moved to Franklin County, Pennsylvania. In the interim in Washington County, Maryland, Jack Imes (b. 1775) married second to Susan Pindle, born August 29, 1795; died 1857, Franklin County, Pennsylvania. Most of the slaves had been sold by 1803.

In 1850, Jack Imes moved to Juniata County, Pennsylvania, with his wife and two sons and there he owned "considerable Land" and had two additional children. Legend has it that his second wife was the daughter of Lord Charles Howard of Baltimore. **Jack Imes** (b. 1775) and Susan Pindle had at least four children:
1. David Imes, b. February 6, 1821, Franklin County, Pennsylvania; d. December 17, 1894, Juniata County, Pennsylvania.
2. Samuel Imes, b. January 14, 1818
3. Henry Imes; m. Elizabeth Cuff; killed at Battle of Dutch Gap, Civil War, in 1864 in Virginia.
4. Elizabeth Imes, b. 1835 (CWH)

David Imes (b. 1821) married first to Adaline Braan; they had five children; married second to Sarah Ann Wilson and they had nine children; owned 1,517 acres in Juniata County, Pennsylvania. His children were:
1. Oliver Imes, b. December 31, 1841, Franklin County; d. November 27, 1914, Carlisle, Pennsylvania; single
2. Sarah Bell Imes, b. November 15, 1843; d. February 6, 1914; m. Benjamin Moore
3. John C. Imes, b. December 14, 1845, Franklin County, Pennsylvania; d. January 5, 1918; m. Caroline Stewart
4. Annie Mariah Imes, b. January 4, 1848; m. Peter Heath
5. Joseph Imes, b. April 8, 1850; d. while on active duty
6. Mary J. Imes b. March 1856, Juniata County, Pennsylvania; d. 1905
7. Wilson David Imes, b. January 1858, Juniata County, Pennsylvania
8. Howard C. Imes, b. December 1859, Juniata County, Pennsylvania
9. Olen Imes, b. November 1861, Juniata County, Pennsylvania
10. Samuel Imes, b. December 1863
11. Emory Imes, b. 1865; d. February 16, 1926
12. Ellie/Ellen Imes, b. 1869, Juniata County, Pennsylvania; d. February 1, 1892
13. Ross Imes, b. 1871; d. 1873
14. Alice Carey Imes, b. August 1873, Juniata County, Pennsylvania

The 1880 Federal Census of Juniata County, Pennsylvania, lists David Imes, age 59, mulatto, b. Maryland); wife Sarah A. Imes, age 48; Oliver Imes, age 38; Sarah Imes, age 36; John C. Imes, age 34; Ann M. Imes, age 32; Joseph Imes, age 30; Mary Ann Imes, age 24; Wilson R. Imes, age 22; Howard C. Imes, age 20; Olin Imes, age 18; Samuel Imes, age 16; Emory Imes, age 14; Ellen Imes, age 11; and Alice Carey Imes, age 6.

Six family groups of Imes are listed in the 1900 Federal Census of Juniata County, Pennsylvania:
1. John C. Imes, age 54, b. Pennsylvania; wife Caroline Imes, age 44; Elmer R. Imes, age 12; Benjamin Imes, age 11; Mary Imes, age 7; May Imes, age 6; and Anna Imes, age 2 months.
2. William Wilson Imes, age 42, b. Pennsylvania; wife Martha A. Imes, age 34; David Imes, age 16; Mary J. Imes, age 15; Joseph Imes, age 14; Jessie Imes, age 12 (a son); Walter Imes, age 7; Sarah B. Imes, age 10; Florence Imes, age 5; and Warren Imes, age 2.
3. Howard C. Imes, age 40, b. Pennsylvania; wife Bettie Imes, age 37; David Imes, age 9; Herman Imes, age 9; Alvin Imes, age 7; Nevan Imes, age 7 (a son); Roda M. Imes, age 5; Hobot Imes, age 2; and William R. Imes, age 1.
4. Olen Imes, age 39, b. Pennsylvania; wife Maggie, age 50; and 4 children.
5. Samuel Imes, age 36, b. Pennsylvania; wife Anna M. Imes, age 31; Sarah Imes, age 8; Mary Imes, age 7; David Imes, age 6; William L. Imes, age 5; Lucian Imes, age 3; and Lincoln Imes, age 8 months.

6. William Imes, age 44, b. Pennsylvania; wife Mildred Imes, age 34; and 4 children.

The 1910 Federal Census of Juniata County, Pennsylvania, listed six Imes family groups:
1. Caroline Imes, age 53, b. Pennsylvania; Benjamin Imes, age 20; Elmer Imes, age 21; Mary E. Imes, age 17; Lillian M. Imes, age 15; and Annie J. Imes, age 10, living with Nancy Barton.
2. John C. Imes (living alone).
3. Wilson D. Imes, age 52, b. Pennsylvania; Martha A. Imes, age 49; Mary J. Imes, age 25; Joseph Imes, age 23; Jesse Imes, age 22; and Sarah B. Imes, age 20.
4. Samuel Imes, age 43, b. Pennsylvania; Malinda M. Imes, age 22; Sarah J. Imes, age 18; Mary B. Imes, age 17; Luther D. Imes, age 16; Lloyd W. Imes, age 15; Lucian Imes, age 12; Foster L. Imes, age 10; Nieman J. Imes, age 9.
5. Emory Imes, age 44, b. Pennsylvania; Theressa Imes, age 29, b. Pennsylvania; Irvin J. Imes, age 11; Ruth Imes, age 9; Thomas Imes, age 8; Henry M. Imes, age 6; and Ellie I. Imes, age 1.
6. William W. Imes, age 53, b. Pennsylvania; Mildred Imes, age 49; Sallie M. Imes, age 12; and Thomas M. Imes, age 10.

The 1920 Federal Census of Juniata County, Pennsylvania, listed four Imes family groups:
1. Caroline Imes, age 66, b. Pennsylvania; Elmer E. Imes, age 29; and Annie J. Imes, age 19.
2. The children of Wilson Imes: David T. Imes, age 25; Mary E. Imes, age 25; William Imes, age 24; and James Imes, age 19.
3. Emery Imes, age 54, b. Pennsylvania; Margaret Imes, age 38; John Imes, age 20; Domas Imes, age 16; Males Imes, age 14 (a son); Elsie Imes, age 11; and Edith Imes, age 9.
4. William Imes, age 61; b. Pennsylvania; Martha Imes, age 59; Walter Imes, age 25; Florence Imes, age 27; and Paul Imes, age 16.

William H. Imes, born ca1815, Washington County, Maryland, son of John "Jack" Howard Imes (b. 1775) and Susan Pendle, married Fannie and they had four children:
1. Charles Imes, b. ca1840
2. Mary E. Imes, b. ca1848
3. William Imes, b. ca1850
4. Margaret Imes, b. ca1855

John Imes, born ca1816, Washington County, Maryland; died June 17, 1854, Franklin County, Pennsylvania, son of John "Jack" Howard Imes (b. 1775) and Susan Pendle, married Elizabeth (b. ca1816, Virginia) and they had six children:
1. David Imes, b. ca1840, Franklin County, Pennsylvania
2. Mary B. Imes, b. ca1842, Franklin County, Pennsylvania
3. James Imes, b. ca1842; d. April 5, 1895; m. October 22, 1891, to Jane Strange
4. Essau H. Imes, b. ca1846; d. November 8, 1907; m. June 17, 1893, to Catherine Ingram, b. ca1846, Watson, Mississippi; d. July 14, 1934, Memphis, Tennessee. Their 5 children were:
   a. Lillie Bell Imes, b. November 4, 1884; d. ca1974; m. James Calvin Borders. Their 2 children were: Imes Borders and Eva Claire Borders, b. October 21, 1907; d. August 1974 in Cleveland.

58

b. Boyd Beverly Imes, b. December 29, 1886; d. August 24, 1961

c. Bennie Lloyd Imes, b. July 27, 1889

d. Carrie Anna Beatrice Imes, b. March 10, 1893

e. Edward Houston Imes, b. November 24, 1895; d. November 27, 1976

5. Caroline Imes, b. ca1847

6. John Imes, b. ca1849.

Samuel Imes, born January 13, 1818, Washington County, Maryland; died February 3, 1893, the son of John "Jack" Imes (b. 1775) and Susan Pendle; married February 22, 1842, to Sarah Moore, born July 31, 1820, Franklin County, Pennsylvania; died January 9, 1894, and they had nine to eleven children:

1. Mary Amanda Imes, b. December 9, 1842, Franklin County, Pennsylvania; d. April 12, 1859

2. George Hazekiah Imes, b. October 8, 1844, Franklin County, Pennsylvania; d. August 24, 1892; m. August 4, 1870, to Lucinda Armstrong Clark, b. January 5, 1843, and they had 5 children:

    a. Aura Channing Imes, b. caMarch 1873, Franklin County, Pennsylvania

    b. Otho Samuel Imes, b. caAugust 1875, Franklin County, Pennsylvania

    c. Amy Allison Imes, b. September 21, 1877, Franklin County, Pennsylvania; d. June 9, 1940, Franklin County, Pennsylvania; m. 1st, January 14, 1896, to Evans Theodore Matthews; m. 2nd, February 26, 1913, to Washeen Robinson.

    d. Jessie Garfield Imes, b. September 26, 1879, Franklin County, Pennsylvania

    e. George Lake Imes, b. October 12, 1883, Franklin County, Pennsylvania; d. ca1957

3. Elizabeth Eveline Imes, b. January 23, 1846, Franklin County, Pennsylvania; d. February 6, 1859

4. Benjamin Albert Imes, b. January 28, 1848, Franklin County, Pennsylvania; d. August 7, 1908; m. 1880 in Oberlin, Ohio, to Elizabeth Rachel Wallace, b. 1852; d. 1944, and they had 3 children:

    a. Elmer Samuel Imes, b. 1883; d. 1941

    b. Albert Lovejoy Imes, b. March 1, 1885

    c. Rev. William Lloyd Imes, b. December 29, 1889

5. Martin Henry Imes, b. May 4, 1850, Juniata County, Pennsylvania

6. Thomas Creigh Imes, M.D., b. March 24, 1852; buried Collingdale, Delaware County, Pennsylvania; first known "black" graduate of Hahnemann Medical College; served as Sunday School Superintendent of Lombard Central Presbyterian Church of Philadelphia, Pennsylvania

7. Sarah Ann Imes, b. January 21, 1854; d. May 24, 1902, buried Lost Creek Cem., McAlisterville, Pennsylvania

8. William W. Imes, b. October 15, 1855; d. March 8, 1925, Detroit, Michigan; m. 1896 to Mildred Thomas, b. June 1862; d. November 1925, Detroit, Michigan; their child was:

    ?a. Sarah Mildred Imes, b. May 9, 1897, Juniata County, Pennsylvania; d. January 1972; m. I. Irving White; their child was LeRoy Glenn White, b. December 12, 1917, and possibly:

    ?b. Thomas Morgan Imes, b. September 9, 1899; d. April 14, 1974; m. November 27, 1918, Detroit, Michigan, to Lillie Woods, b. October 14, 1902, in Alderson, West Virginia.

59

9. John Imes, b. December 16, 1857; d. March 16, 1859
10. Margaret Jane Imes, b. January 24, 1860; d. February 24, 1879
11. David Hunter Imes, b. December 27, 1862

Amy Allison Imes, born September 21, 1877, Franklin County, Pennsylvania; died June 9, 1940, Franklin County, Pennsylvania, daughter of George Hazekiah Imes (b. 1844) and Lucinda Armstrong Clark (b. 1843) married first, January 14, 1896, to Evans Theodore Matthews; she married second, February 26, 1913, to Washeen Robinson (b. ca1887), and she had three children:
1. Stanley Matthews, b. caJuly 1896; d. May 27, 1899
2. Eva Allison Matthews, b. February 14, 1898; m. James E. Braxton, b. July 12, 1896
3. Ivy Markle Matthews, b. February 16, 1899; d. ca1968; m. Virgil A. Stern, b. January 12, 1891; d. January 12, 1963; they had 5 children:
   a. Mary M. Stern
   b. Amy A. Stern
   c. Stanley V. Stern
   d. Eleanor B. Stern
   e. Virginia L. Stern

David Imes, born February 6, 1821, Washington County, Maryland; died December 17, 1894; buried in Ebenezer Cemetery, Juniata County, Pennsylvania; son of John "Jack" Howard Imes (b. 1775) and Susan Pendle; married first, ca1840, to Adaline Braan, born ca1819; died April 15, 1850; married second, December 25, 1854, to Sarah Ann Wilson, born ca1831; died ca1914; buried in Ebenezer Cemetery; they had fourteen children:
1. Oliver Imes, b. December 31, 1841, Franklin County, Pennsylvania; d. November 27, 1914, Carlisle, Pennsylvania; single
2. Sarah Bell Imes, b. November 15, 1843, Franklin County, Pennsylvania; d. February 6, 1914
3. John C. Imes, b. December 14, 1845; Franklin County, Pennsylvania; d. January 5, 1918
4. Ann Mariah Imes, b. January 4, 1848, Franklin County, Pennsylvania
5. Joseph Imes, b. April 8, 1850, Franklin County, Pennsylvania
6. Mary J. Imes, b. March 1856, Juniata County, Pennsylvania; d. 1905
7. Wilson David Imes, b. January 1858, Juniata County, Pennsylvania
8. Howard C. Imes, b. December 1859, Juniata County, Pennsylvania
9. Olen Imes, b. November 1861, Juniata County, Pennsylvania
10. Samuel Imes, b. December 1863, Juniata County, Pennsylvania; d. May 4, 1946; buried Ebenezer Cem.; m. 1st, Anna M. Strong; m. 2nd, December 1909, Malinda Fultz
11. Emory Imes, b. 1865; d. February 16, 1926; buried Ebenezer Cem.; m. Tressa, b. 1881; d. 1938; their son was Miles H. Imes, b. 1905; d. 1994; buried Lower Presbyterian Cem., Academia, Pennsylvania; he m. Clair Benner
12. Ellen Imes, b. 1869, Juniata County, Pennsylvania; d. February 1, 1892
13. Ross Imes, b. 1871; d. 1873
14. Alice Carey Imes, b. August 1873, Juniata County, Pennsylvania

Samuel Imes, born December 1863, Juniata County, Pennsylvania; died May 4, 1946, son of David Imes, born 1821, Washington County, Maryland, and grandson of John "Jack" Howard Imes (b. 1776); married first, Anna M. Strong, born August 15, 1868; died August 9, 1904; married second, December 1909, to Malinda Fultz (HI); his eight children were:

1. Sarah Jane Imes, b. June 1891; d. February 6, 1982; buried McCoysville, Pennsylvania, Cem.; m. Charles Shaffer, b. 1885; d. 1965
2. Mary Belle Imes, b. August 1892; d. April 16, 1944; buried Logantown, Pennsylvania, Cem.; m. 1st, Mr. Glunt; m. 2nd, Mr. Snook
3. David Luther Imes, b. February 23, 1894; d. December 12, 1972; m. Josette Mae Swartswood, b. September 6, 1905; d. June 11, 1980
4. William Lloyd Imes, b. April 1895; d. 1984; buried McCoysville Cem., Juniata County, Pennsylvania; m. Gay, b. 1902; d. 1978
5. Lucian Wilson Imes, b. May 1897; d. November 9, 1919; buried Ebenezer Cem., Juniata County, Pennsylvania
6. daughter, b. 1898; d. seven days later; buried Ebenezer Cem., Juniata County, Pennsylvania
7. Lincoln Foster Imes, b. November 12, 1899; d. July 17, 1973; buried Loganton Cem., Juniata County, Pennsylvania; m. Jenetta, b. 1905; d. 1980; buried St. Paul Cem., Nook, Juniata County, Pennsylvania
8. Jeremiah Neimond Imes, b. February 12, 1901; d. 1993; m. Sylvia Martha Smith, b. 1900; d. 1940; their son, Rev. Harold N. Imes (m. Frances), a contributor to the family history, lived in Mifflintown, Pennsylvania, in 1994.

Albert Lovejoy Imes, born March 1, 1885, Memphis, Tennessee; died January 1, 1976, Cincinnati, Ohio; son of Benjamin Albert Imes (b. 1845) and Elizabeth Rachel Wallace; grandson of Samuel Imes (b. 1818); married September 1, 1913, in Cincinnati, Ohio, to Amy Marian Field, born May 3, 1889, Philadelphia, Pennsylvania; died February 27, 1951, Cincinnati, Ohio; their two children were:

1. Paul Lovejoy Imes, b. January 18, 1918, Cincinnati, Ohio; m. March 10, 1938, Middleboro, Kentucky., to Althea Marie Mills, b. November 4, 1919, Knoxville, Tennessee; lived in Ohio; their 3 children were:
   a. Daniel Mills Imes, b. April 30, 1939; m. April 16, 1966, to Diane Lynn Burbanks; they had 3 children: Tammie Louise Imes, b. May 30, 1969; Daniel Mills Imes II, b. November 10, 1972; and Mimi Nicole Imes, b. September 23, 1975
   b. Edith Marian Imes, b. April 23, 1940
   c. Sylvia Marie Imes, b. December 27, 1941
2. Marjorie Jean Imes, b. October 22, 1928, Cincinnati, Ohio

William Lloyd Imes, born December 29, 1889; died September 6, 1915, a minister; son of Benjamin Albert Imes (b. 1845) and grandson of Samuel Imes (b. 1818); m. September 6, 1915, Dundee, New York, to Grace Virginia Frank, born December 11, 1889; died October 16, 1972; they had three children:

1. Wendell Phillips Imes, b. June 8, 1916; died December 4, 1944; married August 26, 1944, to Anita Lloyd Rogers, b. August 24, 1921
2. Hope Mathilde Imes, b. August 24, 1921; m. January 17, 1945, to George Johnson Haley, b. June 7, 1920
3. Jane Elizabeth Imes, b. July 19, 1924; d. February 6, 1931 (CWH)

Thomas Morgan Imes, born September 9, 1899; died April 14, 1974; son of William W. Imes (b. 1855) and grandson of Samuel Imes (b. 1818); married November 27, 1918, in Detroit, Michigan, to Lillie Woods, born October 14, 1902, Alderson, West Virginia; they had three children:

1. Helen Mildred Imes, b. February 16, 1920, Detroit, Michigan
2. Barbara Jane Imes, b. June 15, 1922, Detroit, Michigan
3. Margaret Ann Imes, b. December 12, 1929, Detroit, Michigan

David Luther Imes, born February 23, 1894; died December 12, 1972; son of Samuel Imes (b. 1863) and grandson of David Imes (b. 1821); married Janetta

Mae Swartwood, born September 6, 1905; died June 11, 1980; they had twelve children:
1. Betty Imes
2. Charles Samuel Imes, b. January 7, 1927
3. Melvin Luther Imes, b. August 14, 1928
4. Blair Wilson Imes
5. Stella Mae Imes
6. Robert Lee Imes
7. David Luther Imes II
8. Lehman Theron Imes
9. Dorothy Lou Imes
10. Mary Kathryn Imes
11. Connie Louise Imes
12. Ronald Earl Imes, b. April 21, 1948; d. March 1971

Eva Allison Matthews, born February 14, 1898, daughter of Amy Allison Imes, born September 21, 1877; granddaughter of George Hazekiah Imes (b. 1844); married James E. Braxton, born January 25, 1918; they had eight children:
1. Richard Benjamin Braxton, b. January 25, 1918, Harrisburg, Pennsylvania; m. October 10, 1938, to Inza Margaret Taylor
2. James E. Braxton
3. Harriet E. Braxton, m. Mr. Logan
4. Ann E. Braxton
5. Floyd M. Braxton, b. April 16, 1928; d. March 4, 1973; m. Dollie Marie Jefferson; their 3 children were:
   a. Cynthia Theresa Braxton
   b. Whitney Imes Braxton
   c. Floyd Matthew Braxton II
6. Mary M. Braxton
7. George L. Braxton, b. August 9, 1934, Harrisburg, Pennsylvania; m. April 30, 1966, Philadelphia, Pennsylvania, to Alice Scott, b. April 10, 1928, Franklin, Virginia; their daughter was: Alison Lynette Braxton, b. April 9, 1960
8. Stanley Gene Braxton, b. September 20, 1935, Harrisburg, Pennsylvania; lived in Wyndmoor, Pennsylvania; president of Jack Imes Family Association which held national meeting in Philadelphia in 1994; m. November 24, 1963, Philadelphia, Pennsylvania, to Virginia Atwell, b. August 1, 1941, Philadelphia; schoolteacher; editor of *Imes Times* family newsletter; contributor to family history; they had 3 children:
   a. Elyse Marie Braxton, b. January 14, 1966, Philadelphia, Pennsylvania
   b. Stanley Hughes Braxton, b. June 7, 1967, Philadelphia, Pennsylvania
   c. Evan Christopher Braxton, b. August 1, 1971, Philadelphia, Pennsylvania (SB)

Sarah Mildred Imes, born May 9, 1897, Juniata County, Pennsylvania; died January 1972; daughter of William W. Imes, (b. 1855); granddaughter of Samuel Imes (b. 1818); married J. Irving White. Their son LeRoy Glenn White, born December 12, 1917; died December 24, 1968; married January 31, 1937, to Hazel Lee Miller, born January 24, 1917; they had two children:
1. LeRoy Glenn White-Wright II, b. December 1, 1941
2. Carmen Henrietta Cecile White-Wright, b. May 20, 1943; family historian, author, and researcher who compiled Jack Imes family history; m.

James Burroughs Harleston, b. October 28, 1940; their 2 children were: Jason B. Harleston and Brandy L. Harleston. (CWH)

Eva Claire Borders, born October 21, 1907; died August 1974, Cleveland, Ohio; daughter of Lillie Bell Imes (b. 1884); granddaughter of Esau H. Imes (b. 1846); married William Francis Good, born January 16, 1908. Their daughter Natacha Jeanne Good, born May 2, 1930, married first, April 5, 1949, to Raymond Franklin Hansbary; married second, to John Chauncey Branham; they had four children:

1. Francine Benita Hansbary, b. February 1, 1950, Cleveland, Ohio; m. David Forrest Slaughter; their 2 children were:
    a. Dawn Marie Slaughter
    b. David Forest Slaughter
2. Natacha Jeanne Hansbary, b. July 23, 1952
3. Cynthia Ranee Hansbary, b. February 7, 1951
4. John Chauncey Branham, b. August 15, 1947; m. Thelma; their 4 children were:
    a. Michelle Branham
    b. Crystal Branham
    c. Brandy Branham
    d. Johnnie Branham

Richard Benjamin Braxton, born January 25, 1918, Harrisburg, Pennsylvania; son of James E. Braxton (b. 1918) and Eva Allison Matthews (b. 1898); grandson of Amy Allison Imes (b. 1877) and Evans Theodore Matthews; great-grandson of George Hazekiah Imes (b. 1844); married October 10, 1938, to Inza Margaret Taylor, born August 19, 1920, Steelton, Pennsylvania; their four children were:

1. Joyce Eileen Braxton, b. April 25, 1939; m. William Forrest Coley; their 3 children were:
    a. William Forrest Coley II, b. July 17, 1963
    b. David Melvin Coley, b. July 2, 1964
    c. Neal Warren Coley, b. February 18, 1966
2. Richard Benjamin Braxton, b. November 23, 1941; m. Joan Ruth Smith, b. December 18, 1941; their 2 children were:
    a. Brian Eric Braxton, b. October 18, 1965
    b. Jeffrey Broderick Braxton, b. September 24, 1970
3. Barraud Imes Braxton, b. June 29, 1944; m. Cheryl Evans; they had 2 children:
    a. Kendea Michelle Braxton, b. September 13, 1972
    b. Dawn Renee Braxton, b. January 19, 1977
4. Juanona Inza Braxton, b. October 20, 1946

William Iiams, Jr., (b. 1670), married August 27, 1696, to Elizabeth Plummer, and they had nine children. The sixth child, John Iiams, married Rebecca Jones and they had eight children: Elizabeth Iiams, Anne Iiams, Mary Iiams, William Iiams, Isaac Iiams, Thomas Iiams, John Iiams (b. ___), and Rebecca Iiams.

This son, **John Iiams** (b.___), fathered a child by a slave woman owned by Joseph Howard of Anne Arundel County, Maryland (CWH), and this son was called John "Jack" Imes (b. January 1, 1775). When the plantation owner, Joseph Howard, died, he gave several of the Howard family slaves, including Jack Imes, to his daughter, Elizabeth Howard.

Elizabeth Howard married William Iiams, the biological uncle of the slave "Jack" Imes (b. 1775). In about 1787, William Iiams and his wife Elizabeth Howard Imes, moved to Washington County, Maryland, and took some of their slaves, including Jack Imes, with them.

In 1782 when Jack Imes was seventeen years old, William Iiams and Elizabeth Howard Iiams decided to move from Washington County, Maryland, so they sold their land and their possessions. Instead of being sold with the other slaves, Jack Imes was given his chance for freedom to choose a new master. This act of freedom is well documented in the Maryland court proceedings of the time.

Jack Imes lived with Andrew Kline for seven years, during which time he married and had three children. According to one version, Jack Imes was sold to Jacob Seibert where he remained for eighteen years. During that time he had ten more children, most of whom were "sold south," and their whereabouts are unknown. Jack Imes' wife died and he then married Susan Pindle, a young slave girl who was also born of a slave mother and a white father.

At that time Maryland law stated that children born of racially mixed parents were to be given freedom at age twenty-one. However, by this time Susan Pendle Imes had given birth to two children destined to remain slaves forever. Jack Imes reasoned with his master and was able to obtain freedom for the entire family eight years later, and they moved from Maryland to Franklin County, Pennsylvania. The family worked on the Christian Negley farm for about five years and then on the Jacob Meyers farm for eleven years. While Jack Imes and Susan Pendle Imes may have had as many as thirteen children, six of the children are known: William Imes, John Imes, Jr., Samuel Imes, David Imes, Henry Imes, and Eliza Imes.

The oldest son of Jack and Susan Pindle Imes, **William Imes**, was born ca1815 in Washington County, Maryland. He married a woman named Fannie (b. 1817 in Virginia), and they appeared in the 1850 and 1860 Census of Montgomery Township, Franklin County, Pennsylvania, with children Charles Imes (b. 1840), Mary E. Imes (b. 1848), William Imes, Jr. (b. 1850), and Margaret Imes (b. 1855). The Dietrich Funeral Home, Greencastle, Franklin County, Pennsylvania, lists a child of William Imes died in August 1854, and that wife Fannie Imes died October 13, 1862. No other information on William Imes and his family has been found.

The second son of Jack and Susan Pindle Imes, **John Imes, Jr.**, born 1816; died June 17, 1854, Franklin County, Pennsylvania, married Elizabeth, born 1816 in Virginia, had six children:
1. David Imes, b. 1840, Franklin County, Pennsylvania
2. Mary B. Imes, b. 1842, Franklin County, Pennsylvania
3. James Imes, b. 1842; d. April 5, 1859; buried Colored Cem., Carlisle, Pennsylvania; m. Jane Strange
4. Esau H. Imes, b. 1848; d. November 8, 1905, in Byhalia, Mississippi; m. June 17, 1883, to Catherine Ingram, b. 1864 in Watson, Mississippi; d. July 14, 1934, in Memphis, Tennessee. They had 5 children, listed below.
5. Caroline Imes, b. 1847; m. Peter Johnson
6. John Imes III, b. 1849

Esau H. Imes (b. 1848) had 5 children: a. Carrie Anne Beatrice Imes, b. March 10, 1893; m. Henry Langford; they had 9 children: Henry Langford, Jr., Samuel Ricardo Langford, d. January 27, 1962; m. January 1936 to Alma Linnese Baker, b. July 15, 1917; they had 3 children, listed below; Margaret Langford; Charles Langford; Mildred Langford, m. 1st, Garland Briggs, m. 2nd, William Duhen; George Langford; Hortense Langford, m. Earl Weaver; their son Earl Weaver, Jr., was b. January 26, 1948; Catherine Langford m. James Stone; and Roland Langford.

Samuel Ricardo Langford (d. 1962) and Alma L. Baker had 3 children:
1. Rosina Visconti Langford, b. July 8, 1937; m. Russell T. Jackson; 2 children: Russell Thomas Jackson, Jr., b. July 18, 1963; and Traci Linnese Jackson, b. August 13, 1965

2. Ricardo Samuel Langford, b. December 13, 1938; m. Mary M. Smith; they had 3 children: Tina Marie Langford, b. May 28, 1939; Toni Lynn Langford, b. October 19, 1967; and Ricardo Samuel Langford III, b. December 6, 1968

3. Raphael Ronald Langford, b. March 16, 1939; m. May 18, 1968, to Susan Hood, b. September 22, 1947; 1 daughter: Dawn Elizabeth Langford, b. January 25, 1972

Lillie Bell Imes, b. November 4, 1884; d. June 1974; buried Highland Park Cem., Cleveland, Ohio; m. James C. Borders; they had 2 children: Imes Borders, d. age 4; buried Mt. Zion Cem., Memphis, Tennessee; and Eva Clair Borders, b. October 21, 1907; d. August 1974, buried Cleveland Ohio; m. 1st, William F. Goode; m. 2nd, Lester P. Circles; 1 daughter: Natacha Jeanne Goode, b. May 2, 1930, who m. 1st, Raymond F. Hansbary; m. 2nd, John C. Branham, Sr.; they had 4 children: 1) John C. Branham, Jr., b. August 15, 1947; m. Thelma, and they had 4 children: Michelle Branham, Crystal Branham, Brandy Branham, and John Branham; 2) Francine Benita Branham, b. February 1, 1950; m. David F. Slaughter, and had 2 children: Dawn Marie Slaughter, and David Forrestt Slaughter; 3) Natacha Jeanne Hansburg, b. July 23, 1952; and Cynthia Raneé Hansburg, b. February 7, 1957.

John Imes, Jr., (b. 1816) also appears in the 1850 Federal Census of Franklin County, Pennsylvania, with wife Elizabeth and six children: David Imes, Mary Imes, James Imes, Esau Imes, Caroline Imes, and John Imes III. By that time, John Imes, Jr. (b. 1816) owned his own farm which he purchased in April 1838 from John McDowell. In April 1844 he also purchased a home on a one-acre lot from Samuel, Thomas, and William Buck and he deeded this property to his parents, Jack and Susan Pindle Imes, on August 27, 1846.

James Imes (b. 1842) served with Company E, 8th Battalion, Pennsylvania Colored Infantry, during the Civil War and was discharged December 20, 1865. He served again in Company K, 9th Infantry, from October 1869 to October 1874. Both Esau Imes (b. 1848) and Caroline Imes (b. 1847) attended Oberlin College in Oberlin, Ohio.

Caroline Imes (b. 1847) married Reverend Peter Johnson and they lived near Topeka, Kansas. Esau Imes (b. 1848) served in the Civil War from August 18, 1864, to September 20, 1865, and later settled in Byhalia, Marshall County, Mississippi.

Edward Houston Imes, born November 24, 1895; died November 27, 1976, lived in Chicago, buried in Lincoln Cemetery, Worth, Illinois, was the fifth child of Esau H. Imes (b. 1848) and Catherine Ingram. He worked as a dining car waiter on the Super Chief, and died in Chicago. Boyd Beverly Imes, born December 29, 1886; died August 24, 1961; buried in Harmony Cemetery, Landover, Maryland. He married several times but had no children; he was the fourth child of Esau Imes (b. 1848). Bernie Lloyd Imes was born July 27, 1889; he was single and lived in Memphis Tennessee.

Henry Imes, born 1825, Franklin County, Pennsylvania; died August 17, 1864; was killed at Dutch Gap during the Civil War. A son of Jack and Susan Pindle Imes, he married January 1855, Franklin County, Pennsylvania, to Elizabeth Cuff.

Eliza Imes, born 1835, Franklin County, Pennsylvania, daughter of Jack and Susan Pindle Imes, was listed in the 1850 census, but her whereabouts are unknown.

Samuel Imes, born January 13, 1818; died February 3, 1893; buried in Lost Creek Cemetery, McAlisterville, Juniata County, Pennsylvania; son of Jack Imes (b. 1775) and Susan Pindle; married February 22, 1842, to Sarah Moore, born July 31, 1820, Franklin County, Pennsylvania; died January 1, 1894; buried in Lost Creek Cemetery, McAlisterville, Pennsylvania. They had eleven children:

1. Mary Amanda Imes, b. February 9, 1842, Franklin County, Pennsylvania

2. George Hezekiah Imes, b. October 8, 1844, Franklin County, Pennsylvania
3. Elizabeth Eveline Imes, b. January 23, 1846, Franklin County, Pennsylvania
4. Benjamin Albert Imes, b. January 28, 1848, Franklin County, Pennsylvania
5. Martin Henry Imes, b. May 4, 1850, Juniata County, Pennsylvania
6. Thomas Creigh Imes, b. March 24, 1852, Juniata County, Pennsylvania
7. Sarah Ann Imes, b. January 21, 1854, Juniata County, Pennsylvania
8. William Warfield Imes, b. October 14/15, 1858, Juniata County, Pennsylvania
9. John Imes, b. December 16, 1857, Juniata County, Pennsylvania; d. March 16, 1859, Juniata County, Pennsylvania; buried Lost Creek Cem., McAlisterville, Juniata County, Pennsylvania
10. Margaret Jane Imes, b. January 24, 1860, Juniata County, Pennsylvania; d. February 24, 1879; buried Lost Creek Cem., McAlisterville, Pennsylvania
11. David Hunter Imes, b. December 27, 1862; m. Elizabeth _____

Details of the families of these children of Samuel Imes (b. 1818) and Sarah Moore follow the short history of Samuel Imes (b. 1818).

Samuel Imes (b. 1818), son of Jack and Susan Pindle Imes, was a farmer and a member of the Presbyterian Church, both in the Mercersburg, Franklin County, Pennsylvania, area and later at the Lost Creek Presbyterian Church, McAlisterville, Juniata County, Pennsylvania, when he became foreman on the Robert McAlister farm, Juniata County, Pennsylvania, in 1848. In 1863 Samuel Imes purchased a large farm in Walker Township, Juniata County, Pennsylvania. The farm remained in the family until 1916, when his son William Imes moved to Detroit, Michigan.

Samuel Imes (b. 1818) had eleven children (see above). Some of these children:
•1. Mary Amanda Imes, b. December 9, 1842, Franklin County, Pennsylvania; d. April 12, 1859; buried Lost Creek Cem., McAlisterville, Pennsylvania
•2. George Hezekiah Imes [b. October 8, 1844, Franklin County, Pennsylvania; d. August 24, 1892; buried Lost Creek Cem., McAlisterville, Pennsylvania; m. August 4, 1870, to Lucinda A. Clark Armstrong, b. Jan. 5, 1843; they had 5 children: a) Otho Samuel Imes, b. ca1875; b) Aura Channing Imes, b. ca1873, Franklin County, Pennsylvania; and c) Amy Allison Imes, b. September 21, 1877; d. June 9, 1940; m. 1st, January 14, 1896, Evans Theodore Matthews, b. 1875; d. July 15, 1903; m. 2nd, February 26, 1913, to Rasheen Robinson, b. 1887; they had 3 children: Stanley Matthews (b. July 1896; d. May 27, 1899); Ivy Merkle Matthews (b. February 16, 1899; d. 1968; m. Virgil Andrew Stern, b. January 12, 1891, and they had 5 children: Mary Muriel Stern, b. March 2, 1921; d. 1931; Amy Anderson Stern, m. 1st, Vernon Smith; m. 2nd, LeRoy Smith, and had 1 daughter, Jane B. Stern. Stanley Virgil Stern, b. 1926; d. 1926; Eleanor Byrd Stern, b. July 15, 1927; m. 1st, July 1944, Charles Forrest; m. 2nd, October 13, 1971, Charles A. Ashley, b. November 22, 1928; she had seven children: Stephanie Forrest, b. May 26, 1947; m. 1st, William Kittrell; m. 2nd, Edward Tucker, and had 2 children: Stacey Kittrell, b. October 9, 1964, and Aaron Kittrell, b. October 11, 1966; Harry Virgil Forrest, b. June 2, 1949; Patrick Arnold Ashley, b. March 17, 1959; m. Rose Tammy Jackson, b. June 18, 1958, and had 1 child: Parrish Aria Ashley, b. April 14, 1982; Frank Leo Ashley, b. April 21, 1960; Cheryl Denise Ashley, b. September 13, 1961, and had a son Damion Anton Ashley; Irving LeRoy Ashley, b. October 13, 1967; Charles Stanley Forrest, b. December 31, 1945; m. Linda Ray; Virginia

Lee Stern, b. September 8, 1929; m. 1st, Stapleton Walker; m. 2nd, George Bains, and had 1 daughter, Villerie Walker, who m. William Matthews); and Eva Allison Matthews (b. February 4, 1898; d. 1958, m. James E. Braxton, b. July 12, 1896, and they had 8 children: Richard Benjamin Braxton, Sr., b. January 25, 1918; m. October 10, 1936, to Inza Taylor, b. August 19, 1920, and they had 4 children: Joyce, who had sons William F. Coley, Jr.; David M. Coley, and Neal Warren Coley. Richard B. Braxton, Jr., b. November 13, 1941; m. Joan Ruth Smith, and they had 2 children: Brian Eric Braxton, b. October 18, 1965; and Jeffrey Roderick Braxton, b. September 24, 1970. Barraud Braxton, b. 1944; m. Cheryl Evans and they had 2 children: Kendra Michelle Braxton, b. September 13, 1972; and Daron Renee Braxton, b. January 19, 1977; and Juanona Braxton. James Edward Braxton, b. March 6, 1922; m. Constance Moon and they had 4 children: 1) Floyd Montgomery Braxton, b. April 16, 1978; d. March 4, 1973; m. Dollie Marie Jefferson and they had 3 children: Cynthia Theresa Braxton, Floyd Matthew Braxton, and Deborah King. 2) George Lake Braxton, b. August 4, 1934, in Harrisburg, Pennsylvania; d. April 30, 1966, Philadelphia, Pennsylvania; m. Alice Scott, b. April 10, 1928, Franklin, Virginia, and they had a child, Alison Lynette Braxton, b. April 9, 1960; Joyce Eileen Braxton, b. April 25, 1939; m. William Forrest Coley, and they had 3 children: William Forrest Coley, Jr., b. July 17, 1963; David Melvin Coley, b. July 2, 1964; and Neal Warren Coley, b. February 18, 1966. Richard Benjamin Braxton, b. January 25, 1918, Harrisburg, Pennsylvania; m. October 10, 1938, to Inza Margaret Taylor, b. August 19, 1920, Steelton, Pennsylvania, and they had four (sic) children: Joyce Eileen Braxton, b. April 25, 1939; m. William F. Coley; Richard Benjamin Braxton, b. November 13, 1941; m. Joan Ruth Smith; Barraud Imes Braxton, b. June 29, 1944; m. Cheryl Evans; and Juannona Inza Braxton, b. October 20, 1946; m. 1976 to Kenneth Montgomery. Harriet Evernia Braxton, b. October 16, 1923; m. April 1952, to Raymond N. Logan; Ann Elizabeth Braxton, b. January 4, 1926; and Floyd Montgomery Braxton, b. April 16, 1928; d. March 4, 1973; m. Dollie Marie Jefferson and had 4 children; Cynthia T. Braxton, who had 2 children: Patrice Miller and Travis Miller; Whitney I. Braxton; Floyd M. Braxton; and Deborah King; Mary Moore Braxton, b. October 30, 1930; George Lake Braxton, b. August 9, 1934; m. April 30, 1966, to Alice ____, b. April 10, 1928, and they had a child, Allison L. Braxton; Stanley Gene Braxton, b. September 20, 1935, Harrisburg, Pennsylvania; m. November 24, 1963, Philadelphia, Pennsylvania, to Virginia Atwell, b. August 1, 1941, Philadelphia, Pennsylvania, and they had 3 children: Elyse Marie Braxton, b. January 14, 1966; Stanley Hughes Braxton, b. June 7, 1967; and Evan Christopher Braxton, b. August 1, 1971). d) Jessie Garfield Imes, b. September 26, 1879; m. Silas Cannon; e) George Lake Imes, b. October 12, 1883; d. 1957; buried Tuskogee Institute, Alabama; m. 1st, Queen Patti Meredith; m. 2nd, January 1, 1940, to Grace McCord, b. December 12, 1876; d. 1956].
•3. Elizabeth Eveline Imes, b. January 23, 1856, Franklin County, Pennsylvania; d. February 6, 1859
•4. Benjamin Albert Imes, b. January 28, 1848, Franklin County, Pennsylvania, lived in Oberlin, Ohio; d. August 7, 1908, Prairie Institute,

67

Alabama; m. 1880 to Elizabeth Wallace, b. 1852; d. 1944, and had 3 children: a) Elmer Samuel Imes, b. 1888; d. 1941; m. Nella Larson; b) Albert Lovejoy Imes, b. March 1, 1885, Memphis, Tennessee; d. January 31, 1976, buried Grove Cem., Cincinnati, Ohio, son of Benjamin A. Imes (b. 1848); m. September 1, 1913, Cincinnati, Ohio; to Amy Marian Field, b. May 3, 1889, Philadelphia, Pennsylvania; d. February 27, 1951; buried Spring Grove Cem., Cincinnati, Ohio, and they had 2 children: [1] Paul Lovejoy Imes, b. January 18, 1918, Cincinnati, Ohio; m. March 10, 1938, Middleboro, Kentucky, to Althea Marie Mills, b. November 4, 1919, Knoxville, Tennessee, and they had 3 children: a[1]) Daniel Mills Imes, b. April 30, 1939; m. April 16, 1966, to Diane Lynn Burbank, b. August 13, 1942, and they had 3 children: Tammy Louise Imes, b. May 30, 1969; Daniel Mills Imes, b. November 10, 1972; and Mimi Nicole Imes, b. September 23, 1975; b[1]) Edith Marian Imes, b. April 23, 1940, Knoxville, Tennessee, m. June 10, 1967, Newport, Kentucky, to Roderick Andrew Bennett, b. October 26, 1948, and they had 2 children: Roderick Lovejoy Bennett, b. December 10, 1968, Petersburg, Virginia; and Nicole Jule Bennett, b. September 7, 1971, Petersburg, Virginia. Sylvia Marie Imes, b. December 27, 1911; m. June 28, 1967, to Harold O'Bannon, b. September 19, 1929; 2) Marjorie Jean Imes, b. October 22, 1928, Cincinnati, Ohio, daughter of Albert Lovejoy Imes (b. 1885); m. June 28, 1952, to Harland Philip Alexander, b. May 9, 1921, and their child, David Imes Alexander, b. July 11, 1954, m. December 18, 1981, Cincinnati, Ohio, to Carol Manuel, b. November 17, 1958]. c)William Lloyd Imes, b. December 29, 1889; d. 1986, Dundee, New York, son of Benjamin A. Imes (b. 1848); m. Grace Virginia Frank, b. December 1, 1889; d. October 16, 1972, Dundee, New York, and they had 3 children: 1) Wendell Phillips Imes, b. June 8, 1916; d. December 4, 1944; buried American Cem., Florence, Italy; m. August 26, 1944, to Anita Lloyd Rogers; 2) Hope Mathilda Imes, b. August 24, 1921; m. January 17, 1945, to George Johnson Haley, b. June 7, 1920, and they had 2 children: Diane Grace Haley, b. December 9, 1954, and James Douglas Haley, b. September 28, 1955; 3) Jane Elizabeth Imes, b. July 19, 1924; d. February 6, 1931; buried Hillside Cem., Dundee, New York.
•5. Martin Henry Imes (b. May 4, 1850, Juniata County, Pennsylvania; m. Mabel R. Lewis)
•6. Thomas Creigh Imes (b. March 24, 1852, Juniata County, Pennsylvania; m. Roxanna Morgan)
•7. Sarah Ann Imes (b. January 21, 1854; d. May 24, 1902; buried Lost Creek Cem., McAlisterville, Pennsylvania)
•8. William Warfield Imes (b. October 14/15, 1855; d. March 8, 1825, in Detroit, Michigan; buried Roselawn Cem., Berkeley, Michigan; m. 1896 to Mildred Thomas, b. June 1862; d. November 1925; buried Roselawn Cem., Berkeley, Michigan; they had 2 children: a) Sarah Mildred Imes, b. May 9, 1897, Juniata County, Pennsylvania; d. January 1972; buried Memorial Cem., Detroit, Michigan; m. 1st, James Irving White, b. July 21, 1886; m. 2nd, William Vaughn; their child was: LeRoy Glenn White, b. December 12, 1917; m. Hazel Lee Miller, b. January 24, 1917; he had 2 children: a 1) LeRoy Glenn White, Jr.-Wright, b. December 1941, Detroit, Michigan; m. December 7, 1979, Syracuse, New York, Betty Jean Gilliam, b. August 9, 1943; their son was Clarence Elliot Wright,

b. January 27, 1980, Syracuse, New York; 2) Carmen Henrietta Cecile White Wright (author and family historian for Jack and Susan Pindle Imes family line), b. May 20, 1943, Detroit, Michigan; m. James Burroughs Harleston, m. April 22, 1972, Washington, D.C.; b. October 28, 1940, Charleston, South Carolina; they had 2 children: Jason Bryon Harleston, b. September 2, 1973, Washington, D.C.; and Brandy Laureen Harleston, b. March 7, 1976, Washington, D.C. Thomas Morgan Imes, b. September 24, 1899; d. April 14, 1974; m. November 27, 1918, Detroit, Michigan, to Lillie Woods, b. October 14, 1902, Alderson, West Virginia; they had 3 children: 1) Helen Mildred Imes, b. February 16, 1925, Detroit, Michigan; m. April 27, 1940, to William Myron Ellington, b. October 7, 1917, Bessmer, Alabama; their 2 children were: a) Helen Elizabeth Ellington, b. July 13, 1943, Detroit, Michigan; who m. September 12, 1965, to Hubert Nelson Flowers, b. October 20, 1942, New Orleans, Louisiana; their 2 children were: Tyrone Nelson Flowers, b. March 15, 1966, Detroit, Michigan, and Michelle Elaine Flowers, b. April 22, 1970, Detroit, Michigan; b) William Imes Ellington, b. November 8, 1940, m. Veda ____ and their children included Cora Ellington, b. September 30, 1970, Grand Bahamas Islands. Barbara June Imes, b. June 15, 1922, Detroit, Michigan; m. George H. Watson; they had 2 children: Harold Watson, whose 2 children were: Karen Imes Watson and Amber Zaire Watson; and Lloyd Watson, whose 3 children were: Steven Watson, Summer Watson, and Winter Watson. Margaret Ann Imes, b. December 12, 1929; m. Russell Livingston; their 5 children were: Arvil Livingston; Shirley Livingston, m. Damon Lowery; Barbara Livingston; Nancy Livingston; and Joel Livingston.
•9. John Imes (b. December 16, 1857; d. March 16, 1859; buried Lost Creek Cem., McAlisterville, Juniata County, Pennsylvania)
•10. Margaret Jane Imes (b. January 24, 1860; d. February 24, 1879; buried Lost Creek Cem., McAlisterville, Pennsylvania)
•11. David Hunter Imes (b. December 27, 1862; m. Elizabeth ____)

David Imes, born February 6, 1821, Washington County, Maryland; died December 17, 1894; buried Ebenezer Cemetery, Juniata County, Pennsylvania; m. 1st, 1840, to Adaline Braan, b. 1819; d. April 15, 1850; buried on the family farm, Juniata County, Pennsylvania; he m. 2nd, December 25, 1854, to Sarah Ann Wilson, b. 1831; d. 1914; buried Ebenezer Cemetery, Juniata County, Pennsylvania.

David Imes (b. 1821) was a highly successful farmer and land owner in Juniata County, Pennsylvania. While married to Adaline Braan with whom he had five children, he purchased a fifty-three-acre farm. After the death of Adaline, he sold the farm (1854) and moved to Juniata County, Pennsylvania, with his five children, his housekeeper, and his elderly father Jack Imes, and bought a new farm.

David Imes (b. 1821) and Sarah Ann Wilson were married in 1854 and had nine additional children. Father Jack Imes (b. 1775) died July 2, 1871, at age ninety-six and is buried in Ebenezer Methodist Church Cemetery near Port Royal, Juniata County, Pennsylvania, also the subsequent burial place of David Imes (b. 1821; d. December 17, 1894).

David Imes was born in Washington County, Maryland, on February 6, 1821, and married twice. His first marriage in 1840 was to Adaline Broun/Braan, born 1819, Richmond, Virginia; died April 15, 1850; buried on the family farm in Juniata County, Pennsylvania. The second marriage, on December 25, 1854, was to Sarah Ann Wilson, born 1831; died 1914, Ebenezer Cemetery, Juniata County, Pennsylvania. David Imes (b. 1821) had at least fourteen children:

1. Oliver Imes, b. December 31, 1841, Franklin County, Pennsylvania; d. November 27, 1914, in Carlisle, Pennsylvania; buried Ebenezer Cem.
2. Sarah Bell Imes, b. November 15, 1843, Franklin County, Pennsylvania; d. February 6, 1914; buried Ebenezer Cem.; m. Benjamin F. Moore, b. October 25, 1833; d. August 16, 1896; their son Benjamin F. Moore, Jr., was b. January 1886 and d. January 1909; buried Ebenezer Cem.
3. John C. Imes, b. December 14, 1845, Franklin County, Pennsylvania; d. January 5, 1918; buried Ebenezer Cem.; m. December 7, 1886, to Caroline Stewart, b. February 12, 1856; d. April 20, 1935; buried Ebenezer Cem.; they had 5 children:
   a. Elmer E. Imes, b. July 1887
   b. Benjamin R. Imes, b. February 1889
   c. Mary Ellen Imes, b. November 1892
   d. Mary E. "Lillian" Imes, b. August 1893
   e. Anna J. Imes, b. March 1900
4. Ann Mariah Imes, b. January 4, 1848, Franklin County, Pennsylvania; m. February 8, 1870, to Peter Keith, b. 1842; they had 7 children:
   a. Anna Keith, b. 1872
   b. David Keith, b. February 1873
   c. Sidney Keith, b. 1875
   d. Howard Keith, b. 1878
   e. Jessie Keith, b. October 1882
   f. Charles Keith, b. October 1886
   g. Charlotte Keith, b. June 1889
5. Joseph Imes, b. April 8, 1850, Franklin County, Pennsylvania
6. Mary J. Imes, b. March 1856, Juniata County, Pennsylvania; d. 1905; buried Ebenezer Cem.; m. Joseph W. Replogle, b. January 1860; they had 4 children:
   a. Samuel Mark Replogle, b. March 1888; m. Lillian Burrows
   b. Eva L. Replogle, b. November 1889
   c. Nellie G. Replogle, b. February 1891
   d. Mary Ethel Replogle, b. August 1894
7. Wilson David Imes, b. January 1858, Juniata County, Pennsylvania; buried Ebenezer Cem.; m. Martha A. Stong, b. October 1860; d. October 1924; they had 9 children:
   a. Jesse Imes, b. September 1887; d. November 1971; m. Florence Rhodes, b. November 1, 1891 (their 5 children described below)
   b. David Imes, b. November 1883
   c. Mary J. "Jenny" Imes, b. July 1884
   d. Joseph Imes, b. May 1886
   e. Sarah Bertha Imes, b. December 1889; m. August Huber
   f. Walter Imes, b. August 1892; d. 1979
   g. Florence Imes, b. July 1894
   h. Warren Imes, b. May 1898; m. Louise J. Metz (their child, Warren Paul Imes is described below)
8. Olin Paul Imes, b. November 12, 1861, Juniata County, Pennsylvania; d. 1937; m. March 12, 1885, to Margaret V. Bollenger, b. May 25, 1852; d. 1928; buried Montgomery Cem., Norristown, Pennsylvania; they had 4 children:
   a. Carrie Ardella Imes, b. June 24, 1886; d. 1945; buried Norristown, Pennsylvania; m. Loon DeHart

70

b. Alda Mae Imes, b. May 13, 1888; d. 1937 in Chicago; m. John Hubert

c. Emmert Glasgow Imes, b. December 12, 1889; d. December 13, 1972; m. 1st, Pearl L. Roland, June 1914; m. 2nd, Ida R. Sagen, (their 4 children are described below)

d. Edgar Reid Imes, b. May 6, 1892; m. April 20, 1920, to Mary Stierly (their 2 children are described below)

9. Howard C. Imes, b. December 1859; m. Nettie Dolby, b. April 1873; they had 16 children:

a. Sherman David Imes, b. July 1890

b. Herman L. Imes, b. July 1890

c. Alvin W. Imes, b. September 1892

d. Nevin C. Imes, b. December 1893

e. Rhoda M. Imes, b. December 1895; m. Edward Wilson

f. Herbert Imes, b. June 1897

g. William Roy Imes, b. February 1899

h. Alice Imes

i. George William Imes, b. August 4, 1903; m. Catherina H. Swicki

j. Bruce Imes

k. Benjamin Imes

l. Augustus Imes

m. Agnes Imes

n. Robert Lafayfette Imes, b. September 26, 1911; m. April 7, 1945, to Edna Foreman; they had a son and a daughter, Sharon Foreman Imes, b. February 16, 1949

o. Chester Imes

p. Virginia Imes

10. Samuel Imes, b. December 1863, Juniata County, Pennsylvania; d. May 4, 1946; m. 1st, Anna Stong, b. August 16, 1868; d. August 9, 1904; m. 2nd, December 1909, to Malinda Fultz; he had 7 children:

a. David Luther Imes, described below

b. Jeremiah Neimond Imes, b. February 12, 1901, described below

c. Mary Belle Imes, b. August 1892, described below

d. Sarah Jane Imes, b. June 26, 1891, described below

e. William Lloyd Imes, b. April 1895, described below

f. Lucian Wilson Imes, b. May 1897; d. November 8, 1919

g. Lincoln Foster Imes, b. November 12, 1899; d. July 17, 1973; m. October 11, 1926, to Lena Snook, b. June 30, 1906

11. Emory Imes, b. December 25, 1865; d. February 16, 1926; buried Ebenezer Cem.; m. November 24, 1897, to Margaret Tressa Hockenberry, b. October 22, 1881; d. May 8, 1938; they had 7 children:

a. James Irvin Imes, b. April 24, 1899; d. February 18, 1967

b. Ruth Viola Imes, b. December 17, 1900; d. March 1976; m.1st, Mark Carnathan; m. 2nd, John Livingston

c. Thomas Scott Imes, b. October 7, 1903

d. Miles Henry Imes, b. October 30, 1905; m. July 22, 1927, to Claire W. Benner, b. August 15, 1907; their 2 children, Faye Elizabeth Imes and Merle Cunningham Imes are described below

e. Elsie Irene Imes, b. June 16, 1908; m. Russell Bufflap

f. Edith Mary Imes, b. February 27, 1910; m. Luther Ritz

g. Margaret Tressa Imes, b. June 24, 1914; d. July 9, 1914

12. Ellen Imes, b. 1869, Juniata County, Pennsylvania; m. February 1, 1892, to Ira B. Shaffer; their children were: Mary Shaffer, Era Shaffer, Homer Shaffer, Florence Shaffer, Jenny Shaffer, Lula Shaffer, and Beulah Shaffer

13. Ross Imes, b. 1871; d. 1873

14. Alice Carey Imes, b. August 1873, Juniata County, Pennsylvania; m. George F. Scholl; their 2 children were Ward Scholl and Penrose Scholl.

The descriptions of the family tree of David Imes (b. 1818) begins from this point to expand the lineage described above, and begins with the offspring of Wilson David Imes (b. 1858), the seventh child of David Imes (b. 1818).

The first son of Wilson David Imes (b. 1858) was Jesse Imes (b. September 1887; d. November 1971; m. Florence Rhodes, b. November 1, 1891; and they had five children: 1) Chester Wilson Imes, b. February 3, 1915; who m. October 1948 to Maud Beck, b. September 11, 1908; 2) Norman Rhodes Imes, b. September 16, 19__; m. Martha Overdorf; 3) Jesse Harold Imes, who m. Louis Schrock; 4) Barbara Louise Imes, b. August 26, 19__; m. Bruce Sheats; and 5) Gerald Imes, b. November 21, 19__, and m. Edith Fye. The eighth child of Wilson David Imes (b. 1858) was Warren Imes (b. May 1898), who m. Louise J. Metz; and whose son was Warren Paul Imes (b. September 23, 1925), who m. Betty Hampton, and who had six children: 1) Warren Michael Imes; 2) Patrick Imes, who m. Karen Jones; 3) Deline Imes, who m. Jonathan Ketcham; 4) Sue Ellen Imes, who m. Joseph Carl; 5) Stephen Imes; and 6) Joseph Imes.

Emmert Glasgow Imes (b. December 13, 1889); d. in Altoona, Pennsylvania, December 13, 1978), the son of Olen Imes (b. 1861) and Margaret V. Bollenger (b. 1852), m. 1st, Paul Larue Roland (b. June 2, 1897; d. February 3, 1973); and m. 2nd, to Ida Rebecca Sagen; had four children by his first wife: 1) Ann Margaret Imes [(b. November 14, 1914), m. May 10, 1945, in Cumberland, Maryland, to Warren Benjamin Worley (b. April 15, 1905; d. January 30, 1982), and had two children: a) Linda Larue Worley (b. September 16, 1948, Altoona, Pennsylvania; m. Wayne Yohn, and their two children were: Jennifer Yohn (b. February 9, 1972), and Valerie Yohn (b. April 16, 1974; and b) Robert Warren Worley (b. June 28, 1951, Altoona, Pennsylvania), m. Bonnie Psahler, and their two children were: Stephanie Worley (b. June 19, 1974) and Amanda Worley (b. October 14, 1977)]. 2) Lucille Georgia Imes (b. December 31, 1915; d. 1921; 3) Robert Faye Imes (b. October 12, 1917) m. December 16, 1942, to Grace Bookhamer (b. June 30, 1920); and 4) George Roland Imes (d. age 14).

Edgar Reid Imes (b. May 6, 1892; m. April 20, 1920, to Mary Stierly, b. June 5, 1892; d. November 23, 1950; buried Augusta Lutheran Cemetery in Trappe, Pennsylvania), also the son of Olen Imes (b. 1861) and Margaret V. Bollenger (b. 1852), had two children: Edgar Robert Imes [(b. November 8, 1922), m. May 3, 1947, to Elizabeth Cressman (b. September 5, 1920), and they had two children: Robert Lee Imes (b. October 3, 1951, who m. September 29, 1979, to Cheryl Beck), and Kenneth Alan Imes (b. November 15, 1955; m. February 10, 1979, to Mary Ann Baker, and their son, Kenneth Allen Imes, Jr., was b. May 28, 1979]; and 2) Margaret Elizabeth Imes [(b. February 16, 1925), m. June 23, 1947, to William J. Love (b. September 7, 1913; d. January 30, 1982); and their daughter Mary Linda Love (b. February 18, 1949), m. December 7, 1968, to Roger L. Schlichter, Jr., had two children: Megan L. Schlichter (b. October 1, 1969) and Roger L. Schlichter III (b. September 7, 1973)].

David Luther Imes (b. February 23, 1894; d. December 12, 1972; buried St. Pauls Cemetery, Nook, Pennsylvania; m. Janetta Mae Swartswood, b. September 6,

1905; d. June 11, 1980; buried at St. Paul's Cemetery); the son of Samuel Imes (b. 1863) had twelve children:

1) Betty Imes (d. infancy);
2) Charles "Samuel" Imes [(b. January 7, 1927), m. July 23, 1953, to Janet Yvonne Hurrell (b. July 23, 1936), and they had four children: a) Treva Diane Imes (b. January 24, 1954); m. June 28, 1975, to Steven Steinberger (b. November 11, 1953); b) Barry Charles Imes (b. June 4, 1956); m. October 23, 1976, to Bonnie Jean Hack, and they had three children: Shelley Reneé Imes, b. February 28, 1977; Charles Matthew Imes, b. December 14, 1978; and Justin Earl Imes, b. August 22, 1980; c) Marlin Imes (b. July 24, 1958; and d) Kimberly Sue Imes (b. March 7, 1960)].
3) Blair Wilson Imes [(b. March 26, 1931, Juniata County, Pennsylvania), m. December 13, 1957, to Laura Susan Hoffman (b. July 2, 1939, Perry County, Pennsylvania) and they had five children: a) Ginger Faith Imes (b. July 17, 1959; m. October 18, 1980, to Abram Herman Stroup, b. February 24, 1956); b) Judy Joann Imes (b. August 6, 1960; m. May 17, 1981, to Donald Edgar Troup); c) Blairene Chris Imes (b. Lewistown, Pennsylvania, April 11, 1962; m. March 12, 1982, to Bradley Arthur Shaeffer, b. November 17, 1959, in Lewisburg, Pennsylvania); d) Angela Marie Imes (b. December 31, 1966); and e) Tracey Beth Imes (b. January 5, 1969)].
4) Melvin Luther Imes [(b. August 14, 1928), m. November 6, 1948, at Hagerstown, Maryland, to Helen H. Burrell (b. May 22, 1932), and they had six children: a) Donald Glen Imes (b. June 19, 1951); m. 1st, Candice Hart; m. 2nd, Barbara Spade, and had son Jason Glen Imes (b. November 15, 1974); b) Barbara Faye Imes (b. July 1, 1957), m. Dean Dressler, and their two children were: Jennifer Sue Dressler (b. January 24, 1976), and John Matthew Dressler (b. October 22, 1981); c) Beverly Rae Imes (b. December 1, 1953), m. Henry Swartz, Jr., and their four children were: Steven Ray Swartz (b. February 16, 1972), Michael Lynn Swartz (b. February 14, 1975), Susan Rae Swartz (b. February 2, 1977), and Matthew Joseph Swartz (b. February 2, 1977); d) Brenda Kay Imes (b. December 20, 1955), m. Lyndon Stimeling, and their daughter Sara Mae Stimeling was b. August 7, 1980; e) Gary Lee Imes (b. May 1, 1950), m. September 13, 1973, to Shirley Beverland, and their child Kelly Lynn Imes was b. October 19, 1980; and f) Melvin Luther Imes, Jr., (b. April 9, 1949), m. April 15, 1968, to Myrna Byner (b. October 12, 1947), and their two children were: Brian Keith Imes (b. October 8, 1968), and Kevin David Imes (b. February 23, 1972)].
5) Stella Mae Imes [(m. Donald R. Brant), and their child Nancy Brant (b. November 25, 19__) m. July 27, 1974, to Marshall Steinberger].
6) Robert Lee Imes [(m. Alice Ammerson) had three children: Deborah Imes, Robert Lee Imes, Jr. (m. Brenda Bryner, and had two children: Timothy Imes and David Lee Imes (b. May 27, 1982), and Stuart David Imes (b. June 20, 1982, and m. Penza Jo Robinson)].
7) David Luther Imes, Jr., [(b. August 27, 1937), m. Judy Meyers, and they had four children: a) Bryan David Imes (b. October 15, 1959; m. Amy Keister); b) Infant son died early; c) Gregory Clark Imes (b. May 10, 1962); d. Sherry Fawn Imes (b. August 29, 1963), and e) Melissa Ann Imes (b. April 30, 1971)].

8) Connie Louise Imes [m. June 20, 1970, to Robert Lester Horst, and their son Robert Lester Horst, Jr., was b. April 4, 197__].
9) Lehman Theron Imes [m. Shirley Noss and they had six children: a) Barry Lee Noss; b) Ricky Lehman Imes (b. July 21, 1959); c) Terry Lynn Imes (b. November 9, 1960); d) Clyde Eugene Imes (b. March 17, 1962); e) Carolyn Kay Imes (b. June 5, 1963); and f) Diane Elaine Imes].
10) Dorothy Lou Imes.
11) Mary Kathryn Imes.
12) Ronald Earl Imes [b. April 22, 1948; d. March 1971; buried at St. Paul's Cemetery, Nook, Pennsylvania].

Jeremiah Neimond Imes (b. February 12, 1901), m. Sylvia Martha Smith (b. September 15, 1900; d. January 5, 1941) was the second son of Samuel Imes (b. 1863) and had six children:1) Charles Foster Imes (b. infant); 2) Vera May Imes (b. December 20, 1926), m. October 27, 1958, to John Guyer; 3) Marian Maxine Imes (b. October 19, 1928), m. Dean Keller; 4) Harold Neimand Imes (b. March17, 1931), m. Frances Ellot; 5) Lena Grace Imes (b. December 7, 1933), m. William Wyrich; and 6) Betty Lou Imes (b. October 28, 1938), m. Robert Glass.

Mary Belle Imes (b. August 1892; d. April 16, 1944) daughter of Samuel Imes (b. 1863) m. 1st, John Samuel Glunt; m. 2nd, Newton Snook; had eight children: 1) John Samuel Glunt, Jr. (b. May 23, 1917; d. 1936); 2) Raymond Luther Glunt [(b. October 25, 1918), m. Pearl Lamey (b. June 5, 1922) and had four children: a) Floyd Allen Glunt (b. September 14, 1940; m. Elizabeth DeArmitt); b) Ruth Mary Glunt (b. April 16, 1942; m. Joseph Casher); c) Howard Raymond Glunt (b. September 8, 1943; m. Brenda Lovine); and d) Paul Richard Glunt (b. September 28, 1944; m. Mary June Parker)]; 3) Kenneth Glunt; 4) Ernest Snook; 5) Lucien Snook; 6) Kathryn Snook; 7) Marlin Snook; and 8) Shelba Snook (m. Mr. Brubaker).

Sara Jane Imes (b. June 26, 1891; d. February 6, 1982; buried McCoysville cemetery), daughter of Samuel Imes (b. 1863); m. January 1915 to Charles Shaffer (b. June 22, 1885; d. June 26, 1965), and they had seven children: 1) Anna Margaret Shaffer; 2) Hilda Mae Shaffer (m. Richie Evitts; had a son Charles Edward Shaffer, b. May 5, 1937); 3) Cloyd Milton Shaffer (b. September 22, 1918); 4) Mary Jane Shaffer [(b. February 21, 1925), m. Harry Burdge, and had five children: a) Rodger Burdge; b) Jane Burdge; c) Linda Burdge; d) Pam Burdge; and e) Wendy Burdge]; 5) Virginia Alice Shaffer (b. November 10, 1927; m. Lewis Clark); 6) Samuel Lewis Shaffer [(b. October 10, 1930), m. Twila Smith, and had three children: a) Cloyd Shaffer; b) Samuel Shaffer; and c) Tina Shaffer]; and 7) Fidellia Grace Shaffer [(b. May 30, 1933), m. Lester Reed, and had two children: a) Patsy Reed, and b) Joyce Reed)].

William Lloyd Imes (b. April 1895; m. Teressa Gay Swartswood), son of Samuel Imes (b. 1863), had eight children: 1) Raymond Lloyd Imes [(b. April 11, 1930), m. October 18, 1951, to Norma Faye "Betsy" Smith (b. July 30, 1932), and had four children: a) Robert David Imes; b) Karen Imes (m. Keith Allen Sweger); c) Kenneth Imes; and d) Michael Imes]; 2) Paul Ritter Imes (b. September 15, 1927), m. February 21, 1951, to Betty Lois Gray, b. June 26, 1923, and their daughter Conal Imes m. Ronald Baumgardner; their other children included Terry D. Imes, Wanda Imes, and Randy Imes]; 3) Herbert Benjamin Imes [(b. February 4, 1934), m. September 15, 1954, to Lois Marie Bennett (b. March 22, 1936), and their son was Steven Imes]; 4) Jack Edward Imes [(b. November 30, 1941), m. March 6, 1963, to June Mae Lamey (b. June 4, 1943), and their children were Angela Marie Imes and Scott Imes)]; 5) William David Imes (b. June 17, 1925); m. Ann Blanche Claybaugh (b. January 28, 1932); 6) Carl Richard Imes (b. October 17, 1936), m. 1st, November 8, 1958, to Joyce Campbell; and m. 2nd, to Theo Mae Biler (b. January 28, 1945); 7)

Anna Louise Imes (b. August 5, 1939; m. October 31, 1959, to Stanley Lee Treaster, b. June 21, 1933); and 8) Floyd Lincoln Imes (b. February 12, 1945; m. August 8, 1964, to Alice Ann Wetzel, b. April 9, 1941).

And finally, Miles Henry Imes (b. October 30, 1905), son of Emory Imes (b. 1865), m. July 22, 1927, to Claire W. Benner (b. August 15, 19__), and they had two children: 1) Faye Elizabeth Imes [(b. October 23, 1942), m. Thomas J. Campbell, and their child was Tennille Campbell (b. December 31, 1976)]; and 2) Merle Cunningham Imes [(b. May 2, 1928), m. December 24, 1953, to Dorothy Keister (b. March 16, 1934), and they had four children: a) Larry Merle Imes (b. July 29, 1955; m. February 14, 1980, to Wendy Jo Shelly); b) Carol Marie Imes (b. December 27, 1956); c) Mary Claire Imes (b. October 18, 1958; m. July 6, 1979, to Michael Ennist); and d) Wayne Edward Imes (b. August 4, 1962)].

Benjamin Albert Imes (b. 1848; d. 1908) compiled an Imes Family History in 1902. Benjamin Albert Imes (b. 1848) was the son of Samuel and Sarah Moore Imes. In this report, Benjamin Albert Imes (b. 1848) declared that "John and William Imes sailed from England to British Guiana in the late 1700s, but moved to Virginia that same year, taking with them a woman servant/slave." John Imes and the slave woman had children, including John or Jack Imes. This Jack Imes later purchased his freedom and with his second wife Susan Pindle, had eight or ten free children, among whom was Samuel Imes (b. January 14, 1816, in Maryland).

A newspaper account from the *Mifflintown* (Pennsylvania) *Record,* relates that John (Jack) Imes, a colored man, was born in Anne Arundel County, Maryland, on January 1, 1775, and died at the home of his son David Imes, in Spruce Hill Township, Juniata County, Pennsylvania, July 2, 1871, and describes this Jack Imes (b. 1775) as the slave of Elizabeth Howard and her husband William Imes, of Washington County, Maryland, where he remained until he was age seventeen, when he was permitted to choose his own master. He chose Andrew Kline, and after working seven years for him, he was purchased by a Jacob Seibert. He had three children while working for Andrew Kline, and ten additional children during the eighteen years he served Jacob Seibert. Many of these children were said to have been "sold South."

By this time Jack Imes (b. 1775) had married his second wife Susan Pindle, and they had two children by the time she was age twenty-one, the age at which she was to become free. Because the children were still considered to be slaves even after their mother was to become free, Jack Imes purchased the children with money that he had saved for thirty years from making rakes and shaking forks, and raising both melons and potatoes with night and Sunday work efforts.

Jack Imes (b. 1775) then served eight years for David Nagle, with the proviso that he would be set free after that period (Washington County, Maryland, Certificate Book A, page 53, March 2, 1824). After obtaining his freedom, he moved to Franklin County, Pennsylvania, with his wife and six children. As a free family Jack Imes (b. 1775) supported them by working for a Christian Negley for five years before moving to the Jacob Myers place on the Conococheague Creek. After eleven more years he bought a home near Greencastle in Franklin County, Pennsylvania, where he lived twelve years and where his wife Susan Pindle was buried.

Jack Imes (b. 1775) moved to Juniata County, Pennsylvania, where he lived for seventeen years, dying in 1871 as the father of twenty-six children (thirteen slave and thirteen free). One of the children was Samuel Imes (b. January 14, 1818, near Mercersburg, Franklin County, Pennsylvania; d. near McAlisterville, Juniata County, Pennsylvania, February 3, 1893). It was the son of this Samuel Imes (b. 1818), Benjamin Albert Imes (b. 1848), who wrote this first account of the family history (1902) so that his "own children may know of their ancestry and the Providential value of that ancestry to them, not in wealth, nor fame, but in industry and moral integrity."

He gives the place of birth of Jack Imes (b. 1775) as near Leonardstown (Lunnentown) on the Eastern Shore, and the parents as being an English planter of some local note and a slave woman from the West African Guinea Coast, a woman of "very strong character and high courage" who protected her son from all harm. This Jack Imes (b. 1775) was much like his mother in character, and by age seventeen was good enough to be a teamster for a six-horse wagon team that carried goods across the mountains between Baltimore and Wheeling. This Jack Imes (b. 1775) was sold as a slave several times before working a settlement, at age forty-nine, for the freedom of his family. His second wife, Susan Pindle, was the daughter of Lord Charles Howard of Baltimore and a slave mother.

After receiving his emancipation papers, Jack Imes (b. 1775) moved from near Hagerstown, Maryland, to near Mercersburg, Franklin County, Pennsylvania, where he purchased a sixty- to eighty-acre farm. This farm eventually became the property of son David Imes (b. 1821), who later became a wealthy property owner in Juniata County, Pennsylvania. This David Imes (b. 1821) married a nineteen-year-old slave "of nearly white blood" from Richmond, Virginia, Miss Adeline Brown/ Braan. Adaline was freed and inherited a sum of $1,000 which was used to improve their Pennsylvania farm.

Like the preceding male members of the Imes family descendants of Jack Imes (b. 1775), Samuel Imes (b. 1818, m. Sarah Moore) was apprenticed to a farmer in the area. Thus, Samuel Imes (b. 1818) worked for a Jacob Brewer, Jr., until age eighteen, and married at age twenty-four to twenty-one-year-old Sarah Moore before going to work for the Scotch-Irish Presbyterian farm family of Josiah McClure. Samuel and Sarah Moore Imes became members of the Presbyterian Church and were favorably impressed by the pastor, Reverend Thomas Creigh. They had been married February 22, 1842, and were able to purchase a small amount of land for $100, later improving and selling the land for $300 in 1848.

Their fourth child, Benjamin Albert Imes (b. 1848) came "into this life with a propensity for books, a thirst for knowledge, and a great desire for the companionship of high minded, good people—such as take delight in the word of God." At the age of six weeks, he moved with his family to near McAlisterville, Juniata County, Pennsylvania, to work for the McAlister family. They were received "not so much as a servant, as a valued acquaintance and friend...." The family remained as tenants at the Fayette Township farm of the McAlisters near Oakland Mills in Juniata County, until 1859 when they became renters of the farm on which they lived. Then on May 20, 1863, the family purchased a farm in Walker Township, Juniata County, from John Tennis for $3,000. While at the McAlister farm, the family had attended the Lost Creek Presbyterian Church.

Son Benjamin Albert Imes (b. 1848) described his early life as one of a desire for learning, and as one of hard farm work. His work included clearing poor farm land, spreading thousands of bushels of lime over the land, serving as teamster in hauling coal, before leaving home at age twenty-one in order to work enough to attend college.

As the other children moved away and the parents grew older, the parents sold the farm and purchased a home in McAlisterville for one hundred dollars. The home was near the Lost Creek Presbyterian Church, so they were able to spend their last days among friends as highly regarded citizens of their community. A dinner prayer, said to be used frequently by the father of Benjamin Albert Imes (b. 1848) is said to have gone like this:

"Great and all-wise God, in whose presence we surround this board to partake of the bounties spread before us, make us thankful for what we are to receive for the nourishment of our bodies. We are dependent creatures upon Thee, look upon us in mercy, forgive our sins, and surround us with Thy favor for Christ's sake. Amen."

In 1870, Benjamin Albert Imes (b. 1848) moved to Ohio, and after a short time in Cleveland, moved to Oberlin where he was admitted to Oberlin College, as was his cousin, Esau Imes. At Oberlin in 1871, he came under the deep religious influence of President Minney and a New York Baptist evangelist, Reverend Doctor Graves, and this experience led to his pursuit of the ministry.

This wonderful biography and early family history of the family of the slave Jack Imes (b. 1775) was provided by Carmen W. Harleston and was composed in 1902 by Benjamin Albert Imes (b. 1848). It speaks of high family values, integrity, honesty, and kindness to fellow man. It acknowledges inheritance and promotes self-worth in terms of honest character, hard work, and determination to succeed, while continuing to acknowledge obedience and submission to God, and to live justly within the community of man. This writing will serve as a legacy to all mankind upon its publication by Mrs. Harleston. As a 1902 text, it represents the first publication of a family history of the Imes family tree, firmly rooted in the early history of colonial Maryland.

*A Biographical Sketch of David Imes**

*This biographical sketch was compiled in 1982 by Carmen W. Harleston. It was based on information gathered from census records, deeds, Benjamin Albert Imes' Sketch of the Family History (written in 1902), The Port Royal Times *(Pennsylvania), and David Imes' memorial.*

David Imes was born February 6, 1821, in Washington County, Maryland. David's parents, John Imes and Susan Pindle Imes, were born to slave mothers by white fathers. John Imes' children from an earlier marriage had been sold away, never to be heard of again; therefore, John was determined that his second family would be free. John Imes made a bargain with his master, David Angle, and after several years obtained freedom for all of his family. By this time the family had grown to six: John, Susan, and the children—William, John Jr., Samuel, and David, who was about age three. The family then moved just across the Maryland state line into Franklin County, Pennsylvania. At first they lived on the Christian Negley farm, and later moved to Jacob Myers' farm on the north branch of the Conococheague Creek.

It was the custom of this time for parents to "bind out" their sons as apprentices to farmers, tanners, mechanics, etc. The apprenticeship usually lasted until the boy reached eighteen years of age. David was "bound out" to Danny Miller, a German farmer, where he was to learn to be a good farmer and to receive schooling as well. Not much is known of the years spent on the Miller farm; however, in view of David's later success as a farmer, one can assume that David learned well.

Later David met Adaline Braan. It is believed that she was originally from Richmond, Virginia, and was born of a slave mother and a white father. When Adaline was given her freedom, she also inherited one thousand dollars. She and David were married sometime around 1840.

In December 1841, Oliver, their first child, was born, followed by a daughter, Sarah Bell, who was born in November 1843.

On March 19, 1844, David Imes purchased a farm from William and Catherine Frye. He paid $900 for the fifty-three acres and 155 perches. The farm was located in Montgomery Township on the northeast side of the West Conococheague Creek.

Over the next six years, David worked hard and greatly improved his land. Three additional children were born: John in 1845, Ann Mariah in 1848, and Joseph in 1850.

On April 25, 1850, less than three weeks after the birth of her fifth child, Adaline Imes died at age thirty-one. Little is known about the four years that followed except that Hannah Green became David's housekeeper.

In March 1854, David sold his farm for $3,000. On April 1, 1854, David purchased a new farm from Henry Buseal. He paid $3,000 for the 110 acres and 96 perches located in Turbett Township, Juniata County, Pennsylvania.

David, his five children, his father, John Imes, Sr., and Hannah Green moved to Juniata County. Later that year David met Sarah Ann Wilson. They were married on December 25, 1854.

The union with Sarah Wilson produced nine children: Mary Jane, Wilson David, Howard, Olen, Samuel, Emery, Ellen, Ross (who died at age two years), and Alice Carey. Throughout his years in Juniata County, David prospered as a farmer, land owner, father, husband, and respected member of the community.

The local papers often made favorable mention of David Imes. In February 1879, *The Port Royal Times* carried an item that David Imes had been selected to serve as a grand juror. The article said, "Mr. Imes is the first of his race that ever served as a juror in the courts of Juniata County. He is an honest, upright, intelligent citizen and is fully qualified to discharge the responsible duties of a grand juror. We congratulate Mr. Imes on having been called to serve his country in such an important capacity."

During his lifetime, David purchased more than 1,500 acres of land, costing him nearly $30,000. The land was left to his children.

David Imes died at age seventy-three on December 17, 1894. He was buried in the Ebenezer Methodist Church Cemetery, Spruce Hill, near Pleasantview, Pennsylvania. Also buried at Ebenezer Cemetery are Sarah Ann Wilson Imes, David's widow (died 1931); John Imes, Sr., his father (died 1871); Ross Imes, his youngest son (died 1873); Hannah Green, his housekeeper from Franklin County (died 1860); and many of David's children, their spouses, and other descendants.

Benjamin Gaither (b. 1712, South River Hundred, Maryland; d. 1793, Prince Georges County, Maryland) and wife Sarah Gaither were among the most affluent of the Gaither familes (*Anne Arundel Gentry*, Newman, 1970, pp. 67-8). Benjamin Gaither (b. 1712) was the son of John Gaither (b. 1668; d. 1739) and Jane Buck, but had no known children of his own marriage. However, in the 1790 Federal Census, Prince Georges County, Maryland, Benjamin Gaither is listed as head of the household that also contains one male between the ages of ten and sixteen, and seventeen Negro slaves. In his will, written June 20, 1791, and probated December 16, 1792, he left "To Benjamin Ijams, son of Sarah Ijams, all land whereon he dwelt with adjoining plantations and the personal estate except the Negroes who were to be set free." The executors of this will were Benjamin Ijams and William Peach, Jr., brother to Benjamin Ijams. The witnesses to the will were Richard Isaac, Joseph Isaac, and Isaac.

This Benjamin Ijams is not otherwise identified, but it is known that he "soon disposed of his possessions." Furthermore, in 1809 law suits were filed by other members of the Gaither family over the ownership of the thirty slaves, based on the executors that were described as "who not being able to execute the trust," and "the personal estate" was sold May 23, 1809, at the store of Wesley Meeke of Prince Georges County, Maryland. In 1814, the court appointed administrator for this sale, Robert McGill, was sued for their share of the estate by the various surviving nieces and nephews of Benjamin Gaither. No court record of the distribution has been found, and the tracing of the Gaither family has been found to be difficult (Chancery Papers 2066, 2074).

The identification of Sarah Ijams, mother of the heir Benjamin Ijams, has never been made with certainty. It has been speculated that Benjamin was born to Sarah Ijams, either before her marriage to Benjamin Gaither, or was sired out of wedlock. Likewise, the relationship of Sarah to William Peach, Jr., brother of Benjamin Ijams, remains unknown. Perhaps related to these persons are Henry Ijams and his designated representative Elizabeth Ijams, who appeared to attempt to claim part of the personal estate of the late Benjamin Gaither (b. 1712).

Work by Carole (Mrs. Stan J.) Paprocki, Columbus, Ohio, has identified Benjamin Ijams (b. ca1775), Maryland; d. ca1802, Maryland or Pennsylvania); m. May 24, 1798, Anne Arundel County, Maryland; Mary (Polly) Mitchell (b. 1780, Maryland; d. February 11, 1863, Monroe Township, Licking County, Ohio; buried at Old Burying Grounds, Johnstown, Ohio), with Mary Mitchell (b. 1780) having married 2nd to Emanuel Hoover. The relationship of this Mary Mitchell Ijams-Hoover (b. 1780) to the Elizabeth Ijams or Henry Ijams mentioned above is not known. The marriage of Benjamin Ijams (b. ca1775) and Mary Mitchell produced one son, William M. Iams, a carpenter with a shady past that included multiple wives and labels of bigamist and adulterer.

William M. Iams (b. ca1800, Maryland; d. ca1863, Shelly County, Memphis, Tennessee, having been murdered). Reported marriages include: 1) February 15, 1820, Licking County Ohio, to Mariah "Marie" Jane Bailey/Bayley; 2) September 13, 1846, Memphis, Tennessee, to Anthior Weed; 3) August 9, 1848, Memphis, Tennessee, to Martha A. Weed; 4) October 29, 1851, Memphis, Tennessee, to Fredonia Underwood; and 5) February 24, 1859, Memphis, Tennessee, to Martha P. Adair. Marriages 2 and 3 are recorded in Vol. 2 of *Early West Tennessee Marriages*, edited by Band B Sistter, Nashville, Tennessee; and marriage 4 has been tentatively assigned by C. S. Paprocki.

The first marriage of Benjamin Ijams (b. ca1775) is recorded by Barnes (Maryland Marriages, 1778-1800), and the first marriage of William M. Iams (b. ca1800) is from Licking County, Ohio, courthouse files. The marriage of William M. Iams (b. ca1800) and his first wife Mariah Bailey (b. ca1804, New York; divorced October 1847; d. February 1849, Delaware County, Ohio; daughter of Isaac Bailey and Hannah Hill) produced seven children:

1) Hannah Jane Iams [(b. January 11, 1821, Monroe Township, Licking County, Ohio; d. 1854, Effingham County, Illinois), m. November 23, 1839, Licking County, Ohio, to John Bradner Carpenter].

2) Benjamin Iams [(b. April 11, 1822, Monroe Township, Licking County, Ohio; a Confederate soldier killed 1863), m. 1) September 26, 1853, Memphis, Shelby County, Tennessee, to Amanda Weed; m. 2) October 18, 1856, Memphis, Tennessee, to Elizabeth Hollingsworth].

3) Isaac Iams (b. 1824, Monroe Township, Licking County, Ohio; d. 1846, Licking County; buried in College Hill Cemetery, Granville Township, Licking County, Ohio; single).

4) Roxanna Iams [(b. November 14, 1825, Monroe Township, Licking County, Ohio; d. after 1880, Effingham, Illinois), m. March 4, 1852, Wolworth County, Wisconsin, to William Riley].

5) Francis Marion Imes [(b. July 27, 1830, Monroe Township, Licking County, Ohio; d. June 17, 1892, Mount Vernon, Knox County, Ohio, and buried in Mound View Cemetery), m. March 3, 1850, in McHenry County, Illinois, to Mary M. Sanders; a Baptist minister who lived in Wisconsin for several years].

6) Mariah A. Iams [(b. October 14, 1837, Delaware County, Ohio; d. after 1880, Tomah, Monroe County, Wisconsin), m. 1st, April 10, 1854,

Memphis, Shelby County, Tennessee, to John L. Weed; m. 2nd, 1863, Tomah, Monroe County, Wisconsin, to Harry Howard; Mariah (b. 1837) is believed to have fled to Wisconsin at the time of the outbreak of the Civil War];

    7) George W. Iams (b. July 12, 1842, Delaware County, Ohio; d. 1863 as a Confederate soldier, presumably while serving with his brother under the command of General Nathan Forest at the Battle of Chattanooga; single).

Francis Marion Iams (b. July 27, 1830, Hartford Township, Licking County, Ohio; d. June 17, 1892, Mount Vernon, Knox County, Ohio, buried Mound View Cemetery), the son of William M. Iams (b. 1800) and Mariah Jane Bailey, was a Congregational minister from 1860 to 1866; a Baptist minister in Illinois in the 1850s; lived in Wisconsin until moving to Mount Vernon, Ohio, November 11, 1875, where they continued their Southern leanings; m. March 3, 1850, McHenry County, Illinois, to Mary M. "Polly" Sanders (b. January 5, 1833, Bakersfield, Vermont; d. December 22, 1897, Bucyrus, Ohio); daughter of Jacob and Hannah Sanders; they had seven children:

    1) Reverend Clayton M. Iams (b. March 5, 1851, Illinois; d. after 1937, Allison Park, Alleghany County, Pennsylvania; m. 1877 in Kentucky to Maggie Taylor);

    2) Loretta Angelia Iams (b. 1853, Illinois; d. August 13, 1919, Berkeley, Alameda County, California; m. June 6, 1976, to William A. Thompson);

    3) Mary Angeline Iams (b. May 1854, McHenry County, Illinois; d. by August 1919; buried at Bucyrus, Ohio; a registered nurse; single);

    4) William Henry Iams [(b. October 11, 1856, Wisconsin; d. April 12, 1913, Bucyrus, Crawford County, Ohio); m. 1st, August 10, 1878, Knox County, Ohio, to S. Galloway; m. 2nd, in Ohio to Ora (buried in Oakwood Cemetery, Bucyrus, Ohio)];

    5) Nellie Jane Iams (b. December 29, 1858, Reedsburg, Sioux County, Wisconsin; d. January 10, 1904, Bucyrus, Ohio, buried at Mount View Cemetery, Mount Vernon, Ohio; single);

    6) Charles Claude Iams [(b. October 23, 1860, Tomah, Monroe County, Wisconsin; d. July 30, 1939, Mount Vernon, Knox County, Ohio; newspaper editor); m. November 25, 1880, Mount Vernon, Ohio, to Katharine Mary Hill];

    7) Frank Curtis Iams [(b. May 16, 1865, Menomonee County, Wisconsin; d. September 25, 1945, Columbus, Franklin County, Ohio; buried at Mound Cemetery, Mount Vernon, Ohio); m. 1890 in Ohio, to Blanche A. Craig]. (CSP)

Charles Claude Iams (b. October 23, 1860, Tomah, Monroe County, Wisconsin; d. July 30, 1939, Mount Vernon, Knox County, Ohio) moved from Wisconsin to Mount Vernon, Ohio, in 1875 (KC) where he first became an apprentice for *Park's Floral Magazine*, became a "devil" (errand boy) by 1877 for the weekly newspaper *Mount Vernon Republican*. He later advanced through newspaper positions of pressman, job printer, foreman, city editor (1887), and then editor (1894). When the newspaper reorganized in 1900, he became vice-president, editor, and manager. He was a Republican; member of the Independent Order of Odd Fellows; member of Ancient Arabia Order of Nobles of the Mystic Shrine, and member of Benevolent and Protective Order of Elks. He m. 1st, November 28, 1880, Mount Vernon, Ohio, to Katharine Margaret Hill (b. January 12, 1862, Mount Vernon; d. February 20, 1926), daughter of James Monroe Hill and Darcus Elizabeth Anders;

m. 2nd to Levia R. Ward; had daughter Edythe Elizabeth Claire Iams [(b. February 17, 1885, Mount Vernon , Knox County, Ohio; d. April 22, 1922, Gainesville, Alachua County, Florida; buried Mound View Cemetery, Mount Vernon, Ohio); m. October 6, 1902, Mount Vernon, Ohio, to Oliver Ray Tucker, Sr. (b. July 1, 1884, Liberty Township, Knox County, Ohio), son of Charles S. Tucker and Almina Jane Willyerd; and Oliver Ray Tucker, Sr., m. 2nd, Ruby Mae Caulkins]. (KC, CSP)

The children of Edythe Claire Iams (b. 1885) and Oliver Ray Tucker, Sr., were:

1) Dorothy Lucille Tucker [(b. December 14, 1902, Mount Vernon, Knox County, Ohio; d. February 10, 1981, Columbus, Franklin County, Ohio); m. November 20, 1920, Campbell County, Kentucky (eloped), to George Daniel Crumley];

2) Charles Arthur Tucker (b. January 26, 1906, Mount Vernon, Ohio; d. October 31, 1978, Cincinnati, Ohio; m. June 16, 1937, to Opal Pickerell);

3) Margaret Edythe Tucker (b. August 23, 1907, Mount Vernon, Knox County, Ohio; m. 1st, August 27, 1929, to George E. Parker; m. 2nd, August 14, 1918, Emlenton, Venango County, Pennsylvania, to Edward E. Green). (CSP)

Dorothy Lucille Tucker (b. December 14, 1902) m. George Daniel Crumley (b. July 1, 1901, Mount Vernon; d. January 12, 1974, Columbus, Ohio; an architect); son of Cloise Hamilton Crumley and Margaret May Brillhart (or Burris), and they had three children:

1) Charles C. Crumley (b. July 28, 1924, Mount Vernon, Ohio; m. May 6, 1944, to Betty Louise Dutro);

2) Constance C. Crumley [b. December 27, 1927, Columbus, Franklin County, Ohio; d. January 26, 1989, Orlando, Orange County, Florida; m. 1st, September 6, 1947, Kentucky (eloped), to John Frank Kramer, Jr.; m. 2nd, October 16, 1965, Columbus, Ohio, to Glendon Gerlach; m. 3rd, April 1, 1972, Lake Forest, Lake County, Illinois, to Alan Gault; m. 4th, January 13, 1976, Daytona Beach, Volusia County, Florida, to John Bidwell];

3) Carole Candace Crumley [(b. March 15, 1930, Columbus, Franklin County, Ohio); m. October 25, 1952, Columbus, Franklin County, Ohio, to Stan John Paprocki (b. July 10, 1922, Chicago, Illinois; a metallurgical engineer); son of Jozef W. Paprocki and Katarzyna Podraza; they had two children: a) Karyn Anne Paprocki [(b. July 24, 1953, Columbus, Ohio); m. September 9, 1978, Columbus, Ohio, to Timothy Paul Rannenbarger (b. February 23, 1953, Harlem Township, Delaware County, Ohio); son of Harold Lowell Rannebarger and Dorothy June Daughters; graduate of Ohio State University; had two children: Sarah Elizabeth Rannenbarger (b. April 13, 1981, West Lafayette, Tippicano County, Indiana), and Daniel Joseph Rannenbarger (b. October 26, 1987, Cape Girardeau, Cape Girardeau County, Missouri)]; b) Paul Patrick Paprocki [(b. July 7, 1957, Columbus, Ohio); m. July 11, 1981, Colorado Springs, El Paso County, Colorado, to Diane Leslie Deshon (b. November 28, 1959, Fort Belvoir, Fairfax County, Virginia); daughter of Raymond Alan Deshon and Livia Jean "Lib" DeAmicis; they had two children: Jeffrey Paul Paprocki (b. July 24, 1983, Colorado Springs, El Paso County, Colorado); and Christina Maria Paprocki (b. December 18, 1986, Colorado Springs, El Paso County, Colorado). Carol Candace Crumley Paprocki (b. 1930), noted genealogist who compiled this branch of the family tree, wrote from her home at 1637 Sussex Cout, Columbus, Ohio,

81

43220, in 1994, that tracing the genealogy of Benjamin Ijams (b. 1775) has been difficult and that others have written that this Benjamin Ijams is "an illegitimate son of who knows who" and who has voiced the interesting thought of writing the ultimate novel of his life that might be called "The Dirty Old Man From Delaware County, Ohio" that could be promised to make Hugh Heffner and others look pale.

William Iiams (b. 1750; d. 1795; m. Mary Hampton) had a son Thomas Iiams [(b. 1784, Pennsylvania; d. April 4, 1855, Shelby County, Ohio), m. Marcia "Mercy" Walton (b. February 1784, New Jersey; d. May 21, 1867)]. The son of Thomas Iiams (b. 1784) was William Iiams [(b. February 13, 1807; d. 1894), m. Martha McClure (b. October 5, 1814; d. June 22, 1896)]; and the son of William Iiams (b. 1807) was also William Iiams [(b. March 24, 1837; d. March 19, 1913, Lima, Allen County, Ohio; m. July 22, 1858, to Martha Ann Moyer (b. December 24, 1841, Port Jefferson, Shelby County, Ohio; d. March 24, 1905)].

A son of this William Iiams (b. 1837) was Charles Riley Iiams [(b. April 12, 1866, Shelby County, Ohio; d. July 9, 1951, Lima, Allen County, Ohio), m. March 15, 1895, to Mary Elizabeth Watkins (b. September 27, 1870, Lima, Ohio; d. March 26, 1955, Lima, Ohio), daughter of Thomas Daniel Watkins and Rebecca Quinn. The daughter of Charles Riley Iiams (b. 1866) was Bernice Cordelia Iiams [(b. August 7, 1901, Lima, Allen County, Ohio; d. July 30, 1984, North Hollywood, California), m. John C. Schwartz, son of John Casimer Schwartz and Julia Rose Gutzwiller. (John C. Schwartz was the son of Fidel Schwartz and Monica Eisley; while Julia Rose Gutzwiller was the daughter of Henry Gutzwiller and Elizabeth Hidismer)]. Their son was John "Jack" Charles Schwartz [(b. August 17, 1917, Lima, Ohio; d. April 15, 1986, Sun Valley, California); m. 1st, December 2, 1937, to Mary Elizabeth Humbert (b. November 1, 1917, Lima, Ohio), the daughter of Henry Edward Humbert and Pearl Weider]. Henry Edward Humbert was the son of Urban (Ruben) Didier Humbert and Mary Henry. Urban Humbert was the son of Jean Nicholas Humbert and Mary Huard. Mary Henry was the daughter of Pierre Paul Henry (Henri) and Frances Grillot. Pearl Weider was the daughter of Henry Clay Weider and Elizabeth Jane Cosart. Henry Clay Weider was the son of Frederick Weider and Mary Campbell. Elizabeth Jane Cosart was the daughter of James Cosart. The daughter of John "Jack" Charles Schwartz (b. 1917) and Mary Elizabeth Humbert (b. 1917) was Janice Lynne Schwartz [(b. May 25, 1939, Lima, Allen County, Ohio); m. 3rd, on December 27, 1968, to Robert Sharp (b. June 24, 1946, Peoria, Illinois)]. Janice Lynne Schwartz Sharp (b. 1939) served as family historian for this portion of the family tree.

EFB has recorded that John Iiams (b. February 1750, Anne Arundel County, Maryland; d. July 24, 1823, West Bethlehem Township, Washington County, Pennsylvania; buried in Franklin Cemetery), m. Elizabeth Gill Hampton (b. April 10, 1763, Anne Arundel County, Maryland; d. September 1, 1836, Washington County, Pennsylvania). John Iiams (b. 1750) was the son of either Thomas Ijams (b. 1708) or John (b. 1708) and Penelope Iiams (JF1, CR1), and the children of John Iiams (b. 1750) were:

    1) William Iiams [(b. February 4, 1792, Washington County, Pennsylvania; d. April 4, 1869), m. June 6, 1816, to Delilah Meeks and their twelve children were: a) Betsy Iiams; b) Miller Iiams (m. Sarah Eggy; lived in Ritchie County, West Virginia; two children: Thomas Iiams, m. 1851 to Nancy Adamson; and James Harvey Iiams, b. 1874; m. Frances D. Davis; their two children were: Hillis D. Iiams, b. 1904; m. Wilda L. Lindawood, with son Jack L. Iiams, b. Washington County, Ohio, in 1929; and Ilda

I. Iiams, b. 1906; m. J. H. Epler; c) James Iiams; d) John Hill Iiams, m. Rebecca McKenna; e) Elisha Iiams, m. Cynthia Garver and lived in Washington County, Pennsylvania; f) Thomas Iiams, m. Sarah Johnson and lived in Greene County, Pennsylvania; g) Isaac Iiams, m. Anne Ferrell and lived in Washington County, Pennsylvania; h) William Iiams, b. 1830, m. 1st, Elizabeth Ferrell and m. 2nd, Mary Swihart; 13 children; i) Delilah Iiams, m. Mr. Johnson, lived in Greene County, Pennsylvania; j) Mary Iiams m. Jacob Bigler; k) Abraham Iiams, d. Civil War; and l) Rachel Iiams, m. Daniel Smith and lived in Washington County, Pennsylvania].

2) Nancy Iiams [(b. 1787 or 1795; d. January 21, 1879); m. December 27, 1821, to Joseph Martin, Sr., and they had six children: a) Morgan Martin (b. 1823); b) Elizabeth Martin (b. and d. 1825); c) John L. Martin (b. 1828), m. Elizabeth Bair; six children: Joseph Martin, Sarah Martin, A. Jackson Martin, Martha Martin, Samuel Martin, and C. W. Martin; d) Joseph Martin (b. 1831); e) Anna Martin (b. 1833), m. A. P. Van Dyke; seven children: LeRoy M. Van Dyke, Nancy Van Dyke, Elizabeth M. Van Dyke, Kate M. Van Dyke, Hannah C. Van Dyke, Thomas Van Dyke and Florence Van Dyke; f) Sarah Martin (b. 1836), m. Neal Zollars; eight children including George Zollars, Ezekial Zollars, and Martha Zollars.

3) Elizabeth Iiams (d. age 21).

4) Anna Iiams (d. age 6).

5) Sabrina Iiams (d. age 4).

6) John H. Iiams (b. 1798; d. April 30, 1846; single).

7) Charity Iiams [(b. 1749; d. 1799), m. John D. Smith; eleven children: a) Martin Smith; b) Thomas Smith; c) Amos Smith (b. 1828); m. Julie Matthews; their daughter Nancy Smith, b. 1843, m. George F. Hyde; d) John Smith; e) Joseph Smith; f) Nathan Smith; g) William Smith; h) Freeman Smith; i) Elizabeth Smith; j) Nancy Smith; k) Isa Smith)].

8) Mary Iiams [(b. 1800 or April 10, 1810; d. September 14, 1849); m. Moses Smith].

9) Sarah Iiams [(b. 1804; d. April 15, 1838), m. Freeman Hathaway].

John Iiams [b. 1712 (REI), 1720 (HWN), 1708 (EFB), or 1716, All Hallow's Parish, Anne Arundel County, Maryland; d. May 18, 1778 (EFB) or before 1778 (MI) in Anne Arundel County (EFB) or Washington County (MI), Maryland]; son of Richard Iiams (b. 1673) and second wife Elizabeth Gaither Iiams (EFB); the children of John Iiams were:

1) Richard Iiams [(b. 1745, New Birmingham Plantation, Anne Arundel County, Maryland; d. 1834, Greene County, Pennsylvania; eldest son and heir; m. 1778 to Eleanor (or Elizabeth) Pottenger (b. 1755, Prince Georges County, Maryland; d. 1834, Greene County, Pennsylvania), daughter of Robert Pottenger (HWN, EFB, RWI)].

2) Thomas Iiams [(b. December 26, 1754, Anne Arundel County, Maryland; d. June 28, 1834 or 1843); purchased the New Birmingham plantation and later settled in Pennsylvania (REI, EFB, HWN); m. November 29, 1785, to Mary Smith (b. 1760) or Catherine Gill Hampton (EFB, LIB), the sister of Joseph Smith, Abraham Smith, Elizabeth Smith, Susan Smith, Dennis Smith, David Smith, Christopher Smith, Sarah Smith, Richard Smith, and Hannah Smith].

3) John Iiams [(b. February 1750 or July 21, 1751; d. July 4, 1823); m. March 12, 1791 to Elizabeth Hampton (MI, EFB, HWN)].

4) William Iiams [(b. 1751; d. February 23, 1795), m. Mary Hampton (MI, EFB, HWN)].

5. Mary Iiams [(b. 1764), m. April 8, 1788, Baltimore, Maryland, to William Penn, and had eleven children (EFB, MI)].

Thomas Iiams (b. 1745 or 1783; d. March 9, 1843, Washington Township, Greene County, Pennsylvania), son of John Iiams (b. 1720) or Richard Iiams (b. 1741) and Mary Smith, daughter of Dennis Smith. The will of Thomas Iiams (Will 1067, Volume 2, page 171, Washington Township, Greene County, Pennsylvania) was probated March 9, 1843 (witnessed by Otho Iams and Benjamin Miller) and left estate to wife Mary Iiams, and upon her death, to sons Thomas Iiams and Dennis (or Dennuce) Iiams, with wife as executor; and also naming son Thomas Iiams, daughter Elizabeth (wife of George Smith), daughter Catherine Iiams, daughter Mary Iiams, and daughter Rachel Iiams. The children of Thomas Iiams and Mary Smith were: 1) Dennis (Demas, Dennuce) Iams [(b. June 2, 1808, Bates Fork, Morris Township, Greene County, Pennsylvania; d. January 7, 1888, Morris Township), m. August 8, 1831, to Matilda Huffman (b. September 26, 1814; d. October 14, 1887; buried at Sycamore, Greene County, Pennsylvania), or to Priscilla Hopkins; owned 1,800 acres; raised sheep for wool; elected deacon in Bates Fork Baptist Church in 1863; related stories of 1818-1820 hunting trips with his grandfather, Richard Iiams, that included hunting deer, wild turkeys, pheasants, squirrels, rabbits, bear, and wolves, with stories including sleeping out at night listening to the wolves and of the description of the log cabin home (WH, EFB)]; 2) Thomas Iams; 3) Elizabeth Iams (m. George Smith); 4) Catherine Iams; 5) Hannah Iams; 6) Mary Iams; 7) Rachel Iams [(b. December 1818; d. December 7, 1858), m. 1835 to Joseph Miller (b. December 25, 1812; d. December 11, 1863)]; and 8) Charity Iams.

EFB has written that Thomas Iams (b. 1781-1790; d. March 1843), m. Mary Smith (b. 1781-7, Washington Township, Greene County, Pennsylvania; d. 1850), daughter of Dennis Smith (b. 1738, Germany; d. August 29, 1829, Greene County, Pennsylvania), who m. November 15, 1771, to Elizabeth Zook (b. May 13, 1756, Pennsylvania; d. August 19, 1895, Clermont County, Ohio). This Thomas Iams (b. 1781-1790) was the son of Richard Iams (b. 1741-9; d. ca1830) and Eleanor Pottinger (b. 1751-60; d. ca1830); and the grandson of Thomas Iams (b. August 7, 1708; d. 1768).

Thomas Iams (b. 1781-1790) had a daughter Rachel Iams (b. 1818; d. caDecember 7, 1858), who m. ca1835 Joseph Miller (b. 1812; d. 1863). A daughter of Joseph (b. 1812) and Rachel Iams Miller (b. 1818) was Margaret Miller (b. March 19, 1854; d. March 16, 1924). Margaret Miller (b. 1854) m. November 30, 1876, to John Vance Scott. John Vance Scott and Margaret Miller Scott (b. 1854) had a daughter Caroline G. Scott (b. December 4, 1898). Caroline G. Scott (b. 1898) m. April 27, 1920, to Bertrum Richard Carson. Bertrum Richard Carson and Caroline G. Scott Carson (b. 1898) had a daughter, Betty J. Carson (b. December 15, 1921). Betty J. Carson (b. 1921) m. Ervin F. Bickley, Jr. of Philadelphia, author of much of the Iams research in this publication.

Per Gertrude Burnham: Joseph Miller (b. 1805) received a pension for his duty during the War of 1812 as corporal in the Capt. William Patterson Company of the Pennsylvania Militia Regiment; lived at Ten Mile, Pennsylvania; enlisted September 25, 1812, was discharged November 24, 1812; was age 80 and living Amwell Township, Washington County, Pennsylvania, April 12, 1885. He had a brother, Benjamin John Miller. Joseph Miller was a member of a company known as the "Ten Mile Marchers." Brother Benjamin Miller served in the same company as did Joseph (War of 1812), but the record was not found. Dr. Benjamin Miller died December 23, 1845, in Greene County, Pennsylvania, leaving two minor children and a widow, Jane (d. December 4, 1848). *The Pennsylvania Archives Third Series*, pages 23, 275, 726, 746, and 807, covering the activities of the Cumberland County Militia during the Revolutionary War dates of 1781 and 1782, include the service record of Benjamin Miller, Sr., who was age about 45 when he died in Greene County, Pennsylvania, in 1799, leaving a widow, Hannah (who m. 2nd, Mr. Day by June 3, 1803). During the Civil War, a Doctor Benjamin Miller (m. Hettie Flick, 1902, of Chanute, Illinois) served with the 2nd Brigade, Co K., Division 23 AC, reported to have served at Loudon, Tennessee, November 8, 1863, under General Burnside; was at USA General Hospital at Camp Butler February 17, 1865, and had some type of paralysis of the left arm. (GB)

Mary Smith (b. 1781) was the daughter of Dennis Smith (b. 1738), who m. Elizabeth _____. Dennis Smith served in the American Revolution, with the pension provided to his widow Elizabeth (b. May 13, 1756; d. August 29, 1829, Greene County Pennsylvania.), with application being made December 29, 1838, from Clermont County, Ohio, having enlisted from Washington County, Pennsylvania. Dennis Smith (b. 1738) served with Captain James Seal's Company of Colonel Thomas Cook's Pennsylvania Regiment. Children of Dennis and Elizabeth Smith were: 1) Elizabeth Smith (b. 1772); 2) Peter Smith (b. 1774); 3) Susan Smith (b. 1776); 4) Joseph Smith (b. August 16, 1779); 5) Mary "Polly" Smith (b. 1781), first wife of Thomas Iams (b. 1780), who m. 2nd, Mr. Jamison; 6) Dennis Smith, Jr. (b. 1783); 7) Sarah Smith (b. 1785); 8) Hannah Smith (b. 1787); 9) Catharine Smith (b. 1788); 10) Christopher Smith (b. 1790); 11) David Smith (b. August 19, 1792); 12) Rachel Smith (b. 1794); and 13) Abraham Smith (b. March 28, 1799).

Dennis Smith, Sr. (b. Gernam 1738; d. Washington Twp., Greene County, Pennsylvania, August 29, 1829), m. Elizabeth Zook (b. May 13, 1756; d. September 19, 1845, Dunkard Township, Greene County, Pennsylvania). The DAR record of Dennis Smith is 372 864, but EFB has found that errors exist in this account.

Dennis Iams (b. June 2, 1808, Washington Township, Greene County, Pennsylvania; d. January 7, 1888, Morris Township, Greene County, Pennsylvania; buried at Bates Fork Cemetery, Greene County, Pennsylvania), son of Thomas Iams (b. 1783) and Mary Smith; m. August 6, 1831, to Matilda Huffman (b. September 26, 1814, Greene County; d. October 14, 1887, Greene County) or Priscilla Hopkins (buried at Sycamore, Pennsylvania). The nine children of Dennis Iams (b. 1808) were:

1) Thomas Iams [(b. July 8, 1833, Morris Township, Greene County, Pennsylvania), m. Lydia Phoebe Penn (or Bell); said to have moved west; 1870 Federal Census of Greene County lists Thomas Iams (age 37), Lidia Iams (age 37), Gemima Iams (age 16), Daniel Iams (age 12), Ross Iams (age 6) and Flora Iams (age 2)].

2) Sarah Iams [(b. June 4, 1837, Morris Township, Greene County, Pennsylvania; d. March 8, 1899), m. 1853 to Daniel Loughman (b. April 25, 1832; d. January 28, 1892), son of Henry Loughman (b. 1802; son of Frederick Loughman, b. February 28, 1768; d. October 25, 1853, and Catherine Hammer, b. May 20, 1774; d. April 7, 1817) and Nancy Smith (b. 1807). They had six children: a) Jack Loughman (m. Emma Hickman); b) Ida Loughman (m. James A. Dunn); c) Dennis Loughman; d) Mary Belle Loughman (b. May 24, 1860; d. August 10, 1839; m. 1880 to George Wiley Hampson, b. January 24, 1859; d. December 24, 1952, son of Wiley and Caroline Hampson); e) George Loughman (m. ___ Pettit); f) Charles Loughman (m. ____ Ingram)].

3) Benjamin Iams [(b. September 4 or 13, 1839, Morris Township, Greene County, Pennsylvania; d. November 5, 1913, Greene County, Pennsylvania), m. February 5, 1860, Greene County, to Maria H. Scott (b. 1840,

Greene County), daughter of Elias Scott and Harriet Kent (b. 1810). Their son Charles Iams had a son, John Iams, whose son Charles V. Iams lived at 424 Beam Drive in Pittsburgh in 1965].

4) Mary Iams [(b. April 24, 1842, Morris Township, Greene County, Pennsylvania; d. June 10, 1924); m. January 1859 to Hiram Scott (b. May 15, 1836, Center Township, Greene County; d. April 22, 1917, Bristoria, Pennsylvania), son of Elias Scott and Harriet Kent (b. November 20, 1810; d. June 14, 1884). Their six children were: a) Thomas Iams Scott (d. March 7, 1933, Sunbury, Ohio; m. Nancy Eli Donahoo; b) Edell Scott; c) Charles Scott; d) Tillie Scott; e) Flora Scott; f) Dennis Scott].

5) Elizabeth Iams (b. January 11 or 19, 1846, Greene County; d. March 19, 1948; single).

6) Dennis Iams, Jr. [(b. May 13, 1848, Morris Township, Greene County; d. July 22, 1919, or May 14, 1927), m. Matilda Mattie Kegley (or Keigley) and they had ten children].

7) Lydia Iams [(b. May 1850, Morris Township, Greene County, Pennsylvania), m. John H. Smith and they had six children: a) Frank Smith; b) Charles Smith; c) Nancy Smith; d) Ora Smith; e) Ocie Smith; and f) Bessie Smith].

8) Amanda Iams [(b. May 24, 1854, Morris Township, Greene County; d. November 24, 1897), m. October 29, 1874, to Charles Adamson (b. 1850; d. March 9, 1926), and they had three children: a) Hiram Ross Adamson; b) Nannie Adamson; and c) Blanche Adamson].

9) Priscilla or Driscilla Iams [(b. October 15, 1859, Morris Township, Greene County, Pennsylvania; d. May 9, 1939, Rogersville, Pennsylvania), m. December 1, 1879, to David M. Hopkins (b. December 10, 1854, Morris Township, Greene County; d. April 22, 1937, Rogersville, Greene County, Pennsylvania). They had six children: a) Jesse Hopkins (b. January 25, 1881; Morris Township; m. September 27, 1902, to Stanley F. Garner, b. December 7, 1889, Morris Township; their child, Margaret Garner, m. Mr. Smith of Claremont County, Ohio); b) Bernice Hopkins; c) Edna Hopkins; d) Eva Hopkins; e) William Hopkins; and f) Ray Hopkins)].

Mary Belle Loughman (b. May 24, 1860; d. August 10, 1939), daughter of Sarah Iams (b. 1837) and Daniel Loughman (b. 1832), m. 1880 to George Wiley Hamson (b. January 24, 1859; d. December 24, 1952), son of Wiley and Caroline Hamson; and their daughter, Nora Ethel Hamson (b. February 9, 1882; d. July 1, 1902) m. 1899 to James Wood Estep (b. October 10, 1879; d. May 16, 1949), whose son, Walter Ralph Estep (b. March 14, 1900) m. December 31, 1919, to Verda Mae Spiker (b. June 28, 1898); and their daughter, Jesse Ethel Estep (b. December 6, 1925) m. David Bailey (genealogy correspondent for family history) and had a daughter, June Estep].

Thomas Iams Scott [(d. March 7, 1933, Sunbury, Ohio), son of Mary Iams (b. 1842) and Hiram Scott (b. 1836), m. Nancy Elizabeth Donahoo (b. December 11, 1861, Greene County, Pennsylvania; d. June 20, 1903, Washington County, Ohio, the daughter of Daniel Gordon Donahoo (b. February 23, 1838, Greene County, Pennsylvania; d. November 4, 1886, Greene County, Pennsylvania) and Sarah Ellen Mitchell (d. January 1, 1838, Greene County, Pennsylvania; d. May 18, 1925, Washington County, Pennsylvania). Thomas Iams Scott and Nancy Elizabeth Donahoo (b. 1861) had a daughter, Bertha Viola Scott (b. May 4, 1893, Washington County, Pennsylvania), who m. Joseph Bonnet]. The 1850 Federal Census of Greene County, Pennsylvania, lists Dennis Iams (age 42, b. Pennsylvania), Matilda Iams (age 36),

Thomas Iams (age 17), Sarah Iams (age 13), Benjamin Iams (age 11), Mary Iams (age 9), and Dennis Iams, Jr., (age 2). The 1880 Census of Greene County lists Dennis Iams (age 72) and Matilda Iams (age 66). The family history of Dennis Iams was provided by Charles R. "Chuck" Iams of 124 Milrose Drive, New Stanton, PA 15672. The parents of Dennis Iams (b. 1808) were said to be Thomas Iams (b. 1783) and Mary Smith (b. 1787). Dennis Iams (b. 1808) was buried in Bates Fork Cemetery, Greene County, Pennsylvania. The 1870 Federal Census of Greene County, Pennsylvania, lists: Dennis Iams (age 62), wife Matilda Iams (age 56), Dennis Iams (age 21), Amanda Iams (age 19), and Priscilla Iams (age 10).

Dennis Iams, Jr. (b. May 13, 1848, Morris Township, Greene County, Pennsylvania; d. July 22, 1919, Morris Township, Greene County), son of Dennis Iams (b. 1808) and Matilda Huffman (b. 1814), m. Matilda "Mattie" J. Kegley (or Keigley), and they had ten children: 1) Oscar Iams [(b. 1875); m. Cora Webster (b. 1878), and they had three children: a) Doane Iams (b. 1902); b) Mabel Iams (b. 1903; m. Charles Estel); and c) Mary Iams (b. 1908; m. John Iams)]; 2) Leah A. Iams (b. 1878; 3) Lydia (or Lidia) M. Iams (b. 1879); 4) Mary Iams (b. 1882); 5) Fannie Iams (b. 1884); 6) Natily Iams (b. 1887); 7) Edith Iams (b. 1889); 8) Erica Iams (b. 1891); 9) Judson Iams (b. 1893); and 10) Louise Iams (b. 1899).

The 1880 Census of Greene County, Pennsylvania, lists: Dennis Iams (age 32, wife Mattie J. Iams (age 27), Oscar Iams (age 5), Leah A. Iams (age 2), and Lida M. Iams (age 1). The 1900 Greene County Census lists: Dennis Iams (age 51), Mattie Iams (age 47), Leah Iams (age 22), Lydia Iams (age 21), Mary Iams (age 18) and Fannie Iams (age 16); also listed Oscar Iams (age 25) in a household with wife Cora Iams (age 23); as well as having a separate listing for a Dennis Iams, Jr., (age 29) as a servant for a Jacob Patterson. The 1920 Census of Greene County lists: Dennis Iams (age 71), wife Mattie Iams (age 67), Fannie Iams (age 36), Louise Iams (age 21), and Judson Iams (age 27); also listed: Oscar Iams (age 44), with wife Cora Iams (age 42), son Doan Iams (age 18), Mabel Iams (age 17), and Mary Iams (age 12).

Benjamin Iams (b. September 4 or 13, 1839, Greene County, Pennsylvania; d. November 15, 1913, Greene County, Pennsylvania), son of Dennis Iams, Sr., (b. 1808) and Matilda Huffman (b. 1814); m. 1860 to Marcia (or Mariah) Scott (b. Febraury 2, 1840, Sycamore, Greene County, Pennsylvania; d. August 15, 1924; buried in Hopewell Cemetery, Greene County), daughter of Elias Scott and Harriet Kent (CRI, LBK), and they had eleven children; 1) Sarah Mabel Iams (b. 1861, Greene County; d. January 29, 1902; m. October 14, 1880, to Isaac Porter Clutter); 2) William R. Iams (b. 1865; d. 1930; m. Siddie Roupe); 3) Franklin Iams (b. March 20, 1867, Center Township, Greene County, Pennsylvania; d. November 30, 1906); 4) Martha A. "Mattie" Iams (b. 1868; d. September 10, 1906 or 1918; m. August 18, 1888, to William H. H. Babbitt); 5) Daniel L. Iams [(b. January 5, 1870, Greene County, Pennsylvania; d. January 31, 1932); m. September 12, 1896, Ninevah, Greene County, Pennsylvania, to Margaret Bell Simpson]; 6) Nancy Pricilla Iams (b. March 2, 1871, Greene County; d. January 4, 1951; m. King G. Porter); 7) Charles "Charley" Iams [(b. April 13, 1873, Center Township, Greene County, Pennsylvania; d. March 16, 1925, Washington, Washington County, Pennsylvania), m. November 13, 1900, Washington, Pennsylvania, to Sarah Alberta Swart]; 8) Cora Iams (b. 1876; d. January 25, 1963; single in 1920); 9) Dennis Iams (b. 1877, Center Township, Greene County; d. July 22, 1919; living at home in 1910); 10) Elza Iams [(b. January 25, 1879, Center Township, Greene County; d. January 6, 1965); m. October 5, 1904, East Waynesburg, Greene County, to Mollie Holmes; and they had two daughters: Ethel Iams (b. 1906) and Lena Iams (b. 1910)]; and 11) Hiram "Harry" Iams (b. February 20, 1881, Center Township, Greene County, Pennsylvania; d. February 1, 1960; single in 1920).

The 1850 Federal Census of Morris Township, Greene County, Pennsylvania, lists Benjamin Iams (age 11) as son of Dennis and Matilda Iams. The 1870 Census lists Benjamin Iams (age 31), wife Mariah Iams (age 29), Sarah Mabell Iams (age 8), William Iams (age 5), Franklin Iams (age 3), Martha A. Iams (age 2) and Daniel Iams (age 5 monthsj). The 1880 Census lists Benjamin Iams (age 42), Mariah Iams (age 39), Sarah A. Iams (age 18), William R. Iams (age 16), Priscilla Iams (age 13), Mattie Iams (age 12), Daniel Iams (age 10), Nancy Iams (age 8), Charley Iams (age 7), Cora Iams (age 5), Dennis Iams (age 4), and Hiram E. Iams (age 2), with Ellie Iams (age 7) listed with grandparents. The 1900 Census lists Benjamin Iams (age 60), Mary Iams (age 63), Priscilla Iams (age 28), Charles Iams (age 27), Cora F. Iams (age 25), Elza Iams (age 21), Harry S. Iams (age 19) and Clide Iams (grandson, age 16); and also listed Daniel L. Iams (age 30), Margaret B. Iams (age 28), Elle Iams (age 2), and Esther Iams (age 4 months). The 1910 Greene County Census lists Benjamin Iams (age 71), Marian Imes (age 69), Cora Iams (age 34), Dennis Iams (age 33), Mary Iams (age 27), and grandson Clyde Iams (age 16); plus Will R. Iams (age 37), wife Lida A. Iams (age 27), son Herman B. Iams (age 8), son Linsey Iams (age 6), George A. Iams (age 3), and son Dona E. Iams (age 1); and also listed Daniel Iams (age 40), wife Margaret Iams (age 36), Effie Iams (age 12), Esther Iams (age 10), Nellie Iams (age 2) and Fred Iams (under age 1). The 1920 Census of Greene County listed 1) Mariah Iams (age 79) living with Clyde Iams (age 26) and Harry Iams (age 38); 2) Elsie Iams (age 40) with wife Mollie Iams (age 33), daughters Ethel Iams (age 14) and Lena Iams (age 10); and also living in Washington County, Pennsylvania, with 3) W. R. Iams (age 56), as father-in-law, with Herman Garner. (CRI)

Charles "Charley" Iams (b. April 13, 1873, Center Township, Greene County, Pennsylvania; d. March 16, 1925, Washington, Pennsylvania), son of Benjamin Iams (b. 1839) and Mariah Scott (b. 1840); m. November 13, 1900, Washington, Pennsylvania, to Sarah Alberta Swart (b. December 29, 1881, Center Township; d. April 20, 1965, Washington, Pennsylvania; buried at Prosperity, Washington County, Pennsylvania), the daughter of John Thomas Swart and Sarah Elizabeth Luellen. The 1920 Federal Census of Washington County, Pennsylvania, lists: Charles Iams (age 40), wife Alberta Iams (age 38), Blanche Iams (age 16), John Iams (age 13), Mary Iams (age 10), son Ross Iams (age 7), and Ruth Iams (age 5). The children of Charles Iams (b. 1873) and Sarah "Alberta" Swart (b. 1881) are otherwise listed as:

1) Blanche Iams [(b. July 25, 1903, Amity, Washington County, Pennsylvania; d. January 13, 1931), m. Clarence Wells, Jr., and their daughter Sarah Margaret Wells (b. January 4, 1931, Washington, Pennsylvania) m. May 29, 1954, Washington, Pennsylvania, to Donald Roy Bell].

2) John Benjamin Iams [(b. July 27, 1906, Amity, Washington County, Pennsylvania; lived at Prosperity, Washington County; d. July 7, 1972, Washington, Pennsylvania), m. April 20, 1929, Pittsburgh, Allegheny County, Pennsylvania, to Catherine "Kathy" Mary Bell];

3) Mary "Margaret" Iams [(b. August 2, 1909, Amity, Washington County, Pennsylvania), m. Roland James Swart; lived in Florida; had six children: a) Margaret Jean Swart (b. July 7, 1929, Washington County, Pennsylvania; m. August 21, 1948, to Albert Dale Irey); b) Elizabeth Blanche Swart (b. November 9, 1930, Niles, Trumball County, Ohio; m. October 8, 1952, Winchester, Virginia, to Dorsey Wade Moats); c) Duane Thomas Swart (b. November 26, 1932; Greene County, Pennsylvania; m. November 14, 1952, to Mary Lee Hughes); d) James Howard Swart (b. December 20, 1934, Greene County, Pennsylvania; m. December 7, 1963, Bethany Presbyterian Church, to Mary Lou Cherry); e)

Ruth Ann Swart (b. December 7, 1941, West Finley Township, Washington County, Pennsylvania; m. Mr. Finney); and f) Ralph Charles Swart (b. September 27, 1943, West Finley Township, Washington County, Pennsylvania; to Nancy Evelyn Moniger)].

4) Ross Charles Iams [(b. June 8, 1912, Amity, Washington County, Pennsylvania; d. September 16, 1980, Washington, Pennsylvania), m. January 12, 1937, to Mabel Pauline Long, and their children were: a) Susan Jane Iams (m. Thomas Schereck); b) stepdaughter Geraldine Iams (m. Bryan Wells; and c) Leanna Iams (m. Pat Napolitan)].

5) Ruth Elizabeth Iams, m. September 29, 1937, to Kenneth Guy Mankey (b. May 4, 1913, Amity, Washington County, Pennsylvania), son of Warren Mankey and Aline Berdine Huffman; and their four children were: a) James Charles Mankey (b. September 29, 1941; m. Karen Eleanor Ashcraft); b) Kenneth Edward Mankey (b. May 6, 1943; m. Paulette Elaine Hickman); c) Susan Ruth Mankey (b. June 18, 1944; m. Paul Lamar Hiestana); and d) Gene Allen Mankey (b. January 29, 1951; m. Rita Karen Shaler)].

6) Martha Marie Iams (b. May 20, 1921, South Franklin Township, Washington County, Pennsylvania; d. 2 days later).

7) Sarah Iams (m. Mr. Bell).

In addition, Duane Thomas Swart (b. November 26, 1932, Greene County, Pennsylvania), son of Mary Margaret Iams (b. 1909) and Roland James Swart; m. November 14, 1952, to Mary Lee Hughes, daughter of Charles Hughes and Ruby Sprowls; they had six children: 1) Thomas Swart (m. Kathy ____; child: Betty Swart); 2) John Swart; 3) Ronnie Swart (m. Mary Watkins; 3 children); 4) Mary Jane Swart (m. Tim Mounts; children: Timmy Mounts, and a daughter); 5) Jean Swart (m. October 1989); and 6) Kenny Swart. (CRI)

John Benjamin Iams (b. July 27, 1906, Amity, Washington County, Pennsylvania; d. July 7, 1972, Washington County, Pennsylvania, son of Charles Iams (b. 1873) and Sarah Alberta Swart (b. 1881); m. April 20, 1929, Pittsburgh, Allegheny County, Pennsylvania, to Kathryn (or Catherine) Mary Bell (b. April 5, 1907, Waynesburg, Greene County, Pennsylvania; d. August 27, 1947, Washington, Pennsylvania), daughter of Alonzo Robert Bell and Lucy Hook Kent (daughter of Spencer B. Kent and Elizabeth Jacobs), and sister of Lucy K. Bell, Mrs. Betty Sharp, Kent R. Bell, and Harold R. Bell. The eight children of John Benjamin Iams (b. 1906) were:

1) Charles Robert Iams [(b. April 13, 1931, South Franklin Township, Washington County, Pennsylvania; lived at New Stanton, Pennsylvania; compiled family tree; m. Jeanne Marie Augustine Palmer (b. February 2, 1933, Geispolsheim, Bas Rhin, Alsace, France), daughter of Laurent Arthur Palmer and Marie Elise Richmann; and they had three children: a) Cynthia Clarisse Elisabeth Iams (b. June 23, 1955, Strasbourg, Bas Rhin, Alsace, France; m. June 2, 1979, Meridian, Butler County, Pennsylvania, to Kenneth Earl Pate, son of Ernest Walton Pate, Sr., and Martha Frances Teachery; and their three children were: Heather Renee Pate, b. June 14, 1986, Kitanning, Armstrong County, Pennsylvania; Danielle Nicole Pate, b. June 7, 1987, Kitanning; and Brittany Milisa Pate, b. May 20, 1989, Kitanning); b) Michelle Nadine Iams (b. August 30, 1967, Pittsburgh; m. May 5, 1988, Salt Lake City, Utah, to Stephen Irl Beechcroft, b. January 8, 1963, Richland, Washington; and their son, Matthew Charles Iams, b. June 29, 1992, Centre

Community Hospital; and c) Lisa Charlene Iams (b. April 17, 1969, Mount Lebanon, Pennsylvania; m. September 1, 1990, Kensington, Montgomery County, Maryland, to Jay Whitney Roberts (b. September 8, 1965, Texas), and their daughter Callianne Elise Roberts, b. April 16, 1993, Farmers Branch, Dallas, Texas].

2) Patricia "Patsy" Ruth Iams (b. September 14, 1932, Washington, Pennsylvania; m. May 1, 1954, to Leo Walter Reichert).

3) Nancy Alberta Iams (b. April 29, 1934, Washington, Pennsylvania; m. 1st, November 5, 1953, Bethel, Washington County, Pennsylvania, to Roy Milton Clovis; m. 2nd, Mr. Valentine).

4) Vernon Lou Iams (b. July 18, 1935, Washington, Pennsylvania, m. 1st, on June 6, 1952, to Robert D. McVay, son of Elisha McVay and Evelyn Knestrick; m. 2nd, November 9, 1955, to James Irvin Pritchard, Jr.

5) Kent Edward Iams (b. December 11, 1936, South Franklin Township, Washington County, Pennsylvania; d, before 1972).

6) Helen Margaret Iams (b. November 12, 1941, Washington County; m. 1st, James Cesky; m. 2nd, Mr. Hemebrick).

7) Betty Kaye Iams (b. April 28, 1943, Washington, Pennsylvania; m. 1st, on July 1, 1960, to Elmer Theodore Cutter; m. 2nd, Mr. Bock).

8) Mildred Ellen Iams (b. October 28, 1946, Washington, Pennsylvania; d. October 28, 1946). (CRI, LBK)

REFERENCES

- (HWN) Harry Wright Newman, *Anne Arundel Gentry* (Maryland, 1933, 1970).

- (LIH) Lois Ijams Hartman, Pasadena, California; personal files.

- (EFB) Ervin F. Bickley, Jr.; personal files and correspondence.

- (REI) Robert Elton Iams, Seattle, Washington; personal correspondence.

- (FEW) F. E. Wright, 1993.

- (MI) Michael P. Iams, Phoenix, Arizona; personal files.

- (CSP) Mrs. Stan J. (Carol Susan) Paprocki, Columbus, Ohio.

- (CWH) Carmen White Harleston, Washington, District of Columbia.

- (HI) Reverend Harold Imes, Mifflintown, Juniata County, Pennsylvania.

- (SB) Stanley Gene Braxton and Virginia Atwell Braxton, Wynnewood, Pennsylvania.

- (KC) *History of Knox County, Ohio* (1890), pp. 449-450.

- (JLS) Janice L. Shart, 23654 Brecklin Road, Definace, Ohio.

- (JFI) John Frederick Iams, Poway, California; personal correspondence.

- (CRI) Charles R. "Chuck" Iams, New Stanton, Pennsylvania; personal works.

- (WH) Reverend William Hannah, p. 201, Greene County, Pennsylvania.

- (GB) Gertrude Burnham; personal communications.

- (LBK) Lois Banks Kent: *Thomas Kent (1748-1835) and His Descendants* (Baltimore, Maryland: Gateway Press, 1995), p. 284.

— CHAPTER 3 —

GEORGE IIAMS

(B. 1676, MARYLAND; D. MARYLAND)

The family of George Iiams (b. 1676) and Elizabeth Basford, Anne Arundel and Prince Georges County, Maryland, whose offspring moved to North Carolina and points beyond.

George Iiams (b. 1676, South River, Anne Arundel County, Maryland; d. 1763, Maryland), the son of Pioneer William Eyams and Elizabeth Cheyney, m. Elizabeth Basford, daughter of Thomas Basford, and they had eight children (HWN): 1) John Iiams (b. November 18, 1725, Anne Arundel County, Maryland; d. Queen Anne Parish, Prince Georges County, Maryland), m. Ariana Worthington; 2) Willliam Iiams (b. December 22, 1723; christened All Hallow's Parish, Anne Arundel County, Maryland, January 18, 1723; d. November 15, 1780, Anne Arundel County, Maryland; m. 1st, Elizabeth ____; m. 2nd, widow Anne Williams, daughter of his Uncle William Iiams; no children); 3) George Iiams, Jr. (baptized 1718, Anne Arundel County, Maryland); 4) Elizabeth Iiams (baptized July 28, 1717, Anne Arundel County, Maryland) 5) Susannah Iiams (m. Mr. Welch); 6) Jacob Iiams (youngest son, swore allegiance to State of Maryland 1778; had a son named William Iiams); 7) Samuel Iiams (baptized February 23, 1721, but birth also given as September 18, 1725; m. February 4, 1779, to Mary Ratcliff); and 8) Mary Iiams (christened August 4, 1728, Anne Arundel County, Maryland).

Contributions to this branch of the Iiams family were provided through the works of Harry Wright Newman, Lois Ijams Hartman, Ervin F. Bickley, Jr., Roberta Iiames, F. E. Wright, Janet Carpenter, Inez Ijames, Morgan Cass Ijames, James Ijames, William A. Ijames, Henry C. Peden; *International Genealogical Index*, and federal census records. FEW also lists the following as being offspring of George Iiams (b. 1676): Elizabeth Ferguson Ijams (illegitimate daughter of Margaret Iiams, b. October 15, 1772); Charity Ijams (m. John Waters); Elizabeth Ijams (m. Benjamin H. Scott); Mary Ijams (m. Richard Wright, December 22, 1726); and Thomas Ijams (m. Ann Neal, November 12, 1780).

George Ijams (b. 1676) received 100 acres of land on the south side of Western Run, Anne Arundel County, Maryland, in the 1703 will of his father, William Iiams. In 1718, he purchased 100 acres termed Bright Seal from James Carroll; later deeding 50 of these acres at the head of the South River and branch of the Patuxent River, November 26, 1751, to his son George Iiams, Jr., and 50 of these acres on June 5, 1752, to son William Iiams. On March 20, 1735, he sold land inherited from his father, Iiams Choice, to Thomas Clark. in his will written September 30, 1745, probated in Anne Arundel County, Maryland, August 12, 1763, he indicated that sons William and George, Jr., should make a Payment of £10 to his son Jacob; the will also provided that his daughters Mary and Susannah should be given equal portions of the personal estate. Not named in his will were children Elizabeth, Samuel, and John. George Iiams, Jr. (b. March 22, 1718) was a bricklayer.

Son William Iiams (b. 1723) m. 2nd, his first cousin Anne Iiams, daughter of William (b. 1670) and Elizabeth Plummer Iiams, and then widow of Richard Williams, Jr. William Iiams (b. 1723) purchased land called Hickory Hills March 11, 1773, from Stockett Williams, and left the land to William Welch in his will; sold his portion of Bright Seal March 26, 1774, to John Conway. In his will, May 11, 1780, William Iiams (b. 1723) left wearing apparel and negro Sam to his brother, Jacob Iiams; negro Priscilla and her two children to Benjamin Williams' daughter Margaret; a negro girl, a cow, a calf, and £500 money to Mrs. Sarah Collins; stallions to Henry Hall's son Edward; and the remaining horses were to be auctioned off, with proceeds divided among William Welch, Edward Holt, and Avis Day-Smith.

John Iiams (b. November 18, 1725, Anne Arundel County, Maryland) m. March or April 1758, to Ariana Worthington-Watkins, daughter of Thomas and Elizabeth Ridgely Worthington, and widow of Nicholas Watkins (whose estate was finally closed March 17, 1761). In 1778, John Iiams (b. 1725) swore allegiance to the State of Maryland, and moved from Anne Arundel County, to Queen Anne Parish in Prince Georges County, Maryland, where he spent his remaining days. On March 23, 1758, as administrator of the estate of her late husband, Ariana Worthington-Watkins deeded the estate to her children, Nicholas Watkins, Jr., John Watkins, and Gassaway Watkins. This transaction also included the 300-acre plantation known as Worthington's Range.

Other children of Ariana Worthington and Nicholas Watkins included: 1) Margaret Watkins (m. 1st, Benedict Dorsey, son of Thomas and Mary Marfield Dorsey; and m. 2nd, Basil Gaither, whose son Nathan Gaither was in the Kentucky Constitutional Convention); 2) Thomas Watkins (became High Sheriff of Anne Arundel County, Maryland; and 3) Elizabeth Watkins. Ariana Worthington-Watkins m. 2nd, John Iiams (b. 1725) and they had six children. John Iiams (b. 1725) is listed in *DAR Patriot Index* (p.1,561, Part 2). Ariana Worthington Watkins Iiams preceeded John Iiams in death, and the death of John Iiams in 1789 resulted in letters of administration being issued to Singleton Wooten, also listed as the largest creditor, with no distribution of the estate made to any heirs in the final account filed by Mr. Wooten on February 7, 1789.

Children of John (b. 1725) and Ariana Worthington Iams were: 1) Vachel Ijams (b. January 1759 in Anne Arundel County, Maryland; served in the American Revolution; d. February 20, 1833, in Lauderdale County, Alabama; m. 1st, Lilah Gaither; m. 2nd, September 19, 1791, Rowan County, North Carolina, to Martha Cunningham; listed below; 2) Brice W. Ijams (b. Anne Arundel County, Maryland; d. Rowan County, North Carolina; m. 1st, March 31, 1803, in Rowan County, to Betsy Anderson; m. 2nd, Polly Smoot; had several daughters and two sons: James Monroe Ijams and William Ijams); 3) Ariana Ijams (b. August 16, 1778, Anne Arundel County, Maryland; d. 1803, Rowan County, North Carolina.); 4) Beale Ijams (b. February 8, 1767, or 1765, in Anne Arundel County, Maryland; m. April 4, 1791, Rowan County, North Carolina), to Elizabeth Little, b. 1770; d. June 25, 1841, 1848, or 1855, Rowan County, North Carolina; listed below; 5) Denton Ijams (m. January 22, 1856, to Margaret E. Wyatt; listed at Edenton, Rowan County, North Carolina, 1790 census, as age 16, with one free white female); and 6) Nicholas W. Ijams (m. Mary ____, who d. 1831, in Davidson County, North Carolina).

Brice W. Ijams, second listed child above, is listed in the 1810 Federal Census of Rowan County, North Carolina, as being between ages 26 and 45, with a female age 16 to 26, a female under age 10, a male under age 10, and one slave. James Munroe Ijams, said to be a son of Brice W. Ijams (b. May 4, 1843, North Carolina); was a Confederate soldier who was in the 5th Carolina Infantry, was captured, later moved to Kansas, and served as the Honorary President of the National Iams Association at age 89, being elected at the 2nd Annual Reunion, Washington, Pennsylvania, on August 27, 1932.

Ariana Ijams Hendron (b. 1778) wrote her will August 13, 1803, as widow Hendron, and named daughter Sally Hendron, daughter Peggy Hendron, son Beele W. Hendron, half-sister Margaret Gaither, half-sister Elizabeth Gaither, brother Sachiel Ijam, and brother Beal Ijam, with Sachiel Ijames as executor, and Basil Gaither, Mary Johnson, and Brice Gaither as witnesses.

Beale Ijams (b. Anne Arundel County, Maryland, February 8, 1767; moved to North Carolina 1781; died Rowan County, North Carolina, July 6, 1855, or 1858), m. Elizabeth Little, April 4, 1791, Rowan County, North Carolina). Elizabeth Little was b. 1770; d. Rowan County, North Carolina, June 25, 1848. Beale Ijams (b. 1767) initially Moved to Iredell County, North Carolina., but this area later became Rowan County, and then Davie County, North Carolina. Beale Ijams (b. 1767) settled near Mocksville, North Carolina. The 1850 Federal Census of Davies County, North Carolina, lists Beal Ijams, age 85, born in Maryland; in household with Matilda Ijames, age 54, and Denton Ijames, Constable, age 37. The 1800 Census of Rowan County, North Carolina had listed Beal Ijams, age 26 to 45, with a female age 26 to 45, 2 males under age 10, and 4 females under age 10. The 1810 Rowan County Census listed Beal Ijams as age 27 to 45, with a female in same age group, 2 males 16 to 26, 1 male under age 10, 3 females age 10 to 16, and 3 females under age 10. The 1830 Rowan County, North Carolina. Census lists Beal/Bruel Ijames as age 50 to 60, a female 50 to 60, a male age 10 to 15, 2 females age 20 to 30, 1 female age 30 to 40, and 1 male slave.

Children of Beale Ijams (b. 1767) and Elizabeth Little were: 1) William Little Ijames (b. Rowan County, North Carolina, January 16, 1792; d. St. Clair County, Mo, February 20, 1864; m. Caty Hanes, February 15, 1812, Rowan County, North Carolina; m. Mary Leonard, June 25, 1831, Davidson County, North Carolina; moved to Kentucky and then to Missouri; 2) John Beale Worthington Ijames (b. May 5, 1793, Rowan County, North Carolina; Moved to Missouri); 3) Ariana Worthington Ijames (b. January 3, 1795); 4) Matilda E. Ijames (b. August 18, 1796, Rowan County, North Carolina; alive 1850); 5) Sarah/Ann Ijames (b. 1798, Rowan County, North Carolina; m. April 23, 1821, Rowan County, to Daniel Levengood; or m. September 18, 1822, Davie County, North Carolina, to Isaac Athon; or m. March 8, 1832, Rowan County, North Carolina, to Wilburn Stonestreet, or to Mr. Beck); 6) Nancy Ijames (b. October 30, 1800, Rowan County, North Carolina; d. October 1805, Rowan County); 7) Jane Bell Ijames (b. January 17, 1803, Rowan County, North Carolina; m. Mr. Smith); 8) Elizabeth Ijames (b. November 20, 1804, Rowan County, North Carolina; d. February 4, 1845); 9) Beal Ijames (b. May 1, 1809; d. September 6, 1888; m. Rachel Clary/Clara Locke, b. 1814; d. 1871); and 10) Denton Ijames (b. September 15, 1811, Rowan County, North Carolina; d. January 9, 1882 or 1892; m. Margaret Coon.

Beal Ijames (b. May 1, 1809; d. September 6, 1888), son of Beale Ijams (b. 1767) above, m. Rachel Clara Locke (b. 1814). The 1880 Federal Census of Callaghan Township, Davie County, North Carolina, lists Beal Ijames as a 71-year-old white male born North Carolina, with daughter Bettie Ijames, age 33, b. North Carolina; son Robert L. Ijames, age 29, born North Carolina; daughter-in-law Margaret Ijames, age 36, b. North Carolina; son Joseph M. Ijames, age 23, b. North Carolina; and granddaughter Mary E. Ijames, age 1, b. North Carolina. The 1870 Census of Callaghan Township lists B. Ijams as a 61-year-old white male, farmer, b. North Carolina; with wife Clara R. Ijams, age 56, b. North Carolina; B. G. Ijams, age 26, b. North Carolina; Margaret A. Ijams, age 22, b. North Carolina; Mary M. Ijams, age 21, b. North Carolina; Robert S. Ijams, age 18, b. North Carolina; and Joseph Ijams, age 15, b. North Carolina.

There are several entries in the Davie County, North Carolina Will and Deed Book that mentioned Beal Ijames. Book 1 (p. 139, November 16, 1839) land was deeded from Daniel Casey to Beal Ijames, trustee, and Joseph W. Rice, for costs as Payment in the Case of the State of North Carolina versus David Casey, in "the bastardly charges for begetting a child in one Mary Swarthlander," based on the decision of Judge Andrew Sain. Fifty-seven acres were deeded from Matthew Locke to Beal Ijams for $300 (Volume 2, p. 309, October 30, 1843). Beal Ijams was given Power of Attorney to act on behalf of Isham Gaither of Iredell County (Volume 2, p. 468, January 27, 1846); the negroes of William F. Griffin, deceased, were divided among Beal Ijams, Wilford Turner, and N. M. Griffin (Volume 2, p. 597, 1846). There were land transfers to Beal Ijams for 126 acres, 156 acres, and 152 acres (Volume 3, pp. 17 and 29, December 24, 1847), and a purchase of 11 acres on Hunting Creek by Beal Ijams (Volume 3, p. 79, March 21, 1848). Also in the same county, James M. Ijams sold 28 acres to Henry Elder for one dollar to pay debts (Volume 1, p. 93, May 5, 1838); sold "personalty" to Newton Frost for one dollar to pay a debt (Volume 1, p. 342, 1850); and paid a debt of one dollar with "personalty" to H. R. Austin (Volume 2, p. 572, September 22, 1847).

Denton Ijames also appears on multiple occasions in these books: Was awarded 20 1/4 acres, resulting from being the highest bidder at a public sale held by Sheriff William B. March for payment of a debt of $18.75 recovered by Joseph Eaton, from Tillman Brogdan, with the sale price being $3.50 (Volume 2, p. 416, February 28, 1845); and Denton Ijams sold 20 acres on Hunting Creek, known as Beals Meeting Place, to John Smith for one hundred dollars (Volume 3, p. 388, February 8, 1848).

The nine children of Beal Ijames (b. 1809) and Rachel Clara Locke were: 1) Joseph Marion Ijames (b. 1855 or 1856, North Carolina; d. 1929; m. Margaret Wellman, b. 1848; d. 1904); 2) Robert L. "Shields" Ijames (b. 1850; d. 1930; m. July 16, 1875, Davie County, North Carolina, to Bell Anderson); 3) Mary "Molllie" Ijames (b. 1848; d. 1931; m. 1st, December 30, 1868, Davie County, North Carolina, to Wilson Hunt; m. 2nd, July 7, 1872, or December 23, 1873, Davie County, North Carolina, to James E. Sain, b. 1847; d. 1933); 4) Betty Margaret Ann Ijames (b. 1846, North Carolina; d. 1931 or 1935; m. July 7 or 25, 1972, to Taylor Gray); 5) Basil Gaither Ijames (b. 1844 or 1845; d. 1934; a Confederate soldier; m. December 12, 1871, to Dorie Alice Brown, b. 1852, d. 1928); 6) Matthew Berry Ijames (b. 1842, a Confederate soldier); 7) James D. Ijames (b. 1841, d. 1887; m. November 19, 1861, Davie County, North Carolina, to Mary E. Coon, b. 1838; d. 1917; a Confederate soldier); 3) Beal Rowan Ijames (b. 1832; d. 1898; m. December 20, 1860, Davie County, North Carolina, to Matilda Jane Coon, b. 1834; d. 1913); and 9) John A. Ijames (b. 1835, a Union soldier).

Joseph Marion Ijames (b. 1855), son of Beal Ijames (b. 1809), m. Margaret Wellman (b. 1848). The 1900 Federal Census of Calahan Township, Davie County, North Carolina, lists Joseph M. Ijames, age 44, b. August 1855, in North Carolina; wife Maggie M. Ijames, age 51, b. August 1848, North Carolina; daughter Mary L. Ijames, age 21, b. May 1879, North Carolina; son William L. Ijames, age 19, b. June 1880, North Carolina; daughter Maggie C. Ijames, age 12, b. October 1887, North Carolina; son John C. Ijames, age 14, b. July 1885, North Carolina; and sister Margaret A. Ijames, age 53, b. November 1846, North Carolina. The 1910 Census of Davie County lists a Marion Ijames, age 56, b. North Carolina; wife Emley C. Ijames, age 50, b. North Carolina; and a stepson John Sink, age 14, b. North Carolina.

Joseph Marion Ijames (b. 1856) had as many as six children: 1) Margaret "Maggie" Ijames (b. 1887; m. H. B. Martin; lived in Salisbury, North Carolina; 2) John L. Ijames (b. 1885; m. Nell Blaylock; lived in Cooleemee, North Carolina; with

John Ijames listed by Social Security as b. July 11, 1885; d. October 10, 1973); 3) Jerry Lucio Ijames (b. 1884; d. 1968; m. Pearl Koontz; b. 1889; d. 1938; lived in Cooleemee, North Carolina; had four children); 4) Sarah Ijames (b. 1881; d. 1950; m. William Billie Powell; lived in Statesville, North Carolina; 5) Mary E. Ijames (b. 1879; d. 1964; m. Carl Strand; lived in Lexington, North Carolina); and 6) William L. Ijames (b. 1880; d. 1919; m. Rose Wells). The 1910 Federal Census of Pitt County, North Carolina, lists a William Imes, age 30, b. North Carolina; with wife Lula Imes, age 31, b. North Carolina; stepdaughter Sudie Pollard, age 13; and stepdaughter Lizie Pollard, age 9, b. North Carolina.

Jerry Lucio Ijames (b. 1884), son of Joseph Marion Ijames (b. 1856), m. Pearl Koontz; with Social Security records giving birth date as January 22, 1884, in North Carolina, and death date as April 1968 in North Carolina. The 1900 Federal Census of Calaghan Township, Davie County, North Carolina, lists Jerry Ijames as age 37, b. North Carolina, with wife Pearl Ijames, age 29, b. North Carolina; daughter Margaret, age 6, b. North Carolina; son Glenn Ijames, age 3, b. North Carolina; and brother-in-law John Kontz, age 43, b. North Carolina.

Jerry Lucio Ijames (b. 1884) had four children: 1) Jerry L. Ijames (b. 1929; m. Edgar McDaniel, b. 1927; had a child: Lou Ann McDaniel, b. 1956); 2) Glenn A. Ijames (b. 1916; m. Hazel Smith, b. September 16, 1916; d. March 1975; had four children); 3) Margaret Ijames (b. 1913; m. Roy Alexander, b. 1914; had two children: Roy F. Alexander, b. 1944; m. Brenda ____; and Margaret Alexander (b. and d. 1940); and 4) Ralph Ijames (b. 1912; d. 1918).

Glenn A. Ijames (b. July 24, 1916), son of Jerry Lucio Ijames (b. 1884), m. Hazel Smith (b. 1916), and they had four children: 1) Richard Lucio Ijames (b. 1950; m. Betty Randall; their child: Diana Ijames); 2) Patricia Ijames (b. 1949; m. Wayne Bray; their child: Amy Bray); 3) James W. Ijames (b. 1940; m. Mary Thompson, b. 1940; prepared part of this George Ijames family line); and 4) Glenda Gladys Ijames (b. 1937; m. Thomas O'Neal; their children were: Julie O'Neal, Jennifer O'Neal, and Thomas O'Neal).

Denton Ijames (b. 1811; d. 1888), the son of Beale Ijames (b. 1767) and Elizabeth Little Ijames, m. Mary Coon (IGI lists marriage to Margaret E. Wyatt, January 22, 1856, Mocksville, Davie County, North Carolina). The 1870 Census of Calahan Township, Davie County, North Carolina, lists Denton Ijams as age 58, b. North Carolina; wife Margaret Ijams, age 44, b. North Carolina; daughter Mary J. Ijams, age 13, b. North Carolina; daughter Betty B. Ijams, age 12, b. North Carolina; son Morgan C. Ijams, age 10, b. North Carolina; and daughter Emma L. Ijams, age 8, b. North Carolina.

Denton Ijames (b. 1811) and Mary Coon had four children: 1) Mary J. Iiams (b. 1857, m. Mr. Leach); 2) Betty B. Iiams (b. 1859; m. Barney Castle); 3) Emma L. Iiams (b. 1862; m. James C. Booc); and 4) Morgan Cass Iiams (b. 1860; d. 1935; m. Nannie Powell; had six children; prepared this portion of the family tree). The six children of Morgan Cass Iiams were: a) Rosa/Rose Cleave Iiams (b. 1893; lived in Merced, Calif.); b) Elias Denton Iiams (b. 1896); c) Marma Duke Iiams (b. 1897); d) Augie Inez Iiams (b. 1901; m. Stacy Chapin); e) Walter Lewis Iiams (b. 1908); and f) Sabia Jane Iiams (b. 1911; m. Mr. Thorpe). The 1900 Federal Census, Calahan Township, Davie County, North Carolina listed Morgan P. Ijames, age 40; b. March 1860, North Carolina; wife Ninnie E. Ijames, age 30; b. August 1869, North Carolina; son Ross C. Ijames, age 7, b. February 1893; son Cline D. Ijames, age 4, b. March 1896, North Carolina; son Marma Duke Ijames, age 2, b. July 1898, North Carolina; and mother Margaret E. Ijames, age 74, b. January 1826, North Carolina.The 1920 Census of Mocksville Township, Davie County, North Carolina, lists M. C. Ijames, age

56, b. North Carolina; wife N. E. Ijames, age 49, b. North Carolina; son Denton E. Ijames, age 25, b. North Carolina; son Dirke M. Ijames, age 22, b. North Carolina; daughter Inez Ijames, age 18, b. North Carolina; son W. L. Ijames, age 10, b. North Carolina; and daughter Seba Jane Ijames, age 8, b. North Carolina. Social Security records give birth date of Elias Ijames as March 25, 1896, North Carolina, with death of May 1969 in North Carolina; and Marma Ijames as born June 13, 1897; d. October 1973, in South Carolina.

James D. Ijames (b. 1841; d. 1887), the son of Beal Ijames (b. 1809) and Rachel Clay Locke, m. November 19, 1861, in Davie County, North Carolina, to Mary E. Coon (b. 1838, North Carolina; d. 1917) and had eight children: 1) James G. Ijames (b. 1867, North Carolina); 2) Beal S. Ijames (b. 1867, North Carolina); 3) Adelia "Bell" Ijames (b. 1869, North Carolina); 4) Cora L. Ijames (b. 1873, North Carolina); 5) George F. Ijames (b. 1876, North Carolina); 6) Emma M. Ijames (b. 1879, North Carolina); 7) Clara A. Ijames (b. 1864, North Carolina); and 8) Garland Ijames (b. 1866, North Carolina). The 1900 Federal Census of Farmington Township, Davie County, North Carolina, lists Garlin Ijames, age 35, b. March 1865, North Carolina; wife Florence Ijames, age 33, b. November 1866, North Carolina; daughter Carrie Ijames, age 10, b. March 1890, North Carolina; son Horace Ijames, age 7, b. June 1893, North Carolina; daughter Mattie Ijames, age 6, b. November 1894, North Carolina; and daughter Dora Ijames, age 1, b. October 1898, North Carolina. The 1880 Federal Census of Jerusalem Township, Davie County, North Carolina listed James Ijames, age 39, b. North Carolina; wife Mary E. Ijames, 41, b. North Carolina; James G. Ijames, age 16, b. North Carolina; Beal S. Ijames, age 13, b. North Carolina; Adelia Ijames, age 10, b. North Carolina; Cora L. Ijames, age 7, b. North Carolina; George F. Ijames, age 4, b. North Carolina; and Emma A. Ijames, age 1, b. North Carolina. The 1870 Federal Census of Callaghan Township, Davie County, North Carolina, listed James Ijames, age 29, farmer; wife Mary Ijames, age 28; daughter Clara A. Ijames, age 6; son Garland Ijames, age 4; son Beal Ijames, age 2; daughter Bell, age 9 months; and Mary Ijames, a 14-year-old black female. In an account by J. D. Wall, on April 11, 1865, James Ijames was working in the fields, reportedly supervising former slaves, when he was confronted and threatened by members of General Stoneman's (Union) Raiders during the close of the Civil War (Lee surrendered at Appomattox April 9, 1865). After he was placed against a tree, the former slaves were able to convince the Union soldiers that they were working on a voluntary basis so James Ijames was released.

Basil Gaither Ijames (b. 1845, North Carolina; d. 1934), son of Beal Ijames (b. 1809), m. Dorie Alice Brown (b. 1852; d. 1928); was a Confederate soldier; they had six children: two infants d. early; one sister m. Willliam Click; one son m. _____ Smoot and lived in Cooleemee, North Carolina; Frank Ijames lived in High Point, North Carolina; and son Boone Ijames lived in New Jersey.

John A. Ijams (b. 1835), a Union soldier and son of Beal Ijames (b. 1809) had nine children: 1) John B. Ijames (b. 1871, Maryland; lived in St. Louis, Mo.; 2) a daughter became Mrs. Wist Connors and lived in East St. Louis, Illinois; 3) Beall Ijames lived in Doniphon, Missouri; 4) Gailand Ijames, d. single; 5) a daughter became Mrs. William Walls and lived in Mocksville, North Carolina; 6) James Ijames; 7) Glen Ijames, lived in High Point, North Carolina; 8) George Ijames, lived in Thomasville, North Carolina; and 9) a daughter became Mrs. Gaither Lathem.

Beall Rowan Ijames (b. 1832; d. 1898), son of Beal Ijames (b. 1809); m. 1860 to Matilda Jane Coon (b. 1834; d. 1913), and had four children: 1) John Iiams (b. 1862, North Carolina; m. Maggie Howard, had two children); 2) Allie Iiams (b. 1865, North Carolina; m. William Godfrey Click, had three children); 3) Josephine

Iiams (b. 1873, North Carolina; m. Mr. Wilson); and 4) Robert Marion Iiams (b. 1869, North Carolina; d. 1934), m. Louise E. Cartner). The 1880 Federal Census of Jerusalem Township, Davie County, North Carolina lists Beal R. Ijames, age 43, b. North Carolina; wife Matilda J. Ijames, age 42, b. North Carolina; son John N. Ijames, age 18, b. North Carolina; and daughter Josephine Ijames, age 7, b. North Carolina. The 1900 Federal Census of Mocksville, Davie County, North Carolina, lists Jane Ijames, age 64, b. July 1836, North Carolina; daughter Allie Ijames, age 34, b. December 1864, North Carolina; son-in-law William G., age 43, b. North Carolina; grandson Eugene C., age 11, b. North Carolina; and granddaughter Elva N., age 6, b. North Carolina.

Allie Iiams (b. 1865, North Carolina), daughter of Beall Rowan Ijames (b. 1832) and Matilda Jane Coon, m. William Godfrey Click; had three children: 1) Clarence Eugene Click (b. September 1888, North Carolina); 2) Elva Neely Click [(b. December 1893, North Carolina), m. A. B. Ramsey and they had two children: a) Charles William Ramsey (b. 1933; m. Anne Hyatt; had four children: Rita Marie Ramsey, b. 1957; Charles Ronald Ramsey, b. 1958; Tina Robin Ramsey, b. 1959; and William Roger Ramsey, b. 1963); and b) Ann Neely Ramsey (b. 1934; m. Ted Cole; had two children: Andrea Michele Cole, b. 1960; and Michael Bradford Cole, b. 1961)]; and 3) Rowan Fletcher Click.

John (H. or N.) Iiams (b. 1862), son of Beall Rowan Ijames (b. 1832), m. Maggie Howard and they had two children: 1) John Howard Iiams (b. 1904, North Carolina); and 2) Galene/Gelene Iiams [(b. 1897, North Carolina), m. H. C. Lane, and had child Henry Clay Lane (m. Rose Emma Oates), who had three children: Henry Clay Lane III, Brenda Galene/Gelene Lane, and Gilbert Oates Lane)]. The 1900 Federal Census of North Main Street, Mocksville, Davie County, North Carolina, lists John M. Ijames, age 37, b. January 1863, North Carolina; wife Maggie L. Ijames, age 34, b. March 1866, North Carolina; with no children. The 1920 Federal Census of Davie County, North Carolina, lists John Ijames, age 57, b. North Carolina; with daughter Galene Ijames, age 22, b. North Carolina; and son Howard Ijames, age 16, b. North Carolina.

Robert Marion Iiams (b. 1869; d. 1934), son of Beal Rowan Ijames (b. 1832), m. Louise E. Cartner, and they had five children: 1) Clyde H. Iiams (b. 1894; d. 1942; m. Ruth Stenhouse); 2) Ivey Iiams (b. 1897; m. J. Frank Miller, b. 1890; d. 1948; and had four children; 3) William Beall Iiams (b. 1901); 4) Herman Iiams [(b. December 31, 1903; d. August 1970, North Carolina), m. Clara Swain (b. 1908), and had two children: a) Jane Carol Iiams (b. 1934, m. Eaton Betts, had daughter Deborah Jane Betts, b. 1953); and b) Marion Iiams Betts (b. 1936; m. Albert Arrington, and had two children: Steven Lee Arrington, b. 1954; and Timothy David Arrington, b. 1954)]; and 5) Inez Iiams [(b. 1906; d. 1943), m. Mr. Bowles, and their child was Rachel Bowles (b. 1943)].

Clyde H. Iiams (b. 1894; d. 1942), son of Robert Marion Iiams (b. 1869) and Louise E. Cartner, m. Ruth Stenhouse, and they had six children: 1) Clyde H. Iiams, Jr. [(b. 1917), m. Catherine Hubbard, and they had three children: a) Peggy Iiams (m. Harold Walker); b) Ruby May Iiams (m. Grady Farmer); and c) Ruth Patricia Iiams (m. Bruce McDade)]; 2) Ruth Geraldine Iiams (b. 1919); 3) Carolyn Louise Iiams [(b. 1921), m. Walter F. Johnston, and they had six children: a) Emily Louise Johnston; b) Richard Thomas Johnston, a twin; c) William Lawrence Johnston, a twin; d) Anne Marie Johnston; e) Jean Carol Johnston; and f) Bruce Norris Johnston, d. at birth)]; 4) Norris G. Iiams (m. Helen Rickey, and their child was Helen Patricia Iiams); 5) William Cartner Iiams (m. Doris King, and they had three children: Barbara Diane Iiams, Susan Elaine Iiams, and William Cartner Iiams, Jr.); and 6) Robert S. Iiams [(b. 1929), m. Gloria Lanier, and they had two children: Robert Kent Iiams and Kelly Louise Iiams]. Social Security Administration records list Ruth Ijames as b. November 1, 1893; and died in South Carolina in November 1975.

Inez Iiams (b. 1897), daughter of Robert Marion Iiams (b. 1869), m. J. Frank Miller (b. 1890; d. 1948), and had four children: 1) Janet Elizabeth Miller [(b. 1916); m. Albert Carpenter and had four children: a) Robert David Carpenter (b. 1941; m. Dortha "Scotty" Stewart, and their child was Krista Kay Carpenter, b. 1965); b) Perry Albert Carpenter (b. 1944; m. Charlene "Deenie" Blackburn, and their child was Marion Michelle Carpenter, b. 1966); c) Janet Carol Carpenter (b. 1949); and d) Linda Susan Carpenter (b. 1954)]; 2) Robert Luther Miller [(b. 1931), m. Ruth Bernhardt, and their three children were: a) Elizabeth Gail Miller (b. 1947); b) Paula Karen Miller (b. 1950; m. Stanley McConnell); and c) Marion Franklin Miller (b. 1951)]; 3) Donald Franklin Miller (b. October 1924); and 4) Rebecca Anne Miller [(b. 1929), m. Norman Warlick, and their four children were: a) David Franklin Warlick (b. 1952); b) Donald Emory Warlick (b. 1954); c) Richard Dennis Warlick (b. 1957); and d) Dennis Clifton Warlick (b. 1965)]. This branch of the family history was compiled by Janet Carpenter (b. 1949).

William Iiams (b. December 22, 1723, All Hallows Parish, Anne Arundel County, Maryland; d. 1780), son of George Iiams (d. 1763) and Elizabeth Bashford; m. 1st, Elizabeth ____; m. 2nd, in 1770, to widow Anne Williams. William Iiams (b. 1723) was deeded 50 acres from his father and later purchased the matching 50 acres from his brother, George Iiams, Jr. (baptized 1718). On June 23, 1769, he paid his mother, Elizabeth Bashford Iiams, the sum of £10 for her dower rights for this plantation, called Bright Seal. By 1764 he had married a woman named Elizabeth, and in 1770 married Anne Williams, widow of Richard Williams, Jr., the daughter of William Iiams (b. 1670) and Elizabeth Plummer. William Iiams (b. 1723) and George Iiams, Sr. (d. 1733) were brothers.

William Iiams (b. 1723) had been the executor for the estate of Richard Williams, Jr. (written March 2, 1769; probated in Anne Arundel County, Maryland, on February 26, 1770). In the filing of the estate of Richard Williams, Sr., May 22, 1771, named children included: Richard Williams, Jr. (deceased), Eleanor Linthicum, Mary Brewer, Priscilla Welch, Elizabeth Linthicum, and Sarah Richardson. Also listed as sons of Richard Williams, Jr., were: Richard Williams III, Joseph Williams, and Stockett Williams. William Iiams (b. 1723) purchased land called Hickory Hills from Stockett Williams for £388 on March 11, 1773. William Iiams (b. 1723) and his brother Samuel Iiams (b. 1721) sold the 100-acre plantation Bright Seal to John Conway for £254.

The final will of William Iiams (b. 1723) was written February 11 (or May 11), 1780, Anne Arundel County, Maryland, and probated there November 15, 1780 (TG No. 1, p. 9). Since his wife Anne Williams Iiams was not named in the will, she had presumably died between 1774 and 1780. Named in the will were brother Jacob Iiams; William Iiams, son of brother Jacob Iiams; Benjamin and Comfort Williams and their daughter Margaret Williams; and William Welch, son of Priscilla Welch. Nephew William Welch, an executor, was given the plantation dwelling, and Edward Hall was also named as an executor. The estate of William Iiams (b. 1723) was appraised at £552 and 6 pence on January 16, 1781, including "14 negroe slaves," eight pictures and old books; and an additional inventory listed four more slaves appraised at £156, 4 shillings, and 10 pence. A final account of the estate was filed on August 24, 1785, and reported a balance of £316 and 1 shilling. No children were listed for William Iiams (b. 1723).

Vachel Ijams (b. January 1759, Anne Arundel County, Maryland; d. January 20, 1833, Laureldale County, Alabama), son of John Ijams (b. 1725) and Ariana

Worthington, m. 1st, 1789, Rowan County, North Carolina to Lilah Gaither; and m. 2nd, September 19, 1791, to Martha "Mary" Cunningham. Lilah Martha Gaither (1st wife) was a daughter of Basil (b. 1757) and Margaret Watkins Gaither. Vachel Ijams has the distinction of serving in the American Revolution, the Flying Camp, serving at a fort in Annapolis, and discharged about December 18, 1776, though that discharge record was later lost. In August 1777 he enlisted in Colonel Dorsey's Maryland Line Regiment, serving under Captain Brogden, and served under General Smallwood in the Battle of Germantown, Pennsylvania, and discharged at White Marsh, Pennsylvania, in October 1777. He moved with his father and family from Anne Arundel County to Prince Georges County, Maryland, between 1777 and 1781. He served five months in the Militia of Prince Georges County, Maryland, from July 1781 to December 1781, but contracted a fever and was first furloughed to his father's farm, then discharged on December 11, 1781. Within the next six months he had moved to Rowan County, North Carolina and there enlisted in Captain Sharp's Company of the 18th North Carolina Regiment commanded by Colonel Lyter. He was discharged in 1783 at the rank of sergeant near Charleston, South Carolina, returning to his home in Rowan County. He was married briefly in 1789 to Lilah Gaither, but after her death married again in 1791 to Martha Cunningham, daughter of Joseph Cunningham, Sr., who later died and left the family land to Martha Cunningham Ijams. Vachel Ijams (b. 1759) and his wife sold 174 1/2 acres of that land to Lawrence Clement in February 1823, and moved to Tennessee for one year before moving on to Lauderdale County, Alabama.

Vachel Ijams (b. 1759) applied for a Revolutionary War pension from Alabama on August 2, 1832, but died January 20, 1833, before it was approved. His will, written February 18, 1832, and probated March 25, 1833, left the home plantation to wife Martha (joint-owned with Samuel C. Ijams); the mare to John D. Ijams, son of Joseph Ijams; and also named eight children, including: Joseph Ijams, Pearson Ijams, Burgess Ijams, Basil Ijams, Wilson Ijams, Anne Ijams, Elizabeth Ijams Herrondean, and Peggy Ijams Edwards. Also named was son-in-law David C. Clannaugh. Vachel Ijams (b. 1759) was buried in a private cemetery near Florence, Alabama. Widow Martha Cunningham Ijams died in 1838.

Eight children of Vachel Ijams (b. 1759) were: 1) Joseph Ijams (m. Elizabeth Baxter; bond filed February 5, 1820, Rowan County, North Carolina); 2) Basil Gaither Ijams (b. August 23, 1801, Rowan County, North Carolina; d. Texas; m. November 12, 1829, to Catherine Woodward, b. April 1, 1812, and they had nine children); 3) Burgess Ijams (b. August 23, 1801, Mocksville, Davie County, North Carolina; m. Catherine Woodward—see note); 4) Wilson Ijams (served as Captain, Second Mississippi Infantry during the Mexican War, and died March 31, 1849, in Marshall County, Mississippi); 5) Pearson Ijams (d. March 4, 1847, in Texas); 6) Nancy Ijams (m. 1st, May 1848 to Ephraim Bolton, who died February 10, 1858; and m. 2nd, David C. Clannaugh); 7) Elizabeth Ijams (m. Mr. Hernden); and 8) Margaret Ijams (m. Mr. Edwards). Rowan County, North Carolina records also show a marriage between Nancy Ijams and John Cicell, December 18, 1812. Family records have recorded the family offspring of Basil Ijams that is nearly identical to the offspring of Burgess Ijams gathered from the IGI and from HWN (1970).

Vachel Ijams (b. 1759) had a Revolutionary War Claim Number S-32337, making an appearance at court in Lauderdale County in Northwestern Georgia, at age 72 or 73, on August 2, 1832. That testimony listed each of his four enlistments. In 1781 he enlisted in Prince Georges County, Maryland, as a substitute in the 4th Regiment under Frenchman LaVah, later commanded by Major Oxborough and Colonel Adams. In Rowan County, North Carolina he also enlisted as a substitute, serving in the 10th Regiment indicated above from July 1782 to July 7, 1783. Son Joseph Ijams, Esquire, wrote letters that are recorded in the Revolutionary War Claims file in 1853 and 1854. Son Wilson Ijams was also said to be a lawyer. The 1810 Federal Census of Rowan County, North Carolina, lists Vachel Ijams as being over age 45; with a female age 26 to 45; one male age 10 to 16; three males under age 10; two females ages 10 to 16; and two females under age 10. The 1830 Federal Census of Rowan County, North Carolina, lists Vatchell Ijams as age over 70, with one male age 60 to 70; two males 50 to 60, one male 30 to 40; one male 15 to 20; one male 10 to 15; 3 males under age 5; and 3 females under age 10.

Basil Gaither Ijams (b. August 23, 1801, Rowan County, now Davie County, North Carolina; d. April 28, 1881, in Michigan or Texas), son of Vachel Ijams (b. 1759) and Martha Cunningham; m. November 12, 1829, in Tennessee, to Catherine Martha Woodward (b. April 1, 1812). Basil Gaither Ijams (b. 1801) had moved to Tennessee by the time of his marriage, but moved to Mississippi in 1831, and in 1850 was living in Tishomingo County, Mississippi. His wife Catharine Woodward Ijams d. July 9, 1896.

Children of Basil Gaither Ijams are listed (family records) as: 1) Vachel M. Ijams [(b. September 30, 1830, in Tennessee; killed in Battle of Helena, Arkansas, July 4, 1864); m. January 6, 1853, to Martha Smith (b. December 15, 1834; d. March 28, 1916), and their son Calvin Taylor Ijams m. Emma Yowt. The child of Calvin Taylor Ijams listed as William A. Ijams (graduated from college in 1900 and went to "Indian Territory," being in Oklahoma at the time of annexation. He returned to Mississippi in 1933, and his son William C. Ijams lived at 3708 NW 28th Street, Oklahoma City, dying at age 56 on September 2, 1965. He had moved to Oklahoma City in 1932 and was sales manager and attorney for the George Townsent Company, a graduate of Oklahoma State University Law School, a 32nd degree Mason; his daughter Barbara Ijams m. Howard R. Sullivan, and they had three sons: Mike Sullivan, Pat Sullivan, and Tim Sullivan)]; 2) Charlotte E. Ijams (b. June 11, 1833, Mississippi; m. December 14, 1852, to J. C. Potts); 3) Benton C. Ijams (b. July 13, 1836; d. December 21, 1875; m. January 26, 1862, to L. C. Burley); 4) Nancy Ann Ijams (b. August 21, 1839; m. A. L. Boon); 5) Gilbert L. Ijams (b. February 10, 1842; m. February 28, 1867, to E. S. Atkins); 6) Joseph C. Ijams (b. May 26, 1844); 7) Louise Clementine Ijams (b. March 6, 1847; m. March 31, 1867, in McMairy County, Tennessee, to M. C. Walker); 8) Mary Catherine Ijams (b. November 22, 1849; d. November 7, 1886; m. Sam. T. Chambers, b. December 23, 1879); and 9) George Allison Ijams (b. June 14, 1852; d. June 13, 1862, of typhoid fever).

Burgess Ijams (b. August 23, 1801, Rowan County, North Carolina; d. April 28, 1881, Tishomingo County, Mississippi), son of Vachel Ijams (b. 1759), m. November 12, 1829, in Tennessee, to Catherine Woodward (b. April 1, 1812, Tennessee; d. July 9, 1896). The 1850 Census of Tishomingo County, Mississippi, lists Burgess Ijams with Vachel Ijams, age 19; Charlotte Ijams, age 16; Benton Ijams, age 14; Nancy Ijams, age 12; Gilbert Ijams, age 9; Joseph Ijams, age 7; Louise Ijams, age 3; and Mary Ijams, age 1. Listed children (see above) of Burgess Ijams (b. 1801) include: 1) Vachel M. Ijams (b. September 30, 1830, Tennessee; killed at Battle of Helena, Arkansas, June 4, 1864); m. January 6, 1853, to Martha Smith (b. December 15, 1834; d. March 28, 1916); 2) Charlotte E. Ijams (b. June 11, 1833, Tishomingo County, Mississippi; m. December 14, 1852, to J. C. Potts); 3) Benton C. Ijams (b. Tishomingo County, Mississippi, July 13, 1836; d. December 2, 1875; m. L. C. Bundy on January 26, 1862); 4) Nancy Ann Ijams (b. Tishomingo County, Mississippi, August 21, 1839; m. January 15, 18__, to A. L. Boon); 5) Gilbert L. Ijams (b. Tishomingo County, Mississippi, Febraury 10, 1842; m. February 28, 1867, to E. S.

Atkins, and lived in Marshall, Saline County, Missouri); 6) Joseph C. Ijams (b. Tishomingo County, Mississippi, May 26, 1844); 7) Louise Clementine Ijams (b. Tishomingo County, Mississippi, March 6, 1847; m. McMairy County, Tennessee, March 31, 1867, to M. C. Walker; lived in Marshall, Saline County, Missouri); 8) Mary Catherine Ijams (b. Tishomingo, Mississippi, November 22, 1849; d. November 7, 1886; m. December 23, 1879, to Sam T. Chambers); and 9) George Allison Ijams (b. Tishomingo County, Mississippi, June 14, 1852; d. June 13, 1862, of a febrile illness).

CHAPTER 4

JOHN IJAMS

(B. 1712, MARYLAND; D. MARYLAND)

John Ijams (b. 1712), the son of William Iiams and Elizabeth Plummer, married Rebecca Jones; was known as Captain John Ijams; they had eight children: Elizabeth, Anne, Mary, William (moved to Fairfield County, Ohio), Isaac Plummer (moved to Ohio), Thomas Plummer (moved to Ohio), John (lived in Maryland), and Rebecca. Offspring moved to Indiana, Nebraska, Iowa, Michigan, Kansas, Oregon, California, Canada, Arizona, Utah, Illinois, Oklahoma, Missouri, Minnesota, North Carolina, and elsewhere.

John Ijams, a son of William Iiams and Elizabeth Plummer, was born at Bridge Hill, Anne Arundel County, Maryland, in 1712. He was christened in All Hallows Parish, Anne Arundel County, Maryland, August 6, 1718; died in Anne Arundel County, Maryland, in 1783; married Rebecca Jones (b. 1712 or 1730; d. 1783 or 1811), daughter of Isaac Jones. John Iiams (b. 1712) was a captain in Provincial Militia at the time of the Revolutionary War, and was given the land of his birth, Bridge Hill, located next to Dodon in Anne Arundel County, Maryland. Records show that he was nominated for the rank of ensign in 1776. By 1742, he had become a member of the prestigious South River Club in Anne Arundel County. This exclusive club was organized in 1740, and 1742 was the first year that records were kept. He was probably a charter member of this club that remains in existence. Membership is limited to twenty-five members, and membership criteria is blood relationship to a prior member. Meetings have been held four times annually.

After the death of Isaac Jones, father of Rebecca Jones, his 800-acre plantation was deeded to Thomas Gibbs, Anne Arundel County, Maryland, on June 23, 1776, with the administration efforts of heirs Captain John Iiams, Rebecca Jones Iiams, Thomas Watkins, wife Elizabeth Watkins, and Mary Jones.

John Iiams (b. 1712) became a merchant of South River, and the first family member to become wealthy. This line of the family is claimed by noted author Lois Ijams Hartman and others. John Iiams (b. 1712) was also reported to be a warden in All Hallows Parish, and to have taken the Oath of Allegiance on March 1, 1778. In 1775, with others, he wrote a petition denying that "tumultous meetings" or "cavaling among negroes" and "misbehavior of Roman Catholics" had been taking place. On July 28, 1744, John Iiams (b. 1712) paid £45 for the 45 acres of Dodon, a tract of land that had been laid out for Plummer Iiams from Stephen Warman of Anne Arundel County. John Iiams (b. 1712) wrote his will in Anne Arundel County, Maryland, October 9, 1782, with witnesses Plummer Iiams, John Iiams (son of Plummer), Joseph Williams, and Christian Parrott. The will was probated April 21, 1783, in Anne Arundel County. Distributions of the estate included £5 each to daughters Elizabeth Lyons and Ann Stockett; 20 shillings to John Ijams and Rebecca Ijams, children of Mary Ijams; negroes to oldest son William Ijams; negroes to son-in-law Thomas

Iiams; negroes to son John Iiams; negroes to son Isaac Plummer Iiams; negroes to son Thomas Plummer Iiams; the plantation to widow Rebecca Jones Iiams, with the plantation to go to minor sons Isaac and Thomas after her death, or to eldest son William Iiams should both Isaac Iiams and Thomas Iiams die without issue. The wife/widow Rebecca Jones Iiams was the executor.

The inventory was filed under the name Captain Iiams and was appraised at £415, 15 shillings, and 2 pence, with Isaac Ijams and Ann Stockett signing as next of kin. There were twelve negroes listed. The horse and Primrose went to son Isaac Iiams. The final estate was filed August 24, 1785, by widow Rebecca Jones Iiams and son John Ijams. The amount of £348, 10 shillings, and 1 pence was distributed to the heirs, and it was written that two cows and sheep had been lost "by the severe winter."

Three of the sons were pioneers in a migration to Fairfield County, Ohio. Sons William Iiams, Isaac Iiams, and Thomas Plummer Iiams were well established in Richland Township, Fairfield County, Ohio, by 1806. Early Fairfield County records list William Iiams, William Iiams, Jr., Isaac Iiams, and Thomas Iiams. The widow Rebecca Jones Iiams moved to Frederick County, Maryland, where some of the children, including Thomas Plummer Ijams, had moved. The will of widow Rebecca Jones Iiams was dated February 12, 1822, and was probated in Frederick County, Maryland (Book RB-1-261). She willed one dollar, and no more, to sons John Iiams, Isaac Iiams, and Thomas Iiams. Legacies were willed to her daughter Elizabeth Fenly, to son William Iiams, and to Elizabeth Iiams, wife of her son Isaac Ijams. Beers (1893) reports John Iams as having been from New Jersey and as owning nearly 1,000 acres in Washington County, Pennsylvania, but the origin of this information is not known. The 1790 Federal Census of Frederick County, Maryland, lists as heads of households: John Ijams, Plummer Ijams, and Richard Ijams. Registered voters for the 1796 presidential election in Frederick County listed: John Ijams, Richard Ijams, Thomas Ijams, and Thomas Ijams, Jr. Revolutionary War pensions to Ijams of Maryland included: John Ijams (to widow Mary Ijams, Frederick County); Vachel Ijams (living in North Carolina, Claim S-32337); and Thomas Ijams (Claim S-8751).

Eight children of Captain John Iiams (b. 1712) and Rebecca Jones are: 1) Elizabeth Ijams (b. 1749, Anne Arundel County; d. April 21, 1783; m. 1st, Mr. Lyons; m. 2nd, Robert Fenlon); 2) Anne Ijams (b. 1751, Anne Arundel County, Maryland; m. June 12, 1762, at All Hallows Parish, Anne Arundel County, to Lewis Stockett); 3) Mary Ijams (b. 1757; m. 1774, to Thomas Iiams, a first cousin and son of Thomas and Elizabeth Imes, whose son John Ijams (b. 1775, was a captain at Fort McHenry in the War of 1812, who m. Rachel Marriott; and whose daughter Rebecca Ijams, b. 1777, Anne Arundel County, m. M. J. Marriott); 4) William Ijams (b. 1760 or 1753 in Anne Arundel County, Maryland; d. 1815 or 1816 in Fairfield County, Ohio; m. in Maryland to Elizabeth Howard; moved to near Rushville, Richland Township, Fairfield County, Ohio, by 1806 with their son William Iiams, Jr.); 5) Isaac Plummer Ijams (b. 1765; d. 1825 in Fairfield County, Ohio; m. August 4, 1795, in Prince Georges County, Maryland, to Elizabeth Beck, widow of William Beck; they moved to Fairfield County, Ohio; the line of Lois Ijams Hartman; 6) Thomas Plummer Ijams (b. April 4, 1773, Anne Arundel County, Maryland; d. August 16, 1847, Muskingum County, Ohio; m. 1st, February 10, 1794, Frederick County, Maryland, to Sarah Duvall; m. 2nd, Mrs. Elizabeth Manley; moved to Fairfield County, Ohio; lived at Hopewell, Muskingum County, Ohio); 7) John Ijams, Jr. (b. 1755, Anne Arundel County, Maryland; d. 1823; m. March 21, 1782, Frederick County, Maryland, to Mary Waters); 8) Rebecca (or Margaret) Ijams, m. Thomas Sunderland.

Frederick County, Maryland, documents include: 1) will of John Ijames, May 5, 1823, with Jacob Ijams, executor, Liber H53, Folio 123; 2) will of Plummer

Ijams, February 23, 1795, with John Ijams, executor; lists children Anna Ijams, Plummer Ijams, Ruth Ijams, Rebecca Ijams, and John Ijams; 3) will of Richard Ijams, Jr., written October 8, 1800; proven November 7, 1800; lists son Thomas Ijams, daughter Nancy Ijams, and Amelia Fisher as daughter of William Ijams (Liber GM 3, folio 414); and 4) a deed statement declared that John Ijams and wife Harriet Ijams of Fairfield County, Ohio, sold their Frederick County, Maryland, land to Thomas Anderson for five dollars; the land had been a gift to Harriet Ijams from her grandfather; exception to the sale was the tobacco on the land which was to go to Joseph H. Ijams, an attorney in Frederick County, Maryland; written and filed May 19, 1823 (Liber JS-18, folio 113).

Fairfield County, Ohio, tax lists include: 1) Isaac Ijams (1800, 1809, 1829, 1838); 2) William Ijams (1800, 1809-1819, 1833-1838); 3) Thomas Plummer Ijams (1809, 1813-1819); 4) Joseph Ijams (1820-1838); 5) Frederick Ijams (1820-1825, 1828); 6) Catherine Ijams (1820-1828); and 7) John Ijams (1820-1828, 1832-1838). The 1830 Federal Census of Fairfield County, Ohio, lists five Ijams as heads of households: 1) Elizabeth Ijams (widow of Isaac, age 60-70, with one male 30-40, 2 males 20-30, and one female 10-15); 2) Catherine Ijams (widow of William, Jr., age 50-60, with one male 15-20); 3) Isaac H. Ijams (age 30-40, with a female 30-40, one male 20-30, and one female 10-15); 4) Joseph H. Ijams (age 30-40, with a female 20-30, and one female 15-20); and 5) William H. Ijams (age 20-30, with a female 20-30, one male under 5, and one female under 5). Fairfield County, Ohio, land records include: 1) sale of a lot in West Rushville from John Ijams, Jr., and wife Harriet, to John Whistler (1818 Vol. M, p. 434); 2) sale of land by John Ijams and wife Ann (Volume L, p. 378); 3) 1824-1843 land records listing John Ijams, Jr., Isaac Ijams, John Iiams, Joseph H. Iiams, F. R. Iiams, William Iiams, John Iiams and wife Elizabeth, Joseph Iiams and wife Mary A., Isaac H. Iiams, and William H. Iiams.

Perry County, Ohio (formed 1817 from Fairfield, Muskingum, and Washington Counties) tax lists include: 1) John Ijams (1828-1838); 2) Joseph H. Ijams (1828-1838); 3) John H. Ijams (1830-1834); 4) William Ijams (1834, 1838); and 5) Isaac H. Ijams (1834-1838). Perry County, Ohio, land deeds include: 1) Sarah Ijams of Fairfield County, Ohio, provided with a land grant (President Monroe) in Section 4 of Perry County, May 13, 1817; 2) Isaac Ijams, Private, Lanabas Company, 3rd Regiment, Infantry, given an Army land grant (President Monroe) on May 6, 1812, Warrant number 12434, 160 acres in Missouri Military Territory (Section 36, Township 56, Range 16), but he sold this 160 acres in Chariton County, Missouri, to William Crest, February 8, 1823 (Isaac Ijams, Jr., and wife Elizabeth); 3) John Ijams, Jr., sold land in Rehoboth, May 13, 1830; 4) John Ijams sold land to the Literary Society of Saint Joseph (lots 18 and 19) to build a Roman Catholic church in Rehoboth (April 5, 1832); 5) John and Mary S. Ijams sold land in Rehoboth to Joseph H. Ijams of Fairfield County (March 30, 1833); 6) John Ijams and William Ijams of Perry County, Ohio, sold land in Rehoboth (July 26, 1837); 7) John and wife Sarah A. Ijams, and William Ijams of Perry County sold land July 28, 1838; 8) John Ijams, Sr., and wife Sarah Ann Ijams of Perry County sold several parcels of land to William Ijams of Perry County, Ohio, August 21, 1841; 9) William Ijams sold Perry County, Ohio, land to John Ijams, December 28, 1841; 10) John and wife Sarah Ann Ijams of Perry County, Ohio, sold several parcels (Rehoboth in Ohio, and 80 acres in Blackford, Indiana) to William Ijams of Perry County, Ohio (May 4, 1842); 11) John and Sarah Ann Ijams sold 98 acres in Perry County, Ohio, to Isaac H. Ijams, July 20, 1843; and 12) John Ijams of Buchanan County, Missouri, sold land in both Rehoboth, Perry County, Ohio, and Blackford County, Indiana, to John Waters of Baltimore on January 21, 1845.

William Ijams (b. 1760 or 1753, Maryland; d. February 1816, Fairfield County, Ohio) was the fourth child and the first son of Captain John Ijams (b. 1712) and Rebecca Jones; m. Elizabeth Howard (b. 1758, Maryland; d. 1835, St. Louis, Missouri); moved to Fairfield County, Ohio, between 1800 and 1810, and lived near Rushville where he farmed and raised tobacco. Some moved to Walton, Indiana; and Elizabeth Howard-Ijams m. 2nd, U. S. Army Major Whisler, St. Louis, Missouri. Elizabeth Howard (b. 1758) was the daughter of Joseph Howard and Rachel Ridgely. William Iiams took the Oath of Allegiance in Maryland March 1, 1778. William Ijams (b. 1760) is buried at West Rushville, Fairfield County, Ohio; his will was written December 27, 1815, Fairfield County, and named son William Ijams, son John Ijams, son Isaac Ijams, son Joseph Ijams, son Frederick Ijams, grandson Richard Ijams (son of his son William Ijams), daughters (no names), with wife as co-administrator with William Wiseman, and with Isaac Ijams, Peter Black, and John Sunderland as witnesses. The eleven children of William Ijams (b. 1760) and Elizabeth Howard were:

1) William Howard Ijams [(b. Fairfield County, Ohio, September 27, 1807; d. August 16, 1894); m. 1st, March 8, 1831, Fairfield County, Ohio, to Mary Chappell, (b. 1808; d. April 10, 1840); m. 2nd, November 25, 1841, Lancaster, Fairfield County, Ohio, to Ann Elizabeth Beall (b. July 6, 1819; d. August 2, 1899, Cass County, Indiana), or b. 1780, Maryland; d. 1820, Fairfield County, Ohio; m. June 20, 1805, Fairfield County, Ohio, to Catherine Ruffner, widow of Peter Ruffner)].

2) John Howard Ijams [(b. 1783, Maryland; d. 1857, Noble County, Ohio, buried Sarahsville Cemetery); m. 1st, 1807, Providence Gassoway, who d. 1815; m. 2nd, November 3, 1815, Perry County, Ohio, Harriet H. Owings; m. 3rd, November 15, 1832, Mary S. Brown (b. 1807; d. May 25, 1837, Rehoboth, Perry County, Ohio); and m. 4th, May 3, 1838, Perry County, Ohio, to Sarah Ann Jasper].

3) Rebecca Ijams (b. 1782; m. 1799 William Wiseman; no children).

4) Rachel Iiams (b. 1784; m. James Turner, August 5, 1802; lived in Fairfield County, Ohio).

5) Mary Iiams (b. 1788, Maryland; m. November 29, 1804, to Walter Teal).

6) Comfort Iiams (b. 1792, Washington County, Maryland; d. 1824); m. Edward Stevenson.

7) Isaac Howard Iiams (b. 1794, Washington County, Maryland; d. 1845, Perry County, Ohio; m. October 5, 1817, Muskingum County, Ohio, to Mrs. Elizabeth Koontz).

8) Joseph Howard Iiams (b. 1797, Washington County, Maryland; lived in Perry County, Ohio; m. September 21, 1828, to first cousin Mary Ann Ijams, daughter of John Ijams; moved to Iowa; d. Iowa City).

9) Sarah Howard Iiams (b. October 6, 1798, Washington County, Maryland; d. February 12, 1829; m. January 25, 1818, to John Jay Jackson).

10) Frederick Rodger Ijams (b. 1800, Washington County, Maryland; single; on Fairfield County, Ohio tax lists of 1820-1825; named in 1845 will of brother Isaac H. Ijams; listed 1850 Federal Census of Union Township, Morgan County, Ohio, as single, age 45, b. Maryland, living with James B. Glassford family).

11) Richard Daniel Ijams [(b. July 12, 1811, Fairfield County, Ohio; d. December 1, 1880, Walton, Indiana); m. October 25, 1838, Fairfield County, Ohio, to Jane E. Alford (b. November 23, 1816, Pennsylvania; d. December 30, 1894, near Walton, Cass County, Indiana)]; and possibly:

12) John Ijams, Sr. (b. 1783, Maryland; d. 1857, Noble County, Ohio; or in Missouri); m. 1st, Mary Waters; m. 2nd, Mary S. Brown; m. 3rd, Sarah

Ann Jasper or Harriet H. Owings)].
13) Thomas Ijams (m. Sarah Duvall).
14) Elizabeth Ijams (m. Robert Fenley).
15) Ann Ijams (m. Louis Stockett; children: John Ijams, William Ijams, Rebecca Ijams, and Ann Ijams).
William Howard Ijams (b. 1807) may have had as many as 16 children:
  a) Jane Elizabeth Ijams [(m. Jacob Dean; their daughter was Christine Dean; they lived near Lancaster, Fairfield County, Ohio); b. December 22, 1828, Fairfield County, Ohio; her first husband may have been Jacob Ivan, m. December 2, 1847)].
  b) William W. "Howard" Ijams [(b. December 1829, Fairfield County, Ohio; d. March 13, 1896, Wayne Township, Muskingum County, Ohio), m. 1st, Harriet Sims, d. 1881 at Fultonsville, Ohio; m. 2nd, March 8, 1884, Rebecca Shiplett, d. April 28, 1937; Private, Company E, 160 Regiment of Ohio Volunteers, May 2, 1864, to September 7, 1864; a merchant; killed on the railroad; d. age 64; discharged from Army with rheumatism, heart disease, right-sided rupture, and piles; Civil War claim made by widow Rebecca Ijams, age 55, of Zanesville, Ohio, and granted February 27, 1892, with widow previously married to Delaney Shiplett on January 11, 1854)].
  c) Samuel J. Ijams (b. July 12, 1832, Fairfield County, Ohio; d. February 16, 1835).
  d) Mary Mathilda Ijams [(b. March 24, 1834, Fairfield County, Ohio; d. 1903, Cass County, Indiana); m. Arthur J. Small (b. 1834; d. 1904); child: Edward Small; family Bible held by Jenny Kay, granddaughter].
  e) Sarah Catherine Ijams (b. September 10, 1837, Fairfield County, Ohio; d. November 17, 1851).
  f) Margaret Ann Ijams [(b. March 24, 1840, Fairfield County, Ohio; d. Walton, Indiana); m. 1st, May 22, 1856, to George Bowyer, son of Washington Lafayette Bowyer of Virginia (b. October 14, 1827); m. 2nd, Joseph Wilson and lived at Idaville, Indiana; they had three children: Washington L. Small, Edward F. Small, and Otho A. Small].
  g) Thomas Howard Ijams [(first child of Ann Beall, daughter of Thomas Beall and Elizabeth Ijams, daughter of Isaac Ijams and Elizabeth Beck Williams); (b. October 1, 1842, Rushville, Ohio; d. February 24, 1896, Grants Pass, Oregon); m. August 19, 1866, Martha Louise Webster (b. April 24, 1843; d. April 3, 1924); their two children were: Louise Ijams (b. April 9, 1868; m. March 7, 1892, to John Milton Orr; and their son John Howard Orr, b. December 12, 1894, m. Lucille Whiting); and Myrtle Ijams (b. April 22, 1872; wrote part of family history; m. December 18, 1895, to Andrew Sydney Hamilton); was Colonel, Company K, 9th Indiana Volunteer Infantry; enlisted as Private and discharged October 1865 as Captain; served in battles of Shiloh, Corinth, Murfeesboro, Chicamauga, Chattanooga, Lookout Mountain, Missionary Ridge, Kennesaw Mountain, Resaca, Peach Tree Creek, Atlanta, Jonesboro, Franklin, Nashville, and others; moved to Kansas City, Missouri, 1888; elected

38th Missouri Legislature; appointed Governor of Northwestern Branch of National Soldiers Home in 1916; returned to Kansas City and made Republican member of Civil Service Board in 1918; member of Fire and Water Board 1919-1921; founding member of GAR; Commander of Farragut Thomas Post, Number 8, from 1919 to 1922; member of Major William Warner's Camp Sons of Veterans; member of Army and Navy Union; honorary member of Spanish American War Veterans; member VFW; member of South Gate Masonic Lodge; died while visiting a daughter in Oregon and buried in family plot of Mount Washington Cemetery, Kansas City, Missouri)].

h) Frank Ijams; single.

i) Isaac Beall Ijams [(b. July 28, 1849, Lancaster County, Ohio; d. October 30, 1902, Walton, Indiana); m. Etta Bickle].

j) Clara E. Ijams [(b. 1860), m. J. W. Wood, lived Galveston, Indiana; had 7 children, including: Ethel Wood (m. Mr. Thomas, lived in Galveston, Indiana); Mabelle Wood, single; Clarence L. Wood (lived in Chicago, Illinois); Geneva Wood (m. Mr. Anderson, lived Veedersburg, Indiana); Mildred Wood (single); and Clara Wood (local family historian)].

k) George Ijams; single.

l) Millard Fillmore Ijams (m. 1st, Sarah Slagle; their son Charles Ijams d. Norfolk, Virginia, in 1931).

m) Åmira Ijams (d. infancy).

n) Lydia Elizabeth Beall Ijams [(b. June 19, 1857, Logansport, Indiana; d. August 1905, Fremont, Nebraska); m. 1st, John W. Chichester (d. 1876, after the birth of John W. Chichester, Jr., b. June 30, 1875, who became a construction foreman and lived at Lincoln, Nebraska, where he had four children; m. 2nd, in 1879 to John R. Smoot, a businessman, and in 1882 they moved from Indiana to Missouri Valley, Iowa, then in 1900 from Iowa to Nebraska, where they farmed and raised three more children: Ray Smoot (b. September 15, 1884, Missouri Valley, Iowa, and whose daughter Ailene Smoot lived in Grant, Nebraska); Roy Thomas Smoot (b. August 24, 1888, Missouri Valley, Iowa; lived at Grant, Pechino County, Nebraska; was World War I Corporal with 341 Machine Gun Battalion of 89th Division in Germany); and Ruth B. Smoot (b. September 8, 1895, Logan, Iowa; m. Emil W. Trojan and lived on large farm in Lehigh, Nebraska)].

EFB has listed the children of William "Howard" Iiams, Jr. (b. 1780; m. Catherine Ruffner) as:

1) Henry Iiams (b. 1809, Fairfield County, Ohio).

2) Richard Daniel Iiams [(b. 1811, Fairfield County, Ohio; d. December 2, 1880, Walton, Indiana); m. October 28, 1838, to Jane E. Alford (b. 1816; d. 1894), and had 8 children: a) William Henry Iiams (b. 1839, Fairfield County, Ohio; d. 1871, Indiana; m. Laura Bishop); b) Thomas Fielding Iiams (b. 1841, Fairfield County, Ohio; d. 1905, Indiana; m. Mary Agnes Jones; c) Daniel Worley Iams (b. 1845, Fairfield County, Ohio; d. 1910, Oregon; m. Virginia Harvey Nace); d) Mary Abigail Iiams (b. 1847, Fairfield County, Ohio; d. 1849, Fairfield County, Ohio); e) Mary Catherine Iiams (b. 1850, Fairfield County, Ohio; d. 1933, Texas; m.

110

James Boyd Burchard; had two children: William Franklin Burchard, b. 1875, Indiana; d. 1963, Texas; and R. Katharine Burchard); f) Laura Victoria Iiams (b. 1854, Cass County, Indiana; d. 1928, Indiana; m. James Monroe Webster); g) Bertha Iams (b. 1858, Cass County, Indiana; d. 1931, Indiana; m. 1st, William Yenna; m. 2nd, Ambrose Bigger); and h) Alford Iiams (b. and d. 1860, Cass County, Indiana)].

   3) William Howard Iiams [(b. 1807, Fairfield County, Ohio; d. 1894, Walton, Indiana); m. 1st, Mary Chappel, who d. 1840; m. 2nd, Ann Elizabeth Beall, and they had 13 children: a) Jane Elizabeth Iiams (b. 1827, Fairfield County, Ohio); b) William W. Iiams (b. 1829, Fairfield County, Ohio; d. 1896, Muskingum County, Ohio; m. 1st, Harriet Dean; m. 2nd, Rebecca Shiplett; c) Samuel J. Iiams (b. 1832, Fairfield County, Ohio); d) Mary Matilda Iiams (b. 1832, Fairfield County, Ohio; d. 1903, Cass County, Indiana); m. Andrew J. Small; e) Sarah Catherine Iiams (b. 1837, Fairfield County, Ohio; d. 1851); e) Margaret Ann Iiams (b. 1840, Fairfield County, Ohio; d. Walton, Indiana; m. 1st, George Bowyer; m. 2nd, Joseph Wilson); f) Thomas Howard Iiams (b. 1842, Fairfield County, Ohio; d. 1926; m. Martha Louise Webster); g) Franklin D. Iiams (b. 1846, Fairfield County, Ohio); h) George Washington Iiams (b. 1844; d. 1845, in Fairfield County, Ohio); i) Amira Iiams (b. 1848; d. 1848, Fairfield County, Ohio); j) Isaac Beall Iiams (b. 1849, Fairfield County, Ohio; d. 1902, Walton, Indiana; m. Etta Rickle); k) Millard Fillmore Iiams (b. 1851, Fairfield County, Ohio; d. 1881, Walton, Indiana); and l) Elizabeth Beall Iiams (b. 1857, Cass County, Indiana; d. 1905, Fremont, Nebraska; m. 1st, John W. Chichester; m. 2nd, Joseph R. Smoot)

   John Howard Iiams [(b. 1783; d. 1857, Noble County, Ohio, veteran of War of 1812; m. 1807 to Providence Gassoway; later m. Mary S. Bloom, and then m. Harriet Owings); and had at least five children: a) a daughter (b. 1824, Perry County, Ohio); b) Caroline Iiams (b. 1831, Perry County, Ohio); c) Louisa Iiams (b. 1838, Perry County, Ohio); d) William Howard Iiams (b. 1836, Perry County, Ohio; d. 1914, Osceola, Iowa; m. 1st, Mary Young; m. 2nd, Mable "Madge" Ijams; two children were: Louise Iiams, b. 1860, Noble County, Ohio, m. Mr. Landon; and Caroline Iiams, b. 1861; m. Mr. Klingenfeld); and e) a son].

   John Iiams [(b. 1783, Maryland; d. 1857, Noble County, Ohio; m. Mary S. Brown, Sarah Ann Jasper, then Harriet Owings Ijams), and had six children: 1) John Iiams, Jr. (b. 1836); 2) a daughter (b. 1837); 3) Clarinda or Cora Charity Iiams (b. 1843, Noble County, Ohio; m. Harrison Shaw); 4) William Iiams (b. 1844, Ohio); 5) Ann Mary Iiams (b. 1854, Ohio); and 6) Theodore J. Iiams (b. 1847, Monroe County, Ohio; d. 1923, Dayton, Ohio; m. Ellen "El" L. Young; and they had seven children: a) Pauline L. Iiams, b. 1874; d. 1875, Noble County, Ohio); b) John Howard Iiams (b. 1878, Noble County, Ohio; d. 1936, Zanesville, Ohio); c) Johanna Iiams (b. 1877; d. 1881, Noble County, Ohio); d) Mabel Young Iiams (b. 1880, Noble County, Ohio; d. Kokomo, Indiana; single); e) William J. Iiams (b. 1882, Noble County, Ohio; d. 1945, Columbus, Ohio; wife Alta M. ___); f) Sarah Jane Iiams (b. 1876; d. 1884, Noble County, Ohio); and g) Vera Iiams (b. 1887, Noble County, Ohio; m. Herman C. Smith)].

   William Ijams, Jr., (b. 1780, Maryland; d. 1820, Fairfield County, Ohio), the son of William Ijams (b. 1753, Maryland) and Elizabeth Howard, m. June 20, 1805, in Fairfield County, Ohio to Catherine Ruffner (b. 1785, Pennsylvania), who had been married previously to Peter Ruffner. The will of Peter Ruffner was filed in Fairfield County, Ohio, April 8, 1805. The Tax Lists of Fairfield County, Ohio, lists William Ijams until 1820, when widow Catherine Ijams was listed (until 1828). In the 1850 Federal Census of Fairfield County, Ohio, widow Catherine Ijams is age 65; born Pennsylvania, living in Fairfield County. She died later that year. Catherine Ijams was the executrix for the estate of William Ijams, Jr., with the will being filed in Fairfield County, Ohio, October 24, 1820. William Ijams, Jr. (b. 1780) and Catherine Ruffner had at least three children: 1) Henry Ijams (b. 1809, Fairfield County, Ohio; d. by 1830); 2) Richard Daniel Ijams [(b. July 12, 1811, Fairfield County, Ohio; d. December 1, 1880, Walton, Cass County, Indiana, and buried in Vernard Cemetery, Walton, Indiana); m. October 25, 1838, Fairfield County, Ohio, to Jane E. Alford (b. November 23, 1816, Pennsylvania; d. December 30, 1894, Walton, Indiana)]; and 3) William "Howard" Ijams [(b. September 27, 1807, Fairfield County, Ohio; d. August 16, 1894, Walton, Indiana; buried Onward Cemetery, Walton, Indiana; m. 1st, March 8, 1827, Glenford, Fairfield County, Ohio, to Mary Chappell (b. 1809; d. April 10, 1840; buried at Rushville, Ohio, cemetery; age 37 years, 7 months, and 7 days); and m. 2nd, November 25, 1851, at Lancaster, Fairfield County, Ohio, to Ann Elizabeth Beall (b. July 6, 1819; d. August 2, 1899, Cass County, Indiana, a cousin.

Richard Daniel Ijams (b. 1811; d. 1880), the son of William Ijams, Jr. (b. 1780) and Catherine Ruffner, m. October 25, 1838, Fairfield County, Ohio, to Jane E. Alford (b. 1816; d. 1894), and they had eight children. The 1850 Federal Census of Richland Township, Fairfield County, Ohio, lists R. D. Ijams (age 38, b. Ohio), J. E. Ijams (age 33, b. Pennsylvania), William H. Ijams (age 10, b. Ohio), Thomas F. Ijams (age 10, b. Ohio); D. Ijams (age 2, b. Ohio), and M. C. Ijams (age 2, b. Ohio). Civil War certificate number 267674 listed widow Jane Ijams as age 71 on July 5, 1888, living in Walton, Indiana. Richard Daniel Ijams was a Private, Company K, 9th Regiment of Indiana Volunteer Infantry, September 10, 1861. The Civil War claims of Richard Daniel Ijams (37628, W C 267674) were filed from Walton, Indiana, beginning June 11, 1866. The pension was approved March 1, 1890, retroactive to the date of the soldier's death of "December 1, 1880, for eight dollars a month." Civil War records show hospitalizations in January 1862 at Rigert Valley and Fetterman, West Virginia. He was at Nashville Barracks in April 1862 with chronic diarrhea and kidney disease and "remained poorly" after the war. He had enlisted at Logansport, Indiana, September 10, 1861; and records list the maiden name of his wife as Alford; he was discharged with disability on October 22, 1863, officially from Chattanooga, Tennessee, after several hospitalizations and home furloughs due to illness. His discharge physical examination listed him as age 40, height 69 inches, sandy complexion, blue eyes, brown hair, and a farmer. He rejoined his unit on September 23, 1863, just prior to his discharge.

Cass County, Indiana, records of Richard Daniel Ijams include: 1) Record No. 1, p. 120; October 19, 1865; Section 12, Township 5, North of Range 2E, 160 acres; paid one dollar for quit claim deed to Martin Ryan for land purchased from William J. Clark by Richard D. Ijams, William H. Ijams, and Daniel W. Ijams, September 16, 1865; sold November 9, 1865, by Richard D. and wife Jane E. Ijams; 2) Record No. Y, page 27, October 19, 1865; William H. Ijams of Cass County, Indiana, granted to Thomas F. Ijams, for the sum of $500, 70 acres in Section 2, Township 25, North of Range 2E, sold November 4, 1864; 3) Record V, page 449, February 16, 1862, Section 2, Township 25, Range 2E; Thomas A. E. McManus to William H. Ijams, et al; 4) Record IV, page 135, September 22, 1854; John M. McGrew to W. H. Ijams, Southeast quarter of Section 36, Township 26, Range 2E; and 5) Record M, page 397, September 23, 1854, to Peter Martin ut ux to William H. Ijams, Northeast quarter of Section 1, Township 25, Range 2E. The will of Richard Daniel Ijams (Volume 3, page 188, Cass County, Indiana) of December 2, 1880, mentions sons William H. Ijams, Thomas F. Ijams, Daniel W. Ijams, and granddaughter Olive

Ijams. The newspaper *Logansport Daily Reporter* of December 3, 1880, reported that R. D. Ijams, Jackson Township, died suddenly of valvular heart disease; that he had lived in Jackson Township for 25 years; and that he left a wife, two sons, and three daughters. The eight children of Richard Daniel Ijams (b. 1811) and Jane E. Alford (b. 1816) were:

1) William Henry Ijams [(b. September 21, 1839, Fairfield County, Ohio; d. January 12, 1871, at Walton, Cass County, Indiana); m. Laura H. Bishop (and their daughter Olive Ijams was b. May 19, 1858; d. March 4, 1931; lived at Logansport and at Anderson; m. 1st, Mr. Allison and m. 2nd, Mr. Williams)].

Richard Daniel Ijams (b. 1811) had a son William Henry Ijams who m. Laura H. Bishop (see above), and they had two children: 1) Leafy Levine Iams (d. infancy); and 2) Olive Iams [m. 1888 to Omri Everett Allison (d. 1912) in Walton, Indiana; and they had two children: a) Karl Leeborn Allison (b. 1899, was a mercantile businessman in Mount Pleasant, Iowa; m. December 25, 1912, to Lucy Early Turner, and they had four children: Jean Allison, d. infancy; Mary Ann Allison, b. 1916; Lucy Caroline Allison, b. 1918; and William James Allison, b. 1921); b) Charlotte Edna Allison (b. 1894; m. Everette John Ackerman on November 13, 1913, in Richmond, Indiana; lived in Richmond, Indiana; had four children: Eugenia Ackerman, d. infancy; Margarette Anne Ackerman, b. 1916; Thomas Fielding Ackerman, b. 1918; and John Allan Ackerman, b. 1929.

2) Thomas Fielding Ijams [(b. May 21, 1841, in Fairfield County, Ohio; d. March 25, 1905 or 1907, at Grove, Indiana), m. November 20, 1880, to Mary Agnes Jones in North Grove, Miami County, Indiana); was a Lieutenant in Civil War. After the war he first went to a college in Wisconsin, and then to Ann Arbor, Michigan, before returning to North Grove, Indiana, setting up a medical office. Civil War files SC 869,381 and 506682 show that he was a member of Company B, 142 Indiana Infantry, and Company K, 9th Indiana Infantry; a graduate of University of Michigan; had no living children on application dated May 4, 1898; had certificate of disability for discharge as a Private from Captain Casille's Company K, 9th Indiana Infantry, from Logansport, Indiana, at age 21. On physical examination on September 8, 1961, he was listed as 68 inches tall, dark complexion, and blue eyes. Because of sickness he was sent to a hospital near Corinth, Mississippi, but was discharged July 30, 1862 (by examination), and September 4, 1864 (official orders), with complaints of being off duty 27 days, having a cough with chest pains and copious sputum, six months of diarrhea, with a weak pulse and with pneumonia. On records of February 1884, he was age 42, having lived in Indiana, Kansas, and Michigan since discharge; was listed as a schoolteacher and as a physician; was affectionately called "Doctor T. F." He was mustered out of the Civil War September 28, 1865, at Camp Stanley, Texas, which reported him as scheduled for discharge with disability September 4, 1862, in Cincinnati, Ohio; but he later enlisted from October 12, 1864, to July 14, 1865, in Company B, 142 Indiana Volunteers, and later was awarded a pension of twelve dollars a month.

3) Daniel Worley Ijams [(b. December 4, 1845, Fairfield County, Ohio, the third son; d. January 6, 1910, Portland, Oregon or Kansas City); m. July 5, 1871, to Virginia "Jenny" Harvey Nance; (Civil War service as a Private

in 118th Regiment of Indiana Volunteers, from July 30, 1863, to May 5, 1864; and as a Corporal in the 111th Regiment of Indiana Infantry from January 23, 1865, to September 19, 1865, being discharged at Nashville, Tennessee; served in Battle of Shiloh and was in reserve lines at Gettysburg); and they had 6 children: a) Richard Lee Ijams (b. August 18, 1873; d. March 24, 1925, Los Angeles, California); b) Laura Ijams (b. August 11, 1879, Portland, Oregon; m. August 13, 1905, to Arthur Porteus Kerron; and their daughter Virginia Kerron was b. June 5, 1910); c) Ethel Ijams (b. August 25, 1881; m. December 5, 1923, to Ridgley C. Force; lived in Seattle, Washington); d) Daniel Leslie Ijams (b. December 29, 1884; served in Company D, 411th Telegraph Battalion, from May 6, 1917, to May 8, 1919, World War I; lived in Eugene Oregon; m. August 25, 1925, to Juda Truand; and their daughter Mary Lee Ijams was b. August 12, 1929); e) Russel Ijams (b. July 7, 1887; d. February 19, 1906, at San Francisco, California); and f) Virginia Evaline Ijams (b. June 30, 1891; m. January 16, 1916, to Joseph Barto, and they had three children: Robert Ijams Barto, b. February 2, 1917; Carolyn Race Barto, b. February 9, 1920; and Joseph Barto, Jr., b. October 17, 1921)].

4) Mary Abigail Ijams (b. August 15, 1846, Fairfield County, Ohio; d. June 14, 1849, Ohio).

5) Mary Catherine or Caroline Ijams [(b. July 1, 1850, Fairfield County, Ohio; d. September 6, 1933, Weatherford, Texas); m. July 15, 1872, James Boyd Burchard (b. 1850, Lincoln, Cass County, Indiana; d. Weathersford, Texas); six children: 1) Arthur Boyd Burchard (a stepson of Mary Catherine Ijams); 2) Lucien Burchard; 3) Lucien Burchard; 4) Monte Burchard; 5) William Franklin Burchard [(b. July 25, 1875, Indiana; d. December 14, 1963, Temple, Texas); m. June 28, 1905, to Mattie Pines; and they had three children: Ruby Katharine Burchard, Donald Reene Burchard, and Helen Patricia Burchard]; and 6) Ruby Burchard].

6) Laura Victoria Ijams [(b. April 24, 1854, Cass County, Indiana; d. 1928, Walton, Indiana); m. James Monroe Webster; one child: Dr. Cash J. Webster, a chiropractor who lived in Edmonton, Alberta, in 1968, at age 93, and who m. twice: first to a German lady, and second to a French Canadian, and had five children: Cash M. Webster, Marcel Webster, Veronica Webster (m. Maurice Brimstead), Margaret Webster (m. Mr. Stewart, and lived on a ranch at Kelorma, British Columbia); and Victoria Webster].

Another source: Laura Victoria Ijams [(d. 1928, Walton, Indiana), m. James Monroe Webster of Logansport, Indiana; and they had three children: a) an infant that died early; b) Clarence Webster (d. 1911); and c) Cassius Webster (a physician in Yorkton, Saskatchewan, Canada, whose wife was Theressa _____)].

7) Bertha Ijams [(b. May 19, 1858, Cass County, Indiana; d. 1931 at Bunker Hill, Indiana), m. 1st, William M. Yenna (d. January 13, 1884) and m. 2nd, Ambrose Bigger, d. June 3, 1928); had three children: 1) Etoile Yenna (b. July 15, 1881; d. nursing home in Peru, Indiana); 2) Raymond Daniel Bigger (b. March 9, 1892; d. June 5, 1965; m. April 4, 1926, to Sarah Sybilla Hung, b. March 10, 1899, and lived in Kokomo, Indiana; had a daughter Sarah Jane Bigger, who was b. August 24, 1929, and m. August 10, 1963, to Albert Morris Christy; lived Wabash Indiana); 3) Lloyd Bigger (b. August 9, 1900; m. Maud Ditto, b. December 25, 1906; had a son Ronald Bigger, b. May 10, 1936, lived in Peru, Indiana)].

Another source: Bertha Ijams [(b. 1857; d. 1931, near Bunker Hill, Indiana), m. 1st, William Yenna and they had a daughter Etoil Yenna; and m. 2nd, Ambrose Bigger (d. 1928; and they had two sons: a) Lloyd Bigger (lived on a farm near Bunker Hill, Indiana); and b) R. D. Bigger (a hog farmer, Bunker Hill, Indiana; served Battery F, 325th Field Artillery, 84th Dro; m. Sarah Bybilla, and their daughter, Sarah Jane Bigger, was b. August 1929)].

    8) Alford Ijams [(b. April 18, 1860, Cass County, Indiana; d. May 9, 1860, Cass County, Indiana)].

William "Howard" Ijams, the third son of William Ijams, Jr. (b. 1780, Maryland) and Catherine Ruffner, was b. September 27, 1807, in Fairfield County, Ohio; d. August 16, 1894, Walton, Indiana, and buried in Onwald Cemetery in Walton; m. 1st, March 8, 1821, Glenford, Fairfield County, Ohio, to Mary Chappell (b. 1809; d. April 10, 1840; buried at Rushville, Ohio); and m. 2nd, November 25, 1841, Lancaster, Fairfield County, Ohio, to Ann Elizabeth Beall (b. July 6, 1819; d. August 2, 1899, Cass County, Indiana); published newspaper in Noble County, Ohio, 1857-8; was a partner in the business with Mr. A. Martin, but was indicted 1857, Sarahsville, Ohio, for selling liquor; had fourteen children:

    1) Jane Elizabeth Ijams [(b. December 22, 1828, Fairfield County, Ohio), m. 1st, December 2, 1847, to Jacob Ivan; m. 2nd, Mr. Dean].

    2) William W. "Howard" Ijams [(b. December 1829, Fairfield County, Ohio; d. March 13, 1896, Wayne Township, Muskingum County, Ohio), m. 1st, Harriet S. Vines (d. Fultonsville, Ohio, 1881); m. 2nd, Rebecca Shiplett March 8, 1884 (d. April 28, 1938); he was a Private, Company E, 160 Regiment O.V.I., May 2, 1864, to September 7, 1864; a merchant; killed on railroad; granted Civil War pension Febrary 27, 1892, for rheumatism, heart disease, right-sided rupture, and piles; wife was formerly married to Delaney Shiplett at Zanesville, Ohio].

    3) Samuel J. Ijams (b. July 12, 1832, Fairfield County, Ohio; d. February 16, 1835).

    4) Mary Matilda Ijams [(b. March 24, 1834, Fairfield County, Ohio; d. 1903; buried Brunner Cemetery, Cass County, Indiana), m. Arthur J. Small (b. 1834; d. 1904); granddaughter Jenny Kay in possession of the family Bible].

    5) Sarah Catharine Ijams (b. September 10, 1837, Fairfield County, Ohio; d. November 17, 1851).

    6) Margaret Ann Ijams [(b. March 24, 1840, Fairfield County, Ohio; d. Walton, Indiana), m. 1st, March 24, 1847, George Bowyers, son of Washington Lafayette Bowyer of Virginia (b. October 14, 1827); m. 2nd, Joseph Wilson (Washington Lafayette Bowyer moved from Virginia to Walton, Tipton Township, Cass County, Indiana, and had several children: Peter Bowyer, d. 1879; Daniel Bowyer, d. 1857; William Bowyer, d. 1875; Andrew Bowyer, d. 1885, age 27; Susanna Bowyer, d. 1897; and Robert Bowyer, b. 1838; d. 1913)].

    7) Thomas Howard Ijams [(b. October 18, 1842, Fairfield County, Ohio; lived in Kansas City, Missouri; d. February 24, 1926, Walton, Indiana); m. Mary Louise Webster].

    8) Franklin D. Ijams (b. May 14, 1846, Fairfield County, Ohio).

    9) George Washington Ijams (b. July 5, 1844, Fairfield County, Ohio; d. April 17, 1845, Fairfield County, Ohio).

    10) Amira Ijams (b. June 27, 1848, Fairfield County, Ohio; d. July 11, 1848, Fairfield County, Ohio).

11) Isaac Beall Ijams (b. July 28, 1849, Fairfield County, Ohio; d. October 30, 1902, Walton, Indiana; m. Etta Rickle).

12) Millard Fillmore Ijams (b. November 4, 1851, Fairfield County, Ohio; d. April 10, 1881, Walton, Indiana; a plasterer and land owner in Tipton Township, Cass County, Indiana; m. Sarah Slagle).

13) Lydia Elizabeth Ijams (b. June 19, 1857, Cass County, Indiana; d. August 1905, Fremont, Nebraska; m. 1st, John W. Chichester; m. 2nd, Joseph R. Smoot).

14) Clara Beall Ijams (b. August 23, 1859, Cass County, Indiana; d. 1942); m. Joe Wood; lived Galveston, Indiana; two children: Mildred Wood and Clarence Wood.

John Howard Ijams (b. 1783, Maryland; d. 1857, Noble County, Ohio; m. Sarah Ann Jasper) is believed by EFB to have had a son Theodore M. Ijams (b. 1838; d. June 7, 1923, Dayton, Ohio; m. October 16, 1872, in West Alexandria, Pennsylvania, to Ella L. Young). Theodore and Ella were divorced, Noble County, Ohio, in April 1894, after Theodore left the state. Ella L. Young was the daughter of William J. Young and Jane McCann. Theodore M. Ijams (b. 1838) served in the Civil War as a Private, Company G, 176 Regiment O.V.I., and was living at 204 North Clark Street, Chicago, Illinois, on June 9, 1904, at the time his pension was filed. He had enlisted September 16, 1864, as a resident of Sarahsville, Noble County, Ohio; and was discharged at Columbus, Ohio, June 14, 1865 (or discharged at Nashville, Tennessee), and moved from Columbus, Ohio, to Chicago in March 1888, working as a carriage driver for a livery in 1908. In his pension application he listed his occupation as tending a hotel; was 5 ft. 8 1/2 in. tall, weighed 150 pounds, had blue eyes and grey hair; said he was not married and that he had no children. On April 25, 1910, he gave a change of address to Department of Interior, and moved to 644 Maple Avenue in Los Angeles, California. Widow Ella L. Ijams filed a petition from Noble County, Ohio, February 16, 1924, and the petition included affidavits from William J. Ijams, age 42, Columbus, Ohio; son Thomas J. Ijams; and son John C. Ijams, age 45.

This Theodore J. Ijams (b. 1838 or November 6, 1847, Morgan County, Ohio; d. June 7, 1923, Dayton, Ohio, buried at National Cemetery, Dayton), m. "Ella," Ellen, or Eleanor L. Young, daughter of William L. Young and Jane McCann. Ella (b. June 1, 1855) divorced Theodore J. Ijams April 1894, Noble County, Ohio, related to his drunkenness; she d. May 21, 1928. Records of Sarahsville, Ohio, 1876, list Theodore J. Ijams as a dealer in dry goods, groceries, and hardware. Theodore J. Ijams and Ella L. Young had seven children:

1) Pauline L. Ijams (b. Sarahsville, Center Township, Noble County, Ohio, October 9, 1874; d. March 18, 1875; buried Old Sarahsville Cemetery).

2) John Howard Ijams (b. March 10, 1878, or October 4, 1878, Noble County, Ohio; d. June 8, 1963, in Zanesville, Ohio; buried Cumberland, Ohio; a pharmacist).

3) Johanna L. Ijams (b. August 25, 1873, Noble County, Ohio; d. April 19, 1881; buried Old Sarahsville Cemetery).

4) Mable Young Ijams (b. October 14, 1880, Noble County, Ohio, lived at 1898 Summit Street, Columbus, Ohio; d. Kokomo, Indiana; single).

5) John W. or William "J" Ijams (b. July 24, 1882, Caldwell, Noble County, Ohio; lived at 1898 Summit Street, Columbus, Ohio, for forty years; d. February 6, 1945, Columbus, at Doctor's Hospital, allegedly following a surgical procedure for duodenal carcinoma; m. Alta ____, who was b. July 24, 1882, Caldwell, Ohio, and d. age 62).

6) Sarah Jane Ijams (b. 1876, Noble County, Ohio; d. 1884).

7) Vera L. Ijams (b. January 6, 1887, Caldwell, Noble County, Ohio; lived in Greenville, Pennsylvania, in 1964; m. February 19, 1913, to Herman C. Smith).

Sarah Howard Ijams (b. October 6, 1798, Washington County, Maryland; d. February 12, 1829); daughter of William Ijams (b. 1753, Maryland) and Elizabeth Howard; m. January 25, 1818, in St. Louis, Missouri, to a soldier, John Jay Jackson. On February 12, 1829, they purchased land in Southern Perry County, Ohio; they lived in Rushville, Fairfield County, Ohio. John Jay Jackson (b. February 7, 1792; d. September 24, 1876), was the son of Lyman and Deidamia Jackson. After the death of his first wife, John Jay Jackson m. 2nd, August 23, 1829, to Mary Cecelia Create, daughter of Joseph and Hannah Create. John Jay Jackson had seven children by his first marriage and six by his second marriage: 1) Deidamia Jay Jackson (b. February 11, 1819; d. February 17, 1819; 2) Elizabeth Comfort Jackson (b. January 5, 1820; d. March 28, 1842); 3) Rosanna Rebecca Jackson (b. September 16, 1821; d. October 14, 1862, in Chickashaw, Iowa); 4) Nancy Ann Jackson (b. February 5, 1823, Perry County, Ohio; d. November 23, 1903; m. Mr. Snider on October 26, 1841, and had four sons and four daughters); 5) Joseph Ijams Jackson (b. June 23, 1825; d. January 7, 1913; m. April 22, 1847; moved to Village Creek, Iowa, and then to Alva, Oklahoma); 6) William Edwin Jackson (b. March 23, 1827; m. 1850; moved to Iowa and then to Red Cloud, Nebraska; 7) Robert Turner Jackson (b. December 20, 1828; d. October 15, 1879; m. 1851; moved to Iowa and the widow moved later to Chicago, where son P. R. Jackson was a businessman; 8) first child of Mary Create, Sarah Catherine Jackson (b. July 10, 1830; d. July 28, 1830); 9) Mary Teresa Jackson (b. July 12, 1831; d. December 2, 1907; m. August 27, 1858); 10) Lyman James Jackson (b. January 13, 1834; d. January 25, 1887; m. February 17, 1863; lived Omaha, Nebraska); 11) Caroline Helen Jackson (b. August 21, 1836; d. October 12, 1913); 12) Clarissa Dalia Jackson (b. August 7, 1839; d. October 8, 1843); 13) Cecelia Clarissa Jackson (b. January 23, 1844; d. April 27, 1899; m. October 12, 1863).

Isaac Beall Ijams [(b. 1849, Fairfield County, Ohio, eleventh child of William Howard Ijams, b. 1807, and second wife Anne Beall; d. 1902, Walton, Indiana); m. Etta Bickle, and they had six children: 1) Lefa Ijams (b. February 8, 1883, Walton, Indiana; m. B. B. Brooks; lived LePorte, Indiana, and then in Saskatchewan, Canada); 2) Belle Ijams (b. January 18, 1892, Walton, Indiana; m. S. J. Johnson and lived Portsmouth, Virginia; 3) Maude Ijams (b. February 8, 1894; m. C. E. Arnold; lived LePorte, Indiana, and Saskatchewan, Canada; and had four children: a) Edward Arnold, b. November 20, 1919, in Canada, and lived at Empress, Alberta; b) Thelma Arnold, b. December 22, 1917, in Saskatchewan, Canada; c) Wayne Arnold, b. October 8, 1821, Canada; and d) Benjamin Arnold, b. September 12, 1923); 4) Eunice Ijams (b. August 28, 1897, Canada; m. W. R. Payne of Lynnhaven, Virginia); 5) Edith Ora Ijams (b. November 26, 1900, in Canada, and lived in Baltimore, Maryland); and 6) William Howard Ijams (b. February 9, 1902, in Canada; and lived in Lynnhaven, Virginia).

Isaac Plummer Ijams [(b. 1765 or 1767, Anne Arundel County, Maryland; d. 1824 or 1825, Fairfield County, Ohio; the fifth child of Captain John Ijams, b. 1712, Maryland, and Rebecca Jones), m. August 4, 1795, Prince Georges County, Maryland, to Elizabeth Beck Williams (daughter of James Beck and Rebecca Walker; and widow of William Williams, who had m. 1st, to Sarah Duvall), and they lived in Frederick County, Maryland, where lawsuits between Isaac Ijams and the Williams family were recorded in 1796; (moved to Rush Creek, Fairfield County, Ohio, by September 5, 1805, with brothers John Ijams and William Ijams; and where widow

Elizabeth Ijams was head of household in 1830; and she d. Logan County, Ohio, January 1856. The 1825 estate records of Isaac Ijams listed sons William Ijams, John Ijams, and Isaac Ijams, Jr.); with the six children of Isaac Plummer Ijams:

1) Isaac H. Ijams (b. 1798, Maryland; d. 1845, Perry County, Ohio; m. December 9, 1832, in Fairfield County, Ohio, to Lucretia Mary Allen)
2) John Wesley Iiams (b. 1805, Fairfield County, Ohio; m. November 17, 1831, Fairfield County, Ohio, to Sarah Ann Vansant, b. 1814; 1850 Census of Fairfield County, Ohio, lists John W. Ijams, age 45, b. Ohio; wife Sarah A. Ijams, age 36, b. Maryland; Louisa Ijams, age 17, b. Ohio; Joseph Ijams, age 15, b. Ohio; Isaac Ijams, age 13, b. Ohio; Elizabeth A. Ijams, age 10, b. Ohio; William Ijams, age 7, b. Ohio; John Ijams, age 5, b. Ohio; and Vinson Ijams, age 2, b. Ohio; and they moved to Missouri).
3) William Iiams [(b. 1800, 1811, or 1815, Ohio), m. Catherine Stevens or Elsie Stevens (b. 1820, Ohio), with 1840 Census of Hopewell Township, Muskingum County, Ohio, listing William Iiams age 20-30, wife age 20-30, a female 15-20, a female under age 5, and a male under age 5; and 1850 census listing of William Iiams, age 39, b. Ohio; wife Elsie Iiams age 30, b. Ohio; Mary A. Iiams, age 12, b. Ohio; William H. H. Iiams, age 10, b. Ohio; Thomas L. Iiams, age 7, b. Ohio; Sarah E. Iiams, age 5, b. Ohio].
4) Rebecca Iiams (b. 1803, Fairfield County, Ohio; m. 1827 to Reverend Samuel J. Bright, and lived in Logan, Ohio).
5) Mary Ann Iiams [(b. 1804, Fairfield County, Ohio), m. September 21, 1821, or 1828, Ohio, to Joseph Howard Iiams, a first cousin (d. 1836, Fairfield County, Ohio; son of William Iiams and Elizabeth Howard); had children: Reverend William Edward Howard (d. in Iowa); Caroline Howard (m. Dana Stone); and Joe Henry Howard (had schools for deaf in Iowa and Tennessee)].
6) Elizabeth Iiams [(b. 1798, Maryland), m. 1818, to Thomas W. Beall, and moved to Mount Pleasant, Ohio].

John Wesley Iiams [(b. 1805, Fairfield County, Ohio), the son of Isaac Plummer Ijams and Elizabeth Beck Williams, m. Sarah Anne Van Sant], and they had eight children:

a) Louise Ijams (b. 1833, Fairfield County, Ohio).
b) Joseph Ijams (b. 1835, Fairfield County, Ohio).
c) Isaac Ijams (b. 1837, Fairfield County, Ohio; m. Sarah Parker).
d) Elizabeth A. Ijams (b. 1840, Fairfield County, Ohio; m. William Harvey, Thomas Beall, and lived in Mount Pleasant, Ohio, where she had ten children including John Beall, M.D., of Lacon, Illinois, who m. Elizabeth "Liz" Zehring of Pennsylvania).
e) William Clayton Ijams (b. 1843, Fairfield County, Ohio; d. September 17, 1854, and buried in Stevenson Cemetery, Richland Township, Fairfield County, Ohio).
f) John Wesley Ijams II [(b. January 2, 1846, Rushville, Fairfield County, Ohio; d. January 11, 1930, in Topeka, Kansas), a Civil War veteran; m. April 28, 1875, in Jefferson County, Kansas, to Elizabeth James (b. 1854; d. 1929); he was a Private, Company E of 21st Missouri and Company F of 39th Missouri, for five years. Civil War records listed his wife as Elizabeth, his mother as Sarah Van Sant, and children as Carrie L. Ijams (b. July 12, 1877); Nellie J. Ijams (b. February 2, 1884); Edwin C.

Ijams (b. January 7, 1886); Sarah Mabel Ijams (b. January 21, 1890), and Ina Ijams (b. November 30, 1895); with John W. Ijams owning a portion of a farm in Ozawkee, Kansas, with a brother and a sister; and, with his mother, ran a hotel in Edina, Missouri].

    g) Vincent Vansant Ijams (b. 1848, Fairfield County, Ohio; d. 1897; m. Ann Lewis and/or Anna Louise England).

    h) Albert Ijams (d. infancy).

    In addition to the information about John Wesley Ijams (b. 1805, Rushville, Fairfield County, Ohio), Lois I. Hartman gives November 17, 1831, Fairfield County, Ohio, as the date of his marriage to Sarah Ann Vansant (b. 1814, Sharpsburg, Maryland; d. 1890, and they had the eight children listed above. Their son Joseph Ijams (d. 1863) was a Civil War soldier; son Isaac Ijams (b. October 15, 1837; d. September 6, 1911, at Hutchinson, Kansas), m. Sarah Parker (b. February 11, 1840; d. April 10, 1879), and they had four children: John Wesley Ijams (b. September 11, 1867; William E. Ijams (b. 1870, Hutchinson, Kansas; d. November 3, 1917), Joseph H. Ijams (b. 1872, Hutchinson, Kansas; d. September 6, 1937); and Emma Etta Ijams (b. Hutchinson, Kansas; d. November 14, 1952).

    John Wesley Ijams (b. 1846, Civil War veteran; d. 1929; the son of John Wesley Ijams, b. 1805, and Sarah Vansant), m. 1875 to Elizabeth "Lib" James (b. March 24, 1854; d. 1829); operated a country store in eastern Kansas. Elizabeth James (b. 1854) was the daughter of John James and Jane Emory of Bath, England, and she was born in Wayne County, New York. John and Jane James also had four other children: Anna James (died young); Mary James (d. young); Josie James (b. 1859); and William James (b. 1861). Their homestead was declared to be "Delaware Indian land" where they settled in 1857, and which was signed by Secretary of Indian Land for President Buchanan, and which Elizabeth James Ijams inherited after the death of her father. John Wesley Ijams (b. 1846) and Elizabeth James (b. 1854) had eight children: Frederick Ijams (b. 1876; d. 1881); Earl Ijams (d. infancy); Roscoe or Reason Ijams (b. 1882; d. 1883); Nell Ijams (b. 1884; d. 1907; m. James Trapp); Edwin Clayton Ijams (b. January 7, 1886; d. January 1933; m. September 12, 1919, to Lillian Round, b. 1897, the line of Lois Ijams Hartman); Carrie Ijams (b. 1882; d. 1981; m. Melvin Manning); Mabel Ijams (b. 1890; d. 1953; m. S. H. Stark, b. 1891; d. 1966); and Ina Ijams (b. 1894; d. 1969; m. J. Fred Bigham).

    Edwin Clayton Ijams (b. January 7, 1886; d. January 1993), the son of John Wesley Ijams (b. 1846) and Elizabeth James (b. 1854), m. September 12, 1919, to Lillian Round (b. 1897); grew up on the homestead Hillcrest in eastern Kansas, five miles from Oskaloosa, where he farmed and wrote poetry and plays for the local schools and churches. Edwin Clayton Ijams (b. 1886) had three children:

    1) Lois M. Ijams [(b. October 2, 1920), m. September 29, 1943, to Warren Hartman (b. October 15, 1920). She is well known as a world authority on the Ijams family, the author of two books on the family, in addition to being a major contributor to this work; originally felt that the name was a variant of James in origin, with the probable first relative being Robert I'Ans of England, Master of Ordnance to Queen Elizabeth and privy Councillor to Ireland for her majesty; author who asked, "Would a stranger care to search for us five hundred years from now?"; a resident of Pasadena, California. Lois and Warren Hartman had four children; a) Margot E. Hartman (b. April 17, 1949); m. 1st, January 7, 1978, to Charles Snyder; and m. 2nd, Steve Mott; and had a child Cameron Mott (b. November 19, 1987); b) Dennis C. Hartman (b. September 5, 1954); m. Heidi Harding, and had a child Kelly T. Hartman

(b. May 3, 1991); c) Lidia M. Hartman (b. in Serbia May 8, 1950, adopted), m. Renee Rivera and had child Anthony Rivera (b. April 19, 1971); and d) Raiko Z. Hartman (b. in Serbia, September 29, 1951, adopted), m. Cathy Hiken and they had two children: Lauren E. Hartman (b. June 21, 1985), and Jonathan R. Hartman b. August 24, 1988)].

    2) Marlin E. Ijams (a twin, b. July 9, 1924; d. 1996), m. 1st, Sue Bearden (b. 1927; d. 1965); m. 2nd, Myrna Wright; m. 3rd, ____; m. 4th to Mercedes Blaylock; had one child with Sue Bearden: Steven Ijams [(b. May 12, 1958, adopted); m. Darlene McGill, and their son: Michael Hartman (b. September 14, 1985)].

    3) Mary Louise Ijams [(a twin, b. July 9, 1924), m. Fred Petrik (b. 1918; d. 1977), and they had two children: a) Nancy Petrik (b. 1947; m. 1st, Russell Kindred, and had child Allison Kindred, b. 1977; and m. 2nd, F. Barajas, with whom she had child Alexis N. Barajas, b. November 8, 1993), and b) Richard Petrik (b. 1950), m. Danna Markham, and had two children: Taylor Petrik (b. December 4, 1990); and Harrison Petrik (b. July 26, 1993)].

    Carrie Ijams (b. 1882; d. 1918), the daughter of John Wesley Ijams (b. 1846), m. Melvin Manning and they had three children: 1) Beth Manning (b. 1899; d. 1922); 2) Earl Manning [(b. 1900; d. 1955); m. Ruth Weaver, and they had five children: a) Rodney Manning (b. 1930); b) Norman Manning (b. 1932; d. 1936); c) Eldon Manning (b. 1936; d. Nancy Manning (b. 1942, a twin); and e) Kevin Manning (b. 1942, a twin)]; and 3) Mildred Manning [(b. 1903; d. 1974); m. Earl Greenwood, and they had two children: a) Donald M. Greenwood (m. Yvonne Gore), who had three children: David Greenwood (b. August 4, 1952); Edward Greenwood (b. October 13, 1955), and Janie Greenwood (b. January 14, 1963); and b) Robert E. Greenwood (m. Jacqueline ____), who had three children: Don Greenwood (b. September 2, 1949); Timothy Greenwood (b. October 29, 1954); and Diana Greenwood (b. February 4, 1952), who m. October 12, 1974, to K. Parypa (b. January 27, 1951)].

    Mabel Ijams (b. 1890; d. 1953), daughter of John Wesley Ijams (b. 1846), m. S. H. Stark (b. 1891; d. 1966), and they had three children: 1) Nola N. Stark (b. 1914); 2) Richard Stark [(b. 1916), m. Mary Myers, and they had four children: Daniel Stark (b. 1957); Jean Stark (b. 1943); Richard Stark, Jr. (b. 1945); and Larry Stark (b. 1951); Jean Stark m. F. Fikken and their two daughters were: Kristen Fikken (b. 1975 and Janna Fikken (b. 1977); Richard Stark, Jr. (b. 1945) m. C. Brandon, and their sons were Michael Stark (b. 1976) and Greg Stark]; and 3) Harwood M. Stark (b. 1957) m. Jean Rozelle, and their children are: a) Kelly Stark (b. 1949; m. Mary Deakers); b) Jeff Stark (b. 1951; m. Peggy Pagano, and their children were: Tyler Stark and Jennifer Stark); and c) Elizabeth Stark (m. Brian Cleary, and their three children were: Erin Cleary (b. 1987; and twin girls Meagan Cleary and Shannon Cleary, b. July 2, 1990)].

    Ina Ijams (b. 1894; d. 1969), daughter of John Wesley Ijams (b. 1846), m. J. Fred Bigham, and they had two children: Helen Bigham [(b. 1916, m. J. Monley (d. 1975), and they had two children: a) Keith Monley (b. September 1, 1948); b) David Monley (b. October 19, 1949); m. December 24, 1973, to Elizabeth Flowers]; 2) Patricia Bigham [(b. 1923), m. 1st, Bryan Gore (d. January 26, 1959), and m. 2nd, Roger Scott (b. November 4, 1960; d. February 18, 1971); and she had two children: a) Dennis Gore (b. July 25, 1945); m. Mary Wardell (b. May 10, 1950; and b) Douglas Gore (b. 1950)].

    Isaac Ijams (b. October 15, 1837), the son of John Wesley Ijams (b. 1805) and Sarah Vansant, m. Sarah Parker (b. February 11, 1840; d. April 10, 1879); and

they had four children. The 1880 Federal Census of Clay Township, Reno County, Kansas, lists Isaac Ijams (age 42; b. Ohio), wife Rebecca Ijams (age 42); son John W. Ijams (age 13, b. Missouri); son William W. Ijams (age 11, b. Iowa); son Joseph Ijams (age 8, b. Kansas), and daughter Emma E. Ijams (age 4, b. Kansas). The 1920 Federal Census of Reno County, Kansas, lists Isaac Ijams (age 72; b. Ohio) living with J. H. Ijams (age 37, b. Kansas); Anna Ijams (age 34, b. Kansas), and Fred Ijams (age 14, b. Kansas). The four children of Isaac Ijams (b. 1837) were:
1) William R. Ijams (b. 1870, Hutchinson, Kansas; d. November 7, 1917); 2) Joseph H. Ijams [(b. 1872, Hutchinson, Kansas; d. September 6, 1937), m. Ann Hedge and they had two sons: a) Fred Ijams (b. November 22, 1896; d. October 1940), m. Gladys M. Mudge; and their daughter Betty Jean Ijams (b. August 22, 1921), m. February 3, 1950, to Raymond B. Petry; and b) Ethel Ijams (b. May 22, 1900)]; 3) John Wesley Ijams [(b. September 11, 1867, Edina, Missouri; d. April 15, 1942); m. Hannah Findley (b. October 16, 1901; d. March 26, 1958), and they had two children: a) Gail F. Ijams (b. June 23, 1906, in Helena, Montana); m. September 24, 1942, to Inez Waldo (b. October 16, 1901; d. March 26, 1958); and b) Paul V. Ijams (b. May 12, 1908, Cashe, Oklahoma); m. September 7, 1933, to Margaret Deitrick (b. September 29, 1908); and their child Janice Ann Ijams (b. December 13, 1935, Topeka, Kansas), m. March 30, 1957, to Gary Miller (b. October 31, 1935), and they had two children: Anne Elizabeth Miller (b. May 29, 1959, Brawley, California), and Jane Elizabeth Miller (b. February 12, 1964, Saint Louis, Missouri)]; and 4) Emma Etta Ijams [(b. August 23, 1876, in Hutchinson, Kansas; d. November 14, 1952), m. 1897, to Charles Gramse (b. May 24, 1875, Ozawkie, Kansas; d. 1947); and they had two children: a) Lucille Gramse (b. September 2, 1900), m. to W. A. McCarthy; and b) Greeta Gramse (b. August 28, 1898; d. 1974), m. August 5, 1922, to A. J. Hay (d. June 7, 1966).
Greeta Gramse (b. 1898; d. 1974) and A. J. Hay (b. August 28, 1896; d. 1966) had three children: 1) Charlene Hay (b. February 13, 1927, Pasadena, California), m. 1st, Wallace Hurst, and m. 2nd, Jack Johnson, and had three children: a) Geraldine Johnson (b. May 15, 1955); b. Stacy Johnson (b. October 9, 1956), and c) Charles Johnson (b. January 18, 1964); 2) Lolita Hay (b. March 6, 1924, Pasadena, California), m. 1st, October 26, 1945, to Robert Foes (d.1975), and m. 2nd, October 1, 1965, to Frederick LaVigne and she had three children: a) Robert Foes, Jr. (b. October 2, 1946); and b) Kristin Gaye Foes [(b. April 25, 1948); m. 1st, Terry Manges; and m. 2nd, Robert Parkhurst; and had two children: Robert Manges (b. September 29, 1968) and Amanda Parkhurst]; and c) Dean Foes (b. January 22, 1954); and 3) Abe "Tim" Hay (b. April 16, 1932, Pasadena, California, m. Tina De Rocher].
Vincent Vansant Ijams (b. 1848; d. 1895), the son of John Wesley Ijams (b. 1805) and Sarah Vansant, m. Ann Lewis England (b. 1863; d. 1922), and they had three children: 1) Leonta Sarah Ijams [(b. 1886; d. 1968), m. 1st, Rodney Courtney; and m. 2nd, John C. Hogue (b. 1881; d. 1964)]; 2) Shelby Howard Ijams [(b. 1890; d. 1942), m. Hazel Jones (b. 1892; d. 1941), and had two children: a) Merle A. Ijams (b. 1917; d. 1937); and b) Virgil Lee Ijams (b. 1924; d. 1933)]; 3) Roy Lee Ijams [(b. 1896; d. 1937), m. April 24, 1926, to Hilda Fritz (b. 1906), and they had four children: a) Roy Lee Ijams, Jr. (b. 1927; d. 1942); b) Dorothy A. Ijams (b. 1932), m. in 1955 to Donald Roberts and they had four children: Brian Lee Roberts (b. 1955); Dawn A. Roberts (b. 1959); Owen S. Roberts (b. 1961); and Holly J. Roberts (b. 1962); c) Charles Vincent Ijams (b. 1934), m. 1st, in 1957 to Judith Medster; m. 2nd, in 1969 to Catherine Springer, and had children Wendeline Ijams (b. 1959), and Roy Lee Ijams (b. 1961); and d) Clayton Dean Ijams (b. 1937), m. 1966 to Barbara W. Stephenson (b. 1938), and they had two children: Jodi K. Ijams (b. 1967); and Clayton

Dean Ijams, Jr. (b. 1969), in addition to the two children of Barbara W. Stephenson by a former marriage: Alan Stephenson and Mark Stephenson)].

William Iiams (b. 1811 or 1815, Fairfield County, Ohio; d. 1845 in Ohio), son of Isaac Plummer Ijams (b. 1765, Maryland) and Elizabeth Beck Williams, m. Catherine Stevens, and they had three children: 1) Edward Talmadge Iiams [(b. April 3, 1846, Logan, Fairfield County, Ohio; d. September 24, 1896, or 1914, Ozawkee, Kansas), m. March 24, 1878, to Elizabeth Unity Gallaspy (b. August 21, 1861; d. in Tucson, Arizona, November 22, 1948), and they had one son, Sheldon L. Iiams (b. 1888) who m. Jesse Maude Hill]; 2) Mary E. Iiams [(b. 1847, Fairfield County, Ohio) lived in Reno County at Hutchinson, Kansas, until 1875; also lived near Nuthall, Oklahoma, and Cushing, Oklahoma; she had three daughters: Mary Ann Iiams, Rebecca Iiams, and Elizabeth Iiams)]; and 3) Laura Ann Iiams (b. 1849, Fairfield County, Ohio, and buried at Pleasant Hill Cemetery at Rushville, Fairfield County, Ohio). Edward Talmadge Ijams (b. 1846) is reported to have died in Whittier, California, December 21, 1914. The 1850 Federal Census of Fairfield County, Ohio, lists William Ijams (age 35, b. Ohio, a merchant); wife Catherine Ijams (age 27, b. Maryland; son Edward T. Ijams (age 4, b. Ohio); Mary E. Imes (age 3, b. Ohio); and Laura Imes (age 1, b. Ohio).

Edward T. Ijams (b. Tombstone, Arizona, March 11, 1911; d. Providence, Utah, November 20, 1993), m. September 10, 1936, to Marianne Mendala Miller. Edward T. Ijams (b. 1911) was the son of Sheldon L. Ijams (b. 1884) and Jessie Maude Hill, with information provided by James O. Ijams of Lennox, California. Edward T. Ijams (b. 1911) had two children: Edward Ijams (m. Anna Kroether, and their daughter was Sabina Ijams), and Elizabeth Ijams (m. Monte Lorrigan, and they had eight children).

Sheldon L. Ijams [(b. April 25, 1884, Safford, Arizona; d. May 5, 1973, Safford, Arizona), son of Edward Talmadge Ijams (b. 1846) and Eliza Unity Gallaspy (the daughter of William J. Gallaspy), m. 1908 to Jessie Maud Hill. Eliza Unity Gallaspy (b. August 21, 1861; m. March 24, 1878; d. November 22, 1948, Tucson, Arizona), was the daughter of William J. Gallaspy (b. November 14, 1810, Georgia; m. December 17, 1839; d. Willcox, Arizona, June 22, 1886), and of Elizabeth Ann Langford (b. February 18, 1823; d. December 12, 1912, Safford, Arizona). Elizabeth Ann Langford (b. 1823)was the daughter of Eli Langford (b. December 30, 1779; m. March 27, 1800) and Mary Edens (b. January 26, 1781; d. January 15, 1862). The seven children of Sheldon L. Ijams (b. 1884) were:

1) Harold Sheldon Ijams (b. Tombstone, Arizona, June 3, 1910), m. July 30, 1938, to Dorothy Elliott, and their two sons were: Donald Ijams and Kirt Ijams; 2) Edward Talmadge Ijams (b. Tombstone, Arizona, March 11 or 26, 1911; d. Providence, Utah, November 20, 1993), m. September 10, 1936, to Marianne Mendala Miller, and their two children are: Elizabeth Ijams and Edward Ijams; 3) Melbourne "Allison" Ijams (b. Fort Lauderdale, Florida, June 14, 1914), m. April 25, 1943, to Era Hickey, and their four children were: Jan Ijams, Linda Ijams, Rex Ijams, and Salina Ijams; 4) Leslie Willcox Ijams (b. Wilcox, Arizona, September 15, 1915), m. 1st, April 11, 1939, to Vida Ruth; m. 2nd, Marly Tiburtius; 5) John William Isaac Ijams (b. Patagonia, Arizona, May or June 5, 1917; d. Arawe, New Guinea, January 16, 1944); 6) James Oscar Ijams (b. Senneca, California, October 15, 1924; family historian), m. September 1, 1946, to Maxine Nelson; and 7) Reverend Carl Phillip Ijams (b. Tombstone, Arizona, August 24, 1928; contributor to family line), m. June 8, 1958, to Anne Kibbe, and their four children were: Michael Ijams, Stephen Ijams, William Ijams, and Andrew Ijams.

Harold S. Ijams (b. Tombstone, Arizona, June 3, 1910), the son of Sheldon L. Ijams (b. 1884) and Jessie Maud Hill; m. July 30, 1938, to Dorothy Elliott, and as outlined by James O. Ijams (b. 1924), had two children: 1) Donald Ijams (m. Kay Wertman, and their daughter was Amy Ijams); and 2) Kirt Ijams (m. 1st, Vivian Pierce, and they had two children: Bennet Ijams and Matthew Ijams; and m. 2nd, Nancy Montoya, and they had a son, Harold E. Ijams).

Elizabeth Ijams, the daughter of Edward T. Ijams (b. 1911) and Marianne Miller, m. Monte Lorrigan and they had eight children: 1) Todd Lorrigan (m. Cindy Bingham, and their daughter was Nicole Lorrigan); 2) Kirk Lorrigan (m. Christine Hodges, and their three children were Tonya Lorrigan, Carli Lorrigan, and Conner Lorrigan); 3) Rebecca Lorrigan (m. David Messer, and their two children were Audrey Messer and Jacob Messer); 4) Catherine Lorrigan (m. 1st, Dale Beaudry, and their child was Corinne Beaudry; and m. 2nd, Lex Sorensen, and their child was Jacqueline Sorensen); 5) Amber Lorrigan (m. David Wiener, and their two children were Darren Wiener and Alexander Wiener); 6) David Lorrigan; 7) William Lorrigan; and 8) Sarah Lorrigan.

Melbourne A. Ijams (b. June 14, 1914, Fort Lauderdale, Florida), the child of Sheldon L. Ijams (b. 1884) and Jessie Maud Hill, m. April 25, 1943, to Era Hickey, and according to James O. Ijams (b. 1924), their four children were: Jan Hickey; 2) Linda Hickey (m. Richard Harris, and their son was Jason Harris); 3) Rex Hickey (m. Brenda Weber); and 4) Salina Hickey (m. Peniamina Sialega, and their children were Mali and Shelli).

Leslie W. Ijams (b. September 15, 1915, Wilcox, Arizona), the son of Sheldon L. Ijams (b. 1884) and Jessie Maud Hill, m. 1st, April 11, 1939, to Vida Ruth (b. 1916; d. 1975); and m. 2nd, Marly Tiburtius; and to his first marriage was b. Gary Ijams (m. Reid Harrington; and their three children were Gary Ijams, Bryon Ijams, and Eric Ijams).

James Oscar Ijams (b. October 15, 1924, Lennox, California; an electrical engineer with Hughes Aircraft in Tucson, Arizona, until retirement in 1989, and a major contributor to the family history), the son of Sheldon L. Ijams (b. 1884) and Jessie Maud Hill, m. September 1, 1946, to Maxine Nelson, a clinical psychologist, and they had three children: 1) Kristin Ijams [(m. 1st, to Paul Hall, and they had a daughter Melinda Ijams, who was b. 1973; d. 1992); and m. 2nd, Raymond Ford (their son was Justin Ford)]; 2) Bronn Ijams (m. Peggy Hansen, and their son was Dylan Maxwell Ijams); and 3) Tracey Ijams (m. Lyslie Bailey, and their son was Corey Wesley Bailey).

Edward Talmadge Ijams [(b. April 3, 1846, Logan, Fairfield County, Ohio; d. December 21, 1914, Whittier, California), the son of William Ijams (b. 1815, Ohio) and Catherine Stevens, m. March 24, 1878, to Elizabeth Unity Gallaspy (b. August 21, 1861; d. November 22, 1948), the daughter of William J. Gallaspy (b. November 14, 1810, Georgia; d. June 22, 1886, Willcox, Arizona) and Elizabeth Ann Langford (b. February 18, 1983; d. December 12, 1912, Safford, Arizona; the daughter of Eli Langford, b. December 30, 1779, and Mary Edena, b. January 26, 1781; d. January 15, 1862), and their son was Sheldon L. Ijams (b. April 25, 1884, Safford, Arizona; d. May 5, 1973), m. July 30, 1908, to Jessie Maude Hill), with history supplied by James O. Ijams and Elizabeth Ijams Lorrigan.

Sheldon L. Ijams (b. April 25, 1884, Safford, Arizona) and Jessie Maude Hill had seven children: 1) Harold S. Ijams (b. March 6, 1910, Tombstone, Arizona; m. July 30, 1938, to Dorothy Elliott) had two children: Donald Ijams (m. Kay Wertman, and their child was Amy Ijams), and Kitt Ijams (m. 1st, Vivian Pearce, and their children were Bennet Ijams and Matthew Ijams; and m. 2nd, Nancy Montoya, and their child was Harold E. Ijams); 2) Edward Talmadge Ijams [(b. March 26, 1911, Tombstone, Arizona; d. November 20, 1993, Providence, Utah; m. September 10, 1936, to Marion Mondale Miller, and their daughter Alice Elizabeth Ijams, a contributor to this family history, m. Monte Lorrigan, and they had seven children: Todd Lorrigan (m. Cindy Bingham, and their daughter was Nicole Lorrigan); Kirk Lorrigan (m. Christine Hodges, and their children were: Tonya Lorrigan, Carli Lorrigan, and Conner Lorrigan); Rebecca Lorrigan (m. David Messer, and their two children were Audrey Messer and Jacob Messer); Catherine Lorrigan (m. 1st, to Dale Beaudry, and m. 2nd, Lex Sorensen, and children were Corinne Beaudry and Jacquelyn Sorenson); David Lorrigan; and Sarah Lorrigan)]; 3) Melbourne A. Ijams; 4) Leslie W. Ijams; 5) John William Ijams (b. June 5, 1917, Patagonia, Arizona; d. January 16, 1944, Arawe, New Guinea); 6) James Oscar Ijams (b. October 15, 1924, Senneca, California); and 7) Carl P. Ijams (b. August 24, 1928, Tombstone, Arizona; m. June 8, 1958, to Anne Kibbe, and their four children were: Michael Ijams, Stephen Ijams, William Ijams, and Andrew Ijams).

Thomas Plummer Ijams [(b. April 4, 1773, Anne Arundel County, Maryland; d. August 16, 1847, Muskingum County, Ohio), the son of Captain John Ijams (b. 1712) and Rebecca Jones; m. February 10, 1794, in Frederick County, Maryland, to Sarah Duvall (b. December 10, 1778; d. September 9, 1811, Ohio), daughter of Lewis Duvall] has been researched by Ervin F. Bickley, Jr. (EFB).

Thomas Plummer Ijams was listed in the Fairfield County, Ohio, tax rolls of 1806, 1809, and 1813-1819. Thomas Plummer Ijams and Isaac Ijams sold land in Frederick County, Maryland, to John Ijams, for 600 pounds (Book 21, Liber 508), which had been previously purchased October 16, 1793, from Jacob Springer, with the land called Duval's Forest and Good Friday, with the sale registered October 8, 1801, while Thomas Plummer Ijams was still a resident of Frederick County, Maryland. John Ijams and wife Mary Ijams sold one half of their land to Plummer Ijams for 500 pounds (Book 25, Liber 307) on January 7, 1804 (41 acres), and Plummer Ijams also purchased three acres of Good Friday from Thomas Plummer Ijams and wife Sarah Ijams, with the transaction also involving Isaac Ijams and wife Elizabeth Ijams (October 17, 1805). Both Thomas Plummer Ijams and Isaac Ijams had moved to Fairfield County, Ohio, by October 1805, and the record of this transaction was also recorded at the courthouse of Fairfield County, Ohio (January 21, 1806).

Thomas Plummer Ijams was elected as a member of the Ohio State Assembly (State Representative) in 1809, 1810, and 1811, as the representative from Fairfield County, and was elected as State Senator in Ohio in 1821 and 1822. He also served as Prosecuting Attorney of Fairfield County, Ohio, from 1822 to 1830. Thomas Plummer Ijams m. 2nd, to Elizabeth Hamilton Manley (b. 1787, Maryland; d. 1850, Ohio), widow of Reverend Robert Manley, the first Methodist itinerate preacher in Ohio.

EFB has indicated that John Ijams and Joseph Ijams were not the sons of Thomas Plummer Ijams, as listed by Newman. The will of Thomas Plummer Ijams was filed in Muskingum County, Ohio, November 2, 1847, after being written June 16, 1847, with Lewis E. Ijams as executor, William F. Ijams as witness, and the estate being left to his widow Elizabeth Hamilton Manley Ijams, with named children Harriet Ijams, Elizabeth Ijams, Charlotte Ijams, Comfort Ijams, Sarah Ijams, Ann Ijams, William F. Ijams, and Lewis Ijams. Several persons have assisted in the compilation of the Thomas Plummer Ijams family, including Dr. James W. Shaw, Ethlyn Bott, and JIH. In the 1850 Census of Muskingum County, Ohio, Elizabeth Ijams was listed as head of household with Ann Olive Ijams (age 10, b. Ohio), and Thomas P. Ijams (age 8, b. Ohio).

Children of Thomas Plummer Ijams (b. 1773) include: 1) John Ijams; 2) Joseph Ijams; 3) Rebecca Ijams (b. 1795; d. by 1847); 4) Lewis Ijams (b. 1796, Frederick County, Maryland; m. February 16, 1826, Muskingum County, Ohio, to Elizabeth Lodman, b. 1810, in Pennsylvania); 5) Harriet Ijams (b. October 27, 1800,

Frederick County, Maryland; d. March 13, 1878; m. Henry Wolf on February 10, 1820, in Muskingum County, Ohio); 6) Elizabeth Ijams (m. January 13, 1825, Muskingum County, Ohio, to Zadock Hall); 7) Comfort Ijams (b. December 31, 1808, in Hopewell Township, Muskingum County, Ohio; d. February 26, 1877, at Minck, Woodford County, Illinois; m. April 13, 1829, Muskingum County, Ohio, to George Evans Dent, son of John Dent; and their daughter Amelia Ann Dent, b. December 18, 1839, m. Jessie Miller Cowan, b. 1834; son of Robert Cowan and Martha Miller); 8) Sarah Ijams m. February 1, 1829, to Joseph Hall); 9) Charlotte Ijams (m. Isaac Springer on May 21, 1826, Muskingum County, Ohio); and three children by second wife; 10) William Fletcher Ijams (b. July 7, 1816, Ohio; d. 1892, McLean County, Illinois; m. in 1837 to Elsie Robinson, b. 1819, Ohio); and 11) Nancy or Ann Ijams (b. February 1819, Muskingum County, Ohio).

Lewis Ijams (b. 1798, Frederick County, Maryland), the son of Thomas Plummer Ijams (b. 1773, Maryland), m. 1826 to Elizabeth Rodman, and they may have had nine children: 1) Thomas Ijams (b. 1830, Ohio); 2) Joseph R. Ijams (b. 1836 or 1837, Ohio; m. Margaret ____; and children included Burt Ijams and Catherine Ijams, born in Illinois); 3) Charlotte Ijams (b. 1839, Ohio; d. 1907; m. 1863 to Reverend John Bennett Colwell, b. 1834; d. 1926); 4) Lewis E. Ijams (b. November 1841 or 1842, Ohio; single); 5) Elizabeth "Jane" Ijams (b. March 1844, Ohio; lived in Bloomington, McLean County, Illinois, with brother Lewis Ijams in 1900); 6) John Spry Ijams (b. November 1845, Ohio; and in 1880 was listed in Census of Liberty Township, Linn County, Kansas, with wife Minewa J. Ijams, age 49, b. Pennsylvania; and daughter Eva Ijams, age 9, b. Ohio); 7) William H. Ijams (b. 1848 or 1849, Ohio); 8) Sarah Ijams (b. 1838; d. 1839); and 9) George Ijams.

The *First Families of America* (Volume 6, p. 151) lists Lewis Ijams (1797-1867) as a member of the Ohio Legislature, Colonel in Ohio Militia, who moved to Bloomington, Illinois, after 1851, who m. Elizabeth Rodman (1808-1899), daughter of Joseph Rodman (1779-1853) and Mary Street (1785-1876) of Zanesville, Ohio, and formerly of Bucks County, Pennsylvania. John Rodman, Jr. (b. 1779) was the son of Joseph Rodman, Sr. (b. 1740) and Mary Allen, and the grandson of John Rodman (1714-1795) and Eleanor Belleijean of Burlington, New Jersey, and Bensalem, Bucks County, Pennsylvania.

Charlotte Ijams (b. 1839, Ohio; d. 1907), the daughter of Lewis Ijams (b. 1798) and Elizabeth Rodman, m. 1863 to Reverend John Bennett Colwell, and they had five children: 1) Lewis William Colwell (b. 1865; m. Grace Ann Stryker); 2) Mary Ellen Colwell (b. 1867); 3) Arthur B. Colwell (b. 1867; d. 1897); 4) Doctor John B. Colwell (b. 1873; m. 1st, Blanche Martin; d. 1918; m. 2nd, Pauline Grover); and 5) Clyde Cornish Colwell [(b. November 28, 1875, Lincoln, Illinois); m. December 8, 1909, to Laura Hoar (b. Henry, Illinois; daughter of Robert Hoar of Cincinnati, Ohio); Clyde Cornish Colwell (b. 1875) was a 1902 graduate of the University of Chicago; recipient of LLB Degree in 1906; a Superintendent of Heyworth, Illinois, schools from 1901-1903; a practicing attorney with Chicago law firm of Bryant, Roberts, Hwass, and Colwell; had a child Robert Clyde Colwell (b. November 17, 1910, Chicago, Illinois), a 1932 recipient of PhD degree from University of Chicago].

Comfort Ijams (b. December 31, 1808, Hopewell Township, Muskingum County, Ohio; d. February 26, 1887, Minok, Woodford County, Illinois), daughter of Thomas Plummer Ijams (b. 1773) and Sarah Duvall, m. April 12, 1829, Muskingum County, Ohio, to George Evans Dent (b. 1806, Monongalia County, West Virginia), the son of John Dent, and their child was Amelia Ann Dent (b. December 18, 1839, Magnolia, Putnam County, Illinois; d. November 3, 1875, Putnam County, Illinois), who m. September 7, 1860, to Jessie Miller Cowan (b. January 2, 1834, Muskingum

County, Ohio; d. September 7, 1890, Hennepin, Illinois), son of Robert Cowan and Martha Miller.

Amelia Ann Dent (b. 1839) and Jessie Miller Cowan had a son Charles Cook Hildreth Cowan (b. June 24, 1861, Magnolia, Illinois; d. March 15, 1934, Trenton, Dade County, Georgia), who m. August 16, 1893, in Illinois, to Mary Pearch Batchelder (b. June 19, 1870; d. October 5, 1947, Springfield, Illinois), daughter of John Jenness Batchelder and Mary Thompson Thorndike. James W. Shaw, M. D., contributed to this family tree. Charles Cook Hildreth Cowan (b. 1861) and Mary Pearch Batchelder had a daughter Amelia Dent Cowan (b. May 3, 1904, Warrensburg, Macon County, Illinois, who m. October 1, 1927, Chicago, Illinois, to James Wallace Shaw, M. D. (b. September 5, 1898, Denison, Jackson County, Kansas), the son of Andrew McLeod Shaw and Mary Elizabeth Reed. Andrew McLeod Shaw also had three other children: 1) Lyle Reid Shaw (b. November 18, 1894, Denison, Kansas; d. November 11, 1967, Topeka, Kansas; m. April 3, 1919, in Holton, Kansas, to Henrietta Mae Mullendore); 2) Martha Elizabeth Shaw (b. July 4, 1897, Denison, Kansas) m. 1st, Roy H. Anderson, and m. 2nd, Clarence Mitts; and 3) Mary Emma Shaw [(b. January 26, 1901, Dennison, Kansas), m. December 30, 1932, in Chicago, to Floyd Wilson Castator, M. D.; and they had 2 children: a) Mary Elizabeth Castator (b. September 21, 1935, Peoria County, Illinois; m. November 1959, to Ron Mercer, and they had two children: Brent Mercer, b. April 1962, Wichita, Kansas; and Chandra Mercer, b. October 1967, California); and b) Floyd Monroe Castator (b. June 1, 1940)].

James Wallace Shaw, Sr., M. D. (b. 1898) and Amelia Dent Cowan had three children: 1) Georgiana Louise Shaw [(b. April 18, 1932, Wichita, Sedgwick County, Kansas), m. June 21, 1958, Wichita, Kansas, to Clifford Dunkin Fales (b. February 17, 1932, Lakeworth, Florida), and they had two children: Peter Shaw Fales, b. April 23, 1960, Atlanta, Fulton County, Georgia; and Ellen Ruth Fales, b. August 18, 1962, Wichita, Kansas]; 2) Richard Cowan Shaw, M. D. [(b. March 21, 1935, Wichita, Kansas), m. August 24, 1957, Kansas City, Kansas, to Ruth Jean Keth (b. December 20, 1934, Omaha, Nebraska), and they had three children: a) Robert Keth (b. July 12, 1960, Kansas City, Kansas); b) James Michael Keth (b. June 2, 1963, San Antonia, Bexar County, Texas); and c) John Wallace Keth (b. April 22, 1964, Munich, Germany)]; 3) James Wallace Shaw, Jr., M. D. [(b. July 17, 1940, Wichita, Kansas), m. May 25, 1968, Hillsboro, Marion County, Kansas, to LaVerna Joyce Penner (b. March 18, 1942, Goessel, Marion County, Kansas), daughter of Alvin Penner and Freda Rempel; and they had two children: a) Kathryn Elizabeth Shaw (b. July 29, 1971, Fort Sill, Comanche County, Oklahoma), and b) Heather Ann Shaw (b. August 30, 1973, Hutchinson, Reno County, Kansas)].

William Fletcher Ijams (b. July 7, 1816, Ohio; d. October 21, 1892), the son of Thomas Plummer Ijams (b. 1773) and second wife Elizabeth Manley (b. 1782, Maryland), m. Elsie Robinson (b. 1818, Ohio; d. March 13, 1904), the daughter of Benjamin Franklin Robinson (b. 1789; d. 1843) and Phoebe Grant (b. 1790; d. 1834); Benjamin Franklin Robinson (b. 1789) was the son of Maximillian Robeson (b. 1758; d. 1831) and Lucinda Gunduff (b. 1753; d. 1832). The 1900 Census of DeWitt County, Illinois, lists Elsie Ijams (age 81, born in Ohio in October 1818) as an aunt of John Kindall family, living in Farmer City, Illinois. In 1850, William Fletcher Ijams and wife Elsie lived in Hopewell Township, Muskingum County, Ohio. In 1950, Evelyn Bott listed the possible children of William Fletcher Ijams as: 1) Eliza Jane Ijams [(b. June 17, 1845, 1848, or 1849; d. July 21, 1927), m. Doctor Newel Patterson (b. October 7, 1835; d. January 1, 1940), and their child was Edith Patterson (b. May 3, 1871; d. June 2, 1942); m. Edwin S. Wisegarver (b. September 2, 1870; d. June 24, 1896), whose child was Ethlyn Wisegarver (m. Doctor Anthony Bott)]; and 2)

Thomas LeRoy "Lee" Ijams (b. June 1842, Ohio; d. August 1908), m. August 18, 1866, to Rosetta "Rose" Walker (b. March 1842, McLean County, Illinois; d. October 1919), daughter of George E. Walker and Harriet Harder.

The 1880 Census of DeWitt County, Illinois, lists Thomas L. Ijams (age 37, b. Ohio); Rosetta Ijams (age 37, b. Illinois); Harold Ijams (age 14, b. Missouri); Hattie Ijams (age 12, b. Illinois); Ida Ijams (age 10, b. Illinois); George E. Ijams (age 8, b. Illinois); Millard Ijams, age 6, b. Illinois); Lewis Ijams (age 3, b. Illinois); and John M. Ijams (age 7 months, b. Illinois. The 1900 Census of Santa Anna Township, DeWitt County, Illinois, listed Thomas L. Ijaims (age 57, b. Ohio); Rosetta Ijaims (age 58, b. March 1842, Illinois); John M. Ijaims (age 20, b. September 1879, Illinois); Ellen S. Ijaims (age 15, b. September 1884, Illinois); Edith H. Ijaims (age 13, b. October 1886, Illinois); and Edna S. Ijaims (age 11, b. May 1889, Illinois). Millard Ijams and wife Nell Scott Ijams lived on the farm with sons Dr. Lynn Ijams, and Scott Ijams. Some (RWI, EFB) have listed other possible children of William Fletcher Ijams (b. 1816), including Mary Ann Ijams (b. 1838); William Henry Harrison Ijams (b. March 6, 1840, Randolph County, Illinois; d. September 24, 1924, Schell City, Missouri; m. November 22, 1862, Muskingum County, Ohio, to Susan Stackey or m. August 11, 1869, Wapella, Illinois, to Henrietta Nettie Williams); Thomas Plummer Ijams (b. 1843; d. 1851); Sarah E. Ijams (b. 1845); and Edith Ijams.

William Henry Harrison Ijams (b. March 6, 1840, Randolph, Illinois; d. September 24, 1924, Schell City, Missouri), m. August 31, 1869, Wapello, Illinois, to Henrietta "Nettie" Williams (b. November 9, 1845, Wapello, Illinois; d. December 10, 1922, Schell City, Missouri), and they had five children, including Lewis Sherman Ijams (b. August 5, 1870, Randolph, Illinois; d. July 14, 1936, Schell City, Missouri; m. December 1894 to Frank Culver); Florence Mignonette Ijams (b. December 14, 1872, Paxton, Illinois; d. August 1956, Schell City, Missouri), and Clyde Elmer Ijams (b. June 12, 1875, Paxton, Illinois; d. May 6, 1954, Schell City, Missouri; m. January 6, 1901, to Mary Elizabeth "Bessie" Thompson, b. August 27, 1871, Schell City, Missouri; d. September 5, 1945, Schell City, Missouri); and they had nine children:

1) Edna Naomi Ijams (b. April 18, 1903, Schell City, Missouri; d. May 28, 1967, Schell City, Missouri); 2) Lilliam Alberta Ijams (b. April 1, 1905, Schell City, Missouri; d. September 6, 1983); 3) Ward "Harold" Hage Ijams (b. March 8, 1907, Schell City, Missouri; d. June 3, 1975, Schell City, Missouri; 4) Ruby "Irene" Ijams (b. July 13, 1910, Schell City, Missouri); 5) Dale Elmer Ijams (b. August 28, 1913, Schell City, Missouri); 6) Leland "Earl" Ijams (b. September 27, 1915, Cambridge, Illinois); 7) Inez LaVonne Ijams (b. March 12, 1918, Cambridge, Illinois); 8) Raymond Lonnie Ijams (b. August 17, 1923, Schell City, Missouri; d. February 12, 1982); and 9) Orval "Ross" Ijams [(b. July 13, 1901, Belvoir or Bevier, Missouri; d. May 21, 1966, Kewanee, Illinois), m. September 3, 1932, to Ethel Christine Wislander (b. September 12, 1907, Cambridge, Illinois); and they had three children: a) Karl Frederick Ijams (b. June 12, 1933, Kewanee, Illinois; m. December 27, 1962, to Judith Elaine Driscoll (b. May 10, 1939, Pittsfield, Massachusetts), and they had two children: Edward Eric Ijams (b. January 27, 1967, Urbana, Illinois), and Joynora "Joy" Lynn Ijams (b. May 27, 1974, Boynton Beach, Florida); b) Alice Christine Ijams (b. March 17, 1937, Kewanee, Illinois), m. August 14, 1965, to Ernest Gustal Soderstrom (b. November 23, 1929, Geneva, Illinois), and they had three children: Kersten Ann Souderstrom (b. October 26, 1967, Saint Charles, Illinois); Merta Lena Soderstrom (b. April 2, 1969, Saint Charles, Illinois); and Lara Elin Soderstrom (b. October 14, 1973, in Saint Charles, Illinois); and c) Charlotte Louise Ijams (b. May 12, 1939, Kewanee, Illinois); m. Kenneth Robert Teleen (b. September 15, 1939,

Kewanee, Illinois), and they had two children: Frederick Crandell Teleen (b. October 20, 1966, Flint, Michigan), and Sarah Louise Teleen (b. December 1, 1969, Minneapolis, Minnesota)].

The sister of Mary Elizabeth "Bessie" Thompson Ijams (b. 1881) was Amanda Louella Thompson (b. August 21, 1879, Schell City, Missouri; d. October 21, 1968, Metz, Missouri), who m. Frank Gordon, and they had two children: Bert Gordon, and Genevieve "Nevis" Gordon. In addition, Amanda Louella Thompson had two earlier children: Roy Sares and Orval "Ross" Ijams (b. 1901), adopted by Clyde Ijams (b. 1875) and Mary Elizabeth Thompson Ijams. Alfred Alonzo "Lou" Thompson (b. August 26, 1877; d. 1950, Girard, Kansas; m. Rose Henderson) was the brother of Amanda Thompson and Mary Elizabeth Thompson and their parents were Alfred Alonzo "Lonnie" Thompson (d. 1873) and Mary Elizabeth "Lady" Westfall (b. August 18, 1841; m. December 27, 1859; d. March 24, 1921, Flat Rock, Missouri).

Thomas LeRoy "Lee" Ijams (b. June 1842, Ohio; d. August 1908), m. August 18, 1866, to Rosetta "Rose" Walker (b. March 1892, McLean County, Illinois; d. October 1919). Thomas Ijams (b. 1842) was the son of William Fletcher Ijams (b. 1816) and Elsie Robinson, though this has been questioned by EFB and others. Thomas Ijams (b. 1842) had ten children:

1) Harvey Lee "Harold" Ijams (b. January 4, 1866, Missouri; d. October 1931, Illinois; m. Corinne "Cosa" Thomas); 2) Hariet "Hattie" Ijams (b. 1868, Illinois; m. Douglas Watson); 3) Ida May Ijams (b. November 9, 1869, Illinois; d. October 1947; m. John W. Kendall, Jr., and they lived in Farmer City, Illinois); 4) George E. Ijams (b. 1872, Illinois; m. Edna _____; he had an automobile dealership with his brother, Harvey Ijams); 5) Millard Ijams (b. October 1873, Illinois; m. Nell Scott, b. December 1876, Illinois); 6) Doctor Lewis Elmer Ijams (b. 1877, DeWitt County, Illinois; m. Ethel Hall); 7) John M. Ijams (b. September 1879, DeWitt County, Illinois; m. Maude Bueschell and they lived in Hollywood, California, where they had a daughter Maude Snow Ijams); 8) Ella Scanlon Ijams (b. September 1884; m. Claude Nichols of Farmer City, Illinois; lived Fort Lauderdale, Florida); 9) Edith Hoysradt Ijams (b. October 1886, Illinois; m. Homer Curtis of Waverly, Illinois; moved first to Des Moines, Iowa, and then to Pomona, California); and 10) Edna Sarah Ijams (b. May 1889, DeWitt County, Illinois; d. 1964; m. George Johnson, and they lived first in Iowa, and later in Bloomington, Illinois).

Doctor Lewis Elmer Ijams (b. 1877, DeWitt County, Illinois), the son of Thomas LeRoy "Lee" Ijams (b. 1842) and Rosetta "Rose" Walker, m. Ethel Hall (who became a Christian Science practitioner); attended business college in Quincy, Illinois; later graduated from College of Osteopathy in Des Moines, Iowa; they had five children: 1) Byron Lewis Ijams (b. March 3, 1906, Champaign, Illinois; m. Bessie Dixon); 2) Walker Hall Ijams (b. February 23, 1908, Des Moines, Iowa; d. December 31, 1974, Oak Park, Illinois; m. 1st, Martha Lapinoja, and they had two children: m. 2nd, Edyth Asheroft, who d. October 12, 1974); 3) Eloise Ethlyn Ijams [(b. August 1, 1911, Marshall, Minnesota); m. Bruce Welliver Caldwell (b. October 27, 1907, Tecumseh, Michigan), and they had two children: Robert Duncan Caldwell (b. August 19, 1945, McPherson, Georgia; m. Brenda Rogers on December 27, 1967, and their child was Sean Brian Caldwell, b. October 29, 1971, in Midland, Michigan); and Joan Elizabeth Caldwell (b. August 8, 1948, Berwyn, Illinois)]; 4) Kermit Williams Ijams [(b. February 17, 1913, Marshall, Minnesota; killed in motorcycle accident August 11, 1944), m. Louise Richardson (she had been previously m. to her cousin, Harold Richardson, and had son Robert Richardson); they had a daughter Judy Ijams (m. David Redo)]; and 5) Lewis Elmer Ijams, Jr. (b. August 27, 1914, Marshall, Minnesota; m. Myrl Chase).

128

Byron Lewis Ijams (b. March 3, 1906, Champaign, Illinois, the son of Lewis Elmer Ijams (b. 1877) and Ethel Hall; m. Bessie Dixon, and they had three children: 1) Billie Virginia Ijams [(b. February 16, 1933, Chicago), m. Fred Haase, Jr. (d. June 1974), and they had two children: Laura Ann Haase (b. December 6, 1959), and Walter William Haase (b. January 29, 1964)]; 2) Jimmy William Ijams [(b. December 7, 1936, Chicago, Illinois), m. April 24, 1964, to Carol Frederickson, and they had two children: Karen Ijams (b. 1967) and Christine Ijams (b. 1970)]; and 3) Richard Ijams (b. November 14, 1940, Chicago).

Walker Hall Ijams (b. February 23, 1908, Des Moines, Iowa; d. December 31, 1974, Oak Park, Illinois), the son of Doctor Lewis Elmer Ijams (b. 1877) and Ethel Hall; m. 1st, to Martha Lapinoja, and they had two children: 1) Walker Lewis "Chip" Ijams; and 2) Lee Stevens Ijams, who m. ____ Sheets, and they had two children: Christine Ijams (b. 1969), and Steven Ijams (b. 1972). Walker Hall Ijams (b. 1908) m. to Edyth Ashcroft (d. 1974), but they are not known to have had children.

Harvey Lee Ijams (b. January 4, 1866, Missouri; d. October 1931, Farmer City, Illinois), the son of Thomas LeRoy "Lee" Ijams (d. 1908) and Rosetta "Rose" Walker; m. February 1890 in Parnell, Illinois, to Corinne Mae "Cosa" Thomas, and they had four children: 1) Samuel LeRoy Ijams (b. May 25, 1893; m. December 1912, to Myrtle McConkey, and they lived at Maroa, Macon County, Illinois); 2) Guy Lyndon Ijams (b. June 20, 1896; d. May 4, 1970, Farmer City, Illinois; m. Imo Hatfield on July 2, 1923, and lived in Chicago); 3) Mabel Kathryn Ijams (b. January 3, 1898; m. 1st, in 1919, to Roy Beaven; and m. 2nd, April 7, 1923, to Kenneth Kindler); and 4) Lucy L. Ijams (b. 1897, Illinois).

Edith Hoysradt Ijams (b. October 1886, Illinois), the daughter of Thomas LeRoy "Lee" Ijams (b. 1842) and Rosetta "Rose" Walker; m. Homer Curtiss, and they had three children: Mary Felicia Curtiss (b. July 17, 1915, Fort Lauderdale, Florida; m. January 24, 1942, to Eric Helmer Patterson); 2) Homer Allen Curtiss [(b. December 13, 1916, Fort Lauderdale, Florida); m. Marian Robinson (b. June 8, 1923), and they had three children: Carol Ann Curtiss (b. September 4, 1945; m. 1st, Bruce Wisser, and m. 2nd, Bill Hendrix, and they had two children); Anita Louise Curtiss (b. July 30, 1955, Pomona, California), and Lynn Eileen Curtiss (b. April 16, 1963)]; and 3) Martha Washington Curtiss [(b. February 22, 1922, Downs, Illinois), m. December 20, 1947, to Herbert Frederick Welch (b. March 30, 1916), and they had three children: Russell Lynn Welch (b. September 11, 1949, Altadena, Pasadena, California); Robert Lee Welch (b. January 30, 1956, Pasadena, California), and Rosemary Welch (b. June 11, 1957, Sierra Madre, California)].

Samuel LeRoy Ijams (b. May 25, 1893), the son of Harvey Lee Ijams (b. 1866) and Corinne Mae Thomas; m. December 1912, to Myrtle McConkey; and they had three children: 1) Vincent Morris Ijams (m. Twila Hearold, and they had three children: James Ijams, Keron Ijams, and a daughter); 2) Robert Delwin Ijams (m. Harriet ____, and they had two children: Billy Joe Ijams and Terrance Ijams); and 3) Barbara Mae Ijams (m. Carli Rainy, and they had four children: Tommy Rainy, Bobby Rainy, Carol Ann Rainy, and Sammy Rainy).

Guy Lyndon Ijams (b. June 20, 1896; d. May 4, 1970), the son of Harvey Lee Ijams (b. 1866) and Corinne Mae Thomas; m. July 2, 1923, to Imo Hatfield, and they had four children; 1) Guy Harvey Ijams (b. 1929; d. May 1, 1968, Dallas, Texas; m. 1961, to Maria Brown); 2) Lyndon Hatfield Ijams (b. 1933; m. 1956 to Babs Gluskoter, and they had two children: David Ijams, and Michael Ijams); 3) Imogene Mildred Ijams (b. 1934; d. age 6 weeks); and 4) Mona Ruth Ijams (b. 1936; m. John Weicimorick; no children).

Ida Mae Ijams (b. November 9, 1869; d. October 1941), daughter of Thomas LeRoy "Lee" Ijams (b. 1908) and Rosetta "Rose" Walker; m. John W. Kendall,

Jr., of South Prairie, Illinois; they had three children: 1) John Thomas Kendall (m. Kitty Robinson, and they had twins: Richard Kendall, who m. Helen Douglas; and Reynole Kendall); 2) Mary Lilly Kendall (b. December 11, 1892, South Prairie, Illinois; m. September 14, 1921, to Roscoe Harget); 3) Lloyd Walker Kendall [(b. November 1894), m. Hulda "Irene" Dennison (b. February 26, 1900), and their child Delores Kendall (b. September 7, 1925), m. April 7, 1944, to Max Hunter Kumler (b. September 13, 1922); with Max Kumler (b. 1922) and Delores Kendall (b. 1925) having a child Cheryl Kumler (b. March 25, 1947), who m. September 27, 1964, to David Howry (and they had two children: Dana Lee Howry, b. February 15, 1968, Yuma, Arizona; and Treva Ann Howry, b. May 6, 1971, Yuma, Arizona)].

Mary Lilly Kendall (b. December 11, 1892, South Prairie, Illinois), the daughter of Ida Mae Ijams (b. 1869), and John W. Kendall, Jr., m. September 14, 1921, to Roscoe Harget (b. August 17, 1888; d. December 14, 1962), and they had four children: 1) Martha Harget [(b. August 8, 1923), m. December 16, 1956, to Milton Strauss, and they had two children: John Michael Strauss (b. March 2, 1959), and Mary Strauss (b. December 1, 1962)]; 2) Jacquiline Harget (b. October 13, 1925; d. March 13, 1935); 3) Roscoe Harget, Jr. [(b. September 30, 1932), m. August 24, 1956, to Beverly Dinger, and they had three children: Lisa Louise Harget (b. November 10, 1957); Linda Lorraine Harget (b. July 17, 1960); and Lincoln Lee Harget (b. March 6, 1962]; and 4) Priscilla Twining Harget [(b. November 2, 1935), m. August 22, 1959, Richard Seth Roberts, Jr., and they had three children: Laura Roberts (b. November 3, 1963); Rhys Harget Roberts (b. July 16, 1966; d. July 26, 1966, Cairo, Egypt); and Wendy Lee Roberts (b. July 19, 1967)].

John Ijams (b. 1755, Anne Arundel County, Maryland; d. May 5, 1823, Frederick County, Maryland), the son of Captain John Iiams (b. 1712) and Rebecca Jones, m. Frederick County, Maryland, March 21, 1782, to Mary Waters, daughter of John and Rachel Waters. According to EFB, Mary Waters Iiams m. 2nd, Thomas Woodward Abraham. The estate of Lt. John Ijams, Frederick County, Maryland, was administered May 13, 1823, by Jacob Ijams. Isaac Ijams held a note and distributions were made to Jane Ijams (wife of Singleton Burgess); Elizabeth Ijams (wife of Thomas Duvall); Mary Ijams (wife of John Montgomery); Ann Ijams (wife of John McLaughlin); son Jacob Ijams; and son John Ijams. Sons John Ijams and Jacob Ijams were given land called Paris. Son Plummer Ijams was given Resurvey. Son Jacob Ijams was given the slave David, among others. Son John Ijams was given the slave Benjamin. Also mentioned in the will were the grandson Plummer Ijams, and daughter Ann McLaughlin (given the slave Grace). Lt. John Ijams had been recommended for the rank of ensign on September 16, 1776, by the Council on Safety of Anne Arundel County; was a second lieutenant in Captain Thomas Watkins' Regiment in the West River Battalion in 1778. John Ijams became a captain and was paid for recruiting duties in 1780 and 1781. Lois I. Hartman, MI, and others have listed John Ijams (b. 1755) as the father of the Howard family slave called Jack Imes, the famous progenitor of the wonderful, closely knit family line that settled in south central Pennsylvania, that flourished and grew as they pursued agriculture as a profession. Jack Imes was born in 1776 and was given his freedom about 1800. His family line is found elsewhere in this book.

John Ijams (b. 1755) and Mary Waters are believed to have had as many as nine children:

1) Jacob Ijams [(b. 1791, Frederick County, Maryland; d. 1823, Frederick County, Maryland) m. March 15, 1814, to Anne Howard, daughter of John Cornelius Howard and Mary Campbell, and they had two children: Rebecca Ijams (b. 1816; d. 1863; m. September 27, 1836, to John Wilcoxon, b. 1807; d. 1883); and Mary Ijams (m. William H. Ijams)].

2) John Waters Ijams [(b. November 21, 1807, Frederick County, Maryland; d. February 16, 1875, Fairfield County, Ohio); license to marry May 25, 1827, Frederick County, Maryland, to Rebecca Marriott Ijams (b. February 4, 1806; d. October 23, 1885), daughter of Captain John Ijams and Rachel Marriott; and they had twelve children: a) John Richard Ijams (b. March 13, 1828; d. November 29, 1831); b) Van Buren Ijams (b. June 28, 1829, Anne Arundel County, Maryland; d. February 10, 1892; m. Florilla Spears); c) Rachel Ann Ijams (b. January 20, 1831, Anne Arundel County, Maryland; d. November 10, 1831); d) Maria Antionette Ijams (b. September 11, 1832, Anne Arundel County, Maryland; d. April 15, 1904); e) Richard William Ijams (b. August 20, 1834; d. June 10, 1889); f) Spragg Homewood Ijams (b. August 19, 1836, Anne Arundel County, Maryland; d. January 4, 1918; m. November 16, 1857, Anne Arundel County, Maryland, to Ann Rebecca Brown); g) Jacob Waters Ijams (b. June 26, 1838; d. 1913; m. Ann Minerva Howard); h) Josephine Ijams (b. October 12, 1842, Anne Arundel County, Maryland; d. November 1925); i) DeWitt Clinton Ijams (b. April 13, 1844; d. October 24, 1862; j) John Barney Ijams (b. September 10, 1844; d. May 27, 1849); k) Victoria Ijams (b. March 15, 1847; d. June 8, 1849); and l) Jane Rebecca Ijams (b. March 3, 1849; d. April 21, 1858)].
3) Plummer D. Ijams.
4) Ann Ijams (m. May 8, 1821, to John McLaughlin).
5) Jane Ijams (m. May 14, 1805, Singleton Burgess).
6) Elizabeth Ijams (b. 1793; m. June 14, 1814, Frederick County, Maryland, to Thomas Duvall).
7) Mary Ijams (m. January 19, 1814, Frederick County, Maryland, to John Montgomery).
8) Rebecca Ijams (b. 1784, Frederick County, Maryland; d. November 10, 1809; m. March 10, 1804, to either Plummer Ijams III or to Thomas Sunderland).
9) William Iiams (m. Elizabeth Howard, and had eleven children); with references provided by EFB, RWI, LIH, HCP, MI, and DAR 76:337, #75899, and #69541.
John Waters Ijams (b. November 21, 1807, Frederick County, Maryland; d. February 16, 1875), the son of John Ijams (b. 1755) and Mary Waters; m. May 25, 1827 (license date), to Rebecca Marriott (b. February 4, 1806; d. October 23, 1885). The 1850 Federal Census of Anne Arundel County, Maryland, lists John W. Ijams (age 43); Rebeca (age 44); Richard (age 16); Sprigg H. (age 14); Jacob W. (age 12); Jane B. (age 2); David C. (age 4); Harriet A. (age 18); and Josephine (age 8); The DAR line 145:36 traces Jacob Waters Iams (b. 1808; d. 1913), m. 1858 to Ann A. Howard (b. 1835; d. 1901), to John Waters Ijams, who m. 1827 to Rebecca Marriott (b. 1807); and then to John Plummer Ijams (m. 1804 to Rebecca Ijams); and finally, to John Ijams (m. Mary Waters). The DAR line 149:69 traces Eva Roberts Hughes (b. 1838; d. 1900), who m. 1864 to Jerusa Ann Ijams (b. 1844; d. 1925); and then to Isaac Plummer Ijams (b. 1812; d. 1877), who m. 1834 to Cecelia Smith Moxley (b. 1813; d. 1887); then to John Ijams (b. 1775; d. 1831), who m. 1794 to Rachel Marriott; and then to Thomas Ijams (m. 1720, to Mary ____); and finally, to John Ijams (b. 1712, a captain, Maryland), who m. Rebecca Jones.
The twelve children of John Waters Ijams (b. 1805) and Rebecca Marriott are:
1) John Richard Ijams (b. March 13, 1828, Anne Arundel County, Maryland; d. November 29, 1831).

2) Van Buren Ijams (b. June 28, 1829, Anne Arundel County, Maryland; d. February 10, 1892).
3) Rachel Ann Ijams (b. January 20, 1831; d. November 10, 1831).
4) Maria Antionette Ijams (b. September 11, 1832, Anne Arundel County, Maryland; d. April 15, 1904).
5) Richard William Ijams (b. August 20, 1834, Anne Arundel County, Maryland; d. June 10, 1889).
6) Sprigg Homewood Ijams (b. August 19, 1836, Anne Arundel County, Maryland; d. January 4, 1918; m. November 16, 1857, to Ann Rebecca Brown).
7) Jacob Waters Ijams (b. June 26, 1838; d. 1913; m. 1858, Ann A. Howard, b. 1835; d. 1901; and their children were Mary L. Ijams, Fanny V. Ijams, John W. Ijams, Ella V. Ijams, and Kate G. Ijams.
8) ?
9) DeWitt Clinton Ijams (b. April 13, 1842; d. October 24, 1862).
10) John Barney Ijams (b. September 10, 1844, Anne Arundel County, Maryland; d. June 8, 1849).
11) Victoria Ijams (b. March 13, 1847, Anne Arundel County, Maryland; d. July 8, 1849).
12) Jane Rebecca Ijams (b. March 3, 1849; d. April 21, 1858). (Reference Harry Wright Newman, *Anne Arundel Gentry*, Volume One, page 314).

Jacob Ijams (b. 17__, Frederick County, Maryland), the son of John Ijams (b. 1755) and Mary Waters, m. March 13, 1814, to Anne Howard (the daughter of John Cornelius Howard and Mary Campbell), and they had two children: 1) Rebecca Ijams (m. September 27, 1836, license date, to John Wilcoxen); and 2) Mary Ijams (m. William H. Ijams). With the death of John Cornelius Howard, the shares of the estate that were to go to Anne Howard Ijams were distributed to both John and Rebecca Ijams Wilcoxen, and to William H. and Mary Ijams. The 1880 Census of Baltimore, Maryland, lists William Henry Ijams (age 57, b. Maryland); Isabella Ijams (age 47, b. Maryland); William Henry Ijams, Jr. (age 25, b. Maryland); George E. Ijams (age 20, b. Maryland); Albert Ijams (age 10, b. Maryland); son-in-law E. T. Drury (age 26, b. Maryland); and Laura Drury (age 23, b. Maryland).

William Ijams (b. 1760, Anne Arundel County, Maryland; d. 1816, Fairfield County, Ohio), the son of John Iiams (b. 1712) and Rebecca Jones, m. Elizabeth Howard [(daughter of Joseph Howard and Rachel Ridgely of Anne Arundel County, Maryland), with Rachel Ridgely Howard giving several slaves to Elizabeth Howard Ijams, March 12, 1785)]. William Ijams left several slaves to his son William Ijams as well, and the son moved to Frederick County, Maryland. William Ijams (b. 1760) took the Oath of Allegiance to State of Maryland March 1778, as "William Ijams, son of John." In 1806, he was taxed in Richland Township, Fairfield County, Ohio, where he and two brothers had settled about 1804. His last will mentioned sons John Ijams, Isaac Ijams, Joseph Ijams, Frederick Ijams, a widow, and unnamed daughters.

Heads of households in the 1830 Federal Census of Richland Township, Fairfield County, Ohio, included William H. Ijams, Joseph H. Ijams, Isaac H. Ijams, Elizabeth Ijams, and Catherine Ijams. The 1840 census of the same area listed heads of households: William H. Ijams, Joseph Ijams, John Ijams, and Richard Ijams. The 1850 census lists heads of households, Richland Township, Fairfield County, Ohio, as: William H. Ijams, William Ijams, John W. Ijams, Catherine Ijams, and B. D. Ijams. William H. Ijams (age 42, b. Ohio); Anne E. Ijams (age 30, b. Ohio); Jane E. Ijams (age 22, b. Ohio); William H. Ijams (age 20, b. Ohio); Mary M. Ijams (age 15, b. Ohio); Sarah C. Ijams (age 13, b. Ohio); Mary Ijams (age 10, b. Ohio); Thomas Ijams (age 7, b. Ohio); Franklin Ijams (age 4, b. Ohio); and Isaac B. Ijams (age 1, b.

Ohio) in one family; William Ijams (age 35, merchant, b. Ohio); Catherine Ijams (age 27, b. Ohio); Edward T. Ijams (age 4, b. Ohio); Mary E. Imes (age 3, b. Ohio); and Laura Imes (age 1, b. Ohio) in a second family; John W. Ijams (age 45, farmer, b. Ohio); Sarah H. Ijams (age 36, b. Maryland); Louisa Ijams (age 17, b. Ohio); Joseph Ijams (age 15, b. Ohio); Isaac Ijams (age 13, b. Ohio); Elizabeth Ijams (age 10, b. Ohio); William Ijams (age 7, b. Ohio); John Ijams (age 5, b. Ohio), and Vinson Ijams (age 2, b. Ohio) as a third family; Catherine Ijams (age 65, b. Pennsylvania) as living alone; and B. D. Ijams (age 38, farmer, b. Ohio); J. E. Ijams (age 33, b. Pennsylvania); William H. Ijams (age 10, b. Ohio); T. F. Ijams (age 9, b. Ohio); Daniel Ijams (age 4, b. Ohio), and Caroline Ijams (age 2 months, b. Ohio) as the other family.

The 1860 Census of Logan Township, Hocking County, Ohio, shows that the merchant William Ijams had moved as was listed as: William Ijams (age 49, merchant, b. Ohio); Catherine Ijams (age 36, b. Maryland); E. T. Ijams (age 14, b. Ohio); Mary E. Ijams (age 14, b. Ohio); James B. Ijams (age 9, b. Ohio); Caroline P. Ijams (age 7, b. Ohio); Elle C. Ijams (age 5, b. Ohio); Frederick S. Ijams (age 3, b. Ohio); and Sally E. Ijams (age 1, b. Ohio). Children of William Ijams (b. 1760, Anne Arundel County, Maryland) and Elizabeth Howard included: 1) William Howard Ijams (b. 1790); 2) John Howard Ijams; 3) Isaac Ijams; 4) Joseph Howard Ijams (b. 1794; m. September 21, 1828, Fairfield County, Ohio, to Mary Ann Ijams, daughter of John Ijams; 5) Frederick Ijams; 6: Richard D. Ijams (m. October 25, 1838, to J. E. Alford); Rebecca Ijams; 8) Rachel Ijams; 9) Mary Ijams; 10) Comfort Ijams; and 11) Sarah Ijams.

Joseph Howard Ijams (b. 1794, Maryland), son of William Ijams (b. 1753, Maryland) and Elizabeth Howard; m. September 21, 1828, Fairfield County, Ohio, to Mary Ann Ijams (daughter of first cousin John Ijams). John Howard Ijams (b. 1794) was a well known merchant of West Rushville, Fairfield County, Ohio, but failed in recession of 1841 and moved to Iowa. He is listed on the Fairfield County, Ohio, tax rolls of 1820 to 1829. Wiseman's *Pioneer Record and Pioneer People of Fairfield County, Ohio,* lists Joseph H. Ijams as the son of Thomas Ijams, and the brother of John Ijams and Frederick Ijams; with Richard Ijams and Howard Ijams as sons of William Ijams; and with Isaac Ijams, John Ijams, and William Ijams as sons of Isaac Ijams. The three Ijams brothers who moved to Fairfield County, Ohio, from Maryland were: Thomas Ijams, William Ijams, and Isaac Ijams. Joseph H. Ijams (b. 1794), merchant, was a partner with William Coulson for a store in West Rushville, Ohio; and also established a store in nearby Baltimore, Ohio, in 1838, with partner Oliver Reed. The children of Joseph Howard Ijams (b. 1794) and Mary Ann Ijams included: 1) an infant (d. 1829); 2) William F. Ijams (b. 1831); 3) Caroline E. Ijams (b. 1834); 4) Mary Victoria Ijams (b. August 9, 1837; d. August 25, 1837; buried West Rushfield, Ohio); 5) Joseph H. H. Ijams (b. 1842); and 6): Frederick Ridgely Ijams (d. July 6, 1840, at age 1 year, 8 months, 17 days, and buried in West Rushville, Ohio).

William Howard Ijams (b. 1790), the son of William Ijams (b. 1760) and Elizabeth Howard, had two sons: 1) Henry Ijams; and 2) Richard Ijams.

Anne Ijams, daughter of John Iiams (b. 1712) and Rebecca Jones, m. June 10 or 12, 1762 or 1763, Anne Arundel County, Maryland, Lewis Stockett (b. August 6, 1724), the son of Thomas Stockett Jr. (b. April 17, 1667; d. 1732). Thomas Stocket Jr. (b. 1667) m. 1st, March 12, 1689, to Mary Sprigg, the daughter of Colonel Thomas Sprigg of West River, Maryland; and m. 2nd, April 9, 1700, to Damaris Welsh, daughter of Major John Stockett, Jr. (b. 1667) had four children: 1) Thomas Stockett III (b. November 18, 1691); 2) Eleanor Stockett (b. December 8, 1693; m. Richard Williams of Calvert County, Maryland, on February 14, 1709); 3) Mary Stockett (m. Jodeph Brewer); and 4) Lewis Stockett (see above, m. Anne Ijams as his second wife).

Plummer Iiams (b. 1716; d. 1792), the son of William Iiams (b. 1670) and Elizabeth Plummer, m. Mary Ruth Childs. Plummer Iiams (b. 1716, baptized All Hallows Parish August 6, 1718; lived South River Hundred, Anne Arundel County, Maryland; d. November 20, 1792); was deeded Dodon by his mother in 1738, which he later sold on July 4, 1744, to John Ijams. Plummer Iiams (b. 1716) m. Ruth Childs (d. December 24, 1794), a descendant of Henry Childs, a Quaker from England (presented certificate to West River Meeting May 11, 1702). On January 31, 1742, Henry Childs of Anne Arundel County, Maryland, a planter, conveyed two tracts of land on Patuxent River in Calvert County, Maryland, called Archer's Hay to Plummer Ijams for 60 pounds. Plummer Iiams (b. 1716) had moved back to Anne Arundel County, Maryland, by November 13, 1751, and Plummer Ijams sold Archer Hays to Lewis Griffith for 60 pounds. On March 12, 1762, he purchased Bridge Hill and Dodon from John Iiams of Anne Arundel County for 100 pounds (93 acres). Plummer Ijams subscribed to Oath of Allegiance and Fidelity to State of Maryland in 1778. The 1770 Census for All Hallows Parish listed Plummer Ijams as a planter, with one man, two women, one child, and fifteen slaves in the household.

The will of Plummer Ijams, dated February 18, 1793, named John Jacobs and Isaac Iiams as witnesses, and gave plantation to wife Ruth Ijams (only one-third if she remarried, and to son Plummer Iiams should she die); slaves and personal effects to daughters Elizabeth Drury and Ann Drury. Ann Stockett and Thomas Ijams were identified as kinsmen. The April 16, 1793, estate inventory totaled slightly over 690 pounds. Ruth Childs Iiams, widow, died intestate 1799, and the estate was not settled until October 23, 1817, when Samuel Drury, as executor, distributed the final total of $199.41 among Plummer Iiams, William Drury, Sr., husband of daughter Elizabeth Iiams), and Samuel Drury, Sr. (husband of daughter Ann Iiams). In addition, Plummer Iiams (b. 1716) is listed as having received the deed for All Hallows Parish church (as Church Warden) from Captain Thomas Gassoway in 1768.

Plummer Ijams (b. 1716 or 1718) moved to Frederick County, Maryland, in January 1785 to an area that became known as Ijamsville, with early settlers from the families of Duvall, Musseter (Lemud and John Musseter later became Ijamsville postmasters); Burgee, Montgomery, and Riggs. The large Ijamsville plantation was called Paradise on the present town site, with the land holdings later expanded by the descendants. Plummer Ijams purchased Ijams Resolution, a plantation of 156 acres in Frederick County, Maryland, in 1787. After the death of Plummer Ijams, the "goods and chattels" of his estate were eventually sold in 1796. Among the things that Ann Ijams purchased were: a Negro Bob for 125 pounds; one cow for 6 pounds; a Dutch oven and two pots for 12 shillings and 6 pence; one wooling wheel for 14 shillings; and a pigeon split for 1 shilling and 10 pence. William Ijams bought a Negro boy Will for 100 pounds. John Ijams bought 300 weight of tobacco, 8 pounds of sugar loaf; 102 pounds of tallow; 11 pounds of coarse yarn; 117 pounds of flax break; and and 11 acres of land for 1 pound, 15 shillings, and 4 pence per acre. Isaac Ijams bought a supply of flannel for 1 pound; the branding iron for 1 shilling and 10 pence. Maureen Duvall bought the money scales for 7 shillings. Maureen Duvall was a famous Huguenot who moved to Maryland in 1659, and whose descendants Thomas Duvall, Benjamin Duvall, and William Duvall, owned large tracts of land including Duvall's Forest next to the Ijams land

On the southwest part of the Ijams land were several log cabins in which the slaves lived. The Ijams spring was later owned by Doctor Reuben Moxley. The local clay was found to be good for making pottery. Eliza Musseter Ijams ran a popular boarding school on the old Ijams homestead from about 1870 to at least 1887. Eliza Musseter, the granddaughter of Captain Christopher Musseter, married her first cousin

Richard Ijams, the son of the founder of Ijamsville, and a lawyer. Eliza Musseter Ijams is credited with promoting the Maryland State School for Deaf after the 1851 death of her husband, and had two deaf children: son Plummer Ijams III and Mary Manning Ijams, known as "Miss Mollie," the first school graduate, who returned to teach at the school from 1872-1917.

C. E. Moylan, author of *Ijamsville: Country Village of Frederick County, Maryland* (published privately) described Plummer Ijams (b. 1718; d. June 14, 1796) as the son of William Ijams (along with brother Thomas Ijams) as the first settler of Ijamsville (moved there in 1785). The Annual Report of the Baltimore and Ohio Railroad referred to the village as "Ijams Mill" (John Ijams built a grist mill that was standing in 1831), and cites the 1831 gift of Plummer Ijams, Jr., of the land for the right of way of the railroad, in exchange for the establishment of a depot (this private depot site was granted September 23, 1833). This reference states that the Ijams family moved from Wales to Maryland in 1650. The post office at Ijamsville was established as "Ijams Mill" on June 22, 1832, with Plummer Ijams, Jr., as the first postmaster. Subsequent postmasters include: James Ijams and Richard Ijams, both sons of Plummer Ijams, Jr. Richard Ijams, a cum laude graduate of Saint Marys College, practiced law in Hedgville, Virginia (now West Virginia), before returning to Ijamsville and purchasing the old homestead. Plummer Ijams was a member of the Maryland Legislature in 1820. The first B. & O Railroad run from Baltimore to Frederick, Maryland, was on Thursday, March 13, 1832, and was drawn by one horse, with eighty passengers when it passed through Ijamsville.

Children of Plummer Ijams (b. 1716 or 1718) and Ruth Childs included:
1) Elizabeth Ijams [(b. December 3, 1750, Anne Arundel County, Maryland) m. William Drury, and they had three sons: Charles Drury, William Drury, and Henry Drury].
2) Margaret Ijams (b. October 1 or 31, 1753) m. Jonathan Selby.
3) Ann Ijams [(b. July 2, 1759) m. Samuel Drury (b. 1753; brother of Charles Drury and son of Charles Drury of the East India Company); lived at Drury's Manor, and had ten children: a) Elizabeth Drury (m. ____ Ward); b) Ruth Drury (m. Benjamin Welsh, and had ten children: Eleanor Welsh, Mary Welsh, Ann Welsh, Eliza Welsh, June Welsh, Robert Welsh, Elizabeth Welsh, Susan Welsh, Benjamin Welsh, and Allen Welsh); c) Mary Drury (m. William Smith and had two daughters and a son); d) Marydell Drury (m. Richard Hill); e) Ann Drury (m. Mr. Gardner); f) Plummer Drury (m. Margaret Cannon); g) Samuel Drury (m. ____ Nolan); h) William Drury (m. ____ Evans); i) Henry Drury (m. Mary Owings); and j) Dr. John Drury (single)].
4) Plummer Ijams, Jr. [(b. October 29, 1748, Anne Arundel County, Maryland; d. February 2, 1793 or 1795, Frederick County, Maryland) m. 1776 to Jemima Welsh (b. October 27, 1760; d. April 16, 1789, Frederick County, Maryland), and their children included: a) Richard Ijams (a postmaster in Ijamsville; a lawyer; purchased old homestead); b) James Ijams (also served as Ijamsville postmaster); and c) Ruth Ijams (m. December 19, 1799, Frederick County, Maryland, to Christopher Musseter, a Captain in War of 1812; and their grandson, Henry P. Musseter was Chief Judge of Orphans Court who lived in the old homestead called Oakdean and who died at age 90 in 1951); and d) Plummer Ijams (b. 1781; d. 1849; m. 1st, Rebecca Iiams, daughter of John Iiams; and m. 2nd, Mary Ann Montgomery)].
5) John Ijams [(b. June 5, 1756; d. September 1791; single); will of 1791 named brother Captain Plummer Ijams as sole heir of 49 acres called

135

Wildcat Hill in Frederick County, Maryland; and housekeeper Elizabeth Sellman as heir of 81 acres called Ijams Resolution in Frederick County, Maryland; enlisted in War of 1812 and served as Captain in Baltimore City Guards; known as one of the "Old Defenders"; build the Ijams Grist Mill that operated for 140 years; built the large home overlooking the mill known as Ijams Homestead and owned later by Howard and Nettie Smith; operated a sawmill for a time]. (Family information from IGI, JFI, EFB, JIH, CEM, HWN, and as indicated.)

Plummer Ijams, Jr. [(b. October 29, 1748, All Hallows Parish, Anne Arundel County, Maryland; d. February 2, 1795, Frederick County, Maryland), son of Plummer Ijams (b. 1718), m. 1776 to Jemima Welsh (b. October 27, 1760; d. April 16, 1789), daughter of Benjamin and Rebecca Welsh. Jemima Welsh Ijams died at age 29, two weeks after the birth of John Ijams, Plummer Ijams, Jr., was an heir to the 1792 will of Plummer Ijams, Sr., and was to receive the plantation upon the death of his mother in 1794, but Plummer Ijams, Jr., died before the settlement was completed. He had given the Oath of Allegiance and Fidelity to the State of Maryland in 1778, and he lived on the parents' plantation of Bridge Hill and Dodon; in 1784 he moved to Frederick County, Maryland, property called Wild Cat Hill, a portion of which later became known as Ijams Resolution. Plummer Ijams, Jr. (b. 1748) owned at least some of his land jointly with his brother John Ijams. Plummer Ijams, Jr. (b. 1748) wrote his will February 2, 1795, and it was probated in Frederick County, Maryland, February 27, 1795, with cousin John Ijams as executor, and with estate value set at 663 pounds, 4 shillings, and 6 pence.

Children of Plummer Ijams, Jr. (b. 1748) and Jemima Welsh include:

1) Richard Ijams.
2) James Ijams.
3) Ruth Ijams [(b. St. Mary's, Maryland, November 13, 1783; d. December 16, 1870), m. December 19, 1799, Frederick County, Maryland, to Christopher Musseter (d. June 6, 1851), and they had 13 children].
4) Anne Ijams (b. September 17, 1778, Anne Arundel County, Maryland; d. March 26, ____, Frederick County, Maryland; m. January 29, 1799, Anne Arundel County, Maryland, to George Sanks).
5) Plummer Ijams III [(b. March 8, 1781, St. Mary's Maryland; d. June 25, 1849, Frederick County, Maryland) m. 1st, October 13, 1804, Rebecca Waters Ijams (daughter of John and Mary Waters Ijams), and had one son: Plummer Ijams IV; and m. 2nd, March 2, 1815, to Mary Ann Montgomery (d. January 7, 1829), and they had six children: John Ijams, James Ijams, Richard Ijams, Rebecca Ijams, Joshua Ijams, and Charles Ijams]; and son James Ijams (b. June 21, 1819; d. June 30, 1871); m. December 4, 1849, to Dorcas Tabb, and their child John Tabb Ijams (b. August 27, 1852, in Virginia; d. July 23, 1923, in New York City, then had a child John Horton Ijams (b. 1885).
6) Rebecca Ijams (b. October 28, 1785, Frederick County, Maryland; d. November 1, 1827), lived with sister Ann Ijams Sanks after the death of her mother.
7) John Ijams [(b. April 3, 1789, Frederick County, Maryland; d. August 31, 1879, Baltimore, Maryland; raised by an aunt, Mrs. Elizabeth Drury, a sister of his father), m. April 22 or 27, 1813 or 1814, to Catherine Barnes, and they had eight children: Elizabeth Ann Ijams, John Ijams, Mary Ijams, Emily Ijams, Jane Ijams, Sarah Jane Ijams, Charles Ijams, and William Henry Ijams (b. October 6, 1822, Baltimore, Maryland; d.

April 9, 1906), m. 1853 to Isabella King (b. December 6, 1832, daughter of John King and Hester Leaf), and they had four children: William H. Ijams, Jr., Laura N. Ijams, Albert B. Ijams, and George Edwin Ijams, m. February 7, 1912; d. 1964].

Ruth Ijams (b. November 13, 1783, Maryland; d. December 16, 1870), daughter of Plummer Ijams, Jr. (b. 1748) and Jemima Welsh; m. December 19, 1799, to Christopher Musseter and they had 13 children:

1) John Musseter [(b. February 24, 1801, Frederick County, Maryland; d. May 16, 1879, Frederick County, Maryland) m. Martha Hyatt of Hyattstown, Maryland, and they had nine children: Ruth C. Musseter, Jane Musseter, Christopher Musseter, Jr., Lemuel Musseter, John Musseter, Ely Musseter, Henry P. Musseter, and Martha Elizabeth Musseter].

2) Rebecca Musseter [(b. May 25, 1802, Frederick County, Maryland) m. January 28, 1820, to Henry Riggs, and they had twelve children: Emily Jane Riggs, John Riggs, Christopher Riggs, Musseter Riggs, Ann Rebecca Riggs, Joseph Charles Riggs, Hester Ruth Riggs, Joel Henry Riggs, Elizabeth Harriet Riggs, Elizabeth Virginia Riggs, Jemima Blanche Riggs, and Mary Isadae Riggs].

3) Elizabeth Musseter (b. September 19, 1803, Frederick County, Maryland; d. July 16, 1879; single).

4) Joel Musseter [(b. June 12, 1805, Frederick County, Maryland) m. Sarah Ann Brice of Allegany County, Maryland, and they had ten children: Ruth Musseter, Mary Musseter, Lemuel Musseter, Jane Musseter, Charles Musseter, Rebecca Musseter, Harriet Musseter, Alice Musseter, William Musseter, and Thomas Musseter].

5) Lemuel Musseter [(b. November 11, 1806, Frederick County, Maryland; d. February 22, 1884, Warsaw, Illinois) m. Hannah Ayers of Warsaw, Illinois, and they had eleven children: John Roberts Musseter, Harriet Ijams Musseter, Lemuel Musseter, Franklin Musseter, Jackson Musseter, Charles David Musseter, Edward Christopher Musseter, Laura May Musseter, Ann Elizabeth Musseter, William Ayers Musseter, and Oliver Ijams Musseter].

6) Harriet Musseter (b. October 30, 1808, Frederick County, Maryland).

7) Henry Musseter [(b. April 4, 1811, Frederick County, Maryland) m. Maria Ann Ream of Van Doren County, Iowa, and they had six children: Charles Musseter, Alma Musseter, Olive Musseter, Minnie Musseter, Margaret Musseter, and Elizabeth Musseter].

8) D. Christopher Musseter (b. August 3, 1812, Frederick County, Maryland; owned land at King and Maple Street in Berkeley County, Virginia; single; d. October 11, 1856).

9) Plummer Ijams Musseter [(b. January 25, 1815, Frederick County, Maryland; d. December 23, 1898, Ijamsville, Frederick County, Maryland) m. 1st, Mary Elizabeth Hedges, daughter of Hezekiah Hedges of Hedgesville, Virginia/West Virginia, and they had seven children: Oliver Plummer Musseter, Charles Harrison Musseter, Edmund Hedges Musseter, John Musseter, Helen Musseter, Hezekiah Musseter, and George Washington Musseter); m. 2nd, in 1865 to Elizabeth Baker of Frederick County, Maryland, and they had a daughter, Florence Musseter, who died in childhood; and her mother died 1881 in Hedgesville, West Virginia); m. 3rd, on December 17, 1884, Beckeley County, West

Virginia, to Theresa Boggs, daughter of John Boggs; she died in Hedgesville, West Virginia, in 1902.

10) Ruth Musseter [(b. April 17, 1819, Frederick County, Maryland) m. Samuel Thomas Buxton of Frederick County, Maryland (and they had nine children: Charles Augustus Buxton, Catherine Virginia Buxton, Clarence Musseter Buxton, Alice B. Buxton, Aldredge Ijams Musseter, Frank Vernon Musseter, Christopher Thomas Musseter, and William Henry Musseter)].

11) Ann Roberta Musseter (b. March 30, 1821, Frederick County, Maryland; d. January 9, 1912).

12) Jemima Welsh Musseter [(b. February 13, 1826, Frederick County, Maryland) m. Abner D. Sanks of Baltimore, a first cousin; and they had two children: Ann Florence Sanks (d. childhood); and Wilbur Sanks (d. childhood)].

13) Eliza Aldridge Musseter (b. December 7, 1830, Frederick County, Maryland).

Ann Ijams (b. September 17, 1778), daughter of Plummer Ijams, Jr. (b. 1748) and Jemima Welsh, m. George Sanks and they had six children: 1) Horatio Sanks, m. Caroline Summers, and they had six children: James Sanks, Caroline Sanks, Sallie Sanks, Horatio Sanks, Eliza Sanks, and George Sanks); 2) Plummer Ijams Sanks (d. April 1872, Frederick County, Maryland) m. Elizabeth Duvall, great-granddaughter of John Ijams and Rebecca Jones, and they had five children: Jane Sanks, Anna Sanks, Ruth Elizabeth Sanks, Mary Sanks, and George Sanks); 3) Ruth Sanks (m. Jonathan Sutton of Harford County, Maryland; no children; 4) Joseph Sanks (m. Rebecca Smith; their son died in childhood); 5) John W. Sanks (d. March 5, 1829, at age 15); 6) Abner D. Sanks (b. January 18, 1822, Baltimore County, Maryland; d. January 7, 1893) m. 1st, Anna P. MacAleese (d. from an accidental kitchen fire); m. 2nd, Jemima Welsh Musseter, daughter of his Aunt Ruth Ijams and Charles Musseter (she d. June 5, 1905); and they had two children: Florence Ann Sanks and Wilbur Sanks (he d. childhood).

Rebecca Ijams (b. October 28, 1785), daughter of Plummer Ijams, Jr., (b. 1848) and Jemima Welsh; m. January 17, 1805, to Benjamin Duvall, and they had eleven children:

1) William Duvall (d. Frederick County, Maryland; single).

2) Jemima Duvall (d. Frederick County, Maryland; single).

3) Eliza Duvall.

4) Frederick Duvall.

5) Mary Elvira Duvall.

6) Ruth Duvall (d. March 1896; m. Arthur De Lashmutt, a widower with several children).

7) Rebecca Duvall [(d. Baltimore) m. Henry Baker (d. February 24, 1896, Baltimore), and among their 13 children were: Fannie Ijams Baker, Harry C. Baker, Benjamin E. Baker (a twin), Elizabeth D. Baker (a twin), Florence Baker, and Edwin Baker].

8) Grafton Duvall [(d. Buckeyetown, Frederick County, Maryland, 1868) m. Columbia Dutrow (who m. 2nd, Reverend Albert Wallis, and they had a son, Albert Wallis, Jr.); and they had four children: Samuel Grafton Duvall; Edward Duvall (d. age 21, Frederick, Frederick County, Maryland); Oliver Duvall (d. childhood, Buckeyetown, Frederick County, Maryland); and Newell Duvall (d. childhood, Buckeyetown, Maryland)].

9) Sarah Duvall.

10) Cordelia Duvall.

11) Benjamin Duvall m. Ann Eichelberger and they had twelve children: Wilbur H. Duvall, Nannie Duvall, Grafton Allen Duvall, Emma Duvall, Benjamin Duvall, Ruth Duvall, James Duvall, Charles Ijams Duvall, Oliver Everett Duvall, Margaret Eichelberger Duvall, Cordelia Duvall, and Sarah Rebecca Duvall.

John Ijams (b. April 3, 1789, Frederick County, Maryland), the son of Plummer Ijams (b. 1748) and Jemima Walsh; m. April 22, 1813, in Baltimore, Maryland, to Catherine Barnes, and they had at least three children:

    1) Elizabeth Ann Ijams [(m. Enoch P. Holden, of Massachusetts), and they had four children: Ann Holden, Kitty Holden, Enoch Holden, and Mary Holden (m. James Landers of California, and they had a child, Annie Landers)].

    2) Mary E. Ijams (d. Baltimore; single).

    3) William Henry Ijams [(d. April 9, 1906, Baltimore) m. Isabella King, and they had four children: William Henry Ijams, Jr. (d. December 15, 1938, Baltimore); Laura Adelaide or Adele Ijams (m. Tilliard Drury, a distant cousin); and they had four children: Isabella Ijams Drury, Violet Drury, William Drury, and a son that d. early; George Edgar Ijams (m. Helen Elizabeth Jordan, and their two children were: Edgar Dudley Ijams, and George Edgar Ijams, Jr.); and Albert Barnes Ijams (m. A. Mann, and their daughter was Mildred Mann Ijams)] (GEI).

William Henry Ijams [(b. October 6, 1822, Baltimore, Maryland; d. April 9, 1906, Baltimore), who m. Isabella King (b. December 6, 1832, daughter of John King and Hester Leaf), was the fourth treasurer of the Baltimore and Ohio Railroad, a company he joined about 1853; he was an auditor in 1866, treasurer in 1869, and retired from B & O Railroad January 17, 1900]. Is also recorded as having children: William Henry Ijams, II (b. October 29, 1854, Baltimore; d. December 15, 1888; single); Laura Adele Ijams [(b. April 1, 1856), m. Edward Tillard Drury, and their four children were: Isabel Drury (m. George Henbeck), Edward T. Drury, William Horner Drury, and Emma Drury (m. William Sipple)]; George Edgar Ijams [(b. July 15, 1859, Baltimore; d. April 25, 1900), m. Helen Elizabeth Jordan, and their two children were: Edgar Dudley Ijams, and George Edgar or Edwin Ijams (b. September 29, 1888, Baltimore; d. March 22, 1964), Director of U. S. Veterans Bureau (later the VA Administration); m. February 7, 1911, to Mary Rawlings Addison]; and Albert Barnes Ijams [(b. February 2, 1870, Baltimore), m. Amelia Mann, and their daughter was Mildred Ijams (m. Charles Reed Johnson)]. George Edwin Ijams (b. 1888) and Mary Rawlings Addison had three children: 1) George Edwin Ijams, Jr., (b. January 8, 1913, Baltimore); 2) Elizabeth Virginia Ijams (b. October 8, 1914, Baltimore), and 3) Barbara Ann Ijams (b. April 12, 1924, Baltimore, Maryland).

George Edwin Ijams (b. 1888) recorded his history (February 24, 1964) in a personal letter, and is also listed in *Who's Who in America* (Volume 4, 1961) and in *New York Times* (obituary, March 23, 1964). He enlisted in Maryland Cavalry (1908); U. S. Army (1917), attained rank of Colonel); served in Mexican Border Activity (1916); World War I (was highly decorated, including Purple Heart, French Chevalier Legion of Honor, Italian Order of Crown, Office of French Academy and French Order of Lafayette); was president and Founder of American; was Director of American Veterans Bureau (1920-1930), and when it became the Veterans Administration, he became the first Assistant (in charge of medical and domicillary care, construction, and supplies); was assigned to War Risk Insurance Bureau during the War (he revolutionized combat insurance, selling over 200 million dollars on the front line, being cited by General Pershing for "exceptional meritorious and conspicious service"); served in France, Italy, North Africa, England, Spain, Portugal, and Switzerland; was a member of the Commission for Study of Economic Conditions of Philippine Islands (World War II, with work leading to creation of War Claims Commission); was Director of National Rehabilitation Services for VFW (1946), and served three terms as Commander-in-Chief of Military Order of World Wars.

Of himself (February 24, 1964), he said that some have become "disgusted with me because I refuse to join all these outfits, eligibility to which comes about through the accident of birth. But I belong to so darned many organizations I just can't see any reason for obligating myself to pay more dues, especially as I became 75 last September and my days are decidedly numbered (he died one month later)." And "too many people...know nothing about the early days of our country and the work of our ancestors performed to make this the greatest country the world has ever seen." He told of an uncle who fought for the South in the Civil War, who was killed at Richmond, but was the writer's favorite relative because he "believed the South was right, and fought in Gray" to support his convictions. He also told a story of a Civil War vet whom he met in 1920 while working in VA Affairs, who remembered finding his wounded uncle, a Union officer, who was lying along the road in Maryland. He claimed that an Isaac Ijams was an original California gold rush '49er who eventually settled in the California San Joaquin Valley. He reflected on the family role in establishing the town of Ijamsville, Maryland; and in helping develop the Baltimore and Ohio Railroad (his grandfather, William Henry Ijams, was the B & O treasurer for 30 years).

Plummer Ijams III (b. March 8, 1781, Dodon, Saint Mary's, All Hallows Parish, Anne Arundel County, Maryland; d. June 28, 1847; buried at Mount Olivet Cemetery, Frederick County, Maryland), the son of Plummer Ijams, Jr. (b. 1748) and Jemima Welsh (b. 1760), m. 1st, March 10 or 15, 1804, Frederick County, Maryland, to Rebecca Waters Ijams; and m. 2nd, February 27, 1815, Frederick County, Maryland, to Mary Ann Montgomery, daughter of John Montgomery, who died at age 32 years, 2 months, and 25 days, on January 7, 1829, and buried in Mount Olivet Cemetery, in Frederick, Maryland. Mary Ann Montgomery was born October 23, 1793. Plummer Ijams III was state legislator from Frederick County, Maryland, for several years. Plummer Ijams III (b. 1781) had one child by his first wife, and six children by his second wife:

1) Plummer Ijams IV [(b. February 26, 1805, Frederick County, Maryland), m. May 27, 1830, Frederick County, Maryland, to first cousin, Harriet Mussetter (d. September 2, 1882, Baltimore, Maryland), daughter of Christopher Ijams and Ruth Ijams: and they had four children: Alfred Ijams (b. 1831); Catherine Rebecca Ijams (b. 1833); Oliver Ijams (b. 1835); and John Plummer Ijams (b. 1837)].

2) John Ijams (b. September 24, 1817, Frederick County, Maryland; d. April 8, 1824, Frederick County, Maryland).

3) James Ijams [(b. June 21, 1819, Frederick County, Maryland; d. June 30, 1871 or 1873, Baltimore, Maryland), m. December 6, 1849, to Dorcas Mitchell Tabb (d. New York City, April 1898)].

4) Richard Plummer Ijams [(b. August 2, 1821, Frederick County, Maryland; d. November 11, 1854, at Ijamsville, Frederick County, Maryland), m. first cousin Elizabeth Aldrige Mussetter, and their three children were: Richard Plummer Ijams (d. single); Mary Ijams (d. single); and Rebecca Ruth Ijams].

5) Rebecca Ijams [(b. November 11, 1822, Frederick County, Maryland; d. August 1, 1849, Ijamsville, Maryland), m. November 24, 1841, to a

cousin, John Montgomery (a carpenter; d. September 19, 1853, Prince Georges County, Maryland), and they had four children: Mary Ann Montgomery, William Henry Montgomery, Mary Montgomery, and Julia Rebecca Montgomery].

6) Joshan Ijams [(b. June 9, 1824, Frederick County, Maryland; d. October 13, 1894), m. May 19, 1847, King Georges County, Maryland, to William Saunders Brown (d. August 2, 1893) of King Georges County, Virginia, and they had eight children: William Wordsworth Brown, Nannie Saunders Brown, Isabelle Brown, Florence Louise Brown, Mary Josephine Brown, Lucy Slaughter Brown, James Frederick Brown, and Mary Symington Brown].

7) Charles Montgomery Ijams (b. December 12, 1827, Frederick County, Maryland; d. June 28, 1828, Frederick County, Maryland).

James Ijams (b. June 21, 1819, Frederick County, Maryland; d. June 30, 1873, Baltimore, Maryland), the son of Plummer Ijams III (b. 1781) and Mary Ann Montgomery; m. Dorcas Susan Mitchell Tabb (b. 1832; d. April 1896), the daughter of John Tabb of Virginia; and they lived in Berkeley County, Virginia, where James Ijams was a merchant and land owner in 1850; but they later moved to Baltimore. After the death of James Ijams, Dorcas Ijams moved to New York City to live with family members. Dorcas Ijams died in New York City, but was buried in Loudoun Park in Baltimore. James Ijams (b. 1819) had nine children: 1) Plummer Montgomery Ijams; 2) John Tabb Ijams [b. August 27, 1852, Berkeley County, Virginia; d. New York City, July 23, 1923); m. April 20, 1881, New York City, to Phoebe Adele Smith (b. December 7, 1852; d. January 4, 1931, New York City]; 3) James Edgar Ijams (d. young); 4) Arabella Janney (Jenny) Ijams (d. young); 5) Raleigh Brown Ijams; 6) Elizabeth Marion Ijams; 7) Marion Turner Ijams (m. Campbell Malcolm; 8) Joshan Ijams; and 9) James Edgar Ijams, the younger.

Elizabeth Aldridge Mussetter (b. 1829) was the daughter of Christopher Mussetter and Ruth Ijams (b. 1783), the sister of Plummer Ijams III (b. 1781).

John Ijams [(b. April 3, 1789, Frederick County, Maryland; d. August 31, 1877, Baltimore County, Maryland), the son of Plummer Ijams, Jr. (b. 1748) and Jemima Walsh; m. April 22, 1813, in Baltimore, to Catherine Barnes. His mother, Jemima Walsh Ijams, died April 16, 1789, when he was two weeks old, and he was taken on horseback from Ijamsville to Anne Arundel County, Maryland. This trip has jokingly been said to have shortened his life (but he lived to age 90). He was raised by an aunt, Mrs. Elizabeth Drury. As a young man he lived in Baltimore. He enlisted August 23, 1813, as private in the 51st Maryland Regiment under Captain Forster, but was discharged a week later on August 30, 1813, when the emergency ended. However, on August 19, 1814, he became a first lieutenant in the same regiment, then commanded by Lt. Col. Henry Amey, and served until November 18, 1814. He is credited with serving in the September 12, 1814, defense of Baltimore and bombardment of Fort McHenry and was later known as the "Old Defender." He remained in the military after the war and was promoted to captain. Under the Act of 1850, he reserved 40 acres of land in Clayton County, Iowa (assigned it to Joshua Barney), and by the Act of 1855, he reserved 120 acres of land in Monroe County, Wisconsin (assigned to Jonathan R. Warner). He applied for a veteran's pension March 7, 1871. He had seven children: Elizabeth Ann Ijams, John Ijams, Mary Ijams, Emily Ijams, Jane Ijams, Sarah Jane Ijams, and William Henry Ijams (b. October 6, 1822; d. April 9, 1906; m. Isabella King, daughter of John King and Hester Leaf).

Richard Iiams (b. 1745 or 1749; d. 1825 or 1833) has been the subject of considerable controversy. Each argument will be presented. Richard Iiams (b. 1745) was the son of Thomas Iiams (b. 1708) and Katy Hampton, a woman named Artridge (HWN), or Richard and Eleanor Iiams (KS). Richard Iiams (b. 1745) m. Eleanor Musgrave (HWN) or Eleanor Pottinger (KS, HWN). May 18, 1778, has been given as the marriage license date for the marriage to Eleanor Pottinger (b. 1755; d. 1834) in Frederick County, Maryland (HL), the daughter of Robert Pottinger and Elizabeth Willett (EFB, BIG), and Eleanor Pottinger died in Greene County, Pennsylvania.

Richard Iiams (b. ca1745) moved from Maryland to Bates Fork, Greene County, Pennsylvania, about 1790; a millwright; was buried in Bates Fork Baptist Cemetery. He had lived in Frederick County, Maryland. Said to be a Revolutionary soldier, by oral tradition he is known to have held military drills in his mill each Saturday. He had been deeded land by his father, John. He subsequently deeded the land to his brother Thomas Iiams, but the deed was not registered. Instead, the deed had been kept in the pocket of Thomas Iiams until it was lost. The Maryland court record said that Richard Iiams was living in Redstone, Washington County, Pennsylvania, during the time the deed was being reconstructed in 1797. Elisha B. Iams, as president of the National Iams Association in 1934, placed Richard Iiams as the son of Thomas Iiams (b. 1710) and Elizabeth Hill, and listed this Richard Jefferson Iiams was born All Hallows Parish, Anne Arundel County, Maryland, in 1745 and died in Morris Township, Greene County, Pennsylvania, about 1825.

In Maryland he had married a woman named Elizabeth ____ and they had moved to Morris Township between 1770 and 1780, where he had erected a mill, and held muster each Saturday afternoon. After the military drills they were said to spend time trading and racing horses. While living in Bates Fork, Greene County, Pennsylvania, he donated the land for the Nineveh school. The IGI lists the husband of Eleanor Pottenger as Richard Iams (b. March 4, 1702). Richard Ijams gave the Oath of Allegiance in Washington County, Maryland, in March 1778, and had left that country by 1790.

Just as there are multiple accounts of Richard Iiams, there is some confusion over his children, which include:

1) John Iams [(b. 1780 or 1781, Washington County, Maryland) m. Ruth Barker of Ninevah, Greene County, Pennsylvania, sister of Squire Barker; lived in Athens County, Ohio (Lecke, EFB); took boat to New Orleans and never returned].

2) Thomas Iams [(b. 1781, Bates Fork, Greene County, Pennsylvania), m. 1807 to Mary "Polly" Smith (b. 1787, daughter of Dennis Schmitt and Elizabeth Zook; with Dennis Schmitt b. 1748; d. August 27, 1829; m. November 14, 1771, to Elizabeth Zook, who was b. May 13, 1756; d. September 19, 1845); purchased three acres, May 3, 1871, Morris Township, Greene County, Pennsylvania; 1860 Census of Greene County, Pennsylvania, lists Thomas Iams (age 72, b. Maryland) living with Martin and Sarah Rush; with children of Thomas Iams being Dennis Iams, Thomas Iams (b. 1822, m. 1848, to Ruth Coy, settled in Wabash, Indiana), Elizabeth Iams (m. George Smith), Catherine Iams (m. Mr. Huffman), Hannah Iams (m. Jesse Church), Mary Iams, Rachel Iams, and Charity Iams; with children of Thomas A. Iams listed as Benjamin Harrison Imes and John Milton Imes].

3) Richard Iams, Jr. (b. 1786, Washington County, Maryland, or Pennsylvania; d. February 20, 1829, Greene County, Pennsylvania) m. 1808 to Mary Shidler (b. 1786; d. February 15, 1868).

4) William Iiams [(b. ca1786; d. 1845), m. 1810 Eleanor Hall; children: William Iiams (b. 1810, single); Richard Iiams (b. 1811, lived Athens County, Ohio; m. Jane Holmes); and John Iiams (moved to Texas)].

5) Rezin (or Reason) Iiams [(b. 1789 or 1791; d. February 19, 1860, age 71, buried Bates Fork Cemetery), m. 1st, 1808 or 1811, to Phoebe Clark (b. June 30, 1781; d. February 2, 1843, Bates Fork, Pennsylvania; daughter of Isaac Clark and Deborah French); m. 2nd, Nancy McClure (b. March 24, 1804; d. January 9, 1876)].

6) Otho Iams [(b. 1791; d. April 27, 1875, Greene County, Pennsylvania), m. 1813 to Nancy Cole (b. 1796); with 1870 Greene County Census showing Otho Iams (age 78) living with Elizabeth Iams (age 42)].

7) Bazil (or Basel) Iams (b. 1795, Morris Township, Greene County, Pennsylvania), a single schoolteacher (Lecke, EBI).

8) Eli Iiams [(b. May 4, 1797, Morris Township, Greene County, Pennsylvania; d. February 6, 1875, Montgomery County, Ohio), m. 1820 to Phoebe Heckathorne (b. 1802), daughter of Martin Heckathorne (d. 1808, Greene County, Pennsylvania) and Catherine Bottenfield (d. Montgomery County, Ohio) and sister of Elizabeth Heckathorne (b. 1780, Maryland; d. Montgomery County, Ohio; m. George Shank), Eve Heckathorne (b. Maryland; m. Jacob Ruse), Daniel Heckathorne (b. June 6, 1785, Frederick County, Maryland; d. Montgomery County, Ohio; m. Mary Boyd), George Heckathorne (b. 1789, Maryland; d. Montgomery County, Ohio), Catherine Heckathorne (m. William Lewis), Jacob Heckathorn (b. 1800, Loudon County, Virginia; d. Ohio; single), and Nancy Heckathorn (b. 1804; d. February 1888, Pennsylvania; m. October 4, 1827, to Paul Huston)].

9) Rachel Iams (m. Benjamin Spruance).

10) Nancy Iiams (b. 1792; d. 1858, Johnson County, Missouri; m. John Ball Cecil), said to be a half-brother of Thomas Musgrave Iiams; b. March 10, 1792, Frederick County, Maryland).

Richard Iiams, the son of Thomas Iiams (b. 1708), m. Eleanor Musgrave, and their children were said to include: 1) Thomas Musgrave Iiams (b. 1774; m. Nancy Carvel; moved to Rowan County, North Carolina, in 1799; a son, "Squire" Iiams, was a Justice of the Peace in Johnson County, Missouri, according to ACK); 2) Nancy Iiams (b. 1792; d. 1858, Johnson County, Missouri; m. John Ball Cecil); and 3) Richard Iiams (m. Elizabeth Pottenger, and they had eight children listed in preceeding paragraph, including: Thomas Iiams, Richard Iiams, Otho Iiams, Rezin Iiams, John Iiams, William Iiams, Bazil Iiams, and Eli Iiams).

Nancy Iiams [(b. March 10, 1792, Frederick County, Maryland; d. February 11, 1858, Johnson County, Missouri), m. December 18, 1812, to John B. Cecil (b. October 9, 1785, Frederick County, Maryland; d. January 21, 1861, Johnson City, Missouri); and she was a daughter of Richard Iiams; John B. Cecil (b. 1785) moved from Frederick County, Maryland, to Rowan (Davidson) County, North Carolina, in 1809; and to Johnson County, Missouri, in 1856 to follow their children; and are buried at Cecil Cemetery, Cornelia, Johnson County, Missouri)] and their ten children are:

1) William B. Cecil [(b. October 22, 1813, North Carolina; d. December 23, 1891, Johnson County, Missouri), m. June 15, 1839, to Isabel Russell (b. May 6, 1821, North Carolina; d. July 28, 1888), daughter of Alexander H. Russell and Eleanor Johnston of Guilford County, North Carolina; and they had twelve children).

2) Thomas Cecil (b. June 17, 1815, North Carolina; d. July 27, 1882, Missouri; m. April 22, 1841, to Nancy Rice).

143

3) George W. Cecil (d. 1849, Missouri; m. January 12, 1841, to Jane Stone).
4) Rachel Cecil (m. Larkin Albertson).
5) Daniel Cecil (b. November 26, 1823; d. April 17, 1906; m. Charity Reece).
6) Andrew J. Cecil (b. 1825; m. February 2, 1842, to Cynthia Stout).
7) Elizabeth Cecil (b. June 4, 1825; d. May 14, 1878; m. October 17, 1851, to Spencer Pope).
8) Phoebe Cecil (b. May 4, 1827; d. December 19, 1855; m. John Hilton).
9) John Cecil (b. 1829; d. 1905; m. 1st, August 29, 1851, to Rachel Burton; m. 2nd, widow Delphine Wood).
10) Richard Cecil (b. March 20, 1831; d. December 24, 1906; m. December 20, 1859, to Charity Roberts).

William B. Cecil [(b. 1813), m. Isabel Russell, and they had 12 children:
1) Josephine Cecil [(b. February 29, 1840, Davidson County, North Carolina; d. October 1, 1892, at home of sister, Louise Poe of Greenfield, Missouri), m. January 12, 1856, to James Taylor (b. May 1842; d. July 28, 1920); and their child John Russell Taylor (b. November 24, 1865, Missouri; d. January 22, 1923, Missouri), m. Elizabeth Stout, and they had two children: Lawrence Russell (b. June 1, 1895), and Sylvia Zelma Russell (b. December 24, 1898; m. Mr. McGrath, and their children were: Maria McGrath and Julia McGrath).
2) John Wesley Cecil
3) Louise Cecil
4) Mary E. Cecil
5) Alexander Russell Cecil
6) Richard F. Cecil
7) Elizabeth J. Cecil
8) Nancy M. Cecil
9) Julia I. Cecil
10) James C. Cecil
11) Henry Clay Cecil
12) David Craig Cecil

Thomas Musgrove Ijams (b. 1774, Frederick County, Maryland; d. 1848, Davidson County, North Carolina), son of Richard Ijams and Eleanor Musgrove; m. 1795 in Maryland, to Nancy Carvel (b. 1778, Maryland; d. 1850, North Carolina); moved to Rowan (Davidson County, North Carolina, after the 1807 death of his father. After the death of Thomas Musgrove Ijams (d. 1848), widow Nancy lived with son George W. Ijams (b. 1817) until her death in 1850. Children of Thomas Musgrove Ijams (b. 1774) included:
1) Henrietta Ijams [(b. July 7, 1796, Maryland; d. May 1, 1846, North Carolina); m. August 13, 1817, Rowan County, North Carolina, to Samuel Cecil (b. 1794, Frederick County, Maryland; d. 1874, Davidson County, North Carolina), son of Philip and Julia Cecil of Maryland].
2) Sarah Ijams [(b. 1798, Maryland; d. Johnson County, Missouri), m. April 23, 1821, Rowan County, North Carolina, to David Levengood (d. Johnson County, Missouri)].
3) Richard Ijams [(b. 1800, Maryland; d. August 25, 1829, or March 12, 1859), m. Ellen Collett (b. 1810, North Carolina; d. 1845, Davidson County)].
4) William Ijams (m. Mary Leonard; both d. North Carolina).
5) Mary Ijams (m. Philip Clinard; both d. North Carolina).
6) Rachel Ijams (d. age 17).
7) Thomas Musgrove Ijams II [(b. July 8, 1812, North Carolina; d. September 11, 1874, Johnson County, Missouri), m. 1st, October 8, 1836,

Davidson County, North Carolina, to Abigale Leonard; m. 2nd, March 29, 1853, Johnson County, Missouri, to Lucinda Cull; m. 3rd, September 13, 1857, to Caroline Taylor (Thomas was a Justice of Peace and was known as "Judge" or "Squire")].
8) Nancy Ijams [(b. May 29, 1815, North Carolina; d. February 8, 1901, Johnson County, Missouri), m. 1836 in North Carolina to Solathal T. "Solly" Stone (b. June 12, 1817, North Carolina; d. May 13, 1910, Johnson County, Missouri)].
9) George Washington Ijams [(b. August 4, 1817, Rowan County, North Carolina; d. Johnson County, Missouri), m. April 22, 1838, to Elizabeth Cecil (b. 1820, North Carolina; d. August 1880, Johnson County, Missouri), daughter of Benjamin Cecil and Ossee Kennedy].
10) Ellen Ijams (d. young).
11) John Ijams (d. young in North Carolina).

Henrietta Ijams [(b. July 7, 1796, Maryland; d. May 6, 1846, North Carolinaj), m. August 13, 1817, Rowan County, North Carolina, to Samuel Cecil (b. 1794, Frederick County, Maryland; d. 1846, North Carolina), the son of Phillip and Julia Cecil of Maryland. Henrietta Ijams (b. 1796) was the daughter of Thomas Musgrove Ijams (b. 1774) and Nancy Carvel. Samuel Cecil had two subsequent wives, with Henrietta Ijams being the mother of the first seven of his nine children]. The seven children of Henrietta Ijams were:
1) Richard Iiams Cecil [(b. August 4, 1818, North Carolina; d. January 16, 1889), m. April 10, 1839, to Suvilla Magdelena Evans (b. 1818); and their children were Sarah E. Cecil (b. 1840; m. Andrew Weaver); Elizabeth Jane Cecil (b. 1842, m. Alpheus Perryman); Samuel Lafayette Cecil (b. 1848; m. Cornelia Burd); John F. Cecil (b. 1848); David King Cecil (b. 1851; m. Chrissie Jane Miller); Rebecca Cecil; James Lee Cecil (b. 1859; m. Julia Leonard); Mary H. Cecil (b. 1853); and Alice R. Cecil (b. 1855)].
2) Isaac A. Cecil [(b. 1825, North Carolina), m. January 9, 1869, to Elizabeth C. Cross, and their children were: Crissie Jane Cecil (b. 1874), and Thomas Cecil].
3) Charles Westley Cecil [(b. August 6, 1827 or 1829; known as "West"; d. 1912, North Carolina); m. 1st, Selonie Craven (b. 1827), and m. 2nd, Elizabeth Holloway; and his children were: George Cecil (b. 1855); William Samuel Cecil (b. 1857); Rebecca Cecil (b. 1859); Ellen Rose Cecil (b. 1863); Richard Franklin Cecil (b. 1860); Mary Lou Cecil (b. 1861); Pauline Cecil (b. 1875), and Elizabeth "Eliza" Cecil (b. 1870)].
4) Julia R. Cecil [(b. 1838), m. Robert Cross, and their children included: Victoria Cross].
5) Nancy J. Cecil [(b. 1833), m. May 9, 1857, to John Welborn Hilton as his second wife, and their children included: Agnes Hilton, Glendora Hilton, John Hilton, and Emory Hilton].
6) Thomas S. Cecil [(b. August 31, 1835, North Carolina), m. Nancy Conner (b. 1835)].
7) Susan E. T. Cecil [(b. 1838, North Carolina), m. August 3, 1868, to James Roly "J.R." Cross, and their three children were: Samuel Alexander Cross (b. 1871); Victoria E. Cross (b. 1873); and James T. Cross (b. 1875)].

Richard Ijams (b. 1800, Maryland; d. August 25, 1829, or March 12, 1859), son of Thomas Musgrove Ijams (b. 1774), m. Ellen Collett (b. 1810, North Carolina; d. 1845, Davidson County, North Carolina), and the 1850 Census of Davidson County, North Carolina, lists Richard Iiams (age 48), Eleanor Iiams (age 38); Faithful Iiams (age 20); John Iiams (age 19); Charles Iiams (age 18); Lucy Iiams (age 16); Margaret Iiams (age 14); William Iiams (age 11); Eleanor Iiams (age 9); Elizabeth Iiams (age 5); and Hiram B. Iiams (age 3). The children of Richard Iiams (b. 1800) include:

1) Lucy Ijams [(b. 1835; d. February 22, 1915; buried at Spring Hill Cemetery, High Point, North Carolina); m. Wilson Cecil, son of Daniel Jerred Cecil; and they lived in Davidson County, North Carolina].

2) Faith Ijams (m. Madison C. Dean, and they lived in North Carolina).

3) John Ijams (single; farmed in North Carolina).

4) Charlie Ijams (m. Alma Peterson, and they lived in Lafayette County, Missouri).

5) Margaret Ijams.

6) Ellen Ijams (m. Mr. Booth and lived in Fayette County, North Carolina).

7) Thomas Ijams (b. 1843).

8) William Ijams [(b. May 1838, Davidson County, North Carolina; d. Johnson County, Missouri), m. June 7, 1874 in Missouri, to Elizabeth Stone (b. July 9, 1848, Missouri), daughter of John Stone and Nancy Lanear of Davidson County, North Carolina; a farmer and carpenter who owned 270 acres in Missouri as a partner with his brother Charles Ijams and his uncle George W. Ijams; had ten children: Richard Ijams (b. April 7, 1876, Missouri); Hale Ijams (b. July 25, 1877, Missouri); Walter Ijams (b. March 24, 1879, Missouri); Sarah Ijams (b. September 30, 1880, Missouri); Thomas Ijams (b. October 16, 1882, Missouri); Margaret Ijams (b. March 15, 1884, Missouri); Charlie Ijams (b. September 10, 1885, Missouri); Isaac Ijams (b. June 15, 1887, Missouri); Lucy Ijams (b. March 1, 1889, Missouri); and Ellen Ijams (b. September 22, 1890, Missouri)].

Thomas Musgrove Ijams II (b. July 8, 1812, North Carolina; d. September 11, 1874, Johnson County, Missouri), son of Thomas Musgrove Ijams (b. 1774) and Nancy Carvel, was married three times: 1st, October 8, 1836, in Davidson County, North Carolina, to Abigail Leonard; m. 2nd, March 29, 1853, Johnson County, Missouri, to Lucinda Cull; m. 3rd, September 15, 1857, Johnson County, Missouri, to Caroline Taylor. A carpenter, millwright, and Justice of Peace, he was known as "Squire" or "Judge." The 1870 Census of Post Oak Township, Johnson County, Missouri, lists Thomas Iiams (age 58); Caroline Iiams (age 42); Nancy Iiams (age 27); Thersia Iiams (age 26); Julius Iiams (age 12); Charles Iiams (age 10); James Iiams (age 8); Sarah Iiams (age 7); Thomas Iiams (age 5); Victoria Iiams (age 5); and Mary Iiams (age 1). The 1880 Census of Post Oak Township lists Caroline (age 45, head of household); Julius Iiams (age 21); Charles Iiams (age 19); James Iiams (age 17); Sarah Iiams (age 16); Thomas Iiams (age 14) Victoria Iiams (age 12); Mary Iiams (age 10); and Ellsworth Iiams (age 8). Children of Thomas Musgrove Ijams II (b. 1812), were:

1) Hiram G. Iiams [(b. March 6, 1840; d. March 30, 1889) m. October 15, 1861, to Phoebe Jane Rice (b. December 8, 1837; d. January 21, 1915); and their infant daughter d. June 10, 1862, and was buried in Cecil Cemetery; and they raised Ed Iiams, son of Franklin M. Iiams].

2) Nancy Iiams (b. 1844; d. 1906, in Johnson County, Missouri; single).

3) Richard H. "Dick" Iiams [(b. 1846; d. 1917, Johnson County, and buried in Grove Cemetery, Simpson Township, Johnson County, Missouri), m. February 23, 1868, to Lucinda Jane "Lucy" Bayless (b. 1851; d. 1883); lived in Post Oak Township; and their three children were: James Iiams (b. 1869); Margaret Iiams (b. 1872); and Mary C. Iiams (b. 1879)].

4) Rebecca Iiams (m. November 19, 1867, to John Hackler).

5) Franklin M. "Whig" Iiams [(b. 1849; d. September 22, 1873, Johnson City, Missouri); m. December 23, 1869, to Sarah E. Bayless, b. June 2, 1853; d. January 2, 1871; buried in Cornelia Cemetery, Cornelia, Missouri; after the birth of son Ed Iiams who was raised by Hiram G. Iiams (b. 1840), a brother of Franklin M. Iiams].

Thomas M. Iiams (b. 1812) had eight children by his third wife, Carolyn Taylor:
1) Julius Iiams (b. 1859; d. 1880; single).
2) Charles G. Iiams (b. December 28, 1860; d. February 1931; single).
3) James McClelland Iiams [(b. 1862; d. May 23, 1943), m. December 23, 1891, to Nevada Doffs (b. January 30, 1871; d. March 1, 1934), and their three children were: Leonard Iiams (b. January 16, 1893; m. March 19, 1916, Bertha Fendley, b. April 4, 1892); Leland Iiams (b. March 31, 1895; m. March 19, 1916, to Daisy Williams, b. July 12, 1898, and their children were: James Marion Iiams, b. January 7, 1918; d. March 13, 1933; Leo Denton Iiams, b. July 22, 1921; m. May 20, 1940, to Leona Wright, and their two children were Katherine Sue Iiams, b. July 29, 1941; and Lawry Dean Iiams, b. June 23, 1943); and Waldon Iiams, b. November 11, 1899].
4) Sarah N. Iiams [(b. December 22, 1864; d. June 25, 1924; buried Cornelia Cemetery, Cornelia, Missouri), m. August 1, 1882, to George W. Howard (b. August 27, 1847; d. January 18, 1929)].
5) Thomas Iiams III [(b. 1866; d. December 31, 1923), m. 1900 to Mary E. Scott (d. January 18, 1950)].
6) Queen Victoria Iiams (m. Sam Foster).
7) Mary "Molly" Celestine Iiams [(b. August 17, 1869; d. May 31, 1941), m. December 24, 1891, to Alonzo Thomas (b. May 31, 1873), and their four children were: Florence Thomas (b. January 29, 1895; m. October 23, 1912, to Ben Williams); John Wesley Thomas (b. August 18, 1900; d. 1965; m. December 6, 1924, to Dorothy Roberts; and their daughter Dorothy Lee Thomas was b. October 21, 1925); Basil Thomas (b. January 16, 1903; m. April 12, 1925, to Mae Mohler, who was b. January 18, 1903); and Elvie Thomas (b. May 27, 1907; m. July 7, 1928, to Leo Whitman, b. July 22, 1907, and their daughter Dela Whitman was b. April 18, 1929)].
8) Ellsworth "Babe" Iiams (b. 1872).

George Washington Ijams (b. August 4, 1817, Rowan County, North Carolina; d. Johnson County, Missouri), son of Thomas Musgrove Ijams (b. 1774) and Nancy Carvel, m. April 26, 1838, Davidson County, North Carolina, to Elizabeth Cecil (b. 1820, Davidson County, North Carolina; d. August 1881, Johnson County, Missouri, the daughter of Benjamin Cecil and Osie or Ossee Kennedy; rented farm land in North Carolina and later purchased a 40-acre farm in North Carolina until June 28, 1858, when he moved to Johnson County, Missouri, and rented a farm eleven miles south of Warrensburg, but later moved to Freedom Township, Lafayette County, Missouri, in 1871 and purchased a farm of 120 acres. They had twelve children: 1) Rachel R. Ijams (b. 1839, North Carolina; single); 2) John C. Ijams (b. 1843, North Carolina; m. Mary Wise, but she moved to Kansas); 3) Annie Ijams (m. John Hurd; lived in Oklahoma); 4) Samuel B. or S. Ijams (b. 1844, North Carolina; m. Mollie Payne; lived in Johnson County, Missouri); 5) Esther Ijams (b. 1848, North Carolina; d. age 23); 6) Preston Ijams (b. 1849, North Carolina; twin; d. April 1893); 7) Calvin Ijams (b. 1849, North Carolina; twin; m. Melinda Wall; lived in Johnson County, Missouri; 8) Melvin Ijams (b. 1856, North Carolina); 9) Hiram Ijams; 10) unnamed child; 11) Nancy Ijams (m. James Ijams; lived in Johnson County, Missouri); and 12) Fathie Ijams (m. Columbus Payne; lived in Texas).

John Ijams (b. 1781; m. Ruth Barker), the son of Richard Iiams (b. 1745) and Eleanor Pottenger; moved to Athens County, Ohio (EFB) in 1810, and they had two children: 1) William Iams (went to New Orleans); and 2) Richard Imes [(b. 1811), m. Jane Holmes and they had four children: a) William Imes (single); b) John A. Iams (m. Nerva Crosson, and their daughter Eva Imes m. Mr. Grant and lived in Kansas); c) Nancy Iams (m. Wallace Marse, and their son Bert Marse later had a son Elbert Marse who lived in Detroit; and d) James O. Iams (m. Frances M. Larry), and they had three children: Richard P. Iams (m. Claire Barid; lived Athens, Ohio; had two sons, Wilbur B. Iams and Richard Iams); LeRoy Iams (m. Farest Weinerman; had three children: James H. Iams, Roger S. Iams, and Mary Lou Iams; lived Denver, Colorado); and Robert H. Iams (single; a telegraph operator for Pennsylvania Railroad)].

Richard Iams, Jr. (b. 1786; d. February 20, 1829, Greene County, Pennsylvania), son of Richard Iams (b. 1745) and Eleanor Pottenger, m. Mary Shidler (b. 1786; d. February 15, 1868), and they had ten children: 1) Sarah Iams [(b. 1807), m. Jesse Grim]; 2) John Iams [(b. April 13, 1809; d. March 9, 1905); lived in Washington County, Iowa; m. Sarah McVey]; 3) Peter Iams [(b. 1806; d. September 2, 1836), m. Mary "Polly" Sellers, and they had two children: Richard Iams (b. 1833), and Sarah Iams (b. 1835; d. December 22, 1879)]; 4) Reason Iams [(b. May 17, 1810); m. Eleanor McCluny or Elinor Riley (b. 1814); lived in Delaware County, Indiana; and they had six children: John Iams (b. 1834); Sarah Iams (b. August 20, 1834); Lydia Iams (twin, b. August 20, 1834); George Iams (b. 1840); and infants that died 1836 and 1838]; 5) Nancy Iams [(b. December 18, 1816); m. 1899 to Roland Hughes]; 6) George Iams [(b. September 28, 1819; d. May 20, 1876)]; 7) Richard Iams (b. June 18, 1821); 8) Susannah Iams (b. September 1, 1825; d. May 5, 1878; 9) William Iams (b. February 1, 1827; d. August 18, 1901); and 10) Mary Iams (b. March 20, 1829; d. April 19, 1863).

Isabel Iams Griffith, Helena, Montana, has recorded that the progenitor William Iams arrived in Maryland in 1645 (d. 1703) after being recognized as a descendant from one of Queen Elizabeth's Court who was appointed to serve in Ireland. The son of this William Iams was William Iams, Jr. (b. 1670; d. 1738). The son of William Iams, Jr. (b. 1670) was Richard Iams (b. March 4, 1702; d. 1761; m. 1st, Anne Cheney and m. 2nd, Elizabeth Gaither); and their son John Iams had the son Richard Iams, Sr. (b. ca1745; d. 1833; m. May 18, 1778, to Eleanor Pottenger, who was b. 1755; d. 1834). The children of Richard Iams, Sr. (b. 1745) were: Richard Iams, Jr. (m. Mary Shidler), Thomas Iams; Otho Iams; Rezin Iams, John Iams, William Iams, Bazel Iams, and Eli Iams. The children of Richard Iams, Jr., were; John Iams (b. April 13, 1809; m. Sarah McVey), Peter Iams, Reason Iams, and Mary Iams. Children of John Iams (b. April 13, 1809; d. March 9, 1905) and Sarah McVey were: Abram Iams (b. March 23, 1843; d. April 16, 1923; m. 1st, in 1866 to Annie Carnahan who d. in 1882; and m. 2nd, June 21, 1891, Ingaborg Belle Haugen, b. October 25, 1857; d. March 16, 1939); Richard Iams (d. young), John Iams (d. young), Catherine Iams (b. July 28, 1835), Mary Iams (b. September 1, 1836), Susan Iams (b. September 6, 1838), Isabelle Iams (b. April 1, 1843), Nancy Iams (b. October 15, 1847), Julie Iams (b. March 7, 1850), and William Iams (b. July 17, 1851). Children of Abram Iams (b. 1843) and second wife Ingaborg Belle Haugen (b. 1857) were: Sarah Iams (b. August 17, 1892; d. July 25, 1991); Augusta Iams (b. March 22, 1895; d. April 3, 1895); and Aaron Iams (b. May 1897; d. November 24, 1989).

Aaron Lewis Iams [(b. May 1897; d. November 24, 1989) was a rancher and farmer until he lost his land during the 1929 Depression. A man of "creative abilities

148

and great charm," he became a builder, a cabinet maker, poet, and author of essays and short stories. Aaron Lewis Iiams (b. 1897) m. September 20, 1928, to Barbara Bader (b. March 30, 1909; d. February 10, 1991), and they raised a family of six, most of whom were teachers, builders, and writers: 1) Isabel Barbara Iams Griffith (family historian); 2) Celeste Lucille Iams Mores; 3) Michael Aaron Iams; 4) Jeffrie Lewis Iams; 5) Sara Beth Iams Swearingen; and 6) Douglas Maynard Iams.

Isabel Barbara Iams Griffith has written: "I think the Iams blood carries a strange bug—one that makes them settle, break the ground, get things profitable, and then the eye strays to the horizon—leave it all and start over. The story of my life, too. It's also hard to admit that as charming and handsome the Iams men were, they carried a large lazy bone. It's why I believe, almost all to a man, they married a strong, hard-working woman. Most of the time, quite socially prominent, too." She describes Abram Iams (b. 1843) as one who became bored with the confinement of the small farm and left Iowa in search of a freer life, that of free range ranching, who owned a farm south of Dickinson, North Dakota, but soon after married and moved on, in the first of many moves as the free range ran out. He is described as having died in a "soddy-dug-out on a ranch bordering the Sioux Indian Reservation near Mandan, North Dakota." The ranch was eventually lost in the 1929 Depression when son Aaron Iams was the occupant. The children of Aaron Iams (b. 1897) and Barbara Bader were:

1) Isabel Barbara Iams [(b. September 21, 1928, Taylor, North Dakota), m. April 6, 1963, Butte, Montana, to Robert James Griffith (b. May 24, 1929, Butte, Montana; and their son was Patrick Michael Griffith (b. January 3, 1970, Helena, Montana)].

2) Celeste Lucille Iams [(b. February 14, 1930, Taylor, North Dakota), m. March 22, 1952, Billings, Montana, to Timothy Renaldo Mares II (b. December 17, 1929, Montana), and they had four children: a) Carmella Louise Mares LeCompte (adopted); b) Timothy R. Mares III (adopted); c) Madolla Mares (b. December 3, 1960; d. August 4, 1970); and Arin Mares (b. September 20, 1964, Billings, Montana; m. August 4, 1988, in Oregon, to Alexander Manton, and their child Jordan Alexander Manton was b. February 18, 1995, Seattle, Washington)].

3) Michael Aaron Iams [(b. February 7, 1931, Taylor, North Dakota), m. Grace Reintsma (later Senn; b. December 5, 1940, Montana), and their two children were: Michele Renee Iams (b. June 4, 1962, Billings, Montana; m. Mr. Medina, and their daughter was Brittnee Lee Medina, b. August 29, 1986, Billings, Montana); and Desiree Lynn Iams (b. July 12, 1964, Billings, Montana; m. March 4, 1989, to David Dolluge)].

4) Jeffrie Lewis Iams [(b. August 16, 1935, Taylor, North Dakota), m. September 27, 1956, Montana, to Adela Ranta (b. April 3, 1936, Red Lodge, Montana), and they had four children: a) Jeffrie Iams, Jr. (b. May 6, 1957, Billings, Montana; had three children: Miriam Iams, b. May 12, 1983, Wyoming; Megan Iams, b. October 22, 1984, Wyoming; and Jessica Iams, b. September 16, 1986, Wyoming); b) Joel Iams (b. April 19, 1958, Billings, Montana; m. June 11, 1994, Bozeman, Montana, to Patti Janacaro); c) Summer Leanne Iams (b. May 29, 1959, Billings, Montana; m. August 16, 1960, Billings, Montana, to Keith Davey, and they had four children: Andrew Davey, b. March 31, 1983, Great Falls, Montana; Eric Davey, b. February 23, 1986, Great Falls, Montana; Caitlen Davey, b. January 23, 1988, Great Falls, Montana); and d) Stephanie Ellen Iams (b. November 14, 1964, Billings,

Montana); m. August 1, 1987, Billings, Montana, to John Lodman, and their first child was Wesley Evan Lodman, b. January 21, 1995, in Salt Lake City, Utah)].

5) Sara Beth Iams [(b. November 24, 1945, Taylor, North Dakota), m. September 23, 1966, California, to Charles Thomas Swearingen (b. November 27, 1946), and they had two children: a) Erika Jane Swearingen (b. May 5, 1967, California; m. July 9, 1994, Houston, Texas, to James Cuellar, b. Pleasantville, Texas); and b) Aaron Iams (b. March 26, 1968, California; m. May 19, 1990, West Virginia, to Beth Childress, b. June 20, 1964, in West Virginia; and their daughter Alyssa Faye Iams was b. December 1, 1993, in Ames, California)].

6) Douglas Maynard Iams [(b. August 13, 1947, Taylor, North Dakota), m. October 1, 1971, Billings, Montana, to Gloria Jean Messer (b. August 1, 1949, in Billings, Montana), and their three children were: a) Michael Douglas Iams, b. April 15, 1974, Billings, Montana; b) Emily Madella Iams, b. November 26, 1975, Billings, Montana; and c) Sarah Cecelia Iams, b. November 10, 1985, Billings, Montana].

7) Thomas Iams [(b. 1783, Bates Fork, Greene County, Pennsylvania; d. 1843, Greene County, Pennsylvania), the son of Richard Iams (b. 1745, Anne Arundel County, Maryland), and Eleanor Pottenger (per Kathryn Shipley), m. November 14, 1801, to Mary Jane "Polly" Smith (b. 1781), the daughter of Dennis Schmit (b. 1748; d. August 29, 1829) and Elizabeth Zook (b. May 13, 1756; d. September 19, 1845); and their daughter Elizabeth Iams (b. 1808, Greene County, Pennsylvania; d. June 10, 1877, Monroe County, Ohio), m. George Smith (b. 1801, Greene County, Ohio; d. September 4, 1869, Monroe County, Ohio), the son of Noah Smith (b. March 20, 1756, New Jersey; d. 1835, Greene County, Pennsylvania) and Ann Hoze (b. April 19, 1754; d. Greene County, Pennsylvania). Noah Smith was the son of Anthony Smith (b. July 26, 1723; d. January 1810, Greene County, Pennsylvania), and Ann Hoze (b. 1759) was the daughter of George Hoze (b. February 6, 1732; m. December 9, 1756; d. 1805, Greene County, Pennsylvania), and Elizabeth Blackledge].

The daughter of George Smith (b. 1801) and Elizabeth Iams (b. 1808) was Elizabeth Smith (b. 1840, Greene County, Pennsylvania; d. 1921, Washington County, Ohio) who m. August 18, 1867, to George Washington Shook (b. February 18, 1822; d. November 3, 1921, Washington County, Ohio), the son of John Shook and Hannah C. Scevat. The son of George Washington Shook (b. 1822) and Elizabeth Smith (b. 1840) was Thomas Franklin Shook (b. May 7, 1868, Trail Run, Monroe County, Ohio; d. February 24, 1934, Washington County, Ohio). The second child of Thomas Iams (b. 1780, Bates Fork Greene County, Pennsylvania) and Polly Smith (b. 1781) was Dennis Iams (b. June 21, 1808; d. January 7, 1888), m. August 6, 1831, to Matilda Huffman (b. September 26, 1814; d. October 14, 1887); and their daughter Priscilla Iams (b. October 15, 1859, m. David Hopkins, and their daughter was Jessie Hopkins (b. January 25, 1881) who m. September 27, 1902, to Stanley F. Garner (b. December 7, 1880), and their daughter Margaret Garner-Smith's National DAR application 372864 was made from Waynesburg, Greene County, Pennsylvania. Margaret Garner-Smith and Henrietta Adamson Conover (National DAR application 289119) linked Dennis Iams (b. 1806) to Thomas Iams (b. 1781; m. Mary "Polly" Smith) and HAC then linked this Thomas Iams to Sgt. Thomas Iams (b. 1754; d. June 24, 1834, Belmont County, Ohio). EFB has added nine additional children to the family of Dennis Iams (b. 1808) and Matilda Hoffman (b. 1814), including:

1) Thomas Iams (b. July 8, 1833; m. Lydia Penn; went west.
2) Sarah Iams (b. June 4, 1837; d. March 8, 1899; m. Dennis Loughman).
3) Benjamin Iams (b. September 4, 1839; m. Mariah Scott; lived at Hunters Cave, Greene County, Pennsylvania).
4) Mary Iams (b. April 24, 1842; d. June 10, 1924; m. Hiram Scott).
5) Lydia Iams (m. John Smith).
6) Amanda Iams (b. May 24, 1854; m. Charles Adamson).
7) Elizabeth Iams (b. January 19, 1846; d. March 19, 1848).
8) Dennis Iams, Jr. [(b. May 13, 1848; d. May 14, 1927; m. Mattie Kegley); and they had ten children: a) Oscar Iams (m. Cora Webster, and their three children: Mabel Iams, m. Charles Estel; Mary Iams, m. John Iams; and Doane Iams); b) Leah Iams (m. Roger Kellsey); c) Mary Iams (b. October 20, 1881; lived Washington, Pennsylvania); d) Lydia Iams (m. Charles Ely); e) Fannie Iams; f) Edith Iams (m. John Robb); g) Nantie Iams (b. January 1886; m. Thomas Dinsmore, and their daughter Margaret Dinsmore m. Oranz Scherick and they lived at Dunns Station, Greene County, Pennsylvania); h) Grace Iams; i) Judson Iams; and j) Louise Iams (m. Homer Sutherland)].

Six additional children of Thomas Iams (b. 1780, Bates Fork, Pennsylvania) and Mary Jane "Polly" Smith (b. 1781) have been added by REI: 1) Thomas Iams, Jr. [(b. 1821; d. 1906); m. Phoebe Penn (b. 1833; d. 1890), or Lydia Penn (b. April 20, 1833; d. November 27, 1890)]; 2) Catharine Iams; 3) Hannah Iams (m. Jesse Church, b. August 15, 1812); 4) Mary Iams (b. January 1, 1814; m. George Huffman); 5) Rachel Iams; and 6) Charity Iams. Hanna has described a detailed hunting trip of Dennis Iiams (b. 1806 or 1808, Bates Fork, Greene County, Pennsylvania; d. Morris Township, Greene County, Pennsylvania, on January 7, 1888); Dennis Iams (b. 1808), the son of Thomas Iiams (b. 1780), m. Matilda Huffman (b. September 25, 1806; d. October 14, 1887), was elected Deacon, Bates Fork Baptist Church, and had eight children:

1) Sarah Iams [(b. June 4, 1837; d. March 8, 1899), m. Daniel Loughman (b. April 25, 1832; d. January 28, 1892) and they had six children: a) Jack Loughman (m. Emma Hickman); b.) Ida Loughman (m. James A. Dunn); c) Dennis Loughman (moved to Oklahoma); d) Bell Loughman (m. George Hampson); e) George Loughman; and f) Charles Loughman].
2) Lydia Iams [(m. John Smith); six children: a) Frank Smith; b) Charles Smith; c) Nancy Smith; d) Cora Smith; e) Ocie Smith; and f) Bessie Smith].
3) Mary Iams [(m. Hiram Scott); six children: Thomas Scott, Clell Scott, Charles Scott, Tillis Scott, Flora Scott, and Dennis Scott].
4) Thomas Iams [(b. 1821, Greene County, Pennsylvania; d. Janauary 7, 1906, Mount Victory, Ohio); m. 1851 to Lydia Phoebe Penn].
5) Mandy Iams [(m. Charles Adamson); three children: Rose Adamson, Fannie Adamson, and Blanche Adamson].
6) Precylla Iams [(m. David Hopkins); six children: Jesse Hopkins, Bernice Hopkins, Edna Hopkins, Eva Hopkins, William Hopkins, and Roy Hopkins].
7) Benjamin Iams (m. Maria Scott).
8) Dennis Iams [(m. Mattie Kegley); ten children: Oscar Iams, Leah Iams, Lydia Iams, Fannie Iams, Mary Iams, Judson Iams, Grace Iams, Nancy Iams, Edith Iams, and Louise Iams].

Otho Iams (b. 1792; d. April 27, 1875, Greene County, Pennsylvania), the son of Richard Iams, m. 1813 to Nancy Cole (b. 1796) and they had eight children:

1) Thomas Iams [(b. 1821; d. February 19, 1881), a judge; m. Delilah Huffman (sister of Matilda Huffman and Rebecca Huffman), and their children included Mrs. J. W. Ray and F. P. Iams];

2) Eleanor "Nellie" Iiams [(b. June 9, 1814, Bates Fork, Greene County, Pennsylvania; d. March 6, 1876), m. April 30, 1835, to Samuel Sanders].

3) Mariah Iiams (b. 1816; m. Mr. Marshall).

4) John Iiams [(b. 1818); m. Rebecca Huffman, and they had nine girls and three sons; moved to Audubon, Iowa; youngest daughter was Mrs. Alice Esbeck].

5) William Iiams [(b. 1825), m. Hannah Wright].

6) Otho Iams [(b. 1829); married and moved to Winterset, Iowa; had three sons].

7) Eli Iams [(b. 1832; m. Clara Douglas, and they had three duaghters: Sadie Iams, Elizabeth Iams, and Catherine Iams].

8) Elizabeth Iams (b. 1823).

The 1850 Census of Greene County, Pennsylvania, lists: Otho Iams (age 59, b. Pennsylvania); wife Nancy Iams (age 59, b. Pennsylvania); Maria Iams (age 34, b. Pennsylvania); Elizabeth Iams (age 27, b. Pennsylvania); William Iams (age 25, b. Pennsylvania); Otho Iams (age 21, b. Pennsylvania); Eli Iams (age 18, b. Pennsylvania) and Westley Iams (age 4, b. Pennsylvania). The February 2, 1872, Greene County, Pennsylvania, will of Otho Iams, listed sons Thomas Iams, John Iams, William Iams, Otho Iams, and Eli Iams; and daughters Eleanor (Iams) Saunders and Maria (Iams) Marshall. In addition, Westley Iams, the son of John Iams was mentioned.

William Iiams (b. 1825, Greene County, Pennsylvania), son of Otho Iiams (b. 1792) and Nancy Cole, m. Hannah Wright (b. 1828) and they had eight children:

1) Thomas Jefferson Iams (b. 1857, Greene County, Pennsylvania; d. 1912), m. Elizabeth Durbin, daughter of Enoch Durbin and Mary M. Stagnal, and they moved to Kansas.

2) Corbley Iams (single; moved to Kansas).

3) Ellsworth Iams (moved first to Kansas, then to California).

4) George B. Iams [(b. 1870, Greene County, Pennsylvania; d. October 19, 1933), m. October 1, 1887, to Ella Bradbury (b. August 31, 1866, West Union, Pennsylvania; d. June 18, 1954, daughter of Cyrus Bradbury and Nancy Moore of Waynesburg College, a Sunday School teacher, church organist, and a ruling elder of Presbyterian Church) and their child Nancy Effie Iams lived in Jefferson, Pennsylvania)].

5) Wesley Iams

6) Dennis Iams (b. 1856; d. August 22, 1930), m. Emma C. Sollar (b. 1856, Pennsylvania) and they lived RD2, Finleyville, Greene County, Pennsylvania).

7) Bell Iams (a twin).

8) Caroline "Cal" Iams [(b. 1857, a twin, single), whose son was Ross Lindsey Iams (b. April 5, 1879, Graysville, Greene County, Pennsylvania; d. March 29, 1952, at U. S. Naval Hospital, San Diego, California; a 32-year Marine Corps veteran and Congressional Medal of Honor winner), who m. Elizabeth Sarah and their two sons were: a) Frederick R. Iams (b. November 14, 1918; lived at Chula Vista California; children included John Iams, Mary Iams, Joan Iams, and Peggy Iams Svatho, whose son was Steve Svatho); and b) Edward E. Iams (b. June 19, 1921; lived in California)]. The 1870 Census of Greene County, Pennsylvania, lists William Iams (age 44, b. Pennsylvania), Hannah Iams (age 39, b. Pennsylvania), Caroline Iams (age 15, b. Pennsylvania), Thomas Iams (age 13, b. Pennsylvania), Delila Iams (age 5, b. Pennsylvania), and George Iams (age 1, b. Pennsylvania). Separately listed in same county

were: Wesley Iams (age 25, b. Pennsylvania), Mary Iams (age 20, b. Pennsylvania), and Frances Iams (age 1, b. Pennsylvania). The 1900 Census of Greene County, Pennsylvania, listed head of household Ross L. Iams (age 19, b. Pennsylvania), and Caroline Iams (age 43, b. Pennsylvania); and a separate household listed George B. Iams (age 30, b. Pennsylvania) and mother Hannah Iams (age 70, b. Pennsylvania).

Ross Lindsey Iams (b. April 5, 1879, Greene County, Pennsylvania) and Elizabeth Sarah, had a son Ross Frederick Iams (b. November 14, 1918, Philadelphia, Pennsylvania; d. November 7, 1990, Rancho Bernardo, California), who m. October 12, 1940, San Francisco, California, to Mary Lou Husung (b. July 2, 1921, in Colorado Springs, Colorado, daughter of William T. Husung and Hazel F. Little), and they had four children: 1) Margaret Elizabeth Iams [(b. July 28, 1944, San Diego, California), m. August 22, 1964, to Alex Svatko, and their son was Steve Svatko]; 2) John Frederick Iams [(b. September 3, 1945, San Diego, California), m. December 30, 1968, to Vonnie Carol Hardesty (b. January 31, 1948, San Diego, California, daughter of Leonard and Mary Hardesty, and granddaughter of Eugene and Iva Hardesty), and their children were: a) Brian Shawn Iams (b. January 18, 1978, San Diego, California); b) Erich Christopher Iams (b. January 5, 1981, San Diego, California); and c) Craig Arthur Iams (b. December 5, 1983, Poway, California)]; 3) Mary Rose Iams [(b. April 11, 1948, San Diego, California), m. October 26, 1967, to James Richardson]; and 4) Joan Cecelia Iams [(b. January 16, 1950, Chula Vista, California), m. January 31, 1970, to Garry Gregory].

The January 19, 1965, issue of *Waynesburg* (Pennsylvania*) Messenger* headline read: "Graysville gave U. S. a Hero," by-line by Jim Moore. The article called Major Ross Lindsey Iams as "the greatest fighting man" from Greene County, a marine who gained national fame and the "coveted Medal of Honor." He was born April 5, 1879, and served 32 years in the Marines. He was awarded the Medal of Honor during the "Banana Wars," for capturing the ancient French Fort Riviera, stronghold for the Caco soldiers at Port-au-Prince in November 1915. In the November 1994 issue of the military history magazine *Command*, appeared an article "Haiti, Been there—Seen It—Done That." Sgt. Ross L. Iams is described as being one of 340 U. S. Marines that went ashore from *the U. S. Cruiser Washington* on July 28, 1915, and bivouaced at the "Camp de Mars" square in the center of Port-au-Prince. He distinguished himself against the indigenous bandit gangs in the battles of Gonaives, Port Capois, and Fort Riviere, and was one of three marines recommended for the Congressional Medal of Honor by the then Assistant Secretary of Navy, Franklin D. Roosevelt (all three were awarded the medal). He had been assigned to the U. S. S. Connecticut when ordered to Haiti because of civil unrest during an election, following a succession of rule by two kings and 23 presidents prior to an election to determine a new chief of state.

The marines had driven the Cacos into their last, and previously unpenetrable stronghold of Fort Riviera, located on top of a 4,000 foot mountain with 25 foot high walls that were up to seven feet wide. However, Sgt. Iams (he worked his way up through the ranks) discovered the mouth of a drain, three feet in diameter, and led 27 marines into the fort for capture. The Lowell Thomas book *Old Gimlet Eye* also credits Sgt. Iams as the leader responsible for this feat, and was the first white man inside the fort in 160 years. The Cacos lost 72 men, including seven chiefs. The fort was blown apart with dynamite; the Caco rebellion was ended, thus "giving Haiti an interlude of peace." As an interesting side light, the commander and one of the few men ever to receive two Congressional medals of honor, Major Smedley Buttes, was being interviewed on a coast-to-coast radio show in 1933 and quoted Sgt. Iams verbatim, "Oh, hell, I'm going through," and this statement resulted in immediate censorship, and the interview was cut off from the network. This event "caused a nationwide sensation, which was reported in all the major newspapers."

Captain Iams retired to San Diego in 1932, but was recalled to active duty as a Major on January 19, 1942, thus serving in three wars, since he also served eleven months in France in 1918-1919. He also had assignments in Mexico, China, Philippines, and Nicaragua. His other decorations included: Philippine Campaign Medal; Nicaraguan Medal, Second Nicaraguan Campaign; Dominican Campaign medal; Expedition Medal with Bronze Star for service in Haiti; Expedition Medal for service in China; Bronze Star; World War I Victory Medal; and World War II Victory Medal. Major Iams died March 29, 1952, at age 71 in U. S. Naval Hospital, San Diego, with few of his family and almost none of his friends aware of his military accomplishments. He was survived by his widow Elizabeth Iams, a son Fred H. Iams, a son Edward E. Iams (WW II disabled veteran). Son Fred H. Iams was a U. S. Navy Signalman during World War II and had a son (John F. Iams) and three daughters (Mary Iams, Joan Iams, and Peggy Iams Svathe, who had a son Steve Svathe). The family lived in Chula Vista, California. Story reported in *Command*, No. 31, Nov.-Dec. 1994, pp. 46-61.

Dennis Iams (b. 1856, Greene County, Pennsylvania; d. August 22, 1930, son of William Iiams (b. 1825) and Hannah Wright, m. Emma C. Sollars, and they had six children: 1) Elizabeth Iams [(b. 1884, Greene County, Pennsylvania), m. 1st, Richard Goslin; and m. 2nd, Carl Tuckel]; 2) James B. Iams (m. Blanche Wright and they lived in Detroit, Michigan); 3) Levi Wesley Iams (b. 1882, Pennsylvania; m. Sadie Closser, and their children included: Edith J. Iams, Mildred Iams, Emma L. Iams, and Bryon S. Iams); 4) Martha L. Iams (b. 1888, Pennsylvania; m. Raymond W. Scott, and they lived at Dunn Station, Greene County, Pennsylvania); 5) John B. Iams (b. 1887, Pennsylvania; single); and 6) William Burns Iams [(b. October 3, 1883), m. Anna E. Green, and their twelve children were: Craig Iams (m. Ann Carroll), James Arthur Iams (b. July 5, 1924), Lena Iams (d. age 9), Ethel Mae Iams-Glendenning, Margaret Iams-Wise, Martha Alberta Iams-Dille, William Wesley Iams, Elmer Raymond Iams, James Arthur Iams, Dennis Iams, Emma Iams, and Oscar Randolph Iams]. James Arthur Iams [(b. July 5, 1924, Washington, Pennsylvania; d. April 22, 1992, Washington, Pennsylvania, buried at Bradock Cemetery, Graysville, Greene County, Pennsylvania), m. April 22, 1950, Washington, Pennsylvania, to Betty Ruth Cumberland (b. January 3, 1938, Holbrook, Pennsylvania; daughter of Frances M. Cumberland and Ellen E. Glover), and their daughter Barbara Lee Iams (b. May 8, 1952, Washington, Pennsylvania; m. May 21, 1981, to Anthony Iannacchione) had three children: Gaetoy James Iannacchione (b. July 30, 1984, Pittsburgh, Pennsylvania), and Stefan Ross Iannacchione (b. May 6, 1989, Pittsburgh, Pennsylvania)]. Family tree provided by Betty Cumberland Iams of Washington, Pennsylvania.

Thomas Jefferson Iams (b. 1857, Greene County, Pennsylvania), son of William Iams (b. 1825) and Hannah Wright, m. Elizabeth Durbin, and their children included:

1) Mary Bell Iams (b. November 15, 1881; d. February 8, 1961; m. Frank Burns).
2) Sadie Iams (b. 1884; m. Emil Tysell).
3) Rosie Iams [(b. 1886), m. Frank Barnes, and they had three children: a) Mildred Barnes (b. june 9, 1913; m. Charles Stilley); b) Jennie Marie Barnes (b. July 30, 1910; m. Bruce Basker, and their son Ronald Basker was b. April 10, 1926; m. Evelyn ____, and had daughter Sherrie J. Basker); and c) Frances LeRoy Barnes (b. August 27, 1915; m. Elvera ____ and their two children were: Harriet Barnes Johnson; had son Jebbie Johnson; and Frances Pearl Barnes Black had a son Michael Black)].

154

4) William Iams [(b. 1889; d. 1960), m. Millie Seley, and they had five children: a) Clara Iams (m. Lester Beetcher); b) Ann Iams; c) Arlene Iams (single); d) Fay Iams; and e) Robert Iams].

5) Corbly "Corb" Iams [(b. June 2, 1894), m. Ruth Seley, and they had four children: a) George William Iams (b. January 6, 1918; m. 1st, Ariel Doty; m. 2nd, Albina ____, and had two children: Arlie Iams, and George Iams; b) Lawrence W. Iams (b. November 25, 1944; m. Deloris Berends); c) Hubert E. Iams (b. December 13, 1931); m. Donna Stockdale; and d) Frank Iams (b. May 18, 1920; m. 1st, Eita Arnett; m. 2nd, Janetta Tice; and had two children: Frank E. Iams, b. 1944; m. 1st, Elizabeth Mesgard; m. 2nd, Pat LaBourdis; and Gary Iams, b. 1946)]. The 1900 Census of Greene County, Pennsylvania, lists Thomas Iams (age 42, b. Pennsylvania); Catherine E. Iams (age 38, b. Pennsylvania); Robert J. Iams (age 18, b. Pennsylvania); Jesse J. Iams (son, age 18, b. Pennsylvania); Mary J. Iams (age 18, b. Pennsylvania); William J. Iams (age 11, b. Pennsylvania); Delsie Iams (age 8, b. Pennsylvania); John Iams (age 6, b. Pennsylvania); and Sally Iams (age 3, b. Pennsylvania).

John Iiams (b. 1818, Greene County, Pennsylvania), son of Otho Iams and Nancy Cole, m. Rebecca Huffman (b. Greene County, Pennsylvania), and according to the youngest of twelve children, Alice Imes Esbik, much information was never recorded. The name was changed to Imes since the mail carriers kept confusing the name with James and Jones. The family moved first from Greene County, Pennsylvania, about 1863 to Mason County, Illinois; then to Logan County, Illinois; and finally in 1870, to Audubon, Iowa. The twelve children of John Iams/Imes were: 1) Delilah Imes (d. age 12); 2) Sarah Imes (d. infancy); 3) Mary Elizabeth Imes (d. infancy); 4) Semantha Imes (d. infancy); 5) Nancy Imes (b. September 26, 1844); 6) Ellen Imes (b. May 20, 1846; d. April 5, 1910); 7) Warren Imes (b. October 28, 1851; lived in Stuart, Iowa; and his son Jason A. Iams lived in Chicago); 8) Keziah Ann "Callie" Imes (b. April 30, 1854, m. Mr. Drury; lived in Audubon, Iowa); 9) Huldah Imes (b. August 31, 1858; d. September 13, 1918); 10) Tilton Imes (b. August 31, 1858; d. 1873); 11) Wesley Imes (b. October 1, 1860; whereabouts unknown); and 12) Alice Bell Imes (b. January 9, 1862 or 1863; she was uncertain of the year).

Thomas Iiams (b. 1821; d. February 19, 1881), the son of Otho Iiams (b. 1792) and Nancy Cole, m. Delilah Huffman, and they had seven children:

1) Benjamin H. Iams (Civil War veteran as 1st Sgt., Company C, 18th Pennsylvania Cavalry under Captain John Hughes; died in Fairfax, Virginia Hospital June 8, 1863, and buried in Old Bates Fork Cemetery, where his photo is recessed in stone marker, listing his age as 19 years, 8 months, and 16 days).

2) Otho Iams [(b. September 4, 1846, Morris Township, Greene County, Pennsylvania; d. October 18, 1927), m. June 1881 in Morris Township to Sarah Jane Bane, daughter of Jasper Bane; and their son Allen A. Iams (b. 1881 or after) m. Nelle Bennett and had three children: a) Mary Lucy Iams (b. December 21, 1917); b) Helen V. Iams (b. July 7, 1922); and c) Hazel Hill Iams (b. May 10, 1925)].

3) James L. Iams [(b. by January 2, 1857; held several Greene County, Pennsylvania, public offices, including County Treasurer and County Associate Judge; was a member of State Democratic Central Committee), m. in 1877 to Belle S. Swart, daughter of Jacob Swart (no children)].

4) Henrietta Iams [(m. Greene County Common Pleas Judge Joseph W. "J.W." Ray), and they had five children: a) Mabel Ray (Librarian in

New York City); b) Irene Ray (m. George Jinkins); c) Lloyd Ray; d) Joseph W. Ray, Jr. (m. Elsie Cooper), an attorney in Uniontown, Fayette County, Pennsylvania; and e) Frank Iams Ray (lived in Akron, Ohio];
5) Franklin P. Iams (an attorney of national repute); lived in Pittsburgh, Pennsylvania; m. socialite Lucy Dorsey.
6) Lucinda Iams (single; lived in Waynesburg, Greene County, Pennsylvania).
7) Jesse Leazer Iams (accidentally killed in 1875 while building the homestead which is on site first settled by Mary Iams Penn and most recently occupied by Allen A. Iams, grandson of Judge Thomas Iams, and known as Knob View farm).
Eleanor "Nellie" Iiams (b. June 9, 1814, Bates Fork, Morris Township, Greene County, Pennsylvania; d. March 6, 1876), daughter of Otho Iiams (b. 1792) and Nancy Cole; m. April 30, 1835, to Samuel Saunders (data from Nellie B. Gilmore, Claysville, Pennsylvania), and they had nine children:
1) Reuben Saunders [(b. August 21, 1836), m. Semantha Hathaway, and they had three children: a) Wylie Saunders (lived in Washington, Pennsylvania); b) Ida Mae Saunders Price (lived in Washington, Pennsylvania); and c) Sarah Jane Saunders Turner (lived in Clinton, Pennsylvania)].
2) Warren Saunders (b. January 26, 1838; d. December 21, 1865; no children).
3) Caroline Saunders [(b. Novembver 28, 1839), m. Silas Saunders of Washington County, Pennsylvania; and they had five children: a) Justice M. Saunders; b) Melvern H. Saunders (lived Claysville, Pennsylvania); c) Samuel C. Saunders (lived in Inglewood, California); d) William B. Saunders (lived Claysville, Pennsylvania); and e) Harry Olney Saunders (lived in Washington, Pennsylvania)].
4) Eleanor Saunders [(b. August 7, 1842; d. January 1925), m. 1st, Jamison Martin (child: Laura Martin-Lyman); m. 2nd, Warren Carroll of West Finley Township, Greene County, Pennsylvania, and had four children: a) Lalla E. Carroll Marse (lived Tampa, Florida); b) Arthur Carroll (lived Claysville, Pennsylvania); c) Robert Iams Carroll (lived Norway, Iowa); and d) Merton Carroll (lived at Cresa, Texas)].
5) Wylie Saunders (b. February 14, 1845; d. 1845).
6) Luvinia Saunders [(b. September 21, 1847; d. July 7, 1919); m. December 20, 1881, to Robert John Gilmore of Greene County, Pennsylvania, and they had four children: Wilbert Ross Gilmore (lived Claysville, Pennsylvania); b) John Robert Gilmore (lived Claysville, Pennsylvania); c) Nellie B. Gilmore (lived Claysville, Pennsylvania; wrote family tree); and d) Glenn E. Gilmore (lived Claysville, Pennsylvania)].
7) James Saunders (b. March 17, 1850; d. June 29, 1864).
8) Nancy E. Saunders [(b. March 30, 1852; d. June 3, 1925); m. May 29, 1879, to J. B. Mitchell of Taylor Station, Pennsylvania, and they had three children: a) Lola M. Mitchell (lived Claysville, Pennsylvania); b) Otto C. Mitchell (lived Washington, Pennsylvania); and c) Bryant Mitchell (lived Taylorstown, Pennsylvania)].
9) Parmelia Almeda Saunders [(b. October 4, 1855), m. October 12, 1882, to A. Mack Smith of Washington, Pennsylvania, and they had two children: a) Harry M. Smith; and b) Mary Eleanor Smith-Grounds (lived Roaring Springs, Pennsylvania)].
Reason (or Rezin) Iams (b. 1789 or 1791; d. February 18, 1860), son of Richard Iiams (b. 1745, Anne Arundel County, Maryland; d. 1825 or 1833) and Eleanor Pottenger (JM), m. Phoebe Clark (b. June 30, 1787; d. June 2, 1845); daughter of

Isaac Clark and Deborah French, and sister of Silas Clark, Abner Clark, and Ezekiel Clark (EBI); and had six children:

1) Reason Iams, Jr. [(b. May 16, 1821; d. January 28, 1850); m. Nancy ____ (b. 1804; d. January 9, 1876, age 71 years, 9 months, 16 days)].

2) Richard Iams [(b. March 6, 1817, Greene County, Pennsylvania; d. August 1893); a driver with routes to East Liberty and to Baltimore; m. January 14, 1842, to Lucinda Fonner; lived at Iams Station, Greene County, on the Waynesburg and Washington Railroad line].

3) Isaac Iams [(b. 1816; d. 1852, Noble County, Ohio), m. Elizabeth Williams, daughter of Abraham Williams and Sarah Hannah; moved to Noble County, Ohio, 1850].

4) Ellen Iams [(b. April 2, 1815; d. February 24, 1907, buried at Union Cemetery), m. Ephriam Conger (Republican, farmer, member of Cumberland Presbyterian Church at West Union), and their son John Conger m. 2nd, Hannah Loughman].

5) John Iams [(b. March 22, 1819; d September 23, 1895), a private in Company F, 22nd PVC who enlisted September 1862 and was discharged June 3, 1856; m. March 5, 1881, to Elizabeth Miller (b. March 28, 1822; d. December 7, 1894)].

6) Deborah Iams [(b. September 27, 1812; d. February 20, 1856), m. 1832 to John Penn (b. June 9, 1808; d. September 5, 1892), and their two children: a) Mary Penn (m. Benjamin Huffman; and b) Margaret Penn m. A. J. Barker, and their three children were Lew Barker (m. ___Farmer), James L. Barker (lived Washington, Pennsylvania), and Richard Barker (lived at Sycamore, Greene County)].

Richard Iams (b. March 6, 1817, Greene County, Pennsylvania; d. August 1893), son of Reason Iams (b. 1789 or 1791) and Phoebe Clark (b. 1787), m. January 14, 1842, to Lucinda Fonner (d. 1883, Kansas) and lived at Iams Station, Greene County, Pennsylvania; bought and sold cattle; was stockholder in Waynesburg and Washington Railroad (narrow gauge) until the Panic of 1877 when both he and his cousin Judge Thomas Iams lost their money; Director of Poor 1870-1875; lived in log cabin until 1877 when he built a fine home from lumber he cut; moved to Kansas in March 1878 and homesteaded NW 1/4 of Section 25, Township 7, Range 3 East, where he farmed until the time of his death; and they had four children: 1) Rezin Iams [(b. November 30, 1844, Greene County, Pennsylvania; d. 1883), m. Emma Reeves, and their two children were: Richard L. Iams (a twin; a miner in Mina, Nevada) and Lilly Iams (a twin, d. age 12)]; 2) Henry B. Iams (b. February 25, 1849, Greene County, Pennsylvania; single; a farmer; d. September 13, 1925, Clay Center, Kansas); 3) Martha Jane Iams (b. March 12, 1851 or 1861; d. age 4 of diphtheria); and 4) James Fonner Iams [(b. November 9, 1865; a farmer, stock raiser, and judge who wrote family history); m. March 28, 1894, to Henrietta Allen; and they moved to Clay Center, Kansas in 1914 where he operated the elevator of Iiams Grain Company; was a grocer until 1921 when he became a Federal Grain Inspector; later sold Nash automobiles in 1931 became Probate Judge of Clay County, Kansas (appointed by Governor Henry Woodring)].

Isaac Iams (b. 1816; d. 1852, Noble County, Ohio), son of Reason Iams (b. 1789 or 1791) and Phoebe Clark, m. 1832, Greene County, Pennsylvania, to Elizabeth Williams (b. Washington County, Pennsylvania), daughter of Abraham Williams; moved to Noble County, Ohio, in 1850; owned 262 acres in Monroe County, Ohio, March 29, 1851; will of Isaac Iams written January 7, 1852, filed from Stock Township, Noble County, Ohio, April 20, 1852, left the estate to his wife and named

157

children Isaac Iams, Rezin Iams, Eleanor Jane Iams, Rebecca Iams, Sarah Iams, and Martha Ann Iams, in addition to son Franklin Iams of Washington County, Pennsylvania; with Richard Iams as witness; and Demer Iams and Richard Iams of Stock Township, Noble County, Ohio, as debtors to the estate; and Isaac Iams died as a wealthy land owner, though his legacy was soon lost throught the guardianship of the heirs. Children of Isaac Iams (b. 1810 or 1816) and Elizabeth Williams were:

1) Eleanor Jane Iams [(b. November 4 or 8, 1835, Washington County, Pennsylvania; died at 91 in Spring Hill, Kansas), m. December 23, 1852, to Armon Price Smith of Carlisle, Noble County, and they had eight children].

2) Abner Iams (d. age 5, buried Bates Fork Cemetery, Greene County, Pennsylvania).

3) George Iams (d. age 14).

4) Isaac Iams, Jr. [(b. October 10, 1842, Greene County, Pennsylvania; d. November 27, 1902, Clay County, Kansas), m. May 30, 1875, Clay County, Kansas, to Mary Spurrier (b. October 1855; d. April 11, 1925) and their four children were: Vaughn Iams (b. April 22, 1875), Virgil Iams (b. September 16, 1878), Audrey B. Iams (b. December 14, 1879), and Stella Iams (d. infancy)].

5) Rebecca Iams [(d. age 60), m. Nimrod Young, lived in Clay County, Kansas, and their five children were: a) William Young; b) Elizabeth Young; c) Charles Young; d) a child that died young; and e) Ted Young].

6) Sarah Iams [(d. Arkansas, age over 40), m. Doctor Wilson and they had two children; a) died young; and b) Jessie Wilson who m. Henry Diffenderfer; lived at Riley, Kansas, and they had two children: a son who studied medicine, and an adopted daughter, Opal Diffendorfer].

7) Martha Ann Iams (b. November 1846, Greene County, Pennsylvania; alive in 1931; single; moved to Green, Clay County, Kansas).

8) Elizabeth Iams (d. infancy and buried Bates Fork, Greene County, Pennsylvania).

9) Rezin Iams (b. January 27, 1850, Greene County, Pennsylvania; d. Clay County, Kansas; over age 60).

10) Richard Iams (d. age 20).

Eleanor Jane Iams (b. November 4, 1835, Washington County, Pennsylvania), daughter of Isaac Iams (b. 1816) and Elizabeth Williams, m. December 3, 1852, at Carlisle, Noble County, Ohio, to Harmon Price Smith, and their eight children were:

1) Franklin Iret Smith [(b. December 2, 1853, Carlisle, Noble County, Ohio); married and had nine children; an active businessman at age over 76 at time of his death in Denver, Colorado].

2) Minerva Jane Smith [(b. June 30, 1855, Noble County, Ohio; d. January 29, 1927, at home in Baldwin, Kansas), m. Charles Wiley and they had one son and one daughter].

3) LeRoy Smith (b. November 29, 1857, Noble County, Ohio; d. January 21, 1916, Paronie Valley County, Oklahoma; single).

4) George B. Smith (b. June 4, 1861, Noble County, Ohio; d. February 2, 1863, Carlisle, Noble County, Ohio).

5) Clara Smith [(b. December 6, 1864, Noble County, Ohio; d. February 13, 1915, Canton, Illinois), m. May 28, 1888, to Doctor E. W. Reagan, a surgeon in U. S. Army, and they had two sons: a) Thomas Harold Reagan (m. a Chicago woman and they had three children); and b) Maurice Ellerslie Reagan (a son who lived in Pittsburgh, Pennsylvania)].

6) William Henry Smith (b. August 9, 1866, Noble County, Ohio; lived at Levelland, Texas).

7) Julia Smith [(b. July 21, 1868, Noble County, Ohio; prepared family history), m. November 10, 1892, Spring Hills, Kansas, to William Herbert Rutter, proprietor of Rutter and Sons Furniture Dealers, Topeka, Kansas, and they had two sons: a) Warren Rutter (b. September 11, 1893; m. August 18, 1921, in Topeka, Kansas, to Vivian Herron, and they had two daughters: Jean Rutter, b. November 6, 1922; and Martha Rutter, b. January 1, 1927); and b) Merril Rutter (b. August 7, 1898; single)].

8) Ella Smith [(b. November 4, 1875, Spring Hill, Kansas), m. Mr. Hoyes; lived in Topeka, Kansas, and their daughter was Alice Hoyes].

Rezin Iams (b. January 27, 1850, Greene County, Pennsylvania), son of Isaac Iams, Sr. (b. 1810), and Elizabeth Williams; m. December 24, 1884, Clay Center, Kansas, to Martha McLaughlin (b. December 26, 1866, Homer, Clay Center, Kansas), daughter of William McLaughlin and Sarah Edwards. Rezin Iams (b. 1850) moved with his family to Noble County, Ohio, as an infant in April 1850, and lived there long enough to begin school at Carlisle before later attending school in Bloomington, Illinois. He taught school for one year and in 1871 moved to Clay County, Kansas, with his brother Isaac Iams, Jr. (b. 1842). Rezin Iams lived at Fancy Creek, Highland Township, Clay County, Kansas, where he raised stock, built a house of stone, eventually owned 1,200 acres before moving to the town of Clay Center, Kansas in 1879, where he engaged in real estate, the loan business, and owned three business blocks in town. Known children of Rezin Iams (b. 1850) and Martha McLaughlin were: 1) Alma Irene Iams (d. age 22 months); 2) Rezin Howard Iams (b. September 1, 1887, Clay County, Kansas); 3) Floyd E. Iams (b. June 1890); and 4) Becil Iams (b. 1896).

Ellen Iams (b. April 2, 1815; d. February 24, 1907; buried in Union Cemetery, Greene County, Pennsylvania), daughter of Reason Iams (b. 1789 or 1791) and Phoebe Clark; m. Ephriam Conger and they had eight children:

1) John Conger [(m. twice, the second to Hannah Loughman); had four children: Ella Conger (single); Emma Conger (m. Doctor Dodd of Amity, Pennsylvania, and they had two children); Agnes Conger; and Ida Conger].

2) Frank Conger [(m. Lena Clutter); had five children: a) Hiram Conger (Spanish American War Veteran in Company H, 10th Volunteer Regiment; m. Cynthia Ferrell and their four children included Lillian Conger, Frank Conger, Russell Conger, and an infant who died young); b) Lawrence Conger (m. Cad Vankirk and they had two children); c) Olive Conger (m. Smith Loughman); d) Mabel Conger (m. William McCullough of Deer Lick, Greene County, Pennsylvania); and e) Albert Conger (m. Lydia Loughman, and their five children were: James Conger, Anna Conger who m. Gilmore Bigler, Mary Conger, Albert Conger, and John Conger)].

3) Elias Conger [(m. Hannah Dunn) and their four children were: a) Elizabeth Conger; b) Sadie Conger; c) Dorothy Conger; and d) William Conger, a meter reader for West Penn].

4) Martha Conger [(m. 1st, William Breece, Sr., and their son was William Breece, Jr.), and (m. 2nd, Joseph Dunn, and their two children were Goldy Dunn and James Dunn who was killed in an auto accident in the West)].

5) Phoebe Conger [(m. Oliver Maddox) and their children were: John Maddox, George Maddox, and Herschel Maddox].

6) Hannah Conger (m. William Penn).

7) Mary Conger (m. Mr. Longdon, and their two children were Fory Longdon, and Inez Longdon, who m. Lee Andrew).
8) Emaline Conger [(m. Hamilton Penn) and their six children were: Franklin Penn (superintendent of Penn Training School at Morganza); Clarence Penn (operated cleaning and dye business in Washington, Pennsylvania); Arthur Penn, Lincoln Penn, and Alice Penn (m. John Clutter)].

Richard Iams (b. 1811, Athens County, Ohio) was the son of William Iiams (m. 1782) and Charity Ryan; and the grandson of Richard Iiams (b. 1745); m. Jane Holmes, and they had four children: 1) William Imes (no children); 2) John A. Imes [(m. Nerva Crosson), and their daughter Eva Imes m. Mr. Grant and lived in Kansas]; 3) Nancy Imes [(m. Wallace Marse) and their son Bert Marse had a child Elbert Marse who lived in Detroit, Michigan]); 4) James Q. Imes [(m. Frances M. Lavrey, lived in Athens, Ohio), and they had three sons: a) Richard P. Imes (m. Clara Baird, and their two sons were Wilbur B. Imes and Richard Imes and lived in Athens, Ohio); b) Leroy L. Imes (m. Forest Weinerman; lived Denver, Colorado, and their three children were; James H. Imes, Roger E. Imes, and Mary Lou Imes); and c) Robert H. Imes (remained single; worked as a telegraph operator for Pennsylvania Railroad)].

John Iams, the son of William Iiams (m. 1782) and Charity Ryan (EBI), went to New Orleans and then to Texas. The Union National Bank of Houston published a story in *Burke's Almanac* which credited Doctor Frank J. Ijams of Houston with information released December 28, 1939, that this John Iiams had two sons: 1) Isaac Iiams (whereabouts unknown); and 2) George Willoughby Iiams, who had three sons: a) George Iams (lived in Houston, and his son Henry Iams was a railroad engineer); b) John Iams [had two sons: a) Doctor Frank J. Iiams; and b) Claxton Iiams (had an insurance agency in Houston); and son Frank Allen Iiams was age 5 at time the above article was written]; and c) Frank Iiams [a cattleman, had four sons, but later disappeared; his sons were Harvey Iiams (a buyer for a firm in Texas); Eugene Iiams (proprietor of a gasoline filling station between the Texas cities of Beaumont and Port Arthur); Melby Iiams (a machinist at Hughes Tool Company of Houston); and William Iiams (who was adopted by the Harrington family of Kansas after the death of his mother and disappearance of his father; he took the Harrington name)].

Eli Iiams (b. May 15, 1790, Washington County, Maryland), the son of Richard Iiams (b. 1745) and Eleanor Pottenger, m. Catherine Crawford (b. 1791, County Donegal, Ireland; d. August 30, 1872, Washington County, Ohio); daughter of John Crawford (b. 1756, Ireland; d. 1805, Washington County, Ohio); and of John Crawford (b. 1756, Ireland; d. 1805, Washington County, Ohio); and of Eleanor Coulter, who d. October 1839. Eleanor Coulter (b. 1760; d. 1839) was the daughter of Thewey Coulter. Eli Iiams is credited by Alice Iams Williams of Tulsa, Oklahoma, as being the first to sign his name Iams, as read from the Eli Iams family Bible. Eli Iams (b. 1790) d. May 26, 1857, at Marietta, Washington County, Ohio, and was buried there in Mound Cemetery. Eli Iams (b. 1790) and Catherine Crawford m. October 12, 1815, at Marietta, and they had eight children: 1) Alfred Ijams (b. August 11, 1816; d. March 24, 1818, Marietta, Ohio); 2) Rufus Putnam Ijams [(b. August 19, 1818, Marietta, Ohio; d. November 26, 1891, Terre Haute, Indiana), m. May 26, 1842, in Marietta, to Mary Whiting Burch (b. January 24, 1824, Virginia; d. January 6, 1899, Terre Haute, Indiana), the daughter of Hiram Burch and Nancy Whiting]; 3) Percival Smith Ijams (b. July 4, 1820; m. at Portsmough, Ohio, in April 1849 to Marionette Oldfields); 4) Sarah Ijams [(b. March 18, 1822; d. April 10, 1879), m. June 29, 1844, Marietta, to Austin Berkeley, and they had three children: a) James Eli Berkeley (b. June 8, 1846); b) Mary Ellen Berkeley (b. June 8, 1849), and c) John Granville Berkeley (d. May 1887, Marietta)]; 5) Frances Maria Ijams [(b. August 19, 1824; d. June

7, 1858, Marietta), m. October 28, 1845, Marietta, to Ephraim "E.C." Wells, and their two children were: a) Charles Elijah Wells (b. October 8, 1846; d. January 14, 1862, at Somerville, West Virginia); and b) John Eli Wells (b. August 18, 1849)]; 6) Eleanor Ijams (b. February 17, 1827; d. February 1, 1883); 7) Mary Wilson Ijams (b. August 23, 1829; d. March 23, 1859, at Marietta); and 8) John Leedham Ijams (b. December 2, 1835; d. May 13, 1836, Marietta). E. B. Iams has reported Eli Iams, son of Richard Iams, as having moved to near Dayton, Ohio, with his wife, Mary Heckathorn. The 1850 Census lists Eli Ijams as a property owner in the First Ward in Marietta, Washington, County, Ohio. Also, other children of John Crawford (b. 1756) were: Sarah Crawford (b. 1790, Ireland; d. 1811); Robert Crawford (b. May 5, 1796, Ireland; d. August 5, 1854, in Ohio); John Crawford (b. May 2, 1798, Brownsville, Pennsylvania; d. September 3, 1852), and William Crawford (b. 1800, in Ohio; d. 1843, Washington County, Ohio). EFB doubts that Eli Iiams (b. 1790) was the son of Richard Iiams (b. 1745), and feels that the Eli Iams of Dayton, Ohio, was the son of Richard Iams, Sr. (b. ca1745) and husband of Phoebe Heckathorn.

Rufus Putnam Ijams (b. August 19, 1818, Marietta, Ohio; named after the famous early Ohio pioneer; d. November 26, 1891, Terre Haute, Indiana), the son of Eli Ijams (b. 1790) and Catharine Crawford (b. 1791); m. May 26, 1842, Marietta, to Mary Whiting Burch (b. January 24, 1824, Virginia; d. January 6, 1899, Terre Haute, Indiana). Mary Whiting Burch (b. 1824) was the daughter of well-known Ohio River boat Captain Hiram Burch (b. October 13, 1796, Newtown, Connecticut; d. November 27, 1882, Marietta), and Nancy Whiting (m. February 18, 1821). Hiram Burch (b. 1796) was the son of William Burch (b. October 16, 1766, Newtown, Connecticut; m. Grace Northrop). William Burch (b. 1766) was the son of William Burch (b. November 13, 1726; d. July 8, 1797, Newton, Connecticut; m. September 27, 1750, to Katherine Hubbell). This William Burch (b. 1726) was the son of Jeremiah Burch (b. June 10, 1699; m. March 24, 1726, to Sarah Beecher), and this Jeremiah Burch (b. 1726) was also the son of a Jeremiah Burch (m. to Elizabeth Wheeler).

Children of Rufus Putnam Ijams (b. 1818) and Mary Whitney Burch (b. 1824) were: 1) Hiram Burch Ijams [(b. May 24, 1843, Marietta, Ohio), served three years as 1st Lt., Company K, First Ohio Light Artillery, 1961-1963, with Civil War pension approved October 7, 1896; d. March 6, 1896, San Antonio, Texas, m. February 28, 1872, to Frances "Frannie" Earle Clark]; 2) William Putnam Ijams [(b. January 18, 1847, Marietta, Ohio; d. March 22, 1922, Terre Haute, Indiana). Listed in *National Encyclopaedia of American Biography*, Volume 31; enlisted as a drummer at age 16; worked as clerk for the Logansport, Crawfordsville, and Southeastern Railroad; then paymaster of Vandalia Railroad; built the Belt Railroad and Stockyard of Indianapolis in 1877 and was president until 1882; organized the Citizens Telephone Company; was president of Terre Haute House and of the Terre Haute Canning Company; helped organize Inland Steel Casting of Terre Haute and Terre Haute Grand Opera House; operated Wabash Cattle Company in Wyoming; was president of American Trotting Association 1899-1922; owned one-mile sulky record holder (2:12), Axtell; m. February 6, 1876, Terre Haute, Indiana, to Sallie Warren (b. December 8, 1855; d. January 12, 1924, Terre Haute), the daughter of Levi Gale Warren (b. January 31, 1816, Terre Haute; d. June 30, 1864, Terre Haute) and Martha Ellen Clake; Levi Gale Warren (b. 1816) was the son of Bernard Miller Warren (b. September 21, 1766, Upton, Massachusetts), who was the son of Samuel Warren (b. November 9, 1729, Westboro, Massachusetts); and William Putnam Ijams (b. 1847) had three children: a) Jesse Warren Ijams (b. 1882, Indiana); b) Alice Warren Ijams (b. December 11, 1882, Terre Haute; m. Richard Wetherill Benbridge); and c) Frank Burch Ijams (b. December 3, 1886, Terre Haute; d. March 11, 1966, Terre Haute); m.

September 15, 1915, Terre Haute, to Helen Pauline Fairbanks, (b. October 7, 1891); a civil engineer, graduate of Yale University; World War I artillery major; president of *Tribune Star* Publishing Company; listed in the 1961 *Who's Who in America*; Chairman of Board of Alton Box Company; Director of Terre Haute First National Bank; Director of Indiana Coke and Glass Company; and had two children: a) Edward Burch Ijams, b. October 16, 1917, Terre Haute; m. February 19, 1941, Alton, Illinois, to Elizabeth Alexander; and b) Emily Alice Ijams, b. January 16, 1922, Terre Haute; m. June 6, 1942, Terre Haute, to John Horter Williams, and lived in Tulsa, Oklahoma.

REFERENCES

- Cemetery and Census Records, Walton County, Indiana.

- (JFI) John Frederick Iams, Poway, California, correspondence.

- Lois Ijams Hartman, Pasadena, California, private research.

- (JM) James Meighen, personal files.

- Cemetery, Land, Wills, and Census Records, Anne Arundel and Frederick Counties, Maryland.

- *Who's Who in America*, various series.

- (MI) Mary Lou Iams, San Diego, California, personal papers.

- *National Cyclopedia of American Biography*.

- Cemetery, Land, Wills, and Census Records of Fairfield County, Ohio.

- County Records, Noble, Perry, and Muskingum Counties, Ohio.

- (HWN) Harry Wright Newman, *Anne Arundel Gentry*, 1933 and 1970.

- (EFB) Ervin F. Binkley, Jr., personal research papers.

- (CEI) Clara E. Ijams, Houston, Texas, 1931.

- (JOI) James Oscar Ijams, personal correspondence, Lennox, California.

- (EWI) Elsie W. Ijams, personal research.

- (AIL) Alice Imes Lorrigan, Tucson, Arizona, correspondence.

- (CPI) Reverend Carl Phillip Ijams, Tucson, Arizona.

- (JWS) James W. Shaw, M. D., Wichita, Kansas, correspondence.

- (EB) Ethlyn Bott, correspondence with EFB.

- *First Families of America*, Volume 6.

- (EC) Eloise Caldwell, personal data.

- (WVS) Winifred Van Seters, personal research.

- Williams: *History of Frederick County, Maryland*, 1880.

- (GEI) George Edwin Ijams, personal papers, 1966.

- (EJ) Eleanor Jones, personal records.

- (BIG) Isabel Barbara Iams Griffith, personal work, Helena, Montana.

- (AAH) Ann Austin Heckathorne, R. R. 3, Earlsville, Illinois, correspondence.

- (GDK) Mrs. G. David Koch, Terre Haute, Indiana, 1967.

- (EBI) Elisha B. Iams, Pennsylvania research.

- (HL) Howard Leckey, personal research, Pennsylvania.

- (KS) Kathryn Shipley, Wheeling, West Virginia, personal research.

— CHAPTER 5 —

WILLIAM IIAMS

(B. 1745, MARYLAND; D. PENNSYLVANIA)

William Iiams (b. ca1745, Maryland), the son of Thomas Iiams (b. 1708) or John Iiams, m. Mary Hampton (one of three sisters to marry an Iiams), and their children were: John, Elizabeth, Mary, Thomas, and Isaac. Many of the family remained in western Pennsylvania, but other family members scattered westward to Ohio, and then to places further west.

William Iiams (b. 1745 or February 23, 1751; d. 1795, Washington County, Pennsylvania), the son of Thomas Iiams (b. 1708) and Katy or Artridge (HWN), m. Mary Hampton, daughter of Thomas Gill Hampton and sister of Elizabeth Hampton and Catherine Hampton (MI, GR, RFI, MJIG, LRI, RI, JBM, JIH, JC, PI, HWN).

Washington County, Pennsylvania, Will Book (Book 1, p. 254) lists the will of William Iiams, written February 20, 1795; probated May 1, 1795; witnessed by Peter Jennings, William Penn, Nathan Meek, and Samuel Moore; names wife Mary Iiams, sons Thomas Iiams and John Iiams, and daughters Elizabeth Iiams and Mary Iiams. Children of William Iiams and Mary Hampton:

1) John Iiams [(b. January 25, 1792, Washington County, Pennsylvania; d. December 12, 1868 or 1866), m. Mary Anna "Anne" Coulson (b. July 25, 1797, Washington County, Pennsylvania; d. November 5, 1868 or 1886, Washington County, and buried at West Finley, Pennsylvania), daughter of Samuel Coulson and Charity Dearth; and the will of John Iiams of West Finley Township, Washington County, Pennsylvania, written April 1, 1862; probated February 13, 1868, mentions wife Anne Iiams, children Thomas Iiams, Esther Ann Iiams, Emma Jane Iiams, Samuel Iiams, Charity Iiams Axtell, and John Iiams; with Samuel Iiams (b. April 8, 1817, Washington County; m. October 29, 1840, to Mary Grimes) as executor];

2) Elizabeth Iiams (b. ca1790; m. Daniel Smith);

3) Mary Iiams (b. ca1794);

4) Thomas Iiams [(b. 1784, Washington County, Pennsylvania; moved to Warren County, Ohio, then to Shelby County, Ohio, in 1835; d. April 4, 1855, Dinsmore Township, Shelby County, Ohio), m. Marcia (Mercia or Mary E.) Walton (b. 1782, Pennsylvania; or February 25, 1784, New Jersey; d. May 21, 1864; buried Toland Cemetery, Shelby County, Ohio)]; and

5) Isaac Iiams [(b. 1794; d. 1838, as per PI), child Robert Iiams (b. 1828; d. 1897); whose child Francis Marion Iiams (b. 1846; d. 1893) had two children: a) Arthur R. Imes (b. 1889; d. 1973; daughter Pauline Imes); and b) Roy Imes (b. October 2, 1882, Monticello, Indiana; d. June 3, 1911; child Roy Imes II d. Chicago, 1974; had a son Richard E. Imes who lived in Algonquin, Illinois)]. (PI)

Isaac Iiams (b. June 5, 1795 or 1794, Pennsylvania; d. 1838 or September 6, 1868, Twin Township, Price Creek, Brennersville, Preble County, Ohio), listed as son of William Iiams (b. 1745) and Mary Hampton by Pauline Imes, is listed as the son of Christophorus Imsen (christened February 18, 1771, Pombsen, Maria-Hammelfahrt Roman Catholic Church), whose immigration record to America has not been found, but where earlier German records include spellings such as Immessen, Imsen, and Imse), the son of Joanne Carolo Imsen and Joannae Fridericae Dissen of Westfalen, Germany.

Child of Isaac Iiams (b. 1795) was Robert Imes (b. October 24, 1822; d. January 29, 1858, Twin Township, Preble County, Ohio), m. November 17, 1844, Preble County, Ohio, to Elizabeth Enoch (b. May 27, 1818; d. June 30, 1901, Twin Township, Preble County, Ohio). They owned 80 acres in Twin Township at the corners of the Easton-Lewisburg, Twin Township and Brennersville-Pymont Roads, and are buried in the family plot on Twin Township Road. Their farm was sold to grandson Samuel Enoch Imes on March 15, 1902, for $12,900, and later sold to John and Brenda Carmony.

The son of Robert Imes (b. 1822) was Francis Marion Imes (b. April 24, 1846, Twin Township; d. May 3, 1893, Twin Township), m. January 27, 1870, to Clarissa Jane Witterman (b. January 8, 1853, Twin Township; d. May 16, 1928, Twin Township), daughter of Emanuel Witterman and Susan Miller; with both buried in Rose Lawn Cemetery, Lewisburg, Ohio.

The son of Francis Marion Imes (b. 1846) was Samuel Enoch Imes (b. April 9, 1871, Twin Township; d. December 14, 1962, Dayton, Ohio; buried at Sugar Grove Cemetery, Lexington, Ohio), m. April 22, 1903, Twin Township, to Clara Alice Ehler (b. January 9, 1879; d. June 4, 1950), daughter of Henry Franklin Ehler and Sarah Catharine Kaylor. They raised six sons and four daughters on the family homestead near the waterfall and grist mill along the south side of Price Creek. Tim Duke of Dayton, Ohio, reported that Samuel Enoch Imes (b. December 10, 1798; d. December 23, 1892) and his wife Elizabeth Hewitt Imes (b. April 28, 1800; d. September 28, 1866) were buried at Sugar Hill Cemetery, West Alexandria, Ohio. As reported by Cochetta Geis, the ten children of Samuel Enoch Imes (b. 1871) and Clara Alice Ehler (b. 1879) were:

    1) Pearl Margurite Imes [(b. August 10, 1909, Twin Township; d. May 1, 1984, Dayton, Ohio), m. February 20, 1933, Eaton, Ohio, to Melvin Wesley Dilke, a neighbor who walked her to school during their early years];

    2) Martha Imes (m. Mr. Pfister; lived at Eaton, Ohio);

    3) Florence Imes (m. Mr. Davis; lived at Lewisburg, Ohio);

    4) Irma Imes (m. Mr. Wright; lived at Lewisburg, Ohio);

    5) Raymond Imes (lived at Dayton, Ohio);

    6) Clyde Imes (lived at Dayton, Ohio);

    7) Roy Imes (lived at Franklin, Ohio);

    8) Howard Imes (lived in Minnesota);

    9) Homer Imes (lived at Brookville, Ohio); and

    10) Everett Imes (lived at Lewisburg, Ohio).

John Iiams (b. January 25, 1792, Washington County, Pennsylvania; d. December 12, 1866, Washington County, Pennsylvania), a millwright, farmer, stockman, owner of 420 acres; son of William Iiams (d. 1795) and Mary Hampton; m. Mary Anna "Anne" Coulson (b. July 25, 1797, Washington County, Pennsylvania; d. November 23, 1866; buried in West Finley, Pennsylvania), daughter of Samuel Coulson and Charity Dearth; and their children were:

    1) Thomas Iiams [(b. February 7, 1829; d. August 30, 1859, buried at Amity Presbyterian Cemetery, Washington County, Pennsylvania), m. September 14, 1854, to Mary Jane Buckingham (b. 1834), and their children

were: Esther Anna Iiams, Emma Jane Iiams, and an infant son that d. September 25, 1839; with the Amity Cemetery tombstone of Thomas Iiams giving his date of death as August 28, 1859, and his age as 80 years, 6 months, and 21 days, making his year of birth as 1779];

2) Samuel Iiams [(b. April 8, 1817; d. August 28, 1894 or 1866, Washington County, Pennsylvania), m. October 29, 1840, to Nancy Grimes (b. August 15, 1817, Greene County, Pennsylvania), daughter of Peter Grimes and Mary Sherwin of Greene County; and three children were: a) John T. Iams; b) Ida B. Iams; and c) Carrie Iams];

3) Charity Iiams [(b. December 20, 1818; d. November 18, 1893), m. November 15, 1842, to Silas Axtell];

4) John Iiams [(b. December 1, 1825; March 25, 1846; or 1816 or 1826; d. August 13, 1807), m. Sarah "Sally" Wright (b. June 27, 1832), daughter of Rezin Wright (b. December 10, 1790; m. April 11, 1819) and Nancy McGlumpy (b. August 8, 1791)]; and

5) William G. Iams (b. September 13, 1815; d. September 20, 1833; buried in Vankirk Cemetery on the Johnson Farm in Washington County, Pennsylvania). (JBM) (RI) (MI) (GIC) (MJIG) (HL) (Harvey) (JI) (RFI)

Samuel Iiams (b. April 18, 1817, Hackneys, Washington County, Pennsylvania; d. August 28, 1894, Greene County or Washington County, Pennsylvania), son of John Iiams (b. 1792) and Anne Coulson; m. October 29, 1840, to Nancy Grimes (b. August 15, 1817, Greene County, Pennsylvania; d. before 1900), daughter of Peter Grimes and Mary Shearin (or Sherwin) of Greene County, Pennsylvania. Samuel Iiams (b. 1817) was a millwright, farmer, member of Methodist church, sheep grower, owned 666 acres near the town of Graysville; moved to Waynesburg 1890; director of F and D Bank; buried in Green Mount Cemetery, Greene County, Pennsylvania. Peter Grimes was a Revolutionary soldier.

The eight children of Samuel Iiams (b. 1817) and Nancy Grimes were: 1) John T. Iams, M.D. (b. March 25, 1846, Mount Morris, Greene County, Pennsylvania; lived in Waynesburg, Pennsylvania; medical practice was called Iams and Ullom); 2) Graham Peter "G.P." "Gra" Iams [(b. September 14, 1852; d. November 26, 1938, farmer, wool dealer, lived in Waynesburg), m. October 2, 1877, to Mary Virginia Patterson (b. April 29, 1858, Greene County, Pennsylvania; d. November 9, 1938), daughter of James Patterson and Elizabeth Spragg]; 3) Charlotte Adeline "Ida" Iams [(b. July 13, 1855; d. November 7, 1926), m. December 26, 1876, to Byron Milton Braddock (b. 1852)]; 4) Nancy Clarissa "Carrie" Iams [(b. June 22, 1857), m. February 28, 1882, Greene County, Pennsylvania, to James R. Throckmorton (b. October 16, 1856, Greene County, Pennsylvania), son of Samuel Throckmorton]; 5) Samuel Shearin Iams [(b. May 18, 1860), m. 1st, September 26, 1890, to Bernice Hawkins (b. August 1872; d. November 29, 1891), m. 2nd, Mary Florence Goodwin]; 6) Mary Ann Iams [(b. January 5, 1842, Greene County, Pennsylvania; d. November 15, 1884, Greene County, Pennsylvania), m. November 2, 1861, Greene County, Pennsylvania, to Simon Buckingham (b. May 21, 1839; d. January 22, 1872), son of John Buckingham and Jane Dalrymple]; 7) Cordelia A. Iams (d. before 1888); and 8) Sarah Kerdella Iams (b. April 29, 1851; d. July 21, 1851). (JBM) (JI) (KK) (GG)

The 1850 Federal Census of Center Township, Greene County, Pennsylvania, lists: Samuel Imes (age 33, b. Pennsylvania), Nancy Imes (age 33), Mary Ann Imes (age 8), John Imes (age 4) and Sarah Imes (age 4 months). The 1870 Census lists: Samuel Imes (age 53, b. Pennsylvania), Nancy Imes (age 52), John Imes, M.D. (age 24), Peter Imes (age 17), Addia Imes (age 14), Clarra Imes (age 12), Samuel Imes (age 10), Martha A. Imes (age 2) and Daniel Imes (age 5 months). The 1880

Census lists: Samuel Iams (age 63, b. Pennsylvania), Nancy Iams (age 62), Carrie Iams (age 22), Shurman (Samuel) Iams (age 20), Charles E. Iams (age 15), Minnie J. Iams (age 13), Ellis Iams (age 7) and Mary Bischanon (age 38, b. Pennsylvania, half sister).

The 1900 Greene County Census lists four families: 1) Peter G. Iams (age 47, b. Pennsylvania), Grace V. Iams (age 42), James E. Iams (age 19), Gale I. Iams (age 18), Samuel Iams (age 15), and Hazel L. Iams (age 5); 2) John W. Iams (age 55, b. Pennsylvania), Mary P. Iams (age 53), and Frank W. Iams (age 30); 3) Samuel S. Iams (age 40, b. Pennsylvania), Clara Iams (age 32), Nellie Iams (age 3), and Glen Iams (age 2); and 4) Daniel L. Iams (age 30, b. Pennsylvania), Margaret B. Iams (age 28), Ella Iams (age 2), and Esther Iams (age 4 months).

Graham Peter Iams (b. September 14, 1852, Graysville, Greene County, Pennsylvania; d. November 26, 1938, Waynesburg, Greene County, Pennsylvania), son of Samuel Iiams (b. 1817) and Nancy Grimes (JI); grandson of John Iiams (b. 1792) and Anne Coulson; and first president (1923) of Graham-Grimes Family Association; m. Mary Virginia Patterson (b. April 29, 1858, Greene County, Pennsylvania; d. November 9, 1938, Greene County, Pennsylvania), eldest daughter of James Patterson (b. February 5, 1832, Greene County, Pennsylvania; d. January 24, 1918) and Elizabeth Spragg (b. December 2, 1833; d. April 25, 1925), and they had four children:

1) John Elbrie Iams (b. June 9, 1880; single; attended Ohio Wesleyan University; worked in automobile business and real estate; lived in Iams home);

2) Isa Gail Iams [(b. January 2, 1882; attended Waynesburg College; d. December 11, 1918), m. April 27, 1913, to Reverend William R. Cowieson (b. Scotland, October 2, 1884; d. November 15, 1921), and their children were: a) Mary Elizabeth Cowieson (b. July 27, 1914; m. May 29, 1937, to John Johnson Page, and their children, born in Milwaukee, Wisconsin, were John English Page and William Page); b) Graham Peter Cowieson (b. November 20, 1915, an undertaker in Washington, Pennsylvania; m. August 27, 1938, to Belldonna Elizabeth Booth; and their son was Clyde Graham Cowieson, b. May 23, 1942); and c) William Reid Cowieson (b. May 2, 1917; m. November 30, 1940, to Florence Edna Pratt; and their daughter was Diana Cowieson)];

3) Samuel Ray Iams [(b. May 14, 1885; attended Ohio Wesleyan University; d. August 17, 1943, Kansas City, Missouri; hobby of woodworking and furniture making), m. September 25, 1909, to Julia Welch (business woman; President Episcopal Women; insurance business in Pittsburgh, Pennsylvania, and Kansas City, Missouri; Executive Director of University Women's Club of Kansas City; attended Ohio Wesleyan University), and their son was James Patterson Iams (b. July 12, 1912; graduate of Antioch College; teacher in American School in Paris, Antioch College, and then Hawaii; hobby of raising orchids; m. Ruth Willard, and they had four children: a) Judith Iams, b. March 6, 1942; b) Jennifer Ruth Iams, b. September 27, 1945, Oakland, California; c) Jean Margaret Iams (b. September 3, 1947); and d) James Willard Iams (b. June 27, 1951)]; and

4) Lucy Hazel Iams [(b. June 27, 1894), m. November 1, 1912, to George Huffman Conner (b. October 3, 1892; a farmer, lived near Waynesburg) and a) Hilda Iams Conner (b. September 10, 1913); m. July 28, 1934, to Clarence Milliken Silvens (b. August 16, 1913; lived in Pittsburgh; a Kaiser-Frazer auto agent); two children: Craig Conner Silvens (b. 1940) and Charles Barry Silvens (b. 1947); b) George Huffman Conner, Jr. (m. Dorothy Gladys Lantz; lived in Pittsburgh; industrial engineer with

Blaroknox; daughter: Nancy Ellen Conner, b. 1939); c) Raymond Ellrie Conner (m. Margaret Ruth Wolfe; lived in Downey, California; worked in personnel division of North American Aviation); and 4) Sarah Virginia Conner]. (JI)

Jennifer Ruth Iams (b. September 27, 1945, Oakland, California), author of Iams family branch; m. Harold Hall Morley; two children: Malia Morley (b. September 9, 1971, San Rafael, California) and Michele Morley (b. October 30, 1973, San Rafael, Marin County, California). Jennifer Ruth Iams (b. 1945) was daughter of James Patterson Iams (b. 1912), and after her divorce lived in Beaverton, Oregon, where she was a successful business woman.

Thomas Iiams (b. 1829), son of John Iiams (b. 1792) and Ann Coulson (JM), m. Mary Jane Buckingham (b. 1834), and they had two children: 1) Esther Anna Iiams [(b. 1854), m. Hector Buys (b. 1853), and they had three children: 1) Earl Romain Buys (b. 1882; m. Jessie Thieny, and their four children were: Marjorie Anna Buys, b. 1910; Richard Ernest Buys, b. 1913; Neal Earl Buys, b. 1915; and Donald Robert Buys, b. 1921); b) Thomas Erwin Buys (b. 1887); and c) Wendel Erwin Buys (b. 1917)]; and 2) Emma Jane Iiams [(b. 1857), m. Charles O. Braden (b. 1857), and they had three children: 1) Anna Iams Braden (b. 1877); b) Lucy Miller Braden (b. 1880; m. Arthur W. Day, and their two children were: Helen Day, b. 1914; and Dorothy Day, b. 1915); and c) Harold Whitney Braden (b. 1883; m. Nellie Covey, and their three children were: Harold Phillips Braden, b. 1904; Miriam Emily Braden, b. 1906; and Ruth Covey Braden, b. 1908)]. (JRB)

John T. Iams, M.D. (b. March 25, 1846, Mount Morris, Greene County, Pennsylvania; d. February 15, 1915, Waynesburg, Pennsylvania), m. May 16, 1872, to Kate E. Harvey (b. November 17, 1852; d. February 7, 1924; buried in Green Mount Cemetery, Waynesburg, Greene County, Pennsylvania), daughter of Samuel Harvey and Sarah I. Throckmorton of Waynesburg. John T. Iams, M.D. (b. 1846) was the son of Samuel Iams (b. 1817) and Nancy Grimes of Greene County. John T. Iams, M.D. attended Waynesburg College and then taught public school for three years before beginning his study of medicine in 1868 at the office of Doctor Gray in Brownsville, Pennsylvania, where he remained for one year before attending Bellevue Medical College in New York City, where he graduated in 1871. Doctor Iams (b. 1846) practiced medicine in Jacksonville, Pennsylvania, until 1874 when he returned to Waynesburg, Pennsylvania, in the practice of Iams and Ulloms. In 1875, Doctor H. S. Burroughs joined the practice. Dr. Iams (b. 1846) was a member of the American Medical Association in 1886, and was the First Assistant Surgeon, 15th Regiment, Pennsylvania National Guard in 1888.

John T. Iams, M.D. (b. 1846) and Kate E. Harvey had three children: 1) Anna Neonetta Harvey "Lonetta" Iams [(b. April 3, 1875; graduate of Waynesburg and Radcliffe College), m. March 4, 1924, to Reverend Thomas Davies Whittier, a Princeton graduate]; 2) Doctor Samuel Harvey Iams [(b. May 30, 1879), m. January 29, 1910, to Elizabeth S. Rouse (b. February 6, 1883, Maryland), daughter of William O. Rouse and Elizabeth Hyatt; and their son was Samuel Harvey "Jack" Iams (b. November 15, 1910)]; and 3) Sarah Graham Iams [(b. May 14, 1889), m. June 19, 1915, Waynesburg, Pennsylvania, to Judge John Inghram Hook, Esquire (b. August 28, 1889), son of George A. Hook and Bertha Kincaid; and their four children were: a) John Inghram Hook (b. September 3, 1916; child: John Hook, an attorney); b) William Harvey Hook (b. August 21, 1918; d. January 13, 1923); c) Robert Aiken Hook (b. February 4, 1924; and d) James Hook (b. October 13, 1928)]. (JB) (RM) (GC) (BG)

The 1880 Federal Census of Greene County, Pennsylvania, lists: John Iams (age 34, b. Pennsylvania), wife Kate Iams (age 27), Netta Iams (age 5) and son Hallie

169

Iams (age 1). The 1900 Federal Census of Greene County lists: J. T. Iams (age 54), wife Catherine Iams (age 47), daughter Neonetta Iams (age 25), and son Samuel Iams (age 21). The 1910 Census lists: Samuel H. Iams (age 30) with wife Elizabeth R. Iams (age 27, born Maryland). The 1920 Census lists Samuel H. Iams (age 40) and wife Elizabeth Iams (age 36). Of interest, the Bellevue School of Medicine graduation address of 1871 was reportedly given by Doctor Oliver Wendell Holmes. Doctor John T. Iams, M.D. did graduate work in Philadelphia, Chicago, and New York City.

Peter G. "GP" Iams (b. 1852), son of Samuel Iams (b. 1817) and Nancy Grimes, m. Mary V. Patterson (JBM) and they had four children: 1) James Elbrie Iams (b. 1880, Greene County, Pennsylvania); 2) Isa "Gail" Iams [(b. 1882), m. William R. Cowleson (or Cowieson), and they had three children: a) Elizabeth Cowleson (b. 1914); b) Peter Graham Cowleson (b. 1915); and c) William Reid Cowleson (b. 1918)]; 3) Samuel Ray Iams [(b. 1885, Greene County, Pennsylvania; d. August 17, 1943, in Kansas City, Missouri, following a surgical procedure; had moved from Pennsylvania in 1915); m. Julia Welch of Delaware, Ohio; and their son was James Iams (United States Naval Officer in World War II; lived at Dunn Station, Greene County, Pennsylvania)]; 4) Lucy Hazelle Iams [(b. 1894), m. George Huffman Conner; and their four children were: a) Hilda Iams Conner (b. 1913), b) George Huffman Conner (b. 1916); c) Raymond Elbrie Conner (b. 1917), and d) Sarah Virginia Conner (b. 1927)].

Charity Adeline Iams (b. July 13, 1855, Greene County, Pennsylvania; d. November 7, 1926), daughter of Samuel Iams (b. 1817) and Nancy Grimes: m. December 26, 1876, to Bryon Milton Braddock (b. July 18, 1853), son of David Braddock and Agnes Carter; and they had six children:

1) Georgia A. Braddock [(b. October 27, 1879, Bristoria, Greene County, Pennsylvania), m. June 24, 1896, to John W. (or M.) Milliken, and they had six children: a) John Russell Milliken (b. December 5, 1899); b) Margaret Adeline Milliken (b. June 27, 1904); c) Dorothy Pauline Milliken (b. January 14, 1907; m. Leo Ailes; two children were: Herbert Byron Ailes and David Ailes); d) Allen Keith Milliken (b. June 16, 1909; m. Edna Keener; their two children were: John Allen Milliken and William B. Milliken); e) Eleanor Braddock Milliken (b. January 20, 1916); and f) Betty Louise Milliken (b. June 19, 1920; m. Samuel P. Weaver, and their three children were: Robert C. Weaver, John R. Weaver, and Ann Weaver)];

2) Samuel Earl Braddock [(b. August 16, 1882), m. September 16, 1903, to Mable M. McNay, and their four children were: a) Mildred Marie Braddock (b. August 5, 1904; d. January 3, 1905); b) Francis Harold Braddock (b. August 27, 1906); c) Robert McNay Braddock (b. April 13, 1909), and d) Elmer Bryon Braddock (b. December 29, 1911)];

3) Mary V. Braddock [(b. October 14, 1884), m. August 21, 1907, to Peter Sutton Kimmel, and their five children were: a) Byron Elwood Kimmel (b. September 1, 1908); b) Edward Augustus Kimmel (b. December 18, 1909); c) Robert Sutton Kimmel (b. January 5, 1916); d) Josephine Iams Kimmel (b. September 5, 1923); and e) Harry Braddock Kimmel (b. November 19, 1926)];

4) Nancy G. Braddock [(b. November 12, 1887; d. April 6, 1921), m. September 26, 1912, to Robert Headley, son of Frank Headley and Belle Burris];

5) Charles G. Braddock [(b. October 29, 1889), m. November 1, 1911, to Nancy Smith, daughter of Samuel Smith and Charity Morris]; and

6) Harry Iams Braddock [(b. August 19, 1891), m. April 19, 1917, to Gail King, daughter of David King and Lizzie Kent; and two children were: a) Paul (or Carl) Milton Braddock (b. April 6, 1918) and b) Ruth Elizabeth Braddock (b. February 1929)]. (JBM) (GB)

Nancy Clarissa Iams (b. June 22, 1857), daughter of Samuel Iiams (b. 1817) and Nancy Grimes, m. February 28, 1882, to James B. Throckmorton (b. October 16, 1856), son of Samuel Throckmorton and Nancy Rees of Rogersville, Arkansas, and a descendant of John and Rebecca Throckmorton who arrived in America with Roger Williams on the ship *Lyons* at Salem in 1630. Roger Williams then moved south and was one of the first 13 settlers of Rhode Island, including Providence.

The five children of Nancy Clarissa Iams (b. 1857) and James B. Throckmorton (b. 1856) were:

1) Harland S. Throckmorton [(b. January 10, 1883), m. March 15, 1911, to Anna Bessie Harvey (b. October 25, 1886), and they had six children: a) Sarah Throckmorton (b. June 30, 1912); b) Margaret Throckmorton (b. August 20, 1913, a twin); c) Marjorie Throckmorton (b. August 20, 1913, a twin); d) James T. H. Throckmorton (b. March 21, 1916); e) Mary Derressa Throckmorton (b. August 18, 1920); and f) Charles Throckmorton (b. 1921)];

2) Charles Loudas S. Throckmorton (b. December 22, 1884; d. January 21, 1916, after a fall from a tree; m. March 28, 1908, to Jennie Blatchley, daughter of Thomas J. Blatchley and Martha Taylor);

3) Ray Iams Throckmorton [(b. December 10, 1886), m. June 10, 1916, to Marcia Story, daughter of Alfred Montine Story and Celeste Thornton (Ray was Professor and Head, Department of Agronomy at Kansas State University at Manhattan), and they had three children: a) Celesta Jane Throckmorton (b. March 31, 1919); b) Ray Iams Throckmorton II (b. March 9, 1914); and c) Marcia M. Throckmorton (b. 1928)];

4) Guy Reese Throckmorton [(b. September 10, 1889), m. 1st, on April 1, 1912, Pearl Fairbee; m. 2nd, Mabel Sprowls, and his child of first marriage was Geraldine Throckmorton (b. November 23, 1913)]; and

5) John Throckmorton [(b. September 11, 1895), m. 1st, on November 6, 1919, to Anna Brown Baramore, and m. 2nd, Florence May Funk; and his child of the first marriage was Elizabeth Caroline Throckmorton (b. October 23, 1921)]. (JBM) (GG)

Samuel Shearn Iams (b. May 18, 1860), son of Samuel Iiams (b. 1817) and Nancy Grimes; m. 1st, September 26, 1890, to Bernice Hawkins and m. 2nd, January 18, 1894, to Mary Florence "Flora" Goodwin (b. October 26, 1867, Rutan, Greene County, Pennsylvania), daughter of Seth Goodwin and Mary Hill; and they had seven chidren: 1) Nellie G. Iams (b. September 9, 1895); 2) Glenn G. Iams [(b. August 22, 1897), m. November 29, 1918, to Kate Orndorff, daughter of William H. Orndorff and Martha Ullom; lived in Waynesburg, Greene County, Pennsylvania; and they had three children: a) Mary Martha Iams (b. December 22, 1920); b) Robert Sherwin Iams (b. 1927; m. April 27, 1963, to Betty J.; lived in San Diego; and their son Kevin R. Iams, b. May 30, 1964, an attorney in Sacramento, m. Christine _____); and c) W. Frederick Iams (b. March 27, 1928)]; 3) Harry Sherwin Iams [(b. October 20, 1900; d. October 6, 1953, Monroeville, Allegheny County, Pennsylvania; Penn State graduate in electrical engineering; worked for Jones and Laughlin Steel Company), m. Edna Mae Von Hedeman, and they had three children: a) Sherwin W. Iams, Sgt., U.S. Marines); b) Charles Iams; and c) Blanche Mae Iams)]. (JBM) (GG)

Mary Ann Iams (b. January 5, 1842; d. November 15, 1889), daughter of Samuel Iams (b. 1817) and Nancy Grimes; m. November 2, 1861, to Simon

Buckingham (b. May 21, 1839; d. January 22, 1872), the son of John Buckingham and Jane Dalrymple; and they had six children: 1) Charles Everett Buckingham [(b. March 21, 1865; corresponded with Howard L. Leckey, describing this family); m. October 27, 1866, to Eva L. Braddock, daughter of Francis Braddock and Maria J. Porter; and they had two children: a) Francis M. Buckingham (b. September 15, 1887; m. April 7, 1920, to Lucy A. Dawes); and b) Ray Buckingham (b. December 17, 1894)]; 2) Minnie J. Buckingham [(b. February 13, 1867; d. October 29, 1895); m. June 21, 1892, to Dr. T. F. Carpenter]; 3) Lilly Buckingham (b. November 5, 1868; d. February 10, 1869); 4) George Edward Buckingham (b. December 22, 1869; d. April 29, 1879); 5) Lucy Monell E. Buckingham (b. March 31, 1871; d. February 16, 1872); 6) Simone Siniore Ella Buckingham [(b. January 20, 1873); m. December 25, 1895, to Harry LeMoyne W. Hawkins; and they had five children: a) Josephine Hawkins (b. January 2, 1897); b) John Iams Hawkins (b. January 27, 1898; m. October 18, 1924, to Margaret Shirk, and their daughter, Wilma Jo Hawkins was b. January 5, 1926); c) Esther Meade Hawkins (b. June 11, 1908); d) Dorothy Hawkins (b. January 20, 1904); and e) Eleanor Hawkins (b. February 8, 1911)]. (JBM) (CEB) (HL)

Charity Iams (b. 1818), daughter of John Iiams (b. 1792) Ann Coulson; m. Silas Axtell, and they had three children: 1) William Allen Axtell [(b. 1843), m. Mary Ella Patterson; and they had four children: a) Homer Axtell (b. 1870); m. Mary Hilton, and their three children were Allen Hilton Axtell (b. 1905), Rowland B. Axtell (b. 1909), and Sarah Jane Axtell (b. 1912); b) May Axtell (b. 1872); c) Gail Axtell (b. 1880); and d) Jay Axtell (b. 1884)]; 2) Sarah Ann Axtell (b. 1846); and 3) Emma Jane Axtell (b. 1848)]. (JBM)

John Iiams (b. December 1, 1825 or 1816 or 1826 or 1846; d. August 13, 1907), son of John Iiams (b. 1792) and Anna Coulson, m. Sarah "Sally" Wright (b. June 22, 1832; d. July 29, 1907), the daughter of Rezin Wright (b. December 10, 1799; m. April 11, 1819) and Nancy McGlumphy (b. August 8, 1799), and they had four children: 1) Levina "Sis" Iams [(b. 1854), m. Daniel Gribben, and they had six children: a) Mary Gribben (m. Mr. Chapman); b) Della Gribben (m. Mr. Poling); c) John Gribben; d) Emma Gribben; e) Elsie Gribben (m. Mr. Wendell); and f) Leona Gribben (m. Mr. Guthrie)]; 2) Mary Jane Iams [(b. 1856), m. Robert Murchland Boles (b. 1856), and they had four children: a) Luella Boles (m. Mr. Richey); b) Albert Boles; c) Elsie Boles (m. Mr. Sanders); and d) Alice Boles (m. Mr. Dowden)]; 3) Thomas Iams [(b. June 12 or 22, 1858, Rutan, Greene County, Pennsylvania; d. July 24, 1900), m. Catherine Clutter (b. March 30, 1861; d. August 27, 1900)]; and 4) Emma "Duck" Iams [m. William Henry Scott, and they had three children: a) Allen Grover Scott (b. 1888; m. Gertrude ___); b) Elsie May Scott (b. 1890; m. Mr. McQuay, and they had two children: Robert McQuay and Irene McQuay); and c) Lloyd Iams Scott (b. 1892) who had two children: a) Harold Scott, and b) Arthur Scott (m. Mildred Orndoff)]. (MI) (JI) (JBM) (WI) (HL) (JNI) (GIC)

Thomas Iams (b. June 22, 1858, Rutan, Greene County, Pennsylvania; d. July 24, 1900), son of John Iams (b. 1825) and Sarah Wright, was photographed and his family picture is included herein; m. Catherine Clutter (b. March 30, 1861; d. August 27, 1900), the daughter of William Clutter and first wife Mary (an "Indian woman") or second wife Polly Sharp [William Clutter was the son of Sophas (or Cephus or Sephas) Clutter and Lany Day; and Sophas Clutter was the son of William (or John) Clutter (b. 1778, New Jersey) and Sarah Rutan]; and they had seven children:

1) John E. Iams, Sr. [(b. 1892; d. 1923), m. Stella Marie Anderson (b. 1898 or 1919; d. 1939, Bellaire, Belmont County, Ohio), daughter of William Anderson and Annie Bourgnine), and they had two sons: a) John Iams (b. November 23, 1916); and b) William Harry Iams (b. January 22, 1919, Bellaire, Ohio; m. January 17, 1944,

in St. Matthew, Calhoun County, South Carolina, to Ruby Ott; b. January 10, 1928, St. Matthews, South Carolina)]; 2) Sarah "Sallie" Iams (m. Allison Hoagland; lived at Rutan, Greene County, Pennsylvania; family historian; researched some of this family tree; and their son, John Hoagland, Jr., lived in Waynesburg, Greene County, Pennsylvania); 3) Robert C. Iams (d. 1900, Rutan, Greene County, Pennsylvania; single); 4) Delsea Iams [(b. September 11, 1891), m. George Winters and lived at Moundsville, West Virginia; had a son Homer Winters (m. Florence ___; lived at Bristol, Virginia) and one daughter Katherine Winters (m. Mr. Ruhoff)]; 5) Mary Jane Iams [(m. Claude Scott and had three children: a) Mildred Scott (m. Mr. Anderson); b) Betty "Mary" Scott (m. Mr. McCord); and c) James Scott]; 6) William "Bill" Patterson Iams (b. 1888; d. 1952); 7) Jesse Cleveland Iams [(b. April 4, 1884, Jacktown, Westmoreland County, Pennsylvania; d. June 5, 1950, Canton, Ohio), m. Frances Etta Yoder or Edith "Etta" Fisher; lived in Canton, Ohio; had seven sons, including three (Glenn C. Iams, Robert Iams, and Bill Iams) living in Canton, Ohio]. (JBM) (HL) (MI) (RF) (JNI) (GIC)

Mary Jane Iams (m. Claude Scott, son of George Scott and Amanda Woods, and grandson of James Scott and Charlotte Strawn), daughter of Thomas Iams (b. 1858) and Catherine Clutter, and they had four children:

1) Betty Jane Scott [(b. August 24, 1924 or August 15, 1923, Washington, Pennsylvania), m. April 8, 1945, in New York City to Stanley Marion McCord (b. June 12, 1924, Washington, Pennsylvania), son of James Henry McCord and Clara Della Brookoven];

2) Mildred Amanda Scott [(b. March 31, 1908; d. March 31, 1937), m. Raymond Floyd Anderson (b. May 19, 1905; d. September 8, 1947), son of James Anderson; worked at Jessop Steel; had two children: a) Norma Jean Anderson (b. September 19, 1932); and b) Raymond Floyd Anderson (b. October 2, 1936 or October 25, 1927, in Washington, Pennsylvania; worked at Brockway Glass)];

3) James Edward Scott [(b. June 17, 1927), m. August 5, 1951, to Alice Louise Kelly (b. April 6, 1931), and they had two children: a) James Claude Scott (b. June 4, 1953; m. December 20, 1975, to Linda Leggett, and they had twins: Bobby Jo Scott and Billy Jo Scott); and b) Gregory Wayne Scott (b. February 4, 1960)]; and

4) Emma Scott [(b. November 21, 1911), m. March 16, 1929, to Albert Thomas (b. July 7, 1902; d. November 21, 1974), and they had four children: a) Albert Thomas, Jr. (b. June 7, 1929; d. August 10, 1968), m. Marilyn Zink (b. November 25, 1932), and they had two children: 1¹) Karen Thomas (b. July 4, 1955); m. Harry Reed (b. August 29, 1952); and their child was Evonne Lynn Reed (b. June 5, 1974); and 2¹) Diane Marie Thomas (b. December 5, 1957); m. Bob Watson (b. June 1, 1953); and their son was Brian Scott Watson (b. November 19, 1973); b) Robert Harlan Thomas (b. November 11, 1932; d. May 4, 1958); c) Helen Marie Thomas (b. May 30, 1937) m. Mr. Lee; and they had three children: 1¹) John Robert Thomas (b. March 3, 1962); 2¹) David Lee (b. August 27, 1968); and 3¹) Richard Lee (b. May 6, 1970); and d) James William Thomas (b. February 19, 1946) m. September 25, 1965, to Janet Teagarden (b. July 25, 1946), and they had four children: 1¹) Robert Joseph Thomas (b. May 25, 1966); 2¹) Marcia Marie Thomas (b. February 17, 1968); 3¹) Jeane Anne Thomas (b. February 20, 1969); and 4¹) Rebecca Susan Thomas (b. July 11, 1970)]. (BM)

Betty Jane Scott (b. August 15 or 24, 1924, Washington, Pennsylvania; lived in Washington, Washington County, Pennsylvania), daughter of Claude Scott and

Mary Jane Iams (daughter of Thomas Iams, b. 1858, and Catherine Clutter), m. April 8, 1945, in New York City, to Stanley Marion McCord (b. June 12, 1924, Washington, Pennsylvania), son of James Henry McCord and Clara Della Brookhaven; and grandson of William Emrod McCord and Delilah Ann Kennedy (Stanley Marion McCord m. 2nd to Clara Dalton of Tennessee), and they had five children:

1) Carol Ann McCord [(b. January 15, 1947, Washington, Pennsylvania), m. August 10, 1968, to Gerald Lee Hanna (b. September 19, 1948, in Washington, Pennsylvania)]; 2) John Wayne McCord [(b. September 20, 1948, Washington, Pennsylvania), m. 1st, __?__, to Patricia Lee Peacock (b. September 5, 1948); m. 2nd, December 22, 1982, Merrely Rennick (b. October 27, 1946); and had two children: a) Jason Scott McCord (b. August 17, 1971); and b) David Allen McCord (b. April 4, 1976), though Merrely Rennick (b. 1946) had two children by a prior marriage: Kenneth Simpson (b. August 27, 1965) and Charity Simpson (b. April 21, 1970)]; 3) James Stanley McCord [(b. April 7, 1951, Monaco, Pennsylvania), m. July 2, 1971, to Drew Louise or Irene Lois Poluda (b. March 29, 1951)]; 4) Rodney Lee McCord [(b. December 1, 1953, Washington, Pennsylvania), m. November 3, 1978, to Linda Morin]; and 5) Mary Jane McCord [(November 29, 1956, Washington, Pennsylvania), m. 1st, October 25, 1974, to Robert Louis Rush (b. January 14, 1953); and m. 2nd, July 1979 to Walter Bursee (b. January 14, 1953, Washington, Pennsylvania)].

Carol Ann McCord (b. January 15, 1947, Washington, Pennsylvania), daughter of Stanley McCord (b. 1924) and Betty Jane Scott (b. 1923), m. August 10, 1968, to Gerald Lee Hanna (b. September 19, 1948, Washington, Pennsylvania), and they had two children: 1) Gerald Lee Hanna, Jr. [(b. December 29, 1969, Washington, Pennsylvania), m. August 24, 19_?_, to Alesha Ann Schwartz (b. July 27, 1970), and their child was Amanda Maria Hanna (b. June 16, 1985)]; and 2) Brian Edward Hanna [(b. February 19, 1971, Wiesbaden, Germany), m. February 7, 1991, Washington, Pennsylvania, to Sarah Supler (b. May 27, 1972, Washington, Washington County, Pennsylvania), and they had two children: a) Brian Andrew Hanna (b. January 5, 1990), and b) Jessica Lynn Hanna (b. November 15, 1992, Sweinbadden, Germany)]; 3) Darren James Hanna (b. January 5, 1975, Anchorage, Alaska); and 4) Jennifer Ann Hanna (b. August 17, 1979, Hollywood, Florida). (BM)

James Stanley McCord (b. April 7, 1951, Monaco, Pennsylvania), son of Stanley McCord (b. 1924) and Betty Jane Scott (b. 1923); m. July 2, 1971, to Irene Lora Paluda (b. March 29, 1951), and they had two children: 1) Jamey Lynn McCord [(b. September 22, 1972, Washington, Pennsylvania), m. Kevin Grant Montgomery (b. November 21, 1970), and they had two children: Victoria Lynne Montgomery (b. April 7, 1990, Washington, Pennsylvania), and James Grant Montgomery (b. 1994, Washington, Pennsylvania)]; and 2) Rebecca Jean McCord (b. January 1, 1979, Fort Leonard Wood, Missouri). (BM)

Mary Jane McCord [(b. November 29, 1956, Washington, Pennsylvania), daughter of Stanley McCord (b. 1924) and Betty Jane Scott (b. 1923) m. 1st, October 25, 1974, to Robert Louis Rush (b. January 14, 1953); m. 2nd, July 1979, to Walter Bursee (b. January 14, 1953, Washington, Pennsylvania; lived in Fayetteville, Arkansas), and had three children: 1) Crystal Lynn Rush [(b. December 1, 1975, Washington, Pennsylvania), m. July 31, 1993, Fort Myers, Florida; m. Robert Petit (b. August 24, 1972), and their child was Christopher James Petit (b. April 8, 1993, in Fayetteville, Arkansas)]; 2) Phillip Anderson Bursee (b. August 31, 1979, Knoxville, Tennessee); and 3) Joseph Dean Bursee (b. May 17, 1981, Washington, Pennsylvania). (BM)

John E. Iams (b. 1892; d. 1923), son of Thomas Iams (b. 1858) and Catherine Clutter, and grandson of John Iiams (b. 1825) and Sarah Wright; m. Stella Marie

Anderson (b. 1898; d. 1939, Bellaire, Belmont County, Ohio), daughter of William Anderson and Anne Bourgine (John E. Iams, Sr., developed "the fever that killed his mother, father, and brother Robert, but recovered and returned to work," according to Geraldine Cheslick), and John E. Iams (b. 1892) had two children: 1) William Harry Iams [(b. January 22, 1919, Bellaire, Belmont County, Ohio), m. January 17, 1944, St. Matthews, Calhoun County, to Ruby Ott (b. January 10, 1928, St. Matthews, South Carolina), daughter of Benjamin Franklin Ott and Daisy Sikes, and granddaughter of Alfred Frank Ott and Mary Crider; and their child was Lillian Darlene Iams (b. Orangeburg, South Carolina, on February 1, 1945) who m. December 22, 1961, to Bobby Weatherford]; and 2) John E. Iams, Jr. [(b. November 24, 1916, Bellaire, Belmont County, Ohio), m. December 5, 1935, Wheeling, West Virginia, to Mary E. Nelson (b. January 7, 1920, Bellaire, Belmont County, Ohio; d. September 19, 1992, Paris, Pennsylvania; buried in Paris Cemetery), daughter of Robert Nelson and Babe Crozier, and granddaughter of Bill Crozier; and they had four children: a) John R. Iams (b. July 1, 1936, Bellaire, Ohio; and child was John Iams); b) Gilbert L. Iams (b. September 17, 1938, Bellaire); c) Pamela M. Iams (b. October 8, 1940, East Liverpool, Columbiana County, Ohio; m. Mr. Farmer); and d) Stephenie Iams (b. September 19, 1950, Steubenville, Jefferson County, Ohio); m. Mr. King]. (JNI) (BC) (GEC)

William Patterson "Bill" Iams, Sr. (b. 1888; d. 1952), son of Thomas Iams (b. 1858) and Catherine Clutter; and grandson of John Iiams (b. 1825) and Sarah Wright; m. Edith Mary Prosser (b. 1891) of Cameron, West Virginia, daughter of Robert L. and Elizabeth Prosser of West Virginia; and their four children were: 1) William Lincoln Iams [(b. Shadyside, Ohio, 1918), m. 1st, Catherine Carlienko; m. 2nd, Anna Gouldsberg, and his two children, both by first wife, were: a) Richard W. Iams (b. 1950; m. Donna Gassaway); and b) Marilyn K. Iams (b. 1852), m. Randall Leggett, and their child was Michael Scott Leggett (b. 1971)]; 2) Geraldine Elizabeth Iams [(b. 1922, Shadyside, Belmont County, Ohio), m. August 2, 1946, Moundsville, West Virginia, to Edward A. Cheslick, Sr. (b. Neffs, Ohio, April 5, 1922), and their two children were: a) Edward Anthony Cheslick, Jr. (b. March 24, 1947, Moundsville, West Virginia; m. 1st, Judy Linsey, and their child was India Cheslick; and m. 2nd, Patty Robinson, and their child was Matthew Lucas Cheslick (b. May 3, 1944); and b) Richard William Cheslick (b. February 11, 1951), m. Lyn Domazor, and their child was Lauren Nicole Cheslick (b. September 12, 1994)]; 3) Harold Prosser Iams [(b. 1909), m. 1st, Olga Perone, and their child was Harold Prosser Iams, Jr.; m. 2nd, Catharine Tweedlie, and their child was Thomas Joseph Iams]; and 4) Catherine Louise Iams [(b. 1912), m. Charles Polinsky, and their four children were: Robert Polinsky, Richard Polinsky, Perry Polinsky, and William Polinsky]. (MJIG) (BM) (GIC) Geraldine Elizabeth Iams Cheslick (b. 1922) assisted Mildred Corbett McKelvey in Iams genealogy search as early as 1935.

Jesse Cleveland Iams (b. April 4, 1884, Jacktown, Westmoreland County, Pennsylvania; d. June 5, 1950, Canton, Ohio; buried in Forest Lawn Cemetery), son of Thomas Iams (b. 1825) and Sarah Wright; m. Frances Etta Yoder (b. March 8, 1886, Wetzel County, West Virginia; d. December 30, 1964, Canton, Ohio; buried in Westlawn Cemetery), the daughter of Zachariah Yoder and Rhoda Lee Fisher. Children of Jesse Cleveland Iams (b. 1884) and Frances Etta Yoder (or Esther "Etta" Fisher, per BM) were:

1) Norman Yoder Iams [(b. August 19, 1916, Midway, Washington County, Pennsylvania; d. March 10, 1955, Canton, Ohio; buried in Forest Hill Cemetery); m. April 18, 1943, in Canton, Ohio, to Dorothy Irene Adams Barr (b. October 27, 1918, Enon Valley, Lawrence County, Pennsylvania), daughter of Vernon Dickey Adams and Laura Belle McNees, and

granddaughter of James Swisher Adams and Clara Adella Bean (the first husband of Dorothy Irene Adams was Melwyn Woodrow Barr), and their two children were: a) Mildred Jean Barr Iams (b. January 20, 1939, in Canton, Ohio; m. February 3, 1956, to Robert Eugene Griffen; correspondent for family tree); and b) Jerry Lee Iams (b. August 6, 1948, Canton, Ohio; m. December 4, 1971, to Kathleen Elizabeth Cairman)];

2) Harlan Cecil Iams [(b. March 28, 1908, Moundsville, West Virginia; d. December 20, 1974, in Canton, Ohio; buried in Forest Hill Cemetery); m. 1st, Irene Nelly Eagel; and m. 2nd, Judy Delassandro; no children];

3) Victor Lee Iams [(b. July 21, 1910; d. October 9, 1978, Plymouth, Massachusetts), m. August 30, 1945, to Beatrice Alice Hunt (b. February 25, 1912, Massachusetts), and their daughter was Kathryn Elizabeth Iams (b. February 15, 1948), who m. August 3, 1974, to Oliver Chamberlain (b. July 19, 1938), and they had three children: James Thomas Chamberlain (b. April 27, 1976), Margaret Emily Chamberlain (b. September 24, 1977), and Carolyn Lee Chamberlain (b. June 5, 1980)];

4) Woodrow Wilson Iams (b. May 17, 1913; d. 1933, Canton, Ohio; buried in Forest Hill Cemetery);

5) Glenn Curtis Iams [(b. October 11, 1919; d. February 22, 1980, Canton, Ohio; buried Forest Hill Cemetery), m. October 11, 1943, to Velma "Jo" Herring (b. July 25, 1924, Texas), and they had three children: a) Stanley Woodrow Iams (b. December 20, 1944); b) James Curtis Iams (b. April 18, 1950, Canton; m. 1st, Vickie Hayes, and their son was Jason Iams; m. 2nd, Diane Lowell); and c) John David Iams (b. March 2, 1961, Canton, Ohio; m. Cynthia Harshberger, and they had three children: Christian John Iams, b. 1984; Lincoln Scott Iams, b. 1986; and Ashley Brooke Iams (b. 1988)];

6) Robert Franklin "Bob" Iams (b. January 23, 1927, Canton, Ohio; a twin; lived in Wooster, Ohio; m. Dorothy Lorraine McClintock; contributor to family tree); and

7) William Henry "Bill" Iams [(b. January 23, 1927, Canton, Ohio; a twin; lived in Canton), m. April 26, 1951, to Nadine Foehrenbach; contributor to family tree]. (MJIG) (RI) (BM) (SI)

Stanley Woodrow Iams (b. December 20, 1944), son of Glenn Curtis Iams (b. 1919) and Velma Jo Herring (b. 1924); a bus driver in Kansas City, Missouri; social worker; oil executive; hospital assistant administrator before becoming a career bus driver. His brother James Curtis Iams (b. 1950) became Superintendent of Education, Bloomsburg, Pennsylvania, after leaving home at age 12 and eventually attending college in Chicago, Illinois.

Sarah Belle "Sallie" Iams (b. September 28, 1895, Greene County, Pennsylvania; d. Rutan, Greene County, Pennsylvania; buried at Rogersville, Pennsylvania), daughter of Thomas Iams (b. 1858) and Catherine Clutter; m. Allison D. Hougland; lived at Rutan, Pennsylvania; had three children: 1) Charles Allison Hougland (b. June 26, 1927, Center Township, Greene County, Pennsylvania; d. June 28, 1927, Greene County); 2) George Eugene Hougland (b. 1932, Center Township, Greene County, Pennsylvania; d. infancy); and 3) John E. Hougland (b. May 21, 1930, Center Township, Greene County, Pennsylvania; m. 1951; lived in Waynesburg, Greene County, Pennsylvania). (GIC) (SI) (RFI) (JIH)

Norman Yoder Iams (b. August 19, 1916, Midway, Washington County, Pennsylvania; d. March 10, 1955, Canton, Stark County, Ohio; buried Forest Hill Cemetery), son of Jesse Cleveland Iams (b. 1884) and Frances Etta Yoder; m. April

18, 1943, to Dorothy Irene Adams (b. October 27, 1918, Enon Valley, Lawrence County, Pennsylvania), daughter of Vernon Dickey Adams and Laura Belle McNees (first husband of Dorothy Irene Adams was Merwyn Woodrow Barr), and they had two children: 1) Mildred Jean Barr-Iams [(b. January 20, 1939, Canton, Ohio; adopted officially in 1950), m. February 3, 1956, Canton, Ohio, to Robert Eugene Griffin (b. November 19, 1937, Canton, Ohio), son of Eugene Joseph Griffin and Hilda Marie Parkam (Robert was a splic tech; a Presbyterian; and the two of them wrote this branch of the family history), and they had three children: a) Richard Robert Griffin (b. September 12, 1956, Canton, Ohio); b) Barbara Ann Griffin (b. December 9, 1959, Canton, Ohio); and c) David Eugene Griffin (b. February 6, 1961)]; and 2) Jerry Lee Iams [(b. August 6, 1948, Canton, Ohio), m. December 4, 1971, Canton, Ohio, to Kathryn Elizabeth Cairns (b. October 8, 1951, Canton, Ohio), daughter of Larry Cairns and Libby Evans, and they had two children: a) Brian Michael Iams (b. January 20, 1977, Canton, Ohio); and b) Elizabeth "Betsy" Ann Iams (b. June 19, 1979, Springfield, Clark County, Ohio)].

Mildred Jean Barr Iams (b. 1939) and Robert Eugene Griffin (b. 1837) had three children: 1) Richard Robert Griffin [(b. September 12, 1956, Canton, Ohio), m. November 8, 1989, in Dania, Broward County, Florida, to Carolyn Burdick Steas (b. February 14, 1956), daughter of Burdick and Ellen Steas; and they had two children: a) Kelly Leigh Griffin (b. May 19, 1977, Norfolk, Virginia), and b) Danielle "Dani" Renee Griffin (b. June 26, 1980, Saint Petersburg, Florida)]; 2) Barbara Ann Griffin [(b. December 9, 1959, Canton, Ohio), m. December 29, 1984, Alexander City, Alabama, to Robert Keith Whaley (b. September 6, 1954), a National Park Ranger, son of Delbert and Vera Whaley; and their daughter was Coleen Amber Whaley (b. May 1, 1986, Atlanta, Georgia)]; and 3) David Eugene Griffin [(b. February 6, 1961, Canton, Ohio), and they had three children: a) Michael Robert "Mike" Griffin (b. October 14, 1982); b) Jason Thomas "Jay" Griffin (b. July 25, 1984); and c) Rebecca Frances "Becca" Griffin (b. April 16, 1986)].

Robert Franklin "Bob" Iams (b. January 23, 1927, Canton, Ohio; a twin) son of Jesse Cleveland Iams (b. 1884) and Frances Etta Yoder; m. July 27, 1959, in Ashland, Ohio, to Dorothy Lorraine McClintock (b. August 26, 1935, Pittsburgh, Pennsylvania), daughter of Steel McClintock and Ellen Nora Wertzel; and granddaughter of both Samuel Thaddeus McClintock and Jane Steel, and of John Wertzel and Bridget Nora McDermot; and they had two children: 1) Douglas Allen Iams (b. July 1, 1960, Ashland, Ohio; single); and 2) Brenda Lynn Iams [(b. August 25, 1962, Ashland, Ohio), m. 1st, September 11, 1982, to Charles Eugene Wagers (b. November 23, 1960), and they had son Todd Anthony Wagers (b. March 14, 1983); m. 2nd to John Joseph Rozborski (b. April 25, 1958), and son Steven Christopher Iams Rozborski was born December 9, 1992]. (MJIG) (DLI)

William Henry "Bill" Iams (b. January 23, 1927, Canton, Ohio, a twin; music teacher; member of Cleveland Philharmonic Orchestra), son of Jesse Cleveland Iams (b. 1884) and Frances Etta Yoder; m. April 26, 1951, to Nadine Foehrenbach (b. May 19, 1930); and their daughter, Sharon Kay Iams (b. January 30, 1952, Canton, Ohio), m. April 2, 1975, Canton, Ohio, to Timothy Michael Haren, and they had three children: 1) Chad Timothy Haren (b. January 15, 1976, Canton, Ohio; 2) Troy Michael Haren (b. July 3, 1978, Canton, Ohio); and 3) Dacota William Iams (b. June 24, 1993, Canton, Ohio). (MJIG) (DLI)

Levina Anna Iams (b. 1854), daughter of John Iiams (b. 1826) and granddaughter of John Iiams (b. 1792); m. Daniel Gribben, and they had six children: 1) Della Gribben (b,. 1875); 2) John Elmer Gribben [(b. 1877), m. Stella Bernice Ross, and they had seven children: a) Clyde Alonzo Gribben (b. 1899; m. Jessie Smith;

177

child: Leon Gribben); b) Lloyd Arthur Gribben (b. 1904); c) Emma Gribben (b. 1906; m. John Morris; child: Dorothy Jane Morris, b. 1930); d) Charles E. Gribben (b. 1908); e) Mildred Marie Gribben (b. 1910); f) Paul Thomas Gribben (b. 1913); and g) Mary Helen Gribben (b. 1916); 3) Emma Gribben (b. 1878); 4) Mary Gribben (b. 1881); 5) Leona Gribben (b. 1886); and 6) Elsie Gribben (b. 1889)]. (JBM)

Mary Jane Iams (b. 1856), daughter of John Iams (b. 1826) and Sarah Wright (b. 1832); m. Robert Murchland Boles (b. 1856) and they had four children: 1) Louella Boles [(b. 1880), m. Henry McCoy Richey (b. 1876), and they had six children: a) Ruth Elva Richey (b. 1900); b) Albert McCoy Richey (b. 1902); c) Clifford Warren Richey (b. 1905); d) William Arthur Richey (b. 1907); e) Harold Iams Richey (b. 1910), and f) Nedra Nesbit Richey (b. 1916)]; 2) Sarah Elsie Boles [(b. 1882), m. William H. Saunders, and they had four children: a) Robert Byron Saunders (b. 1903); b) Mary Margaret Saunders (b. 1907); c) John Iams Saunders (b. 1911), and d) Willa Saunders (b. 1917)]; 3) Albert Elson Boles (b. 1884); and 4) Alice Levina Boles (b. 1884)]. (JBM)

Thomas Iiams [(b. 1784, Washington County, Pennsylvania; d. April 4, 1855, Shelby County, Ohio; buried at Anna Methodist Church, Anna, Shelby County, Ohio, in Toland Cemetery); moved first to Warren County, Ohio, before moving to Shelby County, Ohio, in 1835, where he lived in southwest quarter of Section 17; organized Mt. Gilead M.E. Church in the home of Richard Dill in 1833]; m. Marcia F. "Mercy" Walton (b. 1782 in Virginia, or February 25, 1784, New Jersey; d. Mary 21, 1864, at home of son in Auglaize County, Ohio; buried in Toland Cemetery, Anna, Shelby County, Ohio), daughter of Thomas Daniel Walton and Rebecca Quinn (RWI lists wife of Thomas Iiams as Mercy "Marcy" Bonnell, b. February 25, 1784, New Jersey; d. May 21, 1867); and they had eleven children:

1) William H. Iiams [(b. February 13, 1807, Washington County, Pennsylvania; d. November 15 or October 18, 1844, Shelby County, Ohio; buried in Toland Cemetery, Anna, Ohio), m. Martha McClure (b. May 5, 1814, Warren County, Pennsylvania; d. October 18, 1844, or January 18, 1896, Shelby County, Ohio, or Lima, Allen County, Ohio), and they had seven children];

2) Sarah Iiams [(b. April 6, 1809 or May 6, 1810, Washington County, Pennsylvania; d. September 23, 1875, Jay County, Indiana), m. April 5, 1827, Warren County, Ohio, to George Washington Harford (d. Portland, Jay County, Indiana)];

3) Rebecca Iiams [(b. November 7, 1805, 1808, or 1810, Washington County, Pennsylvania; d. December 24, 1881, St. Johns, Auglaize County, Ohio); m. March 5, 1827 or July 8, 1824, Warren County, Ohio, to Howard Harford (b. 1781, Auglaize County, Ohio; d. 1838, Jay County, Indiana; brother of George W. Harford; moved to Jay County in 1837), and they had five children: a) William Harford (b. 1828); b) Rachel Harford (b. 1832); c) Cynthia A. Harford (b. 1835); d) Mary Harford (b. 1834); and e) Lucinda Harford (b. 1835)];

4) Mary J. Iiams [(b. December 11, 1811, Washington County, Pennsylvania; d. May 4, 1888, Shelby County, Ohio; buried in Toland Cemetery, Anna, Ohio); m. October 11, 1857, Shelby County, Ohio, to Erasmus "E.B." Toland (b. September 29, 1808, Berkley County, Virginia; his third marriage), son of Andrew Toland and Rachel Montgomery (moved to Morgan County, Ohio, 1827)];

5) James Iiams (b. 1812; m. Mary F.);

6) Ann Iiams (b. 1814; m. April 3, 1836, Shelby County, Ohio, to Tom Forshee);

7) John Iiams [(b. November 24, 1816, Washington County, Pennsylvania; d. June 30, 1878, Shelby or Auglaize County, Ohio); m. 1st, December 9, 1841, Shelby County, Ohio, to Debra Ann Scott (b. 1818, New Jersey; and had children Mary E. Iiams, William Iiams, and George Iiams); m. 2nd, January 25, 1853, Auglaize County, Ohio, Margaret Ann Bittner Partlett (b. December 12, 1827, Virginia; her third marriage; d. December 24, 1901, Auglaize County, Ohio), with the first husband of Margaret Ann Baner Partlett listed as James Burden, an ancestor of contributor Linda Amey];

8) Nancy Iiams [(b. 1818 or 1826), m. April 22, 1847, Shelby County, Ohio, to Gabriel Lambert (b. March 19, 1824; d. September 18, 1876, Shelby County, Ohio), and they had four children: a) Sarah Lambert (b. 1849); b) Mary Lambert (b. 1849); c) George Lambert (b. 1854); m. February 2, 1879, to Mary E. Turner); and d) George Lambert (b. 1857); Gabriel and Nancy Iiams Lambert purchased 80 acres from Thomas and Amanda M. Iiams on April 4, 1863; and 80 acres from William Iiams and wife Martha A. Moyer on March 16, 1863];

9) Elizabeth Iiams (b. April 18, 1820, Warren County, Ohio; m. William Frushour);

10) Thomas Iiams [(b. June 2, 1822, Morrow County or Warren County, Ohio; d. March 5, 1888, Jay County, Indiana; buried in Zoar Cemetery, Portland, Indiana); m. 1st, January 25, 1844, Shelby County, Ohio, to Elizabeth Jane Scott; m. 2nd, April 27, 1851, Auglaize County, Ohio, to Amanda M. Woolery (or Ullery); bought land from George Harford; after 1838 death of Howard Harford, his widow Rebecca Iiams moved in with them; moved to Jay County, Indiana, after 1850; the son of Thomas Iiams and first wife Elizabeth Jane Scott was Absolom H. Iiams (b. November 6, 1846, Shelby County, Ohio; d. June 2, 1928, Van Wert, Ohio; m. Sarah Ellen Crawford, and their four children were: a) Percilla Iiams, b. 1868; b) Emma W. Iiams, b. February 11, 1872; m. James S. Snodgrass; c) Mary R. Iiams, b. 1868; and d) Clara Estella Iiams, b. January 1882; m. C. G. Morris, b. October 29, 1869, Elida, Ohio); the three children of Thomas Iiams and second wife Amanda Woolery (or Ullery, or Wolary) were: a) Evan Iiams, b. 1854; b) Nancy W. Iiams, b. 1864; and c) William H. Iiams (b. 1867); and RWI lists the three children of Thomas Iiams as: a) Mary Jane Iiams (b. March 29, 1852; m. Frances J. Edgerly; b) Ivan Roger Iiams (b. November 24, 1853; died young); and c) Elizabeth Georgia Iiams (b. September 22, 1856; m. Mr. Mock);

11) Eleanor Iiams [(b. 1825), m. February 20, 1845, Shelby County, Ohio, to Absalom Scott (b. December 2, 1820; d. May 5, 1883, Auglaize County, Ohio), and their six children were: a) Sarah Scott (b. 1853); b) Jane Scott (b. 1862); c) Mary A. Scott (b. 18_?_, Ohio); d) George Scott (b. 1846, Ohio); m. Amanda ___; children: Minnie Scott, Samuel Scott, and Effie Scott); e) Thomas Scott (b. 1851); and f) Eda Scott (b. 1859, Ohio)];

12) (tentative, per RWI) Charity Iiams [(b. July 7, 1832, Ohio; d. July 15, 1910), m. October 3, 1853, Shelby County, Ohio, to Aaron Lambert (b. 1830), and they had six children: a) Albert Lambert (b. 1854); b) Jane Lambert (b. 1856; m. Robert Turner, and their five children were: Aron Turner (b. April 28, 1881); Augusta Turner (b. August 15, 1889); Edith Turner (b. August 15, 1889); Joseph Turner (b. April 24, 1888), and

Robert Turner (b. November 20, 1882, Shelby County, Ohio; c) Alice Lambert (b. 1859); d) William Lambert (b. 1861; m. December 27, 1892, to Hulda J. Banning); e) Phebe Lambert (b. 1863); and f) Addie Lambert (b. 1864)]. (RWI) (GR) (HL) (LA) (JIH) (EB)

The estate of Thomas Iiams named Mercy Iiams as administrator, with John Iiams and Joseph Park also bonded. The inventory (No. 890) was filed in Shelby County, Ohio, December 5, 1855; and was finalized October 25, 1856; with Mary Iiams named guardian for Francis J. Iams, age 15; Martha C. Iams, age 13; and William W. Iams, age 11, filed on July 1, 1871; and with Willliam Fisher named guardian for Martha C. Imes, age 13, and William W. Imes, age 11, on November 12, 1874; and on July 1874, both Martha Imes, age 16; and William W. Iimes, age 14, lived with William Park, Shelby County, Ohio.

William H. (or R.) Iiams (b. February 13, 1807, Washington County, Pennsylvania; d. November 15, 1844, or October 18, 1844, Shelby County, Ohio; buried Toland Cemetery, Anna, Ohio), son of Thomas Iiams (b. 1784) and Marcia "Mary Walton; m. Martha McClure (b. May 5, 1814, Warren County, Pennsylvania; d. January 19, 1896, Lima, Allen County, Ohio); with the will of William Iiams of Shelby County, probated November 18, 1844, left the estate to wife Martha Iiams; then equally among children Thomas Iiams, John Iiams, and William Morson Iiams, with Martha Iiams named executor; with estate valued at $313.21 after $500 was given to each Martha Iiams, John Iiams, and Thomas Iiams; and serving as witnesses were John Iiams and Thomas Iiams; with inventory filed February 17, 1845; and final settlement filed March 3, 1847.

The 1850 Census of Dinsmore Township, Shelby County, Ohio, listed Thomas Imes (age 18), James (John) Imes (age 16), William Imes (age 14), Richard Imes (age 12), Samuel Imes (age 7), and Jane (James) Imes (age 3). Children of William H. Imes (b. 1807) and Martha McClure were:

1) John Iiams [(b. 1834, Shelby County, Ohio; m. Mary (b. 1838, Shelby County, Ohio), and their daughter Laura Iiams (b. 1859)];

2) William E. Morson Iiams [(b. September 24, 1837, Shelby County, Ohio; d. March 19, 1913, Cridersville, Auglaize County, Ohio); m. July 22, 1858, Shelby County, Ohio, to Martha Ann Moyer (b. December 24, 1841, Ohio; d. March 24, 1905, Allen County, Ohio; lived at Botkins, Shelby County, Ohio), daughter of George and Jane Moyer];

3) Thomas A. Iiams [(b. October 10, 1832, Shelby County, Ohio; d. March 16, 1868, age 35, Dinsmore Township, Shelby County, Ohio; buried at Anna Methodist Cemetery), m. May 18, 1854, to Mary F. Ellis (b. September 9, 1832, Shelby County, Ohio; d. October 3, 1874; buried at Anna Methodist Church between Anna and Botkins, Ohio) and their children were: a) Martha C. "Mattie" Iams (b. July 6, 1858, Shelby County, Ohio; d. December 17, 1880, Shelby County, Ohio; buried at Anna Methodist Church); m. January 31, 1877, Shelby County, Ohio, to Hiram Howard Varner, (b. January 1, 1843, Vinton County, Ohio; d. January 6, 1926, Auglaize County, Ohio); son of Benjamin F. Varner, b. 1809 in southeastern Ohio. They had two children: 1[1]) Wayne Stanley Varner (b. October 6, 1878, Shelby County, Ohio; d. February 11, 1942, Lucas County, Ohio; buried in Greenlawn Cemetery, Wapakoneta, Auglaize County, Ohio), m. Emily Cecilia Griss (b. May 24, 1886; d. August 7, 1972); and 2[1]) Harry Garfield Varner (b. September 9, 1880, Shelby County, Ohio; d. 1889; buried in Anna Methodist Cemetery)] and Hiram Howard Varner (b. 1843) m. 2nd, Clara A. Morgan, and their

son Carl E. Varner (b. March 1, 1901) had a daughter Eileen Varner (m. Mr. Bame; lived in Findlay, Hancock County, Ohio); b) William W. Iiams ((b. July 19, 1860, Shelby County, Ohio; d. October 14, 1927, Dayton, Montgomery County, Ohio; buried in Woodland Cemetery in Dayton); m. 1st, Freda Jaeger; m. 2nd, December 11, 1887, Auglaize County, Ohio, to Angela Catherine Hilbrant, (b. December, 28, 1863, Shelby County, Ohio; d. November 7, 1930, Dayton, Ohio); daughter of Irvin Hilbrant and Jane Collins; and they had two children: 1¹) Guy Harrison Iiams (b. September 1888, Ohio; m. Clara Bentrop, b. 1895, Germany), and 2¹) Clyde Vernon Iiams (b. January 17, 1892, Botkins, Shelby County, Ohio; d. January 29, 1958, Dayton, Ohio; m. Mary Adeline Hill, (b. June 27, 1901, Springfield, Clark County, Ohio; d. September 12, 1982, Dayton, Ohio); and their two children were: Dean Charles Iiams, (b. March 16, 1928; d. November 15, 1938); and Guy Melvin Iiams, (b. April 11, 1930); and c) Frances J. Iiams (b. September 14, 1855); m. November 27, 1873, Auglaize County, Ohio, to Benjamin F. Park (b. March 23, 1848, Ohio; d. November 27, 1877, Ohio), and they had nine children: Charles A. Parks, William C. Parks, Ida M. Parks, Harvey B. Parks, Effie G. Parks, Roy F. Parks, Alger H. Parks, Bertha P. Parks, and Odie N. Parks)];

4) Samuel Iiams [(b. April 20, 1843, Shelby County, Ohio; d. January 30, 1919, Lima, Allen County, Ohio; buried in Woodlawn Cemetery), m. August 27, 1865, to Mary Ann Abbott (b. June 21, 1847, Pennsylvania) and they had eight children];

5) Richard Iiams (b. August 23, 1839);

6) James E. Iiams (b. May 30, 1844, Shelby County, Ohio; d. December 25, 1911, Shelby County, Ohio; single); and

7) Martha J. Iiams [(b. July 8, 1841, Shelby County, Ohio; d. December 8, 1858; Shelby County, Ohio; buried Toland Cemetery, Dinsmore Township)]. Also, children of Guy Harrison Iiams are said to include: a) Neva Mae Iiams (b. 1919, Ohio); b) Dorothy Iiams (b. 1920); c) Robert Dale Iiams (b. May 1925); and d) Catherine Iiams (b. May 1928). (RWI) (BL) (EB)

Martha C. "Mattie" Iiams (b. July 6, 1858, Shelby County, Ohio; d. December 17, 1880, Shelby County, Ohio; buried in Anna Methodist Cemetery), daughter of Thomas A. Iiams (b. 1832) and Mary F. Ellis; m. January 31, 1877, Shelby County, Ohio, to Hiram Howard Varner (b. January 1, 1843, Vinton County, Ohio; d. January 6, 1926, Auglaize County, Ohio; buried Wapakoneta, Ohio), the son of Benjamin F. Varner (b. 1809) and Sarah Abbot. Hiram Howard Varner was a schoolteacher and served in the Civil War with Company C of 20th Ohio Volunteer Infantry; and m. 2nd, May 24, 1881, to Clara Augusta Morgan (b. August 18, 1861, Shelby County, Ohio; d. March 24, 1936, Auglaize County, Ohio; buried in Greenlawn Cemetery, Wapakoneta, Auglaize County, Ohio), daughter of David Elias Morgan and Elizabeth Dresback. The twelve children of Hiram Howard Varner (b. 1843) were: 1) Wayne Stanley Varner [(b.October 6, 1878, Shelby County, Ohio; d. February 11, 1912, Lucas County, Ohio; served with 120th Company, USCA of Spanish American War), m. Emily Cecil Gress (b. May 24, 1886; d. August 7, 1972, Montgomery County, Ohio), and they had two children: a) Winifred Barbara Varner; and b) Blaine Edgar Varner (b. October 3, 1909, Shelby County, Ohio; d. September 8, 1980, Montague, Michigan; m. August 25, 1934, to Helen Spear, and their two children were: Linda Ann Varner and Michael Varner)]; 2) Harry Garfield Varner (b. September 9, 1880,

Shelby County, Ohio; d. 1880; buried Anna Cemetery, Shelby County, Ohio); 3) Lillian Gertrude Varner [(b. May 6, 1882, Shelby County, Ohio; d. November 2, 1956, Auglaize County, Ohio; buried at Wapakoneta, Ohio); m. December 25, 1901, Wapakoneta, Ohio, to Ed Wentz (b. May 14, 1879; d. May 11, 1957)]; 4) Mary Edith Varner [(b. December 25, 1883, Shelby County, Ohio; d. November 30, 1964, Auglaize County, Ohio), m. September 16, 1908, Wapakoneta, Ohio, to Harry Swink (b. July 11, 1882; d. July 26, 1956)]; 5) Chase Gladstone Varner (b. 1885; d. 1885, Shelby County, Ohio); 6) Bertha Hazel Varner [(b. February 22, 1887, Shelby County, Ohio; d. May 23, 1971, Auglaize County, Ohio), m. December 26, 1915, to Charles Alfred Shumate (b. June 15, 1886; d. December 30, 1959)]; 7) Mable Blanche Varner [(b. July 8, 1889, Shelby County, Ohio; d. March 28, 1967, Mercer County, Ohio), m. July 14, 1923, John Lyman Ellis (b. September 26, 1898; d. February 23, 1973)]; 8) William McKinley Varner [(b. September 26, 1891; d. July 9, 1970, Hancock County, Indiana), m. January 11, 1917, Auglaize County, Ohio, to Ethel Wright (b. July 23, 1893; d. June 14, 1978)]; 9) Friend Huber Varner [(b. August 21, 1893, Shelby County, Ohio; d. November 30, 1964, Dade County, Florida), m. May 29, 1913, Monroe County, Indiana, to Loretta Monica Schwartz (b. July 15, 1896; d. October 9, 1963)] 10) Bessie Chloe Varner [(b. June 9, 1896, Shelby County, Ohio; d. March 31, 1986, Mercer County, Ohio), m. June 9, 1917, Wapakoneta, Ohio, to George Leroy "Roy" Beard (b. May 6, 1890; d. December 1, 1959)]; 11) Ralph Edgar Varner (b. June 9, 1896; Shelby Couty, Ohio; d. 1896); and 12) Carl Everett Varner [(b. March 1, 1901, Auglaize County, Ohio; d. May 11, 1968, Hancock County, Indiana); m. September 28, 1921, Auglaize County, Ohio, to Marjorie Dotson (b. March 18, 1902; d. September 27, 1948)]. (EB) Carl E. Varner (b. 1901) had a daughter, Eileen Varner Bane, who lived in Findlay, Ohio.

John Iiams (b. November 21, 1816, Pennsylvania; d. June 30, 1878, Shelby County, Ohio), son of Thomas Iiams (b. 1784) and Marcia Walton (b. 1784); m. 1st, December 9, 1841, Shelby County, Ohio, to Deborah Ann Scott (b. 1818, New Jersey), and m. 2nd, January 25, 1853, Auglaize County, Ohio, to Margaret Ann Bitner (her 3rd marriage; b. December 12, 1827, Virginia; d. December 24, 1901, Auglaize County, Ohio), and John Iiams (b. 1816), had five of his twelve children by his first wife: 1) Mary E. Iiams (b. 1842; m. Henry Bechdolt); 2) William Iiams (b. 1844); 3) George L. Iiams [(b. September 16, 1846, Auglaize County, Ohio; d. February 20, 1908, Cridersville, Auglaize County, Ohio), m. November 21, 1869, Auglaize County, Ohio, to Mary Jane Snyder (b. November 12, 1837; d. January 21, 1921)]; 4) July Iiams (b. March 1850); 5) Sarah Jane Iiams (b. 1851; d. December 6, 1895, Shelby County, Ohio); 6) Margaret Iiams (b. 1855); 7) Debora Iiams (b. 1857; m. May 30, 1883, Auglaize County, Ohio, to Oscar Sands); 8) John Henry Iiams [(b. September 24, 1848, Ohio; d. November 30, 1899, Uniopolis, Ohio), m. January 23, 1881, Shelby County, Ohio, to Della E. Carter (b. 1866, Ohio; d. April 16, 1902, Wapakoneta, Ohio)]; 9) Naomi Iiams (b. July 23, 1861, Auglaize County, Ohio; d. August 18, 1882, Auglaize County, Ohio); 10) Rebecca Iiams (b. 1863, Auglaize County, Ohio; m. April 30, 1882, James Tippie); 11) Minerva Iiams (b. April. 24, 1886, Auglaize County, Ohio; d. October 6, 1872, Auglaize County, Ohio); and 12) Louisa E. Iiams (b. 1869, Auglaize County, Ohio). (RWI)

George L. Iiams (b. September 16, 1846, Auglaize County, Ohio; d. February 20, 1908, Cridersville, Auglaize County, Ohio), son of John Iiams (b. 1816) and Deborah Ann Scott; m. November 21, 1869, Auglaize County, Ohio, to Mary Jane Snyder (b. November 12, 1837; d. January 21, 1921), and they had five children: 1) Lola Emma Viola Iiams [(b. October 24, 1872; d. January 7, 1949), m. April 7, 1891, Auglaize County, Ohio, to Charles E. Morris (b. January 7, 1949)]; 2) Birl Elmer

Iiams [(b. March 13, 1875, Cridersville, Auglaize County, Ohio; d. July 24, 1939, Melrose, Paulding County, Ohio; buried at Cridersville, Ohio); m. October 13, 1913, to Sarah Ann Ingmire (b. January 13, 1889, Franklin County, Ohio; d. September 26, 1962, Lima, Allen County, Ohio; buried at Cridersville, Ohio)]; 3) Joseph William Iiams [(b. March 20, 1877, Cridersville, Auglaize County, Ohio; d. 1942, Cridersville), m. 1st, April 19, 1908, Lima, Ohio, Flossie Fern McLory (b. February 13, 1888, Plattsville, Ohio; d. May 5, 1918, Cridersville, Ohio), daughter of Frederick McLory and Lizzie McLory of Miami County, Ohio; and m. 2nd, Katherine Herr]; 4) Eva Mae Iiams [(b. September 8, 1879, Auglaize County, Ohio; d. November 27, 1952, Wapakoneta, Auglaize County, Ohio), m. July 23, 1898, to George Kaeck]; and 5) Ella Sarah Iiams [(b. 1882; d. 1945, Cridersville, Auglaize County, Ohio), m. Homer Smith (or South)]. (RWI)

Birl Elmer Iiams (b. March 13, 1875, Cridersville, Auglaize County, Ohio; d. July 24, 1939, Melrose, Paulding County, Ohio), son of George Iiams (b. 1846) and Mary Jane Snyder (b. 1847), m. October 13, 1913, to Sarah Ann Ingmire (b. January 13, 1889, Franklin County, Ohio; d. September 26, 1962, Lima, Allen County, Ohio; buried at Cridersville, Ohio), and they had eight children: 1) Elmer William Iiams (b. December 23, 1914, Wapakoneta, Auglaize County, Ohio; m. February 23, 1940, to Irene Wirick Frysinger); 2) Helen Olive Iiams (b. January 19, 1917, Freeport, Michigan; m. May 28, 1938, to Donald L. Shrider); 3) Martin Lewis Iiams (b. September 9, 1919, Lima, Allen County, Ohio; d. September 19, 1919, Cridersville, Auglaize Conty, Ohio); 4) Franklin Carl Iiams [(b. October 9, 1920, Lima, Allen County, Ohio; d. October 31, 1987, Putnam County, Ohio), m. December 20, 1938, to LaDonna Pauline Carrino, and their four children were: a) Helen Marie Iiams (b. January 11, 1942, Lima, Allen County, Ohio); b) Franklin Paul Iiams (b. December 17, 1942, Lima, Allen County, Ohio); c) a daughter (b. March 27, 1949, Lima, Allen County, Ohio), and d) Philip William Iiams (b. March 28, 1954, Auglaize County, Ohio)]; 5) Alice Luella Iiams (b. April 7, 1923, Lima, Allen County, Ohio; m. January 6, 1941, to Calvin C. Moore); 6) Edna Phyllis Iiams (b. May 1, 1925, Lima, Allen County, Ohio; m. July 17, 1943, to Gerald E. White, b. January 19, 1922, Lima, Allen County, Ohio); 7) Louise Catherine Iiams (b. October 12, 1927, Lima, Allen County, Ohio; m. October 20, 1943, to Ben D. King); and 8) Thomas Levi Iiams [(b. November 28, 1932, Lima, Allen County, Ohio; d. May 20, 1976, Westminster, Allen County, Ohio), m. May 21, 1956, to Joyce Webb]. (RWI)

William E. Morson Iiams (b. September 24, 1837, Van Buren Township, Shelby County, Ohio; d. March 19, 1913, Cridersville, Auglaize County, Ohio; buried in St. Mathews Cemetery), son of William R. Iiams (b. 1807) and Martha McClure (b. 1814); m. July 22, 1858, Shelby County, Ohio, to Martha Ann Moyer (b. December 24, 1841, Port Jefferson, Ohio; d. March 24, 1905, Lima, Ohio; lived at Botkins, Shelby County, Ohio), daughter of George Moyer and Ann Consolver; had several children:

    1) Alonzo Phillip Iiams [(b. September 15, 1859, Dinsmore Township, Shelby County, Ohio; a carpenter; d. December 13, 1952, Shelby County, Ohio; buried in Pearl Cemetery), m. November 4, 1880, Shelby County, Ohio, to Ruth Ella Taylor (b. October 1861, Cridersville, Auglaize County, Ohio; d. 1948 or 1954, Shelby County, Ohio)];

    2) Emma "Jane" Iiams [(b. September 22, 1861, Shelby County, Ohio; d. April 11, 1939, Lima, Allen County, Ohio; buried in Memorial Park), m. July 27, 1880, Shelby County, Ohio, to Frank Marion Taylor (b. November 17, 1859, Shelby County, Ohio; d. December 30, 1935, Harold, Allen County, Ohio; buried Memorial Park Cemetery in Lima, Ohio), the son of Samuel Taylor and Lidelia "Lydia" Jane Powell; five

183

children: a) Walter Wilber Taylor (b. June 29, 1881; m. December 12, 1906, Lima, Allen County, Ohio, to Iva Gertrude Loffler); b) Bertha M. Taylor (b. November 7, 1883, Lima, Ohio; m. James E. Morton); c) Charles B. Taylor (b. December 6, 1886, Lima, Ohio); d) Clevely O. Taylor (b. September 10, 1888, Lima, Ohio; d. April 21, 1930, Lima, Ohio; m. Lilly May Wilkins); and e) Eva R. "Evy" Taylor (b. December 21, 1894, Lima, Ohio; m. 1st, Mr. Perry; m. 2nd, Ted Bear; and m. 3rd, Mr. Whitacre)];

3) Elmer Rodifus Iiams (b. 1864, Shelby County, Ohio);

4) Charles Riley Iiams [(b. April 12, 1866, Shelby County, Ohio; d. July 10, 1951, Lima, Allen County, Ohio), m. March 15, 1895, Lima, Ohio, to Mary E. Watkins (b. 1871)];

5) George Milton Iiams [(b. September 17, 1867, Dinsmore Township, Shelby County, Ohio; d. January 25, 1934), m. 1888, Minnie Decker (b. 1872, Bitz, Germany)];

6) William Edward Iiams (b. July 24, 1869, Van Buren Township, Shelby County, Ohio; moved to Marion, Indiana);

7) Joseph N. Iiams [(b. July 17, 1873, Dinsmore Township, Shelby County, Ohio; d. July 9, 1953, Tiffin, Seneca County, Ohio; buried in Memorial Park, Lima, Ohio), m. Alice (or Anna) Mary Hayes (b. 1878; d. March 25, 1954, Tiffin, Ohio)];

8) Ida May Iiams (b. 1876, Shelby County, Ohio; d. California);

9) Cordelia M. "Mattie" Iiams (b. February 25, 1877, Shelby County, Ohio; d. July 24, 1879, Shelby County, Ohio);

10) Lillian Eva Iiams [(b. October 4, 1879, Van Buren Township, Shelby County, Ohio; d. Compton, California), m. June 1879, to James Parsons (b. June 1879, Lima, Ohio), and their two daughters were: a) Ruth Parsons (b. March 1898), and b) Ethel Parsons (b. August 1899)];

11) Harry Early Iiams [(b. April 11, 1882, Shelby County, Ohio; d. November 16, 1918, Lima, Allen County, Ohio; buried in St. Paul Cemetery, Perry Township), m. in Lima, to Evangeline Suzanne "Eva" Peterson-Nusbaum (b. 1832, St. Mary's, Mercer County, Ohio), and their children were: a) Martha Iiams (b.1904; m. Robert Krause; 2 children: Robert Krause, Jr., and Dorothy Krause, who m. Kenneth Jacobs); b) James Earl Iiams (b. September 10, 1907; d. 1970); c) Vesta Florin Iiams (b. 1909; d. 1942; m. Hitz); d) Everett Milton Iiams (b. 1912; d. 1979); e) Alice Evaline Iiams (b. 1916), m. Harry Cressman Gregg (b. 1910; d. 1963, his second marriage; a tanker captain; lived in Toledo, Lucas County, Ohio), and they had two children: 1') Harry C. Gregg, who had three children: Daniel Ray Gregg, Gwendolyn Ann Gregg, and Jonathan Cress Gregg; and 2') Allan Albert Gregg, who had four children: Allen Albert Gregg, Jr., Robert Kennedy Gregg, Cressman David Gregg, and Julia Ann Gregg]; f) Flossie Ruth Iiams (b. 1918; m. Raymond Hess); and g) Nora B. Iiams (b. December 5, 1919, Shelby County, Ohio). (RWI) (BL)

Walter Wilber Taylor (b. June 29, 1881), son of Emma "Jane" Iiams (b. 1861) and Frank Merion Taylor (b. 1859); grandson of William E. Iiams (b. 1837); m. December 12, 1907, Lima, Ohio, to Iva Gertrude Leffler (b. September 19, 1890, Auglaize Township, Allen County, Ohio; d. July 6, 1942, Lima, Ohio; buried in Memorial Park), daughter of John William Leffler and Delilah A. Snider; and they had four children:

1) Donald Maxwell Taylor [(b. June 30, 1907, Lima, Ohio; d. November 27, 1979, Lima, Ohio; buried in Elida Greenlawn Cemetery), m. G.

Mildred Bigelow, and their two children were: a) Shirley Dean Taylor (b. April 20, 1929, Allen County, Ohio; m. Robert Palmer), and b) Judith Jo Taylor (b. 1936, Allen County, Ohio; m. Wayne Bolender)];

2) Mildred Leona Taylor [(b. September 5, 1909, Lima, Ohio), m. July 2, 1927, Mount Vernon, Ohio, to Howard Ryan (b. December 24, 1906, Lucas County, Ohio), and their son, Robert Dean Ryan (b. February 18, 1929, Lucas County, Ohio) m. 1st, JoAn Hutchinson, and m. 2nd, Diane Marie Hattery];

3) Robert Gordon Taylor [(b. October 31, 1912, Lima, Ohio; d. November 2, 1963, Toledo, Ohio; buried in Woodlawn Cemetery), m. Hazel Anna Haney (b. March 5, 1914, Lucas County, Ohio), and their son, Edgar Lee Taylor (b. January 6, 1934) m. 1st, Elaine Delores Conjour, and m. 2nd, Lisa M. Sharp]; and

4) Mellie Josephine "Jo" Taylor [(b. January 26, 1915, Lima, Allen County, Ohio; d. February 21, 1988, Toledo, Ohio; buried in Toledo Memorial Park), m. 1st, February 5, 1945, Toledo, to Harold Gibson; m. 2nd to John Wesley Blackwell (b. November 20, 1903, Glenvar, Virginia; d. October 22, 1958, Cole, Ohio; buried in Sherwood Park), son of John William Blackwell and Olive Eugenia Hill; and she had three children: a) Nancy Carole Gibson (b. June 4, 1938; m. John Frederick Myers); b) Sandra Jean Gibson (b. February 14, 1940, Ohio; m. 1st, Ronald Dale Uphold; and m. 2nd, James Bush); and c) Barbara Jo Blackwell (b. July 25, 1945, Toledo, Ohio), m. 1st, Toledo, to Dennis Gerald Wesenberg; m. 2nd, May 22, 1971, to Gary John Locker (b. April 25, 1946, Toledo; son of John Henry Locker and Meiriem Lois Barber), and their daughter was Amy Jo Locker (b. November 17, 1971, Toledo, Lucas County, Ohio)]. (BTL)

James Earl Iiams (b. September 10, 1907, Lima, Allen County, Ohio; d. January 23, 1970, Toledo, Lucas County, Ohio), the son of Harry Earl Iiams (b. 1882) and grandson of William E. Iiams (b. 1837); m. Rosella Mae Stevens (b. January 13, 1907, Toledo, Ohio; d. December 30, 1965; buried Toledo Memorial Park); and they had two children (he m. 2nd, Margaret Krause; and m. 3rd, Leah Hopkins): 1) James Earl Iiams, Jr. (b. August 16, 1926; d. November 6, 1926, Lucas County, Ohio); 2) Donald Edward Iiams [(b. April 15, 1928, Dayton, Ohio) and he m. five times: a) January 10, 1928, Dayton, Ohio, to Elaine Marie Van Tassel (b. 1931), and they had four children; b) 1958, to Mary Catherine Cramer, and they had two additional children; c) 1968, to Constance Bondy; d) to Shirley Weiker; and e) to Linda ___]. The six children of Donald Edward Iiams (b. 1928) were: 1) Barbara Ann Iiams [(b. January 10, 1948, Lucas County, Ohio), m. March 15, 1968, to James Kent Eichner (b. February 18, 1944, Lucas County, Ohio), and they had five children: a) Amy Lee Eichner (b. May 12, 1970; m. October 9, 1992, to Chad Richard Berg, b. 1971); b) Holly Ann Eichner (b. November 20, 1973, Lucas County, Ohio); c) John Daniel Eichner (b. March 2, 1978, adopted, Toledo, Ohio); d) Ashley Noel Eichner (b. December 25, 1980, Toledo, Ohio); and e) Whitney Rae Eichner (b. September 29, 1983, Toledo, Ohio, adopted)]; 2) Donald Edward Iiams, Jr. [(b. August 16, 1949, Toledo, Ohio), m. 1st, May 19, 1972, Toledo, Ohio, to Jill Klutter (b. November 25, 1951), and they had three children: a) Kelly Anne-Marie Iiams (b. April 15, 1973; m. May 9, 1994, Toledo, to Justin Canfield, b. February 14, 1973, Toledo; and their daughter, Haley Kay Canfield, b. June 17, 1991); b) Andrew Edward Iiams (b. July 4, 1974, Toledo, Ohio); and c) Jessica Lynne Iiams (b. January 22, 1976, Toledo); m. 2nd, 1987, to Tammy Hall, and their daughter, Loren Ashley Iiams (b. November 19, 1990,

Toledo)]; 3) Patrick Michael Frayer-Iiams [(b. November 18, 1957, Toledo), m. January 27, 1979, Monroe, Michigan, to Lisa Carol Della Contrada (b. March 20, 1956, Rome, New York), and their three children were: a) Nicholas James Frayer-Iiams (b. September 3, 1979, Glen Ellyn, Illinois); b) Lauren Avery Frayer-Iiams (b. April 15, 1982); c) Patrick Joseph "PJ" Frayer-Iiams (b. April 27, 1987, Fairhope, Alabama)]; 4) Candace Susan Iiams [(b. September 26, 1953), m. April 24, 1921, to Ronald Baron (b. January 6, 1951, Michigan), and their two children were: a) Tracy Marie Baron (b. November 10, 1970; m. November 3, 1990, Ronald James Riehl, (b. 1969); and their two children were: Britany Christian Riehl, b. February 17, 1990; and Alyssa Sue-Ann Riehl, b. December 28, 1991, Monroe, Michigan)]; 5) Bruce Williams Iiams [(b. May 15, 1958, Toledo, Ohio), m. Marie O'Brian, and their two children were: a) Maura Iiams (b. October 14, 1987, Toledo, Ohio) and b) Erin Iiams (b. October 5, 1989)]; and 6) Sean Stacy Iiams (b. 1960). (BTL)

Alonzo Phillip Iiams (b. September 15, 1859, Shelby County, Ohio; a carpenter; d. December 13, 1952, Shelby County, Ohio), son of William E. Iiams (b. 1837) and Martha Ann Moyer; m. November 4, 1880, to Ruth Ella Taylor (b. October 1861, Cridersville, Auglaize County, Ohio; d. 1948, Shelby County, Ohio), and they had nine children:

1) Ollie C. Iiams [(b. February 20, 1882, Botkins, Shelby County, Ohio), m. October 1, 1903, to Lowell E. Blakeley (b. March 10, 1882, Botkins, Shelby County, Ohio; the son of Adam Blakeley and Emma Cocklin)];

2) Ethel L. "Ertie" Iiams [(b. September 24, 1884, Botkins, Shelby County, Ohio), m. December 29, 1909, in Botkins, to a cousin Harry (or Harvey) B. Parke (b. March 10, 1886, Kettlerville, Shelby County, Ohio, a schoolteacher; d. 1948, Shelby County, Ohio); son of B. F. Parke and Frances Iiams (b. 1855, daughter of Thomas A. Iiams); and they had four children: a) Harold L. Parke (m. Elsie Heiland); b) Emma Parke (m. Gordon Baxter); c) Perry Parke (m. Ruth Lenox); and d) Donald Parke (m. Marian Busse)];

3) Maundy Iiams (b. June 17, 1891, Shelby County, Ohio; d. November 8, 1892, Shelby County, Ohio);

4) Urril Vincent Iiams [(b. May 12, 1886, Lima, Allen County, Ohio; d. December 8, 1965, Shelby County, Ohio), m. March 18, 1920, Shelby County, Ohio, to Pearl Elizabeth Griffis (b. September 5, 1893, Shelby County, Ohio; d. November 27, 1962, Sidney, Ohio; daughter of Ambrose Griffis and Gertrude Latimer); and they had two children (each of whom had three more children): a) Doyle Keith Iiams (b. November 20, 1928; m. Margaret Frances Toller; and their three children were: 1¹) Kurt Allen Iiams, b. April 7, 1954; 2¹) Pamela Lynn Iiams, b. June 21, 1956; and 3¹) Elaine Susan Iiams, b. August 1, 1959); and b) Myron Gale Iiams (b. February 24, 1921; m. Janice Elizabeth Roth; and their three children were: 1¹) Gregory Keith Iiams, b. March 24, 1947; 2¹) James Stephen Iiams, b. December 17, 1954; and 3¹) Thomas Wayne Iiams, b. April 7, 1948)];

5) Winifred Raymond Iiams [(b. August 31, 1890, Allen County, Ohio; d. February 21, 1967, Shelby County, Ohio), m. March 3, 1919, Botkins, Shelby County, Ohio, to Edna Catharine Arnold (b. December 3, 1899; d. 1928), daughter of Henry Arnold and Catharine Gehret, and they had five children: a) Lester Charles Iiams (b. September 30, 1922, Shelby County, Ohio; U.S. Navy in World War II; d. February 22, 1949, buried in Conception Cemetery); b) Gerald Ralph Iiams (b. January 17, 1920, Botkins, Shelby County, Ohio; m. Thelma Pauline Everett, b. April 20,

1933, and d. June 18, 1993; and their son, Richard Lee Iiams, was b. July 24, 1951, Sidney, Shelby County, Ohio); c) an infant (d. age one day, September 11, 1921); d) Elmo R. Iiams (b. September 30, 1921; d. April 24, 1946); and e) Marion Pete Iiams];

    6) Florence L. Iiams (b. 1893);

    7) Martha J. Iiams [(b. October 31, 1893, Botkins, Shelby County, Ohio), m. April 19, 1917, Shelby County, Ohio, Harold N. Daugherty (b. March 14, 1896, Hardin County, Ohio; son of George and Hillery Daugherty of Wapakoneta, Auglaize County, Ohio)];

    8) Alma G. Iiams [(b. May 9, 1898, Botkins, Shelby County, Ohio), m. December 7, 1917, Shelby County, Ohio, to Edward A. Sollman (b. September 8, 1893, Kettlersville, Shelby County, Ohio, son of John Sollman and Katherine Rowall)]; and

    9) Grace Iiams [(b. October 23, 1901, Botkins, Shelby County, Ohio), m. September 24, 1921, Botkins, Ohio, to Edwin Nevin (b. December 4, 1899, New York City; son of Thomas Nevin and Katherine Rowall)]. (BTL)

Emma Jane Iiams (b. September 22, 1861, Shelby County, Ohio; d. April 11, 1939, Lima, Ohio), daughter of William E. Iiams (b. 1837); m. July 27 (or 29), 1880, Shelby County, Ohio, to Frank Marion Taylor (b. November 15, 1859, Shelby County, Ohio; d. December 30, 1935, Harrod, Allen County, Ohio; buried Memorial Park Cemetery), son of Samuel Taylor and Lydia Jane (Ledelia) Powell; and they had five children (on whose birth certificate is written the name Emma Jane James):

    1) Walter Wilber Taylor [(b. June 29, 1881), m. 1st, December 12, 1906, Lima, Ohio, Iva Gertrude Leffler (b. August 19, 1890, Auglaize County, Ohio; d. July 6, 1942, Lima, Ohio); daughter of John William Leffler and Delilah A. Snider (Iva Leffler m. 2nd, Stephen W. Gilmore);

    2) Bertha M. Taylor [(b. November 7, 1883, Lima, Ohio), m. James E. Morton, and their two children were: Miriam Morton and Gae Morton (m. Mr. Beach)];

    3) Charles B. Taylor (b. 1886);

    4) Clevely O. "Pete" Taylor [(b. September 10, 1888, Lima, Ohio; d. April 21, 1930, Lima, Ohio), m. Lilly May Wilkin (b. 1895; d. 1976), and they had three children: a) Laurel E. Taylor (b. 1913); b) Elaine Virginia Taylor (b. 1915; d. 1974; m. Mr. David); and c) Kathleen Wilma Taylor (b. 1918; d. 1975; m. 1st, Mr. Park; m. 2nd, Mr. Hines; and m. 3rd, Mr. Rinehart)]; and

    5) Eva R. "Evy" Taylor [(b. December 21, 1894, Lima, Ohio; d. Lima, Ohio), m. 1st, Mr. Perry (their two children were James Perry and Gene Perry); m. 2nd, Ted Bear; and m. 3rd, Mr. Whitacre]. (BTL)

Walter Wilber Taylor (b. June 29, 1881), son of Emma Jane Iiams (b. 1861; daughter of William E. Iiams, b. 1837); m. December 12, 1906, Lima, Ohio, to Iva Gertrude Leffler (b. August 19, 1890, Auglaize County, Ohio; d. July 6, 1942, Lima, Ohio), daughter of John William Leffler and Delilah A. Snider; and they had four children:

    1) Donald Maxwell Taylor [(b. June 30, 1907, Lima, Ohio; d. 1979), m. 1928 to G. Mildred Bigelow (b. 1911; d. 1983), and they had two children: a) Shirley Dean Taylor (b. 1929; d. 1991; m. Robert Palmer, b. 1929; three children: Kathy Palmer, Dawn Palmer, and Pam Palmer); and b) Judith Jo Taylor (b. 1936; m. Wayne Bolender; three children: Bruce Bolender, Dawn Bolender, and Michael Bolender)];

    2) Mildred Leona Taylor [(b. September 5, 1909, Lima, Ohio), m. July 2, 1927, Mount Vernon, Ohio, to Howard Ryan (b. 1906, d. 1993); and

their son, Robert Dean Ryan (b. 1929), m. 1st, JoAn Hutchinson, and they had three children: a) Robert Dean Ryan, Jr. (b. 1952); b) Vickie Lynn Ryan (b. 1954; m. Mike Conover; two children: Shad Justin Ryan, b. 1970; and Jennifer Conover, b. 1976); and c) Judith Jo Ryan (b. 1958; m. Robert Meining); m. 2nd, Diane Marie Hattery (b. 1956), and their child was d) Stephanie Ann Ryan (b. 1988);

    3) Robert Gordon Taylor [(b. October 31, 1912, Lima, Ohio; d. November 2, 1963, Toledo, Ohio; buried Woodlawn Cemetery), m. Hazel Anna Haney (b. 1914; d. 1964), and their three children were: a) Edgar Lee Taylor (b. 1934; m. 1st, Elaine Dolores Conjour, and their daughter, Laura Lynn Taylor, b. 1960, m. 1st, Randall James Tabor, b. 1953; their children: Christopher Lee Tabor, b. 1984; and Michael Albert Tabor, b. 1986; she m. 2nd, Raymond Charles Sandford); b) Letitia Diane Taylor (b. 1962, m. Charles Calvin Estes, b. 1961; their child: Samantha Diane Estes, b. 1987); and c) Glen Richard Taylor (b. 1969)]; and

    4) Melanie Mellee Josephine "Jo" Taylor [(b. January 26, 1915, Lima, Ohio; d. February 21, 1988, Toledo, Lucas County, Ohio), m. 1st, February 5, 1945, Toledo, Ohio, to Harold Gibson, and they had two children: 1) Nancy Carole Gibson (b. 1938), and b) Sandra Dean Gibson (b. 1940); m. 2nd, John Wesley Blackwell and had one additional child; c) Barbara Jo Blackwell (b. 1945)]. (BTL)

Mellie Melanie Josephine "Jo" Taylor (b. January 26, 1915, Lima, Allen County, Ohio; d. February 21, 1988, Toledo, Lucas County, Ohio), daughter of Walter Wilber Taylor (b. 1881) and Iva Gertrude Leffler (b. 1890); m. 1st, February 5, 1945, Toledo, Ohio, to Harold Gibson, and they had two children:

    1) Nancy Carole Gibson [(b. 1938), m. Paul Frederick Myers, and they had two children: a) Debra Lynn Myers (b. 1953; m. Michael Borysiak, and their two children were: Kathryn Borysiak and Lisa Jo Borysiak), and b) Paul Frederick Myers, Jr. (b. 1960; m. Kathy ___, and their daughter was Amanda Myers)];

    2) Sandra Dean Gibson [(b. 1940); m. 1st, Ronald Dale Uphold, and their three children were: a) Cheryl Dawn Uphold (m. Eric Baker); b) Brenda Dean Uphold (m. Michael Pierce, and their son was Jason Pierce); and c) Donald Dale Uphold; Sandra m. 2nd, James Bush]; Melanie Josephine Taylor (b. 1915) m. 2nd, John Wesley Blackwell (b. 1903; d. 1958), and they had a daughter.

    3) Barbara Jo Blackwell [(b. 1945); author and researcher whose work is documented in this branch of the family tree; m. 1st, Dennis Gerald Wesenberg; m. 2nd, Gary John Locker (b. 1946); their daughter was Amy Jo Locker (b. 1971)]. (BTL)

Charles Riley Iiams (b. April 12, 1866, Shelby County, Ohio; d. July 10, 1951, Lima, Allen County, Ohio), son of William E. Iiams (b. 1837) and Martha Ann Moyer; m. March 15, 1895, Lima, Allen County, Ohio, to Mary E. Watkins (b. 1871), and they had four children:

    1) Cordelia Bernice Iiams [(b. August 7, 1901, Allen County, Ohio), m. February 17, 1917, Lima, Allen County, Ohio, to John Charles Schwartz (b. February 11, 1900, Lima, Ohio), son of John Schwartz and Julia Rose Gutzurle];

    2) Alice Irene Iiams [(b. September 6, 1904, Lima, Allen County, Ohio; d. November 9, 1994, Toledo, Lucas County, Ohio), m. February 8, 1922, to Charles Clyde Hanthorn (b. November 19, 1901, Perry Township,

Allen County, Ohio), and they had seven children: Dorothy Hanthorn, Mary Hanthorn, Delores "Dee" Hanthorn (m. John Garcia), Bertha Hanthorn, Harold E. Hanthorn, Charles C. Hanthorn, and William Hanthorn]:

3) Charles Ralph Iiams (b. December 28, 1907); and perhaps

4) Frank M. Iiams (b. August 1893). (BTL)

William W. Morson Iiams (b. July 19, 1860, Shelby County, Ohio; d. October 14, 1927, Dayton, Montgomery County, Ohio, buried in Woodland Cemetery, or d. March 19, 1913, Auglaize County, Ohio), son of Thomas A. Iiams (b. 1832) and Mary F. Ellis; and the grandson of William R. Iiams (b. 1807) and Martha McClure; and the great-grandson of Thomas Iiams (b. 1784) and Marcia "Mercie" Walton (b. 1782), m. July 22, 1858 or December 11, 1887, to Angela Catherine Hilbrant or Martha Ann Moyer (b. December 28, 1863, Shelby County, Ohio; d. November 11, 1930, Dayton, Ohio, or March 24, 1905), the daughter of George and Jane Moyer or Irvin and Jane Collins Hilbrant; and the children of William W. Iiams (b. 1860) and Angela Catherine Hilbrant (RWI) were:

1) Guy Harrison Iiams [(b. September, 1888, Ohio), m. Clara Bentrop (b. 1885, Germany) and their four children were: Neva Mae Iiams (b. 1919), Dorothy Iiams (b. 1922), Robert Dale Iiams (b. 1925) and Catherine Iiams (b. 1928) and

2) Clyde Vernon Iiams [(b. January 17, 1892, Ohio; d. January 29, 1958, Dayton, Ohio, buried Woodland Cemetery), m. January 11, 1926, in Springfield, Clark County, Ohio, to Mary Adaline Hill (b. June 27, 1901, Springfield, Ohio; d. April 12, 1982, Dayton, Montgomery County, Ohio), and their two children were: Dean Charles Iiams (b. March 16, 1928) and Guy Melvin Iiams (b. April 11, 1930)]; and the two children of William Iiams and Martha Ann Moyer (m. 1858) were: 1) Alonzo P. Iiams [(b. September 15, 1859, Botkins, Ohio; d. October 13, 1952, buried in Pearl Cemetery), m. November 4, 1880, to Ruthella Taylor, daughter of Samuel G. Taylor and Lydia Powell; and their nine children were: a) Ollie C. Iiams (b. February 8, 1882; m. L. E. Blakely; and their child Geraldine Blakeley m. Everett Cole, had a daughter Mary Ann Cole, who m. Mr. Koenig, lived in Botkins, Ohio, and in turn, had a daughter Martha Koenig, who m. Mr. Anspaugh and they lived on Silver Street in Wapakoneta, Auglaize County, Ohio); b) Ertie L. Iiams (b. September 27, 1883; m. H. B. Parke of Sidney, Ohio); c) Urril V. Iiams (b. May 12, 1886, Lima, Ohio; d. December 8, 1965, Fort Laramie, Shelby County, Ohio; m. March 1920, to Pearl Griffin, and their son was Doyle Iiams); d) Winifred R. Iiams (b. August 31, 1888; d. 1967); e) Maude Cecilia Iiams (b. June 17, 1891; d. 1895, buried in Shenbone Cemetery, Auglaize County, Ohio); f) Fern L. Iiams (b. September 1, 1893; m. John Gillian or John Gilliard in Dayton, Ohio); g) Martha J. Iiams (b. October 31, 1896; m. Mr. Daugherty of Sidney, Shelby County, Ohio); h) Alma J. Iiams (b. May 9, 1898; m. Edward Solomon in Sidney, Ohio); and i) Grace B. Iiams (b. October 23, 1901; m. Edward Nevin in Sidney, Ohio)]; and 2) Charles Riley Iiams [(m. Mary Elizabeth Watkins), and their daughter was Bernice Cordelia Iiams, m. John C. Schwartz, son of John Casimir Schwartz and Julia Rose Gutzmiller (John Jr. m. 2nd, Mary Elizabeth Humbert, daughter of Henry Edward Humbert and Pearl Weider), and their daughter was Janice Lynn Schwartz (m. Robert Sharp, son of Robert Sharp and Marie Hollis)]. (MA)

189

Sarah Iiams (b. April 6, 1809, Washington County, Pennsylvania; moved to Shelby County, Ohio, or Warren County, Ohio, with parents in 1820; d. September 23, 1875, Jay County, Indiana), daughter of Thomas Iiams (b. 1784) and Marcia "Mercie" Walton (b. 1782), and the granddaughter of William Iiams (b. 1745) and Mary Hampton; m. April 5, 1827, Warren County, Ohio, to George Washington Harford (b. October 25, 1805; d. November 23, 1875, Portland, Jay County, Indiana), the son of John Harford and Rachel Compton Harford (George and Sarah moved to Jay County with brother Howard Harford and his wife Rebecca Iiams who was also the sister of Sarah Iiams Harford), and their son George Washington Harford, Jr. (b. August 12, 1845, Jay County, Indiana; d. April 4, 1930, Jay County, Indiana), m. Lucretia Burden (a stepdaughter of John Iiams, b. 1816), and they had eleven children. The eleventh child was a son, James Franklin Harford (b. April 24, 1889, Jay County, Indiana; d. May 12, 1952, Logan County, Ohio), m. November 21, 1911, to Rose Zella Toland (b. April 7, 1894, Auglaize County, Ohio; d. April 30, 1934, Logan County, Ohio), daughter of Henry Martin Toland (b. August 14, 1860, Auglaize County, Ohio; d. August 10, 1837, Logan County, Ohio) and Mary Elizabeth Harford (b. February 15, 1863; d. April 3, 1910, Auglaize County, Ohio), and the granddaughter of John W. Toland (b. 1835, Shelby County, Ohio; d. June 10, 1863, Memphis, Tennessee) and Elizabeth Bechdolt (b. 1835, Auglaize County, Ohio; m. June 22, 1856) and the great-great-granddaughter of Erasmus B. Toland and Sarah A. Johnson. Elizabeth Bechdolt (b. 1835) was the daughter of Samuel Bechdolt and Sophia Fours. Mary Elizabeth Harford (b. 1863) was the daughter of Henry Harford (b. December 7, 1832, Warren County, Ohio; d. May 18, 1894) and Mary Bechdolt (b. December 22, 1838, Auglaize County, Ohio; m. June 24, 1860; d. September 17, 1907, Auglaize County, Ohio) and the granddaughter of John Harford and Rachel Compton. Rose Zella Toland (b. 1894) was also the great-granddaughter of E. B. Toland who m. Mary Iiams (b. 1811). James Franklin Harford (b. 1889) and Rose Zella Toland had eleven children. The eleventh child was Lucretia Mary Harford (b. 1931) who m. 1951, to Robert James Searfoss, and they had six children: 1) Linda Searfoss [(b. August 30, 1954), m. 1972 to Richard Lynn Amey (she compiled this branch of the family tree), and they had four children: a) Jeff Amey (b. 1973); b) Sherry Amey (b. 1975); c) Scott Amey (b. 1978); and d) Christy Amey (b. 1982)]; 2) Cindy Searfoss; 3) Penny Searfoss (m. Mr. Placky); 4) Patricia Searfoss (m. Mr. Fletcher); 5) Nancy Searfoss (m. Mr. Pace); and 6) Sandra Searfoss (m. Mr. Hawkins). (LA)

Samuel Iiams (b. April 20, 1843, Shelby County, Ohio; d. January 29, 1919, Lima, Allen County, Ohio; buried in Woodlawn Cemetery), son of William R. Iiams (b. 1807) and Martha McClure (b. 1814), and the grandson of Thomas Iiams (b. 1784, Pennsylvania); m. August 27, 1865, Shelby County, Ohio (served in Civil War, 19th Regiment, Company G, September 26, 1864, to June 8, 1865; a carpenter), to Mary Ann Abbott (b. June 21, 1847, Pennsylvania; d. March 28, 1906, Lima, Allen County, Ohio), daughter of David Abbott (b. 1826, Pennsylvania) and Percilla Brown (b. December 2, 1829, Pennsylvania; d. March 28, 1906, Lima, Ohio), and their children were:

    1) Harvey Enos (or Enis) Iiames [(b. July 5, 1871, Auglaize County, Ohio; d. July 9, 1947, Lima, Allen County, Ohio), m. April 8, 1894, Grove City, Franklin County, Ohio, to Martha Myrtle "Mertie" Drew (b. December 13, 1873, Lima, Allen County, Ohio; d. July 29, 1956, Lima, Ohio), the daughter of Samuel Smith Drew and Rebecca Snodgrass (she m. 2nd, February 19, 1930, Lima, Ohio, to John Horace Shuster, son of John Shuster and Martha Gilber)];

    2) Martha J. "Murthey" Iiams (b. July 11, 1868, Shelby County, Ohio; d. November 13, 1869, Shelby County, Ohio);

3) Minnie E. Iiams (b. August 15, 1874, Shelby County, Ohio); m. 1st, December 31, 1891, to George Anspach; and m. 2nd, Harry Dinsman;

4) James Arthur Iiams (b. February 9, 1877, Sidney, Shelby County, Ohio; d. April 14, 1967, Lima, Allen County, Ohio; m. Myrtle Mae Wood);

5) Thomas E. Iames [(b. December 16, 1878, Shelby County, Ohio; d. August 22, 1933, in Toledo, Lucas County, Ohio; a brakeman on Baltimore and Ohio Railroad), m. April 15, 1900, Lima, Ohio, to Wilma A. Wright (b. August 6, 1882, Lafayette, Indiana; lived in Cincinnati, Ohio), and they had six children: a) Mildred Iames (b. 1902), b) Frank W. Iames (b. 1906), c) Thomas E. Iames (b. 1909), d) Richard H. Iames (b. 1912), e) Gilbert Earl Iames (b. February 13, 1915), and f) Anna Belle Iames (b. July 1, 1920; d. September 19, 1928, Cincinnati, Ohio)];

6) Frank Merle "Tinker" Iames [(b. January 12, 1885, Auglaize County, Ohio; d. December 1, 1972, Lima, Ohio), m. 1st, before 1905, to Minnie D. Betz (b. May 18, 1889, St. Marys, Mercer County, Ohio; d. December 13, 1918, Lima, Ohio); m. 2nd, September 10, 1919, Lima, Ohio, to Estella May Siferd (b. August 25, 1898, Lima, Ohio; daughter of Noah Siferd and Ethel Riese); and m. 3rd, April 3, 1921, Lima, Ohio, to Mayme Tice Sharrits]; and

7) William R. Iiams (b. January 27, 1887, Kenton, Hardin County, Ohio; m. December 22, 1909, Auglaize County, Ohio, to Hazel Lenora "Lizzie" Upperman). (RWI)

Harvey Enos Iiams (b. July 5, 1871, Auglaize County, Ohio; d. July 9, 1947, Lima, Allen County, Ohio), son of Samuel Iiams (b. 1843) and the grandson of William R. Iiams (b. 1807), m. April 8, 1894, Lima, Allen County, Ohio, to Martha Myrtle "Mertie" Drew (b. December 13, 1873, Lima, Allen County, Ohio; d. July 29, 1956, Lima, Allen County, Ohio), daughter of Samuel Smith Drew (b. August 14, 1822, New York; m. February 7, 1850, Ohio) and Rebecca Snodgrass (b. 1834, Ohio; daughter of Robert Snodgrass, b. 1785, Virginia), and the five children of Harvey Enos Iiams (b. 1871) were:

1) Lila Vesta Iiames [(b. April 19, 1895, Lima, Allen County, Ohio), m. October 17, 1914, Lima, Ohio, to Harry Lovett (b. January 22, 1890, Lima, Ohio), and they had three children: Dick Lovett, Ruth Lovett, and Edward Lovett]; 2) Guy Ralston Iiames, Sr. [(b. February 23, 1897, Lima, Allen County, Ohio, as Guy B. Iiames; d. August 12, 1984, Dayton, Montgomery County, Ohio), m. January 3, 1920, Lima, Allen County, Ohio, to Vida Iantha Matson (b. November 7, 1903, Ada, Hardin County, Ohio; d. July 28, 1986, Troy, Miami County, Ohio, or Montgomery County, Ohio), daughter of Thomas Juriah Matson and Mary Ellen Ault]; 3) Irene Adell Iiames [(b. August 31, 1899, Lima, Allen County, Ohio; d. September 7, 1971, Lima, Allen County, Ohio), m. Clyde R. Custer (b. September 18, 1893; d. February 10, 1950, Lima, Ohio)]; 4) Olive Ruth Iiames [(b. March 25, 1904, Lima, Allen County, Ohio); m. 1st, August 13, 1921, Lima, Ohio, to Clarence E. Dohme (b. October 18, 1900), the son of Frederick Dohme and Elizabeth Miller; m. 2nd, February 6, 1926, Lima, Ohio, to Allan O'dell Ireland (b. August 30, 1901), and her child was Evelyn Ruth Dohme (b. May 14, 1922, Lima, Allen County, Ohio)]; and 5) Esther Blanche Iiames [(b. June 17, 1906, Lima, Allen County, Ohio), m. January 22, 1927, Lima, Ohio, to Paul Myron Kelly (b. July 2, 1898, Creidersville, Shelby County, Ohio), and their son was Harold Kelly (m. Eunice Gail Kelly)]. (RWI)

Guy Ralston Iiames, Sr. (b. February 23, 1897, Lima, Allen County, Ohio; d. August 12, 1984, Dayton, Montgomery County, Ohio), son of Harvey Enos Iiams (b. 1871), m. January 3, 1920, Lima, Allen County, Ohio, to Vida Iantha Matson, the four-foot, ten-inch daughter of Thomas Juriah Matson and Mary Ellen Ault; and their sixteen children were:

1) Juanita Vida Iiames [(b. April 6, 1921, Lima, Allen County, Ohio), m. April 4, 1940, to Robert Graham True (b. August 26, 1922, Dayton, Ohio; son of Edward True and Jennie Purcell)];

2) Helen Irene Iiames (b. April 7, 1922, Fort Wayne, Allen County, Indiana, to Roy Hollon);

3) Betty Ruth Iiames (b. June 11, 1923, Lima, Allen County, Ohio; worked at National Cash Register and at Apex Machine Tools); d. August 3, 1995);

4) Guy Ross (Ralston) "Chick" Iiames, Jr. [(b. June 28, 1924, Lima, Allen County, Ohio, as Guy James Iiames, Jr.), m. December 10, 1952, Dayton, Montgomery County, Ohio, to Roberta Evelyn "Bert" Wright];

5) James Edward Iiames (b. November 27, 1926, Fort Wayne, Allen County, Indiana; m. February 17, 1951, Long Beach, California, to Betty Eileen Rist);

6) Ray Leo Iiames (b. October 26, 1927, Fort Wayne, Allen County, Indiana; m. February 14, 1972, Tiajuana, Mexico, Laura Nell McMullen; lived in Ocean Springs, Mississippi; d. January 6, 1996);

7) Joan Iiames [(b. January 30, 1929, Fort Wayne, Indiana), m. 1st, 1949, to Ray Bailey; m. 2nd, Jess Cowgill; m. 3rd, August 23, 1967, Cairo, Illinois, to Eugene Wilson Young (b. August 4, 1934, Chicago, Illinois), and her four children were: Diana Lynne Bailey (b. 1949, Illinois), Donald Bailey (b. 1950, Illinois), Vicki Bailey (b. 1951, Illinois), and Thomas Bailey (b. December 1953, Illinois)];

8) Bonnie Jean Iiames (b. December 1931, Harlan, Illinois; m. Lee Wayne Farley);

9) Lois Ann Iiames [(b. November 10, 1933, Dayton, Ohio), m. August 16, 1952, Dayton, Ohio, to Bernard Lloyd Bise (b. August 29, 1930, Mongahalia, West Virginia)];

10) Robert Wayne Iames [(b. November 29, 1936, Fort Wayne, Indiana), m. February 16, 1957, Holy Family Church, Dayton, Ohio, to Pauline Marie Bauer];

11) Judith Beth Iiames (b. April 5, 1937, Dayton, Montgomery County) Ohio; d. October 26, 1945);

12) William Lee Iiames [(b. March 4, 1940, Dayton, Montgomery County, Ohio), m. June 4, 1963, Dayton, Ohio, to Peggy Kathryn Lucus (b. December 19, 1941), daughter of Oliver G. Lucus and Margaret Louis of Dayton (they were twice married); m. 3rd, Bonna Lorene "Bonnie" Betz; and m. 4th, Eleanor Louise "Lori" Roush; and their daughter, Jennifer Lynn Iiames (b. June 10, 1964, Dayton, Ohio; m. April 1985, to David Priano, b. August 12, 1965, New York); had two children: Casey Lynn Priano (b. June 6, 1986) and Alexandra Maria Priano (b. August 12, 1965, New York)];

13) Linda Lou Iiames (b. April 30, 1941, Dayton, Ohio; m. March 12, 1961, to Benjamin Francis Clark);

14) Samuel Edward Iiames (b. September 4, 1942, Dayton, Ohio; m. April 14, 1962, to Nancy Rose Moore);

15) Barbara Jean Iiames (b. March 14, 1944, Dayton, Montgomery County, Ohio); and

16) Michael Allen Iiames [(b. March 19, 1949, Dayton, Montgomery County, Ohio), m. July 31, 1971, Sidney, Ohio, to Sondia Elaine Glass (b. March 1, 1947, Sidney, Ohio); lived in Troy, Ohio; had three children: a) Chad

Allen Iiames (b. January 15, 1974, Dayton, Ohio); b) Mark Edward Iiames (b. August 1, 1977, Dayton, Ohio); and c) Seth Michael Iiames (b. January 3, 1986, Dayton, Ohio)]. (RWI)

Juanita Vida Iiames (b. April 6, 1921, Lima, Allen County, Ohio), daughter of Guy Ralston Iiames, Sr. (b. 1897) and Vida Matson; m. April 4, 1940, to Robert Graham True (b. August 26, 1923, Dayton, Montgomery County, Ohio; d. November 13, 1990, Dayton, Ohio; buried in Arlington Cemetery), son of Edward True and Jennie Purcell; and they had three children: 1) Barbara Lou True [(b. February 26, 1942, Dayton, Montgomery County, Ohio), m. 1st, Douglas B. Beionly (b. August 27, 1938, Montgomery County, Ohio), m. 2nd, October 11, 1964, Dayton, Montgomery County, Ohio, to Harold Galbraith (b. November 6, 1922, Danville, Kentucky; d. June 13, 1986, Vandalia, Ohio); m. 3rd, March 26, 1983, Dayton, Ohio, to James William Neubauer (b. August 3, 1941); and m. 4th, May 1993, Indiana, to Howard Everett Johnson (b. November 26, 1927, Indiana), and her two sons were: a) Michael Douglas Galbraith (b. December 2, 1961, Dayton, Ohio; m. September 29, 1984, Dayton, Ohio, to Catherine Virginia Grant, b. April 22, 1969); and b) Adam Galbraith (b. April 22, 1969, Dayton, Ohio)]; 2) Danny True (b. August 3, 1943; d. April 19, 1944, Dayton, Montgomery County, Ohio); and 3) Robert G. True [(b. January 22, 1941, Dayton, Ohio), m. March 15, 1969, to Nina Jean Lighthizer Walker (b. February 6, 1949, Dayton, Ohio); m. 2nd, Vickie Lee Ward (b. December 21, 1947); m. 3rd, to Rose ___; and his two children by second wife were: Danie True and Jason True]. (RWI)

Helen Irene Iiames (b. April 7, 1922, Fort Wayne, Allen County, Indiana), daughter of Guy Ralston Iiames, Sr. (b. 1896) and Vida Iantha Matson; m. September 2, 1950, Richmond, Indiana, to Roy Hollon (b. January 27, 1921, Wolfe County, Kentucky; d. September 22, 1985, Middletown, Ohio), the son of Plummer Hollon and Nicy Blankenship (Roy Hollon was a machinist; member U.S. Army Combat Infantry, World War II, July 21, 1941 to November 9, 1943); and their child: Roy Allen Hollon (b. January 27, 1962, Dayton, Montgomery County, Ohio; m. January 18, 1983, Carlisle, Warren County, Ohio, to Angela Banks, b. January 20, 1963, Hazlegreen, Wolfe County, Kentucky; the daughter of Raymond Edward Banks and Delphia Elizabeth Taulbee), and had two children: 1) Rachel Elizabeth Hollon (b. January 26, 1985, Middletown, Butler County, Ohio); and 2) Rebecca Ann Hollon (b. October 26, 1986, Middletown, Butler County, Ohio). (RWI)

Guy Ross "Chick" Iiames, Jr. (b. June 28, 1924, Lima, Allen County, Ohio), son of Guy Ralston Iiams, Sr. (b. 1897) and Vida Iantha Matson; m. December 10, 1952, Dayton, Montgomery County, Ohio, to Roberta Evelyn "Bert" Wright (b. November 7, 1928, Dayton, Montgomery County, Ohio), the daughter of Robert Lee Wright and Helen Susan Hostetter of Indiana (Guy Ross Iiames, Jr. was born as Guy James Iiames, Jr., but used the commonly used name; compiled the extensive family genealogy in a joint effort with his wife; and published *A History of William Iiams, The Immigrant, His Ancestors and Descendants, The Pioneer* in 1996; and the Hostetler (Hostetter) immigrant was Jacob Hochstetter (b. 1736) as recorded by Reverend Harvey Hostetter, D.D., in 1912), and the great-granddaughter of Susan P. Spencer, and great-great-granddaughter of Rachel Stites and Timothy Kibby (Rachel Stites was the daughter of Benjamin Stites, founder of Columbia, Ohio; and Columbia was later incorporated into Losantisville, now known as Cincinnati; where they had moved from Redstone, Washington County, Pennsylvania); and Guy Ross Iiames, Jr. (b. 1924) and Roberta Evelyn Wright (b. 1928) raised three children: 1) William Lee Iiames [(b. June 23, 1950, Dayton, Montgomery County, Ohio), m. December 18, 1971, Dayton, Montgomery County, Ohio, to Carol Ann Frost (b. February 18,

1951, Dayton, Ohio; divorced; children in California), and they had two children: a) Jacob Zacharia Iiames (b. June 20, 1975, Dayton, Montgomery County, Ohio); and b) Amy Elizabeth Iiames (b. January 15, 1979, Dayton, Montgomery County, Ohio)]; 2) Patricia Lynne "Tish" Iiames [(b. November 27, 1953, Dayton, Montgomery County, Ohio), m. May 4, 1989, Covington, Kentucky, to Timothy Alan Couch (b. October 9, 1964, Olney, Illinois), the son of Larry M. Couch and Carolyn Sue Gaede of Illinois]; and 3) George Marcus Edward Trapp [(b. November 14, 1968, Montgomery County, Ohio), m. to Barbara Ann Long, and their two children were: a) Christopher Anthony Trapp (b. March 2, 1992, Ohio); b) Briana Danielle Trapp (b. November 20, 1994, Ohio)].

Guy Ross Iiames, Jr. (b. 1924) enlisted in U.S. Navy at Cincinnati, Ohio, January 2, 1942, and served until August 1947. In March 1942, he "commissioned" the *U.S.S. Essex* at Norfolk, Carrier Air Group 9, Torpedo Group 9, plank owner, holding rank of Radioman First Class and Gunner on an Avenger torpedo plane. His group took aerial photos for the pending raid on Wake Island on May 6, 1943; flew bombing missions; Rabaul, November 11, 1943, Battle of Tarawa, November 11, 1943; raid on Kwajaleim on December 4, 1943; Truk on February 16 and 17, 1944; raid on Saipan, February 22, 1944; after which the *U.S.S. Essex* returned from the Pacific Ocean to the United States and he was assigned to Air Group 12 on the *U.S.S. Randolph*. He also served on VT-9, VT-12, VPB-119, and VP-ML7; receiving World War II Victory Medal, American Area Campaign Medal; Air Medal (two stars), Commendation Medal, Philippine Liberation Medal; Asiatic Pacific Campaign Medal (five stars), and Good Conduct Medal.

Roberta Evelyn Wright Iiames (b. 1928) and Guy Ross Iiames, Jr. (b. 1924) both worked at National Cash Register (NCR) in Dayton, Ohio. Roberta was Manager of Benefits at NCR, retiring in 1992 after over 35 years of service. While enjoying her work, she recalled the sad times between 1972 and 1978 when NCR was changing over from mechanical cash registers to electronic systems, resulting in the loss of several thousand jobs, and again in 1992 when AT&T "took over" NCR, though she acknowledged that corporate takeovers were a way of life in the 1980s and 1990s. Such takeovers resulted in the upheaval of families and destruction of lifetime goals by otherwise loyal employees.

Roberta (b. 1928), a native of Dayton, Ohio, attended Stivers High School and Sinclair Community College. She readily admitted a dislike of flying, and a reluctance to travel by car "unless I know the driver." Roberta (b. 1928) and her husband (Guy Ross Iiames, Jr., b. 1924) had two children: William (Bill) and Patricia, and also raised a Godson, George Trapp. George Trapp was married, had two children, and attended Miami University. Son William (Bill) attended Wright State University, was Supervisor of Montgomery County Human Services, and lists reading, sailing, canoeing, and kayaking as hobbies. Daughter Patricia (Tish) attended Sinclair Community College, was an avid reader, and was Supervisor at Reynolds and Reynolds Company in Dayton, Ohio.

Roberta (b. 1928) described husband Guy Ross Iiames, Jr. (b. 1924) as "one of the best (machinists) around." Guy Ross (b. 1924) worked at NCR until 1975, before working in a small machine shop. Roberta says she "didn't think he would ever retire; he was 68, thought he could work forever." While Guy Ross (b. 1924) seldom reminisced about anything except humorous experiences of his military tour of service from 1942 to 1947, the *Lima (Ohio) News* published the following article, June 8, 1944:

Navy Buddies Call Former Boy "Indestructible"

"Only 19, but Guy R. Iames has taken everything the Japs have thrown at him and he has come back asking for more.

A former Lima resident, Iames, the son of Mr. and Mrs. G. R. Iames, now living in Dayton, and the grandson of Mrs. Myrtle Shuster (she was formerly married to Harvey Enos), is an aviation radioman, second class, serving with the U.S. Navy.

His mates call him "Indestructible Iames," and they have reasons for dubbing him this.

Flying near the Solomon Islands on a bombing mission, the motor of his Grumman Avenger conked out. The plane hit the water and "Indestructible Iames" was tossed from the bomber, his life jacket only partly fastened. Stunned, he swallowed a lot of the Pacific, but managed to hang on until a destroyer picked him up.

It was the first raid on Truk that his plane got caught in a crossfire between a Jap cruiser and a destroyer. "I don't know how we came out of that," he was quoted recently in a national picture magazine. "The flak seemed to be bursting in our ears, but we got back."

Years hence, when "Indestructible" is bouncing young "indestructible"on his knee, he'll be asked time and time again to tell this one: His plane had taken off for a routine raid on Rabaul. They had been in the air only a few minutes when the crew learned that a heavy formation of Jap planes—120 of them—were headed their direction. Although he doesn't go into detail in his description of the ensuing battle, the fighting Navy man does admit that Jap planes fell into the Pacific like "hailstones on a stormy day!"

If the other close shaves were not enough, the former Lima school boy really had the rabbit's foot in his pocket the day his plane ground-looped on the deck of a carrier and tossed him once again into the sea. His jaw broken, James was patched up after 18 stitches were set into the side of his face. But, like the old river, they kept singing about, "Indestructible" came out of that scrape and kept right on rolling along. He participated in several raids after his recovery and is now back in the states for a "breather." (RWI)

James Edward Iames (b. November 27, 1926, Fort Wayne, Allen County, Indiana), son of Guy Ralston Iiames, Sr. (b. 1897) and Vida Iantha Matson, m. February 17, 1951, Long Beach, California, to Betty Eileen Rist (b. October 28, 1926, Ironton, Lawrence County, Ohio), daughter of Charles Leslie Rist and Mary Leona Barton of Ironton, Lawrence County, Ohio; lived in Albuquerque, New Mexico (James Edward Iames served in U.S. Navy in World War II and in Korea), and they had two children: 1) David Leslie Iiames [(b. February 7, 1947, Ironton, Ohio), m. Dayton, Ohio, to Mary Strack (b. July 1, 1947, Dayton, Ohio), and their three children were: Angelique Gabrelle Iiames, Rachel Marie Iiames, and Rebecca Elizabeth Iiames]; and 2) Debra Leone Iiames [(b. December 6, 1953, Ironton, Ohio), m. December 7, 1973, Dayton, Ohio, to Glen Preston Blackwell (b. February 27, 1951, Richmond, Madison County, Kentucky), son of Beverly Broddus Blackwell and Beatrice Earl Durbin (and a U.S. Marine from 1970-1974); and they had two children: a) Rachel Michelle Blackwell (b. August 31, 1976, Hillsboro, Highland County, Ohio; m. July 2, 1994, to Scott Michael Noland, b. February 5, 1974, the son of Steve and Donna Noland), and b) Michael Glen Blackwell (b. July 30, 1977, Hillsboro, Highland County, Ohio)]. (RWI)

Bonnie Jean Iiames (b. December 1931, Harlan, Allen County, Indiana), the daughter of Guy Ralston Iiames, Sr. (b. 1897) and Vida Iantha Matson; m. October 10, 1953, Dayton, Montgomery County, Ohio, to Lee Wayne Farley, b. July 10, 1933, Cookeville, Putnam County, Tennessee), and they had three children: 1) Karen Lynne Farley [(b. July 12, 1956, Dayton, Montgomery County, Ohio), m. October 9, 1983, Burlington, Ontario, Canada, to Michael James Newhauser (b. February 24, 1960, Windsor, Ontario, Canada), and they had two children: a) Adam Michael Newhouser

(b. January 13, 1987, Canada), and b) Timothy Robert Newhouser (b. January 18, 1989, Canada)]; 2) Janet Elaine Farley [(b. January 12, 1959, Dayton, Montgomery County, Ohio), m. August 4, 1979, Dayton, Ohio, to Charles Alan Hicks (b. October 14, 1956, Crestline, Crawford County, Ohio), and their two children were: a) Gail Elaine Hicks (b. May 1, 1982, Dayton, Montgomery County, Ohio), and b) Charles Alan Hicks, Jr. (b. March 3, 1988, Dayton, Ohio)]; and 3) David Lee Farley (b. June 11, 1966, Dayton, Ohio; served several years in U.S. Armed Forces, then attended Ohio State University). (RWI)

Lois Ann Iiames (b. November 10, 1933, Dayton, Montgomery County, Ohio), daughter of Guy Ralston Iiames (b. 1897) and Vida Iantha Matson; m. August 16, 1952, Dayton, Ohio, to Bernard Lloyd Bise (b. August 29, 1930, Mongahelia, West Virginia), son of Burley Bise and Nellie Pearl Fluharty (Bernard Bise had a career in the U.S. Army), and their two children were: 1) Michael Edward Bise [(b. June 13, 1953, Dayton, Ohio) m. April 8, 1975, Dayton, Ohio, to Carol Ann Witzke (b. February 18, 1957), and their three children were: a) Matthew Edward Bise (b. September 9, 1981, Dayton, Ohio); b) Rachel Ann Bise (b. September 25, 1983, Dayton, Ohio; and c) David Michael Bise (b. February 27, 1987, Dayton, Ohio)]; and 2) Beverly Ann Bise [(b. August 14, 1955, Baumholder Army Base, Germany), m. 1st, September 10, 1977, Springfield, Clark County, Ohio, to Douglas Gene Beverly (b. July 1, 1954, Springfield, Ohio); m. 2nd, June 1991, Arizona, to Roy Terry Smith (b. Sulfur Clicasieu County, Louisiana), and her child was Gelene Michelle Beverly (b. January 4, 1979, Dayton, Montgomery County, Ohio)]. (RWI)

Robert Wayne Iames (b. November 29, 1936, Fort Wayne, Allen County, Indiana), son of Guy Ralston Iiames, Sr. (b. 1897) and Vida Iantha Matson; m. February 16, 1957, Dayton, Montgomery County, Ohio, to Pauline Marie Bauer (b. September 18, 1937, Dayton, Ohio), and they had five children: 1) Robert Wayne "Guy" Iiames, Jr. [(b. November 17, 1957, Washington, D.C.), m. November 12, 1983, Eaglewood, Montgomery County, Ohio, to Karen Laureen Strider (b. February 22, 1956); lived in Dayton; active in theater and voice]; 2) Christopher Paul Joseph Iiames (b. November 27, 1958, Dayton, Ohio); 3) Jerome Alan Paul Iiames [(b. February 7, 1961, Dayton, Ohio), m. 1st, August 30, 1980, West Milton, Miami County, Ohio, to Linda Lou Megakey (b. June 23, 1960); m. 2nd, June 8, 1985, Dayton, Ohio, to Deborah Ann Polzay (b. September 16, 1963) and his son, Zachary Alan Iiames (b. December 4, 1989, Dayton, Ohio)]; 4) Richard Thomas Luke Iiames [(b. September 22, 1962, Dayton, Ohio), m. May 5, 1984, West Milton, Miami County, Ohio, to Lisa Marie Weider (b. December 20, 1963, Troy, Miami County, Ohio)]; and 5) Holly Marie Judith Iiames [(b. December 29, 1963, Dayton, Ohio), m. June 20, 1987, West Milton, Ohio, to Kenneth Albert Adams (b. Dayton, Ohio), and their daughter was Michelle Marie Adams (b. October 14, 1988, Dayton, Ohio)]. (RWI)

Linda Lou Iiames (b. April 30, 1941, Dayton, Montgomery County, Ohio), daughter of Guy Ralston Iiames, Sr. (b. 1897) and Vida Iantha Matson; m. March 12, 1961, Indiana, to Benjamin Francis Clark (b. January 23, 1936, Piqua, Miami County, Ohio), the son of Harold William Clark and Frances Lillian Erwin; and their three children were: 1) Teresa Ann Clark [(b. August 20, 1961, Dayton, Ohio), m. October 21, 1989, Trotwood, Montgomery County, Ohio, to Clarence Denny Hunter (b. July 30, 1955, Manchester, Clay County, Kentucky), the son of Lucian Hunter and Lucy May Collins; and their four children were: a) Craig Denny Hunter (b. August 20, 1981, Dayton, Ohio); b) Jason Scott Hunter (b. August 6, 1983, Dayton, Ohio); c) Angela Nicole Hunter (b. May 10, 1986, Fort Pierce, Kentucky); and d) Kyle Matthew Hunter (b. March 12, 1993, Manchester, Kentucky)]; 2) Donald Clark (b. April 30, 1963, Dayton, Ohio); and 3) Robin Clark [(b. August 27, 1964, Dayton, Ohio);

m. 1st, February 14, 1985, Kettering, Ohio, to Steve Fritz (b. August 25, 1953), son of Joseph Fritz and Elaine Bellar; m. 2nd, November 1, 1990, Dayton, Ohio, to Chester Richard Comer, Jr. (b. August 29, 1949, Dayton, Ohio), son of Chester Richard Comer, Sr. and Berneda Mae Whalen; and their son was Andrew Joseph Comer (b. May 6, 1987, Dayton, Ohio)]. (RWI)

Samuel Edward Iiames (b. September 4, 1942, Dayton, Montgomery County, Ohio), son of Guy Ralston Iiames, Sr. (b. 1897) and Vida Ianda Matson; m. April 14, 1962, in Michigan, to Nancy ___ (b. November 24, 1943, Detroit, Michigan). Samuel (b. 1942) served as a staff sergeant in the United States Air Force from 1960-1968, and later rose to the rank of Lieutenant Colonel in the United States Air Force National Guard before retiring in Tucson, Arizona, in 1994; their three children were: 1) Teresa Marie Iiames [(b. September 15, 1963, Detroit, Michigan), m. April 8, 1989, Tucson, Pima County, Arizona, to Christopher R. Marcus (b. May 26, 1966, Aurora, Arapahoe County, Colorado), and their son was Kevin Marcus (b. August 30, 1991, Arizona)]; 2) Gregory Allen Iiames [(b. January 15, 1966, Detroit, Michigan), m. March 30, 1993, Glenoace, Arizona, to Tonya Sue Shank (b. June 18, 1968, Dayton, Ohio)]; and 3) Steven Edward Iiames (b. August 21, 1969, Detroit, Michigan). (RWI)

Barbara Jean Iiames (b. March 14, 1944, Dayton, Ohio), daughter of Guy Ralston Iiames, Sr. (b. 1897) and Vida Ianda Matson, m. 1st, 1962, to Robert Eugene Surface (b. July 26, 1941, Hillsboro, Ohio); m. 2nd, October 16, 1975, Pascagoula, Jackson County, Mississippi, to Stanley Lewis Woodward (b. March 16, 1952, Poplarville, Pear River County, Mississippi), and they had two children: 1) Kimberly Ann Surface [(b. April 8, 1963, Dayton, Ohio), m. James Goresch, and they had three children: a) Jackie Goresch (b. July 27, 1986, Dayton, Ohio); b) Robbie Goresch (b. March 15, 1988, Dayton, Ohio); and c) Katie Goresch (b. June 15, 1991, Dayton, Ohio)]; and 2) Pamela Sue Surface [(b. June 10, 1964, Dayton, Montgomery County, Ohio), m. Douglas Earl Robinson (b. July 24, 1963, Troy, Miami County, Ohio), and they had two children: a) Heather Nicole Robinson (b. May 3, 1985, and b) Lindsey Marie Mandelik (b. June 14, 1991)]. (RWI)

Irene Adell Iiames (b. March 25, 1904, Lima, Allen County, Ohio), daughter of Harvey Enos Iiams (b. 1871) and Martha Myrtle Drew (b. 1873), m. 1st, Lima, Ohio, to Clarence E. Dohme (b. October 18, 1900), the son of Frederick Dohme and Elizabeth Miller; m. 2nd, February 6, 1926, Lima, Ohio, to Allen O'dell Ireland (b. August 30, 1901), and they had thirteen children: 1) Helen Irene Custer [(b. January 18, 1917), m. Edwin Charles Hullinger, Sr., and they had three children: a) Charles E. Hullinger, Jr. (b. June 20, 1938), m. 1st, 1968, Madlyn ___; m. 2nd, Bonita Louise ___; and m. 3rd, Linda J. Borchers Smith); b) Larry Hullinger; and c) Donald Hullinger]; 2) Paul Eugene Custer [(b. February 10, 1919; d. May 31, 1993, Lima, Allen County, Ohio), m. Mary E. Routson]; 3) William Roland Custer [(b. March 27,1920, Lima, Ohio), m. May 14, 1943, Blackstone, Virginia, to Mary Matson (b. March 16, 1923, Lima, Ohio), daughter of William Matson and Grace M. Rockwell, and they had three children: a) David Laurel Custer (b. July 5, 1946, Lima, Ohio; m. May 27, 1966, Lima, Ohio, to Sandra Baker, b. January 3, 1946, to James Price Morris; m. 2nd, September 8, 1971, Lima, Ohio, to Gilbert Russell Michael, and her three children were: Donna Diane Morris, b. September 24, 1966, Lima, Ohio; James Price Morris, b. October 10, 1967, Lima, Ohio; and Crystal Jolene Michael, b. September 22, 1978, Lima, Ohio); and c) Dale Eugene Custer (d. October 29, 1950, Lima, Ohio; age 1 day)]; 4) Donald LeRoy Custer (b. August 1, 1923, Lima, Ohio; d. July 1, 1944, over Florence, Italy, during World War II); 5) Clyde Richard Custer (b. August 31, 1924, Lima, Ohio; d. September 15, 1944, on Guam during World War

II); 6) Mary Elizabeth Custer (b. January 26, 1926, Lima, Ohio); 7) May Custer (b. October 21, 1927, Lima, Ohio; d. same date); 8) Alice Marie Custer (b. July 1, 1929, Lima, Ohio; m. Frederick ___; four children: Sally, John, Carol, and Paula); 9) Dorothy Jeanne Custer [(b. August 10, 1931, Lima, Ohio), m. June 16, 1951, Lima, Ohio, to Carl Reed (b. September 23, 1926), the son of Melvin Earl Reed and Elnora McGinnis; and they had four children: a) Pamela Reed; b) Timothy Reed; c) Cindy Reed; and d) Jeff Reed]; 10) Virginia Eileen Custer [(b. October 6, 1935, Lima, Ohio), m. August 31, 1955, Lima, Ohio, to Richard Hartzog (b. July 9, 1932), the son of Norman Hartzog and Vivian Wilson; and their son was Dennis Hartzog (b. November 20, 1957, Lima, Ohio; m. September 30, 1977, Lima, Ohio, to Catherine Dianne Hubbard (b. June 5, 1959, Granite City, Illinois), daughter of James Edwards Hubbard and Pearl Vincent]; 11) Harold Oliver Custer [(b. January 17, 1973, Lima, Ohio), m. Marlene Hicks, and their two children were: Cheryl Custer and Gary Custer]; 12) Barbara Ann Custer [(b. June 6, 1938, Lima, Ohio), m. Ray Douglas Barnes, and their two children were: Lawrence Barnes and Christine Barnes]; and 13) Margaret Louise Custer [(b. April 22, 1942, Lima, Ohio), m. Gale Everett Kline, and their five children were: a) Valerie Kline; b) James Kline; c) Rebecca Kline (b. March 20, 1963); d) Susan Kline; and e) Joan Kline]. (RWI, sic)

Paul Eugene Custer (b. February 10, 1919), son of Irene Adell Iiames (b. 1904), m. Mary E. Routson, and they had eleven children: 1) Robert Eugene Custer [(b. October 24, 1942), m. 1st, April 9, 1959, to Neta Mae Thompson, daughter of Walter Thompson and Pauline Shaw; m. 2nd, July 19, 1969, to Karen J. Altstraetter, daughter of Eldon J. Altstaetter and Marilyn J. Piper; and they had four children: a) Robert Alan Custer (b. August 20, 1960); b) Rhonda Custer (b. May 20, 1962); c) Pauline Custer (b. May 13, 1966); and d) Victoria Custer (b. February 2, 1968)] 2) Ronald Custer (no date); 3) Paul Leroy Custer, Jr. (b. 1948); 4) Catherine Irene Custer [(b. October 4, 1951), m. 1971, Lima, Ohio, to Larry Dale Snider (b. December 10, 1951, Lima, Ohio)]; 5) Raymond Clyde Custer [(b. September 5, 1953, m. June 12, 1976, Lima, Ohio, to Sheila Ann Fruek (b. November 17, 1958, Lima, Ohio)]; 6) Kenneth Alan Custer [(b. June 22, 1955), m. April 20, 1974, Lima, Ohio, to Ellen Louise Stoody (b. December 16, 1964, Bluffton, Allen County, Ohio), daughter of William Stoody and Velma McKanna]; 7) Paula Rae Custer [(b. July 30, 1956), m. July 7, 1979, Lima, Ohio, to Forest Junior Hale (b. November 19, 1955, Hastings, Michigan), son of Forest Hale and Charlene Campbell]; 8) Russell Dean Custer (b. November 28, 1959); 9) Walter Custer (b. November 1, 1963); 10) Dianne Louise Custer (b. October 26, 1948); and 11) Betty Jo Satterfield Custer (b. May 29, 1947, Lima, Ohio). (RWI)

Minnie E. Iiams (b. August 15, 1874, Shelby County, Ohio), daughter of Samuel Iiams (b. 1843); m. 1st, December 3, 1891, Lima, Allen County, Ohio, to George Anspach; m. 2nd, March 2, 1900, Lima, Ohio, to Harry Disman (b. August 2, 1890, Lima, Ohio; d. June 1958, Lima, Ohio), son of John Dinsman and Sarah Albertson; and their six children were: 1) Harry E. Anspach [(b. May 10, 1892, Lima, Ohio; his son was James Anspach (b. February 1920, Allen County, Ohio)]; 2) Ralph J. Anspach (b. January 21, 1893, Lima, Ohio); 3) Jay R. Anspach (b. 1895); 4) Donald H. Anspach (b. June 12, 1913); 5) James E. Anspach (b. February 22, 1915); and 6) Betty H. Anspach (b. December 30, 1920). (RWI)

James Arthur Iiams (b. February 9, 1877, Sidney, Shelby County, Ohio; d. April 14, 1967, Lima, Allen County, Ohio; buried in Memorial Park Cemetery in Lima), son of Samuel Iiams (b. 1843); and m. April 14, 1906, Lima, Ohio, to Myrtle Mae Wood (b. January 11, 1887, Allen County, Ohio; d. February 11, 1966, Lima, Ohio), daughter of Theodore Wood and Mary Stoner; and they had three children: 1)

Howard Theodore Iiams [(b. October 11, 1907, Lima, Allen County, Ohio), m. December 23, 1928, Lima, Ohio, to Edith Dempster (b. June 21, 1909, Lima, Ohio), daughter of Edmund G. Dempster and Lelia Melville Maxwell; and their daughter, Norma Jean Iiames (b. June 23, 1931, Lima, Ohio; m. June 2, 1952, Lima, Ohio, to Albert James Kihm, b. June 12, 1931, Lorain, Lorain County, Ohio) had a son Gregory Howard Kihm (b. April 18, 1963, Lima, Ohio)]; 2) Raymond Merle Iiames [(b. February 1, 1911, Lima, Ohio; d. January 3, 1981, Lima, Ohio; buried in Memorial Park Cemetery), m. May 16, 1936, Lima, Ohio, to Emerald Geraldine Critchfield (b. November 13, 1916, Lima, Ohio), and they had three children: a) Sharon Rae Iiames (b. July 18, 1938, Lima, Ohio), m. September 16, 1959, Lima, Ohio, to Emil Ralph White (b. December 17, 1937, Wapakoneta, Auglaize County, Ohio) and they had two children: 1[1]) Michael Scott White (b. October 21, 1960, Lima, Ohio; m. December 4, 1988, to Kelly Sarno, b. July 23, 1966, Lima, Ohio; and they had two children: Cory White, b. October 4, 1988; and Emily White, (b. September 16, 1991); and 2[1]) Steven Craig White (b. September 20, 1963, Lima, Ohio); and had child Samone Ellse White, b. July 13, 1988); b) Linda Sue Iiames (b. July 6, 1940, Lima, Ohio); m. 1st, April 1, 1959, to David Lester Becker; m. 2nd, March 20, 1964, Lima, Ohio, to Ronald Gene Staley (b. July 13, 1939, Allen County, Ohio), and she had four children: 1[1]) Wayne David Becker (b. February 11, 1960, Lima, Ohio), m. June 23, 1979, Findlay, Hancock County, Ohio, to Cheri Lynn Eichman (b. March 28, 1961), and they had two children: Drew Michael Becker, (b. August 18, 1988); and Syndi Nicole Becker, (b. April 17, 1991); 2[1]) Timothy Gene Staley (b. October 1, 1964; m. Columbus Grove, Putnam County, Ohio, to Gretchen Sue Fortman, b. June 7, 1966); 3[1]) Daniel Ray Staley, (b. August 29, 1968, Lima, Ohio; m. August 1, 1992, North Baltimore, Wood County, Ohio, to Rhonda Sue Nigh, b. March 20, 1968); and they had two children: Bridgette Gabriel Nigh, b. July 4, 1989; and Jerid Ray Staley, b. March 8, 1992); and 4[1]) Gregory Lynn Staley (b. August 29, 1968, a twin); c) James William Iiames (b. March 22, 1942, Lima, Ohio), m. October 28, 1966, Lima, Ohio, to Iva Joyce Plaugher (b. July 27, 1943, Lima, Ohio), and they had two children: 1[1]) Jeffrey Alan Iiames (b. January 30, 1969, Lima, Ohio; m. December 4, 1993, Lima, Ohio, to Mary Christine Steiner, b. October 11, 1965); and 2[1]) John William Iiames (b. October 8, 1971)]; and 3) Ruth May Iiames [(b. April 12, 1916, Lima, Ohio), m. April 9, 1939, Lima, Ohio, to Donald Eugene Brown (b. May 18, 1918)]. (RWI)

Ruth May Iiames (b. April 12, 1916, Lima, Ohio), daughter of James Arthur Iiames (b. 1877), m. April 9, 1939, Lima, Ohio, to Donald Eugene Brown (served in U.S. Navy in Pacific Theater in World War II; moved to Florida), and they had four children: 1) Kathleen Ann Brown [(b. April 25, 1940, Lima, Allen County, Ohio), m. November 23, 1958, Lima, Ohio, to Eugene Adair (b. January 2, 1939, Continental, Putnam County, Ohio), and they had four children: a) Laurie Lyn Adair (b. October 9, 1959, Lima, Ohio; m. October 18, 1980, Bluffton, Ohio, to Ronald Wayne Matter, b. September 12, 1958; and they had two children: Ryan Wayne Matter, b. July 13, 1984; and Jaclyn Rae Matter, b. July 21, 1987); b) Alison Ann Adair (b. October 6, 1970, Lima, Ohio; m. April 7, 1979, Memphis, Tennessee, to Curtis Bradford Simpson, b. March 5, 1959; and they had two daughters: Kathleen Ann Simpson, b. August 2, 1982; and Meghan Michelle Simpson, b. March 27, 1984); c) Scott Douglas Adair (b. July 21, 1966, Findlay, Hancock County, Ohio; m. February 8, 1992, Lancaster, Fairfield County, Ohio, to Tamara Kay May, b. November 3, 1967; and their son was Joshua Matthew Adair, b. February 23, 1992; d. February 23, 1992); and d) Christopher Allen Adair (b. November 7, 1968, Hamilton, Butler County, Ohio; m. February 10, 1990, Bluffton, Ohio, to Michelle Ann Haines, b. January 24, 1969; and their son was Brandon Christopher Adair, b. July 22, 1993)]; 2) Donald E. Brown II [(b.

199

July 22, 1944, Lima, Ohio), m. August 3, 1973, Webb Air Force Base, Big Spring, Texas, to Jane Ann Cochran (b. December 17, 1946, Lima, Ohio); he had attended Bluffton College and Ohio State University; retired from U.S. Air Force as Lieutenant Colonel where he was Vice Deputy Director for Space Operations, and decorations included Mentorius Service Medal, Air Force Commendation Medal, and Berlin Occupation Medal), and their three children were: a) Donald Eugene Brown III (b. August 4, 1974, Wichita Falls, Texas); b) Judy Ann Brown (b. August 15, 1976; d. October 5, 1977); and c) William Arthur Brown (b. April 3, 1979, U.S. Air Force Hospital, Berlin, Germany)]; 3) Nancy Louise Brown [(b. May 15, 1946, Lima, Ohio), m. April 3, 1966, Beaverdam, Allen County, Ohio, to Michael Diller (b. June 17, 1946, Bluffton, Ohio), and their four children were: a) Alicia Ann Diller (b. October 4, 1968); b) Paul Joshua Diller (b. December 29, 1972); c) Benjamin James Diller (b. July 22, 1975); and d) Rachel Louise Diller (b. December 30, 1971)]; and 4) Richard Michael Brown (b. April 10, 1949, Lima, Ohio). (RWI)

Frank Merle "Tinker" Iiams (b. January 12, 1885, Auglaize County, Ohio; d. December 1, 1972, Lima, Ohio), son of Samuel Iiams (b. 1845); m. 1st, 1904, to Minnie D. Betz (b. May 18, 1889, St. Marys, Mercer County, Ohio; d. December 13, 1918, Lima, Ohio), m. 2nd, Lima, Ohio, September 10, 1919, to Estella May Siferd (b. August 25, 1898, Lima, Ohio), daughter of Noah Siferd and Ethel Riese; m. 3rd, April 3, 1921, Lima, Ohio, to Mayme Tice Sherrits (b. July 5, 1893; d. August 25, 1993), daughter of Harry Sharrits and Eva Brannon; and he had two children: 1) Arthur Ray Iiams (b. January 3, 1905, Lima, Ohio; d. June 3, 1905, Lima, Allen County, Ohio); and 2) Kenneth Milton Iiams [(b. July 7, 1907, Lima, Ohio; d. over China, October 4, 1944, in World War II); m. 1925, Dayton, Ohio, to Edna Rae Frock, and they had four children: Don Iiams, Jackie Lamar Iiams (b. August 2, 1927), Franklin Robert Iiams (b. March 31, 1935) and Terry Joseph Iiams (b. June 5, 1944)]. (RWI)

William R. Iiams (b. January 27, 1887, Kenton, Hardin County, Ohio; d. March 20, 1958, Lima, Ohio), son of Samuel Iiams (b. 1845), m. 1st, December 22, 1909, Auglaize County, Ohio, to Hazel Lenora "Lizzie" Upperman (b. June 20, 1890, St. Marys, Mercer County, Ohio; d. August 28, 1919, Lima, Ohio), daughter of Charles Upperman and Elizabeth Beaty; m. 2nd, August 14, 1935, Lima, Ohio, to Dorothy Lucinda Tarr (b. May 2, 1893, Oil City, Venengo County, Pennsylvania), daughter of Levi Fellers and Eva Ray; and they had three children: 1) William Harold Iiams [b. January 21, 1911, Middlepoint, Van Wert County, Ohio; d. January 26, 1911, Middlepoint, Ohio]; 2) Robert E. Iiams [b. May 28, 1912, Middlepoint, Van Wert County, Ohio), m. 1st, June 10, 1935, Lima, Ohio, to Romain Heite (b. August 20, 1914, Fort Wayne, Allen County, Indiana), daughter of R. M. Heite and Oral McCarty; m. 2nd, June 12, 1942, to Dorothy Henderson (b. September 20, 1918, Beaver, Oklahoma)]; and 3) Valerie Iiams Binkley (b. 1915). (RWI)

REFERENCES

- (HWN) Harry Wright Newman; personal works and correspondence.

- (JC) Reverend Fred Cochran, Greene County, Pennsylvania; personal works.

- (HL) Howard L. Leckey, Waynesburg, Pennsylvania; personal works.

- (PI) Pauline Imes, New Athens, Illinois; personal communication.

- (JH) James Haughland, Waynesburg, Greene County, Pennsylvania.

- (RWI) Roberta W. Iiames and Guy R. Iiames, Sesame Street, Springboro, Ohio; personal communication.

- (JBM) James B. Meighen, author and genealogist, western Pennsylvania.

- (RI) Robert Franklin Iams, Wooster, Ohio; personal research.

- (MJIG) Mildred Jean Barr Iams Griffin, Canton, Ohio; correspondent.

- (RFI) Robert Franklin Iams, Wooster, Ohio.

- (GR) Guy Ross Iiames, Springboro, Ohio; personal research.

- (EFB) Ervin F. Bickley, Jr., New Canaan, Connecticut; personal research.

- (MI) Mildred Jean Barr Iams-Griffen; personal communication.

- (BTL) Barbara J. Taylor Locker; personal contribution and research.

- (CG) Cochetta Geis, Redkey, Indiana; personal communication.

- (TD) Tim Duke, Dayton, Ohio; personal investigation.

- (GIC) Geraldine Elizabeth Iams Cheslick, Moundsville, West Virginia; personal work.

- (Harvey) Harvey's History of Washington County, Pennsylvania.

- (JI) Jennifer Iams, Beaverton, Oregon; personal communication.

- (KK) J. F. Woodrow and L. W. Burke: *Our Kith and Kin*, Denison New Press, Granville, Ohio.

- (GG) Frances Grimes Sitterwood: *The Graham-Grimes Genealogy with Cognate Branches, 1756-1926*, Bloomington, Illinois, 1926.

- (BG) Bates' *History of Greene County, Pennsylvania*.

- (RM) Ruth Iams McCord, Washington, Pennsylvania; personal communication.

- (CEB) Charles Everett Buckingham, Casa Grande, Arizona; personal communication.

- (WI) William and Ruby Iams, St. Matthews, South Carolina; personal work.

- (JNI) John E. Iams, Paris, Pennsylvania; personal contribution.

- (SIH) Sarah "Sallie" Iams Hoagland, Ruten, Pennsylvania; personal contribution.

- (BM) Betty McCord, Washington, Pennsylvania; personal communication.

- (WHI) William Henry "Bob" Iams, Canton, Ohio; contributor.

- (SI) Stanley Iams, Kansas City, Missouri; personal communication.

- (DLI) Dorothy Lorraine McClintock Iams, Wooster, Ohio; personal communication.

- (LA) Linda Amey; personal research and communication.

- (EB) Eileen Bane, western Pennsylvania; personal research.

- (JIH) Joy Iams Hannon, Zanesville, Ohio; personal communication.

- (BL) Barbara Locker; personal family research contribution.

- (MA) Martha Koenig Anspaugh, Wapakoneta, Ohio; personal research.

— *Chapter 6* —

Richard Iiams, Sr.

(b. 1745, Maryland; d. 1834, Pennsylvania)

Richard Iiams (b. ca1745), the son of John Iiams (b. 1720), married Eleanor (or Elizabeth) Pottenger, and they had the following children: Thomas, Richard, John, William, Rezin, Otho, Bazil, Rachel, and Eli. The offspring were born in Maryland and Pennsylvania, but there was a brisk movement westward to Ohio, and then to Indiana, Illinois, Missouri, Kansas, Nebraska, Wyoming, Minnesota, Iowa, Wisconsin, Utah, Texas, Oklahoma, West Virginia, Oregon, Washington, California, and Arizona.

Richard Iiams, Sr. (b. 1745, 1748, or 1749, on Birmingham Plantation, Anne Arundel County, Maryland; d. 1834, Greene County, Pennsylvania), son of John Iiams (or Jeames), (b. ca1720), and grandson of Richard Iiams (b. 1673); m. 1777 or May 18, 1778, to Eleanor or Elizabeth Pottenger at Redstone, Washington County, Pennsylvania (or to Eleanor Jones or Mary ____). Eleanor Pottenger (b. 1755, Prince Georges County, Maryland; d. 1831 or 1834, Greene County, Pennsylvania) was the daughter of Robert Pottenger and Elizabeth Willett. They settled near Nineveh, Pennsylvania; lived at Bates Fork, Pennsylvania; died on a farm later owned by Elias Cary. Richard Iams (b. ca1745) moved to Washington County (then Upper Frederick County), Maryland, before 1776; and on May 18, 1778, deeded his portion of the family plantation New Birmingham to his brother Thomas Iiams. As the story goes, Thomas Iiams stuck the deed in his billfold and carried it around with him until it became lost. It was finally recorded on February 17, 1797, with the help of the court and Richard Iiams (b. ca1745), when Richard Iiams was recorded as living at Redstone, Washington County, Pennsylvania. In March 1778, Richard Iiams (b. 1745) pledged the Oath of Allegiance to the State of Maryland while residing in Washington County, Maryland, a place he remained for the 1790 Federal Census. He moved to western Pennsylvania with several kinsmen and settled in what became Greene County in 1796. The 1830 Census of Greene County, Pennsylvania, listed Richard Iams, Sr., as being between ages 80 and 90; with his wife between ages 70 and 79. He, his wife, and several children are buried at Bates Fork, Greene County, Pennsylvania. EFB considered Redstone to be in Maryland.

The children of Richard Iiams (b. 1745) were: 1) Thomas Iiams [(b. 1780 or 1783, Washington County, Maryland; d. March 1843), m. 1807, Greene County, Pennsylvania, to Mary "Polly" Smith (b. 1781 or 1787; d. after 1850), daughter of Dennis Smith and Elizabeth Rook (or Zook)]; 2) Richard Iiams, Jr. [(b. 1781 or 1787, Washington County, Maryland; d. February 20, 1829, Greene County, Pennsylvania); m. 1805, Greene County, to Mary Shidler (b. 1786; d. February 15, 1868, Indiana). He served as a Private in Captain John Brown's Company, Ferre's Rifles, First Regiment of Pennsylvania militia from March to September, and October to December 12, 1812; lived in Greene County, Pennsylvania. Will of Richard Iiams, Jr., farmer, Morris Township, Greene County, Pennsylvania (Vol. 1, p. 353, No. 618), written December 21, 1828, and probated February 24, 1829, left all personal property to wife Mary Imes, with one thousand dollars to be divided among children as they became of age]; 3) John Iiams [(b. 1778, 1780, or 1785, Washington County, Maryland], m. 1805 to Ruth Baker or Barker (b. 1787; d. November 2, 1845), moved to Athens County, Ohio]; 4) William Iams [(b. 1786, Washington County, Maryland; d. 1845), m. 1810 to Eleanor Hall or Charity (?) Ryan]; 5) Rezin (or Reason, or Resin) Iiams [b. 1789 or 1790, Washington County, Maryland; d. February 19, 1860, Greene County, Pennsylvania), m. 1st, 1811, Phoebe Clark (b. 1787; d. January 12, 1815; or November 2, 1845; m. 2nd, Nancy McClung (b. September 23, 1804; d. January or July 9, 1876)]; 6) Otho Iiams [(b. 1791, Greene County, Pennsylvania; or Washington County, Maryland; d. April 27, 1875, Greene County, Pennsylvania), m. 1813 to Nancy Cole (b. 1796)]; 7) Basel (or Bazel, or Bazil) Iams (b. 1795, Morris Township, Greene County, Pennsylvania; d. 1821; "mentally challenged"); 8) Rachel Iiams (b. 1800, Morris Township, Greene County, Pennsylvania; m. Benjamin Spruance); and 9) Eli Iiams [(b. February or March 4, 1797 or 1799, Morris Township, Greene County, Pennsylvania; d. February 6, 1875); m. September 12, 1820, to Catharine Crawford (b. February 13, 1791; d. August 30, 1872, Marietta, Ohio); or to Phoebe Heckathorn (EFB); and other Eli Iiams birth dates include April 31, 1798 (CRI), and May 15, 1799,Washington County, Maryland (RI)]. (CRI, RI, PI, EFB, LIH, HWN, MI, REI).

John Iiams (b. 1780, Maryland), son of Richard Iiams (b. 1748), m. Ruth Barker (or Bacher), moved to Athens, Ohio, 1810 (EFB), and their two children were: 1) William Iams (went to New Orleans); and 2) Richard Iiams [(b. 1811, Virginia), m. Jane S. Holmes (b. 1807, Virginia), and they had four children: a) William Iams (single); b) John A. Iams (m. Neva Crossen, and their daughter, Eva Iams, m. Mr. Grant and moved to Kansas); c) Nancy Iams (m. Wallace Marse, and their son was Bert Marse); and d) James Q. Iams (b. 1839, Ohio; m. Frances M. Larrey, b. 1851, New York), and they had three sons: 1[1]) Richard P. Iiams (b. 1879, Ohio; m. Clara Baird; lived in Athens, Ohio; had two sons: Wilbur B. Iams and Richard Iams); 2[1]) LeRoy L. Iams (b. 1887, Ohio; m. Farest Weinerman; lived Denver, Colorado; three children: James H. Iams, Roger S. Iams, and Mary Lou Iams); and 3[1]) Robert H. or F. Iams (single; Pennsylvania Railroad telegraph operator)] (FFB). The 1850 Federal Census, Dover Township, Athens County, Ohio, listed: Hannah Iams (age 80, b. New Jersey), who lived with the Isaac Stubblefield family; and also: Benjamin Ornes or Arms (age 32, b. Ohio); Ruth Orms (age 40, b. Ohio), and Martha Orms (age 1, b. Ohio). The 1880 Census of Waterloo Township, Athens, County, Ohio, listed Richard Imes (age 68, b. Virginia), Jane S. Imes (age 73, b. Virginia), James Q. Imes (age 41, b. Ohio), Frances M. Imes (age 29, b. New York, daughter-in-law), Leroy Imes (age 3, b. Ohio, grandson), Rupert F. Imes (age 2, b. Ohio, grandson), and Richard P. Imes (age 4 months, b. Ohio, grandson).

Richard Iams (b. 1751), (?) son of Thomas Iiams (b. 1708), brother of John Iiams (b. 1750) and Thomas Iiams (b. 1754), m. Eleanor Jones and had son Richard Iiams (b. 1781); lived first in Frederick County, Maryland, then Bates Fork in Greene County, Pennsylvania; a millwright; known for holding military muster in the mill on Saturday nights; buried Bates Fork Cemetery; m. Elizabeth or Eleanor Pottenger and had eight children (RI, HWN, GR): 1) Thomas Iiams [(b. 1783; d. 1843, Greene County), m. 1807, to Mary Smith (b. 1787), daughter of Dennis Smith and Elizabeth Zook); and they had eight children: a) Dennis Iams (b. June 2, 1808; d. January 7, 1888; m. July 6, 1831, to Matilda Huffman, b. September 26, 1814; d. October 14, 1887, buried at Sycamore, Greene County, Pennsylvania); b) Elizabeth Iams (b.1810; m. George Smith); c) Catherine Iams (b. 1812); d) Mary Iams (b. January 1, 1814; d. April 28, 1904; m. George Huffman, b. March 20, 1810; d. May 26, 1890); e) Hannah

Iams (b. 1816); f) Rachel Iams (b. 1818; d. December 7, 1858; m. Joseph or Ben Miller); g) Charity Iams (b. 1823) and h) Thomas Iams (b. 1825; m. 1st, Lydia ____; m. 2nd, Phoebe ____)]; 2) Richard Iams (b. 1829, Greene County, Pennsylvania; m. Mary Shidler); 3) Otho Iams [(b. 1791; d. April 27, 1815 or 1825); m. 1813 to Nancy Cole (b. 1796)]; 4) Rezin Iams [(b. 1789 or 1791; d. February 10 or 19, 1860, Bates Fork, Greene County, Pennsylvania); m. 1811 to Phoebe Clark (d. June 2, 1845, Bates Fork), daughter of Isaac Clark and Delilah French]; 5) John Iiams [(b. 1809; d. 1905), m. 1805 to Ruth Barker or Baker; lived in Athens County, Ohio]; 6) William Iiams (b. 1827, moved to Indiana; m. Charity ____); 7) Bazil Iiams (b. 1795; single); and 8) Eli Iiams [(m. Phoebe Heckathorne; in 1870, Montgomery County, Ohio, census lists: Eli Iams (age 71, b. Pennsylvania), Phoebe Iiams (age 66, b. Pennsylvania); and three children]. (PI, ER, RI).

Dennis Iams (b. June 2, 1808; d. January 7, 1888), m. July 6, 1831, to Matilda Huffman (b. September 26, 1814; d. October 14, 1887; buried in Sycamore, Greene County, Pennsylvania), and they had nine children: 1) Thomas Iams (b. July 8, 1833); 2) Sarah Iams (b. June 4, 1837; d. March 8, 1899); 3) Benjamin Iams (b. September 4, 1839); 4) Mary Iams (b. April 24, 1842); 5) Elizabeth Iams (b. January 14, 1846; d. March 19, 1848); 6) Dennis Iams (b. May 13, 1848); 7) Lydia Iams [(b. May 13, 1850; d. December 16, 1940); m. John Hill Smith, son of Jacob Smith (b. February 25, 1811; d. April 21, 1887; m. October 9, 1834) and Nancy Hill (b. January 28, 1817; d. May 1, 1889); grandson of Peter Smith (b. February 14,1774; d. May 6, 1848) and Priscilla Cooper (b. 1785; d. July 4, 1840); great-grandson of Dennis Smith (b. November 15, 1738, Germany; d. August 29, 1829, Greene County, Pennsylvania) and Elizabeth Zook (b. 1756; d. August 19, 1845); and the daughter of Lydia Iams (b. 1869), Bessie Leona Smith (b. January 15, 1891, Ninevah, Greene County, Pennsylvania; d. December 1, 1984, Wheeling, West Virginia), m. Charles M. Swart, and they had two children: Martha Smith Swart (m. Warren E. Gregg; lived Myrtle Beach, South Carolina), and Charles M. Swart, Jr. (d. 1983), member of DAR]; 8) Amanda Iams (b. May 24, 1854); and 9) Priscilla Iams (b. October 15, 1859).

William Iiams (b. 1786, Washington County, Maryland; d. 1845, Columbiana County, Ohio), the son of Richard Iiams (b. 1745), m. 1810 in Pennsylvania, to Eleanor "Ellen" Hall (b. 1792, Pennsylvania), listed in 1830 Census of Columbiana County, Ohio, where they had moved from Greene County, Pennsylvania; had eleven children:
1) Jeremiah H. "Jerry," "Jessie" Iams [(b. July 22, 1832, Columbiana County, Ohio; d. May 10, 1890, Peru, Miami County, Indiana), m. February 14, 1881, Peru, Indiana, to Cynthia Ann Cooper (b. June 4, 1852, Hillsboro, Ohio; d. April 13, 1928, New Waverly Cass County, Indiana, and buried in Mt. Hope Cemetery, Peru); a private in Captain Alexander Hess's F Company, 41st Regiment, 2nd Cavalry, Indiana Volunteers, from September 2, 1861, to October 4, 1864, and the discharge document lists birth place as Columbiana County, age 21, height 73 inches, dark complexion, black eyes, dark hair, and a carpenter on October 4, 1864; m. 1st, October 4, 1858, to Frances A. Jackson, Wabash County, Indiana (she was b. 1839, Columbiana County, Ohio; d. March 3, 1880, Wabash County, Indiana); they had a son Orris B. Iams (b. 1860, Somerset, Waltz Township, Wabash, Indiana; d. 1865); and Jeremiah Iiams (b. 1832) lived in Carthage, Missouri, for a time; 1850 Census of Wabash County, Indiana, lists: Eleanor Iiams (age 58, b. Pennsylvania), Uriah Iiams (age 22, farmer, b. Ohio); Jeremiah H. Iams (age 19, carpenter, b. Ohio); and Eleanor Beurden (age 20, b. Ohio) with Wilson Beurden (age 2, b. Ohio), and the second child of Jeremiah

H. Iams (b. 1832) was Omar Ingerson Iams (b. 1883, Indiana; m. Nora Ann Roher; d. Indiana)].

2) a daughter (m. Mr. Adams, lived in Addica, Indiana).

3) Thomas A. Iams [(b. 1822, Pennsylvania), m. June 10, 1848, to Ruth Gray (b. 1823, Indiana); lived in Wabash County, Indiana].

4) John Imes [(b. February 13, 1814, Pennsylvania; d. June 17, 1877, Carthage, Missouri), m. 1837, Indiana, to Jane Pitman (b. October 1, 1816, Ohio; d. February 7, 1884, Columbus, Nebraska); lived Noble Township, Wabash County, Indiana; and they had five children: a) Freeman Asbury Iiams (b. December 17, 1838; d. March 6, 1839); b) David Pittman Iiams (b. June 16, 1840 or 1841, Ohio; d. March 13, 1867; single); c) Laura Susan Iiams (b. June 23, 1842 or 1843, Ohio); d) Samuel Edwin Iiams (b. April 21, 1844, Middletown, Butler County, Ohio; d. March 9, 1911); and e) Emma J. Iiams (b. 1847, Ohio)].

5) William Imes (b. 1827; m. ____ Faris; lived in Smith Township, Columbiana County, Ohio).

6) Benjamin Imes (b. 1810, was in Genoa, Nevada Territory in 1855).

7) Mary Anna Imes (b. 1832, Ohio).

8) Louise Imes (d. Peru, Indiana).

9) George W. Imes (b. 1821, Pennsylvania; m. Elizabeth ____).

10) Uriah Imes (b. 1828, Ohio).

11) Eleanor Imes (b. 1830, Columbiana County, Ohio; m. Mr. Bearden). (EFB, IJM)

John Iams (b. February 13, 1814, Pennsylvania; d. June 17, 1877, Carthage, Missouri; height 78 inches; lived for a time in Marietta, Ohio), son of William Iiams (b. 1786), m. Jane Pittman (b. October 1, 1816, Urbana, Campaign County, Ohio; d. February 7, 1884, Columbus, Nebraska, at home of her daughter); left Wabash, Indiana, in Spring of 1852, in the company of 90 men and 400 women and children and settled in Winona, Indian Territory of Minnesota, where they had their first meeting May 6, 1852. The 1860 Census of Township 105, Range 9 of Winona, Minnesota, listed: John Iams (age 46, b. Pennsylvania); Jane Iams (age 44, b. Ohio); Laura Iams (age 18, b. Ohio); and Samuel E. Iams (age 16, b. Ohio). John Iams (b. 1814), a carpenter, built the first log home of red oak in Section 7, Township 107, Range 8, using red oak shingles. He is credited with the founding of Minnesota City and Rollingstone in Winona Territory. He was elected to the State Legislature, an honorary position; was road commissioner; was one of founders of the first Baptist Society; was a charter member of Winona and Winnebago Masonic Lodge; was Sheriff of Filmore County from 1853 to 1856; moved to Carthage, Missouri, by 1875. Brothers of John Iams (b. 1814) included Thomas Iams, Richard Iams, Rezin Iams, Eli Iams, Otho Iams, Bazel Iames, and William Iams. On October 22, 1882, widow Jane Iams wrote a letter to her son Samuel Iams with regard to Civil War-connected disability and advised him: "I believe your complaint was commenced when you had the measles in the army. I can testify to that, but be careful not to pay anything till you get it yourself. Your Uncle Jerry Iams did not pay till he got his. He got about $500 and he likely had to pay one." At that time, this Jane Iams was said to be the widow of Eli Iams (denied by EFB); and the majority of this branch of the family tree was compiled by Gertrude Magnusen of the family listed below. The six children of John Iams (b. 1814) and Jane Pitman (b. October 1, 1814) were: 1) Freeman Asbury Iams (b. December 17, 1838; d. March 6, 1939); 2) David or Daniel Pitman Iams (b. June 16, 1840; d. March 13, 1867); single; travelled a lot; 3) Laura Susan Iams (b. June 23, 1842, Ohio; m. Chester Graves; lived in Iowa); 4) Emily or Emma J. Iams (b.

1847, Ohio); 5) a son (died of chloroform asphyxia during surgery on April 21, 1874, age 66 years); and 6) Samuel Edwin Iams [(b. April 21, 1844, Middletown, Butler County, Ohio; worked for a time as wagon maker in Springfield Illinois; Civil War veteran; moved to Fairbault County, Minnesota, at age 14; recipient of letter quoted above), m. Elizabeth C. (b. 1845, New York City); and they had five children.

The five children of Samuel Edwin Iams (b. 1844) were: 1) Mrs. E. F. Magnusen (lived to age 94); 2) Reverend Francis E. Iams [(b. 1874; d. November 22, 1956); lived in Prairie View, Illinois; taught school; served missions in Argentina, Brazil, and England; had 15 Baptist pastorates in United States; had eight children: a) Grace Iams; b) Evelyn Iams (m. Erick F. Magnusen, family historian; reported in 1962 about "Uncles Eel, Bazzle, Rezin, and Oatha," that the mother of William Iiams was a Shidler, and that the Dutch spelling was Shodlin; that the father of William Iiams was Richard Iiams, Greene County, Pennsylvania, in 1829; and that children of William Iiams included William A. Iiams (a lawyer) and that a son-in-law, Charles Hartman, was a Probate Judge in Bozeman, Montana, at age 25); c) William Charles Iams; d) Benjamin M. Iams (a soldier; lived in Washington, D. C.); e) Basel Iams (a mechanic; lived in Treon, Wisconsin); f) George Iams (lived in Cambridge, Minnesota); g) a daughter (m. Mr. La Rue; lived in Chicago, Illinois); and h) Myra Iams (m. Mr. Schultz; lived in Prairie View, Illinois)]; 3) Ida M. Iams (b. 1868); 4) Martha J. Iams (b. 1870); and 5) Charles Iams (b. 1883). In 1954 Gertrude Burnam gave John Iams to be the father of Francis E. Iams. (EFB)

Ervin F. Bickley, Jr., has described his family tree with spelling variations including Böckle, Bocklin, Boeckle, Boecle, Bickley, and Beckley, the *Pennsylvania German Pioneers* (Vol. 1, pp. 59-61) indicate that the family landed at Philadelphia on August 11, 1732, on board the ship *Samuel*. Hans Jacob Böckly of Germany was born 1686 and died in Philadelphia ca1733. Hans (b. 1686) m. in Germany in 1710 to Barbara ____ (b. 1690, Germany; buried in Philadelphia January 4, 1753). Their son Henry Bickley, Sr., was born in Germany in April 1716; was buried in Philadelphia August 17, 1782. Henry Sr. (b. 1716) m. October 30, 1750, to Anna Margaret Berendahler (b. 1730, d. ca1789). Henry, Sr. (b. 1716) and Ann Margaret (b. 1730) had a son Henry Bickley, Jr. They had a son John George Bickley (b. May 18, 1769, in Philadelphia; buried in Philadelphia, December 1, 1807) who m. 1798-1800, Mary Maggy (b. ca1775; lived to 1822). Mary Maggy (b. ca1775) m. 2nd, February 15, 1810, Philip Felton. John George Bickley (b. 1769) had a son George Bickley (b. April 27, 1804, Cheltenham Township, Montgomery County, Pennsylvania; d. April 18, 1883, Philadelphia), who m. January 2, 1826 to Mary Williams (b. June 9, 1809, Philadelphia; d. March 19, 1874, Philadelphia). Mary Williams (b. 1809) was the daughter of Andrew and Jane Williams.

The *DAR Lineage Book 160*, page 170, lists a Henry Bickley (b. 1746 in Europe; d. 1807). Listings for the War of 1812 list Jacob Bickley/Beckley as born about 1790 in Chambersburg, Pennsylvania, and whose wife's name was Susannah Mortimer. Horning Bickley was a relative but not a direct ancestor.

The 1800 Census for Philadelphia County, Pennsylvania, lists: Jacob Beckley (age 26-45), with females 45, 26-45, 10-16 under 10, under 10; and 6 males under 26; Adam Buckley (age 26-45), with females 26-45 and under 10; and males 10-16 and under 10; George Bickley (Oxford Township) (age 26-45), with females 26-45 and under 10; Widow Buckley (Southwork) (age over 45), with females 10-16, 10-16, under 10, under 10, under 10, and 1 male 26-45; Isaac Beckley (over 45) with 1 female 26-45; the 1804 County Tax List of Cheltenham Township, Montgomery County, Pennsylvania, lists George Bickley. The 1870 Reconstructed Census, 23rd Ward of Philadelphia, lists George Bickeily (age 66), Mary Bickerly (age 61), and Lilly Bickerly (age 18). The 1871 Philadelphia City Directory lists 19 Bickley households: Albert, Charles, Daniel, David, Elizabeth Frederick, Frederick, Frederick M., George, Hannah (widow of Joseph), Henry, Henry E., Howell W., Lloyd W., Mary W. (widow of Henry), William (2), and William H. (2).

Jeremiah H. "Jerry" Iams (b. July 22, 1832, Columbiana County, Ohio; d. May 10, 1890, Peru, Miami County, Indiana), son of William Iams (b. 1786, Washington County, Maryland), m. 1st, October 14, 1858, Wabash, Indiana, to Frances A. Jackson (b. 1839, Columbiana County, Ohio; d. March 3, 1880, Wabash County, Indiana), and their son Orris B. Iams (b. 1860, Somerset, Watts Township, Wabash County, Indiana); died 1865); m. 2nd, February 14, 1881, Peru, Indiana, to Cynthia Ann Cooper (b. June 14, 1852, Hillsboro, Ohio; d. April 13, 1928, New Waverly, Cass County, Indiana), who m. 2nd, November 2, 1892, Miami County, Indiana, to William H. Green (d. March 5, 1908); and m. 3rd, November 29, 1914, to James K. Chaplin (d. April 4, 1926).

Jeremiah H. Iams (b. 1832) enlisted at Wabash, Indiana, September 12, 1861; was honorably discharged October 7, 1864; served in Company F of 41st Indiana Cavalry; on June 24, 1878, as a resident of Carthage, Jasper County, Missouri, at age 50, declared himself to be a Civil War pensioner who had enrolled at Fort Wayne, Indiana; was awarded six dollars per month for Civil War disability resulting from a gunshot wound (gsw) in right ankle at Shelbyville, Tennessee, on July 1, 1862, when he was thrown from a horse; and his widow Cynthia Ann Cooper declared for widow's pension July 2, 1890, Miami County, Indiana, at age 39; and after the death of her second husband James K. Chaplin, she filed for his remarried widow's pension on May 10, 1926. The child of Jeremiah H. Iams (b. 1832) and Cynthia Ann Cooper Iams Green Chaplin (b. 1852) was Omer Ingersol Iams [(b. August 26, 1883, Peru, Miami County, Indiana; alive in 1966), m. June 9, 1908, Peru, Indiana, to Nora Anora Rober (b. 1890; d. January 3, 1960, Mexico, Indiana); no children; provided family tree information at age 83]. (OII)

Rezin (or Reason) Iams (b. 1781, 1789, or 1790; d. February 19, 1860 or 1880), son of Richard Iams (b. ca1745, Maryland), m. 1st, 1808, to Phoebe Clark (b. 1787, June 30, 1789, or June 30, 1800; d. November 2, 1845); m. 2nd, 1848, to Nancy McClung (b. March 4, 1804; d. January 9, 1876); with Rezin Iams and Phoebe Clark buried at Old Bates Fork Baptist Church Cemetery, Fonner's Run, Greene County, Pennsylvania. The 1850 Federal Census of Morris Township, Greene County, Pennsylvania, lists: Reason Iams (age 60, b. Pennsylvania); Nancy Iams (age 40, b. Pennsylvania); Martha Iams (age 10, b. Pennsylvania); and son Bazell Iams (age 1, b. Pennsylvania). The 1850 Census of Monroe County, Ohio, lists Isaac Iams (age 41, b. Pennsylvania, farmer); Elizabeth Iams (age 38, b. Pennsylvania; Elenor Iams (age 14, b. Pennsylvania); George Iams (age 12, b. Pennsylvania); Rebecca Iams (age 10, b. Pennsylvania); Isaac Iams (age 8, b. Pennsylvania); Sarah Iams (age 7, b. Pennsylvania); and Dennis Iams (age 25, farmer, b. Pennsylvania). The 1860 Census of Monroe County, Ohio, lists Isaac Iams (age 31, b. Ohio, a schoolteacher); Lucinda Iams (age 30, b. Ohio); Byron Iams (age 5, b. Ohio); Olive Iams (age 4, b. Ohio); Caroline Iams (age 3, b. Ohio); and Marion Iams (age 10 months, b. Ohio), as the only Iams in Monroe County, and the only Isaac Iams in Ohio. The six children of Rezin (or Resin, or Reason) Iams (b. 1790) and Phoebe Clark (b. 1787) were:

1) Reason (or Rezin) Iams, Jr. [(b. May 16, 1821 or 1817, Greene County, Pennsylvania; d. January 28, 1850, Greene County, Pennsylvania; buried at Old Bates Fork Cemetery), m. Margaret Reeves]; 2) Richard "Dick" Iams [(b. March 6, 1817, Greene County, Pennsylvania; d. August 1893, Greene County, Pennsylvania), m. January 14, 1842, to Lucinda Fonner (or Fenner) who d. 1883; moved March 1878 to

Kansas; had four children: a) Reason or Rezin Iams (b. November 30, 1844, Greene County, Pennsylvania; d. 1883; m. Emma Reeves); b) Henry B. Iams (b. February 25, 1849; d. September 13, 1925, Clay, Kansas; single); c) Martha Jane Iams (b. March 12, 1861; d. 1865); and d) James Fenner Iams (b. November 11, 1865); m. March 28, 1891, to Henrietta Allen; was Probate Judge, Clay County, Kansas; 3) Isaac Iams [(b. 1809 or 1816, Pennsylvania), m. Elizabeth Williams (b. 1812, Pennsylvania); moved to Ohio in 1850]; 4) Ellen Iams [(b. April 2, 1815, Greene County, Pennsylvania, at Crane Creek; d. February 24, 1907, Greene County, Pennsylvania); m. Ephraim Conger (d. 1893) and they had seven children: Hiram Conger, Elias Conger, Albert Conger, Mary Conger (m. Mr. Longden), Mrs. Olive Mattox, Mrs. Joseph Dunn, and John Conger (m. 2nd, Hannah Loughman)]; 5) John or Otha Iams [(b. March 22, 1819; d. September 23, 1895), m. March 5, 1841, to Elizabeth Miller (b. March 28, 1822; d. December 7, 1894); 1850 Census of Greene County, Pennsylvania, lists John Iams (age 29, b. Pennsylvania); Elizabeth Iams (age 28); Abner Iams (age 7); Jane Iams (age 6); Phoebe Iams (age 4); Samuel Iams (age 2); and Richard Iams (age 4 months); 1870 Census lists: John Iams (age 51); Elizabeth Iams (age 48); Jane Iams (age 25); Nancy Iams (age 18); Margaret Iams (age 15); John Iams (age 12); Deborah Iams (age 12); and George Iams (age 5); and 1900 Census of Washington County, Pennsylvania, lists: George B. Iams (age 35, b. Pennsylvania); Ella Iams (age 33); and Effie N. Iams (age 11); and 1910 Census of Greene County, Pennsylvania, lists: George B. Iams (age 44); wife Ella B. Iams (age 43); and daughter Effie M. Iams (age 20)]; and 6) Deborah Iams [(b. September 27, 1812; d. February 20, 1856); m. 1832 to John Penn (b. June 9, 1809; d. September 5, 1892)].

Richard "Dick" Iams (b. March 6, 1817, Bates Fork Morris Township, Greene County, Pennsylvania; d. August 1893, Kansas), son of Reason Iams (b. 1790) and Phoebe Clark (b. 1787); m. January 14, 1842, Greene County, Pennsylvania, to Lucinda Fonner (b. Greene County, Pennsylvania, June 30, 1789; d. Kansas, November 2, 1848). The 1850 Federal Census of Morris Township, Greene County, Pennsylvania, lists: Reason Iams (age 60); wife Nancy Iams (age 40), daughter Martha Iams (age 10); son Bozell Iams (age 1); and Richard Iams (age 35); Lucinda Iams (age 36); Reason Iams (age 6); and Henry Iams (age 2). The 1870 Census of Greene County lists Richard Iams (age 53); wife Lucinda Iams (age 49); son Rezzin Iams (age 25); Henry Iams (age 21); Emily Iams (age 20); Margaret Iams (age 13); and James Iams (age 4). Richard Iams (b. 1817) moved to Kansas in March 1878. James Iams (b. 1866), a son, was Probate Judge in Clay County, Kansas. The 1880 Census of Clay Center, Clay County, Kansas, lists Rezin Iams (age 34, b. Pennsylvania); wife Emma Iams (age 30, b. Virginia); son Richard L. Iams (age 8, b. Pennsylvania); and daughter Lilly Iams (age 8, b. Pennsylvania). The 1900 Clay County, Kansas, census lists Rezin Iams (age 50, b. Pennsylvania); wife Martha B. Iams (age 33, b. Illinois); Howard R. Iams (age 12, b. Kansas); Floyd Iams (age 9, b. Kansas); and Carol M. Iams (age 4, b. Kansas); and in a separate household: Henry B. Iams (age 50, b. Pennsylvania; living alone); and also, a Martha Iams (age 53, b. Pennsylvania) was listed as a sister-in-law with Nimrod Young household that included George H. Iams (age 9, a grandson), and James Iams (age 34, b. Pennsylvania).

Isaac Iams (b. 1809, Greene County, Pennsylvania; moved to Monroe County, Ohio, in 1850; d. 1852, Noble County, Ohio), son of Rezin Iams (b. 1790); m. Greene County, Pennsylvania, to Elizabeth Williams (b. 1812, Pennsylvania); and their children were:

1) Eleanor Iams [(b. November 8, 1835, Greene County, Pennsylvania; d. age 91); m. December 23, 1852, Carlisle, Noble County, Ohio, to Harmon Price Smith, and their eight children were: a) Frank Iret Smith (b. December 2, 1853); b)

Minerva Jane Smith (b. June 30, 1855; d. January 21, 1927); c) LeRoy Smith (b. November 29, 1857; d. January 21, 1876; d) George B. Smith (b. June 14, 1861; d. February 2, 1863); e) Clark Smith (b. December 6, 1864; d. February 13, 1915, Illinois); f) William Henry Smith (b. August 9, 1866); g) Julia Smith (b. July 21, 1868; m. November 10, 1892); and h) Ella Smith (b. November 4, 1875)]; 2) George Iams (b. 1838, Greene County, Pennsylvania; m. _____ Young); 4) Isaac Iams, Jr. [(b. October 10, 1842, Greene County, Pennsylvania; d. November 22, 1902, Clay County, Kansas), m. May 30, 1875, Clay County, Kansas, to May E. Spurrier (b. October 1855, Iowa; d. April 11, 1925, Green, Clay County, Kansas), and they had three children: a) Stella Vaughn Iams (b. April 22, 1877); b) Audrey B. Iams (b. December 4, 1879); and c) Virgil M. Iams (b. September 16, 1891)]; 5) Sarah Iams (b. 1843, Greene County, Pennsylvania; m. Mr. Wilson; 6) Abner Iams (d. age 4); 7) Martha Iams (b. November 1846; single); 8) Elizabeth Iams (d. infancy; buried at Bates Fork, Greene County, Pennsylvania); and 9) Rezin Iams [(b. January 1850, Greene County, Pennsylvania; d. age over 60); lived on 7th Street, Clay Center, Kansas, in 1880; m. Martha B. _____ (b. December 1866, Illinois); and their three children: a) Howard R. Iams (b. September 1887, Kansas); b) Floyd E. Iams (b. June 1890, Kansas); and c) Cecil M. Iams (b. April 1896, Kansas)].

The deed in Monroe County, Ohio, filed March 28, 1851, for 200 acres to Isaac Iams, formerly of Greene County, Pennsylvania, and recently of Stock Township, Noble County, Ohio, was purchased for $4,000 from Nimrod and Cassandra Pumphrey of Mason County, Virginia. The will of Isaac Iams (b. 1809), written April 20, 1852, Stock Township, Noble County, Ohio, has the spelling of the subject Isaac Iams spelled in different ways (Iams, Iames, Iiams, and Imes), with the 254-acre farm left to his widow; with named sons including Isaac Iams and Rezin Iams; and daughters Eleanor Jane Iams, Rebecca Iams, Sarah Iams, and Martha Iams; with "only" five dollars to son Benjamin "Franklin" Iams of Washington County, Pennsylvania. Witnesses were Richard Iams and Timothy Smith; and listed debtors including Richard Iams, Demas Iams of Stock Township; with receipts to the estate by Elizabeth Iams ($240.10) and H. B. Smith, husband of Eloner J. Imes ($575).

The 1880 Census of Highland Township, Clay County, Kansas, lists: Isaac Iams (age 38, b. Pennsylvania); May E. Iams (age 24, b. Iowa); Stella V. Iams (age 3, b. Kansas); Audrey B. Iams (age 6 months, b. Kansas); and brother-in-law Joseph Spurrier (age 7, b. Kansas). The 1900 Census of Highland Township, Clay County, Kansas, lists Isaac Iams (age 57, b. Pennsylvania); Mary E. Iams (age 44, b. Iowa); daughter Banion Iams (age 23); Audrey B. Iams (age 20, b. Kansas); and daughter Virgil M. Iams (age 9, b. Kansas). The 1910 Census of Clay County, Kansas, lists only Isaac Iams (age 72, b. Ohio). Isaac Iams (b. 1842) Civil War Pension application, lists him as a member of Company C, 196 Ohio Volunteer Infantry; enlisted at Barnesville, Belmont County, Ohio, March 8, 1865; discharged in Baltimore September 11, 1865; affidavit issued in Clay County, Kansas, May 30, 1892; age 51; height 66 inches; fair complexion, light hair, blue eyes, 159 pounds; suffering from corpulancy, rheumatism, and Bright's disease; with April 5, 1902, declaration from Clay County, Kansas. At age 60, as a resident of Green with brother Rezin Iams as attorney; given $8.00 per month pension; had moved from Noble County, Ohio, to Kansas in 1871. Declaration filed September 6, 1916, by widow Mary E. Iams, age 60, of Green, Clay County, Kansas, for widow pension with witness being Martha A. Iams, age 68 of Green, Clay County, Kansas, sister of the late Isaac Iams.

Isaac Iams, Jr. (b. October 10, 1842, Greene County, Pennsylvania; lived at Carlisle, Noble County, Ohio; d. November 27, 1902, Green, Clay County, Kansas), son of Isaac Iams (b. 1809) and Elizabeth Williams; m. May 30, 1875, Clay Center,

Clay County, Kansas, to Mary "May" E. Spurrier (b. October 1855, Iowa; d. April 11, 1925, Green, Clay County, Kansas); and they had three children: 1) Stella Vaughn or Baugh Iams (b. April 22, 1877, Kansas); 2) Audrey B. Iams (b. December 4, 1879, Kansas); and 3) Virgil M. Iams (b. September 16, 1891, Kansas).

John Iams (b. March 22, 1819, Greene County, Pennsylvania; d. September 23, 1895, Greene County, Pennsylvania), son of Rezin Iams (b. 1790), and they had ten children): 1) Abner Iams (b. 1843, Greene County, Pennsylvania); 2) Jane Iams (b. 1844, Greene County, Pennsylvania); 3) Phoebe Iams (b. 1846, Greene County, Pennsylvania); 4) Samuel Iams (b. 1848, Greene County, Pennsylvania); 5) Richard Iams (b. 1850, Greene County, Pennsylvania); 6) Nancy Iams (b. 1852, Greene County, Pennsylvania); 7) Margaret Iams (b. 1855, Greene County, Pennsylvania); 8) John Iams (b. 1858, Greene County, Pennsylvania); 9) Deborah Iams (b. 1858, Greene County, Pennsylvania); and 10) George Iams (b. 1865, Greene County, Pennsylvania.

The 1850 Census of Morris Township, Greene County, Pennsylvania, lists John Iams (age 29, b. Pennsylvania); Elizabeth Iams (age 28, b. Pennsylvania); Abner Iams (age 7); Jane Iams (age 6); Phoebe Iams (age 4); Samuel Iams (age 2); and Richard Iams (age 4 months). The 1870 Census of Morris Township, Greene County, Pennsylvania, lists John Iams (age 51); Elizabeth Iams (age 48); Jane Iams (age 25); Nancy Iams (age 18); Margaret Iams (age 15); John Iams (age 12); Deborah Iams (age 12); and George Iams (age 5). (EFB, REI, FC, JBM)

Thomas Iams (b. 1783, Washington County, Maryland; lived in Greene County, Pennsylvania; d. 1843, Greene County, Pennsylvania), the son of Richard Iiams (b. 1745, Maryland); and Eleanor or Elizabeth Pottenger, m. 1807 to Mary Jane "Polly" Smith (b. 1751; d. after 1807), daughter of Dennis Smith (b. 1748, Germany; d. August 29, 1829, Pennsylvania) and Elizabeth Zook (m. November 14, 1771; b. September 19, 1815; d. May 13, 1756), and Thomas Iams (b. 1783) had eight children:

1) Dennis Iams [(b. June 2, 1808, Greene County, Pennsylvania; d. January 7, 1888, Sycamore, Greene County, Pennsylvania) m. August 6, 1831, Greene County, Pennsylvania, to Matilda Huffman (b. September 26, 1814, or August 16, 1826, Greene County, Pennsylvania; d. October 14, 1887, buried Bates Fork Greene County, Pennsylvania) and they had nine children (family Bible): a) Benjamin Iams (b. 1839, Pennsylvania); b) Thomas Iams (b. 1833, Pennsylvania); c) Sarah Iams (b. 1837; d. 1899; d. Mary Iams (b. 1842); e) Elizabeth Iams (b. 1846; d. 1848); f) Dennis Iams (b. 1848); g) Lydia Iams (b. 1850); h) Amanda Iams (b. 1854); and i) Priscilla Iams (b. 1859)]; 2) Thomas Iams [(b. 1821, 1825, or 1828, Greene County, Pennsylvania; d. January 7, 1906, Mount Victory, Logan County, Ohio; buried in Rushylvania, Ohio, cemetery) m. December 5, 1850, to Phoebe Penn (or to Delilah Huffman) and they had six sons and three daughters; with two sons and one daughter who died young; moved to Logan County, Ohio, and bought a farm near Big Springs in 1870; moved to Dakota Territory for about two years and then back to the Ohio farm where Phoebe Penn died and he m. 2nd, Mrs. Sarah Douglass]; 3) Elizabeth Iams [(b. 1808 or 1810, Greene County, Pennsylvania; d. June 10, 1877; Monroe County, Ohio) m. 1830 to George Smith (b. 1801; d. September 4, 1869, Monroe County, Ohio), the son of Noah Smith (b. March 20, 1756, New Jersey; d. 1835, Greene County, Pennsylvania) and Ann Hoge (b. April 19, 1759; d. Greene County, Pennsylvania), daughter of George Hoge (b. February 6, 1732; d. 1805, Greene County, Pennsylvania); and grandson of Anthony Smith (b. July 26, 1723) and Lydia Willetts (b. January 16, 1724; d. January 3, 1798, Greene County, Pennsylvania)]; 4) Catherine Iams (b. 1811, Greene County, Pennsylvania; m. Mr. Huffman (or William McCracken); 5) Mary Iams (b. January 1, 1814; d. April 28, 1904; m. George Huffman, b. 1813; d. 1890); 6) Rachel

Iams [(b. December 1818; d. December 7, 1858) m. 1835 to Joseph Miller (family line of the children of Ervin F. Bickley, Jr.)]; 7) Charity Iams [(b. 1823, Pennsylvania; d. 1900, Logan County, Ohio) m. Harvey (or Henry) Gardner (b. October 18, 1820, Pennsylvania)]; and 8) Hannah Iams [(b. 1817; d. 1895) m. Jesse Church (b. 1812)]. (FC, NI, CRI, EFB, REI, MI, HWN). The DAR Line 372864 by Margaret Gainer Smith listed Thomas Iams (b. 1780, Maryland; d. Washington Township, Greene County, Pennsylvania, March 19, 1843, and refers to Will 1067 (Book 2, p. 171) and Will 636 (Book 1, p. 362) for the son of Richard Iams. Thomas Iams (b. 1783) and Mary had a son Thomas Iams (b. 1828) who later sold the family farm to Elias Cary. The Greene County, Pennsylvania, Will No. 1067 indicated that Thomas Iams had a daughter Rachel Iams, a son Dennis Iams, a son Thomas Iams, a daughter Elizabeth Iams (m. George Smith), a daughter Catherine Iams, a daughter Mary Iams, a daughter Hannah Iams, and a daughter Charity Iams. Will No. 3677 shows that this Dennis Iams d. 1888.

Dennis Iams (b. June 2, 1808, Greene County, Pennsylvania; d. January 7, 1888, Sycamore, Greene County, Pennsylvania), son of Thomas Iiams (b. 1783, Greene County, Pennsylvania), m. August 6, 1831, Greene County, to Matilda Huffman (b. September 26, 1814, or August 16, 1826, Greene County, Pennsylvania; d. October 14, 1887, Greene County, and buried in Bates Fork Cemetery, Greene County, Pennsylvania), daughter of Benjamin Huffman and Sarah Woods. Hannah's *History of Greene County, Pennsylvania* (pp. 200-204), quotes Dennis Iams as saying that his grandfather Richard Iiams came to western Pennsylvania from Maryland in 1780 and settled first in what is Ninevah, and later at Bates Fork, both in Greene County. Richard Iiams had a son Thomas Iiams and lived on the family farm where Dennis Iams was born. Dennis Iams was described as "Quiet, easy going but industrious" and who would be considered a prime mover in today's world, who owned 1,800 acres, who had been a successful wool grower for 30 years, who was elected Deacon in the Baptist Church, and who recalled the 1818-1820 hunting expeditions with his grandfather, Richard Iams. As he said, "Deer were already scarce, but sometimes found them in the early morning; also hunted wild turkey, pheasants, squirrels, rabbits, some bear"; (described as "fat, lazy, complacent since farmers grew corn"); wolves would howl at night, giving eerie feelings. "Grandfather had bear skins on the cabin walls." Children of Dennis Iams (b. 1808) and Matilda Huffman were:

1) Thomas Iams (b. July 8, 1833, Greene County; m. Lydia Bell); 2) Sarah Iams (b. June 4, 1837, Greene County; d. March 7, 1899; m. 1853 to Daniel Loughman); 3) Mary Iams (b. April 24, 1842, Greene County; d. June 10, 1924; m. Hiram Scott); 4) Elizabeth Iams (b. January 14, 1846, Greene County; d. March 19, 1848); 5) Dennis Iams, Jr. (b. May 13, 1848; d. July 22, 1919; m. Matilda Keighey); 6) Lydia Iams (b. May 1850, Greene County; m. John H. Smith); 7) Amanda Iams (b. May 24, 1854; Greene County; d. November 24, 1897; m. Charles Adamson); 8) Priscilla Iams (b. October 15, 1859, Greene County, Pennsylvania; d. May 9, 1939; m. David Hopkins); and 9) Benjamin Iams [(b. September 13, 1839, Greene County; d. November 15, 1913, Greene County, Pennsylvania); m. 1860, Greene County, to Mariah (or Maria) Scott (b. February 2, 1840, Greene County; d. August 15, 1924, Greene County; buried at Hopewell Cemetery in Greene County), daughter of Elias Scott and Harriet Kent]. Elias Scott (DBK), Esquire (b. August 7, 1811, Greene County, Pennsylvania; d. August 20, 1884; buried Hopewell Cemetery, Center Township, Greene County, Pennsylvania), the son of John Scott, Jr., and Susan Nyceswanger; farmed in Center Township. Harriet Kent (b. 1815, Franklin Township, Greene County, Pennsylvania; d. June 14, 1884, and buried in Hopewell Cemetery) was the daughter of Thomas Kent, Jr. [(fourth child of Thomas Kent and Ann Ralston) who was (b. November 15,

1783, Franklin Township, Greene County, Pennsylvania; d. December 30, 1862, Franklin Township)] and Olive Smith (b. 1785, Franklin Township, Greene County; d. January 1864, Franklin Township), daughter of Thomas Smith, Jr., and Mary Williams. Elias Scott (b. 1811) and Harriet Kent (b. 1815) had eight children: 1) Thomas Scott; 2) Susanna Scott; 3) Hiram Scott; 4) Maria Scott; 5) Sarah Scott; 6) Mattie Scott; 7) Nancy Scott; and 8) Mary Jane Scott. (DBK)

Benjamin Iams (b. September 13, 1839, Greene County, Pennsylvania; d. November 15, 1913, Greene County, Pennsylvania), son of Dennis Iams (b. 1808), m. 1860, Greene County, Pennsylvania, to Maria Scott (b. February 2, 1840, Sycamore, Greene County, Pennsylvania; d. August 15, 1924, Greene County, Pennsylvania; buried Hopewell Cemetery, Greene County, Pennsylvania), daughter of Ellis Scott and Harriet Kent; and they had eleven children:

1) Sarah Iams (b. 1861, Greene County, Pennsylvania; d. January 29, 1902; m. October 14, 1880, to Isaac Porter Clutter, son of Christopher and Elizabeth Clutter); 2) William R. Iams [(b. 1865, Greene County, Pennsylvania; d. 1930) m. Siddie Roupe (b. April 13, 1873, Greene County, Pennsylvania; d. April 1944; buried Washington, Pennsylvania, cemetery)]; 3) Franklin Iams (b. March 20, 1867, Center Township, Greene County; d. November 30, 1906; single); 4) Martha A. "Mattie" Iams [(b. 1868, Greene County, Pennsylvania; d. September 10 or 16, 1918; buried Green Mount Cemetery, Greene County, Pennsylvania) m. August 18, 1888, to William H. H. Babbitt (b. 1869; d. 1934; buried in Green Mount Cemetery), son of James H. and Lucy F. Babbitt; had a daughter who became a singer and worked in New York City]; 5) Daniel Iams [(b. January 5, 1870, Greene County, Pennsylvania; d. February 2, 1932) m. September 12, 1896, in Greene County, to Margaret Bell Simpson]; 6) Nancy "Priscilla" Iams [(b. March 2, 1871, Greene County; d. January 4, 1951) m. King G. Porter]; 7) Cora Iams [(b. 1876, Center Township, Greene County; d. January 25, 1963), single; and her son Clyde Iams (lived in Rutan, Greene County) had three children: a) Clyde Iams, Jr. (had a daughter Evelyn Iams who m. September 11, 1955, to John G. Burns, son of Norris Burns); b) Duane B. Iams (m. Ruth Elizabeth Braddock, daughter of Harry I. Braddock); worked at Peoples Glass in Washington, Pennsylvania; and c) Ruth Iams (a medical technologist; lived on Long Island, New York)]; 8) Dennis Iams (b. 1877, Center Township, Greene County; d. July 22, 1919; single); 9) Elza "Elzie" H. Iams [(b. January 25, 1879, Center Township, Greene County; d. January 6, 1965); m. 1st, October 5, 1904, Greene County, to Mollie Holmes (d. November 24, 1927), daughter of William and Sarah E. Holmes; m. 2nd, Amy Tharp (d. January 16, 1964); had two children by first marriage: a) Ethel Iams (m. Mr. Cole); and b) Lena Iams (m. Mr. Werton)]; 10) Hiram "Harry" Iams (b. February 20, 1881, Center Township, Greene County; d. February 1, 1960; single); and 11) Charles "Charley" Iams (b. April 13, 1873; d. March 16, 1925; m. November 13, 1900, Washington County, Pennsylvania, to Alberta Swart). (CRI, EI).

William R. Iams (b. 1865, Greene County, Pennsylvania; d. 1930) son of Benjamin Iams (b. 1839) and Mariah Scott; m. Sadie "Siddie" Roupe (b. April 13, 1873, Greene County; d. April 1944; buried in Washington Cemetery, Washington County, Pennsylvania), and they had four children: 1) Albert H. "Bert" Iams [(b. September 15, 1891, Greene County; d. September 15, 1952; buried in Washington County); m. Hazel H. Collins (b. June 14, 1892, or September 15, 1914, Washington County; d. February 5, 1985, or September 15, 1952; buried in Washington Cemetery, Washington County), sister of Mary Collins Reillo and daughter of Hugh Collins and Elizabeth Schwear]; 2) Raymond Iams (b. January 10, 1893, lived in Amity, Washington County; m. Florence Fatman); 3) Georgia Iams [(b. September 15, 1896, Greene County) m. Herman Garner (b. June 11, 1914; d. July 20, 1973)];

213

4) Donald E. Iams [(b. April 23, 1899, Greene County; d. December 27, 1964, Washington County; worked at Hazel Atlas Glass in Washington, Washington County) m. June 1922 to Myrl M. Hillberry (b. March 1900; d. December 21, 1990 or 1964), daughter of Lafayette and Lenora Hillberry; sister of Logan Hillberry, Homer Hillberry, William Hillberry, Edward Hillberry, Emma Hillberry (m. Mr. Kuhn), Ida Hillberry (m. Mr. Hammett), Bell Hillberry (m. Mr. Beddow), Dora Hillberry (m. Mr. Diest), Margaret Hillberry (m. Mr. Tiderman), and Mary Hillberry; worked at Hazel Atlas Glass; served as 8th Ward Chairman in Washington, Pennsylvania; worked as a model for Lang's Furs and Beckers Shoes; and Donald E. Iams (b. 1899) had five children: a) Donald E. Iams, Jr.; b) Juanita Iams (m. Mr. Nesbitt); Myrl Dean Iams (m. July 7, 1962, to Paul Jusko, b. January 10, 1930; d. June 22, 1991; son of Paul Jusko, Sr., and Inez McCown of Charleston, West Virginia; worked at Ball Glass Company; was Commander of American Legion Post 175; brother of Mary Jusko (m. Mr. Gura) and Arabella Jusko (m. Lee Holmes) of Washington, Pennsylvania; d) Dora Iams (m. July 7, 1961, to Mr. Evans); and e) Carol Iams (m. Ken Bails or Bell)]. (CRI, RHI)

Daniel Iams (b. January 5, 1870, Greene County, Pennsylvania; d. February 2, 1932), son of Benjamin Iams (b. 1839) and Maria Scott (b. 1840); m. September 12, 1896, in Greene County, Pennsylvania, to Margaret Bell Simpson; and they had five children; Effie Iams (m. Mr. Wood), Esther Iams (m. Mr. Pounds), Nettie Iams (m. Mr. Gilbert), Mark Iams, and Fred Iams (b. October 4, 1909).

Charles "Charley" Iams (b. April 13, 1873, Center Township, Greene County, Pennsylvania; d. March 16, 1925, Washington County, Pennsylvania), son of Benjamin Iams (b. 1839) and Maria Scott (b. 1840); m. November 13, 1900, Washington County, Pennsylvania, to Sarah Alberta Swart (b. December 29, 1881, Greene County, Pennsylvania; d. April 20, 1965, Washington County, Pennsylvania), daughter of John Thomas Swart and Sarah Elizabeth Luellen; and they had six children: 1) Blanche Iams [(b. July 25, 1903, Washington County, Pennsylvania; d. January 13, 1931) m. Clarence Wells, and their daughter Sarah Margaret Wells (b. January 4, 1931, Washington County, Pennsylvania), m. May 29, 1954, Washington County, Pennsylvania, to Donald Roy Bell]; 2) John Benjamin Iams [(b. July 27, 1906, Washington County, Pennsylvania, "a mean cuss"; d. July 7, 1972, Washington, Pennsylvania); m. April 20, 1929, Allegheny County, Pennsylvania, to Catherine Mary Bell (b. April 5, 1907, Greene County, Pennsylvania; d. August 27, 1947, Washington County, Pennsylvania), daughter of Alonzo Robert Bell and Lucy Hook Kent; and they had eight children: a) Charles Robert Iams (b. April 13, 1931, Washington County; m. Jeanne Marie Augustine Palmer, b. Alsace, France, February 2, 1933; daughter of Laurent Arthur Palmer and Marie Elise Richmann); b) Patricia Ruth Iams (b. September 14, 1932; m. May 1, 1954, to Leo Walter Reichert); c) Nancy Alberta Iams (b. April 29, 1934, Washington County; m. November 5, 1953, to Roy Milton Clovis); d. Verna Lou Iams (b. July 18, 1935, Washington County; m. November 19, 1955, to James Irvin Pritchard, Jr.); e) Kent Edward Iams (b. December 11, 1936, Washington County; d. January 11, 1937); f) Helen Margaret Iams (b. November 12, 1941, Washington County; m. James Cesky); g) Betty Kaye Iams (b. April 28, 1943, Washington County; m. July 1, 1960, to Elmer Theodore Clutter; and h) Mildred Ellen Iams (b. October 28, 1946; d. October 28, 1946)]; 3) Mary Margaret Iams [(b. August 2, 1909, Washington County, Pennsylvania) m. Roland James Swart (b. March 9, 1907), son of John Thomas Swart and Lillian Frances Supler; and they had six children: a) Margaret Jean Swart (b. July 7, 1929, Washington County; m. August 21, 1948, to Albert Dale Irey); b) Elizabeth Blanche Swart (b. November 9, 1930, Niles, Trumbull County, Ohio; m. October 8, 1952, Winchester, Virginia, to

Dorsey Wade Moats); c) Duane Thomas Swart (b. November 26, 1932, Greene County, Pennsylvania; m. November 14, 1952, West Finley, Pennsylvania, to Mary Lee Hughes); d. James Howard Swart (b. December 20, 1934, Greene County, Pennsylvania; m. December 7, 1963, to Mary Lou Cherry); e) Ruth Ann Swart (b. December 7, 1941, Pennsylvania; m. Mr. Finney); f) Ralph Charles Swart (b. September 27, 1943, West Finley, Pennsylvania; m. March 13, 1965, Washington County, to Nancy Evelyn Moniger)]; 4) Ross Charles Iams [(b. June 8, 1912, Amity, Washington County, Pennsylvania; d. September 16, 1980, Washington County, Pennsylvania); m. January 12, 1937, Wheeling, West Virginia, to Mabel Pauline Long (her second; b. August 20, 1915, West Virginia; d. December 12, 1996); and Mabel (b. 1915) had a daughter by her first marriage, Geraldine Livingood (b. September 31, 1932; m. Jerry Thomas, who d. July 21, 1988; buried in Upper Buffalo Township), and an adopted daughter, Susan Livingood (b. March 7, 1948). The story was that neither Mabel (b. 1915) nor Ross (b. 1912) spoke to each other for many years; and that Ross (b. 1912) didn't speak to his brother John Iams for several years, a result of an event explained by Ross (b. 1912) as being over a dispute over "when to harvest hay!"]; 5) Ruth Elizabeth Iams [(b. November 17, 1914, Washington County, Pennsylvania); m. September 29, 1937, to Kenneth Guy Mankey (b. May 4, 1913, Amity, Washington County, Pennsylvania), and they had four children: a) James Charles Mankey (b. September 21, 1941, Washington County; m. Karen Eleanor Ashcraft), b. December 29, 1949); b) Kenneth Edward Mankey, (b. May 6, 1943, Washington County; d. November 29, 1983, m. Paulette Elaine Hickman); c) Susan Ruth Mankey (b. June 18, 1944, Washington County; m. Paul Lamar Hiestand, d. December 25, 1981); and d) Gene Allen Mankey (b. January 29, 1951, Washington County; m. Rita Karen Shaler)]; 6) Martha Marie Iams (b. May 20, 1921, South Franklin Township, Washington County, Pennsylvania; d. May 22, 1921). (CRI)

Charles Robert Iams (April 13, 1931, Washington County, Pennsylvania), son of John Benjamin Iams (b. 1906) and Catherine Mary Bell (b. 1907); grandson of Charles Iams (b. 1873) and Sarah Alberta Swart (b. 1881); m. Jeanne Marie Augustine Palmer (b. February 2, 1933, Alsace, France), daughter of Laurent Arthur Palmer and Marie Elise Richmann; and they had three children: 1) Cynthia Clarisse Elizabeth Iams [(b. June 23, 1955, France) m. June 2, 1979, Butler County, Pennsylvania, to Kenneth Earl Pate (b. October 25, 1956, Butler County, Pennsylvania); and they had three children: a) Heather Renee Pate (b. June 14, 1986, Kitanning, Armstrong County, Pennsylvania); b) Danielle Nicole Pate (b. June 7, 1987, Kitanning, Armstrong County, Pennsylvania); and c) Brittany Milisa Pate (b. May 20, 1989, Kitanning, Armstrong County, Pennsylvania)]; 2) Michelle Nadine Iams [(b. August 30, 1967, Pittsburgh, Allegheny County, Pennsylvania) m. May 5, 1988, Salt Lake City, Utah, to Stephen Irl Beecroft (b. January 8, 1963, Richland, Washington), and their sons were Matthew Charles Beecroft (b. June 29, 1992, State College, Pennsylvania), and Sean James Beecroft, b. February 14, 1995, at State College)]; and 3) Lisa Charlene Iams [(b. April 14, 1969, Mt. Lebanon, Pennsylvania), m. September 1, 1990, Montgomery County, Maryland) to Jay Whitney Roberts (b. August 8, 1965), and their children were: Callianne Elise Roberts (b. April 16, 1993, Dallas, Texas, and Jace Hardison Roberts (b. September 12, 1995, at American Fork, Utah)]. Family tree compiled by Charles Robert Iams (b. 1931).

Thomas Iams (b. 1821, Morris Township, Greene County, Pennsylvania; d. January 7, 1906, Mount Victory, Hardin County, Ohio; buried at Rushylvania, Logan County, Ohio; as compiled by Ervin F. Bickley, Jr.), the son of Thomas Iams (b. 1783) and Mary Smith; or of Dennis Iams and Matilda Huffman (RI); m. 1851, to Lydia Phoebe Penn (b. 1833; d. 1898); moved from Greene County to Logan County in 1870, and he bought a farm near Big Spring; moved to Dakota Territory for two years and then moved back to the Logan County farm. Thomas Iams donated land for M P Church near Big Spring. The 1880 Federal Census of Richland Township, Logan County, Ohio, lists: Thomas Iams (age 50, b. Pennsylvania); Phoebe Iams (age 48, b. Virginia); George Iams (age 19, b. Pennsylvania); Dennis Iams (age 17, b. Pennsylvania); John Iams (age 15, b. Pennsylvania), and Heath J. Iams (age 10, b. Ohio). Lydia Phoebe Penn (b. 1833) was the daughter of John Penn (b. 1808; d. 1892) and Deborah Iams (b. 1812; d. 1856); and granddaughter of William Penn (b. 1762) and Mary Iams (daughter of Thomas Iams (b. 1708, and Elizabeth Hill); and Thomas Iams (b. 1821) had nine children:

1) Frank Iams (m. Mariah Hughes; lived at McGuffey, Hardin County, Ohio); 2) an infant son; 3) Dennis Iams (lived in Hardin County); 4) Heath (or Heth) Iams (lived first in Hardin County), and in 1935, lived at Stevens Point, Wisconsin); 5) a son, died young; 6) Margaret Iams (m. Mr. Titus; lived at Big Springs, Logan County); 7) a daughter, died young; 8) John Iams (was living in Shelton, Nebraska, in 1935); and 9) George W. Iams [(b. June 7, 1860, Waynesburg, Greene County, Pennsylvania; d. March 11, 1935, Wood River, Hall County, Nebraska), m. December 31, 1889, Greene County, Pennsylvania, to Nancy Sunday Longdon (b. March 14, 1862, Washington County, Pennsylvania; d. November 29, 1941, Wood River, Nebraska), daughter of Daniel Longdon (b. March 22, 1829; d. May 21, 1896), and Judith Crumrie; and granddaughter of Nimrod Longdon and Mary Houghton; moved from Greene County, Pennsylvania, to Superior, Nebraska, in 1905 and later to Wood River, Nebraska. Their three sons each served in World War I; and their four children were: a) a daughter died in infancy; b) Thomas Iams (lived in Wood River, Nebraska); c) John Iams (m. Mary ____; lived in Sheldon, Nebraska, Colorado, and California); and d) Bryan Jennings Iams (b. November 3, 1895, Washington County, Pennsylvania; d. April 9, 1956, Kenai Penninsula, Alaska; buried in Tacoma, Washington; m. September 15, 1919, in Grand Island, Nebraska, to Hilda Emma Wiese). (EFB, RI)

Bryan Jennings Iams (b. November 3, 1895, Washington County, Pennsylvania; d. April 9, 1956, Kenai Peninsula, Alaska; buried in Tacoma, Washington), son of Thomas Iams (b. 1828) and Lydia Phoebe Penn; m. September 15, 1919, Grand Island, Nebraska, to Hilda Emma Wiese (b. September 20, 1896, Hall County, Nebraska; d. November 25, 1974, Tacoma, Washington), daughter of Henry W. Wiese (b. March 17, 1860, in Germany; m. November 15, 1887, Grand Island, Nebraska; d. October 17, 1935, Hall County, Nebraska) and Rebecca Marie Schultz (b. December 18, 1866, Rugen, Germany; d. February 24, 1946, Hall County, Nebraska), daughter of Karl Schultz (b. 1817, Germany; d. 1897, Germany; m. 1857, Germany) and Marie Schwieger (b. September 1, 1832, Germany; d. August 26, 1914); and Henry W. Wiese (b. 1860) was the son of Joashin Wiese (b. 1834; d. 1909) and Katherine Sampf.

Bryan Jennings Iams received his name because of the strong Democratic ties of his parents, but preferred to be called BJ; died in an airplane crash while working on a government contract in Alaska. A family story tells of how Emma (b. 1896) spilled her plate on her lap at a restaurant in Grand Island, Nebraska, on her wedding day and how she was teased about that for many years thereafter. Also, how she was the first high school graduate in her German immigrant family, having been a member of a high school class of nine members and known for the first class to wear caps and gowns, a phenomenon that created a problem because of the need to obtain a dollar for the cap and gown rental, and how they kept the cap and gown wearing secret until the curtain was drawn at the graduation ceremonies. Also in the class was Mae Spohn, who later married Thomas Iams, brother of Bryan Jennings Iams. Emma Wiese (b. 1896) drove a horse and buggy six miles each way to school;

passed the Nebraska College entrance exam; was accepted at University of Nebraska but accepted a teaching job first with the job located near Sidney, Nebraska, in a sod prairie hut that consisted of five children of a Mennonite family. She later taught school at District 44, where she had attended as a child and where she taught her nieces Althea Taylor and Opal Taylor while she boarded at their old homestead home.

Bryan Jennings Iams (b. 1895) completed the eighth grade but failed the high school entrance exam. In World War I he went to France as a member of the newly organized Army Air Corps and was stationed in Belgium, Luxembourg, and Germany. During their early marriage years he farmed rental land, operated the Iams Garage with his brother "Pete" Iams. He worked as a "Raleigh man" then moved to Casper, Wyoming, where he worked for Standard Oil, for Kellogg Construction, sold Christmas trees, sold Willys automobiles, operated a steam shovel, worked on the Platte River Dam project at Alcova, Wyoming. He then moved to Provo, Utah, to build the General Steel Plant before moving to Tacoma, Washington, where he worked on several Federal projects, including Grand Coulee Dam. He was killed during a heavy fog while working in the Aleutian Islands, Alaska, when his airplane crashed into a mountain. Bryan Jennings Iams (b. 1895) and Hilda Emma Wiese had three children:

1) Naomi Mae Iams [(b. August 10, 1920, Wood River, Nebraska), m. December 30, 1945, First Methodist Church, Tacoma, Washington, to Frank Charles Snider (b. April 25, 1922)]; 2) Robert Elton Iams [(b. November 25, 1925, Wood River, Nebraska), m. July 12, 1953, Goldendale, Washington, to Shirley Ann Branten (b. July 4, 1927, Goldendale, Washington), with both being highly regarded librarians who have received numerous national awards, who compiled this branch of the family tree, and who have also researched the Wiese family in great detail]; 3) Donald James Iams [(b. June 28, 1930, Casper, Wyoming), m. 1st, July 21, 1950, to Nancy Ann Green (b. May 2, 1930); m. 2nd, July 2, 1975, to Kay Danforth Franklin (b. August 10, 1941); graduated Tacoma High School; worked for Tacoma City Light; moved to Eatonville, Washington, after retirement; had three children (with Nancy Ann Green), including: a) Kirk Wayne Iams (b. March 28, 1953, Tacoma; m. June 2, 1973, to Beverly Baublets, b. February 5, 1953; and they had two children: Bryan K. Iams, b. January 31, 1980; and Kevin B. Iams, b. April 25, 1983; a budding genealogist who received A+ on his school paper with the help of Uncle Robert Elton Iams); b) Glenn Bruce Iams (b. August 13, 1956; m. 1st, March 6, 1977, to Annette Carlson, b. October 15, 1977; m. 2nd, February 14, 1992, to Ray Lowe, b. August 14, 1955; and had four children: Sarah Marie Iams, b. September 15, 1983; Chester Ariel Iams, b. September 5, 1992; Jennifer Lowe, a stepdaughter; and Brian Lowe, a stepson; and c) Karl Bryan Iams (b. December 30, 1958; m. 1st, August 30, 1980, to Linda Marie Hogenson; m. 2nd, April 7, 1988, to Zelda ____, b. July 22, 1961; and had three children: Leanne Nicole Iams, b. November 25, 1984; Zachary Allen Iams, b. October 21, 1990; and Deziree Iams)].

Naomi Mae Iams (b. August 10, 1920, Wood River, Nebraska), daughter of Bryan Jennings Iams (b. 1895) and Hilda Emma Wiese; m. December 30, 1945, Tacoma, Washington, to Frank Charles Snider (b. April 25, 19__, "a secret"); with Naomi Mae Iams attending first grade in Wood River, where she was known for taking her class across the street to her home to view her newborn brother, but was rebuffed by "Aunt Lizzie," thus leaving the spectacle of Robert Elton Iams' first public appearance "died aborning." Naomi later graduated from Natrona County High School, Casper, Wyoming, Class of 1938; attended Chillicothe, Missouri, Business School and later worked in the medical field in Casper, Denver, Salt Lake City, and Tacoma. In Salt Lake City she met Frank Charles Snider, then the handsome soldier in uniform." Frank Snider later worked at Boeing Aircraft in Seattle before retiring to Reston, Washington. They had two children:

1) Nancy Lynn Snider [(b. August 2, 1949, Seattle, Washington; a graduate of Western State University; a schoolteacher; m. December 6, 1969, to Glenn Coye (b. October 17, 1947), and their son was Aaron Coye (b. June 7, 1970, Tacoma, Washington]; and 2) Larry Paul Snider [(b. June 28, 1952, Tacoma, Washington); served in U. S. Army; attended University of Washington; m. 1st, September 20, 1980, to Julie Ann Clark (b. November 20, 1958), and they had two children; m. 2nd, September 21, 1990, to Gerry Cahill (b. June 8, 1955); lived in Tucson, Arizona; two children were: a) Frank Scott "Frankie" Snider (b. November 14, 1984, Tacoma); and b) Tara Ann Snider (b. August 28, 1986)].

Robert Elton Iams (b. 1925), son of Bryan Jennings Iams (b. 1895); m. July 12, 1953, Goldendale, Washington, to Shirley Ann Branton (b. July 4, 1927, Goldendale, Washington); were both librarians listed in the 1970 edition of *The Biographical Directory of Librarians in the United States and Canada* (Lee Ash, Editor). Robert Elton Iams (b. 1925) was a graduate of Natrona High School, Casper, Wyoming; served as a Hospital Mate First Class with U. S. Navy in the Marianna Islands of the South Pacific during World War II; received B. A. in English at University of Washington in Seattle in 1949, and B. A. in Librarianship from the same institution in 1950. He was librarian in public libraries of Tacoma, Camos, and Seattle, Washington. He and his wife, Shirley Ann Branton (b. 1927) retired after 29 years in Seattle Library System. Shirley Ann Branton (b. 1927) graduated from Goldendale High School, from Central Washington University with B. A. degree in 1949; B. A. in Librarianship in 1950 from University of Washington; worked in Tacoma library and then taught school in Camas, Washington, before beginning her long and distinguished career in Seattle; served on Washington State Library Board 1955-1959, and was treasurer from 1957-1959; a descendant of John Branton (and Susannan Burgess) who came across the Oregon Trail in 1850; and of Samuel Snyth, Tacoma City Clerk of the 1890s.

Frank Iams (b. ca1853), son of Thomas Iams (b. 1821, Greene County, Pennsylvania; d. 1906, Logan County, Ohio, and Lydia Phoebe Penn (b. 1833); m. Mariah Hughes, and they had seven children: 1) James M. "JM" Iams [(b. August 14, 1880, Logan County, Ohio; d. Hardin County, Ohio), m. November 26, 1902, Hardin County, Ohio, to Della Ayle (b. June 17, 1879, McGuffey, Hardin County, Ohio), daughter of John Wilson Ayle and Dimor Armentrout)]; 2) Stella Iams (m. Mr. McClure); 3) John Iams; 4) Harvey Iams; 5) Edna Iams (m. Howard Dolph); 6) Cory Iams (m. Mr. Berry); and 7) Vesta Iams (m. Mr. Curl).

James M. "JM" "Jim" Iams (b. August 14, 1880; d. McGuffey, Hardin County, Ohio), m. November 26, 1902, Hardin County, Ohio, to Della Ayle (b. June 17, 1879, Hardin County, Ohio), daughter of John Wilson Ayle and Dimor Armentrout; and they had seven children: 1) Roy Allen Iams [(b. September 22, 1905; schoolteacher), m. Mary Dattorio; and their daughter, Beth Elizabeth Iams (b. November 15, 1941), m. Mr. Culbertson and they had two children: Jay Culbertson (b. March 19, 1972) and Jack Culbertson (b. April 15, 1973)]; 2) Pearl Elizabeth Iams (b. June 16, 1908; m. Frank Kelly; lived in Ada, Ohio; no children); 3) Wright Iams (b. September 9, 1910; d. as child); 4) Nellie Iams [(b. December 22, 1912), m. Venon Dodds, and they had one daughter, Connie Dodd (m. Meryl Smith; lived in Canton, Ohio)]; 5) Glesna Iams [(b. December 18, 1914), m. Melvin Sutherly; lived in Lima, Ohio; seven children]; 6) Lavern Iams [(b. June 19, 1919), m. Joseph Chalfin; lived Bucyrus, Ohio; four children]; 7) Ray Eugene Iams (b. April 19, 1916, McGuffey, Hardin County, Ohio; lived in Ada, Ohio), m. September 4, 1936, Kenton, Ohio, to Beulah Lavon Ellison (b. September 30, 1919), daughter of Joseph Ellison and Clara Dunson, and they had two children: a) Dennis Ray Iams (b. June 6, 1942, Lima,

218

Ohio; lived in Devine, Texas; m. four times; children were: Dennis Robert Iams and Will Bob Iams); b) Valera Jane Iams (b. May 16, 1937, McGuffey, Hardin County, Ohio; m. James Kistler; lived in Elyria, Ohio, and they had three children: Michelle "Shelley" Marie Kistler, b. December 3, 1959; James "Jimmy" Dennis Kistler, b. November 9, 1961; and Rebecca "Becky" Jane Kistler, b. May 30, 1966)]. (RI)

Charity Iams (b. 1823, Greene County, Pennsylvania; d. 1900; buried in Rushlyvania, Logan County, Ohio), daughter of Thomas Iams (b. 1783) and Mary Smith; m. in Greene County, to Harvey Henry Gardner (b. October 13, 1920, Greene County; d. November 14, 1889, Rushlyvania, Logan County, Ohio; a farmer); moved from Greene County, Pennsylvania, to Big Springs, Logan County, Ohio, in 1854; and they had four children: 1) Caroline Gardner [(b. October 28, 1849, Greene County; d. February 15, 1936, Rushlyvania, Logan County, Ohio); m. 1878, Logan County, to Nelson Williams]; 2) Thomas Gardner [(b. June 6, 1851, Greene County; d. 1937, Logan County, Ohio), m. Virginia Jasinsky]; 3) Jane "Jennie" Gardner [(b. April 29, 1859, Logan County, Ohio; d. February 18, 1936, Ohio), m. January 1, 1876, to Benjamin J. Hatcher (b. 1854; d. 1930)]; and 4) Mary "Mollie" Gardner [(b. January 1, 1852, Logan County; d. June 16, 1939, Logan County, Ohio), m. 1st, June 6, 1869, to Henry Roberts (b. 1849, Ohio; d. May 12, 1876, Ohio); m. 2nd, William Jesse Oder].

Mary "Mollie" Gardner (b. January 1, 1852, Logan County, Ohio; d. June 16, 1939, Rushlyvania, Logan County, Ohio), daughter of Harvey Henry Gardner (b. October 13, 1820, Greene County, Pennsylvania; d. November 14, 1889, Rushlyvania, Logan County, Ohio) and Charity Iams (b. 1823, Greene County, Pennsylvania; d. 1900, Rushlyvania, Logan County, Ohio); m. 1st, June 6, 1869, Logan County, Ohio, to Henry Roberts (b. 1849, Ohio; d. May 12, 1876, Ohio); m. 2nd, William Jesse Oder (no issue), and her three children were: 1) Harvey S. Roberts (b. September 18, 1870; d. October 30, 1956; m. Emma ____); 2) Nellie Ellen Roberts (b. May 6, 1873, Logan County; d. February 13, 1962, Logan County; m. December 5, 1893, to William I. Patterson); and 3) Gertrude Ida Roberts [(b. January 20, 1871, Logan County; d. August 6, 1938, Logan County), m. February 2, 1887, Covington, Kentucky, to Henry Siegel Hall (b. December 3, 1863, Hardin County, Ohio; d. September 11, 1953); owned hotel in Huntsville, Logan County; she was known for homemade preserves; had four children: a) Gardner Calvin Hall (b. November 14, 1896, Henry County, Ohio; d. November 23, 1964, Logan County, Ohio; m. October 10, 1925, to Eva Anna Buckingham); b) Herbert Frederick Hall (b. October 18, 1905, Ohio; m. June 28, 1929, Visalia, California, to Edna Marie Fullerton); c) Myrtle Hall (b. November 4, 1909, Ohio; d. 1992, Logan County, Ohio; m. November 30, 1927, to Harold Mullen); and d) Mary Ellen Hall (b. December 15, 1887, Henry County, Ohio; d. October 19, 1979, Bellefontaine, Logan County, Ohio; m. December 12, 1900, Logan County, Ohio, to Abram Walter King, b. June 16, 1887, Bellefontaine; d. April 22, 1965, Bellefontaine). Abram Walter King (b. 1887) was the son of Hiram Joseph King and Mary Mumphrey. Mary Ellen Hall (b. 1887) attended school in Huntsville; taught school; and taught piano. They had three children: 1[1]) Lawrence Henry King (b. December 21, 1910, Logan County; d. September 3, 1971, Logan County; m. May 17, 1941, to Frances Leighninger, who was killed in an automobile accident with his son); 2[1]) Kathryn Louise King (b. July 27, 1915, Logan County; m. March 6, 1942, to Charles Ezra Shoots); and 3[1]) Robert Humphry King (b. January 16, 1913, Logan County, Ohio; moved to California in 1949).

Robert Humphrey King (b. January 16, 1913, Logan County, Ohio), son of Abram Walter King (b. June 16, 1887) and Mary Ellen Hall (b. 1887); m. 1st, June 22, 1934, Covington, Kentucky, to Irene Elizabeth Jones (b. November 3, 1915; Wyandot County, Ohio; daughter of Orris Ray Jones and Christina Belle Uncaphers;

m. 2nd, September 15, 1956, to Ruthella Souder; lived in Havasu Lake, California; had two children: 1) Neil Edward King [(b. November 14, 1940, Logan County, Ohio), m. Delores Shannon, had two children: Mark Shannon King (b. May 10, 1966) and Michael Joseph King (b. April 7, 1968)]; 2) Sally Irene King [(b. November 13, 1934, Hardin County, Ohio), m. February 12, 1955, Las Vegas, Nevada, to Jack Irby Ross, Jr. (b. September 2, 1927, Wichita, Texas), son of Jack Irby Ross, Sr., and Gretchen Emma Shoemaker; and Sally (b. 1934) graduated from Beverly Hills High School; attended UCLA; lived in Long Beach, California; compiled branch of family tree; and they had three children; a) Robert Neil Ross (b. September 30, 1955, Santa Monica, California); m. August 20, 1977, Orange County, California, to Laura Jean Unfried (b. May 26, 1956, Los Angeles); daughter of Hugh Frederick Unfried and Beverly Jean Albertine. Robert (b. 1955) graduated from California State Long Beach University; was Lt. Colonel in United States Air Force in 1995; they had three children; 1¹) Kristin Brianne Ross, b. April 9, 1980, Long Beach; 2¹) Tracy Lynn Ross, b. December 25, 1982, Honolulu, Hawaii; and 3¹) Kelli Devon Ross, b. February 26, 1991, Scott AFB, Illinois); b) Gretchen Irene Ross (b. March 2, 1957, Santa Monica, California; m. May 16, 1981, Long Beach, to Keith Fergus Kerr (b. December 30, 1952, Ventura, California; son of Bruce Gibson Kerr and Reita Camp; had two children: 1¹) Trevor Bruce Kerr, b. October 15, 1984, Long Beach; and 2¹) Brent Ross Kerr, b. September 23, 1988, Long Beach); and c) James Alan Ross (b. September 12, 1958, Santa Monica; m. June 20, 1992, Florida, to Christine Marie Martin, b. November 14, 1962, California). James (b. 1958) graduated from Air Force Academy in 1980; lived in San Diego; worked as stockbroker; and Christine (b. 1962) was daughter of Harold H. and Lyda Jean Martin, and had a son, Matthew Ryan Langley, from prior marriage to Timothy Langley. (SIKR)

George W. Iams (b. June 7, 1860, Greene County, Pennsylvania; d. March 11, 1935, Wood River, Nebraska), the son of Thomas Iams (b. 1828) and Lydia Phoebe Iams; m. December 31, 1889, to Nancy Sunday Longdon (b. March 19, 1862, Washington; d. November 28, 1941, Wood River, Nebraska), the daughter of David Longdon (b. March 22, 1829; d. May 21, 1896, Pennsylvania) and Judith Crumrie; and granddaughter of Nimrod Longdon (d. 1875) and Mary Houston; moved to Nebraska in 1906; had four children; 1) Bryan Jennings "BJ" Iams [(b. November 3, 1895; d. April 9, 1956, Alaska), m. September 15, 1919, Grand Island, Nebraska, to Hilda Emma Wiese (b. September 20, 1896, Hall County, Nebraska; d. November 25, 1974), daughter of Henry W. Wiese (b. March 17, 1860, Germany) and Rebecca Marie Schultz (b. December 8, 1866)]; 2) Thomas Penn Iams (d. 1942); 3) Mary Ann Iams (d. infancy); and 4) John "Pete" Iams (considered the "black sheep" due to absence of family contact from 1945 to 1970; m. Helen Mitchell; son was Donald Iams). (REI)

Richard Iams (b. 1787; d. February 20, 1828 or 1829, Greene County, Pennsylvania, in barn raising accident), son of Richard Iams (b. 1745, Maryland) and Eleanor Pottenger; m. 1808, Greene County, Pennsylvania, to Mary Shidler (b. 1786; d. February 15, 1868, Monticello, Indiana. Richard Iams (b. 1787) moved to Washington County with his parents; was in War of 1812; later moved to Morris Township, Greene County; purchased 310 acres in Morris Township on April 17, 1817; will in Greene County dated September 1, 1828, and probated February 24, 1829, left the personal estate to his wife Mary, with the estate to be divided into thirds should Mary die or remarry; and as many as ten children were born to them:

1) William Iams (or Imes) [(b. February 1, 1827, Greene County, Pennsylvania; d. August 18, 1901, California); lived in Monticello, Indiana, on February 12, 1886, when he wrote to Samuel E. Iams, Delavan, Minnesota, stating that William

Iams' father was Richard Iams of Greene County, Pennsylvania; and that the large family had included "Rezin, John, Oath, Bazle, Eli, and William"; and the 1870 Census of Greene County, Pennsylvania, lists William Iams (age 44, b. Pennsylvania); Hannah Iams (age 89, b. Pennsylvania); Carolina Iams (age 15); Thomas Iams (age 13); Dennis Iams (age 11); Corbly Iams (age 9); Delila Iams (age 5); and George Iams (age 1)]; 2) Mary Iams (b. March 20, 1829, Greene County, Pennsylvania; d. April 19, 1863, Monticello, Indiana); 3) John Iams [(b. April 13, 1809, Greene County, Pennsylvania; d. March 9, 1905, Washington County, Iowa); m. September 12, 1828, probably in Washington County, Pennsylvania, to Sarah McVey; lived in Delaware County, Indiana; line of Charles Iams Cherney, M.D.]; 4) Reason (or Rezin) Iams [(b. May 17, 1810, Greene County, Pennsylvania; d. September 10, 1868, Granville, Delaware County, Indiana), m. Elenor ____]; 5) Peter Iams [(b. 1811, Greene County, Pennsylvania; d. September 2, 1836, Greene County, Pennsylvania), m. Mary "Polly" Sellars]; 6) Richard Iams [(b. June 18, 1821, Greene County, Pennsylvania), m. November 23, 1843, to Mary Ann Orr (b. November 6, 1816, Greene County, Pennsylvania); farmed in Union Township until selling the farm in 1862; then owned 200 acres in Marion Township; lived in White County, Indiana]; 7) George Iams (b. September 28, 1819, Greene County, Pennsylvania; d. May 20, 1876, White County, Indiana; m. Elizabeth ____); 8) Susanna Iams (b. September 1, 1825, Greene County, Pennsylvania; d. May 5, 1878, White County, Indiana; m. William Tarier); 9) Sally Iams (b. 1813, Greene County, Pennsylvania; lived Monroe County, Ohio; m. Jesse Grim); 10) Nancy Iams (b. December 18, 1816, Greene County, Pennsylvania; d. 1899; m. Roland Hughes)]. (REI, MI, EFB, HWN)

Richard Iams [(b. June 18, 1821, Greene County, Pennsylvania), son of Richard Iams (b. 1787) and Mary Shidler and was grandson of Richard Iams (b. 1745); m. November 23, 1843, to Mary Ann Orr (b. November 6, 1816, Greene County, Pennsylvania), and they had eight children: 1) Mary E. Iams (b. October 24, 1844); 2) George W. Iams (b. October 24, 1846); 3) Jasper N. Iams (b. August 11, 1848); 4) Letitia M. Iams (b. February 7, 1850); 5) Melissa J. Iams (b. March 17, 1852); 6) Melinda C. Iams (b. August 21, 1853); 7) Alice C. Iams (b. November 2, 1855); and 8) Susan Iams (b. May 23, 1858). (MI, EFB)

Eli Iams (b. May 15, 1790, Washington County, Maryland; d. May 26, 1857; buried in Mound Cemetery, Marietta, Washington County, Ohio), son of Richard Iiams (b. 1745); m. October 15, 1815, Marietta, Ohio, to Catherine Crawford (b. February 13, 1791, Ireland; d. August 30, 1872, Marietta, Ohio), daughter of John Crawford and Eleanor Coulter of Ireland; Eli had moved to Washington County, Pennsylvania, by 1800; moved to Washington County, Ohio, as a young man. John Crawford (b. 1756, County Donegal, Ireland; d. 1805, Washington County, Ohio), m. Eleanor Coulter (b. September 1760, Ireland; d. October 1837), daughter of Thewey Coultier; and their other children were: Sarah Crawford (b. 1790); Robert Crawford (b. 1796); John Crawford (b. 1798, Brownsville, Pennsylvania), and William Crawford (b. 1800, Pennsylvania; d. 1843, Washington County, Ohio). The 1830 Census of Washington County, Ohio, lists both Eli Iams and Jerry Iams of First Ward in Marietta. Jerry Ijams was "colored male," age over 55 years, and died March 23, 1846, in Marietta, at age 77; he was described as "a respectable colored man" who had at least one daughter, and owned at least 160 acres in the area. The 1850 Census of Washington County, Ohio, lists Eli Iams, First Ward in Marietta, (age 60, b. Maryland); Catherine Iams (age 59, b. Ireland); and Mary W. Iams (age 20, b. Ohio). Also in First Ward was Rufus Iames (age 31, merchant, b. Ohio); Mary W. Iames (age 25, b. Virginia); William Iames (age 3, b. Ohio); and Hiram B. Iames (age 7, b. Ohio). The eight children of Eli Iams (b. 1790) and Catherine Crawford, as listed in the family Bible, are:

221

1) Alfred Iams (b. August 11, 1816; d. March 24, 1818); 2) Rufus Putnam Iams [(b. August 19, 1818, Marietta; moved to Terre Haute, Indiana, in 1882; d. November 26, 1891, Terre Haute; and buried in Highland-Laron Cemetery, merchant and Clark Streets, Marietta, Ohio), m. May 26, 1842, Terre Haute, to Mary Whiting Burch (b. January 25, 1824 or 1825, Virginia); d. January 6, 1899, Terre Haute, Indiana, daughter of Hiram Burch and Nancy Whiting); and their two children were: a) Hiram B. Iames (b. May 25, 1843; d. January 4, 1849, Terre Haute); and b) William Putnam Iames (b. January 18, 1847, in Marietta, Ohio)]; 3) Percival Smith Iams (b. July 4, 1820, Marietta, Ohio; m. April 1849, Portsmouth, Ohio, to Marionette Oldfield); 4) Sarah Iams [(b. March 22, 1822, Marietta, Ohio; d. April 10, 1879), m. June 20, 1844, Marietta, Ohio, to Austin Beckley (or Berkley); and their two children were: a) John Grinville Beckley, (d. May 2, 1887, Washington County, Ohio); and b) Mary Ellen Beckley (b. June 5, 1848)]; 5) Frances Maria Iams [(b. August 19, 1824, Marietta, Ohio; d. June 7, 1858), m. October 28, 1845, Marietta, Ohio, to Ephraim C. Wells of Wellsburg, Virginia (West Virginia), and their three children were: a) John E. Wells; b) Albert S. Wells; and 3) Charles Elijah Wells (b. October 1846, Washington County, Ohio)]; 6) Eleanor "Ellen" Iams [(b. February 17, 1827; d. February 1, 1883); will was written in Cincinnati, Ohio, in 1883; was probated February 12, 1883, and left property in Marietta, Ohio, to Robert Wells and others]; 7) Mary Wilson Iams (b. August 23, 1829; d. March 30, 1860 or 1857, Marietta, Ohio; buried in Mound Cemetery, Marietta); and 8) John Leedham Iams (b. December 20 or 25, 1835; d. May 13, 1836). (RI, MI)

Rufus Putnam Iams [(b. August 19, 1818, Marietta, Washington County, Ohio; d. November 26, 1891, Terre Haute, Indiana), m. May 26, 1842, Terre Haute, Indiana, to Mary Whiting Burch (b. January 25, 1825, or 1825, Virginia; d. January 4, 1849, Terre Haute, Indiana), daughter of Hiram Burch and Nancy Whiting (b. 1827, Belpre, Ohio; d. January 6, 1899, Terre Haute, Indiana), daughter of Joseph Whiting (a Revolutionary War soldier from Boston who was present at the defeat of St. Clair, and who moved to Belpre, Ohio, after the Indian wars). Rufus Putnam Iams (b. 1818) was the son of Eli Iams (b. 1790) and Catherine Crawford; was active in Marietta Methodist Church (Superintendent of Sunday School; member of Official Board, and member of Centenery Church); the 1860 Census of Marietta, Washington County, Ohio, listed Hiram B. Iams, William Iams, Kate Iams, and Mary Moore Iams; and the four children of Rufus Putnam Iams (b. 1818) were:

1) Hiram Burch Iams [(b. May 24, 1843, Terre Haute, Indiana; d. March 6, 1896, San Antonio, Texas), m. February 28, 1872, to Frances Earle "Fannie" Clark; he was a second lieutenant, Battery K, 1st Ohio Volunteer Light Infantry; an $8.00 per month pension for widow Frances C. Iams approved October 7, 1896, and dropped November 25, 1901, after there was failure to claim payment, with her last address given as 1549 24th Street, Ogden, Utah; they had also lived in Cheyenne, Wyoming; had enlisted in Marietta, Ohio, September 15, 1861; was promoted to second lieutenant on March 27, 1862; was discharged May 11, 1863; d. San Antonio, Texas, with age given as 52, birthplace, Ohio, death from tuberculosis of three years' duration; body buried in Highland Larin Cemetery, Terre Haute, Indiana, on March 10, 1896]; 2) William Putnam Iams [(b. January 18, 1847, Marietta, Ohio; d. March 22, 1922, Terre Haute), m. February 6, 1876, to Sallie Warren (b. December 8, 1855; d. January 12, 1924, Terre Haute, Indiana); daughter of Levi Gale Warren and Martha Ellen Clark; lived in Terre Haute where William Putnam Iams (b. 1847) was Superintendent of Belt Railroad and Union Stockyards; then President of Belt Railroad; one of founders of the American Trotting Association; president and owner of the famous horse Axtell, which was purchased for a record $105,000; executive

222

and co-founder of several companies, including Citizens Telephone Company and Indiana Steel Company; and they had three children: a) Jesse "Warren" Iams (b. 1882, Indianapolis; m. Katharine _____); b) Alice Warren Iams (b. December 1884, Terre Haute; m. Richard Benridge); and c) Frank "Burch" Iams (b. December 3, 1886, Terre Haute; m. September 15, 1915, to Helen Fairbanks; and their daughter Alice Iams m. Mr. Williams and lived in Tulsa, Oklahoma]; 3) Mary Katherine "Kate" Iams (b. February 2, 1851, Marietta, Ohio; d. September 1937, Terre Haute; single; corresponded with E. B. Iams, president of Iams Association, in 1931; a letter dated October 8, 1931, to her described that he believed the original spelling to to have been Ievans; then I'ans in Wales; then Eyones and Iams in Maryland; and then to variations such as Ijams, Iams, Imes, Ijames; that Ievans was an old Welch or Saxon king in 1040 A.D.; that the first National Iams Association meeting was held August 1931 (Washington County, Pennsylvania); and that in 1931 there were about 20 Iams, Iiams, etc, clans in American; and 4) Edward Lewis Iams (b. August 5, 1860, Marietta; d. November 21, 1860). (RI)

Alternately , (EFB, Beers, PI) Eli Iams (b. March 4, 1799, Greene County, Pennsylvania; moved to Ohio 1833; d. February 6, 1875, Madison Township, Montgomery County, Ohio; buried in Woodland Cemetery, Dayton, Ohio), son of Richard Iams (b. 1745) and Eleanor Pottenger; m. September 12, 1820, to Phoebe Heckathorn (b. 1800 or 1801, Loudon County, Virginia; d. July 11, 1880, Madison Township, Montgomery County), daughter of Martin Heckathorn and Catherine Bottenfield of Virginia; and Eli Iams (b. 1799) was Justice of Peace in Montgomery County; owned a farm near Trotwood, Madison Township, Montgomery County, Ohio; 1860 Census of Madison Township lists Eli Imes (age 62, b. Pennsylvania); Phebe Imes (age 58, b. Pennsylvania); Joseph Imes (age 30, b. Ohio); Harvey H. Imes (age 25, b. Ohio; he and Joseph being schoolteachers); Martha M. Imes (age 21, b. Ohio); Lawrence S. Imes (age 18, b. Ohio); Martin H. Imes (age 39, farmer, b. Ohio); George W. Imes (age 8, b. Indiana); and Josephine Imes (age 6, b. Indiana); and also listed in the same township were: Alfred Iams (age 32, b. Ohio); Susan Imes (age 26, b. Maryland); Ellen Iams (age 8, b. Ohio); Martha Imes (age 6, b. Ohio); Oliver C. Iams (age 3, b. Ohio); and Inez Iams (age 1, b. Ohio). The 1850 Census lists: Eli Iams (age 52, b. Pennsylvania); Phebe Iams (age 49, b. Virginia); Jacob Iams (age 21, b. Ohio); Harvey Iams (age 17, b. Ohio); Martha Iams (age 12, b. Ohio); and Lauren Iams (age 9, b. Ohio). Children of Eli Iams (b. 1799) and Phoebe Hackathorn were:

1) Martin H. Iams (b. 1821, Pennsylvania); 2) Richard Iams (b. March 12, 1822, Pennsylvania, or December 3, 1823, Washington County, Pennsylvania; m. December 3, 1841 or 1849, to Phoebe Jane Thompson of Montgomery County, Ohio); 3) George Iams (PI); 4) Alfred Iams [(b. 1825, Montgomery County; d. December 20, 1891; buried Woodland Cemetery, Dayton, Ohio), m. Susan Neibert (b. 1832, Washington County, Maryland; d. January 13, 1905, buried in Woodland Cemetery)]; 5) Martha M. Iams (b. 1828 in Montgomery County); 6) David Iams (PI); 7) Jacob Iams [(b. April 27, 1830, Montgomery County, Ohio); m. 1871 to Charlotte Sanders, daughter of Richard Sanders; Jacob Iams (b. 1830) was Justice of Peace for 12 years in Madison Township, Montgomery County; manufactured "hubs, spokes, and felloes" until after the "panic of 1872" when the business failed; was a schoolteacher at age 20; had only a few months of formal schooling himself; ran a saw mill; had an address of "P. O. Iamton, Montgomery County, Ohio"; had three children: Elsie V. Iams, Pearle or Mary B. Iams, and Alvin Iams]; 8) Harvey H. Iams (b. 1833, Montgomery County, Ohio; a merchant in Harrisburg, Randolph Township, Montgomery County, Ohio); 9) Lawrence B. Iams [(b. 1841, Montgomery County, Ohio), m. Salome Fouts and they had three children: Harry E. Iams, Howard Iams, d.

infancy; and Ruth M. Iams, m. Harry Patten; and this Harry E. Iams had three children: Mary Iams (b. 1913, m. Branch Rickey, Jr., baseball executive); Paul Iams (founder of Iams Pet Food; m. Jane Landrum or Hendron); and Nancy Iams (m. Howard Epbert, and their son Howard Epbert, Jr., m. Susan Park)]; (PI, Beers-1882, EFB); 10) Pitt Iams; 11) an infant girl; and 12) Howard Iams. (PI)

Richard Iams (b. March 12, 1822, Washington County, Pennsylvania), son of Eli Iams (b. 1799) and Phoebe Heckathorn; m. December 13, 1848, to Phoebe Jane Thompson of Montgomery County, Ohio; owned a farm about two miles south and east of Plain City, Madison County, Ohio; date of birth also (Chapman, 1892) listed as December 3, 1823, as son of Eli Iams (native of Maryland; moved to Pennsylvania age 12 with parents listed as Richard Iams and Ellen Patterngard; moved to Ohio in 1823 to 700-acre farm in Darby Township, Madison County, Ohio, in 1856; a Quaker; family of Phoebe were Dunkards; had 8 sons and 3 daughters). In 1847 Richard Iams (b. 1822) was in the grain business (Reuben Brown, Dayton, Ohio, as partner); entered grocery business two years later; served as contractor and railroad superintendent; built his large, beautiful home on his Madison County farm for $4,000; had five children: 1) Alfred Iams (lived in Franklin County, Ohio); 2) Richard Iams, Jr. (lived in Madison County, Ohio); 3) Charles Iams (lived in Madison County, Ohio); 4) Alvan Iams (lived in Madison County, Ohio); and 5) Howard Iams (remained on the Madison County, Ohio, farm)]. (EFB, Beers 1883, Chapman 1892)

Alfred Iams (b. 1825, Montgomery County, Ohio; d. December 20, 1891; buried Woodland Cemetery, Dayton, Ohio), son of Eli Iams (b. 1799) and Phoebe Hackathorn; m. Susan Neibert (b. 1832, Washington County, Maryland; d. January 13, 1905; buried in Woodland Cemetery), and they had seven children: 1) Lauren "Lenren" C. Iams (b. 1865, Montgomery County, Ohio; d. March 13, 1876; buried in Woodland Cemetery); 2) Susan M. Iams (b. 1875, Montgomery County; d. August 3, 1875; buried in Woodland Cemetery; 3) Mimmie Iams (b. 1871, Montgomery County; d. July 13, 1872; buried Woodland Cemetery); 4) Harriet Iams (b. 1861, Montgomery County; d. September 21, 1864; buried Woodland Cemetery); 5) Inez Iams (b. 1862 or 1869, Montgomery County; d. December 19, 1891; buried in Woodland Cemetery); 6) Ellen Iams (b. 1852); 7) Martha Iams (b. 1852); and 8) Oliver C. Iams (b. 1851).

Jacob Iams (b. April 27, 1830, Montgomery County, Ohio); son of Eli Iams (b. 1799); m. 1871 to Charlotte Sanders, daughter of Richard Sanders; a grocer in Englewood, Montgomery County; had three children: 1) Elsie V. Iams; 2) Pearl or Mary B. Iams; and 3) Alvin A. Iams (b. January 31, 1874; d. March 13, 1960, Oakwood, Montgomery County, Ohio, by self-inflicted .32 revolver; retired railroad worker).

John Iams (b. April 13, 1809, Greene County, Pennsylvania; d. March 9, 1905, Washington County, Iowa), son of Richard Iams (b. 1829) and Mary Shidler; m. September 12, 1828, to Sarah McVey (b. December 25, 1811, Washington County, Pennsylvania; d. January 18, 1903, Washington County, Iowa); moved from Pennsylvania to near Newark, Licking County, Ohio, by 1831; lived in Iowa long enough to be declared Iowa's oldest living couple; but in 1836 John Iams (b. 1809) was working in a tannery in Delaware, Delaware County, Ohio; moved to Washington County, Iowa, by 1838, and settled on Dutch Creek; married 74 years; had nine children:

    1. Richard Iams [(b. April 2, 1831, Licking County, Ohio; lived in Delaware County, Ohio, Iowa, and St. Paul, Nebraska; m. December 3, 1856, to Susan Crawford (b. October 19, 1832, Columbiana County, Ohio), the daughter of William Crawford and Harriet Henrietta Lightfoot; and granddaughter of Samuel Crawford and Sarah Allen. (Harriet Henrietta Lightfoot was the daughter of Solomon and Susan Lightfoot of Beaver County, Pennsylvania); and the ten children of Richard Iams (b. 1831) were:

1) Frank Iams (b. 1858, lived in St. Paul, Howard County, Nebraska);
2) Charlie Iams (b. 1859, lived in Howard County, Nebraska;
alive age 65; had daughter Gladys Iams, b. 1879); 3) Rose Iams
[(b. 1861; d. before 1942); m. Mr. Abraham and they had seven
children: a) Ralph Abraham (lived in Natal, South Africa); b)
Richard Abraham (lived in San Francisco); c) M. Keith Abraham
(lived in Portland, Oregon); d) Paul Abraham (lived in
Richmond, Virginia); e) Major D. D. Abraham (lived in Wichita
Falls, Texas); f) G. W. Abraham (lived in Mojave, California);
and g) Dr. V. R. Abraham (had two children: Kenneth Abraham,
lived in Portland Oregon; and Virginia Abraham, m. Mr.
Howard; lived in Campbell, California)]; 4) John Williams Iams
(b. 1869); 5) Etta Iams [(b. 1865; d. by 1942); m. Cassius B.
Manuel (b. 1860, McKean County, Pennsylvania), the son of
Benjamin F. Manuel; and they had three children: a) Bessie
Manuel (lived in Palo Alto, California); b) Ruth Manuel (m.
Mr. Wade; lived in Kearney, Nebraska); and c) Ruby Manuel
(m. Mr. Schoonover; lived in Chicago, Illinois)]; 6) Perry Iams
(b. 1863; d. March 14, 1942, in Everett, Washington; served in
Spanish American War); 7) George Iams [(b. January 2, 1871,
Keokuk, Iowa; d. October 2, 1939, Vancouver, Clark County,
Washington; buried Hill Cemetery, Vancouver); served in
Company B, 2nd Nebraska Infantry, Spanish American War;
m. Elizabeth Emma Dahlke]; 8) Minnie Iams (b. 1867; m. Mr.
Stewart); 9) Bessie Iams; and 10) Gaybrella "Gary" Iams (b.
1873; m. Mr. Stewart; lived in Viroqua, Wisconsin). William
Crawford and Harriet Henrietta Lightfoot (parents of Susan
Crawford, b. 1832) had a total of eight children: 1) Samuel
Crawford [(m. Mrs. Mary McNeil); their three children were:
a) William Crawford; b) Winnie Crawford; and c) Hattie
Crawford]; 2) Saul Crawford (a bachelor); 3) George Crawford
(a bachelor); 4) William Crawford (d. young); 5) Mary Crawford
(m. Elijah Stucker; had a large family); 6) Kizzie Crawford (m.
Elijah Triggs; had a large family); 7) Elizabeth Crawford (m.
Jonathan Brown; had a large family); and 8) Susan Crawford
(m. Richard Iams, b. 1831; see above). (CIC, MI)

Charles Iams Cherney, M.D., of Zanesville, Ohio (1994) wrote that Richard
Iams (m. Mary Schidler or Shidler) was his gt-gt-gt-grandfather; that John Iams [(b.
Greene County, Pennsylvania, April 13, 1809; d. March 9, 1905, Washington County,
Iowa); m. September 12, 1828, Washington County, Pennsylvania, to Sarah McVey
(b. December 25, 1810, Washington County, Pennsylvania; d. January 18, 1903,
Washington County, Iowa), was his gt-gt-grandfather; and that Richard Iams (m.
Mary Schidler or Shidler) was listed in Jefferson County, Ohio, in the 1830 census.
He was in Licking County, Ohio, by 1831, and in Delaware County, Ohio, by 1835.
Richard Iams, the son of John Iams and Sarah McVey, b. April 3, 1831, in Licking
County, Ohio. In 1838, John Iams and wife Sarah, with son Richard Iams, moved to
Washington County, Iowa, where they lived at Dutch Creek and raised nine children.
Although not directly connected to this lineage, early records in Jefferson County,
Ohio, show: a) a Court of Common Pleas case of April 1, 1806, described where
Richard Ranning sued a John Iams for $131.50; b) In September 1806, the home of
John Iiams is described as being located on Cross Creek near Forsythe Mill; c) a

January 28, 1812, newspaper article in the *Western Herald* (page 4) declared that Mary Iiams, wife of John Iiams, was an adulteress; and d) 1818 and 1819 County Tax Lists described John Iiams as owning 252 acres (Range 2, Township 1, Section 10), and Richard Iiams as owning 194 acres (Range 2; annual tax $3.29). The 1820 Census of Jefferson County, Ohio, lists Jonathan Iams as living alone; and lists Jonathan Iams, Jr., as living in household with his family that included one older woman. The Steubenville, Jefferson County, Ohio, Land Office Records show two entries for John Iiams: On August 10, 1801 (Section 3, Township 6, Range 2) a warrant was issued to John Jiams; and on December 21, 1804, (Warrant 1177) and May 16, 1805 (Warrant 1414), John Jiams is listed as being a resident of Brook County, Virginia.];

2) John Iams (b. 1832, Delaware County, Ohio);

3) Catherine Iams (b. July 23, 1833, Delaware County, Ohio);

4) Mary E. Iams (b. September 1, 1836, Delaware County, Ohio; m. Billy Moats);

5) Susan Iams [(b. September 6, 1838, Washington County, Iowa); m. Mr. Shepler];

6) Isabel Iams [(b. April 1, 1843, Washington County, Iowa); m. Mr. Jenks];

7) Abraham Iams [(b. March 23, 1845, Washington County, Iowa); m. _____ Young];

8) Nancy Iams [(b. October 15, 1847, Washington County, Iowa; d. April 1, 1876); m. Franklin Singmaster]; and

9) William Iams (b. July 17, 1851, Washington County, Iowa).

The 1880 Federal Census of Dutch Creek, Madison County, Iowa, lists: John Iiams (age 71, b. Pennsylvania); Sarah Iiams (age 69, b. Pennsylvania); and granddaughter Fannie Singmaster (age 5, b. Iowa). The 1880 Census of Clear Creek Township, Keokuk County, Iowa, lists: Richard Iams (age 49, b. Ohio); Susan Iams (age 47, b. Ohio); Frank Iiams (age 22, b. Iowa); Chester Iams (age 21, b. Iowa); Rose Iams (age 19, b. Iowa); Perry Iams (age 17, b. Iowa); Ettie Iams (age 15, b. Iowa); Minnie Iams (age 13, b. Iowa); John Iams (age 11, b. Iowa); George Iams (age 9, b. Iowa); and Gary Iams (age 7, b. Iowa); with mother-in-law Harriet Crawford (age 71, b. Pennsylvania). The 1880 Census for Athens Township, Ringgold County, Iowa, lists: Abram Iams (age 35, b. Iowa); Anna Iams (age 37, b. Pennsylvania); Edwin Iams (age 14, b. Iowa); Joseph Iams (age 12, b. Iowa); and William Iams (age 3, b. Iowa). EFB disputes the origin of this line.

George Iams (b. January 2, 1871, Keokuk County, Iowa; d. October 2, 1939, Vancouver, Clark County, Washington; buried Park Hill Cemetery, Vancouver), son of Richard Iams (b. 1831) and Susan Crawford; m. January 6, 1900, Iowa, to Elizabeth Emma Dahlke (b. April 30, 1879, Iowa; d. June 17, 1843); was a member of Company B, 2nd Nebraska Infantry, in Spanish American War (enlisted in Nebraska May 9, 1898; discharged October 24, 1898); lived in Medford, Oregon, for ten years; sent a declaration by mail from Jackson County, Oregon, November 22, 1909, at age 36; sent an affadavit from Hall County, Nebraska, June 1, 1922, at age 51; lived in Grand Island, Nebraska, for five years; mailed a questionnaire as resident of St. Paul, Nebraska, August 26, 1922; and on both June 13, 1930, and on July 25, 1933, was reported to be living at 410 West 17th Street, Vancouver, Washington; had at least two children: 1) Hazel Leola Iams (b. July 19, 1902); and 2) Raymond Frank Iams (b. October 6, 1903).

Richard Iams (b. April 2, 1831, Licking County, Ohio; d. May 23, 1912, St. Paul, Howard County, Nebraska), son of John Iams (b. 1809) and Sarah McVey; m. December 3, 1856, to Susan Crawford (b. October 19, 1832, Columbiana County, Ohio; d. St. Paul, Nebraska), daughter of William Crawford and Harriet Henrietta

Lightfoot; moved to Delaware County, Ohio, by 1836; to Washington County, Iowa, by 1838; to Tallyrand Keokuk County, Iowa, by 1865 (operated a general store and tavern); to St. Paul, Nebraska, after 1890 retirement to be near sons Frank Iams and Charles Iams. He was described as having a long white beard and as needing something to do after retirement and selling the store, he sold utensils and gadgets door-to-door in St. Paul; had ten children:

1) Frank Iams [(b. September 9, 1857, Washington County, Iowa; d. October 21, 1918, South Dakota), m. Ella Jenks; was a dealer in horses; travelled worldwide to purchase houses for sale in Nebraska while living in St. Paul; in business with his brother Charles Iams, and after the 1912 sinking of the Titanic, left all overseas trips to his brother; and with the advent of the tractor, sold his business and moved to South Dakota to enter the cattle business, but died shortly thereafter]; 2) Charles Iams [(b. June 9, 1859, Dutch Creek Township, Washington County, Iowa, to Mary Alice Lemley; learned to enjoy buying and selling horses as a child; was in business with his brother, Frank Iams, in St. Paul, Howard County, Nebraska]; 3) Rose Iams [(b. February 21, 1861; d. June 26, 1923); m. Vestel Abraham]; 4) Perry Iams [(b. November 7, 1862; d. March 14, 1942), m. Grace May Fry (per JLI)]; 5) Sarah Etta Iams [(b. September 7, 1864; d. September 27, 1935), m. Cassius Manuel]; 6) Minnie Iams [(b. December 31, 1867; d. before 1960), m. Frank Street]; 7) John William Iams (b. December 19, 1868; d. June 28, 1918); 8) George Iams (b. January 2, 1871; d. before 1942; m. Lizzie); 9) Gabrilla Iams (b. March 24, 1873; d. before 1960; m. John Stewart); and 10) Bessie Iams (b. May 22, 1876; d. January 4, 1879). (CIC)

Charles Iams (b. June 9, 1859, Dutch Creek Township, Washington County, Iowa; d. October 2, 1946, St. Paul, Howard County, Nebraska), son of Richard Iams (b. 1831) and Susan Crawford; m. October 25, 1893, at Grace Hill, Washington County, Iowa, to Mary Alice Lemley; was Past Master of Masonic Lodge; was a dealer in horses who retired after his brother and partner died; served as horse show judge for several years; member of Cemetery Board; member of School Board for 12 years; served as St. Paul mayor for 4 years; ran for sheriff. Their child was Gladys Genevieve Iams (b. November 3, 1899, St. Paul, Howard County, Nebraska; d. July 23, 1991); m. June 12, 1923, to Ernest F. Cerney (d. December 25, 1978); she was a "natural leader and pillar of the community"; valedictorian at St. Paul High School; completed University of Nebraska Normal School and returned to St. Paul to teach kindergarten; retired from teaching following her marriage, but returned to teaching during the teacher shortage of World War II; was a teacher and school principal; active in local theater, reading, bridge clubs, piano, First Presbyterian Church, church choir, member of Presbyterian Session; church treasurer for 15 years; Past Matron, Treasurer, and 49-year member of Eastern Star; President of American Legion Auxiliary; received Bachelor of Science from University of Nebraska in 1953; bought a Conoco Station and motel in 1957; ran a nursery school until 1973; served as St. Paul Community Centennial Queen in 1972; celebrated 50th wedding anniversary in 1973; awarded Distinguished Service Award for 52 years at St. Paul schools in 1989; had a scholarship established in her honor at St. Paul High School; and their only child was Charles Iams Cherney, M.D., a specialist in internal medicine who served as family historian; has composed a history of medicine of the Zanesville, Muskingum County, Ohio, area, and composed the branch of the family history; practiced internal medicine in Zanesville, Ohio, in 1994.

Perry Iams (b. November 7, 1862, Dutch Creek Township, Washington County, Iowa; d. March 14, 1942), son of Richard Iams (b. 1832) and Susan Crawford; m. Grace Mae Fry; and their son was William Daniel Iams [(b. November 15, 1913, Marion, Ohio; d. February 7, 1970, Sullivan, Franklin County, Missouri); m.

Virginia Leigh Utz (b. July 24, 1911, St. Joseph, Missouri; d. February 7, 1970), daughter of Amos Logan Utz and Edith Katherine Hunt; and their son James Leigh Iams (b. October 16, 1947, Washington, Franklin County, Missouri), m. June 6, 1970, to Christine Carmain (no children), and they lived in Berkeley, California, in 1995, serving as family tree correspondent.]

Otho Iams (b. 1791, Washington County, Maryland; d. April 27, 1875, or before 1871, Morris Township, Greene County, Pennsylvania), son of Richard Iiams (b. ca1745) and Eleanor Pottenger; m. Morris Township, Greene County, Pennsylvania, to Nancy Cole (b. 1795 or 1796, Virginia; d. before 1870). Bates, 1888, states that the family of Otho Iams had moved from New Jersey in 1790; settled in Morris Township; became one of the most prominent and successful farmers. In 1797, he was living in Redstone, Washington County, Pennsylvania; and in the 1790 Census of Washington County, Maryland, the family of Richard Iiams had been enumerated. The will of Otho Iams, written February 2, 1872, named sons Thomas Iams, John Iams (and son Wesley Iams), William Iams, Otho Iams, Eli Iams; and daughters Eleanor Sanders and Mariah Marshall; with J. Wesley Iams offering testimony about the death of Otho Iams May 11, 1875, at 7:20 p.m., with the inventory subsequently filed on June 11, 1875 (Greene County, Volume 5, page 17, 1875). The 1850 Census of Morris Township, Greene County, Pennsylvania, lists Otho Imes (age 59, b. Maryland); Nancy Imes (age 54, b. Virginia); Mariah Imes (age 34, b. Pennsylvania); Elizabeth Imes (age 27, b. Pennsylvania); William Imes (age 25, b. Pennsylvania); Otho Imes (age 21, b. Pennsylvania); Eli Imes (age 18, b. Pennsylvania); and Westley Imes (age 16, b. Pennsylvania). The 1870 Census of Madison County, Iowa, lists Otha Iams (age 40, farmer, b. Pennsylvania); Mary Iams (age 30, b. Pennsylvania); John W. Iams (age 8, b. Pennsylvania); Florenzer Iams (age 7, b. Iowa); and Charles W. Iams (age 2, b. Iowa). The 1900 Census of Madison County, Iowa, lists Otho Iames (age 70, b. Pennsylvania); Mary Iames (age 60, b. Pennsylvania); Charles M. Iames (age 32, b. Iowa). The 1920 Census of Polk County, Iowa, lists Charles Iams (age 51, b. Iowa); Ida M. Iams (age 46, b. Iowa); stepson James F. Schloesser (age 20, b. Iowa). The eleven children of Otho Iams (b. 1791) and Nancy Cole, or other wife, were:

1) Thomas "Dennis" Iams [(b. 1821 or 1822, Morris Township, Greene County, Pennsylvania; d. February 19, 1881 or 1888), m. before 1843; to Delilah "Matilda" Huffman (b. 1824, Morris Township; d. after 1870, Morris Township; daughter of Benjamin and Sarah Huffman; a will of a Dennis Iams was filed in Greene County, Volume 6, p. 200, 1888; a Demas Iams was drafted June 28, 1864, Company B, 126 Reg., O.V.L., Belmont County, Ohio; 1900 Census of Greene County lists Delilah Iams (age 75, b. Pennsylvania), with daughter Lucinda Iams (age 41)]; 2) William Iams (b. 1825, Pennsylvania; m. Hannah Wright; their two children were: Mrs. J. W. Iams and F. F. Iams); 3) Neal Iams; 4) Nancy Iams (b. March 20, 1828, Morris Township; d. February 21, 1848, Morris Township; 5) Richard Iams; 6) Isaac Iams; 7) Mariah Iams (b. 1816); 8) Elizabeth Iams (b. 1823 or 1825, Morris Township); 9) Otho Iams (b. October 1829, Morris Township); m. Mary ____ (b. January 1840, Pennsylvania; moved to Iowa); 10) Eli Iams (b. 1832, Morris Township; m. Clarissa ____; 3 children: Madge Iams, b. 1867; Sarah Iams, b. 1872; and Evelyn Iams, b. 1877); 11) Westley Iams (b. 1834); 12) John Iams (b. 1818; m. Rebecca Huffman; moved to Audubon, Iowa; had a son Wesley Iams); and 13) Eleanor Iams (b. June 9, 1814; m. April 30, 1835; m. Sam Saunders). (EFB, MI, Bates, 1888).

Thomas "Dennis" Iams (b. 1821, Greene County, Pennsylvania; d. February 19, 1881, Greene County, Pennsylvania), son of Otho Iams (b. 1791), m. June 30, 1842, Greene County, Pennsylvania, to Delilah "Matilda" Huffman (b. 1824, Morris

Township, Greene County, Pennsylvania), daughter of Benjamin Huffman and Sally Wood, or (James B. Meighen) fourth child of John Huffman (b. 1802; d. 1883) and wife Anna (other children): James Huffman, George Huffman, Joseph Huffman, Nancy Huffman, Rebecca Huffman, and Elizabeth Huffman); a judge; lived at Ruff Creek in Greene County; a Democrat; elected to several county offices including Treasurer; Greene County Associate Judge; one of eleven founders of the Washington and Waynesburg Railroad (narrow gauge); and their seven children were: 1) Benjamin H. Iams [(b. September 23, 1843, Morris Township, Greene County; d. June 8, 1863, in Fairfax, Virginia Union Army Hospital); a member of the 18th Cavalry under Captain John Hughes]; 2) Otho Iams [(b. September 4, 1846, Ruff's Creek, Morris Township, Greene County, Pennsylvania), m. June 1881, Greene County, to Sarah Bane, daughter of Jasper Bane; lived at Swart, Greene County; attended Waynesburg College; member of State Democratic Central Committee; owned 600 acres of land in Morris Township]; 3) James L. "JL" Iams (b. January 2, 1856, Morris Township, Greene County); lived at Swart, Greene County; farmer and stock grower; schoolteacher; attended Waynesburg College; member State Democratic Central Committee; in 1877, Morris Township, m. Bell S. Swart (b. 1849), daughter of Jacob Swart]; 4) Frank Pierce Iams (b. July 20, 1852; d. December 3, 1925); a lawyer in Pittsburgh; 5) Lucinda Henrietta Iams [(b. March 20, 1859, Pennsylvania; d. May 14, 1936), m. May 18, 1875, to Joseph W. Ring (or Ray) of Waynesburg, Pennsylvania]; 6) Jesse Lazear Iams (b. November 9, 1854, Morris Township; d. November 9, 1871); and 7) Henrietta Iams [(b. February 19, 1850, Greene County, Pennsylvania; d. April 18, 1938, Waynesburg, Greene County, Pennsylvania), m. May 18, 1878, Morris Township, to J. Warren Ray of Waynesburg]. The 1850 Federal Census of Greene County, Pennsylvania, lists Thomas Imes (age 29, b. Pennsylvania); Delila Imes (age 26, b. Pennsylvania); Benjamin Imes (age 7, b. Pennsylvania); Otho Imes (age 4, b. Pennsylvania); and Henrietta Imes (age 4 months). The 1870 Census lists Thomas Iams (age 48, b. Pennsylvania); Delila Iams (age 46, b. Pennsylvania); Otho Iams (age 23, b. Pennsylvania; Jesse Iams (age 15, b. Pennsylvania); James Iams (age 13, b. Pennsylvania); and Lucinda Iams (age 10, b. Pennsylvania). The 1880 Census lists Thomas Iams (age 58); Delilah Iams (age 55); Otho Iams (age 33); Lucinda Iams (age 21); and nephew Thomas Iams (age 23, b. Pennsylvania); with James Iams (age 23) and wife Belle V. Iams (age 21) living nearby. The 1900 Census includes James L. Iams (age 43); Belle Iams (age 41); and near was Otho Iams (age 53) with wife Sarah J. Iams (age 44) and son Allen Iams (age 16). The 1910 Census lists Otho Iams (age 63) with wife Sarah J. Iams (age 54) and son Allen Iams (age 25). And the 1920 Census lists Allen A. Iams (age 35) with wife Nellie B. Iams (age 27); daughter Mary B. Iams (age 3); daughter Lucy M. Iams (age 2); father Otho Iams (age 75, listed as b. Ohio); and mother Sarah J. Iams (age 64, b. Pennsylvania). (JBM, MI)

Otho Iams (b. September 4, 1846, Ruff's Creek, Morris Township, Greene County, Pennsylvania), son of Thomas Iams (b. 1821) and Delilah Huffman; m. June 1881 to Sarah Jane Bane, daughter of Jasper Bane; lived at Swart in Greene County; a farmer and stockman; member of Democratic State Committee; had a son Allen A. Iams (b. May 11, 1884, Morris Township; d. March 1, 1957, Morris Township, Greene County), an early promoter of Greene County Extension Association (member of Executive Board with office of Secretary for 20 years); Morris Township Tax Collector for 12 years and Assessor for 8 years; Greene County Tax Appraiser for 6 years; m. December 1, 1915, to Nellie Bennet, and they had four children: 1) Mary Iams (single); 2) Lucy Iams (m. Clarence Oradorff; lived at Harrisburg, Pennsylvania); 3) Helen Iams (m. A. C. Bogush; lived at Manchester, Connecticut; and 4) Hazel Iams (m. Robert Stein; lived at Meadville, Pennsylvania).

William Iiams (b. 1755, Anne Arundel County, Maryland; d. 1809, Greene County, Pennsylvania), son of Thomas Iiams (b. 1708); m. Charity Ryan, and their four children were: 1) William Iams, Jr. (b. 1783, Anne Arundel County, Maryland; had a son, George Iams); 2) John Iams [(b. 1785, Anne Arundel County); moved to Greene County, Pennsylvania, and then to Ohio; had 7 children: 1) a child, b. 1811, Greene County; 2) Andrew Iams (b. 1811, Greene County); 3) Henry Iams (b. 1820, Greene County); 4) John Iams, Jr. (b. 1821, Greene County); 5) Anna Iams (b. 1826); 6) Mary Iams (b. 1831); and 7) William Iams (b. Ohio)]; 3) Isaac Iams (b. 1795, Anne Arundel County, Maryland); and 4) Mary Iams [(b. December 1784, Maryland; d. October 1851, Greene County, Illinois), m. 1805, Washington County, Pennsylvania, to John Heaton (b. 1780; d. 1844); moved to Illinois after 1830; a family letter from Illinois to Texas in 1850 referred to "Uncle John Iams"]. (EFB)

John Wesley Iams (b. 1850, Greene County, Pennsylvania; d. 1926); m. Mary Elizabeth Patterson (b. 1852; d. 1924), the sister of Matthew Patterson, Mark Patterson, and John Patterson. He was Greene County Superintendent of Schools; member of Waynesburg College faculty; believed to be the son of Thomas Iams and Mary Smith, and grandson of Richard Iams (b. 1748, Maryland); moved first to Hagerstown, Maryland, area; and to Greene County, Pennsylvania, in 1794. The child of John Wesley Iams (b. 1850) was Frank Victor Iams [(b. 1872; d. 1945), a lawyer; 1901 graduate of Waynesburg College; moved to New Martinsville, Wetzel County, West Virginia, at the onset of the "oil boom"); m. Mary Elizabeth Harker (b. 1880, Wadestown, West Virginia; d. 1961, New Martinsville, West Virginia), and they had five children: 1) William Archibald Iams (b. and d. 1905, New Martinsville, West Virginia; alive 1967; compiled branch of family tree); and the two children were: Frank Victor Iams (b. 1945, New Martinsville)]; and 5) Ruth Ann Iams (m. Mr. Cochran and their son Mark Iams Cochran, b. 1949). (JVI, EFB)

Franklin Pierce Iams (b. July 20, 1852, Morris Township, Greene County, Pennsylvania; d. March 11, 1917, Pittsburgh, Allegheny County, Pennsylvania; son of Judge Thomas Iams (b. 1821) and Delilah Huffman; m. August 12, 1877, Waynesburg, Pennsylvania, to Lucy Virginia Dorsey (b. November 13, 1855, Oakland, Garrett County, Maryland; d. October 26, 1924, Sheraden, Allegheny County, Pennsylvania; buried in Allegheny Cemetery), daughter of James Francis Dorsey and Charlotte Hook. They had two children: 1) Jesse Dorsey Iams (b. August 8, 1844; lived in Tulsa, Oklahoma); and 2) Doctor Jay Donald Iams [(b. December 1879, Waynesburg, Greene County, Pennsylvania); m. May 21, 1904, to Grace Forrester Donnan (b. May 8, 1883, Washington, Washington County, Pennsylvania; d. May 18, 1861, Washington, Pennsylvania), daughter of Alvan Donnan and Lucy Alexander Murdock, and they had four children: 1) Charlotte D. Iams (lived in Washington, Pennsylvania); 2) Franklin Pierce Iams [(b. 1915, Pittsburgh; d. November 18, 1986, Sarasota, Florida; buried St. Johns Episcopal, King Georges County, Virginia); graduated from Washington and Jefferson University; lived in Washington, Pennsylvania; U. S. Army in 1941; M.A. in Hospital Administration from University of Minnesota in 1948; Assistant Director of Rhode Island University Hospital; Administrator New York University Bellevue Medical Center; President and Chief Executive Officer of Fairfax, Virginia, Hospital; President of Committee on United States Health in Lyndon Baines Johnson administration; member of President's Commission on Emergency Preparedness; an uncle of Jay D. Iams, M.D., of Columbus, Ohio; and of Mrs. John McDaniel of Brownsville, Texas]; 3) Alexander M. Iams, M.D. [(d. February 1984; lived in Madison, Wisconsin); and his two children were: William M. Iams (lived in Madison, Wisconsin) and Jay D. Iams, M.D. (lived Columbus, Ohio; faculty at Ohio State University)]; and 4) Alvin Donnan Iams (d. young). (MI, JDI)

Franklin Pierce Iams (b. 1852; lawyer; listed *Cyclopedia of American Biography* (8:305, 1965) as son of Thomas Iams and Delilah Huffman; grandson of Otho Iams and Nancy Cole; great-grandson of Richard Iams and Eleanor Pottenger; great-great-grandson of Richard Iams, Revolutionary soldier from Maryland; graduate of Waynesburg College and University of Michigan School of Law; admitted to Bar in 1876; known for successful defense in McCausland murder case in which his client, but not other defendants, was acquitted by a reversal of the lower court on appeal to Supreme Court; was District Attorney of Greene County, Pennsylvania; a Burgess of Waynesburg and Pittsburgh (Sheradan); helped organize First National Bank of Sheradan; served as Bank Director; member of Democratic State Central Committee. He married Lucy Virginia Dorsey (b. 1855), a notable in her own right.

Lucy Virginia Dorsey (b. 1855) is listed in *Notable American Women* (pp. 249-251) and in *Who's Who in America* (1915). She devoted her time as a Pittsburgh welfare worker and leader of reform legislation; a graduate of Waynesburg College (B.A., 1873); taught in public schools; served as court stenographer; participated in legal field activities; worked with Allegheny County Civic Club; Vice-President and then Chairman of Social Science Department and Legislative Committee; served as Chairman State Federation of Pennsylvania Women; Chairman of Consumer League of Western Pennsylvania; served on Committee of Associated Charities of Pittsburgh; Committee on Pennsylvania and Allegheny County Child Labor; made outstanding contributions in areas of housing, health, women and child welfare, and correctional institutions; said to be ranked "among the best practitioners of reform politics in the early twentieth century"; is credited with the initiation and development of housing authorities, building codes, town planning association of Federal Children's Bureau, school health programs, and health programs for women.

Lucy Virginia Dorsey (b. November 13, 1855; d. October 25, 1924), m. August 1877 to F. P. Iams; was daughter of James Dorsey, M.D. (also a Methodist minister) and Charlotte Hook (d. January 21, 1866), who were m. December 21, 1848; was the sister of Elbert Charles Dorsey (b. 1852); and Charlotte Hook (b. 1866) was the daughter of Jesse Hook (son of James Hook and Charlotte Morris) and Lucy Burbridge. Other children of Dr. James Dorsey and Charlotte Hook, were: 1) Jesse Dorsey (b. 1849; d. 1914; m. Emma Chalfont); 2) Larken Edward Dorsey (b. 1852); and 3) Sarah Frances Dorsey (b. 1856; d. 1891; m. Levi Atkins). Other children of Jesse Hook and Lucy Burbridge were: 1) Catherine M. Hook (b. and d. 1826); 2) James Burbridge Hook [(b. 1830; d. 1884); m. November 1, 1849, to Elizabeth Blaine (b. 1835; d. 1914)]; 3) John Inghram Hook [(b. September 14, 1834; d. June 25, 1896), m. February 7, 1858, to Rebecca S. Aiken (b. 1828; d. April 4, 1920); 4) Catherine Hook (m. October 30, 1856, to Morgan R. Wise, son of Joseph Wise and Pamela Barnard); 5) Thomas J. Hook (b. February 3, 1837; d. January 26, 1858); 6) Enos Hook (b. 1839; d. 1865); 7) Francis M. Hook (b. 1840; d. January 29, 1866; m. M. S. Kingsland); and 8) Benjamin F. Hook (b. May 24, 1844).

Larkin Edward Dorsey (b. September 23, 1852, Waynesburg, Greene County, Pennsylvania), the son of Dr. James Dorsey (b. 1825) and Charlotte Hook (b. 1828; d. January 21, 1866), is known for often changing his name. He first changed his name to Elbert Charles Forest and left the home area of Waynesburg, Pennsylvania. In 1890 he was reported to be living in Utah, and his youngest daughter, Beulah Forest-Johnson (b. 1911) reported that in the interim he had gone to Texas and drove cattle along the trails to Dodge City, Kansas, and later moved to Utah and to Oklahoma, and died in Boise, Idaho, on September 10, 1950. Other known aliases include: Edwin Dorsey, Elmer Charles Dorsey, C. E. Dorsey, Elmer Dorsey, Edwin Forest, and Charles Elbert Forest. He had told his children that he was the son of a

231

minister, but had been orphaned while a child in Greene County, Pennsylvania. He is believed to have m. 1st, Mary Elizabeth Coleman (b. May 1, 1870, in Cumberland County, Illinois; d. June 13, 1953, in Twin Falls County, Idaho), and m. 2nd, January 20, 1891, to Eva Rebecca Seely. The nine known children of Larkin Edward Dorsey-Forest (b. 1852) were:

1) Charles LeRoy Forest (b. August 6, 1891, Emery County, Utah; d. March 23, 1923; m. May 27, 1912, to Reba Gibson); 2)Nellie Murl Forest (b. December 3, 1894, Woodward County, Oklahoma; m. 1924 to Mae Etheridge); 4) Wiley Forest (b. October 19, 1897, Woodward County, Oklahoma; m. 1923 to Grace Hildreth); 5) Oloff James Forest (b. July 18, 1900, Woodward County, Oklahoma; m. February 9, 1921, to Frances Dolon); 6) Carl Forest (b. November 7, 1902, Woodward County, Oklahoma; m. 1924 to Emma Uptain); 7) Harold Forest (b. November 7, 1902, Woodward County, Oklahoma; m. 1928 to Mae Etheridge Forest); 8) Melvin Forest (b. May 14, 1905, Woodward County, Oklahoma; d. July 25, 1994; m. April 23, 1928, to Eva Velva Jewell); 9) Beulah Forest (b. November 16, 1911, Woodward County, Oklahoma; m. November 1931, to Ammond Johnson). Melvin Forest (b. 1905) had a son Robert Theodore Forest (b. 1929) who reported this branch of the family tree; reported that Charles Elbert D. Forest (b. 1852) moved to Oklahoma in 1894 and lived in a dugout before building "a nice sod home which they lived in for several years," and by 1920 their ranch had grown to 4,400 acres and was known for large orchards and gardens before they sold the farm and moved to Colorado. (RTF)

Robert Theodore Forest (b. May 21, 1929, Lewis, Montgomery County, Colorado, a geologist and son of Melvin Forest (b. 1905, Oklahoma) and Elva Velva Jewell (b. 1910); m. November 21, 1951, LaMesa, San Diego County, California, to Vivian LaVerne Zimmerman (b. December 23, 1925, Lucerne Mines, Indiana County, Pennsylvania), daughter of George Emery Zimmerman and Vivian Genevieve Straw, a graduate of Indiana University of Pennsylvania; a schoolteacher; and they had three children: 1) Carol Denise Forest (b. February 3, 1954, Denver, Colorado; m. April 7, 1979, to Dennis Lee Buonanoma); 2) Michael Melvin Forest (b. August 7, 1957, Chuquicamata, Autofagasta Province, Chile, South America; m. June 28, 1980, to Patricia Lynn Gialy); and 3) Mark Emery Forest (b. January 23, 1959, Denver, Colorado; m. May 26, 1979, to Theresa Rose Young). Other children of Melvin Forest (b. 1905) were: Doris Marie Forest (b. November 29, 1930, Lewis, Colorado; m. August 11, 1951, to John J. Butler); Donald Eugene Forest (b. June 22, 1933, Lewis, Colorado; m. July 4, 1956, to Bonnie Joan Rogers); and Patricia Ann Forest (b. August 14, 1939, Lewis, Colorado; m. August 1, 1959, to William Clements). (RTF)

Jesse Dorsey Iams (b. August 8, 1884, Pittsburgh, Allegheny County, Pennsylvania; d. January 15, 1973, Taos, New Mexico), son of Franklin Pierce Iams (b. 1852) and Lucy Virginia Dorsey; m. 1920 in Tulsa, Oklahoma, to Margaret Shannon Laubach (b. November 19, 1895, Scranton, Lackawanna County, Pennsylvania; d. February 14, 1991, Taos, New Mexico), daughter of Charles Crissman Laubach and Sarah Cathrine Shannon; and they had three children: John Dorsey Iams (b. December 30, 1921); 2) Kathrine Virginia Iams (b. December 23, 1925, Tulsa, Oklahoma); and 3) Donald Richard Iams [(b. February 9, 1932, Tulsa, Oklahoma; d. March 5, 1992, Phoenix, Arizona); m. 1st, July 24, 1958, Denver, Colorado, to Gail Cynthia Shepherd (b. April 29, 1937, Denver Colorado), daughter of Jack Harlow Shepherd and Phyllis Regina Ormsby; m. 2nd, in Phoenix, Arizona, to Donna Lyn Jones (b. September 14, 1947, San Antonio, Bexar County, Texas), daughter of Willard Jefferson Jones and Mabel Nell Davis; and the six children of Donald Richard Iams (b. 1932) were: a) Richard Iams (b. September 9, 1960; d. September 11, 1960, Phoenix, Arizona); b) Mark Shannon Iams (b. January 23, 1962, Phoenix, Arizona); c)

Christopher Shepherd Iams (b. December 22, 1963, Phoenix, Arizona); d) Michael Dorsey Iams (b. April 30, 1968, Palo Alto, Santa Cruz County, Arizona; graduate of American Univeristy; wrote family history); e) Jonathan Alexander Iams (b. October 26, 1982, Chandler, Maricopa County, Arizona); and f) Stephen Donald Iams (b. January 28, 1986, Chandler, Maricopa County, Arizona)]. (MI)

Frank Victor Iams (b. March 27, 1872, Greene County, Pennsylvania; d. September 7, 1945, New Martinsville, West Virginia), son of John Wesley Iams (b. 1850; d. 1926; Superintendent of Greene County, Pennsylvania, Schools); m. December 23, 1903, to Mary Elizabeth Halken (or Hacker) (b. April 8, 1880; d. December 6, 1961), and they had two children: 1) John Victor Iams [(b. December 16, 1913; d. April 25, 1981), m. Louise Morris (b. September 26, 1911); owner of Iams Funeral Home in Moundsville, West Virginia; (served in World War II where he befriended a black medic by same name who relayed the story that the King of England released two of his personal guards, both named Ijames to come to America, and these two Ijames were believed to have settled in the South, had large farms, and kept some slaves); had two children: a) Frank Victor Iams II; lived in New Martinsville, West Virginia; m. Ann Priesten (and they had three children: Thomas Victor Iams, Misty Dawn Iams, and Dane Roswell Iams); and b) Ruth Ann Iams (b. March 4, 1918); m. Noel Philip Cochran (b. March 28, 1915), and they had two children: Gina Renee Cochran (b. May 3, 1971; had child Zachary Glover, b. February 12, 1992), and Angela Dawn Cochran (m. Mr. McIsaac; she was b. October 20, 1970; child was Clayton McIsaac, b. June 22, 1993)]. (RAIC)

Descendants of Doctor Lake Iams of Johns Hopkins Hospital report that he had told John V. Iams (b. 1913) that the Imes had been body guards for King James I, and that two of the guards or two of the sons of guards came to America in 1796. One of the immigrants purchased 400 acres of land to the west of Philadelphia, Pennsylvania, about 30 miles west of Jamesville. The other immigrant married, had four sons, and one of these four sons moved to Washington County, Pennsylvania; one of the sons moved to Greene County, Pennsylvania; one of the sons moved to Monroe County, Ohio (or Pennsylvania); and the fourth of the sons moved to Indiana. One of the original immigrants married at the age of 35, but prior to getting married, fathered three children "with a high yellow slave," with the mother and children moving to Baltimore, one being the direct ancestor of Dr. Lake Imes (or Iams).

James Franklin "Frank" or "Frank James" Imes (b. 1869, Ohio), son of Solomon H. Imes (b. 1846; buried September 21, 1885, Vesuvius, Lawrence County, Ohio), and Nancy Sharp (marriage said to have been anulled in 1872 following her act of adultery), but as Allen D. Bare has reported, "This is no game. I want to be correct, no doubt;" and James Franklin Imes (b. 1869), m. April 13, 1885, in Wayne, West Virginia, to Anna Queen (b. April 12, 1871; d. Becco, Logan County, West Virginia), daughter of Samuel and Sarah Elizabeth Queen; and they had ten children: 1) Asa Imes (b. November 26, 1897, Lincoln County, West Virginia); 2) Alice Imes (b. April 1898, Logan County, West Virginia); 3) Lola Imes (b. March 3, 1900, Lincoln County, West Virginia); 4) Stella Iams (b. April 30, 1902, Amherstdale, Lincoln County, West Virginia; d. March 20, 1989, Logan County, West Virginia); 5) Ossie Imes (b. March 19, 1904, Lincoln County, West Virginia; d. September 20, 1971); 6) Ora Imes (b. July 13, 1913, Lincoln County, West Virginia; d. 1977); 7) William "Bill" Imes (b. June 3, 1906, Lincoln County, West Virginia; d. July 27, 1950, Logan County, West Virginia); 8) Roy Imes (b. February 15, 1909, Atenville, Lincoln County, West Virginia); 9) Frank Imes (b. October 3, 1910, Atenville, Lincoln County, West Virginia; d. May 29, 1991, Logan County, West Virginia); and 10) Helen Imes (b. June 3, 1919, West Virginia; d. May 14, 1974, Amherstdale, Logan County, West Virginia). (ADB)

Paul F. Iams, Sr. (b. 1915), founder of Iams Pet Foods of Dayton, Ohio, and his family have constructed their family tree. Eli Iams (b. 1779, Greene County, Pennsylvania; d. 1855, Trotwood, Ohio), son of Thomas Iams of Greene County, Pennsylvania; is famed for walking from Erie, Pennsylvania, to Trotwood, Montgomery County, Ohio, with a brother in the early 1800s; m. Phoebe Jane Heckathorn, and they had twelve children: 1) Martin Iams (b. 1820); 2) Richard Iams (b. 1823); 3) George Iams; 4) Alfred Iams; 5) Jacob Iams; 6) David Iams; 7) a girl; 8) a girl; 9) Harvey Iams; 10) Martha Iams; 11) Howard Iams, and 12) Loren Iams [(b. 1840, Trotwood, Montgomery County, Ohio); a farmer; at 73 inches, the shortest of the brothers; m. 1880 to Salome Fouts (b. 1860; operated a millinery shop; d. 1942), and they had three children: a) Harry Eli Iams (b. 1881; d. 1966; m. Carrie Alice Falknor, b. 1890; d. 1978); b) Howard Iams (b. 1886; d. 1887); and c) Ruth Iams (m. Harry Patton, and their daughter was Mary Patton)].

Harry Eli Iams (b. 1881) and Carrie Alice Falknor (b. 1890) had three children: 1) Mary Elizabeth Iams [(b. 1913, Dayton, Ohio), m. Branch Rickey, Jr. (b. January 13, 1914; d. April 11, 1961), and they had three children: a) Caroline Rickey; b) Nancy Rickey; and c) Branch Rickey III]; 2) Paul Falkner Iams, Sr. (b. August 11, 1915; m. April 23, 1948, to Harriet Jane Landrum, b. January 27, 1925); and 3) Nancy Lee Iams (b. 1923; m. Howard Egbert, Jr., b. 1920; they had two children: Susan Egbert, d. 1989; and Howard Egbert].

Paul Falkner Iams (b. 1915), the founder of Iams Pet Food Company of Dayton, sold the company in 1982 and settled in Sun City, Phoenix, Arizona; m. April 23, 1948, to Harriet Jane Landrum (b. January 27, 1925), daughter of Ralph Garret Landrum (b. March 28, 1896; m. August 23, 1922; d. October 14, 1968) and Dorothy Hamilton (b. October 27, 1901); and sister of a) Willamae Landrum [(b. July 28, 1923), m. 1st, March 12, 1945, to Fred G. Addis (b. April 17, 1914; d. June 20, 1982), and m. 2nd, January 14, 1985, to Dr. Josephus Brown III; and she had two children: 1[1]) Fred David Addis (b. August 8, 1945; m. October 6, 1974, to Nancy K. Smith, b. January 4, 1951, daughter of Con and Nancy Smith); and had three children: Amy Amber Addis (b. December 18, 1975), Ashley Addson Addis (b. February 7, 1977), and Alyx Ayn Addis (b. February 10, 1978); and 2[1]) Jodi Jane Addis (b. January 5, 1948; m. March 24, 1978, to Donald C. Sleeper, b. November 26, 1956)]; 2) Ralph Garrett Landrum, Jr. (b. November 2, 1929); and 3) Jeffrey Earl Landrum (b. December 21, 1939).

The *Million Dollar Directory* (1994) lists the Iams Company as employing 500 workers, with their main plant in Dayton, Ohio, and sales of 201 million dollars annually. The 1995 *Standard and Poor's Registry* lists sales of between 200 and 500 million dollars and 800 employees. Paul F. Iams, Sr. (b. 1915) has described the oral history of the Iams family as having begun the westward movement during the Revolutionary War when two Iams brothers (Thomas and James) of Maryland wanted to cross a river being guarded by two Hessian soldiers, but when the two Hessians were killed, the Iams boys became too afraid to return home so they walked to Erie (or Greene County), Pennsylvania. It was from Greene County, Pennsylvania, that Eli and his brother (sons of Thomas Iams and P. James Iams) walked to Trotwood, near Dayton, in Montgomery County, Ohio, about 1811. The early Iams family of Ohio has been described as consisting of large members, and as "a big family with great industrial size and a love for fighting," and Paul Iams, Jr., adds that I take credit for advertising the family name." The three children of Paul Falknor Iams, Sr. (b. 1915) and Harriet Jane Landrum were:

1) Paul Falknor Iams, Jr. [(b. June 3, 1949, Dayton, Ohio), m. June 30, 1972, in Evanston, Illinois, to Mary Elizabeth Martin (b. August 27, 1950, Evanston,

Illinois), the daughter of George William Martin and Mary Elizabeth Knudson; and granddaughter of Fred David Martin and Elizabeth Fulmer Frances Long; lived in Wilmette, Illinois, in 1995; had two children: a) Elizabeth Martin Iams (b. June 25, 1980, Evanston, Cook County, Illinois), and b) Paul Falknor "Beep" Iams III (b. February 14, 1984, Evanston, Cook County, Illinois; a child prodigy who played the son of Kurt Russell and Rebecca DeMornay in the 1991 movie "Backdraft")]; 2) Barbara Kay Iams [(b. December 27, 1953), m. July 9, 1976, to James Korein (b. January 25, 1953), son of Julius Korein and brother of Beth Korein and John Korein; had three children: (a) Alison Lee Korein (b. January 3, 1978); b) Leslie Korein (b. February 3, 1980); and c) Joanna Korein (b. February 11, 1987)]; and 3) Carrie Beth Iams [(b. March 22, 1956), m. October 18, 1986, to Greg Masami Terada (b. February 29, 1960), son of Masami and Shirley Terada; brother of Sherry Terada; and their son was Christopher Terada].

The 1870 Census of Madison Township, Montgomery County, Ohio, listed Eli Iams (age 71, b. Pennsylvania); Phebe Iams (age 61, b. Pennsylvania); Jacob Iams (age 32, teacher, b. Ohio); Lauren Iams (age 24, laborer, b. Ohio); and George W. Iams (age 18, b. Maryland); and in another household nearby was Alfred Iams (age 45, b. Ohio); Susan Iams (age 38, b. Michigan); Ellen Iams (age 18, b. Ohio); Martha Iams (age 16, b. Ohio); Oliver C. Iams (age 13, b. Ohio); Inex Iams (age 11, b. Ohio); Lauren Iams (age 5, b. Ohio); and Eli Jacob Iams (age 3 months, b. Ohio).

The 1830 Census of Madison Township, Montgomery County, Ohio, shows Eli Iams as head of household, with wife and six children that included 5 boys. In the 1850 Census of Montgomery County, Ohio, Eli Iams was 32, b. Pennsylvania; Phoebe (age 47, b. Virginia); Jacob (age 21, b. Ohio); Harry (age 17, b. Ohio); Martha (age 12, b. Ohio); Lauren (age 9, b. Ohio), and Mary E. (age 11, b. Ohio).

The 1860 Census of Madison Township, Montgomery County, Ohio, lists: Eli Iams (age 62, b. Pennsylvania); Phoebe (age 58, b. Pennsylvania); Jacob (age 30, b. Ohio); Harvey (age 25, b. Ohio); Martha M. (age 21, b. Ohio); Lauren S. (age 18, b. Ohio). Also listed in Madison Township, Montgomery, Ohio, are: Martin H. (age 39, b. Ohio); George W. (age 8, b. Indiana); Josephine (age 6, b. Indiana); and in a third household: Alfred (age 32, b. Ohio); Susan (age 26, b. Maryland); Ellen (age 8, b. Ohio); Martha (age 6, b. Ohio); Oliver (age 3, b. Ohio); and Inez (age 1, b. Ohio).

The 1900 Census of Montgomery County, Ohio, listed: Lauren S. Iams (age 58, b. Ohio); Salomia (age 39, b. Ohio; Harry E. (age 18, b. Ohio); and Ruth A. (age 7, b. Ohio); and also listed: Harvey H. Iams (age 65, b. Ohio); Martha E. (age 63, b. Ohio); Jeremiah P. (age 33, b. Ohio); and Louise B. (age 30, b. Ohio). The 1910 Census of Montgomery County, Ohio, listed: Lauren S. (age 69, b. Ohio); Salome (age 49, b. Ohio); and Anna R., (age 17, b. Ohio); and listed: Harvey M. Iams (age 74, b. Ohio); Jeremiah (age 42, b. Ohio); and Louie O. (age 38, b. Ohio); and also listed: Harry E. Iams (age 28, b. Ohio) as living in Daniel Mason household. The 1920 census of Montgomery County, Ohio, listed five Iams households: 1) Lauren (age 79, b. Ohio) and Salomod (age 59, b. Ohio); 2) Ella Iams (age 67, b. Ohio), with sister Martha (age 63, b. Ohio); 3) Martha, a sister, with Otha Iams; 4) William Iiams (age 59, b. Ohio); Angie (age 56, b. Ohio); Clyde (age 27, b. Ohio); MIL Jane Alvin (age 45, b. Ohio, and grandniece Winfried Varner (age 12, b. Ohio); and 5) Guy Iams (age 31, b. Ohio); Clara (age 25, b. Ohio); and Mae (age 1, b. Ohio).

Ten Mile Country, by H. Leckey (p. 482) lists Richard Iams as having lived in Frederick County, Maryland, where he m. Elizabeth Pottenger (?Eleanor Jones or Eleanor Pottenger) and moved to Bates Fork, Greene County, Pennsylvania, in 1790, with some children. Their children included: Eli (m. Phebe Heckathorn); Thomas (m. Mary Smith); Richard (m. Mary Shidler); Otho (m. Nancy Cole); Rezin (m. Phoebe Clark); John (m. Ruth Barker); William (m. Charity ____), and Bazel, who was single.

Portrait and Biographical Record of Fayette, Pickway, and Madison Counties, Ohio, 1892, p. 875, by Chapman Brothers, Chicago, states that Eli Iams (b. Maryland) moved to Pennsylvania with his parents when he was 12 years old. His parents were Richard Iams and Ellen Pattengood (Pottenger). Eli Iams m. Phoebe Heckathorn (b. Loudon County, Virginia, but raised in Pennsylvania), the daughter of Martin and Catherine Duttonfield Heckathorn. Eli Iams and Phoebe Heckathorn had a son Richard Iams (b. Washington County, Pennsylvania, December 3, 1822), who moved to Montgomery County, Ohio, with his family in 1823. Eli Iams died in Montgomery County at age 79 and Phoebe at age 80. Eli Iams and Phoebe Heckathorn had eleven children (8 sons), with 9 growing to adulthood. This Richard Iams (b. 1822) m. 1849 to Phoebe June Thompson of Montgomery County, Ohio. The enterprising Richard Iams was reasonably successful for a time in several businesses in Montgomery County, Ohio, before moving to a farm in Madison County, Ohio. After much work the farm, located 2 miles from Plain City, was described as being beautiful and consisted of 700 acres. They moved to the farm in 1856. The children of Richard Iams and Phoebe Thompson included: Alfred Iams (lived Franklin County, Ohio); Richard Iams (lived Madison County, Ohio); Charles Iams (lived Madison County, Ohio) Alva Iams (lived Madison County, Ohio); Howard Iams (lived on Richard Iams' farm); and Martha H. Iams. EFB discounts the past two lineages.

Branch Rickey "The Mahatma" (b. Stockdale in rural Pike County, Ohio, December 20, 1881; d. Columbia, Maryland, December 9, 1965); a member of Baseball Hall of Fame; best remembered for breaking the baseball color barrier by bringing Jackie Robinson to the Brooklyn Dodgers in 1947. An accomplished baseball executive, he built championship baseball teams for the St. Louis Cardinals (6 pennants, four World Series titles); Brooklyn Dodgers (2 pennants); and Pittsburgh Pirates. He was a catcher for a short time with the Cincinnati Reds (1904); St. Louis Browns; and New York Yankees (1907). He later was scout, club secretary, manager, vice president, and finally general manager of the St. Louis Browns before becoming president. He was later manager of the St. Louis Cardinals where he introduced the concept of the "farm system" for developing players in 1919. He was later vice president and general manager of the St. Louis Cardinals before becoming president and general manager of the Brooklyn Dodgers in 1942. He was a devout Methodist and did not attend Sunday ball games. In 1904 he graduated from Ohio Wesleyan University (A.B.), Delaware County, Ohio, and remained a loyal benefactor to that institution. He later graduated from University of Michigan Law School and practiced law after it was apparent that his playing days were limited, but before his baseball executive abilities had become manifest.

Branch Rickey (b. 1881) was the son of Jacob Franklin Rickey and Emily Brown (d. May 1935) and on June 1, 1906; m. Jane Moulton. Branch Rickey (b. 1881) and Jane Moulton had six children: 1) Mary Emily Rickey; 2) Branch Rickey, Jr. (m. Mary Elizabeth Iams (b. 1913); 3) Jane Ainsworth Rickey; 4) Mabel Alice Rickey; 5) Sue Moulton Rickey; and 6) Elizabeth Ann Rickey. They lived at 3 Warson Lane, Ladue, St. Louis, Missouri.

Mary Elizabeth Iams (b. 1913, Dayton, Ohio), m. Branch Rickey, Jr. (b. January 13, 1914; d. April 11, 1961), the son of Branch Rickey, Sr. (b. 1881) and Jane Moulton; grandson of Jacob Franklin Rickey and Emily Brown.

Mary Elizabeth Iams (b. 1913) was the sister of Iams Pet Food founder Paul F. Iams, Sr., and the daughter of Harry Eli Iams (b. 1881) and Carrie Alice Falkner.

Branch Rickey, Jr. (b. 1914) was best known for being a close friend and confidant of his father, for developing major league baseball farm systems, and for signing Jackie Robinson to a minor league baseball contract to play for the Montreal

Royals in October 1945. Branch Rickey, Jr., called "Twig" by his friends, died of complications of diabetes melletus and hepatitis at age 47 in Pittsburgh. He graduated from Ohio Wesleyan University (1935) in Delaware, Ohio, and attended University of Michigan Law School. Described by biographer Harvey Frommes as "a wonderful human being, religious and fair minded," he is credited by General Manager Joe Brown with much of the success of the 1960 World Champion Pittsburgh Pirates victory that culminated in the Series ending home run by second baseman Bill Mazeroski. His first transaction, when moving to the Pirates, had been to claim Roberto Clemente from the Dodgers for a mere $8,000.00. Branch Rickey, Jr., officially began his baseball career in 1935 as business manager of the St. Louis farm club in Albany, Georgia; then became Brooklyn Dodgers farm director from 1941 to 1947 when he became assistant general manager; and then joined the Pirates in 1950 when the Pirates were in last place and the farm system unproven.

Children of Mary Elizabeth Iams (b. 1913) and Branch Rickey, Jr.: 1) Carolyn Rickey; 2) Nancy Rickey; and 3) Branch Rickey III.

References

- (LIH) Lois Ijams Hartman, Pasadena, California; personal work.

- (REI) Robert Elton Iams, Seattle, Washington; personal files.

- (MI) Michael Dorsey Iams, b. 1968, Arizona; correspondence.

- (CRI) Charles Robert Iams, New Stanton, Pennsylvania; personal works.

- (EFB) Ervin F. Bickley, Jr., New Canaan, Connecticut; personal communication.

- (RHI) Ruth Iams, Ten Mile, Washington County, Pennsylvania.

- (HWN) Harry Wright Newman: *Anne Arundel Gentry*, 1933 and 1970.

- (GRI) Guy Ross Iiames, Jr., and Roberta Ross Iiames; personal communications.

- (JEL) John E. Loughman, family Bible, Sycamore, Pennsylvania.

- Federal Census Records, 1790 to 1920.

- (GB) Gertrude Burnam; personal research, 1954.

- (DAR) Lineage Books, DAR Library, Washington, D.C.

- (RI) Roy Iams, Ida, Ohio; personal files.

- (SIKR) Sally Irene King Ross, Long Beach, California; personal files.

- (JM) James B. Meighan, western Pennsylvania; personal files.

- *History of Madison County, Ohio* (Beers and Company, Chicago, 1883).

- (PI) Paul F. Iams, Jr., Sun City, Arizona; personal communication.

- *History of Montgomery County, Ohio* (Beers and Company, Chicago, 1882).

- (CIC) Charles Iams Cherney, M.D., Zanesville, Ohio; personal files.

- (EJM) Reverend E. J. Magnuson, RR1, Hartland, Minnesota; correspondence.

- (OII) Omar Ingersol Iams, Peru, Indiana; personal correspondence, 1966.

- (FC) Reverend Fred Cochran; personal files; Greene County, Pennsylvania.

- (NI) Nell Iams; personal files and correspondence.

- (DBK) Doris Banks Kent, *Thomas Kent: 1748-1835* (Gateway Press, Baltimore, 1995).

- Pennsylvania Archives, Multivolume, State House, Harrisburg, Pennsylvania.

- Beers, *History of Madison County, Ohio* (Beers Publishing, Chicago, 1883).

- Beers, *History of Montgomery County, Ohio* (Beers Publishing, Chicago, 1882).

- Chapman, *History of Madison County, Ohio* (Chapman Publishing, 1892).

- Boston Transcript #905, July 25, 1921.

- (JLI) James Leigh Iams, Berkeley, California; personal correspondence.

- *History of Greene County, Pennsylvania* (Bates, Waynesburg, Pa., 1888).

- (JVI) John Victor Iams, New Martinsville, West Virginia; personal files.

- (JDI) Jay D. Iams, M.D., The Ohio State University, Columbus, Ohio; correspondence.

- (RTF) Robert T. Forest, Sparks, Nevada; personal communcations.

- J. W. Hook, *Captain James Hook of Greene County, Pennsylvania.*

- (RAIC) Ruth Ann Iams Cochran, HC 60, Box 95, New Martinsville, West Virginia; correspondence.

- (ADB) Allen D. Bare, Macon, Georgia; personal correspondence.

- (PFI Sr.) Paul F. Iams, Sr., Sun City, Arizona; personal correspondence.

— CHAPTER 7 —

JOHN IIAMS

(B. 1750, MARYLAND; D. 1823, PENNSYLVANIA)

John Iiams (b. 1750, son of John Iams (b. ca1720, EFB) or Thomas Iiams (b. 1708), m. Elizabeth Gill Hampton (one of three sisters to marry into the family), and they had nine children: Nancy (author), William, Elizabeth, Anna, Sabina, John, Charity, Mary, and Sarah; with offspring moving to West Virginia, Ohio, Indiana, Iowa, and other states, though most remained in Pennsylvania.

John Iiams (b. July 2, 1750, All Hallows Parish, Anne Arundel County, Maryland; d. July 4, 1823, Bethlehem Township, Washington County, Pennsylvania; buried in Franklin Cemetery, Washington County), son of John Iams (b. ca1720) or Thomas Iiams (b. 1708), m. March 12,1791, to Elizabeth Gill Hampton (b. April 10, 1763, Anne Arundel County, Maryland; d. September 1, 1836), daughter of Thomas Gill Hampton of Maryland, and sister of Catherine Hampton and Mary Hampton. (HWN, EFB, JBM, JFI, CRI, PZI, RI, HL, GRI, HLL, EBH).

John Iiams (b. 1750), was a private, First Maryland Regiment, in Captain John Stone's Revolutionary War regiment; enlisted June 2, 1779; discharged November 1, 1780 (Maryland Archives, Volume 18, p. 126). In 1783 he purchased Rhyneland patent in Washington County, Pennsylvania, and moved there with his brothers. He later purchased land called Industry and reportedly "tomahawked" adjacent land, utilizing an Indian ceremonial process which included bartering. He owned 350 acres in Washington County, Ten Mile, area. A millwright, he purchased land from Mr. Key, with land originally patented by a Mr. Kelly, and this became known as Iams Mill, and later as Bissell P. O. at Ten Mile. He was reportedly active in the Whiskey Rebellion of 1794. He eventually owned one thousand acres in West Bethlehem and Amwell Townships of Washington County, Pennsylvania. His Washington County, Pennsylvania, will (Vol. 4, p. 9, 1823) left the mill to his wife, Elizabeth Iiams, along with the farm, land called Industry and land called Rhyne (RI).

There are some disagreements about the first ownership of land in southwestern Pennsylvania. Although the first land warrants were issued in 1784, the 1768 Indian peace Treaty resulted in the agreement that the Indians would remain west of the Ohio, relinquishing land east of the Ohio River, including land in what is now Washington and Greene Counties, Pennsylvania. Also, Virginia opened a land office April 13, 1769, and sold this land of Washington and Greene Counties. Virginia remained owner of this land until 1781. Amwell Township, Washington County, was organized July 1, 1781, but the Mason-Dixon Line was not established below the area of what is now Greene County, Pennsylvania, until November 18, 1784. Official records show a 1785 patent for Rhyme (351 3/4 acres) to John Woodwine, and an 1814 land patent to John Jiames. On the other hand, the 1791 Tax Duplicate for Amwell Township, Washington County, Pennsylvania, lists the bill for John Jiames as being 4 shillings and 6 pence. The 1793 Tax List of Washington County, Pennsylvania, lists John Iams; and the 1793 census lists both John Iams and William Iams. The 1810 Federal Census of Amwell Township, Washington County, Pennsylvania, lists John Iams (age over 45) in household with a woman in same age group, two younger males each in 10 to 16 and 16 to 26 age groups, and two females, each in 10 to 16 and under 10 age groups. When John Iiams (EBI) purchased the 1783 tract of land called Rhyne, the land was part of Monongahela County, Virginia.

John Iiams, then single, returned to Maryland, was married, and returned with his bride. The mill of John Iiams was the first grist mill west of the Monongahela River, with the stone burrs having been carried from Maryland, and remained in place until at least 1932. The mill burned in 1839 but was rebuilt by John Iiams, Jr. Washington County. A road petition number 11, in 1798, described a road from Bartholomew's to Muddy Creek Road through the lands of John Iiams, John Miller, Thomas Moore, Nathaniel McGriffen, and Joseph Evans. Road Petitions in 1802 and 1820 also involved the John Iiams Merchant Mill on Ten Mile Creek. The John Iiams mill was sold to John Iiams, Jr., in 1839 and to Joseph Martin (husband of Nancy Iiams, subject of *Nancy Martin: Country Gal*) on May 31, 1844, and then more recently to Morgan Martin and W. R. Martin, with subsequent name change to Martin's Mill. The mill may have been originally built by a Mr. Keyes. Isaac Lindsay "Ike" Iams and wife Ruth Hand Iams lived on 154 acres of land in the Ten Mile area in 1996, with ownership of the land traceable to William Iams and wife Delilah Meeks. The ten children of John Iiams (b. 1750) and Elizabeth Hampton were:

1) Nancy Iams [(b. January 10, 1787, or 1795, Washington County, Pennsylvania; d. January 21, 1871, or 1879; buried in Franklin Cemetery, Washington County, Pennsylvania) was the second wife (m. December 27, 1821, Washington County) of Joseph Martin (b. March 15, 1790; d. December 25, 1850, or 1859; buried in Franklin Cemetery, son of James Martin and Anna McIntyre; whose first wife had been Elizabeth Haiden, daughter of Miles Haiden; and they had five children: a) Elizabeth Martin (d. infancy); b) John Martin; c) Ann Martin (m. Andrew Van Dyke); d) Sarah Martin (m. Neal Zollars); and e) Joseph Martin (b. 1830; d. 1852)]; 2) William Iams [(b. February 4, 1782, or 1792, near Martin's Mill, Amwell Township, Washington County, Pennsylvania; d. April 4, 1869; buried in Franklin Cemetery), m. June 6, 1816, Washington County, Pennsylvania, to Delilah M. Meeks (d. September 6, 1876, or 1877, age 84 or 93; buried Franklin Cemetery, Washington County, Pennsylvania), daughter of Elisha Meeks]; 3) Elizabeth Iams (d. age 21, buried Franklin Cemetery); 4) Anna Iams (d. age 6); 5) Sabina Iams (d. age 4); 6) John H. Iams, Jr. [(b. August or December 1797 or 1798, Washington County, Pennsylvania; d. March 30, 1846; buried Franklin Cemetery); single; operated Iams/Martin Mill that went to his sister, Nancy Iams Martin, when he died]; 7) Charity Iams [(b. 1799, Pennsylvania; d. January 19 or March 12, 1876; buried in Franklin Cemetery), m. John D. Smith (b. 1795; d. March 12, 1876)]; 8) Mary B. Iams [(b. April 10 or 20, 1800, 1806, or 1810; d. September 5, 1848, 1849, or 1859; buried in Franklin Cemetery); m. Moses Smith (b. 1806; d. September 14, 1848; and they had four children: a) John Smith (d. a member of Union Army at Battle of Fair Oaks); b) Moses Smith, Jr., Civil War veteran (b. April 22, 1842; d. April 11, 1924; buried Ten Mile Baptist Church); m. Phoebe Jewell (b. July 24, 1847; d. February 26, 1924; buried Ten Mile Baptist Church); and their four children were; 1[1]) Ethel Smith (schoolteacher, m. A. G. Bane); 2[1]) Fonny Josephine Smith (single; b. September 27, 1873; d. February 16, 1965); 3[1]) Carl Evarts Smith (b. December 16, 1878; d. May 16, 1892); and 4[1]) an infant son who died young); c) Sarah Smith (b. January 22, 1840; d. April 16, 1910), m. George Washington Huffman (his second marriage; b. October 25, 1840; d. February 20, 1907; buried North Ten Mile); and d) Joseph Smith (b.

January 11, 1847; d. November 25, 1941; buried at North Ten Mile), m. Elizabeth Ann Wise (b. July 26, 1847; d. March 30, 1910; buried at North Ten Mile Baptist Church); and they had five children: 1¹) Joe Edwin or Edward Smith (b. January 21, 1881; d. December 25, 1958; single); 2¹) Alice Smith (b. April 20, 1888; d. February 3, 1979); m. W. D. Elliott, and they had two children: Kenneth Elliott and Lenore Elliott; 3¹) Hannah May Smith (b. January 20, 1885; d. July 6, 1971), m. John Thomas "JT" Donneher (b. June 19, 1874; d. April 15, 1972); and their child was; Lloyd Donnehoo; 4¹) Sarah Grace Smith (b. November 21, 1886; d. July 15, 1972), m. Blaine Charles Bigler; and their child was Keith Bigler; and 5¹) Odessa Mildred Smith (b. September 29, 1889; d. September 28, 1976), m. Curtis Chalmar Cowan (b. April 24, 1887; d. February 3, 1974), and their child was Chalmer Cowan]; and 9) Sarah "Sallie" Iams [(b. 1804, Pennsylvania; d. April 16, 1876, or April 15, 1838, at age 34; buried in Franklin Cemetery), m. William H. Hathaway (owned flour mill in Clarktown; early postmaster); no children].

William Iams (b. February 4, 1792, or 1782; d. April 4, 1868, or 1869); son of John Iiams, Sr. (b. 1750 or 1751) and Elizabeth Hampton; m. June 6, 1816, to Delilah Meeks (b. June 6, 1793, Pennsylvania; d. September 6, 1876, or 1877), daughter of Elisha Meeks, an early settler at Ruff Creek, Greene County, Pennsylvania, and of Mary Miller. William Iams (b. 1792) became wealthy, but because of his kind generosity as a surety for bonds and for notes for his friends and neighbors, he lost much of his wealth. He was also a noted Bible scholar. The twelve children of William Iams (b. 1792) and Delilah Meek were:

1) Elizabeth "Betsy" Iams (b. and d. 1817); 2) Miller James Iams [(b. July 14, 1811, Greene County, Pennsylvania; d. 1880, Ritchie County, West Virginia); Justice of Peace in Morgan Township, Greene County, Pennsylvania, 1863 to 1868; moved to Ritchie County by 1890 (Beers, 1893); a farmer; m. October 29, 1843, West Bethlehem Township, Washington County, Pennsylvania, to Sarah Ann Eggy, a cousin]; 3) James Iams (d. infancy, 1826); 4) John Hill Iams [(b. June 2, 1821, Pennsylvania; d. February 26, 1890; buried Franklin Cemetery, Washington County, Pennsylvania), m. Rebecca McKinney McKenna; no children]; 5) Elisha Iams [(b. December 16, 1822, West Bethlehem Township, Washington County, Pennsylvania; d. April 14, 1898; buried in Franklin Cemetery); m. February 20, 1848, to Cynthia Garber (b. May 6, 1828; d. October 11, 1877), daughter of William Christian Garber and Elizabeth Weaver; William Christian Garber is the son of Jonathan Garber and Elizabeth Hufford, daughter of Christian Hufford, Sr.]; 6) Thomas P. Iams [(b. September 24, 1824; d. June 2, 1902, or April 30, 1907; buried Ruff Creek Cemetery, Greene County, Pennsylvania); m. December 23, 1851, to Sarah Johnson (b. June 28, 1831; d. April 30, 1907), daughter of Zeneas Johnson and Sarah Crayne; and their nine children were: a) Margaret Iams (m. John Jewell; child: Maude Jewell; lived Waynesburg, Pennsylvania); b) Sarah D. Iams (b. November 26, 1854; d. January 3, 1926; buried North Ten Mile Cemetery); m. James Bigler Greenlee, (b. July 9, 1859; d. October 24, 1955; buried North Ten Mile Cemetery); two children were: 1¹) Frances Greenlee, b. December 19, 1890; d. September 20, 1979; m. Howard Keys; and 2¹) Florence Helen Greenlee, b. March 29, 1894, West Bethlehem Township; d. November 14, 1980, West Bethlehem Township; single; graduate of Waynesburg College; schoolteacher; c) Zeneas Iams (m. Elizabeth Dunn, daughter of Washington Dunn, and granddaughter of Joseph Dunn and Jane Martin); d) James Iiams; e) Flora Iiams; f) Mary E. Iiams (b. 1862; d. August 26, 1864; buried Franklin Cemetery); g) Lewis Iiams (lived at Jefferson, Greene County, Pennsylvania; h) Miller Iiams (b. 1855; d. June 4, 1862; buried Franklin Cemetery); and i) William Iiams (b. 1862; d. September 13, 1863, at age 10 months; buried in Franklin Cemetery,

Washington County, Pennsylvania)]; 7) Isaac Iams [(b. February 25 or July 28, 1828; d. July 24, 1901; buried Lone Pine Cemetery, Washington County, Pennsylvania), m. September 27, 1852, to Ann Farrell (b. October 4, 1832; d. March 26, 1905); lived in Amwell Township, Washington County, Pennsylvania]; 8) William Iams [(b. March 2, 1830; d. 1905), a carpenter; m. 1st, Elizabeth Ferrell (b. 1836; d. 1863); m. 2nd, Caroline Gantz; and m. 3rd, Mary Magdalene Swihart (b. 1845; d. 1921; buried North Ten Mile Cemetery]; 9) Delilah Iams [(b. September 24, 1831, or 1832, or September 24, 1834), m. James Johnson-Loudon, and lived in Greene County, Pennsylvania]; 10) Mary Iams [(b. 1834 or April 24, 1835; d. 1889; buried at North Ten Mile Cemetery); m. Jacob Bigler (b. February 6, 1836; d. 1932), a third cousin and great-grandson of Mary Iiams and William Penn; and who m. 2nd, Lila Swihart, b. 1841; d. 1910; eight children: a) Mrs. Homer Lewis; b) Mrs. Sarah Ulray; c) Mrs. Elizabeth Richardson; d) unknown; e) Nannie Bigler (b. September 9, 1875; d. March 2, 1976; lived at Bentleyville, West Bethlehem Township, Washington County, Pennsylvania; member First Baptist Church; m. William J. Crawford; d. January 1919; two children: 1[1]) Stanley Crawford; 2[1]) Mary Crawford, who m. Welling Randolph); f) Emma Bigler (b. August 2, 1865; d. 1957; buried at North Ten Mile Cemetery; m. October 14, 1883, to John Austin Rose; two children: 1[1]) Ida Mary Rose, b. May 30, 1902; d. December 8, 1989; m. Harry Blaker, who d. July 15, 1962; and their children were Roseleta Blaker, m. Edwin Taylor; and Kermit R. Blaker, and 2[1]) Ella Rose Barr); g) Ella M. Bigler (b. 1870; d. 1889; buried at North Ten Mile Cemetery); and h) Abraham Hill Bigler (b. 1863; d. 1921, North Ten Mile; m. Martha Crispin; and their two children were: Ray Bigler and Anna Bigler; 11) Abraham Iams [(b. September 24, 1836; d. 1862); single; "shot through the breast" at Battle of Fair Oaks, and died one day later]; and 12) Rachel J. Iams [(b. April 11, 1839, Washington County, Pennsylvania); m. Daniel R. Smith (b. April 30, 1840, Washington County, Pennsylvania; d. April 3, 1925, or April 11, 1929; buried in North Ten Mile Cemetery, Washington County, Pennsylvania); son of George Smith or Israel Smith (b. 1814, Washington County, Pennsylvania; d. March 29, 1892, Washington County, Pennsylvania), and Hannah Grable (b. 1820; d. August 27, 1884; Washington County, Pennsylvania); daughter of Daniel Grable and Susan Byler; with Israel Smith (b. 1814) the son of George and Mary Magdalene Smith; and the child of Daniel R. Smith (b. 1840), Lida Belle Smith (b. February 18, 1871; d. June 23, 1962, Washington County, Pennsylvania), who m. December 30, 1895, to Joseph Columbus Phillips (b. September 6, 1863; d. October 14, 1953, Washington County, Pennsylvania); son of William James Phillips and Elizabeth Greene].

Elizabeth Iams (b. 1817). An Elizabeth Iams was an early settler in Wolf Pen Run at Den Run, Ritchie County, West Virginia, with her son Thomas Hill, the son of a "Thomas Hill who went west," and had moved from their Greene County, Pennsylvania, home. Some records say that Elizabeth Iams and Thomas Hill had been married. Elizabeth Iams moved to Ritchie County about 1848, and purchased 200 acres on Indian Creek. Son Thomas Hill d. August 1, 1891; buried at King Knob, Ritchie County, West Virginia. Thomas Hill (d. 1891) had m. December 11, 1852, to Belinda Sinnett (b. December 11, 1832; d. April 2, 1913; buried at King Knob), the daughter of Abel Sinnett. Eleven of the twelve children of Thomas Hill and Belinda Sinnett were born in the one-room cabin built by mother Elizabeth Iams:

1) Elizabeth P. Hill (b. 1853; m. Harmon Nottingham); 2) Miller I. Hill [(b. 1855; d. 1936), m. _____ Hammer, daughter of Jacob Hammer]; 3) Margaret E. Hill (b. 1857; d. 1904); 4) Sarah Catherine Hill [(b. 1861; d. 1922), m. William Lewllyn]; 5) William E. Hill (b. 1861; d. 1922); 6) Lucinda A. Hill (m. Benton McCann); 7) George W. Hill (b. 1862; d. 1932); 8) Abel T. Hill (b. and d. 1866 at age 3 months

when he was "killed by lightning"); 9) Mary Rebecca Hill (m. Philip Wagner); 10) Jacob Lewis Hill; 11) Florence M. Hill (m. Daniel Givens); and 12) Jennie M. Hill (m. James Hedge).

Rachel Iams (b. April 11, 1839), daughter of William Iiams (b. 1792) and Delilah Meeks, m. Daniel Smith (a carpenter; son of Israel Smith and grandson of George Smith; lived West Bethlehem Township, Washington County, Pennsylvania; and buried in North Ten Mile Cemetery), and they had eight children: 1) Abraham Smith (m. Elizabeth Bigler; and their daughter Cora Smith m. Ross Whitfield); 2) Jack Smith (m. Alfreda Knestrick, and their four children were; Daniel Smith, Freeman Smith, Lovea Smith, and Frona Smith); 3) John Smith (m. ____ Grable, and they had four children: Clarence Smith, Charles Smith, Edna Smith, and Violet Smith); 4) Lyda Smith (m. Joseph Phillips; lived at Marianna, Pennsylvania, and had two children: Abraham Phillips, and Harry Phillips; 5) Hannah Smith (m. Henry Montgomery, and they had two children: Archie Montgomery, and Earl Montgomery); 6) Israel Smith (m. Etta Fair, and their three children were: Clell Smith, Kenneth Smith, and Mildred Smith; 7) Mary Florence Smith (m. Hugh Montgomery, and had three children: Winona Montgomery, Relda Montgomery, and Huetta Mongtomery; and 8) Samuel H. Smith [(m. June 12, 1909, Waynesburg, Pennsylvania, to Lucy Vaughn Pollock, daughter of John L. Pollock and Emma Jane Baker); lived in Marianna, Pennsylvania; a carpenter; and their son Merle F. Smith (b. August 11, 1916; a business contractor; d. April 18, 1981, Waynesburg, Pennsylvania; World War II veteran; owned S. H. Smith and Son for 44 years; m. January 2, 1937, to Nellie Mae Booth); had three children: a) Merle F. Smith, Jr.; b) Donald Wayne Smith; and c) Donna Mae Smith (m. Anthony Mercante of Marianna, and their two children were Sherry Mercante and Tony Mercante)].

Mary Iams (b. April 24, 1834), daughter of William Iiams (b. 1792) and Delilah Meeks, m. Jacob Bigler, and they had six children: 1) Abraham Bigler [(m. Martha Crispin) had two children: Ray Bigler (civil engineer; World War I veteran; lived at Bentleyville, Pennsylvania), and Anna Bigler (a schoolteacher in Bentleyville)]; 2) Elizabeth Bigler [(a pianist), m. Winfield Richardson, and their child was Adaire Richardson]; 3) Nancy "Nannia" Bigler [(b. September 9, 1875, West Bethlehem Township, Washington County, Pennsylvania); lived to age 100; m. 1904 to William Crawford (operated grocery store in Bentleyville; tax collector; charter member of Bentleyville Baptist Church); two children: Stanley Crawford and Mary Crawford (m. Mr. Welling)]; 4) Sarah Bigler (m. Joseph Ullery, and their child was Charles Ullery); 5) Emma Bigler (m. John Rose); and 6) Hannah Bigler (m. Homer Lewis, and their child was Kirk Lewis); (RI, EBI). Jacob Bigler (m. Mary Iams, above) was the son of Israel Bigler (b. 1811; d. 1887) and Elizabeth Smith (b. 1812; d. 1893). Israel Bigler (b. 1888) was the son of Jacob Bigler (b. 1778; d. 1849) and Nancy Penn (b. 1789; d. 1835); and Jacob Bigler (b. 1778) was the son of Israel Bigler (b. 1747; d. 1838) and Catherine (b. 1738; d. 1839); and finally, this Israel Bigler (b. 1748) was the son of Mark and Catrina Bigler of Switzerland, who moved via Germany to Philadelphia, Pennsylvania, in 1733.

Delilah Iams (b. September 24, 1832, Pennsylvania), the daughter of William Iiams (b. 1792) and Delilah Meeks (b. 1793), m. James Johnson-Loudon. James Johnson-Loudon was born near Loudonville, Ohio, where his mother died shortly after giving birth, and James didn't get along with his eventual new mother (by marriage). James Johnson-Loudon left home at age 10, adopted his mother's maiden name of Johnson (father's name was Loudon) and ended up in western Pennsylvania, where he worked for, and was raised by, the Silas Clark family. James Johnson-Loudon kept his identity a secret until late in life. Both James Johnson-

Loudon and his wife Delilah Iams are buried at Ruff's Creek Cemetery, Greene County, Pennsylvania, and they had six children: 1) George Johnson (a hotel proprietor); 2) Miller Johnson; 3) Alice Johnson; 4) Susie Johnson (single); 5) Rachel Johnson (single); and 6) Thomas Johnson [(m. Alice Brewer); lived in Waynesburg, Pennsylvania; and had three children: a) Marie Johnson (m. Arthur L. Mitchell; had four children: Ray Mitchell, Lowrena Mitchell, Thomas Mitchell, and Delilah Mitchell); b) Incas Johnson (m. John Inghran; and their three children were: Paul Inghram, Helen Inghran, and Ray Inghram); and c) Austen Johnson (m. Mary Pettit; and their two children were: Alvin Johnson and Kenneth Johnson)].

Isaac Iams (b. February 25 or July 28, 1828; d. July 24, 1907; buried in Lone Pine Cemetery, Washington County, Pennsylvania), son of William Iiams (b. 1792) and Delilah Meeks (b. 1793), m. Anne Ferrell (b. 1832; d. March 20, 1905), daughter of Zebulon Ferrell and Katherine Shrontz, and they lived in Amwell Township, Washington County, Pennsylvania. Isaac Iams (b. 1828) owned 303 acres in the Ten Mile area, and the 1870 Federal Census listed Isaac Iams (age 43), wife Ann Iams (age 38), daughter Ann Elizabeth Iams (age 7), daughter Hannah E. Iams (age 4), and daughter Emma B. Iams (age 1). The 1880 Census lists Isaac Iams (age 52), Ann Iams (age 48), William M. Iams (age 22), James D. Iams (age 19), Ann-Elizabeth Iams (age 17), Hannah C. Iams (age 15, Emma Iams (age 11), and Maggie Iams (age 8). The 1900 Census lists Isaac Iams (age 72), Ann Iams (age 67), William Iams (age 42) and Hannah E. Iams (age 34). PZI lists Isaac Iams (b. March 1, 1799; d. Gratis, Ohio; m. Elizabeth _____) with children: Robert Iams, Margaret Iams, Mary F. Iams, John L. Iams, and James S. Iams, with each born Preble County, Ohio.

RI, JSI, MI and others list the eight children of Isaac Iams (b. 1828) and Anne Ferrell (b. 1832) as: 1) Catherine "Kate" Delilah Iams (b. August 7, 1853; d. October 29, 1876, buried Lone Pine Cemetery); 2) Zebulon Ferrell Iams [(b. March 10, 1856, Amwell Township, Washington County, Pennsylvania; d. June 20, 1927; buried in Lone Pine Cemetery, Washington County, Pennsylvania); m. January 13, 1877, to Elizabeth Ann Crile (b. May 20, 1858; d. March 28, 1939; buried in Lone Pine Cemetery), daughter of Conrad Crile and Mary Ann Garrett, and their four children were: a) Daley V. Iams (a daughter; d. age 11); b) Isaac "Weller" Iams (b. January 10, 1874 or 1878; d. January 8, 1953; m. Ida Ruth Edgar; b. April 7, 1872; d. December 27, 1941, the daughter of John Edgar and Mary A. Keys); had five children: 1[1]) Idalia Ruth Iams; b. March 1905; d. March 1906; 2[1]) an infant son; 3[1]) an infant daughter; and 4[1]) Evelyn Morrison Iams, b. July 31, 1903; d. January 11, 1962; buried North Ten Mile Cemetery, Washington County, Pennsylvania; and 5[1]) Minnie Katherine Iams (b. April 9, 1905; d. October 17, 1987), m. James C. Maley; c) Permelia Belle "Minnie" Iams (b. May 27, 1880; d. February 4, 1955; buried Lone Pine Cemetery), m. May 23, 1901, to Charles Wray Grayson Allender (b. September 6, 1879; d. December 2, 1956); four children: Clarence Weller Allender (b. March 9, 1903; d. November 4, 1967); Edna Dale Allender (b. December 31, 1905; d. March 26, 1993); Ruth Dolly Allender (b. January 11, 1914; d. March 30, 1985); and Orville Iams (b. March 16, 1916; d. January 26, 1979); and d) Katy Mae "Mary" Iams (b. August 20, 1880; d. August 29, 1947; buried Washington Cemetery), m. August 25, 1906, to Clarence Gibson Donahoo (b. June 27, 1879; d. January 12, 1963; buried Washington Cemetery); no children; 3) William Montgomery Iams (b. May 20, 1858; d. July 10, 1926; single; buried Lone Pine Cemetery); 4) James Dorsey Iams [(b. December 11, 1860; a merchant and teacher; d. 1943; buried in Lone Pine Cemetery); m. April 25, 1885, to Sarah F. McClelland (b. August 3, 1859; d. 1942); and a child was: a) Charles Shirk Iams (b. November 24, 1891; a schoolteacher; d. August 5, 1936), m. Florence Lewis, also a schoolteacher)]; 5) Anna Eliza Iams [(b. March 31,

1863; d. April 6, 1934), m. July 23, 1882, to William Fulton (b. December 4, 1862; d. April 4, 1938), a merchant at Dunn's Station; and they had four children: a) James D. Fulton (b. March 5, 1890, Greene County, Pennsylvania; a merchant at Dunn's Station; graduate of Waynesburg Business College; a postmaster and station agent for Waynesburg and Washington Railroad for 45 years; m. Clara Louise Mollenaur); b) Olive Mae Fulton (m. Doctor O. G. Lewis, a well-known surgeon; veteran of World War I, and treasurer of National Iams Association; and they had two children: Anna Lewis (d. young) and Evelyn Lewis); c) Queen E. Fulton (b. June 21, 1896; d. March 12, 1978; buried Washington City, Pennsylvania; m. Dr. O. G. Lewis after death of her sister, Olive Mae Fulton, and had two children: William Lewis and Orville Lewis); and d) Rose F. Fulton (b. November 20, 1898; a schoolteacher; d. August 4, 1979; m. June 14, 1931, to Ralph Hickman (d. December 12, 1952); and their child was: Fulton F. Hickman, who married and had a daughter, Amy Elizabeth Hickman)]; 6) Hannah Elizabeth Iams [(b. September 26, 1865 or 1866; d. April 11, 1906; buried Lone Pine Cemetery), m. George Austin M. Bovier (b. 1879; d. July 7, 1948; buried North Ten Mile Cemetery); no children]; 7) Emma Beatrice Iams [(b. January 16, 1869; d. April 1, 1928; buried in Lone Pine Cemetery, Lone Pine, Washington County, Pennsylvania), m. Allison Dupont Swart (d. October 11, 1863, in a western state), and two children were: a) Hiram Swart, who went west; and b) Anna Swart (m. Walter Hall)]; and 8) Margaret "Maggie" Florence Iams [(b. January 30, 1872, Amwell Township; d. November 29, 1934; buried at Lone Pine Cemetery), m. September 19, 1895, to Joseph Ganman Barr (b. August 2, 1870, West Bethlehem Township, Washington County, Pennsylvania; d. October 20, 1938; buried in Lone Pine Cemetery), and two children were: a) Margaret Elizabeth Barr (b. February 18, 1904; d. December 4, 1991), m. October 15, 1929, to Robert E. Hill, b. October 3, 1900; d. February 4, 1978), and b) Charles Frederick Barr (b. July 20, 1896; d. September 13, 1986; m. August 17, 1923, to Mildred Evelyn Hindman; and their daughter, Joan Evelyn Barr, m. October 5, 1954, to Palli "Paul" C. "Cliff" Ostergaard, and they had 3 children: 1^1) Paul Ostergaard, b. June 29, 1955; 2^1) Dale Ostergaard, b. October 5, 1956, in Idaho; and 3^1) Judy Ostergaard, b. August 10, 1961)].

Conchetta Geis, Ridley, Indiana, places Isaac Imes (b. June 5, 1795, Pennsylvania) as the son of Christophorus Imsen (christened at Pombsen, at the Maria-Hammelfahrt Roman Catholic Church, Germany, on February 18, 1771), and the grandson of Joanne Carolo Imsen and Joannae Fridericae Dissen of Westfalen, Germany. According to Pauline Z. Imes, Isaac Iams (b. 1794), the son of William Iiams (b. 1792) and Delilah Meek had the following five children: 1) Robert Imes (b. October 22, 1822; d. November 17, 1884); m. January 29, 1852, at Gratis, Preble County, Ohio, to Elizabeth Enoch); 2) Margaret Imes (b. 1833; m. January 13, 1883, to Isaac Hewitt Enoch); 3) Mary E. Imes (b. 1841; d. 1909; m. February 24, 1863, to Henry Glaze); 4) John L. Imes (b. 1830; d. June 23, 1849, at Gratis, Ohio, of cholera); and 5) James S. Imes (b. 1835; d. April 10, 1848, at Gratis, Ohio).

Robert Imes (b. October 22 or 24, 1822; d. January 29, 1852, or 1858, at Gratis, Twin Township, Preble County, Ohio), the son of Isaac Iams (b. 1794); m. November 17, 1894, to Elizabeth Enoch (b. January 3, 1818, Preble County, Ohio), the daughter of Samuel Enoch and Elizabeth Hewitt; and they owned 80 acres at Brennersville, at the corner of the Eaton-Lewisburg, Twin Township, and Brennersville-Pyrmont Road intersection in Preble County, Ohio; and their four children were: 1) Ann Elizabeth Imes (b. 1845 or 1850, Preble County, Ohio; m. Mr. Hapner); 2) Francis Marion Imes (b. April 24, 1846, Twin Township; d. May 3, 1893, Twin Township), who m. January 27, 1870, Lewisburg, Preble County, Ohio, to Clarissa "Clara" Jane Witterman; 3) Oscar Winfield Fitzallen Scott Imes [(b. Janu-

247

ary 12, 1852, Preble County, Ohio; d. September 15, 1939, Jay County, Indiana, and buried at Hillcrest Cemetery, Redkey, Indiana), m. January 28, 1880, Jay County, Indiana, to Martha Minerva Racer, and while they lived at Redkey, Jay County, Indiana, they returned annually to Lewisburg, Ohio, for the Imes-Enoch Family Reunion at Imes Park, adjacent to the original home of the Iams Pet Food Company/ Imes Cat Food Factory]; and 4) Robert Joseph Adalaska "Joe" Imes [(b. December 2, 1855, Preble County, Ohio; d. September 21, 1941, Jay County, Indiana), who m. January 1, 1888, to Amelia Booker]. (PZI, SGL and CG)

Francis Marion Imes (b. April 24, 1846, Twin Township, Preble County, Ohio; d. May 3, 1893, Preble County, Ohio), son of Robert Imes (b. 1822) and Elizabeth Enoch, m. January 27, 1870, in Lewisburg, Preble County, Ohio, to Clarissa "Claia" Jane Witterman (b. January 8, 1853, Twin Township, Preble County, Ohio; d. May 16, 1928; buried Roselawn Cemetery, Lewisburg, Ohio); daughter of Emanuel Witterman and Susan Miller; and they had nine children: 1) Almeda Imes (m. William Davidson; d. from childbirth); 2) Samuel Enoch Imes [(b. April 9, 1871, Twin Township, Preble County, Ohio; d. December 14, 1962, Dayton, Ohio; buried Sugar Grove Cemetery, Lexington, Ohio); m. April 22, 1903, Twin Township, Preble County, Ohio, to Clara Alice Ehler]; 3) Bertha F. Imes [(b. August 28, 1881, Twin Township, Preble County, Ohio; d. March 10, 1966), m. 1906 to Charles Deisher; lived in Lewisburg, Ohio]; 4) Myrtle Imes (m. Harvey Maddock); 5) Jesse Paul Imes (b. 1874; d. 1955; single); 6) Viola "Vida" M. Imes (m. John Curry; lived Brookville, Indiana); 7) Elsie May Imes (m. Walter Waggoner); 8) Arthur Ray Imes [(b. July 4, 1889; d. February 3, 1976); m. February 12, 1919, to Elma Zela Eck; lived in Johnsville, Ohio]; and 9) Flora D. Imes [(b. February 28, 1877); m. February 28, 1897, to James Richards; lived at Lewisburg, Ohio]. (PZI, CG)

Samuel Enoch Imes (b. April 9, 1871, Twin Township, Preble County, Ohio; d. December 14, 1962, Dayton, Ohio; buried Sugar Grove Cemetery, Lexington, Ohio), son of Francis Marion Imes (b. 1846) and Clarissa Jane Witterman; m. April 22, 1903, Twin Township, to Clara Alice Ehler (b. January 9, 1879; d. June 4, 1950), daughter of Henry Franklin Ehler and Sarah Catharine Kaylor; lived in two-room farmhouse on Price Creek, Preble County, Ohio, near a set of waterfalls and an old grist mill where they raised ten children: 1) Martha Imes (m. Mr. Pfister; lived at Eaton, Ohio); 2) Pearl Marguerite Imes [(b. August 10, 1909, Twin Township; d. May 1, 1884, Dayton, Ohio), m. February 20, 1933, Eaton, Ohio, to Melvin Wesley Duke, a childhood friend]; 3) Florence Imes (m. Mr. Davis; lived at Lewisburg, Ohio); 4) Irma Imes (m. Mr. Wright); 5) Raymond Imes (lived Dayton, Ohio); 6) Clyde Imes; 7) Roy Imes (lived at Franklin, Ohio); 8) Howard Imes (lived in Minnesota); 9) Homer Imes (lived at Brookfield, Ohio); and 10 Everett Imes (lived at Lewisburg, Ohio). (CG)

Arthur Ray Imes (b. July 4, 1889, Preble County, Ohio; d. February 3, 1976, New Lebanon, Ohio), son of Francis Marion Imes (b. 1847) and Clarissa Witterman; m. February 12, 1919, at Lewisburg, Preble County, Ohio, to Elma Zela Eck (b. July 10, 1896, Twin Township, Preble County, Ohio; d. March 19, 1953, at Grandview Hospital, Dayton, Ohio), daughter of Edward Eck and Ida Bell; lived in New Lebanon, Montgomery, Ohio; buried at Sugar Grove Cemetery, New Lexington, Ohio; and they had nine children: 1) Allen Edward Imes (b. October 5, 1923, Preble County, Ohio; m. Pearlie Buck in Richmond, Indiana); 2) Betty Lucille Imes (b. October 12, 1924, Preble County, Ohio; d. November 4, 1987; buried at Enon, Ohio; m. Thurman Daniels); 3) James Robert Imes (b. April 1925, Preble County, Ohio; single); 4) Geraldine Elizabeth Imes (b. July 1, 1927, Preble County, Ohio; d. January 8, 1986; buried at Sugar Grove Cemetery, New Lexington, Ohio; single); 5) Maybelle Imes (b. July 19, 1928; d. January 2, 1929; buried in Sugar Loaf Cemetery); 6) Ruth Marie

Imes (b. August 24, 1929; m. June 2, 1979, Ohio; m. Forrest Miller); 7) Joseph Ray Imes (b. May 14, 1931; m. in Hawaii to Marsha ____); 8) William Roger Imes (b. October 19, 1935; d. June 24, 1978, Dayton, Ohio; single); and 9) Pauline Zelma Imes [(b. August 2, 1939, Good Samaritan Hospital, Dayton, Ohio); family genealogist and correspondent].

Oscar Winfield Fitzallen Scott Imes (b. January 12, 1852, Preble County, Ohio; d. September 15, 1939, Jay County, Indiana; buried in Hillcrest Cemetery, Redkey, Indiana), son of Robert Imes (b. 1822) and Elizabeth Enoch, m. January 28, 1880, Jay County, Indiana, to Martha Minerva Racer (b. June 27, 1862, Jay County, Indiana; d. September 9, 1944, Jay County, Indiana), the daughter of Davis Racer and Mary Jane Whitaker; and they had five children: 1) Henry Rufus Imes (b. April 1883, Jay County, Indiana; d. January 13, 1964; m. Ethel Lee); 2) Ernestine Imes (b. November 1884; Jay County, Indiana; d. 1949; m. W. Boltz); 3) Roscoe D. Imes (b. February 1887, Jay County, Indiana; d. 1918; m. Hazel Barr); 4) Frances Ann Imes (b. 1880; d. 1883); 5) Almeda Elizabeth Imes [(b. March 12, 1889, Jay County, Indiana; d. February 28, 1965, Richmond, Indiana), m. June 18, 1913, Jay County, to Lyman Cleveland Stephen (b. October 27, 1886, Jay County, Indiana; d. April 27, 1954, Jay County, Indiana; buried in Hillcrest Cemetery, Redkey, Indiana), son of Samuel C. Stephen and Lucinda Murphy; and they had five children: 1) Lewis Hedrick Stephen (b. September 3, 1917, Jay County, Indiana; m. November 23, 1939, to Glenna Armstrong); 2) Jesse Madison Stephen (b. March 6, 1921, Jay County, Indiana; m. July 10, 1932, to Marion Arnold); 3) Louise Helen Stephen (b. January 12, 1924, Jay County, Indiana; d. January 23, 1924); 4) Richard Frederick Stephen (b. May 15, 1931, Jay County, Indiana; m. July 3, 1951, to Norma Lloyd); and 5) Conchetta Delight Stephen (b. September 24, 1919, Jay County, Indiana; m. May 25, 1942, Indiana, to Martin W. Geis), correspondent and contributor].

Conchetta Delight Stephen (b. September 24, 1919, Jay County, Indiana), the daughter of Lyman Cleveland Stephen (b. 1886) and Almeda Elizabeth Imes; m. May 25, 1942, Indianapolis, Indiana, to Martin W. Geis (b. October 1, 1910, Indianapolis, Indiana; d. September 20, 1963, Hammond, Indiana), son of Martin P. Geis and Grace M. Westover, and they had two children; 1) Teresa Emily Geis [(b. September 30, 1952, Grand Rapids, Michigan), m. September 23, 1978, to Ronald Horner, and they had four children: a) Lizabeth Kay Horner (b. December 9, 1979, Hammond, Indiana); b) Sara Lynn Horner (b. November 11, 1981, Columbus, Ohio); c) Leslie Ann Horner; and d) Martin Robert Horner (b. November 9, 1984, Columbus, Ohio)] and 2) Suzanne Elaine Geis [(b. September 30, 1948, Marion, Indiana), m. January 24, 1976, to Thomas R. Long; and they had two children; a) Eric V. Long (b. December 20, 1978, Hammond, Indiana); and b) Elaine M. Long (b. May 26, 1980)]. Conchetta Delight Geis (b.1919) tells of travels from Redkey, Indiana, to Lewisburg, Ohio, for the Imes-Enoch family reunions at Imes Park, south of Lewisburg. The trip, along dirt roads in the "Model T," and later "Model A," was a much-dreaded trip made in one car with grandparents Oscar and Martha Imes, parents Lyman and Almeda Stephen, and the three children, Conchetta, Richard, and Louise Stephen. The picturesque park with the rock bottom creek and waterfall made the trip memorable, (SGL, CSG) and remains a beautiful place.

Zebulon Ferrell Iams (b. March 10, 1856, Washington County, Pennsylvania; d. June 20, 1927; buried North Ten Mile Cemetery, West Bethlehem Township, Washington County, Pennsylvania), son of Isaac Iams (b. 1828) and Ann Ferrell; m. January 10, 1877, to Elizabeth Ann Crile (b. May 20, 1858; d. March 28, 1939), the daughter of Conrad Crile and Mary Ann Garrett. The 1880 Washington County, Pennsylvania, Census lists: Zebulon (age 23, b. Pennsylvania); wife Elizabeth Iams

249

(age 22, b. Pennsylvania); son Isaac C. Iams (age 1, b. Pennsylvania); and daughter Permilia Iams (age 1 month); and the 1900 Census lists: Gabulern Iams (age 44); wife Lizzie A. Iams (age 48); son Isaac N. Iams (age 22); daughter Minnie Iams (age 20); daughter Katie May Iams (age 14); and daughter Daby Iams (age 5); while the 1920 Census lists only Zeb F. Iams (age 63) with wife Lizzie Iams (age 61).

The four children of Zebulon Ferrell Iams (b. 1856) and Elizabeth Ann Crile were: 1) Isaac Weller Iams [(b. January 10, 1874; d. January 8, 1953; buried North Ten Mile Cemetery), m. June 18, 1902, Castile, Pennsylvania, to Ida Ruth Edgar (b. April 7, 1872; d. December 27, 1941; buried at North Ten Mile Cemetery, Washington County, Pennsylvania), daughter of John Edgar and Mary A. Keys; and their four children were: a) Idalia Ruth Iams (b. March 14, 1905; d. July 14, 1906); b) Minnie Katherine Iams (b. April 9, 1908; d. October 17, 1987); c) John Edgar Iams (b. October 13, 1910; d. October 14, 1910); and d) an infant daughter (b. and d. June 15, 1915); and Evelyn Morrison Iams, a son (b. July 31, 1903; d. January 11, 1962; buried North Ten Mile Baptist Church Cemetery, Washington County, Pennsylvania)]; 2) Permelia "Belle" or "Minnie" R. Iams [(b. May 27, 1880; d. February 4, 1955; buried at Lone Pine Cemetery, Lone Pine, Washington County, Pennsylvania), m. May 23, 1901, to Charles R. Wray Grayson Allender (b. September 6, 1879; lived in Denver, Colorado; d. December 2, 1956, when hit by a car; buried Washington, Pennsylvania, cemetery), son of John Alexander and Levinia Andrew; five children: a) Clarence Weller Allender (b. March 9, 1903; d. November 4, 1967; buried in Washington, Pennsylvania); m. Evelyn Charity Lorraine Fogle (b.. July 21, 1905); b) Edna Dale Allender (b. December 31, 1905; d. March 26, 1993; m. Robert A. Neal); c) Ruth Dolly Allender (b. January 11, 1914; d. March 30, 1985; m. Lee B. Finch); and d) Orville Iams (b. March 16, 1916; d. January 26, 1979)]; 3) Katie Mae "May" Iams [(b. August 20, 1885; d. August 29, 1947; buried in Washington, Pennsylvania), m. August 25, 1906, to Clarence Gibson Donahoo (b. June 27, 1879; d. January 12, 1963; buried Washington, Pennsylvania)]; and 4) Daley V. "Dale" Iams (b. 1894; d. 1905 of "lock jaw from vaccination"; buried in Lone Pine Cemetery, Washington County, Pennsylvania). (RI)

Isaac Weller Iams (b. January 10, 1874, lived near Zollarsville, Pennsylvania; d. January 8, 1953; buried North Ten Mile Baptist Church, Washington County, Pennsylvania), son of Zebulon Ferrell Iams (b. 1856) and Elizabeth Ann Crile; m. June 18, 1902, at Castile, Pennsylvania, to Ida Ruth Edgar (b. April 7, 1852, West Bethlehem Township, Washington County, Pennsylvania; d. December 27, 1941; buried in North Ten Mile Cemetery); daughter of John Edgar and Mary A. Keys; sister of D. A. Edgar of Bentleyville; Mrs. J. H. Lewis of Castile, Pennsylvania; Mrs. H. R. Murray of Washington, Pennsylvania; W. K. Edgar of Castile, Pennsylvania; J. M. Edgar of Pittsburgh, Pennsylvania; Mrs. T. M. Reese of Rogersville, Pennsylvania; Clarence Edgar of Waynesburg, Pennsylvania; and Herman Edgar of Washington, Pennsylvania. Isaac Weller Iams (b. 1874) and Ida Ruth Edgar had five children:

1) Evelyn Morrison Iams [(b. July 31, 1903, Amwell Township, Washington County, Pennsylvania; d. January 11, 1962; buried North Ten Mile Cemetery); m. July 18, 1930, in Washington, Pennsylvania, to Dorothy Elizabeth Harden (b. October 26, 1914; d. June 11, 1990, in Maryland), and m. November 30, 1940, to Gertie Elder or Gertie Toland; lived in Amwell Township; farmer; member of Bethel Presbyterian Church]; 2) Idaliah Ruth Iams (b. March 14, 1905; d. July 14, 1906, of typhoid fever); 3) Minnie Katherine Iams [(b. April 9, 1908; d. October 17, 1987; buried Washington, Pennsylvania), m. May 16, 1925, to James Claude Maloy (b. June 24, 1905), and had two children: a) Richard Weller Maloy (b. October 20, 1926), m. 1st, August 10, 1948, to Emma Lou Fluke (b. August 5, 1920), and they had three

children: 1¹) Christy Ann Maloy (b. September 2, 1957), m. Duane Stauffer, and their child Tharissa Rae Stauffer, b. March 2, 1975; 2¹) Mary Jane Maloy (b. February 10, 1956); and 3¹) Judy Catherine Maloy (b. October 28, 1858), and had a daughter, Cynthia Judy; m. 2nd, September 15, 1972, to Ruth Frantz Cook; and m. 3rd, November 12, 1983, to Sonja ____; and b) James Walter Maloy (b. February 15, 1944), m. 1st, on June 19, 1966, to Rosella Louise Guthrie (b. September 24, 1943), and had child: Amy Beth Maloy (b. September 11, 1968); and then m. 2nd, July 17, 1976, to Sharon Kay Stutter (b. March 25, 1948), and their child was James Ronald Maloy, (b. January 26, 1978)]; 4) John Edgar Iams (b. October 13, 1910; d. October 14, 1910; buried in North Ten Mile Cemetery); and 5) an infant daughter (b. and d. June 15, 1915; buried in North Ten Mile Baptist Cemetery, Washington, Pennsylvania). (MI, RI)

Evelyn Morrison Iams (b. July 31, 1903; d. January 11, 1962; buried in North Ten Mile Cemetery, Washington County, Pennsylvania), son of Isaac Weller Iams (b. 1874) and Ida Ruth Edgar; m. 1st, July 18, 1930, in Washington, Pennsylvania, to Dorothy Elizabeth Harden (b. October 26, 1914; d. June 11, 1990, in Maryland); m. 2nd, November 30, 1940, to Gertie Mae Elder (b. March 28, 1896, at Time, Greene County, Pennsylvania; d. September 18, 1976, Washington, Washington County, Pennsylvania), who had been m. 1st, J. Arley Elder (d. 1938). Gertie Mae Elder was the daughter of Frank Toland and Phoebe Ewing; and the sister of Olive Toland (m. Harry Amos of West Alexander, Pennsylvania); Wilma Toland; Minnie Toland (m. George Miller of West Alexander, Pennsylvania); Lula Toland (m. Morgan Stollar of West Finley, Pennsylvania); Vesta Toland (m. Raymond Yoders of Washington, Pennsylvania); Annabelle Toland (m. Arthur Daily of Waynesburg, Pennsylvania); Bernice Toland (m. Donald Hewitt of Greenville, South Carolina); Clarence Toland (of West Finley, Pennsylvania); Marvin Toland; Howard Toland; Kenneth Toland; and Franklin Toland.

Evelyn Morrison Iams (b. 1903) and Dorothy Elizabeth Harden had one son, Isaac Lindsey Morrison Iams [(b. April 3, 1933, Washington, Pennsylvania; lived at 81 Ike's Road, Marianna, Ten Mile, Washington County, Pennsylvania), m. August 2, 1953, to Ruth Eleanor Hand (b. February 15, 1937, Claysville, Pennsylvania), daughter of Howard Edward Hand and Helen Elaine Kerns; and had four children: William Isaac Iams, David Lindsey Iams, James Morrison Iams, and Richard Weller Iams. Isaac Lindsey Morrison "Ike" Iams (b. 1933) and Ruth Eleanor Hand lived on the family farm (a "century farm") at 81 Ike's Road, North Ten Mile, Amwell Township, Washington County, Pennsylvania. The home may be found on the top of the mountain, and except for the Log Cabin Fence Company, owned by a son, is the only home on the road. Surrounding the farm buildings may be found graders and other road equipment belonging to Amwell Township, reflective of the township responsibilities of Ike and Ruth. Both are Amwell Township Supervisors; and he served as the Chairman/President of the Board, and Ruth served as Secretary/ Treasurer. By 1996, Ike had been elected to the Board of Supervisors consecutively for over 30 years, and he also doubles as the Road Commissioner. Ruth's duties also included those of church organist; choir director of the historic North Ten Mile Baptist Church; church historian; a member of the County Covered Bridge preservation Commission; and an H and R Block tax consultant. Ike and Ruth Iams have a working farm where they raise black angus cattle, and their 174-acre Pennsylvania "Century Farm" (a designation designed to promote the importance of the Pennsylvania rural tradition) has been in the family since it was owned by William Iiams (b. 1830) prior to 1868. Ike and Ruth Iams are pillars of the community and have been active in historical and genealogical projects, including this book.

Isaac Lindsey Morrison Iams (b. April 3, 1933, Washington, Pennsylvania), son of Evelyn Morrison Iams (b. 1903) and Dorothy Elizabeth Harden, m. August 2,

1953, Triadelphia, at Roney's Point, West Virginia, to Ruth Eleanor Hand (b. February 15, 1937, Claysville, Pennsylvnia), daughter of Howard Edward Hand and Helen Elaine Kerns; had four children: 1) William Isaac Iams [(b. May 25, 1957, Washington County, Pennsylvania), m. November 15, 1975, East Bethlehem Baptist Church, Washington County, Pennsylvania, to Judith Angeline Rhodes of Deemston, Pennsylvania (b. March 12, 1957), daughter of Louis R. Rhodes, and sister of Mrs. Linda Sauers and Richard Rhodes; and they had two children: a) Clinton William Iams (b. February 29, 1980, Washington, Pennsylvania); and b) Charity Melysia Iams (b. December 29, 1981, Washington, Pennsylvania)]; 2) David Lindsey Iams [(b. July 25, 1960, Washington, Pennsylvania), m. December 29, 1980, Parisburg, Virginia, to Trudy Kimberly Sheets of Lancaster, Ohio (b. February 2, 1957), and they had two children: a) Jacob Lindsey Iams (b. July 6, 1983, Lancaster, Ohio); and b) Joseph Isaac Iams (b. June 3, 1985, Lancaster, Ohio)]; 3) James Morrison Iams [(b. February 27, 1963, Washington, Pennsylvania), m. July 10, 1983, North Ten Mile Baptist Church, Washington County, Pennsylvania, to Mary Elizabeth Cooke (b. April 12, 1962, Virginia), and they had two children: a) Contessa Mary Iams (b. December 7, 1983, Washington County, Pennsylvania); and b) Joshua James Iams (b. January 3, 1986, Washington, Pennsylvania)]; and 4) Richard Weller Iams [(b. July 22, 1965, Washington County, Pennsylvania), a graduate of Washington Institute of Technology, m. September 7, 1985, at Saint Mary's and Ann Church in Marianna, Pennsylvania, to Lisa Marie Colcombe (b. April 12, 1967), daughter of Albert and Kathleen Colcombe of Marianna, Pennsylvania; and sister of Michael Colcombe, Daniel Colcombe, Deborah Colcombe, Brian Colcombe, Karan Colcombe, Lynn Colcombe, Krista Colcombe, Albert Colcombe, Douglas Colcombe, and Mrs. Donna Kelsch; and they had five children: a) an infant son (d. November 20, 1986); b) Felecia Brooke Iams (b. December 23, 1988); c) Drew Richard Iams (b. January 22, 1990); d) Rachel Faith Iams (b. July 1, 1993); and e) Stephen Joseph Iams (b. August 9, 1995).

According to Ruth Eleanor Hand (b. 1937), William Hand (b. June 22, 1817; d. March 6, 1900), brother of John A. Hand and Thomas Hand; m. Sarah Ann Rogers (b. May 7, 1829; d. January 7, 1913; buried at Stone Church Cemetery, West Virginia, and they had six children: 1) Mary Jane Hand [(m. John Roseberry), and they had seven children: a) Anna Roseberry (m. Hud Creighton and they had three children: Bessie Creighton, Kenneth Creighton, and Arbie Creighton); b) Wiley Roseberry (single); c) Herman Roseberry; d) Melvin Roseberry; e) Eddie Roseberry; f) Harry Roseberry; and g) Mary Belle Roseberry (m. John Porter and their three children were: Nellie Porter, Bernice Porter, and John Porter)]; 2) Sarah Rachela Hand [(m. James Huff) and they had three children: a) Lena Huff (m. Edward Vance; no children); b) John Huff (m. Sadie Stricklin), and daughter Mildred Huff m. Edward Clark, and their two children were: Jean Clark (m. Richard Lastman) and James Huff; c) Anna Huff (m. Mr. Smith)]; 3) Annabelle Hand (m. Moses White); 4) William Roger Hand (d. as an infant); 5) William Milton Hand (d. as an infant); and 6) John Theodore Hand [(b. April 2, 1855; d. August 10, 1928, Stone Church Cemetery), m. June 1, 1881, at Windy Gap Church, West Finley, Pennsylvania, to Mary Elizabeth McDaniel (b. January 24, 1861; d. February 28, 1963; buried at Stone Church Cemetery); and they had four children: a) Pearl Hand (b. October 25, 1882; d. January 31, 1883; buried at Stone Church Cemetery); b) Elsie Doane Hand (b. August 12, 1895; d. July 9, 1962; buried Stone Church Cemetery; m. October 26, 1913, to Edward Blake); c) Edna Blanche Hand (b. March 16, 1898; m. March 3, 1917, Wheeling, West Virginia, to William Howard Shook); and 3) Oliver Walter Hand (b. March 15, 1885; d. October 8, 1962; buried at Stone Church Cemetery; m. April 20, 1914, to Anna Marie Denilson Baron, and they had four children).

Elsie Doane Hand (b. August 12, 1895; d. July 9, 1962; buried in Stone Cemetery), m. October 26, 1913, to Edward Blake (b. January 1, 1885; d. July 30, 1944; buried Stone Church Cemetery), and they had four children: 1) Ellis Cracroft Blake [(b. October 30, 1914; d. September 11, 1978; buried Stone Church Cemetery), m. May 31, 1937, to Ethel Connor (b. November 14, 1912; d. February 8, 1974; buried in Stone Church Cemetery), and they had six children: a) Mary Ellen Blake (b. October 17, 1938; m. Gary Wallace, and son John Robert Blake was b. September 25, 1956); b) Victoria Lynn Carpenter (b. September 13, 1939; and daughter Victoria Lynn Carpenter was b. September 13, 1959); c) Ellis Edward Blake (m. 1st, Patricia Croskin and their daughter was Lorie Elizabeth Blake; m. 2nd, Susan Gee Williams, and second child ws Debra Gee Blake); d) Robert Lee Blake (b. 1944); e) Alma Louise Blake (b. October 20, 1948; m. Thomas Joseph Manning, Sr., and their three children were: Thomas Joseph Manning, Jr., Susan Janeen Manning, and Gregory Manning); and f) Martha Mae Blake]; 2) Ellen Nerine Blake [(b. November 12, 1917; d. August 21, 1979; buried at Stone Church Cemetery), m. "J.W." Corwin Van Kirk (d. 1943; buried in Washington, Pennsylvania), and their son James Edward "Lacy" Van Kirk (b. August 19, 1941; d. August 1971) had a son David Van Kirk (b. 1963)]; 3) Mary Geneva Blake (b. May 8, 1920; m. Mr. Cusick or Couley; no children); 4) Edward Ferrell Blake [(b. March 23, 1922; d. March 12, 1950; buried Stone Church Cemetery), m. Alice Volka, and their daughter Norma Jean Blake (b. December 12, 1948), m.1st, December 2, 1967, to Jack Tyras, and had four children (later adopted by sister Mildred Blake Seaman): a) Kathleen Sue Tyras (b. January 16, 1969); b) Joan Tyras (b. February 2, 1970); c) Jack Tyras, Jr. (b. September 7, 1975); and d) Tina Marie Tyras (b. April 18, 1977)]; 5) Mildred Elsie Blake (b. March 24, 1926; m. John Seaman); 6) Vina Virginia Blake [(b. September 26, 1929), m. 1st, Mr. Riley; m. 2nd, Mr. Woods; had three children: a) Valerie Lynn Wood; b) Victor Lee Riley; and c) Jesse Lee Riley (b. 1960)]; and 7) Betty Jean Blake [(b. January 8, 1932); lived in Springvale, Utah; m. 1st, Philip Hebner; and m. 2nd, Mr. Crandall; children: a) Patricia Hebner; b) Edward Hebner; c) Rebecca Hebner; d) Robin Hebner; e) Candy Hebner; f) Sue Ann Hebner; g) Diane Hebner; h) Mark Hebner; and i) John Blake Hebner].

Edna Blanche Hand (b. March 16, 1898; d. October 18, 1996); m. March 3, 1917, to William Howard Shook (b. April 16, 1893; d. June 23, 1944), and they had nine children: 1) Martha Elizabeth Shook [(b. October 4, 1918; d. April 8, 1971; buried Claysville, Pennsylvania), m. October 20, 1936, to Charles Oliver Rothwell (b. November 5, 1912), and their son was William Lee Rothwell (b. June 7, 1941), who m. April 22, 1961, to Carol Ann Westfall (b. July 13, 1945) and their three children were: Kim Wynona Rothwell (b. November 9, 1961), Kreed William Rothwell (b. March 28, 1963), and Kena Wryn Rothwell (b. October 4, 1964; m. August 26, 1989, in Maryland, to Maynard L. Cowell, and their daughter was Amanda Lynn Cowell, b. February 1994)]; 2) Virginia Grace Shook (b. March 31, 1920; d. February 15, 1921; buried in Stone Church Cemetery); 3) Clarence William Shook [(b. June 26, 1921; d. June 16, 1991); buried in Claysville, Pennsylvania; m. Joan Columbia Zappi (b. October 12, 1927), and their four children were: a) Gary William Shook (b. July 2, 1952; m. June 25, 1971, to Audrey Lynn Evans, and they had four children: Cornia Lynn Shook, b. March 31, 1973; Gary Evans Shook, b. December 7, 1976; Justin William Shook, b. November 24, 1980; and Jeremi Robert Shook, b. October 18, 1982); and b) Karen Lea Shook (b. November 14, 1953; m. December 2, 1972; m. Randall Dallas Frye, b. March 20, 1952; and they had three children: John Day Frye, b. July 19, 1974; Hollie Ann Frye, b. August 19, 1976; and Autume Lea Frye, b. August 8, 1978); c) Michael Ray Shook (b. October 13, 1954; m. September

253

26, 1981, to Carol Jean Riggle, b. July 27, 1968; and their four children were: Matthew Ray Shook, b. November 25, 1983, Wheeling, West Virginia; Natalie Rose Shook, b. December 30, 1985; Sarah Jean Shook (b. October 14, 1989); and Andrew Michael Shook (b. 1990); and d) Lorie Lynn Shook (b. June 26, 1959; m. May 1986, to Robert John Seamon)]; 4) Ethel Eileen Shook [(b. March 31, 1923), m. August 24, 1946, to Edward Olshinsky (b. April 21, 1911; d. August 10, 1983), and their two children were: a) Donna Lee Olshinsky (b. April 19, 1954), m. August 16, 1960, to John Joseph Parks (b. July 19, 1951), and their two children were: Heather Michelle Parks (b. July 11, 1975), and Robin Renee Parks (b. May 1, 1981); and b) Leo Edward Olshinsky (b. December 31, 1957; m. October 1993)]; 5) John Robert Shook [(b. October 29, 1924; d. November 13, 1991); m. May 4, 1946, to Margaret Jane Newman (b. November 5, 1924), and their five children were: a) Shirley Ann Shook (b. December 18, 1946; m. 1st, Joseph Huffman; and m. 2nd, July 21, 1979, to Ronald Steven Foseman); b) Nancy Jane Shook (b. October 26, 1948; m. January 28, 1965, to Patsy Anthony Andy, Jr., b. June 21, 1941; and d. August 1975; and their children were: Sharon Marie Andy, b. December 9, 1967; Patsy Anthony Andy III, b. April 11, 1969; and Jack Michael Jacob, b. January 30, 1977); c) John Michael Shook (b. November 29, 1956, m. December 28, 1974, to Debra Marie Andrews, b. September 18, 1956; and their two children were: Anissa Marie Shook, b. June 9, 1979, and Andrew "Adam" Michael Shook, b. June 19, 1984); d) Mark William Shook (b. March 25, 1958); and e) Philip Wayne Shook (b. July 6, 1959; m. July 19, 1980, to Michelle Griffin)]; 6) Opal Elaine Shook [(b. February 7, 1927), m. October 24, 1949, to Charles Eugene Keller (b. April 18, 1921; d. January 23, 1989), and they had four children: a) Gregory Eugene Keller (b. October 31, 1950; m. September 9, 1972, to Norma Jean McFear, b. July 27, 1949; and their child was Christopher Michael Keller, b. July 27, 1976); b) Jeffrey Keller (b. October 26, 1953); c) Bambi Lynn Keller (b. June 14, 1957; m. May 22, 1976, to Timothy Lee Hardin, b. May 14, 1954; and their two children were: Sean Timothy Hardin, b. April 4, 1980; and Michelle Hardin, b. February 9, 1985); and d) Tracy Ann Keller (b. September 13, 1958; m. 1st, April 10, 1976, to James A. Blair; m. 2nd, April 10, 1978, to Lee Wiltsey, b. April 29, 1953; and their two children were: Brandy Lynn Wiltsey, b. June 10, 1978; and Elizabeth Marie Wiltsey, b. October 25, 1979)]; 7) Mabel Lucille Shook (b. March 13, 1931; d. from tornado at Taylorstown, Pennsylvania, with her father, on June 23, 1944, and buried at Stone Church Cemetery); 8) Nellie Marie Shook (b. September 3, 1933; d. May 24, 1934; buried in Stone Church Cemetery); 9) Delmar Lee Shook [(b. March 8, 1935), m. October 14, 1954, to Wilma Jean Scott (b. November 29, 1936), and their four children were: a) Randy Lee Shook (b. October 2, 1955; m. 1st, March 20, 1980, to Diane Elizabeth Guthrie, b. February 16, 1957); b) Mimi Louise Shook (b. February 2, 1957; m. September 13, 1987, to Edward Joseph Brittner); c) Hope Ann Shook (b. December 4, 1963; m. April 30, 1983, Taylorsville, Pennsylvania, to David Howard "Doc" Miller, b. October 17, 1959; and their two children were: Nicole Ilene Miller, b. February 25, 1984, in New Jersey; and Dana Lee Miller, b. May 21, 1991); and d) Dianna Jo Shook (b. November 29, 1964; m. July 1955, to Vernon Charles Curtis, and their two children were: Sadie Jo Curtis, b. February 21, 1990; and Levi Edward Curtis, b. May 29, 1991)]; and 10) Paul Russell Shook [(b. February 28, 1940; d. September 19, 1993; buried Oak Springs Cemetery), m. January 12, 1960, Winchester, Virginia, to Carol Ann Roupe (b. January 20, 1943), and they had four children: a) Jody Lynn Shook (b. May 3, 1961; m. October 16, 1981, to Robert William Mary, b. June 9, 1960, and their child was Ashley Lynn Mary, b. November 6, 1984); b) Paul Craig Shook (b. July 24, 1962; m. March 25, 1982, in Oklahoma, to Robin Lea Lane, daughter of Robert Lane, b. January 24, 1961; and their two children were: Paul Robert Shook, b. September 23, 1986; d. November 14, 1986, in Pennsylvania; and Robert Paul Shook, b. June 29, 1990; d. August 26, 1990); c) Aaron Wayne Shook (b. June 19, 1966); and d) Joy Leiah Shook (b. December 16, 1972)].

Oliver Walter Hand (b. March 15, 1885; d. October 8, 1962; buried in Stone Church Cemetery), son of John Theodore Hand (b. 1855) and Mary Elizabeth McDaniel; m. April 20, 1914, to Anna Marie Danielson Baron (b. September 20, 1880; d. February 21, 1977; buried in Stone Church Cemetery); and they had four children: 1) Pearl Hand (b. October 25, 1882; d. January 31, 1883); 2) Elsie Doane Hand (b. August 12, 1895; d. July 9, 1962); 3) Oliver Walter Hand (b. March 15, 1885; d. October 8, 1962); and 4) Edna Blanche Hand (b. March 16, 1898; m. March 3, 1917, in Wheeling, West Virginia to William Howard Shook (b. April 16, 1893; d. June 23, 1944, in tornado). The father of Anna Marie Danielson (b. September 20, 1880, in Denmark) was Peter Danielson, who m. in Denmark to Hannah Jepson, who migrated to Wheeling, West Virginia. The children of Peter Danielson were: 1) Earl Danielson, Sr. [(b. Pittsburgh, Pennsylvania; d. February 5, 1981), m. Marie Kahel and their two children were: Earl Danielson, Jr., and Harry E. Danielson]; and 2) Anna Marie Danielson [(b. September 20, 1880, in Denmark; d. February 21, 1977, in Wheeling, West Virginia; and buried in Stone Church Cemetery); m. 1st, Harry Baron (b. 1880; d. 1913; buried in Mt. Zion Cemetery); and their three children were: a) Harry B. Baron (b. January 20, 1906; d. February 9, 1949; buried in Mt. Zion Cemetery, Wheeling, West Virginia); b) Frank Baron (b. 1908; d. November 19, 1973; buried in Mt. Zion Cemetery); and c) Kenneth C. Baron (b. January 22, 1910), m. Margaret Griffin, and their three children were Dolores Baron, Charles Baron, and Amelia Baron, who m. Donald Porter); and Anna Marie Danielson Baron (b. 1880); m. 2nd, April 20, 1914, to Oliver Watter (b. March 15, 1885; d. October 8, 1962)].

Children of Oliver Walter Hand (b. 1885) and Anna Marie Danielson Baron (b. 1880) were: 1) Paul Russell Hand [(b. April 20, 1915; d. August 9, 1949; buried Stone Church Cemetery), m. November 25, 1937, to Pearl Frances Barstow (b. December 23, 1913), and their two children were: a) Lois Pauline Hand (b. October 22, 1938; m. September 12, 1958, to Reverend Charles Ray Gipson, b. October 28, 1938; and their five children were: 1[1]) Debora Lynn Gipson, b. and d. May 25, 1959; buried at Cedar Lawn, Philadelphia, Mississippi; 2[1]) Linda Gaye Gipson, b. June 28, 1960; m. June 22, 1979, to Ronald M. Pell, in Indiana, b. July 1, 1957; m. 2nd in April 1989 to Scott D. Gates, b. September 26, 1963, and their son was Brandon Scott Gates, b. May 8, 1989; 3[1]) Paula Raye Gipson, b. May 27, 1961; d. February 7, 1967; buried in Cedar Lawn Philadelphia, Mississippi; 4[1]) Paul Ray Gipson, b. August 7, 1964; and 5[1]) David Martin Gipson, b. July 26, 1971); and b) Gerald Dennis Hand (b. September 13, 1940; m. September 30, 1960, to Sandra Sue DuBois, b. October 23, 1941; and they had three children: 1[1]) Gerald Dennis Hand, Jr., b. October 28, 1961, Anderson, Indiana; m. June 5, 1984, to Cherie Dawn Miller, b. June 9, 1964; lived in Orlando, Florida; 2[1]) Tracy Samuel Hand, b. April 3, 1963, Anderson, Indiana; m. April 16, 1988, to Karen Sue Brady, b. February 21, 1964; and 3[1]) Cecelia Sue Hand, b. March 20, 1964; m. July 19, 1986, to Kevin Clark Shell, b. February 21, 1959; and they had two children: Lenzi Rae Hand, stillborn November 10, 1985, Anderson, Indiana; and Tyler Jay Snell, b. July 1, 1987, in Warsaw, Indiana)]; 2) Howard Edward Hand [(b. December 9, 1917; d. December 30, 1992), m. 1st, March 9, 1936, to Helen Elaine Kerns (b. September 13, 1918; d. September 27, 1988, West Alexander, Pennsylvania); m. 2nd, May 27, 1965, to Helen Louise Burris Kaufman (b. May 12, 1920; d. September 14, 1992); and their four children were: a) Ruth Eleanor Hand (b. February 15, 1937, Claysville, Pennsylvania; m. August 2, 1953, Roncy's Point, to Isaac Lindsay Iams, b. April 3, 1933, Washington County, Pennsylvania; son of Evelyn Morrison Iams, b. 1903, and Dorothy Elizabeth Harden); b) Elaine Lenora Hand (b. January 23, 1938, at Middle Wheeling Creek, West Virginia; m. February 1, 1957, Dallas Pike, West Virginia, to Clarence James Bambarger, b. February 4, 1933; d. March 2, 1991, at West Alexander, Pennsylvania; and their three children were: 1¹) Greg Edward Bambarger, b. August 22, 1959, Wheeling, West Virginia; 2¹) Kent Everett Bambarger, b. January 18, 1962, Wheeling, Virginia; m. March 21, 1981, at Roney's point, to Kelly Jo Caldwell, b. June 13, 1961, and their son was Lukas James Bambarger, b. February 13, 1992; and 3¹) Karen Sue Bambarger, b. November 7, 1964, Wheeling, West Virginia; m. October 1, 1988, at Roney's Point, to Aubrey William Ward); c) William Howard Hand (b. August 11, 1939, Middle Wheeling Creek, West Virginia; m. November 8, 1958, to Bonnie Jane Strawn, and their five children were: a) Kimberly Sue Hand, b. April 16, 1960, Wheeling, West Virginia; m. 1st, September 22, 1979, to Gregg L. Newman; m. 2nd, March 3, 1988, Key Largo, Florida, to Jerry Pennington; and their three children were: 1¹) Allen Scott Pennington, b. May 17, 1988; 2¹) Nathan Robert Pennington, b. July 5, 1989; and 3¹) Keydea Sue Pennington, b. April 18, 1991; b) Jeffrey Howard Hand, b. April 26, 1962, Wheeling, West Virginia; m. September 7, 1991; c) Bradley William Hand, b. August 28, 1963, Wheeling, West Virginia; m. December 10, 1983, to Rhoda Louise "Lisa" Ready, b. September 27, 1960; and their two children were:1¹) Jocelyn N. Hand, b. August 14, 1987; and Megan Renee Hand, b. September 29, 1988; d) Scott Allan Hand, b. January 4, 1968, Wheeling, West Virginia; m. April 4, 1992, to Corrie Jean Wimer; and e) William Lee Hand, b. January 8, 1969, Wheeling, West Virginia); d) Raymond Eugene Hand (b. August 10, 1940, Wheeling, West Virginia; d. August 11, 1940, Wheeling, West Virginia; buried at Stone Church Cemetery); and e) Robert James Hand (b. February 26, 1954, Alliance, Ohio; adopted; d. February 13, 1985)]; 3) Oliver Theodore Hand [(b. May 19, 1923), m. January 17, 1944, Triadelphia, West Virginia, to Rose Marie Farmer (b. November 17, 1922), and their two children were: a) Donald Clifford Hand (b. May 14, 1945; m. May 15, 1965, to Cheryl Ann Herbert, b. May 2, 1946; and their three children were: 1¹) April Michelle Hand, b. April 1, 1968; 2¹) Laurie Christine Hand, b. July 4, 1970; and 3¹) Kerry Alexis Hand, b. March 28, 1981); and b) Becky Lee Hand (b. September 15, 1948; m. 1st, December 24, 1968, to David M. Quill; m. 2nd, May 24, 1985, to Gerald R. Freeze, and their three children were: David, John, and Stefanie Quill)]; and 4) Mildred Hand [(b. June 3, 1921; m. January 8, 1940, to William Earl Dickson, b. June 4, 1912; and they had three children: a) Ronald LeRoy Dickson (b. August 28, 1942); m. 1st, December 27, 1965, Rockville, Maryland, to Betty Louise Diller, b. September 20, 1946; m. 2nd, November 2, 1985, to Vivien Pinedana, b. October 18, 1959; and he had two children: 1¹) Tiffany Ann Dickson, b. November 16, 1969; and 2¹) Ronald William Dickson, b. March 1, 1973); b) Carol Jean Dickson (b. March 9, 1945; d. December 1989; buried at Halacon Hills; m. May 6, 1968, at Elm Grove, West Virginia, to Bruce Alan Forinash, b. December 8, 1945; and their son was Robert Alan Forinash, b. October 2, 1970); and c) Gary William Dickson (b. July 1, 1960; m. June 8, 1985, Wheeling, West Virginia, to Victoria Holm Meyer, b. September 20, 1960; and their two children were: 1¹) William Bruce Dickson, b. August 29, 1987; and 2¹) Hannah Holm Dickson)].

Permilia Belle Iams (b. May 27, 1880; d. February 4, 1955; buried at Lone Pine Cemetery, Washington County, Pennsylvania), daughter of Zebulon Ferrell Iams (b. 1856), m. 1st, Charles Wray Grayson Allender; m. 2nd, John Melvin Edgar (b. November 10, 1879; d. August 2, 1955; buried in South Side Cemetery, Pittsburgh, Pennsylvania), and their three children were: 1) Clarence Weller Allender [(b. March 9, 1903; d. November 4, 1967; buried in Washington, Pennsylvania), m. March 12,

1925, to Evelyn Charity Lorraine Fogel, b. July 21, 1907; and their four children were: a) June Evalee Allender (b. June 7, 1926; m. November 7, 1940, to Verne Duane Keenan, b. September 2, 1919; and their two children were: 1¹) William Darl Kennan, b. February 14, 1947; and daughter was Lisa Marie Kennan, b. May 27, 1967; and 2¹) April Lee Kennan, b. March 5, 1955); b) Clarence Weller Allender, Jr. (b. July 4, 1927; m. Virginia Gigliotti, b. March 28, 1935; and their four children were: 1¹) Danny Lee Allender, a twin, b. April 16, 1953; 2¹) Mary Evelyn Allender, a twin, b. April 16, 1953; 3¹) Michael Jay Allender, b. April 24, 1955; and 4¹) Joseph Darl Allender, b. December 13, 1967; m. October 22, 1990, at Fairhill Manor, to Jamie S. Salvaggi); c) Earle William Allender (b. July 14, 1931; m. June 7, 1954, to Lois Carolyn Blacka, b. June 27, 1936; and their four children were: 1¹) Linda Lou Allender, b. April 16, 1955; 2¹) Luanne Allender, b. October 2, 1956; 3¹) Susan Lee Allender, b. November 29, 1957; and 4¹) Earl William Allender, b. July 17, 1960); and d) Darlene Lorraine Allender (b. February 18, 1938; d. October 23, 1942; buried in Washington, Pennsylvania)]; 2) Edna Dale Allender [(b. December 31, 1905; d. March 26, 1993; buried Washington Cemetery), m. June 10, 1925, Pittsburgh, Pennsylvania, to Robert Alexander Neal, b. February 18, 1906; d. July 2, 1967, Washington Cemetery, Washington, Pennsylvania), and their daughter Edna Mae Neal (b. August 18, 1926), m. June 8, 1946, to Fred Andrew Simpson (b. March 1, 1925), and they had two children: Fred Andrew Simpson (b. July 17, 1948) and Catherine Ann Simpson (b. May 1, 1951; m. Ronald Dyson)]; 3) Ruth Dolly Allender [(b. January 11, 1914, Denver, Colorado; d. March 30, 1985; buried Memorial Cemetery, Washington, Pennsylvania), m. June 1, 1829, to Leroy Beatty Finch (b. July 23, 1906; d. October 31, 1975; buried in Memorial Cemetery), and they had three children: a) Rodell Ruth Finch (b. May 31, 1931; m. March 31, 1950, to Richard Hazlett Lewis, b. July 9, 1926; and they had two children: 1¹) Richard Lee Lewis, b. February 14, 1952; m. Darla Faber, and their children were: Cristopher Lewis and Ashley Lewis; and 2¹) Paula Marie Lewis, b. December 13, 1955; m. Ralph E. Ferry, and their daughter Michelle Ferry, b. August 28, 1981); b) Robert Lee Finch (b. November 29, 1932; m. June 5, 1953, to Wilma Marlene Mounts, b. October 9, 1935; and their five children were: 1¹) Jody Lynn Finch, b. February 19, 1954; m. John Cowan; 2¹) Cynthia Lea Finch, b. July 25, 1956; m. James Andrew Beattie; 3¹) Jeffrey Scott Finch, b. May 16, 1958; m. May 12, 1964, to Martha J. Ahens, b. June 15, 1959; daughter of Henry Arns; and their four children were: a¹) Jeffrey Scott Finch II, b. August 21, 1975; b¹) Aaron Michael Finch, b. September 5, 1978; c¹) Jamie Lee Finch, b. June 21, 1988; and d¹) Jonathan Weir Finch, b. January 19, 1990; 4¹) Toni Jill Finch, b. November 20, 1963; m. Stephan Keller; and 5¹) Robert Finch, b. August 26, 1972); c) Beverly Ann Finch (b. September 8, 1938; m. September 24, 1955, to Samuel Guy Miller, b. May 21, 1935; and they had four children; 1¹) Kenneth Guy Miller, b. June 23, 1958; 21) Ruth Ann Miller, b. December 24, 1959; d. September 11, 1961; 3¹) Douglas Samuel Miller, b. April 16, 1961; and 4¹) Susan Renee Miller, b. July 6, 1967)]; and 4) Orville Iams (b. March 16, 1916), son of Permilia Belle Iams (b. 1880) and second husband John Melvin Edgar; (d. January 26, 1979; buried at Lone Pine Cemetery, Washington County, Pennsylvania), m. March 8, 1938, to Eleanor Corinne Barney (b. December 21, 1917; m. 2nd, Ralph Eckels); and their three children were: a) David Warren Iams [(b. July 5, 1939), m. September 26, 1960, to Judith Ann Tunney (b. October 31, 1942); and their four children were: 1¹) Cheryl Renee Iams (b. June 27, 1961; m. 1st, Jeffrey Lynn Ames; m. 2nd, May 1981, Ronald Harry Wise, b. December 18, 1981; and her children were: David Jay Ames, b. August 7, 1980; and Melissa Renee Wise, b. December 7, 1918); 2¹) David Lee Iams (b. January 20, 1963; m. 1st, October 1985, to Marion Jean Gorby, m. 2nd, May 1990, to Nancy Sue Tennant, and his two children were: Lottie Marie Iams, b. September 29, 1986, Hopewell, Virginia; and Courtney Lea Iams, b. June 1990); 3¹) Kimberly Ann Iams (b. December 17, 1963); and 4¹) Scott Douglas Iams (b. December 27, 1964; m. August 21, 1992, to Cindy Lou Tennant, b. May 8, 1972)]; b) Donald Orville Iams [(b. February 26, 1941), m. June 2, 1961, to Barbara Ilene Mazzie (b. October 28, 1941), daughter of James V. and Thelma Mazzie; and their three children were: 1¹) Donald M. Iams (b. September 12, 1964; worked at Jessop Steel in Washington, Pennsylvania; m. September 12, 1989, to Kristen L. Wolf, a beautician and daughter of G. Marvin and Janice Wolf, and sister of Amy Wolf, Stacey Wolf, and Craig Wolf); 2¹) Darrin Mark Iams, b. July 14, 1970; and 3¹) Steven James Iams, b. November 29, 1972); and c) Robert Gene Iams [(b. November 18, 1942), m. July 22, 1966, to Diana Ruth Walker (b. March 1, 1947), and they had three children: 1¹) Robert Todd Iams (b. September 6, 1968, and in September 1995, became engaged to Jana S. Rush, daughter of Gary and Becky Rush of Washington, Pennsylvania); 2¹) Stacy Lynn Iams (b. October 4, 1970); and 3¹) Melinda Iams]. (RI, ILMI)

Annie Eliza Iams (b. March 31, 1863; d. April 6, 1934; buried in Washington Cemetery, Washington, Pennsylvania), daughter of Isaac Iams (b. 1828) and Anne Ferrell, m. July 23, 1882, to William Fulton (b. December 4, 1862; d. April 14, 1938; buried in Washington Cemetery, Washington, Pennsylvania), and they had four children: 1) Olive May Fulton [(b. July 31, 1884; d. June 25, 1920; buried in Washington, Pennsylvania, cemetery), m. February 22, 1904, to Doctor Orville Garrett Lewis (b. October 7, 1877; d. March 22, 1946); and their two children were: a) Annie Elizabeth Lewis (b. July 4, 1906; d. March 22, 1913; buried in Washington Cemetery); and b) Evelyn Fulton Lewis (b. April 17, 1916), m. February 14, 1940, to Doctor Paul Phillips Riggle (b. October 1, 1902; d. March 8, 1979; buried in Washington Cemetery); and their two children were: 1¹) Jane Phillips Riggle (b. February 17, 1970; m. September 22, 1962, to John Clark Van Aken II, b. November 11, 1939; and their three children were: John Clark Van Aken III, b. September 22, 1964; David Riggle Van Aken, b. April 4, 1967; and Andrew Lewis Van Aken, b. August 9, 1969); and 2¹) Susan Lewis Riggle (b. November 13, 1946); m. July 1, 1967, to Lloyd Norman Roupe, b. April 14, 1946; and their two children were: Christopher Lloyd Roupe (b. March 15, 1970) and Peter John Roupe (b. December 22, 1973)]; 2) James Dorsey Fulton [(b. March 5, 1890; d. January 10, 1974; buried in Washington Cemetery), m. June 25, 1912, to Clara Mollenaver (b. December 21, 1889; d. December 15, 1974; buried in Washington Cemetery); and their son was James Orville Fulton (b. December 25, 1912; d. October 19, 1939; buried in Washington Cemetery, Washington, Pennsylvania; single)]; 3) Queen Elizabeth Fulton [(b. June 21, 1896; d. March 12, 1978; buried in Washington Cemetery), m. June 1, 1921, to Doctor Orville Garrett Lewis (his second; b. October 7, 1877; d. March 22, 1946; buried in Washington Cemetery); and they had two children: a) William Franklin Lewis (b. October 5, 1926; m. May 1, 1944, to Mary Alice Forney, b. October 11, 1926; and their three children were: 1¹) William Forney Lewis, b. May 11, 1945; m. May 24, 1964; to Catherine Lou Ritz, b. April 30, 1948; 2¹) Rebecca Ann Lewis, b. November 21, 1948; m. September 7, 1968, to Roy Allen Hartmacher, b. September 30, 1947; and 3¹) Richard Wayne Lewis, b. August 13, 1951; m. January 13, 1973, to Carol Jean Miller, b. April 18, 1951); and b) Doctor Orville Garrett Lewis, Jr., D.V.M. (b. December 18, 1929)]; and 4) Rose Anna Fulton [(b. November 20, 1898; d. August 4, 1979; buried Washington Cemetery), m. June 14, 1931, to Ralph Fulton Hickman (b. July 28, 1896; d. December 16, 1952; buried Washington Cemetery), and their son Fulton Fordyce Hickman (b. April 28, 1932), m. November 11, 1960, to Marilyn Bane (b. December 1, 1938), had a daughter, Amy Elizabeth Fulton (b.

February 26, 1970)]. Hannah Elizabeth Iams (b. September 25, 1865; d. November 11, 1960; m. George Austin Bovier (b. 1877; d. July 7, 1948).

Emma Beatrice Iams (b. January 16, 1869; d. April 1, 1928; buried in Lone Pine Cemetery, Washington County, Pennsylvania), daughter of Isaac Iams (b. 1828) and Anne Ferrell; m. Allison Dupont Swart (b. October 11, 1863; went west); and they had two children: Hiram Imes Swart (b. December 11, 1887) and Anna Catherine Swart (b. June 16, 1892). Hiram Imes Swart (b. December 11, 1887), m. Effie Mary Breese (b. July 18, 1887; d. November 13, 1967; buried in Prosperity Cemetery, Washington County, Pennsylvania), and they had four children: 1) Ruth Elizabeth Swart [(b. June 18, 1909), m. June 30, 1936, to Thomas Viran Ong (b. January 24, 1905)]; 2) Louis Hiram Swart [(b. April 23, 1912; d. January 13, 1978; buried in Newton Falls Cemetery), m. August 19, 1936, to Freda Stanley (b. January 14, 1915), and their two children were: a) Karen Ruth Swart (b. September 11, 1947; m. June 20, 1970, to Bert Ross, b. March 3, 1946; and their son Bradley Allen Ross, b. January 5, 1978); and b) Stanley Lewis Swart (b. October 2, 1941; m. August 7, 1971, to Janice Hunt, b. December 6, 1946)]; 3) William Alton Swart [(b. June 29, 1914), m. Lois Dea Hirby (b. September 27, 1912); and they had two children: a) Sue Ann Swart (b. August 5, 1950; m. August 8, 1971, to Roger Lucas and their two children were: Julie Ann Lucas, b. December 1, 1972; and Nicolo Lucas); and b) William Daniel Swart (b. July 9, 1952)]; 4) Bruce Phillip Swart [(b. May 25, 1917), and had four children: a) Mary Swart (m. Mr. Luden, and their three children were: John Luden, David Luden, and Steven Luden); b) Judy Swart (m. Mr. Noland, and their two children were: Paula Noland and Darla Noland); c) Nancy Swart (m. Mr. Carlson, and their three children were: Robert Carlson, Kari Carlson, and Chad Carlson); and d) Bruce Swart (married; child was Jeremy Swart)].

Anna Catherine Swart (b. June 16, 1892; a schoolteacher; d. June 2, 1976; buried in Washington Cemetery), m. December 26, 1924, to Walter Cleveland Hall (b. September 26, 1884; d. April 27, 1969; buried in Washington Cemetery, Washington, Pennsylvania); and they had three children: 1) Robert Swart Hall [(b. January 12, 1926), m. May 27, 1950, to Delores Albanese (b. May 31, 1927); lived in Western Springs, Maryland; two children: a) Stephan Swart Hall (b. October 28, 1952); and b) Eric Robert Hall (b. July 24, 1957), m. September 8, 1985, to Dawn Seymour]; 2) James M. Hall [(b. April 3, 1914, a stepson; d. May 16, 1990; buried in Washington Cemetery), m. March 25, 1939, to Ruth Morris (b. October 6, 1915); and they had three children: a) Judith Mildred Hall (b. June 15, 1940), m. Wallace Bishop, and their child was Matthew Bishop; b) Ruth Ann Hall (b. September 30, 1941), m. 1st, Mr. Francis; and m. 2nd, Ronald Smith; and her two children were: Scott Allan Francis and Michael David Francis; and c) Rebecca Jane Hall (b. February 16, 1945), m. Lloyd Kennan]; and 3) Mildred Louise Hall [(b. August 5, 1912; lived in Washington, Pennsylvania), m. November 29, 1939, to Boone Hall Morrison (b. February 8, 1915; d. May 15, 1978; buried in Washington, Pennsylvania); and they had three children: a) Phyllis Ann Morrison (b. December 3, 1942; m. July 16, 1966, to Charles Leonard Anderson, b. September 11, 1942; and their two children were: Kristen Joy Anderson, b. January 16, 1971; and Brian Charles Anderson, b. December 11, 1972); b) Nancy Louise Morrison (b. February 1, 1945; m. June 7, 1967, to David Ashley Samson, b. July 26, 1945; and their three children were: 1') Amy Louise Samson, b. July 25, 1971; 2') Laura Elizabeth Samson, b. December 27, 1974; and 3') Erin Elaine Samson, b. May 14, 1973); and c) Martha Jean Morrison (b. June 10, 1950; m. January 29, 1972, to Curtis Ray Kerns, b. September 17, 1950; and their two children were: 1') Samuel Curtis Kerns, b. June 10, 1977; and 2') Christopher Morrison Kerns, b. July 10, 1979)].

James Dorsey Iams (b. December 11, 1860, or 1868; d. 1943; buried in Lone Pine Cemetery, Washington County, Pennsylvania), the son of Isaac Iams (b. 1828) and Ann Ferrell, was a merchant and teacher; m. April 25, 1885, to Sarah Frances McClelland (b. August 3, 1859; d. 1942); lived in Green County, Pennsylvania in 1900; and had five children: 1) Daisy Mabel Iams [(b. March 1886; d. August 28, 1964, Tucson, Arizona), m. 1st, Henry Conger; m. 2nd, Carlson Weiss; m. 3rd, Ward Mollohan; and her four children were: a) Francis Conger (m. ____ Corbitt); b) Mary Conger (m. Fred Baumberger, Sr.; and their son was Fred Baumberger, Jr.); c) Dorsey Conger (m. ____ Payette); and d) Sarah Conger]; 2) William Allison "Allie" Iams, Sr. [(b. October 15, 1888; d. January 7, 1963; buried in Ruff Creek Cemetery, Greene County, Pennsylvania); a railroad engineer; m. May 11, 1912, to Eva "Evie" Sarah Shirk (b. April 29, 1892; d. May 25, 1973; buried Ruff Creek Cemetery); and their three children were: a) Ralph C. Iams; b) James Benjamin Iams (m. August 29, 1941, to Ruth E. Jones, b. March 6, 1920; d. October 12, 1970; and their child, James L. Iams, was b. August 25, 1942; d. December 22, 1977); c) James Shirk Iams (b. December 1, 1930; m. Helen Margaret Sargent, b. July 20, 1931; and their two children were: 1¹) Kathy Lynn Iams, b. January 3, 1956; m. Doctor Larry E. Orwig; and their child, Kathryn Lynn Orwig, b. August 24, 1980; and 2¹) Tammy Renee Iams, b. February 26, 1959); and d) William Allison Iams, Jr.]; 3) Charles Shirk Iams [(b. November 24, 1891; d. July 16 or August 5, 1936; buried at Lone Pine Cemetery, Washington County, Pennsylvania), m. November 20, 1915, to Florence Lewis (b. April 1, 1893; d. November 3, 1971; buried in Lone Pine Cemetery; she m. 2nd, September 27, 1947, to Moine Minor, b. March 27, 1889)]; 4) Sarah "Sadie" Edna Iams [(b. September 15, 1895, Ruff Creek, Greene County, Pennsylvania; a twin; d. May 27, 1962; buried in Washington Cemetery, Washington, Washington County, Pennsylvania), m. August 30, 1915, at North Ten Mile Baptist Church, Washington County, Pennsylvania, to Isaac Herman Edgar (b. August 17, 1891; d. April 6, 1962; buried in Washington Cemetery), the son of John Edgar and Mary Keys, and the brother of Clarence Edgar, W. R. Edgar, Herman Edgar, and Minnie Edgar (b. February 20, 1884; d. October 20, 1960; m. April 12, 1911, to Thomas M. Rees, a teacher who attended Waynesburg College; and their three children were: Thomas R. Rees, Miriam Rees, and Margaret Rees); and they had three children: a) Mary Kathleen Edgar (b. September 20, 1916), m. September 3, 1939, to Harry George Haviland (b. August 30, 1915; d. April 13, 1971; lived in Pittsburgh); and they had two children: 1¹) Richard Byron Haviland (b. June 13, 1945), m. December 27, 1967, to Sandra Lee Smith (b. July 20, 1948), and their child, Rebecca Jean Haviland (b. January 30, 1969; m. May 1992 to Keith Moore), had a daughter April Christine Moore (b. November 11, 1992); and 2¹) Kathleen Carol Haviland (b. December 7, 1946), m. August 16, 1969, to Henry Edward Hess II (b. September 22, 1942); and their three children were: Christine Carol Hess, b. August 21, 1970; Henry Edward Hess III, b. January 25, 1973; and Mary Kathleen Hess, b. August 2, 1974); b) Robert Iams Edgar (b. April 26, 1926), m. June 28, 1962, to Ruth Laurella Plymire (b. July 9, 1925), and their child was David Robert Edgar (b. September 28, 1963); and c) Carol Ann Edgar (b. August 3, 1936), m. 1952 to Edward Lee "Prigg" Prince (b. June 14, 1934); m. 2nd, William George Myers II; and her six children were: 1¹) Jacqueline Jolane "Bunny" Myers (b. April 5, 1953), m. December 12, 1970, to Steven Douglas Means, Sr. (b. August 4, 1951); and their four children were: Stacey Ann Means (m. October 27, 1990, to Jonathan Sexton); Lori Kay Means (b. September 16, 1974); Stephanie Diane Means (b. December 22, 1982); and Steven Douglas Means, Jr. (b. June 22, 1985); 2¹) William George Myers III (b. April 1, 1957); 3¹) Bradley Stephen Myers (b. June 18, 1959); 4¹) Brian Jeffrey Myers (b. August 3, 1960; m. Cynthia ____; and their two children were: Kristal Myers and Paige Myers); 5¹) Barry Douglas Myers (b. August 5, 1962); and 6¹) Jennifer Sue Myers (b. September 21, 1965)]; and 5) James Dorsey Iams, Jr. [(b. September 15, 1895, a twin; d. May 27, 1962; buried in Washington Cemetery), m. December 21, 1929, to Thelma Rush (d. July 25, 1960)].

William Allison "Allie" Iams, Sr. (b. October 15, 1888, Marianna, Washington County, Pennsylvania; d. January 7, 1963, Washington; buried in Ruff Creek Cemetery, Greene County, Pennsylvania); a railroad engineer; son of James Dorsey Iams (b. 1860) and Sarah F. McClelland of Greene County, Pennsylvania; and m. May 11, 1912, at Ruff Creek, to Evie "Eva" Sarah Shirk (b. April 29, 1892; d. May 25, 1973; buried in Ruff Creek Cemetery); and their four children were: 1) Ralph Charles Iams [(b. March 7, 1914, Ruff Creek; lived in Brownsville, Pennsylvania, in 1995); m. December 21, 1940, Ruff Creek Baptist Church, to Blanche Dunn (b. November 14, 1914; and their daughter Eva Marie Iams (b. March 3, 1943), m. James Piazzi (b. June 14, 1943; lived in Upper Marlboro, Maryland, in 1995) and they had two children: James "Jamie" Piazzi, b. September 20, 1863; and Michelle Piazzi (b. March 5, 1967)]; 2) James Benjamin Iams [(b. October 6, 1920, Waynesburg, Pennsylvania); operated a trucking company in Washington, Pennsylvania, for a time; operated "Ralph's Superette" in Washington, Pennsylvania; owned first K.O.A. camping franchise in Washington, Pennsylvania, area (d. December 13, 1984, Washington, Pennsylvania); m. August 29, 1941, to Ruth E. Jones (b. March 6, 1920, Ligonier, Pennsylvania; d. October 12, 1976); and their son James L. Iams (b. August 25, 1942, Washington, Pennsylvania; d. October 12, 1976, or December 22, 1977, Washington, Pennsylvania)]; 3) Jack Shirk Iams [(b. December 1, 1930, Washington, Pennsylvania; lived in Riverdale, Michigan, and since 1965 in Silver Spring, Maryland), m. October 28, 1951, Washington, Pennsylvania, to Helen Margaret Sargent (b. July 20, 1931, Washington, Pennsylvania; d. October 9, 1993, Silver Spring, Maryland; buried at Ruff Creek), daughter of Melvin L. Sargent and Leona M. Mundel; and they had two children: a) Kathy Lynn Iams (b. January 3, 1956, U. S. Naval Base, Guantanamo Bay, Cuba), m. December 2, 1979, to Doctor Larry E. Orwig; and their child was Kathryn Lynn Orwig (b. August 24, 1980); and b) Tami or Tammy Renee Iams (b. February 26, 1959, Charleroi, Pennsylvania; single)]; and 5) William "Allan" Allison Iams, Jr. [(b. July 31, 1925, Waynesburg, Greene County, Pennsylvania), m. June 3, 1944, at Waynesburg Baptist Church, to Margaret Jean Spitznogle, daughter of Gar Spitznogle and Ola B. Condit; and their daughter was Barbara "Jan" Iams (b. February 28, 1950, Waynesburg, Pennsylvania), m. Ben Costello, a lawyer; lived in Washington, Pennsylvania).

Charles Shirk Iams (b. November 24, 1891; a schoolteacher; d. July 16, 1936; buried in Lone Pine Cemetery, Washington County, Pennsylvania); son of James Dorsey Iams (b. 1860) and Sarah F. McClelland; m. November 20, 1915, Ida Florence Lewis (b. April 1, 1893; d. November 3, 1971; buried in Lone Pine Cemetery; m. 2nd, September 27, 1937, to Moine Minor), daughter of Jacob H. Lewis and Margaret E. Edgar [(m. September 16, 1892); she was the daughter of John Edgar and Mary Keys of Castile; (Jacob and Margaret Edgar Lewis had eight children: Harry Lewis, Florence Lewis Iams, John Lewis, Challen W. Lewis, Mrs. Stuart (Rachel Lewis) Simms, Paul Lewis, Mrs. J. D. (Margaret Lewis) Reed, and Roy Lewis); while John and Mary Kay Edgar had five children: Margaret Edgar Lewis; Mrs. Thomas Reese of Rogersville, Pennsylvania; Mrs. Howard Murray of Washington, Pennsylvania; Daniel Edgar of Eighty-Four, Pennsylvania; Clarence Edgar of Waynesburg, Pennsylvania; and Herman Edgar of Washington, Pennsylvania]; and Charles Shirk Iams (b. 1891) had four children: 1) Sarah Margaret Iams [(b. July 12, 1916; lived in Waynesburg, Pennsylvania, and Crucible, Michigan), m. Charles

261

Joseph Ross, Jr. (b. May 25, 1942; m. November 25, 1966, to Shirley Ann Wilson, b. July 13, 1944; and had two children; Leica Jo Ross, b. April 16, 1967; m. September 30, 1991, to Alan Keith Snyder; and Douglas Charles Ross, b. April 21, 1973); and on October 1, 1947, Sarah Margaret Iams Ross m. 2nd, Paul Edwin Cain, b. May 24, 1910; d. February 11, 1991; buried at Oakmont Cemetery in Pittsburgh; and her next children were: b) Emma Christine Cain (b. May 14, 1948; m. May 8, 1982, to Roger Charles Kuha, b. October 20, 1943); c) Larry Paul Cain (b. July 13, 1949; m. April 4, 1976, to Mary Alice Koweleski, b. February 10, 1957; lived at Crucible, Pennsylvania; daughter Becky Marie Cain, b. October 10, 1978); and d) Phyllis Ann Cain, b. July 24, 1957; m. July 4, 1956, to Claude Augustus "Gus" Donowho, b. March 6, 1946; and daughter Sarah Christine Donowho, b. July 17, 1988)]; 2) Charles Lewis Iams (b. April 26, 1919; m. 1st, Penny Owens; m. 2nd August 16, 1965, in Cumberland, Maryland, to Audrene Margaret Longstreth, b. May 15, 1921, in Carlisle, Pennsylvania; d. December 12, 1991, Waynesburg, Pennsylvania; buried in Pleasant Hill Cemetery); 3) Mary Helen Iams [(b. June 27, 1926), m. William R. McKay, and they had four children: a) Rosella Iams McKay (b. September 20, 1947; m. Charles Waiveras, and their two children were: John Waiveras and Katie Waiveras); b) James S. McKay (b. August 18, 1949); c) Leslie Marie McKay (b. August 6, 1951; m. Nathan Levine); and d) Heather Elizabeth McKay (b. March 23, 1966)]; and 4) James Dorsey Iams [(b. April 23, 1932), m. February 17, 1956, to Carol Lorraine Blake-Huelbert (b. July 11, 1927), and they had three children: a) James Dorsey Iams II (b. May 4, 1957; m. July 11, 1981, to Debra Ann Furlong, b. June 27, 1958; and their child was Brian Iams, b. June 25, 1982); b) Charles Stuart Iams (b. December 15, 1958; d. July 4, 1988; m. June 6, 1981, to Susan Marie Behrend, b. July 5, 1962; and their daughter was Elizabeth Sarah Iams, b. December 30, 1982); and c) Christopher Joseph Iams (b. December 23, 1960; d. August 19, 1992; buried in Mentor Cemetery; m. December 12, 1980, to Darlene Faith Pratt; and their son, Charles Ray Iams, b. September 3, 1991, m. Mitzi Miller.

Mary "Elizabeth" Iams (b. 1769; d. 1850; buried Amity Cemetery, Washington County, Pennsylvania), daughter of Thomas Iiams (b. 1708), m. April 8, 1788, Baltimore County, Maryland, to William Penn (b. 1762), son of John Penn of Baltimore; Captain in Captain Ezekial Rose's Company of the Fifth Battallion of Washington County militia that had been recruited from the Pigeon Creek section of the county, and which was engaged in the Sandusky Expedition, 1782; signed a quit claim deed in Baltimore in 1799, and returned to Greene County, Pennsylvania, where he obtained a land warrant in Morris Township on McClelland Fork of the Ten Mile Creek); and they had eleven children:

1) Richard Penn [(War of 1812) m. Sarah Mary McCullough, sister of Eynon McCullough, and they had five children: a) George Penn; b) William Penn; c) Mary Penn; d) Sarah Penn; and e) Hannah Penn]; 2) Nancy Penn (m. Jacob Bigler or Biegler, and they had two children: Israel Bigler and Hannah Bigler); 3) Mary Penn [(b. 1794; d. 1870), m. Thomas Shidler, and they had five children: a) David Shidler; b) Nancy Shidler (m. James Pence); c) John Shidler (m. Susannah ____); d) Sarah Shidler; and e) Susannah Shidler (m. John Pence)]; 4) William Penn [(b. March 1, 1799; d. February 25, 1891), m. Phoebe Bane (b. 1807); lived in Greene County, Pennsylvania; had eight children: a) Jacob Penn (b. August 3, 1825); b) John N. Penn (b. May 18, 1824, or 1829); c) Mary Penn (b. August 24, 1830; m. Mr. Post); d) Clarissa Penn (b. March 10, 1832); e) Hamilton Penn (b. January 10, 1834); f) Hiram Penn (b. February 23, 1836); g) Thomas Penn (b. October 27, 1837); and h) William H. Penn (b. September 3, 1841; m. Elizabeth ____; lived in southwestern Iowa; had three children: infant son, d. June 24, 1807; Mary Bertha Penn, d. age 4 months on November

6, 1879; and T. Homer Penn, b. January 1, 1882; d. January 28, 1889)]; 5) Nathan Penn [(b. 1801), m. Rachel McCullough, sister of Mary McCullough; had six children: a) Rachel Penn; b) Nancy Penn; c) Jennie Penn; d) Mary Penn; e) Ruth Penn; and f) Samuel Penn (b. December 30, 1831; d. September 18, 1903; m. Minerva Miller, b. January 15, 1833; d. February 21, 1907; buried in Mount Herman Cemetery; son John Penn (b. August 22, 1856; d. May 28, 1932; buried in Pleasant Hill Cemetery; m. Emma Bradbury (b. January 12, 1863; d. October 21, 1927); and had two children: John Howard Penn (b. September 12, 1893; d. June 5, 1978; buried in Pleasant Hill Cemetery; m. December 24, 1916, to Myrtle Katural Dunn, b. October 2, 1891; d. May 6, 1959; buried Pleasant Hill Cemetery; had five children: Mildred Katural Penn; m. Mr. Miller; infant son; Olive Kathryn Penn, m. Mr. Plymire; Herman Ray Penn; and John Walter Penn); and Gwendola Olive Penn (m. January 12, 1918, to Russell Bryan Pettit)]; 6) John Penn [(b. June 9, 1808; d. September 5, 1892), m. 1st, Deborah Iams (d. February 20, 1856; buried in Bates Fork Cemetery, Greene County, Pennsylvania); m. 2nd on October 3, 1866, to Rebecca Condit; had six children: a) Phoebe Penn (b. April 24, 1833; d. November 27, 1890; m. December 5, 1850, to Thomas Iams); b) Mary Penn (b. July 28, 1834; d. December 28, 1884; m. Benjamin F. Huffman, son of John Huffman and Elizabeth Smith; had two children: 1¹) Sarah A. Huffman; and 2¹) Phoebe Jane Huffman, m. Thomas William Fonner; and their son, Earl Ross Fonner, m. December 29, 1895, to Jane Elizabeth Myers; and their daughter, Dorothy Elizabeth Fonner, m. December 14,1946, to Charles Gratton Martell); c) Ellinor Penn (b. March 29, 1837; m. Fred Fonner); d) Margaret Penn (b. April 10, 1839; d. May 2, 1885; m. A. J. Barker); e) John H. Penn (b. June 5, 1845; d. April 27, 1864); and f) Emma Penn (b. April 13, 1873, by second marriage; lived in Ridgeway, Ohio; family historian who provided information; m. Guy Terrill)]; 7) Margaret Penn [(m. 1st, James Riley or Remley; m. 2nd, William Milliken); had five children: Martha Remley, Sarah Remley, Mary Remley, John Remley, and George Remley]; 8) Sarah Penn [m. James Pierson, and their two children: Vincent Pierson and William Pierson]; 9) Susannah Penn [(b. July 26, 1797; d. February 26, 1872), m. John Rogers (b. March 26, 1800; d. March 14, 1879), from Rogersville, Pennsylvania]; 10) Matilda Penn [(b. March 26, 1805; d. March 18, 1898), m. Daniel Hill]; and 11) Thomas Penn [(d. May 24, 1838), m. Sarah Moore, and their two children: Carie Penn and William Penn]. (JBM, MI, EP)

Jacob Penn (b. August 3, 1825), the son of William Penn (b. 1799) and Phoebe Bane, worked in "Penn Flouring Mill" and "Carding Machine" on Ten Mile Creek, Pennsylvania, owned by the father; m. November 19, 1846, to Emaline McCloy; had five children: 1) William H. H. Penn (b. 1854, Washington County, Pennsylvania; moved to Nebraska City, Nebraska, in 1860, with his father); 2) Anna E. Penn (d. young); 3) Mary E. Penn (d. young); 4) Abner B. Penn (d. young); and 5) John V. Penn (d. young).

John Newton Penn (b. May 18, 1824, or 1829, Pennsylvania; d. 1896, in Sidney, Iowa), the son of William Penn (b. 1799) and Phoebe Bane; m. October 17, 1848, Greene County, Pennsylvania, to Emilie Richie (d. 1917; studied merchandising at Waynesburg College); moved to Ohio in 1854 and to Fremont County, Iowa, in 1856; with John Newton Penn (b. 1824) serving as an examining Army doctor for the Civil War; had seven children: 1)Alphonso V. Penn [(b. 1857; a pharmacist; lived at least 88 years); m. Mary Z. Grey (b. 1857; d. 1920); had a son Alfonso V. Penn, Jr. (owned Penn Drug Store in Sidney, Iowa; and had a son, William Penn)]; 2) Jacob Penn [(b. August 3, 1825; d. 1890); migrated to Nebraska]; 3) Abner Penn (b. September 27, 1827; killed as a boy in Pennsylvania); 4) Mary Penn (b. April 24, 1830; m. Mr. Post); 5) Clarisa Penn (b. March 10, 1832; m. in Pennsylvania, to

263

Joshua Cooper); 6) Hamilton Penn (b. 1834, in Pennsylvania; m. _____ Conger); and 7) Hiram Penn [(b. 1836, Pennsylvania; d. 1939 at age 103); owned farm in southwest Iowa at Randolph; m. 1st, Rachel Hitchcock (on October 16, 1862; and had twelve children); m. 2nd, Cynthia Crevino (d. 1938)].

Susannah Penn (b. July 26, 1797; d. February 26, 1872), the daughter of William Penn and Mary Iiams (b. 1769); m. John Rogers (b. March 26, 1800; d. March 14, 1879; lived in area of Greene County, Pennsylvania; later named Rogersville, after him); the son of William Rogers; had nine children: 1) Levi Munce Rogers (b. 1838; killed in Civil War, as Captain in 58th Pennsylvania Regiment); 2) Thomas P. Rogers (b. 1842; Corporal in 58th P.V.I.; killed on August 16, 1864, at Deep Bottom, Virginia; 3) William Rogers (b. 1824; d. 1899; m. Catherine Meegan); 4) James Albert Rogers [(b. October 2, 1826; d. March 1903); m. November 1, 1849, to Luvina Sellars (b. October 24, 1830; d. October 2, 1914)]; 5) Doctor Timothy Ross Rogers (b. 1833; d. October 4, 1904; m. Emma Frantz); 6) Mary Rogers (b. 1836; d. 1846); 7) Nancy Rogers (b. December 18, 1822; d. November 5, 1903; m. George Sellars); 8) Captain John Rogers (b. 1832; d. 1917; m. Cairie McCormrick); and 9) Cephas Coe Rogers (b. 1829; d. 1852).

Matilda Penn (b. March 26, 1805; d. March 8, 1896), daughter of William Penn and Mary Iiams (b. 1769), m. Daniel Hill (b. February 5, 1803; d. August 5, 1882), son of Rees Hill and Nancy Heaton; had five children: 1) Mary Hill (b. March 16, 1832; d. September 16, 1914; m. April 4, 1854, to Seth Goodwin); 2) Rees Hill (b. December 12, 1833; d. July 15, 1910; m. Sarah Price); 3) William Hill (b. June 5, 1830; d. April 27, 1924; m. Mariah Tinsman); 4) Thomas Hill (b. November 22, 1839; d. July 11, 1928; m. Adelaide Peake); and 5) John Hill (b. May 24, 1850; d. May 2, 1856).

James Albert Rogers (b. October 2, 1826; d. March 1903), son of John Rogers (b. 1800) and Susannah Penn (b. 1797), daughter of Mary Iiams (b. 1769) and William Penn; m. November 1, 1849, to Luvina Sellers (b. October 24, 1830; d. October 2, 1915); and they had six children: 1) Sarah Rogers (b. 1850; m. Robert Watson); 2) John Rogers (b. 1854; m. Minerva Stockdale); 3) Susannah "Annie" Rogers [(b. December 11, 1856; d. December 21, 1924); m. June 19, 1881, to George Donahoe Huffman (b. May 15, 1853; d. 1933)]; 4) George Rogers (b. 1860; m. Ann Dillie); 5) Emma Rogers (b. 1865; m. Daniel Bailey); and 6) James Albert Rogers II (b. August 13, 1874; d. 1910; m. Blanch Orndoff).

Susannah "Annie" Rogers (b. December 11, 1856; d. December 21, 1924), the daughter of James Albert Rogers (b. 1826) and Luvina Sellers, m. June 19, 1881, to George Donahoe Huffman (b. May 15, 1853; d. 1933), and they had three children: 1) James William Huffman (b. February 1, 1886; d. July 21, 1973); 2) Mary Luvina Huffman [(b. February 17, 1888; d. July 14, 1973), m. March 11, 1912, to Frank Whittlatch Meighen (b. March 30, 1886; d. November 7, 1960); and had two children: a) Anna Gordon Meighen (b. February 25, 1913; schoolteacher; single); and b) James Brice Meighen (b. April 21, 1915; author and contributor; m. June 23, 1944, to Helen Elizabeth Murdock, b. March 15, 1917); and 3) Edna Huffman [(b. Februay 11, 1890; d. April 26, 1976); m. Joseph Monroe Chilcote (b. August 2, 1884; d. November 7, 1946)].

John Huffman, m. Elizabeth Smith (b. 1776; d. April 11, 1853, daughter of Dennis Smith and Elizabeth Zook, had nine children including: Benjamin F. Huffman (m. Mary Penn, daughter of John Penn and Deborah Iams); Matilda Huffman (m. Dennis Iams); James Huffman; Nancy Huffman; Rebecca Huffman (m. John Iams); Joseph Huffman (m. Nancy Reader); George Huffman (m. Mary Iams); John Huffman; and Delilah Huffman [(m. June 30, 1842, to "the Democrat" Thomas Iams); they owned 600 acres; had three children: 1) Benjamin H. Iams (b. September 4, 1846, Ruff's Creek, Greene County, Ohio; was 1st Sergeant in Company G of 18th Pennsylvania Cavalry in Civil War); 2) Otho Iams (also a Democrat; m. June 1884, to Sara Bane, daughter of Jasper Bane of Swart, Greene County, Ohio); and 3) James L. Iams (m. Belle Swart; their four children were: F. P. Iams, James Iams, Mort Iams, and Ike Iams)].

Charity Iams (b. February 12, 1799; d. January 18, or March 12, 1876; buried in Franklin Cemetery, Washington County, Pennsylvania), daughter of John Iiams (b. 1752) and Elizabeth Hampton; m. John D. Smith (b. August 8, 1795; d. November 12, 1876; buried in Franklin Cemetery); and they had eleven children:

1) Martin Smith [(b. March 21, 1824; a painter; d. December 12, 1890); m. Calista Wright; and their child, Matilda Smith, m. W. A. Davis and lived in Fairview, West Virginia]; 2) R. D. Thomas Smith (b. 1826; d. October 3, 1827); 3) John D. Smith (b. November 20, 1832; d. March 16, 1917; single; buried in Franklin Cemetery); 4) Joseph Smith (b. March 21, 1835; d. January 17, 1906; a minister; m. Jennie P. Boyd); 5) Nathan R. Smith (b. April 8, 1837; d. July 23, 1912; a farmer; m. Catherine Moore); 6) William Freeman Smith (b. October 4, 1839; d. March 20, 1915; a farmer; m. Caroline A. Adams); 7) Freeman Smith; 8) Elizabeth "Betty" Smith (b. November 17, 1830; d. April 12, 1909; single; buried in Franklin Cemetery); 9) Nancy Smith (b. April 20, 1843; d. November 12, 1884; 10) Ira Smith (b. August 5, 1845; d. April 5, 1868); and 11) Amos Smith [(b. April 20, 1828; d. April 10, 1894), m. Julia Matthews, and they had ten children: a) Charity A. Smith (b. December 20, 1848; d. May 10, 1907; single); b) Nancy Smith (b. November 17, 1851; d. April 21, 1926; m. George F. Hyde; and they had four children: Lotta Hyde, Helen Hyde, Howard Hyde, and George Hyde); c) Lewis M. Smith (b. December 13, 1853; lived in Anaheim, California; m. Margaret Sulser; and their child, Edith Smith, m. R. W. McCool and lived in Long Beach, California); d) Lucinda Smith (b. April 28, 1856; d. April 22, 1902; m. W. R. Scandretti; and their three children were Lulu Scandretti; Milton Scandretti; and Bernice Scandretti); e) John D. Smith (b. September 12, 1858; d. April 9, 1908); f) William M. Smith (b. January 20, 1861; d. April 18, 1890; m. Ella Gaghagan; and their son was Paul H. Smith); g) Amos Calvin Smith (b. October 31, 1863; d. April 18, 1889); h) Mary Smith (b. December 8, 1865; m. William K. June; and their three children were: Charles K. June, Franklin M. June, and Lewis William June); i) Julia E. Smith (b. February 29, 1868; m. J. E. Craven; and their four children were: Bayard Craven, Elsie Craven, Bessie Craven, and John Craven); and j) Matthew S. Smith (b. January 2, 1871; m. Susie Spooner; and their three children were: Francis Smith, Stanley Smith, and Austin Smith)]. (EBI)

Nancy Iams (b. January 10, 1787, or 1795; d. January 21, 1871, or 1879; buried in Franklin Cemetery, Washington County, Pennsylvania), daughter of John Iiams (b. 1751) and Elizabeth Hampton of Iams Mills, Amwell Township, Washington County, Pennsylvania), m. December 27, 1821, to Joseph Martin, his 2nd marriage (b. March 15, 1790; d. December 25, 1859), the son of James Martin and Anna McIntyre (Elizabeth Harden, the first wife of Joseph Martin, died shortly after their marriage). Children of James Martin and Anna McIntyre of New Jersey were: Thomas Martin (m. 1821 to Mary Bradbury); Joseph Martin (b. 1821); Zephaniah Martin (m. Belle Hood); Jane Martin (m. Joseph Dunn and had seven children); Sarah Martin; and Elizabeth Martin. The father of James Martin was Zephaniah Martin, a blacksmith who moved from Morris County, New Jersey, to Pennsylvania. The seven children of Nancy Martin (b. 1787) and Joseph Martin (b. 1790) were:

1) Morgan Martin [(b. October 19, 1823; d. March 5, 1909; buried in Franklin Cemetery, Washington County, Pennsylvania); m. September 18, 1856, to Anna Rees

(b. October 22, 1833; d. July 18, 1913; buried in Franklin Cemetery)]; 2) Elizabeth Iams Martin (b. November 24, 1825; d. December 13, 1825; buried in Franklin Cemetery); 3) John Iams Martin [(b. February 8, 1828; d. November 8, 1892); m. November 30, 1851, to Elizabeth Bair Barr; and their seven children were; Joseph Martin, Sarah Martin (m. William Keys); A. Jackson Martin (m. ____ Buckingham); Martha Martin (m. Van Voorhes); Samuel Martin (m. ___ McCuen); Clarion W. Martin (m. ____ Bennington); and Morgan Martin (m. Anne Sutherland-Reese)]; 4) Joseph Martin, Jr. (b. April 2, 1831; d. May 13, 1853; buried in Franklin Cemetery); 5) Anna Martin [(b. July 23, 1833; d. March 13, 1918); m. January 25, 1855, to Andrew P. Van Dyke (b. June 19, 1831; d. November 30, 1918; buried Amity Cemetery, Washington County, Pennsylvania); and they had seven children: a) Leroy Martin Van Dyke, b. October 22, 1855; d. October 6, 1923; buried Amity Cemetery; m. Lydia Gibson); b) Nancy Caroline Van Dyke (b. February 15, 1858; d. July 7, 1940; m. David Herman Swart); c) Sarah Elizabeth Van Dyke (m. Troal C. Bebout); d) Katie McFarland Van Dyke (b. August 6, 1862; d. 1931; buried Amity Cemetery; m. Grant B. McCola); e) Hannah Clare Van Dyke (b. 1863; d. August 22, 1887; buried in Amity Presbyterian Church; m. M. J. Allen); f) Thomas McFarlane Van Dyke (b. April 3, 1864; d. July 1, 1956; buried Amity Presbyterian Cemetery; m. Anne E. Crawl); g) Florence Anna Van Dyke (m. James Oscar)]; 6) Sarah Martin [(b. February 1, 1836), m. Neal Zollars; had eight children, including: George Zollars, Ezekial Zollars, Martha Zollars, Joseph Zollars, Grant Zollars, Nancy Zollars, and Kate Zollars (m. Harry Richards)]; and 7) Jacob Martin.

Morgan Martin (b. October 19, 1823, Washington County, Pennsylvania; d. March 5, 1909; buried Franklin Cemetery, Washington County, Pennsylvania; a Methodist; operated John Iiams Mill (Martin Mill); son of Joseph Martin (b. 1790) and Nancy Iams (b. 1787); m. September 18, 1856, to Anna Rees (b. October 22, 1833; d. July 18,1913; buried in Franklin Cemetery); and they had eight children:

1) Sanford Martin [(b. June 18, 1857; d. September 15, 1889; buried Franklin Cemetery), m. March 9, 1882, to Alice Bigler]; 2) William R. Martin (b. December 28, 1862; d. June 12, 1958; buried Franklin Cemetery; single); 3) Anna Martin (b. December 17, 1864; d. December 8, 1946; buried Franklin Cemetery); 4) Sarah Martin (b. June 8, 1867; d. July 21, 1967; single); 5) Elizabeth Jane Martin [(b. December 19, 1859; d. August 22, 1885; buried in Franklin Cemetery), m. October 13, 1883, to William S. Bigler; and two children were: Israel Gilmore Bigler (b. August 11, 1884; m. Anne Conger); and Estella Bigler (b. February 11, 1887; m. George Cowan)]; 6) Mary Ellen Martin (b. September 6, 1872; d. December 30, 1885; buried in Franklin Cemetery); 7) Lucy Martin [(b. October 10, 1874; lived in original John Iiams home), m. Adam McCullough; and they had four children: a) Guy McCullough (m. Ruth Hindman); b) Harold McCullough (m. Alma Hufford); c) Lela McCullough (m. C. I. Reynolds); and d) Edith McCullough; single)]; and 8) Nancy Martin [(b. August 12, 1869; author of *Nancy Martin: Country Gal*, Christopher Publishing House: Boston, 1950: d. February 1956), m. February 13, 1896, to Joseph William Shidler (b. February 26, 1868; d. May 2, 1957; buried Washington Cemetery); son of Jacob Shidler and Sarah Ward (Jacob Shidler and son Daniel Shidler "went West and never returned," leaving Sarah with two infants: Daisy Shidler, who was raised by John Iiams Martin; and J. Walter Shidler, who was raised by John D. Smith, Jr., and became a physician); and they had six children: a) Dorothy Martin Shidler; b) Marjorie Mae Shidler (m. Stuart Murphy); c) Virginia Shidler (m. Russell Horn); d) Leroy Shidler; e) Lenore Shidler (m.Mr. Jacques); and f) Katherine Shidler]. Dorothy Martin Shidler (b. November 9, 1898; d. May 21, 1981; buried Washington Cemetery), m. 1st, December 15, 1934, to Carl S. Sundin (d. June 22, 1943), m. 2nd,

June 27, 1944, to Albert Skyrmes. Marjorie Mae Shidler (b. July 1, 1900; d. July 26, 1995; buried Washington Cemetery), m. August 4, 1927, to Stuart Ellsworth Murphy (b. May 17, 1899; d. May 3, 1970; buried Washington Cemetery); adopted Joseph Leroy Murphy (b. July 1, 1928). Leroy Beatty Shidler (b. January 11, 1902; d. May 12, 1985; buried Washington Cemetery), m. December 30, 1929, to Mildred Hawn (b. March 31, 1901; d. April 25, 1981); no children. Anna Virginia Shidler (b. October 20, 1903; d. September 17, 1993), m. November 24, 1924, to Russell J. Horne (d. 1961; buried Washington Cemetery); two children: Marjorie Jean Horne [(b. September 1, 1929; an RN), m. 1st, 1954, to Richard Bowles; m. 2nd, James Spencer; four children: Gena Rae Bowles (b. December 11, 1956; d. 1994; m. Mr. Martin); Russell Thomas Bowles (b. December 18, 1958); Virginia Kay Bowles (b. April 26, 1960); and Randall James Spencer (b. August 22, 1969)]; and William Stuart Horne [(b. December 6, 1931; d. October 29, 1985), m. September 27, 1957, to Mona Jean Huston (b. July 13, 1934); two children: Scott William Horne (b. December 24, 1959); and Susan Elaine Horne (b. December 6, 1961)]. Sarah Katheryn Shidler (b. October 28, 1905; d. 1992; buried in Huntington, Texas), m. Mr. Mohler. Lenore Seaman Shidler (b. February 19, 1909; d. 1994; buried Washington Cemetery; m. January 6, 1939, to Doctor William Horbaly). Twins Mary Shidler (b. February 2, 1910; d. February 10, 1910), and Ruth Shidler (b. February 2, 1910; d. February 7, 1910); both died early.

William Iiams (b. March 2, 1830, Ten Mile, Amwell Township, Washington County, Pennsylvania; lived in West Bethlehem Township; d. May 14, 1899, or 1905); son of William Iiams (b. 1792) and Delilah Meeks; m. 1st, February 9, 1854, to Eliza Ferrell (b. May 6, 1836; d. July 8, 1863; buried Lone Pine Cemetery, Washington County, Pennsylvania); m. 3rd, February 13, 1870, to Mary Magdalene Swihart (b. July 29, 1845; d. May 22, 1921; buried North Ten Mile Baptist Cemetery); daughter of Jacob and Elizabeth Swihart; owned 127 acres of original John Iiams homestead; a carpenter and farmer; charter member of Clarkstown Masonic Lodge; was elected to township offices; probably m. 2nd, to Caroline Gantz; but they had no children; and William Iams (b. 1830) had thirteen children (four by Elizabeth Ferrell); 1) Sarah "Sadie" F. Iams [(b. November 22, 1854; d. February 25, 1909; buried North Ten Mile Baptist Cemetery); m. October 16, 1873, to James Hufford or Samuel Greenlee (James Hufford, b. February 12, 1848; d. July 29, 1935; buried North Ten Mile Cemetery); m. 2nd, Marie Piatt Doty)]; 2) John H. Iams (b. August 21, 1856; d. October 28, 1876; buried Lone Pine Cemetery; single); 3) Laura A. Iams [(b. 1862, Amwell Township; d. 1894; buried Lone Pine Cemetery); m. Samuel B. Greenlee (b. 1867; lived Amwell Township; d. 1939; buried North Ten Mile Baptist Cemetery)]; 4) an infant (d. February 23, 1860; buried Lone Pine Cemetery); 5) Etta Rose Iams [(b. June 7, 1871, or 1874; d. April 11, 1890; buried North Ten Mile Baptist Cemetery)]; 6) Lizzie Bell Iams (b. November 1873; d. February 21, 1874, or February 24, 1876; buried in Franklin Cemetery); 7) William J. Iams (b. May 12, 1874; d. September 24, 1950; buried North Ten Mile Baptist Cemetery; 8) Mary E. Iams (b. 1876; m. Vern Sampson); 9) Miller Addison Iams [(b. June 28, 1877, Washington County, Pennsylvania; d. August 10, 1940, Elizabeth, West Virginia); m. Sadie _____ (b. 1875); m. 2nd, March 24, 1917, to Merlie May Pribble]; 10) Clark Joseph Iams [(b. March 8, 1879; d. May 3, 1962; buried North Ten Mile Baptist Cemetery); m. Viola Kerns (b. 1886); and their child, Romaine Iams, m. Leo Eckenrod]; 11) Isaac Walter Iams (b. 1878; m. Ida R. _____); 12) Charles P. Iams (b. June 28, 1886; d. January 7, 1957; buried North Ten Mile Baptist Cemetery); and 13) Iris M. Iams (b. 1888; m. Ambrose Bradley). William Iiams (b. 1830) may also have m. Caroline Gantz (RI).

267

Sarah "Sadie" F. Iams [(b. November 22, 1854; d. February 25, 1909; buried North Ten Mile Baptist Cemetery), m. October 16, 1873, to James Hufford (b. February 12, 1848; d. July 29, 1935; buried North Ten Mile Cemetery; he m. 2nd, Marie Piatt Doty)], the daughter of William Iiams (b. 1830) and first wife Elizabeth Ferrell; and had two children: 1) Laura B. Hufford [(b. August 23, 1880; d. February 10, 1931), m. William A. Young; and they had five children: Laura Young (d. infancy); Beatrice Pearl Young (m. Mr. Longstreth); William Arleigh Young; David Young; and Vernon Young]; and 2) Ida Hufford [(b. February 18, 1875; d. February 18, 1945), m. Baker H. Watson (b. March 20, 1872; d. June 20, 1949); and their child, Jason C. Watson (b. December 30, 1895; d. September 5, 1957; buried North Ten Mile Cemetery; m. Margaret Alice Stenhouse; b. May 24, 1895; d. June 25, 1976); had three children: Esther Watson (died after swallowing a nail); Gerta Watson (m. Melvin Deyell); and Jason C. Watson, Jr.].

Miller Addison Iams (b. June 28, 1877, Washington County, Pennsylvania; d. August 10, 1940; buried in Elizabeth, West Virginia); son of William Iiams (b. 1830) and third wife Mary M. Swihart (b. 1845); m. March 24, 1917, Wellsbury, Brook County, West Virginia, to Merlie May Pribble (b. March 6, 1892, Standing Stone, West Virginia; d. April 13, 1958, Parkersburg, West Virginia), daughter of Alfred Pribble and Mary Elizabeth Wyer; with 1910 Census of Washington County, Pennsylvania, listing: Miller A. Iams (age 32); wife Sadie L. Iams (age 34); Leona M. Iams (age 12); Addison Iams (age 10); daughter Caffie M. Iams (age 9); Hazel I. Iams (age 7); and Pearl V. Iams (age 3); and with son John Frank Iams (b. June 8, 1928, Elizabeth, West Virginia; m. 1st, June 10, 1949, to Gladys June Scott; lived in Mentor-on-the-Lake, Ohio; composed family information used here). (JFI, RI, MI, CRI, JRI)

Miller Iams (b. July14, 1819, Greene County, Pennsylvania; d. after 1880, Ritchie County, West Virginia, at Harrisville; buried in IOOF Cemetery, Harrisville, West Virginia), son of William Iiams (b. 1792) and Delilah Meeks; m. October 29, 1843, to Sarah Anne Eggye/Eggy (b. March 28, 1823; d. after 1884); Justice of Peace of Morgan Township, Greene County, Pennsylvania; a farmer; moved to Ritchie County by 1880 Census; listed as druggist while in Pennsylvania; with Sarah Ann Eggy the daughter of Jacob Eggy and Mary "Polly" Iiams (daughter of Thomas Iiams, b. 1754; and Catherine Gill Hampton); and they had five children: 1) Thomas Morgan Iams [(b. January 8, 1851, Pennsylvania; d. Waynesburg, Pennsylvania; buried Jefferson Cemetery); m. 1871, Greene County, Pennsylvania, to Nancy Margaret Adamson (b. 1855, Pennsylvania; lived at Ruff Creek, Pennsylvania; d. 1901); and children listed as James Iams, Alonzo Iams, and Frank Iams]; 2) Mary Ann Iams (b. 1854 or 1855; d. New Martinsville, West Virginia); 3) Harvey Jackson Iams (b. 1860; d. January 25, 1862; buried in Bethlehem Baptist Cemetery, Greene County, Pennsylvania); 4) William Lyman Iams (m. Hannah Margaret Harkinson); and 5) Joseph Martin Iams (b. 1848; m. Susan Piatt; moved to Knoxville, Tennessee; son Thomas Iiams lived in Knoxville, Tennessee). (JLI, JIK, JIH, MJKS, EFB)

Thomas Morgan Iams (b. January 8, 1851, Greene County, Pennsylvania; d. Waynesburg, Pennsylvania; buried at Jefferson Cemetery), son of Miller Iams (b. 1811) and Sarah Ann Eggy (b. 1823); m. 1871, Greene County, Pennsylvania, to Nancy Margaret Adamson (b. 1855; d. 1901); moved from Greene County, Pennsylvania, to Ritchie County, West Virginia, about 1880; a blacksmith; m. 1901 to Laura Randolph (d. 1938, Waynesburg, Pennsylvania); and Thomas Morgan Iams (b. 1851) had four children: 1) James Harvey Iams [(b. June 22, 1873, Windridge, Greene County, Pennsylvania; d. January 27, 1964, Marietta, Ohio; buried Valley Cemetery, Marietta, Washington County, Ohio), m. December 21, 1898, Greene County, Pennsylvania, to Frances Dora Davis (b. September 5, 1877, Rutan, Greene County,

Pennsylvania; d. June 5, 1945, Marietta, Ohio); moved from Greene County, Pennsylvania, to Warwood, West Virginia, for a year, and then to Marietta, Ohio, where he worked as a clerk in a steel mill until the mill closed; then worked at Otto Brothers department store in Marietta, before working in a dairy; was a singer)]; 2) Barnet Iams (b. 1878; d. 1881); 3) Alonzo Miller Iams (b. June 9, 1881, Greene County, Pennsylvania; d. 1978, at McDonald, Washington County, Pennsylvania); m. Washington County, Pennsylvania, to Rose Forester, and they lived in Carnegie, Pennsylvania); and 4) Francis "Frank" Iams (b. and d. 1881). (MJKS, MI). Marian Jeanne Kilmer Starkey (b. 1926) contributed family history; reported that a "parlor melodian" of Laura Randolph was in her possession (1994), and that one of her wooden clocks was owned by David Kilmer.

James Harvey Iams (b. June 22, 1873, or 1874, Windridge, Greene County, Pennsylvania; d. January 27, 1964, Marietta, Washington County, Ohio), son of Thomas Morgan Iams (b. 1851) and Nancy Margaret Adamson; m. December 21, 1898, Greene County, Pennsylvania, to Frances Dora Davis (b. September 5, 1877, Rutan, Greene County, Pennsylvania; d. June 5, 1945, Marietta, Ohio); the daughter of George Washington Davis (b. 1847, Greene County, Pennsylvania; d. 1905, Greene County), and Julianna Ross (b. May 24, 1846, Rutan, Greene County, Pennsylvania; d. November 15, 1915, Greene County, Pennsylvania). George Washington Davis (b. 1847) was the son of William Davis and Sela Lavina. Julianna Ross (b. 1846) was the daughter of Peabody Atkinson Ross and Maria Matthews. The children of James Harvey Iams (b. 1873) were:

1) Marian Ross Iams [(b. June 1, 1900; d. September 25, 1978); m. Henry David Kilmer (b. October 29, 1893; d. June 3, 1964)]; 2) Francis Alonzo Iams [(b. October 22, 1902, Washington, Washington County, Pennsylvania; a display designer who attended certification school in Pittsburgh); m. 1st, in Orlando Florida, to Lois ____; m. 2nd, in Orlando, Florida, to Dorothy Bellenhaus; and child by first marriage was Allen Iams (b. 1929); and by second marriage was Nancy Iams]; 3) Hillis Del Ray Iams [(b. December 15, 1904, Washington, Pennsylvania; a sales-man; d. December 24, 1993, Marietta, Ohio); m. Washington County, Ohio, to Wilda L. Lindawood (b. March 12, 1909; d. Marietta, Ohio; buried in Mound Cemetery); and child was Jack Lewis Iams (b. June 1, 1929, Marietta, Ohio; architect; contributor to family history)]; and 4) Ilda Iantha Iams [(b. August 6, 1906, Washington, Pennsylvania; d. April 7, 1991, Marietta, Ohio; buried in East Lawn Cemetery); m. December 21, 1932, at Marietta, to John H. Epler (a widower; b. September 1893; d. February 11, 1976; buried in East Lawn Cemetery, Marietta, Washington County, Ohio; a singer; worked as clerk in county treasurer's office; two children by previous marriage were: William Epler and Jean Epler); both sang in a local well-known quartet]. (JLI, JIH, JIK)

Marian Ross Iams (b. June 1, 1900, McKees Rock, Allegheny County, Pennsylvania; d. September 25, 1978, Marietta, Ohio); daughter of James Harvey Iams (b. 1873) and Frances Dora Davis; m. August 30, 1922, Trinity Methodist Church, Marietta, Ohio, to Henry David Kilmer (b. October 29, 1893; d. June 3, 1964; and Marian Iams (b. 1900); worked for a dentist and a photographer prior to her marriage; and as a homemaker, enjoyed travel and cooking); they had three children:

1) Marcella Jane Kilmer [(b. July 6, 1923, Marietta, Ohio), graduate of Marietta High School; office manager; m. Trinity Methodist Church, Marietta, July 6, 1944, to Edward Eugene McCauley (b. August 19, 1925); and their daughter was Nancy Jo McCauley (b. March 10, 1947; m. 1967, to David Dee Spindler, b. 1946; whose adopted daughter was Regan Dee Spindler, b. December 7, 1977)]; 2) Marian Jeanne Kilmer [(b. February 14, 1926; receptionist for K. F. Bennett, M.D., for 25

years); m. Donald Lee Starkey (b. May 30, 1924)]; and 3) David Henry Kilmer [(b. January 10, 1931, Marietta, Ohio; graduate of Marietta High School; U. S. Air Force during Korean War; plumber and pipefitter); m. 1st, 1951, to Ona McElroy; m. 2nd, June 1964, to June Wallace (b. 1927; d. 1968); m. 3rd, in 1974 to Mary J. Stewart; m. 4th, 1977, to Patricia Reed; and he had two children: a) David Dennis Kilmer (a twin, b. February 19, 1966); and b) Daniel James Kilmer (a twin, b. February 19, 1966; m. Alisha ____; and they had two sons: Joshua Kilmer, b. September 22, 1989; and Matthew Kilmer, b. January 7, 1994)].

Marian Jeanne Kilmer (b. 1926), family genealogist, and Donald Lee Stanley (b. 1924) had one daughter, Jennifer Lynn Starkey (b. March 25, 1947, Marietta, Ohio), graduate of Marietta High school; attended Martha Washington and Marietta Colleges; accomplished pianist; graduate of University of South Florida; worked as a parent coordinator of Head Start in Head Start in Marietta; became Certified Public Accountant); m. February 12, 1966, in North Carolina, to William Lee Burton (b. April 28, 1946); and they had two children: a) Lynlee Sue Burton (b. August 9, 1966, Orange County, California); m. December 22, 1990, Christ United Methodist Church in Marietta, to Kenneth Donald Frampton (b. January 17, 1966); lived in St. Petersburg, Florida, for grades 1 to 3; graduated Marietta High School; played flute and piccolo; graduate of Hollins College; MBA from Virginia Polytechnical Institute); and b) Donald William Burton (b. June 9, 1988). (MJK)

Elisha Iams (b. December 16, 1822, West Bethlehem Township,Washington County, Pennsylvania; d. April 14, 1899, West Bethlehem Township; buried in Franklin Cemetery); the son of William Iiams (b. 1792) and Delilah Meeks; was a carpenter; a Baptist; a Democrat; and one of the founders of the Clarkstown Masonic Lodge, located in what is now the village of Ten Mile; m. February 20, 1848, to Cynthia "Sinthy" Garber (b. May 6, 1828, West Bethlehem Township; d. October 11, 1877, West Bethlehem Township), the daughter of William Garber and Elizabeth Weaver; and they had 10 children:

    1) Elizabeth Iams [(b. December 22, 1848, West Bethlehem Township; d. January10, 1899, Greene County, Pennsylvania); m. John Mills Cowan (b. (1839; d. 1910; buried in Mount Zion Castile Cemetery); and they had two children: Flora Cowan (m. Albert Fulton); and Edith Cowan (m. Stephen Fulton)];

    2) Delilah Iams [(b. July 24, 1850, West Bethlehem Township; d. August 19, 1943; buried North Ten Mile Baptist Cemetery, Washington County, Pennsylvania); m. Peter Voorhes (b. 1848; d. 1918; buried North Ten Mile Baptist Cemetery); and they had six children; a) Andrew Voorhes (b. April 15, 1877; d. August 17, 1916; buried in North Ten Mile Baptist Cemetery); b) Homer or Harry Voorhes (b. February 20, 1887; d. September 25, 1912; buried in North Ten Mile Baptist Cemetery); c) William E. Voorhes (b. February 18, 1872; d. March 25, 1892); d) Lucy Voorhes (b. June 8, 1889; d. December 25, 1965; m. Ambrose G. Patterson); e) Ruben Voorhes; and f) Clyde Voorhes; or Delilah may have married James Johnson Loudon (EFB)];

    3) Demas Garber Iams [(b. October 15, 1850; d. March 8, 1925; buried in North Ten Mile Baptist Cemetery); m. November 3, 1881, to Elizabeth Anne "Anna" Dunn (b. November 25, 1861; d. June 24, 1936); with 1910 Federal Census of Washington County, Pennsylvania, showing Demas Iams (age 58); Anna Iams (age 48); Margaret Iams (age 23); Elisha Iams (age 18); Howard Iams (age 13); and Clifford Iams (age 9); and with family records showing six children: a) Winifred Scott Iams

(b. September 18, 1882; d. 1955; m. Mabel Phillips and lived in Clarksburg, West Virginia); b) William Wylie Iams (b. October 31, 1883; d. December 2, 1970; m. Laura Steele); c) Sarah Margaret Iams (b. October 26, 1886; d. 1963; m. Merl P. Rush); d) Elisha Bernard Iams (b. April 17, 1892; d. December 31, 1944; buried in North Ten Mile Baptist Cemetery; genealogist; family leader and founder of Iams National Association in 1931; served as first Iams president with meeting held at North Ten Mile Baptist Church attended by 500 persons from dozens of cities and states; a World War I U. S. Navy veteran; with tombstone marked as "Cook and Baker"; m. Rowena Denman); e) John Howard Iams (b. April 10, 1897; d. May 25, 1964; noted artist with national reputation featured at numerous art exhibits, including The White House); and f) Clifford Haldon Iams (b. July 11, 1903; d. 1973; m. Bertha Waugomen)];

4) William Owen Iams [(b. October 19 or 29, 1855, West Bethlehem Township; d. December 29, 1937; buried North Ten Mile Baptist Cemetery); m. November 14, 1880, to Catherine Luzarbo Shidler (b. March 14, 1865, or 1862; d. March 29, 1949)];

5) Emma Mary Iams [(b. October 4, 1853, or 1859; d. March 14, 1916); m. August 19, 1877, to William Smith Hufford, son of Levi Hufford, grandson of Peter Hufford, and great-grandson of Christian Hufford, Sr.; with William Smith Hufford, (b. August 3, 1850; d. November 12, 1901), and their child: Meta E. Hufford, b. 1883; m. October 10, 1901, to Theodore Kelly];

6) Margaret Pleasant Iams [(b. March 10, 1858; d. 1936); m. Lebrius G. Garrett (described as an inventor, a genius, a musician); and their four children (all said to be an NBC artist) were: a) L. Guy Garrett (professor; professional musician); b) Martha or Bertha Garrett (a musician); c) Ina Garrett (a "genius at piano forte"); and d) Tillie Garrett (m. D. Hunter)];

7) Reuben Isaac Iams (b. November 6, 1861; d. June 4, 1864; buried in Franklin Cemetery, Washington County, Pennsylvania);

8) Cynthia Anabel Iams [(b. November 24, 1863; d. June 7, 1950; buried in North Ten Mile Baptist Cemetery); m. 1st, Henry Fulton (b. March 2, 1860; d. November 10, 1890; buried in North Ten Mile Baptist Cemetery; and daughter Mary Elizabeth Fulton m. Frank Earnest); and m. 2nd, to Norton Earl Reese, Sr. (b. May 22, 1861; d. September 6, 1909; buried in North Ten Mile Cemetery; former husband of Clara Iams); and they had five additional children: a) Herman Reese (d. Idaho; m. 1st, to Helen Jackson; m. 2nd, to Mildred ____; m. 3rd, to Viola ____; no children); b) Norton Earl "Norte" Reese, Jr. (b. June 14, 1900; d. November 17, 1949; buried North Ten Mile Baptist Cemetery; farmer; cattle drover); c) Mark Reese (b. December 11, 1901; d. June 4, 1909; buried in North Ten Mile Baptist Cemetery); d) Ionabelle "Ima" Reese (b. December 12, 1894; d. December 11, 1966; m. Walter E. Rauber; b. 1887; d. May 18, 1954; and their two children were: Louie Rauber and Virginia Rauber); and e) Earnest Reese (b. August 12, 1903; d. August 30, 1903; buried in North Ten Mile Baptist Cemetery)];

9) Lucy Idamay Iams (b. March 20, 1866; d. December 30, 1878; buried in Franklin Cemetery); and

10) Clara Iams (b. March 27, 1868; d. January 12, 1892; buried in North Ten Mile Baptist Cemetery); (EBI, RI, MI, EFB)

William Garber (b. December 16, 1796; d. February 9, 1868, Miami County, Indiana), m. 1820 to Elizabeth Weaver (b. May 27, 1803; d. August 12, 1858, Indiana); daughter of Peter Weaver and Pleasant Best; and they had eleven children: Demas Garber (b. December 3, 1820); Jonathan Garber (b. February 22, 1823); Pleasant Garber (b. August 25, 1825; d. July 23, 1869, West Bethlehem Township); Cynthia Garber (b. 1828; m. Elisha Iams, b. 1822); Sarah Garber (b. July 29, 1830); Margaret Garber (b. January 4, 1833); William Garber (b. October 8, 1935; d. August 30, 1863, Civil War; killed at Morris Island, South Carolina); Isabel Garber (b. February 18, 1838; d. March 1872); Simon Garber (b. January 24, 1840; d. November 10, 1903; Los Angeles); Silas C. Garber (b. June 20, 1843; d. July 19, 1865); and Reuben Garber.

William Garber (b. 1796) was the son of Jonathan Garber (b. 1775; d. July 10, 1850, West Bethlehem Township, Washington County, Pennsylvania), and Elizabeth Hufford, daughter of Christian Hufford. Jonathan Garber (b. 1775) was the son of Jacob Garber (b. Switzerland; moved to Maryland). Christian Hufford (b. July 2, 1846, Lancaster County, Pennsylvania; father of Elizabeth Hufford; d. May 24, 1826, West Bethlehem Township), was the son of Matthais Hufford or Huffer (b. August 24, 1718, Klein Hannigan, Basle Canton, Switzerland; landed in Philadelphia September 2, 1743; m. Mary W. Wohlwindu; lived at Manheim, Lancaster County, Pennsylvania.

Delilah Meek was the daughter of Elisha Meek (b. 1770; d. October 1843, Washington Township, Greene County, Pennsylvania) and May Miller, and sister of John Meek (b. April 8, 1792; d. February 8, 1878; m. Elizabeth Boyd), Elizabeth Meek, Susannah Meek, Mary Meek, Nancy Meek, and Jane Meek. The father of Elisha Meek (b. 1770) was Nathan Meek (b. 1735, Maryland; m. ____ Barnes; settled in Ten Mile area when it was part of Virginia; a member of Captain Farley's Company, who mustered out November 2, 1781).

William Dunn (b. January 30, 1830, Greene County, Pennsylvania; d. January 21, 1867, from wounds received while serving under Colonel Joseph Sack, Company A, 16th Pennsylvania Regiment), the father of Ann Elizabeth Dunn; m. 1857, to Elizabeth Stout, daughter of Abraham Stout and Elizabeth Allen of Jefferson, Greene County, Pennsylvania; and the seven children of William Dunn (b. 1830) were: an infant; Ambrose Dunn (b. December 1, 1854); Sarah Dunn (b. March 10, 1853; d. January 12, 1928; m. January 16, 1873, to George Denston); Martin Dunn (b. October 28, 1856; d. January 25, 1927); William Dunn (b. February 26, 1866); Anne Elizabeth Dunn (see above); and James Montrose Dunn (b. September 5, 1864; d. September 29, 1921, Montrose, Colorado). William Dunn (b. 1830) was the son of Joseph Dunn (b. 1788, Greene County, Pennsylvania; d. 1865) and Jane Martin (m. May 1817), the daughter of James and Ann Martin. Thomas Gill Hampton (b. 1730, Maryland; d. West Bethlehem Township, Washington County, Pennsylvania), m. Mary Gill, members of North Ten Mile Baptist Church; had six children: Thomas Hampton, Jonathan Hampton, John Hampton, Elizabeth Hampton (m. John Iams), Mary Hampton (m. William Iams) and Catherine Hampton (m. Thomas Iams; d. Belmont County, Ohio).

Demas Garber Iams (b. October 15, 1851, West Bethlehem Township, Washington County, Pennsylvania; d. March 8, 1925, Washington County; buried in North Ten Mile Baptist Cemetery); the son of Elisha Iams (b. 1822) and Cynthia Garber; m. November 3, 1881, to Elizabeth Anne Dunn (b. November 25, 1861; d. June 24, 1936); daughter of William Dunn and Elizabeth Stout; was a carpenter; Democrat; prohibitionist; and deacon in North Ten Mile Baptist Church, and later the Washington Baptist Church; considered an excellent role model to whom son Elisha dedicated his writings; had six children:

    1) Winfield "Scott" Iams [(b. September 18, 1882, West Bethlehem Township; d. April 15, 1955); m. October 29, 1908, to Mabel Alice Phillips

(b. February15, 1887, Library, Pennsylvania; d. February 5, 1975, Parkersburg, West Virginia)];
2) William Wylie "Wiley" Iams [(b. October 31, 1883, West Bethlehem Township; an auditor for Hazel Glass Company; d. December 2, 1970); m. Annie Laura Steele (b. March 23, 1895); lived in Washington, Pennsylvania];
3) Sarah Margaret Iams [(b. October 28, 1886; d. December 1963); m. September 12, 1921, to Merle P. Rush (b. 1883; d. 1958, an insurance broker)];
4) Elisha Bernard "E.B." "Elijah" Iams [(b. April 17, 1892; d. December 31, 1944); a contractor; genealogist; founder and first president of National Iams Association in 1931); m. Rowena Denman and lived in Washington, Pennsylvania);
5) John Howard Iams [(b. April 10 or 17, 1897, Washington County, Pennsylvania; d. May 25, 1964, Marion, Ohio; buried in Washington Cemetery); m. July 1, 1939 to Margaret Lewis (lived in Marion, Ohio, in 1994); internationally acclaimed painter and artist]; and
6) Clifford Haldon Iams [(b. July 11, 1903, Washington, Pennsylvania); m. January 25, 1930; to Bertha Waugeman (b. April 10, 1906); a merchant; had two children: a) Dorothy May Iams (b. May 15 or 19, 1931; m. George Charles Sollinger; b. August 30, 1931; lived in East Aurora, New York; had daughter Ellen Marie Sollinger, b. April 30, 1956; and b) Lois Ellen Iams (b. August 3, 1932; m. Frederick John Novak; b. August 5, 1932; lived at Industry, Washington County, Pennsylvania; had three children: Frederick John Novak, Jr., b. August 2, 1955, or 1956; Kathy Diane Novak, b. December 25, 1957; and Ellen Novak)].
(EBI, MI, RI)

Winfield "Scott" Iams [(b. September 18, 1882, West Bethlehem Township; d. April 15, 1955), the son of Demas Garber Iams (b. 1850) and Elizabeth Dunn (b. 1861), m. October 29, 1908, to Mabel Alice Phillips (b. February 15, 1887, at Library, Pennsylvania; d. February 5, 1975, Parkersburg, West Virginia; buried in Washington, Pennsylvania, cemetery); daughter of Warren J. Phillips and Lillian J. Ewing; an auditor for West Virginia Public School System; graduate of Ohio Northern University; member of Parkersburg First Baptist Church; Mabel was a member of WCTU and an accomplished pianist; and they had six children:
1) Doctor Malcolm Phillips Iams (b. August 9, 1909; m. Pauline Coffindoffer; lived in Parkersburg, West Virginia); 2) Lyman or Layman H. or R. Iams (b. February 14, 1912; m. Claire Moore; lived in Akron, Ohio; daughter Helen Claire Iams, b. March 17, 1943, m. David Clingerman, and they had two children: Kim Clingerman, and a daughter); 3) Victor G. or S. Iams (b. November or December 7, 1917; m. Virginia Jarvis, b. November 30, 1921; lived in Akron, Ohio); 4) Bernie May "Mae" Iams (b. February 5, 1923; m. O. Glenn Wilson; lived in Parkersburg, West Virginia; their two children were: Robert Glenn Wilson, b. July 23, 1953; and Pamela Ann Wilson, b. April 16, 1964; m. Kevin Farr); 5) Rosemary Iams (b. July 2, 1924; m. Dale E. Rausch, b. August 18, 1928; lived at Plain City, Ohio; had two children: Susan Marie Rausch, b. July 8, 1961; and Philip Scott Rausch, b. May 19, 1964; and 6) Sarah Louise Iams [(b. March 29, 1930; m. June 26, 1952), to Earl C. Woods (b. December 29, 1929), Library, Pennsylvania; d. January 5, 1981); and their child was Kelly Ann Woods (b. September 23, 1967); m. February 14, 1989, to Dwayne Edward Allen].

William Wylie "Wiley" Iams (b. October 31, 1883; d. December 2, 1970), the son of Demas Garber Iams (b. 1850) and Elizabeth Ann Dunn; m. Annie Laura "Laurri" Steele (b. March 23, 1895), and they had four children: 1) Edna May Iams [(b. June 8, 1916), m. Virgil A. Miller (b. September 22, 1907); and their child was Susan Amy Miller (b. April 1960)]; 2) Paul C. Iams [(b. August 6, 1907, Washington, Pennsylvania); m. January 15, 1944, in Pittsburgh, to Dorothy McCullough (b. June 8, 1916, Pittsburgh, Pennsylvania); daughter of James M. McCullough and Edna Maeges (daughter of John Maeges and Emma Wall), and they had two children: Doctor William James Iams (b. December 24, 1946, Pittsburgh, Pennsylvania; m. Marie LeMessurier; lived in Newfoundland; no children); and Dr. Keith Paul Iams (b. January 5, 1951, Pittsburgh; single; lived in Indiana)]; 3) Ruth Ann Iams [(b. March 18, 1921), m. Russell William Justin (b. May 18, 1919); and they have five children: a) James Richard Justin (b. September 25, 1956; d. September 30, 1956); b) Patricia Louise Justin (b. October 21, 1947; m. Lyle Gene Feiock, b. December 18, 1949; and their child Russell William Feiock, b. September 14, 1968); c) Terrence Lee Justin (b. April 10, 1949); d) Thomas Russell Justin (b. July 3, 1952); and e) Kathleen Joyce Justin (b. January 16, 1955)]; and 4) Martha Jane Iams [(b. July 30, 1925); m. Edward B. Stewart (b. June 21, 1919); and their two children were: a) Rebekah Jane Stewart (b. July 15, 1952; m. Robert Mikita); and b) Edward Blair Stewart (b. July 1, 1955)]. (PCI, MI, RI)

William Owen Iiams (b. October 19, 1855), son of Elisha Iiams (b. 1822) and Cynthia Garber, m. 1881 to Katherine L. Shidler; daughter of Jacob Shidler (the son of early settlers Jacob Shidler and Eilizabeth Wise); operated a whiskey distillery on a North Bethlehem Township, Washington County, farm owned by the Hildebrans; a farmer, carpenter, and sheep raiser who raised Percheron horses in partnership with his brother, Demas G. Iams; a Democrat; held several public offices; and their children were: 1) Frank Iams (d. young); 2) Demas G. Iams [(m. Grace Heinman of Ada, Ohio); a design engineer with Pennsylvania Railroad; graduate of Ohio Northern University; veteran of World War I; had four children: Sue Iams, Ruth Iams, Betty Iams, and Ned Iams]; 3) Grace Iams [(d. 1913), graduate of California State University of Pennsylvania; buried North Ten Mile Baptist Cemetery; m. Thomas Weaver of Scenery Hill, Washington County, Pennsylvania]; 4) Nevada Iams [(graduate of California State University of Pennsylvania/California Normal Teachers College); m. George A. Bovier, a Baptist minister; and their son Owen Bovier studied for the ministry]; and 5) Byard Owen Imes (an educator with Master's Degree in Education from Washington and Jefferson College).

Delilah Iams (b. July 24, 1850, West Bethlehem Township, Washington County, Pennsylvania; d. August 19, 1943; buried in North Ten Mile Baptist Cemetery, Washington County, Pennsylvania); daughter of Elisha Iams (b. 1822) and Cynthia Garber; m. Peter Voorhees (b. 1848; d. 1918); and they had seven children: 1) William Elisha Voorhes (single); 2) Reuben Voorhes [(m. Della Nichols); and they had four children: a) William Ellery Voorhes (m. Daisy Stockton; and their daughter was Virginia Voorhes); b) Francis Earl Voorhes (m. Myrtle Hilbert); c) Harry Stephen Voorhes (m. Mamie McVey; and their two children were: Charles Voorhes and Mamie McVey Voorhes); and d) Mary Hazel Voorhes (m. Robert Bauman; she was a stenographer at Washington County, Pennsylvania, Court House; and their child was Peggy Bauman)]; 3) Andrew Voorhes (m. Lenora Filby); 4) Clyde Voorhes [(m. Jennie Supler); and their eight children were: Claude Voorhes, Kenneth Voorhes, Clarence Voorhes, Dessie Voorhes, Mary Voorhes, Roger Voorhes, DeLoyd Voorhes, and Clyde Voorhes, Jr.]; 5) Homer Voorhes (d. young); 6) Lucy Voorhes [(m. Ambrose Patterson; lived in Washington, Pennsylvania); and their eleven children were: Albert Ambrose Patterson, Charles William Patterson, Delilah Isophena Patterson, Edna May Patterson, Robert Voorhes Patterson, John Andy Patterson, Lucy Annabel Patterson, Florence Lenora Patterson, Clarence Raymond Patterson, Ruth Elizabeth

Patterson, and Roy Richard Patterson]; and 7) Harry Voorhes (m. Louise Fithian; and their four children were: Lucy May Voorhes, Alonzo Voorhes, Joseph Voorhes, and Martha Voorhes).

The children of William Owen Iams (b. 1855) and Katherine Luzarbo Shidler were:

1) Byard Owen Iams [(b. April 28, 1900, Ten Mile, Washington County, Pennsylvania; d. December 18, 1957; buried in North Ten Mile Baptist Cemetery); m. June 1, 1935, to Elsie Leona White (b. March 18, 1905, Clarksville, West Virginia; d. January 16, 1993, West Bethlehem Township, Washington County, Pennsylvania); and they had three children: a) William Owen Iams (b. September 27, 1939); b) Mary Kathryn Iams (b. September 6, 1942; m. August 26, 1967, North Ten Mile Baptist Church, to George Thomas Dobich, b. January 18, 1943; and their adopted child was Sean Robert Dobich, b. April 3, 1963; m. October 31, 1985, at Connellsville, Pennsylvania, to Cinthia Ana McCutchen, b. December 6, 1965); and c) Ruth Elaine Iams (b. September 4, 1948; m. October 16, 1971, at North Ten Mile Baptist Church, to Robert Charles Fell, b. July 10, 1950; and their four children were: Beth Ann Fell, b. March 28, 1973; Robert Owen Fell, b. May 27, 1974; Bonnie Kathryn Fell, b. November 16, 1982, a twin; and Rebeka Maran Fell, b. November 16, 1982, a twin)];

2) George Demas Iams [(b. February 22, 1882, Ten Mile; d. January 16, 1961, Washington, Pennsylvania; buried North Ten Mile Baptist Cemetery); m. December 25, 1907, Ada, Ohio, to Grace Elva Hyndman (b. September 1, 1881, at Ada, Ohio; d. February 6, 1965, at Washington, Pennsylvania); he was one of the leading civil engineer highway construction officers and land appraisers of southwestern Pennsylvania; Washington County surveyor; Washington County engineer; Bachelor's and Master's degrees from Ohio Northern University; taught school two years; worked in Mexico as construction engineer; engineer for Pittsburgh Coal Company; Marianna construction of coal buildings for Buffalo Coal Company; worked for Fort Pitt Bridge Company; First Lieutenant in Quartermaster Corps of Engineer; Pennsylvania Railroad engineer (1918-1932); United States land appraiser; Director of Works Progress Administration (WPA); played four years of college football at Ohio Northern University; and they had five children: a) Sue Kathryn Iams (b. September 20, 1909; Marianna, Pennsylvania); m. March 3, 1934, to Andrew Dran (b. November 19, 1906, Cleveland, Ohio; d. May 7, 1988, Washington, Pennsylvania); and they had three children: 1^1) Jack Andrew Dran (b. March 1, 1935); m. April 4, 1959, North Ten Mile Baptist Church, to Doris Jean Stopka (b. September 18, 1940) and they had three children: a^1) Jeffrey Jack Dran (b. September 10, 1964; m. Stacey Renee Burgess, b. September 30, 1969); b^1) Ward Iams Dran (b. November 1, 1937); m. April 30, 1965, at North Ten Mile Baptist Church, to Cindy Sue Ircy (b. January 4, 1942); and they had two children: Marcus Eli Dran (b. September 12, 1968; and Amy Jo Dran (b. December 13, 1970); and c^1) Reverend George Stephen Dran (b. February 12, 1945); m. November 24, 1967, in North Franklin Township, to Sandra Jean Sumney (b. May 27, 1947); and they had two children: James Andrew Dran (b. December 12, 1968; m. December 1993); and Charity Sue Dran (b. September 19, 1972); b) Ruth Evangeline Iams

(b. April 28, 1911, Marianna, Pennsylvania; d. May 17, 1994, in Maine-Crem), m. June 17, 1933, in Pittsburgh, Pennsylvania, to John Myer Roth (b. January 30, 1910; d. 1986, in Oakland, Maine); and their child John Reese Roth (b. September 17, 1937; m. January 14, 1972, to Helen Marie De Crane; and their two children were: Nancy Ann Roth, b. May 23, 1975; and John Alexander Roth, b. November 13, 1978); c) Betty Pearl Iams (b. June 20, 1913, Marianna); m. January 17, 1936, Washington, Pennsylvania, to Henry Adam Weaver (b. June 11, 1912, Scenery Hill, Washington County, Pennsylvania; d. May 7, 1981, Washington, Pennsylvania; son of Charles E. Weaver and Zoe Evans; an engineer; graduate of Beckley School of Engineering of Harrisburg; worked for Brockway Glass Company; member of Lone Pine Fire Department; and they had one child: 1¹) Henry Linn Weaver (b. August 24, 1937; m. October 25, 1958, to Shirley Mae Mounts, b. May 24, 1938; and they had four children: Robert Weaver, Christy Lynn Weaver, Barry Allan Weaver, and Darla Sue Weaver); (whose child was Nicole Marie Burns, b. December 27, 1984); d) Ned Hyndman Iams (b. October 11, 1917, Houston, Pennsylvania; d. June 2, 1974; buried Forest Lawn Cemetery; m. September 9, 1944, to Betty Jane Bryner, b. February 14, 1924; and their child Sandra Lee Iams, b. August 24, 1945; d. August 13, 1994; m. November 24, 1966, to Edwin Craig Moyer; and the child of Sandra Lee Iams was Edwin Craig Moyer, Jr., b. September 30, 1969; and e) Esther Kirkland Iams (b. September 10, 1920; d. September 10, 1920; buried in Franklin Cemetery, Washington County, Pennsylvania);

3) Nevada Iams [(b. September 26, 1885; d. January 23, 1961; buried in North Ten Mile Baptist Cemetery); m. 1st, in 1909, to George Austin Bovier (b. 1877; d. July 7, 1948); m. 2nd, to Homer Hedge; and had one child: Owen Leland Bovier (b. December 17, 1912; d. January 10, 1992; m. July 23, 1936, to Edna Mae Cline, daughter of Harry Cline and Jessie Mae Kunkel, b. June 6, 1917; d. March 29, 1989), who had three children: a) Sonia Mae Bovier (b. October 9, 1939; m. November 23, 1963, to William Dibrell Jones II; and they had two children: 1¹) William Dibrell Jones III, b. June 19, 1967, Atlanta, Georgia; m August 28, 1990, to Anna Mae Johns; and 2¹) Julia Mae Jones, b. August 25, 1969); b) Owenna Lea Bovier (b. September 29, 1942; m. 2nd, on March 23, 1986, to Jeff Eichvold Donstone; and m. 1st, to Robert Gerry); and c) Sophia Sue Bovier (b. August 21, 1947; m. August 17, 1975, to Charles G. Williams, and their daughter Tiffany Bovier Williams, b. April 15, 1980, Monterey, California)];

4) Grace Iams [(b. January 17, 1887; d. July 1913; buried North Ten Mile Baptist Cemetery), m. June 1912, to John Thomas Weaver (b. 1882; d. 1970); and their child Ruth Eleanor Weaver (b. June 26, 1913; d. January 8, 1975; buried in North Ten Mile Baptist Cemetery)];

5) Franklin Iams (b. November 25, 1887; d. 1889; buried in Franklin Cemetery, Washington County, Pennsylvania); and

6) Esther Kirkland Iams (b. 1920; stillborn).

Sarah Margaret Iams (b. October 28, 1886, Ten Mile, Pennsylvania; d. December 1963; buried in Washington, Pennsylvania Cemetery); daughter of Demas Iams (b. 1851) and Ann Elizabeth Dunn; m. September 12, 1912, to Merrell P. Rush (b. 1883; d. October 11, 1958); an insurance broker in Washington, Pennsylvania; and they had six children: 1) Jeanne "Gene" Anne "Jean Ann" Rush (b. January 26, 1916); 2) Hilda Lois Rush (b. October 31, 1918); 3) Mel Iams Rush (b. December 4, 1920); 4) Mira Avis Rush (d. January 12, 1915); 5) Wynne Dale Rush (d. September 17, 1918); and 6) Ina Mary Rush (d. November 30, 1924).

Elisha Bernard "Elijah" "EB" "Elisha B" Iams (b. April 17, 1892, West Bethlehem Township, Washington County, Pennsylvania; d. December 31, 1944; buried at North Ten Mile Baptist Church Cemetery, Washington County, Pennsylvania); son of Demas Garber Iams (b. 1850) and Elizabeth Ann Dunn; m. October 1916, to Rowena E. Denman (b. September 14, 1894; d. January 12, 1974; buried Washington Cemetery); daughter of Samuel O. Denman and Frances M. Grem; and Elisha (b. 1892) was a contractor; author; noted genealogist; organizer and first president of National Iams Association that met with 500 attendees at Ten Mile Baptist Church for the first reunion in 1931; attended California State Teachers College; taught in Washington County, Pennsylvania school system for a few years; better known as an engineer; was a civilian member of the United States Army Corps of Engineers; member of First Baptist Church; trustee of American Baptist Historical Society; member of Sons of American Revolution; member of American Genealogical Society; member of Masonic Lodge; author of *Genealogy of Iams Clans in America Since 1670*; was genealogist for Upper Ohio Valley Genealogical Association; was archivist for Washington County; collected the "Iams Manuscript Collection" now at Citizens Library in Washington, Pennsylvania; life member of New York Genealogical Biographical Society; member of American Order of Pioneers. (EBI, MI, RI, EJI, PCI).

REFERENCES

- (JBM) James B. Meighan Jr., Monongahela, Pennsylvania, personal files.

- (JFI) James Frank Iams, Mentor-on-the-Lake, Ohio, personal files.

- (CRI) Charles Iams, New Stanton, Pennsylvania, files.

- (PZI) Pauline Z. Imes, personal files of Ohio and Western Pennsylvania.

- (EFB) Ervin F. Bickley Jr., New Canaan, Connecticut, files.

- (LIH) Lois Ijams Hartman, Pasadena, California, author.

- (GRI) Guy Ross Iiams Jr., personal files, Ohio.

- (HLL) Howard L. Leckey, Ten Mile, author of *Ten Mile Country and Its Pioneer Families* (1977).

- (FBH) F. B. Heitman, Historical Register of Offices of Continental Army, 1893.

- (JIK) Jeanne Iams Kilmer, personal file.

- (HWN) Harry Wright Newman, Anne Aruadel Gentry, 1933 and 1970.

- (EBI) E. B. Iams, President Iams Association, Washington, Pennsylvania.

- (RI) Ruth Iams, Ten Mile, Pennsylvania, personal files.

- (SR) Sally I. Ross, Long Beach, California, personal file.

- *Amwell Township: Rural Reflections, Washington County, Pennsylvania* (1976), Isaac L. Iams and Ruth Iams, Chairmen.

- Federal Census, Pennsylvania, Washington and Greene Counties.

- Beers, *History of Washington County, Pennsylvania* (1893).

- Citizens Library, Washington, Pennsylvania, vertical files.

- (EAI) Elisha A. Iams, Western Pennsylvania, personal file.

- (JSI) Jack Shirk Iams, personal files, Silver Spring, Maryland.

- (CG) Conchetta Geis, Redkey, Indiana, personal files.

- (SGL) Suzanne Geis Long, Hammond, Indiana, personal files.

- (SIC) Sarah Iams Cain, personal file, Crucible, Missouri.

- (WAI) William Allen Iams, personal files.

- Nancy Martin Shidler, *Nancy Martin: Country Gal* (Christopher House Publishers, Boston, 1930).

- (JLI) Jack L. Iams, personal files.

- E. B. Iams, *Genealogy of Demas Garber Iams and Elizabeth Ann Dunn* (1940).

- *Pennsylvania Archives, Sixth Series*, Volume 2, page 167.

- (PCI) Paul C. Iams, Washington, Pennsylvania, personal file.

- (EJI) E. Jay Iams, personal files, Washington, Pennsylvania, 1930-6.

- L. C. Walkinshaw, *Annals of Southwestern Pennsylvania* (1939).

- Marian Jeanne Kilmer Starkey, personal communication.

- Elisha B. Iams, *Genealogy of Demas Garber Iams and Elizabeth Ann Dunn* (1940).

- L. C. Walkinshaw, *Annals of Southwestern Pennsylvania* (Lewis Publishing Company, New York, 1939).

— CHAPTER 8 —

THOMAS IIAMS (1754-1836)

Thomas Iiams, born in Anne Arundel County, Maryland, on December 26, 1754, later moved to western Pennsylvania, and then to Belmont County, Ohio, where he died in 1836. His magnificent tombstone may be found in Richland Township, just south of St. Clairsville, near where he died. A Revolutionary War soldier, he has been used frequently for linking memberships for eligibility into such organizations as the Daughters of American Revolution (DAR).

Thomas Iiams (b. Anne Arundel County, Maryland, December 26, 1754; d. in Richland Township, Belmont County, Ohio, June or July 24, 1834, or 1836; and was buried in Old Dutch (Ault) Cemetery, Richland Township, Belmont County, Ohio). The cemetery is reached by going south from St. Clairsville on Ohio Route 9 for a distance of one mile, then turning left toward Glencoe, Ohio, on Belmont County Road 5 (old Belmont County Road 125) for about one-half mile, then turning right into a small housing development on Evelyn Drive in Richland Acres. The cemetery is on the right, on the far hill, in a cow pasture (unmaintained 1995; with maintenance refused by county commissioner in spite of money allocated in old Iams will). Grave is located in Row 8, Grave 13, by official plot map located in Belmont County, Ohio, court house, under the name "Dutch Hill Cemetery." The tombstone stands nine feet high and is topped on its four sides by corn, peaches, pears, plums, grapes, and flowers. The tombstone lists Thomas Iiams (died at age 80, June 21, 1834); Catherine Iiams, wife of Thomas Iiams (died May 12, 1838, age 72); Samuel Iiams (died August 21, 1860, age 65 years, five months, and 20 days); and wife Elizabeth Iiams (died November 15, 1867, in her fiftieth year). The grave has been acknowledged by official government records and has been used for DAR certification.

Newman (1970) lists Thomas Iiams (b. 1754) as the son "of John, of Richard," born at New Birmingham in Upper Patuxent area of Anne Arundel County, Maryland; later Prince George's County, Maryland; and who purchased 100 acres of Richard Iiams of Washington County, Maryland, on May 18, 1778, which Richard Iiams had inherited from his father, John Iiams. It was here that he and his bride Catherine Gill Hampton initially settled, before they moved to Bethlehem Township, Washington County, Pennsylvania, in 1793, where his brother Richard Iiams had settled, and before they moved to Richland Township, Belmont County, Ohio, in 1798 (according to his Revolutionary War pension claim No. S-8751).

Thomas Iiams' pension claim of March 1834 was eventually approved, but he died before he was able to benefit from the payment. The pension was approved May 12, 1834. As a Revolutionary War soldier he enlisted on January 10, 1777, and was discharged January 1, 1780 (Maryland Archives), though it has been written that "he served seven years under George Washington." Thomas volunteered for three months of duty as a private in the Maryland Militia and was later promoted to sergeant under Colonel Thomas Dorsey, Lieutenant William Spurrier, and Ensign Nicholas Ridgley. He later served for two months in Baltimore, then two more weeks in Baltimore, then served three months in the Maryland Militia. He was a sergeant in Richard Stringer's Company, Second Regiment, Army of the Maryland Line.

Thomas Iiams (b. 1754) has been considered to be the son of John (b. 1720), and also of Thomas (b. 1708) and Elizabeth Hill (b. 1730); the son of William (b. 1670) and Elizabeth Plummer Iiams of South River, Anne Arundel County, Maryland. John Iiams (b. 1720) m. Penelope _____ (or other), while a John Iiams (b. 1708) purchased Duvall's Delight in Anne Arundel County, Maryland, April 17, 1703, from Charles Carroll for 25 pounds, 18 shillings, and 6 pence; and wrote his will on October 27, 1766, and divided his estate among his four sons: John (b. 1750), Thomas (b. 1754), Richard, and William; and later added a codicil which named daughter Susannah Pumphreys; the codicil was added before his death in 1768. In 1770, at the final settlement of his will, there were seven heirs named.

Thomas Iiams (b. 1754) and each of his brothers, John Iiams and William Iiams, married Hampton sisters: Catherine, Elizabeth, and Mary Hampton, daughters of Thomas Gill Hampton. Each settled in Washington County, Pennsylvania, with another brother, Richard Iiams, and a sister, Susannah Iiams (m. William Penn, a relative of the original founder of Pennsylvania). The Hamptons were related to General Wade Hampton, later famous as a member of the Confederate Army in the War Between the States/Civil War.

Thomas Iiams (b. 1754) m. November 29, 1785 (1791 in official Continental Army Record), in Baltimore, Maryland, to Catherine "Katy" Gill Hampton, daughter of Thomas Gill Hampton. They moved to the Ten Mile Valley, Washington County, Pennsylvania, in 1793 and the Anne Arundel County, Maryland, Chancery Court, February 17, 1797, recorded that Richard Ijams (b. ca1745) of Washington County, Pennsylvania; and Thomas Iiams (b. 1754) of Pennsylvania, deeded the plantation New Birmingham to John Snowden of Anne Arundel County, Maryland. A Thomas Iams voted for George Murdock, "Republican Presidential Electorate," Frederick County, Maryland, November 19, 1776. The family line from Thomas (b. 1754) is much clearer than is the generation immediately preceeding this Thomas (b. 1754). It seems certain that he was a Revolutionary soldier and that he serves as a major focal point for those that wish to obtain membership in one or more of the various patriotic organizations.

Story recorded in Maryland Archives: May 1777, while in charge of a recruiting party of Revolutionary War soldiers, he is said to order "fire and fix bayonets." Maryland Council of Safety 1777-8 records May 13, 1777: "We are obliged to you for the trouble you took in stating the officers. We understand Sergeant Iiams conduct in so full and circumstances in manner, he is not yet come to town; we expect him and shall make proper inquiry and act accordingly. We are sorry that there should happen ground for complaint, but shall surely duly attend to anything that is well founded." In that same journal was recorded: "Thomas Iiames, the person mentioned (in previous sentence) in the letter of Mr. Christopher Loundes, dated the 21st, as the officer of the recruiting party therein mentioned appeared before the council according to order and confessed that he had ordered the men of his party to fire and afterwards to fix bayonets nearly in the manner and on the occasion mentioned in the said letter. It is with sufficient security in the sum of 100 pounds currency for his appearance at Prince Georges County Court, to be held in Upper Marlboro the 3rd Tuesday Inst. to answer for his conduct toward and in the presence of the said Christopher E. B. Lownes, Registrate in the execution of his office." The record of July 11, 1778, states that the orders had been justified and "that the commissary of stores deliver to Thomas Iiams strip linen for two pairs trousers and two jackets, white linen for two shirts, blouse linen for coats (sic) and trimmings suitable."

Dailey, in the book *The Official Roles of the Soldiers of the American Revolution Buried in the State of Ohio, Daughters of American Revolution of Ohio*, lists:

1) James Iams, buried in Belmont County, Ohio; was a private in Captain Walker's Company of Colonel Dorsey's Regiment of the Maryland Line; applied for pension from residence in Richland Township, Belmont County, Ohio, in March 1834. Said to have been born in Anne Arundel County, Maryland, in 1754, where he enlisted; moved to Bethlehem Township, Washington County, Ohio, where he lived for five years. He was entered on the Ohio rolls on March 26, 1834. Papers were sent to Wilson Shannon of Saint Clairsville, Richland Township, Belmont County, Ohio (Maryland Pension Claim S-8751); and 2) Thomas Iiams (or Imes), buried in Belmont County, Ohio; served in 2nd Maryland Regiment; discharged January 1, 1780; was born in Maryland in 1754; buried in 1834 (or May 12, 1838), in Ault Cemetery, Richland Township, Belmont County, Ohio; married November 29, 1791, in Maryland to Catherine Hampton (SAR 52601, reported by William Pettit).

The 1800 Federal Census of Washington County, Pennsylvania, lists Thomas Iiams (age over 45, with female 26-45, 3 females under 10, one boy 10-16, and two boys under 10). The 1810 Census lists Thomas Iiams over age 45, 1 woman over 45, 1 16-27, 2 10-16, 2 under 10, 3 males 10-27, 1 male 10-16, and 1 male under 10. The 1830 Federal Census of Belmont County, Ohio, listed Thomas Iiams 1 male age 40-50; 1 female, age 20-30; 1 female, age 5-10; and 1 female under age 5); and Thomas Iiams (1 male, age 20-30; 1 female age 60-70; 1 female age 20-30; 1 female, age 15-20; and 1 male age 70-80). The 1820 Federal Census of Belmont County, Ohio, had listed both Richard Imes (1 male, age 26-45; 1 female, age 16-26; 1 male, age 16-26; and 3 males, under age 10); and Samuel Imes (1 male, age 26-45; and 1 female, age 26-45). The 1840 Census of Richland Township, Belmont County, Ohio, listed only Samuel Ijames (1 male, age 40-50; 1 female, age 40-50; 1 female, age 15-20; and 1 male, age 10-15). The 1850 Census of Richland Township, Belmont County, Ohio, listed Samuel Iimes (age 55, farmer, born Pennsylvania); Elizabeth Iimes (age 61, born Pennsylvania); adopted son Isaac Iimes (age 27, born in Ohio); Elizabeth Myers (age 25, born in Ohio); Susannah Myers (age 5, born in Ohio); Calvin Myers (age 2, born in Ohio); and a laborer, Elias McCloud (age 33, born Pennsylvania).

H. W. Newman (1970) has also listed a Thomas Ijams (b. 1708) that is often considered to be the progenitor of this branch of the Iams family, even though the early date of birth makes this relationship unlikely, according to many researchers. This Thomas Ijams (from All Hallows Parish, Anne Arundel County, Maryland, August 7, 1708); will probated November 28, 1768, in Anne Arundel County, Maryland). This Thomas Ijams (b. 1708) was joint executor with brother John Ijames of his father's 1738 will in which he was named the "contingent heir" of the family farm and was given a legacy of only five shillings. On April 17, 1730, he purchased part of Duvall's Delight in Anne Arundel County, Maryland, from Charles Carrol. The origin of his wife Artridge is not known. On May 16, 1741, he purchased an additional 100 acres of Duvall's Delight, this time from Charles Hogan, for one hundred pounds.

One Thomas Iams wrote his last will and testament on October 27, 1766, in the presence of John Iiams and Mary Iiams; later adding a codicil with John and Plummer Iiams as witnesses. The will left equal portions of the real estate to sons John, Thomas, Richard, and William Iiams, with "all unnamed children" to share the personal estate on an equal basis. The will also referred to his daughter, Susanna Pumphries.

This Thomas Ijams (b. 1708) had no slaves and the inventory of his personal estate (July 4, 1769) was approved by Elizabeth Ijams and John Ijams. On June 13, 1770, the balance filed with the court totaled 97 pounds, 10 shillings, 1 pence; with each of seven unnamed children receiving 13 pounds, 18 shillings, 4 pence. Newman admits that the children were not listed, but feels that there were eight children: Elizabeth (b. 1732), Sarah (b. 1734), Artridge (b. 1736), Charity (b. 1739), Susanna (b. 1742), Thomas (b. 1745; m. Mary Iiams and Sarah Marriott); John (b. 1747; m. Susannah Watkins); and Richard (b. 1749; m. Eleanor Musgrove). It would have been nice if families used a wider variety of names for their offspring, but "that would make the work of genealogy research too easy."

Children of Thomas Iiams (b. 1754) and Catherine Gill Hampton:

1) John Iiams, d. "young," 1856, a bachelor;
2) Elizabeth Iiams [(b. Anne Arundel County, Maryland, 1788; d. Richland Township, Belmont County, Ohio, 1868, age 86; buried Old Dutch (Ault or Dutch Hill) Cemetery, Richland Township, Belmont County, Ohio). However, the 1880 Census of Ritchie County, West Virginia, lists an Elizabeth Iiams, age 77, born Pennsylvania, parents both born in Maryland, and has perhaps led LIB to suggest that this Elizabeth Iiams as b. October 2, 1802; d. October 10, 1886, Ritchie County, West Virginia];
3) Samuel Iiams [(b. March 1, 1795, Washington County, Pennsylvania, or February 25, 1795 (EFB); d. August 21, 1860, Richland Township, Belmont County, Ohio; buried Old Dutch (Ault, Dutch Hill) Cemetery, Richland Township); m. Elizabeth Meek (b. 1786; d. November 18, 1866; age 80; buried Old Dutch Cemetery), of Belmont County, Ohio; no children except for an adopted son, Isaac Bennett-Iiams. They lived in or near the home of the parents of Samuel Iiams (b. 1795). The will of Elizabeth Iiams (Belmont County, Ohio, Volume K, page 280) and inventory (Volume 2, page 211; and Volume 3, page 650) written on February 11, 1866, as Elizabeth Iames, and probated on November 23, 1867, written as the widow of Samuel Iiams and mentions adopted son Isaac Iiams, who was left one dollar in addition to that willed him by the deceased Samuel Iiams. She also left four hundred dollars to nephew Thomas Ault; four hundred dollars to Columbia Myers, a boy she raised; four hundred dollars to Henry Meek, a son of Joseph Meek, for his kindness to her; four hundred dollars to her friend William Seeley (or Feeley) to whom she also gave the farm, providing they take care of her; and of the balance of the estate, one-third was to go to niece Christie Ann Ault; one-third to Maggie Bell, and one-third to Wallace Myers (perhaps children of Susan Crow).

Samuel Iiams (b. 1795) purchased a farm in Section 34, Township 5, Range 3, Belmont County, Ohio, in 1815, and purchased 5 acres for $350 from Isaac Iiams on October 2, 1857, also in Section 34, Township 5, Range 3 (Book 3, Belmont County, Ohio, Deeds).

The Belmont County, Ohio, 1820 land Duplicate Tax List lists Samuel Iiams as having two parcels (80 acres; 26 acres) that were taxable. Both parcels were in Range 3, Township 5, in the northwest and northeast portions of Section 36, land that was originally deeded to Robert Mills, and which were taxed at $1.14 and $1.62, respectively.

Samuel Iiams and his wife Elizabeth Meek did not have children of their own. They did adopt a boy, Isaac Bryant or Bennett, who changed his name on March 17, 1848.

The will of Samuel Iiams (Belmont County Will Book I, page 295, Case 4599) was written January 15, 1859, and probated September 8, 1860, provided $100 to the county for the care of the cemetery; $600 to their adopted son Isaac Iiams; $600 to Columbus C. Myers, a boy they raised; $100 to Susan Myers, a girl they raised; $300 to Samuel J. Wilson, son of Jacob Wilson; 2/3 of the estate to his brothers and sisters and their heirs; with adopted son Isaac Iiams and Samuel Wilson as executors.

Book A, Deeds, Belmont County, Ohio, lists 81 acres (Section 34, Township 5, Range 3) purchased for $200 from Uriah Hartesty on August 4, 1822; 34 acres (Section 34, Township 5, Range 3) purchased from Henry Meeks for $100 on August 24, 1822; and 55 acres (Section 35, Township 5, Range 3) purchased from Charles Mason for $300 on May 24, 1833.

The Belmont County Common Pleas Court, page 527, for August 1841, lists a case where Joshua T. Iiams and Samuel Iiams won a judgement of $848.24 for debt plus $100 damages as carryover bond from September 21, 1839, against a John Inskeep.

On September 8, 1849, Samuel Iiams deeded land in Richland Township, Belmont County, Ohio; Section 34, Township 5, Range 3, for the purpose of building a school building, to Richland Township School District in District number 20, for the sum of one dollar.

The 1830 Census of Richland Township, Belmont County, Ohio, lists Samuel Jimes, age 55, a farmer with an estate valued at $5,000, who was born in Pennsylvania; and who was enumerated with his wife Elizabeth, age 61, born in Pennsylvania; with Isaac Jimes, age 22, born in Ohio; and with others living in the household. The 1820 Federal Census listed both Samuel Iams and his wife as age 26 to 45];

4) Charity Iiams [(b. August 12, 1805, in Washington County, Pennsylvania; d. 1886); m. December 5, 1832, in Belmont County, Ohio, by J. P. George Meeker, to Jacob Myers, son of Daniel Myers and Elizabeth Swagler. Their eight children: a) Catherine Myers; b) Elizabeth Myers (m. Isaac Berg); c) Andrew Jackson Myers (m. Mary Elizabeth Weir); d) Daniel Myers (m. Sarah McGanaghey or Caughly); e) Caroline Myers (m. Elisha Higgins Lucas); f) Mary Myers (m. Uletas Moore); g) Thomas Myers (d. age 12); and h) Mathias Myers (m. Anna Ault)];

5) Thomas Iiams [(b. 1786 or 1790, Anne Arundel County, Maryland; d. February 14, 1862, Morrow County, Ohio; buried at Baptist Cemetery, south of West Point, Morrow County, Ohio); m. August 6, 1822, in Belmont County, Ohio, to Mary "Polly" Hardesty of Belmont County (b. December 1806); daughter of Obediah Hardesty (b. 1757; d. 1830, Glencoe, Belmont County, Ohio, a Revolutionary War soldier who served under Lafayette) and Mary "Polly from Paris" (m. in Virginia; lived to age 102; buried at Morristown Cemetery, Belmont County, Ohio). The 1810 Federal Census of Bethlehem Township, Washington County, Pennsylvania, lists: Thomas Jimes, age 16-26; one female 16-26; 3 females under age 10; and one male under age 10. In Morris Township, Greene County, Pennsylvania, the 1810 Federal Census lists: Thomas Iams, age 26-45; a female age 26-45; one female under age 10; 1 male age 10-16, and one male under age 10. At this same place in the 1820 Federal Census was a Thomas Iams age 26-45; and also in Washington County, Pennsylvania, was a Thomas Iiams age 26-45. Thomas (b. 1786) and his wife Mary "Polly" Hardesty moved to Morrow County, Ohio, in 1835, where they owned a farm of 235 acres near Whitstone. It is believed they had 13 children, but other variations have been suggested];

6) William Iiams [(b. September 8, 1793, or October 10, 1794, Anne Arundel County, Maryland, d. April 30, 1859; buried at Amity Cemetery,

Washington County, Pennsylvania); lived at Amity, Pennsylvania; m. Susannah "Susan" Sharp (b. April 27, 1795; d. February 6, 1883; buried at Amity Cemetery). William Iiams (b. 1793) was the only child of Thomas Iiams (b. 1754) to remain in western Pennsylvania (TI). See chapter on Wesley Iams (b. 1828) for additional information. Their children included:

  a) Charity Iiams (b. 1830); m. Sebastian Eliot (Elliott), and their two children were: Reverend John Alonzo Eliot, and Siddle Eliot (b. 1861; d. 1865);

  b) Delilah Iiams (b. 1825); single;

  c) Eleanor "Ellen" Iiams (b. 1819); m. Daniel Eller;

  d) Elizabeth Iiams (b. 1838); m. Reverend John Seth Baldwin;

  e) Salem Iiams (b. 1817); m. Elizabeth Ann Deems;

  f) Franklin F. "F F" Iams, (b. 1834); m. Mary Ellen Bane;

  g) John "Wesley" Iams (b. 1828); see separate chapter; and

  h) Jehu or Jonathan Iams (b. 1822); m. Phoebe McCracken];

7) Mary "Polly" Iiams [(b. Washington County, Pennsylvania); m. Jacob Eggy of Washington County, Pennsylvania (b. 1798; Pennsylvania; d. 1884, Ritchie County, West Virginia); members of Pleasant Valley Christian Church organized in 1840. The will of Jacob Eggy, Will Book 2, March 18, 1884, Ritchie County, West Virginia, named deceased son David Eggy and his widow Jane Eggy; his son A. J. Eggy; and his daughter Catherine Eggy McKenna. Miller Iams, a son-in-law, was named executor. Daughter Catherine Eggy is also believed to have married a Richardson; daughter Sarah Ann Eggy to have married Jackson James, M.D., of West Virginia; and a daughter Mary may have married a Freer (Phaer)];

8) Richard Iiams (Iimes) [(b. 1787 or 1789, Anne Arundel County, Maryland; d. 1844); m. Frances "Fannie" C. Meeks, daughter of William Meeks of Monroe County, Ohio. They moved to Richland County, Ohio, about 1818.

The 1820 Duplicate Tax Record of Richland Township, Belmont County, Ohio, showed that Richard Iiams owned 61 acres in Range 3, Township 5, Section 35 NE, originally owned by John Barcourt and which was taxed $0.78.

The Belmont County Common Pleas Court, March 1815 term, pages 65 and 66, lists a case by Richard Iiams against Benjamin Burdette for $100 to pay for meat, drink, clothing, washing, and lodging.

The 1820 Federal Census of Belmont County lists Richard Imes (age 26 to 45) with one female of same age, one male 16-25, 1 male 16-18, and 3 males under age 10.

Book A, Belmont County, Ohio, General Index of Deeds, listed five land transfers for Richard Iiams from 1819 through 1823: 52 acres (Section 36, Township 54, Range 3) to Crawford Welch for $270 on March 27, 1819; a lot (33-65) in Barnesville, Belmont County, Ohio, from James Barnes for $100 (July 3, 1819); and to Amos Wyman for $200 (August 22, 1820); 124 acres (Section 36, Township 5, Range 3) from James Smith for $900 on May 22, 1823.

Richard Iiams and his wife were early members of the Pleasant Hill Methodist Church of Morrow County, Ohio; and the congregation met initially in their home. Their children are listed later in this chapter.];

9) Rezin/Reason Iiams [(b. December 18, 1807, Bethlehem Township, Washington County, Pennsylvania; d. November 17, 1873; buried at Bell

Cemetery, Olive Township, Noble County, Ohio); m. in Belmont County, Ohio, on November 29, 1831, by J. P. George Meehan, to Mary Myers (b. April 10, 1808, or 1809 (LIB), in Belmont County, Ohio; and died October 10, 1904); the daughter of Daniel Myers and Elizabeth Swagler of Smith Township, Belmont County, Ohio. EBI has recorded the marriage to Mary Iiams, daughter of Daniel Iiams and Elizabeth Swagler, but close relatives have refuted this alignment. Marriage Records of Belmont County, Ohio (Volume 3, 1830-1833, page 87) lists marriage of Reason Imes to Mary Myres of Smith Township, Belmont County, Ohio, by J. P. George Meek, October 12, 1831. They were both buried at Bell's Cemetery, Olive Township, Noble County, Ohio. Mrs. Helen Parks Nesselroad, great-granddaughter of Rezin Iiams (b. 1807) became a member of DAR, Amanda Parker Devin Chapter, McConnellsville, Ohio, February 1, 1971 (National Number 556505); and Lois Iams Blake of the same line was admitted to DAR June 5, 1973, Marietta, Ohio (National Number 579812). Daniel Myers (b. 1782; d. April 2, 1866; buried in Warnock Cemetery, Smith Township, Belmont County, Ohio). Wife Elizabeth Swagler (b. 1784; d. May 25, 1867); daughter of Jacob Swagler (d. 1806) and Sophia Huffman, daughter of Rudolph Huffman and Dorothea Weiss.]

The children of Rezin Iiams (b. 1807) and Mary Myers (b. 1808) included:

a) John C. Iiams [(b. August 17, 1832, Belmont County, Ohio; d. at age one year, 1833)];

b) Daniel Iiams [(b. 1834, Belmont County, Ohio, died 1924 (LIB) or 1928, Gary, Indiana; and buried in Olive Cemetery, Noble County, Ohio); m. October 31, 1861, to Sarah Ellen Jennings (b. February 28, 1841, in Ohio; d. October 25, 1917; buried at Olive Cemetery, Noble County, Ohio); daughter of Abraham M. Jennings of Ohio and Louisa Foreman of West Virginia. The 1860 Federal Census of Olive Township, Noble County, Ohio, lists Daniel Iams (age 26, carpenter; b. Ohio); Thomas Iams (age 23, b. Ohio; a farmer); Jefferson Iams (age 20, schoolteacher; b. Ohio); Sarah Iams (age 19; b. Ohio); Rebecca Iiams (age 8; b. Ohio); Mary Iams (age 35; b. Ohio) with George and wife Elizabeth Shepard (both age 35; b. Ohio). The 1880 Census lists Daniel Iams (age 45; b. Ohio); Sarah E. Iams (age 39, b. Ohio); Mary L. Iams (age 17; b. Ohio); John E. Iams (age 15; b. Ohio); Abraham M. J. Iams (age 6; b. Ohio). They moved to near Gary, Indiana, 1910];

c) Catherine Iiams [(b. 1835, Belmont County, Ohio; d. 1921; m. October 7, 1858, to Joseph Begley/Bigley; their eight children were: a) James Bigley (b. 1859); b) John R. Bigley (b. 1861); c) Mary M. Bigley (b. 1863); d) Wiley H. Bigley (b. 1864); e) Jefferson Bigley (b. 1867); f) Amy C. Bigley (b. 1869); g) Joseph Vance Bigley (b. 1861) and h) Hettie M. Bigley (b. 1879)];

d) Thomas Iiams [(b. 1837 or August 28, 1838, Belmont County, Ohio; d. November 20, 1914; buried at Bell's Cemetery, Olive Township, Noble County, Ohio); m. October 5, 1862, to Mary/ Nancy Jane Parks (b. 1844, Morgan County, Ohio; d. 1921, Noble County, Ohio; buried in Bell's Cemetery, Olive Township, Noble

County, Ohio); daughter of Jonathan Parks and Rosanna Foraker. The 1860 Federal Census of Noble County, Ohio, lists: Thomas Iiams (age 23, b. Ohio; farmer); Jefferson Iiams (age 10; b. Ohio); Sarah Iiams (age 19; b. Ohio); Mary A. Iiams (age 17; b. Ohio); Sophia Iiams (age 13; b. Ohio); Charity Iiams (age 11; b. Ohio); Rebecca Iiams (age 8; b. Ohio), and Mary Iiams (age 35; b. Ohio); The 1880 Census lists: Thomas Iams (age 39; b. Ohio); Nancy J. Iams (age 35; b. Ohio); Madison Iams (age 16; b. Ohio); Lydia A. Iams (age 14; b. Ohio); Olive M. Iams (age 12; b. Ohio); Charity Iams (age 9; b. Ohio); John Iams (age 7; b. Ohio); Mary Iams (age 5; b. Ohio); and Roseanna Iams (age 3; b. Ohio). The 1900 Federal Census of Sharon Township, Noble County, Ohio, lists: Thomas Iams (age 61; b. Ohio); Nancy J. Iams (age 55; b. Ohio); Pez/John Iams (age 17; b. Ohio); and Alta Iams (age 15; b. Ohio). The 1920 Census lists: Nancy J. Iams (age 75; b. Ohio); Alta B. Iams (age 34; b. Ohio) and grandson Carlos Iams (age 1; b. Ohio)];

e) Jefferson M. Iiams [(b. August 1, 1849, Morgan County, Ohio; d. 1927, Noble County, Ohio); m. Laura L. Wilson on April 1, 1879 (b. about October 1853 (LIB) or 1855; d. 1936); lived in Olive Township, Noble County, Ohio; and their two children were: Lillian "Lillie" C. Iiams (b. September 8, 1886, Noble County, Ohio; d. 1968; m. Lawrence C. Jordan); and Cora M. Iiams (b. May 1881, Noble County, Ohio; d. 1978; m. James Antill)];

f) Charity Iiams [(b. 1847, Morgan County, Ohio; d. 1934); m. November 22, 1874, to Ezra Caldwell (b. 1845; d. 1887); one child, a son];

g) Elizabeth Iiams [(b. 1839, Morgan County, Ohio; d. 1924); m. April 3, 1862, to Isaac Keyser (b. 1841, Belmont County, Ohio; d. 1922, and their two children were: Anna Keyser (b. 1863; d. 1914); and Andrew J. Keyser (b. 1868; d. 1934)];

h) Sarah Ann Iiams [(b. Morgan County, Ohio, 1841; d. 1932); m. October 2, 1862, to Martin V. Sailor. They moved to Kansas; and their eight children were: Clement Laird Sailor (b. 1863); Emma Frances Sailor (b. 1865); Laura Elizabeth Sailor (b. 1867); Mary Lillian Sailor (b. 1869); Hettie May Sailor (b. 1873); Flora Blanche Sailor (b. 1872); Luella Irene Sailor (b. 1877); and Walter Edmund Sailor (b. 1879)];

i) Sophia Jane Iiams [(b. Morgan County, Ohio, 1845; d. 1921); m. October 26, 1865, to Josiah Elliott (b. 1843; d. 1927). They were buried in Sharon Cemetery, Sharon Township, Noble County, Ohio; and their four children were: Minnie Elliott (b. 1867); Myrtle Bell Elliott, twin (b. 1882; d. 1962)]; Lawrence Elliott (b. 1875; d.1958); and Mamie Blanche Elliott (b. 1882; d. 1962)];

j) Rebecca Iiams [(b. Noble County, Ohio, 1851; d. 1930; single; died of breast cancer]; and

k) Mary Anne Iiams [(b. Morgan County, Ohio, 1843; d. 1908); m. April 9, 1868, to John Wheeler (b. 1844; d. 1918); and their four children were: Ruth Wheeler (b. 1868; d. 1963), m. William Crouch); Ellis Wheeler; Mary Wheeler; and Harold Wheeler (b. 1884; d. 1964; m. Minnie Keyser)];

10) Rebecca Iiams [(b. Washington County, Pennsylvania); m. Jacob Wilson of Belmont County, Ohio, and their four children were: Elizabeth Wilson (m. Fred Mellott); Samuel Wilson (m. Sarah Elizabeth Moore); Robinson Wilson (m. Samantha Hart); and Sarah Ann Wilson (m. Melanathan Watts)];

11) Catherine Iiams [(b. January 25, 1812, Washington County, Pennsylvania; d. May 8, 1880, Richland Township, Belmont County, Ohio; buried Ault/Old Dutch Cemetery, Richland Township); m. March 10, 1831, Belmont County, Ohio, by E. M. Workman, J. P., and sworn by Rezin Ijams, to Michael Ault of Richland Township, son of Michael and Christina Ault, ancestors of the Fultons who moved to Ohio in 1817. Michael Ault's father was born in Germany and Michael Ault, Sr., was born in Pennsylvania in 1777 and died in Belmont County, Ohio, January 13, 1849; while wife Christina Ault was born 1767 and died at age 87 on October 17, 1854. Michael Ault, Jr., was a miller who owned one or more flour mills in Glencoe, Belmont County, Ohio. Michael Ault, Jr., was born October 9, 1806, Washington County, Pennsylvania; d. September 18, 1892, or 1848; buried in Ault/Old Dutch Cemetery, Richland Township, Belmont County, Ohio; and their ten children were: Thomas Ault (m. Mary Trimble); Charity Jane Ault (m. Austin Clark Warren); Isaiah Ault (m. Kate Clark); Wilson Samuel Ault (m. Anna Moffett); Mary Adaline Ault (m. William Thomas Mitchell); Alexander Ault (m. Mary Elizabeth Edson); Christine Sarah Ault (b. 1831; d. 1910; single; Elizabeth Ault; and Michael Alonzo Ault, Jr. (b. May 29, 1853; d. February 25, 1854). In addition, children John Ault, Adam Ault, and Sarah Ault may have been raised in this family.];

12) Sarah Iiams [(m. Henry Meek (EFB)]; and

13) Dennis/Demas Iiams [(b. 1806, Greene County, Pennsylvania, per JBM)].

Thomas Iiams (b. 1786, Anne Arundel County, Maryland; d. February 14, 1862, Morrow County, Ohio) and Mary "Polly" Hardesty (b. December 1806, Belmont County, Ohio), had several children. Among these children were:

1) Thomas Iiams (b. 1836, Morrow County, Ohio; lived in Williams County, Ohio); 2) Violet Iiams [(b. 1844, Morrow County, Ohio); a schoolteacher; m. W. A. McClenathan; lived in Morrow County; buried in Baptist Congress Cemetery in Morrow County]; 3) Rebecca Iiams [(b. 1830, Belmont County, Ohio), m. 1st, Eli Bateman; m. 2nd, Joseph Wilson; four children: Elizabeth Wilson (m. Fred Mellott); Samuel Wilson (m. Sarah Moore); Robinson Wilson (m. Samantha Hall); and Sarah Ann Wilson (m. Milanathan West)]; 4) Nancy Elizabeth Iiams (b. 1831, Belmont County, Ohio; lived in Kansas); 5) Matilda Iiams (b. 1828, Belmont County, Ohio; single; lived at home); 6) Martha Iiams (b. 1838, Morrow County, Ohio); 7) Lydia Iiams (b. 1846, Morrow County, Ohio); 8) Samuel Iiams (b. 1837, Morrow County, Ohio; lived in Kansas); 9) Elizabeth Iiams (b. 1825, Belmont County, Ohio); 10) Mary Iiams (b. 1840, Morrow County, Ohio); 11) Dennis Iiams (F. C. proposal); 12) Polly Iiams (F. C. proposal); 13) Catherine Iiams (d. young); 14) Rachel Iiams (F. C. proposal); 15) Charity Iiams (F. C. proposal); 16) Hannah Iiams (F. C. proposal); 17) Mary "Sarah" Iiams (b. 1842, Morrow County, Ohio); 18) Jane Iiams (b. 1823, Belmont County, Ohio); and 19) Franklin Iiams [(b. 1833, Morrow County, Ohio; d. August 19, 1919, Morrow County, Ohio, or Upper Sandusky in Wyandotte County, Ohio), m. Mary A. ____ (b. 1833, Pennsylvania); and they had seven children: William Thomas Iiams (b. 1860, Ohio); m. September 1, 1881, to Fannie "Annie" Emma Brewer); Seth Iiams (b. 1863, Ohio); Maude Iames (b. 1863, Ohio); Melvin Iames

(b. 1867, Ohio); Franer Iames (b. 1869, Ohio); Minnie Iames (b. December 5, 1870, Wyandotte County, Ohio); and Charles Edgar Iames (b. 1872, Wyandotte County, Ohio; d. March 2, 1948, Ohio); m. Gertrude E. Ralya (b. January 3, 1875, Antrim, Guernsey County, Ohio; d. July 14, 1962); lived on a farm in Upper Sandusky, Ohio; seven children.]

William Thomas Iames or Iiams (b. 1860, Ohio), and Fannie "Annie" Emma Brewer of Morrow County, Ohio, had a son John L. Iiams/Iames, who m. Mable Florence Albright, daughter of Fred W. Albright and Caroline Weirtzbacker of Germany, who owned an ice cream parlor in Caledonia, Marion County, Ohio. John L. Iiams had three children: Garnet Iiams, Violet Iiams, and Hoyt Iiams. Hoyt Iiams [(b. 1909, Marion County, Ohio), m. 1st, in 1928, Detroit Michigan, to Kathryn Wood, daughter of Plia Wood and Essie McCullough of Gilboa, Putnam County, Ohio; m. 2nd, in 1975 to Kenneth Foos (b. 1909), her second marriage; and he had two sons: 1) Elgin Iiams (b. 1929; lived in Florida; had a son); and 2) Robert Iiams (b. 1930; lived in Florida; had three sons and four daughters)]. Kenneth Foos (b. 1909) was the daughter of Carroll Foos and Sybil Underwood, and the sister of both Russell Foos and Helen Foos. Carroll Foos was the son of Hiram Foos and Minerva Clark of Morrow County, Ohio. Sybil Underwood was the daughter of Saben A. Underwood and Loretta Hipsher of Caledonia, Morrow County, Ohio. Saben A. Underwood was the son of Benjamin Underwood and Marie Miller. Loretta Hipsher was the daughter of Silas and Sarah Hipsher of Caledonia, Ohio. Kennetha Underwood Foos m. 1st in 1936 to Wallace G. Coulter (d. 1971), son of William Coulter and Lydia Mason; had a daughter, Carolyn Kay Coulter (b. 1946; m. 1966 to James Emory, son of Earl Emory and Cecille Restoule of Caledonia, Ohio), who had two children: Jennifer Emory (b. 1970, Morrow County, Ohio) and Benjamin Emory (b. 1976, Morrow County, Ohio).

Charles Edgar Iams (b. 1872, Ohio; d. March 2, 1948, Ohio, son of Franklin and Mary A. Iiams; m. Gertrude E. Ralya (b. January 3, 1875, Antrim, Guernsey County, Ohio; d. July 14, 1962); and they had seven children before they were divorced:

1) Harley F. Iams [(b. 1895, Wyandotte County, Ohio; World War I veteran; a security guard in Dayton, Ohio; d. 1950); m. Daisy ____; and their daughter was JoAnne Iams]; 2) Ralph George Iams [(b. May 4, 1899; lived in Mansfield, Ohio, area; d. February 15, 1972; m. Nola ____; and had two children: Evelyn Iams and Janice Iams]; 3) Herbert Iams (b. 1902, Ohio; lived in Wyandotte County, Ohio; single; worked on railroad and was killed in a work-related accident); 4) Robert S. Iams [(b. 1906, Ohio; worked on railroad; lived in Mansfield, Ohio, and in Crestline, Ohio); m. Myrtle Earp; and their son was Charles Edgar Iams]; 5) Frances Iams [(b. October 12, 1912; lived in Upper Sandusky, Ohio; d. March 30, 1990); m. Arthur Mercer; and their daughter was Barbara Mercer]; 6) Gladys Iams (b. 1915, Ohio; d. 1978), m. 1935 to Frederick Newell; lived in Upper Sandusky, Ohio; had two children: Norita Newell and Richard Newell]; 7) Lester Charles Iams [(b. May 10, 1897, Upper Sandusky, Wyandot County, Ohio; d. May 27, 1948, Marion, Marion County, Ohio), worked at Marion Steam Shovel Company; served in Motorcycle Corps in World War I; m. March 18, 1918, Monroe, Michigan, to Ruby Fern Miller (b. February 22, 1900, Wyandot County, Ohio; d. February 24, 1979, Marion, Ohio), daughter of Jacob A. Miller and Dollie Mouser of Little Sandusky, Ohio; (Ruby m. 2nd, 1958, to Fred R. Heisel); and they had three children: Dolores Carmen Iams (b. 1921); Charles Edgar Iams (b. 1925); and Harold Eugene Iams (b. 1929)].

Dolores Carmen Iams [(b. July 31, 1921, Marion, Ohio), daughter of Lester Charles Iams (b. 1897); m. 1941 to William F. Freshour (b. October 13, 1941); and had two children: 1) Donald William Freshour (b. October 13, 1914; lived in

Mobile, Alabama); and 2) David Paul Freshour (b. July 28, 1944; m. Judy Shenefield; and they had two children: Paul Freshour and Amy Freshour)].

Charles Edgar Iams (b. October 6, 1925; lived in Marion, Ohio), m. November 24, 1946, Marion, Ohio, to Jane Louise Young (b. May 27, 1926); he was Marion County Engineer 1944-1946; worked at Marion Reserve Power Plant and at Ohio Edison from 1946-1990; and Jane Louise Young was the daughter of Troy Young and Mary Louise Grubb, as well as the sister of Virginia Young and Raymond Young. Charles Edgar Iams (b. 1925) had two children: 1) Charles Gary Iams [(b. July 26, 1950, Marion, Ohio; contributed significantly to family history), m. June 14, 1975, to Denise Lee Zucker (b. September 7, 1951, Columbus, Franklin County, Ohio), daughter of Joseph Stanley Zucker and Betty Jo White; and the granddaughter of Meyer Zucker and Beatrice Blum; and Charles Gary Iams (b. 1950) graduated from Capital University School of Music; received his M.A. in Music from The Ohio State University; was Coordinator of Music Education in Marion City Schools; a member of Music Educators National Conference; member of National School Orchestra Association; a member of Marion Noon Kiwanis; member of Marion County Youth Foundation; founder of the Delion Quartet; and Director of Marion Civic Chorus and Orchestra]; and 2) Carolyn Louise Iams [(b. July 11, 1960, Marion, Ohio), a graduate of Bowling Green State University; m. May 24, 1986, to Mark Henry Green; she worked for Ohio Theater, Ballet Metropolitan, and the Columbus Symphony; and they had a daughter: Emily Ann Green (b. May 25, 1995)].

Harold Eugene Iams (b. August 22, 1929, Marion, Marion County, Ohio), son of Lester Charles Iams (b. 1897); m. 1st, Marion, Ohio, to Mary A. Smith; m. 2nd to Naomi ____; had four children: 1) Rebecca Iams [(b. May 14, 1949); husband was killed in 1980; four children]; 2) R. Craig Iams [(b. January 19, 1951); m. August 21, 1971, to Janis L. Tesenier (or Tesenear)(b. June 1, 1950, Galion, Ohio); daughter of James D. Tesenear and Lorraine Ross; and they had two children: a) Matthew C. Iams (b. May 31, 1974, Galion, Ohio; and Jeffrey C. Iams (b. September 20, 1977, Galion, Ohio)]; 3) Shelly Iams (b. June 30, 1952; married; three children); and 4) Robin Iams (a son; b. November 23, 1957).

William Iiams (b. July 19, 1829, Belmont County, Ohio; d. October 16, 1894, Orange Township, Noble County, Indiana), the son of Richard Iiams (b. 1787, Anne Arundel County, Maryland) and Frances C. "Fanny" Meeks; grandson of Thomas Iiams (b. 1754, Anne Arundel County, Maryland, and Catherine Gill Hampton; m. March 1, 1849, Morrow County, Ohio, to Jane Hafferty (b. May 7, 1827), daughter of William Hafferty and Elizabeth Luther of Richland County, Ohio; lived in Monroe County, Ohio; moved to Noble County, Indiana, in 1850; was Noble County Assessor for several years; served two terms as Noble County Commissioner; had seven children:

1) Thomas L. Iiams [(b. December 3, 1849, Ohio; d. Indiana), m. March 13, 1873, at "Altar of Hyman," to Mary C. Hoster (b. January 21, 1848, Morrow County, Ohio), daughter of Samuel R. Hoster and Barbara Keifer; sister of John Henry Hoster, William W. Hoster, Margaret M. Hoster (d. young), and Barbara Ella Hoster (b. 1861) of Pennsylvania; and their daughter was Mabel M. Iams (b. 1873; Indiana; d. March 20, 1894)]; 2) William A. Iiams [b. May 3, 1854, Noble County, Indiana; a schoolteacher; lived at old homestead); m. October 12, 1883, Kendallville, Indiana, to Barbara Ella Hoster (b. June 22, 1861; daughter of Samuel R. Hoster and Barbara Keifer); and they had two children: a) Roy A. Iiams (b. August 1884; m. Mary K. Huston; and their two children were: Robert H. Iiams, b. 1912; and Warren A. Iiams, b. 1914); and b) Ortho/Orlo/Otho H. Iiams (b. May 1894), m. Lucile M. Fairbanks; and they had one child: Thomas Iiams (b. 1920, Noble County, Indiana; lived at Brimfield,

Indiana; a major contributor to family tree; graduate of Purdue University; two children: Thomas "Tom" Iiams, Jr., and Cindy Iiams]; 3) John H. Iiams (b. February 1851, Noble County, Indiana; farmer; single; lived in Orange Township); 4) James P. Iiams (d. age 27, Noble County, Indiana); 5) Mary E. Iiams (b. Noble County, Indiana; m. William W. Hoster, son of Samuel R. Hoster and Barbara Keifer); 6) Milton Iiams (b. Noble County, Indiana; d. age 39); and 7) Isabella Iiams (b. Noble County, Indiana; m. Enos Bricker). The 1900 Federal Census of Orange Township, Noble County, Indiana, listed William A. Imes (age 46, b. Indiana, May 1854); wife Ella B. Iams (age 38, b. Indiana, June 1861); son Roy Iams (age 15, b. Indiana, August 1884); and son Orla H. Imes (age 6, b. Indiana, May 1894). The 1920 Federal Census of Noble County, Indiana, lists Orlo H. Imes (age 25, b. Indiana) and wife Lucile M. Imes (age 21, b. Indiana).

The Accelerated Name Search lists both John Imes and Francis Imes, Perry Township, Richland County, Ohio, marriages include Joan L. Iiams to Robert Edgecomb (January 1, 1856); Rhoda Iiams to David Graham (September 1, 1851); and Rachel Iiams to Isaac M. Roos (September 4, 1856).

John F. Ijams (Civil War Certificate Number 312676) of Morrow County, Ohio, d. June 16, 1865, leaving his widow Harriet Elizabeth Webb, formerly the widow of Samuel Webb who was killed in a railroad accident in Morrow County, Ohio, July 4, 1857. On July 16, 1890, she was listed as age 60, living in Columbus, Franklin County, Ohio; John F. Iiams and Harriet Eliza Webb were married April 11, 1861. Jane, the first wife of John F. Iiams, died September 1, 1860. John F. Iiams was a Major in the 36th Ohio Cavalry, and a Major in the 5th Battalion of Ohio Independent Cavalry; enlisted July 9, 1863, and discharged February 15, 1864.

The 1880 Federal Census, Noble County, Indiana, listed Thomas Imes (age 30, b. Ohio); Mary Imes (age 30, b. Ohio); and daughter Mable Imes (age 6, b. Indiana); Absalom Imes (age 34, b. Ohio); Sarah E. Imes (age 31, b. Ohio); Mary R. Imes (age 12, b. Indiana); and Emma V. Imes (age 7, b. Ohio). The 1910 Federal Census of Orange Township, Noble County, Indiana, lists Jane Imes (age 73, b. May 1827 in Ohio, as mother-in-law of Joseph Bailey). The 1900 Federal Census of Orange Township, Noble County, Indiana, lists: Thomas L. Imes (b. Ohio, December 1849, age 50); and wife Mary C. Imes (b. Ohio, January 1848, age 52). The 1920 Census of Noble County, Indiana, lists Thomas L. Imes (age 70, b. Ohio); and wife Mary E. Imes (age 71, b. Ohio); and living alone was Sarah C. Imes (age 66, b. Indiana); and Edith M. Imes (age 35, b. Indiana).

Daniel Iiams (b. 1834, Belmont County, Ohio; d. Indiana); the son of Rezin Iiams (b. 1807); m. October 31, 1861, to Sarah Ellen Jennings (b. February 28, 1841, Ohio; d. October 25, 1917, Noble County, Ohio); and they had four children: 1) Mary Louise Iams (b. 1862); 2) John Ellsworth Iams (b. 1864); 3) Martha B. Iams (b. 1885; m. Warren; DAR 205395; and 4) Abraham Miley J. Iiams (b. 1874, Noble County, Ohio; d. 1924); m. Cleo Smith (b. 1864, Ohio), the granddaughter of both John and Mary Smith, and of Daniel and Margaret (Young) Moore; and great-granddaughter of Reverend Joseph Smith and Hannah Greene (daughter of American Revolutionary General Nathaniel Greene, for whom Greene County, Pennsylvania, was named); and they had two children: a) Ines McCain Iiams (b. 1902, Ohio); and b) Marshall Iams (b. 1911, Indiana; m. Miriam Howard), who had two children: Margaret Iams and Howard Marshall Iams].

Marshall Iams (b. 1910, Indiana), son of Abraham Miley J. Iiams (b. 1874, Noble County, Ohio) and Cleo Smith (b. 1864, Ohio), m. Miriam Howard, daughter of Talcott Howard and Martha Mathilda Briley (daughter of William Briley and Mathilda Riley); and they had two children: 1) Margaret Iams; and 2) Howard Marshall

Iams, Ph.D. (b. July 8, 1945, Gary, Indiana; lived in Bethesda, Maryland); m. December 21, 1969, Evanston, Illinois, to Ella Weingarten (b. March 5, 1946, Schenectady, New York); daughter of Samuel Weingarten and Sarah Kramer; granddaughter of both Ellis or Eli Joel Weingarten of Poland, and Ethel or Esther Gales of Lithuania; and of Samuel Kramer and Jenny Frisch Miransky; contributor to family history; and they had two children: Joel Marshall Iams (b. January 30, 1979, Washington, District of Columbia); and Sarah Miriam Iams (b. March 22, 1982, Washington, District of Columbia). The 1920 Census of Lake County, Indiana, lists Miley Iams (age 45, b. Ohio; living on Adams Street in Gary, Indiana); wife Cleo Iams (age 45, b. Ohio); daughter Inez L. Iams (age 18, b. Ohio); and Marshall Iams (age 9, b. Indiana).

Thomas Iiams (b. 1837, Belmont County, Ohio; d. 1914, Noble County, Ohio); son of Rezin Iiams (b. 1807) and Mary Myers (b. 1808); m. October 5, 1862, to Mary (or Nancy Jane) Parks (b. 1844, Ohio); and they had ten children:

1) William McClelland Iiams (b. 1863, Sharon Township, Noble County, Ohio; d. 1865 following a fall from a cradle);

2) Madison J. Iiams [(b. 1864, Noble County, Ohio; d. 1942, Noble County, Ohio); m. April 14, 1876, to Leutitia "Tish" Morrison (b. May 1864, Ohio; d. 1944)];

3) Lydia Iiams [(b. 1866, Noble County, Ohio; d. 1942), m. March 6, 1892, to William Coombs (d. 1937); seven children];

4) Olive May Iiams [(b. 1868, Noble County, Ohio; d. 1959), m. June 23, 1888, to James Walters (b. 1864; d. 1940); five children];

5) Charity Iiams [(b. 1869, Sharon Township, Noble County, Ohio; d. 1960), m. April 19, 1880, to Hiram Ellison (b. 1864; d. 1936); three children];

6) John Moody Iiams [(b. April 1872, Sharon Township, Noble County, Ohio; d. 1958), m. July 23, 1893, to Cora M. Teeters (b. March 1871; d. 1920; buried in Olive Cemetery, Olive Township, Noble County, Ohio); had six children: Mabel Ethel Iams (b. 1893); Glenn Columbus Iams (b. 1895); Jennie Hazel Iams (b. 1898); Molly May Iams (b. 1900), Ruby Pearl Iams (b. 1902); and Cash Harold Iams (b. 1904)];

7) Mary Iiams [(b. 1874, Noble County, Ohio; d. 1956), m. 1st, Delbert Woodford on September 7, 1892; m. 2nd, June 20, 1925, to Ray Frye; two children];

8) Roseanna "Anna" Iiams [(b. 1878, Noble County, Ohio; d. 1937), m. February 8, 1899, to Vernon Foster (b. 1878; d. 1928); ten children];

9) Rezin Erwin Iiams [(b. September 8, 1882, Sharon Township, Noble County, Ohio; d. February 7, 1970, Caldwell, Noble County, Ohio; buried in Sharon Cemetery, Sharon Township, Noble County, Ohio), m. February 25, 1905, to Alta Jane Parrish (b. February 26, 1883, Noble County, Ohio; d. September 2, 1973, Caldwell, Noble County, Ohio; buried in Sharon Cemetery), daughter of Thomas E. Parrish and Elizabeth Ann Marquis; and they had four children: Burl Blake Iams (b. March 3, 1906, Sharon Township, Noble County; d. August 20, 1908, of cholera); Thomas Bliss Iams (b. 1908); Helen Lois Iams (b. 1910; associate editor of this book); and Lewis Dale Iams (b. March 5, 1915, Sharon Township, Noble County, Ohio; d. February 25, 1922, Wilm's tumor)]; and

10) Alta Bell Iiams [(b. 1884, Noble County, Ohio; d. 1967), m. September 1, 1920, to William Spears; two children: Zail E. Spears (b. 1921, Noble County, Ohio; m. Sheila Cain; lived in Noble County); and Carlos Ivan Iams (b. July 3, 1909; Noble County, Ohio; d. January 4, 1978, Canton,

Ohio); m. September 1930, Sharon Township, Noble County, Ohio, to Anna Lucetti Archibald (b. August 18, 1908, Sharon Township; d. August 5, 1991, Canton, Ohio; buried in Sharon Cemetery, Sharon Township, Noble County, Ohio), daughter of Frank W. Archibald and Anna McFarland; granddaughter of Hezikiah Archibald and Aurelia Wiley; and their child was Betty Annabelle Iams (b. April 3, 1931, Sharon Township, Noble County, Ohio), m. April 30, 1960, Canton, Ohio, to Edward J. Kromi; and they had five children: Regina Ann Kromi; Brian Edward Kromi; David Joseph Kromi; Susan Iams Kromi; and Linda Marie Kromi]. Zail E. Spears (b. 1921) served World War II.

Glenn Columbus Iams (b. August 30, 1895, Caldwell, Noble County, Ohio; drove supply wagon in World War I; a farmer; d. April 13, 1964, Caldwell, Ohio); son of John Moody Iiams (b. 1872, Noble County, Ohio); m. August 11, 1917, to Mary Burdell McGlashan (b. March 18, 1897, Cumberland, Guernsey County, Ohio; d. October 10, 1979, Caldwell, Ohio); daughter of John C. McGlashan and Martha McGlashan; and they had five children:

1) Martha Mae Iams [(b. March 1, 1918, Caldwell, Ohio; d. June 8, 1991, Cincinnati, Ohio); m. June 2, 1939, to William Ode Devoll (b. August 18, 1915, Caldwell, Ohio); son of William Ode Devoll, Sr., and Zora Wescott; and had three children: a) Jonathan Earl Devoll (b. March 13, 1941, Marietta, Washington County, Ohio); b) Marianna Devoll (b. July 19, 1944, Richmond, Indiana); and c) David Calvin Devoll (b. October 16, 1949, Hamilton, Ohio; m. January 20, 1975, to Fabriola Lersunder)];

2) John Winder Iams [(b. June 20, 1920, Caldwell, Ohio; lived in South Bend, Indiana); m. May 12, 1943, Caldwell, Ohio, to Helen R. Schott, daughter of Clarence George Schott and Pearl Margaret Zwick; cousin of the husband of the "not so lovable" Marge Schott (owner of Cincinnati Reds National League Baseball Club, and Cincinnati automobile dealership, pending current legal actions); and granddaughter of both Nicholas Schott and Philomena Smithberger, and of Joseph Zwick and Margaret Burkhardt; had several children: a) Barbara Jane Iams (b. August 8, 1945, Boston, Massachusetts; m. August 19, 1967, South Bend, Indiana, to Robert Linn Herr, b. May 28, 1945, South Bend, Indiana; two children: Michael Robert Herr, b. July 11, 1968; and Kathryn Dougherty Herr, b. September 30, 1970, South Bend, Indiana); b) Marcia Ann Iams (b. October 25, 1946, Marietta, Ohio; m. April 3, 1971, South Bend, Indiana, to Daniel Robert Jones, b. November 1, 1945, South Bend, Indiana, son of George Francis Jones and Mary Ann Frash; four children: Stephen Daniel Jones, b. February 5, 1972, South Bend; Matthew Joseph Jones, b. February 28,1973, South Bend; John Francis Jones, b. September 30, 1975, South Bend; and Mary Margaret Jones, b. January 14, 1978, South Bend, Indiana); c) John Anthony Iams (b. February 22, 1950, Columbus, Ohio; d. April 25, 1991, Indianapolis, Indiana; m. August 24, 1974, Edgewater Park, New Jersey, to Mary Susan Morgan Magoon, b. January 3, 1951, Dover, New Hampshire, daughter of Ernest Howard Magoon and Margaret Ann "Margery" Driscoll; four children: Christopher John Iams (b. November 12, 1975, Indianapolis, Indiana; Timothy Patrick Iams, b. February 27, 1979, Indianapolis, Indiana; Amy Elizabeth Iams, b. April 2, 1981, Indianapolis, Indiana; and Andrew Jacob Iams, b. February 18, 1987, Louisville, Kentucky); d) Mary Catherine Iams (b. November 6, 1953, Hamilton, Ohio; m. June

24, 1978, South Bend, Indiana, to Todd August Hannert, b. August 6, 1953, Detroit, Michigan; son of Dale Hannert and Jane Ann Sutherland; one daughter: Adrienne Jane Hannert, b. October 22, 1981, Lansing, Michigan); e) Joseph Thomas Iams (b. December 6, 1954, Hamilton, Ohio; m. June 2, 1979, South Bend, Indiana, to Ann Marie Thomas, b. December 30, 1955, Akron, Ohio; daughter of Joseph Kenneth Thomas and Marie Ann Selby; four children: Benjamin Joseph Iams, b. June 24, 1980, South Bend; Sean Michael Iams, b. January 11, 1982, South Bend; Matthew Kenneth Iams, b. June 6, 1985, South Bend; and Daniel Patrick Iams, b. October 12, 1988, South Bend, Indiana); f) George Edward Iams (b. October 5, 1958, Hamilton, Ohio; m. August 2, 1980, in South Bend, to Tracy Ann Troeger, b. December 7, 1958; daughter of Thomas Albert Troeger, M.D., and Patty Lou Borden/Bourdon; and granddaughter of Carl Edward Troeger and Esther Steiner; four children: Tyler Andrew Iams, b. June 12, 1984, South Bend; Wade Thomas Iams, b. November 7, 1985, South Bend; Brady Patrick Iams, b. September 5, 1988, South Bend; and Corey John Iams, b. December 12, 1991, South Bend); and g) Martha Elizabeth Iams (b. May 16, 1961, Hamilton, Ohio; m. November 24, 1984, South Bend, Indiana, to Johnnie Roosevelt Johnson, b. April 19, 1964, Marion, Arkansas; son of Robert Lee Johnson and Willie Beatrice Clay; one son: Johnnie Robert Johnson, b.(?) July 24, 1986, Willimantic, Connecticut);
3) Peggy Florence Iams [(b. July 8, 1921, Caldwell, Noble County, Ohio; d. August 4, 1962, Alliance, Stark County, Ohio); m. September 6, 1941, Caldwell, Ohio, to George Edgar Brown (b. March 16, 1921, New Lexington, Perry County, Ohio; d. July 24, 1991, Alliance, Ohio, and buried at Sebring, Mahoning County, Ohio); m. 2nd, Martha Jane Wang; four children: a) Rebecca Ann Brown (b. September 6, 1946, Wichita Falls, Texas; m. September 14, 1968, Cleveland, Ohio, to Norbert John Leszez, b. June 6, 1941, Cleveland, Ohio; son of Walter Leszez and Mary Kuczek; two children: Brian Edward Leszez, b. July 13, 1969, Garfield Heights, Ohio; and John Patrick Leszez, b. May 14, 1971, Garfield Heights, Ohio); b) Benjamin Loy Brown (b. October 4, 1950, Wheeling, West Virginia; m. June 1974, to Pamela Marie Hanna, b. September 21, 1949; one son: Zachary Joseph Brown, b. June 8, 1980; c) Martha Lou Brown (b. November 10, 1957, Alliance, Ohio; single); and d) Cora Mae Brown (b. November 10, 1957, Alliance, Ohio; m. July 6, 1985, Massachusetts, to Paul Claude Arsenault, b. May 28, 1961, Moncton, New Brunswick, Canada; son of Alphee Joseph Arsenault and Dina Marie Breau; two children: Jacob Daniel Arsenault, b. February 19, 1989, Stoneham, Maryland; and Peter Gregory Arsenault, b. July 16, 1991, Stoneham, Maryland)];
4) Ruth Ann Iams [(b. February 11, 1924, Caldwell, Noble County, Ohio), m. June 3, 1944, Caldwell, to Rosario Charles Laudicina (b. July 2, 1918, Framingham, Massachusetts), son of Nicholas Laudicina of Sicily, and Gaetanand Calamosa; four children: a) Rosario Charles Laudicina, Jr. (b. November 20, 1945, Marietta, Washington County, Ohio); b) David Iams Laudicina (b. January 18, 1949, Boston, Massachusetts; m. June 13, 1970, Wabash, Indiana, to Rebecca Jane Ridlon, b. January 3, 1947, Wabash; daughter of Kenneth Ridlon and Mary Emmaline Enycart; and their child was Rose Anna Laudicina, b. July

27, 1988); c) Betsy Ann Laudicina (b. September 20, 1952, Boston; m. October 4, 1975, Marlboro, Massachusetts, to Charles Freeman Anastas, b. September 7, 1951, Boston; and their two children were: Sassha Marie Anastas, b. June 10, 1983, Aspen, Pitcan County, Colorado; and Nicholas Freeman Anastas, b. October 20, 1988, Aspen, Pitcan County, Colorado); and d) Tana Marie Laudicina (b. November 5, 1956, Boston; m. 1st, Herbert Holmes; m. 2nd, July 15, 1989, Aspen, Pitcan County, Colorado, to William Joseph Rinaldi, b. Allentown, Pennsylvania; son of Joseph William Rinaldi and Joan Mahan; three children were: Elli Mayre Rinaldi, b. March 23, 1990, Aspen, Colorado; Haley Michelle Rinaldi, b. September 30, 1991, Aspen, Colorado; and Dominic William Rinaldi, b. May 4, 1994, Aspen, Pitcan County, Colorado)];

    5) Mary Lou Iams [(b. April 7, 1927, Caldwell, Noble County, Ohio; d. January 22, 1995, Zanesville, Muskingum County, Ohio), m. December 31, 1946, Caldwell, Noble County, Ohio, to Vere Harper Miller (b. June 19, 1923, Marietta, Washington County, Ohio), son of James Otis Miller and Althea Harper; and they had four children: a) Glenn O. Miller (b. October 2, 1947, Marietta, Ohio; m. December 28, 1969, Zanesville, Ohio, to Susan Thomas, b. February 7, 1947, Asheville, North Carolina; daughter of Garvia Harrison and Virginia Rose Thomas; one child: Melissa Miller, b. November 15, 1970, Torrance, California); b) Mary Suzanne Miller (b. April 30, 1955, Columbus, Franklin County, Ohio; m. May 17, 1975, to Larry Eugene Dailey); c) Vere Harper Miller (b. August 26, 1963, Zanesville, Ohio; m. May 11, 1991, Duncan Falls, Ohio, to Diane Lynn Dietz, b. June 23, 1963, Zanesville, Ohio; one child: Elizabeth Sierra Miller, b. January 10, 1995, Middletown, Ohio); and d) Van McGlashan Miller (b. August 26, 1963, Zanesville, Ohio; m. June 3, 1993, West Chester, Ohio, to Rita Jane Brady, b. August 23, 1969, Hamilton, Ohio, daughter of Gerald Leon Brady and Deanna Joyce Holt)].

    Martha Mae Iams (b. March 1, 1918, Caldwell, Noble County, Ohio; d. June 8, 1991, Cincinnati, Ohio), daughter of Glenn Columbus Iams (b. August 30, 1895, Caldwell, Ohio) and Mary Burdell McGlashan; m. June 2, 1939, to William Ode Devoll (b. August 18, 1915, Caldwell, Ohio), son of William Ode Devoll, Sr., and Zora Wescott; had three children: 1) Jonathan Earl Devoll [(b. March 13, 1941, Marietta, Ohio; m. May 23, 1964, to Patricia Thoma (b. November 14, 1943, Cincinnati, Ohio), daughter of Louis Thoma of Romania, and Adelaide Koelker; and they had three children: a) Mary Elizabeth DeVoll (b. October 16, 1966, Philadelphia, Pennsylvania); b) David Louis DeVoll (b. November 2, 1969, Wilmington, Delaware; m. November 27, 1993, to Christina Renaldi); and c) Matthew William DeVoll (b. February 7, 1971, Wilmington, Delaware)]; 2) Marianna DeVoll [(b. June 19, 1944, Richmond, Indiana), m. June 2, 1967, Indiana, to David Lowell Garrett; three children: a) David John Garrett (b. March 18, 1970, Cincinnati, Ohio); b) Joseph Lowell Garrett (b. January 10, 1972, Cincinnati, Ohio); and c) Martha Catherine Garrett (b. June 3, 1973, Cincinnati, Ohio)]; and 3) David Calvin DeVoll [(b. October 16, 1949, Hamilton, Ohio), m. January 20, 1975, to Fabriola Lersunder].

    Jennie Hazel Iams (b. May 12, 1898, Caldwell, Noble County, Ohio; d. May 4, 1976, Caldwell, Noble County, Ohio), daughter of John Moody Iams (b. April 1872) and sister of Glenn Columbus Iams (b. 1895); m. October 3, 1918, Caldwell, Ohio; to Frank Elmer Boyd (b. August 30, 1894, Enoch Township, Noble County, Ohio; and they had two children: 1) Dwight Iams Boyd [(b. May 24, 1920, Caldwell, Ohio), m. April 18, 1942, Columbus, Ohio, to Betty Jane Weaver (b. July 20, 1920,

Dover, Tuscawaras County, Ohio, daughter of Harry William Weaver and Mary Elizabeth Calland; and they had three children: a) David Thomas Boyd (b. January 6, 1948, Columbus, Ohio; d. January 8, 1948); b) Brent Dwight Boyd (b. July 27, 1949, Columbus, Ohio; m. June 3, 1972, Union, Missouri, to Mary Jane Kroeger, b. December 18, 1949, Union, Missouri, daughter of Harry Kroeger and Pearl Lucille Kreft; and their child was Catlin Elizabeth Boyd, b. September 2, 1992, St. Louis, Missouri); c) Scott Douglas Boyd (b. September 15, 1951, Osaka, Japan; m. September 10, 1983, Tolona, Illinois, to Lynda Kay Garrett, b. June 30, 1959, Champaign, Illinois, daughter of Lee Elwood Garrett and Dortha Sean Fleener; and their two children were: Craig Garrett Boyd, b. April 3, 1987, St. Louis, Missouri; and Grant Garrett Boyd, b. December 21, 1990, St. Louis, Missouri); and d) Brian Kent Boyd (b. January 5, 1957, San Juan, Puerto Rico; m. August 9, 1980, St. Louis, Missouri, to Laura Ann Owens, b. October 3, 1958, Cincinnati, Ohio, daughter of Raymond Owens and Lucille Brennan; and they had two children: Christopher Brian Boyd, b. August 16, 1983, Columbia, Missouri; and Michael Owens Boyd, b. May 11, 1988, Springfield, Missouri)]; and 2) Annabelle Boyd [(b. December 7, 1927, Caldwell, Noble County, Ohio), m. 1st, Walter Lee Johnson; m. 2nd, Harold Slate].

Cash Harold Iams (b. October 3, 1904, Noble County, Ohio), son of John Moody Iams (b. April 1872, Sharon Township, Noble County, Ohio, and Cora M. Teeters; m. February 18, 1928, Marietta, Washington County, Ohio, to Goldie Juanita Fogle (b. April 24, 1909, Belle Valley, Noble County, Ohio; d. September 18, 1978, Zanesville, Ohio), daughter of Ellis Fogle and Elizabeth Barnhouse; three children:

    1) Cash Iams, Jr. [(b. July 17, 1931, Massillon, Stark County, Ohio), m. April 6, 1952, Massillon, Ohio, to Patty June Fouts (b. February 9, 1934, Massillon, Ohio); and they had three children: a) Deborah Iams (b. May 16, 1954, Almagordo, New Mexico; m. September 22, 1973, Massillon, Ohio, to Richard Reale, b. June 5, 1953; and their two children were: Jennifer Juanita Reale, b. January 1, 1979, Massillon, Ohio; and Matthew Gintz Reale, b. May 11, 1981, Massillon, Ohio); b) Nancy Iams (b. October 18, 1955, Almagordo, New Mexico; m. Michael Ream; divorced, taking maiden name; moved to Florida; one son: Travis Scott Ream, b. March 26, 1977, Massillon, Ohio); and c) Michael Cash Iams (b. December 10, 1956, Massillon, Ohio; m. September 10, 1983, Massillon, Ohio, to Karen Lynette Medure, b. November 4, 1954, Massillon, Ohio; her second marriage; had a son Aron James Gayheart, b. April 27, 1979, by first marriage; two children: Justin Michael Iams, b. March 24, 1984, Massillon, Ohio; and Kayleigh Frances Iams, b. June 11, 1990)].

    2) George Richard Iams [(b. October 7, 1932, Massillon, Ohio), m. August 20, 1952, Massillon, Ohio, to Joan Marie Hindley (b. July 31, 1932, Massillon, Stark County, Ohio), daughter of Elmer "Honey" Hindley and Frances Lydia Wilson (George Richard Iams contributed significantly to the family tree), and they had four children: a) Gregory Allen Iams (b. February 19, 1955, Massillon, Ohio; single); b) Bradley Richard Iams (b. April 25, 1961, Massillon, Stark County, Ohio; an attorney; m. May 29, 1982, Canton, Stark County, Ohio, to Ronda Jo Risher, b. February 27, 1959, Massillon, Ohio, daughter of Ronald Eugene Risher, Jr., and Joann Kandle Pfaus; and they had two children: Kathleen Marie Iams, b. January 4, 1986, Canton, Ohio; and Stephanie Diana Iams, b. October 18, 1989, Canton, Ohio); c) Leslie Ann Iams (b. April 25, 1961, Ashland, Ohio; an attorney; m. November 12, 1994, to Lee David Kuntz); and d) Philip Bryon Iams (b. February 28, 1964,

Grand Rapids, Michigan)]; and 3) Wanda Jean Iams [(b. November 4, 1936, Massillon, Stark County, Ohio); single; lived in Caldwell, Noble County, Ohio].

Thomas Bliss Iams (b. March 3, 1908, Sharon Township, Noble County, Ohio), son of Rezin Erwin Iams (b. September 8, 1882, Sharon Township, Noble County, Ohio), grandson of Thomas Iams (b. 1837) and Nancy Jane Parks; m. April 26, 1929, to Bertha "Ethel" Wiley (b. 1905), daughter of Bruce Wiley and Maggie Parks; and they had three children: 1) Eva Jane Iams [(b. 1930; d. 1932)]; 2) Wava Joy Iams [(b. 1934; lived in Hillsboro, Oregon); m. August 1955 to Neal Dutton, son of Clem Dutton and Marguerite McKee; and they had two children: a) Beverly Annette Dutton (b. 1956; m. Michael Mills; three children: Heather Mills, Holly Mills, Hillary Mills, Helena Mills, and Haley Mills, who d. infancy); and b) Bryant Bliss Dutton (b. 1960)]; and 3) Walter Roger "W.R." Iams [(b. March 22, 1942, Sharon Township, Noble County, Ohio); vocational agriculture teacher in Hamilton, Ohio; m. June 1965, to Nadine Lee Rideout (b. December 8, 1942), daughter of Stanley Leo Rideout and Vivian Lenore Miley; lived on Isabella Lane in Hamilton; (Stanley Lee Rideout was the son of Harvey James Rideout and Rose Saguin; Vivian Lenore Miley was the daughter of Alva Miley and Laura Pitcher); two children: a) Rachel Lee Iams (b. January 18, 1969, Zanesville, Muskingum County, Ohio; m. Matthew Peacock); and b) John Roger Iams (b. December 9, 1971, Findlay, Hancock County, Ohio; m. Lisa Clary)].

Helen "Lois" Iams (b. August 13, 1910, Sharon Township, Noble County, Ohio); native of Caldwell; co-editor and inspiration for this family history; m. February 25, 1937, to Robert C. Blake (b. 1912; d. June 4, 1964, of cancer). Lois Iams (b. 1910) was the daughter of Rezin Erwin Iams (b. September 8, 1882, Sharon Township, Noble County, Ohio); and the granddaughter of Thomas Iams (b. 1837, Belmont County, Ohio; d. 1914, Noble County, Ohio) and Nancy Jane Parks (b. 1844). Lois Iams Blake (b. 1910) began the study of Iams genealogy at the age of 14 as a high school student, and has completed several family histories. She has been historian for the Noble County, Ohio, Historical and Genealogical Society; and is a member of the DAR. She collected items of the Iams family history for E. Jay Iams of Donora, Pennsylvania; for E. B. Iams of Washington, Pennsylvania, and for the early Iams work of Ervin F. Bickley, Jr., of Philadelphia, Pennsylvania, and New Canaan, Connecticut. She attended the Iams National Family Reunion when it was held in Noble County, Ohio, in 1932; and also when it was held in Washington County, Pennsylvania; in Wheeling, West Virginia; and in New Martinsville, West Virginia, during the 1930s. She was among the first to claim the connection between the Iams/Iiams of America and the Imes or I'ans of England and the Innes of Scotland. Lois Iams and Robert C. Blake had two children:

1) Rebecca Iams Blake [(b. November 16, 1939, Caldwell, Noble County, Ohio; d. 1981), m. 1st, June 1960, to Earl Atwood; and after they divorced in 1962 she m. 2nd, October 1, 1965, to Benjamin Sheets, son of Clair Sheets and Merledean Mildred Baker of Paden City, West Virginia; lived in Heath, Licking County, Ohio; two children: a) Cathryn Elaine "Kati" Sheets (b. June 20, 1968); and b) Victoria Faye "Viki" Sheets (b. September 28, 1970)]; and 2) Robert C. Blake II [(b. March 19, 1950), m. June 24, 1972, to Diane M. Adams, daughter of Herbert and Dorothy Adams; both have Ph.D. and work in cancer biomedical research; both received B.S. from Ohio State in 1972; Ph.D. from University of Illinois in 1977; worked at University of Michigan, Meharry Medical College, Xavier University, and Tulane University; had two children: a) Robert C. "Robbie" Blake III (b. January 8, 1981); and b) Elizabeth Adams "Liz" Blake (b. May 8, 1984)].

Carlos Ivan Iams (b. July 3, 1909, Noble County, Ohio; d. January 4, 1978, Canton, Ohio; m. September 1930, Sharon Township, Noble County, Ohio, to Anna

Lucetti Archibald (August 18, 1908, Sharon Township, Noble County, Ohio; d. August 5, 1991, Canton, Ohio; buried in Sharon Township); daughter of Frank W. Archibald and Anna McFarland; granddaughter of Hezekiah Archibald and Aurelia Wiley; lived near Leesville Lake, Ohio; had one child: Betty Annabelle Iams (b. April 3, 1931, Sharon Township, Noble County, Ohio), who m. April 30, 1960, Canton, Ohio, to Edward J. Kromi (Betty Iams Kromi was a member of the Deaf Advisory Committee; a public schoolteacher for sign language; was Deaf Woman of the Year in 1982; a member of the Senior Citizens Bible Group of Carrollton, Ohio; a highly regarded babysitter; and a contributing editor for this work on Iams history); had five children: 1) Regina Ann Kromi [(b. October 15, 1961; worked at General Electric Capital in Canton, Ohio; m. J. Kelly Dickes, and they had three children: a) Jennifer Dickes (b. 1982, Canton, Ohio); b) Jack Dickes (b. 1985, Canton, Ohio); and c) Ivan Dickes (b. 1994)]; 2) Brian Edward Kromi [(b. March 10, 1963); worked at a printing company in Canton, Ohio; m. Kelly R. Volkert; had three children: a) Mark Kromi (b. 1984); b) Rachel Kromi (b. 1988); and c) Jessica Kromi (b. 1990)]; 3) David Joseph Kromi [(b. July 30, 1965); owner of Beldon Village Carpet; m. Kelly Ann Notch; had two children: a) Adam Kromi (b. 1988); and b) Steven Kromi (b. 1994)]; 4) Susan Iams Kromi [(b. July 10, 1967); graduate of Bowling Green State University; a fashion model for K-Mart; single]; and 5) Linda Marie Kromi [(b. August 30, 1969); worked at General Electric Capital, Canton, Ohio, while working on degree in Medical Laboratory Technology].

REFERENCES

- E. Jay Iams, personal papers of family history. Westen Pennsylvania, 1931-1938.

- Tom Imes, personal papers of family history, Kendallville, Indiana, 1995.

- Ervin F. Bickley, Jr., personal papers of Iams families, New Canaan, Connecticut, 1954-1995.

- Harry Wright Newman, personal papers, correspondence, and writings, Annapolis, Maryland.

- Joy I. Hannon, family history, personal papers, Zanesville, Ohio, 1992-1995.

- Guy Ross and Roberta Iiames, personal papers of family history, Springboro, Ohio, 1992-1996.

- Howard Leckey, writings and personal papers of James B. Meighen, western Pennsylvania; and *Ten Mile Country* (The Bookmark, Kingstown, New York, 1977).

- James B. Meighen, personal papers of Iams family history, Monongahela, Pennsylvania, 1992-1996.

- Lois Iams Blake, personal papers of Iams family, Caldwell, Ohio, 1992-1995.

- Michael Iams, personal file of Iams family, Phoenix, Arizona, 1994-1995.

- C. Gary Iams, personal file of family history, Marion, Indiana, 1994-1995.

- Howard Iams, personal history of Iams family, Bethesda, Maryland, 1995.

- Betty Kromi, personal files of family history of Iams family, Canton, Ohio, 1995-1996.

- Joan Marie Hindley Iams, personal history of Iams family, Canton, Ohio, 1995.

- Fred Cochran, personal files in Greene County Historical Center, Waynesburg, Pennsylvania, 1995.

- Federal Census Records, 1790-1920, National Archives, Washington, D.C.

- *Maryland Archives*, Volumes XVII (p. 126); XVIII; and XXI (pp. 159, 252), Annapolis, Maryland.

- Court House Records, Belmont County Court House, Saint Clairsville, Ohio.

- Maryland Council of Safety 1777-1778 (p. 268), Annapolis, Maryland.

- *History of Morrow County* (Morrow County, Ohio, Historical Society, 1880).

- Records of Deeds, Maryland Archives, Annapolis, Maryland.

- Revolutionary War Pension Claims and Rosters of Revolutionary War Soldiers buried in Ohio, National Archives, Washington, D.C.

— CHAPTER 9 —

WILLIAM IIAMS

(B. 1755, MARYLAND; D. MARYLAND)

William Iiams (b. 1755, Maryland; d. 1831, Allegany County, Maryland), son of Richard Iiams (EFB), had his will filed in both Allegany County, Maryland, and Bedford County, Pennsylvania, because his estate was located in each location. His wife was not mentioned in his will, though the Federal Census of Allegany County, Maryland in 1830 listed both William Iiams and a woman in the household as being between 70 and 80 years of age; and a Bedford County, Pennsylvania, land transfer (M-162, December, 13, 1800) lists the name of his wife as Charity. The Bedford County, Pennsylvania, deed (d-638, June 7, 1798) transferred land called Spurgeon's Choice to his youngest son, Hugh Iiams of Bedford County, Pennsylvania, for £150.

The will of William Iiams was probated in Allegany County, Maryland, on August 10, 1831. On March 1, 1779, William Iiams of Frederick County, Maryland, purchased 140 acres in Allegany County, Maryland (1-349) from Jacob Kaplinger. Jacob Kaplinger or Kaplinger also sold 14 acres of Resurvey on Wildcat Hill to Plummer Ijams of Frederick County, Maryland (8-370) for 19 pounds, 5 shillings, in March 1780; and 98 1/2 acres (9-437) of the same area for 147 pounds, 15 shillings, on September 2, 1790. The will of Plummer Ijams of Frederick County, Maryland (13-372, January 12, 1793) listed John Iiams as executor, and resulted in the sale of 100 acres of Resurvey on Wild Cat Hill or also called Iiams Resolution to Christopher Musseter, Sr., for 170 pounds, 13 shillings, 4 pence.

On October 17, 1805 (28-190), Plummer Ijams of Frederick County, Maryland, received lands called Duvall's Forrest and Good Fryday from a joint deed transfer action by Thomas Plummer Ijams (and wife Sarah) and Isaac Ijams (and wife Elizabeth) of Fairfield County, Ohio. A later will of Rebecca Ijams mentions Isaac Ijams and wife Elizabeth as well as their three sons—Isaac Ijams, John Ijams, and Thomas Ijams—specifically leaving William Ijams the sum of one dollar. The land purchased by William Iiams of Frederick County, Maryland (for 1700 pounds), included Strow's Burrick on Colection Creek (71 acres), Resurvey on Turkey Range (39 1/2 acres, and Resurvey (36 acres).

William Iiams had purchased 147 acres in March 1779 from Jacob Keplinger, and this land consisted of The Resurvey on Turkey Ridge, and Strow's Burrick; and he sold this land to Jacob Stringer for £300 on December 7, 1790 (WR9-543, Frederick County, Maryland) while living in Washington County, Maryland. On May 7, 1795, William Iiams purchased Duvall's Delight from Benjamin Penn of Hopewell, Bedford County, Pennsylvania, for £100 (HWN). On December 30, 1785, William Iiams and his wife, Charity Iiams, deeded Anne Arundel County land previously owned by Thomas Iiams to Thomas Iiams (HWN). William Iiams, son of John Iiams and Rebecca Jones, moved from Anne Arundel County, Maryland, to Frederick County, Maryland, where he married Elizabeth Howard, daughter of Joseph Howard and Rachel Ridgely. The name William Iiams appears in Frederick County, Maryland; Allegany County, Maryland;

Fairfield County, Ohio; Bedford County, Pennsylvania; and Washington County, Maryland, all within the same era.

William Iiams, son of Richard Iiams (b. 1673), and second wife, Elizabeth Gaither (HWN), settled in Washington County, Maryland, by March 5, 1787; and in Allegany County, Maryland, by October 1, 1792, where he deeded land to John Snowden. By 1803, William Iiams had sold his land holdings in Washington County, Maryland (HWN). Washington County, Maryland, record review shows that William Iiams of Frederick County, Maryland, purchased 140 acres in four tracts called Resurvey of Turkey Lands, Hole Hill, Shaw-Burial and Good Wife, for £1,700 on March 1, 1779 (W-11, 349), from Jacob Kaplinger. On March 30, 1793 (H-393), the 250 acres on which William Iiams lived, called Chance, was purchased from Thomas Worley for £80. This land, as well as other land, Hole in the Rock, Resurvey, and Addition to Chance was sold by William Iiams, Jr., and wife Elizabeth for £1,882 and 10 shillings to Abraham Ditto (P-280). EFB has stated that this is a different William Iams line.

On April 5, 1742, William Jiams had purchased 50 acres in Allegany County, Maryland, called New Birmingham from Richard Snowden; and his son, William Jiams, sold part of this land to John Snowden on October 1, 1792. The 1830 Census of Allegany County, Maryland, lists William Iiams, Amos Iiams, and Jesse Iiams each as heads of households. William Iiams (age 70 to 80) is listed with a woman (age 70 to 80), a male (10 to 15), and a female (age 30 to 40). Amos Iiams (age 40 to 50) is listed with a female (age 40 to 50), two males (age 5 to 10), two males (age 15 to 20), and one female (age 20 to 30). Jesse Iiams (age 30 to 40) is listed with a female (age 30 to 40), one male (age under 5), one female (age under 5), two males (age 5 to 10), one male (age 10 to 15), and one male (15 to 20).

On March 20, 1808, in Allegany County, Maryland, both William Iiams and William Iiams, Jr., were witnesses to the will of Moses Lewman. Land purchased from Thomas Worley, 1793, Washington County, Maryland, by William Ijams, was sold to Abraham Pitt in 1803. William Ijams and wife Elizabeth Howard moved to Fairfield County, Ohio, in 1803. A land transaction, Bedford County, Pennsylvania, December 9, 1799 (M-159) transferred 275 acres called Bridge Water on the Shoups Mill Branch in Hopewell Township (now Huntingdon County) to William Iiams, Morgan Township, Greene County, Pennsylvania; and on December 13, 1800 (M-162), 161 of these acres were sold by William and Charity Iiams (listed as a blacksmith of Greene County, Pennsylvania) to John McIlvaine of Hopewell Township.

On June 7, 1798 (D-638), William Iiams of Bedford County, Pennsylvania, transferred 0.5 acres of Spurgeon's Choice in Bedford County, to Hugh Iiams of Bedford County, Pennsylvania; and on December 12, 1834 (R-384), this land was transferred by Hugh and Mary Ann Iiams of Jackson Township, Sandusky County, Ohio, to Michael Huff of Southampton Township, Bedford County, Pennsylvania. On April 2, 1800, 74 acres on Flintstone Creek, Bedford County, Pennsylvania, were transferred from John and Ann Iiams of Bedford County to Abraham Ash of Washington County (AA5-52). On May 9, 1794, 75 acres in Bedford County, Pennsylvania (25-649), were transferred to William Iiams, who had previously (22-212) received 100 acres in Collerain Township, Bedford County, Pennsylvania. On August 5, 1843 (25-551), 60 acres in Bedford County were transferred to William Ieiams; and in 1783 (22-264), 90 acres in the Cumberland Valley of Bedford County, Pennsylvania, were deeded to John Iiams.

The will (HWN) of William Iiams, dated June 2, 1824, Allegany County, Maryland, and probated August 10, 1831 (1-313) listed 256 acres called William's Farm, 60 acres called Partnership, and a tract originally obtained from Thomas Mayhew of Bedford County, Pennsylvania, and these lands were designated for both the eldest son, Amos Iiams, and the youngest son, Jesse Iiams, with son William Iiams, Jr., given the land on Town Creek in Bedford County, Pennsylvania. Daughter Rachel Iiams was given $130; daughter Rebecca Iiams, $130; Mary Gordon was given $80; and Isabel Sloan (and her two children) to have "full use of the dwelling for three months after his death."

In the award-winning book, *The Chaneysville Incident*, by David Bradley (Harper and Row, New York, 1981), and in C. L. Blockson's, *The Underground Railroad* (Hippocrine Books, New York, 1994, pp. 116-117), the Bedford County Iames/ Iiames/Imes are described as being involved in the underground railroad, and with the presumably associated suicide and burial in the Iames family cemetery, of thirteen slaves trapped in a huntdown in Southern Bedford County, just south of Chaneysville. In the novel, David Bradley refers to Lester V. Iames (p. ix), to the Ames family (p. 236), to Richard Iiames as one of the thirteen original settlers of Southampton Township, Bedford County (p. 236), and the slave movement of 1846 as described by Joseph Powell. The Iames family graveyard is described on page 376. In the book, the diary of C. K. "Brobdingniz" Washington, husband of Bijou and father of Lamen Washington, ended on December 23, 1859. Lamen Washington married Cora Alice O'Reilly and they had a son, Moses Washington, about whom Mr. Bradley wrote.

Blockson has written that, while the exact truth will never be known, it was known that even though the Bedford County, Pennsylvania, area was very dangerous for slaves, that many still attempted to pursue freedom through these deep mountains and valleys leading from Maryland up through Bedford County, and that the Iames were sympathetic and supportive of the underground railroad. It was here that thirteen slaves died and were buried on the Iames farm, with crude rough-cut fieldstones without names. In the novel, the Iames had provided shelter for the slaves, but in their attempt to move further to the north, they were surrounded, and rather than be killed by the slave hunters, elected for suicide. Their burial place on the Iames farm may still be seen by first locating the sawmill on Route 326, about four miles below Chaneysville. Just below the sawmill, a lane goes back through the trees and up the slight grade near the creek, a distance of about one-third of a mile. The stones remain and are clearly visible in the clearing of the woods.

The children (EFB) of William Iiams (d. 1831, Maryland) were: 1) Amos Iiams (b. 1783, Maryland; d. 1851, Allegany County, Maryland; m. 1st, Elizabeth ___; m. 2nd, December 1, 1836, to Harriet Beall); 2) Mary Iiams (b. 1784; m. Thomas Gordon); 3) William Iiams, Jr. (b. 1785; d. January 26, 1858, Southampton Township, Bedford County, Pennsylvania; m. Ruth ___); 4) Rachel Iiams (b. 1792; m. Thomas Hart); 5) Rebecca Iiams (b. 1789, Pennsylvania; m. Michael Crow); 6) Jesse Iiams [(b. August 8, 1794, Maryland; d. June 12, 1874, Clark County, Iowa), buried in Union Cemetery; m. 1st, 1815, to Mary Cherry (b. 1799, Maryland), m. 2nd, Barbara ___; moved to Holmes County, Ohio, by 1840, when he decided to deed land in Allegany County, Maryland (AB-798), to Daniel Wolford]; 7) John Iiams (b. 1780, Pennsylvania; m. Ann ___); 8) Juart Iiams (b. 1797, Pennsylvania); and 9: Hugh Iiams (b. 1788; m. Mary Ann Huff; moved to Ohio, then to Iowa).

Amos Iiams (b. 1783, Maryland; d. 1851, Allegany County, Maryland), son of William Iiams (b. 1755), m. 1st, to Elizabeth ___; m. 2nd, December 1, 1836, to Harriet Beall. The Allegany County, Maryland, will (B-39), written on August 6, 1851, and probated November 11, 1851, lists Lewis Iiams, executor; Harriet Iiams as widow of Amos Iiams; Hiram Iiams, Israel Iiams, and John Iiams as sons; and Sarah Davis, Rachel Sloan, and Mary Easter as daughters. The 1820 Federal Census of Bedford County, Pennsylvania, lists Amos Iiams (age 26 to 45, head of household), one female (age over 45), two males (under age 10), one female (age under

305

10), and one female (age 10 to 16). In the 1830 census, Amos Iiams is listed in Allegany County, Maryland. Children of Amos Iiams (b. 1783) were: 1) Israel Iiams [(m. December 8, 1838, to Mary Sarah Twigg), 1900 Census of Bedford County, Pennsylvania, lists Israel Imes (age 57, b. Pennsylvania) and Mary Imes (age 53); and in 1920, Israel Imes (age 68) lived with father-in-law Arthur Robinette]; 2) John Iiams; 3) Hiram Iiams [(d. 1855), m. Ede Ann; Will (B-92) written March 1, 1855; probated April 12, 1855; named brother Lewis Iiams, executor; Ede Ann Iiams as wife, and three children: Emma Cornelia Iiams, Hiram Milton Iiams, and Thornton Iiams]; 4) Lewis Iiams; 5) Sarah Iiams (m. Mr. Davis); 6) Rachel Iams (m. Mr. Sloan); and 7) Mary Iiams (m. Mr. Easter).

William Iiams, Jr. (b. 1785, Maryland; d. January 26, 1858, Bedford County, Pennsylvania), son of William Iiams (b. 1755), m. Ruth ___ (b. 1784; d. before 1855) was living in Bedford County, Pennsylvania, in 1824, when the will of his father was written in Allegany County, Maryland (A-313). An 1854 Bedford County, Pennsylvania, court document names the children of William Iiams, Jr. as Moses Iiams, Aaron Iiams, William Iiams, Isaac Iiams, John Iiams, Richard Iiams, and Henry Iiams. William Iiams, Jr. received ownership of the land on Town Creek in Bedford County, Pennsylvania, from his father. Children of William Iiams, Jr. (b. 1785) were: 1) Moses Iiams [(b. September 1, 1817; d. December 12 or 18, 1896, age 79; buried Mt. Zion Cemetery, Chaneysville, Pennsylvania), m. Amy ___ (b. April 8, 1817; d. April 13, 1891)]; 2) Aaron Iiams/Jeames/ Jiames/Imes (b. 1819; d. July 6, 1869, Bedford County; m. Mary ___); 3) William Iiams III; 4) Isaac Iiams (b. 1811; m. Mary ___); 5) John Iiams [(d. intestate, 1858); had daughter May and granddaughter Sarah; organized first Sunday School at Fairview Church in Flintstone, Maryland; m. April 1, 1853; member of Board of Managers]; 6) Richard Iiams; and 7) Henry Iiams (DDI).

Moses Iames (b. September 1, 1817; d. December 18, 1896, Southampton Township, Bedford County, Pennsylvania), son of William Iiams, Jr. (b. 1785), m. Amy ___ (b. April 8, 1817; d. April 13, 1891, buried in Mt. Zion Cemetery, Southampton Township, Bedford County, Pennsylvania). In 1905, the family had the name officially changed from Iames to Imes through legal action transacted at the Bedford County, Pennsylvania, courthouse. The 1860 Census of Bedford County lists Moses Imes (age 42, b. Pennsylvania), Amy Imes (age 42), Nathaniel Imes (age 15), Israel Imes (age 11), Masinda Imes (age 7), George Imes (age 4), Alfred Imes (age 2), and Jesper Imes (age 4 months); and the 1870 census lists Moses Imes (age 53), Amy Imes (age 52), Nathaniel Imes (age 23), Israel Imes (age 20), Emmanuel Imes (age 16), George Imes (age 14), Alfred Imes (age 12), and Jasper Imes (age 10).

Children of Moses Imes (b. 1817) were: 1) Alfred Imes [(b. November 17, 1857, Bedford County, Pennsylvania; d. 1927), m. October 3, 1879, to Nancy ___ (b. April 1, 1861; d. October 16, 1925; both buried at Chaneysville Cemetery, Bedford County, Pennsylvania)]; 2) Nathaniel Imes (b. 1845, Pennsylvania); 3) Israel Imes [(b. 1849, Bedford County, Pennsylvania); 1900 Census of Bedford County lists Israel Imes (age 57) and Mary Imes (age 53)]; 4) Marinda Imes (b. 1853); 5) George Imes [(b. 1856); the 1920 Census of Bedford County lists George Imes (age 64), Ruth Imes (age 60) and Roy Imes (age 22)]; 6) Jasper Imes [(b. 1859); 1920 Bedford County census lists Jasper Imes (age 54) with sister Marinda Imes (age 60)]; 7) John Imes (b.1843); and 8) Susannah Imes (b. 1847) (DDI).

Alfred Imes (b. November 17, 1857, Southampton Township, Bedford County, Pennsylvania; d. 1921), son of Moses Imes (b. 1817), m. October 3, 1879, to Nancy ___ (b. April 1, 1861; d. October 16, 1925; both buried in Chaneysville Cemetery, Bedford County, Pennsylvania), and 1920 Bedford County census lists Alfred Imes (age 62) and Nancie Imes (age 58). Their children were: 1) Edgar F. Imes [(b.

October 31, 1884, Chaneysville, Bedford County, Pennsylvania; d. February 25, 1955, Cumberland, Maryland; buried in Chaneysville Cemetery, Bedford County, Pennsylvania), m. Alice Walters (b. October 31, 1884, Bedford County; d. August 13, 1937, Chaneysville)]; and 2) Amanda Imes (b. September 13, 1880, Chaneysville; m. Samuel Bowman). (DDI)

Edgar F. Imes (b. October 31, 1884, Chaneysville, Bedford County, Pennsylvania; d. February 25, 1955, Cumberland, Maryland; buried in Chaneysville Cemetery), m. Alice Walters (b. October 31, 1884, Bedford County, Pennsylvania; d. August 13, 1937, Chaneysville), daughter of Hezekiah (b. May 1848; d. February 1924) and Rachel A. Walters (b. October 1859; d. February 1940; buried in Chaneysville Cemetery); and the six children of Edgar F. Imes (son of Alfred Imes, b. 1857) were: 1) Chalmer M. Imes [(b. April 14, 1906, Chaneysville; d. April 8, 1987), m. December 24, 1926, to Alice Morgan]; 2) Melvin Imes (b. February 3, 1908, Chaneysville; d. April 9, 1982); 3) Myrtle Imes [(b. October 6, 1910, Chaneysville; d. October 10, 1990), m. Hobart Redinger (d. June 12, 1964)]; 4) Goldie Imes (b. April 10, 1913, Chaneysville; d. September 18, 1961); 5) Elva Imes [(b. June 7, 1922, Chaneysville; alive 1995), m. William Spencer (d. October 1994)]; and 6) Dorotha Imes (b. October 6, 1925; m. Eddie Shannon). (DDI)

Chalmer M. Imes (b. April 14, 1906, Chaneysville, Southampton Township, Bedford County, Pennsylvania; d. April 8, 1987), the son of Edgar F. Imes (b. 1884), m. December 24, 1926, to Alice Morgan, and their son was Donald D. Imes [(b. March 14, 1929, Somerset County, Pennsylvania; lived at Roaring Springs, Pennsylvania; compiled this branch of family history), m. in Frederick County, Virginia, September 24, 1948, to Margaret I. Myers (b. September 6, 1929, Roaring Spring, Blair County, Pennsylvania), the daughter of Wilson Myers and Anna McKnight; and the granddaughter of Wesley Myers and Margaret Daniels) and Donald D. Imes (b. 1929) had four children: 1) G. Michael Imes [(b. February 24, 1949, Roaring Spring, Pennsylvania), m. January 1, 1987, to Nancy Martin]; 2) David D. Imes [(b. August 17, 1950, Roaring Spring), m. March 17, 1973, to Janet Quarry]; 3) Ann M. Imes (b. November 8, 1951, Roaring Spring); and 4) Gregory L. Imes [(b. April 10, 1953, Roaring Spring), m. August 19, 1975, to Martha Pickel].

Aaron Iiams (b. 1819; d. July 6, 1869, Bedford County, Pennsylvania), son of William Iiams, Jr. (b. 1785), m. Mary or Sophia ___ (b. 1820). The 1850 Federal Census of Southampton Township, Bedford County, Pennsylvania, lists Aaron Iiams (age 25, farmer, b. Pennsylvania), Sophia Iiams (age 22), Daniel Iiams (age 6), Mary A. Iiams (age 5), and Julia Iiams (age 2). The 1860 census lists Aaron Imes (age 40, b. Maryland), Sophia Imes (age 40), Daniel Imes (age 14), Mary Ann Imes (age 13), Julia Imes (age 11), Martha Jane Imes (age 9). Catherine Imes (age 7), Talitha Imes (age 6), and Amos Imes (age 5). The 1870 census lists Sophia Imes (age 53), Mary Ann Imes (age 23), Martha Imes (age 20), Catherine Imes (age 17), Amos Imes (age 15), and Ephriam Imes (age 9). The 1870 Mortality Record shows that Aaron Iiams died at age 50 of consumption. The 1880 census lists Sophia Imes (age 60), Martha Imes (age 28), Upton Imes (age 19), Alice Imes (age 8), Jesse Lee Imes (age 46), and Wilson Imes (age 6); and also listed as head of household in 1880 was Amos Imes (age 25), with wife Susannah Imes (age 20), Lulu B. Imes (age 4), Rebecca Imes (age 2), and A. Edward Imes (age 4 months). In his will (4-598), filed in Bedford County, Pennsylvania, Aaron Imes (b. 1819) left the estate to wife Sophia Imes, with a cow and calf given to Caroline (Catherine) Imes, a heifer given to Julia Imes, a calf given to Amos Imes, $50 given to Upton Imes (plus one colt or $86 at age 20; and also named were daughters Martha Jane Imes and Catherine Imes; with will probated on July 5, 1869.

307

Children of Aaron Imes (b. 1819) were: 1) Daniel Imes (b. 1845); 2) Mary Jane Imes (b. 1846); 3) Julia Imes (b. 1848); 4) Martha Jane Imes (b. 1851); 5) Catherine Imes (b. 1853); 6) Talitha Imes (b. 1854); 7) Amos Imes [(b. 1855), m. Susanna; their children included: Lula Belle Imes (b. 1876), Rebecca Imes (b. 1878), and Aaron Edward Imes (b. 1879)]; 8) Upton Ephraim Imes [(b. 1861), m. Louisa ___ (b. 1873) and their four children were: Stella Imes (b. 1894), Lester Imes (b. 1895), Marshall Imes (b. 1896), Kelly Imes (b. 1898), Percy Imes (b. 1901), and Regis Imes (b. 1913)].

Amos Imes (b. 1855, Pennsylvania), the son of Aaron Imes (b. 1819), m. Susannah ___ (b. 1860), and their children were: 1) Lulu B. Imes (b. 1876), 2) Rebecca Imes (b. 1878), 3) A. Edward Imes (b. 1879), 4) Esta R. Imes (b. 1883), 5) Emaline Imes (b. 1885), 6) Daniel W. Imes [(b. 1887, Pennsylvania), m. Mary ___ (b. 1887), and their child Arvil Imes (b. 1903, in Maryland)], 7) Narah Imes (b. 1889), 8) Amanda M. Imes (b. 1891), 9) Abner R. Imes (b. 1894), 10) Rosa L. Imes (b. 1896), 11) Huldah Imes (b. 1899), and 12) Olivia Imes (b. 1902). The 1900 Census of Bedford County, Pennsylvania, lists: Amos Imes (age 45, b. Pennsylvania), Susan Imes (age 41, b. Pennsylvania), Esta R. Imes (age 17), Emaline Imes (age 15), Daniel W. Imes (age 13), Narah Imes (age 11), Amanda M. Imes (age 9), Abner R. Imes (age 6), Rosa L., Imes (age 4), and Huldah Imes (age 1).

Upton Imes (b. 1861, Pennsylvania), the son of Aaron Imes (b. 1819) m. Louisa ___ (b. 1873), and their six children were: 1) Stella Imes (b. 1894, Pennsylvania), Lester Imes (b. 1895, Pennsylvania), Marshall Imes (b. 1897), Kelly Imes (b. 1899), Percy Imes (b. 1901), and Regis Imes (b. 1913, Pennsylvania). The 1920 Census of Southampton Township, Bedford County, Pennsylvania, lists Upton Imes (age 59), Louise Imes (age 47), Lester Imes (age 24), Marshall Imes (age 23), Kelly Imes (age 21), Percy Imes (age 19), and Regis Imes (age 7).

Isaac Imes (b. 1811, also spelled Iames, Iiams), the son of William Iiams, Jr. (b. 1785), m. Mary ___ (b. 1815), and their seven children were: 1) Mary Imes (b. 1835, Bedford County, Pennsylvania), 2) Barbara Imes (b. 1839), 3) Michael Imes (b. 1841), 4) John Imes (b. 1847, Bedford County, Pennsylvania). The 1860 Census of Bedford County, Pennsylvania, lists: Isaac Imes (age 50, b. Pennsylvania), Mary Imes (age 26, b. Pennsylvania), Michael Imes (age 22), Priscilla Imes (age 18), and David Imes (age 16).

David Iames (b. 1842, Bedford County, Pennsylvania), the son of Isaac Iams (b. 1810), m. Emma or Ann ___ (b. 1844), and their three children were: 1) Thomas H. Imes [(b. December 4, 1864, Bedford County, Pennsylvania; d. March 9, 1934, Bedford County, Pennsylvania; buried in Pleasant Grove Cemetery, Cumberland, Maryland), m. Emma Elizabeth Cooper (b. June 26, 1873; d. June 18, 1920)]; 2) Martha E. Iames (b. 1867); and 3) William C. Iames (b. 1875). The 1860 Census of Southampton Township, Bedford County, Pennsylvania, lists David Iams to be the son of Isaac Iams (b. 1810) and Mary Iams (b. 1812), with Isaac Iams (age 50, b. Pennsylvania), Mary Iams (age 46), Michael Iams (age 22), Priscilla Iams (age 18), and David Iams (age 16). David Iames (b. 1842) is buried on the family farm in Southampton Township, Bedford County, Pennsylvania, that includes twelve graves of slaves caught up in their escape during the days of the "Underground Railroad" on the Lester Iames farm on Route 326 along Town Creek, south of Chaneysville, and served as the basis for the award-winning book, *The Chaneysville Incident*, by University of Pennsylvania and Temple University professor, David Bradley.

Thomas Iames (b. December 4, 1868 or 1864; d. March 9, 1934; buried in Pleasant Grove Cemetery, Baltimore Pike, Cumberland, Maryland), the son of David Iames (b. 1842), m. Emma Elizabeth Cooper (b. June 26, 1873; d. June 18, 1920).

The 1880 Census of Bedford County, Pennsylvania, lists David Iames (age 38), Ann Iames (age 36), Thomas Iames (age 16), Martha Iames (age 13), and William O. Iames (age 5). David Iames (b. 1842) is buried on the Lester Iames farm and has GAR marker from Co. 101, PVL, 1861-1865. The 1920 Census of Allegany County, Maryland, lists Thomas Imes (age 49, b. Pennsylvania), Emma E. Imes (age 46, b. West Virginia), Percy A. Imes (age 23, b. Pennsylvania), McKinley Imes (age 16, b. Pennsylvania), Besta Imes (age 12, b. Pennsylvania), and Silva Imes (age 5, b. Maryland). The seven children of Thomas Iames (b. 1868) and Emma Elizabeth Cooper (b. 1873) were: 1) Grace E. Iames [(b. February 2, 1895; d. June 2, 1992), m. May 18, 1918, to Roy Miller]; 2) Percy A. Iames [(b. May 16, 1896; d. February 28, 1934), m. Mary Virginia Iliff]; 3) Dolsie Iames Baines (b. December 10, 1897); 4) Lester Iames (b. March 18, 1900; d. March 8, 1901); 5) McKinley Iames (b. August 10, 1903; d. August 8, 1944); 6) Vista Iames Meister (b. January 12, 1908), and 7) Sylva Iames Crabtree (b. November 28, 1915). (WI)

Percy A. Iames (b. May 16, 1896; d. February 28, 1934), son of Thomas Iames (b. 1868), m. Mary Virginia Iliff (She is buried in Greenmont Cemetery in Cumberland, Maryland); he is buried at Mt. Zion Cemetery, Cumberland, Maryland, following a fatal accident while working as a conductor on the Baltimore and Ohio (B and O) Railroad at Sandpatch, Pennsylvania. The two children of Percy A. Iames (b. 1896) were: 1) Jean Virginia Iames (b. April 2, 1917; m. Donald R. Corbett); and 2) William P. Iames (b. July 8, 1924; m. Betty M. Stallings). (WI)

Jean Virginia Iames (b. April 2, 1917), daughter of Percy A. Iames (b. 1896), m. at Hancock, Maryland, to Donald R. Corbett, and they had four children: 1) Donald F. Corbett [(b. September 17, 1939), m. Wilma Jean Dival (b. May 30, 1940), lived in Hancock, Maryland; had four children: a) Donald F. Corbett, Jr. (b. October 19, 1963); b) Steve B. Corbett (b. May 1, 1959); c) Michael B. Corbett (b. November 22, 1966); and d) Cathy Jo Corbett (b. September 2, 1973)]; 2) Mary Ann Corbett [(b. August 21, 1942), m. Marvin Leslie Golden (b. May 4, 1941), lived in Hancock, Maryland; had four children: a) Tammy A. Golden Smith (b. January 27, 1963); b) Marvin Golden III (b. May 21, 1965); c) Randall Lee Golden (b. March 5, 1970), and d) Julie A. Golden (b. March 8, 1977)]; 3) Ronald Lee Corbett [(b. November 12, 1944), m. Donna Sue Pettit (b. June 22, 1948), lived in Hancock, Maryland; two children were: a) Stephanie Sue Corbett (b. December 28, 1972), and b) Melisha Dawn Corbett (b. January 3, 1978)]; 4) Marilyn Jean Corbett [(b. January 26, 1948), m. Harold Neil Walls (b. May 28, 1944), lived in Hancock, Maryland; had four children: a) Teresa Jean Walls (b. September 17, 1965); b) Harold Neil Walls, Jr. (b. May 19, 1968); c) Sandi Kay Walls (b. December 10, 1973); and d) Susie Marie Walls (b. July 2, 1970)]. (WPI)

William P. Iames, M.D. (b. July 28, 1924), the son of Percy A. Iames (b. May 16, 1896) and Mary Virginia Iliff; m. at Cooks Mills, Hyndman, Pennsylvania, to Betty M. Stallings; lived at 948 Bedford Street, Cumberland, Maryland; compiled family line; practiced medicine in Cumberland, Maryland; had four children: 1) Sandra Rae Iames [(b. August 26, 1948), m. 1st, Mr. Shircliff; m. 2nd to John Cullen; lived in Rawlings, Maryland; had two children: a) Julia M. Shircliff (b. August 28, 1970), and b) Jonathan C. Cullen (b. February 22, 1991)]; 2) William P. Iames II [(b. April 17, 1952), m. Karen S. Geatz (b. September 22, 1953); lived in Cumberland, Maryland; three children: a) William P. Iames III (b. November 11, 1975); b) Brian Iames (b. November 20, 1980); and c) Karen Ann Iames (b. August 3, 1987)]; 3) Judith Marie Iames [(b. August 24, 1954), m. Thomas McBee (b. September 26, 1950); lived at Fort Ashby, West Virginia; two children: a) Jason Thomas McBee (b. October 16, 1977); and b) Sharon Michael McBee (b. July 30, 1980)]; and 4) Christopher

Alan Iames [(b. March 15, 1963), m. Pamela J. Harman (b. March 8, 1967), lived in Fort Ashby, West Virginia; child: Brooke Ann-Marie Iames (b. February 13, 1993)].

Hugh Iiams (b. 1788), son of William Iiams (b. 1755), m. Mary Ann Huff; moved to Ohio, then Iowa; Children: 1) Mahala Iiams (m. Mr. String); 2) Sally Iiams (m. Henry Haven); 3) Priscilla Iiams (m. Mr. Inke); 4) Harriet Iiams; 5) Rachel Iiams; 6) Mary Ann Iiams; 7) Jesper Iiams; 8) Hugh Iiams, Jr.; 9) Jestine Iiams; and 10) John Iiams. On June 7, 1798, William Iiams of Bedford County, Pennsylvania, farmer, for £150 sold a tract of land called Spurgeon's Choice on Town Creek, Bedford County, Pennsylvania, to Hugh Iiams. The will of Hugh Iams, June 10, 1838, of Sandusky, Ohio, named the wife and children as listed.

Moses Iames (b. September 1, 1817; d. December 18, 1896, buried in Mt. Zion Cemetery, Southampton Township, Bedford County, Pennsylvania), m. Amy ___ (b. April 8, 1817; d. April 13, 1891, buried in Mt. Zion Cemetery, Southampton Township, Bedford County, Pennsylvania. They had a son Alfred Iames (b. November 17, 1857, Bedford County, Pennsylvania; name officially changed to Imes April 1905, at Bedford County Courthouse.

Alfred Iames (b. November 17, 1857, Bedford County, Pennsylvania: d. 1927, Bedford County, Pennsylvania; buried in Chaneysville Cemetery), m. October 3, 1879, to Nancy ___ (b. April 1, 1861; d. October 16, 1925, Bedford County, Pennsylvania; buried in Chaneysville Cemetery) and they had two children: 1) Edgar F. Imes [(b. October 31, 1884, Chaneysville, Bedford County, Pennsylvania; d. February 25, 1955, Cumberland, Maryland; buried in Chaneysville Cemetery, Southampton Township, Bedford County, Pennsylvania), m. Alice Walters (b. October 31, 1884, Bedford County, Pennsylvania; d. August 13, 1957, Chaneysville, Bedford County, Pennsylvania; buried in Chaneysville Cemetery), daughter of Hezekiah Walters (b. May 1848; d. February 1924; buried in Chaneysville Cemetery, Bedford County, Pennsylvania) and Rachel A. Walters (b. October 1859; d. February 1940; buried in Chaneysville Cemetery, Bedford County, Pennsylvania), and they had six children]; and 2) Amanda Imes (b. September 13, 1880, Chaneysville, Southampton Township, Bedford County, Pennsylvania).

The six children of Edgar F. Imes (b. 1884) and Alice Walters (b. 1884) were: 1) Chalmer M. Imes [(b. April 14, 1906, Chaneysville, Bedford County, Pennsylvania; d. April 8, 1987), m. December 24, 1926, to Alice Morgan]; 2) Melvin Imes (b. February 3, 1908; d. April 9, 1982); 3) Myrtle Imes [(b. October 6, 1910, Chaneysville, Bedford County, Pennsylvania; d. October 10, 1990), m. June 12, 1964, to Hobart Nedinger]; 4) Goldie Imes (b. April 10, 1913; d. September 18, 1961); 5) Elva Imes [(b. June 7, 1922, Chaneysville, Bedford County, Pennsylvania; alive in 1993), m. William Spencer (d. October 1994)]; and 6) Dorotha Imes [(b. October 6, 1925, Chaneysville, Southampton Township, Bedford County, Pennsylvania), m. Eddie Shannon].

Chalmer M. Imes (b. April 14, 1906) and Alice Morgan had a son, Donald D. Imes [(b. March 14, 1929, Somerset County, Pennsylvania), m. September 24, 1948, Frederick County, Virginia, to Margaret Myers (b. September 6, 1929, Roaring Spring, Pennsylvania), daughter of Wilson Myers and Anna McKnight; and granddaughter of Wesley Myers and Margaret Daniels; and they had four children: 1) G. Michael Imes [(b. February 24, 1949, Roaring Spring, Blair County, Pennsylvania), m. January 1, 1987, to Nancy Martin]; 2) David D. Imes [(b. August 17, 1950, Roaring Spring, Pennsylvania), m. March 17, 1973, to Janet Quarry]; 3) Ann M. Imes (b. November 8, 1951, Roaring Spring, Pennsylvania); and 4) Gregory L. Imes [(b. April 10, 1953, Roaring Spring, Pennsylvania), m. August 19, 1975, to Martha Pickel].

MOTHER ELIZABETH SETON, AMERICAN SAINT (1774-1821)

Thanks to the efforts of The Reverend Lucy Ijams, Amelia I. Atkinson, and Monsignor Seton, the Ijams connection with the first American Saint, "Mother Seton," has been firmly established. Much has been written about Elizabeth Ann Bayley Seton ("Mother Seton"). Born in 1774 or 1779, she was a Roman Catholic for about sixteen years and lived most of that time in poverty of relatively remote areas. As a child in New York, she learned piano, French, and "other refinements appropriate to young women of the upper classes."

After her 1797 marriage to William Seton (d. 1803) at Trinity Episcopal Church in New York, they had five children with a large household staff which permitted her to participate in the social life of New York City and to assist in the 1797 founding of the Society for the Relief of Poor Widows with small children. However, in 1800 the family business went bankrupt, and her husband, William Seton, died of tuberculosis in 1803.

Elizabeth Seton (b. 1774) became a Roman Catholic in 1805 and attempted to support her young family by teaching school and by taking in boarders. In 1808, a Baltimore college president suggested that she start a Catholic school for girls. She did accept the challenge and eventually died at the school in 1821. The school, initially called the "Paca Street House" in Baltimore, eventually moved to the town of Emmitsburg, Maryland, where the results of that beginning remain as a monument to Mother Seton. The school became known as Saint Joseph Academy and later became Saint Joseph College. The student population and the nucleus of her Sisters of Charity grew rapidly. Today there are six branches of "Mother Seton's Daughters," with "Motherhouses" in Emmitsburg, New York City, Cincinnati, Nova Scotia, and at Seton Hill College in Greensburg, Pennsylvania. Her cause for canonization was proposed in 1907; her virtues declared "heroic" in 1959; title of "Venerable" conferred also in 1959; her beatification with title "Blessed" bestowed in 1963; and was proclaimed "Saint Elizabeth Ann Seton" by Pope Paul VI on September 14, 1975.

Her sons went to boarding school at Georgetown in 1806, and the girls remained with their mother. The sons were later schooled at Leghorn (Livorno) near Pisa on the coast of Italy. The scripture passage believed responsible for much of the influence of the life of Mother Seton was, "My grace is sufficient for thee, for my power is made perfect in weakness." About death, she wrote: "All I know is that we must all be ready for this dear, dearest thief who is to come when least expected."

Elizabeth Ann Bayley (b. August 28, 1774, New York, New York; d. January 4, 1821, Emmitsburg, Maryland), m. January 25, 1794, New York's Trinity Episcopal Church, to William Magee Seton (b. 1768; d. December 21, 1803, in Italy), the son of William Seton, Sr. [(b. 1746; d. 1798) and Rebecca Curson (m. 1767), daughter of Richard Curson and Elizabeth Rebecca Baker], an importer, founder of Bank of New York and founder of Seton, Maitland, and Company. Children of William Seton, Sr. (b. 1746) and Rebecca Curson included: 1) William Magee Seton [(b. 1768; d. 1803); m. 1794 to Elizabeth Ann Bayley ("Mother Seton," Saint Elizabeth Ann Seton)]; 2) James Seton [(b. 1770), m. 1798 to Mary Hoffman, daughter of Nicholas Hoffman and Sarah Ogden]; 3) John Curson Seton [(m. 1st, 1799, to Mary Wise; m. 2nd to ___ Gorham)]; 4) Henry Seton (Lieutenant, United States Navy); and 5) Ann Marie Seton (m. 1790, U.S. Senator John Middleton Vining of Delaware). William Seton, Sr. (b. 1746) m. 2nd, in 1776, to his sister-in-law, Anna Marie Curson (d. 1812), and their children included: 6) Rebecca Seton (b. 1780; d. 1804); 7) Mary Seton (m. Josiah Ogden Hoffman); 8) Charlotte Seton [(b. 1786; d. 1852);

m. 1800, to Gouverneur Ogden, law partner of Alexander Hamilton]; 9) Elizabeth Seton [(b. 1779; d. 1807); m. 1797 to James Maitland, and serves as the Ijams line of decendency]; 10) Cecelia Seton (b. 1791; d, 1810); 11) Harriet Seton (b. 1787; d. 1809); 12) Edward Augustus Seton (b. 1790; lived in Louisiana); and 13) Samuel Waddington Seton [(b. 1789; d. 1869), Superintendent of New York City Public Schools].

Elizabeth Bayley Seton (b. 1774) was the daughter of Richard Bayley, M.D. (b. 1744; d. 1801) and Catherine Charlton (d. 1777), the daughter of Reverend Richard Charlton of Saint Andrew's Episcopal Church, Richmond, Long Island, New York. (He m. 2nd, 1778, to Charlotte Amelia Barclay, daughter of Andrew Barclay and Helena Roosevelt). Other children of Richard Bayley (b. 1744) and Catherine Charlton were: 1) Mary Magdalen Bayley (b. 1768; m. Dr. Wright Post); 2) Catherine Bayley (b. 1777; d. 1778); and children of Richard Bayley (b. 1744) and second wife, Charlotte Barclay, were: 3) Charlotte Amelia "Emma" Bayley (b. 1805; m. William Craig); 4) Mary Fitch Bayley (m. Sir Robert Henry Bunch); 5) William Augustus Bayley (d. 1818); 6) Richard Bayley [(b. 1781; d. 1815; m. 1812, to Catherine White]; 7) Andrew Barclay Bayley (d. 1811); 8) Guy Carlton Bayley [(b. 1786; d. 1859; m. 1813, to Grace Roosevelt, and were parents of Archbishop of Baltimore James Roosevelt Bayley]; and 9) Helen Bayley [(b. 1790, d. 1848), m. 1818, to Samuel Craig]. Richard Bayley, M.D. (b. 1744) was considered to be an authority on yellow fever, and while he was the health officer for the Port of New York, in 1796, established the Staten Island quarantine station.

Children of William Magee "Willy" Seton, Jr. (b. 1768) and Elizabeth Ann Bayley ("Mother Seton," Saint Elizabeth Ann Seton) were: 1) Anna Maria Seton [(b. 1795, New York City; d. March 12, 1812, Emmitsburg, Maryland), and her death at age 16 was a significant, depressing event in the life of her mother]; 2) William Seton III [(b. 1796, New York City; d. 1868), m. 1832, to Emily Prime (b. 1804; d. 1854); served in U.S. Navy from 1818 to 1834]; 3) Prime Seton (b. New York City, served in U.S. Navy); 4) Richard "Ricksey" "Dicksey" Seton [(b. 1798, New York City; d. 1823), member of U.S. Navy in 1822 and 1823]; 5) Catherine Josephine Seton (b. 1800, New York City; d. 1891); and 6) Rebecca "Bec" Seton [(b. 1802, New York City; d. 1816, Emmitsburg, Maryland); a death taken as a mere temporary separation by Mother Seton, rather than as a major loss].

Elizabeth Seton (b. 1779), daughter of William Seton (b. 1746, Scotland) and Anna Maria Curzon and double first cousin of Elizabeth Ann Bayley (b. 1774), m. James Maitland, and their daughter, Rebecca Seton Maitland m. Benjamin Porter. The son of Benjamin Porter and Rebecca Seton Maitland, Robert Hobart Porter, m. Annie Metcalfe Dwight, whose son was Henry Hobart Porter (m. Katharine Porter). The daughter of Henry Hobart Porter and Katharine Porter was Margaret Seton Porter, who m. John Horton Ijams, Sr. (b. 1884), the son of John Tabb Ijams (b. 1852) and Phoebe Adele Smith; the grandson of James Iiams (b. 1818) and Dorcas Susan Mitchell Tabb; the great-grandson of Plummer Ijams (b. 1780) and Rebecca Ijams (daughter of John Iiams and Mary Waters); the great-great-grandson of Plummer Ijams and Jemima Welch; and the great-great-great-grandson of Plummer and Ruth Ijams. The children of John Horton Ijams, Sr. (b. 1884) and Margaret Seton Porter (daughter of Henry Hobart Porter and Katharine Delano Porter) were: 1) John Horton Ijams (b. 1918); 2) Seton Ijams [(b. 1922), m. Anne Mellen, and their four children included author Lucy Ijams (b. 1955); 3) Maitland Tabb Ijams (b. 1926); and 4) Porter Ijams (b. 1930).

Henry Wright Newman (1970) has outlined the lineage of the Ijams family to the point that it intersects the family line of Elizabeth Ann Bayley Seton ("Mother Seton," Saint Elizabeth Ann Seton). Plummer Ijams (b. October 29, 1748, All

Hallows Parish, Anne Arundel County, Maryland; will probated February 27, 1795, Frederick County, Maryland), son of Plummer Ijams (baptized August 6, 1718, All Hallows Parish, Anne Arundel County, Maryland) and Ruth Childs; m. Jemima Welsh (b. October 27, 1760; d. April 16, 1789), daughter of Benjamin and Rebecca Welsh; and in 1784, moved to Wild Cat Hill in Frederick County, Maryland, with some of the land later called Ijams Resolution. The children of Plummer Ijams (b. 1748) and Jemima Welsh (b.1760) were: 1) Anne Ijams [(b. September 17, 1778), m. January 29, 1799, Anne Arundel County, Maryland, to George Sacks]; 2) Plummer Ijams (b. March 8, 1781), m. 1st, Rebecca Ijams, daughter of John Ijams and Mary Waters Ijams; m. 2nd, Mary Montgomery]; 3) Ruth Ijams [(b. November 13, 1783), m. December 19, 1799, to Christopher Mussetter]; Rebecca Ijams [(b. October 28, 1785), m. Benjamin Duvall]; and 5) John Ijams [(b. April 3, 1789), m. Catherine Barnes].

This Plummer Ijams (baptized March 8, 1781, Doden, All Hallows Parish, Anne Arundel County, Maryland; d. June 25, 1849), m. 1st, (license date) March 15, 1804, to Rebecca Ijams (d. November 10, 1809) and their child was: 1) Plummer Ijams [(b. February 26, 1805); m. Harriet Mussetter]; and m. 2nd, in 1815 (license issued February 27, 1815, Frederick County, Maryland) to Mary Ann Montgomery [(b. October 22, 1796; d. January 7, 1829, buried Mt. Olivet Cemetery, Fredericksburg, Maryland), daughter of John Montgomery], and they had five additional children]; 2) John Ijams (b. 1817; d. 1824); 3) James Ijams, the Mother Seton line, [(b. June 21, 1819, Frederick County, Maryland; d. June 30, 1873, Baltimore, Maryland), m. December 6, 1849, to Dorcas Susan Mitchell Tabb (d. April 1896, New York City), daughter of John Tabb of Berkeley County, Virginia]; 4) Richard Ijams [(b. August 2, 1821), m. Elizabeth Aldridge Mussetter]; 5) Joshan Ijams [(b. June 9, 1825), m. May 19, 1847, Frederick County, Maryland, to William Saunders Brown of King George County, Virginia]; and 6) Charles Montgomery Ijams (b. 1827; d. 1828). During this time, Plummer Ijams (b. 1781) was a member of the Maryland State Legislature, representing Frederick County, Maryland, from the village of Ijamsville.

This James Ijams (b. 1819) and Dorcas Susan Mitchell Tabb had nine children: 1) Plummer Montgomery Ijams (b. December 12, 1850; d. November 26, 1901); 2) John Tabb Ijams [(b. August 27, 1852, Berkeley County, Virginia; d. July 23, 1923, New York City); m. April 20, 1881, New York City, to Phoebe Adele Smith (b. December 7, 1852; d. January 4, 1931, New York City)]; 3) James Edgar Ijams (b. December 9, 1854; d. September 22, 1862); 4) Arabella Janney Ijams (b. May 2, 1856; d. April 14, 1864); 5) Raleigh Brown Ijams (b. September 12, 1858; d. April 8, 1887); 6) Elizabeth Ijams (b. November 25, 1859; d. December 23, 1947); 7) Martin Turner Ijams (b. February 25, 1861; d. March 17, 1892); 8) Joshan Ijams [(b. September 6, 1864; d. June 26, 1895), m. James Cambell Malcolm, Sr.]; and 9) James Edgar Ijams, the younger (b. August 6, 1865 d. December 23, 1938).

John Tabb Ijams (b. August 27, 1852, Berkeley County, Virginia; d. July 23, 1923, New York City), son of James Ijams (b. 1819) and Dorcas Tabb; m. April 20, 1881, New York City, to Phoebe Adele Smith (b. December 7, 1852; d. January 4, 1931, New York City), daughter of Isaac H. Smith, and their two children were: 1) Adele Ethel Ijams (b. April 16, 1883; d. April 16, 1883); and 2) John Horton Ijams [the Mother Seton connection (b. November 20, 1884, New York City; d. March 11, 1957, New York City), m. May 8, 1915, New York City, to Margaret Seton Porter (b. August 11, 1895, New York City; d. June 16, 1987, New York City; buried in Hewlett, New York), daughter of Henry Hobart Porter and Katharine Delano and the granddaughter of Robert Hobart Porter; and they had four children: a) John Horton Ijams (b. 1918); b) Seton Ijams (d. 1922); c) Maitland Tabb Ijams (b. 1926); and d) Porter Ijams (b. 1930)].

John Horton "Jack" Ijams (b. August 27, 1918, Lawrence, Nassau County, Long Island, New York; d. over North Africa during World War II, January 12, 1943). Seton Ijams [(b. October 9, 1922, Lawrence, Long Island, Nassau County, New York; d. July 17, 1993, Bath, Maine; buried in Hewlett, New York), m. June 9, 1951, Cedarhurst, New York, to Anne Seymour Clark Mellen (b. May 14, 1922, New York City), daughter of Joseph Manley Mellen and Sylvia Belden Wigglesworth and granddaughter of Chase Mellen; and they had four children: Lucy Manley Ijams (b. 1955), John Horton Ijams (b. 1956), William Seton Ijams (b. August 23, 1957, New York City), and Henry Wigglesworth Ijams (b. May 4, 1961, New York City; m. November 11, 1990, High Point, North Carolina, to Virginia Clay Corpening, and they had a son, Chase Mellen Ijams, b. November 3, 1993, in New York City)]. John Horton Ijams [(b. August 1, 1956, New York City), m. September 24, 1983, South Dartmouth, Massachusetts, to Sarah Howell Blatchford (b. August 20, 1957, South Dartmouth, Massachusetts), daughter of John Blatchford and Susan Brown; and their two children were: Katharine Seton Ijams (b. April 26, 1987, Greenwich, Connecticut) and Phoebe Lord Blatchford Ijams (b. November 3, 1989, Bridgeport, Connecticut)]. Maitland Tabb Ijams [(b. September 1, 1926, Lawrence, Nassau County, Long Island, New York; summer theater producer; member of Wall Street), m. Alexander Ainsworth Bunn; and they had two children: 1) Margaret Ditson Ijams [(b. September 4, 1954, New York City), m. October 6, 1984, Hewlett, New York, to Wayne A. Josephson, and their three children were: Bradford Delano Josephson (b. October 29, 1987), William Seton Josephson (b. September 18, 1992), and Margaret Ijams Josephson (June 1993)]; and 2) Maitland Tabb Ijams (b. September 14, 1951, New York City). Porter Ijams [b. December 24, 1930, New York City), a correspondent for this branch of the family tree, m. Jean Drummond; and he had three children: 1) Rachel Lee Ijams (b. 1958; m. J. Peter Schmader at Princeton, New Jersey, and they had two children: Samuel Drummond Schmader, b. August 18, 1989; and Edward Schmader); 2) Allison Drummond Ijams (b. 1960; m. September 8, 1984, Princeton, New Jersey, to Thomas Sargent; and they had three children including Katharine Sargent and William Sargent); and 3) Katharine Porter Ijams (b. 1962).

The New York Times reported the June 19, 1987, obituary of Margaret Seton Porter Ijams (b. August 11, 1895, New York City; d. June 16, 1987, New York City), wife of John Horton Ijams (b. 1884; d. 1957), as follows: "Margaret Seton Ijams, a former vice-president of the Community Service Society, New York's oldest family welfare organization, died Tuesday in her Manhattan apartment. She was 92 years old and also lived in Lawrence, Long Island. Mrs. Ijams was a collateral descendant of Mother Elizabeth Bayley Seton, the first native-born American to become a saint. In 1917, she joined the board of the Virginia Day Nursery, which her mother helped found in 1879, and remained on the board until her death. She was also active on the board of the Community Service Society and the Federation of Protestant Welfare Agencies. She is survived by three sons: Seton of Bowdoinham, Maine; Maitland of Barneveld, New York; and Porter of Locust Valley, Long Island; nine grandchildren and one great-grandchild."

Lucy Manley Ijams (b. February 10, 1955, New York City), daughter of Seton Ijams (b. October 9, 1922; d. July 17, 1993) and Anne Seymour Mellen (b. 1922, New York City) has worked as a co-author on this important portion of the Ijams family history. Currently serving as a Unitarian Universalist parish minister in Meriden, Connecticut, she received her Master of Divinity in 1994 from Andover Newton Theological School; interned in 1995 at Emerson Unitarian Church of Houston, Texas; described herself as a feminist and activist; served as student minister, youth leader, chaplain, adult leader and counselor, freelance writer, U.S. Census enumerator, worker for Area Agency on Aging, owner of a house cleaning enterprise, customer service representative for L. L. Bean; obtained BA from Hofstra University after first attending University of Hartford and Wykeham Rise School of Washington, Connecticut; with special interests in drama, sculpture, creative writing, anthropology, and sociology; served as President of Oratorio Chorale; was chair for Nuclear Freeze; editor of Peace Center Newsletter; ran political campaign fund raising and telemarketing efforts; drove an airport limousine; worked as an occupational therapist; taught classes for retarded adults; performed several personal musical and thespian concerts and plays; has traveled in France, Italy, Mexico, and Jamaica; and has personal interests in public radio, singing, music, movies, drama, reading, television, aerobic exercises, peer counseling, support groups and workshops. She is of the belief that the Ijams may have come from the Frisian (Friesian) Islands off the northern coast of Netherlands and Germany as a "Teutonic Tribe." In support of this, she has pointed out that the Dutch are one of the few who use "I" and "J" as adjacent letters in some of their works. the "Zuider Zee" is also known as "Ijsslmeer." "Ijssel" is a river in Holland, and Ijmuiden is a town in the Netherlands. These ideas about the origin of the family that migrated to America in the seventeenth century are as good as any others, though the theories of Lois Ijam Hartman of Pasadena, and as expressed in the Harry Wright Newman publication of a British Isles origin have been widely accepted to date.

REFERENCES

- Kelly E. and Melville A., eds, Elizabeth Seton: *Selected Writings* (Paulist Press, New York, 1985).

- Monsignor Seton, *An Old Family—The Setons in Scotland and America* (New York, 1899).

- Mrs. Guy Atkinson, East 46th Street, New York City; personal research.

- Lucy Ijams, Bath, Maine; personal research and communications.

- Harry Wright Newman, *Anne Arundel Gentry* (privately published 1937 and 1970).

- *Collier Encyclopedia*, Volume 5 (P. F. Collier Corporation, New York, 1955), pp. 31-32.

- Robert I. Dirvin, *Mrs. Seton: Founder of American Sisters of Charity* (Farrah, Straus, and Giroux Pub., New York, 1962).

- Marey Heidesh, *Miracles: A Novel About Mother Seton* (New American Library Pub., New York, 1984).

- *New York Times*, obituary section, June 19, 1987.

- (EFB) Ervin F. Bickley, Jr., personal communications, 1994.

- (HWN) Harry Wright Newman, *Anne Arundel Gentry* (1933, 1970).

- Court House Records, Bedford County, Pennsylvania; Allegany County, Maryland.

- David Bradley, *The Chaneysville Incident* (Harper Row, New York, 1981).

- (DDI) Donald D. Imes, Cumberland, Maryland; personal files, Roaring Springs.

- (WI) Doctor William Iames, Cumberland, Maryland; personal files.

— CHAPTER 10 —

WILLIAM IAMS (1793-1859)

Thomas Iiams (b. Maryland, December 26, 1754; d. 1834, Belmont County, Ohio) and his family, except for son William (b. 1793), moved from Washington County in western Pennsylvania, to Ohio and made their home on a road leading from Ohio Route 147, between Key and Jacobsburg, near Glencoe, in Belmont County. He was granted a Revolutionary War pension (Claim 58751), but died before he received it. Thomas (b. 1754) and two of his brothers (John and William) each had married one of the Hampton sisters and settled in Washington County, Pennsylvania. A son of William Iams (b. 1793) was John Wesley "Wesley" Iams (b. 1828), who moved first to Belmont County, Ohio, and then to land he owned in Ritchie County, West Virginia. A daughter of Wesley Iams (b. 1828) was Iola Ellen Iams (b. 1879). Iola and her brothers and sisters grew up in Ritchie County, West Virginia, and serve as the subjects of this section. Iola Iams (b. 1879) married William Milton "Milton" Corbett, and one of their daughters was Edna Louise Corbett born near Caldwell, Noble County, Ohio, June 29, 1906), who grew up in Mead Township, Belmont County, Ohio, married Ray Campbell Reynolds (b. December 4, 1904; d. December 26, 1988), the father of Ralph D. Reynolds, M.D. and Robert W. Reynolds, and died March 9, 1997.

Thomas Iiams, believed to be the son of John Iiams (b. 1720) or Thomas Iiams (1708-1768), was born December 26, 1754, in All Hallows Parish, Anne Arundel County, Maryland, and his tombstone in Old Dutch Cemetery, near St. Clairsville and Glencoe, Belmont County, Ohio, indicates that he died June 21, 1834. He was a Revolutionary War soldier and his records erroneously list death date as May 12, 1838. He was a member of the Presbyterian Church and worked as a miller, owning his own business in Glencoe, Ohio. He married Catherine "Katy" Gill Hampton, November 29, 1785, in Anne Arundel County, Maryland, Catherine Hampton was born about 1766 and died May 12, 1838, being buried in the same Old Dutch Cemetery in Richfield Township, Belmont County, Ohio. Thomas Iiams (b. 1754) was described as one of the "community's most esteemed citizens." He "served seven years under George Washington in the Revolutionary War."

After leaving Maryland, Thomas Iiams (b. 1754) settled in the Ten Mile Valley in southern Washington County, Pennsylvania; and later moved to Glencoe in Belmont County, Ohio. He enlisted as a private in the Maryland Line on June 10, 1777. He was later promoted to sergeant and received his discharge January 1, 1780. Official records show he was pensioned May 12, 1834, but it is said that he died before he was paid. On November 19, 1796, voting records of Frederick County, Maryland, show that he voted for George Murdock as the Republican Presidential Electorate. One recorded official account lists Thomas Iiams (b. 1754) as being in charge of a Revolutionary War recruiting party in May 177, when he allegedly ordered his troops to "fire and fix bayonets." There is no report of any damage being done. Charges were brought against Thomas Iiams (b. 1754), but it is believed that these charges were dropped after he made a court appearance. Three of the children of Thomas and Catherine Gill Hampton were said to have been born in Maryland before their move to western Pennsylvania. Of their children, only William Iiams (b. 1793) failed to move from western Pennsylvania to Ohio. The tombstone of Thomas and Catherine Hampton, in the abandoned Old Dutch Cemetery about a quarter of a mile south of the road between Saint Clairsville and Glencoe in Belmont County, Ohio, is a magnificent structure about nine feet tall (photo inclosed) with the top of each of the four sides decorated (ear of corn on the south; grapes on the west; flowers on the east, and peaches, pears, and plums on the north). The marker serves both Thomas and Catherine Iams and their son and wife, Samuel and Elizabeth Meek Iiams. (References: DAR Records, E. B. Iiams, Mildred McKelvey, and others). Children of Thomas Iiams (b. 1754):

1) William Iiams [(b. September 6, 1793; d. April 30, 1859, Amity, Washington County, Pennsylvania), m. Susanna Sharp (continued)];
2) Richard Iiams [(m. Fanny Meeks, daughter of William Meeks of Monroe County, Ohio, and said to live in Richland County, Ohio, in 1818];
3) Thomas Iiams, Jr. [m. either Mary "Polly" Hardesty, daughter of Obidiah and Mary "From Paris" Hardesty in Virginia, 1789, or first cousin Mary Iams. Lived in Belmont County, Ohio; marriage certificate issued August 2, 1823, by J. P. Crawford, with Solomon Hardesty providing voucher, with Jams as spelling on wedding certificate. "Polly" lived to age 102; was a Quaker; buried at Morristown, Belmont County, Ohio. They had a daughter, Keziah "Cassy" Iams];
4) Samuel Iiams [(b. caMarch 1, 1801, or in 1795; d. August 21, 1866; buried in Old Dutch Cemetery, Richland Township, Belmont County, Ohio; m. Elizabeth Meek (d. November 18, 1866). In 1815 they purchased a farm in Section 34, Township 5, Range 3, in Belmont County, Ohio. They had no children and lived with his parents];
5) Polly Iams [m. Jacob Eggy. Polly was the grandmother of Mary Iams Freer];
6) John Iiams [believed to be a single son (inconclusive)];
7) Elizabeth Iiams [a single daughter; died at age 86 and buried in Old Dutch Cemetery, Belmont County, Ohio. The 1880 West Virginia Census of Ritchie County lists her as being age 77, born in Pennsylvania, with both of her parents having been born in Maryland];
8) Charity Iiams [(b. 1805), m. December 5, 1832, by J. P. George Meade, to Jacob Myers of Smith Township, Belmont County, Ohio];
9) Rezin or Reason (among other spellings) Iiams [(b. December 18, 1807; d. November 17, 1873, and buried in Bell's Cemetery, Olive Township, Noble County, Ohio), m. November 29, 1831, in Belmont County, Ohio, to Mary Myers, daughter of Daniel and Elizabeth Swaggler Myers];
10) Rebecca Iiams (m. Jacob Wilson in Belmont County, Ohio);
11) Catherine Iiams [(b. January 25, 1812; d. May 8, 1880; buried in Old Dutch Cemetery), m. March 10, 1831, to Michael Ault (b. Washington County, Pennsylvania; d. 1848) of Richland Township, Belmont County, Ohio, and sworn by Rezin Iiams; Michael Ault was a prominent citizen; a Presbyterian; owned mills in Glencoe, Ohio].

William Iiams (b. September 6, 1793; d. April 30, 1859, Amity, Pennsylvania); m. Susannah "Susan" Sharp (b. April 27, 1795; d. February 6, 1883, and buried in Amity M.E. Cemetery, Washington County, Pennsylvania). The 1859 will of William Iiams names his eight children, listed below. Crumrine's *History of Washington County, Pennsylvania* (page 661) lists: "William Iams, son of Thomas Iams, Revolutionary War soldier. The Methodist Protestant Church of Amity, Amwell

Township, was organized in 1832 by the Monongahela Circuit. William Iams and Joel Woods, of Amity, invited the Reverends John Wilson and Israel Thorp, itinerant ministers of the church, to preach at Amity in the fall of 1831. Early in January 1832, a class was organized at the house of William Iams, which consisted of the following persons: Joel Wood, William and Susannah Iams, N. B. Clutter, and Mary Thompson. Soon after, the Society purchased for fifty dollars the old log church used by the Presbyterians, since that group was about to erect a new one. A lot was donated by William Iams upon which they erected a house using the logs of the old church. This was used as a place of worship until 1851 when, at a cost of $500.00, they erected on the same site a neat frame house in which they worshipped until 1867. Since they needed a larger house, they sold the old church and erected another frame building in which they still continue to worship. In 1882 there was a membership of one hundred and thirty-three."

The Amity, Washington County, Pennsylvania, cemetery contains several Iams tombstones, including: William (September 8,1793-April 30, 1857) and Susannah Iams (April 27, 1795-February 6, 1883); Delilah Iams (April 23,1823-June 28, 1866); Jehu Iams (June 30, 1822-April 11, 1903) and Phoebe McCracken (August 22, 1825-January 30, 1909); Franklin F. Iams (July 11, 1836-May 3,1906, Civil War veteran; and Mary E. Iams (February 11, 1839-July 26, 1913). Mary E. Iams was Mary Ellen Bane and wife of Franklin F. Iams. The 1850 Federal Census of Washington County, Pennsylvania, included William Iams, age 57; Susannah Iams, age 55; John Iams, age 28; Salem Iams, age 35; Delila Iams, age 25; Wesley Iams, age 22; Charity Iams, age 18; Franklin Iams, age 15; and Phoebe Iams, age 23. The 1860 Census listed Susannah Iams, age 64, born in Maryland, in the household with Franklin Iams, age 24, and Delilah Iams, age 30. The 1870 Census listed Susannah Iams, age 74, again in the Franklin Iams household.

William Iams owned at least 109 acres in the Ten Mile region. In January 1832 the Methodist Church of Amity, Pennsylvania, first met as a class in his home. He later donated land for a log cabin church. Then, in 1851 on the same site, a frame church was built for five hundred dollars. In 1867 the building was sold to Doctor S. S. Strouse and the congregation built a larger (38 x 33 feet) church.

The will of William Iams (Volume 8, page 132, Washington County, Pennsylvania) was written March 26, 1859, and probated May 2, 1859. The estate was left to his widow Susannah Iams with the request that he be buried at the MP Cemetery in Amity, Pennsylvania. The residual estate was to be divided equally among the children: Salem Iiams, Eleanor Iiams, Jehu Iiams, Delilah Iiams, Wesley Iiams, Charity Iiams, Jane Iiams, and Franklin Iiams. George Swart was a witness to the will. The will of Delilah Iiams of Amwell Township, Washington County, Pennsylvania, was probated June 19, 1866 (Volume 9, page 197). Sister Jane Baldwin was given twenty-five dollars and Flora Baldwin, daughter of Jane Baldwin, was given "the saddle," with the remainder to be equally divided among three brothers: Wesley Iiams, John Iiams, and Franklin Iiams, and with a sister, Charity Elliott. The children of William Iiams (b. 1793) and Susannah Sharp were:

1) Charity J. Iiams [(b. April 23, 1825, or November 23, 1830; d. December 13, 1921; buried at Amity, Pennsylvania); active in Missionary Society; m. Sebastian B. Elliott (b. March 28, 1835, or November 28, 1825; d. August 22, 1909); their children were: Reverend John Alonzo Elliott (1869-December 15, 1917); Siddie Elliott (1861-1865); William Elliott; Clark Elliott; Eva Elliott (m. Tom Frazer); and Elizabeth Elliott (m. Herbert McAfee)];
2) Delilah Iiams [(b. April 23, 1825; d. June 28, 1866; buried at Amity, Pennsylvania; single];

3) Eleanor "Ellen" Iiams [(b. December 26, 1819); m. Daniel Eller; no children];
4) Elizabeth Jane "Jane" Iiams [(b. June 26, 1835, or June 6, 1838; d. 1878; buried Washington, Pennsylvania), m. Reverend John Seth Baldwin; their children were: Collier Baldwin and Flora Baldwin (m. W. L. Milne)];
5) Salem Iiams [(b. April 6, 1817; d. January 17, 1887, or January 11, 1789; buried at Beallsville, Pennsylvania); m. May 8, 1955, to Elizabeth Ann Deems (b. October 29, 1823, or 1833, at Clarksville, Greene County, Pennsylvania; d. April 1892); owned land in Ritchie County, West Virginia); continued];
6) Franklin F. "F.F." "Frank" Iiams [(b. July 11, 1826, or 1834; d. May 3, 1906; buried with GAR marker at Amity, Pennsylvania); m. Mary Ellen Bane (b. February 11, 1839; d. July 13, 1913); their children were: William H. Iiams (b. February 10, 1866; d. February 2, 1877); George L. Iiams (b. February 28, 1868; d. February 17, 1913); and Ella Iiams (b. 1869];
7) John "Wesley" Iiams [(b. March 8, 1828; d. September 23, 1894; buried Chevauxdefrise Methodist Church, Ritchie County, West Virginia); m. 1st, to Caroline or Catherine Scales; m. 2nd, to Nancy McKelvey (continued)];
8) Jehu or John or Jonathan Iiams [(b. June 30, 1822; d. April 11, 1903); m. Phoebe McCracken (b. August 22, 1825; d. November 30, 1909); purchased land from I. M. Wilson on "waters of the Chevauxdefrise, Virginia," Ritchie County, West Virginia, in 1847; children were: Alice Iams (m. Mr. Cook); Florence Iams, single; Elizabeth Iams (m. Mr. Ernest); Martha Iams (m. Mr. Menzer); George Iams; and Frank Iams].

Salem Iiams (b. West Bethlehem Township, Washington County, Pennsylvania; b. April 6, 1817; d. January 11, 1887; buried at Beallsville, Pennsylvania); m. Washington County, Pennsylvania, May 8, 1955, to Elizabeth Ann Deems (b. October 29, 1823; d. April 1892). Salem Iiams (b. 1817) was the son of William Iiams (b. 1793). Children of Salem Iiams and Elizabeth Ann Deems were:

1) Neva Eugenia Iiams [(b. September 25, 1860); m. Joseph A. Huffman; no children];
2) Elmer Jay Iiams [(b. Washington County, Pennsylvania, April 30, 1865); m. August 21, 1890, Anna Laurena Camp; worked at Washington County, Pennsylvania, court house; compiled an early Iiams family genealogy and a founder of National Iiams Association which held national reunions in the 1930s, including reunions at Ten Mile Baptist Church, Amwell Township, Amity, Ten Mile, Washington County, Pennsylvania; their five children were; a) Sarah Malverne Iiams (b. February 18, 1892); b) Amber Eugenia Iiams (b. November 23, 1898), m. June 28, 1924, to Thomas Nuttall; c) Harrison Jay Iiams (b. November 15, 1895), m. December 24, 1920, to Christine McDougal; buried in Monongahela Cemetery; two children: 1¹) Edward E. Iiams (b. 1909); 2¹) Viola Jane Iiams (b. March 11, 1924); 3¹) Elmer Duncan Iiams (b. April 13, 1922); d) Irene Camp Iiams (b. January 3, 1903); m. March 22, 1924, to Peter Gerard; their children were 1¹) Mary Laurena Gerard (b. Donora, Pennsylvania, October 3, 1924), m. Charleroi, Pennsylvania, March 22, 1947, to Clarence LeRoy Matson (b. Charleroi, Pennsylvania, January 10, 1923; d. March 30, 1989, Charleroi, Pennsylvania; buried Monongahela Cemetery); contributed to history; a¹) Edward Clarence Matson (b. March 9, 1948, North Charleroi, Pennsylvania); m. March 1966 to Linda Silbaugh; b¹) Nancy Laurena Matson (b. March 3, 1950, North Charleroi,

Pennsylvania); m. December 12, 1970, to John L. Avay/Avau (b. October 16, 1949, Charleroi, Pennsylvania), son of John G. Avau and Ann M. Christinis, and grandson of Leon Avau and Susan Hauths; children:1) Michael John Avau (b. Feb. 19, 1976); 2) Carolyn Suzanne Avau; c[1]) Carol Lee Matson (b. July 25, 1953, North Charleroi, Pennsylvania), m. October 1975 to Bruce Weitzmer; e) Edward E. Iiams (b. March 3, 1900; d. March 9, 1909; buried Monongahela, Pennsylvania)];

    3) Tard Samuel Iiams [(b. December 17, 1869; d. August 30, 1931); single].

    Franklin F. "F.F." "Frank" Iams (b. July 11, 1834), son of William Iiams (b. 1793), was a Justice of the Peace in Amwell Township, Washington County, Pennsylvania, on March 21, 1877. He owned 21 acres of land near Amity, Pennsylvania, about 1878, and was a Civil War veteran, serving in the 140th Pennsylvania Infantry, being wounded at Petersburg, Virginia, near the close of the war. At Cold Harbor on June 5, 1864, Company D was on the left flank when F.F. Iams and his buddy John Clauser became overly curious and wandered forward beyond the enemy line of the left flank. They discovered a Confederate group in the process of organizing an attack. The Confederates discovered the adventurers and began to retreat. As they retreated, they fired their weapons and the noise alerted the other Union troops, thus saving the day for Company D.

    The 1850 Federal Census of Washington County, Pennsylvania, listed Franklin as age 15, born in Pennsylvania, son of William and Susannah Iams. In the 1860 Census, Franklin, age 24, is listed as a teacher and in the household headed by Susannah Iams, age 64. Nearby was the household of John or Job Iams, age 37, with wife Phoebe Iams, age 35, and children Elizabeth Iams, age 9; Mary Iams, age 8; Sarah Iams, age 6; William Iams, age 5; George Iams, age 3; and Lorena Iams, age 1. The 1870 Census lists Franklin Iams as age 33; Mary E. Iams, age 31; William H. Iams, age 4; George L. Iams, age 2; and mother Susannah Iams, age 75. In the 1880 Census of Washington County, Pennsylvania, is listed Frank Iams, age 43; Mary E. Iams, age 41; William Iams, age 14; George L. Iams, age 12; Mary F. Iams, age 5; and mother Susannah Iams, age 85. In the 1900 Census Franklin F. Iams was listed as age 63; Mary E. Iams, 63; and daughter Mary F. Iams, age 24. George Iams is a head of household, age 32; with wife Rachel Iams, age 29; son William J. Iams, age 8; and son Henry F. Iams, age 4. The 1910 Census of Washington County, Pennsylvania, lists G. L. Iams as age 41; wife Ella R. Iams, age 40; son William J. Iams, age 18; and son Henry F. Iiams, age 14. Children of Franklin F. Iams were:

    1) William H. Iams [(b. February 10, 1866; d. February 2, 1887; buried at Amity Methodist Cemetery, Washington County, Pennsylvania)];

    2) George L. Iams [(b. February 28, 1868, Washington County, Pennsylvania; d. February 17, 1913; lived at Amity, Pennsylvania), m. Ella Wolf (b. Greene County, Pennsylvania, on July 31, 1869); daughter of Hiram H. Wolf and Elizabeth Ann Tucker; both are buried at Amity, Washington County, Pennsylvania; other children of Hiram H. Wolf were James Wolf, George B. Wolf, Katherine (Wolf) Garner, and Margaret (Wolf) Ward. Children of George L. Iams and Ella Wolf were: a) William J. Iams; lived at Laboratory, Washington County, Pennsylvania; d. December 2, 1958; m. November 17, 1915, at Houston, Pennsylvania, to Olive Anderson (b. December 15, 1884, Houston, Pennsylvania; d. April 15, 1991, Washington, Washington County, Pennsylvania); daughter of James H. Anderson and Elizabeth Buckingham; members of First United Methodist Church, Washington, Pennsylvania; their children were: 1[1]) Catherine Iams, lived in Washington, Pennsylvania; m. William. A.

Dennison, and had the following children: Reed Dennison; Robert Dennison; Cathy Dennison; b) Henry F. Iams (b. Amity, Pennsylvania, January 12, 1896; d. in Southern Pacific Railroad Hospital in San Francisco, California, April 18, 1947); lived at Amity, Pennsylvania, until 1945 and then moved to California; member Amity Methodist Church, Amity, Washington County, Pennsylvania; m. Nell Bradley; and their children were: 1¹) Virginia Iams, m. H. W. Wright of Amity, Pennsylvania; and 2¹) William J. Iams, lived in Washington County, Pennsylvania];
3) Florence Iams [(b. 1862; d. 1938); buried in same area].

Ritchie County, West Virginia (Virginia) Land Transfers:

1) April 5, 1847 - Between J. M. Wilson and wife Sarah; and John Imes of Washington County, Pennsylvania; John paid $800 for 50 acres on Chevauxdefrise Creek, adjacent to Wilson land.

2) November 18, 1852 - From John Iiams and wife, to Salem Iiams, for 50 acres on Chevauxdefrise. Jehu (John) and wife Phebe appeared at Washington County, Pennsylvania, Court House, April 2, 1852, to sign for their part in the transfer of the Ritchie County land for $275.00. Wesley Iiams served as a witness.

3) December 9, 1852 - From Isaac Clark and wife Catherine to Salem Iiams, for $50.00; a parcel of land along Chevauxdefrise, land adjacent to current holding of Salem Iiams.

4) December 6, 1852 - Wesley Iiams purchased 162 acres of land from Isaac Clark adjacent to land owned by Salem Iiams, on Chevauxdefrise Creek, Ritchie County, Virginia, for $162.00.

5) June 22, 1853 - 262 acres on Chevauxdefrise, a branch of Indian Creek, from Isaac Clark and wife Katherine; and Ransom Kendall.

6) December 16, 1861 - 50 acres of land on Chevauxdefrise Creek from Salem Iiams (and wife Elizabeth) of Somerset Township, Washington County, Pennsylvania, to Wesley Iiams of Belmont County, Ohio, for $600.00.

7) Wesley Iiams land was surveyed, plotted, and registered Ritchie County, West Virginia, August 19, 1884, for 253 acres and 42 p; land on Chevauxdefrise.

8) Wesley Iiams deed - 162 acres; July 4, 1885, graveyard plot church; a centennial church declared 1963.

9) Tax receipt - 1870, Ritchie County; 280 acres ($6.29 tax) + $283 personal property (tax $3.43); Tax receipt - 1869 - Ritchie County; 280 acres ($0.73 tax) +$257 personal property (tax $0.25).

10) February 14, 1887 - Payments made for Cemetery, Methodist Church, Chevauxdefrise, Ritchie County, West Virginia.

11) May-November 1928 - Estate settlement of Nancy McKelvey Iams, Ritchie County, West Virginia. The estate settlement of Nancy McKelvey Iams of $903.57, Charles V. Iams, Executor; May-November 1928 includes names of: Charley Iams, for labor, $12.00 on June 12, 1928; Martha Maud Iams, part of amount willed, $110.00, June 19, 1928; Jennie Iams, part of amount willed, $100.00 May 29, and part of deceased estate $10.00, May 3, 1928; Martha Maud Iams, part of share of estate $49.32, on November 1, 1928; and $10.00 on May 3, 1928; Viola Iams Corbett, willed by deceased, $1.00 on June 18, 1928; Jennie Iams $1.82 part of estate on November 1, 1928, and $11.00 in goods June 21, 1928; $1.00 willed by deceased June 18, 1928; C. V. Iams, $44.00 commission on October 19, 1928; $57.49 to Jennie Iams, part of estate, October 19, 1928; $1.00 to Roxie Hall October 8, 1928, part of estate; Violet Iams $17.50 on May 3, 1928 and $10.50 on May 28, 1928, for labor; $11.00 to Martha Maude Iams June 2, 1928, household goods; John Iams $1.00 June 1, 1928, willed by mother; $1.00 to Ida Corbett, June 2, 1928, willed by mother.

John "Wesley" Iams (b. March 3, or 8, 1828, Washington County, Pennsylvania; died September 23, 1894; buried Methodist Cemetery on Chevauxdefrise, Ritchie County, West Virginia). Wesley Iams (b. 1828) was the son of William Iiams (b. 1793) and Susannah Sharp (b. 1795). He married twice, first to Caroline Scales of Monroe County, Ohio, on March 8, 1855, Belmont County, Ohio; and second to Nancy McKelvey, December 12, 1867, Monroe County, Ohio. There were two children from the first marriage and eleven from the second marriage. Wesley Iams (b. 1828) moved from Washington County, Pennsylvania, to Belmont County, Ohio, when he met and married Caroline Scales (tombstone in Bethel Cemetery, Key, Ohio, gives death date as 1858). The license was issued in Belmont County, Ohio, to Wesley Imes on February 26, 1856. Wesley Iams (b. 1828) was a carpenter known for his barn building ability; he also wrote music. The 1860 Federal Census of Mead Township, Belmont County, Ohio, lists Wesley Iams. The 1870 Federal Census of Mead Township lists the children of Wesley (b. 1828) and Caroline Scales Iams as attending school and living with Thomas Scales (age 66, b. Pennsylvania) and Elizabeth Scales (age 60, b. Ohio); with their daughter Nancy Scales (age 29, b. Ohio); William Thomas Iams (b. 1858, age 12); and Isabelle "Anna Belle" "Anne" Iams (b. 1856, age 14);

Anna Belle Iams married Mr. Myers and their daughter Sarah Myers married Conrad "Con" Hagemeier. Wesley Iams (b. 1828) married second on December 12, 1867, Monroe County, Pennsylvania, to Nancy McKelvey (b. Monroe County, Ohio, September 20, 1846; d. April 27 or 29, 1928, and buried at Methodist Cemetery on the Chevauxdefrise, Ritchie County, West Virginia). The announcement of the death of John Wesley Iams (b. 1828) in the *Wetzel Republican* of Wheeling, West Virginia, October 28, 1894, stated that the Iams family had moved from Hagerstown, Maryland, to western Pennsylvania in 1794. Nancy McKelvey Iams (b. 1846) was the daughter of George C. McKelvey and Eliza Fulton. George C. McKelvey was born in Tyrone County, Ireland, and migrated to Ohio in 1840 with other family members.

Wesley Iams (b. 1828) lived in Mead Township, Belmont County, Ohio, in 1860. He was born in Washington County, Pennsylvania, and moved to Ohio before moving to land he had purchased from an Isaac Clark in Ritchie County, West Virginia. The 1880 Federal Census of Ritchie County, West Virginia, lists Wesley Iams as age 53, a farmer; born Pennsylvania; (father b. Pennsylvania; mother b. Pennsylvania); wife Nancy, age 33, born Ohio; (father b. Ireland; mother b. Ohio); children: John Iams (age 11, b. West Virginia); Edison Iams (age 10, b. West Virginia); Charles Iams (age 6, b. West Virginia); Ida Iams (age 4, b. West Virginia); Isa Iams (age 3, b. West Virginia); and Iola Iams (age 1, b. West Virginia). Wesley Iams (b. 1828) had purchased 99 acres (Range 3, Township 5, Section 27) in Belmont County, Ohio, from Amos L. Jones for $18.00 on April 29, 1856; and sold the land to Jim Hammond on March 13, 1860, for $25.00.

An account of the death of Wesley Iams appeared in the Wheeling (West Virginia) *Wetzel Republican* as follows: "Mr. Iams came from one of the pioneer families of this country. His ancestors moved from Normandy to England in the eleventh century, and were soldiers under William the Conqueror. When the sovereign divided up the lands of England, they were among the grantees. Some of his ancestors moved to Maryland before 1706 and received land grants from Lord Baltimore. They were originally Catholics but became Methodists under the preaching of John Wesley. They removed from Hagerstown to Pennsylvania in 1794." Submitted by Harley Iams, Rancho Bernardo, California, to Lois Iiams Hartman, Pasadena, California, May 4, 1978. The article had been published in the Wheeling newspaper in 1894.

Nancy McKelvey (b. September 30, 1846; m. Wesley Iams; d. April 29, 1928; buried at Chevauxdefrise Methodist Church, Ritchie County, West Virginia); was the daughter of George C. McKelvey/McElvey (b. 1819, Omah County, Tyrone, Ireland; a farmer who lived in Green Township of Monroe County, Ohio, in 1860; buried at Belmont Church, Key, Ohio); m. Eliza Fulton, sister of Isabella Fulton. George C. McKelvey (b. 1819) was the son of Robert McKelvey and Ann Boyd.

George C. McKelvey (b. 1819) m. 1st, to Elizabeth Fulton (d. by1860); and m. 2nd, to Mahola Stonebraker of Belmont County, Ohio. After working as a laborer on the "National Pike," he entered into a partnership with a brother and purchased land in Mead Township, Belmont County, Ohio. In 1876 he moved to Green Township in Monroe County, Ohio, and purchased two farms. He died in Monroe County, Ohio, in 1891 at age 81 and was buried at Belmont Church, east of Key, Mead Township, Belmont County, Ohio. Children of George C. McKelvey included: 1) George C. McKelvey, Jr. [(a twin; schoolteacher; farmer (m. 1st, to Nettie McMahon of Monroe County, Ohio, who d. 1889 after birth of Forrest McKelvey; m. 2nd, to widow of K. F. Jeffers and farmed the Jeffers Farm west of Bellaire, Belmont County, Ohio; and had two more children: Earl McKelvey and Lucille McKelvey)]; 2) Lizzie McKelvey (a twin; m. Mr. Clegg of Monroe County); 3) Mary Ann McKelvey (b. 1848; m. Mr. Watkins); 4) Isabella "Bell" McKelvey (b. 1848; m. Mr. Sykes of Monroe County); 5) Emily "Emma" McKelvey (b. 1850; m. Mr. Holmes of West Virginia); 6) Nancy McKelvey (b. September 30, 1845, Monroe County, Ohio; d. Chevauxdefrise, Ritchie County, West Virginia, April 29, 1928; m. Wesley Iams; buried at Chevauxdefrise Methodist Cemetery); 7) Violet McKelvey (b. 1854); 8) William McKelvey (b. 1852); 9) David McKelvey (b. 1841); and 10) Margaret McKelvey (b. 1840).

Other children of Robert McKelvey, Sr. (b. Ireland) and Ann Boyd were: 1) Weir McKelvey (b. Ireland, 1818; d. 1887; m. Eliza ____; b. 1822; d. 1884); 2) Thomas McKelvey (b. Ireland March 14, 1793; d. February 16, 1882; buried Belmont U.P. Church, Key, Ohio; m. Mary ____, b. 1838; d. 1870); 3) James McKelvey (b. Ireland 1793; d. Monroe County, Ohio); 4) Joseph B. McKelvey (b. Ireland 1815; d. 1887; buried Belmont U. P. Church, Key, Ohio; m. Ann ____; (b. 1828; d. 1967); 5) Elizabeth McKelvey; and 6) Samuel McKelvey [b. Ireland, March 18, 1909; d. 1892; m. 1842 to Linda Creamer, b. 1823; d. 1885; had five children: a) J. O. McKelvey (b. 1854; m. Ida B. King; daughter of James and Margaret King); b) David McKelvey (b. 1843); c) Robert McKelvey (b. 1845); d) Mary E. McKelvey (b. 1847); and e) Nancy E. McKelvey (b. 1849)].

An Iams family reunion was held May 15, 1993, after a hiatus for this group of over 50 years. The reunion was held at the old Wesley Iams (b. 1828) home, now owned by Dale and Orpha Iams and located on Chevauxdefrise, Ritchie County, West Virginia. The site contained the old homestead of Wesley and Nancy (McKelvey) Iams as well as the old Chevauxdefrise Methodist Church founded by Wesley Iams and others of the area. Thirty-two relatives attended, including: Edna Louise Corbett Reynolds, Ralph and Norita Reynolds, Jim and Lois McKelvey Neely of North Carolina, Paul and Julia McKelvey, John and Chris McKelvey, John and Karen (McKelvey) Lackey with daughters Maria Lackey and Kate Lackey, Paul and Naomi Federkiel and daughter Judy Nutter, Cornelius and Johanna Hall, Lloyd and Wilma Bircher, Opal Hamilton, Carol Ginanni, Paul and Ruth Villers with children Larry Villers, Paula Webb, Nicholas Webb, Alicia Webb, hosts Dale and Orpha Iams, Russell and Lois Hall.

Robert McKelvey, Sr. (b. Omah, County Tyrone, Ireland) and Ann Boyd (b. Ireland 1827; d. Ohio 1857) had eight children, including seven sons. All of the sons migrated to the United States in 1839 and later brought their mother and sister to the

United States. The boys worked on the National Road (U.S. Route 40). Three of the brothers moved to Monroe County, Ohio. The oldest son of Robert McKelvey, Sr., and Ann Boyd was Robert McKelvey, Jr. (b. 1814); d. Janaury 7, 1858), who m. Isabella Fulton, daughter of George and Isabella McClarean Fulton of County Tyrone, Ireland, and who migrated to the United States in 1816 after their 1812 attempt failed. Robert McKelvey, Jr. (b. 1814) and Isabella Fulton had a son Thomas McKelvey who m. Mary McMillan (b. 1839; d. 1871). Thomas McKelvey and Mary McMillan (b. 1839) had four children:

1) Bruce McKelvey, who m. Mary "Mollie" Hatcher, daughter of one of the first Belmont County, Ohio, constables, Joshua Hatcher. Bruce McKelvey and Mollie Hatcher had two children: Clyde McKelvey, b. 1900; m. Mildred Corbett; and Lillian McKelvey, m. Sam Finley; 2) William F. McKelvey, lived in Eugene, Oregon; 3) Ida McKelvey (b. November 2, 1861; lived in Pasadena, California); and 4) Josephine McKelvey (m. Mr. Brady; lived in Columbus, Ohio. The second son of Robert McKelvey, Sr., and Ann Boyd was George C. McKelvey (m. Eliza Fulton, as described above) who had eight children: Margaret McKelvey (b. 1840); David McKelvey (b. 1841); Nancy McKelvey (b. 1845; m. Wesley Iams, above); Emily "Emma" McKelvey (b. 1850; m. Mr. Holmes); Isabella McKelvey (b. 1848; m. Mr. Sykes); William McKelvey (b. 1852); and Violet McKelvey (b. 1852).

The children of Wesley Iams (b. 1828) and Caroline Scales were:

1) William Thomas Iams [(b. October 10, 1857, or 1858; d. April 15, 1950); no children. The 1870 Federal Census of Mead Township, Belmont County, Ohio, lists William T. Iams (and Anne B. Iams, age 14), age 12, as attending school and living with Thomas Scales (age 66, b. Pennsylvania), and his wife Elizabeth Scales (age 60, b. Ohio); with single daughter Nancy Scales (age 29, b. Ohio). A book currently owned by H. Dale Iams, Ritchie County, West Virginia, entitled *Domestic Medicine*, written in 1848 by Horton Howard, is inscribed by William Iams];

2) Isabella "Anna Belle" "Anne" Iams (b. November 28, 1855, or 1856); m. Mr. Myers. Their daughter Sarah Ann Myers (d. November 1954) m. Conrad "Con" Hagemeier (d. August 21, 1934) of Bellaire, Ohio; a farmer and carpenter. Children of Sarah and Conrad Hagemeier included: 1) Rosella Hagemeier (m. Fred Daly), known as "Ringy," and lived west of Saint Clairsville, Ohio, along the south side of U. S. Route 40; 2) Mildred Hagemeier (m. Alonzo Beck; had a son Lon Allen "Lonnie" Beck; operated Beck Funeral Home in Saint Clairsville, but after death of her husband Mildred Hagemeier Beck worked for the telephone company before retiring to Wesley Glen, 5155 North High Street, Columbus, Ohio, where she lived in 1996); 3) Roberta Hagemeier (m. Mr. Workman; had two children: Thomas Workman and April Workman, who m. Gary Kinser); 4) Lester Eugene Hagmaier (d. age 14, March 28, 1932); and 5) Conrad Charles Hagemaier (b. November 9, 1910; d. February 27, 1963; m. Alma Wells and had four children: 1) Elaine Connie Hagmaier (m. William Hickox); 2) Conrad Eugene Hagmaier (m. Nancy _____); 3) Roger Arland Hagmaier (b. September 7, 1941, at Lloydsville, Ohio; lived at Hudson, Ohio; m. November 16, 1962, to Alma Faye Doan who was b. May 7, 1937, at Mount Vernon, Kentucky; and had a child: Derek Conrad Hagmainer who was b. in Jackson, Michigan, February 9, 1973)].

Conrad Charles Hagmaier (b. 1910) and Alma Walls lived near Warren, Ohio. Rosella "Ringy" Hagmaier and Fred Daley had two children: 1) Bonnie Alice Daley; and 2) Robert E. Daley, Ph.D. (Director of Cardiac Rehabilitation of Eastern Ohio Regional Hospital of Martins Ferry, Belmont County, Ohio). Robert E. Daley had two children: 1) Shirley Daley (m. Gary Miller; had a son Robert Allen Miller, b. May 12, 1988); and 2) Mary Daley (m. Richard Moore; had two children: Elice Moore and Aaron Moore.

Children of Wesley Iams (b. 1828) and Nancy McKelvey:
3) John Franklin Iams (b. September 22, 1868, Ritchie County, West Virginia; d. February 17, 1930, following an automobile accident east of San Diego, California; buried at Greenwood Mausoleum, San Diego); m. Mary "Josephine" Conrad (b. 1871; d. February 16, 1930, in automobile accident that claimed her husband's life and critically injured their son Harley A. Iams).

Josephine Conrad was the sister of Mrs. J. W. Smith of Charleston, West Virginia; Mrs. J. D. Bennett of Conneaut, Ohio; Mrs. J. L. Hennan of Burton, West Virginia; Mrs. O. Schutz; and Mrs. R. E. Case, of San Diego, California. John Franklin Iams was a telegrapher. Children of John Franklin Iams (b. 1868) and Josephine Conrad were: a) Gertrude May Iams (d. 1975), m. Merle P. Bennett; they lived at 5105 Hawley Boulevard., San Diego, California. They had one son, Robert Bennett, who lived in Idaho (m. 1st to Mary Louise ____; and m. 2nd to Jeanette ____); b) Harley Ambrose Iams (b. March 13, 1905; d. December 3, 1984, San Diego, California, lived at 11933 Bernardo Center Court, San Diego, California); m. December 27, 1935, to Margaret E. Redwell in New Jersey. They had one daughter, Margaret "Margie" Elizabeth Iams (b. January 27, 1944), who m. Larry Kennedy and they had two sons: William Joseph Kennedy (b. August 4, 1963), and Michael John Kennedy (b. July 3, 1964). They lived in Apple Valley, California; and m. 2nd, November 27, 1993, in Colorado, to James Colleran.

Harley Ambrose Iams (b. 1905) is featured elsewhere in this book because of his acknowledged place in history, based on his work in the invention of television, and for his work as a rocket scientist with Hughes Aircraft. In additon, he maintained an interest in family history and contributed significant information to this work through the cooperation with his good friend and noted author Lois Iiams Hartman. Harley Iams also supplied a western Pennsylvania newspaper clipping dated August 23, 1931, regarding the First Iams Family Reunion for Descendants of William Iiams which read, "The name was spelled Ians in early England—Iiams in early Maryland—and now the name has changed in various ways. Many have retained the Iiams; those of Maryland now spell it Ijams; those of North Carolina, Alabama, Mississippi, and Tennessee spell it Ijames."

In 1931, Harley A. Iams, E. B. Iiams, and Ida Iams Charter proposed the following family line: 1) William Eyams/Iiams, South River Hundred, Anne Arundel County, Maryland (d. 1703); 2) Richard Iiams (b. 1673; d. 1761), South River Hundred; 3) John Iiams (b. 1710; d. 1776), South River Hundred; 4) Thomas Iiams (b. 1754; d. 1834), born in Anne Arundel County; moved to Frederick County, Maryland; then to Washington County, Pennsylvania; and finally, to Belmont County, Ohio; 5) William Iiams (b. 1793), who remained at Amity, Washington County, Pennsylvania; 6) John Wesley Iiams (b. 1824 at Amity, Pennsylvania; d. 1894), who lived in Washington County, Pennsylvania; then in

Belmont County, Ohio; and finally, near Harrisville in Ritchie County, West Virginia; 7) John Franklin Iiams (b. 1864; d. 1930), who moved from Ritchie County, West Virginia, to San Diego, California, in 1908; and 8) Harley Ambrose Iams (b. 1905 in West Virginia), who lived in Pittsburgh, Pennsylvania, in New Jersey, in Los Angeles, and finally, in San Diego, California. Harley Iams graduated in engineering from Stanford University, Palo Alto, California, in 1927. He then worked in western Pennsylvania (Westinghouse) before moving to New Jersey (RCA), where he met and married Margaret E. Redwell. They moved back to California in 1947 and lived in such beautiful sounding places as Venice, Pacific Palisades, Malibu, and San Diego. Mrs. Harley A. (Margaret) Iams lived in nearby Spring Valley, California, in 1995.

Harley Ambrose Iams (b. March 12, 1905, Lorentz, West Virginia; d. December 3, 1985, California); m. December 27, 1935, to Margaret E. Redwell on a snowy day in Yuma, Arizona. Margaret had traveled from New York where she had completed nursing training at Bellevue Hospital, by Greyhound bus to San Francisco, and then San Diego, to Yuma, Arizona, for the wedding, and then to Pasadena, California, for the Rose Bowl; then they returned to New Jersey. Harley Iams (b. 1905) was the son of John Franklin Iams (b. 1866), himself a telegrapher and house contractor/builder. Harley Iams (b. 1905) is described by noted television historian Albert Abramson as a "kind and gentle man" whose "contribution to television is remarkable," and whose professed career reads like a storybook from the land of television, modern rocketry, and electronic systems such as radar. On July 25, 1983, after suffering his second stroke but continuing to be bright and insightful, Harley Iams (b. 1905) wrote: "My ability to read and write has been mediocre, but I do better with visual thoughts. My (current) thinking is about all the people in the Earth (and a desire for more) understanding about the structure of our planet; learning how to make the magma below generate geothermal powers, to make quiet and comfortable electric vehicles which will reduce smog; to offer ample pure water, and to dispose of trash—all at once." There is no doubt in this writer's mind that Harley Iams (b. 1905) would have accomplished each of these challenges, had he been permitted more than his allotted seventy-nine years.

Considered by some as "The Father of Television," Harley Iams (b. 1905) graduated from Stanford in 1927 with a degree in Engineering, after receiving his A.A. degree from San Diego State in 1924. He went to work for Westinghouse in Pittsburgh, Pennsylvania, with Vladimir K. Zworykin, and obtained his first of sixty-three U. S. patents for television on December 12, 1930 (Pat. No. 2, 141, 789, entitled: "Photoelectric Cell Oscillation Current," after designing and building the first six home electronic sets in 1929. Between 1931 and 1939, while working in New Jersey for General Electric, he invented TV camera tubes and carried them to production. Furthermore, while working as Director of Research for Hughes Aviation in California, he developed rapid scanning radar, guided missles, and rockets that were sent to the moon. At Hughes Aircraft, he became the director for all research before retiring in 1970. His accomplishments have been chronicled by Albert Abramson in *The History of Television* (McFarland: Jefferson, N. C., 1987), and *Zworykin, Pioneer in Television* (University of Illinois, 1994).

An amateur wireless operator (W6BKH), Harley Iams (b. 1905) was a Life Fellow in IEEE; author of eighteen articles (including "Television Today" in *Stanford Review* 41:23-31, 1940); consultant to both Cal Tech and MIT; was honored as early as 1934 as a pioneer for the development of the cathode ray television; Fellow in Institute of Radar Engineers; Phi Beta Kappa (Stanford); Sigma XI; recipient of the Joint Award in 1940 as a "Modern Pioneer"; and was a select member of the World War II Selective Service Advisory Committee on Scientific Engineers and Specialized Personnel.

In April 1931, Harley Iams (b. 1905) advised RCA in Camden (VK2) that a photosensitive surface would not be harmed by an electronic beam. He was asked to prove it, and did just that. Also in 1931, Harley Iams and Ogloblinsky made the first dogleg iconoscope, using an eight-inch diameter spherical housing and a large mica surface, with a big lens to gather light. In 1933, Harley Iams (b. 1905) was transferred by RCA to Harrison, New Jersey, to make iconoscopes. In 1937, Harley Iams (b. 1905), Morton, and Zworykin revealed the development of the image iconoscope; and with Albert Ross, developed the Orthocon in 1938. Under his guidance as Director of the Hughes Guided Missle Laboratory, successful rocket landings were made to the moon and also to Mars. Margaret Iams, a descendant of Sir William Drake, brother of Sir Francis Drake, lived in Spring Valley, California, in 1995.

The child of Harley Iams (b. 1905) and Margaret Conrad was: 1) Margaret Elizabeth "Margie" Iams (b. January 27, 1944, Princeton, New Jersey); m. 1st in Pacific Palisades, California, to Larry Kennedy; m. 2nd, November 27, 19__, in Lewis, Colorado, to James Collison. Children of Margaret Iams (b. 1944) and Larry Kennedy were: a) William Joseph "BJ" Kennedy (b. August 4, 1963, Los Angeles, California); a surveyor; lived Apple Valley, California; b) Michael John Kennedy (b. July 3, 1964, Los Angeles, California), an off-road racer; lived in Apple Valley, California.

In 1993, Lois Ijams Hartman recalled pleasant memories of Harley Iams of Rancho Bernardo, California, and reported that he had died in 1984 and considered him to be "a fine man." Harley Iams had furnished Lois Ijams Hartman with an announcement report from the *Wetzel Republican*, announcing the death of John Wesley Iams on October 26, 1894, at Wheeling, West Virginia.

4) David Edson/Edison "Ed" "Edward" Iams (b. March 25, 1870; d. October 22, 1900, or 1901, buried Chevauxdefrise Methodist Church, Ritchie County, West Virginia), m. 1st to Emma Jane Wilson (b. 1870 or 1872; d. October 17, 1953; buried at Chevauxdefrise Methodist Church); she m. 2nd to ____ Cornell. Child of David Edson Iams and Emma Jane Wilson: a) Roxanne R. "Roxy/Roxie" Iams (b. September 21, 1896, Chevauxdefrise, Ritchie County, West Virginia; d. November 9, 1968; buried at Chevauxdefrise Methodist Church), m. 1st to Jesse Clarence Lamp (b. October 10, 1892), and lived at Cairo, West Virginia; m. 2nd on March 4, 1922, in Cairo, West Virginia, to Neal Ray Hall (b. November 16, 1887, or 1888; d. February 4, 1959; buried at Chevauxdefrise Methodist Church).

Three children of Roxy Iams and Jesse Clarence Lamp were:

1¹) Jessie "Opal" Lamp (b. November 4, 1914, Beatrice, Ritchie County, West Virginia; d. December 16, 1993, Harrisville, West

Virginia), m. 1st, on December 24, 1932, to Thomas A. Pittman (b. 1906; d. 1972); and m. 2nd, on February 23, 1974, to Hosea/ Hacie Hamilton (b. December 23, 1920, Ritchie County, West Virginia; d. 1986), son of William Hamilton and Laura Reed. Opal operated The Sandwich Shop in Harrisville for over 20 years. She was a member of Harrisville Garden Club, Royal Neighbors, St. Luke's United Methodist Church, and Ladies Auxillary of Post 3554 VFW. She had four children: a¹) Don Pittman of Harrisville, Ritchie County, West Virginia; m. Charlene Wass; lived Harrisville, West Virginia; b¹) William "Bill" Pittman of Richmond, Virginia; m. twice; had a son by each marriage; c¹) Martha Pittman of Lakefront, Mississippi; m. Lawrence Morris of Smithville, West Virginia; d¹) Betty Pittman Adams of Harrisville; m. 1st, Tom Bailey; they had two sons and a daughter; m. 2nd, Mr. Park; m. 3rd, Mr. Bird; m. 4th, Mr. Collins; m. 5th, Mr. Adams; lived 820 South Spring Street, Harrisville, West Virginia; operated a business called The Store, adjacent to The Sandwich Shop operated by her mother.

2¹) Emmen Darrell Lamp (b. October 7, 1916, West Virginia; d. 1917; age 6 months);

3¹) Wilma Iona Lamp (b. February 22, 1917, Eaton, West Virginia), m. in Cairo, West Virginia, December 12, 1936, to Lloyd Bircher (b. July 25, 1912), son of Milburn Bircher and Alice Cornell; their two children were (lived 214 Orchard, Harrisville): a¹) Emma Jean/Emogene Bircher (b. Mahone, West Virginia, April 19, 1938); m. 1st, in 1960 to Robert Zerick of Smithville, West Virginia; they had two children: 1¹¹) William Robert "Bill" Zerick, M.D., a neurosurgeon; (b. July 17, 1961), who attended Harrisville, West Virginia, schools; then University of Virginia, West Virginia University, and trained in Norfolk, Virginia; Charleston, West Virginia; Tucson, Arizona, and Columbus, Ohio; served as Chief of Staff at Children's Hospital, Ohio State University, Columbus, Ohio; single in 1994; 2¹¹) Allen Lloyd Carpenter (b. October 27, 1966); m. _____ Richards of Kentucky; their child: Ryan Taylor Carpenter (b. June 17, 1994); b¹) Shirley Ann Bircher (b. Mahone, West Virginia, September 25, 1939), m. February 12, 1960, to Claire Perkins (b. October 5, 1931, of Parkersburg, West Virginia); lived at Dog Run, Route 1, Harrisville, West Virginia; 1¹¹) Angela "Angie" Dawn Perkins (b. March 27, 1961), m. June 21, 1986, to Ricky Lee Gant (b. July 28, 1958, of Parkersburg, West Virginia; a) Rebecca Nicole Gant (b. July 12, 1988); b) Rachel Elaine Gant (b. April 5, 1995); 2¹¹) Teresa Ann Perkins (b. July 20, 1962); m. December 10, 1983, to Rodney Ray Smith (b. March 9, 1959); lived Parkersburg, West Virginia; a) Chase Alexander Smith (b. May 5, 1987; b) Kaycee Ann Smith (b. May 27, 1989; 3¹¹) Matthew Claire Perkins (b. 1966), m. Christine "Cristie" Watson; a) Austin Matthew Perkins (b. March 1994, Parkersburg, West Virginia; c¹) Patsy Belle Bircher (b. Mahone, West Virginia, December 29, 1941); m. March 17, 1960, to Rodney Jack McCloy (b. Ritchie County, West Virginia, July 29, 1936); son of Harvey McCloy and Clyde Jones McCloy; lived in Parkersburg; retired from American Cyanimid; 1^{11}) Rodney Allen McCloy, Ph.D. in industrial psychology; m. Washington, D.C., on August 12, 1993, to Christine Matthews; 2^{11}) Larry McCloy, who m. briefly; no children.

The eight children of Roxy Iams (b. 1896) and Neal Ray Hall were:

4^1) Comilla Esther Hall (b. January 7, 1923, Greenwood, West Virginia; m. November 9, 1953, at Kingsland, Camden County, Georgia, to Roland Pete Hines, her second marriage (b. July 25, 1921, Baker County, Florida; d. November 8, 1979); son of William Hines and ____ Deese. Comilla and Roland Pete Hines lived in Toronto, Ohio, in 1995. Children of Comilla Esther Hall were: a^{11}) Vickie Kaynickefoose (b. October 31, 1946, in Parkersburg, West Virginia); m. February 21, 1964, to Mark E. Mohn; their children were: 1) Darla Kay Mohn (b. May 18, 1965, at Steubenville, Ohio); 2) John Edward Mohn (b. June 5, 1967, at Steubenville, Ohio); m. ____ and had two children: Marcus Shane Mohn (b. November 1988 in Steubenville, Ohio); and Tiarri Rei-Lani Mohn (b. June 9, 1994, in Steubenville, Ohio); b^{11}) Nessa Claudine Hines (b. December 20, 1954, in Steubenville, Ohio), m. 1st, to Mr. Lindsay; m. 2nd, April 29, 1995, Mr. Robinson; children: Kaitlyn Daron Lindsay (b. July 7, 1988, Fairfield, Butler County, Ohio); and Kelsey Maureen Robinson (b. May 21, 1993, in Fairfield, Butler County, Ohio); c^{11}) Comilla Dawn Hines (b. September 9, 1961, in Steubenville, Ohio), m./divorced Mr. Piatt; their child: Derrick Stephen Piatt (b. July 3, 1982, in Steubenville, Ohio); d^{11}) Roland Pete Hines (b. June 15, 1964, in Steubenville, Ohio); single in 1995.

5^1) Corene/Carien/Coreine Emma Hall (b. October 3, 1924, Greenwood, West Virginia; d. 1969); m. Ritchie County, West Virginia, to Bernard Skidmore (b. 1924) of Harrisville;

6^1) Claridon Ernest "Ernie" Hall (b. August 26, 1926, Parkersburg, West Virginia; d. September 12, 1969), m. in Wierton, West Virginia, February 12, 1948;

7^1) Clearance Emcil/Ensil Hall (b. July 3, 1928, Parkersburg, West Virginia; d. November 23, 1973), m. in Wierton, West Virginia; m. Betty Grimes;

8^1) Cornelies Ellsworth Hall (b. April 13, 1930, Parkersburg, West Virginia), m. August 1, 1952, to Joan Meadows; lived in Cincinnati, Ohio;

9^1) Russell Lee Ray Hall (b. May 26, 1931, Smithville, West Virginia), m. 1st, in Canton, Ohio, to LaisyArnold; m. 2nd, August 9, 1984; lived in Pullman, Ritchie County, West Virginia;

10^1) Wayne Douglas Durl Eugene Hall (b. October 4, 1933, Harrisville), Ritchie County, West Virginia; d. May 13, 1976, or April 11, 1968);

11^1) Blondene Jane Hall (b. June 12, 1934, Cairo, West Virginia), m. Cairo, West Virginia, June 12, 1953, to Cleon Marshall; lived in Ishpeming, Michigan.

5) George H. Iams [(b. February19, 1872; d. June 2, 1875); born and buried at Chevauxdefrise, Ritchie County, West Virginia];

6) Charles "Charley" V. Iams (b. November 8, 1873, Chevauxdefrise, Ritchie County, West Virginia; d. December 25, 1949; buried at Chevauxdefrise Methodist Episcopal Cemetery, Ritchie County, West Virginia), m. March 26, 1903, to Stella Eckard (b. January 10, 1882; d. July 8, 1964, at Pullman, West Virginia; buried at Chevauxdefrise Methodist Episcopal Cemetery). Charley Iams liked to claim that his middle initial "V" stood for vinegar, but it is believed that the initial had no other designation. Charley Iams (b. 1873) owned the home of Wesley Iams (b. 1828), his father, but did not live there after 1919. He was a Methodist and attended the Chevauxdefrise Methodist Church. Stella Eckard was the daughter of John Eckard and Sarah Cokeley. Charles Iams (b. 1873) was a farmer, but also owned a store at Five Forks in Ritchie County, West Virginia. He also owned a farm on Isaac's Fork and in 1963, after his death, his widow Stella Eckard Iams and their son Dale Iams (b. 1912) moved from the farm to the town of Pullman, West Virginia. The four children of Charles V. Iams (b. 1873) and Stella Eckerd were:

a) Ruben or Reuben Renzy Iams (b. December 21, 1904; d. January 14, 1942; lived at Isaac's Fork; buried at Chevauxdefrise Cemetery); single; used crutches for severe rheumatoid arthritis;

b) Isa "Violet" Iams (b. October 31, 1906; d. November 6, 1983; buried at Pullman, Ritchie County, West Virginia); m. Ralph Frank Prunty on August 14, 1943. She and Ruth Prunty wrote the 1980 version of the Iams history for the *Ritchie County History* book. While they had no children of their own, they raised their neice, Naomi Prunty, after her sister Gladys's death.

c) Gladys Mae Iams (b. Isaac's Fork, Ritchie County, West Virginia, September 15, 1909; d. April 13, 1932; buried at Pullman, Ritchie County, West Virginia); m. September 1928 to William Glen Prunty (b. December 4, 1900, Pullman, West Virginia; d. March 23, 1953, Pullman, West Virginia); members of Methodist Church. Gladys Iams (b. 1909) d. 1932 after childbirth). William Glen Prunty (b. 1900) was the son of James William "Willie" Prunty and N. Dell Cox.

Gladys Mae Iams and William Glen Prunty had two daughters: 1¹) Ruth Marie Prunty (b. May 12, 1929); was raised by her father and her Prunty grandparents. She attended business college and served as City Clerk of Pennsboro, West Virginia; member Church of Christ; m. Paul Lewis Villers of Pennsboro, West Virginia, on September 4, 1948 (Paul was b. August 13, 1929, son of Russell Villers and Naomi Stull).

Ruth Marie Prunty (b. 1929) and Paul Lewis Villers (b. 1929) had five children: a¹) Carol Ann Villers, R.N. (b. January 26, 1952; was a nurse at St. Joseph's Hospital, Parkersburg, West Virginia), m. September 17, 1968, to Eric Joseph Ginanni (b. February 16, 1951; d. July 19, 1980), son of Joseph Ginanni and Jean Ball (Humphrey); lived in Parkersburg, West Virginia; and had two children: Eric Joseph Ginanni II (b. February 26, 1970) and Lori Ann Ginanni (b. May 29, 1974); Carol Villers was a nurse at St. Joseph's Hospital, Parkersburg, West Virginia; b¹) Michael Villers (b. March 26, 1954; an industrial engineer as head of Energy Department of Union Carbide, lived

Marietta, Georgia), m. May 24, 1984, to Pamela Wingfield, daughter of Bill and Carol Parsons Wingfield. They had three children: Sheena Renee Villers (b. April 21, 1983), Melissa Rae Villers (b. September 1, 1984), and Cameron Villers (b. May 1, 1989); c[1]) Paula Jean Villers (b. December 2, 1956, m. June 8, 1975, to Richard "Rick" Webb, son of Edward Webb and Kathleen Todd; lived in Pennsboro, West Virginia; two children: Nicolas Prunty Webb (b. January 14, 1980), and Alicia Nicole Webb (b. April 27, 1982); d[1]) David Dean Villers (b. December 15, 1958; attended West Virginia University; a chemical engineer); m. October 3, 1987, to Karen Robertson, daughter of Robert T. Robertson and Shirley Reed; lives Pennsboro, West Virginia; children: Alex Villers (b. September 24, 1989), and Leandra Villers (b. March 25, 1992); and Garrett Villers (b. April 4, 1994); e[1]) Larry Alan Villers (b. June 17, 1961; attended Ohio Valley College).

2[1]) Naomi Lee Prunty (b. March 29, 1932; a schoolteacher and administrator; retired from Berlin Heights, Ohio, schools in 1986), m. June 21, 1968, to Paul Harmon Federkiel (b. August 28, 1928, Sandusky, Ohio). They lived at 18 Olive Street, Norwalk, Ohio, 44857, in 1995; Methodist. As an educator, she was both an elementary school teacher and a school principal. Paul Harmon Federkiel (b. 1928) was the son of George and Jeannell Federkiel. They had a daughter, Judy Lee Federkiel (b. March 28, 1969) who m. April 7, 1990, to Jon Nutter, son of Kenneth Nutter and Joan McMorrow. Judy Lee Federkiel and Jon Nutter had a daughter, Audrey Lee Nutter (b. August 1995).

d) Howard "Dale" Iams (b. February 3, 1912, Isaac's Fork, Ritchie County, West Virginia), m. December 7, 1965, to Orpha Marie Ferrebee Tanzy, and they lived in Pullman, Route 1, Box 177, Harrisville, West Virginia, 26321, in 1996. Orpha was born in Dodridge County, West Virginia, as the oldest of ten girls. She had three grown children at the time of her marriage to Dale Iams: a beautician in Harrisville, West Virginia; a truck driver in Dallas, Texas, and a mechanic in Harrisonville, West Virginia. Dale Iams (b. 1912) and Orpha remodeled the old home of Wesley Iams (b. 1828) on the Chevauxdefrise Creek, Ritchie County, West Virginia, in 1967. The Chevauxdefrise Church and cemetery are now owned by local residents, through the generosity of Dale Iams, who serves as a trustee. He refurbished the church and cares for the cemetery. The church was designated as a West Virginia Centennial Church on the occasion of the West Virginia Centennial celebration. The church was painted in 1984. Except for weddings, there have been no services in the church since 1916.

The Prunty family was among the most influential and colorful families of West Virginia, serving several terms in state legislature bodies and serving the local communities in various public service positions. The first of the Prunty family to move into what is now West Virginia, as outlined by Floyd O. Prunty (b. 1903), was the legendary John Prunty. John Prunty (b. 1750; d. 1848) was born in Hampshire County, Virginia, and was the first man to move to what is now the junction of U. S. Route 50 and U. S. Route 250, at what was first called crossroads, later to be officially named Williamsport, and since 1845 has been known as Pruntytown, the county seat of Taylor County, West Virginia. Also settling in the area about the same time was a brother, David Prunty.

It is believed that the name change to Pruntytown was an effort to appease the Irishman with the picturesque language and salty character, John Prunty (b. 1750). John Prunty (b. 1750) had opposed the formation of the new county of Taylor by saying, "It is so ____ small I can stand on one edge and spit across it." Legend refers to him as "tempestuous by nature and possessed of a sulfurous, profane vocabulary." He was the sheriff of the then Harrison County, Virginia, and served several terms in Richmond as a state legislator. He is known to have been jailed after refusing to post bail after contempt of court resulting from his outspoken, foul language, objection to the unilateral action of the court in calling witnesses without going through the office of the sheriff. Instead, as a man of principle, John Prunty is quoted to have said, "The court and attorney and the whole bunch are ____ fools and a set of ____ scoundrels." After "repeated contempt and abuse of this court," John Prunty was fined at a rate of eighty-three cents per oath for "seven oaths sworn in the hearing and presence of this court," and the same rate for "fifteen oaths in the presence of William Robinson, Justice of the Peace." The court later failed in its attempt to have John Prunty reappointed as sheriff, and he also later served twenty years in the state legislature at Richmond, Virginia. His greatest act was the privilege of voting for the constitution of the United States. Children of John Prunty (b. 1750) were:

1) Jacob Prunty [(b. Pruntytown, West Virginia [Virginia], 1784; served in Virginia General Assembly; d. 1860; buried at White Oak, near Pullman, Ritchie County, West Virginia); m. July 18, 1811, in Pruntytown, to Mary McKinney, daughter of Michael McKinney (d. 1865; buried at White Oak Cemetery). They moved to Lynn Camp, Ritchie County, about 1830, where they founded a community. He returned to Pruntytown between 1842 and 1851 and was described as being like his old man, with a "rough and ready" order to him. During his many years as a legislator, several pleasing anecdotes have been told of his travels to and from Richmond on the back of his gray "superannuated" horse. Jacob Prunty (b. 1785) and Mary McKinney had eight children. The family of Jacob Prunty (b. 1784) is described below]:

2) Samuel Prunty [m. Ellen Taylor, who was the sister of Isaiah Wells. They had a son, Samuel Prunty, Jr., who moved to Sumner, Missouri, where he died.];

3) Joseph Prunty [m. Rosanna Whitehair];

4) Isaac Prunty [m. May 24, 1792, to Phoebe Bartlett];

5) David Prunty [the earliest known civil engineer in Taylor County, West Virginia, m. September 20, 1790, to Anne Carroll];

6) John Prunty, Jr. [m. February 12, 1792, to Darius Plummer, daughter of Robert Plummer];

7) Elizabeth/Roanna Prunty [m. October 1, 1789, to George Arnold of Lewis County, Virginia. Their daughter, Roanna Arnold, married June 15, 1817, to Samuel L. Hayes, a United States congressman. Their sons Warren Hayes and French Hayes served in the Virginia Assembly. Elizabeth Prunty and George Arnold purchased land in Harrison County, Virginia];

8) Jesse Prunty [m. March 20, 1807, to Susan McKinney].

Children of Jacob Prunty (b. 1784) and Mary McKinney were:

1) Wilson K. Prunty [lived near Goff, West Virginia; described as "a great talker on common, general subjects];

2) Felix Prunty [(d. 1895), a pioneer of upper South Fork, West Virginia; m. Emily Greathouse (b. Ritchie County, 1820), was a member of West Virginia House of Delegates. They had ten children. One son, Marshall Neal Prunty (b. September 11, 1852, Ritchie County; d. February 14, 1946), m. August 30, 1877, to Flora Odell Lawson (b. November 4, 1861), daughter of Bushrow Washington Lawson and Anna Pritchard. They had eight children: 1) Sylvester O. Prunty (b. July 17, 1878; d. February 7, 1950); 2) Anna Prunty (b. August 5, 1881; d. December 11, 1956); 3) Felix Prunty (b. April 20, 1883; d. Nerkirk, Oklahoma, August 29, 1967); 4) Jesse Prunty (b. July 18, 1885; d. March 21, 1967, at Falls Church, Virginia); 5) May Prunty (b. February 10, 1887; d. December 28, 1925); 6) Raymond Cleo Printz (b. August 11, 1892; d. September 29, 1963; buried Lakeview Cemetery, Cleveland, Ohio); 7) Carl Prunty (b. and d. May 11, 1896); 8) Marshall Erlo Prunty (b. March 25, 1900; lived Lexington, Kentucky; m. Genevieve Cordray. The second listed son of Felix Prunty (b. 1895) and Emily Greathouse (b. 1820). Alexander Prunty (b. 1841; d. 1901) was both a member of the State Legislature of West Virginia, and Sheriff of Ritchie County. Frank Prunty, M.D., and Shirley Prunty, M.D., both children of Alexander Prunty (b. 1841) were "prominent members of the West Virginia medical profession." Grandsons of Alexander Prunty (b. 1841) included M. R. Lowther, a state legislator, and Judge J. O. Prunty, a prominent jurist of Harrisville, Ritchie County, West Virginia];

3) Jacob Prunty [(b. 1844; d. 1917)];

4) Emily Prunty [(b. 1820), m. Alexander K. Lowther, Jr., of Parkersburg. Their son, M. R. Lowther, was a state senator];

5) Rachel Prunty [m. William (or Thomas) Maley of Rock Camp, West Virginia];

6) Katherine Prunty [m. Stephen Clayton of White Oak, West Virginia];

7) Fannie Prunty [m. Bushrod Lawson, Jr. (his 2nd marriage); they are buried near Rivesville, West Virginia, on Parker farm];

8) Elmore Prunty[(b. 1832, Lynn Camp, Ritchie County, West Virginia; d. at Turtle Run on South Fork of Hughes River in 1892, and is buried at White Oak Cemetery near Pullman, Ritchie County, West Virginia, with his two wives. Elmore Prunty m. 1st, in 1861 to Ingiby Clayton, daughter of Elijah M. Clayton. Ingiby Clayton d. at age 21 and was buried at the White Oak Methodist Cemetery on grounds donated by her father for the church. Elmore Prunty m. 2nd, in 1863, to Mary Katharine Strahin (b. 1841; d. 1913), daughter of James (b. 1802; d. 1882) and Sarah Lee (b. 1809; d. 1888) Strahin of Preston County, West Virginia. They lived near Lynn Camp until the 1870s when they moved to the headwaters of Turtle Run. Sometime after Elmer Prunty's death, the widow Mary Katherine Strahin moved to Pullman and built a new home. The J. W. Prunty family later lived in this home].

The twelve children of Elmore Prunty (b. 1872) and Mary Katharine Strahin were:

1) James Willie Prunty [(b. July 11, 1864; d. 1949), a schoolteacher; m. October 1895 to N. Dell Cox (b. April 18, 1814; d. January 6, 1956), daughter of Floyd and Eliza Fox Cox, and they lived in Pullman, Ritchie County, West Virginia. They had four children: a) Ralph F. Prunty (b. 1896; d. June 5, 1962), m. Violet Iams of Pullman in 1942 (see Iams

family description); b) Boyd C. Prunty (b. 1897; a banker), m. Emma Jane Robey; c) W. Glen Prunty (b. 1900; mayor and town recorder; d. March 23, 1953), m. Gladys Iams of Pullman (see Iams family description); d) Floyd O. Prunty (b. 1903; schoolteacher and principal), m. August 16, 1930, Eunice Heltzel, author and source of most of this Prunty family history section; Michael Villers and Ruth Prunty also contributed];
2) Ellis Prunty [(b. 1866; d. 1939), m. Janie Davis (b. 1872; d. 1966). They had eight children: a) Flossie Prunty (b. 1894; d. 1967; m. Mr. Hebert); b) Leo Anderson Prunty (b. 1896; d. 1975); c) Kittie Prunty (b. 1900; m. Mr. Gaughan); d) Carl Prunty (b. 1902; d. 1963); e) Harold Prunty (b. 1907); f) Myrle Prunty (b. 1909; m. Mr. Kirma); g) Marie Prunty (b. 1914; m. Mr. Grimm); g) Wanema Amos Wiblin Prunty (b. 1916)];
3) Porter M. Prunty [(b. 1868; d. 1843), m. Julie Claiborn; no children];
4) Hattie Prunty [(b. 1869), m. Samuel Milroy Grimm. They had two children: a) Earl Grimm and b) Orval Grimm];
5) Homer Milton Prunty [(b. 1871; d. 1957), m. Lenna Jones (b. 1872; d. 1946). They had six children: a) Roxie Pearl Prunty (b. 1894; d. 1963); b) Mary Lenora Prunty (b. 1896); c) Laura I. Prunty (b. 1900); d) Opal B. Prunty (b. 1903); e) Olin J. Prunty (b. 1905; d. 1964); and f) Dulcie Juanita Prunty (b. 1915)];
6) Calvin Prunty [(b. 1873; d. 1925); single];
7) Laura Prunty [(b. 1875; d. 1899); single];
8) Harvey Wilson Prunty [(b. 1878; d. 1910), m. Ethel Jones. They had three children: a) Eva Prunty; b) Edna Prunty; and c) Hazel Prunty];
9) Emma Prunty [(b. 1880), m. Clem Grimm. They had four children: a) Lester Grimm; b) Ruby Grimm; 3) Clarence Grimm; and 4) Dale Grimm. Emma Prunty Grimm m. 2nd, to M. Mead Squires, and they had one child: Winfred Squires];
10) Creed Prunty [(b. 1882; d. 1912 in India, where he was buried)];
11) Edith Prunty [(b. 1884; d. 1955), m. Frank Broadwater; no children];
12) Aggie B. Prunty [(b. 1886; d. 1947), m. Claud H. Watson (b. 1874; d. 1953). They had seven children: a) Loran M. Watson (b. 1905; d. 1949); b) Ulla Norine Watson (b. 1907; d. 1953); c) Ruby Geraldine Watson (b. 1909); d) Hayward Earl Watson (b. 1910); e) Herman O. Watson (b. 1913; d. 1945; killed in action in World War II); f) H. Pauling Watson (b. 1920); and g) William R. Watson (b. 1922; d. 1945; killed in action in World War II)].

Sylvester Orval Prunty (b. July 17, 1878; d. February 7, 1956), son of Marshall Neal Prunty (b. 1852) and Flora O'Dell Lawson (b. 1861), obtained his law degree from Ohio Northern University in 1904, then moved to Cairo, Ritchie County, West Virginia, where he also was mayor and taught school before joining the law practice of Freer amd Robinson in Harrisville, Ritchie County, West Virginia. After forming a partnership with Samuel A. Powell, he became the Third Circuit Judge from 1925 to 1944, with jurisdiction over Ritchie, Pleasants, and Doddridge Counties, West Virginia. He also served three terms as Mayor of Harrisville and President of Board of Education. He married 1st, to Mabel Kester and they had two children: 1) a son Orean Prunty and 2) a daughter Frances Prunty. After a divorce, he married 2nd, August 13, 1913, to Elsie D. Haddox (b. May 21, 1889), daughter of Jonathan Hewey Haddox and Safronia Collins), but they had no children.
7) Ida May Iams [(b. September 27, 1875, Ritchie County, West Virginia; d. May 31, 1962; buried in Mount Zion Cemetery, Key, Belmont County,

Ohio); she was single for many years before marrying December 9, 1918, at home of Mrs. R. H. Freed of Harrisville, West Virginia, to Charles A. Charter. They had no children; lived in Belpre, Ohio, and later in Cleveland, Ohio. Charles A. Charter, age 58 in 1918, was a widower, born in Dodridge, West Virginia];

8) Isa Jane "Jennie" Iams [(b. May 11, 1877, Ritchie County, West Virginia; d. December 23, 1930, Ritchie County, West Virginia; buried in Chevauxdefrise Methodist Cemetery, Ritchie County, West Virginia; single];

9) Iola Ellen "Ola" Iams [(b. March 9, 1879, Ritchie County, West Virginia; d. April 15, 1959, Ohio State University Hospital, Columbus, Ohio; buried at Bethel Presbyterian Church, Key, Belmont County, Ohio); m. Thanksgiving Day, November 24, 1898, Ritchie County, West Virginia, to William "Milton" Corbett (b. at Heath, Mead Township, Belmont County, Ohio, February 6, 1867; d. June 24, 1954; buried at Bethel Presbyterian Church, Key, Ohio); continued as expanded family at the end of this chapter];

10) Martha "Maud" "Mattie" Iams [(b. March 4, 1881, Ritchie County, West Virginia; d. March 4 or 5, 1949; buried Mount Zion Cemetery, Key, Belmont County, Ohio); single];

11) Homer D. Iams [(b. February 10, 1883, Ritchie County, West Virginia; d. August 9, 1904; buried Chevauxdefrise Methodist Cemetery, Ritchie County, West Virginia); single; birth record reads: Homer Clifton Iams, born October 10, 1883].

12) Earl Iams [(b. November 20, 1884; d. April 16, 1907; buried at Chevauxdefrise Methodist Cemetery, Ritchie County, West Virginia); single];

13) Fern Iams [(b. October 18 or 20, 1886, Ritchie County, West Virginia; d. May 30, 1970; buried in Old Wegee Cemetery, Mead Township, Belmont County, Ohio), m. September 26, 1912, to Emmitt Clarence Corbett (b. November 26, 1876 at Wegee, Mead Township, Belmont County, Ohio; d. March 2, 1956). They owned and lived on a 106-acre farm on Winding Hill, Bellaire, Ohio. Emmitt Clarence Corbett (b. 1876) was the son of John Corbett (b. Belmont County, Ohio, 1836; and grandson of Samuel Corbett). Their five children were:

   a) Walter Clyde Corbett (b. July 27, 1913, rural Shadyside, Belmont County, Ohio; d. September 9, 1987; m. February 15, 1937, to Wilda Angus (b. January 13, 1917; lived in Belmont County, Ohio); their two children were: 1¹) Walter Clarence Corbett (b. April 14, 1942); m. Judy Hertzman; 2¹) Nancy Lee Corbett (b. March 9, 1939); m. February 7, 1959, to Robert Krupinski (b. July 7, 1931); their three children: a¹) Barbara Ann Krupinski (b. August 10, 1960); m. April 24, 1982, to Jeffrey Alan Storm (b. December 10, 1960); b¹) Robert Alan Krupinski (b. August 23, 1962); c¹) Stella Mae Krupinski (b. October 1, 1964); m. January 3, 1987, to Jack Heric.

   b) Charles Robert Corbett (b. September 16 or 26, 1916; d. 1992, Bellaire, Ohio); m. May 9, 1970, to long time friend and neighbor Charlotte Margaret Shockey (b. August 12, 1914); daughter of Henry Shockley and Cora Lehman "a next door neighbor"; dairy farmer and raised beef cattle. Charlotte was a teacher and contributor.

   c) Mildred Lucille Corbett (b. January 18, 1920, Pultney Township, Belmont County, Ohio); m. July 6, 1943, to Clyde Donley

Johnston (b. August 25, 1917; d. May 23, 1972); their two children: 1¹) Bradley Johnston (b. March 24, 1956); m. Marnee Earls (b. April 7, 1962); 2¹) Waltzie Johnston (b. October 19, 1946); m. Bonn Arenas of Negrus Oriental Islands (b. May 25, 1942); their two children: a¹)Laura Arenas (b. July 12, 1972, Negrus Oriental Islands); b¹) Eric Arenas (b. August 18, 1978, Phillipines);

   d) Lila Mae Corbett (b. June 23, 1930, Bellaire, Ohio); m. May 14, 1950, to Floyd Underwood (b. August 11, 1928); lived near Bellaire; their four children: 1¹)Donley Floyd Underwood (b. January 4, 1951); m. Bertie Elizabeth (b. December 16, 1952); their two children: a¹) Christopher Don Underwood (b. August 22, 1976); b¹) Nathaniel Brock Underwood (b. March 19, 1980); 2¹) Dennis Dale Underwood (b. August 25, 1952); m/div. 1st to Sherie ____; his daughter: a¹) Amy Underwood (b. November 4, 1976); 3¹) Randy Lee Underwood (b. May 5, 1955); m. Jacquiline Marie Dorff (b. May 26, 1964); their two children: a¹) Randy Lee Underwood (b. September 22, 1983; b¹) Joshua Paul Underwood (b. January 26, 1988); 4¹) Rodney Lynn Underwood (b. July 27, 1960); single;

   e) John Wesley Corbett (b. November 3, 1915, Shadyside, Belmont County, Ohio; d. November 3, 1915, Shadyside, Belmont County, Ohio)].

Family of Iola Ellen "Ola" Iams

Iola Ellen "Ola" Iams (b. March 9, 1879, Chevauxdefrise, Ritchie County, West Virginia; lived in Mead Townnship, Belmont County, Ohio; d. April 15, 1959, Ohio State University Hospital, Columbus, Ohio; buried at Bethel Presbyterian Church Cemetery, Key, Mead Township, Belmont County, Ohio). Iola Ellen Iams (b. 1879) was the ninth child of Wesley Iams (b. 1828) and seventh child by his second wife, Nancy McKelvey (b. 1846). Iola Ellen "Ola" Iams married on Thanksgiving Day, November 24, 1898, in Ritchie County, West Virginia, to William "Milton" Corbett (b. February 6, 1867, at Heath, Stone Coal Creek, Wegee, Mead Township, Belmont County, Ohio; d. June 24, 1954, at their 120-acre farm on Crozier Ridge, Key, Mead Township, Belmont County, Ohio. They belonged to Old Wegee Church in 1920, and attended Bethel Presbyterian Church, Mead Township, Belmont County, Ohio, in later years. Iola Ellen "Ola" Corbett (b. 1879) and Milton Corbett (b. 1879) and Milton Corbett (b. 1867) operated a general farm and had four children. Except for one disappointing year in Noble County, Ohio, Milton Corbett lived his entire life in Mead Township, Belmont County, Ohio.

Letters of the 1890s courtship of Iola Ellen Iams and William "Milton" Corbett have been preserved and some have been reserved for this volume. William Milton and Iola Iams Corbett lived along Wegee Creek, Mead Township, Belmont County, Ohio, for about four years and were members of the Lower Wegee Methodist Church, later lost in one of the rare but infamous floods of Wegee Creek. William Milton and Iola Iams Corbett were then convinced by one of the Methodist ministers (later a bishop) to move to near Caldwell, Noble County, Ohio, to operate a farm of the preacher. After a very unhappy year they moved back to Mead Township, where they spent the remainder of their married life.

They lived at the Old Myers Place before moving to their 120-acre homestead on Crozier Ridge. They attended Old Wegee Methodist Church from 1908-1920; and later were members of the Bethel Presbyterian Church in Key, Ohio. Their general farm included a coal mine, orchard, grape arbors, horses, cattle, pigs, chickens, wheat fields, oat fields, hay fields, corn fields, and large gardens.

Threshing and butchering seasons were big social events in the neighborhood, with the meal at threshing time being the largest, and perhaps the best, of home cooking ever experienced. Horses did the plowing and pulled the heavy wagons. Milk was separated for the butter and placed in ten-gallon cans in the spring house until taken to the dairy. Apples were gathered and taken to the cider press. Cutting hay often gave youngsters unexpected pleasures by exposing young rabbits that could be chased and caught by hand. Hickory nuts, walnuts, and wild honey were plentiful. Fields were full of blackberries, strawberries, and elderberries. Root bark of the sassafras tree served as a special treat for making tea. Deer, turkeys, bears, foxes, wolves, and other wild animals were almost unheard of, but conservation measures are rapidly replenishing these creatures, often to the dismay of the serious farmer. Rabbits, squirrels, and groundhogs were always plentiful, and Milton Corbett was one of the best marksmen in the county.

Only later in life did Milton and Iola Iams Corbett forego the surrey or the horse and wagon for the Model A with the crank-up engine, or the jitney, used for hauling heavy loads, much as the common pickup is used today. Iola Ellen Iams Corbett became an expert chef, cooking great delicacies on her large woodburning kitchen stove that also provided hot water for cooking, bathing, and cleaning.

Water came from the well in the yard (always uphill from the barnyard) that required priming with water in order to make the hand pumping mechanism work. A community cup and a bucket of water were always at the pump, ready to provide a quick drink. The smokehouse out back always had ham and sides of bacon ready for use. The old dark earthen floor basement kept the canned goods cool and contained the canned (packed) beef and bags of potatoes to last the year.

Electricity was unheard of, but kerosene lanterns provided adequate light to read the latest *Ohio Farmer* or passages from the Bible. The cold bedrooms were made cozy by the large straw tick mattress, and the heavy, wonderfully stitched quilted comforters on the beds. Urgent trips to the outhouse in the middle of the night were made unnecessary by the placement of the essential chamber pot beside each person's bed.

Milking the cows by hand was a task entrusted only to the talents of Iola Iams Corbett, who considered the cow Buttercup to be the best milk producer of the entire herd of three cattle. The barnyard was always a favorite place to walk in your bare feet on warm summer days, though not recommended for sanitary reasons in this day and age. A bent safety pin served as a satisfactory fishing hook to land the few small fish of the local streams. The small, shallow, rocky streams often afforded to catch both small fish and hard shell crayfish by hand.

Sundays were always special and provided a much needed respite for attending church, visiting friends, and hosting neighbors and families that found their way back down the unpaved "red-dog" road to the country farm. Education was not always a high priority item on the farm, and it was only due to the individual persistence and diligence of the children that led them to complete their schooling and pursue a professional career.

(William) Milton Corbett (b. February 6, 1867) was the brother of Sarah "Sade" Corbett (m. Trueman E. Keyser); Margaret "Maggie" Corbett (m. Frank Trigg); Amos Corbett (m. Louise Wagner); Ida Mae Corbett (m. James Keyser); Bertha Corbett (d. age 24, single); Pearl Corbett (m. Ulysses S. Day); and Ami Corbett (m. Flossie Ickes). Children of Sarah Corbett Keyser: John Keyser, David Keyser, Lane Keyser, and Mary Keyser. Children of Amos Corbett: Clarence Corbett, Walter Corbett, and Ralph Corbett. Children of Pearl Corbett Day: Mansell Day, Lowell Day, Harold Day, and Clyde Day. Child of Ami Corbett: Woodrow Corbett.

Milton Corbett was a successful general farmer, church supporter, and outdoorsman. His cattle, horses, hogs, and chickens were among the finest in the county. They raised sufficient corn, hay, wheat, and oats to maintain the needs of the family as well as the livestock. He was the son of George W. Corbett and Mary Marietta Morton Corbett (b. 1842; d. 1944). George W. Corbett (b. June 29, 1832; d. 1917) was one of fourteen children of James Corbett and Mary Crow Corbett. Other children included: Elizabeth Ann Corbett (b. June 22, 1825); Samuel Corbett (b. April 14, 1827; Joseph Corbett (b. December 7, 1828; d. July 28, 1908); Sarah Ann Corbett (b. August 13, 1830; d. April 15, 1864); James Corbett (b. February 21, 1836; d. 1918); John Corbett (b. November 24, 1837; d. August 13, 1915); William G. Corbett (b. January 5, 1840; d. October 18, 1861); Jane Corbett (b. January 3, 1842); Susan Corbett (b. February 29, 1844; d. January 10, 1863); Rebecca Corbett (b. May 9, 1846; d. March 17, 1861); Charley(?) Corbett (b. August 1, 1848; d. January 31, 1861); and Margaret Corbett (b. September 28, 1850).

James Corbett (b. January 27, 1803; d. February 19, 1877) was m. August 19, 1824, to Mary Crow (b. January 27, 1805; d. March 10, 1879). James Corbett (b. 1803) was one of three children of Samuel Corbett (b. ca1760; d. 1839) and Catherine Jenkins Corbett. Other children included John Corbett (b. 1807; d. 1873; m. Nancy Lashley on January 17, 1838) and Sarah Corbett. It was this Samuel Corbett who brought his family from Harford County, Maryland, to western Pennsylvania and to Belmont County, Ohio, prior to 1820 and settled along Wegee Creek. Iola Ellen Iams (b. 1879) and Milton Corbett (b. 1867) had four children: Mildred Corbett, Edna Louise Corbett, Olive Corbett, and Lane "Meek" Corbett.

    1) Mildred Corbett (b. November 12, 1901, Wegee, Mead Township, Belmont County, Ohio; lived in Lebanon, Ohio, in 1996); m. June 5, 1923, and lived in Shadyside, Belmont County, Ohio, to Clyde McKelvey (b. April 5, 1900, Lamira, Belmont County, Ohio; d. June 6, 1968). Clyde McKelvey (b. 1900) was the son of Bruce and Mary "Mollie" Hatcher McKelvey. Mildred Corbett McKelvey served most of her working adult life as the initial and highly respected librarian at Shadyside, Ohio, with the library occupying a portion of the Shadyside High School building, where both of her children graduated. A noted historian and educator, she is credited with influencing several young students to pursue excellence through the media of reading. The editor recalls that as a young boy of six or eight years of age, he was both encouraged to visit the library and to check out several books at a time for future reading. This was a special treat related to the kindness of the librarian, since the editor lived several miles away in a separate township and school district. As a young girl, Mildred Corbett worked with her mother performing household chores, while her sister Edna Corbett helped her father with tasks in the fields and other outdoor farm chores. Mildred Corbett McKelvey has been credited with being the first member of her immediate family to be interested in the family genealogy, and was responsible for inspiring her children, Lois McKelvey and Paul McKelvey, to attempt to complete this task. The children of Mildred Corbett McKelvey and Clyde McKelvey were:

        a) Lois Lorraine McKelvey (b. March 2, 1924, a registered nurse; trained in Washington, D.C.; born at Shadyside, Ohio); m. December 6, 1947, at Methodist Church, Shadyside, Belmont County, Ohio, to James Curtis Neely (b. April 10, 1924, Birmingham, Alabama, son of John Douglas Neely). Children of Lois Lorraine McKelvey and James Curtis Neely:

1) Jo-Anna Neely (b. September 28, 1948, Garfield Memorial Hospital, Washington, D.C.), m. May 27, 1972, Durham, North Carolina, to Reverend Michael Drew Solomon (b. July 16, 1949, Durham, North Carolina; attended Duke University; was graduate of Renaselier Poly; graduated from South East Baptist Seminary, Wake Forest, North Carolina). They lived at Roxboro, North Carolina, and had four sons: a[1]) Benjamin Michael Solomon (b. July 3, 1973, Lee County Hospital, Sanford, North Carolina); b[1]) David Neely Solomon (b. July 3, 1974, Glenn R. Frye Memorial Hospital, Hickory, North Carolina; served in United States Navy until April 1995); c[1]) Timothy James Solomon (b. December 23, 1977, at Glenn R. Frye Memorial Hospital, Hickory, North Carolina); d[1]) Jared Andrew Solomon (b. June 5, 1980, at Glenn R. Frye Memorial Hospital, Hickory, North Carolina).

2) Jeannette "Jeannie" Elaine Neely (b. December 6, 1954, Garfield Memorial Hospital, Washington, D.C.; an engraver; m. December 10, 1977, at Light House Church, Indian Harbor, Florida, to Ronnie "Ron" Neil Snider (b. October 17, 1954, at Saint Francis Hospital, Miami Beach, Florida); a[1]) Chad Nathan Snider (b. November 25, 1980, Durham, North Carolina); b[1]) Heather Noll Snider (b. October 24, 1982, Durham, North Carolina).

b) Paul Laverne McKelvey (b. December 27, 1925, Shadyside, Belmont County, Ohio; graduated from Ohio State University in dairy technology; dairy executive, Dayton, Ohio; World War II veteran, U.S. Army in Europe, 1943-46), m. June 29, 1957, to Julia Curtis (b. April 5, 1927).

Children of Paul Laverne McKelvey (b. 1925) and Julia Curtis:

1) Alan Curtis McKelvey (b. March 29, 1958, Dayton, Ohio; graduate of Ohio Northern University School of Pharmacy; Director of Pharmacy, Fred A. White Center at Wright State University, Dayton, Ohio, 1985-____); m. May 21, 1983, to Linda Beckley; children: a[1]) Jennifer Irene McKelvey (b. July 11, 1985); b[1]) David Alan McKelvey (b. March 9, 1990);

2) John Kenneth McKelvey (b. April 26, 1960; graduated from Fairmont East High School, Kettering, Ohio, 1978; Metallurgical Engineer; graduate of Wright State University, Dayton, Ohio; hobby as a model; employed by McDonnell Douglas Aerospace), m. September 10, 1983, to Christine Mosconi; three children: a[1]) Rachel Jeanne McKelvey (b. June 22, 1989); b[1]) Drue Marie McKelvey (b. September 15, 1991); c[1]) Kevin Logan McKelvey (b. June 4, 1994);

3) Kathleen "Kathy" Ann McKelvey (b. May 11, 1961; a 1980 graduate of Fairmont East High School, Kettering, Ohio; graduated as chemistry major from Butler

University, 1984; worked as analytical laboratory coordinator); m. November 23, 1985, to John David Blaine; their child: a[1]) Amanda Blaine (b. November 16, 1987).

4) Karen Sue McKelvey (b. November 21, 1963; 1982 graduate of Fairmount East High School, Kettering, Ohio; member of track team and graduate of Purdue University College of Pharmacy in 1987; a registered pharmacist); m. August 22, 1987, to John Lackey, an engineering graduate of Purdue University (summa cum laude, Electrical, Master's Degree); lived in Columbus, Ohio; a[1]) Marie Kathleen Lackey (b. September 8, 1990); b[1]) Kathryn Nicole Lackey (b. August 17, 1992); c[1]) Nathan Andrew Lackey (b. April 11, 1995).

Edna Louise Corbett Reynolds (b. June 29, 1906) was born near Caldwell in Noble County, Ohio. Her family had moved there to farm on the advice and recommendation of their minister, Rev. Danford, but found the circumstances to be less than was expected. After two years they returned to a farm in Mead Township, Belmont County, Ohio. Edna helped her father on the farm and he called her "Ed." Her memories are recorded as part of her autobiography elsewhere in this book. An elementary school teacher, she was an active community leader and served her church well. Her thirty years as a school teacher included assignments at Bell Hill in York Township, Belmont County; Glendale in Mead Township, Belmont County; Warnoch, Smith Township, Belmont County; Obetz, Hamilton Township, Franklin County; Brookfield and Hartford, Trumbull County; Youngstown Schools, Mahoning County; Mifflin Township, Franklin County; and Huntsville, Logan County, all in Ohio. She was Past Worthy Matron and fifty-year member of Caplina Chapter 489 Order of Eastern Star at Powhatan Point, Ohio; Assistant Deaconess of Powhatan Methodist Episcopal Church; member of Powhatan Women's Club; member Worthington United Methodist Church; 1928 graduate of Muskingum College; Superintendent of Powhatan Methodist Church Sunday School; church pianist at Centerville Methodist Church.

Edna (b. 1906) attended grade schools in Mead Township, Belmont County, Ohio, including the one-room school of Dauntless, and then graduated from Bellaire High School, Belmont County, Ohio, in 1924. After completing Normal School in Bellaire in 1925, she graduated from Muskingum College, New Concord, in 1928. It was there that she met her future husband, Ray C. Reynolds. She began her teaching career in 1926 at Glendale, a one-room school in Mead Township, Belmont County, Ohio, and eventually specialized in the teaching of third and fourth grade. Edna was raised in a farm in Belmont County, Ohio, where she needed to travel fifteen miles by horseback and by narrow gauge railroad (Ohio River and Western) to attend high school, a process which took much persuasion on her part. She was a talented, though modest, musician who learned to play the piano and organ without benefit of any formal lessons. She died March 9, 1997, Columbus, Ohio; buried at Glens Rest, Reynoldsburg, Ohio.

Ray Campbell Reynolds (b. 1904; d. Columbus, Ohio, December 26, 1988; buried Glens Rest, Reynoldsburg, Ohio) was the son of Reverend Neff J. Reynolds (b. 1879) and Mary Hobbs Reynolds; and the brother of Fred Reynolds, Carl Reynolds, Roger Reynolds, Leanna Reynolds Steiner, and Elizabeth Reynolds. Ray C. Reynolds (b. 1904) attended schools in Belmont County, Ohio, graduating from Somerton High School in 1923. A good basketball and baseball player, he was the Ohio Conference batting champion while attending Muskingum College in 1930. He earned his

Bachelor's Degree from Muskingum College and his Master's Degree from the University of Pittsburgh. He taught and coached at Powhatan Point, Ohio, coaching boys' and girls' basketball, boys' baseball, and American Legion baseball, having several championship teams. He served as Superintendent of Smith Township Schools in Belmont County, Ohio, from 1942 until 1945, when he assumed a similar post at Hamilton Township in Franklin County, Ohio. In 1948, he became Superintendent of Hubbard Village Schools in Trumbull County, Ohio; and in 1954 became Executive Head of Jefferson Township Schools in Gahanna, Franklin County, Ohio. In 1963, he became Superintendent of Logan County Schools. His special expertise was in building school systems and new facilities. A polished public speaker, he was active in numerous youth and community organizations. He was a 32nd degree Mason; a Shriner; life member in National Education Association; member Worthington Methodist Church; Franklin County and Ohio State Teacher's Association; Past Worthy Patron and Golden Anniversary Member of Captina Chapter 489 Order of Eastern Star; Past-Master of Mariah Masonic Lodge 105 of Powhatan; member of Ohio, Franklin, Trumbull, and Logan Counties Superintendent's Association; Powhatan ME Church Sunday School teacher; Ohio High School State High School Official's Association; Boy Scouts of America Scoutmaster; Chairman, Council Commissioner; and Silver Beaver Awards. He returned after forty-two years in public school systems, having started his teaching at Shucks School in Muskingum County, Ohio, and then in Pleasant Hill School in York Township in Belmont County, Ohio.

A noted educator, community leader, and sportsman, Ray was the son of Reverend Neff J. Reynolds (b. July 26, 1879, Belmont County, Ohio; d. July 21, 1966; buried in Sewellsville, Kirkwood Township, Belmont County, Ohio), and Mary Hobbs Reynolds (b. Somerset Township, Belmont County, Ohio, June 7, 1881; d. November 1971), who were married October 23, 1901. Neff J. Reynolds, a Methodist minister, schoolteacher, postmaster, notary public, and well known local merchant, was the son of Job Reynolds (b. Kirkwood Township, Belmont County, Ohio, February 12, 1854; d. February 21, 1946) and Sadie Todd (b. June 1859; d.1942), who were m. October 8, 1878. Job Reynolds (b. 1854), a local minister and merchant in Fairview, Ohio, was the son of Reuben Reynolds (b. September 3, 1824; d. October 10, 1915) and Nancy Perkins (b. November 18, 1825; d. December 27, 1911), who were m. February 1, 1849. Reuben Reynolds (b. 1824) was the son of early Belmont County pioneer Richard Barnard Reynolds (b. August 31, 1790, Lancaster County, Pennsylvania; d. Belmont County, Ohio, August 3, 1829) and Esther Sidwell (b. 1792, Lancaster County, Pennsylvania; d. 1874; buried at Sewellsville, Ohio), who were m. April 16, 1812. Richard Barnard Reynolds (b. 1790) was a Quaker; migrated from near Nottingham, Lancaster County, Pennsylvania, in 1817; and lived for a short time in Jefferson County, Ohio, before settling in northern Kirkwood Township, Belmont County, Ohio.

Ray Campbell Reynolds (b. 1904) had three brothers and two sisters. Sister Sarah Leanna Reynolds was b. April 11, 1903; d. Powhatan Point, Ohio, January 1, 1994; m. in 1926 Amos Steiner, and lived in Powhatan Point, Belmont County, Ohio. Sister Elizabeth Reynolds (b. April 1911); d. of meningitis at age 9. Brother Fred Hubert Reynolds (b. Londerry Township, Guernsey County, Ohio, August 4, 1907; d. Fairfield November 25, 1995), m. November 24, 1927, Fairview, Ohio, Wilma Luellan (b. February 26, 1908, of Key, Ohio; d. Fairfield August 12, 1982; buried Fairview Cemetery, Fairfield, California), and was a popular physics and chemistry teacher at Bellaire and Shadyside High Schools; farmer; sawmill operator; developer of the local telephone system; public school superintendent and administrator, who operated a plumbing and heating business during the Alaskan oil boom. He later became a leader in the California senior citizens movement and was nominated for Muskingum College Distinguished Alumni Award in 1992. Children of Fred (b. 1907) and Wilma Reynolds included Fred Ray Reynolds, Alice Reynolds, Jeanette Reynolds, James Hubert Reynolds, and Audrey June Reynolds. Brother Carl Reuben Reynolds (b. Richmond Township, Belmont County, Ohio, May 29, 1910; d. Seminole, Florida, May 23, 1988), m. at Buffalo, Ohio, in 1928 to Mildred Harding (b. February 1, 1912; lived in Seminole, Florida, in 1996).

Carl R. Reynolds (b. 1910) graduated from Muskingum College and then pursued a career as teacher, principal, and public school superintendent at Senecaville, New Concord, and Garfield Heights, Ohio, before retiring to Seminole, Florida. Children of Carl and Mildred Reynolds included Carl Henry Reynolds, Jr., Harold Richard Reynolds, and Mark Alan Reynolds. Brother Clarence "Roger" Reynolds was b. October 9, 1912. Roger (b. 1912) m. 1st to Emma Cherry (b. April 10, 1912), daughter of Michael and Julia Cherry; and their child, Patricia Jean Reynolds (b. April 22, 1934) m. 1st on August 25, 1956, to Marshall Hallock Brenner (b. May 27, 1933; d. July 7, 1974), and m. 2nd to William Ehrler, PhD. Children of Patricia Reynolds (b. 1934) were 1) Michele Annette Brenner (b. October 12, 1962; m. August 25, 1984, to William Dodds); and 2) Cynthia Allyn Brenner (b. March 13, 1964). Patricia Reynolds (b. 1934) and her husband, Dr. William "Bill" Ehrler, lived in San Diego, California, in 1996. Clarence Roger Reynolds (b. 1912) m. 2nd to Dorothy Grandy and they had three children: 1) Barbara Reynolds (lived in Dixon, Illinois; m. Mr. Morrison and lived in Moline, Illinois); 2) Nancy Ruth Reynolds (m. Mr. Masters); and 3) Bonnie Reynolds (m. Mr. Ryan; their child: Sean Ryan). Children of Edna Louise Corbett (b. 1906) and Ray Campbell Reynolds were: Ralph D. Reynolds, and Robert W. Reynolds.

a) Ralph Duane Reynolds, M.D. (b. February 22, 1934, Powhatan Point, York Township, Belmont County, Ohio), m. 1st, June 15, 1957, Gibsonia, Pennsylvania, to Gertrude Elaine Manifold (b. February 13, 1936, Cleveland, Ohio), daughter of George O. Manifold and Mary Fargo; m. 2nd, November 6, 1982, St. Mary's Episcopal Church, Napa, California, to Norita Rose Sholly Otte (b. April 18, 1935, Le Mars, Iowa), the daughter of Harry B. Sholly (b. March 2, 1891, Lebanon, Pennsylvania; m. Guttenberg, Iowa, June 10, 1923; d. January 4, 1960, Cherokee, Iowa), and Stella Rose Weber (b. January 7, 1901, Clayton County, Iowa; d. March 3, 1974, Sioux City, Iowa, and buried in Marcus, Iowa).

Norita Rose Sholly had two children by a former marriage: 1) Nancy Lee Otte (b. March 22, 1955, Cherokee, Iowa; m. August 12, 1978, Santa Cruz, California, to Frank Howard Anson, who was b. October 15, 1946, son of Frank Anson and Virginia Wilson); children: Tressa Leigh Anson (b. August 9, 1983, Columbia, Missouri), and Zachary Frank Anson (b. April 19, 1988, Springfield, Massachusetts); graduated from Solano College School of Nursing, Fairfield, California; and graduated from University of Massachusetts School of Nursing, Amherst, Massachusetts; and 2) Susan Lee Otte Robbins (b. August 19, 1956); m. 1974 to David Robbins; professional office design, Boston.

The children of Harry B. Sholly and Stella Weber were: 1) Vincent George Sholly [b. October 23, 1923; d. May 25, 1984; m. Eileen Fangman; five children: Michael James Sholly (b. 1941); Roxanne Kay Sholly (b. 1953); Edward Lee Sholly (b. 1954); Louis Patrick Sholly (b. 1955), and Deborah Kathryn Sholly (b. 1959)]; 2) Clarence Anthony Sholly [(b. January 17, 1925, Cherokee, Iowa; d. April 16, 1961,

Sutherland, Iowa; m. September 24, 1951, to Zelma Mae Otte; seven children: Patricia Ann Sholly (b. 1952); Clarence Anthony "Tony" Sholly (b. 1955); Sandia Marie Sholly (b. 1956); David Lee Sholly {(b. 1952); and Jerome Francis Sholly (b. 1961)]; 3) Kenneth Francis Sholly [(b. March 14, 1926, Cherokee County, Iowa); m. June 24, 1953, Sutherland, Iowa, to Phyllis Katherine Miller; lived in Eagle Grove, Iowa; five children: Bruce Rodrick Sholly (b. 1954); Denise Marie Sholly (b. 1955); Maureen Annette Sholly (b. 1957); Melissa Jean Sholly (b. 1963); and Kevin Francis Sholly (b. 1965)]; 4) Richard Joseph Sholly [(b. May 27, 1927, Cherokee County, Iowa; m. November 23, 1957, Storm Lake, Iowa, to Agatha Ann Jansen; lived in Stanchfield, Minnesota; five children: Jean Marie Sholly (b. 1959); Robert John Sholly (b. 1960); Helen Elizabeth Sholly (b. 1961); Karen Ann Sholly (b. 1962); and Sharon Lee Sholly (b. 1965)]; 5) Kathleen Theresa Sholly [(b. November 6, 1928, Cherokee County, Iowa; d. Sioux City, Iowa, August 9, 1988); m. June 22, 1948, Marcus, Iowa, to Raymond Alfred Kass; lived at Marcus, Iowa; four children: a) Linda Marie Kass (b. 1949); b) Larry Joseph Kass (b. 1952); c) Ronald Raymond Kass (b. 1956); and d) Beverly Ann Kass (b. 1960)]; 6) Edna May Sholly [(b. April 5, 1930, Cherokee County, Iowa; m. November 3, 1951, Sioux City, Iowa, to Vernon Henry Binder; lived at San Marcos, Texas; five children: Barbara Jean Binder (b. 1952); Donna Lynn Binder (b. 1954); Nicholas Harry Binder (b. and d. 1955); Mary Kay Binder (b. 1958); and Verna Rose Binder (b. 1959)]; 7) Cletus Edward Sholly [(b. May 3, 1932, Le Mars, Iowa; m. May 4, 1979, California, to Doris "Jean" Woodward; child: Brian Edward Sholly (b. 1969, Concord, California)]; 8) Duane Anthony Sholly [(b. October 11, 1933, Le Mars, Iowa); a professional boilermaker; single in 1996; lived in Fairfield, Solano County, California)]; 9) Norita Rose Sholly [(b. April 18, 1935, Sacred Heart Hospital, LeMars, Iowa; m. 1st, Evan Otte; m. 2nd, Ralph D. Reynolds, M.D.; active in children's shelter; homeless programs; Brownies; Girl Scouts, Women's Cancer Control Program (treasurer); Women's Health Program; Ellis Fischel Cancer Center Hospital Guild (treasurer); founder of Four Seasons Gift Shop at Cancer Center; Twigs of Columbus Children's Hospital (local president); Worthington Hills Garden Club; Liberty Presbyterian Church; Holy Spirit Catholic Church; Jenkins Arboretum of Philadelphia; Kirksville (Missouri) Osteopathic Medical Center; Adair County Historical Society and Sholly Family historian]; 10) Rosemary Elizabeth Sholly [(b. November 5, 1938, LeMars, Iowa; m. April 12, 1958, Washington, D.C., to Troy Knott of Oklahoma; lived in Fairfield, California; four children: Brenda Elizabeth Knott (b. 1966; adopted); Deanna Marie Knott (b. 1966); Tammy Louise Knott (b. 1968); and Jennifer Christine Knott (b. 1974)].

Ralph Duane Reynolds (b. 1934) attended public Schools at Powhatan and Centerville, Smith Township, Belmont County, Ohio; Obetz and Hamilton Township, Franklin County, Ohio, and Hubbard, Trumbull County, Ohio; graduated from Muskingum College in 1956; the Ohio State University School of Medicine in 1960; internship from Madigan General Hospital, Tacoma, Washington, in 1961; internal medicine residency and Hematology Oncology Fellowship from Wilford Hall Medical Center, San Antonio, Texas, in 1965; served as Colonel, United

States Air Force Medical Corps, 1959-1983; President of Society of Air Force Physicians; Chief of Hematology Oncology Service at David Grant Medical Center, Travis AFB, California, 1965-1983; Professor of Medicine, University of California, Davis School of Medicine and University of Missouri Columbia School of Medicine; Chairman, Department of Medicine, Ellis Fischel Cancer Center; Director of Clinical Research, Cancer Research Center; Medical Director, Women's Cancer Control Program; Associate Director Oncology Research, Adria Laboratories in Columbus, Ohio; Senior Director of Research and Development, U. S. Bioscience; Cancer Research Investigator for National Cancer Institute; Director of Oncology, Kirksville Osteopathic Medical Center; pioneered work in biological response modifiers; chemotherapy for cancer; and the use of effective protector agents in the treatment of cancer. Children of Ralph Duane Reynolds:

    1) Daniel Ralph Reynolds (b. October 21, 1960, Madigan General Hospital, Tacoma, Washington); m. 1st, August 28, 1982, to Cathlyn Lee Stephenson (b. July 4, 1963); daughter of Bud and Dorie Stephenson of Vacaville, California); m. 2nd, May 20, 1993, Maui, Hawaii, to Susan Marie Crews (b. April 7, 1966, Stuttgart, Germany), daughter of Roy Crews (b. July 20, 1933, in Chesterfield, Missouri) and Ann Smith (b. September 4, 1941, in Fort Towsow, Oklahoma); and sister of Michael Eric Crews (b. March 3, 1965, Tacoma, Washington). A child of the first marriage was Thomas Daniel Reynolds (b. November 22, 1989, Berkeley, California); and children of the second marriage were Nicholas Logan Reynolds (b. February 10, 1995, Los Gatos, California); and Matthew Davis Reynolds (b. November 14, 1996). Daniel Ralph Reynolds (b. 1960) graduated with honors from Vacaville High School, Solano County, California, where he played basketball and baseball, serving as team captain for each. He was all-league in both sports, being a high-scoring guard on the basketball team and both undefeated pitcher and league leading hitter (league record) on the baseball team. He graduated from University of California Berkeley, and became a Certified Public Accountant with Arthur Anderson of San Francisco and San Jose, California. While at the University of California, he played baseball and basketball; a pitcher on the baseball team and captain; leading scorer; leader in free throw and field goal percentage on the junior varsity basketball team.

    2) Barry Duane Reynolds (b. March 31, 1962, Wilford Hall Medical Center, San Antonio, Texas); graduated from Vacaville High School, Solano County, California, earning letters in football, basketball, and baseball, serving as captain of the latter two sports; achieving All-American honors in Pop Wamer football and All-State high school honors in baseball; graduated from University California Berkeley, with Bachelor of Science Degree in computer science, electrical engineering, and nuclear engineering, where he finished with a 4.0 grade-point ratio and was named outstanding university student. He later graduated from the same university with a Master's Degree in Electrical Engineering; and later from Stanford University Business

School, with a Master's Degree in Business Administration as top graduate in his class, Arjay Miller, and also the Henry Ford Scholar; played rugby at both University of California Berkeley and at Stanford Business School, leading his business school to final four in 1992. He worked first for General Electric, then with Bain and Company of San Francisco, and then a short employment with Texas Pacific before returning to Bain and Company, where he engineered the purchase of several highly regarded California wineries, including Beringer of Napa Valley. He m. August 13, 1988, in San Jose, California, to Jill Kanani Peterson (b. February 8, 1961), daughter of Gordon and June Peterson of San Jose. Jill Peterson graduated from San Jose State University with a degree in Business Administration, and pursued a career in Marketing. Gordon Kanani Peterson (b. January 8, 1934, Honolulu), m. January 5, 1960, to June Marie Meyers (b. January 2, 1941, Bakersfield, California), and their children included: Garland Lani Peterson (b. May 18, 1962); Eric Gordon Peterson (b. September 3, 1967); Cindy Louise Peterson (b. October 19, 1963; m. October 2, 1983, to John Matranga, who was b. Febraury 26, 1951); and Jennel Marie Peterson (b. April 29, 1965; m. October 7, 1989, to Theodore Nicholas Pappas, who was b. February 3, 1964). Cindy Louise Peterson and John Matranga had three children: Sarah Louise Matranga (b. September 14, 1985; Jennifer Kanani-Marie Matranga (b. September 17, 1989); and Kimberly Nicole Matranga (b. May 22, 1990). Barry Reynolds and Jill Peterson, living in Danville, California, had a son McKinley Duane Reynolds (b. April 3, 1996).

3) Ronald Arthur Reynolds (b. March 20, 1966, David Grant Medical Center, Travis Air Force Base, California) graduated with honors from Vacaville High School, Solano County, California in 1984; and with a Bachelor's Degree from University of California Berkeley in 1989; was an outstanding athlete who won honors in both football and baseball and also participated well in both basketball and track. As a heralded high school football running back, he led his team in rushing offense; was credited by his coaches as breaking open several big games; was named to the Helms All American Football Team, and to the Northern California Football Scholar-Athlete Hall of Fame. As a speedy baserunner and outstanding hitter, he won All-State honors, leading his Senior Babe Ruth team to the California State Championship. Ronald Arthur Reynolds pursued a career as an executive accountant with Chevron Corporation; and m. May 29, 1993, in the Napa Valley of California, to Laura Lynn Bischoff (b. March 12, 1968), the daughter of Marshall Bischoff, M.D. (b. August 23, 1940, in Michigan, a pathologist), and Noyce Snow (b. June 16, 1940, in Jamestown, Kentucky). Laura Lynn Bischoff was the sister of Stephanie Cheryl Bischoff (b. July 7, 1970), m. Gary McIver, August 8, 1992. Laura Lynn Bischoff graduated with a bachelor's degree from Fresno State University, Fresno, California, in 1990; then performed work

toward a Master's Degree before working at Chevron USA as an accountant. Ronald Arthur Reynolds and Laura Lynn Bischoff lived in Fairfield, California, after their marriage; expected a child 1998.

b) Robert Wayne Reynolds (b. April 5, 1937, Powhatan Point, York Township, Belmont County, Ohio); graduated from Gahanna Lincoln High School, Jefferson Township, Franklin County, Ohio, in 1955; and from Ohio University, Athens, Ohio, with a Bachelor of Science in Mechanical Engineering in 1960. He was high school valedictorian and an outstanding athlete, earning multiple varsity letters in football, basketball, and track; earning all-state honors in track where he was the record holder and district champion in the high jump; was the record holder district and state champion in the long jump. He also established the school record in the hundred yard dash (10.0 seconds), and was the leading ground gainer on the football team. At Ohio University, he played football and track, winning the greatest distinction in track as a long jumper. He held the school, stadium, Mid-American Conference records, and won the prestigious Drake Relays and IC4A meet championships. His olympic hopes ended when he suffered a severe compound fracture of the lower leg while helping paint the family homestead. He pursued a career in engineering as the major production engineer of television tubes in the world, working for Owens-Illinois (later OI-NEC). He was eventually plant manger of the large television tube manufacturing facility in Wilkes Barre, Pennsylvania, during which time he also obtained his Master's Degree in Business Administration from Wilkes College.

Robert Wayne Reynolds (b. 1937) m. 1st, to Baiba Folkmanis (b. March 26, 1940, Latvia); m. 2nd, to Mary Kern (b. January 21, 1951, Wilkes Barre, Pennsylvania); daughter of Mr. and Mrs. Louis Joseph Kern, Sr. Their children were: 1) Jeffrey Wayne Reynolds (b. January 2, 1962, in Ohio), m. October 5, 1985, in Reynoldsburg, Franklin County, Ohio, to Leah Pusecker (b. December 26, 1962; daughter of Charles Nicholas Pusecker and Mary I. Abernathy). Their child: Ian Jeffrey Reynolds (b. June 20, 1992, in Columbus, Ohio. Jeffrey Wayne Reynolds (b. 1962) attended schools in Columbus, Ohio, and Wilkes Barre, Pennsylvania, before graduating from Ohio University, Athens, Ohio; and pursuing a career with the Environmental Protection Agency (EPA). Leah Pusecker (b. 1962) attended Reynoldsburg High School, then graduated from Ohio University before pursuing a career as a commercial artist for the Ohio Department of Natural Resources (ODNR), and also with her own company. Jeffrey and Leah Reynolds made their home in Grandview, Franklin County, Ohio. 2) Steven Robert Reynolds (b. April 22, 1965; graduated from The Ohio State University after attending Grandview High School, where he was a wrestler, an engraver, and a serious candidate for city council in his home town. He later pursued a career as an executive with a large real estate appraisal firm, later forming his own successful company in Grandview, Franklin County, Ohio, where he also made his home. 3) Joshua Robert Reynolds (b. June 20, 1995, in Louisiana, adopted).

Other children of Nick Pusecker (b. 1933) and Mary Ann Abernathy were: 1) Aline Pusecker (b. Columbus, Ohio, June 12, 1957); 2) Michael Pusecker (b. June 15, 1958); 3) Theodore Pusecker (b. April 13, 1961); 4) Daniel Pusecker (b. September

15, 1968); and 5) Cara Pusecker (b. January 30, 1971). Nick Pusecker (b. 1933) was the son of Ivan "Fatso" Pusecker, famous local painter, and Margaret Corbett. Ivan Pusecker and Margaret Corbett also had four other children: 1) Reta Pusecker; 2) Thomas Pusecker, who owned an art and frame shop in the town of Bexley, Franklin County, Ohio; 3) Robert Pusecker, who made furniture and did antique restoration; and 4) Ivan "Butch" Pusecker, Jr., known for being senior class president and "in the money business." The parents of Mary Ann Abernathy (b. 1936) were Henry "Hank" and Madge Abernathy. Leah Pusecker (b. 1962) pursued a successful career in graphic arts.

The children of Patrick and Bridget Sweeney Kern were: 1) Louis Kern; and 2) Genevive Kern (m. Martin Gilbary). The other children of Louis Kern and Mildred Randozza were: Linda Kern (b. January 5, 1955; m. November 1977, James Dessoye; two children: 1) Jillian Dessoye, b. September 1978; and 2) James "Jimmy" Dessoye, b. March 1982); 2) Paul Kern (b. May 1940; m. Sheila Ackerman; children: 1) Paulette Kern; and 2) Jeffrey Kern, b. January 21, 1972); and 3) Louis Kern II, (b. August 22, 1944; m. Ann Cawley; children: 1) Louis Kern III, b. 1968; and 2) Lisa Kern, b. 1969; m. Richard "Rick" M. Guericks, with their son Jonathan Joseph Guericks, b. 1988).

The other children of Norman Randazza and Theresa Saporita were: Mildred Randazza; 2) Louis Randazza; 3) Joseph Randazza; 4) Pauline Randazza; 5) Norma Randazza; 6) Rosa Randazza; 7) Norman Randazza; and 8) Lillian Randazza.

3. Lane Meek Corbett (b. July 9, 1915, Mead Township, Belmont County, Ohio; d. July 27, 1997), m. September 10, 1938, Key, Ohio, to Alberta Marie "Dolly" Brown (b. July 12, 1919, daughter of Mr. and Mrs. Arthur "Coon" Brown of Key, Belmont County, Ohio). Meek Corbett (b. 1915) lived on the Corbett family homestead on Crozier Ridge near Key, Belmont County, Ohio. Known for his generosity and his large piles of firewood, Meek Corbett (b. 1915) was the pillar of the community. He worked for the Roads Department of the township and operated his own sawmill. He was known for his strength and dedication to the principles of truth and honesty. At 6 ft. 3 in. and 240 pounds, he presented a commanding presence, and his lively, friendly demeanor gained him the trust and friendship of those who knew him.

    a) Lane Meek "Buddy" Corbett (b. May 30, 1939, Mead Township, Belmont County, Ohio); m. 1st, June 8, 1963, to Darlene Myers; and m. 2nd to Sue Goff (b. July 20, 1949); children: 1) Jim Corbett (b. April 2, 1964); 2) Misty Corbett (b. June 30, 1967); lived in Columbus, Ohio; 3) Carla Corbett (b. July 1, 1968); lived in Columbus, Ohio; 4) Richard Corbett (b. January 27, 1972).

    b) Hazel Corbett (b. December 6, 1946, Mead Township, Belmont County, Ohio), m. May 7, 1972, to William "Bill" Dillon (b. June 19, 1950); children: 1) Dorothy "Dot" Dillon (b. January 4, 1973); 2) Minnie Dillon (b. September 30, 1978).

    c) Dorothy Corbett (twin, b. January 15, 1951, Mead Township, Belmont County, Ohio), m. October 8, 1972, to James "Jim" Bennett (b. December 3, 1950); children: 1) Lorrie Ann Bennett (b. December 3, 1973); 2) Jennifer Bennett (b. December 14, 1978); 3) Angie Bennett (b. November 8, 1981); 4) James Joseph Bennett (b. March 15, 1988).

    d) Delores Corbett (twin, b. January 15, 1951), Mead Township, Belmont County, Ohio), m. November 1, 1984, to Dennis LeMasters (b. 1956), and lived in Bridgeport, Belmont County, Ohio; child: 1) Dennis LeMasters, Jr. (b. September 21, 1985).

4) Sarah Olive Corbett (b. November 25, 1908, Mead Township, Belmont County, Ohio; d. July 7, 1933, of drowning in Captina Creek, Belmont County, Ohio, while a second year nursing student).

REFERENCES

- Lewis Clark Walkinshaw, *Annals of Southwestern Pennsylvania* Volume 4 (Lewis Historical Publishing Co., New York, 1939), pp. 102, 103, 269.

- Washington County and City Directory, City Directory, 1877, 1878, 1886, 1894, 1896, 1897, 1899, 1901, 1902, 1903, 1907, 1917, 1926.

- *The Morning Observer (*Washington, Pennsylvania, August 31, 1931, and August 26, 1933).

- Federal Population Censuses, 1790 through 1920, as available, National Archives, Washington, D.C.

- Tax Lists, Fairfield County, Ohio; Perry County, Ohio; Belmont County, Ohio.

- Sharon J. Doliante, *Maryland and Virginia Colonials: Genealogies of Some Colonial Families.*

- Marriage Records, Frederick County, Maryland; Percy County, Ohio; Muskingum County, Ohio; Belmont County, Ohio; Ritchie County, West Virginia; Noble County, Ohio.

- Wills, Frederick County, Maryland; Belmont County, Ohio; Ritchie County, West Virginia.

- F. G. Witherwood, *The Graham-Grimes Genealogy and Complete Branches, 1756-1926* (Bloomington, Illinois, 1926).

- Court Abstracts, Frederick County, Maryland; Licking County, Ohio.

- Archives of State of Maryland, Annapolis, Maryland.

- International Genealogical Index (IGI), Salt Lake City, Utah, 1984, 1988.

- Revolutionary War Pensioners, Frederick County, Maryland; National Archives, Washington, D.C.

- Voters in Presidential Election of 1796, Frederick County, Maryland.

- Deeds, Fairfield County, Ohio; Perry County, Ohio; Noble County, Ohio; Belmont County, Ohio.

- N. N. Hill, *History of Licking County, Ohio* (1881), p. 481.

- L. H. Watkins, *History of Warren County, Ohio* (1886), p. 496.

- W. T. Martin, *History of Franklin County, Ohio (1858)*, pp. 228, 446.

- Cemetery Records, New Lexington, Ohio; Noble County, Ohio; Belmont County, Ohio; Cass County, Indiana; Noble County, Ohio; Fairfield County, Ohio.

- Elsie Iams, The Elsie Iams Narrative, from *The Tower*, North Ten Mile Baptist Church, March 1972, pp. 29-31.

- C. M. L.Wiseman, *Pioneer Records and Pioneer People of Fairfield, Ohio* (F. J. Heer Printing Company, Columbus, Ohio, 1901).

- Harvey Scott, *A Complete History of Fairfield County, Ohio, 1877.*

- O. L. Baskin, *History of Morrow County, Ohio, 1880*, p. 689.

- Connelly *History of Kansas* (Volume 4, 1928), p. 2032.

- D. E. Allen, *Zimmerman, Waters and Allied Families*, p. 54.

- Charles E. Moylan, *Ijamsville: The Story of a Country Village of Frederick County, Maryland* (privately published, from *Frederick* (Maryland) *News*; February 17, 24, and March 3, 10, and 17, 1951).

- Harry Wright Newman, *Anne Arundel Gentry* (published privately, Vol. 1, 1970; Vol. 2, 1971).

- Harry Wright Newman, *Anne Arundel Gentry* (published privately, 1933).

- Harry Wright Newman, *Mareen Duvall of Middle Plantation* (published privately, 1952).

- Harry Wright Newman, *To Maryland From Oversees* (Genealogical Publisher, Baltimore, Maryland, 1985).

- Lois Ijams Hartman, *Remembered in this Land* (Hillcrest Books, Pasadena, 1978); *In His Steps* (Hillcrest Books, Pasadena).

- Iams Manuscript Collection of Elisha B. Iams for Greene County, Pennsylvania, Waynesburg, Pennsylvania.

- E. Jay Iams, collection of Papers of E. Jay Iams, Washington County, Pennsylvania, 1938.

- Howard L. Leckey, *Ten Mile Country and Its Pioneer Families: A Genealogical History of the Upper Monongahela Valley* (Greene County Historical Society, The Bookmark, Kingstown, New York, 1977).

- Harry Wright Newman, *To Maryland From Overseas* (Genealogical Publishing Company, Baltimore, Maryland, 1988).

- J. D. Warfield, *The Founders of Anne Arundel and Howard Counties, Maryland* (Kohn and Pollock Publishers, Baltimore, Maryland, 1905).

351

- F. B. Heitman, *Historical Register of Officers of the Continental Army During the War of the Revolution, April 1775 to December 1783* (Washington, 1893).

- Bob and Mary Clossen, *Index to Washington County, Pennsylvania, Wills, 1781-1900* (1981).

- Samuel E. Alvord, *History of Noble County, Indiana* (B. F. Bower Pub., Logansport, Indiana, 1902).

- W. H. Beers, *History of Montgomery County, Ohio* (W. H. Beers Co., 1882); *History of Sandusky and Ottawa Counties, Ohio, 1896*; *History of Madison County, Ohio, 1883*.

- John Malcolm Bulloch, *The House of Gordon* (Volume 1, New Spalding Club, Aberdeen, 1903), pp. 173-282.

- C. L. Blackson, *Hippocrene Guide to Underground Railroad* (Hippocrene Books, New York, 1994).

- Grace M. Biggs, *John Biggs, Revolutionary War Veteran and Allied Families* (Jessup, Maryland, 1972).

- L. H. Watkins, *History of Noble County, Ohio* (Chicago, Illinois, 1887).

- Brant and Fuller, *History of Upper Ohio Valley* (Brant and Fuller, Madison, Wisconsin, 1890).

- Vertical File, Jefferson County Historical Society, Steubenville, Ohio, 1986.

- J. A. Magruder, Jr., *Index of Maryland Colonial Wills, 1634-1777* (Genealogical Publishing Company, Baltimore, Maryland, 1986).

- J. H. Beers, *Commemorative Biographical Record of Washington County, Pennsylvania* (J. H. Beers Company, Chicago, Illinois, 1893).

- William Hanna, *History of Greene County, Pennsylvania* (1882).

- F. E. Wright, *Anne Arundel County Church Records of the 17th and 18th Centuries, Annapolis, Maryland* (Family Line Pub., Westminster, 1993).

- I. M. Ochsenbein and C. F. Fedorchak, *Belmont County, Ohio, Before 1830* (1977).

- Gust Skordas, *The Early Settlers of Maryland* (Genealogical Publishing Company, Baltimore, Maryland, 1968).

- Clayton Torence, *Old Somerset on the Eastern Shore of Maryland* (Regional Publishing Co., Baltimore, Maryland, 1966).

- R. B. Clark, *Genealogies of Virginia Families* (Genealogical Publishing Co., Baltimore, Maryland, 1981).

- Proceedings of the Council of Maryland, Annapolis, Archives of Maryland, 1752-1761.

- Floyd O. Prunty, *History of the Prunty Family of Pruntytown and Taylor County* (1978).

- Minnie Kendall Lowther, *Ritchie County In History and Romance.*

- Ritchie County Historical Society, *The History of Ritchie County, West Virginia, to 1980* (Taylor Publishing Co., Salem, West Virginia, 1980).

- Ruth Iams; Isaac L. Iams; Norma Bayne; Fred Cochran, *Rural Reflections of Amwell Township, Washington County, Pennsylvania* (4 volumes, 1977).

- Richard G. and Malvine B. Zollars, *Marriages Compiled from Greene County, Pennsylvania, Records 1780-1885* (Waynesburg).

- Helen Reynolds, *Marriage Records from the Green County Court House.*

- Everhart, *History of Muskingum County, Ohio* (1882).

- Sutton, *History of Shelby County, Ohio* (1883).

- Washington County Chapter, Daughters of American Revolution: Lists of Revolutionary Soldiers Buried in Washington County, Pennsylvania.

- Samuel P. Bates, *History of Greene County, Pennsylvania* (Nelson, Richford and Company, Chicago, Ilinois, 1888).

- Waterman, Watkins and Company, *History of Bedford, Somerset, and Fulton Counties, Pennsylvania* (Chicago, 1884).

- Andrew J. Waychoff, *Local History of Greene County and Southwestern Pennsylvania* (Greene County Historical Society, 1975).

- Daughters of American Revolution of Ohio: The Official Roster of the Soldiers of the American Revolution Buried in the State of Ohio.

- S. E. Clements, and F. E. Wright, *The Maryland Militia in the Revolutionary War* (Family Line Publications, Silver Spring, 1987).

- Ellen T. Berry and David A. Berry, *Early Ohio Settlers: Purchasers of Land in Southeastern Ohio, 1800 to 1840* (Genealogical Publishing Co., Baltimore, Maryland, 1985).

- John Thomas Gurney III, *Cemetery Inscriptions of Anne Arundel County, Maryland* (Bookcrafters, Inc., Chelsea, Michigan, 1982).

- Henry C. Peden, Jr., *Revolutionary Patriots of Anne Arundel County, Maryland* (Family Line Publication, Westminster, Maryland, 1992).

- Ralph D. Reynolds, *John Hobbs, 16__-1731* (Quaint Pub., Naples, Florida, 1994).

- Ohio Extension Homemakers; Belmont County History, 1988, Wadsworth Press, Salem, West Virginia, 1988.

- Raymond B.Clark, Jr., *Index to Anne Arundel County, Maryland, Wills* (Arlington, Virginia, 1981).

- Bettie Stirling Carothers, 1776 Census of Maryland, Luthersville, Maryland.

- James Drake Iams, *Bayside Impressions: Maryland's Eastern Shore and the Chesapeake Bay* (paintings) (Tidewater Publishers, Centreville, Maryland, 1984).

- Nancy Martin Shidler, *Nancy Martin: Country Gal* (Christopher Publishing House, Boston, Massachusetts, 1950).

- Albert Abramson, *Zworykin: Pioneer of Television* (University of Illinois Press, Urbane, 1995).

- Albert Abramson, *The History of Television, 1880 to 1941* (McFarland and Company, Jefferson, North Carolina, 1987).

- David Bradley, *The Chaneysville Incident* (Harper and Row Pub., New York, 1981).

- *Pedigree Chart Index*, Citizens Library, Washington, Pennsylvania, Vol. 4:534; 5: 740, 14:1207, 14:1208, 14:1246.

- *Portrait and Biographical Record of Johnson and Pettis Counties, Missouri*, pp. 213-214, Chicago, 1895. (G.W. Iams)

- Elisha B. Iams, *Genealogy of Demas Garber Iams and Elizabeth Ann Dunn. A compendium prepared by E. B. Iams, 1940.*

- Guy R. Iiames, Jr., and Roberta Wright Iiames, *The Iiames Family Genealogy* (Springboro, Ohio, 1994).

- Elisha B. Iams, "The Genealogy of the Western Pennsylvania Iiams/Iams" (An unpublished manuscript written by E. B. Iams between 1930 and 1932, Washington, Pennsylvania.

- Geoffrey Skelton, *Haiti: Been There...Seen It...Done That. Command: Military History, Strategy, and Analysis* 31;46-53 (November-December), 1994.

- Clara L. Pascoe, *Artists Work Commemorates the Whiskey Rebellion. Southwestern Pennsylvania Scene*, 24; 70-72 (November-December), 1984.

- John Howard Iams (1897-1964), in *Southwestern Pennsylvania Painter*, Paul A. Chew, ed., Collection of Westmoreland Museum of Art, Greensburg, Pennsylvania, 1989, pp. 61-65.

- *Portrait and Biographical Record of Fayette, Pickaway, and Madison Counties, Ohio* (Chapman Brothers, Chicago, 1892).

- Records of Virginia Company 1607-1622, Vol. 3, p. 328, Entry for June 22, 1620.

- *Atlas of Belmont County, Ohio* (H. C. Mead and Company, Philadelphia, Pennsylvania, 1988).

- R. B. Clark, *Index to Anne Arundel County Wills 1650-1777*, Arlington, Virginia, 1981.

- R. B. Clark, *Maryland Revolutionary, Petitioners*, Arlington, Virginia, 1982.

- Betty S. Carothers, *1776 Census of Maryland*, Luthersville, Maryland.

- J. F. Woodrow and L. W. Burke, *Our Kith and Kin* (Denison University Press, Granville, Ohio).

- *Artist's Work Commemorates The Whiskey Rebellion*, by Clara L. Pascoe, in Southwestern Pennsylvania Scene, 24:70-72 (November-December) 1994.

- P. A. Chew, ed, *Southwestern Pennsylvania Painters Collection of Westmoreland Museum of Art*, Greensburg, Pennsylvania, 1989, pp. 61-65.

- *Plains Indians and Pioneer Historical Foundation, Woodward County* (Oklahoma.) *Pioneer Families Before 1915* (Woodward, Oklahoma., 1975).

- Jane Dowd Dailey, Chairman, The Official Roles of the Soldiers of the American Revolution Buried in the State of Ohio, Daughters of the American Revolution of Ohio.

- Carmen W. Harleston, *A Brief History of the Imes Family–1660-1916*, personal files, Silver Spring, Maryland, 1996.

- Benjamin Albert Imes, *Sketch of the Family History, listed in Imes Family—1660-1916* by Carmen W. Harleston, above, 1962.

- (Mrs.) Virginia A. Braxton, *Imes Times*, 8501 Hull Drive, Wyndmoor, PA 19118, 1995.

- George Johnson Haley, Drawing of Samuel Imes and Sarah Moore Imes; and drawing of David Imes and Sarah Wilson Imes; provided by Carmen W. Harleston.

- Joy I. Hannon, personal files, Zaneville, Ohio.

- Evelyn Bott, personal files, compliments of E. F. Bickley, Jr.

- C. E. Moylen, Ijamsville, *A Country Village of Frederick County, Maryland* (published privately).

- Eloise Caldwell, personal files.

- George Edwin Ijams, personal files.

- Isabel Barbara Iams Griffith, personal files, Helena, Montana.

- Doug Iams, personal files.

- Kathryn Shipley, personal files.

- Howard Leckey, *Ten Mile Country*.

- James B. Meighen

- Clara E. Ijams, personal files, Indiana.

- James Oscar Iiams, personal files, Lennox, California.

- Alice Ijams Lorrigan, Alice Ijams, personal files.

- Elsie Warfield Ijams, Elsie personal files.

- Reverend Carl Phillips Ijams, personal files, Tucson, Arizona.

- Dr. James B. Shaw, personal files.

- Daughters of American Revolution, Application 372864, Margaret Garner Smith, Waynesburg, Pennsylvania.

- Daughter of American Revolution, Application 289199, Henrietta Adamson Conover, Waynesburg, Pennsylvania.

- Betty Ruth Iams, personal files, Washington, Pennsylvania.

- *National Cyclopedia of American Biography*, Vol. 31, p. 368.

- *Who's Who of America*, Vol. 4, p. 481, 1961; 51st ed., 1997.

- County Records, Cass County, Indiana; Anne Arundel County, Maryland; Frederick County, Maryland; Cumberland County, Maryland; Bedford County, Pennsylvania; Washington County, Pennsylvania; Greene County, Pennsylvania; Ritchie County, West Virginia; Fairfield County, Ohio.

Documents, Photos, and Letters

Documents,
Photos, and Letters

The will of William Eyams, November 10, 1703, Anne Arundel County, Maryland (Liber 11, folio 359). William Eyams/Iiams was the husband of Elizabeth Cheney. Translation by James W. Shaw, M.D.

In the name of God, Amen, the Last Will and Testament of William Eyams of the County of Anne Arundel in the Province of Maryland, viz;

First, I bequeath my soul to the hands of the Great God who hath given me a being in the world and many other things that are necessary for the support of my body in the same for all which blessed be His name I therefore being of sound mind and perfect memory at this present do bequeath my goods and estate as followeth and then my body to be decently buried at the discretion of my executors as hereafter shall be named viz,

Imprimis, I give and bequeath to my eldest son William, Jr., the sum of 5 shillings

Item, I give and bequeath to my son Richard Eyams 100 acres of land lying near Patuxent River in Prince George's County to him and his heirs forever, I give and bequeath to my daughter Elizabeth Duvall 5 shillings.

Item, I give and bequeath to my youngest son, George Eyams 100 acres of land it being an equal parts of the land that I bequeathed to my son Richard and lying on the South side of the Western Run to him and his heirs forever.

Item, As to what personal estate I have in general, I reserving my wife and heirs, I leave it to the discretion of my executrix to dispose of among my two sons Richard and George, and my two daughters Hester and Susanna as though shall be convenient.

Item, It is my will that my dear and loving wife, Elizabeth Eyams, shall be whole and sole executrix of this my Last Will and Testament and by these presents do revoke all former Will and Testaments. In witness whereof I have hereunto set my hand and seal February 16, 1698. Signed: William Eyams

Signed, sealed, and acknowledged in the presence of use, Tester Clement, David and Richard R. Cheney, John Robertson, Robert R. D. Daviss. On the back of the foregoing will was this written viz, November 10, 1703. Then came the within witnesses Clement Daviss and Richard Cheney two of the witnesses to the within will and made oath on the Holy Evangels that they saw William Eyams sign, seal, publish, and declare the within written will as his last Will and Testament and that all the doing thereof to the best of his knowledge the said testator was of sound, perfect sense, and memory. W. Taylard, Deputy

The will of William Iiams, Jr., May 18, 1738, Anne Arundel County, Maryland (Liber 21, folio 878). William Iiams was the husband of Elizabeth Plummer. Translation by James W. Shaw, M.D.

The Last Will and Testament of William Jiams, dated June 28, 1734, was probated in Anne Arundel County on May 17, 1738, by Richard William, Richard Welsh, John Nicholson, Jr., and Richard Williams, Jr. Wills, Liber 21, folio 878.

In the name of God, Amen: I, William Jiams, of Anne Arundel County in the Province of Maryland Planter being of perfect mind and memory and calling to mind the mortality of my body knowing it is appointed for all men once to die, do make constitute and ordain this my Last Will and Testament in the following manner and form:

Imprimis: I bequeath my soul unto the hands of God that gave it me, and my body to the earth to be buried in a Christian like and descent manner at the discretion of my executors hereafter named and touching such worldly goods as it hath pleased God to bestow upon me, after my just debts being paid, I give devise and dispose of them as follows:

Item, I give and bequeath to my beloved wife, Elizabeth Jiams, during her natural life all my personal estate whatsoever except the following legacies, provided my said wife lives single and remains unmarried but in case she thinks proper to marry again, then I bequeath all the personal estate aforesaid except as before excepted, to be equally divided immediately after such marriage, between my son John Jiams, my son Plummer Jiams, and my daughter Anne Jiams.

Item, I give and bequeath to my son William Jiams and his heirs forever a certain tract or parcel of land called Cheney's Resolution containing 100 acres lying in Anne Arundel County aforesaid also the sum of five shillings current money.

Item, I give and bequeath to my son Richard Jiams and Thomas Jiams also to my daughter, Elizabeth, Mary, and Charity each of them the sum of five shillings current money.

Item, I give and bequeath unto my son, John Jiams, and his heirs forever after his mother's decease a certain tract or parcel of land lying in Anne Arundel County called Bridge Hill containing 100 acres being the greater part of my dwelling plantation and if my son John die without issue lawfully begotten of his body then I bequeath the aforesaid land and Bridge Hill to my son Plummer and his heirs forever and further if my son, Plummer, die without lawful heirs begotten of his body then I give and bequeath the aforesaid land unto my son Thomas and his heirs forever.

Item, I give and bequeath unto my son Plummer and his heirs forever, after his mother's decease, a certain parcel of land adjoining Bridge Hill aforesaid containing 64 acres called Dodon lying in Anne Arundel County aforesaid.

Now if my son Plummer die without heirs lawfully begotten of his body then I give the said parcel of land called Dodon to my son John Jiams his heirs forever and if my son, John, die without heirs lawfully begotten of his body then I give the said land unto my son Thomas and his heirs forever.

Item, I give and bequeath to my daughter Ann, one negro girl named Bean and her increase and in case my daughter Anne die without lawful heirs then I give the said negro girl and her increase to my son John Jiams aforesaid.

Lastly, I constitute and ordain my sons, Thomas and John, executors of this my Last Will and Testament, and I do utterly disallow, revoke, and annul all and every other former testaments, wills, legacies, and executors by me in anywise named, willed, and bequeathed ratifying this and no other to be my Last Will and Testament in witness thereof I have hereunto set my hand and seal this June 28 Anno Domini 1734. Sealed, published, pronounced, and declared to be the Last Will and Testament of said William Jiams in the presence of us: Richard Williams, John Nicholson, Jr., Richard Welsh, Richard Williams, Jr.

Signed: William Jiams.

On the back of the foregoing will was written, viz: May 17, 1738 Richard Williams, John Nicholson, Jr., being only sworn severally deposed and swear that they saw the testator, William Jiams sign and seal the foregoing instrument and hear him publish and declare the same to be his Last Will and Testament that at the time of his so doing he was to the best of their judgement of sound and disposing mind and memory and that they severally subscribed their names to the said will in the presence of the testator as witnesses; 7 lives, sworn to before me, D. Dulaney, County Deputy

On May 11, 1739, John Iiams, as acting executor of his father's estate filed an account with the court when he accounted for a value of the personal estate of 356 pounds 10/10 plus the tobacco crop of 4,335 pounds tobacco. Five shillings each were distributed to the following: Thomas Iiams, Elizabeth Watkins, William Iiams, Mary Waters, and Richard Iiams as contained in the Administration Account, Liber 17, folio 128.

360

The will of Elizabeth Plummer Ijams/Iiams, May 5, 1762, Anne Arundel County, Maryland. Elizabeth Plummer Ijams was the widow of William Ijams/Iiams (b. 1670, d. 1738). Translated by James W. Shaw, M.D.

Will of Elizabeth Ijams May 5, 1762

In the name of God, Amen. I, Elizabeth Ijams, of Anne Arundel County in the Province of Maryland being of perfect mind and memory and calling to mind the mortality of my body knowing it is appointed from me once to die do make this my Last Will and Testament in the following manner and form.

Imprimis, I bequeath my soul unto the hands of God that gave it me and my body to the earth to be buried in a Christian like and decent manner at the discretion of my executors hereafter named and together with such worldly goods as it hath pleased God to bestow upon me after my just debts being paid, I give devise and dispose of them as following. That is to say notwithstanding it was my deceased husband, William Ijams, will that all the effects that I should die possessed with should be equally divided between my sons John Ijams and Plummer Ijams and my daughter Anne Williams, it is my will that they should so do it and dispose of it in the manner and form following:

It is my will that the Negroes should not be divided between my three children aforementioned until the first day of December next but to be kept on the Plantation for the benefit of my son John Ijams and my provision to be for the use of the family, my best bed and furniture and the great looking glass to my son, John Ijams, also my wearing apparel to my daughter, Anne Williams and all my earthen ware and my side saddle and bridle to my daughter-in-law, Ruth Ijams also my desire is that my son John Ijams and Plummer Ijams and my daughter Anne Williams should give my son, Thomas Ijams, ten pounds current money a piece in case the Negroes should live until the time of the division and if any part of them should die they are to give him what sum they think proper and the small looking glass to my son, Plummer Ijams, and all the remaining part of my estate is to be equally divided between my sons, John Ijams and Plummer Ijams and my daughter, Anne Williams except that is to say if any one of the rest of my children or there are at law should have a rite to any part of my estate I give each of them one shilling sterling but I think they have no rite by my deceased husbands will.

Lastly I constitute and ordain my son John Ijams executor of this my Last Will and Testament but in case he should die before this my last will is executed, then I appoint my son, Plummer Ijams, to execute the same in witness thereof I have hereunto set my hand and seal

May 5, 1762. Signed, sealed, published, pronounced, and declared to be the Last Will and Testament of the said Elizabeth Ijams. Elizabeth, her mark, Ijams

In the presence of Richard Harwood, Jr., John, his mark, Phelps, Ariana Ijams, Mary Tull.

September 22, 1762, came Richard Harwood, Jr., and John Phelps and made oath on the Holy Evangels of Almighty God that they saw the testatrix Elizabeth Ijams make her mark to the within will and saw her seal the same and heard her publish and declare the same to be her Last Will and Testament and that at the time of her so doing, she was of a sound disposing mind and memory to the best of her apprehension and that they and Ariana Ijams and Mary Tull signed their respective names as witnesses to the said will in the presence of the testatrix and at her request. Sworn before John Davidge, Deputy Clerk, Anne Arundel County

The original administration bond of the widow in the value of 700 pounds, dated August 18, 1738 is on file at Annapolis, with the name spelled as Jiams and written as Jiams, by the son, John. The original inventory of the personal estate is likewise on file with the sons, William and Plummer, using the orthography of Jiams. His estate was of considerable affluence for the times, being appraised at 356 pounds 10 shilling and 10 pence including six Negro slaves record found in the Testamentary papers box 41, folder 6.

The extant original Last Will and Testament of Elizabeth Iiams, sic, is on file at Annapolis and was written by Richard Harwood, Jr., one of the witnesses. Her heirs were children: John Iiams, Plummer Iiams, Anne Williams, and Thomas Iiams, also her daughter-in-law, Ruth Iiams. Quoting from the instrument, "...not withstanding it was my deceased husband, William Jiams, sic, will that all the effects I should die possessed with should be divided equally between my sons John and Plummer and my daughter Anne Williams," therefore were to settle and dispose of the personal property between them. "...Negroes not to be divided between my three children until December 1, next but to be kept on the plantation for the benefit of my son John and my provisions to be for the use of the family."

Wearing apparel was bequeathed to her daughter, Anne Williams, and her side saddle and bridle to her daughter-in-law, Ruth Jiams. Her children, John, Plummer and Anne were to give their brother "my son" Thomas 10 pounds. Her other children, if they were entitled to any part of her estate, were to have one shilling each. She named her son, John, as executor while the will was signed by Richard Harwood, Jr., Ariana Ijams, Mary Tull and John X. Phelps. It was written on May 5, 1762, and probated in Anne Arundel County on September 22, 1762.

A copy of a blueprint of the Iams/Iiams family tree emphasizing the Western Pennsylvania branch from the Revolutionary War soldier, Thomas Iiams (b. Maryland, December 26, 1754; d. in Belmont County, Ohio, June 24, 1834). Compiled by E. Jay Iiams, Donora, Pennsylvania, March 14, 1934.

363

The family of Isaac and Ruth Iams, Ten Mile, Amwell Township, Washington County, Pennsylvania, including excerpts from their publication *Rural Reflections of Amwell Township* (four volumes), a Bicentennial publication. Included are photos of the North Ten Mile Baptist Church (site of the first Iams/Iiams/Ijams, etc., national reunion in 1931), stories and photos of the Martin Mill (originally Iiams Mill, until Nancy Iiams married Joseph Martin), and an early official map of the first road to the Iiams Mill (Martin's Mill) in 1802.

Isaac Weller Iams and wife Ida Ruth Edgar.

Zebulon Iams and wife Lizzie Crile.

Zebulon Iams, wife Lizzie Crile, and their minister, at home in Pancake, Pennsylvania.

Grandchildren of Isaac and Ruth Iams,
photo taken in 1987.
Back row: Clifton, Josah, and Charity
Front row: Contessa, Joshua, and Jacob

Isaac and Ruth Iams

Sons of Isaac and Ruth Iams and their families.

Kim and David with sons Jacob and Joseph.

Mary holding Joshua; James; and Contessa
Iams, January 1989.

From left rear: Richard holding Drew; Lisa holding Rachel; and Felicia Iams, January 1994.

From left, clockwise: Charity, Clinton, Bill, and Judy Iams, January 1989.

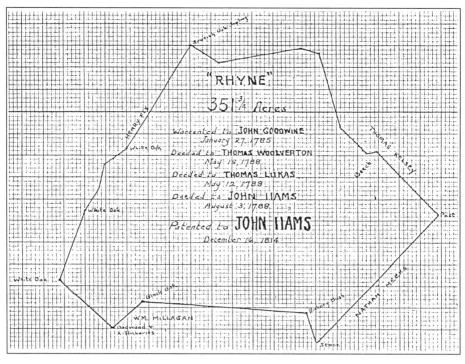

RURAL REFLECTIONS
of
AMWELL TOWNSHIP

Washington County
Pennsylvania

Vol. II of IV

The present North Ten Mile Baptist Church building erected in 1904.

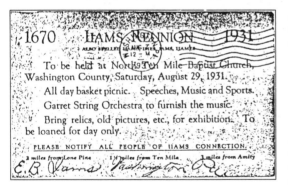

Announcement of the first Iiams Reunion, 1931, signed by (Elisha) E. B. Iams, Washington, Pennsylvania.

1670 IIAMS REUNION 1931

ALSO SPELLED IAMS, IMES, IAMS, UAMES

To be held at North Ten Mile Baptist Church,
Washington County, Saturday, August 29, 1931.
All day basket picnic. Speeches, Music and Sports.
Garret String Orchestra to furnish the music.
Bring relics, old pictures, etc., for exhibition. To
be loaned for day only.

PLEASE NOTIFY ALL PEOPLE OF IIAMS CONNECTION.

2 miles from Lone Pine   1½ miles from Ten Mile   1 miles from Amity

E. B. (Iiams)   Washington, Pa.

A news account describing the local area near Pullman, Ritchie County, West Virginia, along a small stream and valley known as Chevauxdefrise.

CHEVAUXDEFRISE

There is only one instance of a foreign word being used as place name in Ritchie County. Spelled a variety of ways on different maps—Chevaudefrise, Chevaux de Frise, and Shiverdyfreese. The various spellings and pronunciations lead to two ideas of origin.

The French term, Chevaux de Frise, actually is the name for a piece of wood filled with iron spikes once used as a weapon, by certain Indians. One of these weapons, legend tells us, was found along the stream and gave rise to it bearing such a name.

Another story relates that two hunters spent the night along the stream, near the settlement area where they almost "shivered and froze" to death. Afterward the creek gained the title of "Shiverdy."

368

The Morning Observer, Washington, Pennsylvania
August 31, 1931

The Ijams Family Reunion

The first national reunion of the Ijams clan, descendants of
William Iiams, who came to the United States from Wales was held at
the North Ten Mile Baptist Church Saturday. About 500 persons, representing Iamses from various sections of the United States, attended.
The forenoon was spent in exchanging greetings and visiting places of
interest about the vicinity, after which dinner was served. At 2 o'clock
members of the clan assembled in the church, and were entertained by
the Garrett orchestra, who are members of the clan, also a local quartet
and speakers from Kansas, North Carolina, Tennessee, Florida, West
Virginia, Ohio, and Pennsylvania. There were many of the clan present
who have won distinction in their various professions. Members of the
Iiames clan have participated in every war of this country.

William Iiams, a descendant of the royal family of England,
settled in Maryland in 1670, had three sons, and from whom there are
thousands of descendants. These sons migrated to North Carolina, Pennsylvania, and the Middle West, and from them members of the clan
have migrated to every state in the union. A number of representatives
from each branch were present. In the Civil War, those of the clan who
settled in the North joined the Union Army and those of the South fought
as Confederates. On each side some were killed in action, others
wounded and a number died in prison. A representative from the South
told of an interesting experience that his father had with his slaves.
When he dismissed his slaves and told them they were to take care of
themselves and look after their own business, they refused to leave.
Homes were erected for them on the plantation where they lived the
remainder of their lives. They were buried at their master's feet, which
was the custom of the south.

At the business session a National Organization known as the
Iams Association was effected. A board of directors representing each
of the three main branches of the clan met and elected the following
officers: President, B. B. Iames; Secretary, Mrs. C. A. Bovier; Treasurer, Dr. O. C. Lewis. Each local association is to elect and maintain
its own officers.

369

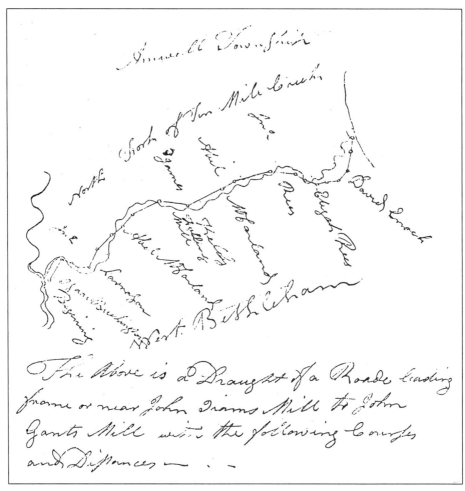

#3 1802. *Road from John Iams Merchant Mill at the south of the North Fork of Ten Mile Creek, up said Creek to where it will intersect with the Muddy Creek Road near John Gantz's Mill, four miles distant. It will pass by a saw and fulling mill. Petitioners: John Iiams, William Reynolds, Daniel Gardner, and others.*

Martin's Mill

Martin's Mill

370

Pictorial family tree of Charles B. Iams of New Stanton, Pennsylvania

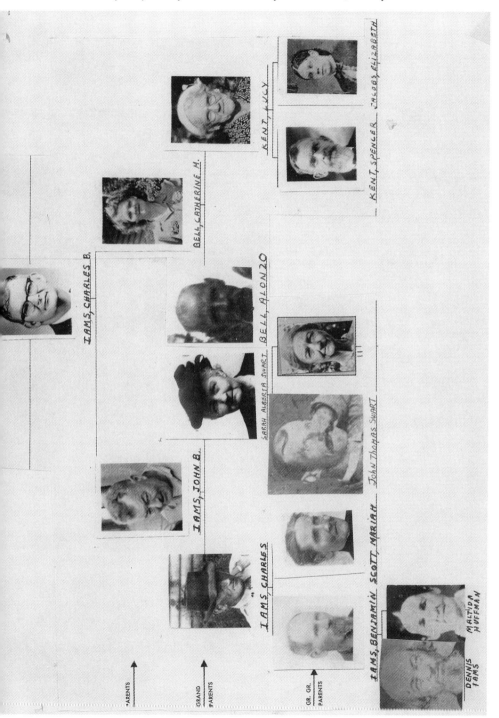

371

Front Row: Matilda Huffman Iams, Dennis Iams, and Mariah Scott Iams

Mariah Scott Iams, wife of Benjamin Iams.

Benjamin Iams

372

Catherine Mary Bell, wife of John B. Iams.   *The Swarts: Duane, Peggy, Jim, and Bea.*

Benjamin and Mariah Iams family. Seated: Benjamin. Standing: Cora, Clyde, Priscilla, Mariah, Harry, and Elgie.

Benjamin Iams, father of John B. Iams.

Charles Iams

Minnie Iams Maloy

Morrison Iams

John Tucker, Mary Iams, four unknowns, Fred Mackay, Ross Iams, and unknown.

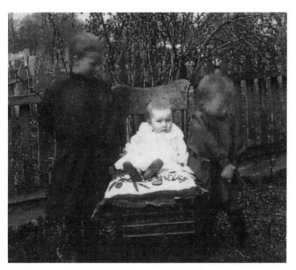

Blanche, Mary, and John Iams

Ross Iams

375

The Charles Iams family of New Stanton, Pennsylvania (1994). Front Row: Daniel Pate (held by Chuck Iams), wife Jeanne Iams (holding Matthew Beacroft), and Brittany Pate in front of Heather Pate. Middle Row: Chuck Iams, Cynthia Iams Pate, and Kenneth Pate (husband of Cynthia). Back Row: Callie Ann Roberts (held by Lisa Iams Roberts), John Whitney Roberts (husband of Lisa), Stephen Beacroft, and Michelle Iams Beacroft (wife of Stephen).

376

Wesley Iams Family (b. Pennsylvania 1828)

Nancy McKelvey Iams (b. 1846, Ohio), daughter of George C. McKelvey (b. 1818, Ireland) and wife of Wesley Iams (b. 1828, Pennsylvania).

John Franklin Iams (b. 1868), wife Josephine, and children Harley Iams and Gertrude Iams, at home in California.

Josephine Iams and daughter Gertrude Iams.

Earl Iams portrait, son of Wesley Iams.

Wesley Iams Family (b. Pennsylvania 1828)

John Iams (b. 1868) and Josephine Iams, married ca1900).

GRESS, FRIDAY, MARCH 28, 1930

Harley Iams
Recovering From Injuries

Harley Iams, who with his parents, Mr. and Mrs. John F. Iams, 4038 Ohio street, was in the automobile accident which resulted in his parents' death two months ago, was removed from the hospital last week to the home of his brother-in-law and sister, Mr. and Mrs. Merle P. Bennett, 5105 Hawley boulevard, and is fast regaining his strength and will soon be able to receive visitors. When fully recovered Mr. Iams expects to go to Camden, N. J., to continue his work on television and picture transmission by radio under R. C. A. For the past two years Mr. Iams has been with the Westinghouse Electrical company in Pittsburgh, working with Zworykin, who has gained fame in the electrical world, and has just incorporated with Radio Corporation of America. Mr. Iams demonstrated the picture transmission in several eastern cities. He also holds four patents for electrical apparatus inventions. The many friends of the young man and his late parents will be pleased to learn of his ultimate recovery from what was at first believed to have been fatal injuries.

Story, Friday, March 28, 1930, San Diego Progress, *of recovery of Harley Iams. He had been riding in the car that crashed in southern California and resulted in the death of both of his parents. The injuries to Harley Iams were serious enough to threaten his life. His eventual recovery permitted him to return to the task of inventing and perfecting "television and picture transmission by radio." By this time, Harley Iams had already been credited with building the first television sets and in demonstrating television to viewers along the east coast of the United States.*

378

Wesley Iams Family (b. Pennsylvania 1828)

John Franklin Iams, wife Josephine Iams, Harley Iams, and Gertrude Iams, in California.

Ida May Iams Charter (b. 1875) married Charles A. Charter and was daughter of Wesley Iams.

Isa Jane "Jenny" Iams (b. 1877), daughter of Wesley Iams.

Harley Iams and Gertrude Iams.

John Iams (father), Harley Iams (son, inventor of television), Gertrude Iams (daughter), and Josephine Iams (mother), California, 1908.

379

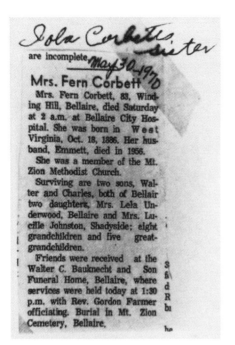

An older picture of Isa Jane "Jenny" Iams sitting in a chair in the tulip bed.

Obituary of Fern Iams (b. 1886), married Emmett Corbett, and was daughter of Wesley Iams.

Joanne Neely being held by her grandmother Mildred Corbett McKelvey, Lois McKelvey Neely, Ida May Iams Charter, and Edna Louise Corbett Reynolds.

Charles V. (for "vinegar," according to legend) Iams, in a resting moment.

Wesley Iams Family (b. Pennsylvania 1828)

Playful Meek Corbett throwing a cup of water while Ida May Iams Charter watches from near the pump at the old catalpa tree in the yard of Milton and Iola Iams Corbett.

Ida May Iams Charter, Fern Iams Corbett, Martha "Mattie" Iams (b. 1881), Iola Ellen Iams Corbett, and Stella Eckard Iams (b. 1882, wife of Charles V. Iams).

Horse of Nancy McKelvey Iams, widow of Wesley Iams, being sold at auction after her death in Ritchie County, West Virginia, in 1928.

Wesley Iams Family (b. Pennsylvania 1828)

Friend Morgan Watson and Charles V. Iams, at home, Chevauxdefrise, Ritchie County, West Virginia.

Martha "Mattie" Iams, single daughter of Wesley Iams.

Charles V. Iams on his horse.

Emmett Corbett and Fern Iams Corbett.

Family (children) of Wesley Iams.

Wesley Iams Family (b. Pennsylvania 1828)

Dale Iams and wife, Orpha Marie Ferrebee Tanzy Iams.

School photo, Ritchie County, West Virginia, includes Dale Iams, in front row right.

Wesley Iams Family (b. Pennsylvania 1828)

The Chevauxdefrise Methodist Episcopal Church, Ritchie County, West Virginia, 1993. The church was built by Wesley Iams (b. 1828) and neighbors in 1863.

The Wesley Iams (b. 1828) home on the Chevauxdefrise, West Virginia. Inspecting the "free perpetual gas lantern" is James Curtis Neely (b. 1924).

384

William E. Iiames (b. September 24, 1837) and his wife Martha Ann Moyer. This portrait, taken about 1905, shows the son of William R. Iiames (b. 1807) and Martha McClure; the grandson of Thomas Iiams (b. 1784); the great-grandson of William Iiams; and the great-great-grandson of Thomas Iiams (b. 1708).

Family of Guy R. Iiames, Hillsboro, Ohio

Picture Identification

Back Row (left to right): 1. Henry Taylor; 2. Alonzo Iiames, son of William Iiams and Martha Moyer, who married Ella Taylor; 3. James Taylor; 4. Frank Taylor, married Emma Jane Iiams, daughter of William Iiams and Martha Moyer; 5. Winfred Iiames; 6. Lon Taylor; and 7. Ted Bear (Eva's husband).

Front Row (left to right): 8. Bertha Morton (Cleve's sister); 9. Ella Taylor Iiames (Frank's sister, Alonzo's wife); 10. Bertha Taylor (James' wife); 11. Miriam Morton (daughter of Bertha); 12. Lilly May Taylor (wife of Cleve, mother of Laurel); 13. Gae Morton (daughter of Bertha); 14. Emma Jane Taylor (Frank's wife, sister to Alonzo Iiams); 15. Alda Taylor (Lon's wife); 16. Grace Iiams; 17. Eva Bear (Cleve's sister); and 18. Cleve Taylor and son 19. Laurel. The picture was taken at 1212 E. Market Street, Lima, Ohio.

Copies of old photographs provided by Neal O. Shortz of Indianapolis, as representative pictures of the Thomas Imes (b. 1800, South Carolina; lived in Lawrence County, Ohio) family.

Anson Hiram Curtis, wife Elizabeth Imes Curtis (b. 1838, Lawrence County, Ohio; daughter of Thomas Imes), son Charles A. Curtis and son Llewelyn Curtis. This family group picture was taken in Wintereset, Madison County, Iowa, when the family lived nearby in Adel, Dallas County, Iowa; and before they moved to Pattonsburg on the Grand River, Daviess County, Missouri.

An "Imes child," believed to be Nora Curtis, daughter of Elizabeth Imes Curtis.

"Imes children" photographed by G. C. Acker, Olathe, Kansas.

Will of Thomas Plummer Ijams/Iiams, June 16, 1847, Muskingum County, Ohio. Thomas Plummer Ijams was the son of Captain John Ijams (b. 1712). Translated by James W. Shaw, M.D.

In the name of God, Amen. I, Thomas Ijams, do make and publish this my Last Will and Testament.

Item 1, I give and devise to my beloved wife all my horses, cattle, sheep, hogs, and any other livestock on the farm; also all the bedsteads, beds, and bedding, and all the household and kitchen furniture.

Item 2, The fifty acres of land more or less on which I now reside and on which my wife holds a dower during her lifetime, after the decease of my wife I desire my executors to sell the same either at private or public sale, as in their judgment they may deem most advantageous, and the proceeds thereof to be divided into seven equal shares between my daughters Harriet, Elizabeth, Charlotte, Comfort, Sarah, Ann, and the heirs of my daughter Rebecca, now if any of my daughters should decease and also fail of heirs before this division is made, then this property to be equally divided in the aforementioned manner among the remainder of them or their heirs.

Item 3, I request my sons Lewis and William F. to pay the expenses of my last sickness and also my funeral expenses.

Item 4, I do hereby nominate and appoint my sons Lewis Ijams and William F. Ijams, executors of this my Last Will and Testament.

In testimony whereof, I have hereunto set my hand and seal this June 16, 1847. Signed and acknowledged by said Thomas Ijams, a his Last Will and Testament in our presence, and signed by us in his presence: John Thompson, Thomas A. Woolf, and George W. Donphfin. Signed Thomas Ijams, his seal.

Plummer Imes, taken about 1863.
Courtesy of Joy I. Hannon

Sarah Ann McDaniels, wife of Plummer Imes,
taken about 1863. Courtesy of Joy I. Hannon

The Lester Iames and Regia Imes family of Chaneysville, Pennsylvania. Other family members are not identified. Courtesy of Joyce Trail, Sweet Roots Crafts, Chaneysville, Pennsylvania.

Family of Thomas Morgan Iams (b. Western Pennsylvania, 1871, son of Miller Iams [b. Pennsylvania, 1811]). Front: Alonzo Iams, Thomas Morgan Iams, and James H. Iams (b. 1873). Back: Nancy Margaret Adamson (wife of Thomas, and Frances D. Davis Iams). Courtesy of Jack Louis Iams, Columbus, Ohio

The John Iams Family (from left to right): John Iams (b. 1868, son of Wesley and Nancy McKelvey Iams), Harley Iams (television pioneer), Gertrude Iams, and Josephine Iams.

David Edson "Ed" Iams (b. 1870, son of Wesley and Nancy McKelvey Iams).

Emma Iams (wife of Ed Iams, 1942 photo).

Family of Iola Ellen Iams (b. 1879, Ritchie County, West Virginia)

Edna Corbett, Olive Corbett, and Mildred Corbett, children of Iola Iams and Milton Corbett.

William Milton Corbett and Iola Ellen Iams, married 1899, Ritchie County, West Virginia.

Mildred Corbett McKelvey, Edna Corbett Reynolds, and Olive Corbett, on horse in Bellmont County, Ohio, 1912.

Olive, Meek, and Edna Corbett.

Olive, Edna, Mildred, Iola, and Milton Corbett, holding Meek.

Family of Iola Ellen Iams (b. 1879, Ritchie County, West Virginia)

Edna, Olive, Meek, and Mildred Corbett.

Iola Ellen Iams Corbett

Milton Corbett and Iola Ellen Iams Corbett at home, about 1950.

Meek Corbett, Iola Ellen Iams Corbett holding Buddy Corbett, Paul McKelvey, Marie Brown Corbett, Edna Corbett Reynolds, Ray Reynolds with Ralph Reynolds and Robert Reynolds in front.

Iola Iams Corbett, Fern Iams Corbett, and Ida Iams Charter in Belmont County, Ohio in 1948.

Wedding photo (1914) of Roxy Iams and Jesse Clarence Lamp. Roxy Iams (b. 1896) was the daughter of David Edson "Ed" Iams and Emma Jane Wilson. Roxy and Jesse Clarence Lamp were the parents of Opal, Emmen, and Wilma Lamp, all of Ritchie County, West Virginia.

Roxanne R. "Roxie" Iams (b. 1896), daughter of David Edson "Ed" Iams and Emma Jane Wilson; with husband Jesse Clarence Lamp.

Wilma Dona Lamp Bircher (b. 1917) and Opal Lamp Pittman (b. 1914) at the Iams Reunion on the Chevauxdefrise in 1993.

Roxie Iams Lamp Hall children: Opal Lamp, Wilma Lamp, Comilla Hall, Corene Hall, and Claridon Hall.

Top left clockwise: Emogine Bircher (daughter of Wilma Lamp Bircher), Patsy Bircher (daughter of Wilma Lamp Bircher), Shirley Bircher (daughter of Wilma Lamp Bircher), and Martha Pitman Morris (daughter of Opal Lamp Pitman).

395

John Howard Iams, b. 1897, Bethlehem Township, Washington County,
Pennsylvania; d. 1964, Marion, Ohio

John Howard Iams was the descendant of early pioneers who built many of the water and grist mills around the town of Washington in southwestern Pennsylvania. After World War I he worked as a carpenter to earn enough money to attend Carnegie Institute of Technology's College of Fine Arts where he studied painting and illustration from 1919 to 1921. His studies continued at the Art Student's League in New York from 1922 to 1924. Like his friend and neighbor Malcolm Parcell, Iams was fascinated with the landscape and history of Washington County and, after a few years in New York, both returned to paint scenes of their native Pennsylvania countryside.

Iams had his first show in 1926 at the annual exhibition of the Associated Artists of Pittsburgh at the Carnegie Institute. His first major oil painting was *The Pack Train* painted under the auspices of the Public Works of Art Project. His works were commended for their sense of reality, incisive draughtsmanship, compact design and austere color. These qualities and the ability to portray atmospheric conditions were constant elements in Iams' work.

Because of his interest in the history of southwestern Pennsylvania, Iams often chose for his subjects structures, houses, farms or mills related to the region's history and development. His oil of the *LeMoyne House* in Washington, Pennsylvania, after being hung with the PWAP show at the Corcoran Gallery in Washington, D.C., was described as a "genuinely distinguished piece of work" by Edward Bruce, head of the national project. President Franklin D. Roosevelt selected it to be hung in the White House offices.

Perhaps Iams' single most ambitious project, one which led him to spend five years in research, travel and artwork, was his series of four large oils, fourteen pastels and twenty-two linoleum blocks depicting the old houses of the principal participants and locations of events of the Whiskey Insurrection (the famed late eighteenth century tax revolt centered in West Virginia, western Pennsylvania, and Ohio). Iams considered the Whiskey Insurrection as important historically as the Boston Tea Party. He stated in an interview of 1934 that "Whiskey was the medium of exchange when money was scarce and seldom seen on the frontier. It cost twenty-five cents a gallon to produce and fifty cents a gallon to transport to Philadelphia where it sold for a dollar, whereas in Pittsburgh it just barely brought the cost price of twenty-five cents. It meant starvation to the pioneers when the tax of twenty-five cents was placed on each gallon, and they naturally revolted." The Westmoreland Museum of Art is very fortunate to have this series in its entirety in its collection.

In 1939 Iams married and moved to Harrisburg where he was employed as a free-lance artist. After having been hired as a mechanical draughtsman by the Sinclair Pipe Line Company he moved to Mechanicsburg, Pennsylvania in 1947. One year later he moved to Marion, Ohio. His paintings have been shown in exhibitions around the United States, including the National Academy of Design in New York, the Chicago Art Institute, the Pennsylvania Academy of Fine Arts in Philadelphia, the Corcoran Gallery in Washington, D.C., and the Houston Museum of Fine Arts. He was also well known and praised by the art critics in Paris.

Thomas Marshall Tavern. This tavern was in Fredericktown, Pennsylvania, during the time of the Whiskey Rebellion (1794), and was owned by one of the leaders against the excise tax.

Mingo Church. The site of many protest meetings during the Whiskey Rebellion, and eventual site of the burial of the leaders of the rebellion including: John Holcroft (John the Tinker), John Hamilton, David Hamilton, Benjamin Parkinson, John Gaston, and James McFarlane.

397

The Board of Trustees of the
Westmoreland Museum of Art

and

The Steering Committee of the
Whiskey Rebellion Bicentennial Task Force

Cordially Invite You to Attend
A Preview Reception and Dinner

For an Exhibition of Works by

J. Howard Iams and Ray Forquer.

Commemorating

the

Whiskey Rebellion (1791-1794)

Friday, April 24, 1992
6:00 p.m. to 9:00 p.m.

Westmoreland Museum of Art
221 North Main Street
Greensburg, Pennsylvania

R.S.V.P. by April 20
No Phone Reservations

Cash Bar
One Complimentary Drink
Per Person

Terrible Night (Dreadful Night)
by J. Howard Iams (1897 - 1964)

The Terrible (Dreadful) Night occurred on November 13, 1794. To quell the insurrection, President Washington had called up nearly 13,000 troops to march into the Western country under the command of General "Light Horse Harry" Lee. Fearing the exodus of Rebels, troops arrested suspects and witnesses in the middle of the night. Some men were dragged out of bed, half clothed, and marched through the sleet and mud to cold, makeshift prison quarters. At least one man died from exposure.

398

Iams Family Crest. This version was composed and painted by the celebrated artist J. Howard Iams in 1933.

In his first letter, Milton writes, "some what upon our former acquaintance I hope to be pardoned for this little note which is to ask permission to correspond with you and also to have the pleasure of calling on you at your home. Anxiously awaiting a favorable reply, I am truly your friend." (s) Milton Corbet. This beautiful letter apparently opened the door to his true love's heart.

In a reply, she wrote, "Mr. Corbet, kind friend. I seat myself this rainy Sabbath afternoon to answer your ever welcome letter, which came to hand some time ago. This is a very rainy, dreary day; and I am very concerned there are plenty of places to go today, as there are preaching all around; but it is too rainy for me today. I am very thankful to you to offer to pay my way up there and back, but it is so that I can't go now, as Mother needs me at home now. I will look for you down (here) any time. I would like you to let me know when you are coming and I will try to make arrangements to meet you at the (train) depot. I will bring my letter to a close as news are scarce, so this is all for this time. I hope I may hear from you in a near future. As ever, your friend Ola. Good bye." They were married several months later on November 24, 1898, and raised their family in Belmont County, Ohio. (Edited by RDR)

Wedding portrait, November 24, 1898, Ritchie County, Virginia, of Iola Ellen Iams (b. 1879) and William Milton Corbett (b. 1867).

401

1899 photo of Thomas Iams (b. 1858) family, compliments of his grandson John E. Iams (b. Bellaire, Ohio, 1916) and Ruth McCord of Washington, Pennsylvania. The father of John E. Iams was John Iams (b. 1892). The quilt backdrop contains initials of members of the Iams family. Front row: John E. Iams (b. 1892), father Thomas Iams (b. 1858), Sallie Iams, Katherine/Catherine Clutter (mother, b. 1861), Delsie Iams, and Bill Iams. Back row: Robert Iams, Mary Iams, and Jesse Iams.

Delsie Iams, Mary Scott, and Sally Hougland.

Four generations of John E. Iams (top) family. Left: son John Iams; right: grandson John R. Iams; front: John Iams (John E., b. 1916).

402

The Imes of Lewisburg, Ohio, and Red Key, Indiana. Photos courtesy of Conchetta Stephen Geis of Red Key.

Oscar Imes and wife, Martha Imes, 1937. He died in 1939, she in 1944.

Imes-Enoch Reunion, Imes Park, Lewisburg Ohio. Third from left is Oscar Imes, and fifth is Arthur Imes. Others are brothers and cousins.

Imes-Enoch Reunion, Imes Park, Lewisburg, Ohio. Cousin Richard (left) and Conchetta Stephen (Geis).

Charlie Imes and wife Carrie Gordon Imes of Chaneysville, Pennsylvania. Mrs. Imes is holding Brenda Lee Shaffer. Courtesy of Joyce Trail of Sweet Roots Crafts, Chaneysville, Pennsylvania.

Harley Iams (March 13, 1905 to December 3, 1984); Pioneer in Television, Radar, Guided Missles, and Interplanatory Projectiles.

Article taken from Television: Journal of the Royal Television Society, *April 1985, page 100.*

Dr. Albert Abramson, the distinguished American television historian and member of the Society, has written an appreciation of the life and work of Harley Iams, who died on 3 December 1984, aged 79. His contribution to television is remarkable.

Harley Iams started with Westinghouse Electric in East Pittsburgh in August 1927. He was assigned to work with Dr. Vladimir K. Zworykin on his development of facsimile and sound recording. Late in 1928 Harley was assigned to work on the deflection circuits of the newly developed Zworykin "Kinescope," the first practical picture tube in television history. In 1929, Harley was part of a team that designed and built the first six all-electronic television receivers in the world. Due to ill health, Harley left Westinghouse late in 1929 and returned to San Diego, California, to recuperate.

On 24 April 1931, he rejoined Dr. Zworykin and his Television Research Group at the RCA Victor plant in Camden, New Jersey. Along with Gregory N. Ogloblinsky, Sanford E. Essig, and Lesley E. Flory, he was responsible for developing the first high-velocity camera tube, the single-sided Iconoscope which made our present system of television possible. In 1933 he went on to become a manager of the RCA Tube Works at Harrison, New Jersey, where Iconoscopes were being built for experimental purposes.

He participated in the development of the first Image Iconoscope, a more sensitive tube. He was then joined by Dr. Abert Rose early in 1937 and started work on the first low-velocity scanning tubes. This included research on photo-conductive as well as photo-emissive and photo-voltaic surfaces. His work with Dr. Rose culminated with the introduction of the Orthicon, the first practical low-velocity camera tube, late in 1938. This was the predecessor of the Image Orthicon camera tube which was later developed by RCA.

From 1939 to 1947 he worked on rapid-scanning radar systems. He left RCA in 1947 to become part of North American Aviation. In 1949 he joined Hughes Aircraft Research Labs as an Associate Director of Research. Here he participated in a variety of guided missile projects until his retirement in 1970.

Harley Iams had some 63 US Patents issued to him. Included were many improvements in the design of the Iconoscope, the first patent for a Monoscope and many low-velocity camera tubes. He had written 12 important articles on television, electronics and micro-wave radar.

Harley Iams was a kind and gentle man of many talents. He was loved and admired by a host of friends and co-workers. His wife Margaret shared his long and fruitful life. He will be missed by all who knew him.

Life Fellow Harley Iams dies; television pioneer

IEEE Life Fellow Harley Iams, who was deeply involved in the early development of television, died Dec. 3, 1984, at the age of 79.

Iams began his career in 1927, when he went to work for Westinghouse Electric Co. in Pittsburgh, Pa., under the direction of Vladimir K. Zworykin.

Iams helped build the deflection circuits of the Zworykin "kinescope," one of the first working television picture tubes. In 1929, he and other Westinghouse engineers built the first six all-electronic television receivers.

In 1931, Iams relocated along with Zworykin and his television research group to the RCA Victor plant in Camden, N.J. There Iams helped develop the "iconoscope," the first high-velocity camera tube and a forerunner of the modern television tube.

Over the next several years, Iams

In this 1977 photograph, the late Harley Iams (1905–1984) holds an iconoscope, a prototype of modern television picture tubes, which he built while working under Vladimir K. Zworykin at RCA in 1933.

participated in building increasingly advanced picture tubes, including the image iconoscope and the "orthicon," the first practical low-velocity television tube.

In 1939, just before World War II, Iams switched from television to radar research and development. In 1949 he joined Hughes Aircraft Research Laboratories, where he participated in a variety of guided missile projects until his retirement in 1970.

Autobiography of Edna Louise Corbett Reynolds

(Written 1993, Columbus, Ohio, at age 87)

I, Edna L. (Corbett) Reynolds, was born on June 29, 1906, on a dairy farm about one mile north of Caldwell, Ohio. My parents were William Milton Corbett and Iola Ellen (Iams) Corbett. At my birth, I had an older sister Mildred, age four years and four months. The farm on which we lived was owned by a Reverend Danford, a Methodist minister and later a district superintendent for the Methodist Church in eastern Ohio. My dad had to have help in the fields in the summertime, and Lane Keyser often came to help during that time. Lane was my first cousin, the second son of my father's sister Sadie. In the wintertime Lane attended high school in Bellaire, Ohio. It was while working on our farm during the summer that Lane met and fell in love with Olive Dye. They were married several years later.

After living on that farm for a few years, my folks decided that they would be better off if they moved back to Belmont County, Ohio, near where my dad and his family had lived for nearly one hundred years. It was also where he had met and fallen in love with my mother. At the time my parents met, my dad was working on a neighboring farm during the summer. It was on that farm that my mother came to visit her uncle.

My mother was born in West Virginia (Ritchie County) and was living there (Chevauxdefrise Creek near Harrisville) at the time she was visiting in Belmont County, Ohio, at the farm of George McKelvey, her uncle. My mother and father wrote many letters back and forth to each other, and finally decided to get married. A few of those letters have been preserved and are in the possession of my brother, Meek Corbett, who continues to live (1993) on the family homestead on Crozier Hill Road, Mead Township, Belmont County, Ohio. My dad continued to work for Uncle George McKelvey after they were married, until Reverend Danford offered my dad and mother the opportunity to rent a second farm from him, this time along Wegee Creek at the mouth of Stone Coal Creek, a smaller creek leading into Wegee Creek in the southern part of Mead Township. My dad and mother later bought seven acres of land with a four-room house and a basement. My dad then added other buildings such as a chicken house, barn, etc.

My dad's father, George Corbett, lived up Stone Coal Creek about one-half mile. He was very old and unable to work, so Dad and Mother bought his sixty acres, and Dad farmed that land for many years. My grandfather and my grandmother, Mary Marietta Morton Corbett, lived apart. While Mary Corbett lived to be 102 years old, Grandfather George lived with us for several years before he died. We had moved to the Myers place by the time of his death.

My younger sister Olive and my brother Meek were both born during the time we lived along Wegee Creek. Olive was two years younger than me, and my brother Meek was eight years younger. My sister Mildred attended Dauntless School, as did our first cousins David and May Keyser, the brother and sister of Lane Keyser mentioned earlier. I often visited the home of my cousins while they were at school. Their parents were Uncle Trueman Keyser and Aunt Sade (Corbett) Keyser. I often went across Wegee Creek to their home while Cousin Mary was at school because she had such pretty dolls and other things to play with. Aunt Sade didn't care if I played with the dolls, but when Cousin Mary got home from school she would say, "I know who has been here today." But really, she didn't seem to care since we were such good friends.

When we moved to Wegee in 1908, no one ever dreamed of a coal mine going to be built within a half-mile of where we lived. Dad and Uncle Trueman Keyser helped build several houses that were needed for some of the mine folks to live in. Dad also used his team of horses to work in the township roads when needed. After finishing the day working as a carpenter, building homes for people working at the Webb mine, Dad would often bring home small ends of boards which varied in length from two inches to maybe eight inches in length. These small boards or blocks served as endless entertainment for me and my sister Olive. By that time Olive was old enough to play outside and we built many buildings from those blocks, and without using any nails. We also played along Wegee Creek, which was never very deep but which did have small fish. We would dig a hole in the sand and catch minnows to put in the hole, but we always put them back in the creek before going to the house.

407

We also had guinea fowl and Rhode Island Red chickens. The guineas always seemed to lay their eggs away from the buildings, often in a brush pile. After they would lay an egg, they would make a lot of noise, so that is the way we knew where to look for the eggs.

In the summertime, the cows were taken to the pasture on the sixty-acre farm up along Stone Creek, formerly owned by my grandfather George Corbett. It was the chore of sister Mildred and myself to get them home in the evening. Sometimes they would be easy to find by being close to the gate in the pasture, but other evenings they would be hard to find.

My dad and mother were very careful to provide watchful care for us, especially after the mine became operational. There were two other families that lived farther up Stone Coal Creek valley, and almost every evening we would meet one gentleman going to work, because the trail down the creek was a short way for him to get to work at Webb mine. My parents would not permit my sister or myself to go alone to bring the cattle home. It was the close proximity to the mine that eventually led to a move from this farm in an attempt by my dad and mother to distance their family from these influences.

I remember also that in the early spring we would be able to find some white strawberries growing along the creek bank, and I remember that these were very good tasting. They were the only ones I ever saw. After the mine was producing well, a reservoir was built on Stone Coal Creek to supply water for the mine, but we had moved away by then. The reservoir has since been destroyed, but the landmarks and white strawberries can no longer be found.

As I became old enough for school, I also began to attend the Dauntless School above Wegee Creek in Mead Township. We walked to and from school every day, but when the snow was real deep my dad would walk ahead of us to make the walking easier for me and my sisters. I remember that we always took our lunch to school and that we carried it in a tin lunch pail.

The O.R. and W (Ohio River and Western Railroad; also called B.Z. and C., for Bellaire, Zanesville, and Cincinnati; at another time nicknamed "Old Rickety and Worn," "Bent, Zigzagged and Crooked," etc.), a narrow gauge train, passed close enough to where we lived for us to see it when it went by. There were two round trips of the passenger train, six days a week, between Bellaire and Zanesville. My folks sold butter and eggs in Bellaire, and when I became about ten years old, I took the butter and eggs to Potts Grocery in Bellaire. The grocery store was close to the train station, and I often returned with coffee, beans, sugar, or whatever my mother told me to get. One reason I was permitted to do that was because I could ride the train for half-fare because of my age. I also remember other events about this train. Since it had a relatively steep climb up the Wegee Creek Valley toward the town of Key, it would move very slowly, and people would often get off and walk beside the train. There were also some very dangerous high, somewhat unstable, trestles along the route, so one had to be careful at times. In the fall when the grass was dry, the train would also create fires along the way. These fires were put out by the passengers, who would jump off and stomp out the fires while they were still small.

When the Webb mine was built along Wegee Creek, by the time it was ready to send coal to market, more railroad tracks were laid for a larger train by the Pennsylvania Railroad. This train came to Webb mine to get coal, but there was also a passenger train that came that far up the Wegee Creek five days a week to take men to and from work. We three girls, Mildred, Olive, and myself (Edna), rode that train to Bellaire on one cold December day so that we could go to the five-and-ten-cent store to shop for a very few toys for us for Christmas. As my sons Ralph and Robert know, five-and-ten-cent stores are still my favorite place to shop.

When I was ten years old we moved to a very large rented farm known as the Myers Place, where Dad raised crops and got only a share of the profits. Since it was such a large farm, some of the pasture land could be rented for horses to graze. A farmer from the town of Belmont had many horses and they would bring in six or eight or more at a time, then take as many, more or less, out of the pasture. It was my duty to keep account of this so that at the end of each month the renters would know how much they owed, because they paid a certain amount per horse per day. Sister Mildred and I helped in the fields until a short time after we moved to the Myers Place, when Mildred went to Wheeling to attend Elliott School. I remember that she would come home some weekends and sometimes I would take her in a horse-driven cart, as far down the creek to the town of Shadyside. At other times Mildred would return to school by train on Monday morning.

While we lived by Wegee Creek and I was quite small, sister Mildred and I would go to Sunday School in Shadyside; Aunt Sade and Uncle Trueman would take us. Then they sold their house and moved to Shadyside, then we went to the Wegee Church on the hill. After a few months there was a large store built on the Keyser property. The store had a nice large basement, so we began going there to Sunday School in the morning. On days that weren't too cold we went to the Wegee Church, too. There had been a church along the valley floor of Wegee Creek, but it had been destroyed. That church body moved to Shadyside, but it was before my time. There is still a small graveyard from this church congregation remaining along Wegee Creek. The Wegee Church on the hill is often called Old Wegee, and is the one we attended. Mother and Dad sometimes went there too. We would get to the church by walking up the path of a very steep hill above the creek. Before we left each Sunday morning, Mother would give us a few pennies for the collection plate.

After we moved to the Myers Place, we attended Mount Zion Church. We all went to that church in a surrey drawn by two fine work horses. When Dad couldn't go, sometimes Mildred or I (mostly me) would drive the horses to church. That was the first church in which I became an active member. Later, my sister Olive and I attended church at the Key Presbyterian Church, now called Bethel Church.

After living on the Myers Place for a few years, Dad and Mother decided to buy a farm on Crozier Ridge, about two miles from the Key Post Office, the railroad station, Bethel Church, etc. We moved in the middle of winter. I remember that I was very sick with "quinsy," but was able to drive a road wagon full of chickens to our new home while Dad drove our cattle along the dirt roadway. I lived at this farm until June 1927, when I married Ray Reynolds.

I was still living along Wegee Creek when I began attending first grade classes at the Dauntless School, on top of the hill above Wegee Creek. We lived in the valley. We moved to the Myers Place when I was in the fourth grade. While we were in elementary school we always loved our noons and recesses. I remember playing such games as "black man," "prisoner base," "hit the can," "ante-over," "hide and seek," etc. Schools of that day were one-room schools with a pot-bellied stove in the center of the room to keep us warm. Sometimes the teacher also took care of starting the fire and did other janitorial work at the school. At other times, for a very few dollars, one of the older boys or a nearby neighbor would be hired for this task.

The name of the school I attended, beginning in the fourth grade, was Vallonia. The school was in the valley community known by that same name, along Wegee Creek, and we now lived up on top of the hill. There was a senior citizen-type gentleman who had a small store nearby; he also had an interest in the Vallonia School. I remember that there were times when one school would decide to compete against another school in contests such as a spelling bee. The elderly gentleman would invite the older students into his home for some spelling practice. He had never married and lived with his sister, who was also single. The effort he made on behalf of the children was an expression of his interest in helping the students learn.

The Myers Place, though mostly up on the hill, also extended down to the valley of the Wegee Creek, and there was an O.R. and W. train that went along the valley. Sometimes it would cause the grass to catch on fire and we would have to put it out by using an old broom to beat the flames. At one time it got completely out of control and burned all the way to the top of the pasture land on the Myers Place. It then spread across two more large fields and came within a few yards of our house. I remember that it was a scary time, and it seemed as if the fire would never stop spreading. The only thing that stopped the fire was when my dad took the horses and plowed some of the ground in furrows in front of the spreading fire until it could be contained. This had succeeded when all else that we had tried failed. I remember that my nose was bleeding and that I was plenty dirty.

While living on the Myers Place I remember that we had a large fireplace in a very large kitchen where we spent most of our time while indoors. Grandpa George Corbett had the room next to the kitchen and that room also had a fireplace. There were lots of chestnut trees on the farm, so every fall we would gather sugar sacks full of chestnuts and keep them in one of the rooms upstairs that was not used for much else. There were four rooms upstairs and five rooms downstairs in this large farmhouse. We would roast the chestnuts in the hot coals of the fireplace and would also pop corn over these hot coals. There was a large orchard on the farm so we had lots of apples and some other kinds of fruit. We would often put apples outside in the cold weather so they could freeze, since we all liked frozen apples.

One of our good neighbors had given a Rhode Island rooster to me as a gift. Some time later, General Pershing of the Army was coming to visit Wheeling, West Virginia, and I wanted to go see him. However, I had no money, so I sold the rooster and was able to get enough money to make the trip. Since my sister Mildred was attending the Elliott School in Wheeling, studying stenography, I was able to stay the night with her.

Quinsy is an illness I dreaded, which seemed to cause a life-threatening situation to me on more than one occasion. The first time I had quinsy was when we lived on the Myers farm. My throat was so swollen that my parents were very worried about me. They were worried enough that dad went down the road until he came to a telephone and called a doctor in the largest neighboring town of Bellaire, which was five or six miles away. The snow was deep and the road to the main highway could not be used by a car (called machines at that time), but my dad talked the doctor into coming up from the valley to meet him at the end of the secondary roads, over a mile from our house. Dad said he would meet the doctor on a sled. When the doctor agreed to come, Dad hitched the team of horses to a sled and brought the doctor to see what was wrong. The doctor lanced my throat and soon the fluid, swelling, heat, and pain was gone. I had other attacks similar to that one in later years, but my mother had found out how to treat it. When detected in the early stages, the process seemed to be minimized by wrapping turpentine-soaked cloths around the neck. Of course, this is not recommended today. After I had taught school for one year and had earned a little money of my own, I had my tonsils removed and was never bothered by quinsy again.

Another incident that happened while we lived on the Myers farm was when Dad had driven a road wagon into a building with a single large door on old fashioned hinges. The wind was blowing hard and I was sent to close the door to the shed. Before I got the door closed it came off the hinges and fell on me, knocking me backwards to the ground. Dad had already taken the horses to the barn so he was not nearby. My mother saw it happen and called for help to get the door off me. I wasn't hurt very much, but I guess it left quite an impression on me, since I still remember it after seventy-five years or so.

Still another incident that I remember well was when my mother sent me to a building closer to the house while we were living near Key. She sent me to close the door of the building because a storm was near and there were little chickens in the building. Just as I got the door closed a bolt of lightning came within a few feet of where I was standing. My mother was on the porch and she thought I was surely hurt badly. They had me go to bed for awhile, but I survived that, too.

The first car I ever saw was when I was about seven years old, in 1913. We lived along Wegee Creek at the time and I remember that it looked like an old fashioned buggy with no horses or sides. It rather frightened both my sister Olive and I as we were playing under a sycamore tree on the other side of the creek from the house. The first car I ever rode in was a Maxwell. It belonged to my Uncle Ami Corbett, my dad's younger brother, who was a blacksmith. This was about 1915. The first car my folks owned was an Overland, made by Willys.

Family of Edna Louise Corbett (b. 1906, Noble County, Ohio)

Edna Corbett, 1924

Edna Corbett, 1923

Edna Louise Corbett and Ray Campbell Reynolds, married 1927.

Ray Campbell Reynolds and Edna Louise Corbett.

411

Family of Edna Louise Corbett (b. 1906, Noble County, Ohio)

Edna Corbett with son Ralph and
husband Ray C. Reynolds.

*Edna Corbett and Ray Reynolds,
1943.*

*Edna Corbett Reynolds, Obetz, Ohio,
schoolteacher, 1946.*

Edna Corbett Reynolds at Logan
Elm, 1947.

Family of Edna Louise Corbett (b. 1906, Noble County, Ohio)

Columbus, Ohio, 1987, 60th Wedding Anniversary of Ray C. Reynolds and Edna Louise Corbett. Christine McKelvey, Daniel Reynolds, Leah Reynolds, Jeff Reynolds, Karen Lackey, Barry Reynolds, Cathy Reynolds, Ron Reynolds, Steve Reynolds, John Lackey, and John McKelvey.

Families of Mildred Corbett McKelvey and Edna Corbett Reynolds: Back: John Lackey, Karen McKelvey Lackey, Paul McKelvey, Julia Curtis McKelvey holding granddaughter Maria Lackey, Lois McKelvey Neely, James Neely, Norita Reynolds, Ralph Reynolds, Kathy McKelvey Blaine, Christine McKelvey holding daughter Rachel McKelvey, and John McKelvey. Front: Mildred Corbett McKelvey and Edna Corbett Reynolds.

Norita Rose Sholly Reynolds, holding Maria Lackey, and Karen McKelvey Lackey, Columbus, Ohio, 1991.

Dayton, Ohio, 1989: Edna Louise Corbett Reynolds, standing; and Mildred Corbett McKelvey, sitting.

413

Family of Edna Louise Corbett (b. 1906, Noble County, Ohio)

Iams Reunion, Chevauxdefrise, Ritchie County, West Virginia, 1993: Edna Louise Corbett Reynolds (b. 1906), Ralph D. Reynolds, M.D. (b. 1934), Paul Federkiel (b. 1928) and Naomi Lee Prunty Federkiel (b. 1932).

Columbus, Ohio, 1990: Ralph D. Reynolds, M.D., Edna Louise Corbett Reynolds, Lois McKelvey Neely, and James Neely.

Dayton, Ohio, 1993: Christine Mosconi and John McKelvey, with children Rachel Jeanne McKelvey and Drue Marie McKelvey.

Milton and Iola Iams Corbett Homestead, Key, Mead Township, Belmont County, Ohio: Edna Louise Corbett Reynolds, Marie Brown Corbett, Ralph D. Reynolds, M.D., and Meek Corbett.

Photo of Mark Reynolds, wife Paula, and Melissa Brook Reynolds, 1979.

Hall and King Family Group, 1911. Left to right (back): Gertrude Roberts Hall (mother, 1871-1936), Gardner Calvin Hall (son, 1896-1964), Mary Hall King (daughter, 1887-1979). Front: Myrtle Hall Mullen Griffen (daughter, 1909-1992), Henry Seigal Hall (father, 1863-1953), Herbert Frederick Hall (son, b. 1905), Abram Walter King (son-in-law, 1887-1964), and Lawrence Henry King (grandson, 1910-1971). Submitted by Sally Irene King Ross.

Five-generation picture, April 1935. Left to right: Robert Humphrey King (b. 1913); Mary Gardner Roberts Oder (1852-1939), daughter of Harvey Gardner; Gertrude Roberts Hall (1871-1938); Mary Hall King (1887-1979). Submitted by Sally Irene King Ross.

Sally Irene King Ross (b. November 13, 1934) and Jack Irby Ross, Jr. (b. September 2, 1927), taken February 2, 1995, on occasion of his 50th high school class reunion, and their 40th wedding anniversary, Long Beach, California.

Portrait of Howard "Dale" Iams (b. 1912), son of Charles "Charley" V. Iams (b. 1873) of Chevauxdefrise, Ritchie County, West Virginia.

Howard Dale Iams (b. 1912), host of 1993 Iams Reunion on the Chevauxdefrise, and Edna Louise Corbett Reynolds (b. 1906).

417

Family of Meek Corbett (b. 1915, Mead Township, Belmont County, Ohio)

Meek Corbett with tie, hat, and coat.

Meek Corbett, in hat, with flag and gun.

Meek Corbett with daughter Hazel Corbett.

Marie Brown, at marriage to Meek Corbett, 1938.

418

Family of Meek Corbett (b. 1915, Mead Township, Belmont County, Ohio)

Meek Corbett

Marie "Dollie" Brown Corbett, with son Meek "Buddy" Corbett.

Aunt Mildred Corbett McKelvey, nephew Meek "Buddy" Corbett (son of Meek Corbett, b. 1915), and Aunt Edna Corbett Reynolds.

Family of Meek Corbett (b. 1915, Mead Township, Belmont County, Ohio)

Twins Delores and Dorothy Corbett (b. 1951).

Delores (left) and Dorothy Corbett.

Meek Corbett (b. 1915) on steps of Bethel Methodist Church in Key, with daughter Dorothy Corbett and her new husband, James Bennett, 1972.

420

Family of Meek Corbett (b. 1915, Mead Township, Belmont County, Ohio)

James Bennett family with wife Dorothy Corbett Bennett and children Laura (age 15), Jennifer (age 10), Angela (age 7), and James Joseph Bennett, 1988.

The James Bennett Family, 1995, Salem, Ohio: Laura, Jenny, Angela, and little James Joseph.

Meek Corbett talking to Paul McKelvey at back porch of old Milton Corbett homestead, near Key, Ohio.

Meek Corbett, in ball cap, with Barry Duane Reynolds, Marie Brown Corbett, Norita Rose Sholly Reynolds, and Edna Louise Corbett Reynolds.

Hatcher Family, 1922. Left to right: Charlotte Hatcher (daughter, 1880-1974), Jane Gardner Hatcher (mother, 1859), Loren Hatcher (son, 1877-1969), and Benjamin Hatcher (father, ca1854-ca1930). Submitted by Sally Irene King Ross.

Family of George E. Iams, South Bend, Indiana, 1994. George E. Iams (b. 1958), Mishawaka, Indiana, is the son of John Winder Iams (b. Caldwell, Ohio, June 2, 1920; and the grandson of Glenn Iams and Mary McGlaskey). Pictured are George E. and Tracey Iams, with their children Tyler age 10, Wade age 9, Brady age 6, and Corey age 3.

Family of Lois Ijams Hartman

Edwin Clayton Ijams

Mabel Stark, Edwin Ijams, Elizabeth, and J. W. Ijams.

Edwin C. Ijams and Lois in 1923.

424

Family of Lois Ijams
Hartman

John Wesley Ijams
Ozawkie, Kansas

Ina Ijams

Nell Ijams

425

Family of Lois McKelvey Neely (b. 1924)

*Mildred Corbett McKelvey retired after 36
years as the first and only Shadyside, Ohio,
librarian, on January 23, 1970.*

*Mildred Corbett McKelvey and
daughter Lois McKelvey Neely.*

*Lois McKelvey as graduate
nurse in Washington, D.C., with
her aunt Edna Corbett Reynolds
and cousins Ralph Reynolds and
Robert Reynolds.*

*Mildred Corbett McKelvey and
daughter Lois McKelvey Neely.*

426

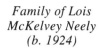

Lois McKelvey Neely
and James Neely, with
daughters JoAnne Neely
and Jeannie Neely.

Wedding photo of
JoAnne Neely and
Michael Solomon
in 1972.

Jeannie Neely and her new husband Randy
Baker were married 1973.

JoAnne and Jeannie Neely with
their grandmother Mildred
Corbett McKelvey, 1958.

The James and Lois Neely Family—
Rear: Ron Snyder (husband), Jeannie
Neely Snyder, JoAnne Neely Solomon,
Michael Solomon (husband), David
Solomon, and Ben Solomon. Front:
Heather Snyder, Lois McKelvey Neely,
Chad Snyder, Jared Solomon, and Timmy
Solomon, 1989, in North Carolina.

427

Family of Paul LaVerne McKelvey (b. 1925)

Lois McKelvey Neely, Paul McKelvey, and Mildred Corbett McKelvey.

A "family tree" of Paul McKelvey, Lois McKelvey Neely, Ralph Reynolds, and Robert Reynolds, at Centerville, 1941.

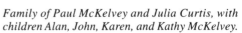

Paul McKelvey and Julia Curtis were married 1957.

Family of Paul McKelvey and Julia Curtis, with children Alan, John, Karen, and Kathy McKelvey.

428

Family of Paul LaVerne McKelvey (b. 1925)

Children of Paul and Julia Curtis McKelvey: John, Karen, Kathy, and Alan McKelvey.

Paul McKelvey behind his wife Julia Curtis, and Lois McKelvey Neely in front of her husband James Neely.

Alan McKelvey and Linda Beckley were married in 1983.

Paul LaVerne McKelvey (b. 1925) and wife Julia Curtis, at the Iams Reunion on the Chevauxdefrise, 1993.

429

Dated March 26th, 1859. "In the name of God Amen. I William Iiams of Amity, Amwell Township, Washington County, Pennsylvania, being of infirm body, but sound and proper mind, do make my last will and testament as follows: I resign my Soul to my creator God, through Jesus my Saviour, and mortal body to my mother, Earth, my remains to be laid in grave in M.P. Burying in Amity, in a decent and becoming habliment for the dead, and a neat tombstone to mark the place where I lay. My funeral and grave expenses to be first paid out of my estate, then my debts after a legal settlement with those that I owe, and then the Court charges and other expenditures necessary for arranging and settling my worldly business in a proper manner, the remainder of my Estate to my affectionate wife, Susannah as long as she remains my widow or as long as she lives, for her support down the steps of time, to be used for her ease, and comfort, but not to be wasted or squandered, and her funeral and grave expenses to be paid, as my own after her decease. The balance of my Estate then to be equally divided between our children. Children Salem, Eleanor, John, Delilah, Wesley, Charity, E. Jane, and Franklin F. Except Delilah who is to have twenty dollars more than the rest, unless her mother gives her a cow before the final settlement of my Estate, then to be equal and Charity's share to be laid out in a piece of land of her own choosing and a title to be made in her name, She to have and to hold the same during her life the decend to legal heirs. Eleanor and E. Jane to receive their shares as their own. In testimony whereof I have set my hand and seal the day and year above written."

Signed by William Iiams, and attested by George Swart, Washington County.

"Be it remembered, that on this 2nd day of May 1859, before me came W. J. Vankirk, Register for the probate of wills and granting settlers of administration in and for said county came George Swart and James A. Jackson, the subscribing witnesses to the foregoing will of William Iiams deceased, who after being duly qualified according to law, depose and say that they were both present and heard the said testator acknowledge the signature hereto attached to be his genuine signature and that the said instrument was his last will and testament and that in his presence, and in the presence of each other, they subscribed their names as witnesses thereto, and that at the time of so doing the said testator was of sound and disposing mind, memory, and understanding, to the best of their judgment, observation, and belief." Sworn to and subscribed before me, W. J. Vankirk, Registrar, and signed by witnesses George Swart and J. A. Jackson. Then, also on May 2, 1859, "the will admitted to probate and the widow renouncing as her paper filed, setlers [sic] of administration with the will annexed issued to Salem Iiams, who on same day was duly sworn. Signed by W. J. Vankirk, Registrar.

Family of Ralph D. Reynolds (b. Powhatan Point, Ohio, 1934)

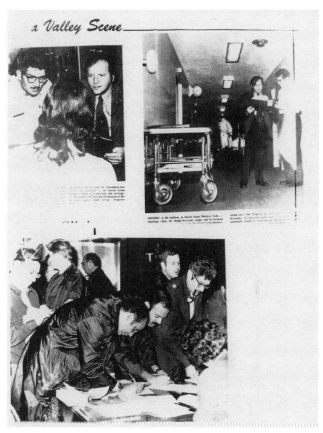

Signing in at an Air Force Physicians Clinical Research Meeting (1970): William Strauss, M.D. (Peter Bent Brigham, Boston), Jerry Reeves, M.D. (Pediatric Oncology, president of South West Medical), Monte B. Miller, M.D. (Air Force Surgeon General), Barry Zaret, M.D. (Professor of Medicine, Chairman Cardiology Yale University), William Howiler, M.D. (Cardiology), and Ralph D. Reynolds, M.D.; featured newspaper article of area's first cancer clinic, David Grant Medical Center, with Ralph D. Reynolds, M.D., and Bernard R. Greenberg, M.D. (Professor and Head, Oncology Services, University of Connecticut).

431

Family of Ralph D. Reynolds
(b. Powhatan Point, Ohio, 1934)

Norita Sholly and Ralph Reynolds,
charcoal portrait.

Ralph D. Reynolds and Norita Rose
Sholly Otte, married 1982.

Norita Rose Sholly Reynolds at a
very happy moment.

Norita Rose Reynolds in the Four Seasons Gift
Shop at Ellis Fischel Cancer Center. (She
founded the gift shop in 1984.)

Ralph and Norita Sholly Otte Reynolds,
with daughter Susan Otte Robbins and
Edna Louise Corbett Reynolds.

432

Family of Ralph D. Reynolds (b. Powhatan Point, Ohio, 1934)

Bridge of Madison County: The Imes Bridge, built 1870, St. Charles, Iowa. Ralph D. Reynolds, M.D., standing in front of the covered bridge, 1988. Made famous by the novel of Robert James Waller, Bridges of Madison County, *1992.*

Portrait of Barry Duane Reynolds, Ronald Arthur Reynolds, and Daniel Ralph Reynolds, California, 1967.

Graduation of the third son from University of California at Berkeley, 1989: Daniel Ralph Reynolds, Ronald Arthur Reynolds, Barry Duane Reynolds, and Ralph Duane Reynolds, M.D.

California, 1993: Barry Reynolds (the Stanford University Business School Rugby player), Ron Reynolds (in Stanford Rugby jersey), and Dan Reynolds (in Stanford Business School jersey).

Family of Ralph D. Reynolds (b. Powhatan Point, Ohio, 1934)

Family portrait of Frank Howard Anson, Nancy Lee Otte Anson, Zachary Anson, and Tressa Leigh Anson, 1995.

Edna Louise Corbett Reynolds and her family, Napa, California, at wedding of Ron and Laura Reynolds, 1993. Robert Wayne Reynolds, Jeff Reynolds holding son Ian Reynolds, Steve Reynolds, Ronald Arthur Reynolds, Daniel Ralph Reynolds with son and ring bearer Thomas Daniel Reynolds, Barry Reynolds, and Ralph D. Reynolds, M.D.

San Jose, California, 1994: Ron Reynolds and wife Laura Bischoff Reynolds.

Napa, California, 1993: Bill Smith, Gertrude Elaine Manifold Reynolds Smith, and Ronald Reynolds.

Ralph and Norita Reynolds Sugar Train, Maui, 1997

Family of Ralph D. Reynolds (b. Powhatan Point, Ohio, 1934)

San Francisco at Golden Gate Bridge, 1994: Susan Crews Reynolds, wife of Daniel Ralph Reynolds.

San Jose, California, 1994: Susan Crews Reynolds and husband Daniel Ralph Reynolds, at home, Christmas, holding trophy for scoring a hole-in-one.

White House, Washington, D.C., 1994: Daniel Ralph Reynolds giving a ride to son Thomas Daniel Reynolds.

Milpitas, California, 1991. Thomas Daniel Reynolds and Norita Sholly Reynolds.

435

Family of Ralph D. Reynolds (b. Powhatan Point, Ohio, 1934)

Barry Duane Reynolds and Jill Peterson Reynolds, California coast, 1989.

Barry Reynolds and Jill Peterson, wedding, San Jose, California, 1988.

Seattle, Washington, 1991: Barry Duane Reynolds and Ronald Arthur Reynolds, attending NCAA Final Four.

Stanford Business School Graduation, 1992, with a display of the family inherited trait of touching the tip of the tongue to the tip of the nose. Dan Reynolds, Barry Reynolds (1st in his class, wearing California Bears baseball cap) holding Thomas Reynolds.

Family of Robert W. Reynolds (b. Powhatan Point, Ohio, 1937)

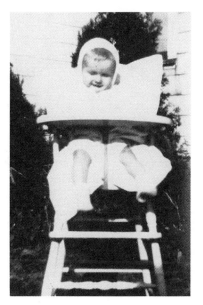

Robert Reynolds, 1938

Robert Reynolds, Junior High

Robert Reynolds as high school graduate, 1955.

Robert Reynolds as an All American long jumper at Ohio University, 1960.

Family of Robert W. Reynolds
(b. Powhatan Point, Ohio, 1937)

Robert W. Reynolds and wife Mary Kern.

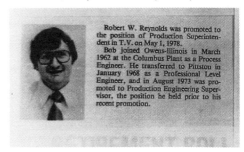

Robert W. Reynolds was promoted to the position of Production Superintendent in T.V. on May 1, 1978.
Bob joined Owens-Illinois in March 1962 at the Columbus Plant as a Process Engineer. He transferred to Pittston in January 1968 as a Professional Level Engineer, and in August 1973 was promoted to Production Engineering Supervisor, the position he held prior to his recent promotion.

Robert W. Reynolds and wife Mary Kern, married Wilkes Barre, Pennsylvania, 1978.

Announcement of promotion (1978) of Robert W. Reynolds to Production Superintendent in TV (later named Plant Manager) in Pittston/Wilkes Barre, Pennsylvania.

Robert and Baiba Folkmanis Reynolds with sons Jeff Reynolds and Steve Reynolds.

Ray C. Reynolds and wife Edna Corbett Reynolds, with their son Robert W. Reynolds, and his sons Jeff Reynolds and Steve Reynolds.

Family of Robert W. Reynolds (b. Powhatan Point, Ohio, 1937)

Steve and Jeff Reynolds.

The grandsons of Edna Louise Corbett Reynolds: Steve Reynolds, Jeff Reynolds, Ron Reynolds, Dan Reynolds, and Barry Reynolds, in Columbus, Ohio, 1966.

Oxford looking Jeff Reynolds, Robert Reynolds, and Steve Reynolds.

Steve Reynolds as Ohio State University graduate.

Tuxedo clad Jeff Reynolds, Robert W. Reynolds, and Steve Reynolds.

Family of Robert W. Reynolds (b. Powhatan Point, Ohio, 1937)

Jeff Reynolds, as Ohio University graduate.

Jeff Reynolds and Leah Pusekar, married 1985.

First birthday, Ian Reynolds, Columbus, Ohio.

Mary Kern Reynolds, with Ian Reynolds and Ian's mother Leah Pusekar Reynolds.

Columbus, Ohio, 1993: Jeffrey Reynolds, Leah Reynolds, Steve Reynolds, Ralph Reynolds, and Robert Reynolds. Front: Edna Corbett Reynolds and Ray Campbell Reynolds.

440

Left to right front: father, Ulysses Grant Imes and mother, Mary Hester Rose Imes. Children back row left to right: Verna Yost, Jessie Orren Imes, Grace Sutton, William Imes, Inez Mautz, and Clarence Aaron Imes. Photo taken about 1922. Courtesy of Joy I. Hannon

Left to right: Grace Sutton, William Imes, Inez Mautz, Jesse Orren Imes, Verna Yost, and Clarence Aaron Imes. Children of Ulysses Grant Imes and Mary Hester Rose Imes. Photo taken in 1949. Courtesy of Joy I. Hannon

442

Husband and family of Inez Imes Mautz: 1979. Back: Myron Mautz, Dale Mautz, Roger Mautz, Gene Mautz, Front: Glen Mautz, Henry Mautz, Marjorie Mautz Dixon.

Imes Cousins: 1991
From left: Marjorie Mautz Dixon, guest, Glen Mautz, Gene Mautz, Joy Imes Hannon, Theda Yost Clemans, Dale Mautz, Roger Mautz, Carolyn Imes, Janet Imes Davis, Jerry Imes

Mautz-Imes Reunion, July 30, 1983.
First Row: Gene Mautz, Jessie Mautz, Edith Imes, Jesse Imes, Karl Yost, Henry Mautz, Phil Clemans, and Theda Yost Clemans.
Second Row: Jeff Dixon, Melissa Cale Kent, Keith Kent, Loren Mautz, Yvonne Martin, Dale E. Mautz, Kay Mautz, Kathy Mautz, Kevin Peters, Jason Peters, Shirley Mautz Peters, Amy Peters, Beth Peters, Bonnie Dixon, Jennifer Dixon, Teri Carter, Dennis Carter, Bruce Carter, Jesse Mercer, and Jan Mautz Mercer.
Third Row: Rita Yost Martin, Jason Mautz, Glen Mautz, Suzi Mautz, Linda Mautz Carter, Carolyn Imes, Jerry Imes, Ray Dixon, Debbie Martin Boughner, Joy Imes, Cale Hannon, Scott Boughner, Jack Hannon, Stacy Rausch, Mark Rausch, Kristie Clemans Rausch, Donna Mautz Young, Kevin Levstek, _____, Sharon Clemans, and Matt Clemans.
Back Row: Juanita Mautz, Dale Mautz, Marjorie Mautz Dixon, Jodi Clayton, Kass Imes, Robert Mautz, and Bonnie Weber.

All Hallows Parish Church, established in 1692, Anne Arundel County, Maryland. Located near the South River Club, this church was the home church of the earliest Iams family members.

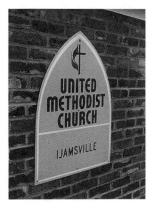

Ijamsville Methodist Church
Ijamsville, Maryland

Old Wegee United Methodist Church, founded 1823, home church for Iams-Corbett family, above Wegee Creek, Mead Township, Belmont County, Ohio.

Ralph Reynolds, M.D. and Paul McKelvey at tombstone monument of Revolutionary soldier Thomas Iams (b. 1754), Old Dutch Cemetery between St. Clairsville and Glencoe, Belmont County, Ohio.

The home church of Bethel Presbyterian Church at Key, Mead Township, Belmont County, Ohio, where Iola Iams, Milton Corbett, Olive Corbett, and Caroline Scales are buried.

Old Dutch Cemetery, Belmont County, Ohio. Samuel Iiams (d. August 21, 1869, age 65 years, 5 months, and 26 days) and wife Elizabeth (d. November 1, 1869); Thomas Iiams (d. June 24, 1834, aged 80), and wife Catherine (d. May 13, 1838).

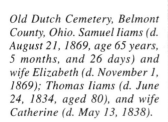

446

Tombstone of first wife of Wesley Iams, Caroline Scales, died August 14, 1888, and buried at Bethel Presbyterian Church Cemetery, Key, Belmont County, Ohio.

Chevauxdefrise Cemetery, Ritchie County, West Virginia; Wesley Iams (b. March 3, 1828; d. September 23, 1894).

Chevauxdefrise Methodist Cemetery, Ritchie County, West Virginia. Grave marker of George H. Iams, son of Wesley and Nancy Iams (b. February 19, 1872; d. June 2, 1875).

Chevauxdefrise Cemetery, Ritchie County, West Virginia: Nancy McKelvey Iams, second wife of Wesley Iams and mother of eleven of his children (b. September 20, 1846, Monroe County, Ohio; d. April 27, 1928).

Tombstone of Harvey Gardner (b. October 13, 1820; d. November 14, 1889), and wife Charity Iiams (1823-1900) on reverse side. Submitted by Sally Irene King Ross.

Chevauxdefrise Methodist Church Cemetery, Ritchie County, West Virginia Grave marker of David E. Iams (b. March 25, 1870; d. October 22, 1901) and Emma Jane Wilson-Iams-Cornell (b. 1870; d. 1955).

448

Chevauxdefrise Methodist Cemetery: Earl Iams (b. November 20, 1884; d. April 16, 1907) and his brother Homer D. Iams (b. February 10, 1883; d. August 9, 1904).

Bethel Presbyterian Church Cemetery, Mead Township, Key, Belmont County, Ohio. William Milton Corbett (b. February 6, 1867; d. June 24, 1954) and his wife Iola Ellen Iams (b. March 9, 1879; d. April 15, 1959).

Chevauxdefrise Methodist Cemetery: Charles V. Iams (b. November 8, 1873; d. December 25, 1949) and Stella Eckard (b. January 10, 1882; d. July 8, 1964).

Slave graveyard on the farm of Lester and Charles Imes in a wooded area, east of Pennsylvania Route 326, near a sawmill, south of Chaneysville, Bedford County, Pennsylvania. The death of the slaves was the subject of a novel The Chaneysville Incident, by David Bradley of the University of Pennsylvania (Harper and Row Publishers, 1981). Photo courtesy of Joyce Trall.

From 13 Graves, A Hometown Novel

CHANEYSVILLE, Pa. (AP) — Stand on the hill where rough-hewn stones mark their graves.

You can almost hear the sounds the 13 runaway slaves might have made, their feet stumbling and lungs struggling, as they fled before their pursuers 122 years ago.

Then, the awful moment of truth—no escape save one. A spiritual sums it up: "And before I'll be a slave, I'll lie buried in my grave, and go home to my Lord, and be free."

One by one, author David Bradley believes, the 13 slew themselves.

In a novel that pulls no punches about the cruelties suffered by such runaways and their descendants in his nearby hometown of Bedford, Bradley has brought the 13 slaves back to live.

Drawing fiction from a local legend, he examines their flight and the unraveling of fate that brought them to be buried here, in a white family's mountainside graveyard high above Blue Gap Run.

Their story, passed down from generation to generation in this isolated southwestern Pennsylvania valley, now comes to a larger audience in *The Chaneysville Incident,* Bradley's second novel, published April 8 by Harper & Row.

It is the story of a young, black college professor's search for self. In trying to understand why his father, an eccentric moonshiner, died, he discovers the death was linked to the deaths of the runaway slaves more than a century earlier.

The book has created a sensation in Bradley's hometown, population 3,200 and peacock-proud of its past. The novel is sold out at the Bedford bookstore, despite—or maybe because of—the jabs it takes at the community's history.

"It's caused talk, let's put it that way," said storeowner Doris Atkinson. "It did open my eyes a little bit."

A boyhood friend of Bradley's, Bill Clark, is now sports editor of the *Bedford Gazette.* Clark, who is white, said he felt the novel portrays prejudice in the town more starkly than he remembers.

"There's things in there I didn't know growing up side-by-side with him," Clark said.

In the story, Bedford is referred to as "the Town," a site of political corruption, segregated eating places, barbers who won't cut the hair of blacks and a lynching.

The novel also says that it was at the colonnaded Bedford Springs Hotel, just outside town, that the Supreme Court justices holed up, with their magnesia water and black servants, before handing down the infamous Dred Scott decision.

That's the one that said, in effect: once a slave, always a slave. It held that a slave's residence in free territory did not make him or her free and denied citizenship rights to the descendants of slaves.

450

The book spans 250 years of history and local landmarks and institutions are recognizable in its pages. Bedford residents say. "I used the things that I knew," Bradley acknowledged.

He was not always kind. His treatment of the town combines nostalgia with anger.

The mixture also comes through in conversation. He speaks affectionately of the old people in town and their endless stories, but the voice grows taut when he recalls his years as one of a small knot of blacks in the local high school. "Sheer, unadulterated terror," he said. "Somebody beat me up every day."

But overall, "they're very good people," he said. "One of the reasons that I didn't use the name of the town in the book was because what happened there could have happened anywhere."

Reconstructing the past is Bradley family tradition. The author's mother, Harriette Bradley, is a history buff. So was his father, the Rev. David Bradley, who died last year.

It was while helping prepare a history of Bedford County in 1969 that Mrs. Bradley heard the legend of the runaway slaves.

She traced the tale to the "south county," near Chaneysville, and finally found the unmarked stones in the graveyard of the Iames clan, one of the county's founding families.

"They put them in their family cemetery. They must have been some quite good people at that time," Mrs. Bradley said.

Bradley, by then studying creative writing at the University of Pennsylvania, was fascinated by the story. He promised himself to write about the slaves fleeing their masters and passing through here on the Underground Railroad.

Bradley's mother said she heard the slaves were killed by sympathetic whites at the slaves' request when they realized capture was imminent. But the author dismisses that part of the story, saying anyone who killed slaves was liable for their value and punishable under law.

He thinks suicide by the band was a more likely explanation, saying that slave suicides were common and widely documented.

"Their idea of death was different," he said. "When these people found themselves in an untenable position, they would simply escape. Instead of escaping North, they would escape in a different direction.'

Bradley in Chaneysville family graveyard.

ERVIN F. BICKLEY, JR.

110 Sleepy Hollow Road
New Canaan, Conn. 06840

August 26, 1970

Dear Mr. Newman:

Thank you very much for your letter of August 14 and for the proof sheets which you sent with it. Needless to say I found these of the greatest interest and have spent several hours looking over them. I can only wish that we had an opportunity to compare notes prior to your finalizing your material, as I think between us we might have closed some still remaining gaps.

The following thoughts and comments occurred to me, based on my review up to this point. I am sure I will have some further questions and ideas as I read the other parts of your book when I receive it.

1. On Page 323 I think there could be at least some question whether Richard, baptized September 1712, was the one who married Mary Nichols. Richard, senior mentioned children of both marriages in his original will dated 1747, but did not mention Richard. Also, in the deed for the land transferred from Richard of Pennsylvania to Thomas of Pennsylvania, John is listed as the eldest son and heir of Richard, senior. If Richard, baptized 1712, was still alive, then he would almost certainly be older than John and the statement in the deed would not be true.

The other possibility is that John really was the son of the first marriage but that the second wife had acted as the mother in the family for so many years that she was so described in the codicil in Richard, senior's will. In any case there seems to be some loose end here.

2. On Page 325 you place John as the one who approved the value of his father's personal estate. You are much more familiar with Maryland law of those years than I, so my question is was it not the usual practice for kinsmen other than those directly involved in the estate to be the ones to approve such papers? If that is the case, then I believe the John who did the approving was probably Captain John, a cousin rather than a son.

3. On Page 325 you place Thomas of Pennsylvania definitely as the brother of Richard, and of course then also as the son of John. I believe this may be open to some question and would be very much interested in your thinking regarding the definite placement of Thomas here.

There is no question that Thomas was the brother of William since he was named as such in William's will in Washington County, Pennsylvania.

4. Page 326 which discusses William, son of Richard, Sr., includes a very interesting note about the deed which this William signed in 1792 describing himself as of Allegheny County, Maryland. I would like very much to have a copy of that deed, and if you would be kind enough to send me one naturally I would send you a check for any cost involved. If this William went to Allegheny County, Maryland, then he certainly had to be the father of the William, Jr., who settled out there as so far as I have been able to determine only one branch of the family ever located in that county. If tax lists for those years of Allegheny County are still available, I wonder if we could get them checked to try to pin down that particular point.

With further reference to William, son of Richard, Sr., the William who settled in Washington County, Maryland and purchased personalty there from John Donnachy, was listed in the 1790 census there, purchased land of Thomas Worly there and in 1803 sold land to Abraham Ditto was not William the son of Richard. The William of Washington County was the one who married Elizabeth Howard and about 1803 left there to settle in Fairfield County, Ohio. I have spent untold hours on this particular branch of the family in an effort to help Mrs. Williams locate the parents of her ancestor Eli, and I am certain that the above statement is accurate.

5. On Page 326 you give the birth date for Richard, son of John, as 1745. I would like to have the documentation for that date, as I have never been able to determine it definitely.

With further reference to the same Richard on Page 327 you mention both a Richard and a Richard, Jr., who took the Oath of Allegiance in Washington County, Maryland during March 1778. I wonder who the Richard, Jr. was, as I have been unable to identify him.

Also on Page 327 you show as one of the sons of Richard and Eleanor Pottenger Iams the Eli who married Catherine Crawford (and who was the ancestor of Mrs. Williams).

I have tracked down the Eli who went to Montgomery County, Ohio and who was the one who married Phebe Hackathorn. The date of his birth corresponds to the census records for Richard and his children, while the date of birth for the Eli who married Catherine Crawford does not. Also, in a biography of the Eli who went to Montgomery County, Ohio he is listed as the son of Richard and Ellen Iams. I am afraid that we still have not identified the parents of the Eli who married Catherine Crawford.

6. At this point I believe we are uncertain about the ancestry of Eleanor Pottenger. The records about Robert Pottenger do not list any child of that name. My tentative conclusion is that she was a child of one of Robert's brothers, as the name Eleanor was placed in the family through the marriage of an earlier generation.

7. On Page 328 you mention that Samuel Iams wrote to William Imes and on Page 329 you indicate that William was the writer of the letter. I have a copy of the letter but have not yet been able to dig it out of my large collection of papers, but I believe the first item is correct in that Samuel wrote to William rather than the other way around.

8. On Page 329 I located an old family record which said that Catherine Iams, widow of Sergeant Thomas, died in 1838 in Belmont County, Ohio. I cannot guarantee that date, but it seems to be reliable.

9. On Page 329 you list the children of Richard, Jr., son of Richard and Eleanor Pottenger Iams. His wife was Mary Shidler who died February 15, 1868 in Monticello, Indiana. Their children were as follows:

1. John, born April 13, 1809
2. Reason, born May 17, 1810, died Sept. 10, 1868 at Granville, Delaware County, Indiana; married Eleanor.
3. Peter, born ca1811, died Sept. 2, 1836 Greene County, Pennsylvania
4. Nancy, born Dec. 18, 1816, died 1899, married Roland Hughes
5. Sally, born about 1817/1818
6. George, born Sept. 28, 1819, died May 20, 1876
7. Richard, born 1821
8. Susannah, born Sept. 1, 1825, died May 5, 1878 Indiana
9. William, born Feb. 1, 1827, died Aug. 18, 1901 in California
10. Mary, born March 20, 1829, died April 18, 1863 at Monticello, Indiana

453

I hope the above comments will be of interest and will be helpful. I am most anxious to read the rest of your book and would particularly appreciate any thoughts or reactions you have regarding some of the questions I have listed above.

I still am hoping that somehow we can find the answer to Mrs. Williams' problem.

With kindest regards,

Sincerely yours,

Harry Wright Newman

EFB/pp

Mr. Harry Wright Newman
640 Americana Drive - Apt. 202
Water Gate Village
Annapolis, Maryland 21403

Norddeutscher Lloyd Bremen   an Bord "Bremen"
                                                         4 September 1970

My dear Mr. Blickley:
    Your letter was handed to me as I was leaving for New York and it was
read after I was safely planted on ship board. I am enroute to Britain to see first
hand what is holding up the printing of the book which was originally promised
for May and then July. Naturally I do not have my manuscript with me to reply to
your negations. But what proof do you have for the varied questions which you
raise. I always maintain an open mind, if my conclusions are incorrect—but proof
should be shown to the contrary.
    While in Europe I am taking the opportunity of attending the Interna-
tional Congress of Genealogy in Vienna and shall return to the States early in
October.

                                          Very sincerely yours,
                                          Harry Wright Newman

640 Americana Drive
Annapolis, MD 21403

1933		1970

Name   DOB

Children of: Children of:

William and Elizabeth Cheyney   William and Elizabeth Cheyney

1. William Iiams   1670......................................William Iiams b. 1670
   m. Elizabeth Plummer   m. Elizabeth Plummer

2. Richard Iiams   1673 (P414)..........................Richard Iiams
   m. 1) Anne Cheyney   m. 1) Anne Cheyney
   b. Mary Iiams m. Richard Wright
   c. Richard Iiams m. Mary Nichols
   d. Rachel Iiams
   e. William Iiams
   f. Cheney Iiams
   m. 2) Elizabeth   m. 2) Elizabeth Gaither
   g. John Iiams
   h. Charity Iiams
   i. Sarah Iiams
   j. Aaron Iiams bp 6-24-1721

3. Elizabeth Iiams   Elizabeth Iiams
   m. 1) Daniel Clark   m. 1) Daniel Clark
   m. 2) Samuel Duval   m. 2) Samauel Duval
      MD June 18, 1697

4. George Iiams   ? (P416)   George Iiams (291)
   m. Elizabeth ____   m. Elizabeth Bashford
   1. Jacob Iiams...In the 1970 edition, Jacob has a son
                                     William Ijams.
   2. Susannah...She marries a "Welch"
   3. Elizabeth Iiams bap 1717
   4. George Iiams bap 1718...............................Styles himself as a bricklayer
   5. Samuel Iiams bap 1721/2
   6. William Iiams b. 1723 m. Anne ?..................Marries Elizabeth
      m. 2x no issues matured   and the widow Williams
   7. John Iiams b. 1725....................................Marries Arina Worthington and
                                     Martha Cunningham
   8. Mary Iiams b. 1728

5. Hester Iiams   ?   Hester Iiams
   m. John Nicholson   m. John Nicholson
      MD Dec. 23, 1708

6. Susannah Iiams   ?   Susannah Iiams
   m. Thomas Fowler   m. 1) Thomas Fowler
      MD Oct. 15, 1696   m. 2) Mark Brown

William and Elizabeth Plummer   William and Elizabeth Plummer

1. Elizabeth Iiams   6-15-1697   Elizabeth Iiams b. 6-15-1697
                                      m. Gassaway Watkins

2. William Iiams   12-22-1699 (P396)   Williams b. 12-22-1699
   m. Elizabeth Jones   m. Elizabeth Jones
   a. Willliam Iiams b. 11-22-1721   William Iiams b. 11-22-1721
   b. Cassandra Iiams b. 9-20-1722   Cassandra Iiams b. 9-20-1722
      m. Henry Leeke 12-16-1736   m. Henry Leeke 12-16-1736
   c. Margaret Iiams b. 8-13-1724   Margaret Iiams b. 8-13-1724
   d. Thomas Iiams m. Mary Iiams*(P401) Thomas Iiams Extant 1775 no marr.
      i. John Ijams Capt. (P409)
        m. Rachel Marriott (Capt)

```
          1. Franklin Lafayette Ijams
             m. Harriet Brown
          2. Rebecca Marriott Ijams
             m. John Ijams
          3. Richard William Ijams
             m. Rebecca Marriott
          4. Isaac Plummer Ijams
          5. Joshua Barney Ijams went west
          6. Rachel Maria Ijams
             m. Voltaire Willett
          7. Ann Homewood Ijams
             m. Benjamin Brown
       ii. Rebecca Ijams
          m. Joseph Marriott
          MD 3-25-1796
    e. Sarah Iams                                    Sarah Iams unmarried in 1774

3. Richard Iiams              3-4-1702              Richard Iiams b. 3-4-1702

4. Mary Iiams                 May 1705             Mary Iiams b. 5-1705
   m. John Waters                                  m. John Waters

5. Thomas Iiams              8-7-1708 (P397)       Thomas Iiams b. 8-7-1708 (293)
                                                    m. Artridge ____
    a. John Iiams                                   John Iiams b. 10-20-1747
       m. Elizabeth Hampton (P401)                  m. Susannah (Watkins) (296)
          i. William Iiams b. 1792
             m. Deliah Meeks
          ii. Nancy Iiams b. 1795
             m. Joseph Martin
          iii. John Iiams b. 1798 dsp 1846
          iv. Charity Iiams b. 1799
             m. John D. Smith
          v. Sarah Iiams b. 1804
             m. Freeman Hathway
          vi. Mary Iiams b. 1806
             m. Moses Smith
    b. Thomas Iiams b. 1754 (P402/3)                Thomas Iiams b. 1745 d. 1805
       m. Catherine Hampton                         m. Mary Iiams & Sarah Marriott
          i. John Iiams                             i. John Iiams m. Rachel Marriott
          ii. Elizabeth Iiams dsp
          iii. Samuel Iiams b. 1795
             m. Elizabeth Meek
          iv. Charity Iiams b. 1805
             m. Jacob Meyer
          v. Thomas Iiams
             m. Mary Hardesty
          vi. Richard Iiams m. Fanny Meek
          vii. Polly Iiams m. Jacob Eggy
          viii. William Iiams m. Susannah Sharp
          ix. Resin Iiams m. Mary Iiams
          x. Rebecca Iiams m. Jacob Wilson          Rebecca Iiams m. Joseph Marriott
          xi. Catherine Iiams m. Michael Ault
    c. Richard Iiams m. Eleanor ____(P404)          Richard Iiams m. Eleanor Musgrove
          i. Richard Iiams.......................................This Richard is not listed as a child
                                                    of Richard and Eleanor
             m. Elizabeth Pottenger (P410)
             1. Thomas Iiams m. Mary Smith
             2. Richard Iiams m. Mary ?
             3. Otho Iiams m. Nancy Cole
             4. Resin Iiams m. Phoebe Clark
             5. John Iiams m. Ruth Barker
                              457
```

6. William Iiams m. Charity
7. Bazil Iiams dsp
8. Eli Iiams m. Phoebe Heckathorn

                ii. Thomas M. Iiams

Thomas Musgrove Ijams m. Nancy Carvel
   iii. Nancy Iiams   Nancy Ijams m. John B. Cecil
d. William Iiams m. Mary Hampton (P405)   Wm. Iiams m. Charity Ryan
   i. Elizabeth Iiams m. Daniel Smith   No children listed
   ii. Mary Iiams
   iii. Thomas Iiams m. Mercia Walton**
   iv. John Iiams OK
e. Susannah Iams m. ? Pumphreys   Susanna Iiams m. ? Pumphreys
f. Mary Iiams m. William Penn   Mary Iiams m. Thomas Ijams
g. One un-named child   Artridge Iiams b. 2-6-1736
                           Added Sarah Iiams b. 12-8-1734
                           Added Charity Iiams b. Jan. 15, 1739
                           Added Elizabeth Iiams b. 8-19-1732

6. John Iiams   1712 (P398)   John Iiams (293)
  m. Rebecca Jones   m. Rebecca Jones
  a. Elizabeth Iiams m. Robert Fenley   Elizabeth Iiams m. R. Fenley
  b. Ann Iiams m. Lewis Stockett   Anne Iiams m. L. Stockett
    MD June 10m 176?
  c. William Iiams   Wm. Iiams
    m. Eliz Howard (398)   m. Eliz Howard (298)
  d. Mary Iiams m. Thomas Iiams*   Mary Iiams m. Thomas Iiams
    i. Richard D. Iiams   Richard D. Ijams m. J. E. Alford
    ii. William Howard Iiams   Wm. Howard Ijams m.
    iii. Rebecca Iiams   Rebecca Iiams
    iv. Rachel Iiams   Rachel Ijams
    v. Comfort Iiams   Comfort Ijams
    vi. Sarah   Sarah Ijams
    vii. John Iiams   John Ijams
    viii. Joseph Iiams   Joseph Ijams m. Mary Ann Ijams
    ix. Frederick Iiams   Frederick Ijams
  e. Isaac Iiams   (P406)   Isaac Iiams
    m. Elizabeth (Beck) Williams   m. Elizabeth (Beck) Williams
    i. Isaac Iiams m. Lucretia Allen
    ii. John Wesley Iiams m. Sarah Vansant
    iii. William Iiams m. Catherine Stevens
    iv. Rebecca Iiams m. Samuel S. Bright
    v. Elizabeth Iiams m. Thomas Beall
    iv. Mary Ann Iiams m. Joseph H. Iiams
  f. Thomas Plummer Iiams b. 4-4-1773 (P406/7)   Thomas Plummer Iiams
    m. 1) Sarah Duval 2) Elizabeth Manly   m. 1) Sarah Duval Manly not listed
    i. John Iiams
    ii. Joseph Iiams
    iii. Rebecca
    iv. Lewis Iiams
    v. Harriet Iiams
    vi. Elizabeth Iiams
    vii. Charlotte Iiams
    viii. Comfort Iiams
    ix. Sarah Iiams
    2) Plummer and Manly
     x. William F. Iiams m. Elsie Robins
    xi. Nancy Iiams
  g. John Iiams m. Mary Waters (P407)   John Iiams m. Mary Waters
    i. Jacob Iiams m. Anne Howard (P410)
    1. Rebecca Iiams m. John Wilcoxen
    2. Mary Ijams m. William H. Ijams
    ii. John Waters Iiams (P411)

m. Rebecca M. Iiams
1. Maria A. Iiams b. 1832
2. Richard Iiams b. 1834
3. Sprigg Iiams b. 1836
4. Jacob W. Iiams b. 1838
5. Josephine Iiams b. 1842
6. Dewitt Iiams b. 1844
7. Jane B. Iiams b. 1848
  iii. Plummer Iiams
  iv. Ann Iiams m. John McLaughlin
  v. Jane Iiams m. Singleton Burgee
  vi. Elizabeth Iiams m. Thomas Duval
  vii. Mary Iiams m. John Montgomery
h. Rebecca Iiams m. Thomas Sunderland

Rebecca Iiams m. T. Sunderland
William Iiams m. Elizabeth Howard

7. Plummer Iiams bap. 8-6-1718 (P400)
m. Ruth Childs
a. Plummer Iiams b. 10-29-1748 (P408)
m. Jemina Welsh
  i. Ann Iiams b. 9-17-1778
  m. George Sanks
  ii. Plummer Iiams b. 1781 (P412)*
   m. 1) Rebecca Iiams*
   1. Plummer Iiams
    m. Harriet Mussetter
    2) Mary A. Montgomery*
   2. John Iiams b. 9-1817, d. 1824
   3. James Iiams b. 6-21-1819 m. Dorcas Susan
    Mitchell d. of John Tabb
   4. Richard Iiams b. 8-2-1821
    m. Elizabeth Aldridge
   5. Rebecca Iiams m. John Montgomery Carpenter
   6. Joshan Iiams m. Wm. Saunders Brown
   7. Charles Montgomery Iiams
    b. 1827, d. 1828
  iii. Ruth Iiams b. 11-13-1783
   m. Christopher Mussetter
  iv. Rebecca Iiams b. 9-18-1785
   m. Benjamin Duval
  v. John Ijams m. Catherine Barnes
   1. Elizabeth Ijams
   2. John Ijams
   3. Mary Ijams
   4. Emily Ijams
   5. Jane Ijams
   6. Sarah Jane Ijams
   7. William Henry Ijams b. 10-6-1822
    m. Isabella King
b. Elizabeth Iiams b. 12-3-1750
m. William Drury
c. Margaret Iiams b. 10-31-1753
m. Jonathan Selby
d. John Iiams b. 6-5-1756 dsp 1791
e. Ann Iiams b. 7-2-1759
m. Samuel Drury

Plummer Iiams bap 8-6-1718
m. Ruth Childs
Plummer Iiams b. 10-29-1748
m. Jemina Welsh

v. John Iiams m. Cath Barnes
1. Elizabeth
2. John
3. Mary
4. Emily
5. Jane
6. Sarah
7. William H. Ijam
  m. Isabelle King
b. Elizabeth Iiams
  m. William Drury
c. Margaret Iiams
  m. Jonathan Selby
d. John Iiams dsp 1791
e. Ann Iiams
  m. Samuel Drury

8. Charity Iiams
m. John Waters

8. Charity Iiams
m. John Waters

9. Anne Iiams
m. Richard Williams

9. Anne Iiams
  m. Richard Williams and
  Wm. Iiams of George

459

12642 Parkwood
Sun City West, Ariz. 85375

Dear Sir,

This is the story that has come down in our family and may not be true—during
the Revolutionary War there were two brothers James and Tom Iiams living in
Maryland who wanted to cross a river. There were two Hessian soldiers guarding
the crossing and they would not permit the brothers to cross. An argument ensued
and the brothers killed the Hessians. The brothers didn't go back but kept on till
they come to Erie, PA. Tom had a son Eli who walked to Trotwood, Ohio and got
160 acres of good land for a song. He had nine boys, Martin, Richard, George,
Alfred, Jacob, David, Harvey, Howard, and Loren plus three girls whose names are
not known. My Grandfather was Loren who was 6 foot one and was the smallest
one of the bunch. They were all big powerful men and I guess they raised a lot of
hell according to some people I have talked to.

I have given the name some publicity since I started the Iams pet food Co. who
have advertised the name pretty extensively. I wish I could be of more help but
this is the extent of my knowledge.

Yours truly,

Paul Iams

Compliments Of:

Easter Operations
P.O. Box 862
Lewisburg, OH 45338
(513) 962-2624

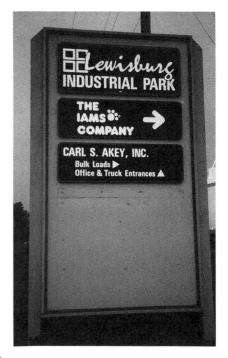

*Iams Pet Food Plant - 1195, Lewisburg, Ohio, one
of six plants in the United States and abroad.*

February 16, 1995

Dear Ralph,

Trying to place the Iiams genealogy correctly takes a Philadelphia lawyer. I have been trying to compare the works of Harry Wright Newman, 1933 and 1970 editions and then pick up on Howard Leckey's (Jimmy Meighen) works.

Most of the genealogy and family ties in Harry Wright Newman's are fine up to Thomas of 1708 (son of William and Elizabeth Cheyney), and Richard Iiams 2, son of William and Elizabeth Cheyney.

Harry Wright Newman	Howard Leckey
Elizabeth Iiams b. 8-19-1732	
Sarah Iiams, b. Dec. 8, 1734	
Artridge Iiams b. Feb. 6, 1736	
Charity Iiams b. Jan. 15, 1739	
Susanna Iiams b. Dec. 15, 1742	Susannah Iiams
m. ? Pumphries	m. ? Pumphries
Thomas Iiams, b. Apr. 20, 1745	Thomas Iiams Dec. 26, 1754
m. 1) Mary Iiams,	m. Catherine Hampton
m. 2) Sarah Marriott	
John Iiams b. Oct. 20, 1747	John Iiams b. 1751,
m. Susannah Watkins	m. Elizabeth Hampton
Richard Iiams b. Feb. 15, 1749	Richard Iiams b. 17??
	m. Eleanor Jones
Mary Iiams b. June 10, 1752	Mary Iiams
m. Thomas Iiams	m. William Penn
William Iiams, b. Nov. 26, 1755	William Iiams
m. Charity Ryan	Mary Hampton

If you compare the lists of siblings as follows, you will see that they are the same but of different parents.

Richard Ijams (son of John, son of Richard & Elizabeth Cheyney) b. 1745, d. 183? m. Eleanor Pottenger	Richard Iams (son of Thomas & Artridge)
Their Children:	Their Children:
Thomas Iams m. Mary Smith	Thomas Iams m. Mary Smith
Richard Iams m. Mary Shidler	Richard Iams m. Mary Shidler
Otho Iams m. Nancy Cole	Otho Iams m. Nancy Cole
Resin Iams m. Phoebe Clark	Resin Iams m. Phoebe Clark
John Iams m. Ruth Baker	John Iams m. Ruth Barker
William Iams m. Charity?	William Iams m. Charity
Bazil Iams	Bazil Iams
Eli Iams m. Catharine Crawford	Eli Iams m. Phoebe Heckathorn

If you haven't had the time to review these works in detail, I thought you might like to have the above. It is very difficult to try to connect a family line unless documents can be found to correct the above. Perhaps, by now, in the historics that

461

people are sending you may have the answer to this troubling matter (or at least troubling to me).

I still am not sure of our Thomas of 1784/6 back to his parents. I put him in as the son of William and Mary Hampton, who was the son of William Iams, son of Thomas, but that is only temporary until I can come up with the correct parents.

I am enclosing some other pieces of data that I have found on the Iiams family just in case you don't have them.

About the picture! I will try and have a copy made from one that is of Guy and I. It was taken several years ago and is probably one of the better pictures. I am normally the person taking the pictures and rarely have my picture taken. Saves on the cameras!

Sincerely,
Roberta Iiames

Guy R. Jr. Iames
150 Sesame St.
Springboro, OH

400 North Broad Street
P.O. Box 8263
Philadelphia, PA 19101

April 20, 1995

Dear Dr. Reynolds:

Belatedly, I am sending you a copy of the family history my father Samuel Harvey ("Jack") Iams, Jr., prepared for my brother, sister and myself about 10 years before his death in 1990. It is a good read, as they say in journalism, particularly on the Rouse side. The Rouses are still active in Maryland commerce. Bill Rouse, of Liberty Place fame, is one of them.

How John T. Iams fits into the Iams who moved west from Maryland is as yet unclear. I am slowly working on this through the census documents on file at the Historical Society of Pennsylvania.

I am also working on the original name, phonetically spelled once as Eyoms. I have gotten in touch with Britain's General Registry of names in Merseyside and they are sending me the necessary papers to make a further inquiry. As I think I told you, the name sounds fascinatingly similar to the name Ioms, which appears among the Cromwellian group, the Levellers.

Thanks for your material.

Yours truly,

David Iams

Dl:/ms

PS: Just looked at your note of March 3 (am I ever behind schedule!) and note it ties in with the 1900 census and the family history. Will keep in touch.

463

David Aveling Iams (born Pittsburgh 1938), society editor for *The Philadelphia Inquirer*, submitted an Iams family history that was compiled in 1980 by his father, Samuel Harvey "Jack" Imes, Jr. (1910-1990). Jack Iams was born in Baltimore November 15, 1910, and died while enroute from London to New York January 27, 1990. Jack Iams was a well-known journalist, *Newsweek* editor, and novelist who was editor of *Atlas* magazine (later called *World Press Review*), and authored thirteen books, eight of which were crime novels including: *Death Draws the Line*, *Do Not Murder Before Christmas*, *A Shot of Murder*, *What Rhymes With Murder?*, *Nowhere With Music*, *Table for Four*, and *Prematurely Gay*.

David Aveling Iams (born March 18, 1938, Pittsburgh) is listed in *Who's Who in America* as a journalist and columnist, son of Samuel Harvey Iams and Dorothy Aveling, who married July 20, 1960, to Dorothy McLaughlin, and to whom was born two children: Anthony Laughlin Iams and Sarah Aveling Iams. David Iams (b. 1938) graduated from Princeton in 1959; attended Breck School in Minneapolis, 1960-61; was a journalist for *Baltimore Sun*, 1965-67; worked for *Stars and Stripes* in Germany, 1968-70; society columnist for *Philadelphia Inquirer* since 1978; was co-author of the history of *The Princeton Tiger* "Roaring at 100*;" a member of American Press Institute, Princeton Club of New York, and the Franklin Inn.

The 1850 Federal Census of Greene County, Pennsylvania, lists head of household: Samuel Iams, age 33, born Pennsylvania; wife Nancy, 33, born Pennsylvania; daughter Mary Ann, 8, born Pennsylvania; son John, 4, born Pennsylvania, and daughter Sarah, age 4 months, born Pennsylvania. The 1880 Census of Greene County, Pennsylvania, lists head of household: John Iams, 34, born in Pennsylvania; wife Kate, age 27, born Pennsylvania; daughter Netta, age 5, born Pennsylvania; and son Hallie, age 1, born Pennsylvania. The 1900 Census of Greene County, Pennsylvania, lists the same family including head of household: Dr. J. T. (John) Iams, age 54, born Pennsylvania; wife Catherine, age 47, born Pennsylvania; daughter Neonetta, age 25, born Pennsylvania; son Samuel H., age 21, born Pennsylvania; and daughter, age 11, born Pennsylvania.

The 1910 Census of Greene County, Pennsylvania, lists: Samuel Iams, age 30, born Pennsylvania; and wife Elizabeth R., age 27, born Maryland. The 1920 Census of Waynesburg, Greene County, Pennsylvania, lists Samuel H. Iams, age 40, born Pennsylvania; wife Elizabeth, age 36, born Maryland; son Jack S., age 9, born Maryland, thus completing the link between David Iams, noted society editor of *The Philadelphia Inquirer* and his early Iams ancestors.

The family histories of "The Iamses" and "The Rouses," written by the well-known author, Samuel Harvey "Jack" Iams (1910-1990) in 1980, for his three children (including David Iams) follows:

Index

Grayson, 250, 256
Allender, Clarence Weller, 246, 250, 256
Allender, Clarence Weller, Jr., 257
Allender, Danny Lee, 257
Allender, Darlene Lorraine, 257
Allender, Earl William, 257
Allender, Edna Dale, 246, 257, 250
Allender, Evelyn Charity Lorraine, 250, 257
Allender, Jamie S., 257
Allender, Joseph Darl, 257
Allender, June Evalee, 257
Allender, Linda Lou, 257
Allender, Lois Carolyn, 257
Allender, Luanne, 257
Allender, Mary Evelyn, 257
Allender, Michael Jay, 257
Allender, Minnie, 250
Allender, Permelia, 250
Allender, Permelia Belle, 256
Allender, Permelia Belle "Minnie," 246
Allender, Ruth Dolly, 246, 250, 257
Allender, Susan Lee, 257
Allender, Virginia, 257
Allison, Charlotte Edna, 113
Allison, Jean, 113
Allison, Karl Leeborn, 113
Allison, Lucy Caroline, 113
Allison, Lucy Early, 113
Allison, Mary Ann, 113
Allison, Olive, 113
Allison, Omri Everett, 113
Allison, William James, 113
Alstaetter, Eldon J., 198
Alstaetter, Marilyn J., 198
Alstraetter, Karen J., 198
Alvin, Jane, 235
Ames, Cheryl Renee, 257
Ames, David Jay, 257
Ames, Jeffrey Lynn, 257
Amey, Christy, 190
Amey, Henry, Lt. Col., 141
Amey, Jeff, 190
Amey, Linda, xxiv, 179, 190, 202
Amey, Richard Lynn, 190
Amey, Scott, 190
Amey, Sherry, 190
Ammerson, Alice, 73

Ammons, Matilda, 14
Amos, Harry, 251
Amos, Olive, 251
Anastas, Betsy Ann, 296
Anastas, Charles Freeman, 295
Anastas, Nicholas Freeman, 296
Anastas, Sassha Maria, 296
Anders, Darcus Elizabeth, 80
Andersen, Carolyn Rae, 20
Andersen, Robert Thomas, 20
Andersen, Scott Robert, 20
Andersen, Susan Lynn, 20
Anderson, Andrew Michael, 47
Anderson, Anne, 175
Anderson, Annie, 172
Anderson, Arthur, 345
Anderson, Bell, 96
Anderson, Betsy, 94
Anderson, Brian Charles, 259
Anderson, Charles Leonard, 259
Anderson, Cynthia Lynne, 47
Anderson, Eleanor, 44
Anderson, Elizabeth, 321
Anderson, Ella, 40
Anderson, Ellen, 40
Anderson, Geneva, 110
Anderson, James, 173
Anderson, James H., 321
Anderson, Kristen Joy, 259
Anderson, Lewis, 40, 44
Anderson, Martha Elizabeth, 126
Anderson, Mildred, 173
Anderson, Mildred Amanda, 173
Anderson, Norma Jean, 173
Anderson, Olive, 321
Anderson, Phyllis Ann, 259
Anderson, Raymond Floyd, 173
Anderson, Richard, 47
Anderson, Roy H., 126
Anderson, Stella Marie, 172, 174, 175
Anderson, Thomas, 107
Anderson, William, 172, 175
Andrew, Inez, 160
Andrew, Lee, 160

Andrew, Levinia, 250
Andrews, Debra Marie, 254
Andy, Nancy Jane, 254
Andy, Patsy Anthony, III, 254
Andy, Patsy Anthony, Jr., 254
Andy, Sharon Marie, 254
Angle, David, 77
Angus, Wilda, 336
Anson, Frank, 343
Anson, Frank Howard, 343, 434
Anson, Nancy Lee, 343
Anson, Nancy Lee Otte, 434
Anson, Tressa Leigh, 343, 434
Anson, Virginia, 343
Anson, Zachary, 434
Anson, Zachary Frank, 343
Anspach, Betty H., 198
Anspach, Donald H., 198
Anspach, George, 37, 191, 198
Anspach, Harry E., 198
Anspach, James, 198
Anspach, James E., 198
Anspach, Jay R., 198
Anspach, Minnie E., 37, 191, 198
Anspach, Ralph J., 198
Anspaugh, Martha, 189
Anspaugh, Martha K., xxiv
Anspaugh, Martha Koenig, 202
Anthony, Mark, 10
Anthony, Mark, xvii
Antill, Cora M., 288
Antill, James, 288
Archibald, Anna, 294, 299
Archbiald, Anna Lucetti, 294, 298, 299
Archibald, Aurelia, 299
Archibald, Frank W., 294, 299
Archibald, Hezekiah, 299
Archibald, Hezikiah, 294
Arenas, Bonn, 337
Arenas, Eric, 337
Arenas, Laura, 337
Arenas, Waltzie, 337
Armentrout, Dimor, 218
Arms, Benjamin, 204
Armstrong, Glenna, 249
Armstrong, Laura, 18
Armstrong, Lucinda A.

Clark, 66
Arnett, Eita, 155
Arnold, Benjamin, 117
Arnold, C. E., 117
Arnold, Catharine, 186
Arnold, E. E., xiv
Arnold, Edna Catharine, 30, 186
Arnold, Edward, 117
Arnold, Elizabeth, 333
Arnold, George, 333
Arnold, Henry, 186
Arnold, Laisy, 330
Arnold, Marion, 249
Arnold, Martha, 20
Arnold, Maude, 117
Arnold, Richard, 20
Arnold, Roanna, 333
Arnold, Sarah, 11, 20
Arnold, Thelma, 117
Arnold, Wayne, 117
Arns, Henry, 257
Arrington, Albert, 99
Arrington, Marion Iiams, 99
Arrington, Steven Lee, 99
Arrington, Timothy David, 99
Arsenault, Alphee Joseph, 295
Arsenault, Cora Mae, 295
Arsenault, Dina Marie, 295
Arsenault, Jacob Daniel, 295
Arsenault, Paul Claude, 295
Arsenault, Peter Gregory, 295
Ashcraft, Karen Eleanor, 89, 215
Ashcroft, Edyth, 129
Asheroft, Edyth, 128
Ashley, Charles A., 66
Ashley, Cheryl Denise, 66
Ashley, Damion Anton, 66
Ashley, Eleanor Byrd, 66
Ashley, Frank Leo, 66
Ashley, Irving LeRoy, 66
Ashley, Parrish Aria, 66
Ashley, Patrick Arnold, 66
Ashley, Rose Tammy, 66
Athon, Ann, 95
Athon, Isaac, 95
Athon, Sarah, 95
Atkins, E. S., 102, 103
Atkins, Levi, 231
Atkins, Sarah Frances, 231
Atkinson, Amelia I., 311
Atkinson, Doris, 450

Atkinson, Guy, Mrs., 316
Atwell, Virginia, 62, 67
Atwood, Earl, 298
Atwood, Rebecca Iams, 298
Ault, Adam, 289
Ault, Alexander, 289
Ault, Anna, 285, 289
Ault, Catherine, 41,289, 318, 457
Ault, Catherine Iiams, xxvii
Ault, Charity Jane, 289
Ault, Christie Ann, 284
Ault, Christina, 289
Ault, Christine Sarah, 289
Ault, Elizabeth, 289
Ault, Isaiah, 289
Ault, John, 289
Ault, Kate, 289
Ault, Mary, 289
Ault, Mary Adaline, 289
Ault, Mary Elizabeth, 289
Ault, Mary Ellen, 191, 192
Ault, Michael, xxvii, 41, 289, 318, 457
Ault, Michael, Jr., 289
Ault, Michael, Sr., 289
Ault, Michael Alonzo, Jr., 289
Ault, Sarah, 289
Ault, Thomas, xxvii, 284, 289
Ault, Wilson Samuel, 289
Austin, H. R., 96
Autry, Denise, 49
Avau, Ann M., 321
Avau, Carolyn Suzanne, 321
Avau, John G., 321
Avau, John L., 321
Avau, Leon, 321
Avau, Michael John, 321
Avau, Susan, 321
Aveling, Dorothy, 464
Axtell, Allen Hilton, 172
Axtell, Charity, 167, 172
Axtell, Charity Iiams, 165
Axtell, Emma Jane, 172
Axtell, Gail, 172
Axtell, Homer, 172
Axtell, Jay, 172
Axtell, Mary, 172
Axtell, Mary Ella, 172
Axtell, May, 172
Axtell, Rowland B., 172
Axtell, Sarah Ann, 172
Axtell, Sarah Jane, 172
Axtell, Silas, 167, 172

Axtell, William Allen, 172
Ayers, Hannah, 137
Ayle, Della, 218
Ayle, Dimor, 218
Ayle, John Wilson, 218

— B —

Babbitt, James H., 213
Babbitt, Lucy F., 213
Babbitt, Martha A. "Mattie," 87, 213
Babbitt, Mattie, 87, 213
Babbitt, William H. H., 87, 213
Bacher, Ruth, 21, 204
Bader, Barbara, 149
Bailey, Betty Pittman, 329
Bailey, Corey Wesley, 123
Bailey, Daniel, 264
Bailey, David, 86
Bailey, Diana Lynne, 192
Bailey, Donald, 192
Bailey, Edward, 48
Bailey, Emma, 264
Bailey, Hannah, 79
Bailey, Isaac, 79
Bailey, Jesse Ethel, 86
Bailey, Joan, 36, 192
Bailey, Joseph, 292
Bailey, Juanita Marie, 48
Bailey, Lyslie, 123
Bailey, Margaret, 48
Bailey, Mariah "Marie," 79
Bailey, Ray, 36, 192
Bailey, Thomas, 192
Bailey, Tom, 329
Bailey, Tracey, 123
Bailey, Vicki, 192
Bails, Carol, 214
Bails, Ken, 214
Baines, Dolsie Iames, 309
Bains, George, 67
Bains, Virginia Lee, 67
Bair, Elizabeth, 83
Baird, Clara, 160, 204
Baker, Alma Linnese, 64
Baker, Benjamin E., 138
Baker, Cheryl Dawn, 188
Baker, Edwin, 13
Baker, Elizabeth, 137
Baker, Elizabeth D., 138
Baker, Emma Jane, 245
Baker, Eric, 188
Baker, Fannie Ijams, 138

467

Bell, Janet, 49
Bell, Kathryn Mary Bell, 89
Bell, Kathy, 88
Bell, Ken, 214
Bell, Kent R., 89
Bell, Lucy Hook, 89, 214
Bell, Lucy K., 89
Bell, Lydia, 212
Bell, Lydia Phoebe, 85
Bell, Maggie, 284
Bell, Mariah, 15
Bell, Rhudy, 49
Bell, Sarah, 89
Bell, Sarah Margaret, 88, 214
Bellar, Elaine, 197
Bellejean, Eleanor, 125
Bellenhaus, Dorothy, 269
Benbridge, Alice Warren, 161
Benbridge, Richard Wetherill, 161
Benner, Clair, 60
Benner, Claire W., 71, 75
Bennet, Nellie, 229
Bennett, Angela, 421
Bennett, Angie, 348
Bennett, Dorothy, 348, 420, 421
Bennett, Edith Marian, 68
Bennett, Gertrude May, 326
Bennett, Isaac, 284
Bennett, J. D., Mrs., 326
Bennett, James, 420, 421
Bennett, James "Jim," 348
Bennett, James Joseph, 348, 421
Bennett, Jeanette, 326
Bennett, Jennifer, 348, 421
Bennett, Jenny, 421
Bennett, K. E., M.D., 269
Bennett, Laura, 421
Bennett, Lois Marie, 74
Bennett, Lorrie Ann, 348
Bennett, Mary Louise, 326
Bennett, Merle P., 326
Bennett, Nelle, 155
Bennett, Nicole Jule, 68
Bennett, Robert, 326
Bennett, Roderick Andrew, 68
Bennett, Roderick Lovejoy, 68
Bennett-Iiams, Isaac, 284
Benridge, Alice Warren, 223
Benridge, Richard, 223

Bentrop, Clara, 28,181, 189
Berendahler, Anna Margaret, 207
Berends, Deloris, 155
Berg, Amy Lee, 185
Berg, Chad Richard, 185
Berg, Elizabeth, 285
Berg, Isaac, 285
Berkeley, Austin, 160
Berkeley, James Eli, 160
Berkeley, John Granville, 160
Berkeley, Mary Ellen, 160
Berkeley, Sarah, 160
Berkley, Austin, 222
Bernhardt, Ruth, 100
Bernheimer, Helen, 12
Berry, Cory, 218
Best, Pleasant, 272
Betts, Deborah Jane, 99
Betts, Eaton, 99
Betts, Jane Carol, 99
Betts, Marion Iams, 99
Betz, Bonna Lorene "Bonnie," 192
Betz, Bonnie, 192
Betz, Minnie D., 37, 191, 200
Beurden, Eleanor, 205
Beurden, Wilson, 205
Beverland, Shirley, 73
Beverly, Beverly Ann, 196
Beverly, Douglas Gene, 196
Beverly, Gelene Michelle, 196
Bickerly, George, 207
Bickerly, Lilly, 208
Bickerly, Mary, 207
Bickle, Etta, 110, 117
Bickley, Albert, 208
Bickley, Anna Margaret, 207
Bickley, Betty J., 84
Bickley, Charles, 208
Bickley, Daniel, 208
Bickley, David, 208
Bickley,Elizabeth Frederick, 208
Bickley, Ervin F., Jr., vii, xiv, xxxv, xxxvi, xxxvii, 22, 42, 52, 84, 91, 93, 124, 201, 207, 212, 215, 238, 278, 298, 300, 316, 452, 455
Bickley, Frederick, 208
Bickley, Frederick M., 208
Bickley, George, 207, 208

Bickley, Hannah, 208
Bickley, Henry, 208
Bickley, Henry, Jr., 207
Bickley, Henry, Sr., 207
Bickley, Henry E., 208
Bickley, Horning, 207
Bickley, Howell W., 208
Bickley, Jacob, 207
Bickley, John George, 207
Bickley, Joseph, 208
Bickley, Lloyd W., 208
Bickley, Mary, 207
Bickley, Mary W., 208
Bickley, Susannah, 207
Bickley, William, 208
Bickley, William H., 208
Bidwell, Constance C., 81
Bidwell, John, 81
Biegler, Jacob, 262
Biegler, Nancy, 262
Biel, Dana Leigh, 18
Biel, Jack Harold, 18
Biel, James Gordon, 18
Biel, Nancy Ann, 18
Biel, Tracy Elizabeth, 18
Bigelow, G. Mildred, 185
Bigger, Ambrose, 111, 114, 115
Bigger, Bertha, 111, 114
Bigger, Lloyd, 114, 115
Bigger, Maud, 114
Bigger, R. D., 115
Bigger, Raymond Daniel, 114
Bigger, Ronald, 114
Bigger, Sarah, 115
Bigger, Sarah Jane, 114, 115
Bigger, Sarah Sybilla, 114
Bigham, Fred, Mrs., xxxii
Bigham, Helen, 120
Bigham, Ina, 119, 120
Bigham, J. Fred, 119, 120
Bigham, Patricia, 120
Bigler, Abraham, 245
Bigler, Abraham Hill, 244
Bigler, Alice, 266
Bigler, Anna, 159, 244, 245
Bigler, Anne, 266
Bigler, Blaine Charles, 243
Bigler, Catherine, 245
Bigler, Catrina, 245
Bigler, Elizabeth, 245
Bigler, Elizabeth Jane, 266
Bigler, Ella M., 244
Bigler, Emma, 244, 245
Bigler, Estella, 266

Bigler, Gilmore, 159
Bigler, Hannah, 245, 262
Bigler, Israel, 245, 262
Bigler, Israel Gilmore, 266
Bigler, Jacob, 26, 83, 244, 245, 262
Bigler, Keith, 243
Bigler, Mark, 245
Bigler, Martha, 244, 245
Bigler, Mary, 26, 83, 244, 245
Bigler, Nancy, 245, 262
Bigler, Nancy "Nannia," 245
Bigler, Nannie, 244
Bigler, Ray, 244, 245
Bigler, Sarah, 245
Bigler, Sarah Grace, 243
Bigler, William S., 266
Bigley, Amy C., 287
Bigley, Catherine, 287
Bigley, Hettie M., 287
Bigley, James, 287
Bigley, Jefferson, 287
Bigley, John R., 287
Bigley, Joseph, 287
Bigley, Joseph Vance, 287
Bigley, Mary M., 287
Bigley, Wiley H., 287
Biler, Theo Mae, 74
Binder, Barbara Jean, 344
Binder, Donna Lynn, 344
Binder, Edna May, 344
Binder, Mary Kay, 344
Binder, Nicholas Harry, 344
Binder, Verna Rose, 344
Binder, Vernon Henry, 344
Bingham, Cindy, 123, 124
Binkley, Ervin F., Jr., 163
Binkley, Valerie Iiams, 200
Bircher, Alice, 329
Bircher, Emma Jean, 329
Bircher, Emogene, 329
Bircher, Emogine, 395
Bircher, Lloyd, 324, 329
Bircher, Milburn, 329
Bircher, Patsy, 395
Bircher, Patsy Belle, 329
Bircher, Shirley, 395
Bircher, Shirley Ann, 329
Bircher, Wilma Iona, 329
Bircher, Wilma, xxiii, 324
Bird, Betty Pittman, 329
Bischanon, Mary, 168
Bischoff, Laura Lynn, 346, 347

Bischoff, Marshall, M.D., 346
Bischoff, Noyce, 346
Bischoff, Stephanie Cheryl, 346
Bise, Bernard Lloyd, 36, 192, 196
Bise, Beverly Ann, 196
Bise, Burley, 196
Bise, Carol Ann, 196
Bise, David Michael, 196
Bise, Lois Ann, 36, 192, 196
Bise, Matthew Edward, 196
Bise, Nellie Pearl, 196
Bise, Rachel Ann, 196
Bishop, Judith Mildred, 259
Bishop, Laura, 110
Bishop, Laura H., 113
Bishop, Matthew, 259
Bishop, Wallace, 259
Bitner, Margaret Ann, 38, 182
Black Prince, xix
Black, Caroline, 46
Black, Frances Pearl Barnes, 154
Black, Michael, 154
Black, Peter, 108
Blacka, Lois Carolyn, 257
Blackburn, Charlene "Deenie," 100
Blackburn, Deenie, 100
Blackburn, Gladys, xxx
Blackburn, Thomas, 41
Blackledge, Elizabeth, 150
Blackwell, Barbara Jo, 185, 188
Blackwell, Beatrice Earl, 195
Blackwell, Beverly Broddus, 195
Blackwell, Debra Leone, 195
Blackwell, Glen Preston, 195
Blackwell, Jo, 185, 188
Blackwell, John Wesley, 185, 188
Blackwell, John William, 185
Blackwell, Melanie Josephine, 188
Blackwell, Mellie Josephine "Jo," 185
Blackwell, Michael Glen, 195

Blackwell, Olive Eugenia, 185
Blackwell, Rachel Michelle, 195
Blaine, Amanda, 341
Blaine, Elizabeth, 231
Blaine, John David, 341
Blaine, Kathleen "Kathy" Anne, 340
Blaine, Kathy McKelvey, 413
Blair, Betty Joe, 17
Blair, Charles B., 17
Blair, Dwight, 17
Blair, James A., 254
Blair, Ruth Ann, 17
Blair, Tracy Ann, 254
Blake, Alice, 253
Blake, Alma Louise, 253
Blake, Betty Jean, 253
Blake, Debra Gee, 253
Blake, Diane M., 298
Blake, Edward, 252, 253
Blake, Edward Ferrell, 253
Blake, Elizabeth Adams "Liz," 298
Blake, Ellen Nerine, 253
Blake, Ellis Cracroft, 253
Blake, Ellis Edward, 253
Blake, Elsie Doane, 252, 253
Blake, Ethel, 253
Blake, Helen "Lois," 298
Blake, John Robert, 253
Blake, Lois, 298
Blake, Lois Iams, vii, xi, xii, xiv, xxxvi, 287, 298, 300
Blake, Lorie Elizabeth, 253
Blake, Martha Mae, 253
Blake, Mary Ellen, 253
Blake, Mary Geneva, 253
Blake, Mildred Elsie, 253
Blake, Norma Jean, 253
Blake, Patricia, 253
Blake, Rebecca Iams, 298
Blake, Robert, xxxiii
Blake, Robert C., 298
Blake, Robert C., II, 298
Blake, Robert C. "Robbie," III, 298
Blake, Robert Lee, 253
Blake, Susan Gee, 253
Blake, Vina Virginia, 253
Blake-Huelbert, Carol Lorraine, 262
Dlakclcy, Adam, 186

471

Bradbury, Nancy, 152
Braddock, Agnes, 170
Braddock, Bryon Milton, 170
Braddock, Byron Milton, 167
Braddock, Charity Adeline, 170
Braddock, Charles G., 170
Braddock, Charlotte Adeline "Ida," 167
Braddock, David, 170
Braddock, Elmer Byron, 170
Braddock, Eva L., 172
Braddock, Francis, 172
Braddock, Francis Harold, 170
Braddock, Gail, 171
Braddock, Georgia A., 170
Braddock, Harry I., 213
Braddock, Harry Iams, 171
Braddock, Ida, 167
Braddock, Mable M., 170
Braddock, Maria J., 172
Braddock, Mary V., 170
Braddock, Mildred Marie, 170
Braddock, Nancy, 170
Braddock, Nancy G., 170
Braddock, Paul (Carl) Milton, 171
Braddock, Robert McNay, 170
Braddock, Ruth Elizabeth, 171, 213
Braddock, Samuel Earl, 170
Braden, Anna Iams, 169
Braden, Charles O., 169
Braden, Emma Jane, 169
Braden, Harold Phillips, 169
Braden, Harold Whitney, 169
Braden, Lucy Miller, 169
Braden, Miriam Emily, 169
Braden, Nellie, 169
Braden, Ruth Covey, 169
Bradley, Ambrose, 267
Bradley, David, 305, 316, 449, 450
Bradley, David, Rev., 451
Bradley, Eleanor, xl
Bradley, Harriette, 451
Bradley, Iris M., 267
Bradley, Nell, 322
Brady, Deanna Joyce, 296
Drady, Gcrald Lcon, 296

Brady, Josephine, 325
Brady, Karen Sue, 255
Brady, Rita Jane, 296
Brandon, C., 120
Branham, Brandy, 63, 65
Branham, Crystal, 63, 65
Branham, Francine Benita, 65
Branham, John, 65
Branham, John C., Jr., 65
Branham, John C., Sr., 65
Branham, John Chauncey, 63
Branham, Johnnie, 63
Branham, Michelle, 63, 65
Branham, Natacha Jeanne, 63, 65
Branham, Thelma, 63, 65
Brannon, Eva, 200
Brant, Donald R., 73
Brant, Nancy, 73
Brant, Stella Mae, 73
Branten, Shirley Ann, 217
Branton, John, 218
Branton, Shirley, 25
Branton, Shirley Ann, 218
Braseur, Benjamin, 8
Braseur, Marie, 8
Brasseur, Susannah, 8
Braxton, Alice, 62, 67
Braxton, Alison Lynette, 62, 67
Braxton, Allison L., 67
Braxton, Ann E., 62
Braxton, Ann Elizabeth, 67
Braxton, Barraud, 67
Braxton, Barraud Imes, 63, 67
Braxton, Brian Eric, 63, 67
Braxton, Cheryl, 63, 67
Braxton, Constance, 67
Braxton, Cynthia T., 67
Braxton, Cynthia Theresa, 62, 67
Braxton, Daron Renee, 67
Braxton, Dawn Renee, 63
Braxton, Dollie Marie, 62, 67
Braxton, Elyse Marie, 62, 67
Braxton, Eva Allison, 60, 62, 67
Braxton, Evan Christopher, 62, 67
Braxton, Floyd M., 62, 67
Braxton, Floyd Matthew, 67

Braxton, Floyd Matthew, II, 62
Braxton, Floyd Montgomery, 67
Braxton, George L., 62
Braxton, George Lake, 67
Braxton, Harriet E., 62
Braxton, Harriet Evernia, 67
Braxton, Inza, 67
Braxton, Inza Margaret, 62, 63, 67
Braxton, James E., 60, 62, 67
Braxton, James Edward, 67
Braxton, Jeffrey Broderick, 63
Braxton, Jeffrey Roderick, 67
Braxton, Joan Ruth, 63, 67
Braxton, Joyce, 67
Braxton, Joyce Eileen, 63, 67
Braxton, Juannona Inza, 67
Braxton, Juanona, 67
Braxton, Juanona Inza, 63
Braxton, Kendea Michelle, 63
Braxton, Kendra Michelle, 67
Braxton, Mary M., 62
Braxton, Mary Moore, 67
Braxton, Richard B., Jr., 67
Braxton, Richard Benjamin, 62, 63, 67
Braxton, Richard Benjamin, Sr., 67
Braxton, Stanley, xxiv
Braxton, Stanley Gene, 62, 67, 91
Braxton, Stanley Hughes, 62, 67
Braxton, Virginia, xxiv, 62, 67, 355
Braxton, Virginia Atwell, 91
Braxton, Whitney I., 67
Braxton, Whitney Imes, 62
Bray, Ann, 97
Bray, Patricia, 97
Bray, Wayne, 97
Breau, Dina Marie, 295
Breece, Martha, 159
Breece, William, Jr., 159
Breece, William, Sr., 159
Breese, Effie Mary, 259
Brennan, Lucille, 297
Brenner, Cynthia Allyn, 343

473

Casey, David, 96
Casher, Joseph, 74
Casher, Ruth Mary, 74
Cass, Elizabeth, 8
Castator, Floyd Monroe, 126
Castator, Floyd Wilson, M.D., 126
Castator, Mary Elizabeth, 126
Castator, Mary Emma, 126
Castle, Barney, 97
Castle, Betty B., 97
Castor, Anna, 15
Caughly, Sarah, 285
Caulkins, Ruby Mae, 81
Cawley, Ann, 348
Cecil, Alexander Russell, 144
Cecil, Alice R., 145
Cecil, Andrew J., 144
Cecil, Benjamin, 145, 147
Cecil, Charity, 144
Cecil, Charles Westley, 145
Cecil, Chrissie Jane, 145
Cecil, Cornelia, 145
Cecil, Crissie Jane, 145
Cecil, Cynthia, 144
Cecil, Daniel, 144
Cecil, Daniel Jerred, 146
Cecil, David Craig, 144
Cecil, David King, 145
Cecil, Delphine, 144
Cecil, Elizabeth, 27, 144, 145, 147
Cecil, Elizabeth C., 145
Cecil, Elizabeth "Eliza," 145
Cecil, Elizabeth J., 144
Cecil, Elizabeth Jane, 145
Cecil, Ellen Rose, 145
Cecil, George, 145
Cecil, George W., 144
Cecil, Henrietta, 27, 144, 145
Cecil, Henry Clay, 144
Cecil, Isaac A., 145
Cecil, Isabel, 143, 144
Cecil, James C., 144
Cecil, James Lee, 145
Cecil, Jane, 144
Cecil, John, 27, 144
Cecil, John B., 21, 22, 458
Cecil, John Ball, 143
Cecil, John F., 145
Cecil, John Wesley, 144
Cecil, Josephine, 144
Cecil, Julia, 144, 145

Cecil, Julia I., 144
Cecil, Julia R., 145
Cecil, Louise, 144
Cecil, Lucy, 146
Cecil, Mary, 458
Cecil, Mary E., 144
Cecil, Mary H., 145
Cecil, Mary Lou, 145
Cecil, Nancy, 21, 22, 27, 143, 145
Cecil, Nancy J., 145
Cecil, Nancy M., 144
Cecil, Osie, 147
Cecil, Ossee, 145, 147
Cecil, Pauline, 145
Cecil, Philip, 144
Cecil, Phillip, 145
Cecil, Phoebe, 144
Cecil, Rachel, 144
Cecil, Rebecca, 145
Cecil, Richard, 144
Cecil, Richard F., 144
Cecil, Richard Franklin, 145
Cecil, Richard Iiams, 145
Cecil, Samuel, 27, 144, 145
Cecil, Samuel Lafayette, 145
Cecil, Sarah E., 145
Cecil, Selonie, 145
Cecil, Susan E. T., 145
Cecil, Suvilla Magdelena, 145
Cecil, Thomas, 143, 145
Cecil, Thomas S., 145
Cecil, West, 145
Cecil, William B., 143, 144
Cecil, William Samuel, 145
Cecil, Wilson, 146
Cerney, Ernest F., 227
Cerney, Gladys Genevieve, 227
Cerney, James Iams, M.D., xxiii
Cesky, Helen Margaret, 90, 214
Cesky, James, 90, 214
Chalfin, Joseph, 218
Chalfin, Lavern, 218
Chalfont, Emma, 231
Chamberlain, Carolyn Lee, 176
Chamberlain, James Thomas, 176
Chamberlain, John, xxx
Chamberlain, Kathryn Elizabeth, 176
Chamberlain, Margaret

Emily, 176
Chamberlain, Oliver, 176
Chambers, Mary Catherine, 102, 103
Chambers, Sam T., 102, 103
Chapin, Augie Inez, 97
Chapin, Stacy, 97
Chaplin, Cynthia Ann, 208
Chaplin, James K., 208
Chapman, Janice Irene, 48
Chapman, Mary, 172
Chapman, Stefen Rhys, 48
Chappel, Mary, 111
Chappell, Ann Elizabeth, 115
Chappell, Mary, 108, 112, 115
Charlton, Catherine, 312
Charlton, Richard, Rev., 312
Charter, Charles A., 336, 379
Charter, Ida Iams, 326, 393
Charter, Ida May, 336
Charter, Ida May Iams, 379, 380, 381
Chase, Myrl, 128
Cheney, Anne, 148
Cheney, David, 358
Cheney, Elizabeth, xxxiii, 358
Cheney, Isiah, xvi
Cheney, Lewis, 4
Cheney, Mary, 4
Cheney, Richard, 4
Cheney, Richard R., 358
Cherney, Charles Iams, M.D., 221, 225, 227, 238
Cherry, Emma, 343
Cherry, Julia, 343
Cherry, Mary, 305
Cherry, Mary Lou, 88, 215
Cherry, Michael, 343
Cheslick, Edward A., Sr., 175
Cheslick, Edward Anthony, Jr., 175
Cheslick, Geraldine, 175
Cheslick, Geraldine E. I., xxiv
Cheslick, Geraldine Elizabeth, 175
Cheslick, Geraldine Elizabeth Iams, 175, 201
Cheslick, India, 175
Cheslick, Judy, 175

480

481

Dillon, Bill, 348
Dillon, Dorothy "Dot," 348
Dillon, Dot, 348
Dillon, Hazel, 348
Dillon, Minnie, 348
Dillon, William "Bill," 348
Dinger, Beverly, 130
Dinsman, Harry, 191
Dinsman, John, 198
Dinsman, Minnie E., 191, 198
Dinsman, Sarah, 198
Dinsmore, Margaret, 16, 151
Dinsmore, Nantie, 151
Dinsmore, Thomas, 151
Dirvin, Robert I., 316
Disman, Harry, 198
Dissen, Joannae Fridericae, 166, 247
Ditto, Abraham, xvi, xxxvii, 453
Ditto, Maud, 114
Dival, Wilma Jean, 309
Dixon, Bessie, 128, 129
Dixon, Bonnie, 444
Dixon, Bonnie Lou, 49
Dixon, Christena Mae, 49
Dixon, Cynthia Jane, 49
Dixon, Erin Rachel, 49
Dixon, Jeff, 444
Dixon, Jeffrey Alan, 49
Dixon, Jennifer, 444
Dixon, Jennifer Marie, 49
Dixon, Marjorie, vii, xiv
Dixon, Marjorie Inez, 49
Dixon, Marjorie Inez Mautz, 53
Dixon, Marjorie Mautz, 443, 444
Dixon, Mike, 49
Dixon, Ray, 444
Dixon, Raymond Earl, 49
Dixon, Raymond Michael "Mike," 49
Dixon, Roy Albert, 49
Dixon, Stephanie Ann, 49
Dixon, Susan Ruth, 49
Doan, Alma Faye, 325
Dobich, Cinthia Ana, 275
Dobich, George Thomas, 275
Dobich, Mary Iams, xxiii
Dobich, Mary Kathryn, 275
Dobich, Sean Robert, 275
Dodd, Connie, 218

Dodd, Emma, 159
Dodds, Michele Annette, 343
Dodds, Nellie, 218
Dodds, Venon, 218
Dodds, William, 343
Dodson, Mary Rose, 18
Doffs, Nevada, 147
Dohme, Clarence E., 36, 191, 197
Dohme, Elizabeth, 191, 197
Dohme, Evelyn Ruth, 191
Dohme, Frederick, 191,197
Dohme, Irene Adell, 197
Dohme, Olive Ruth, 36, 191
Dolby, Nettie, 71
Dolluge, David, 149
Dolluge, Desiree Lynn, 149
Dolon, Frances, 232
Dolph, Edna, 218
Dolph, Howard, 218
Domazor, Lyn, 175
Donahoo, Clarence Gibson, 246, 250
Donahoo, Daniel Gordon, 86
Donahoo, Katie Mae "May," 250
Donahoo, Katy Mae "Mary," 246
Donahoo, May, 250
Donahoo, Nancy Eli, 86
Donahoo, Nancy Elizabeth, 86
Donahoo, Sarah Ellen, 86
Donald, Agnes H., 15
Donaldson, Mary, 4
Donaldson, Mary A., 28
Donaldson, Thomas, 56
Donnachy, John, xvi, xxxvii, 56, 453
Donnan, Alvan, 230
Donnan, Grace Forrester, 230
Donnan, Lucy Alexander, 230
Donneher, Hannah May, 243
Donneher, Thomas "JT," 243
Donnehoo, Lloyd, 243
Donowho, Claude Augustus, 262
Donowho, Gus, 262
Donowho, Phyllis Ann, 262
Donowho, Sarah Christine, 262

Donphfin, George W., 388
Donstone, Jeff Eichvold, 276
Donstone, Owenna Lea, 276
Dooley, Heather Janelle, 49
Dooley, Johnny Lee, 49
Dooley, Pamela Arlene, 49
Dooley, Rachel Caryn, 49
Dooling, Michell, 35
Dooling, Terrence John, 35
Dooling, Vera Elizabeth, 35
Dorff, Jacquiline Marie, 337
Dorsey, Benedict, 94
Dorsey, C. E., 231
Dorsey, Charlotte, 230, 231
Dorsey, Col., 283
Dorsey, Edwin, 231
Dorsey, Elbert Charles, 231
Dorsey, Elmer, 231
Dorsey, Elmer Charles, 231
Dorsey, Emma, 231
Dorsey, Eva Rebecca, 232
Dorsey, James, Dr., 231
Dorsey, James, M.D., 231
Dorsey, James Francis, 230
Dorsey, Jesse, 231
Dorsey, Larken Edward, 231
Dorsey, Lucy, 156
Dorsey, Lucy Virginia, 230, 231, 232
Dorsey, Margaret, 94
Dorsey, Mary Elizabeth, 232
Dorsey, Mary Marfield, 94
Dorsey, Sarah Frances, 231
Dorsey, Thomas, xxix, 94
Dorsey, Thomas, Col., 281
Dorsey-Forest, Larkin Edward, 232
Dotson, Marjorie, 182
Doty, Ariel, 155
Doty, Marie Piatt, 267, 268
Douglas, Clara, 152
Douglas, Helen, 130
Douglass, Sarah, 211
Dowden, Alice, 172
Drake, Francis, Sr., 328
Drake, William, Sr., 328
Dran, Amy Jo, 275
Dran, Andrew, 275
Dran, Charity Sue, 275
Dran, Doris Jean, 275
Dran, George Stephen, Rev., 275
Dran, Jack Andrew, 275
Dran, James Andrew, 275
Dran, Jeffrey Jack, 275

Duvall, Mareen, 5, 7, 8
Duvall, Margaret Eichelberger, 139
Duvall, Mark B., 16
Duvall, Mary Elvira, 138
Duvall, Mary Rita, 16
Duvall, Maureen, 134
Duvall, Melvin Richard, 16, 17
Duvall, Nannie, 139
Duvall, Newell, 138
Duvall, Oliver, 138
Duvall, Oliver Everett, 139
Duvall, Orville Russell, 16
Duvall, Rebecca, 138, 313
Duvall, Rebecca Ijams, xxviii
Duvall, Rita, 16
Duvall, Ruth, 138, 139
Duvall, Sammye, 17
Duvall, Samuel, xl, 1, 5, 7, 8
Duvall, Samuel Grafton, 138
Duvall, Samuel John, 16
Duvall, Sarah, 7, 106, 109, 117, 124, 138
Duvall, Sarah Rebecca, 139
Duvall, Susan, 16
Duvall, Susanna, 6, 7
Duvall, Susannah, 6, 7, 8
Duvall, Tanya Jeannette, 17
Duvall, Thomas, 130, 131, 134
Duvall, Wilbur H., 139
Duvall, William, 134, 138
Dwight, Annie Metcalfe, 312
Dye, Olive, 407
Dyson, Catherine Ann, 257
Dyson, Ronald, 257
Dzurian, Eleanor Vivian, 17

— E —

Eagel, Irene Nelly, 176
Earl of Murray, xx, 2
Earls, Marnee, 337
Earnest, Frank, 271
Earnest, Mary Elizabeth, 271
Earp, Myrtle, 290
Easter, Mary, 305, 306
Eaton, Joseph, 96
Eby, John, M.D., 15
Eby, Lucy Crayne, 15
Eby, Mary, 15

Eck, Edwrd, 248
Eck, Elma Zela, 248
Eck, Ida, 248
Eckard, John, 331
Eckard, Sarah, 331
Eckard, Stella, 331, 449
Eckels, Eleanor Corinne, 257
Eckels, Ralph, 257
Eckenrod, Leo, 267
Eckenrod, Romaine, 267
Edena, Mary, 123, 122
Edgar, Carol Ann, 260
Edgar, Clarence, 250, 260, 261
Edgar, D. A., 250
Edgar, Daniel, 261
Edgar, David Robert, 260
Edgar, Herman, 250, 260, 261
Edgar, Ida Ruth, 246, 250, 251, 364
Edgar, Isaac Herman, 260
Edgar, J. M., 250
Edgar, John, 246, 250, 260, 261
Edgar, John Melvin, 256, 257
Edgar, Margaret E., 261
Edgar, Mary, 260, 261
Edgar, Mary A., 246, 250
Edgar, Mary Kathleen, 260
Edgar, May Kay, 261
Edgar, Minnie, 260
Edgar, Permelia Belle, 256
Edgar, Permilia Bell, 257
Edgar, Robert Iams, 260
Edgar, Ruth Laurella, 260
Edgar, Sadie, 260
Edgar, Sarah "Sadie" Edna, 260
Edgar, W. K., 250
Edgar, W. R., 260
Edgecomb, Joan L., 292
Edgecomb, Robert, 292
Edgerly, Frances J., 39, 179
Edgerly, Mary Jane, 39, 179
Edmund Plantagenet, Sir, xix
Edson, Mary Elizabeth, 289
Edward III, King of England, xix
Edwards, Margaret, 101
Edwards, Margaret Ijams, xxix
Edwards, Peggy Ijams, 101

Edwards, Sarah, 159
Egbert, Howard, 234
Egbert, Howard, Jr., 234
Egbert, Nancy Lee, 234
Egbert, Susan, 234
Eggy, A. J., 286
Eggy, Catherine, 286
Eggy, David, 286
Eggy, Jacob, 268, 286, 318, 457
Eggy, Jane, 286
Eggy, Mary, 286
Eggy, Mary "Polly," 286
Eggy, Polly, 286, 318, 457
Eggy, Sarah, 26, 82
Eggy, Sarah Ann, 243, 268, 286
Eggy, Sarah Anne, 268
Eggye, Sarah Anne, 268
Ehler, Clara Alice, 166, 248
Ehler, Henry Franklin, 166, 248
Ehler, Sarah Catharine, 166, 248
Ehrler, Patricia Jean, 343
Ehrler, William "Bill," Dr., 343
Ehrler, William, Ph.D., 343
Eichelberger, Ann, 139
Eichman, Cheri Lynn, 199
Eichner, Amy Lee, 32, 185
Eichner, Ashley Noel, 32, 185
Eichner, Barbara Ann, 32, 185
Eichner, Holly Ann, 185
Eichner, James K. Kent, 32
Eichner, James Kent, 185
Eichner, John Daniel, 185
Eichner, Whitney Rae, 32, 185
Eirrons, Elizabeth, x
Eirrons, William, x
Eisen, Anna, 47
Eisley, Monica, 82
Ekey, William, 41
Elder, Gertie, 250
Elder, Gertie Mae, 251
Elder, Henry, 96
Elder, J. Arley, 251
Eliot, Bastian, xxxix
Eliot, Charity, 286
Eliot, Charity J., xxxix
Eliot, John Alonzo, xxxix
Eliot, John Alonzo, Rev., 286

487

Force, Ridgley C., 114
Forcum, Cecil Loy, 29
Forcum, Cora Ellen, 28
Forcum, Edith May, 28
Forcum, Eva Leona, 29
Forcum, Margaret Eliza, 29
Forcum, Martha Cleo, 28
Forcum, Phyllis Ann, 29
Forcum, Wilbur Malcolm, 28
Forcum, William Henry, 28
Forcum, William Richard, 29
Ford, Harriet E., 33
Ford, Justin, 123
Ford, Kristin, 123
Ford, Raymond, 123
Foreman, Edna, 71
Foreman, Louisa, 287
Forest, Beulah, 232
Forest, Bonnie Joan, 232
Forest, Carl, 232
Forest, Carol Denise, 232
Forest, Charles Elbert, 231
Forest, Charles Elbert D., 232
Forest, Charles LeRoy, 232
Forest, Donald Eugene, 232
Forest, Doris Marie, 232
Forest, Edwin, 231
Forest, Elbert Charles, 231
Forest, Elizabeth, 7
Forest, Elva Velva, 232
Forest, Emma, 232
Forest, Eva Velva, 232
Forest, Frances, 232
Forest, Harold, 232
Forest, Lucy, 7
Forest, Mae Etheridge, 232
Forest, Mark Emery, 232
Forest, Melvin, 232
Forest, Michael Melvin, 232
Forest, Nathan, Gen., 80
Forest, Nellie Murl, 232
Forest, Oloff James, 232
Forest, Patricia Ann, 232
Forest, Patricia Lynn, 232
Forest, Reba, 232
Forest, Robert T., xxiv, 239
Forest, Robert Theodore, 232
Forest, Theresa Rose, 232
Forest, Vivian LaVerne, 232
Forest, Wiley, 232
Forest, William, 7
Forest-Johnson, Beulah, 231

Forinash, Bruce Alan, 256
Forinash, Carol Jean, 256
Forinash, Robert Alan, 256
Forner, Lucinda, 27
Forney, Mary Alice, 258
Forney, William Forney, 258
Forrest, Charles, 66
Forrest, Charles Stanley, 66
Forrest, Eleanor Byrd, 66
Forrest, Harry Virgil, 66
Forrest, Linda, 66
Forrest, Stephanie, 66
Forrester, Rose, 269
Forshee, Ann, 178
Forshee, Tom, 178
Foseman, Ronald Steven, 254
Foster, Anna, 293
Foster, Queen Victoria, 147
Foster, Roseanna "Anna," 293
Foster, Sam, 147
Fours, Sophia, 190
Fouts, Patty June, 297
Fouts, Salome, 223, 234
Fowler, Ann, 6
Fowler, Barbara, 52
Fowler, Benjamin, 6
Fowler, Benoni, 6
Fowler, Elizabeth, 6
Fowler, Evaline, 44
Fowler, Frank, 28
Fowler, Harry O., 29
Fowler, Hester, 456
Fowler, Howard M., 29
Fowler, Ida Leila, 29
Fowler, James, 29
Fowler, Jeremiah, 6
Fowler, John, 6
Fowler, Mary, 6
Fowler, Richard, 6
Fowler, S. Emma, 28
Fowler, Samuel, 6
Fowler, Susan, 6, 29
Fowler, Susanna, 6
Fowler, Susannah, 1, 6
Fowler, Thomas, 1, 6, 456
Fowler, William, 6
Foxworthy, Alice, 33
Foxworthy, Jefferson Harper, 33
Frampton, Kenneth Donald, 270
Frampton, Lynlee, 270
Francis, Michael David, 259
Francis, Michell, 34

Francis, Ruth Ann, 259
Francis, Scott Allan, 259
Frank, Catharine, 28
Frank, Grace Virginia, 61, 68
Franklin, Kay Danforth, 217
Franklin, Rachel, 20
Frantz, Emma, 264
Frash, Mary Ann, 294
Frayer-Iiams, Lauren Avery, 186
Frayer-Iiams, Lisa Carol Della, 186
Frayer-Iiams, Nicholas James, 186
Frayer-Iiams, Patrick Joseph "PJ," 186
Frayer-Iiams, Patrick Michael, 186
Frazer, Eva, 319
Frazer, Tom, 319
Frazier, Barbara, 19
Frazier, Helen Mae, 19
Frazier, John Douglas, 19
Frazier, John Harry, 19
Frazier, Robert Lee, 19
Frederickson, Carol, 129
Freed, R. H., Mrs., 336
Freeman, Caroline A., 265
Freer, Mary, 286
Freer, Mary Iams, 318
Freeze, Becky Lee, 256
Freeze, Gerald R., 256
French, Deborah, 143, 157
French, Delilah, 205
Freshour, Amy, 291
Freshour, David Paul, 291
Freshour, Donald William, 290
Freshour, Judy, 291
Freshour, Paul, 291
Freshour, William F., 290
Frey, Jacqueline, 34
Friel, Anita Louise, 48
Friel, Brian Matthew, 48
Friel, Kenneth Francis, 48
Friel, Kimberly Lynn, 48
Frier, Mary, 26
Frier, Romeo, 26
Friesinger, Elsie, 47
Fritz, Elaine, 197
Fritz, Hilda, 121
Fritz, Joseph, 197
Fritz, Robin, 196, 197
Fritz, Steve, 197
Frock, Edna Mae, 200
Frock, Edna R., 37

Frommes, Harvey, 237
Frost, Carol Ann, 36, 193
Frost, Newton, 96
Fruek, Sheila Ann, 198
Frushour, Elizabeth, 39, 179
Fry, Grace Mae, 227
Frye, Autume Lea, 253
Frye, Catherine, 77
Frye, Hollie Ann, 253
Frye, John Day, 253
Frye, Karen Lea, 253
Frye, Mary, 293
Frye, Randall Dallas, 253
Frye, Ray, 293
Frye, William, 77
Frysinger, Irene Wirick, 183
Frysinger, Marjorie, 38
Fullerton, Edna Marie, 219
Fulton, Albert, 270
Fulton, Amy Elizabeth, 258
Fulton, Anna Eliza, 246
Fulton, Annie Eliza, 258
Fulton, Clara, 258
Fulton, Clara Louise, 247
Fulton, Cynthia Anabel, 271
Fulton, Edith, 270
Fulton, Eliza, 323, 324, 325
Fulton, Elizabeth, 324
Fulton, Flora, 270
Fulton, George, 325
Fulton, Henry, 271
Fulton, Isabella, 324, 325
Fulton, Isabella McClarean, 325
Fulton, James D., 247
Fulton, James Dorsey, 258
Fulton, James Orville, 258
Fulton, Mary Elizabeth, 271
Fulton, Olive Mae, 247
Fulton, Olive May, 258
Fulton, Queen E., 247
Fulton, Queen Elizabeth, 258
Fulton, Rose Anna, 258
Fulton, Rose, F., 247
Fulton, Stephen, 270
Fulton, William, 247, 258
Fultz, Malinda, 60, 71
Funk, Florence May, 171
Furlong, Debra Ann, 262
Fye, Edith, 72

— G—

Gadack, Charles Stanley, 34
Gadack, Mike James, 35

Gaede, Carolyn Sue, 194
Gaghagan, Ella, 265
Gaither, Basil, 94, 95, 101
Gaither, Benjamin, 78, 79
Gaither, Brice, 95
Gaither, Elizabeth, 1, 5, 7, 55, 95, 148, 304, 456
Gaither, Isham, 96
Gaither, Jane, 78
Gaither, John, 55, 78
Gaither, Lilah, xxix, 94
Gaither, Lilah Martha, 101
Gaither, Margaret, 94, 95
Gaither, Margaret Watkins, 101
Gaither, Nathan, 94
Gaither, Sarah, 78, 79
Galbraith, Adam, 193
Galbraith, Barbara Lou, 193
Galbraith, Catherine Virginia, 193
Galbraith, Harold, 193
Galbraith, Michael Douglas, 193
Gales, Esther, 293
Gales, Ethel, 293
Gallaspy, Eliza Unity, 122
Gallaspy, Elizabeth Ann, 122, 123
Gallaspy, Elizabeth Unity, 122, 123
Gallaspy, William J., 122, 123
Galloway, John, 11
Galloway, S., 80
Gant, Angela "Angie" Dawn, 329
Gant, Caroline, 267
Gant, Rachel Elaine, 329
Gant, Rebecca Nicole, 329
Gant, Ricky Lee, 329
Gantz, Caroline, 244, 267
Gantz, John, 370
Garber, Cynthia, 26, 243, 272, 274
Garber, Cynthia "Sinthy," 270
Garber, Demas, 272
Garber, Elizabeth, 243, 270, 272
Garber, Isabel , 272
Garber, Jacob, 272
Garber, Jonathan, 243, 272
Garber, Margaret, 272

Garber, Pleasant, 272
Garber, Reuben, 272
Garber, Sarah, 272
Garber, Silas C., 272
Garber, Simon, 272
Garber, William, 270, 272
Garber, William Christian, 243
Garcia, Dee, 189
Garcia, Delores "Dee," 189
Garcia, John, 189
Gardner, Ann, 135
Gardner, Caroline, 219
Gardner, Charity, 212, 219, 448
Gardner, Daniel, 370
Gardner, Harvey, 212, 416, 448
Gardner, Harvey Henry, 219
Gardner, Henry, 212
Gardner, Jane "Jennie," 219
Gardner, Jennie, 219
Gardner, Mary "Mollie," 219
Gardner, Mollie, 219
Gardner, Thomas, 219
Gardner, Virginia, 219
Garlow, Vera, 35
Garner, Georgia, 213
Garner, Herman, 88, 213
Garner, Katherine (Wolf), 321
Garner, Margaret, 86
Garner, Stanely F., 150
Garrett, Bertha, 271
Garrett, David John, 296
Garrett, David Lowell, 296
Garrett, Dortha Sean, 297
Garrett, Ina, 271
Garrett, Joseph Lowell, 296
Garrett, L. Guy, 271
Garrett, Lebius G., 26
Garrett, Lebrius G., 271
Garrett, Lee Elwood, 297
Garrett, Lynda Kay, 297
Garrett, Margaret Pleasane, 26
Garrett, Margaret Pleasant, 271
Garrett, Marianna, 296
Garrett, Martha, 271
Garrett, Martha Catherine, 296
Garrett, Mary Ann, 246, 249
Garrett, Tillie, 271
Garver, Cynthia, 83

Gassaway, Donna, 175
Gassoway, Providence, 108, 111
Gaston, John, 397
Gates, Brandon Scott, 255
Gates, Elizabeth, 11
Gates, Linda Gaye, 255
Gates, Scott D., 255
Gaughan, Kittie, 335
Gault, Alan, 81
Gault, Constance C., 81
Gayheart, Aron James, 297
Geatz, Karen S., 309
Gehret, Catharine, 186
Geis, Cochetta, 166, 201
Geis, Conchetta, xxiii, 247, 248
Geis, Conchetta Delight, 249
Geis, Conchetta Stephen, 403
Geis, Conchetta, xxiii, 247, 248
Geis, Martin P., 249
Geis, Martin W., 249
Geis, Suzanne Elaine, 249
Geis, Teresa Emily, 249
Gerard, Mary Laurena, 320
Gerard, Peter, 320
Gerlach, Constance C., 81
Gerlach, Glendon, 81
Gerry, Owenna Lea, 276
Gerry, Robert, 276
Gialy, Patricia Lynn, 232
Gibbs, Thomas, 105
Gibson, Harold, 185, 188
Gibson, Jo, 185, 188
Gibson, Lydia, 266
Gibson, Mellie Josephine "Jo," 185
Gibson, Mellie Melanie Josephine "Jo," 188
Gibson, Nancy Carole, 185, 188
Gibson, Reba, 232
Gibson, Sandra Dean, 188
Gibson, Sandra Jean, 185
Gigliotti, Virginia, 257
Gilbary, Genevive, 348
Gilbary, Martin, 348
Gilber, Martha, 190
Gilbert, Nettie, 214
Giles, Elizabeth, 20
Giles, John, 20
Gill, Mary, 272
Gilliam, Betty Jean, 68
Gillian, Fern L., 189

Gillian, John, 189
Gilliard, Fern L., 189
Gilliard, John, 189
Gilmore, Eva, 187
Gilmore, Glenn E., 156
Gilmore, John Robert, 156
Gilmore, Luvinia, 156
Gilmore, Nellie B., 156
Gilmore, Robert John, 156
Gilmore, Stephen W., 187
Gilmore, Wilbert Ross, 156
Ginanni, Carol, 324
Ginanni, Carol Ann, 331
Ginanni, Eric Joseph, 331
Ginanni, Eric Joseph, II, 331
Ginanni, Jean Ball, 331
Ginanni, Joseph, 331
Ginanni, Lori Ann, 331
Gipson, Charles Ray, Rev., 255
Gipson, David Martin, 255
Gipson, Debora Lynn, 255
Gipson, Linda Gaye, 255
Gipson, Lois Pauline, 255
Gipson, Paul Ray, 255
Gipson, Paula Raye, 255
Givens, Daniel, 245
Givens, Florence M., 245
Glass, Betty Lou, 74
Glass, Robert, 74
Glass, Sandra Elaine, 36
Glass, Sondia Elaine, 192
Glassford, James B., 108
Glaze, Henry, 247
Glaze, Mary E., 247
Glendenning, Ethel Mae Iams, 154
Glenn, Anna "Annie," 15
Glenn, Clara, 15
Glenn, John, 1
Glenn, John C., 15
Glenn, John H., Jr., 5, 155
Glenn, John H., Sr., 15
Glenn, Mary, 15
Glennen, Emma Morris, 13
Glennen, Walter, 13
Glover, Ellen E., 154
Glover, Zachary, 233
Glune, Elizabeth, 74
Glunt, Brenda, 74
Glunt, Floyd Allen, 74
Glunt, Howard Raymond, 74
Glunt, John Samuel, 74
Glunt, John Samuel, Jr., 74
Glunt, Kenneth, 74

Glunt, Mary Belle, 61, 74
Glunt, Mary June, 74
Glunt, Paul Richard, 74
Glunt, Pearl, 74
Glunt, Raymond Luther, 74
Glunt, Ruth Mary, 74
Gluskoter, Babs, 129
Goff, Sue, 348
Golden, Julie A., 309
Golden, Marvin, III, 309
Golden, Marvin Leslie, 309
Golden, Mary Ann, 309
Golden, Randall Lee, 309
Goldsmith, Blanche, 10
Good, Eva Claire, 63
Good, Natacha Jeanne, 63
Good, William Francis, 63
Goode, Eva Clair, 65
Goode, Natacha Jeanne, 65
Goode, William F., 65
Goodwin, Flora, 171
Goodwin, Mary, 171, 264
Goodwin, Mary Florence, 167
Goodwin, Mary Florence "Flora," 171
Goodwin, Seth, 171, 264
Gorby, Marion Jean, 257
Gordon, Adam Byron, 14
Gordon, Adam Randolph, 14
Gordon, Adam S., 14
Gordon, Agnes H., 15
Gordon, Alexander, 2
Gordon, Alice, 15
Gordon, Alice D., 16
Gordon, Alice Ellen, 16
Gordon, Allen, 15
Gordon, Amanda, 13
Gordon, Amanda Louella, 128
Gordon, Ankrom, 14
Gordon, Annabella, xx
Gordon, Ara, 13
Gordon, Basil, 15
Gordon, Basil Jennings, 15
Gordon, Belle, 15
Gordon, Bert, 128
Gordon, Brian Lee, 14
Gordon, Carolyn Jean, 14
Gordon, Carrie Lee, 13
Gordon, Cassandra, 12, 13, 14, 15, 16
Gordon, Catherine, 15
Gordon, Charlotte, 14
Gordon, Clarence, 14
Gordon, Cora, 14

492

Greene, Elizabeth Greene, 244
Greene, Hannah, 292
Greene, Nathaniel, Gen., 292
Greenlee, Florence Helen, 243
Greenlee, Frances, 243
Greenlee, James Bigler, 243
Greenlee, Laura A., 267
Greenlee, Sadie, 267
Greenlee, Samuel, 267
Greenlee, Samuel B., 267
Greenlee, Sarah "Sadie" F., 267
Greenlee, Sarah D., 243
Greenwood, David, 120
Greenwood, Diana, 120
Greenwood, Don, 120
Greenwood, Donald M., 120
Greenwood, Earl, 120
Greenwood, Jacqueline, 120
Greenwood, Janie, 120
Greenwood, Mildred, 120
Greenwood, Robert E., 120
Greenwood, Timothy, 120
Greenwood, Yvonne, 120
Gregg, Alice Evaline, 184
Gregg, Allan Albert, 33, 184
Gregg, Allen Albert, Jr., 184
Gregg, Bonnie Lou, 33
Gregg, Cressman David, 184
Gregg, Daniel Ray, 184
Gregg, Evaline Alice, 33
Gregg, Gwendolyn Ann, 184
Gregg, Harry C., 184
Gregg, Harry Cressman, 33, 184
Gregg, Jonathan Cress, 184
Gregg, Julia Ann, 184
Gregg, Martha Smith, 205
Gregg, Robert Kennedy, 184
Gregg, Warren E., 205
Gregory, Garry, 153
Gregory, Joan Cecelia, 153
Grem, Frances M., 277
Gress, Emily Cecil, 181
Greulich, Barbara, 48
Greulich, Edward, 48
Greulich, Kathleen Marie, 48
Grey, Mary Z., 263
Gribben, Charles E., 178
Gribben, Clyde Alonzo, 177
Gribben, Daniel, 172, 177

Gribben, Della, 172, 177
Gribben, Elsie, 172, 178
Gribben, Emma, 172, 178
Gribben, Jessie, 177
Gribben, John, 172
Gribben, John Elmer, 177
Gribben, Leon, 178
Gribben, Leona, 172, 178
Gribben, Levina Anna, 177
Gribben, Levina "Sis," 172
Gribben, Lloyd Arthur, 178
Gribben, Mary, 172, 178
Gribben, Mary Helen, 178
Gribben, Mildred Marie, 178
Gribben, Paul Thomas, 178
Gribben, Sis, 172
Gribben, Stella Bernice, 177
Griffen, Jean, xxiii
Griffen, Mildred Jean Barr, 176
Griffen, Myrtle Hall Mullen, 415
Griffen, Robert Eugene, 176
Griffey, B. W., 29
Griffey, Sarah Jane, 29
Griffey, Valeria Eileen, 29
Griffin, Barbara Ann, 177
Griffin, Carolyn Burdick, 177
Griffin, Danielle "Dani" Renee, 177
Griffin, David Eugene, 177
Griffin, Eugene Joseph, 177
Griffin, Hilda Marie, 177
Griffin, Jason Thomas "Jay," 177
Griffin, Kelly Leigh, 177
Griffin, Margaret, 255
Griffin, Michael Robert "Mike," 177
Griffin, Michelle, 254
Griffin, Mildred Jean, 177
Griffin, Mildred Jean Barr Iams, 201
Griffin, N. M., 96
Griffin, Pearl, 189
Griffin, Rebecca Frances "Becca," 177
Griffin, Richard Robert, 177
Griffin, Robert Eugene, 177
Griffin, William F., 96
Griffis, Ambrose, 186
Griffis, Pearl E., 30
Griffis, Pearl Elizabeth, 186
Griffith, Arthur, 40
Griffith, Isabel B. Iams, xxiv

Griffith, Isabel Barbara, 149
Griffith, Isabel Barbara Iams, 149, 164, 356
Griffith, Isabel Iams, 148
Griffith, Lewis, 134
Griffith, Patrick Michael, 149
Griffith, Robert James, 149
Grillot, Frances, 82
Grim, Jesse, 148, 221
Grim, Sally, 221
Grim, Sarah, 148
Grimes, Betty, 330
Grimes, Emma, 16
Grimes, Mary, 165, 167
Grimes, Mary Iams, xxiii
Grimes, Nancy, 27, 167, 169
Grimes, Peter, 167
Grimm, Clarence, 335
Grimm, Clem, 335
Grimm, Dale, 335
Grimm, Earl, 335
Grimm, Emma, 335
Grimm, Emma Prunty, 335
Grimm, Hattie, 335
Grimm, Lester, 335
Grimm, Marie, 335
Grimm, Orval, 335
Grimm, Ruby, 335
Grimm, Samuel Milroy, 335
Griss, Emily Cecilia, 180
Grounds, Mary Eleanor Smith, 156
Grover, Pauline, 125
Grubb, Mary Louise, 291
Guericks, Jonathan Joseph, 348
Guericks, Lisa, 348
Guericks, Richard "Rick" M., 348
Guinn, Ella, 13
Guinn, Eva, 13
Guinn, Haddie, 13
Guinn, Joe, 13
Guinn, Leasure, 13
Guinn, Linnie, 13
Guinn, Sarah Ann, 13
Gundstaff, James, Mrs., 43
Gunduff, Lucinda, 126
Gunterman, Elizabeth, 8
Gunterman, Henry, 8
Gunterman, Katherine, 9
Gunterman, Nancy, 8
Gunterman, Peter, 8
Gunterman, Sarah, 9
Gura, Mary, 214

496

Hartzog, Catherine Dianne, 198
Hartzog, Dennis, 198
Hartzog, Norman, 198
Hartzog, Richard, 198
Hartzog, Virginia Eileen, 198
Hartzog, Vivian, 198
Harvey, Anna Bessie, 171
Harvey, Elizabeth A., 118
Harvey, Kate E., 169
Harvey, Samuel, 169
Harvey, Sarah I., 169
Harvey, William, 118
Harwood, Richard, Jr., xvi, xxix, xxvii, xxviii, 10, 362
Hatcher, Benjamin, 422
Hatcher, Benjamin J., 219
Hatcher, Charlotte, 422
Hatcher, Jane Gardner, 422
Hatcher, Jane "Jennie," 219
Hatcher, Jennie, 219
Hatcher, Joshua, 325
Hatcher, Loren, 422
Hatcher, Mary "Mollie," 325
Hatcher, Mollie, 325, 339
Hatfield, Imo, 129
Hatfield, James, 16
Hatfield, Sadie E., 16
Hathaway, Freeman, 83
Hathaway, Sarah, 83
Hathaway, Sarah "Sallie," 243
Hathaway, Semantha, 156
Hathaway, William H., 243
Hathway, Freeman, 457
Hathway, Sarah, 457
Hattery, Diane Marie, 185, 188
Hatton, John, 4
Hatton, Sarah, 4
Haugen, Ingaborg Belle, 148
Haughland, James, 201
Hauths, Susan, 321
Haven, Henry, 310
Haven, Sally, 310
Haviland, Harry George, 260
Haviland, Kathleen Carol, 260
Haviland, Mary Kathleen, 260
Haviland, Rebecca Jean, 260
Haviland, Richard Byron, 260

Hawkins, Bernice, 167, 171
Hawkins, Dorothy, 172
Hawkins, Eleanor, 172
Hawkins, Esther Meade, 172
Hawkins, Harry LeMoyne W., 172
Hawkins, John Iams, 172
Hawkins, Josephine, 172
Hawkins, Margaret, 172
Hawkins, Sandra, 190
Hawkins, Simone Siniore Ella, 172
Hawkins, Wilma Jo, 172
Hawn, Mildred, 267
Hay, A. J., 121
Hay, Abe "Tim," 121
Hay, Charlene, 121
Hay, Greeta, 121
Hay, Lolita, 121
Hay, Sally, 14
Hay, Tim, 121
Hay, Tina, 121
Hayes, Alice Mary, 30, 84
Hayes, Anna Mary, 184
Hayes, French, 333
Hayes, Roanna, 333
Hayes, Samuel L., 333
Hayes, Vickie, 176
Hayes, Warren, 333
Headley, Belle, 170
Headley, Frank, 170
Headley, Helen, 17
Headley, Nancy G., 170
Headley, Robert, 170
Headrick, Ginger Lee, 34
Hearold, Twila, 129
Heath, Annie Mariah, 57
Heath, Peter, 57
Heaton, John, 230
Heaton, Mary, 230
Heaton, Nancy, 264
Hebert, Flossie, 335
Hebner, Betty Jean, 253
Hebner, Candy, 253
Hebner, Diane, 253
Hebner, Edward, 253
Hebner, John Blake, 253
Hebner, Mark, 253
Hebner, Patricia, 253
Hebner, Philip, 253
Hebner, Rebecca, 253
Hebner, Robin, 253
Hebner, Sue Ann, 253
Heckathorn, Catherine, 223
Heckathorn, Jacob, 143

Heckathorn, Martin, 223
Heckathorn, Mary, 161
Heckathorn, Nancy, 143
Heckathorn, Phebe, 235
Heckathorn, Phoebe, 21, 27, 161, 204, 223, 236, 458, 461
Heckathorn, Phoebe Jane, 234
Heckathorne, Ann A., xxiv
Heckathorne, Ann Austin, 164
Heckathorne, Catherine, 143
Heckathorne, Daniel, 143
Heckathorne, Elizabeth, 143
Heckathorne, Eve, 143
Heckathorne, George, 143
Heckathorne, Martin, 143
Heckathorne, Mary, 143
Heckathorne, Phoebe, xxxvii, 143, 205
Hedge, Ann, 121
Hedge, Homer, 276
Hedge, James, 245
Hedge, Jennie M, 245
Hedge, Nevada, 276
Hedges, Conrad M., 42
Hedges, Hezekiah, 137
Hedges, Marti, 48
Hedges, Mary Elizabeth, 137
Heidesh, Marey, 316
Heiland, Elsie, 186
Heiland, Elsie L., 30
Heinman, Grace, 274
Heisel, Fred R., 290
Heisel, Ruby Fern, 290
Heite, Oral, 200
Heite, R. M., 200
Heite, Romain, 37, 200
Heitman, F. B., 278
Helms, Vickie, 47
Heltzel, Eunice, 335
Hemebrick, Helen Margaret, 90
Henbeck, George, 139
Henbeck, Isabel, 139
Henderson, D., 37
Henderson, Dorothy, 200
Henderson, Eva Leona, 29
Henderson, Homer Glen, 29
Henderson, Rose, 128
Hendren, Ariana Ijams, xxviii
Hendrix, Bill, 129
Hendrix, Carol Ann, 129

498

501

504

505

507

511

513

515

Iiams, Harriet, 111, 305, 310, 458, 459
Iiams, Harriet E., 33
Iiams, Harriet Owings Ijams, 111
Iiams, Harrison Jay, 320
Iiams, Harry Early, 30, 31, 184
Iiams, Harvey, 160, 460
Iiams, Harvey Enis, 36
Iiams, Harvey Enos, 191
iams, Harvey Enos (Enis), 190
Iiams, Hattie, 47
Iiams, Hazel L., 37
Iiams, Hazel Lenora "Lizzie," 191, 200
Iiams, Helen, 99
Iiams, Helen Blanche, 35
Iiams, Helen Marie, 38, 183
Iiams, Helen Olive, 38, 183
Iiams, Helen Patricia, 99
Iiams, Henry, 39, 110, 306
Iiams, Henry F., 321
Iiams, Herman, 99
Iiams, Hester, 1, 2, 5, 6, 456
Iiams, Hettie Rose, 28
Iiams, Hillis D., 40, 82
Iiams, Hiram, 305, 306
Iiams, Hiram B., 146
Iiams, Hiram G., 146, 147
Iiams, Hiram Milton, 306
Iiams, Howard, 460
Iiams, Howard, Jr., 110
Iiams, Howard Leslie, 35
Iiams, Howard Theodore, 199
Iiams, Hoyt, 290
Iiams, Hugh, 303-305, 310
Iiams, Hugh, Jr., 310
Iiams, Huldah Jane, 28
Iiams, Ida Leila, 29
Iiams, Ida May, 30, 184
Iiams, Ilda I., 40, 82, 83
Iiams, Ines McCain, 292
Iiams, Inez, 99, 100
Iiams, Ira Russell, 28
Iiams, Irene Camp, 320
Iiams, Irene Wirick, 183
Iiams, Iris M., 40
Iiams, Iris Rebecca, 39
Iiams, Irum Turner, 35
Iiams, Isaac, 26, 27, 40, 63, 83, 106, 134, 160, 165, 166, 284, 285, 306, 308, 458

Iiams, Isaac Beall, 111
Iiams, Isaac H., 107
Iiams, Isaac Howard, 108
Iiams, Isaac Plummer, 106
Iiams, Isaac W., 40
Iiams, Isabella, 292
Iiams, Israel, 305, 306
Iiams, Iva Gertrude, 184
Iiams, Ivan Roger, 39, 179
Iiams, Ivey, 99
Iiams, J. E., 458
Iiams, Jack L., 82
Iiams, Jackie Lamar, 37, 200
Iiams, Jacob, 93, 94, 100, 456, 458, 460
Iiams, Jacob W., 459
Iiams, Jacqueline, 34
Iiams, Jaime Lynn, 35
Iiams, James, 40, 83, 146, 178, 243, 312, 459, 460
Iiams, James Arthur, xvii, 191, 198
Iiams, James Donald, 34
Iiams, James E., 37, 181
Iiams, James Earl, 32, 184, 185
Iiams, James Earl, Jr., 185
Iiams, James Frank, 2
Iiams, James H., 40
Iiams, James Harvey, 82
Iiams, James Marion, 147
Iiams, James McClelland, 147
Iiams, James Oscar, 356
Iiams, James P., 292
Iiams, James Stephen, 30, 186
Iiams, Jane, xxvi, 142, 183, 184, 289, 291, 292, 319, 320, 459
Iiams, Jane B., 459
Iiams, Jane Carol, 99
Iiams, Jane E., 110
Iiams, Jane Elizabeth, 111
Iiams, Jane S., 204
Iiams, Janet Kay, 34
Iiams, Janice Elizabeth, 30, 186
Iiams, Jeff, xxvi
Iiams, Jefferson, 288
Iiams, Jefferson M., 288
Iiams, Jeffrey Allan, 35
Iiams, Jehu, xxvi, 319, 320
Iiams, Jemina, 459
Iiams, Jennifer, 34
Iiams, Jeremiah, 205

Iiams, Jeremiah H., 205
Iiams, Jesper, 310
Iiams, Jesse, 304, 305
Iiams, Jesse Cleveland, 177
Iiams, Jesse Maude, 122
Iiams, Jessica Lynn, 32
Iiams, Jessica Lynne, 185
Iiams, Jessie Nevada, 33
Iiams, Jessie Pearl, 34
Iiams, Jestine, 310
Iiams, Jill, 32, 185
Iiams, Joan L., 292
Iiams, Johanna, 111
Iiams, John, xi, xiii, xviii, xxvi, xxvii, xxviii, 6, 9, 11, 12, 21, 22-25, 27, 38-41, 43, 55, 56, 63, 82-84, 93, 94, 98, 106, 107, 111, 142, 143, 146, 152, 160, 165, 166, 172, 175-177, 179, 180, 182, 190, 203-205, 226, 241, 242, 265, 272, 281-284, 303, 305, 306, 311, 312, 317, 318, 320, 322, 326, 362, 370, 430, 456-459, 461
Iiams, John, Jr., xxx, xxxi, 26, 41, 106, 111, 242
Iiams, John, Sr., xxx, 41, 243
Iiams, John, II, 40
Iiams, John C., 287
Iiams, John Christian, 34
Iiams, John David, 34
Iiams, John F., 292
Iiams, John Franklin, 327
Iiams, John H., 40, 83, 99, 292
Iiams, John Henry, 38, 182
Iiams, John Hill, 26, 83
Iiams, John Howard, 99, 111
Iiams, John L., 290
Iiams, John Moody, 293, 294
Iiams, John Murray, 29
Iiams, John N., 99
Iiams, John T., M.D., 169
Iiams, John Waters, 458
Iiams, John Wesley, 118, 326, 458
Iiams, John "Wesley," 320
Iiams, Jonathan, 320
Iiams, Josefina Andreasdotter, 33
Iiams, Joseph, 458
Iiams, Joseph Daniel, 34

520

Ijams, Charlotte, 124, 125, 388
Ijams, Charlotte E., 102
Ijams, Charlotte Louise, 127
Ijams, Chase Mellen, 314
Ijams, Chip, 129
Ijams, Christine, 129
Ijams, Christopher, 140
Ijams, Clara Beall, 116
Ijams, Clara E., 110, 163, 356
Ijams, Clara R., 95
Ijams, Clayton Dean, 121
Ijams, Clayton Dean, Jr., 121, 122
Ijams, Clyde, 128
Ijams, Clyde Elmer, 127
Ijams, Comfort, xxix, 124, 125, 133, 388
Ijams, Corinne "Cosa," 128
Ijams, Corinne Mae "Cosa," 129
Ijams, Cosa, 128, 129
Ijams, D., 112
Ijams, Dale Elmer, 127
Ijams, Daniel, 133
Ijams, Daniel Leslie, 114
Ijams, Daniel W., 112
Ijams, Daniel Worley, 113
Ijams, Darlene, 120
Ijams, David, 129
Ijams, David C., 131
Ijams, Denton, xxviii, 94, 96
Ijams, Dewitt Clinton, 43, 131, 132
Ijams, Donald, 122, 123
Ijams, Dorcas, 136
Ijams, Dorcas Mitchell, 140
Ijams, Dorcas S. M., 42
Ijams, Dorcus Susan Mitchell, 141, 313
Ijams, Dorothy, 122, 123
Ijams, Dorothy A., 121
Ijams, Dylan Maxwell, 123
Ijams, E. H., xxxi
Ijams, E. T., 133
Ijams, Earl, 119, 127
Ijams, Edgar Dudley, 139
Ijams, Edith, 127
Ijams, Edith Hoysradt, 128, 129
Ijams, Edith Ora, 117
Ijams, Edna, 128
Ijams, Edna Naomi, 127
Ijams, Edna Sarah, 128
Ijams, Edward, 122

Ijams, Edward Burch, 162
Ijams, Edward Eric, 127
Ijams, Edward T., 122, 123, 133
Ijams, Edward Talmadge, 122, 123
Ijams, Edwin, xxxii, 424
Ijams, Edwin C., vii, 118
Ijams, Edwin Clayton, 119, 424
Ijams, Edyth, 128, 129
Ijams, Eleanor, 41, 161, 284, 461
Ijams, Eleanor L., 116
Ijams, Eli, 161
Ijams, Eliza Jane, 126
Ijams, Eliza Musseter, 134, 135
Ijams, Eliza Unity, 122
Ijams, Elizabeth, xl, xv, xix, xviii, xxix, xxxvii, xxviii, 1, 7, 21, 79, 93-95, 101, 105-109, 117, 118, 122-125, 130-135, 145-147, 162, 283, 284, 303, 313, 362, 388, 424, 459
Ijams, Elizabeth A., 42, 118
Ijams, Elizabeth Aldridge, 140, 313
Ijams, Elizabeth Aldridge, 313
Ijams, Elizabeth Ann, 136, 139, 141
Ijams, Elizabeth Beck, 109,117, 118
Ijams, Elizabeth Ferguson, 93
Ijams, Elizabeth Hamilton, 124
Ijams, Elizabeth Howard, 108, 132
Ijams, Elizabeth "Jane," 125
Ijams, Elizabeth Jones, 11
Ijams, Elizabeth "Lib," 119
Ijams, Elizabeth Marion, 141
Ijams, Elizabeth Plummer, 10, 361
Ijams, Elizabeth Unity, 123
Ijams, Elizabeth Virginia, 139
Ijams, Ella L., 116
Ijams, Ella Scanlon, 128
Ijams, Ella V., 132

Ijams, Elle C., 133
Ijams, Ellen, 27, 144, 145, 146
Ijams, Ellen L., 116
Ijams, Eloise Ethlyn, 128
Ijams, Elsie, 125, 126, 128
Ijams, Elsie W., xxiv, 163
Ijams, Elsie Warfield, 356
Ijams, Emily, 136, 141, 459
Ijams, Emily Alice, 162
Ijams, Emma, 12, 102
Ijams, Emma E., 121
Ijams, Emma Etta, 119, 121
Ijams, Emma L., 97
Ijams, Era, 122, 123
Ijams, Eric, 123
Ijams, Esther, 147
Ijams, Ethel, 114, 121, 128
Ijams, Ethel Christine, 127
Ijams, Etta, 110, 116, 117
Ijams, Eunice, 117
Ijams, Eva, 125
Ijams, Eva Roberts, 131
Ijams, Faith, 146
Ijams, Fanny V., 132
Ijams, Fathie, 148
Ijams, Fayette, 12
Ijams, Florence Mignonette, 127
Ijams, Florilla, 43, 131
Ijams, Frances "Frannie" Earle, 161
Ijams, Frances E., 43
Ijams, Frances Maria, 160
Ijams, Frank, 110
Ijams, Frank Burch, 161
Ijams, Frank J., Dr., 160
Ijams, Franklin, 12, 132
Ijams, Franklin D., 115
Ijams, Franklin Lafayette, 22, 25, 457
Ijams, Frannie, 161
Ijams, Fred, 121
Ijams, Frederick, xvi, xxix, 107, 108, 119, 132, 133
Ijams, Frederick Ridgely, 133
Ijams, Frederick Rodger, 108
Ijams, Frederick S., 133
Ijams, Gail F., 121
Ijams, Gary, 123
Ijams, George, xxvii, xxviii, xxix, 25, 93, 110, 125
Ijams, George Allison, 102, 103

524

529

533

Jewell, Elva Velva, 232
Jewell, Eva Velva, 232
Jewell, John, 243
Jewell, Margaret, 243
Jewell, Maude, 243
Jewell, Phoebe, 242
Jiames, Aaron, 306
Jiames, John, 241
Jiames, Mary, 306
Jiams, Ann, 360
Jiams, Anne, 359
Jiams, Charity, 9, 359
Jiams, Elizabeth, 9, 359
Jiams, Elizabeth Cheyney, 9
Jiams, John, 9, 359, 360
Jiams, Mary, 9, 359
Jiams, Plummer, 9, 359
Jiams, Richard, 9, 359
Jiams, Thomas, 359, 360, 9
Jiams, William, 9, 304, 359
Jimes, Elizabeth, 285
Jimes, Isaac, 285
Jimes, Samuel, 285
Jimes, Thomas, 285
Jinkins, George, 156
Jinkins, Irene, 156
Joan Maid of Kent, xix
John Duke of Bedford, xix
Johns, Abraham, viii
Johns, Anna Mae, 276
Johnson, Alice, 246
Johnson, Alvin, 246
Johnson, Ammond, 232
Johnson, Annabelle, 297
Johnson, Austen, 246
Johnson, Barbara Lou, 193
Johnson, Belle, 117
Johnson, Beulah, 232
Johnson, Caroline, 64
Johnson, Charlene, 121
Johnson, Charles Reed, 139
Johnson, Charles, 121
Johnson, Chris Harwood, 34
Johnson, Crystal Rae, 34
Johnson, Delilah, 83
Johnson, Edna Sarah, 128
Johnson, George, 128, 246
Johnson, Geraldine, 121
Johnson, Harriet Barnes, 154
Johnson, Howard Everett, 193
Johnson, Incas, 246
Johnson, Jack, 121
Johnson, Jebbie, 154
Johnson, Jessie Nevada, 33

Johnson, Johnnie Robert, 295
Johnson, Johnnie Roosevelt, 295
Johnson, Kenneth, 246
Johnson, Marie, 246
Johnson, Martha Elizabeth, 295
Johnson, Mary, xxviii, 95, 246
Johnson, Mildred, 139
Johnson, Miller, 246
Johnson, Peter, 64
Johnson, Rachel, 246
Johnson, Robert Lee, 295
Johnson, S. J., 117
Johnson, Sarah, 26, 83, 243
Johnson, Sarah A., 190
Johnson, Stacy, 121
Johnson, Susie, 246
Johnson, Thomas, 246
Johnson, Walter Lee, 297
Johnson, Willie Beatrice, 295
Johnson, Zeneas, 243
Johnson-Loudon, James, 245
Johnson-Loudon, Delilah, 244, 245, 246
Johnson-Loudon, James, 244
Johnston, Anne Marie, 99
Johnston, Bradley, 337
Johnston, Bruce Norris, 99
Johnston, Carolyn Louise, 99
Johnston, Clyde Donley, 336, 337
Johnston, Eleanor, 143
Johnston, Emily Louise, 99
Johnston, Jean Carol, 99
Johnston, John William, 19
Johnston, Marnee, 337
Johnston, Mary Alice, 19
Johnston, Mildred Lucille, 336
Johnston, Richard Thomas, 99
Johnston, Walter F., 99
Johnston, Waltzie, 337
Johnston, William Lawrence, 99
Johnston, William Quay, 19
Jones, Ada Alice, 39
Jones, Amos L., 323
Jones, Christina Belle, 219

Jones, Daniel Robert, 294
Jones, Donna Lyn, 232
Jones, Eleanor, xxiv, 21, 23, 25, 203, 204, 235, 461
Jones, Eleanor, 164
Jones, Elinor, 23
Jones, Elizabeth, xviii, xix, 4, 5, 11, 456
Jones, Elizabeth "Liza," 10
Jones, Ethel, 335
Jones, George Francis, 294
Jones, Hazel, 121
Jones, Irene Elizabeth, 219
Jones, Isaac, xviii, 11, 105
Jones, John, x
Jones, John Francis, 294
Jones, Julia Mae, 276
Jones, Karen, 72
Jones, Lenna, 335
Jones, Mabel Nell, 232
Jones, Marcia Ann, 294
Jones, Margaret, 17
Jones, Mary, 105
Jones, Mary Agnes, 110, 113
Jones, Mary Ann, 294
Jones, Mary Margaret, 294
Jones, Matthew Joseph, 294
Jones, Orris Ray, 219
Jones, Quincy Arthur, 17
Jones, Rebecca, xv, xviii, xxvii, xxviii, xxix, 11, 12, 25, 63, 105, 117, 124, 131, 138, 303, 458
Jones, Richard, xxvii
Jones, Ruth E., 260, 261
Jones, Sonia Mae, 276
Jones, Stephen Daniel, 294
Jones, Susannah, 8
Jones, Willard Jefferson, 232
Jones, William, 10
Jones, William, Dr., 8
Jones, William, Sr., 4
Jones, William Dibrell, 276
Jones, William Dibrell, III, 276
Jordan, Helen Elizabeth, 139
Jordan, L. C., xxxviii
Jordan, Lawrence C., 288
Jordan, Lillian "Lillie," 288
Josephson, Bradford Delano, 314
Josephson, Margaret Ditson, 314
Josephson, Margaret Ijams, 314

534

536

Lane, Henry Clay, III, 99
Lane, Robert, 254
Lane, Robin Lea, 254
Lane, Rose Emma, 99
Lanear, Nancy, 146
Langford, Alma Linnese, 64
Langford, Carrie Anne Beatrice, 64
Langford, Catherine, 64
Langford, Charles, 64
Langford, Dawn Elizabeth, 65
Langford, Eli, 122, 123
Langford, Elizabeth Ann, 122, 123
Langford, George, 64
Langford, Henry, 64
Langford, Henry, Jr., 64
Langford, Hortense, 64
Langford, Margaret, 64
Langford, Mary, 122, 123
Langford, Mary M., 65
Langford, Mildred, 64
Langford, Raphael Ronald, 65
Langford, Ricardo Samuel, 65
Langford, Ricardo Samuel, III, 65
Langford, Roland, 64
Langford, Rosina Visconti, 64
Langford, Samuel Ricardo, 64
Langford, Susan, 65
Langford, Tina Marie, 65
Langford, Toni Lynn, 65
Langley, Ann, xl
Langley, Matthew Ryan, 220
Langley, Timothy, 220
Lanier, Gloria, 99
Lanning, Effie J., 39
Lantz, Dorothy Gladys, 168
Lapinoja, Martha, 128, 129
Lapping, Cora, 19
Lapping, Emma Inghram, 16
Lapping, Frank, 16
Lapping, John, 16
Larrey, Frances M., 204
Larry, Frances M., 148
Larson, Dolores N., xiv
Larson, Nella, 68
Lashley, Nancy, 339
Lastman, Jean, 252
Lastman, Richard, 252
Lathem, Gaither, Mrs., 98

Latimer, Gertrude, 186
Laubach, Charles Crissman, 232
Laubach, Margaret Shannon, 232
Laubach, Sarah Cathrine, 232
Laudicina, Betsy Ann, 295
Laudicina, David Iams, 295
Laudicina, Gaetanand, 295
Laudicina, Nicholas, 295
Laudicina, Rebecca Jane, 295
Laudicina, Rosario Charles, 295
Laudicina, Rosario Charles, Jr., 295
Laudicina, Rose Anna, 295
Laudicina, Ruth Ann, 295
Laudicina, Tana Marie, 296
LaVigne, Frederick, 121
Lavina, Sela, 269
Lavrey, Frances M., 160
Lawson, Bushrod, Jr., 334
Lawson, Bushrow Washington, 334
Lawson, Fannie, 334
Lawson, Flora O'Dell, 335
Lawson, Flora Odell, 334
Lawson, Lois Rosaline, 33
Lawson, Wallace, 33
Leach, Mary J., 97
Leaf, Hester, 137, 139, 141
Leake, Cassandra, 12
Leake, Henry, 12
Lecke, Howard, 18
Leckey, Howard, vii, xvii, xviii, xxxv, 22, 300, 356, 461
Leckey, Howard L., 172, 201, 278
Leckrone, Bonnie, 47
Leckrone, C., 46
Leckrone, Carl, 46
Leckrone, Carnet Paul, 46
Leckrone, Cleno, 46
Leckrone, Edgar, 46
Leckrone, Eloise, 47
Leckrone, Ezra, 46
Leckrone, Faye, 46
Leckrone, Gladys, 46
Leckrone, Jacob, 46
Leckrone, Kathleen, 46
Leckrone, Margurite, 46
Leckrone, Merle, 46
Leckrone, Ralph, 46

Leckrone, Rosa, 46
Leckrone, Rose, 46
Leckrone, Vera Marie, 46
Leckrone, Willard, 46
LeCompte, Carmella Louise Mares, 149
Lecroke, Ezra, 46
Lecrone, Ezra, 46
Lee, Barbara, 35
Lee, David, 173
Lee, Ethel, 249
Lee, Helen Marie, 173
Lee, Richard, 173
Leeke, Ann, 12
Leeke, Cassandra, xix, 12, 456
Leeke, Henry, xix, 12, 456
Leeke, Henry, III, 12
Leeke, Henry, Sr., 12
Leeke, Joseph, 12
Leeke, Mary, 12
Leeke, Obed, 12
Leffler, Delilah A., 184, 187
Leffler, Iva Gertrude, 131, 84, 187, 188
Leffler, John William, 184, 187
Leggett, Linda, 173
Leggett, Marilyn K., 175
Leggett, Michael Scott, 175
Leggett, Randall, 175
Lehman, Cora, 336
Leighninger, Frances, 219
LeMasters, Delores, 348
LeMasters, Dennis, 348
LeMasters, Dennis, Jr., 348
LeMessurier, Marie, 274
Lemley, David, 15
Lemley, Emma, 15
Lemley, Mary Alice, 227
Lenox, Ruth, 30, 186
Lent, David, Rev., 11
Leonard, Abigail, 146
Leonard, Abigale, 145
Leonard, Bonnie Lou, 33
Leonard, Julia, 145
Leonard, Mary, 27, 95, 144
Lersunder, Fabiola, 294
Lersunder, Fabiola, 296
Leszez, Brian Edward, 295
Leszez, John Patrick, 295
Leszez, Mary, 295
Leszez, Norbert John, 295
Leszez, Rebecca, 295
Leszez, Walter, 295
Levengood, Ann, 95

538

539

Lorrigan, Nicole, 123, 124
Lorrigan, Rebecca, 123, 124
Lorrigan, Sarah, 123, 124
Lorrigan, Todd, 123, 124
Lorrigan, Tonya, 123, 124
Lorrigan, William, 123
Loudon, James Johnson, 270
Loudon-Johnson, Delilah, 26
Loudon-Johnson, James, 26
Loughman, Bell, 151
Loughman, Catherine, 85
Loughman, Charles, 85, 151
Loughman, Daniel, 85, 86, 151, 212
Loughman, Dennis, 85, 151
Loughman, Emma, 85,151
Loughman, Frederick, 85
Loughman, George, 85, 151
Loughman, Hannah, 157, 159, 209
Loughman, Henry, 85
Loughman, Ida, 85, 151
Loughman, Jack, 85, 151
Loughman, John E., 238
Loughman, Lydia, 159
Loughman, Mary Bell, 86
Loughman, Mary Belle, 85
Loughman, Olive, 159
Loughman, Sarah, 85, 86, 151, 212, 169
Loughman, Smith, 159
Louis, Margaret, 192
Loundes, Christian, x, xi
Loundes, Christopher, 282
Loundes, Christopher E. B., xxvi
Love, Margaret Elizabeth, 72
Love, Mary Linda, 72
Love, William J., 72
Lovell, Harry, 36
Lovell, Lila Vesta, 36
Lover, Cleno, 46
Lovett, Dick, 191
Lovett, Edward, 191
Lovett, Harry, 191
Lovett, Lila Vesta, 191
Lovett, Ruth, 191
Lovine, Brenda, 74
Lowe, Brian, 217
Lowe, Jennifer, 217
Lowe, Ray, 217
Lowell, Diane, 176
Lowery, Damon, 69
Lowery, Shirley, 69

Lowndes, Christopher, xxxiii
Lowndes, Christopher E. B., xxxiv
Lownes, Christopher E. B., 282
Lowrie, Margurite, 46
Lowther, Alexander K., Jr., 334
Lowther, Emily, 334
Lowther, M. R., 334
Lucas, Bernard, 41
Lucas, Caroline, 285
Lucas, Elisha Higgin, 285
Lucas, Julie Ann, 259
Lucas, Nicolo, 259
Lucas, Roger, 259
Lucas, Sue Ann, 259
Lucus, Margaret, 192
Lucus, Oliver G., 192
Lucus, Peggy K., 36
Lucus, Peggy Kathryn, 192
Luden, David, 259
Luden, John, 259
Luden, Mary, 259
Luden, Steven, 259
Luellan, Wilma, 342
Luellen, Sarah Elizabeth, 88, 215
Luman, Ada Lillian, 50
Luther, Elizabeth, 291
Lyman, Laura Martin, 156
Lyons, Elizabeth, 105, 106

— M —

Maartin, Elizabeth Iams, 266
MacAleese, Anna P., 138
Maccubbin, Nicholas, xv
MacGregor, Deborah Sue, 50
MacGregor, Peter, 50
Mackelfish, Susannah, 3
Mackelfish, Thomas, 3
Maddock, Harvey, 248
Maddock, Myrtle, 248
Maddox, George, 159
Maddox, Herschel, 159
Maddox, John, 159
Maddox, Oliver, 159
Maddox, Phoebe, 159
Maeges, Edna, 274
Maeges, Emma, 274
Maeges, John, 274
Maggy, Mary, 207

Magnusen, E. F., Mrs., 207
Magnusen, Erick F., 207
Magnusen, Evelyn, 207
Magnusen, Gertrude, 206
Magnuson, E. J., Rev., 238
Magnuson, Evelyn, xxiii
Magoon, Ernest Howard, 294
Magoon, Margaret Ann "Margery, 294
Magoon, Margery, 294
Magoon, Mary Susan Morgan, 294
Mahan, Joan, 296
Maitland, Elizabeth, 312
Maitland, James, 312
Maitland, Rebecca Seton, 312
Majors, Nettie Leitch, xiv
Makenzie, Path, 2
Malcolm, Campbell, 141
Malcolm, James Cambell, Sr., 313
Malcolm, Joshan, 313
Malcolm, Marion Turner, 141
Maley, James C., 246
Maley, Minnie Katherine, 246
Maley, Rachel, 334
Maley, Thomas, 334
Maley, William, 334
Maloy, Amy Beth, 251
Maloy, Christy Ann, 251
Maloy, Cynthia Judy, 251
Maloy, Emma Lou, 250
Maloy, James Claude, 250
Maloy, James Ronald, 251
Maloy, James Walter, 251
Maloy, Judy Catherine, 251
Maloy, Mary Jane, 251
Maloy, Minnia Iams, 374
Maloy, Minnie Katherine, 250
Maloy, Richard Weller, 250
Maloy, Rosella Louise, 251
Maloy, Ruth Frantz, 251
Maloy, Sharon Kay, 251
Maloy, Sonja, 251
Mandelik, Lindsey Marie, 197
Manges, Kristin Gaye, 121
Manges, Robert, 121
Manges, Terry, 121
Manifold, George O., 343

540

Manifold, Gertrude Elaine, 343
Manifold, Mary, 343
Mankey, Aline Berdine, 89
Mankey, Gene Allen, 89, 215
Mankey, James Charles, 89, 215
Mankey, Karen Eleanor, 89, 215
Mankey, Kenneth Edward, 89, 215
Mankey, Kenneth Guy, 89, 215
Mankey, Paulette Elaine, 89, 215
Mankey, Rita Karen, 89, 215
Mankey, Ruth Elizabeth, 89
Mankey, Susan Ruth, 215
Mankey, Warren, 89
Manley, Elizabeth, 106
Manley, Elizabeth Hamilton, 124
Manley, Robert, Rev., 124
Manly, Elizabeth, 458
Mann, A., 139
Mann, Amelia, 139
Manning, Alma Louise, 253
Manning, Beth, 120
Manning, Carrie, 119, 120
Manning, Earl, xxxii, 120
Manning, Eldon, 120
Manning, Gregory, 253
Manning, Kevin, 120
Manning, Melvin, 119, 120
Manning, Mildred, 120
Manning, Nancy, 120
Manning, Norman, 120
Manning, Rodney, 120
Manning, Ruth, 120
Manning, Susan Janeen, 253
Manning, Thomas Joseph, Jr., 253
Manning, Thomas Joseph, Sr., 253
Mansfield, Thomas, 41
Manton, Alexander, 149
Manton, Arin, 149
Manton, Jordan Alexander, 149
Manuel, Benjamin F., 225
Manuel, Bessie, 225
Manuel, Carol, 68
Manuel, Cassius, 227
Manuel, Cassius B., 225
Manuel, Etta, 225

Manuel, Ruby, 225
Manuel, Ruth, 225
Manuel, Sarah Etta, 227
Maple, Adam, 16
Maple, Basil, 16
Maple, Cassancra, 16
Maple, Elijah, 16
Maple, Hamilton, 16
Maple, Harvey, 16
Maple, Ida, 16
Maple, Lafayette, 16
Maple, Lyde, 16
Maple, Mark, 16
Maple, Mary, 16
Maple, Raymond, 16
Maple, Sadie, 16
Maple, Sarah, 16
Maple, Sidney, 16
Maple, Susan, 16
March, William B., 96
Marcus, Christopher R., 197
Marcus, Kevin, 197
Marcus, Teresa Marie, 197
Mares, Arin, 149
Mares, Carmella Louise, 149
Mares, Celeste Lucille, 149
Mares, Madolla, 149
Mares, Timothy R., III, 149
Mares, Timothy Renaldo, II, 149
Margaret Jean, 19
Markham, Danna, 120
Marquis, Elizabeth Ann, 293
Marriott, Ann, 25
Marriott, Anne, 22
Marriott, Joseph, 22, 25, 43, 457
Marriott, Joshua, 22, 25
Marriott, M. J., 106
Marriott, Rachel, 12, 22, 25, 43, 106, 131, 456, 457
Marriott, Rebecca, 22, 25, 43, 106, 457
Marriott, Rebecca H., 22, 25
Marriott, Sarah, 21, 22, 25, 284, 457, 461
Marse, Bert, 148, 160, 204
Marse, Elbert, 148, 160
Marse, Lalla E. Carroll, 156
Marse, Nancy, 148, 160, 204
Marse, Wallace, 148, 160, 204
Marshall, Blondene Jane, 330
Marshall, Cleon, 330

Marshall, Maria, 152
Marshall, Mariah, 152, 228
Martell, Charles, xvii
Martell, Charles Gratton, 263
Martell, Dorothy Elizabeth, 263
Martill, Charles, 10
Martin, A., 115
Martin, Alice, 266
Martin, Ann, 242, 272
Martin, Anna, xxxi, 83, 242, 265, 266
Martin, Anne, 26, 266
Martin, Belle, 265
Martin, Benjamin Whitmer, 50
Martin, Blanche, 125
Martin, C. W., 83
Martin, Christine Marie, 220
Martin, Clarion W., 266
Martin, Deborah Sue, 50
Martin, Eleanor, 156
Martin, Elizabeth, xxxi, 26, 83, 242, 265
Martin, Elizabeth Bair, 266
Martin, Elizabeth Fulmer Frances, 235
Martin, Elizabeth Jane, 266
Martin, Fred David, 235
Martin, Gena Rae, 267
Martin, George William, 235
Martin, H. B., 96
Martin, Harold H., 220
Martin, Jack Anthony, 50
Martin, Jackson, 266
Martin, Jackson, 83
Martin, Jacob, xxxi, 266
Martin, James, 242, 265, 272
Martin, Jamison, 156
Martin, Jane, 243, 265, 272
Martin, John, xxxi, 242
Martin, John Iams, 266
Martin, John Iiams, 26, 266
Martin, John L., 83
Martin, Joseph, xxx, xxxi, 26, 83, 242, 265, 266, 364, 457
Martin, Joseph, Jr., xxxi, 266
Martin, Joseph, Sr., 83
Martin, Karl Whitmer, 50
Martin, Laura, 156
Martin, Lucy, 266
Martin, Lyda Jean, 220

541

McDade, Ruth Patricia, 99
McDamrock, Nancy Ijams Bollen, xxix
McDaniel, Edgar, 97
McDaniel, Jerry L., 97
McDaniel, John, Mrs., 230
McDaniel, Lou Ann, 97
McDaniel, MaryElizabeth, 252, 255
McDaniel, Sarah Ann, 45, 46
McDaniels, Sarah Ann, 389
McDermot, Bridget Nora, 177
McDermott, Grace M., 15
McDermott, Virginia, 15
McDermott, William C., 15
McDowell, John, 65
McElroy, Ona, 270
McElvey, George C., 324
McFarland, Anna, 294, 299
McFarlane, James, 397
McFear, Norma Jean, 254
McGanaghey, Sarah, 285
McGill, Darlene, 120
McGill, Robert, 78
McGinnis, Elnora, 198
McGlashan, John C., 294
McGlashan, Martha, 294
McGlashan, Mary Burdell, 296
McGlashan, MaryBurdell, 294
McGlaskey, Mary, 423
McGlumphy, Alice Margaret, 18
McGlumphy, Brian Edward, 19
McGlumphy, Debra Ann, 19
McGlumphy, Delores Jean, 19
McGlumphy, Earl Gordon, 19
McGlumphy, Earl Gordon, II, 19
McGlumphy, Earl Gordon, III, 19
McGlumphy, Elzie Lee, 18
McGlumphy, Faynella, 19
McGlumphy, Helen Mae, 19
McGlumphy, John Ralph, 19
McGlumphy, Kathleen, 19
McGlumphy, Kelly Jean, 19
McGlumphy, Mary Alice, 19
McGlumphy, Nancy, 172
McGlumphy, Naomi Ruth, 19

McGlumphy, Patricia Ann, 19
McGlumphy, Vera Lucinda, 19
McGlumphy, William Lee, 19
McGlumpy, Nancy, 167
McGrath, Julia, 144
McGrath, Maria, 144
McGrath, Sylvia Zelma, 144
McGriffen, Nathaniel, 242
McIlvaine, John, 304
McIntyre, Anna, 242, 265
McIsaac, Angela Dawn, 233
McIsaac, Clayton, 233
McIver, Cheryl, 346
McIver, Gary, 346
McKanna, Velma, 198
McKay, Heather Elizabeth, 262
McKay, James S., 262
McKay, Leslie Marie, 262
McKay, Mary Helen, 262
McKay, Rosella Iams, 262
McKay, William R., 262
McKee, Marguerite, 298
McKelvey, Alan Curtis, 340
McKelvey, Alan, 428, 429
McKelvey, Ann, 324, 325
McKelvey, Bruce, 325, 339
McKelvey, Chris, 324
McKelvey, Christine Mosconi, 414
McKelvey, Christine, 340, 413
McKelvey, Clyde, 325, 339
McKelvey, David Alan, 340
McKelvey, David, 324, 325
McKelvey, Drue Marie, 340, 414
McKelvey, Earl, 324
McKelvey, Eliza, 323, 324, 325
McKelvey, Elizabeth, 324
McKelvey, Emily "Emma," 325
McKelvey, Emma, 325
McKelvey, Forrest, 324
McKelvey, George, 407
McKelvey, George C., 323, 324, 325, 377
McKelvey, George C., Jr., 324
McKelvey, Ida, 325
McKelvey, Ida B., 324
McKelvey, Isabella, 325

McKelvey, J. O., 324
McKelvey, James, 324
McKelvey, Jennifer Irene, 340
McKelvey, John Kenneth, 340
McKelvey, John, 324, 413, 414, 429
McKelvey, Josephine, 325
McKelvey, Julia Curtis, 413, 429
McKelvey, Julia, 324, 340, 428
McKelvey, Karen, 428, 429
McKelvey, Karen Sue, 341
McKelvey, Kathleen "Kathy" Anne, 340
McKelvey, Kathy, 428, 429
McKelvey, Kevin Logan, 340
McKelvey, Lillian, 325
McKelvey, Linda, 324, 340, 429
McKelvey, Lois Lorraine, 339
McKelvey, Lois, 339, 426
McKelvey, Lucille, 324
McKelvey, Mahola, 324
McKelvey, Margaret, 324, 325
McKelvey, Mary, 324, 325
McKelvey, Mary "Mollie, 325
McKelvey, Mary "Mollie" Hatcher, 339
McKelvey, Mary E., 324
McKelvey, Mildred, 318, 325, 339
McKelvey, Mildred C., xxiii
McKelvey, Mildred Corbett, 175, 339, 380, 392, 414, 419, 426, 427, 428
McKelvey, Mollie, 325
McKelvey, Nancy, 320, 323, 324, 325, 326, 337
McKelvey, Nancy E., 324
McKelvey, Nettie, 324
McKelvey, Paul L., vii
McKelvey, Paul Laverne, 340
McKelvey, Paul LaVerne, 428, 429
McKelvey, Paul, 324, 339, 393, 413, 421, 428, 429, 446
McKelvey, Rachel, 413, 324

545

Meighen, John Murdock, 18
Meighen, John Price, 20
Meighen, John, 17, 18
Meighen, Laura, 18
Meighen, Leslie Ann, 19
Meighen, Lucinda, 17, 18
Meighen, Lucy Elizabeth, 18
Meighen, Lucy Holland, 18
Meighen, Lyn Ann, 18
Meighen, Margaret E., 18
Meighen, Margaret Jean, 19
Meighen, Mark, 18
Meighen, Mary Catherine, 18
Meighen, Mary Elizabeth, 18
Meighen, Mary Frances, 20
Meighen, Mary Luvina, 18, 264
Meighen, Mary Rose, 18
Meighen, Michael, 18
Meighen, Nancy Ann, 18
Meighen, Olive, 18
Meighen, Olive P., 19
Meighen, Patricia, 18
Meighen, Patrick James, 19
Meighen, Robert Frank, 18
Meighen, Robert Pattison, 19
Meighen, Sandra, 18
Meighen, Sharon Ann, 19
Meighen, William Edward, 19
Meighen, William, 18
Meining, Judith Jo, 188
Meining, Robert, 188
Meister, Vista Iames, 309
Mellen, Anne, 312
Mellen, Anne Seymour, 314
Mellen, Anne Seymour Clark, 314
Mellen, Chase, 314
Mellen, Joseph Manley, 314
Mellen, Sylvia Belden, 314
Mellott, Elizabeth, 288, 289
Mellott, Fred, 289
Menzer, Martha, 320
Mercante, Anthony, 245
Mercante, Donna Mae, 245
Mercante, Sherry, 245
Mercante, Tony, 245
Mercer, Arthur Francis, 48
Mercer, Arthur, 290
Mercer, Barbara, 290
Mercer, Brent, 126
Mercer, Chandra, 126

Mercer, Frances, 290
Mercer, Jan Mautz, 444
Mercer, Janice Irene, 48
Mercer, Jesse, 444
Mercer, Mary Elizabeth, 126
Mercer, Ron, 126
Merder, Jesse Aaron, 48
Meredith, Queen Patti, 67
Mesgard, Elizabeth, 155
Messer, Audrey, 123, 124
Messer, David, 123, 124
Messer, Gloria Jean, 150
Messer, Jacob, 123, 124
Messer, Rebecca, 123, 124
Metz, Louise J., 70, 72
Meyer, Charity, 457
Meyer, Jacob, 457
Meyer, Victoria Holm, 256
Meyers, Jacob, 64
Meyers, Judy, 73
Meyers, June Marie, 346
Michael, Crystal Jolene, 197
Michael, Gilbert Russell, 197
Michael, Sandra, 197
Mikita, Rebekah Jane, 274
Mikita, Robert, 274
Miley, Alva, 298
Miley, Laura, 298
Miley, Vivian Lenore, 298
Miller, Anne Elizabeth, 121
Miller, Ben, 205
Miller, Benjamin, 84
Miller, Benjamin John, 84
Miller, Benjamin, Dr., 84, 85
Miller, Benjamin, Sr., 85
Miller, Beverly Ann, 257
Miller, Carol Jean, 258
Miller, Cherie Dawn, 255
Miller, Chrissie Jane, 145
Miller, Dana Lee, 254
Miller, Danny, 77
Miller, David Howard "Doc," 254
Miller, Diane Lynn, 296
Miller, Doc, 254
Miller, Dollie, 290
Miller, Donald Franklin, 100
Miller, Douglas Samuel, 257
Miller, Edna May, 273
Miller, Elizabeth Gail, 100
Miller, Elizabeth Sierra, 296
Miller, Elizabeth, 17, 42, 157, 191, 197, 209
Miller, Elizabeth, 42
Miller, Floyd, 17

Miller, Forrest, 249
Miller, Gary, 121, 326
Miller, George, 251
Miller, Gladys, xxxii
Miller, Glenn O., 296
Miller, Grace E., 309
Miller, Hannah, 85
Miller, Harriet, 17
Miller, Hazel Lee, 62, 68
Miller, Hettie, 85
Miller, Hope Ann, 354
Miller, Inez, 100
Miller, Ivey, 99
Miller, J. Frank, 99, 100
Miller, Jacob A., 290
Miller, James Otis, 296
Miller, Jane, 85
Miller, Jane Elizabeth, 121
Miller, Janet Elizabeth, 100
Miller, Janice Ann, 121
Miller, John, 242
Miller, Joseph, 84, 205, 212
Miller, Kenneth Guy, 257
Miller, Margaret, 84
Miller, Marianne Mendala, 122
Miller, Marianne, 123
Miller, Marie, 290
Miller, Marion Franklin, 100
Miller, Marion Mondale, 123
Miller, Martha, 125, 126
Miller, Mary Suzanne, 296
Miller, Mary, 17, 243
Miller, May, 272
Miller, Melissa, 296
Miller, Mildred Katural, 263
Miller, Minerva, 263
Miller, Minnie, 251
Miller, Mitzi, 262
Miller, Monte B., M.D., 431
Miller, Nicole Ilene, 254
Miller, Patrice, 67
Miller, Paula Karen, 100
Miller, Phyllis Katherine, 344
Miller, Rachel, 84, 205, 212
Miller, Rebecca Anne, 100
Miller, Richard, 17
Miller, Rita Jane, 296
Miller, Robert Allen, 326
Miller, Robert Luther, 100
Miller, Roy, 309
Miller, Ruby Fern, 290
Miller, Ruth, 100
Miller, Ruth Ann, 257

Miller, Ruth Marie, 249
Miller, Samuel Guy, 257
Miller, Shirley, 326
Miller, Susan Amy, 274
Miller, Susan Renee, 257
Miller, Susan, 166, 248, 296
Miller, Travis, 67
Miller, Van McGlashan, 296
Miller, Vere Harper, 296
Miller, Virgil A., 274
Miller, Virginia, 17
Milligan, Margaret, 43
Milliken, Allen Keith, 170
Milliken, Betty Louise, 170
Milliken, Dorothy Pauline, 170
Milliken, Edna, 170
Milliken, Eleanor Braddock, 170
Milliken, Georgia A., 170
Milliken, John Allen, 170
Milliken, John Russell, 170
Milliken, John W. (M.), 170
Milliken, Margaret, 263
Milliken, Margaret Adeline, 170
Milliken, William B., 170
Milliken, William, 263
Mills, Althea Marie, 61, 68
Mills, Beverly Annette, 298
Mills, Haley, 298
Mills, Heather, 298
Mills, Helena, 298
Mills, Hillary, 298
Mills, Holly, 298
Mills, Michael, 298
Mills, Robert, 284
Milne, Flora, 320
Milne, W. L., 320
Milner, Hugh W., 34
Milner, Lois Maude, 34
Minor, Florence, 260
Minor, Moine, 260, 261
Minton, Bonnie Jean, 19
Minton, Carol, 19
Minton, Catherine Jane, 19
Minton, Christine, 19
Minton, Dorothy, 19
Minton, Edward Douglas, 19
Minton, Edward M., 19
Minton, Evelyn, 19
Minton, Inez, 19
Minton, James W., 19
Minton, Jerry L., 19
Minton, Jody, 19

Minton, John Gordon, 19
Minton, Linda, 19
Minton, Lisa, 19
Minton, Mildred, 19
Minton, Patricia, 19
Minton, R. Frank, 19
Minton, Robert Lynn, 19
Minton, Robert Lynn, Jr., 19
Minton, Sharon Kay, 19
Minton, Susan Arlene, 19
Minton, Wahnetta, 19
Minton, William H., 19
Minton, William, 19
Miransky, Jenny Frisch, 293
Mitchell, Arthur L., 246
Mitchell, Bryant, 156
Mitchell, Delilah, 246
Mitchell, Dorcas Susan, 459
Mitchell, Helen, 220
Mitchell, J. B., 156
Mitchell, Lola M., 156
Mitchell, Lowrena, 246
Mitchell, Marie, 246
Mitchell, Mary (Polly), 79
Mitchell, Mary Adaline, 289
Mitchell, Nancy E., 156
Mitchell, Otto C., 156
Mitchell, Polly, 79
Mitchell, Ray, 246
Mitchell, Sarah Ellen, 86
Mitchell, Thomas, 246
Mitchell, William Thomas, 289
Mitts, Clarence, 126
Mitts, Martha Elizabeth, 126
Moats, Billy, 226
Moats, Dorsey Wade, 88, 215
Moats, Elizabeth Blanche, 88, 214, 215
Moats, Mary E., 226
Mock, Elizabeth Georgia, 39, 179
Moffett, Anna, 289
Mohler, Mae, 147
Mohler, Sarah Katheryn, 267
Mohn, Darla Kay, 330
Mohn, John Edward, 330
Mohn, Marcus Shane, 330
Mohn, Mark E., 330
Mohn, Tiarri Rei-Lani, 330
Mohn, Vickie, 330
Molerum, William, 2
Mollenaur, Clara Louise, 247

Mollenaver, Clara, 258
Mollohan, Daisy Mabel, 260
Mollohan, Ward, 260
Monely, David, 120
Monggomery, Huetta, 245
Moniger, Nancy Evelyn, 89, 215
Monley, Elizabeth, 120
Monley, Helen, 120
Monley, J., 120
Monley, Keith, 120
Montgomery, Earl, 245
Montgomery, Archie, 245
Montgomery, Bazil, 16
Montgomery, Bernice, 16
Montgomery, Erving, 16
Montgomery, Florence, 16
Montgomery, Grace, 15
Montgomery, Hannah, 245
Montgomery, Henry, 245
Montgomery, Hugh, 15, 245
Montgomery, James Grant, 174
Montgomery, Jamey Lynn, 174
Montgomery, John, 130, 131, 140, 141, 313, 459
Montgomery, Juannona Inza, 67
Montgomery, Julia Rebecca, 141
Montgomery, Kenneth, 67
Montgomery, Kevin Grant, 174
Montgomery, Margaret, 15
Montgomery, Mary A., 459
Montgomery, Mary Ann, 135, 136, 140, 141, 313
Montgomery, Mary Florence, 245
Montgomery, Mary Ijams, xxviii
Montgomery, Mary, 130, 131, 141, 313, 459
Montgomery, Mavis, 16
Montgomery, Michael G., 16
Montgomery, Nancy, 15
Montgomery, Pauline, 16
Montgomery, Rachel, 178
Montgomery, Rebecca, 141
Montgomery, Relda, 245
Montgomery, Susan W., 16
Montgomery, Terry, 16
Montgomery, Thomas, 15
Montgomery, Thomas F., 15

548

Murdock, George, xxxiv, 282, 317
Murdock, Helen Elizabeth, 18, 264
Murdock, Lucy Alexander, 230
Murphy, Helen Blanche, 35
Murphy, Ivan, 35
Murphy, Joseph Leroy, 267
Murphy, Lennie, 35
Murphy, Lucinda, 249
Murphy, Marjorie, 266
Murphy, Marjorie Mae, 267
Murphy, Olive P., 19
Murphy, Stuart, 266
Murphy, Stuart Ellsworth, 267
Murphy, Tynne Ivana "Lennie," 35
Murray, Gwen, 48
Murray, H. R., 250
Murray, Howard, 261
Murray, Mildred, 19
Musgrave, Eleanor, 142, 143
Musgrave, Elinor, 23
Musgrove, Eleanor, 21, 22, 284, 457
Musseter, Aldredge Ijams, 138
Musseter, Alice, 137
Musseter, Alma, 137
Musseter, Ann Elizabeth, 137
Musseter, Ann Roberta, 138
Musseter, Charles David, 137
Musseter, Charles Harrison, 137
Musseter, Charles, 137, 138
Musseter, Christopher Thomas, 138
Musseter, Christopher, 134, 135, 136, 137
Musseter, Christopher, Jr., 137
Musseter, Christopher, Sr., 303
Musseter, D. Christopher, 137
Musseter, Edmund Hedges, 137
Musseter, Edward Christopher, 137
Musseter, Eliza Aldridge, 138
Musseter, Eliza, 134

Musseter, Elizabeth, 137
Musseter, Ely, 137
Musseter, Florence, 137
Musseter, Frank Vernon, 138
Musseter, Franklin, 137
Musseter, George Washington, 137
Musseter, Hannah, 137
Musseter, Harriet, 137
Musseter, Harriet Ijams, 137
Musseter, Helen, 137
Musseter, Henry, 137
Musseter, Henry P., 135, 137
Musseter, Hezekiah, 137
Musseter, Jackson, 137
Musseter, Jane, 137
Musseter, Jemima Welsh, 138
Musseter, Joel, 137
Musseter, John Roberts, 137
Musseter, John, 134, 137
Musseter, Laura May, 137
Musseter, Lemud, 134
Musseter, Lemuel, 137
Musseter, Margaret, 137
Musseter, Maria Ann, 137
Musseter, Martha Elizabeth, 137
Musseter, Martha, 137
Musseter, Mary, 137
Musseter, Mary Elizabeth, 137
Musseter, Minnie, 137
Musseter, Olive, 137
Musseter, Oliver Ijams, 137
Musseter, Oliver Plummer, 137
Musseter, Plummer Ijams, 137
Musseter, Rebecca, 137
Musseter, Ruth, 135, 136, 137, 138
Musseter, Ruth C., 137
Musseter, Theresa, 138
Musseter, Thomas, 137
Musseter, William Ayers, 137
Musseter, William Henry, 138
Musseter, William, 137
Mussetter, Christopher, 313
Mussetter, Christopher, 459
Mussetter, Elizabeth Aldridge, 140, 141, 313
Mussetter, Harriet, 140, 313, 459

Mussetter, Ruth, 313, 459
Mussetter, Ruth Ijams, xxviii
Mutlicte, William, xxxviii
Myers, Amanda, 188
Myers, Andrew Jackson, 285
Myers, Anna Belle, 323, 325
Myers, Anna, 285, 307, 310
Myers, Barry Douglas, 261
Myers, Bradley Stephen, 260
Myers, Brian Jeffrey, 260
Myers, Bunny, 260
Myers, Calvin, 283
Myers, Carol Ann, 260
Myers, Caroline, 285
Myers, Catherine, 285
Myers, Charity, 318
Myers, Columbia, 284
Myers, Columbus C., 284
Myers, Cynthia, 260
Myers, Daniel, 285, 287, 318
Myers, Darlene, 348
Myers, Debra Lynn, 188
Myers, Elizabeth, 283, 285, 287
Myers, Elizabeth Swaggler, 318
Myers, Isabella "Anna Belle" "Anne," 325
Myers, Isabelle, 323
Myers, Iva, xxxiii
Myers, Jacob, 75, 77, 285, 318
Myers, Jacqueline Jolane "Bunny," 260
Myers, Jane Elizabeth, 263
Myers, Jennifer Sue, 261
Myers, John Frederick, 185
Myers, John Iams, Rev., xxx
Myers, John, Rev., xxx
Myers, Kathy, 188
Myers, Kristal, 261
Myers, Margaret, 307, 310
Myers, Margaret I., 307
Myers, Mary, 120, 285, 287, 293, 318
Myers, Mary Elizabeth, 285
Myers, Mathias, 285
Myers, Nancy Carole, 185, 188
Myers, Paige, 261
Myers, Paul Frederick, 188
Myers, Paul, Jr., 188
Myers, Sarah Ann, 325

Myers, Sarah, 285, 323
Myers, Susan, 285
Myers, Susannah, 283
Myers, Thomas, 285
Myers, Wallace, 284
Myers, Wesley, 307, 310
Myers, William George, II, 260
Myers, William George, III, 260
Myers, Wilson, 307, 310
Myres, Charity, 41
Myres, Jacob, 41
Myres, Mary, 41, 287

— N —

Nace, Virginia Harvey, 110
Naegle, Phillinda K., xiv
Nagle, David, 75
Nance, Jenny, 113
Nance, Virginia "Jenny" Harvey, 113
Napolitan, Leanna, 89
Napolitan, Pat, 89
Neal, Ann, 93
Neal, Edna Dale, 250, 257
Neal, Edna Mae, 257
Neal, Robert A., 250
Neal, Robert Alexander, 257
Nedinger, Hobart, 310
Nedinger, Myrtle, 310
Neely, James, 413, 414, 427, 429
Neely, James Curtis, 339, 384
Neely, Jeannette "Jeannie" Elaine, 340
Neely, Jeannie, 340, 427
Neely, Jim, 324
Neely, Jo-Anna, 340
Neely, Joanne, 380
Neely, JoAnne, 427
Neely, John Douglas, 339
Neely, Lois Lorraine, 339
Neely, Lois M., xxiii
Neely, Lois McKelvey, 324, 380, 413, 414, 426, 427, 428, 429
Negley, Christian, 64, 75, 77
Neibert, Susan, 223, 224
Nelson, Babe, 175
Nelson, Mary E., 175
Nelson, Maxine, 122, 123
Nelson, Robert, 175
Nesbitt, Juanita, 214

Nesselroad, Helen Parks, 287
Neubauer, Barbara Lou, 193
Neubauer, James William, 193
Neville, Catherine, xix
Neville, Edward, xix
Neville, Eleanor, xix
Neville, Frances, xix
Nevin, Edward, 189
Nevin, Edwin, 31, 187
Nevin, Grace, 31, 187
Nevin, Grace B., 189
Nevin, Thomas, 187
Newell, Frederick, 290
Newell, Gladys, 290
Newell, Norita, 290
Newell, Richard, 290
Newhauser, Karen Lynne, 195
Newhauser, Michael James, 195
Newhouser, Adam Michael, 195
Newhouser, Timothy Robert, 196
Newman, Gregg L., 256
Newman, H. W., 283
Newman, H. W., xxxvii
Newman, Harry Wright, xiv, xviii, xxx, xxxv, xxxvi, 1, 12, 22, 43, 52, 91, 93, 132, 163, 201, 238, 278, 300, 312, 315, 316, 454, 455, 456, 461
Newman, Kimberly Sue, 256
Newman, Margaret Jane, 254
Nichols, Claude, 128
Nichols, Della, 274
Nichols, Ella Scanlon, 128
Nichols, Ida, 16
Nichols, Mary, xxxvii, 10, 23, 452, 456
Nichols, Melvin, 16
Nicholson, Benjamin, 6
Nicholson, Esther, 5
Nicholson, Hester, 1, 5, 6, 456
Nicholson, John, 1, 5, 6, 456
Nicholson, John, Jr., 6, 9, 359, 360
Nicholson, Joseph, 6
Nicholson, Nicholas, 6
Nicholson, Rachel, 3, 6

Nicholson, Rebecca, 6
Nicholson, Richard, 6
Nicholson, Sarah, 6
Nigh, Bridgette Gabriel, 199
Nigh, Rhonda Sue, 199
Nixon, Richard M., Pres., xvii
Noland, Darla, 259
Noland, Donna, 195
Noland, Judy, 259
Noland, Paula, 259
Noland, Rachel Michelle, 195
Noland, Scott Michael, 195
Noland, Steve, 195
Norris, Sarah Waters, 20
Northrop, Grace, 161
Noss, Barry Lee, 74
Noss, Shirley, 74
Notch, Kelly Ann, 299
Nottingham, Elizabeth P., 244
Nottingham, Harmon, 244
Novak, Ellen, 273
Novak, Frederick John, 273
Novak, Frederick John, Jr., 273
Novak, Kathy Diane, 273
Novak, Lois Ellen, 273
Nowell, Elizabeth, 12
Nowell, John, Rev., 12
Nuez, Olivia, 12
Nuttall, Thomas, 320
Nutter, Audrey Lee, 332
Nutter, Joan, 332
Nutter, Jon, 332
Nutter, Judy Lee, 332
Nutter, Judy, 324
Nutter, Kenneth, 332
Nyceswanger, Susan, 212

— O —

O'Bannon, Harold, 68
O'Bannon, Sylvia Marie, 68
O'Brian, Maria, 32
O'Brian, Marie, 186
O'Neal, Glenda Gladys, 97
O'Neal, Jennifer, 97
O'Neal, Julie, 97
O'Neal, Thomas, 97
O'Reilly, Cora Alice, 305
Oams, Ross, 375
Oates, Rose Emma, 99
Oberlies, Helen Elta, 34
Ochsenbein, Grace, xiv

Ochsenbein, Irene M., 42, 53
Ochterlony, Isabel, xx
Oder, Mary "Mollie," 219
Oder, Mary Gardner Roberts, 416
Oder, Mollie, 219
Oder, William Jesse, 219
Ogden, Gouverneur, 312
Ogden, Sarah, 311
Oggessen, Margaret, 12
Oggessen, Walter, 12
Ogilvie, Janet, xx
Ogloblinsky, Gregory N., 405
Oldfield, Marionette, 222
Oldfields, Marionette, 160
Olshinsky, Donna Lee, 254
Olshinsky, Edward, 254
Olshinsky, Ethel Eileen, 254
Olshinsky, Leo Edward, 254
Ong, Ruth Elizabeth, 259
Ong, Thomas Viran, 259
Opperlander, Judy, 48
Oradorff, Clarence, 229
Oradorff, Lucy, 229
Orms, Martha, 204
Orms, Ruth, 204
Ormsby, Phyllis Regina, 232
Orndoff, Blanch, 264
Orndoff, Mildred, 172
Orndorff, Edith M., 17
Orndorff, Elizabeth, 17
Orndorff, Florence, 17
Orndorff, George B., 17
Orndorff, Harriet, 17
Orndorff, Kate, 171
Orndorff, Martha, 171
Orndorff, Mary, 16
Orndorff, Ralph, 17
Orndorff, Ruth, 17
Orndorff, William H., 171
Ornes, Benjamin, 204
Orr, John Howard, 109
Orr, John Milton, 109
Orr, Louise, 109
Orr, Lucille, 109
Orr, Mary Ann, 221
Orr, Mary Catherine, 28
Orwig, Kathryn Lynn, 260, 261
Orwig, Kathy Lynn, 260, 261
Orwig, Larry E., Dr., 260, 261
Osacr, Florence Anna, 266
Oscar, James, 266

Ostergaard, Dale, 247
Ostergaard, Joan Evelynn, 247
Ostergaard, Judy, 247
Ostergaard, Palli "Paul" C. "Cliff," 247
Ostergaard, Paul, 247
Ott, Alfred Frank, 175
Ott, Benjamin Franklin, 175
Ott, Daisy, 175
Ott, Mary, 175
Ott, Ruby, 173, 175
Otte, Evan, 344
Otte, Nancy Lee, 343
Otte, Norita Rose, 344
Otte, Norita Rose Sholly, 343, 432
Otte, Zelma Mae, 344
Ouada, Deborah Lea, 34
Ouada, Gregory Thomas, 34
Ouada, Janet Kay, 34
Ouada, Julie Ann, 34
Ouada, Steven, 34
Ouada, Susan Elaine, 34
Overdorf, Martha, 72
Owen, Megan, 50
Owens, Laura Ann, 297
Owens, Lucille, 297
Owens, Penny, 262
Owens, Raymond, 297
Owings, Harriet, 111
Owings, Harriet H., 108, 109
Owings, Mary, 135

— P —

Paap, Bob, 50
Paap, Melissa Lynn, 50
Pace, Nancy, 190
Pagano, Peggy, 120
Page, John English, 168
Page, John Johnson, 168
Page, Mary Elizabeth, 168
Page, William, 168
Palmer, Dawn, 187
Palmer, Jeanne Marie Augustine, 89, 214, 215
Palmer, Kathy, 187
Palmer, Laurent Arthur, 89, 214, 215
Palmer, Marie Elise, 89, 214, 215
Palmer, Pam, 187
Palmer, Robert, 185, 187
Palmer, Shirley Dean, 185, 187

Paluda, Irene Lora, 174
Pappas, Jennel Marie, 346
Pappas, Theodore Nicholas, 346
Paprocki, C. S., 79
Paprocki, Carol C., xxiv
Paprocki, Carol Susan, 91
Paprocki, Carole Candace, 81
Paprocki, Carole, 79
Paprocki, Christina Maria, 81
Paprocki, Diane Leslie, 81
Paprocki, Jeffrey Paul, 81
Paprocki, Jozef W., 81
Paprocki, Karyn Anne, 81
Paprocki, Katarzyna, 81
Paprocki, Paul Patrick, 81
Paprocki, Stan J., Mrs., 79
Paprocki, Stan John, 81
Parcell, Malcolm, 396
Park, Benjamin F., 181
Park, Betty Pittman, 329
Park, Joseph, 180
Park, KathleenWilma, 187
Park, Susan, 224
Park, William, 180
Parkam, Hilda Marie, 177
Parke, B. F., 186
Parke, Donald Emerson, 30
Parke, Donald, 186
Parke, Elsie L., 30
Parke, Emma, 186
Parke, Erma Eileen, 30
Parke, Ertie Leona, 30
Parke, Frances, 186
Parke, Gerald Paul, 30
Parke, H. B., 189
Parke, Harold L., 186
Parke, Harold Ralph, 30
Parke, Harry B., 186
Parke, Harvey B., 30, 186
Parke, Heiland, 186
Parke, Marian, 30, 186
Parke, Perry, 186
Parke, Ruth, 30, 186
Parker, George E., 81
Parker, Glen, 49
Parker, Iris Rebecca, 39
Parker, Margaret Edythe, 81
Parker, Mary June, 74
Parker, Sarah, 118, 119, 120
Parker, Shirley Ann, 48, 49
Parker, Willis Allen, 39
Parkhurst, Amanda, 121
Parkhurst, Kristin Gaye, 121

Phillips, William James, 244
Phipps, Adam Duane, 48
Phipps, Bruce, 48
Phipps, Christopher Duane, 48
Phipps, Judith Ann, 48
Phipps, Megan Denise, 48
Phipps, Tracy Maureen, 48
Piatt, Comilla Dawn, 330
Piatt, Derrick Stephen, 330
Piatt, Sarah, 26
Piatt, Susan, 268
Piazzi, Eva Marie, 261
Piazzi, James "Jamie," 261
Piazzi, James, 261
Piazzi, Michelle, 261
Pickel, Martha, 307, 310
Pickerell, Opal, 81
Pierce, Brenda Dean, 188
Pierce, Michael, 188
Pierce, Vivian, 123
Pierse, Jason, 188
Pierson, James, 263
Pierson, Sarah, 263
Pierson, Vincent, 263
Pierson, William, 263
Pindle, Susan, 56, 57, 64, 75, 76
Pinedana, Vivien, 256
Pines, Mattie, 114
Piper, Marilyn J., 198
Pipes, Henry, 15
Pipes, Mary, 15
Pitcher, Laura, 298
Pitcock, Alberta, 13
Pitcock, Bertha, 13
Pitcock, Brice, 13
Pitcock, Maria, 13
Pitcock, Owen, 13
Pitcock, Plezzy, 13
Pitcock, Ray, 13
Pitcock, William, 13
Pitman, Jane, 206
Pitt, Abraham, 304
Pittman, Bill, 329
Pittman, Charlene, 329
Pittman, Don, 329
Pittman, Jane, 206
Pittman, Jessie "Opal, 329
Pittman, Martha, 329
Pittman, Opal, 329
Pittman, Opal Lamp, 395
Pittman, Thomas A., 329
Pittman, William "Bill," 329
Placky, Penny, 190
Plantagenet, Elizabeth, xx

Plantagenet, Richard, xix
Plantagenet, Thomas, xx
Plaugher, Iva Joyce, 37, 199
Ploummer, Elizabeth, xxvi
Plummber, Robert, 333
Plummer, Darius, 333
Plummer, Elizabeth Yates, 9
Plummer, Elizabeth, xvii, xviii, xix, xxvi, xxviii, xxxiii, 1, 5, 7, 9, 10, 20, 21, 63, 100, 359, 456
Plummer, J. W., 46
Plummer, Margaret, xvii, xix, 10
Plummer, Mary, xvii, xix, 10
Plummer, Susanna, xvii, xix, 10
Plummer, Thomas, xvii, xix, 5, 7, 9, 10
Plummer, Thomas, Jr., 10
Plummer, William, 456
Plymire, Olive Kathryn, 263
Plymire, Ruth Laurella, 260
Podraza, Katarzyna, 81
Poe, Louise, 144
Poling, Della, 172
Polinsky, Catherine Louise, 175
Polinsky, Perry, 175
Polinsky, Richard, 175
Polinsky, Robert, 175
Polinsky, William, 175
Polk, Sharon Kay, 49
Pollard, Lizie, 97
Pollard, Sudie, 97
Pollock, Emma Jane, 245
Pollock, John L., 245
Pollock, Lucy Vaughn, 245
Poluda, Drew Louise, 174
Poluda, Irene Lois, 174
Polzay, Deborah Ann, 196
Pope, Elizabeth, 144
Pope, Spencer, 144
Porter, Amelia, 255
Porter, Annette Mae, 18
Porter, Annie Metcalfe, 312
Porter, Benjamin, 312
Porter, Bernice, 252
Porter, Carol Jean, 18
Porter, Charles, 16
Porter, David Edward, 18
Porter, Donald, 255
Porter, Eleanor Kay, 18
Porter, Emma Inghram, 16
Porter, Glenn Edward, 18

Porter, Henry Hobart, 312, 313
Porter, Jennie, 16
Porter, John, 252
Porter, Katherine, 16, 312
Porter, Katherine Delano, 312
Porter, King G., 87, 213
Porter, Lucy Holland, 18
Porter, Margaret Seton, 312, 313
Porter, Maria J., 172
Porter, Mary Belle, 252
Porter, Nancy Pricilla, 87
Porter, Nellie, 252
Porter, Priscilla, 213
Porter, Rebecca Seton, 312
Porter, Robert Hobart, 312, 313
Porter, Thomas, 16
Porter, William A., 16
Post, Mary Magdalen, 312
Post, Mary, 262, 263
Post, Wright, Dr., 312
Pottenger, Eleanor, 10, 21, 23, 83, 142, 148, 150, 203, 204, 228, 231, 235, 453, 461
Pottenger, Elizabeth, xxxviii, 83, 26, 143, 203, 204, 235, 457
Pottenger, Ellen, 236
Pottenger, Robert, 83, 203
Pottinger, Eleanor, 84, 142
Pottinger, Elizabeth, 23, 142
Pottinger, Robert, 142
Potts, Charlotte E., 102
Potts, J. C., 102
Potts, Margaret, 24
Potts, Tracy Maureen, 48
Pounds, Esther, 214
Powell, Joseph, 305
Powell, Lidelia "Lydia" Jane, 183
Powell, Lydia, 183, 189
Powell, Lydia Jane (Ledelia), 187
Powell, Nannie, 97
Powell, Samuel A., 335
Powell, Sarah, 97
Powell, William Billie, 97
Powers, Cassandra Holland, 12
Pratt, Darlene Faith, 262
Pratt, Florence Edna, 168
Priana, Jennifer Lynn, 192

Reese, Cynthia Annabel, 26
Reese, Doris Jean, 14
Reese, Earnest, 271
Reese, Elizabeth, 14
Reese, Helen, 271
Reese, Herman, 271
Reese, Ima, 271
Reese, Ionabelle "Ima," 271
Reese, Mark, 271
Reese, Mary Jane, 14
Reese, Mildred, 271
Reese, Nancy, 14
Reese, Nort, 14
Reese, Norte, 271
Reese, Norton, 26
Reese, Norton Earl "Norte,"
    Jr., 271
Reese, Norton Earl, Sr., 271
Reese, T. M., 250
Reese, Thomas, 261
Reese, Viola, 271
Reeves, Emma, 157, 209
Reeves, Jerry, M.D., 431
Reeves, Margaret, 208
Reichert, Leo Walter, 90,
    214
Reichert, Patricia "Patsy"
    Ruth, 90
Reichert, Patricia Ruth, 214
Reillo, Mary Collins, 213
Reilly, Hugh, 10
Reilly, Margaret, 10
Reintsma, Grace, 149
Remley, George, 263
Remley, James, 263
Remley, John, 263
Remley, Margaret, 263
Remley, Martha, 263
Remley, Mary, 263
Remley, Sarah, 263
Rempel, Freda, 126
Renaldi, Christina, 296
Rennick, Merrely, 174
Replogle, Eva L., 70
Replogle, Joseph W., 70
Replogle, Mary Ethel, 70
Replogle, Mary J., 70
Replogle, Nellie G., 70
Replogle, Samuel Mark, 70
Restoule, Cecille, 290
Reynolds, Alice, 343
Reynolds, Audrey June, 343
Reynolds, Baiba, 347
Reynolds, Barbara, 343
Reynolds, Barry Duane, 25,
    345, 421, 433, 436

Reynolds, Barry, 346,
    413, 434, 436, 439
Reynolds, Bonnie, 343
Reynolds, C. I., 266
Reynolds, Carl Henry, Jr.,
    343
Reynolds, Carl Reuben, 343
Reynolds, Carl, 341
Reynolds, Cathlyn Lee, 345
Reynolds, Cathy, 413
Reynolds,   Clarence
    "Roger," 343
Reynolds, Clarence Roger,
    343
Reynolds, Dan, 436, 439
Reynolds, Daniel, 413
Reynolds, Daniel Ralph, 25,
    345, 433, 434, 435
Reynolds, Dorothy, 343
Reynolds, Duane Reynolds,
    344
Reynolds, Edna Corbett,
    xxiii,   392,   393,
    44, 426, 438, 439, 440
Reynolds, Edna Louise, 24,
    25, 317, 343, 407, 411,
    412, 413
Reynolds, Edna Louise
    Corbett, xxvi, 324, 341,
    380, 413, 414, 417,
    432, 434
Reynolds, Elizabeth "Liz"
    Esther, 44, 45
Reynolds, Elizabeth, 341,
    342
Reynolds, Emily, 44
Reynolds, Emma, 343
Reynolds, Esther, 342
Reynolds, Folkmais, 438
Reynolds, Fred Hubert, 342
Reynolds, Fred Ray, 343
Reynolds, Fred, 341, 343
Reynolds, George, 44
Reynolds, George, Jr., 44
Reynolds, Gertrude Elaine,
    343
Reynolds, Harold Richard,
    343
Reynolds, Ian, 434, 440
Reynolds, Ian Jeffrey, 347
Reynolds, James Hubert,
    343
Reynolds, Jane, 44
Reynolds, Jeanette, 343
Reynolds, Jeff, 413, 434,
    438, 439, 440

Reynolds, Jeffrey, 440
Reynolds, Jeffrey Wayne,
    347
Reynolds, Jill Kanani, 346
Reynolds, Jill Peterson, 436
Reynolds, Job, 342
Reynolds, Joshua Robert,
    347
Reynolds, Laura Bischoff,
    434
Reynolds, Laura Lynn, 346
Reynolds, Leah Pusekar,
    440
Reynolds, Leah, 347, 413
Reynolds, Lela, 266
Reynolds, Liz, 44, 45
Reynolds, Louis, 44
Reynolds, Louise Corbett,
    421
Reynolds, Margaret, 44
Reynolds, Mark, 414
Reynolds, Mark Alan, 343
Reynolds, Mary Hobbs,
    342
Reynolds, Mary Kern, 438,
    440
Reynolds, Mary, 44, 347
Reynolds, MaryHobbs, 341
Reynolds, Matthew Davis,
    345
Reynolds, McKinley Duane,
    346
Reynolds, Melissa Brook,
    414
Reynolds, Mildred, 343
Reynolds, Nancy, 342
Reynolds, Nancy Ruth, 343
Reynolds, Neff J., Rev., 341,
    342
Reynolds, Nicholas Logan,
    345
Reynolds, Norita Rose, vi,
    344, 432
Reynolds, Norita Rose
    Sholly, 343, 421
Reynolds, Norita S., xxiv
Reynolds, Norita Sholly, 435
Reynolds, Norita, 324, 413,
    434
Reynolds, Patricia Jean, 343
Reynolds, Paul, 414
Reynolds, Ralph D., 25, 343
Reynolds, Ralph D., M.D.,
    vi, 317, 344, 414, 430,
    431, 432, 433, 434,
    435, 436

557

Rutter, Merril, 159
Rutter, Vivian, 159
Rutter, W. H., Mrs., xxxii
Rutter, Warren, 159
Rutter, William Herbert, 159
Ryan, Bonnie, 343
Ryan, Charity, xv, xxix, 21,
    204, 230, 458, 461
Ryan, Diane Marie, 185, 188
Ryan, Howard, 185, 187
Ryan, JoAn, 185, 188
Ryan, Judith Jo, 188
Ryan, Martin, 112
Ryan, Mildred Leona, 185,
    187
Ryan, Robert Dean, 185, 188
Ryan, Robert Dean, Jr., 188
Ryan, Sean, 343
Ryan, Stephanie Ann, 188
Ryan, Vickie Lynn, 188
Ryan,Shad Justin, 188
Ryman, My, x
Ryman, Richard, x

— S —

Sack, Joseph, Col., 272
Sacks, Anne, 313
Sacks, George, 313
Sacksd, Anne Ijams, xxviii
Sagen, Ida R., 71
Sagen, Ida Rebecca, 72
Saguin, Rose, 298
Sailor, Clement Laird, 288
Sailor, Emma Frances, 288
Sailor, Flora Blanche, 288
Sailor, Hettie May, 288
Sailor, Laura Elizabeth, 288
Sailor, Luella Irene, 288
Sailor, Martin V., 288
Sailor, Mary Lillian, 288
Sailor, Sarah Ann, 288
Sailor, Walter Edmund, 288
Sain, Andrew, 96
Sain, James E., 96
Sain, Mary "Mollie," 96
Sain, Mollie, 96
Salloway, Anthony, 10
Salloway, Martha, 10
Salt, George W., 44
Salt, Ruth, 44
Salvaggi, Jamie S., 257
Sammons, Elizabeth, 17
Sammons, Gordon, 17
Sammons, James Jones, 17
Sammons, Katherine, 17

Sammons, Margaret, 17
Sampf, Katherine, 216
Sampson, Mary E., 267
Sampson, Vern, 267
Samson, Amy Louise, 259
Samson, David Ashley, 259
Samson, Erin Elaine, 259
Samson, Laura Elizabeth,
    259
Samson, Nancy Louise, 259
Sanders, Charlotte, 223, 224
Sanders, Eleanor, 228
Sanders, Eleanor "Nellie,"
    152
Sanders, Elsie, 172
Sanders, Hannah, 80
Sanders, Jacob, 80
Sanders, Mary M., 79
Sanders, Mary M. "Polly,"
    80
Sanders, Nellie, 152
Sanders, Polly, 80
Sanders, Richard, 223, 224
Sanders, Samuel, 152
Sands, Debora, 182
Sands, Deborah, 38
Sands, Oscar, 38, 182
Sanford, Laura Lynn, 188
Sanford, Raymond Charles,
    188
Sanks, Abner D., 138
Sanks, Ann Florence, 138
Sanks, Ann, 138, 459
Sanks, Anna, 138
Sanks, Anna P., 138
Sanks, Anne, 136
Sanks, Caroline, 138
Sanks, Eliza, 138
Sanks, Elizabeth, 138
Sanks, Florence Ann, 138
Sanks, George, 136, 138,
    459
Sanks, Horatio, 138
Sanks, James, 138
Sanks, Jane, 138
Sanks, Jemima Welsh, 138
Sanks, John W., 138
Sanks, Joseph, 138
Sanks, Mary, 138
Sanks, Plummer Ijams, 138
Sanks, Rebecca, 138
Sanks, Ruth, 138
Sanks, Ruth Elizabeth, 138
Sanks, Sallie, 138
Sanks, Wilbur, 138
Sapington, Frances, 7

Saporita, Theresa, 348
Sappington, Jane, 44
Sappington, Phillip, 44
Sarah, Elizabeth, 152, 153
Sares, Roy, 128
Sargeant, John, 24
Sargeant, Patience, 24
Sargent, Allison Drummond,
    314
Sargent, Ellen, 24
Sargent, Helen Margaret,
    260, 261
Sargent, Jeremiah, 24
Sargent, John, 24
Sargent, Katharine, 314
Sargent, Leona M., 261
Sargent, Margaret, 24
Sargent, Mary, 24
Sargent, Melvin L., 261
Sargent, Prudence, 24
Sargent, Thomas, 314
Sargent, William, 314
Sarno, Kelly, 199
Sato, Carol Sue, 14
Sauers, Linda, 252
Saulsberry, Rhoney Ray, 29
Saulsberry, Valeria Eileen,
    29
Saunders, Caroline, 156
Saunders, Eleanor, 152, 156,
    228
Saunders, Eleanor "Nellie,"
    156
Saunders, Harry Olney, 156
Saunders, Ida Mae, 156
Saunders, James, 156
Saunders, John Iams, 178
Saunders, Justice M., 156
Saunders, Luvinia, 156
Saunders, Mary Margaret,
    178
Saunders, Melvern H., 156
Saunders, Nancy E., 156
Saunders, Nellie, 156
Saunders, Parmelia Almeda,
    156
Saunders, Reuben, 156
Saunders, Robert Byron, 178
Saunders, Sam, 228
Saunders, Samuel, 156
Saunders, Samuel C., 156
Saunders, Sarah Elsie, 178
Saunders, Sarah Jane, 156
Saunders, Semantha, 156
Saunders, Silas, 156
Saunders, Warren, 156

Saunders, Willa, 178
Saunders, William B., 156
Saunders, William H., 178
Saunders, Wylie, 156
Sayers, Grace, 15
Scales, Caroline, 320, 323, 325,446, 447
Scales, Catherine, 320
Scales, Elizabeth, 323, 325
Scales, Nancy, 323, 325
Scales, Thomas, 323, 325
Scandretti, Bernice, 265
Scandretti, Lucinda, 265
Scandretti, Lulu, 265
Scandretti, Milton, 265
Scandretti, W. R. 265
Scevat, Hannah C., 150
Schereck, Susan Jane, 89
Schereck, Thomas, 89
Scherick, Margaret, 151
Scherick, Oranz, 151
Schidler, Mary, 225
Schlichter, Mary Linda, 72
Schlichter, Megan L., 72
Schlichter, Roger L., III, 72
Schlichter, Roger L., Jr., 72
Schloesser, James F., 228
Schmader, Edward, 314
Schmader, J. Peter, 314
Schmader, Rachel Lee, 314
Schmader, Samuel Drummond, 314
Schmit, Dennis, 150
Schmit, Elizabeth, 150
Schmitt, Dennis, 142
Schmitt, Elizabeth, 142
Scholl, Alice Carey, 72
Scholl, George F., 72
Scholl, Penrose, 72
Scholl, Ward, 72
Schoonover, Ruby, 225
Schott, Clarence George, 294
Schott, Helen R., 294
Schott, Marge, 294
Schott, Nicholas, 294
Schott, Pearl Margaret, 294
Schott, Philomena, 294
Schrock, Louis?, 72
Schuck, Ruth Lippencott, 13
Schultz, Carin, 48
Schultz, Karl, 216
Schultz, Marie, 216
Schultz, Myra, 207
Schultz, Rebecca Marie, 216, 220

Schutz, O., Mrs., 326
Schwartz, Alesha Ann, 174
Schwartz, Bernice Cordelia, 82, 189
Schwartz, Cordelia Bernice, 31, 188
Schwartz, Fidel, 82
Schwartz, Jack, 82
Schwartz, Janice Lynn, 189
Schwartz, Janice Lynne, 82
Schwartz, John, 188
Schwartz, John "Jack" Charles, 82
Schwartz, John C., 82, 189
Schwartz, John Casimer, 82
Schwartz, John Casimir, 189
Schwartz, John Charles, 31, 188
Schwartz, Julia Rose, 189
Schwartz, Julia Rose, 82
Schwartz, Loretta Monica, 182
Schwartz, Mary Elizabeth, 82, 189
Schwartz, Monica, 82
Schwear, Elizabeth, 213
Schwieger, Marie, 216
Scott, Absalom, 39, 179
Scott, Alice, 62, 67
Scott, Alice Louise, 173
Scott, Allen Grover, 172
Scott, Amanda, 173, 179
Scott, Arthur, 172
Scott, Benjamin H., 93
Scott, Bertha Viola, 86
Scott, Betty "Mary," 173
Scott, Betty Jane, 173
Scott, Billy Jo, 173
Scott, Bobby Jo, 173
Scott, Caroline G., 84
Scott, Charles, 86, 151
Scott, Charlotte, 173
Scott, Claude, 173
Scott, Clell, 151
Scott, Deborah A., 38
Scott, Debra Ann, 179
Scott, Dennis, 86, 151
Scott, Duck, 172
Scott, Eda, 179
Scott, Edell, 86
Scott, Effie, 179
Scott, Eleanor, 39, 179
Scott, Elias, 86, 87, 212
Scott, Elizabeth, 93
Scott, Elizabeth Jane, 39, 179

Scott, Ellis, 213
Scott, Elsie May, 172
Scott, Emily, 44
Scott, Emma, 173
Scott, Emma "Duck," 172
Scott, Flora, 86, 151
Scott, George, 173, 179
Scott, Gertrude, 172
Scott, Gladys June, 268
Scott, Gregory Wayne, 173
Scott, Harold, 172
Scott, Harriet, 86, 87, 212, 213
Scott, Helen M., 13
Scott, Henry, 44
Scott, Hiram, 86, 151, 212, 213
Scott, James Claude, 173
Scott, James Edward, 173
Scott, James, 173
Scott, Jane, 179
Scott, John Vance, 84
Scott, John, Jr., 212
Scott, Linda, 173
Scott, Lloyd Iams, 172
Scott, Marcia, 87
Scott, Margaret Miller, 84
Scott, Margaret, 14
Scott, Maria H., 85
Scott, Maria, 151, 212, 213
Scott, Mariah, 87, 151, 212, 213
Scott, Martha L., 154
Scott, Mary, 86, 151, 173, 212, 402
Scott, Mary E., 147
Scott, Mary Jane, 173, 213
Scott, Mary A., 179
Scott, Mattie, 213
Scott, Mildred Amanda, 173
Scott, Mildred, 172, 173
Scott, Minnie, 179
Scott, Nancy Eli, 86
Scott, Nancy Elizabeth, 86
Scott, Nancy, 213
Scott, Nell, 128
Scott, Patricia, 120
Scott, Raymond W., 154
Scott, Roger, 120
Scott, Samuel, 179
Scott, Sarah, 179, 213
Scott, Susan, 212
Scott, Susanna, 213
Scott, Thomas Iams, 86
Scott, Thomas, 151, 179, 213

Shaw, Mary Emma, 126
Shaw, Pauline, 198
Shaw, Richard Cowan, M.D., 126
Shawler, Patricia Elaine, 34
Shearin, Mary, 167
Sheats, Barbara Louise, 72
Sheats, Bruce, 72
Sheets, Benjamin, 298
Sheets, Cathryn Elaine "Kati," 298
Sheets, Clair, 298
Sheets, Kati, 298
Sheets, Merledean Mildred, 298
Sheets, Rebecca Iams,298
Sheets, Trudy Kimberly, 252
Sheets, Victoria Faye "Viki," 298
Sheldon, Effie Mabel, 35
Shell, Cecelia Sue, 255
Shell, Kevin Clark, 255
Shelly, Wendy Jo, 75
Shenefield, Judy, 291
Shepard, Elizabeth, 287
Shepard, George, 287
Shepherd, Gail Cynthia, 232
Shepherd, Jack Harlow, 232
Shepherd, Phyllis Regina, 232
Shepler, Susan, 226
Sherrard, Robert, 40
Sherrits, Mayme Tice, 200
Sherwin, Mary, 167
Sherwin, Mary, 167
Shidler, Anna Virginia, 267
Shidler, Catherine Luzarbo, 271
Shidler, Daisy, 266
Shidler, Daniel, 266
Shidler, David, 262
Shidler, Dorothy Martin, 266
Shidler, Edith, 266
Shidler, Elizabeth, 274
Shidler, J. Walter, 266
Shidler, Jacob, 266, 274
Shidler, John, 262
Shidler, Joseph William, 266
Shidler, Katherine, 26, 266
Shidler, Katherine L., 274
Shidler, Katherine Luzarbo, 275
Shidler, Lenore, 266
Shidler, Lenore Seaman, 267
Shidler, Leroy, 266

Shidler, Leroy Beatty, 267
Shidler, Marjorie Mae, 266, 267
Shidler, Mary, xxxvii, 21, 27, 142, 148, 203, 205, 220, 225, 262, 267, 461
Shidler, Mildred, 267
Shidler, Nancy, 262
Shidler, Nancy Martin, 279
Shidler, Ruth, 267
Shidler, Sarah, 262, 266
Shidler, Sarah Katheryn, 267
Shidler, Susannah, 262
Shidler, Thomas, 262
Shidler, Virginia, 266
Shiplett, Delaney, 109, 115
Shiplett, Rebecca, 109, 111, 115
Shipley, Kathryn, xiv, xxiv, 150, 164, 356
Shipman, Jesse, 29
Shipman, Julia Myrtle, 29
Shipman, Sarah, 29
Shircliff, Julia M., 309
Shircliff, Sandra Rae, 309
Shirk, Eva "Evie" Sarah, 260
Shirk, Evie "Eva" Sarah, 261
Shirk, Margaret, 172
Shockey, Charlotte Margaret, 336
Shockley, Cora, 336
Shockley, Henry, 336
Shoemaker, Gretchen Emma, 220
Sholly, Agatha Ann, 344
Sholly, Brian Edward, 344
Sholly, Bruce Rodrick, 344
Sholly, Clarence Anthony, 343
Sholly, Clarence Anthony "Tony," 344
Sholly, Cletus Edward, 344
Sholly, David Lee, 344
Sholly, Deborah Kathryn, 343
Sholly, Denise Marie, 344
Sholly, Doris "Jean," 344
Sholly, Duane Anthony, 344
Sholly, Edna May, 344
Sholly, Edward Lee, 343
Sholly, Eileen, 343
Sholly, Harry B., 343
Sholly, Helen Elizabeth, 344
Sholly, Jean, 344

Sholly, Jean Marie, 344
Sholly, Jerome Francis, 344
Sholly, Karen Ann, 344
Sholly, KathleenTheresa, 344
Sholly, Kenneth Francis, 344
Sholly, Kevin Francis, 344
Sholly, Louis Patrick, 343
Sholly, Maureen Annette, 344
Sholly, Melissa Jean, 344
Sholly, Michael James, 343
Sholly, Norita Rose, vi, 343, 344, 432
Sholly, Patricia Ann, 344
Sholly, Phyllis Katherine, 344
Sholly, Richard Joseph, 344
Sholly, Robert John, 344
Sholly, Rosemary Elizabeth, 344
Sholly, Roxanne Kay, 343
Sholly, Sandia Marie, 344
Sholly, Sharon Lee, 344
Sholly, Stella Rose, 343
Sholly, Stella, 343
Sholly, Tony, 344
Sholly, Vincent George, 343
Sholly, Zelma Mae, 344
Shook Aaron Wayne, 255
Shook, Adam, 254
Shook, Andrew "Adam" Michael, 254
Shook, Andrew Michael, 254
Shook, Anissa Marie, 254
Shook, Carol Ann, 254
Shook, Carol Jean, 254
Shook, Clarence William, 253
Shook, Cornia Lynn, 253
Shook, Debra Marie, 254
Shook, Delmar Lee, 254
Shook, Diane Elizabeth, 254
Shook, Dianna Jo, 254
Shook, Edna Blanche, 252, 253
Shook, Elizabeth, 150
Shook, Ethel Eileen, 254
Shook, Gary Evans Shook, 253
Shook, Gary William, 253
Shook, George Washington, 150
Shook, Hannah C., 150
Shook, Hope Ann, 254

564

Shook, Jeremi Robert, 253
Shook, Joan Columbia, 253
Shook, Jody Lynn, 254
Shook, John, 150
Shook, John Michael, 254
Shook, John Robert, 254
Shook, Joy Leiah, 255
Shook, Justin William, 253
Shook, Lorie Lynn, 254
Shook, Mabel Lucille, 254
Shook, Margaret Jane, 254
Shook, Mark William, 254
Shook, Martha Elizabeth, 253
Shook, Matthew Ray, 254
Shook, Michael Ray, 253
Shook, Michelle, 254
Shook, Mimi Louise, 254
Shook, Nancy Jane, 254
Shook, Natalie Rose, 254
Shook, Nellie Marie, 254
Shook, Opal Elaine, 254
Shook, Paul Craig, 254
Shook, Paul Robert, 255
Shook, Paul Russell, 254
Shook, Philip Wayne, 254
Shook, Randy Lee, 254
Shook, Robert Paul, 255
Shook, Robin Lea, 254
Shook, Sarah Jean, 254
Shook, Shirley Ann, 254
Shook, Thomas Franklin, 150
Shook, Virginia Grace, 253
Shook, William Howard, 252, 253, 255
Shook, Wilma Jean, 254
Shoots, Charles Ezra, 219
Shoots, Kathryn Louise, 219
Shortz, Neal O., 387
Shrider, C., 46
Shrider, Donald L., 38, 183
Shrider, Helen Olive, 38, 183
Shriver, Adam, 13, 15
Shriver, Allen William, 14
Shriver, Cassandra, 15
Shriver, Cassie Sarah, 14
Shriver, Cecil Donley, 14
Shriver, Charles Ray, 14
Shriver, Delilah, 13, 15
Shriver, Edward Paul, 14
Shriver, Elijah, 15
Shriver, Eliza, 15
Shriver, Elizabeth Gordon, 15

Shriver, Isaac, 13
Shriver, Jane, 15
Shriver, John, 14
Shriver, Lucy, 13
Shriver, Margaret, 15
Shriver, Mark Gordon, 15
Shriver, Martha, 15
Shriver, Mary, 15
Shriver, Michael, 15
Shriver, Rachel, 15
Shriver, Rose, 14
Shriver, Russell James, 14
Shriver, Solomon, 15
Shriver, Susannah, 15
Shrontz, Katherine, 246
Shultz, Eliza, 15
Shultz, Hannah, 16
Shultz, Sadie Ocie, 16
Shumate, Bertha Hazel, 182
Shumate, Charles Alfred, 182
Shuster, John, 190
Shuster, John Horace, 190
Shuster, Martha, 190
Shuster, Martha Myrtle "Mertie," 190
Shuster, Mertie, 190
Shuster, Myrtle, 195
Sialega, Mali, 123
Sialega, Peniamina, 123
Sialega, Salina, 123
Sialega, Shelli, 123
Sider, Tara Ann, 218
Sidler, Mary, 453
Sidwell, Esther, 342
Siebert, Henry J., 42
Siferd, Estella May, 191, 200
Siferd, Ethel, 191, 200
Siferd, Noah, 191, 200
Sikes, Daisy, 175
Silbaugh, Linda, 320
Silvens, Charles Barry, 168
Silvens, Clarence Milliken, 168
Silvens, Craig Conner, 168
Silvens, Hilda, Iams, 168
Simms, Rachel, 261
Simms, Stuart, 261
Simpson, Alison Ann, 199
Simpson, Ann, 44
Simpson, Catherine Ann, 257
Simpson, Charity, 174
Simpson, Curtis Bradford, 199
Simpson, Edna Mae, 257

Simpson, Fred Andrew, 257
Simpson, Kathleen Ann, 199
Simpson, Kenneth, 174
Simpson, Margaret Bell, 87, 213, 214
Simpson, Meghan Michelle, 199
Sims, Harriet, 109
Singmaster, Fannie, 226
Singmaster, Franklin, 226
Singmaster, Nancy, 226
Sink, John, 96
Sinnett, Abel, 244
Sinnett, Belinda, 244
Sipple, Emma, 139
Sipple, William, 139
Sistter, Band B., 79
Skidmore, Bernard, 330
Skidmore, Carien Emma, 330
Skidmore, Coreine, 330
Skidmore, Corene Emma, 330
Skrable, Edna, 35
Skrable, James, 35
Skrable, Mary Lou, 35
Skyrmes, Albert, 267
Skyrmes, Dorothy Martin, 267
Slagle, Sarah, 110, 116
Slate, Annabelle, 297
Slate, Harold, 297
Slaugherhaupt, Nancy, 15
Slaughter, David F., 65
Slaughter, David Forest, 63
Slaughter, David Forrestt, 65
Slaughter, Dawn Marie, 63, 65
Slaughter, Francine Benita, 63, 65
Sleeper, Donald C., 234
Sleeper, Jodi Jane, 234
Sloan, Isabel, 305
Sloan, Rachel, 305, 306
Small, Andrew J., 111
Small, Arthur J., 109, 115
Small, Edward, 109
Small, Edward F., 109
Small, Mary Mathilda, 109
Small, Mary Matilda, 111, 115
Small, Otho A., 109
Small, Washington L., 109
Smith, A. Mack, 156
Smith, Abraham, 83, 85, 245
Smith, Alfreda, 245

Spears, Sheila, 293
Spears, William, 293
Spears, Zail E., 293
Spencer, Elva, 307, 310
Spencer, James, 267
Spencer, Marjorie Jean, 267
Spencer, Randall James, 267
Spencer, Susan P., 193
Spencer, William, 307, 310
Spiker, Verda Mae, 86
Spindler, David Dee, 269
Spindler, NancyJo, 269
Spindler, Regan Dee, 269
Spitznogle, Margaret Jean, 261
Spitznogle, Gar, 261
Spitznogle, Ola B., 261
Spohn, Mae, 216
Spooner, Susie, 265
Spragg, Carl, 14
Spragg, Elizabeth, 167, 168
Spragg, Ethel, 14
Spragg, Frances, 16
Spragg, Joann, 14
Spragg, Kathryn, 16
Sprigg, Mary, 133
Sprigg, Thomas, Col., 133
Springer, Catherine, 121
Springer, Charlotte, 125
Springer, Isaac, 125
Springer, Jacob, 124
Sproat, Charlotte, 14
Sproat, Clara, 15
Sprowls, Mabel, 171
Sprowls, Ruby, 89
Spruance, Benjamin, 143, 204
Spruance, Rachel, 143, 204
Spurrier, Joseph, 210
Spurrier, Mary, 158
Spurrier, Mary "May" E., 211
Spurrier, May, 211
Spurrier, May E., 210
Spurrier, William., Lt., 281
Squires, Emma Prunty Grimm, 335
Squires, M. Mead, 335
Squires, Winfred, 335
Stackey, Susan, 127
Stafford, Mary, xix
Staggers, Carolyn Rae, 20
Staggers, Carolyn, 20
Staggers, David Lee, 20
Staggers, Donna Joe, 20
Staggers, Herbert R., 20

Staggers, Janice, 20
Staggers, Melissa Lynn, 20
Staggers, Peggy Ann, 20
Staggers, Ralph Lynn, 20
Staggers, Richard H., 20
Staggers, Sarah Sue, 20
Stagnal, Mary M., 152
Staley, Daniel Ray, 199
Staley, Donald G., 37
Staley, Gregory Lynn, 199
Staley, Gretchen Sue, 199
Staley, Jerid Ray, 199
Staley, Linda Sue, 37, 199
Staley, Rhonda Sue, 199
Staley, Ronald Gene, 199
Stallings, Betty M., 309
Stanley, Donald Lee, 270
Stanley, Freda, 259
Stanley, Marian Jeanne, 270
Stansby, Anne, 10
Stansby, John, Dr., 10
Stansell, Charles, 14
Stansell, Lydia, 14
Stark, C., 120
Stark, Daniel, 120
Stark, Elizabeth, 120
Stark, Greg, 120
Stark, Harwood M., 120
Stark, Jean, 120
Stark, Jeff, 120
Stark, Jennifer, 120
Stark, Kelly, 120
Stark, Larry, 120
Stark, Mabel, xxxii, 119, 120, 424
Stark, Mary, 120
Stark, Michael, 120
Stark, Nola N., 120
Stark, Peggy, 120
Stark, Richard, 120
Stark, Richard, Jr., 120
Stark, S. H., xxxii, 119, 120
Stark, Tyler, 120
Starkey, Donald Lee, 270
Starkey, Jeanne K., xxiii
Starkey, Jennifer Lynn, 270
Starkey, Marian Jeanne, 270
Starkey, Marian Jeanne Kilmer, 269, 279
Stauffer, Christy Ann, 251
Stauffer, Duane, 251
Stauffer, Tharissa Rae, 251
Steas, Burdick, 177
Steas, Carolyn Burdick, 177
Steas, Ellen, 177
Steel, Jane, 177

Steele, Annie Laura, 273
Steele, Annie Laura "Laurri," 273
Steele, Laura, 26, 271
Stein, Hazel, 229
Stein, Robert, 229
Steinberger, Marshall, 73
Steinberger, Nancy, 73
Steinberger, Steven, 73
Steinberger, Treva Diane, 73
Steiner, Amos, 342
Steiner, Esther, 295
Steiner, Leanna Reynolds, 341
Steiner, Mary C., 37
Steiner, Mary Christine, 199
Steiner, Sarah Leanna, 342
Stenhouse, Margaret Alice, 268
Stenhouse, Ruth, 99
Stephans, Emma, 16
Stephen, Almeda, 249
Stephen, Almeda Elizabeth, 249
Stephen, Conchetta, 249
Stephen, Conchetta Delight, 249
Stephen, Glenna, 249
Stephen, Jesse Madison, 249
Stephen, Lewis Hedrick, 249
Stephen, Louise, 249
Stephen, Louise Helen, 249
Stephen, Lucinda, 249
Stephen, Lyman Cleveland, 249
Stephen, Lyman, 249
Stephen, Norma, 249
Stephen, Richard Frederick, 249
Stephen, Richard, 249
Stephen, Samuel C., 249
Stephenson, Alan, 122
Stephenson, Barbara W., 121, 122
Stephenson, Bud, 345
Stephenson, Cathlyn Lee, 345
Stephenson, Dorie, 345
Stephenson, Mark, 122
Stern, Amy A., 60
Stern, Amy Anderson, 66
Stern, Eleanor B., 60
Stern, Eleanor Byrd, 66
Stern, Ivy Markle, 60, 66
Stern, Jane B., 66
Stern, Mary M., 60

568

571

Thomas, Albert, Jr., 173
Thomas, Alonzo, 147
Thomas, Ann Marie, 295
Thomas, Basil, 147
Thomas, Blanche, xxxiii
Thomas, Corinne "Cosa," 128
Thomas, Corinne Mae "Cosa," 129
Thomas, Cosa, 128, 129
Thomas, Diane Marie, 173
Thomas, Dorothy, 147
Thomas, Dorothy Lee, 147
Thomas, Elvie, 147
Thomas, Emma, 173
Thomas, Ethel, 110
Thomas, Florence, 147
Thomas, Floyd, Jr., 50
Thomas, Geraldine, 215
Thomas, Helen Marie, 173
Thomas, James William, 173
Thomas, Janet, 173
Thomas, Jeane Anne, 173
Thomas, Jerry, 215
Thomas, Jessie G., 17
Thomas, John Robert, 173
Thomas, John Wesley, 147
Thomas, Joseph Kenneth, 295
Thomas, Karen, 173
Thomas, Lawrence, 20
Thomas, Lois, 20
Thomas, Lowell, 153
Thomas, Mae, 147
Thomas, Marcia Marie, 173
Thomas, Marie Ann, 295
Thomas, Marilyn, 173
Thomas, Martha, 20
Thomas, Mary "Molly" Celestine, 147
Thomas, Mildred, 59, 68
Thomas, Molly, 147
Thomas, Rebecca Gail, 50
Thomas, Rebecca Susan, 173
Thomas, Robert Harlan, 173
Thomas, Robert Joseph, 173
Thomas, Virginia Rose, 296
Thomas, Susan, 296
Thompson, Alfred Alonzo "Lou," 128
Thompson, Amanda Louella, 128
Thompson, Bessie, 127, 128

Thompson, Della Blanche, 34
Thompson, Dorothy, 19
Thompson, Earnest, 14
Thompson, Floyd, 14
Thompson, John, 388
Thompson, John Wilbur, 19
Thompson, Loretta Angelia, 80
Thompson, Lou, 128
Thompson, Lucy, 14
Thompson, Margaret, 14
Thompson, Mary, 97, 319
Thompson, Mary Elizabeth "Bessie," 127, 128
Thompson, Nancy, 19
Thompson, Neta Mae, 198
Thompson, Pauline, 198
Thompson, Perry, 14
Thompson, Phebe Jane, 27
Thompson, Phoebe Jane, 223, 224
Thompson, Phoebe June, 236
Thompson, Rose, 128
Thompson, Walter, 198
Thompson, William A., 80
Thonpson, Lonnie, 128
Thorndike, Mary Thompson, 126
Thornton, Celeste, 171
Thorp, Israel, Rev., 319
Thorpe, Sabia Jane, 97
Throckmorton, Anna Bessie, 171
Throckmorton, Anna Brown, 171
Throckmorton, Carrie, 167
Throckmorton, Celesta Jane, 171
Throckmorton, Charles Loudas S., 171
Throckmorton, Charles, 171
Throckmorton, Elizabeth Caroline, 171
Throckmorton, Florence May, 171
Throckmorton, Geraldine, 171
Throckmorton, Guy Reese, 171
Throckmorton, Harland S., 171
Throckmorton, James B., 171

Throckmorton, James R., 167
Throckmorton, James T. H., 171
Throckmorton, Jennie, 171
Throckmorton, John, 171
Throckmorton, Mabel, 171
Throckmorton, Marcia, 171
Throckmorton, Marcia M., 171
Throckmorton, Margaret, 171
Throckmorton, Marjorie, 171
Throckmorton, Mary Derressa, 171
Throckmorton, Nancy, 171
Throckmorton, Nancy Clarissa, 171
Throckmorton, Nancy Clarissa "Carrie," 167
Throckmorton, Pearl, 171
Throckmorton, Ray Iams, 171
Throckmorton, Ray Iams, II, 171
Throckmorton, Rebecca, 171
Throckmorton, Samuel, 171
Throckmorton, Sarah, 171
Throckmorton, Sarah I., 169
Tiburtius, Marly, 122, 123
Tice, Janetta, 155
Tiderman, Margaret, 214
Tinsman, Mariah, 264
Tippie, James, 182
Tippie, James, 38
Tippie, Rebecca, 38, 182
Titus, Margaret, 216
Tkasch, Walter, xvii
Todd, Kathleen, 332
Todd, Sadie, 342
Toland, Andrew, 178
Toland, Annabelle, 251
Toland, Bernice, 251
Toland, Clarence, 251
Toland, E. B., 190
Toland, Elizabeth, 190
Toland, Erasmus B., 37, 190
Toland, Erasmus "E.B.," 178
Toland, Frank, 251
Toland, Franklin, 251
Toland, Gertie, 250
Toland, Henry Martin, 190
Toland, Howard, 251
Toland, John W., 190

573

Vining, John Middleton, Sen., 311
Voght, Edith Caroline, 51
Volka, Alice, 253
Volkert, Kelly R., 299
Von Hedeman, Edna Mae, 171
Voorhees, Delilah, 26, 274
Voorhees, Homer, 274
Voorhees, Peter, 26, 274
Voorhes, Alonzo, 275
Voorhes, Andrew, 270, 274
Voorhes, Charles, 274
Voorhes, Clarence, 274
Voorhes, Claude, 274
Voorhes, Clyde, 270, 274
Voorhes, Clyde, Jr., 274
Voorhes, Daisy, 274
Voorhes, Delilah, 270
Voorhes, Della, 274
Voorhes, DeLoyd, 274
Voorhes, Dessie, 274
Voorhes, Francis Earl, 274
Voorhes, Harry Stephen, 274
Voorhes, Harry, 270, 275
Voorhes, Homer, 270
Voorhes, Jennie, 274
Voorhes, Joseph, 275
Voorhes, Kenneth, 274
Voorhes, Lenora, 274
Voorhes, Louise, 275
Voorhes, Lucy May, 275
Voorhes, Lucy, 270, 274
Voorhes, Mamie, 274
Voorhes, Mamie McVey, 274
Voorhes, Martha, 266, 275
Voorhes, Mary, 274
Voorhes, Mary Hazel, 274
Voorhes, Myrtle, 274
Voorhes, Peter, 270
Voorhes, Reuben, 274
Voorhes, Roger, 274
Voorhes, Ruben, 270
Voorhes, Van, 266
Voorhes, Virginia, 274
Voorhes, William E., 270
Voorhes, William Elery, 274
Voorhes, William Elisha, 274

— W —

Wade, Ruth, 225
Wagers, Brenda Lynn, 177

Wagers, Charles Eugene, 177
Wagers, Todd Anthony, 177
Waggoner, Elsie May, 248
Waggoner, Walter, 248
Wagner, Louise, 338
Wagner, Mary Rebecca, 245
Wagner, Philip, 245
Waiveras, Charles, 262
Waiveras, Katie, 262
Waiveras, Rosella Iams, 262
Waiveris, John, 262
Waiveris, John W, 262
Waldegrave, Catherine, xix
Waldegrave, Edward, xix
Waldegrave, Frances, xix
Waldegrave, Nicholas, xix
Waldo, Inez, 121
Walker, Capt., 283
Walker, Diana Ruth, 258
Walker, George E., 127
Walker, Harold, 99
Walker, Harriet, 127
Walker, Louise Clementine, 102, 103
Walker, M. C., 102, 103
Walker, Nina Jean Lighthizer, 193
Walker, Peggy, 99
Walker, Rebecca, 117
Walker, Rose, 128
Walker, Rosetta "Rose," 127, 128
Walker, Stapleton, 67
Walker, Villerie, 67
Walker, Virginia Lee, 67
Walkinshaw, L. C., 279
Wall, Emma, 274
Wall, J. D., 98
Wall, Melinda, 147
Wallace, Bess, xxxix
Wallace, Elizabeth, 68
Wallace, Elizabeth Rachel, 59, 61
Wallace, Gary, 253
Wallace, June, 270
Wallace, Mary Ellen, 253
Waller, Robert James, 433
Wallis, Albert, Jr., 138
Wallis, Albert, Rev., 138
Wallis, Columbia, 138
Walls, Harold Neil, 309
Walls, Harold Neil, Jr., 309
Walls, Marilyn Jean, 309
Walls, Sandi Kay, 309
Walls, Susie Marie, 309

Walls, Teresa Jean, 309
Walls, William, Mrs., 98
Walters, Alice, 307, 310
Walters, Hezekiah, 307, 310
Walters, James, 293
Walters, Olive May, 293
Walters, Rachel A., 307, 310
Walton, Marcia, 182
Walton, Marcia "Mary," 180
Walton, Marcia "Mercy," 82
Walton, Marcia F. "Mercy," 178
Walton, Marcie, 165
Walton, Mary, 180
Walton, Mary E., 165
Walton, Mercia, 165
Walton, Mercia, 22, 27, 458
Walton, Mercy,178
Walton, Rebecca, 178
Walton, Thomas Daniel, 178
Wang, Martha Jane, 295
Ward, Aubrey William, 256
Ward, Elizabeth, 135
Ward, Karen Sue, 256
Ward, Levia R., 81
Ward, Lucy, 33
Ward, Margaret (Wolf), 321
Ward, Sarah, 266
Ward, Vickie Lee, 193
Wardell, Mary, 120
Warfield, Vachel, 21
Warlick, David Franklin, 100
Warlick, Dennis Clifton, 100
Warlick, Donald Emory, 100
Warlick, Norman, 100
Warlick, Rebecca Anne, 100
Warlick, Richard Dennis, 100
Warman, Stephen, 105
Warner, William, 110
Warren, Albert, 19
Warren, Austin Clark, 289
Warren, Bernard Miller, 161
Warren, Charity Jane, 289
Warren, Edward T., Jr., 19
Warren, Frederick, 19
Warren, Levi Gale, 161, 222
Warren, Martha Ellen, 161, 222
Warren, Sallie, 161, 222
Warren, Samuel, 161
Warren, Sara Leanne, 19
Washington, Bijou, 305
Washington, Brobdingniz, 305

576

577

Wetzel, Alice Ann, 75
Whalen, Berneda Mae, 197
Whaley, Barbara Ann, 177
Whaley, Coleen Amber, 177
Whaley, Delbert, 177
Whaley, Robert Keith, 177
Whaley, Vera, 177
Wheeler, Elizabeth, 161
Wheeler, Ellis, 288
Wheeler, Harold, 288
Wheeler, John, 288
Wheeler, Mary, 288
Wheeler, Mary Anne, 288
Wheeler, Minnie, 288
Wheeler, Ruth, 288
Whipkey, Evelyn, 19
Whisler, Elizabeth, 108
Whistler, Harriet, 107
Whistler, John, 107
Whitacre, Eva R. "Evy," 184, 187
Whitaker, Mary Jane, 249
White, Annabelle, 252
White, Betty Jo, 291
White, Beverly Ann, 19
White, Catherine, xix, 312
White, Cory, 199
White, Edna Phyllis, 38, 183
White, Elsie Leona, 275
White, Emil Ralph, 37, 199
White, Emily, 199
White, Frances, xvii, xix, 10
White, Gerald E., 38, 183
White, Hazel Lee, 62, 68
White, Irving, 59
White, J. Irving, 62
White, James Irving, 68
White, Jane, 15
White, Kelly, 199
White, LeRoy Glenn, 59, 62, 68
White, Lueata Eulalie, 35
White, Mary, 15
White, Michael Scott, 199
White, Moses, 252
White, Omer D., xxx
White, Ray Douglas, 19
White, Richard, xix
White, Samone Ellse, 199
White, Sarah Mildred, 59, 62, 68
White, Sharon Rae, 37, 199
White, Steven Craig, 199
White, Thomas, 15
White-Wright, Betty Jean, 68

White-Wright, Carmen Henrietta Cecile, 62
White-Wright, LeRoy Glenn, II, 62
White-Wright, LeRoy Glenn, Jr., 68
Whitehair, Rosanna, 333
Whitfield, Cora, 245
Whitfield, Ross, 245
Whiting, Joseph, 222
Whiting, Lucille, 109
Whiting, Nancy, 160, 161, 222
Whitlatch, Ara, 13
Whitlatch, Barnet, Rev., 13
Whitlatch, Margaret Maria, 17
Whitman, Dela, 147
Whitman, Elvie, 147
Whitman, Leo, 147
Whittier, Anna Neonetta Harvey "Lonetta," 169
Whittier, Lonetta, 169
Whittier, Thomas Davies, Rev., 169
Whittington, Elizabeth, 20
Wiener, Alexander, 123
Wiener, Amber, 123
Wiener, Darren, 123
Wiener, David, 123
Wiese, Henry W., 216, 220
Wiese, Hilda, 25
Wiese, Hilda Emma, 216, 217, 220
Wiese, Joashin, 216
Wiese, Katherine, 216
Wiese, Rebecca Marie, 216, 220
Wigglesworth, Sylvia Belden, 314
Wilcoxen, John, 132, 458
Wilcoxen, Rebecca, 132, 458
Wilcoxon, John, 130
Wilcoxon, Rebecca, 130
Wiley, Aurelia, 294
Wiley, Bertha "Ethel," 298
Wiley, Bruce, 298
Wiley, Charles, 158
Wiley, Ethel, 298
Wiley, Maggie, 298
Wiley, Minerva Jane, 158
Wiley, Aurelia, 299
Wilkins, LillyMay, 184, 187
Willard, Ruth, 168
Willett, Elizabeth, 142, 203

Willett, Rachel Maria, 22, 25, 457
Willett, Voltaire, 22, 25, 457
Willetts, Lydia, 211
Williams, Abraham, 157
Williams, Alice, xiv, xxxix, 223
Williams, Alice Iams, 160
Williams, Andrew, 207
Williams, Ann, 9
Williams, Anna, 93
Williams, Anne B., 11
Williams, Anne, xxvi, 100, 361, 362, 459
Williams, Anne Ijams, xxix
Williams, Ben, 147
Williams, Benjamin, 4, 94, 100
Williams, Caroline, 219
Williams, Charles G., 276
Williams, Comfort, 100
Williams, Daisy, 147
Williams, Eleanor, 133
Williams, Elizabeth, 27, 157, 158, 209
Williams, Elizabeth (Beck), 458
Williams, Elizabeth Beck, 109, 117, 18
Williams, Ethel Clesta, 29
Williams, Florence, 147
Williams, Henrietta Nettie, 127
Williams, Jane, 207
Williams, Jeremiah, x
Williams, Jerome, x
Williams, John Horter, 162
Williams, Joseph, 100, 105
Williams, Margaret, 94, 100
Williams, Mary, 20, 207, 213
Williams, Nelson, 219
Williams, Nettie, 127
Williams, Obadiah, 42
Williams, Olive, 113
Williams, Richard, 9, 11, 133, 359, 360, 459
Williams, Richard, III, 100
Williams, Richard, Jr., 9, 94, 100, 359, 360
Williams, Richard, Sr., 100
Williams, Roger, 171
Williams, Sarah, 117, 157
Williams, Sophia Sue, 276
Williams, Stockett, x, 20, 94, 100

578

Williams, Susan Gee, 253
Williams, Tiffany Bovier, 276
Williams, William, 117
Willis, Anne B., 11
Willis, Richard, 11
Willyerd, Almina Jane, 81
Wilson, Bernie May "Mae," 273
Wilson, Christena Mae, 49
Wilson, Doctor, 158
Wilson, Edward, 71
Wilson, Elizabeth, 288, 289
Wilson, Emma Jane, 328, 394
Wilson, Frances Lydia, 297
Wilson, I. M., 320
Wilson, J. M., 322
Wilson, Jacob, 285, 289, 318, 457
Wilson, James, 42
Wilson, Jessie, 158
Wilson, Joann Hanna, 13
Wilson, John, Rev., 319
Wilson, Joseph, 41, 109, 111, 115, 289
Wilson, Josephine, 99
Wilson, Laura L., 288
Wilson, Margaret Ann, 109, 111, 115
Wilson, O. Glenn, 273
Wilson, Pamela Ann, 273
Wilson, Rebecca, 289, 318, 457
Wilson, Rhoda M., 71
Wilson, Robert Glenn, 273
Wilson, Robinson, 289
Wilson, Sally, 41
Wilson, Samantha, 289
Wilson, Samuel, 285, 289
Wilson, Samuel J., 285
Wilson, Sarah, 158, 310, 289, 322
Wilson, Sarah Ann, 57, 60, 69, 78, 289
Wilson, Sarah Elizabeth, 289
Wilson, Virginia, 343
Wilson, Vivian, 198
Wiltsey, Brandy Lynn, 254
Wiltsey, Elizabeth Marie, 254
Wiltsey, Lee, 254
Wiltsey, Tracy Ann, 254
Wimer, Corrie Jean, 256
Windsor, Eleanor, xix

Wingfield, Bill, 332
Wingfield, Carol Parsons, 332
Wingfield, Pamela, 332
Winters, Delsea, 173
Winters, Florence, 173
Winters, George, 173
Winters, Homer, 173
Winters, Katherine, 173
Wise, Anna Helen, 19
Wise, Catherine, 231
Wise, Cheryl Renee, 257
Wise, Elizabeth, 274
Wise, Elizabeth Ann, 243
Wise, Joseph, 231
Wise, Lee W., 19
Wise, Margaret Iams, 154
Wise, Mary, 147, 311
Wise, Melissa Renee, 257
Wise, Morgan R., 231
Wise, Pamela, 231
Wise, Ronald Harry, 257
Wise, Sara Leanne, 19
Wisegarver, Edith, 126
Wisegarver, Edwin S., 126
Wisegarver, Ethlyn, 126
Wiseman, Rebecca, 108
Wiseman, William, 108
Wislander, Ethel Christine, 127
Wisser, Bruce, 129
Wisser, Carol Ann, 129
Witterman, Clarissa, 248
Witterman, Clarissa "Claia" Jane, 248
Witterman, Clarissa "Clara" Jane, 247
Witterman, Clarissa Jane, 166, 248
Witterman, Emanuel, 166, 248
Witterman, Susan, 166, 248
Witzke, Carol Ann, 196
Wohlwindu, Mary W., 272
Wolary, Amanda, 39, 179
Wolf, Amy, 258
Wolf, Craig, 258
Wolf, ElizabethAnn, 321
Wolf, Ella, 321
Wolf, G. Marvin, 258
Wolf, George B.,321
Wolf, Harriet, 124, 125
Wolf, Henry, 125
Wolf, Hiram H., 321
Wolf, James, 321
Wolf, Janice, 258

Wolf, Kristen L., 258
Wolf, Stacey, 258
Wolfe, Margaret Ruth, 169
Wolford, Daniel, 305
Wood, Alice D., 16
Wood, Carlos G., 16
Wood, Clara, 110
Wood, Clara Beall, 116
Wood, Clara E., 110
Wood, Clarence, 116
Wood, Delphine, 144
Wood, Donald G., 16
Wood, Effie, 214
Wood, Emma, 16
Wood, Essie, 290
Wood, Ethel, 110
Wood, Geneva, 110
Wood, Gordon B., 16
Wood, Isaac, 16
Wood, J. W., 110
Wood, Joe, 116
Wood, Kathryn, 290
Wood, Linda, 16
Wood, Mabelle, 110
Wood, Margaret, 16
Wood, Mary, 198
Wood, Mildred, xiv, 110, 116
Wood, Myrtle Mae, 37, 191, 198
Wood, Nancy, 16
Wood, Plia, 290
Wood, Rita Mae, 16
Wood, Sadie Ocie, 16
Wood, Sally, 229
Wood, Theodore, 198
Wood, Valerie Lynn, 253
Wood, William, 16
Wood, William R., 16
Woodbine, John, 241
Woodford, Delbert, 293
Woodford, Mary, 293
Woodman, Jill, 48
Woodring, Henry, Gov., 157
Woodrow, Martha, 15
Woods, Amanda, 173
Woods, Earl C., 273
Woods, Joel, 319
Woods, Kelly Ann, 273
Woods, Lillie, 59, 61, 69
Woods, Sarah Louise, 273
Woods, Sarah, 212
Woods, Vina Virginia, 253
Woodward, Barbara Jean, 197

581